## DATE DUE

| | | | |
|---|---|---|---|
| | | | |
| | | | |
| | | | |
| | | | |
| | | | |
| | | | |
| | | | |
| | | | |
| | | | |
| | | | |
| | | | |
| | | | |
| | | | |
| | | | |
| | | | |
| | | | |
| | | | |

# JOHN KEATS

*The Making of a Poet*

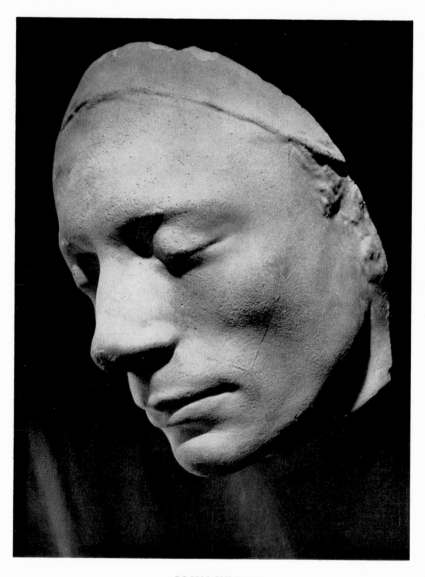

I JOHN KEATS

From the life mask by B. R. Haydon, 1816,
Keats Memorial House, Hampstead

# JOHN KEATS

*The Making of a Poet*

BY AILEEN WARD

THE VIKING PRESS

NEW YORK

Published simultaneously in Canada by The Macmillan Company of Canada Limited

Library of Congress catalog card number: 63-15218

Second Printing January 1964
Third Printing July 1964

M B G
Set in Baskerville and Bulmer types
Printed in the U.S.A. by Vail-Ballou Press, Inc.

To Marjorie Hope Nicolson

and the memory of

Victoria Louise Schrager

# Contents

# Plates

Plates I and VII are photographs by Christopher Oxford from the collection in Keats Memorial House, reproduced by permission of the Hampstead Borough Council. The source of each of the other plates appears with the plate.

# Preface

A NEW LIFE OF KEATS requires a word of explanation. The story has been told many times before and will be told again, as new facts about his life continue to be brought to light and critical re-valuation clarifies and redefines his place in English poetry. But a new biography of Keats should attempt more than to present new information or synthesize recent criticism: it should try to convey a new sense of the meaning of his life. Keats's life has in fact meant something new to each generation that has reflected on it, for it was an extraordinary life, both in the intensity with which he lived it and in the unconscious eloquence with which he recorded it. Indeed, it has that representative quality, that fullness of significance, of which Keats himself was thinking when he wrote, "Shakespeare led a life of Allegory: his works are the comments on it." As Lionel Trilling has suggested, it was a life cast in the heroic mould. A close reading of Keats's poems and letters reveals the allegory that he himself sensed in it; his recurrent image for his own endeavour in poetry is a voyage of exploration across uncharted seas. He died thinking he had not reached his goal; yet in spite of the interruption of his work just as he attained maturity, his life shows a significant completion—the achievement of identity, the self-making which, according to Otto Rank, is the most important act of any artist's career. Keats's own remark on Milton may then be applied to him: "There was working in him as it were that same sort of thing as operates in the great world to the end of a Prophecy's being accomplished."

In our time Keats has been regarded increasingly as the man of his letters: so much so that F. R. Leavis has had to remind us sharply that our final concern must be with his poetry. In my view of Keats his greatness as a man is something distinct from, yet at the same time significantly related to, his greatness as a poet; his life was essentially a process of integrating these two aspects of his nature. The profound and delighted and ultimately tragic insight into human life which Keats communicated so immediately and directly in his letters was

ix

something he learned only slowly to express in his poetry as he re-shaped his poetic medium to convey it. Slowly—that is, in three years of the most concentrated effort in our literature. My account of his life, therefore, is concerned primarily with the development of his character as a poet—that audacious act of self-creation which he de-scribed in connection with the writing of *Endymion*. Where his previous biographers have viewed him against the long tradition of English poetry or his day-to-day study of the poets from whom he learned his art, or against the wide backdrop of Regency society or the minutiae of his daily existence, I have tried to convey something of the inner drama of his creative life as it is recorded in his poems and letters. Inevitably this has limited my critical focus. The interpretation of Keats's poetry in the following pages is offered not as the detailed and rounded criticism which can alone do justice to the individual poem, but as a study, chiefly through his imagery, of the process by which his goal in poetry became clear to him, in that miraculous unfolding which John Middleton Murry has called the mystery of Keats. The mystery remains beyond analysis in the end, and fortunately so: for it is the compelling reason for us to continue reading Keats.

It is a pleasure to record the obligations incurred in writing this book. My first thanks are due to Elizabeth Ames and the Yaddo Corporation, for hospitality of the most constructive sort in the early stages of my work. I am also grateful to the American Association of University Women for the award of a Shirley Farr Fellowship which helped me to continue it.

The staffs of the New York Public Library, the Pierpont Morgan Library, the Skidmore College Library, the Harvard University Library, the Cambridge University Library, the British Museum, and the Keats Memorial Library of the Hampstead Borough Council have extended me many courtesies. For permission to examine manuscripts and other documents relating to Keats, I owe especial thanks to Signora Vera Cacciatore, Curator of the Keats-Shelley Memorial House in Rome; Mr. J. H. Preston, former Curator of the Keats Memorial House and Museum in Hampstead; and most of all to Miss Mabel A. E. Steele, Curator of the Keats Collection of the Harvard University Library, who has generously and knowledgeably answered countless questions about the Keats documents in her charge. I am also grateful to all the present owners and custodians of Keats's letters for answering my inquiries regarding them.

The Keats Memorial Library of the Hampstead Borough Council has kindly granted permission to use on the title page a drawing after that by Joseph Severn, found in Charles Brown's copy of *Endymion,* of the

Greek lyre which Keats asked to have engraved on his tombstone. For permission to reproduce the illustrations in this book I am grateful to the Houghton Library of Harvard University, the Keats Memorial House in Hampstead, the Keats-Shelley Memorial House in Rome, the Radio Times Hulton Picture Library of London, the Victoria and Albert Museum, and the National Portrait Gallery, London.

In my effort to work as completely as possible from Keats's own writings and those of his friends, I am profoundly indebted to Keats's editors—Harry Buxton Forman, Maurice Buxton Forman, H. W. Garrod, and Hyder Edward Rollins. I am also keenly aware of what I owe to the researches of many scholars in the field of Keats and his circle, especially to Keats's previous biographers, Sir Sidney Colvin, Miss Amy Lowell, Miss Dorothy Hewlett, and Mr. Robert Gittings. On several earlier occasions I have expressed my disagreement with certain aspects of Mr. Gittings' interpretation of Keats's life, particularly Keats's relations with Isabella Jones and the influence of Burton's *Anatomy of Melancholy* on his work. I would like to take this opportunity to record my admiration of many other aspects of Mr. Gittings' research and of the manner in which he has set it forth.

In the interest of general readability, I have kept the documentation of this book to a minimum. It is assumed that students of Keats will be familiar with his poems and letters in the editions of H. W. Garrod and H. E. Rollins and with the documents collected by Professor Rollins in *The Keats Circle* and *More Letters and Papers of the Keats Circle*. Therefore, except where a reference is obscure or a point controverted, I have not given notes to these primary sources in the life of Keats. I hope that my general indebtedness to the previous biographers of Keats and his friends will also be immediately apparent to students of the period and will be sufficiently acknowledged in the bibliography. Again for the sake of a readable narrative, I have quoted freely from Keats's letters without indicating omissions and have sometimes transposed the order of sentences; I have taken care, however, not to distort Keats's meaning in the process, and I trust that the close reader of Keats will recognize and accept these occasional condensations of the text. Wherever I have departed from the established text in my quotations, the emendations are indicated in detail.

Miss Dorothy Hewlett graciously answered a number of questions I asked her concerning Keats's life, and Mr. A. J. Liebling provided some valuable information about boxing in the nineteenth century. For other information I am indebted to Mr. W. R. LeFanu, Librarian of the Royal Society of Surgeons of England; Mr. William Lichtenwanger, Assistant Head of the Reference Section, Library of Congress; Mr. Cyril E. R. Platten, Town Clerk of the Borough of Enfield; Miss

Ellen Shafer, Librarian of the Rare Book Department, Free Library of Philadelphia; Mr. Lawrence E. Tanner, Keeper of the Muniments and Sub-Librarian, Westminster Abbey; and Mr. A. W. Wheen, Keeper of the Library of the Victoria and Albert Museum. I wish also to thank Professor Willard Bissell Pope, of the University of Vermont, and Professor Charles W. Hagelman, Jr., of the Lamar State College of Technology, for permission to cite from their unpublished doctoral dissertations. I am especially grateful to Dr. Erik H. Erikson for sending me a copy of his monograph, "The Problem of Ego Identity," prior to its publication in the *Journal of the American Psychoanalytic Association;* and to Dr. Frederick Wyatt for reading and commenting on the early chapters of my manuscript.

My greatest thanks are due to my editors, Marshall A. Best, Malcolm Cowley, and especially Catharine Carver, whose patience and skill have contributed immeasurably to the final form of this book.

It is a pleasure also to record the names of friends who have helped in many different ways during the course of my work: First, Kirsten Scott, for invaluable assistance in typing my manuscript; Mary Jane Holmes Baillie, Sylvia Berkman, Daphne Wilson Ercoli, Emma M. E. Hess, Mrs. Searle F. Holmes, Carter Harman, Kenneth Lewars, Lawrence Lieberfeld, Helen Drusilla Lockwood, Jean Baker Read, my colleague Robert Wagner, my student Elizabeth Caffrey, and last but not least, my parents, Aline Coursen and Waldron Merry Ward.

A. W.

*New York City*
*April* 1963

# JOHN KEATS

*The Making of a Poet*

*Chapter One*

---

# Close to the Source

I N the summer of 1803 the threat of invasion hung over England like a thunder-cloud. All along the shores of Kent and Sussex red-coated troops were pitching camp. A chain of Martello towers was being thrown over the hills of the southeast coast, and a defence canal dug across Romney Marsh; even the fishing boats were arming for conflict. In the coastal towns nervous civilians refused to undress at night, and petitions for deliverance from the foe were read aloud in every church of the land. Out at sea the squadrons of the Royal Navy stalked up and down before the French naval ports of Brest and Rochefort and Toulon, while a detachment of cruisers patrolled the Channel; on the cliffs of Dover sentries stood watch around the clock. Twenty miles across the strait the chalk cliffs of the French coast gleamed quietly in the summer sun; but in the crowded harbor of Boulogne the air rang with the sound of shipwrights' hammers. On the beaches the "Army of England," a hundred and fifty thousand veterans of the Revolutionary Wars, practised landing manœuvres  and waited for their commander's orders. Napoleon Bonaparte had broken the Treaty of Amiens, signed with England only the year before. First Consul in France and virtual master of the Continent, he needed only to bring the British to their knees to rule unchallenged over Europe.

London meanwhile seethed with activity. On intercepting Bonaparte's plans for invasion, the Government had declared war in March, calling up the militia and setting the press gangs to work to man the fleet. Government agents slipped out of Whitehall, bound for France with plots against the First Consul's life. George

III, autocratic as ever though now only intermittently sane, had dismissed the great Tory leader Pitt in 1801 and brought in the ineffectual Addington as Prime Minister, thus making it easier to play the Tory factions off against each other. The Prince of Wales, who had broken with Princess Caroline several years before to return to his first but illegal wife, Mrs. Fitzherbert, was now on the point of finally breaking with her. Fat, silly, extravagant, universally unpopular, he dabbled in Whig politics mainly, it was said, to annoy his father.

Yet the nation as a whole was united by the menace of invasion as it had not been since the days of the Armada. The Army might be corrupt and inefficient—a collection of dissipated young bluebloods commanding troops drawn from the scum of society, who were kept in line mainly by the lash—but the citizens of England rallied proudly to her defence. When nearly half a million recruits answered the call for volunteers, the Government was so short of muskets that it had to issue pikes instead. There was hardly an able-bodied man in the whole country who did not join some military unit or other. Up in Westmoreland, William Wordsworth, who had been carried away by republican ardor in the early years of the French Revolution, now marched in a red coat with the Grasmere volunteers and poured out sonnets calling England to "Victory or Death!" In London a young whippersnapper named Leigh Hunt paraded gaily in the fashionable St. James Regiment at Burlington House, then pranced off to wine-parties or the theatre afterward. The wave of patriotic fervor reached its height that summer with a grand muster of twenty-seven thousand volunteers in Hyde Park.

All this while, in a quiet northern suburb of London off City Road, a small boy was playing with his brothers—John Keats, seven and a half years old. No more than any boy of the time could he have escaped the tide of military excitement that was sweeping over England. Beside their hoops and tops and kites, English lads of 1803 had toy guillotines to play with, toy cannons to fire with real gunpowder, and great English victories to act out in their games. Their hero was Nelson, who had whipped the Spanish off Cape Saint Vincent, the French at the Nile, and the Danes in the Baltic; "Boney" was the ogre who, they were told, would carry them off if they misbehaved. Parades became commonplace in London that summer, but small boys were always ready to cheer

a line of soldiers marching by to drums and trumpets, led by officers with white plumes and drawn swords on prancing chargers.
The Clerkenwell Volunteers drilled in a field near Keats's home in
Craven Street; the Honourable Artillery Company practised on
their grounds close to his father's stable on Finsbury Pavement.
Keats's father, an accomplished horseman, most likely joined a
cavalry unit, perhaps the Clerkenwell cavalry, which rode out in
smart leather breeches and magnificent bearskin helmets.[1] * Keats's
uncle, Midgley John Jennings, was a lieutenant in the Marines
and had fought in the battle against the Dutch off Camperdown in
1797. In his old school at Enfield it was a legend that his tallness
had made him a special mark for enemy fire, which he coolly
ignored, and that the Dutch commander had afterward remarked
on his courage to Admiral Duncan.

In this time of mobilization and suspense, John Keats confronted an anxious future of his own—the traditional first trial of
manhood in England. He was to be sent away to his uncle's old
school, the Clarke academy at Enfield. What he felt at leaving the
safe haven of family and home is not a matter of record. But years
later, when he faced the last separation of his life—leaving the
country and the girl he loved, to die in a foreign land—these days
stirred in his memory. With the thought of the journey waking
him up each morning at dawn, he nerved himself to leave England,
he wrote, "as a soldier marches up to a battery." The image is
significant. From the time of his first encounter with the world,
life was to seem a test of whatever fortitude he could bring to it.

⋙ ⋘

In later years Keats almost never mentioned his boyhood. Indeed, for the first twenty of his twenty-five years, there is no personal record except for a handful of short poems of uncertain date.
Beside these remain a few bare facts, some of them disputed, about
his parentage and schooling, and the fragmentary and often conflicting impressions of four or five of his contemporaries, mostly
recalled a quarter-century after his death and distorted by bias or
clouded by sentiment. Nevertheless most of his biographers have
assumed—perhaps on the analogy with nations that have no history—that his boyhood was a happy one. Keats's silence on this

* Superior numbers refer to Notes, pp. 416–440.

point may raise a doubt; yet his first seven or eight years do seem to have been remarkably happy, though in an unremarkable way.

His father, Thomas Keats, had come up as a boy from the west of England to make his way in London. From the little that is known of him, he was a likeable young man, energetic, intelligent, short but strongly built and good-looking—"a man much above his station in life," as he was later described. He had sprung from humble people and first worked as a groom in the London stables. By twenty he had become head ostler at the Swan and Hoop, a prosperous livery establishment in Moorfields owned by one John Jennings; and there, like the industrious apprentice of legend, he won the love of his master's daughter. Frances Jennings was a headstrong girl of nineteen, with a fine figure and a pretty face a little spoiled by too wide a mouth. She was evidently a flirt; one of her neighbours remembered her habit of picking up her skirts in crossing a muddy street to show off her good-looking legs, and another—an unsympathetic witness—reported "her passions were so ardent that it was dangerous to be alone with her." [2] If she risked her parents' disapproval in marrying her father's foreman, she was not one to be deterred. In October 1794 she and Thomas Keats were married at St. George's in Hanover Square, a fashionable West End church several miles from her own parish. Neither of her parents was present to sign the register; but whether they merely refused to indulge her whim of a Mayfair wedding, or whether she needed to keep the marriage a secret till after the event, remains a mystery. There is some uncertainty about the exact birth date of her oldest son, and some reason for thinking it occurred only seven or eight months after her marriage.[3] But her parents cannot have greatly disapproved of the match, for the young couple returned to the parental roof and the family business, and their first child, John, was born in their rooms over the stable. At his baptism the following December, the date of his birth was given as October 31, 1795, and this apparently is the date Keats regarded as his birthday—though, we are told, he always disliked having it celebrated. Three brothers followed him—George in February 1797, Thomas in November 1799, and Edward in April 1801; then a sister, Frances Mary, in June 1803.

From the little evidence we have, it was a lively and affectionate family to grow up in. John Jennings was all a grandfather should be. Hearty and confident like most self-made men, he was riding the great wave of English prosperity in the later eighteenth century. Road transport, shipping, commerce, agriculture, and industry—all were expanding at an unprecedented rate. It was the great age of coaching, between the surfacing of the turnpikes and the advent of the railway; the new crack coaches cut travelling time to a quarter of what it had been in the mid-century. A stable such as the Swan and Hoop, well located near the center of the city, could make a small fortune for its owner. Yet for all his business acumen, John Jennings had a generous nature—too generous and gullible, according to his grandson George Keats, for him to become really rich. He loved good food and drink; it was said that the women of his household spent four days out of the week roasting and baking for Sunday dinner—though this may only reflect the fact that he was an innkeeper or "victualler" as well as a stable-keeper.[4] Alice Jennings, his wife, was a more sober character, sensible, kindly, and warm-hearted, well liked by her neighbours and adored by her grandchildren. She was the kind of woman to whom people instinctively turn in distress, one to take care of orphans and befriend country girls in the city. In the family background there were a few shadowy cousins and aunts and uncles, most of them apparently small merchants in London; in the foreground a crowd of little boys laughed and tumbled and scrapped, watched with indulgent eyes by their parents.

Frances Jennings had been an ardent young girl in love; as a mother she poured out affection unrestrainedly. Like her father, she had a great gusto for life. It is said she was "passionately fond of amusement" and paid no attention to hours or seasons or even pregnancies in pursuing it.[5] Her son George remembered her chiefly for her "doting fondness" and her recklessness with money —a trait which her sons inherited. According to George, John, the firstborn, was her favourite child, the one most like her in appearance and temperament, whom she humoured in all his whims. As Freud ( a favourite son himself) once remarked, "A man who has been the indisputable favourite of his mother keeps for life the feeling of a conqueror, that confidence of success which frequently induces real success." From the beginning John seems to have been a boy of intense feelings and a vivid imagination, fiercely devoted to his mother. Once, it is told, when she fell ill and absolute quiet was ordered, John found an old sword and took up his post outside her door with the blade bared, forbidding anyone to enter. The family atmosphere was one of warmth and freedom, in which the brothers grew up knit by unusually close bonds of loyalty; and for his young sister Keats was to develop an almost fatherly tenderness. Perhaps their first experience of loss, when Edward, the youngest boy, died in infancy, drew them still closer together.

Not long after his daughter's marriage, John Jennings, already ailing with gout, retired from active control of his business and moved with his wife to the country. Thomas Keats was then left in charge of the Swan and Hoop, which became his property in 1803. By about 1800 he had prospered enough to move his growing family from the rooms over the stables to a house in Craven Street, half a mile to the north in Shoreditch. Still it was the Swan and Hoop that gave John Keats his first glimpse of the world, and the colour and clamour of those earliest impressions must have sunk deep in his memory. The stableyard was the scene of constant comings and goings, of shouts and neighs and clattering hoofs, of jingling harness and gleaming horseflesh, of strong smells and swift movement that would fill a small boy with delight. Thomas Keats, though he was described as an unostentatious man, loved good horses and kept a remarkably fine one for his own use; he cut a handsome figure when he rode out on Sundays to the meets at Highgate and Highbury. Among the tall men astride their powerful horses who were Keats's first image of splendour and mastery, his own father must have seemed the most magnificent.

Their new home in Craven Street, a backwater of neat brick houses not far from Charles Square, marked a step up in the world. The Keatses were prospering, and their sons must have felt the force of their parents' ambitions for them. When it came time to think of the boys' schooling, there was talk of sending them to Harrow. It was an impractical idea, though not impossible. The lines that divided one class from another in England were as sharply drawn as ever at that time, and the public schools were far fewer in number and less open to middle-class pupils than they later became. The son of a tailor in the Strand is remembered as the one boy whom Shelley fought and whipped at Eton; there was a place in that world for the sons of the owner of the Swan and Hoop, but they would have had to fight for it. At Harrow, Keats would probably have missed making the acquaintance of the young Lord Byron, who was seven years his senior; he would have gained a perfunctory training in Latin and Greek and a more thorough one in cricket and fives, but little else. Studies in the public schools then were narrow and poorly directed; games took more of the boys' time than work; discipline was brutal, bullying and dissoluteness common. However, the question of Harrow did not have to be answered till Keats reached twelve or thirteen. His parents decided to start his education at Mr. Clarke's academy at Enfield, and they chose better than they knew.

→»«←

John Clarke had started out in the law but soon found teaching more congenial. After a few years as classics master in the famous Dissenting academy in Northampton then headed by the eminent Baptist minister John Collett Ryland, he married Ryland's daughter and moved to Enfield to set up a school of his own. A stocky, square-headed man of liberal convictions, he remained unshaken in his beliefs when public opinion turned toward reaction in the 1790s. He was a friend of John Cartwright, the Parliamentary reformer, and of Joseph Priestley, the great scientist, Unitarian minister, and radical, whose house and laboratory were wrecked by the Birmingham mob in 1791. Through these men Clarke was aligned with a small but significant minority who, even after England went to war with France in 1793, continued to uphold the principles of political democracy and religious freedom which had triumphed in America and inspired the early days of the French Revolution. In 1794 twelve of the leading Reformers were indicted for high treason in a wave of anti-Jacobin hysteria; but though the Government failed to win a conviction, it managed to stifle effective protest for many years afterward, and it was a brave man who openly maintained his faith in the principles of reform in those oppressive years.

Clarke had enlightened theories of education, which, like his liberal stand in politics, were rare in schoolmasters of his day. He thought that a school should bring out the good in boys, not merely hold the bad in check. Instead of caning his pupils into learning their lessons, he set up rules enforced by rewards rather than by punishments and encouraged voluntary extra work with special prizes. The school was evidently modelled on the Dissenting academies of the time, which offered a much more modern and rounded curriculum than the public schools, including history, science, and modern languages as well as the classics. Keats later complained that French had been crammed down his throat as though he were a young jackdaw, but he never regretted his ability to read Voltaire or Ronsard in the original. Mr. Clarke also encouraged hobbies; he provided garden plots, for instance, for the boys who wanted to work in them. His system left the pupils far freer to develop in their own directions and at their own rates than most schools of the day; it was a good soil for John Keats to take root and grow in.

The village of Enfield lay about twelve miles north of London, among rolling fields and shady woods, the remains of the old Enfield Chase. It was a pleasant countryside for half-holiday rambles, and the New River provided good swimming for the boys. The schoolhouse was a handsome, airy residence, with a classical façade garlanded with flowers and fruits and heads of cherubim. Behind it lay the playground, bordered with poplars, and gardens and a pasture. A fine pear tree stood in the playground, and a morello cherry tree grew against the courtyard wall; strawberry beds were planted beside the pond, and the boys who watered them were given the berries when they were ripe. Here Keats must have sampled his first "antiquated cherries full of sugar cracks" and acquired the weakness for "pear-tasting—plum-judging —apricot nibbling—peach scrunching—Nectarine-sucking and Melon-carving" to which he later confessed. Probably he too had his garden plot to tend, for he developed a close and loving knowledge of flowers, to judge from the drawings of pinks and violets scattered up and down the margins of one of his lecture notebooks. Beyond the school the meadows stretched away to the dark edges of the forest, from which the song of nightingales unfurled endlessly in the still May nights.

Here Keats arrived in the summer of 1803. Cowden Clarke, the fifteen-year-old son of the headmaster, remembered him only dimly in his first year as the smallest of the seventy or eighty pupils, still wearing the frilled dress of a little boy. His brother George either came with him or followed not long afterward, and they were later joined by Tom, the youngest. From the beginning there was some confusion about the brothers' ages. Even as a boy John was unusually short, and George soon outgrew him; as a result, Cowden Clarke, who later became his close friend, always took

Keats as George's junior and thought him a year younger than he actually was.

Whatever the ordeal of separation from home, Keats must have soon surmounted it, for he rapidly became popular with his schoolmates and a favourite of Mrs. Clarke. Cowden Clarke's first clear recollection of Keats was "his brisk, winning face"—a mobility of expression that was to become striking in his young manhood. There was every reason for him to be happy at Enfield. His grandparents lived only a few miles away in Ponders End; his uncle occasionally returned to his old school to dine with the headmaster; and his father and mother often drove out for a Sunday visit. Thomas Keats impressed John Clarke as a man of "fine commonsense and native respectability," unaffected by his rapid rise to prosperity. It is true that Cowden Clarke, who reported this verdict, was eager to prove that Keats's family was not merely respectable but "estimable." Yet his own recollection of Thomas Keats's "lively and energetic countenance, when seated in his gig and preparing to drive his wife home," gives a glimpse of a forceful and attractive man, one whose image must have sunk deep into his young son's mind.

The family's future looked bright; then disaster struck out of a clear sky. On April 15, 1804, Thomas Keats, riding home late at night from Southgate, was thrown when his horse slipped on the pavement in City Road, and fractured his skull against the railings. He was alive but speechless when the watchman found him and carried him home; the next morning he died. A week later he was buried at St. Stephen's Church in Coleman Street.

Frances Keats was now left alone in London with four young children to support and a busy livery stable to manage. Her parents were a dozen miles away in Middlesex, her father past seventy and ill. As an attractive young widow with a thriving business, she was a desirable match, especially under the law of those times by which a woman's property became her husband's at marriage. It is not difficult to see why a suitor presented himself almost immediately, but it is hard to understand her acceptance of him barely two months after Thomas Keats's death. Neither loneliness nor a sense of helplessness, nor even her passionate nature, can quite account for the haste of this remarriage; and her motive in being married a second time in St. George's Church, on June 27, 1804, is still harder to fathom. But most obscure of all is her

reason for choosing William Rawlings as her second husband.
A bank clerk in the City, with no property of his own, he seems
to have taken a far keener interest in the Swan and Hoop than in
his new wife and family.

The marriage did not last. Frances Rawlings soon found life
with her new husband so intolerable that she left him, even
though, under the law of the time, she thereby lost all claim to her
property and all legal control of her children. Alice Jennings, who
had disapproved of the marriage from the start, then took the
grandchildren to live with her—whether on Rawlings' insistence
or her own initiative does not matter. Rawlings sold the stable
at the beginning of 1806 and thereupon dropped out of Keats's
life for good; [6] while his mother, according to the only account
of her life, disappeared for several years, taking to brandy, it is
hinted, and living "as the wife of a Jew at Enfield, named Abraham." [7]

Keats's biographers have usually mentioned this story of his
mother only to deny it and maintain that she went to live with her
mother and her children on leaving Rawlings, but the evidence
is against them. In a jingle describing his boyhood which he later
wrote to amuse his sister, Keats mentioned their "Granny good"
but, significantly, not their mother; indeed, he never referred to
her in all his letters to Fanny. Once, however, he guardedly told
a close friend that "his greatest misfortune" since childhood was
that "he had no mother." [8] George Keats recalled his mother only
dimly, while Fanny hardly ever mentioned her in all her later
voluminous writings about her childhood. And the fact that for
four years Mrs. Rawlings did not collect an annuity of fifty pounds
bequeathed her by her father in 1805 [9] strongly implies that she
was estranged from her family after leaving her second husband,
if not also living on the support of another man. None of the
children ever spoke of their stepfather, though Keats may have
had him in mind in his cryptic mention, years later, of "earlier
Misfortunes" preceding his mother's death. So complete was his
silence on the events of his early life that his later friends were
astonished to learn of them after his death.[10] His reserve has been
laid to his diffidence about being born over a livery stable, but
it was far more probably due to an insoluble conflict of emotions
about his mother.

His father's death and his mother's remarriage would be staggering blows to any boy of eight or nine; their effect on John Keats can hardly be exaggerated. In two short months the very foundations of his security had been knocked out from under him. Some writers have taken these losses as mere "unpropitious occurrences," brief interruptions in the happy course of Keats's boyhood; [11] but it is worth recalling another tragedy very similar to his. "But two months dead!" The parallel with Hamlet's situation is startling, and it helps illuminate the welter of incommunicable emotion which young John Keats felt against his faithless mother and his father's usurper. The timing of these two blows was also particularly unfortunate. Keats lost his father at the stage in a boy's development when his earlier jealous rivalry begins to yield to proud identification with his male parent; as a result, he was to search for an idealized father in one older man after another throughout his life. He had also barely reached the end of the period of intense possessiveness about his mother—marked dramatically for an English boy by his being sent off to school— when his former rival disappeared and a new and hateful one took his place. But still harder for Keats to accept must have been his mother's subsequent disappearance and mysterious disgrace. The idealized woman of his crucial early experience, beautiful and recklessly affectionate, had betrayed and abandoned him in a manner beyond his understanding, and forever afterward he was haunted by the fear that any woman he loved would play him false and then leave him. The boy began to develop a wariness in his dealings with others, beneath his instinctive openness and spontaneity. "All my life I have suspected every Body," Keats later wrote; and though his biographers have discounted this statement, he had good reason for making it.

Yet the immediate effect of this tragedy was not to plunge Keats into a Hamlet-like paralysis: quite the reverse. Almost overnight, it seems, he changed from an affectionate child into a rebellious schoolboy, protesting against the world by the only means he had —his fists. Fifteen years later Keats still remembered the glory of winning his first battle—like being "lifted from the tribe of Manessah"; and in spite of his small size he soon established himself as the pluckiest and scrappiest fighter in the school. Fighting was "meat and drink to him," as Edward Holmes, one of his first friends, recalled; "he would fight anyone, morning, noon or night." Such pugnacity must have had a driving force deeper than mere ambition to win a place in the schoolboy world. Some of it must have sprung from half-conscious rage against his stepfather and his errant mother. Some of it came more consciously from another source: identification with his heroic uncle, Lieutenant (later Captain) Midgley Jennings of the Royal Marines. "Their sailor relation was always in the thoughts of the brothers," Holmes remembered, "and they determined to keep up a family reputation for courage." Regrettably it appears that the story of Jennings' intrepidity under fire at Camperdown was mostly invented [12]— perhaps by his own nephews. Yet the fact that Cowden Clarke believed it suggests that Keats had more than the average small boy's talent for boasting. With the death of his father he desperately needed an image of manhood on which to pattern himself; and in an England whose Navy had saved it from Napoleon and whose national idol was Nelson, Keats's choice of his uncle as hero was inevitable.

Less than a year after his father's death one more link with his childhood snapped when his grandfather died in March 1805. The old man had laboured well for his family. John Jennings left more than £13,000—a respectable estate in those days—to be divided among his wife, his sister Mary Sweetingburgh, his son Midgley, his daughter Frances Rawlings, and his four Keats grandchildren. The will was badly drawn, and as a result much of the estate was later entangled in Chancery proceedings; but for the present the family was comfortably provided for. Mrs. Jennings received a moderate income of £200, and Mrs. Rawlings the annuity of £50 mentioned earlier. The grandchildren inherited £250 each in trust, and much more of the estate was eventually to come to them. With the breakdown of their mother's second marriage soon afterward, however, they were left less well off than John Jennings could have foreseen. When Rawlings sold the Swan and Hoop, pocketed the money, and disappeared, all the dreams of a Harrow education for the Keats boys vanished with him.

But Alice Jennings immediately picked up the broken pieces of their lives. Soon after her husband's death she took a house in Edmonton, a village about four miles from Enfield, and here Keats found a second home. Mrs. Jennings became a second mother to him, winning from him a devotion very different from the love he had felt for his mother, yet almost as deep. The fact that Keats had two mothers during his boyhood—one young, beau-

tiful and unreliable, the other much older, equable and affectionate—is worth noting. It helps explain a division in his nature
which appeared later in many forms, one being a tendency to be
drawn toward two quite different types of women—flirtatious
young beauties and serious young ladies, sexually much less challenging, often several years older than himself.

No doubt the new home lacked some of the warmth of the old
one, but it gave the Keats children a stability they needed. Here
Fanny grew up into a shy little girl, quiet and well behaved—
her grandmother's child rather than her mother's, and the pet of
her three older brothers. And here no doubt Keats enjoyed himself in all the ways that boys did at that time: "played cricket," as
his friend Haydon described his own boyhood, "rode a black pony
about the neighbourhood; pinned ladies' gowns together on market days and waited to see them split; knocked at doors by night
and ran away; swam and bathed, heated myself, worried my parents, and at last was laid on my back by the measles." [13] From
Keats's later poems and letters we catch glimpses of him in those
years at home or on half-holidays at school, roaming the meadows,
climbing trees, watching the clouds overhead drift into fantastic
figures, sailing homemade boats on the ponds, and thus becoming
acquainted with "the whole tribe of the Bushes and the Brooks"—
"Gold-finches, Tomtits, Minnows, Mice, Ticklebacks, Dace, and
Cock-salmons." The "Song About Myself" he later wrote for his
sister recalls his habit of bringing fish home to keep in the washing-
tubs—"In spite Of the might Of the Maid"—

> O he made
> 'Twas his trade
> Of Fish a pretty Kettle
> A Kettle—A Kettle
> Of Fish a pretty Kettle
> A Kettle!

At school there was little to mark him off from the other boys
except the very intensity of his boyishness. From all accounts he
was as thoughtless, impulsive, boastful, and self-centred as any
growing lad. Years later Keats wrote, "The most unhappy hours
in our lives are those in which we recollect times past to our own
blushing," and singled out his schooldays as those he would like
most to forget. From the first—or from the time he acquired a
stepfather—he cared conspicuously little for the good opinion of

the masters but scrambled through his lessons with no visible effort. He took all a boy's usual delight in jokes and pranks, and in sports he was outstanding. Like any schoolboy of his age he learned to ride, swim, box, row, and play cricket—a game he was still keen on a dozen years later. But it was as a fighter that he made his name. The older boys came to look on him as a kind of pet gamecock, while the younger boys who wanted to win his friendship had to prove themselves in battle. Apparently there was a histrionic streak in him—some more than usually vivid sense of playing a noble part. Cowden Clarke reports that when his fighting temper was up Keats resembled no one so much as the great Shakespearean actor Edmund Kean in one of his dramatic transports. Once, Clarke recalled, when Tom Keats spoke saucily to one of the junior teachers and was cuffed for it, John rushed up to the defence of his frail young brother and struck out in a fury at the astonished usher, who was twice his size. Mr. Clarke was so touched by this bravado that he could not bring himself to punish Keats when the boy was haled up before him.

Yet under these gestures appears a certain nervous instability, evidence of the emotional conflict still latent. Keats was plagued by violent swings of mood; Holmes remembered him as always between "outrageous fits of laughter" and "passions of tears," and Clarke recalled that his temper was sometimes almost uncontrollable. In his dark moments he used to lash out savagely at his younger brother. George, a far more even-natured lad, seems to have inherited their father's self-assurance and stability, while John took after their mother, and it was also George, the taller and heavier, who usually won their battles. Clarke reports that George used to pin John down by main force and laugh while John raged against him—a humiliating defeat to take from one's younger brother. Nevertheless George remained the closest companion of his boyhood. According to Holmes, Keats made few of the warm attachments that most schoolboys form at this age; evidently the mysterious disgrace hanging over his family life made friendship difficult. Yet he was an attractive lad, with his curly reddish-gold hair, large hazel-coloured eyes, and trim athletic build; and, with his daring and generosity of character, he was universally liked. Holmes summed him up forty years later as "a boy whom anyone from his extraordinary vivacity & personal beauty might easily have fancied would become great—but," he added significantly, "rather in some military capacity than in literature."

For Keats's schooldays were played out against a steadily darkening background of war. For two long years after 1803 England remained poised to meet the French invasion, while Napoleon crowned himself Emperor, reorganized his government, and revised his strategy. In the summer of 1805 the French fleet slipped out of its blockade at Toulon, then was cornered by the British off Cape Trafalgar. There, with Nelson's death, England won decisive command of the seas; yet war on the Continent was to drag on for another decade. On hearing of the defeat of the Third Coalition at Austerlitz in December, 1805, the ailing Pitt cried, "Roll up that map of Europe—we shall not need it these twenty years." A few weeks later he died, followed shortly by Charles James Fox, the great Whig leader and the last liberal spokesman in Parliament. After Austerlitz came more disasters at Jena and Wagram; by 1810 Napoleon's empire extended from the Baltic to the Straits of Messina, from the Niemen River to Cape Finisterre. The war simmered down to a struggle between rival blockades and endless skirmishing in Spain. Under the blockade English landowners' fortunes rose as food prices soared, and the enterprising new factory owners prospered with them; but the wages of the workers on the farms and in the mills sank to the starvation level. To muffle their discontent the Government outlawed trade unions and political societies, prosecuted its critics for sedition, and forbade meetings of protest. In 1811, Keats's last year at school, George III became hopelessly insane and his dissolute and unstable son was appointed Prince Regent.

Keats's own life grew darker during these years. At the end of 1807 his uncle Midgley, whom he worshipped, was stricken with consumption. The following year he died at Huntington at the age of thirty-one,[14] leaving Keats, at thirteen, the oldest male member of his family. Far more disturbing was his mother's reappearance not long afterward. At last she returned to her family in Edmonton, an ill woman, bedridden in her early thirties, evidently broken in both body and spirit. To Keats, on the threshold of adolescence, the sight of her faded beauty and dimming vitality must have been a deeply troubling experience. Then in 1809 her illness changed disastrously for the worse: she too developed signs of consumption.

This was merely the last stage in an illness that must have been advancing unchecked for several years. Tuberculosis * was epidemic in England at that time, taking the life of one person out of every four in London,[15] yet almost nothing was understood about its cause or cure. It was thought to be hereditary, and there was no way of diagnosing it with certainty till its final symptoms appeared, when it was too late. First came a low fever, barely detectable, alternating with periods of good health and spirits; then lassitude, pallor, and loss of weight; later a persistent cough with blood-spitting; then finally a sudden decline and wasting of the body. This was the change Keats had to watch taking place in his mother, and it shook him to the depths. All the devotion he had felt to her as a child came surging back, redoubled by the passion of early adolescence. During his holidays at home he insisted on taking over the whole task of nursing her. He cooked her meals and administered her medicine; he read novels to her by day and sat up nights in an armchair, watching by her bed.[16] On returning to Enfield he must have cheered himself along with dreams of her recovery, for when the news of her death came, in March 1810, it was a sudden and staggering blow. On March 20 he followed one more coffin out of St. Stephen's and stood by one more grave in the churchyard at Coleman Street. Back at school, he was overcome by the loss for weeks afterward. Attacks of grief used to seize him during study hours; then he would hide behind the master's desk to fight it out alone, while the schoolroom was hushed in sympathy.

→»» «««

Poetry, Cyril Connolly has said, comes from the ferment of an unhappy childhood working through a noble imagination. Keats is no exception to this rule, though the painful experience of his childhood took a special form—intense happiness suddenly shattered by his father's death and his mother's defection. The tragedy of his mother's death not only upset whatever equilibrium he had managed to recover in his schooldays but added a far more complicated experience of bereavement to the earlier one. Just as he

---

* This term was not used till the end of the nineteenth century. In Keats's time the disease was called phthisis or, in its final stages, consumption.

lost his father at the age when he needed him most keenly, he found and then lost his mother again at the time of his sexual reawakening, when the unusual physical intimacy with her would have been especially disturbing. These losses did not, of course, make Keats a poet, but they laid a burden of emotion on him which would later seek an outlet, and they shaped the ways in which he received and interpreted his later experience just as surely as Byron's humiliating deformity and Calvinistic upbringing and Shelley's persecution at school formed their sensibility. By comparison with them, Keats seems to have reacted more straightforwardly to his experience, much as any healthy child would have done; so, rather than distorting his view of life, his bereavement appears at first only to have given it precocious depth and clarity. The line seems to run straight from his early experience to his later vision of

> Beauty that must die;
> And Joy, whose hand is ever at his lips
> Bidding adieu; and aching Pleasure nigh,
> Turning to poison while the bee-mouth sips. . . .

The intensity of the beauty, the joy, the pleasure, and the bitterness of their loss: this "knowledge of contrast, feeling for light and shade," which he spoke of in the last letter he ever wrote as "necessary for a poem," was the lesson of his boyhood. The experience of his adolescence, however, was to shape his later life in ways more obscure than this, which would become apparent only with the passing of the years.

His mother's death seems to have transformed Keats even more dramatically than his father's death six years before. All at once the aggressive and irresponsible boy who had taken such delight in jokes and brawls became a silent adolescent, concentrated, aloof, passionately absorbed in reading. Before this time he had shown no interest in books; now he would be up and at work before seven in the morning. Driven out by the masters to play cricket, he would walk up and down the garden with a book; at supper he ate with a folio propped between him and the table. Almost overnight he seems to have lost his taste for fighting; his battle with the world appears to have turned in on himself. George testified that from this time on he and John "never passed an opposing word" [17]—surely an exaggeration, but still some sign of

change. The fiery spirit portrayed by Holmes turned melancholy
and fretful, given, according to his brother, to "bitter fits of hypo-
chondriasm."

This was apparently not the usual melancholy moodiness of
early adolescence but a deep and prolonged depression in which
the experience of death was compounded, as it often is for sensi-
tive children, with a feeling of guilt. For Keats's absorption in
his studies, at first a way of withdrawing from a world which had
become too painful to deal with, soon became an endeavour to
win the adult approval he had scorned before, and thus perhaps
to fend off an obscure sense of responsibility for his mother's
suffering. Life suddenly became a serious affair. Already he had
to face the question of his future career, for only one more year
of school lay ahead. Then, probably within a few months of his
mother's death, he was confirmed.[18] This experience must have
raised large issues of human nature and destiny at a time when
they would have been most troubling to him. Behind all these
questions lay the greatest riddle of all—his mother. She had not
been a good woman; yet he had loved her. She had betrayed him,
then, betrayed herself, had returned to him; he had devoted himself to caring for her, then she had died. The dilemma of her nature, the irony of his failure, the meaning of death itself—all were
problems that he could neither solve nor keep from posing themselves.

Keats may have retreated into books as a refuge from painful
reality, but they soon became an imaginary world that almost
made up for the one he had lost. He went headlong through the
school library, devouring everything from *Robinson Crusoe* and
*The Arabian Nights* to Captain Cook's voyages and Robertson's
histories of Scotland and the reign of Charles V. Some of his
pocket money went on the thrillers popular with schoolboys of
his time, such as Beckford's *Vathek* and the novels of Monk Lewis
and Mrs. Radcliffe. Shakespeare, on first reading, appealed to
the same thirst for excitement, for Holmes recalled Keats's saying of *Macbeth* that no one would dare read it alone in a house
at two o'clock in the morning. History satisfied another deep
need, for heroes to worship. "The memory of great men" was to
be a constant theme of Keats's early poems, especially the champions of freedom such as Brutus and Milton, William Tell and
William Wallace, and King Alfred, whose portrait appears on the

seals of many of his early letters.[19] Years later this hero-worship-ping tendency led Keats on an out-of-the-way expedition to copy a letter of Nelson's—"very much to his honor"—to show his friends.

Something else drew him to the world of mythology and the wanderings of Aeneas—the first stirrings of a sense of beauty and pathos. Years later Cowden Clarke recalled Keats at this time as poring over a handbook of classical mythology till he knew it by heart; but this picture appears to be an elderly schoolmaster's sentimental exaggeration—unless Keats was fascinated, as was Leigh Hunt at the same age, by the alluring illustrations of the goddesses.[20] Yet as a voluntary task in his last year at school he undertook a prose translation of the entire *Aeneid*. Books now became a new world to conquer, and he threw himself into his studies with the same energy he had given to games and fighting. In his last two or three terms at school he won first place for volun-tary work each time, emerging with a miscellaneous assortment of prizes—Kauffman's *Dictionary of Merchandise,* Robertson's *History of America,* and Bonnycastle's *Introduction to Astron-omy.* The first made no impression on him, but the other two were to send his imagination on distant journeys.

In discovering this new world Keats also found the first and most important friend of his youth. Cowden Clarke, the head-master's son, was eight years his senior and had tutored him in his first lessons at Enfield. But with Keats's sudden intellectual de-velopment the gap between their ages began to narrow, and Clarke took an increasingly warm interest in his pupil. He was a born teacher, enthusiastic and generous, with a keen feeling for poetry and a gift for bringing the past to life; years later he was to make his name as a lecturer and writer on Chaucer and Shakespeare. Tall, sturdy, with bristly hair and a hearty laugh, he was also a first-rate cricketer and subsequently wrote a popular book on the game. He loved music and played the piano well; in the dormitory upstairs Keats used to lie awake nights listening to him practise Mozart and Handel. One evening Clarke found young Edward Holmes listening to him on the stairs, and on learning of the boy's passion for music agreed to give him lessons; Holmes grew up to be an accomplished pianist and to write the first biography of Mozart in English. Clarke encouraged Keats by lending him books from his own shelves and discussing his interests, in politics as well as literature, with him. Bishop Burnet's *History of My Own Time*, the folio volume which Clarke remembered Keats reading at supper, gave the boy his first glimpse of the long struggle for freedom in England. Keats also started borrowing *The Examiner*, the leading liberal magazine of the day, from Mr. Clarke, and from it he began to form a vivid picture of the contradictions and injustices of the world around him.

Soon enough he would have to come to grips with that world, in one of its more uncompromising aspects. Mrs. Jennings, who was now nearly seventy-five, realized she needed help in providing for her grandchildren's future. Shortly after her daughter's death she appointed two London merchants, John Rowland Sandell and Richard Abbey, to be their guardians and made over to them the money left her by her husband to hold in trust for the children. Sandell played a minor part in this responsibility; six years later he got into financial difficulties and fled from his creditors to Holland, where he later died. But Abbey, who had come from the same Yorkshire village as Mrs. Jennings and had known her family in London, readily assumed the role of authority in the Keats children's lives.

In all England it would have been hard to find a more solid pillar of the established order than Abbey—prosperous tea broker in Pancras Lane, landowner and churchwarden in Walthamstow, member of the Port of London Committee and the Honourable Company of Girdlers, Steward of the City of London National Schools Examinations, and twice Master of the Honourable Company of Patten Makers. Stout, conscientious, unimaginative, he was as old-fashioned in his dress as in his opinions and kept on wearing the white cotton stockings, breeches, and half-boots of the mid-eighteenth century for years after they had gone out of style. The prudence one looks for in a trustee took some strange forms with Abbey, however. The Sunday School Committee in Walthamstow, of which he was a member, awarded a guinea to every poor pupil who, after leaving the school, remained for a year in his first employment. But when Abbey became chairman he required that, in order to receive their guineas, the pupils produce the Bibles and prayer books they had been given on leaving school, to prove they had not sold them.[21] As Master of the Patten Makers, Abbey cut down on the Company's dinners, which had been noted for their conviviality, and outlawed the serving of

wine. It was Abbey who disapprovingly described Frances Jennings as a flirtatious young girl and dissolute young widow. He
thought she had married beneath her and suspected there was bad
blood in the family; but he resolved to do his duty, as he saw it,
by his four charges.

On becoming their guardian, Abbey must have discussed the
question of careers with John and George at some length. With
their limited resources, it was important they get off to a good
start. At fourteen or fifteen, it would seem, a boy hardly knows
who he is, much less what he wants to do with his life; yet this was
the usual age for middle-class lads to leave school and start work.
George apparently had no trouble making up his mind; Abbey
offered to take him into his counting-house and, as far as can be
known, he accepted without hesitation. But the tea brokerage,
or any other business, had little appeal for John. His record at
Mr. Clarke's suggested a professional career, but in what? He
could have entered the law by way of an apprenticeship, or have
followed the example of Cowden Clarke and gone into teaching;
but evidently neither of these possibilities tempted him. Advance-
ment in the Army required wealth and social position; as for a
naval career like his uncle's, he came three inches short of the
height required of an officer.[22] If Keats felt any disappointment
at giving up what may well have been the ambition of his boyhood, there is no record of it. The change which his mother's illness and death had made in him reached deep, for it is the only
explanation of his final choice of career. He decided to become
a doctor.

This decision has astonished so many of Keats's later readers
that it is often assumed that his guardian forced it on him. But
Cowden Clarke, his closest friend at the time, always understood
it was "his own selection" and not Abbey's.[23] Certainly from Abbey's point of view a medical career was a sensible choice. The
boy could not hope to become a physician—the topmost rank of
the profession, which required years of advanced study; but he
could easily qualify as an apothecary or surgeon, the equivalent
at that time of a general practitioner. This involved a shorter and
less expensive course of training, quite within John's reach—an
apprenticeship of some years to a local doctor, perhaps followed
by a year's study in a London hospital to qualify for the Surgeons'
Examination. Moreover, Mr. Thomas Hammond, the surgeon

of Edmonton, needed an apprentice in the summer of 1811. Hammond lived in Church Street, not far from Keats's own home, and often paid calls at the Clarke school; Mrs. Jennings must have known him, and it is probable that he tended Mrs. Rawlings in her last illness. He was the inevitable choice for Keats's master.

What Keats felt at the transfer of authority from John Clarke to Thomas Hammond is not known. Hammond was respected in the neighbourhood; he is said to have kept two apprentices, which suggests that his practice was large. Over and above the usual apprenticeship fee of £40, he charged a premium, as was customary—but of £200, a fairly high figure for a country doctor.[24] For this sum he provided his apprentice with room and board as well as training. Keats on his part had to promise in the traditional indentures not to "waste the goods of his said Master nor lend them unlawfully to any," or "commit fornication nor contract Matrimony within the said Term," or "play at Cards or Dice Tables or any other unlawful Games," or "haunt Taverns or Playhouses nor absent himself from his said Master's service day or night unlawfully," but to obey his master faithfully in everything he commanded.[25] The indentures were duly signed and the fees duly paid. The long, irresponsible years of boyhood were over. At the end of the summer term in 1811, not yet sixteen, Keats left Mr. Clarke's to serve as bound apprentice to Hammond for five years.

>>>————————————————————————————<<<

## Chapter Two

# The Widening Stream

M R. Hammond lived in a square-built, three-storied brick house on Church Street, standing back from the road in a front garden enclosed by a brick wall. A gate at the side led to the surgery, a small building in the back garden, where the doctor received his patients. Keats took his meals in the house; he studied and slept in a little room above the surgery with two narrow windows set under the roof. It was a cramped, airless place. On summer afternoons, with the sun beating down on the roof, he thought longingly of the half-holidays he had spent swimming in the New River or chasing the fish in the shady ponds at Enfield. Winter evenings, sitting in front of his fire with a book, he was sometimes overwhelmed by the "blue devils," the melancholy fits that used to plague him at school. Yet at first his new work left little time for moodiness or ruminations. His tasks were menial to start with: driving Hammond on his rounds, running errands, sweeping out the shop, keeping accounts, and helping with patients in the surgery. At the same time he was beginning his study of anatomy and physiology and the *materia medica*. Later he would make up pills and potions, and, under Hammond's direction, learn how to bleed and vaccinate, dress wounds, set bones, pull teeth, and apply leeches and cups and poultices—the sum of the accomplishments of most country doctors of that time.

Keats's choice of medicine as a career seems a puzzle only if one reads his life backward, from the standpoint of his later poetry, not forward; considering the possibilities that were open to him at fifteen, it was a good choice he made. Medicine in his day was being slowly revolutionized, like English society as a whole, by middle-class energy breaking through the traditional system. For centuries the practice of medicine had been divided among three distinct groups—physicians, surgeons, and apothecaries. In Keats's time the field was still dominated by the physicians, a small and conservative group trained at the universities, who alone took the title of "Doctor" and charged fees that only the wealthy could pay. They did little to meet the growing demand for medical care, however; as late as the beginning of Victoria's reign there were fewer than three hundred licensed physicians in all Britain, as compared with eight thousand surgeons.[1] It was the surgeons who tended most of the country's sick, consulting the physicians only in special cases; and their development of new medical techniques helped immeasurably to raise the general level of health, and with it the population, in the later eighteenth century. Before that time medicine was hardly a profession in the modern sense, and surgery was hardly a science; quacks were everywhere, and surgeons were not considered gentlemen. Not until 1745 did the surgeons break away from the medieval guild of the Barbers and Surgeons and begin to establish professional standards and qualifications of their own; not until 1800 were they granted a charter for their own Royal College. The apothecaries, the lowest rank in the medical hierarchy, soon followed suit. In the eighteenth century they were still classed as tradesmen and were forbidden by the physicians to dispense medical advice along with their drugs; in actuality they were the doctors of the poor. Only in 1815 did they finally win their independence of the physicians by an act of Parliament empowering the Society of Apothecaries to license candidates for general medical practice. By this time it was becoming customary for apothecaries also to qualify as surgeons by a year of "walking the hospitals" after the usual apprenticeship. Thus the modern system of medical training began to emerge and the various practices to draw together in a single profession.[2]

Keats could look forward, then, to a comfortable and respectable existence as a small-town doctor. But a boy of his talents does not choose his career for practical reasons alone; other important though more obscure motives must also have been at work. There was a strong admixture of idealism in his nature. Years later he confessed—not once but several times—that he was "ambitious of doing the world some good." Medicine must have first appealed to him, as it does to many medical students, as an opportunity to relieve suffering. But it is still more significant that he chose medicine of all careers in the year after the deeply affecting experience of his mother's death. His taking on the responsibilities for her care during her illness is a touching reminder of the possessive little boy guarding her sickroom with a sword; but it was also an experience which helped transform Keats from a thoughtless, brawling schoolboy into a sober and purposeful youth. In nursing his mother Keats seems to have been making amends for the rage he had felt at her remarriage; perhaps in taking up medicine after her death he was trying to relieve an unconscious sense of guilt for having failed to save her. On a more conscious level, his decision expressed the same sturdy resolution to face and subdue the harsh realities of the world, rather than retreat from them, that he had shown as a belligerent schoolboy at the time of his father's death. Whatever the reasons for his choice, Clarke tells us that he felt a deep satisfaction in his new work and that his apprenticeship was "the most placid period of his painful life."

Yet Clarke's picture of Keats as the industrious apprentice is, like his recollection of the prize-winning student, a little too schoolmasterish to be the whole truth. Keats was never placid by nature; his brother George described him at this time as "nervous" and "morbid." He appears to have been lonely in Edmonton. George, still his closest friend, was now working a dozen miles away in London. His schoolboy world seems to have broken up almost at once, for none of his Enfield acquaintances figured in his later life, and evidently he made no real friends for several years. As for girls, they remained remote and magical beings, glimpsed from afar and endlessly dreamed over, but never approached. Yet for all his shyness Keats was a healthy lad, with the sap of adolescence rising in his veins; this isolation, apparently self-imposed, is a sign that he had not really made his peace with the world.

In his loneliness he turned increasingly to his books or went rambling in the woods and fields around Edmonton. The sense of beauty was growing in him, and from his later writings it is plain how great a weight of emotion displaced from its lost human objects was now transferred to the natural world around him. The imagery of his later poems and letters suggests that what moved him most deeply in this world was its very apartness, the

wild secret life which he sensed going on far from human awareness. The birds singing without a thought of being heard, the
small bright-eyed animals running their errands through the
underbrush, "fruit ripening in stillness,"

> the birth, life, death
> Of unseen flowers in heavy peacefulness, . . .

offered him a world in which he could forget his own isolation.
He would lie for hours stretched out in a thicket or a nest of tall
grass, close to the moist and fertile earth, listening to the "little
noiseless noises" that betrayed the life stirring all around him.
Yet from this refuge close to the ground he was constantly looking
upward "into the fair and open face of heaven." The sky was the
field of freedom, where larks soared or pigeons tumbled in the
clear summer air; but he also imagined that it held mysterious
presences in its depths, angels and departed spirits. The blueness
of noon seemed to smile down on him, and the faces of the dead
peered out of the clouds at sunset; he lay awake at night, staring
up at the stars, which seemed to gaze unblinkingly down on the
earth below. With this sense of a mysteriously animated world
his solitude became an element in which he could escape from the
emptiness of the world around him.

Another refuge from loneliness was the world of books which
Cowden Clarke had opened up to him. On leaving Enfield, Keats
realized that his schooling was still far from complete, and both
the Clarkes, father and son, encouraged him to continue. As quick
a student as ever, he soon found he had plenty of time to spare
from his medical studies. During his first year with Hammond
he completed the prose translation of the *Aeneid* he had begun at
school, and perhaps it was to reward him for this effort that Mr.
Clarke gave him a scholarly edition of Ovid's *Metamorphoses*,
which Keats signed with a flourish, "John Keats emer [itus] 1812."
The same sprawling signature appears in a large, handsomely
illustrated edition of *Paradise Lost* which he had acquired two
years earlier: [3] already he was building up a small library. After
the *Aeneid*, Keats rounded out his knowledge of classical poetry
with Vergil's *Eclogues* and Ovid and Terence and Horace—all
of whom he could quote with effect years later—and continued
his reading of the French historians and philosophers, among

whom Voltaire became his favourite. Clarke recalled that he "translated and copied an immense quantity" during his time at Hammond's; he "devoured" books rather than read them. Naturally he was also reading the great English authors—Bacon and Addison and Swift and Locke, Shakespeare and Milton and Pope, Fielding and Smollett and Sterne. Though Pope's translation of Homer made a lasting impression on him,[4] most of Milton and Shakespeare was evidently still above him, as Leigh Hunt tells us they were for him at this time.[5] History was still Keats's absorbing interest, a field in which he "made himself learned for his age," according to his later friend Charles Brown.

Only one story survives from the early years of his apprenticeship, and it is probably apocryphal. One winter day Keats went with Hammond on a call at Mr. Clarke's in Enfield. As he waited outside with the horse, word went round the schoolyard that John Keats, the famous fighter, was sitting out front in the doctor's gig. Keats was deep in a book and did not notice the knot of younger boys that gathered to see him. Then one lad whispered a dare to another, and a snowball hit Keats square in the back. He whirled around to see his attacker take to his heels, leaped up to give the boy a thrashing, then—to the disappointment of the others— thought better of it and went back to his book. Somehow, they must have felt, he had changed.

Soon Keats began slipping out of the surgery once or twice every week with a book under his arm, to trudge four miles across the fields for an afternoon of talk with Cowden Clarke at Enfield. His old tutor was a link with the past and a guide to the future. He gave Keats the intellectual direction he needed; at the same time his humour and energy must have been a healthy counterpoise to Keats's spells of gloom. Keats still addressed him deferentially as "sir," but the constant sharing of interests drew them close together. Clarke was a keen theatre-goer and used to walk fifteen miles into London to see John Kemble or Mrs. Siddons—the sun already setting on her magnificence—play Shakespeare at Covent Garden. His enthusiasm was infectious. On summer afternoons the two young men used to sit in an arbour on the far side of the school grounds reading the plays aloud, or wander through the shaded lanes of Enfield debating some point of literature or history. Often their talk ran on after supper, when Clarke would play

a Mozart sonata or two and Keats would pick out another book
from his shelves; then they would walk halfway to Edmonton together, to part with a handshake in the middle of the fields.

"Nothing is finer for the purposes of great productions," Keats
later wrote, "than a very gradual ripening of the intellectual
powers." It is striking that he did not show any real interest in
poetry till late adolescence—till nearly eighteen, in fact. All the
elements were there—the sensitivity to language, the intensity of
feeling, the sensuous response to the natural world; but they did
not fuse in one great moment of discovery till Clarke introduced
him to Spenser. One afternoon, probably in the summer of 1813,
Clarke read the "Epithalamion" aloud and looked up to see Keats's
face transfigured with pleasure. This was poetry of a kind he had
never heard before: all the joyous bustle of the wedding morning,
the noisy procession to the church, the bride blushing with down-
cast eyes, the feasting and dancing, the wine splashing the walls,
the bells clanging through the town, then at last nightfall and
the silent consummation, recalling the love of Cynthia and Endymion, of Jupiter and Alcmena, and of Maia, the mother of
Hermes,

> whenas Jove her took
> In Tempe, lying on the flowery grass
> Twixt sleep and wake, after she weary was
> With bathing in the Acidalian brook.

This encounter with Spenser was a turning point. Up to this time
Keats had never borrowed a book of poetry from Clarke; that night
he went home with the first volume of *The Faerie Queene*. Clarke
thought it was "mere boyish ambition" that led him to ask for it;
but the next time they met he found that Keats had gone through
the book "like a young horse through a spring meadow—ramp-
ing."

*The Faerie Queene* led Keats into a new world of bright colour
and honied language, of romantic adventure and chivalric devotion far above the level of actual life. He never quite recovered
from this first discovery; the most significant poetry he later wrote
was an attempt to set this world of imagination in clear perspective against the world of sober experience. But for Keats at eighteen, with the best of life lying before him, the boundaries between
dream and reality were still unclear, and Spenser's poetry was

a trumpet call to rouse the sleeping figures of his own imagination. Such a discovery is no more, or less, mysterious than falling in love; the only question is why one poet and not another should touch it off. The supple music of Spenser's verse had a strong appeal to him, and the painterly effects of his description. But Clarke specifically mentioned Keats's "ecstatic" expression as he listened to "the more passionate passages" of the "Epithalamion"; apparently the innocent yet exuberant sensuality of Spenser's wedding song opened up a realm of poetic experience which had previously existed for Keats only in dream. His narrow life at Hammond's had dammed up all his longings for an ideal beauty, bright and sweet and soft and fair; now they burst out into this new channel. Almost overnight his life acquired a direction it had lacked before.

John Clarke was surprised and even amused to hear of Keats's new enthusiasm, but Cowden Clarke, a versifier himself, did all he could to encourage it. His tastes in poetry were typical of a well-read young schoolmaster of his time, broad but not revolutionary; it is doubtful, for instance, that he yet knew the work of Wordsworth, who was still unrecognized and largely unread in 1813.[6] He introduced Keats to the principles of poetry held by the eighteenth century, with its carefully distinguished styles and clearly defined forms and moralizing bias, and, except for Spenser and Shakespeare, their reading at first kept to the standard authors, from Milton to Gray—the limits established by Johnson's *Lives of the English Poets*. From Spenser it was an easy move to Spenser's eighteenth-century imitators, Thomson and Shenstone and Beattie, and then to Milton's early poems and the more introspective and elegiac poets of the mid-century, Gray and Collins and Cowper. Yet despite the great deal of uninspired poetry Keats read at the start, he rapidly developed a fresh and perceptive taste of his own. The passages he marked in his copy of *The Faerie Queene* show a love of precisely observed colour and light and sound and movement, and an image compressed into a single explosive epithet filled him with an almost physical delight. One day he and Clarke read together a passage of Spenser describing the monsters of a magic sea-storm:

> All dreadful portraits of deformity,
> Bright Scolopendraes, arm'd with silver scales,

> Great whirlpools, which all fishes make to flee,
> Spring-headed Hydras, and sea-shouldering whales. . . .*

As Clarke recalled, Keats "hoisted himself up, and looked burly and dominant, as he said, 'What an image that is—sea-shouldering whales!'" For a moment he was himself shaking the weight of oceans from his back. From the beginning poetry was an intensely physical experience for him, felt almost literally in every nerve and along every fibre of his body.

Spenser did more than open Keats's eyes to poetry: he led him to write his first poem. From our vantage point we can see all his past and future converging on this act; to Keats himself it must have seemed a miracle, an event lifted out of time. The "Imitation of Spenser" is a strangely unpromising first performance, full of clumsy syntax and overblown imagery, written in a worn-out eighteenth-century idiom. But though Keats later destroyed much of his early poetry, he included the "Imitation" in his first volume and acknowledged it as his first poem: somehow it meant a great deal to him. If it is true that a writer often reveals himself more directly in his first work than he ever does again, this poem may offer a clue not merely to Keats's idea of poetry at the start of his career, but also to his deeper reasons for writing it. At first glance the "Imitation" recalls one of Keats's favourite passages from *The Faerie Queene,* the description of the Bower of Bliss, a Circean paradise of crystal streams and laurel groves. Yet a closer reading reveals something very different from mere imitation. Spenser's landscape is a clear-cut allegory of sensual temptation to be overcome; Keats's is a vision of almost indescribable beauty, transfigured with inexpressible meaning like a dream.

But what is he dreaming of? It is a morning in spring; the rising sun lights up flower-spangled hills surrounding a placid lake. An island overgrown with roses lies in its midst, golden-scaled fish circle in its depths, and on its surface floats a single swan. The scene is a romantic stage-set; and yet Keats insists it is far more than this:

> Ah! could I tell the wonders of an isle
> That in that fairest lake had placed been,
> I could e'en Dido of her grief beguile;
> Or rob from aged Lear his bitter teen:

---

* *Faerie Queene,* II.xii.23. I take the liberty of transposing the second and fourth lines of the quatrain.

> For sure so fair a place was never seen,
> Of all that ever charm'd romantic eye:
> It seem'd an emerald in the silver sheen
> Of the bright waters; or as when on high,
> Through clouds of fleecy white, laughs the cœrulean sky.

It is a scene strikingly similar to his first view of Lake Windermere, some four years later, which stunned him into silence. But why did it move him so? A dream cannot be pressed too far for its meaning, yet a meaning is always there. For all the staleness of its phrasing, the freshness of the morning in this poem evokes the wonder of another dawn—the new-created world of early childhood. It is significant that the swan at the centre of the scene, floating proudly on the bosom of the lake, appears in several of Keats's other early poems as an explicit symbol for the poet—Bryon, his friend Mathew, himself. If this swan represents—below the level of conscious intention—Keats himself in his dawning consciousness, the lake on which he floats, ringed about with hills and arched over by a sky smiling with light, seems a dreamlike re-creation of the child's first horizons, the circle of his mother's arms and the meridian of his father's gaze. It is curious how this swan encircled by sky and water—two primordial symbols for male and female—calls up another image from Keats's earliest memories: the painted sign of a swan in a hoop that no doubt hung outside his grandfather's stable.[7]

Another interesting cluster of images is the trio of flower, fish, and swan, for Keats used these same three images a year later as explicit symbols of the spiritual growth of a young poet, in a passage which strikingly suggests the processes of conception and embryonic development he had learned in his medical texts:

> For thou wast once a flowret blooming wild,
> Close to the source, bright, pure, and undefil'd,
> Whence gush the streams of song: in happy hour
> Came chaste Diana from her shady bower,
> Just as the sun was from the east uprising;
> And, as for him some gift she was devising,
> Beheld thee, pluck'd thee, cast thee in the stream
> To meet her glorious brother's greeting beam.
> I marvel much that thou hast never told
> How, from a flower, into a fish of gold
> Apollo chang'd thee; how thou next didst seem
> A black-eyed swan upon the widening stream;

> And when thou first didst in that mirror trace
> The placid features of a human face. . . .

Perhaps it is significant, then, that the swan in the first poem still has sole possession of the lake, while in the last stanza the water rippling in delight up the side of the rose-strewn island evokes a contentment still closer to the oceanic consciousness of the infant.

This does not mean that Keats intended even half-consciously to describe the child's first inexpressible felicity in these stanzas. Rather it appears that, in trying to paint the most beautiful scene he could imagine, he drew on certain unconscious images of his own childhood experience and thus cast over the landscape an aura of feeling derived from his earliest memories—the serenity of the swan at the center of the scene, the happy unity of water and earth and sky around him, and the beauty of the flowers drenched by stream or tide in the kind of joyous intermingling which Keats was later to describe as "moistened and bedewed with Pleasures." Clearly this landscape was no Bower of Bliss to be destroyed, but a paradise to be regained. Keats seems to have regarded even the Bower of Bliss in this spirit, for he later repeated to a friend in love the very advice which Spenser intended his hero to refuse:

> "So passeth, in the passing of a day,
> Of mortal life the leaf, the bud, the flower;
> Ne more doth flourish after first decay,
> That erst was sought to deck both bed and bower
> Of many a lady, and many a paramour.
> Gather therefore the rose, whilst yet is prime,
> For soon comes age, that will her pride deflower:
> Gather the rose of love, whilst yet is time,
> Whilst loving thou mayst loved be with equal crime."

For Keats at eighteen the passing of beauty "in the passing of a day" was all too vivid a recollection. His first poem suggests not only how deep the experience of childhood happiness, once enjoyed to overflowing and then suddenly snatched away, had sunk into his mind; it also suggests that the discovery of poetry was so momentous an event to him because it pointed out a road back to that lost paradise of sensuous and emotional delight.

→»·«←

Between work and study and his new absorption in poetry, Keats's life may well have seemed placid to Cowden Clarke. But Clarke did not know the whole truth: Keats did not tell him of his first efforts to write poetry, nor did he mention his growing restiveness in his work. For reasons which are not clear, Keats began to rebel against his master. "Seven years ago," he wrote in 1819, thinking of the constant renewal of the body's tissues, "it was not this hand that clench'd itself against Hammond." This gesture seems to have been no mere flare-up of temper but a settled antipathy. In later years Keats was almost as silent about his apprenticeship as about his boyhood; when he did mention his days with Hammond, it was to regret he had undergone "a one of them." Clearly Hammond was no John Clarke; perhaps he was a neglectful master. It was not uncommon for masters to collect large fees from apprentices and give them little training in return; and even Abbey came to think that Hammond "did not conduct himself as he ought to have done to his young pupil." Perhaps Keats also struck Hammond as an unsatisfactory pupil, with his habit of slipping off on afternoons and returning late with a book under his arm. A nameless fellow apprentice described him as "an idle loafing fellow," and this may well have echoed Hammond's own opinion. But the real trouble seems to have been a conflict of personalities or opinions. Hammond and his pupil did not agree, Clarke later recalled rather vaguely; "Keats's tastes [were] totally opposed to his master's." [8]

One wonders what subjects were discussed around Hammond's dinner table. It is improbable that Hammond would have had any opinions on poetry, for few surgeons at that time had any literary education; a much likelier topic is politics. Keats's rebellion against Hammond may have been only one phase of his growing quarrel with the established order, on which the evidence is clear. The temperature of political debate was rising in England as the war drew to an end. The year 1812 marked the turning point, with Napoleon's retreat from Moscow; with his abdication after the fall of Paris in April 1814, it seemed that peace had come at last. Yet England was more bitterly divided than it had been for over a century. The gap between the rich and poor had steadily widened under the pressures of twenty years of war. The average worker paid out over half of his meagre earnings in in-

direct taxation, but under a corrupt and antiquated voting system neither he nor the middle-class citizen had any real voice in
Parliament. Factory hands in the Midlands, driven out of work
by the new cotton-spinning machines, began smashing them in
despair; Parliament replied with a Frame-Breaking Bill which
punished these acts with hanging. In protesting against the bill
in his maiden speech in the House of Lords, young Lord Byron
described the wretchedness of the factory towns as worse than the
most squalid provinces he had seen in his travels in Turkey. But
the countryman's lot was no better. Cut off from the land by
enclosures, pauperized by the parish dole, the farm worker faced
starvation as food prices rose; but if he went poaching to feed his
children, he risked being transported to the colonies. Yet all this
while the gentry were living more comfortably than ever in their
fine country houses; and in London the fashionable world was
entering a new era of extravagance and dissoluteness centered at
Carlton House. Here the Prince Regent squabbled publicly with
his wife, whom he had accused of bearing an illegitimate child
while living abroad, and managed in 1813 to deprive her of the
custody of the young princess. Small wonder that he was hissed
by a London mob in 1814 as he led a procession of the Allied
sovereigns at the celebrations for the Peace of Paris.

It is easy to guess how a quick-witted and idealistic lad of
seventeen or eighteen would react to these events, and it is not
surprising that of the nine or ten poems Keats wrote during his
apprenticeship at Hammond's, four dealt with political themes.
Injustice and autocracy ruled in England no less than in Europe;
in the end, there seemed little to choose between the tyranny of
Napoleon and that of the despots who opposed him. Such, at
least, was the view which Keats absorbed from his regular reading
of *The Examiner,* the most articulate liberal voice of the time.
This magazine was a red rag to the John Bulls of the day. When
Abbey learned that Keats had begun reading it at Mr. Clarke's,
he swore that "if he had fifty children he would not send one of
them to that school." [9] Keats laughed when he told the story to
Cowden Clarke, but it shows him already in secret revolt against
his guardian. It was a time for taking sides—between conservative
or liberal, faith in the Thirty-Nine Articles or in human perfectibility, the complacencies of the aristocracy or the reforming
zeal of the middle-class intellectuals. In the front ranks of the

struggle was the youthful editor of *The Examiner,* Leigh Hunt, who was leading an attack on Tory oppression that drew the attention of all England at this time.

Here was a man to turn any young idealist's head: poet, critic, polemicist, wit, and something of a dandy to boot. Born in 1784, the son of a fashionable London preacher from Barbados, Hunt was a precocious lad who at sixteen published a facile little volume of verse which went through four editions in as many years. From this he turned to more original work in theatre criticism while clerking in the War Office, then joined his older brother to set up *The Examiner* in 1808. John Hunt was a sober and courageous journalist, dedicated to upholding traditional English liberty against government encroachment. He acted as manager and news editor of the new weekly, giving his mercurial brother most of the political commentary as well as the reviews of art and music and literature to write. At once the paper was attacked as pro-Bonapartist, and soon it ran afoul of the Tory censorship. Three times in its first three years the Hunts were haled into court for discussing such touchy subjects as the sale of army promotions by the Duke of York's mistress, the unpopularity of George III's ministers, and the flogging of soldiers; but all three prosecutions were dismissed. The trials succeeded merely in raising *The Examiner*'s circulation and adding glitter to Leigh Hunt's reputation.

So when, in March 1812, *The Morning Post* hailed the Regent on his fiftieth birthday as the "Glory of the People" and an "Adonis in Loveliness," Hunt rose gaily to the challenge. "Now no one can accuse me of not writing a libel," he remarked to Charles Lamb, and a few days later his article on "Princely Qualities" appeared. No Adonis but "a corpulent man of fifty," the Regent was described as "a violator of his word, a libertine over head and ears in disgrace, a despiser of domestic ties, and the companion of gamblers and demireps." A fourth indictment was promptly issued against the Hunts; eight months went by while the Regent tried to buy them off; then at last they were tried before a jury packed with Government officials. Public interest was unprecedented: ten thousand copies of *The Examiner* were sold in the hour after the verdict was published. It was, of course, Guilty. On February 3, 1813, the sentence was pronounced. It was a stiff one: each of the brothers was to serve two years in a separate prison, pay a fine of £500, and provide £500 security for good behaviour for the five years following. Undaunted, Leigh Hunt rolled off in a hackney coach to the Horsemonger Lane Gaol with his head still high, dressed in his natty best, and carry-ing a slim volume of the neo-Latin poet Erycius Puteanus.

Imprisonment made Hunt's name as a martyr to the liberal cause. Tom Moore wrote him verses of glowing tribute, and young Percy Shelley sent him £20 to help meet the fine. A repentant juror later offered him £500, which Hunt refused—a quixotic gesture he could hardly afford, since he was already deep in debt. Nevertheless he borrowed several hundred pounds with which to turn his two prison rooms into a snug apartment papered with trellised roses and furnished with bookcases, busts of his favourite poets, and a piano. Nothing was overlooked that could disguise the reality of the situation. Venetian blinds hid the bars of his win-dows, the prison yard outside was planted with pansies and sweet-briar, and the ceiling of his living room was painted with a blue sky and fleecy clouds. While his brother John served his term quietly at Coldbath Fields, Leigh Hunt moved his wife and children into his apartment and began receiving his admirers—James Mill and Jeremy Bentham, Henry Brougham the great Whig lawyer and his defence counsel, Thomas Barnes of *The Times,* Benjamin Haydon the historical painter, William Godwin the radical phi-losopher, Maria Edgeworth the novelist, William Hazlitt, Charles and Mary Lamb, and many others. The guests were allowed to stay till ten in the evening. Tom Moore brought Byron with him, who was so taken with "the wit in the dungeon" that he gave a dinner party in the cell. So Hunt's evenings were spent in pleasant conversation on Elizabethan literature and Italian poetry, which he had begun to translate; the days sped by in reading and writing, strumming on the piano, playing battledore and shuttlecock with his children, and dashing off political commentary for *The Ex-aminer,* which he continued to edit through his term. In fact, his imprisonment only brought new lustre to the paper, since Barnes and Hazlitt were now regular contributors, with Lamb and Haydon occasionally joining in.

Echoes of this excitement arrived in Edmonton with every Saturday's *Examiner;* but Keats was beginning to follow Hunt's adventures at closer range. Cowden Clarke had met Hunt at a musical party in London in 1812 and had been dazzled by his jaunty charm. Now he went each week to visit Hunt in jail, bringing him fruit and eggs from Enfield and joining in the discussions around the fireside. His reports of these expeditions crystallized Keats's political loyalties. Hunt supplied him with just the example of bravado he needed in his smouldering rebellion against Hammond and Abbey. The distant glories of Camperdown and Trafalgar faded from his mind. Now the Government itself became the enemy, backed up by its red-coated troops and the machinery of Church and State; and the hero of his time was an elegant young man discoursing on Spenser and writing ironic editorials from a prison cell. Hunt's poetry gave Keats a new model for his own, while *The Examiner* continued to guide his opinions. In the second poem of Keats that has come down to us, a stilted sonnet "On Peace," we find him closely following *The Examiner's* editorial line of the spring of 1814. At that time Hunt hoped that the Peace of Paris might bring about constitutional monarchy in Europe, and so Keats echoed him: [10]

> O Europe! let not sceptred tyrants see
>     That thou must shelter in thy former state;
> Keep thy chains burst, and boldly say thou art free;
>     Give thy kings law—leave not uncurbed the great;
>     So with the horrors past thou'lt win thy happier fate!

Though these hopes were soon to be dashed, for a few months it seemed that the liberal cause, at home as well as abroad, might carry the day.

All this while another current was beginning to run under the surface of Keats's existence, one still less visible to Clarke than his rebellion against Hammond. The opposite sex was beginning to exert its tidal pull on Keats's life, even though he seems to have long resisted its force. Evidently his deep-seated reserve and the half-monastic isolation of his life at Hammond's made him shy and awkward on his first ventures into society. Keats later confessed that he had made almost all his friends through his brother George, who, it appears, lost no time in forming a circle of new acquaintances in London after leaving school. Most of these friends—Briggs, Peachey, Kirkman, Archer, Squibb, Frith, Parker, Beilby—remain mere names. But a few—William Haslam, a young law clerk, and Henry and Charles Wylie, two spruce young lads with a warmhearted mother, the widow of an infantry officer, and a shy but charming younger sister—were to play important parts in both brothers' lives. On his occasional visits to town Keats began to slip into this circle; but here he found a new difficulty. George was turning into a handsome young fellow who could bring a smile and a blush to a pretty girl's face; but John was often taken for George's younger brother, just as in his schooldays. For this his height was chiefly to blame. At his full growth he reached not quite five foot one—not remarkably short in those days, when five foot six was the average and five foot ten was tall, but still about ten inches shorter than George, who was growing nearly as tall as their famous uncle. So on his first meetings with young ladies Keats had to struggle against a feeling of physical insignificance, even though, from all accounts, he was a good-looking young man. Yet all his self-consciousness could not stifle his susceptibility to beauty; rather his stand-offishness only encouraged his boyish tendency to idealize women. "When I was a Schoolboy," he wrote some years later, "I thought a fair Woman a pure Goddess, my mind was a soft nest in which some one of them slept though she knew it not." Now, at closer contact, he scented danger—the risk both of rebuff and of dis-illusionment. If he must fall in love—and at his age it was in-evitable—far safer to choose some unattainable beauty whom he could worship from a safe distance in secret.

This is a common adventure at seventeen or eighteen; what was uncommon in Keats's experience was both the distance and the duration of the involvement. It began casually one summer evening in 1814 during the riotous Peace celebrations in London, when he went for a fling at Vauxhall, the public gardens in Southwark, which were then at the height of their popularity. And there a chance encounter with a nameless young woman fired what seems to have been the first real passion of his life. The meeting itself was nothing: for half an hour or so he watched her as she talked with friends over a table, enthralled by her every gesture, waiting for a smile of recognition she never quite gave him. The verses he wrote afterward—"Fill for me a brimming bowl"—seem lighthearted enough, mere conventional protesta-tions of longing and despair. Yet the emotion which the experi-ence kindled somehow survived and grew to a talismanic sig-nificance in Keats's mind. For, he maintained in two sonnets of 1818, it still haunted him four years later:

> Time's sea hath been five years at its slow ebb;
>   Long hours have to and fro let creep the sand;
> Since I was tangled in thy beauty's web,
>   And snared by the ungloving of thine hand. . . .*

The remembrance of her beauty, he claimed, had stood between him and every other woman he had met in those years; still more, her power over him had come to mean a fulfilment in love which at twenty-two he feared he would die without attaining:

> And when I feel, fair creature of an hour!
>   That I shall never look upon thee more,
> Never have relish in the faery power
>   Of unreflecting love!—then on the shore
> Of the wide world I stand alone, and think
> Till love and fame to nothingness do sink.

It is always a delicate task to gauge the weight of biographical implication in a poem, though it may be said that Keats's poems in general have a more direct relation to his life than the work of most poets. Yet even if in these sonnets he was more interested in working out a theme than in expressing an emotion, still they imply that the casual experience of 1814 had become a refuge from troubling actuality for him—whether he understood the exact nature of his feelings or not. And the early lyric already hints at a recurrent theme of his later work: beauty as a rare and unearthly visitant, who appears and then departs as suddenly as she came, leaving a chill of premonition in the air behind her.

-»»-«««-

As 1814 drew on, Keats's life darkened again. His grandmother, Alice Jennings, now seventy-eight, fell ill; in the middle of December she died. Nothing is known of her illness; but however she died, it was a painful loss for Keats. For ten years she had been a second mother to him and an example of gentle selflessness he could never forget. About a week after her death he wrote a sonnet to her memory ("As from the darkening gloom a silver dove"), fervently asserting his faith in her soul's reward in heaven. So deep were his feelings about her that he apparently never showed the

---

* Keats in 1818 had either forgotten the precise date of the encounter or preferred the euphony of "five" to "four" in the first line.

poem to anyone till two years later and then would not tell even his brothers to whom he had written it.[11] He kept his grief, as he did his other emotions, to himself. Besides, he was now head of the family, to whom the younger ones would look for support. With Mrs. Jennings' death the pattern of their life together was finally broken up. Fanny, now eleven years old, was taken off to live in the stale respectability of the Abbey household in Walthamstow. A letter which George wrote her that winter from Pancras Lane, asking her to make him an eyeshade to wear at work, gives a glimpse of her as a shy and dutiful little girl struggling to improve in her music and skipping rope in the cold weather to stave off chilblains. Tom was taken out of school and set up beside George on a stool in Abbey's counting-house; Keats was left alone in Edmonton.

A deep depression now overtook him, from which he could escape only through poetry. A few stilted stanzas addressed "To Hope" express the mood of numb despair, all too familiar at nineteen, in which the world appears too large and indifferent even to struggle against. Grief for his parents, anxiety about his future, doubts of his ability to win a woman's love, misgivings for the cause of freedom—these evidently were the thoughts that assailed him as he sat before his solitary fire or wandered through the woods in the early winter evenings. He found companionship only in the verse of two young poets—Byron, the pale mysterious exile of *Childe Harold,* nursing his secret sorrow, and Chatterton, "the marvellous boy" who, rather than face failure, poisoned himself in a London garret at seventeen. With them, at least in imagination, Keats could share his moods. In the poems he wrote during these dark months the world seemed a prison, and death at times the only release; poetry itself was a kind of communication with the immortal dead, or of the dead with one another, and the poet a birdlike figure who escapes the bonds of earth to join them. These are the outpourings of an unhappy adolescent; yet they sound two central motives of Keats's later work—a sense of the constant hovering regard of the dead, and the attempt to reach a transcendent realm of the spirit through poetry. By some healthy instinct, Keats seems to have kept these melancholy poems to himself; [12] but, locked within his own gloom, he could not have found his loneliness easier to bear.

At last this spell was broken, by a real release from a real prison.

Leigh Hunt's two-year term was to expire on February 2, 1815. This was a glorious event, a vindication of both the liberal spirit and the poetic mind; and Keats decided to commemorate it in verse. The resulting sonnet was a tame echo of Tom Moore's lines to Hunt; yet it expressed something of Keats's sense of vicarious liberation. For, he asserted, even in prison a spirit like Hunt's was far freer than the "minion of grandeur" who bolted him in:

> In Spenser's halls he strayed, and bowers fair,
>   Culling enchanted flowers; and he flew
> With daring Milton through the fields of air:
>   To regions of his own his genius true
> Took happy flights. Who shall his fame impair
>   When thou are dead, and all thy wretched crew?

Imprisoned at Hammond's, Keats caught a glimpse through Hunt of a liberty of the imagination that only poets know, and an immortality of fame more triumphant even than that of the soul.

In his enthusiasm, he decided that the time had come for him to speak out as clearly as Hunt had done. Cowden Clarke, he knew, was going up to London to congratulate Hunt on his release; Keats met him in the fields and walked with him a good part of the way. At the last gate he stopped to say good-bye to Clarke, hesitated, then handed him the sonnet to Hunt. Clarke was surprised: this was the first he knew of Keats's writing poetry. Yet he sensed at once the significance of the moment. He would never forget—or so he said years later—the "conscious look" with which Keats gave him the poem. In the excitement of his release, the sonnet evidently made no impression on Hunt; [13] but it represented an important step forward for Keats. He had declared himself a poet to the man who was his one link with the world of poets, and committed himself to Hunt's side in politics —an act with more consequences than he could yet glimpse.

At about the time he worked up his courage to show his sonnet to Clarke, Keats found another friend to share his interest in poetry. George Felton Mathew, one of the young men Keats met through George in London, seems at first an unlikely companion. Mathew later described himself as "of a serious and tender nature," "thoughtful beyond his years," and "diffident to the last degree." The son of a prosperous textile dealer with a home in the fashionable new Regent's Park, he was then clerking in the firm of a West India merchant, "a secular and uncongenial employment" which he found a trial to his "weak nerves and trembling feelings." Mathew's enthusiasms in poetry ran to longwinded romantic epics such as *Ossian* and Wieland's *Oberon,* and saccharine lady versifiers such as Mary Tighe. A few years later Keats found it almost impossible to believe that he had once enjoyed such stuff; but now, in the pleasure of finding a "genius-loving heart" like his own, he identified his tastes with Mathew's and exalted their friendship into a "brotherhood in song" like that of Beaumont and Fletcher. The evenings they spent reading their verses to each other must have been a decided change from his sessions with Clarke; but Mathew gave Keats what his old tutor could not—the admiration of a contemporary and the stimulus of a fellow craftsman.

Mathew belonged to a large family, and Keats was soon drawn into this circle. Mathew's sister Mary took an interest in her brother's "poetical friend" and copied his verses in the album which, like most young ladies of the day, she kept for her friends' literary efforts. So did her cousins Ann and Caroline Mathew, at whose house in Goswell Street George Keats had first introduced his brother to the set. They were not a lively clan, the Mathews. Both families were earnestly evangelical, and one of their cousins became a famous "apostle of temperance." Neither Ann nor Caroline ever married; instead, they grew into sour spinsters, full of pious horror at their youthful frivolities. These were innocent enough—"little domestic concerts and dances," as Mathew described them, at which the young ladies tinkled on the pianoforte and attempted arias from *Don Giovanni* and the young gentlemen perspired through the quadrille. If Keats did not shine in this part, his talent for writing new words to the young ladies' favourite tunes was highly appreciated. He soon learned to string together the clichés of the most popular poets of the times in graceful little lyrics; at the same time, it appears, some of his shyness began to wear off.

It is hard to imagine Ann or Caroline Mathew as one of the goddesses who slumbered in Keats's mind during his lonely years at Edmonton; but there was a dark-haired bright-eyed beauty in this little circle who evidently filled the place. Mary Frogley held the center of the stage at the Mathews' parties; all the young men flirted with her in turn, including George Keats and even Mathew himself. If three sonnets "On Woman" which Keats wrote at about this time [14] were inspired by her, as many of his early poems were said to be, Keats was struck almost speechless by her beauty:

> Light feet, dark violet eyes, and parted hair;
>> Soft dimpled hands, white neck, and creamy breast,
>> Are things on which the dazzled senses rest
> Till the fond, fixed eyes forget they stare. . . .

Yet this dazzling apparition, he at once realized, could also be "flippant, vain, Inconstant, childish, proud, and full of fancies." In her impulsive gaiety, which offered to release him from the constrictions of his own shyness, a woman like Mary elated him yet disturbed him profoundly. Torn between longing and timidity, he felt far safer with young ladies like the Mathew sisters, of "lovely modesty and virtues rare," who combined "dove-like" innocence and "mild intelligence."

> Ah! who can e'er forget so fair a being?
>> Who can forget her half retiring sweets?
>> God! she is like a milk-white lamb that bleats
> For man's protection, . . .

he exclaimed, in lines which, it is astonishing to learn, moved him to tears at the time he wrote them.[15] This division within his feelings—the belle matched against the bluestocking—clearly echoes the earlier and deeper one between the two very different women who had dominated his boyhood—his mother and his grandmother. In the fascination of a vivacious and unpredictable beauty like Mary he must also fear rejection or even betrayal; evidently he could trust himself only in a non-sexual relationship. So Ann and Caroline became the first of several pairs of sisters, usually older than himself, with whom Keats was to carry on a kind of semi-serious platonic affair, safe in the company of one of his brothers.

This friendship with the Mathew sisters inspired what are certainly the feeblest of all his early poems. In the summer of 1815 Keats wrote two sets of verses to thank them for sending him "a beautiful dome-shaped shell" from the seaside. Cast in the jingling measures of Tom Moore, they mix nightingales and cherubs, sylphs and moonbeams and dewy flowers with platonic compliments to the sisters' "elegant, pure, and aerial minds." Keats drew on their favourite poem, Wieland's *Oberon,* to describe the shell as "the work of a fay," a magic canopy under which the fairy king crept, when deserted by Titania, to strum sad songs on his lute:

> In this little dome, all those melodies strange,
>     Soft, plaintive, and melting, for ever will sigh;
> Nor e'er will the notes from their tenderness change;
>     Nor e'er will the music of Oberon die. . . .

In style and sentiment, these poems are atrocious; yet they merely show Keats following the worst poetic fashions of his day. It was not an easy time to be a young poet. After the great achievement of Dryden and Pope, English poetry had long since run dry in the sandy flats of didactic verse or settled in the marshes of sentimentalism. The poets who appeared at the end of the eighteenth century to give it a new voice and new substance had hardly yet won a hearing. Meanwhile the lilting sentimentalities of Moore, the patriotic flutings of Campbell, and the elegant inanities of Rogers held the stage, along with the tireless chivalrics of Scott and the melancholy posturings of the young Byron.

It should be no surprise, then, that at nineteen Keats had not surmounted the mediocre poetry that was in him and all around him. He was not one of those rare poets who are born, not made. He lacked the endowments or opportunities with which the other great poets of his time started—Blake's unerring ear for word-music, for instance, or Wordsworth's experience of the French Revolution, or Byron's exotic adventures in the Mediterranean, or Shelley's wide knowledge of the classics. As Carlyle said of Burns, "Every genius is an impossibility till he appear"; but Keats seems one of the greatest impossibilities of all. He was to rise above his own narrow background by stubborn ambition and hard work, making himself a poet by studying the best examples of poetry he could find and absorbing what he could from them, one after another; but as yet he had hardly begun. His verses to the Mathew sisters merely mark the depth from which his climb upward must be measured.

With his new friendships in London, Keats had still more reason to chafe against the narrow limits of his life at Hammond's; but the excitement of the spring of 1815 was enough to make any young man restless. The news that Napoleon had escaped from Elba burst like a thunderclap on the Congress of Vienna at the beginning of March. The Hundred Days had begun. While Louis XVIII scurried to Belgium for refuge, the Emperor swept triumphantly up from Cannes to Paris, welcomed by his people on every side. England at once despatched Wellington to the Low Countries while the Allies regrouped their forces. With the odds mounting against him, Napoleon struck out in mid-June, and at last the game ended at Waterloo. But for many English liberals this was no real victory. William Hazlitt described it as "the sacred triumph of kings over mankind." [16] Even Leigh Hunt, an advocate of constitutional monarchy, had come out for Napoleon that spring, disillusioned by the sovereigns' betrayal of their promises to their peoples at Vienna.[17] When the Emperor arrived at Plymouth to seek political asylum with the English, huge crowds gathered on the shore to cheer him. Keats's reaction to these events may be gathered from a little poem which he wrote at the height of the Hundred Days, when the bells were rung all over England on May 29 to commemorate Charles II's restoration.[18] "Infatuate Britons," he burst out angrily—why should they celebrate their "direst, foulest shame" and forget the martyrs of freedom, the heroes of his schoolboy reading of Bishop Burnet, whom Charles had put to death?

> Ah! while I hear each traitorous lying bell,
> 'Tis gallant Sydney's, Russel's, Vane's sad knell,
> That pains my wounded ear.

Keats's protest against the rule of mere legitimacy sprang from deep conviction but also from his growing awareness of the resistance which a man of talent would meet in trying to rise above the level of his birth and education in the society of that day. He was no warm admirer of Napoleon, but the triumph of "the divine right gentlemen" whom he despised must have sharpened his own sense of oppression.

Revolt was in the air; and in the summer of 1815 Keats saw his chance to escape from Hammond's authority. After a year of wrangling between the Society of Apothecaries and the Royal College of Physicians, Parliament finally passed the Apothecaries Act. Under its regulations no one could now practise as an apothecary without attending a prescribed course of lectures in a London hospital and then passing an examination set by the Society.[19] At first it appeared that this would merely add an extra year of training to his five-year apprenticeship, but Keats wondered. Could he not cut his term short and try for the Apothecaries' Examination in another year? It was not unheard of to break one's indentures, and evidently he felt he had learned all that Hammond could teach him. He would have to win Abbey over, but it should be easy to persuade him to any plan for avoiding the extra expense. So Keats must have thought, and so he acted. Somehow he won both his guardian's and his master's consent. Hammond wrote out a statement that Keats had satisfactorily completed his apprenticeship, and Keats, armed with this certificate of good behaviour, packed his belongings in the middle of September and went up to London to enter the United Hospitals of Guy's and St. Thomas's.

*Chapter Three*

# The Dark City

THE United Hospitals stood on the edge of the Borough of Southwark, a jumble of narrow streets, sunless alleys, and tenements swarming with the poorest of London's million inhabitants. To reach the hospital from the City, one had to cross London Bridge, dodging the long whips of the draymen coming up from Kent with their wagon-loads of vegetables, then pick one's way through the filth of Borough High Street and turn left into St. Thomas's Street. Here stood the ancient foundation of St. Thomas's Hospital, surrounded by a few fine houses left above the rising tide of the slums. A new wing had been added to the hospital in 1814, containing an anatomical museum, a large dissecting room, and a handsome lecture theatre. Guy's Hospital, founded a century before by an enterprising publisher of Bibles, stood across the street—a group of well-proportioned Georgian buildings facing on a central courtyard behind an imposing iron gate. Here Keats presented himself on October 1, 1815, signed the register of Surgeons' Pupils, and paid a matriculation fee of £1.2. The next day, according to the register, he paid his tuition of twenty-four guineas for a twelve-month term; then work started in earnest.

It must have been a busy and exciting time, that first week or two—the beginning of a year of new friends, new experience, new and demanding work. A full-fledged medical student, he was free at last from the surveillance of Hammond and on his own in the greatest city in the world. In a few weeks he would be twenty, and by the end of the next summer he would be ready to practise medicine for himself. Almost at once he made his first new friend, a younger student named John Spurgin who, after two years at St. Thomas's, was about to enter Cambridge to train as a physician.[1] Spurgin, an odd, enthusiastic young man, was a fanatical Swedenborgian, and he may have fastened on Keats at first with the idea of converting him. He was to lend Keats books and write him long letters from Cambridge in the months ahead; and evidently he was glad to show him around the Borough in the first few days. He may also have helped Keats find lodgings near the hospital. Once settled, Keats bought himself the necessary equipment—a collection of medical texts, a case of surgical instruments, and a supply of two-shilling notebooks, whose pages he neatly numbered. Then he plunged into his new routine.

The day began early, with a lecture on midwifery at seven-thirty in the morning. From that time on there was a steady round of lectures to attend, operations to watch, hospital wards to visit, dissections to perform. His first day in the dissecting room must have been an ordeal, even with the two pints of beer which, by tradition, each new student had to supply. Here, in a clutter of macerating tubs and jars of anatomical specimens, pipkins and syringes, sawdust underfoot and formaldehyde in the air, he faced the fact of death in its most literal form. The subjects were stolen from nearby graveyards, doubled up stark naked in sacks, and smuggled in at the dead of night by body-snatchers—"resurrection men," as they were called—who were paid three or four guineas for each corpse. Their silent company did not keep the students from using the place as their common room, where they cooked their suppers over the grate, played dice or cards in their spare hours, and drank and joked together. Sometimes their jokes turned into horseplay up and down the rows of dissecting tables; but this ghoulish humour must have helped nerve them against the living horrors of the operating theatre.

Keats apparently met the test of initiation as well as the next man. Yet after the first week or two, when Spurgin left for Cambridge, he found himself lonely and depressed in his new surroundings—to judge from a sonnet he wrote at the time.[2]

> O Solitude! if I must with thee dwell,
>   Let it not be among the jumbled heap
>   Of murky buildings; climb with me the steep,—
> Nature's observatory—whence the dell,

Its flowery slopes, its river's crystal swell,
   May seem a span; let me thy vigils keep
   'Mongst boughs pavillion'd, where the deer's swift leap
Startles the wild bee from the fox-glove bell. . . .

Imprisoned in the Borough, he was suddenly homesick for the summer woods and fields of Edmonton. Keats was no real Londoner, and the noisome streets and smoky skies of the city must have oppressed him more as autumn drew on and the days grew shorter. Most of all he missed "the sweet converse of an elegant mind," * as his sonnet unhappily put it, which was not to be found in the dissecting room. Who the "kindred spirit" was with whom he longed to share his solitude we can only guess—perhaps Spurgin, or Cowden Clarke sixteen miles away in Enfield, or Mathew, to whom he sent a copy of the sonnet; perhaps some ideal companion he had not yet discovered.

But just as he had done five years before at school, Keats conquered his depression by throwing himself into his work. His ability must have soon caught the notice of his superiors, for within four weeks he won a real distinction. An assistantship under one of the surgeons, a Mr. William Lucas, became vacant; Keats applied and was appointed—the first man in his group of students to be assigned to such a post. In the register of Guy's it was noted on October 29 that six guineas were returned to John Keats, "he becoming a dresser," and beside the October 2 entry of his name was added "6 Mo." Since on starting his work as a dresser in the spring term Keats would pay his fee directly to Mr. Lucas, the difference between the full-year tuition and the half-year fee of eighteen guineas was refunded to him, and in the following March his name was entered under "Dressers to the Surgeons" for a twelve-month term.[3] The dressers were a group apart from the ordinary students, with special privileges and responsibilities. Each of the three staff surgeons at Guy's had four dressers serving under him, along with one or two apprentices or private pupils—young men destined for outstanding careers. Besides the honour, the position also represented a heavier financial commitment for Keats. The dresser's fee would be fifty pounds; in addition he would have to pay an extra half-year's living expenses before he would be ready to take the Surgeons'

---

* The reading of the autograph version (*The Poetical Works of John Keats*, ed. H. W. Garrod, 2nd ed. [1958], p. 43).

Examination a year from the following spring. The change of plan shows a serious ambition on Keats's part, for Abbey probably objected to the added drain on his inheritance.

It is not known how Keats came to apply for the dressership, but it seems likely that he was recommended by Astley Cooper, the distinguished surgeon who was his professor of anatomy and physiology. Cooper was at any rate interested enough in Keats early in the term to ask two of his young assistants to look after him. Immediately they invited Keats to move into their lodgings at 28 St. Thomas's Street—a welcome change from his previous solitude. Keats now had two of the most serious and promising students at Guy's for company: Frederick Tyrrell, Cooper's apprentice and later a staff surgeon at St. Thomas's; and George Cooper (apparently no relation), his dresser. Tyrrell had spent the previous summer in the army hospitals at Brussels, tending the wounded from the battle of Waterloo,[4] and his stories of this adventure must have stirred Keats to a new sense of dedication to his work.

All this left little time for poetry, at least for a while. It was not often he could spend an evening or a Sunday with Mathew, and when he did his friend sensed a change in him. For one thing, Keats's new independence, his new friends, the new experiences of medical school, all seem to have plunged him from adolescence into manhood in a matter of weeks—such is the difference between his poems of the summer and of the fall of 1815. For another, Keats had recently discovered some poets of the early seventeenth century—Michael Drayton and William Browne— beside whom Mathew's enthusiasms began to seem pallid indeed. Evidently troubled by the gap opening between them,[5] Mathew wrote some "Lines to a Poetical Friend," urging Keats not to let his medical studies interfere with his writing or turn him from the poetry they had enjoyed together—Wieland's romantic "tales of the elf and the fay" and "captures and rescues and wonderful loves." He could not have guessed that "the music of Oberon" was indeed fading for Keats. The very poem in which Keats answered Mathew's "Lines" shows him shaking off his friend's influence and practising a sober masculine style patterned on Drayton's verse-letters. Already Keats realized that their "brotherhood in song" would have to yield to his new responsibilities, and hinted at this as gracefully as he could. Not only was he too busy

to write; he was also becoming aware of the contrast between his
own experience of life and Mathew's poetic version of it:

> Too partial friend! fain would I follow thee
> Past each horizon of fine poesy; . . .
> But 'tis impossible; far different cares
> Beckon me sternly from soft "Lydian airs", . . .
> [And] might I now each passing moment give
> To the coy muse, with me she would not live
> In this dark city, nor would condescend
> 'Mid contradictions her delights to lend.

The contradictions were all too clear: the stark realities of the
dissecting room set against the fairy rings and moonlit groves of
Mathew's verse. Yet Keats still believed with him that writing
poetry required the inspiration of "some flowery spot, sequester'd,
wild, romantic," and the stimulus of a sympathetic friend; lacking
these, he could only be silent.

So he buckled to the serious business of lecture hall and hospital
ward. Day after day, dressed in a dirty linen gown, Keats worked
at one of the tables in the dissecting room, following his outline
of anatomy from chapter to chapter—bones, muscles, joints, internal organs, blood vessels, nerves. A pleasant change from this
work came with the weekly lectures in *materia medica* or medical
botany at the Herb Gardens of the Apothecaries' Society in
Chelsea. This course was sometimes supplemented by trips to the
meadows outside London to gather specimens—a real holiday.
Gradually Keats's brown leather-covered notebooks, one of which
has survived, filled up with close-packed summaries of lectures,
with here and there a few drawings of skulls and fruits and flowers
in the margins. At times, it appears, Keats found note-taking
tedious—as well he might, since it was the custom to repeat each
statement three times for the benefit of the slower students.
Compared with the careful notes which a fellow student, Joshua
Waddington, kept in three thick volumes now in the library at
Guy's, Keats's are sketchy and disjointed. This may mean that
Keats was quicker-witted and more retentive than Waddington,
or simply that his detailed transcription of his lecture notes—
which every student was expected to make [6]—has not survived.

The lecturers at the United Hospitals were for the most part
the leading men in their fields; their lectures would have been
thoroughgoing but rarely dull. Astley Cooper was the most bril-

liant of the lot, a fashionable surgeon whose practice earned him about £20,000 a year and, eventually, a baronetcy. A handsome, energetic man of great charm and warmth, something of a fop but also a hero to his students, Cooper was a daring innovator in operative technique. In the spring of 1816 he was to perform the first ligation of the aorta for aneurysm—an astonishing surgical feat. Every Tuesday and Friday, when he visited his surgical patients in the ward at Guy's, the students swarmed around him, hanging on every remark, then jammed into his lectures at St. Thomas's. Speaking in a broad Norfolk twang and giving an odd snort of appreciation at his own jokes, Cooper enlivened his talk with observations from his own surgical experience and anecdotes from the affairs of the day. Once Keats noted with curious interest "Mr. C's" sarcastic remark on physicians, that "in disease medical men guess; if they cannot ascertain a disease, they call it nervous." Another time he recorded Cooper's account of the division of the sciatic nerve in a wound suffered by Kosciusko, the champion of Polish independence who had fought under Napoleon and whom Keats later commemorated in a sonnet.

Cooper was not only a great doctor who more than anyone else in his time made surgery an esteemed profession; he was also a well-read man with a taste for poetry and liberal leanings in politics. Like other adventurous young Englishmen in 1792, including William Wordsworth, he had been drawn to France and become involved in the Revolution, though he had had to give up his Jacobin connections when he was appointed staff surgeon at Guy's in 1800. A number of other members of the staff at Guy's had liberal or unorthodox convictions, and the intellectual atmosphere must have encouraged freethinking among the students as well as a sturdy belief in scientific progress. Mathew, a timid conservative, was alarmed to find Keats becoming a more and more outspoken advocate of reform and "a fault-finder with everything established," and their discussions evidently became heated.

His new friend Spurgin was also distressed by Keats's growing scepticism about religion. In answer to one of his theological harangues, Keats had confessed that he was in a "mazy Mist" of doubt about Christian belief. Thereupon Spurgin, who had in the meantime gone up to Cambridge, wrote him a long letter expounding the principles of Swedenborg, from the purpose of

Creation to the imminence of Christ's coming, laying special stress on the doctrine of the Trinity. "In every page of the Bible," he pleaded, "we may find that there is One God in Essence and in Person, in whom is a divine Trinity, the same as may be seen in a Glass (as it were) in Man: (viz) Soul, Body, and Operation, the whole of which I will prove from Passages out of the Bible. . . . Dear Keats," he added several closely written pages later, "I FEEL, I PERCEIVE, and acknowledge thereby the Truth and Sanctity of these Writings, and . . . the Love which I am led and taught to bear to my Fellow Creatures, leads me to wish you as a Part thereof a Partaker of those Blessings and Sound and lasting Felicity which an Obedience to the Laws of God can and does most liberally bestow." [7]

Yet Spurgin's exhortations had no apparent effect. Perhaps by way of reaction Keats, who had taken to scribbling doggerel verses in the notebooks of his fellow students to amuse them during lectures, dashed off the following irreverent lines in the syllabus of his friend Henry Stephens:

> Give me women, wine and snuff
> Until I cry out 'hold, enough!'
> You may do so sans objection
> Till the day of resurrection;
> For bless my beard they aye shall be
> My beloved Trinity.

From this it would seem that Keats was fitting comfortably into the life of the average medical student. His friends at Guy's, if they ran true to type, were tough-skinned, level-headed young men, hardened against the physical and mental rigours of their work. Probably it was in their company that Keats acquired his taste for claret and snuff and cigars, learned to play billiards and whist and brag, a kind of poker, and began going to boxing matches, cockfights, and even the bear-baitings at Southwark— the amusements London offered to young men with shillings to jingle in their pockets but not guineas to squander over the tables at White's or Boodle's. No doubt Vauxhall drew him back on other visits. Even the pious Spurgin missed the freedom of the Borough and complained there was "no female Society" in Cambridge.

What kind of female society the Borough offered can only be guessed. In a scrap of would-be Middle English prose cataloguing

the charms of a sleeping maiden which Walter Cooper Dendy, another medical-school acquaintance, tells us Keats tossed off during
an evening lecture, we see him at least posing as a gay dog. Yet,
looked at more closely, these scrawls suggest not a change so much
as a conflict between two aspects of his nature which he could not
yet resolve: his aspirations in poetry and his struggle to come to
terms with the realities of life around him. Keats kept up his
friendship with Mathew through the winter but never introduced
him to his friends at Guy's; [8] he must have sensed that the two
worlds could not be joined. Perhaps the rowdy lines he scribbled
for his fellow students were, like the strained and sentimental
verses he wrote to the Mathew sisters, merely efforts to break out
of the isolation he still felt in his inmost self from the world outside.

>>>·<<<

With the start of his second term, in March 1816, Keats's load
of work grew heavier. He began attending Cooper's evening lectures in surgery, in addition to his other courses; [9] and as dresser
to Mr. Lucas he had many new responsibilities at the hospital.
Every Wednesday, which was "taking-in day" at Guy's, he went
round the wards with his master, carrying the tin plaster-box
which was the badge of his rank and noting Lucas's instructions
for each new case. After their first visit the surgeons rarely saw
their patients again but left the dressers in charge. The nurses
gave them little help, for they were illiterate handywomen who
kept busy scrubbing floors, emptying pans, and making up linseed
poultices when they were not boiling mutton for broth in the
middle of the wards. Cleanliness was rudimentary; one of the
highest-paid members of the hospital staff was the bug-catcher.
Since antiseptic techniques were still unknown, wounds constantly festered and dressings had to be changed at least once a
day. Besides his daily rounds, each dresser took his turn every few
months at living in the hospital for a week as dresser-in-charge,
a kind of resident intern. During this time he supervised all the
wards, attended to accident cases, drew teeth, and dressed out-
patients in the surgery, calling on his superior only in emer-
gencies. It was hard work, but valuable training for a committed
student. It must also have tested a young man's emotional endur-

ance. Guy's had been established as a charity hospital for incur-
ables—patients who were too poor and too ill to be taken in elsewhere.[10] There was no better place to learn the limitations of
medical science in those days—the mystery that still surrounded
most forms of disease and the helplessness of doctors to deal with
it most of the time.

If Keats could have served under Cooper, he might have become
a great surgeon, but Mr. William Lucas, Jr.—"Billy," the students
called him—was not a man to encourage a brilliant pupil. Tall,
stooped, shuffling, deaf, he was good-natured and undemanding
but dull as an instructor and evidently several generations behind
Cooper in surgical technique. Faulty diagnoses and even worse
blunders on the operating table were attributed to him, and one
of the favourite stories circulated at Guy's told that once he forgot from which direction he was amputating a leg and neatly
finished off the discarded end while leaving the raw bone projecting from the stump.[11] Lucas must have put Keats's interest in
surgery to a severe test. Since the dressers assisted at operations,
they saw at close range what was a nerve-shaking spectacle for
many of the students packed in the operating theatre behind
them. Ether was not to be introduced for another thirty years; so
the patient was usually carried in half-stupefied with drink and
strapped down on the table while the operation was performed
as rapidly as possible. As Cooper put it, the surgeon needed "an
eagle's eye, a lady's hand, and a lion's heart" for his work.[12] Yet
even with as skilled an operator as he, the strain was gruelling.
Every now and then one of the students would be overcome and
stagger out into the corridor, half fainting from the foul air and
the groans of the patient under the knife. Perhaps a scene from
these days flashed through Keats's memory several years later when
he described the anguish of the fallen Titans in *Hyperion:* [13]

> Next Cottus: prone he lay, chin uppermost,
> As though in pain; for still upon the flint
> He ground severe his skull, with open mouth
> And eyes at horrid working. . . .

No matter how well he may have acquitted himself under Lucas,
these experiences of helpless agony seared his memory.

At the start of his appointment as dresser, his room-mates Tyrrell and George Cooper finished their course at Guy's and left
—Cooper to enter practice near London and Tyrrell to go to

Edinburgh for further study. Keats then gave up their set of rooms and moved in with Henry Stephens and his friend George Wilson Mackereth, who had an apartment in the same house on St. Thomas's Street. His new companions were a decided change from Cooper and Tyrrell, for Mackereth was to fail his examinations at Guy's, and Stephens later turned from medicine to the manufacture of ink. Stephens had a mild interest in poetry and the theatre, however, and soon became Keats's closest friend at the hospital. Yet they were never intimate; Keats told him nothing of his family life, and Stephens later recalled only vaguely that he was an orphan.

Nevertheless, his new room-mate left a revealing picture of Keats at this time, taken at close range and from an unflattering angle. Stephens himself was a practical and self-possessed young man of conventional tastes; he admired Pope, whom Keats was learning to despise, and found Keats's enthusiasm for Spenser slightly ridiculous. When they read their own poems to each other, Keats let him know that he thought little of Stephens' efforts. This was galling; but Stephens was still more nettled by George and Tom Keats, who on their visits to St. Thomas's Street boasted that their brother would "exalt the family name." Stephens had his revenge, however, when Henry Newmarch, an old acquaintance of Keats training at St. Bartholomew's, dropped in for an evening. Newmarch was a good classical scholar as well as a lighthearted, bantering fellow, and he and Keats often discussed Latin poetry together; but when Keats showed him his verses, Newmarch gave them rough critical treatment, which set off violent quarrels. In Stephens' eyes, Keats had too much the air of "one of the Gods mingling with mortals," and some occasional ridicule was required to bring him down to the level of "mere Medical students." Yet apparently it succeeded only in driving Keats back on himself. With Stephens he became quiet and "unsocial"; in their rooms he would often sit abstractedly by the window, staring out into space. Once off the subject of poetry, Stephens conceded, he could be "agreeable and intelligent," and was always "gentlemanly in his manners." Yet when Stephens took him on a visit to some of his friends in the country, the occasion was not a success. Keats could not easily unbend, Stephens noted, "unless he was among those who were of his own tastes, and who would flatter him."

Some of the "pride and conceit" which irritated Stephens may have been only the impact of a first-rate mind on a second-rate one. But there was more to it than that. From many signs it appears that Keats was torn that spring by a division within himself that he could not understand, an estrangement from himself that estranged him from everyone else. Each of the accounts of him at this time describes him differently, agreeing only on the point of his alienation. Mathew, the serious and sentimental, began to find him too readily amused with "the frivolities of life" and indifferent to the true pathos of poetry. He noted disapprovingly that Keats's eye never filled, his voice never broke as they read together; rather he seemed pleased only with "external decorations" such as imagery. Stephens, representing the average medical student, found him standoffish and conceited. Dendy, an older student who stayed on at the hospital as a junior demonstrator, was struck by Keats's growing inattention at lectures. It would seem that Keats was entering a crisis encountered by many young men at his age: a deep uncertainty about his own nature and purposes at the very moment of undertaking his role in life.

The fact that his friends' impressions of him were blurred suggests that Keats himself was uncertain of his own identity—a term which, it is interesting to note, he later used many times in a sense strikingly close to its present-day meaning, to describe the firm sense of selfhood which he now began to realize he lacked.[14] Normally by the age of twenty the individual is ready at last to come to terms with himself, to weld all his previous aspirations and conflicting impulses and various potentialities into enduring decisions for work and marriage, and to achieve a settled character or identity underwriting these commitments. But at just this crucial point in Keats's development the effect of the hidden psychic damage he had suffered in the deaths of his father and mother began to be manifest. Under the strain of his life at Guy's he became increasingly unsure of who he was or what he might become. Wherever he looked for an image of himself— in the eyes of a woman, at the medical students around him, even within his own inner self—the reflection that returned seems to have filled him with doubt and anxiety.

Evidently he had reached a crisis in his relations with women. It is significant that after writing some shyly amorous lyrics in the early months of 1816, Keats suddenly stopped and, except for one brief interlude, wrote no more real love poetry for almost three years.[15] In a man of twenty, responsive as Keats was to a woman's charm—and few English poets seem to have been so deeply affected by the sheer physical beauty of women as Keats—this about-face needs explaining. There may be a clue in the fact that apparently the last of these love poems was a valentine addressed to Mary Frogley,[16] the belle of the Mathews' balls, praising her bright eyes and graceful gait and dark luxuriant hair. Years later it was said that she had been "an old flame" of his; at some time, it appears, and most probably this winter, a romance flickered up between them and was suddenly snuffed out. Keats did not even send the valentine himself; instead his brother George copied it out and sent it to Mary in his own name. Whether this represents one more battle which Keats fought and lost to his enterprising younger brother cannot be known for sure, any more than whether it was a rebuff from Mary Frogley that silenced his love poetry. But something happened at this time that drove him to the sidelines and left him brooding over his dream of a perfect woman. Whatever it was, it still rankled two and a half years later, when Keats confided to a close friend that he had been "disappointed since Boyhood" in his affairs with women. Years of humiliation lie behind the savage remark with which he then attempted to dismiss the subject: "I do think better of Womankind than to suppose they care whether Mister John Keats five feet high * likes them or not." Perhaps an echo of this experience may be caught in a wistful sonnet he wrote that winter at Guy's, beginning "Had I a man's fair form." [17] As Henry Stephens, who chose to call him "little Keats," dryly noted, "He would have been pleased to find himself admired by the Fair Sex, for his Genius, but not for his person." In his physical self, Keats had become convinced he could never win the love of a woman he desired; as for his genius, he had written nothing yet that proved it.

The transition from boyhood to manhood is especially uncomfortable for a young man convinced that he has great abilities but aware that the world is not convinced of them. Bernard Shaw has described his own uneasy sense at this age of living under false pretences till at last he began to realize his potentialities and forced the world to acknowledge them. Till then, he noted, young men of talent are "tormented by a shortcoming in themselves; yet they irritate others by a continual overweening." [18] Besides irritating Stephens and his friends, Keats was also beginning to won-

* Keats in his haste actually wrote "Five feet hight."

der how much scope for his potentialities he would find in the career he had chosen. Suddenly that spring his dedication to medicine began to flag. He started cutting lectures for several weeks at a time and, when present, sat lost in abstraction or working out a sonnet instead of taking notes. Once he told Stephens that he thought medicine at best merely a way "to live in a workaday world." [19] This is a remarkable change from the energy and ambition Keats had shown in the fall. One cause must have been his disillusionment with Lucas; perhaps another was his feeling of superiority to most of his fellow students, destined for the prosaic existence of small-town surgeons. Surely life held more than this!

Yet it also appears that Keats's overweening, like Shaw's, concealed a gnawing suspicion of shortcoming. He confided to Stephens that he was not sure whether he could "keep up the strain" of surgery. Apparently he was encountering a difficulty which is a frequent cause of failure in medical school—an excessive identification with the patient, arising from the student's inability to develop a sense of detachment from suffering early in his career.[20] Several years later Keats admitted he was often disturbed by profound and unconquerable anxiety in close contact with an invalid, especially when alone with him.[21] Probably this vulnerability to suffering began to trouble him when he started assisting Lucas at operations and serving as dresser in the wards. Here he would have encountered one hopeless case of consumption after another—a daily reminder of his mother's last illness. Try as he might to struggle against it, the memory of that time was returning to haunt him. This seems the only meaning, at any rate, of some strangely revealing lines describing a sickroom which he wrote later in 1816. This passage, which occurs near the end of a long poem eventually entitled "I Stood Tiptoe upon a Little Hill," has no logical connection with the rest of the poem; in fact its very irrelevance suggests that it sprang from one of the deepest levels of his mind:

> The breezes were ethereal, and pure,
> And crept through half closed lattices to cure
> The languid sick; it cool'd their fever'd sleep,
> And soothed them into slumbers full and deep.
> Soon they awoke clear eyed: nor burnt with thirsting,
> Nor with hot fingers, nor with temples bursting:
> And springing up, they met the wond'ring sight
> Of their dear friends, nigh foolish with delight;

Who feel their arms, and breasts, and kiss and stare,
And on their placid foreheads part the hair.

Taken in itself, the passage may seem insignificant; but this scene is only the first of several such scenes in Keats's poetry, which acquire a greater weight of meaning with each recurrence. It is a vision of a return to life from a deathlike sleep, the kind of dream which one often dreams after the death of a beloved person, and which may well have been the recurrent dream of a boy who had watched at his dying mother's bedside but not witnessed her death. In dream language it states the vain hope of her miraculous recovery, which, it now appears, was probably another deep though unrecognized motive in Keats's original choice of a medical career. As a level-headed medical student of twenty, he should have been able to dismiss the fantasy as absurd; but the need to cling to it in the face of his daily experience of death must have been a strong motive in his growing revulsion from a medical career. The growing hold which the fantasy seems to have taken over him suggests something of his reasons for withdrawing from his friends to stare gloomily out the window on St. Thomas's Street.

Alienated from the part he was playing in the outer world, Keats looked inward; and here again he must have felt a stranger to himself. Not only was he disturbed by the discrepancy between "little Keats," whom Stephens and Newmarch found so easy to ridicule, and his own proud sense of himself; it would seem that he had no clear image of the self he struggled to assert. There were more sides to his nature than could be contained within any single personality. The disasters of his early experience apparently had produced discontinuities in his development which he could not bridge. The sober, withdrawn adolescent, dedicated to serving the world as a doctor, was very different from the high-spirited rebellious boy who appeared destined for military greatness, like his uncle, and each seemed unrelated to the happily indulged child he had been, the favourite of his doting mother. A few years later Keats became acutely aware of this inner division and described it in various terms: as the alternation of what he called energy and indolence, or the active and passive sides of his nature; as his vacillation between "a Life of Sensations" and "of Thoughts"; or as the battle of the claims that love, ambition, and poetry made on him, as he felt one with Troilus longing for Cressida, Achilles shouting in the trenches, or Theocritus singing in the vales of

Sicily. These doubts and conflicts assail many young men as they face the transition from the freedom of youth to the commitments of adulthood; but for Keats, lacking the support of parents or other enduring patterns of maturity, the conflicts reached deeper and the resolution was more difficult than for most. At the threshold of manhood, he halted in uncertainty.

From this uncertainty there was one refuge—a character deliberately assumed to cover up the lack of identity he felt. He would become a poet. It was a part into which he had been drifting all through the year, and it is impossible to tell at what point the resolve became conscious. Not that it implied giving up medicine, for obviously he needed his profession as a livelihood. Yet however slowly or suddenly it appeared, the resolution transformed Keats from the lonely youth who "sighed out sonnets to the midnight air," into a man dedicated to the task of asserting his own being to the world through his poems and of measuring himself against the great poets of the past. It is significant that, from the spring of 1816 on, Keats's poetry is addressed primarily to men, deals with masculine preoccupations—chiefly, for a year at least, the writing of poetry itself—and challenges comparison with the most serious poets of the day. So overpowering did this ambition become that he reportedly told his brothers at about this time that if he did not succeed he would kill himself.[22] Poetry was already becoming what he later called his "only life." Otto Rank has described the psychological mainspring of creative achievement as the "will to self-immortalization" arising from the universal fear of death—a fear which the average man meets by immersing himself in life through his family and his work.[23] But Keats at twenty found himself blocked in his first strivings toward sexual love and increasingly disturbed in his work by its daily reminders of illness and death. Just as six years before he had escaped from painful reality by retreating into study, now he threw himself into his other life of poetry with the energy almost of despair.

Again it was Henry Stephens who marked the change. Keats informed him that poetry was "the only thing worthy the attention of superior minds," and that to rank among the poets was "the chief object of his ambition." At first this involved striking a pose; as Auden has remarked, we are all actors who cannot become something before we have first pretended to be it. So, Stephens noted,

Keats began to appear "with his neck nearly bare à la Byron," his shirt collar turned down and tied with a black ribbon instead of trussed up to his chin with the customary neckerchief. Sometime during 1816 he also took to wearing a kind of loose trousers like a sailor's and a short seaman's jacket, which Byron had affected in protest against the dandiacal fashion of the times; he let his own thick curls grow even longer than Byron's, and experimented with a set of moustaches. There was nothing remarkable in Keats's behaviour, though it was intended to appear remarkable. He was only following the usual course of the young artist, who, before any real act of creation, must appoint himself an artist and create his own creative personality by patterning himself on the stereotype of the artist in his society.[24] The parts most men play are slipped on as easily and attract as little attention as a ready-made suit of clothes. But the young artist in assuming his role hurls a challenge at the world, which he is then obliged to justify by exceptional achievement. Before he makes good his claim, he can only appear ridiculous to prosaic young men like Henry Stephens. Even George Keats, who bragged that his brother would "exalt the family name," later admitted that John had been "a little infected" with the "cockney affectations" of Leigh Hunt at this time.

For Hunt, still more than Byron, was Keats's exemplar of the poet. Sometime that spring Keats decided he must take the crucial step of submitting a poem for publication, and this meant, inevitably, sending one in to *The Examiner*. No doubt he looked over his poems with much anxious deliberation before finally choosing his sonnet "To Solitude." He mailed it in signed only with his initials, then waited. On May 5 the new *Examiner* arrived, and there, at the bottom of an inside page full of miscellaneous foreign despatches, he found it—his own poem published. In all his twenty years he could have felt no more glorious moment than this recognition by Hunt, the champion of freedom, the spokesman of the new poetry. It was the first tangible proof that he might fulfil his claim to being a poet, and a long stride toward his goal. He showed the paper to Stephens, not bothering to hide his delight, and Stephens was impressed. He must also have shown it to Mathew. But to Mathew, who disapproved of everything *The Examiner* stood for, Keats's achievement can have seemed only one more sign of the distance growing between them.

Happily Keats made a new friend this spring who was eager to accept him on his own terms, if his other friends were not. Joseph Severn, an acquaintance of his school friend Edward Holmes,[25] was a struggling young painter whose father, a tyrannical music-master, had bitterly opposed his choice of career and apprenticed him to a copper-engraver. Severn detested this occupation and held stubbornly to his ambition, attending night classes at the Royal Academy while making water-colour portraits at half a guinea each to buy the oils he needed. A good-looking young man, thin with delicately chiselled features, fair hair which he wore in straggling curls, and a mouth almost girlish in its beauty, he was still rather unsure of himself, but he had a natural good humour that opened out in congenial company. Meeting Keats raised Severn "to the third heaven," as he later wrote, and filled him with new hope for his own career. It appears that from the start Severn set more store on their friendship than Keats; he did not become one of Keats's intimates until over four years later. Yet each had much to give the other. From his father Severn had acquired some skill as a pianist, and he introduced Keats to the world of painting. Together they began to visit the British Institution, where Severn pointed out his favourite Titians and Poussins and Claudes; on other holidays they talked of books, for which Severn had little time in the long drudgery of his apprenticeship. He was not only a gay companion but an appreciative one. Evidently he matched Keats's mood that spring far better than the melancholy Mathew, and his admiration must have reflected back to Keats the image he sought of the rising young poet.

As spring turned into summer they began to go for long walks together on Hampstead Heath. Once away from the city and out in the fields, Keats's spirits always soared, and Severn was struck by his vivid response to every sight and sound. Nothing escaped him, Severn later recalled—the distant note of a thrush answering its mate in a nearby hedge, the rustle of a stoat in the underbrush, the foxlike expression of a passing tramp, the sway of meadow flowers in the breeze. His greatest delight was the sight of the wind rippling over a field of wheat and the sound it made like rushing water as it surged through the branches of oaks and chestnuts. Evidently his boyhood absorption in the hidden life of nature had only been intensified by his training in close observation as a medical student. Severn on his side was studying Keats with the eye of a portrait-painter, noting the trim but muscular body with its narrow hips, long trunk, and small skull poised above broad shoulders, watching the play of emotion across his face. He was puzzled when he saw Keats fall into one of his taciturn moods, gripped by "a profound disquiet which he could not or would not explain." Then he noted how in his outgoing moods Keats seemed taller than his real height, partly because of his erect bearing and a characteristic backward toss of the head, but still more because of "a peculiarly dauntless expression, such as may be seen on the face of some seamen." [26] It was a significant resemblance that he caught.

Evidently, with the end of the term at Guy's, Keats found more time for tramping on the heath with Severn, swimming in the New River with Stephens, or, best of all, spending a whole afternoon by himself, reading in the tall grass or working out a sonnet. Writing still did not come easily to him: his early drafts are full of false starts and stops, of wrenched syntax and misplaced accents and bad rhymes,[27] of painful searching for the right word and angry scratching out of lines at a time. Still he kept at it, driven by an unconquerable determination to struggle through awkwardness and inexactness and inanity to some perfect utterance which he dimly sensed as his goal. His worst difficulty was still a tendency toward mawkishness and verbosity: only here and there in his sonnets did he achieve the noble chiselled line toward which he was groping.

Another difficulty, revealed in his sonnet "How many bards gild the lapses of time," was the echoes of other poets' work that began chiming in his head whenever he started a poem of his own. This June he was full of a new discovery, *The Story of Rimini,* which Leigh Hunt had published that spring, retelling the episode of Paolo and Francesca from the *Inferno.* Though Hunt had turned Dante's noble and laconic tragedy into a long-winded sentimental romance, the poem scored an instant success with the poetry-reading public. The Tory critics could sneer, but ladies wept over it; Byron, to whom it was dedicated, called it "devilish good," while Haydon the painter thought it "the sweetest thing of our time." Keats was swept off his feet by it. Hunt's easy conversational tone and his lush descriptions of woods and gardens and secret bowers brought the knights and ladies of romance down to a recognizable earth and present. At once Keats wondered—

could he not do the same? Starting a long poem was taking a great dare, but his appearance in *The Examiner* had given him the courage. He took a subject from Spenser—the youth of Calidore, one of the heroes of *The Faerie Queene*—and began: "Lo! I must tell a tale of chivalry." [28] At once he was overwhelmed by his own presumption. Interrupting his tale to write a preliminary "Induction," he apologized to Spenser for daring to follow in his footsteps and begged Hunt, his "lov'd Libertas," to intercede for Spenser's favour.

But with July this project was cut short. The Apothecaries' Examination was coming up, and Stephens, for one, was sure that Keats would not pass. Only a few weeks were left in which to make up for the hours dreamed away in the lecture room. But, as Stephens admitted, Keats was "quick and apt at learning, when he chose to give his attention to any subject." The examination stressed the terminology of medicine, and here Keats's knowledge of Latin gave him an edge. When he and Stephens and Mackereth went up to the Apothecaries Hall on July 25, Mackereth was "ploughed" and Keats, to everyone's surprise, passed. As his certificate recorded, John Keats, "of full age," having served as apprentice to Thomas Hammond and attended the required courses of lectures at the United Hospitals, was examined by Mr. Brande of the Worshipful Masters and found qualified "to practise as an Apothecary in the Country"—that is, throughout England and Wales though not in London. It erred in stating that he was twenty-one—unless, of course, his baptismal record was mistaken—and that he had completed a five-year term with Hammond; but these errors merely underscore his achievement. For all the doubts and distractions of his first year at Guy's, Keats had successfully qualified as an apothecary in the shortest possible time and at the earliest possible age.[29]

—»»•«««—

Two months now lay ahead before the start of the fall term. Keats had earned a carefree holiday for himself, but he was worried about his younger brother. Apparently Tom had not been well for some time. He had grown into a tall, narrow-shouldered, high-strung lad of sixteen, with a build that doctors then described as "consumptive." From the time he began clerking for

Abbey his health had suffered from the long hours and the smoke and fog of London. Sometime during the previous winter he had been sent to Lyons for its milder climate and perhaps also to learn the hat trade, in which Abbey had an interest. Now back in London, he still looked pale and thin, and Keats decided that a vacation by the sea would do him good. So they packed up and went off to Margate, a popular resort on the Kentish coast, complete with the usual ballrooms and cardrooms, a sandy beach for swimming, and a promenade from which to watch the yacht races.

The two brothers were good company for each other. The four-year gap between their ages made little difference now, and Tom, gifted, as Keats later said, with "an exquisite love of life," was developing as great an appetite for books as his older brother. According to George, Tom understood Keats better than anyone else. While George was in most ways John's antithesis, practical, gregarious, a steady balance-wheel to his wide swings of mood, Tom had much of Keats's own delicacy of feeling and playful imagination, as his few surviving letters show. Tom had his moods too, and this summer it appears that he was unhappily in love with a mysterious young Frenchwoman named Amena, an acquaintance of his school friend Charles Wells, with whom he was carrying on a long sentimental correspondence. Wells, a precocious red-haired fellow and a great joker, now a junior clerk in a solicitor's office, was also vacationing at Margate. He had already developed an interest in the theatre which in a few years was to lead him into playwriting; now he was eager to cultivate Keats's acquaintance. His company must have livened up their holiday, besides making it possible for Keats to spend some longed-for time by himself.

For he had come on this vacation primarily to write, to see what he could do in a month or more away from the responsibilities of the hospital. Day after day he went tramping along the coast with a book or a half-finished poem in hand, drinking in every new sight and sound. Apparently this was his first visit to the seaside, and it seemed he could never tire of watching the line of a gull's flight, the slow curve and crash of a wave, the shadows stretching across the fields at evening, the flash of a falling star across the night sky. Almost at once the vast openness of the scene, with its endless motion and glimmer, entered into his poetry, adding a new dimension to the earthy, enclosed, overshadowed world of his earlier poems. But these "wonders of the sea and sky," as he called them in a sonnet he sent to George shortly after arriving, did more:

> The ocean with its vastness, its blue green,
>   Its ships, its rocks, its caves, its hopes, its fears,—
>   Its voice mysterious, which who so hears
> Must think on what will be, and what has been, . . .

sank deep into his consciousness and merged there with the unanswered question of the winter. What was his life to be? What place could he find in it for poetry? As yet he could not glimpse an answer; but as he stood on the cliff at Margate, staring at the wide plain of water beneath him, an image began to take form in his mind. His future seemed to lie spread before him like an uncharted sea. Where was he going? When would he set out? The question made him restless. But for the present he could put it out of his mind by stretching out in the oat fields along the cliff's edge, now bright with poppies, to read or work on his poems.

It was here that he picked up the long verse-narrative of Calidore's boyhood which he had started in the spring. For about a hundred lines all seemed to go well; then he ran into difficulties. He could not make anything happen. His young hero rows across a lake in the evening to welcome two knights and ladies who have ridden up to his castle; he helps the ladies off their horses, embraces them with delight, escorts his guests to a chamber—and there the story breaks off. Much of the poem merely describes the same scenery of lake and island as the "Imitation of Spenser"; yet a comparison with the early poem suggests a reason for Keats's failure to finish it. It is significant that Calidore crosses the lake to emerge from the maternal element of water into real human life. The guests whom he meets in the castle constitute a small society, an older and a young couple.[30] The older knight is Calidore's lord and generous benefactor; the younger knight is a visitor, almost a stranger, whose exploits the boy longs to hear recounted and perhaps to emulate. He is the mighty horseman who appears in several other of Keats's early poems, wielding a stout lance, proud in the possession of a beautiful lady, admired from a distance by the boy-poet. The reminders of Keats's father and grandfather are striking; even the castle courtyard, with the horses

"slanting out their necks with loosened rein" as their riders dis-
mount, seems a recollection of his childhood home. Whatever
Keats's original intention for his narrative, it has apparently been
drawn into the orbit of boyish fantasy. This may explain the excessive emotion which Calidore feels on greeting his guests, and
perhaps also account for Keats's sudden faltering at the end, when
the knights retire with their ladies to bed. Though "Calidore"
is a fantasy of rebirth, of emergence into a masculine world, not
of mere retreat as was the "Imitation of Spenser," it shows Keats
still closely tied to half-remembered early experience, not yet
ready for the full freedom of mature creation.

Keats himself was aware that "Calidore" was not going right,
and in July he wrote a long verse-letter to George describing his
discouragement. This artless confession suggests another reason
for his failure: Keats was looking for a vision. Lying in the grass,
staring up into the sky at sunset, he was listening for a "spherey
strain," striving "to think divinely." He still clung to a notion
which he attributed to Spenser and Hunt, that poetry was a kind
of supernatural insight into some transcendental realm, a matter
of seeing knights on white coursers in the clouds and the clash
of their combat in the sheet-lightning along the horizon at dusk.
If writing poetry was as mysterious a process as this, then what
marvellous beings poets were, and what folly for him to hope to
become one! Yet still more awe-inspiring was the poet's responsibility to society, his power to move men to noble deeds or instruct
them in true wisdom, which won him the reward of an immortal
name after death. The more Keats thought about becoming a
poet, the more exalted the role came to seem—one that would
absorb his whole being and require all his energies, not merely
what he could give it after his daily work was done. But this was
madness. For all the pleasure his poems might give, or even the
good he might do in speaking out for freedom and justice, he had
been trained for another part. "Ah, my dear friend and brother,"
he burst out,

> Could I, at once, my mad ambition smother,
> For tasting joys like these, sure I should be
> Happier, and dearer to society.

The world needed good doctors, and he needed a livelihood. And
why should he delude himself for a moment that he would ever

join the ranks of the great poets whose faces he seemed to glimpse in the feathery clouds of sunset?

His verses limped; the promise in the sunset faded; but he did not quite give up. For even as he wrote, his purposes began to clarify. He had brought with him on vacation two small volumes of poetry by Wordsworth,[31] whom, it appears, he had not heard of till Hunt printed a few of his sonnets in *The Examiner* that winter. This was one of the significant discoveries of Keats's career. Almost at once he recognized Wordsworth as the greatest of the living poets, and the one who had most to teach him. It was to take Keats another year or more to grasp Wordsworth's full meaning; but already this summer echoes of the older poet's sonnets began to appear in his own lines—especially Wordsworth's magnificent images of the sea and the night sky. And already he found in "Tintern Abbey" and the ode on "Intimations of Immortality" an eloquent expression of his own response to the beauty of the natural world. As Wordsworth described the poet, he was no romantic visionary but "a man speaking to men" of their own most deeply felt experience; a man "who rejoices more than other men in the spirit of life that is in him" and "in the goings-on of the Universe around him," where he finds a life like his own, sharing his own "passions and volitions." The deep organic bond between the poet and the world of nature, the slow, plantlike unfolding of the poet's mind, the mysterious ebb and flow of his imagination: these were the doctrines that Keats absorbed with each rereading of Wordsworth and which were soon to transform his whole conception of poetry.

As "Calidore" began to sound hollow to his ears he turned back to another poem he had started in June, a long and wandering description of the sights and sounds of a summer's day he had observed from a little hill on Hampstead Heath. The poem had no name, no theme when he began it, not even a clear sense of direction; but that seemed not to matter. He let it run on from morning to evening, double back on itself to round out the cycle of the hours, then run on again, full of his delight in the blossoming world around him. For the earth had never seemed more beautiful than it did that summer, nor the sweep of the heavens above the plain of the sea, nor—most of all—the moon, which he watched starting her climb as he walked along the Margate cliff after sunset. Now the moon became a presence in his poetry as though he had never seen it before, lighting up a field of broken clouds like white bean-blossoms, gliding from behind a dark cloud like a swimmer into water, or

> Floating through space with ever loving eye
> The night crowned queen of ocean and the sky.[32]

Why should this beauty move him so deeply? He did not quite know. But as he read and walked and pondered, he began to see more clearly what he was trying to say. There was more to it than listing all the sights and sounds of a summer's day, however beautiful. The ocean spoke with a "voice mysterious," the moon gazed down on the earth with an "ever loving eye"; everywhere in nature the poet looked, he found, as Wordsworth had said, "relationship and love"; and this, Keats now began to see, was the stuff of poetry, not the fancied visions of his sunset musings. The poem which he had started so simply on a June morning on Hampstead Heath began to move in a new direction, though he still could not quite see his goal.

The August sunlight thinned into September, and Keats's vacation was drawing to a close. Then a piece of welcome news arrived. George wrote that Cowden Clarke had moved to the city. His father was about to retire from the Enfield school, and Clarke had decided to try his luck in publishing. Keats had been out of touch with his old tutor during his year at Guy's, though he had evidently gone out to Enfield to see him early in the summer. That must have been a pleasant reunion, with Keats's appearance in *The Examiner* and Clarke's growing friendship with Hunt to talk over. Now as he looked forward and then back on their friendship, Keats was struck by how much he owed to the older man for opening up the world of poetry to him. Yet he had never expressed his gratitude, just as he had not yet dared show Clarke most of his poems. He decided to write him a verse letter of thanks; yet no sooner than he began he was overcome by the same discouragement as he had felt in writing George. The distance between his present achievement and his ambition as a poet was so vast that he hardly had the courage to start:

> Whene'er I venture on the stream of rhyme,
> With shatter'd boat, oar snapt, and canvass rent,
> I slowly sail, scarce knowing my intent. . . .

But his sails filled as the poem moved on, swelling out in praise of Clarke, of poetry, of freedom, of friendship, of Leigh Hunt, whom Keats shyly hinted he would like to meet—Hunt

> who elegantly chats, and talks—
> The wrong'd Libertas,—who has told you stories
> Of laurel chaplets, and Apollo's glories;
> Of troops chivalrous prancing through a city,
> And tearful ladies made for love, and pity:
> With many else which I have never known.

The tribute was sincere, but the tone of slack-limbed sentimentality unerringly caught from *Rimini* suggests that closer acquaintance with Hunt might not be all for the good.

Soon after he finished this epistle to Clarke it was time for Keats to return to London—his two long poems still incomplete, his questions about the future still unanswered. He and Tom took rooms together in Dean Street near the hospital,[33] for Keats had decided that Tom was still not well enough to go back to work for Abbey. He picked up his own tasks at Guy's again, but most of the time his thoughts were elsewhere. At the first chance he had to slip off, he went to look up Clarke at his sister's in Clerkenwell, two miles away on the other side of the city, and took him the poetry he had written over the last few months. Clarke was delighted to see him and impressed by his poems. He asked Keats about his work at the hospital and was surprised to hear him speak of it with dislike, as though he had to keep at it against his will.[34] Then Clarke made a suggestion which must have sent the blood rushing to Keats's forehead. He would take the poems to show to Leigh Hunt on his next visit and see whether an invitation could be arranged.

Not long after his release from prison Hunt had moved from London to the Vale of Health, just outside of Hampstead. At that time Hampstead was a pleasant country village, four miles from the northernmost suburbs of London, famous for its clear air and mineral springs and the view of half a dozen counties from the top of its hill. In his cottage on the edge of the Heath, Hunt held a kind of literary court while editing *The Examiner* and turning out gossipy essays and poems on the pleasures of rural life. Cowden Clarke was one of the company invited out for conversational evenings around the fire or family picnics on the Heath or those "sweet forest walks" which Keats had heard about with a touch of envy. Knowing Hunt's enthusiastic spirit, Clarke was sure Keats's poems would be well received. But he was taken by surprise when Hunt, after reading for only a minute, burst out in genuine admiration. This was real poetry, he exclaimed—immature, perhaps, but was the man only twenty? Horace Smith, a fashionable writer and wit who happened to be visiting Hunt that morning, was equally impressed. He read aloud to Hunt the sonnet "How many bards gild the lapses of time," repeating the next-to-last line, which struck him as especially well turned for so young a writer. Hunt quizzed Clarke about his protégé, then asked him to bring Keats along on his next visit. Back in London, Clarke forwarded the invitation at once, and Keats replied in jubilation. "The busy time has just gone by," he wrote on October 9, shortly after the beginning of the term, "and I can now devote any time you may mention to the pleasure of seeing M$^r$ Hunt— 't will be an Era in my existence." He began copying out some of his poems, then in a moment of despair tossed half of them into the fire. The verse-letter to Mathew was perhaps good enough to show Hunt, but nothing he had written earlier.

The appointed day came. As they started out early on their walk to Hampstead, Keats was in such high spirits that his expression caught the attention of the passers-by. He fell silent as they started up the long hill together, but did not slacken his pace. At the porch of his white-painted cottage, Hunt met them with a warm grasp of the hand—a tall, slender, good-looking man in his early thirties, his dark eyes shining with the liquidity of short-sightedness, and a full-lipped smile lighting up his pale and rather softly moulded features. His welcome had all the grace of a man who had rarely if ever doubted his own charm, his talents, or the rightness of his convictions. Hunt led them into the parlour, which also served as his study, a small neat room hung with prints of mythological scenes and lined with bookcases and busts of his heroes, with a pianoforte in one corner and a baize-topped desk with a small vase of flowers in the other. Clarke watched him putting Keats immediately at his ease—the great man deferring to the young one, drawing out his opinions, dazzling him with a burst of eloquence, then dissolving the effect in a joke. But Clarke also saw that Keats was holding his own, and that Hunt warmed to his enthusiasm. The two were hitting it off perfectly. Their visit stretched out to three times the length of a proper call and ended with Hunt's inviting Keats to come again, and often.

As Keats foresaw, this meeting opened a new era in his life. Hunt urged him to bring out more of his poetry and praised it almost to extravagance. At once his friend the painter Haydon, who was taking a fortnight's holiday in Hampstead, begged to be introduced and was so delighted with Keats on their first meeting that he immediately invited him for Sunday dinner in his Hampstead lodgings. Keats agreed—though it may be with some embarrassment when he learned that Hunt was not to be included. Haydon, however, wished to introduce him to a protégé of his own, the poet John Hamilton Reynolds. Only a year older than Keats, Reynolds had just published his third volume of verse, *The Naiad,* a romantic tale in the style of Hunt, and dedicated it to Haydon. Sworn to secrecy about the dinner, Reynolds may have come with some misgivings mingled with curiosity

> To meet John Keats, who soon will shine
> The greatest, of this Splendid time,
> That e'er has wooed the Muses nine—

as Haydon put it in his rhymed invitation. Reynolds must have scented a rival, and perhaps Keats was overawed by the young poet whose work had won the attention of Wordsworth and the praise of Byron, and who was dramatic critic of *The Champion* and man about town as well. The two young men had much in common; but since they met as respective disciples of Hunt and Haydon, their friendship proceeded rather cautiously at first.[35] Yet this acquaintance was one more sign to Keats of the glorious world that was opening up before him.

The air was still electric with adventure when, one evening later in October, Clarke invited him up to Warner Street to share a discovery. A friend of Hunt's had loaned him a 1616 folio of George Chapman's translation of Homer, a treasure in the days when much Elizabethan literature had not been reprinted and was hard to come by. Both Keats and Clarke knew Homer only through Pope's translation, which tailored the long, swinging hexameters of the Greek to the neat proportions of the balanced couplet. As they searched Chapman for some of the great passages —Helen's conversation with Priam on the walls of Troy, the descriptions of the shield of Diomed, the chariot of Neptune—they

found a free-striding verse that matched Homer's own, and a hard
masculine strength of phrase that made Pope's elegant abstractions
seem thin and bloodless. Where Pope had described the ship-
wrecked Ulysses as he staggered up on the Phaeacian shore, streaming with salt water:

> his knees no more
> Perform'd their office, or his weight upheld:
> His swoln heart heav'd, his bloated body swell'd:
> From mouth to nose the briny torrent ran,
> And lost in lassitude lay all the man,
> Deprived of voice, of motion, and of breath,
> The soul scarce waking in the arms of death, . . .

Chapman showed him

> both knees falt'ring, both
> His strong hands hanging down, and all with froth
> His cheeks and nostrils flowing, voice and breath
> Spent to all use, and down he sank to death.
> The sea had soak'd his heart through. . . .

As Clarke recalled, Keats shouted with delight at this last line.
This was what it was to lead a band of heroes against Troy and
voyage homeward through long years of misadventure and lie half
drowned on a lonely beach; this was what Homer had been saying
all along—or so he thought; * this was poetry of a kind that had
not been written in England for two hundred years.

All night they turned the pages of the great calf-bound book
together. When Keats tore himself away at last it was almost six.
He walked home through the empty streets under the fading
planets, with the lines of a sonnet beating in his head. The storm
of that night's excitement had stirred up the very depths of his
mind; things he had seen and felt and read in the last few months
and six or eight years ago were washing up together on the shores
of his consciousness. The sea which he had stared at from the cliffs
of Margate, the stars he had watched and the moon

> lifting her silver rim
> Above a cloud, and with a gradual swim
> Coming into the blue with all her light, . . .

the Mediterranean islands and the new vistas of poetry which he
had glimpsed that evening with Clarke: all these were jostling in

---

* The line that especially pleased Keats was an interpolation of Chapman's: see the
literal translation by A. T. Murray in the Loeb Classical Library *Odyssey*, p. 203.

his mind with phrases from Shakespeare and Wordsworth and recollections more distant still—passages from Bonnycastle and Robertson describing Herschel's discovery of the planet Uranus and Balboa's discovery of the Pacific and Cortez's first view of Mexico City, which recalled a painting by Titian which Severn may have pointed out to him that summer. When he reached Dean Street at dawn he took a piece of paper, marked lines down the right-hand margin to guide him in his rhymes, and wrote out the poem that had been taking shape in his head.* When it was done, he made a copy and sent it off by messenger to Clarke, who found it on his breakfast table when he came down that morning:

ON THE FIRST LOOKING INTO CHAPMAN'S HOMER

Much have I travell'd in the Realms of Gold,
   And many goodly states and kingdoms seen,
   Round many Western islands have I been
Which bards in fealty to Apollo hold.
Oft of one wide expanse had I been told,
       deep
   Which ~~low~~-brow'd Homer ruled as his Demesne:
   Yet could I never judge what Men could mean,
Till I heard Chapman speak out loud and bold.

Then felt I like some Watcher of the Skies
   When a new Planet swims into his Ken,
Or like stout Cortez, when with wond'ring eyes
   He star'd at the Pacific, and all his Men
Look'd at each other with a wild surmise—
   Silent upon a peak in Darien.[36]

It is not hard to imagine Clarke's amazement as he read the sonnet over. The poem was a miracle; not simply because of its mastery of form, or because Keats was only twenty when he wrote it, or because he wrote it in the space of an hour or two after a night without sleep. Rather because nothing in his earlier poetry gave any promise of this achievement: the gap between this poem and his summer work could be leaped only by genius. He had still to rework a phrase here and there before he was quite satisfied; he overlooked a false rhyme in the sixth line and a historical slip in the eleventh which went unnoticed till Tennyson pointed it out years later. But the unity of form and feeling that begins in the first line and swells in one crescendo of excitement to the final crashing silence was instantaneous and unimprovable. After the

---

* This draft is reproduced as Plate X.

reverberation of that ending has died away, something new appears to our eyes. The sonnet, we realize, is not about Chapman, or Homer, or even Keats's reading of Chapman's translation. It is about something much larger, more universal, the rapture of discovery itself—of a new star in the vast heavens, of a sea where none was known before. Cortez standing on his peak is Keats himself on the cliff at Margate, staring at the sea and thinking "on what will be, and what has been"; the poem as a whole expresses his rising excitement of the previous weeks, from the moment Clarke promised to introduce him to Hunt. Saluted by Hunt and his friends, his eyes opened to new kingdoms of poetry, Keats felt the horizons of his world expanding beyond all expectation. It was the limitless possibilities of his own future that he saw spread out before him that morning, shining with the promise of El Dorado.

*Chapter Four*

---

# The Green Shore

A W E E K or two later Keats turned twenty-one. The event seems to have gone unmarked, perhaps because of his queer dislike of having his birthday celebrated, perhaps because he was too busy at the hospital. Apparently he did not even receive his inheritance at this time, for it was found necessary to look up an old servant who could testify to the exact date of his birth.[1] Yet in the most important sense he had already come into his own: in writing the Chapman sonnet he had proved his title as poet. Though nothing that he wrote for months afterward was to sound quite the same note, in this sonnet he had spoken out at last in his own poetic voice. Leigh Hunt at once caught the unmistakable accent. He must have stared with at least a moment's wonder at this work of his new protégé, but he lost no time in praising it to his friends. Hazlitt and Godwin, dining at Hampstead not long afterward, were shown the sonnet and agreed it was as extraordinary as he had thought, a work which "announced the new poet taking possession." Hunt could not have put it better. For almost a year the idea of becoming a poet had been the stuff of Keats's dreams, the object of his most determined efforts, even the subject of much of his writing; now he had done the actual deed. From this time on Hunt began to introduce him in his circle as the young man to watch.

It was an interesting and often brilliant group that gathered at Hunt's, all men who had made their mark in one way or another. They included Horace Smith, the stockbroker, a minor novelist and master parodist; Thomas Barnes, the *Times'* dramatic critic

and soon its editor-in-chief; John Scott, the editor of the new
liberal weekly *The Champion;* Vincent Novello, a distinguished
conductor and organist who introduced Haydn's and Mozart's
religious music to England; William Godwin, the ageing author
of the once notorious *Political Justice,* the Bible of the radicals
of the 1790s; Haydon, Hazlitt, Lamb, and many lesser names from
the compact London world of letters, affairs, the theatre, and the
arts. Hunt's genius for hospitality and his eager interest in everyone and everything attracted men of many different temperaments
and abilities. Yet he also had a wit that could cut both ways—
against his friends as well as his enemies. He was especially fond
of quizzing Haydon, a stout believer in the Bible as the literal
Word of God and the Duke of Wellington as the defender of
civilization; and eventually they had to agree never to argue on
religion or Napoleon. Because of his airy manners and unorthodox opinions, Hunt's opponents found it easy to sneer at his
"vulgarity." Yet Barry Cornwall, the poet, a man who set great
store by politeness, declared Hunt was "essentially a gentleman." [2]
Perhaps the point needed stressing, for Hunt was something of a
Bohemian before his time, and his style as a writer is marred by
a misplaced informality which, then as now, many readers found
distasteful who did not know his charm as a man.

Few men have displayed the defects of their virtues more
flamboyantly. Things always seemed to come easily to Hunt. As
he once gracefully remarked, he found it as delightful to be
obliged to a friend as to oblige him; but, having no head for
finances, he usually ended up on the debit side. Generous in
paying tribute to others, he was shamelessly fond of praise himself
—especially from the ladies, to the distress of his bachelor friends.
Hunt had ideas about freer relations between the sexes that few
men of his time could accept; [3] and, between his literary sister-
in-law Elizabeth Kent and his pretty but scatterbrained wife
Marianne, his household was a queer mixture of the bluestocking
and the sentimentalist. His friendliness was irresistible, but, as
his son Thornton later said, "he invested his personal friends with
ideal attributes"—a risky business—and thus "seldom viewed anything as it really was." Even while serving his prison term for
speaking unpopular truths, he had begun to narrow his gaze more
and more to what he called "the sunny side of things." On leaving
his rose-trellised cell he went through some kind of nervous crisis;

London life seemed so "hideous" that he fled to Hampstead to escape it. His political enthusiasms were cooling, his literary tastes becoming more dilettantish; and *The Champion* was beginning to challenge the popularity of *The Examiner*. In fact, though no one yet suspected it, by 1816 Hunt had passed his peak. The fate of the child prodigy, the early fading of an early-blooming talent, was overtaking him.

If none of Hunt's friends could see this change, still less could Keats. Meeting Hunt was the great turning point of his life. As Severn said, it "intoxicated him with an excess of enthusiasm" for months afterward.[4] Hunt's friendship was a dream come true, Hunt's interest in his work the proof of his wildest ambition. He began to steal more and more time away from the hospital for what Hunt called his "evenings joco-serio-musico-pictorio-poetical," when his friends gathered at the cottage and the wine went round. The talk ranged in all directions—from Wordsworth's merits to the principles of punning, from the life of Petrarch to the latest *Political Register;* then it would break off as Hunt went to the piano and accompanied himself in an aria of Mozart's or played a flute sonata with one of his guests. If it turned to art, Hunt would take down one of his portfolios and "read" a painting, as he called it, scanning a print of Titian or Raphael or Poussin for its mythological implications. All this was Keats's first taste of good conversation, and it left him almost drunk with delight. Even the eight-mile walk back to the Borough, across the Heath under the frosty stars, seemed nothing after such an evening.

As Hunt's protégé, he was content at first to sit on the sidelines and listen. Clarke pictured him in a characteristic pose at these debates, sitting with one leg crossed over the other while absent-mindedly smoothing his ankle with his hand. He impressed the modish Horace Smith as "a loose, slack, not well-dressed youth," his manner "shy and embarrassed, as of one unused to society." [5] In England then, even more than now, dress and diction were unmistakable badges of class; and for Keats, who spoke with a trace of a Cockney accent,[6] his first acquaintance with such men as Smith may well have heightened his natural diffidence. Only with Clarke and Hunt could he feel quite at ease. Hunt began calling him "Junkets," a nickname which he apparently accepted in good humour, along with Hunt's other whimsicalities. These

ranged from birthday celebrations for men of genius, alive or
departed, to sonnet-writing contests, often with a time limit of
fifteen minutes. At these Keats made his mark with one of his
most successful poems that winter. One snug evening when a
cricket began chirping on the hearth, Hunt proposed they match
wits on the subject of "The Grasshopper and the Cricket." They
set to, and Keats finished first, under the time limit and in top
form. As he read out his first line, "The poetry of earth is never
dead," Hunt exclaimed over the promising start, then interrupted
with "Bravo Keats!" at his modulation from the drowsiness of
summer to the silence of frost near the end. Not to be outdone,
Keats insisted to Clarke on their way home that Hunt's sonnet
was much better than his own, and Clarke smiled to himself at
each man's eagerness to find everything admirable in the other.

Keats's adulation of Hunt could not last, of course, and while
it did it had some regrettable effects. With the publication of
*Rimini,* Hunt had become the leader of a kind of "New Poetry"
movement which aimed at breaking the lingering hold of Dryden
and Pope over English verse while it also managed to trivialize
Wordsworth's revolutionary attempt to make poetry out of the
real experience and language of men. So Hunt encouraged Keats's
own tendency to think of poetry as a kind of exquisite indulgence
in poetic sensations, a matter of almond blossoms, nightingales,
and white-handed nymphs; he also sanctioned all the qualities
Keats most needed to discipline in his work—vagueness of thought,
looseness of language, extravagance of sentiment. Yet, for all his
dilettantism, Hunt had the widest range of taste of any critic of
his day, and the keenest ear for the new talent of his time. To his
credit, he pointed out to Keats many poets of the past who were
to contribute significantly to his work, and convinced him that
English poetry was entering on a great new age. Still better, he
introduced Keats to an audience worthy of his gifts, and helped
turn his imagination in a significant new direction.

In the fall of 1816 Hunt was pursuing a new enthusiasm for
Greek mythology, fired by Wordsworth's discussion of myth in
*The Excursion* which, Hunt felt, had rescued the myths from the
inanities of neo-classic verse and restored them to their true esti-
mation. Hunt now planned to write a series of poems retelling the
Greek legends in the style of *Rimini* and was already at work on
the story of Hero and Leander.[7] At this, it seems, Keats's scattered

intentions suddenly came to a focus. In the myths, Hunt told him, the early poets were attempting to express their sense of the beauty of the natural world through some equally beautiful human form. For Hunt, they were mere "lovely tales" and nothing more, and for Keats at this point that was all the justification they needed. The old stories which he had mused over in his schoolbooks now sprang to new life, especially when Hunt showed them transmuted into poetry by the Elizabethans—Spenser and Chapman and Fletcher and Sandys, whose translation of Ovid was a treasure-house of classical legend. Now at last he glimpsed his goal in the long poem he had started in June, standing "tiptoe upon a little hill." The beauty of the myths sprang from no mere fancy but from something as real as what he experienced rambling over the Heath—all the shifting moods of nature, from the springlike joy of the story of Psyche to the desolation of Pan baffled by the fleeing Syrinx. So he would retell these stories: best of all, he would recount the legend of Cynthia and Endymion. This myth explaining the mysterious disappearance and reappearance of the moon—"Peace ho! the moon sleeps with Endymion And would not be awaked"—had always moved him more deeply than he could explain. No other tale could better convey the sense of unearthly loveliness he had felt in his moonlit walks at Margate, the lingering notion of a realm of transcendent joy achieved by the poet, or, perhaps, the still uncommunicated vision of the "fair goddess" sleeping in his mind. It was an idea which Hunt must have approved wholeheartedly.[8]

Yet just as the future began to take new shape the past tugged unexpectedly at his sleeve. In October, George Felton Mathew's "Lines to a Poetical Friend" were published in *The European Magazine*. This gesture, probably intended to revive their failing friendship, could only have reminded Keats of enthusiasms he could no longer share. The cruel truth was that he was moving ahead at a pace that his friend could not follow. If Mathew opposed everything that Leigh Hunt stood for, it was Hunt's world that Keats had cast his lot with. Sometime that fall they apparently had an argument in which Keats's "sceptical and republican" convictions flared up, and which left Mathew shocked and hurt. "I respected Keats's opinions, because they were sincere," he later wrote, "and only asked him to concede with me the fallibility of human judgment; while he, on his part, expressed regret on finding that he had given pain or annoyance by opposing with ridicule or asperity the opinions of others." Evidently Keats was tactless in talking Mathew down, though he did not consider their friendship broken. But Mathew withdrew, salving his vanity with the conviction of his own righteousness.

Mathew blamed Hunt for Keats's irreligious notions, but this was no passing phase. Keats's scepticism had troubled his friend Spurgin a year before, and later friends were to find his religious opinions "extraordinary and revolting." [9] He had evidently emerged from his year at Guy's a thoroughgoing deist, believing in a Supreme Power who created the world but denying the divinity of Christ and all the other supernatural aspects of the Christian faith. Keats's rejection of Christianity was rooted deep in his past, however, as appears from an angry sonnet "In Disgust of Vulgar Superstition" which he wrote one Sunday morning this winter. The church bells which broke in on his reading of the poets—"converse high of those with glory crown'd"—sent "a chill as from a tomb" down his back, wakening the memory of bells tolling at five funerals within his own family. Yet there was more to his protest than mere bitter association. The Church of England at that time was a hollow shell of form without real belief, of dogma unsupported by reason, to which few intelligent men could wholeheartedly subscribe; it was also a pillar of the established order which Keats hated, venal, complacent and reactionary. His private image of orthodoxy may well have been Richard Abbey, the prosperous churchwarden haggling with his Sunday-school pupils over their rightful guinea.

Hunt gave Keats a glimpse of another kind of religion, which he insisted was true Christianity as distinct from "Christianism," or the faith of the Thirty-Nine Articles. From his father, a Unitarian minister, Hunt had derived a kind of aesthetic Unitarianism, which opposed the church and its doctrines with all the fervor of Voltaire, while affirming the human goodness of Christ and the benevolence of the Creator,

> Who we know, from things that bless,
> Must delight in loveliness,
> And who, therefore, we believe,
> Means us well in things that grieve, . . .

as he wrote that spring in a hymn that soon became famous, "To the Spirit Great and Good." Keats seems to have had some such

religion in mind when he ended his sonnet with the prophecy of
a happier faith in time to come, when

> . . . fresh flowers will grow,
> And many glories of immortal stamp.

Yet by "glories" he may also have meant the poetry which, half
a century later, Matthew Arnold thought would replace religion
as an interpretation of life. As Keats put it a few months later,
at the end of an argument on religion, "Shakspeare is enough for
us." At twenty-one, full of hope for the future and delight in the
world around him, he demanded no more explanation of existence than Hunt's easy tribute to its "loveliness."

Yet, from the beginning of Keats's friendship with Hunt, a
powerful force was drawing him in another direction. Benjamin
Haydon had been greatly impressed by Keats on their first meeting
in Hampstead. Soon after returning to London early in November
he invited Cowden Clarke to bring him for Sunday breakfast in
his studio. Keats was exultant. "Very glad am I at the thoughts of
seeing so soon this glorious Haydon and all his Creation," he exclaimed in his reply to Clarke. His first glimpse of Haydon's
painting-room at 41 Great Marlborough Street was a revelation.
It was a small room, crowded with casts and sketches of heads
and torsos, with the half-finished canvas of "Christ's Triumphal
Entry into Jerusalem" blocking one entire wall. Haydon had been
working on this picture, which he counted on to make his fortune,
for over two years, but still only four or five characters in the
foreground were completed, and the central figure of Christ on
a donkey was being repainted in one of these repeated transforma-
tions which, his friends uneasily noticed, only heightened its
uncanny resemblance to Haydon himself.[10]
More chaos than creation, the place must have seemed, but
Haydon was the indisputable god at work. Short-legged, bull-
throated, broad-browed, his hair worn long like Raphael's, he
looked the very embodiment of the energy and determination
which, he believed, were the chief requisites of greatness. With
his loud voice and a laugh like the trumpet of Jericho, he radiated
confidence; nothing in his appearance betrayed the occasional
flashes of misery and doubt which he confided only to his diary.
Haydon had had to make his way against poverty, parental opposi-

tion, and a nagging physical handicap of weak eyesight. Other handicaps were his fiery temper and his unmitigable egotism. What he described in his journals as "irresistible, perpetual, continued urgings of future greatness" used to shoot through him with such intensity that he could only "lift up his heart and thank God" for these assurances of divine favour. Taste was turning against the outsized heroic paintings which Haydon believed were the highest form of art; yet he not only continued to paint one huge canvas after another, but quarrelled with his patrons and even the Royal Academy. Turner, Constable, Blake: these are the names in the English art of his time that live today. But Haydon had only scorn for landscape painting—"Think what *I* am doing," he once remarked to Constable—and evidently knew nothing of Blake's work.[11]

By the sheer force of his enthusiasm, Haydon persuaded most of his contemporaries to take him at his own estimate as a great painter; he also persuaded them that it was he who prevailed on the British Government to purchase the Elgin Marbles. These sculptures, which Lord Elgin had salvaged from the Parthenon for his private collection, had left Haydon thunderstruck on his first view in 1808. Official taste of the time took the effeminate Belvedere Apollo and the insipid Medici Venus as the high points of classical art; by contrast, the Parthenon statues seemed mere "Phidian freaks." It is forever to Haydon's credit that he immediately grasped the difference between the imitation and the original. From his long study of anatomy he recognized at once the profound knowledge underlying the effortless nobility of the sculptures, from the articulation of the wrist of Cecrops' daughter to the ripple of muscle across Theseus' back.[12] He spent months sketching the Marbles, though never quite capturing the secret of their strength; then, when Elgin offered to sell them to the British Government in 1811, he hurled himself into the resulting controversy. Hellenophiles such as Byron protested that Elgin was no better than a thief; connoisseurs insisted that the works were not Greek at all but late Roman copies. Haydon wrote, wrangled, buttonholed, bullied; but not until 1815, when the archaeologist Visconti and the sculptor Canova declared the Marbles genuine, did the tide of opinion turn. Early in 1816 a Government committee heard the recommendations of seven leading British painters that the sculptures be purchased. Haydon, who had played a very minor part in the hearings, was determined to get his word in; accordingly he published a stinging attack in *The Examiner* on Payne Knight, a director of the British Institution, who had testified against the authenticity of the Marbles. When the committee at last decided for the purchase, Haydon was convinced—and convinced his friends—that his article had won the case, and extravagant tributes to his victory, including sonnets from Wordsworth and Hunt, poured in from all sides.[13]

Keats had met Haydon in the very week that Hunt was hailing him in *The Examiner* as the successor of Michelangelo and Raphael, and his first impression of Haydon as the champion of the Marbles struck deep. At once he wrote a sonnet praising Haydon but also—and this is noteworthy—congratulating all those who had shared his belief:

> How glorious this affection for the cause
> Of stedfast genius, toiling gallantly! . . .
> Unnumber'd souls breathe out a still applause,
> Proud to behold him in his country's eye.

This shows a remarkable sense of proportion in a man of twenty-one, which Keats maintained on closer acquaintance. On November 19 he visited Haydon in his studio again. It was a memorable evening, full of Haydon's discoursings on art and literature, past and present; but it seems they also talked of Keats's future, and Haydon made a sketch of Keats in profile. From the start he had been struck as much by the modelling of Keats's head as by his poetry, and now he proposed to paint Keats as one of the spectators in "Christ's Entry," along with Wordsworth and Hazlitt, Newton and Voltaire. The next day Keats wrote him tersely: "Last Evening wrought me up, and I cannot forbear sending you the following." It was another sonnet, "Great spirits now on earth are sojourning," praising his heroes Wordsworth and Hunt along with Haydon,

> whose stedfastness would never take
> A meaner sound than Raphael's whispering, . . .

then soaring into a prophecy of the future of English poetry:

> And other spirits there are standing apart
> Upon the forehead of the age to come;
> These, these will give the world another heart,
> And other pulses. Hear ye not the hum

Of mighty workings in a distant mart?
Listen awhile ye nations, and be dumb.

Haydon answered at once, suggesting that Keats shorten the next-to-last line, then announcing he would send the sonnet to Wordsworth. To Wordsworth! "The Idea," Keats replied, "put me out of breath—you know with what Reverence—I would send my Wellwishes to him." What Haydon did, however, was to take the sonnet around to show to his young friend Reynolds, who replied the next morning with one of his own in praise of Haydon —fourteen fulsome lines to Keats's two:

Haydon!—Thou'rt born to Immortality!—
I look full on;—And Fame's eternal star
Shines out o'er Ages which are yet afar;—
It hangs in all its radiance over thee! . . .

Weak though it was in comparison to Keats's, Haydon had Reynolds' tribute printed two days later in *The Champion*. Six weeks passed, however, before he sent Keats's sonnet to Wordsworth, who wrote back at the end of January that it "appears to be of good promise." [14]

Keats may well have smiled wryly when he saw Reynolds' sonnet in print. Yet—as he wrote a year later to a friend who had been wounded by another display of Haydon's egotism—"As soon as I had known Haydon three days I had got enough of his character not to have been surprised at such a Letter as he has hurt you with." This may be the wisdom of hindsight; yet both Keats's sonnets to Haydon present him in clearer perspective than either Hunt's or Reynolds', and they give the painter his due in twice describing him as "stedfast." Divided as he still was between two vocations, Keats found in Haydon an example of hard-working devotion to art very different from Hunt's dilettantism. "I begin to fix my eye upon one horizon," he announced to Haydon on November 21, while thanking him for his praise of the second sonnet.

This remark has been taken to indicate some kind of break in Keats's work at Guy's, since he and Tom had left Dean Street only a few days earlier to move into lodgings with George at 76 Cheapside, over a mile from the hospital. Yet the record shows that Keats continued to attend lectures and perform his duties at Guy's all through the winter.[15] The reason for the move to Cheapside seems to be quite simply that the three brothers wanted to live together after their five-year separation. They found rooms over the archway of Bird-in-Hand Court, a few steps from the Mermaid Tavern and Bow Church of the immemorial bells, and around two corners from Abbey's counting-house in Pancras Lane, where George still worked. It was a pleasant arrangement, as appears from a sonnet Keats wrote on the evening of Tom's seventeenth birthday, November 18, while listening to the crackling of coals in the grate and watching Tom absorbed in a book. This was the nearest thing to a home of their own they had had for years, and at this point in his life Keats could not imagine a happier existence.

Still it is clear that poetry was the "one horizon" on which Keats told Haydon he was fixing his gaze; and two weeks later it lit up with a portent. On the first of December, Hunt published an article praising Keats's poetry to the world. Under the title of "Young Poets," he welcomed three recruits to the "new school" of poetry championed by *The Examiner*. The first of these was Percy Bysshe Shelley, a virtually unknown young writer who in 1813 had privately printed a long philosophical poem, *Queen Mab,* which no one had read, and then early in 1816 had published an allegorical poem, *Alastor,* which had been dismissed by two or three of the reviews as "sublime obscurity" and "delightful nonsense." In October, Shelley had sent his "Hymn to Intellectual Beauty" in to *The Examiner* under the pseudonym "Elfin Knight"; then, when a month went by and nothing happened, he evidently wrote Hunt again to ask about it. Hunt, who had mislaid the manuscript, made his amends by praising Shelley in his review as "a very striking and original thinker." It is one of the ironies of criticism that, next to encouraging Keats, Hunt did no better service to poetry than calling attention to Shelley's talent in this roundabout fashion. After discussing Reynolds' *Naiad* at greater length, Hunt then gave Keats pride of place at the end of the article, as the youngest of the three aspirants and the most promising. "He has not yet published anything except in a newspaper," Hunt remarked, "but a set of his manuscripts was handed us the other day, and fairly surprised us with the truth of their ambition and ardent grappling with Nature." Then he concluded, with unerring effect, by quoting the sonnet on Chapman's Homer. The article was all that a young writer needed

to send his hopes soaring. Its effect on Keats was succinctly described by Henry Stephens: "This seald his fate."

For shortly afterward he nerved himself to an important resolve.
Urged by Hunt, encouraged by his brothers, he decided to bring
out a book of his poems. It was a gamble on which he risked his
whole sense of himself as a poet, but the stakes for which he was
playing were high, and his chances seemed good. There was a
large audience for poetry in those days. Fashionable poets such as
Sir Walter Scott and Tom Moore could ask, and get, three thous-
and pounds or more for a long verse narrative; Byron's *Corsair*
sold ten thousand copies the day it appeared, in a London of about
one-eighth its present population. Keats had enough poetry on
hand—sonnets, lyrics, epistles, and several fragments of longer
poems—to work up into a little book like Hunt's and Byron's
first volumes, and Hunt already had a publisher for him. His
friend Charles Ollier, an amateur musician and poet, had just
decided to enter publishing with his older brother, James, and
was eager to take Keats on as one of his first authors.[16] Keats's
own reasons for the decision went deeper. With each step he had
already taken toward becoming a poet, he saw more clearly what
he wanted. Not fame alone, though he dreamed of it as much as
any man of twenty-one; not money either, though the wild hope
had already crossed his mind that his books might earn him a
release from medicine; but rather to join the ranks of the great
poets, the finest of human beings—so he believed—who somehow
served the highest of human purposes. Publishing was a decisive
act of commitment and a necessary step toward his goal.

In these last months of 1816 Keats was "standing on the top of
golden hours," at that extraordinary moment in life when all the
dreamed-of future begins to become actual. Two portraits made
of him at this time catch him in the flush of decision. As Hunt
once described Keats's face, it showed "energy and sensibility
remarkably mixed up"; and these two sides of his nature, the
dream of achievement and the determination to realize it, were
captured in striking contrast by Severn and Haydon. Severn's
pencil sketch of Keats in three-quarter profile, made one evening at his rooms in Cheapside, presents the young disciple of
Hunt, with his hair worn long and curling, his throat bare above
the turned-down collar. It is Keats seen through the eyes of a
sentimental miniature-painter, the features softened to effeminacy,

the nose lengthened, the chin shortened, the lips almost quivering. The portrait is a falsification except where, by some magic about the eyes, it suggests the dazzling mobility of Keats's expression, which all his friends mentioned at one time or another. But sometime early in December, Haydon made a cast of Keats's face, as he did with the other friends whom he was putting into "Christ's Entry," and this life mask gives the enduring truth of Keats's appearance. The wet plaster slowly hardening over his features stilled their intense expressiveness; but it recorded all the lean masculine strength of the low brow and the hollow cheeks, the compact nose, the stubborn jaw, and the wide mouth which Hunt found too pugnacious for his taste. The energy seems poised, purposeful; the sensuousness hinted at in the long curve of the lips is controlled.*

But Keats left his own record of the moment when his purpose finally crystallized—that long, rambling, ecstatic poem called "Sleep and Poetry." One evening at Hampstead the conversation ran on so late that Hunt offered to put him up overnight on the sofa in his study. Keats was too excited to sleep, and as he lay there, conscious of the great names surrounding him on Hunt's crowded shelves, he had a kind of waking dream of his own destiny. It was a moment such as Shelley had experienced as an unhappy schoolboy, when he walked out into the fields one May morning and vowed to struggle all his life against tyranny; or such as Wordsworth had known, when, near thirty, he revisited the countryside around Tintern Abbey and came to understand the change which the years had worked in him. For Keats that night his sense of the all-engrossing present expanded to a vision not only of his own future but also of the past of English poetry and their intersection in the moment at which he stood. He thought of the greatness of Chaucer and Shakespeare and Milton and the triviality, as he felt it, of Pope and his successors; then of Chatterton and the new poets, led by Wordsworth, in whose ranks Hunt had told him—Keats's blood raced at the recollection—he would be numbered. Thought crowded on thought, and a poem began to take shape in his mind.

As he gazed into the darkness, a painting which he and Hunt may have studied that very evening—Poussin's "Empire of Flora" —flashed on the screen of his imagination.[17] In the foreground

---

* These portraits are reproduced as Plates VIII and I.

lay the garden of Flora, thronged with nymphs and lovers of classical legend; high above them Apollo in his golden chariot lashed his horses across the skies. The painting became an image of his own career: the poetry which he was writing at present, full of the "o'erwhelming sweets" of youth, which he now saw he must leave behind for a goal which still lay out of sight—a poetry that dealt with "the events of the wide world," that faced "the agonies, the strife of human hearts" and wrested another kind of beauty from them. As yet he could envisage this poetry only in the dimmest fashion, as "shapes of delight, of mystery, and fear"; but someday, somehow, he knew he would write it. As he lay on his narrow bed between sleep and waking, line followed on line with the miraculous ease of dream, and when the light began to glimmer at the window he could not believe morning had come so soon. He rose up, full of the energy of a man with a task which he is eager to start.

"Sleep and Poetry" inevitably fell short of Keats's experience that night. Built on the very movement of his mind between fatigue and excitement, hope and despair, much of it is a jumble of confused images and wildly shifting moods. In essence, the poem was a challenge to the conservative tradition symbolized by Pope and a proclamation of Hunt's notion of poetry—that

> they shall be accounted poet kings
> Who simply tell the most heart-easing things.

Yet at the same time Keats was groping toward a more arduous and significant ideal—a poetry that took on itself the Wordsworthian "burthen of the mystery." "Sleep and Poetry" has been called "an attempt to express in the style of *Rimini* something of the spirit of 'Tintern Abbey' "; [18] but in some ways it comes closer to another far greater poem of dedication—Milton's "Lycidas." In each the young poet hesitates between the joys of the senses, which other young men seize without a thought, and the uncertain rewards of "the thankless Muse":

> Were it not better done as others use,
> To sport with Amaryllis in the shade,
> Or withe the tangles of Neaera's hair? *

---

* "Withe" (*NED, with, withe:* to twist or plait) seems to have been Milton's intended meaning in this line.

For Milton, however, the decision "to scorn delights and live laborious days" raised no troubling doubts; for Keats it was much more of a problem. Sleep and poetry, the rather odd set of contrasts on which he built his poem, were, as he saw, not an antithesis but a necessary ebb and flow of poetic power, the alternation of what he later described as "indolence" and "energy." Time after time the poet must surrender to the health-giving delights of the body, give rein to its hungers and draw new strength from their satisfactions in order to rise again to the discipline of art. More than this, Keats was also beginning to grasp something which words hardly yet existed to describe—the creative activity of the unconscious mind in dream, as it fashions

> many a verse from so strange influence
> That we must ever wonder how, and whence
> It came. . . .

Yet Keats had as strenuous a notion as Milton of a great purpose to be achieved through poetry, a goal higher even than individual fame. Like most young men, they could define their purpose best in terms of what they were opposed to—the outworn tradition of eighteenth-century poetry for Keats, the corruptions of the English Church for Milton. And for each the sense of his mission took on an unexpected urgency from the thought of death. While in his earlier poems death was a mere abstract possibility for Keats, a fact of someone else's life, he now refers to it repeatedly as something that will happen to him. It seems that to fully admit his ambition raised a haunting fear that life would not be long enough to achieve it.

> O for ten years, that I may overwhelm
> Myself in poesy; so I may do the deed
> That my own soul has to itself decreed. . . .

Life was a precarious matter, as he knew all too well; his father had died at thirty, his mother at thirty-six. At twenty-one, he could not think a decade was too much to ask.

→»«←

In deciding to publish his poems, Keats tapped a new spring of creative energy. In the four or five weeks that followed, he wrote

half a dozen new sonnets, completed "Sleep and Poetry," and
turned back to his long poem on nature and myth, which he now
called "Endymion." He was reaching the climax of the poem,
a retelling of the moon goddess's love for the young shepherd
whom she visited nightly in his sleep. Yet here unexpectedly he
ran into trouble. As he started to describe the hushed beauty of
their bridal night another scene unaccountably interposed itself
—the miraculous recovery of a sick woman, waking "clear-eyed"
and feverless from a deep sleep, and her reunion with the anxious
watchers by her bedside, "nigh foolish with delight." This is the
dream which, as was suggested, had haunted his imagination for
years and returned to trouble him at Guy's; and only the wild
logic of dream can relate this episode to the scene of erotic fulfilment which follows. Yet, as he went on to recount the final
episode of Cynthia's wedding, Keats faltered and broke off with
four lines of apology for his inadequacy. He could only hint at
some deeper significance in these events:

> Cynthia! I cannot tell the greater blisses,
> That follow'd thine, and thy dear shepherd's kisses:
> Was there a Poet born?—but now no more,
> My wand'ring spirit must no further soar.—

Around the original core of his myth were gathering meanings
which he was still struggling to formulate to himself: the birth
of the poetic consciousness, now somehow linked with a dream
of fulfilment in sexual love.

At the end of these four lines Keats stopped in indecision, added
a dash, then wrote the date, "Decr. 16," in the margin. The poem
was incomplete, but for the time being he did not know quite
what to do with it.[19] The next day he wrote in discouragement to
Clarke: "I have done little to Endymion lately—I hope to finish
it in one more attack." Clarke, who was to visit him that very
evening, was evidently following his progress with the book almost
from day to day. There was much to be done. After assembling
his poems from his jumbled copies, Keats had to decide which to
leave out and which to include, then polish off their rough edges.
Tom began copying the poems into a notebook as he revised them,
and Hunt later went through this copy and suggested some corrections.[20] Reworking a poem in cold blood Keats found a tiresome task. While the revisions in the manuscripts of his later

poems show an assured craftsman at work, in these early poems he was often merely saving himself from blunders. Yet he was also learning how to sharpen an image or tighten a phrase or cut out an internal rhyme. He spotted the one lame line in his Chapman sonnet—"Yet could I never judge what Men could mean," which struck him as "bald and too simply wondering"— and with a sure hand changed it to its present form, "Yet did I never breathe its pure serene." Slowly Tom's copy-book filled up and the volume began to take actual shape before Keats's eyes.

In the meantime a new character made a dramatic entrance on the Hampstead scene. Shelley, touched by Hunt's tribute to him in *The Examiner,* wrote him from Bath a glowing letter of thanks. As "an outcast from human society," he confessed, he had become discouraged in his attempts "to interest or improve mankind" through his poetry. But now his faith was restored: "With you, and perhaps some others (though in a less degree I fear) my gentleness and sincerity find favour, because they are themselves gentle and sincere." Shelley had indeed been an outcast for most of his twenty-four years—as a tormented schoolboy at Syon House, as "The Atheist" at Eton, as the author of a pamphlet on *The Necessity of Atheism* which got him expelled from Oxford, and now as the rebellious heir to a baronetcy and a fortune who had eloped at nineteen with the daughter of a tavernkeeper and then run off to Switzerland three years later with Mary Godwin, the daughter of the philosopher. Far more radical than Hunt in his political and religious opinions, Shelley had a correspondingly greater capacity for idealizing his friends and then becoming disillusioned with them. But the friendship that began on December 12, when he presented himself at Hunt's cottage, was to become central in both men's lives. On the thirteenth Hunt invited several of his friends, including Keats and Horace Smith, to meet the newest member of the circle. The stockbroker immediately noted Shelley's Etonian manners and well-cut clothes, which he wore with an air of abstracted untidiness, and was impressed by his conversation on Plato.[21] Here, he realized, was a gentleman and a scholar. From this pleasant introduction to the Vale of Health, Shelley returned to Bath the next day to learn that Harriet, the young wife he had deserted two years before, had drowned herself in the Serpentine. He immediately returned to Hunt's to straighten out his affairs in London. A letter he wrote to Mary Godwin on the sixteenth makes uncomfortable reading. Immediately accepting a slanderous account of the circumstances of Harriet's suicide, Shelley found "little to regret" in her death beyond "the mere shock of so hideous a catastrophe having fallen on a human being once so nearly connected with me." Everyone, he added, "bears testimony to the upright spirit and liberality of my conduct to her," while Hunt sustained him in his painful contemplation of the "vice and folly and hardheartedness" of Harriet and her family.[22]

All during the last two weeks of December, while Shelley began the battle to gain legal possession of his two children, he and Mary —whom he married on the twenty-ninth—stayed with Hunt. The friendship so tragically interrupted at its start was now cemented. Though Shelley was already carrying the financial burdens of his friend the novelist Thomas Love Peacock and his new father-in-law, William Godwin, he immediately offered Hunt assistance, which Hunt, deeper in debt than ever, agreed at once to take. A year later, in fact, as he was "proud to relate" in his *Autobiography*, Hunt received £1400 from Shelley to settle his debts. But though Hunt came to regard Shelley as the finest character he had ever met, few of his friends shared his admiration. Lamb, Hazlitt, Haydon, Reynolds, Crabb Robinson the diarist, even Godwin, all found reasons for distrust or even dislike. It is true that Shelley was under great emotional stress this winter; it is also true that for years he had suffered from delusions bordering on paranoia that put a severe strain on his friendships. With Hunt he lived on a level of radiant idealism; to Hazlitt, he had "a fire in his eye, a fever in his blood, a maggot in his brain, a hectic flutter in his speech, which mark out the philosophic fanatic." Shelley loved to set up questions for debate that had more than merely philosophic interest for most men. With his high-pitched voice, girlish complexion, narrow shoulders, and nervous mannerisms, he appeared a harmless adversary; but, after advancing the most outrageous opinions with studied casualness, he would fall on his unsuspecting opponents with crushing logic.

Keats managed to avoid tangling with him except on one occasion, which he did not forget. While at Hunt's in December, Shelley read over Keats's poems, then took him for a walk on the Heath and advised him not to publish. Perhaps this was wise counsel, for Shelley's first poems had been drubbed by the Tory critics, but Keats could hardly be expected to agree. He politely declined Shelley's advice, and thereafter kept his distance in a manner that Shelley could not quite understand. The reasons are plain: the clash of Shelley's unconscious patronizing with Keats's fierce pride; a profound difference of temperament; most important of all, perhaps, a disagreement about poetry itself. The didacticism of much of Shelley's work was becoming more and more alien to Keats. As Shelley admitted, he hoped to create the world anew by "familiarizing the highly refined imaginations of the more select classes of poetical readers with beautiful idealisms of moral excellence." Keats, as Hunt remarked, could not follow him in these "Archimedean endeavors to move the globe with his own hands" [23]—nor did he care to. He was still feeling his way toward the kind of poetry he wanted to write; but disagreement with Shelley, it appears, helped sharpen his sense of direction.

Shelley, it was later said, also offered Keats help, presumably financial, in getting his first volume published. This is very doubtful,[24] but if he did the offer could only have stiffened Keats's new-won sense of independence. He very soon became aware that Hunt was accepting Shelley's largesse, and though he was in no position to impress Shelley as being well off himself, that is precisely what he managed to do. Half a year later Shelley, in writing Hunt to explain that he could send him no more money at the time, suggested, "But there is Keats, who certainly can." Keats certainly could not. It is almost impossible to untangle the truth of his financial affairs from the conflicting figures and contradictory statements which he and his friends left behind. The one sure fact is that money matters depressed him so much that he never looked closely into his own accounts, with the result that he usually assumed he had more money than he actually did. Curiously, however, there was some truth in this assumption. Under the terms of his grandfather's will, Keats should have received by reversion or direct bequest about three thousand pounds on reaching twenty-one.[25] But Abbey, for reasons of his own, apparently told him that he had inherited only a fifteen-hundred-pound legacy from his grandmother, a sum which his medical training had reduced to a thousand pounds or less. It was not much, though for a while it allowed Keats to feel that he had money both to spend and to lend: so much so that within the next two or three years he loaned nearly two hundred pounds to various friends, and a larger figure to his brothers. Tom was in poor health and earning nothing; George was an extravagant spender, especially on clothes; and, so long as they were under age, they had only their older brother to turn to when they ran over their incomes. After he came of age Keats managed to keep his own expenses down to nearly a hundred pounds a year [26]—a very "moderate subsistence" for a young bachelor; even so, he was constantly dipping into his principal. But at twenty-one, full of confidence in the future, he must have felt that his money would last as long as he needed it.

The early months of 1817 were filled with hopeful work and mounting excitement. After his poems were sent off to the printer, there was the task of proofreading—no task at all but the heady delight of seeing page after page of his poetry in print for the first time. Keats was too busy in January and February to write more than a few new sonnets, but Hunt printed two of these in *The Examiner* during February to whet his readers' interest in the forthcoming volume. Probably about this time Haydon got him a ticket to the British Museum Reading Room, where he might continue what he called his "study"—his intense and eager reading of the older English poets from whom he was learning his craft, noting with an increasingly expert eye the fine points of diction and versification, structure and imagery. But Keats did not make much use of this ticket—perhaps because he had already discovered the Abbey Library at Westminster, formerly the chief public library of London and now a half-forgotten treasure-house of old books where he could browse in cloistered solitude.[27] All this while he was finding his way around a new London, a city of bookstores and printshops, galleries and theatres. This winter he became a regular theatregoer with Clarke and Reynolds, and for the best of all reasons: Edmund Kean was now appearing regularly at Drury Lane, electrifying the London audience with his new style of acting, natural, intimate, full of Elizabethan fire—"like reading Shakespeare by flashes of lightning," as Coleridge described it.

We catch echoes of evening parties in Keats's rooms off Cheapside, lively with wine and wit and disputation, at which Keats once dumfounded Severn by maintaining that Milton was not a great poet. He was developing a habit of what his friends called rodomontade—upholding the worse side of an argument for the sake of the intellectual drama that ensued. The shyness which Horace Smith had noticed disappeared with his growing confidence in his abilities and among friends of his own choosing. He was rapidly becoming good friends with Reynolds, who now introduced him to his own family: his father, the mathematics and writing master at Christ's Hospital; his mother, a writer of sorts and a conversationalist who could hold her own with Charles Lamb; and his four sisters. Keats at once struck up a brotherly chaffing relationship with Jane, the eldest, four years his senior, a rather humourless young lady on the verge of spinsterdom. Mariane Reynolds, two years younger than he, seems to have shone for a while in the eyes of his brother George—but not dazzlingly, for George was already more than half in love with Georgiana Wylie, the young sister of his friends Henry and Charles, the "nymph of the downward smile and sidelong glance" to whom Keats wrote a sonnet of praise that winter. Keats was also going with Clarke and his old schoolmate Edward Holmes to the famous musical evenings at Novello's, the organist and friend of Lamb and Hunt. In his rose-painted living room overlooking Hyde Park, writers and musicians and painters gathered from all over London to drink "Lutheran beer" and listen to Novello playing Bach and Purcell on his chamber organ. Holmes remembered Keats on one of these occasions joking with Hunt about Bach fugues, that they were like nothing so much as two dogs chasing each other through the dust.[28]

But a still more memorable experience for Keats this winter was meeting William Hazlitt at Hunt's—an enigmatic, many-talented, much disappointed man, an unreconstructed Bonapartist and a great but still unrecognized critic whose trenchant articles on politics and the theatre Keats had long admired in *The Examiner*. One wonders if he was also at Hunt's on February 9, when, as Mary Shelley noted in her diary, the guests stayed on for "a discussion until three in the morning with Hazlitt concerning Monarchy and Republicanism." For Shelley was usually to be found at Hunt's now, arguing on every conceivable topic from vegetarianism to the national debt. Keats also spent many evenings at Haydon's studio, talking about painting and poetry and reading Shakespeare aloud—whom, Haydon once said, he enjoyed more with Keats than with any other man. Yet despite his fervent

admiration for Haydon, Keats's opinions struck the older man as
dangerously wrongheaded. One evening, evidently after an argument on religion, he walked over to the canvas of "Christ's Entry,"
where, next to Wordsworth bowing in reverence before Christ,
Haydon had painted Voltaire as a smiling scoffer. Before this portrait, whose hideous sneer Hunt had bitterly criticized, Keats put
his hand on his heart, bowed, and said, "There's the being I will
bend to!"

Haydon had his reasons, then, for being troubled by Hunt's
hold over Keats. With Shelley's appearance, a curious four-cor-
nered battle of friends and disciples was joined. It is revealing
to note that Hunt, in his sonnets at least, immediately began addressing Shelley as "Percy"—a rare intimacy in those days—while
Keats remained "Young Keats" or, conversationally, "Junkets."
On his side Keats, who was scrupulous about these matters, continued to call him "Mr. Hunt," though he dropped this formality
with Haydon a few weeks after their meeting. The first open
skirmish in the battle took place at Horace Smith's one afternoon
in January. As Haydon came in late to dinner, Shelley, carving
a piece of broccoli with elaborate care, remarked in a gentle tone,
"As to that detestable religion the Christian—" Haydon, not having met Shelley before, looked around in astonishment and saw
Hunt and his wife and sister-in-law smiling in anticipation; he
then pitched in and at once found himself cornered. Shelley,
backed by Hunt, maintained that the moral code of the Old
Testament was inconsistent with the New; Haydon flatly contradicted them. The question shifted to whether Shakespeare had
believed in Christianity; Shelley and Hunt asserted he had not,
while Haydon shouted them down by quoting passage after passage from the plays. Logic evaporated in the heat of the argument,
and argument gave way to insult. Meanwhile Keats sat silent with
Smith and the other guests. Haydon finally retired into the next
room to cool off, and the discussion ended; but Hunt could not
keep from making one last dig. When the ladies went to get their
cloaks, he asked, "Are these creatures to be damned, Haydon?"
What a morbid view of Christianity, Haydon retorted, but decided then and there to avoid Hunt and his arguments in the future.

Keats kept up his acquaintance with the Shelleys until they left
London in the middle of March, but the afternoon at Smith's

must have set him thinking. Intellectually he stood with Hunt against Haydon, on the liberal and sceptical side of most questions. But he had seen enough of life already to sense that the truth was more complicated than it appeared from Shelley's black-and-white view of the universe, and more serious than Hunt's largely aesthetic interest in ideas would admit. Nor was he willing to risk a friendship for mere argument's sake, as Hunt did so blithely. When at their first meeting he saw Shelley drawing Severn into a debate on the Christian miracles, Keats stepped in to take Severn's side. A year later he was to admit, "I shall never be a Reasoner because I care not to be in the right." One wonders how much Shelley's obsession with being in the right fostered this scepticism, or whether Keats had heard enough disputations at Hunt's that winter to begin to doubt the power of reason to settle every issue.

Keats was beginning to look on Hunt with more detachment than in the first days of their friendship; yet he still realized how much he owed to Hunt's encouragement. One evening in February, when a last-minute note came from Ollier, asking if his book was to have a dedication, Keats sat down in the middle of a party in his Cheapside rooms and wrote a sonnet "To Leigh Hunt, Esq.," which he sent off to the printer with the final proof-sheets. "Glory and loveliness have passed away," it began; the early-morning walker finds no nymphs on Hampstead Heath, no incense rising from pagan altars. Yet Hunt could offer his friends "delights as high as these," Keats averred, and

> in a time, when under pleasant trees
> Pan is no longer sought, I feel a free
> A leafy luxury, seeing I could please
> With these poor offerings, a man like thee.

The apology in the last line is conventional enough; but at the last minute Keats added a real one. In a prefatory note he let it be known that "the Short Pieces in the middle of the Book, as well as some of the Sonnets, were written at an earlier period than the rest of the Poems." Why he had decided to include some of his earliest and poorest poems, dating back to his friendship with Mathew, we can only guess; the fact is that at the last moment he had some misgivings.

This dissatisfaction with poems he had written a year and a

half before is one more sign of Keats's extraordinary development since the previous fall. But the final revisions of his recent poems, in which he tried to prune the lusher sentimentalism of his style,[29] also suggest that he was becoming aware of something he could not yet openly admit—that he was outgrowing Hunt's influence as surely as he had outgrown Mathew's. Almost from the beginning of their friendship Hunt's idea of the poet and of poetry satisfied only one part of Keats's double nature—that curious mixture of energy and sensibility which Hunt himself had noted. Now he felt increasingly drawn toward Haydon's conception of art. Haydon stood for the heroic manner and the grand scale, where Hunt represented the sentimental and intimate; Haydon worshipped Shakespeare, while Hunt preferred Spenser; Haydon gloried in Homer's virile Greek, while Hunt—who had had little taste for Homer from the time an irate schoolmaster knocked out one of his teeth with a copy of the *Iliad*—delighted in the romantic fantasies of Tasso and Ariosto.

All through this fall and winter Keats tried to keep these two allegiances in balance, but the conflict between them may be read in the poems he wrote at this time. His earliest notion of poetry as a return to the idyllic world of childhood or a release from hated imprisonment and a flight to some supernal realm soon gave way to a set of images describing it as a retreat to some delightful and quite earthy refuge—a bower, a pavilion of boughs, a lair of wavy grass, the bosom of a leafy world. This was the direction in which Hunt's verse pulled him, with its "places of nestling green, for Poets made" *—the realm of Flora, which, even as he described it in "Sleep and Poetry," Keats knew he must leave behind. Toward the end of 1816 his conception of poetry began to take a very different metaphorical colour. One is struck by the many images of height scattered through the poems of this period: Cortez on his peak in Darien, for instance, Endymion on Latmos's top, Wordsworth on the summit of Helvellyn, or Keats himself standing more modestly "upon a little hill." "For what a height my spirit is contending!" he exclaimed of the dizzy excitement he felt on the first evenings at Hunt's cottage. This upward aspiration, reflected in a whole vocabulary of compounds—"upborne," "upcast," "upcurl'd," "upflown," and so forth—suggests that Keats

---

* A quotation from Hunt which Keats later used as the epigraph for "I Stood Tiptoe upon a Little Hill."

was unconsciously finding in poetry a compensation for his small stature.

Yet the height he sought was only a vantage-point from which to survey the task before him, the great poetry he must some day write. The image in which he conveyed this idea is significant. The boy who devoured stories of exploration and identified with his uncle in the Marines, who seemed to give promise of greatness "in some military capacity," re-emerged in the young poet who imagined his life work as a sea voyage. Earlier, in his epistles to Mathew and Clarke, Keats had described poetry in terms of sailing; it was by the sea at Margate, standing on the cliff and listening to the ocean's "voice mysterious," that he began to think of devoting his life to poetry; and the Chapman sonnet started with a voyage to the Spanish Main and reached its climax with the discovery of the Pacific, in an image recalling Keats himself on the cliff at Margate. In "Sleep and Poetry," where he finally committed himself to his vocation, the sea is the metaphorical warp of the entire poem. Poetry is "the grand sea," to whose "mighty winds" and "gathering waves" he gives himself; "a vast idea" of his future "rolls" before him, "an ocean dim" whose "widenesses" he must explore through "many days" and "desperate turmoil." The appearance of this imagery at this time suggests a subtle psychological transformation taking place. Not merely was Keats's sense of the poet's nature, derived from his earlier identification with Hunt, beginning to change and enlarge as he came to see Hunt in clearer perspective. All the events of the winter—his acceptance into Hunt's circle, his decision to publish, his meeting with Shelley—were turning him away from merely playing the part of the young poet, toward a new awareness of the unique creative individual he might become. In this search for his own identity he began half consciously to draw on the resources of his early experience, to see his life again in terms of the first image he had formed of himself in his battle with the world—the naval hero.

The call to action came sooner than he perhaps expected. Ever since the end of December he had been mulling over plans for his next effort in poetry. In spite of his dissatisfaction with "Endymion," he had finally sent it off to the printers unfinished as it was, for he had decided to write another and longer poem on the legend. Accordingly he dropped the title of "Endymion" and, unable to think of another, substituted an epigraph from *Rimini* instead—with the awkward result that the poem has been called by its first line, "I stood tiptoe upon a little hill," ever since. Then Shelley, sometime before leaving London in March, announced his plans for his next work, a long narrative poem on an imaginary revolution in the Middle East, and suggested to Keats that they write their poems in a friendly competition over the summer.[30] Each poem was to run to four thousand lines and be finished in six months' time. It was a breath-taking proposal. The new *Endymion* would be twice the length of Hunt's *Rimini,* over ten times the length of his *Hero and Leander.* Nothing Keats had written so far showed the strength for such an effort. But his mettle was up, and he accepted Shelley's challenge.

The time of decision had come at last, the point toward which he had been moving irreversibly for almost a year. He would give up medicine. *Endymion* would require all his time, all his powers; there was no other way to achieve his goal. When the Surgeons' Examination was held on February 7 and his friends Stephens and Newmarch went up and passed, Keats was not with them.[31] One reason may have been the fact that, though he had already completed his term with Lucas, he still lacked eight months of the age of twenty-two required to qualify as a surgeon. But far more important were his overpowering ambition in poetry and his steadily growing revulsion from surgery. At last the strain of operating became too much for him. One day at the hospital as he was opening a man's temporal artery he found himself overwhelmed by the thought of the disaster that would result from a possible slip of his lancet. With a great effort he went on and performed the ligation neatly, but all the while he seemed to be standing outside himself and watching his own dexterity with disbelief. The conflict between the cool scientific detachment required of a surgeon and the sensibility and warmth of feeling instinctive to him as a poet had reached its crisis. When he laid down his instruments at the end he realized he could never operate again.

On the face of it, throwing up a secure profession to risk everything on his still unproved abilities as a poet was sheer foolhardiness, as at least one of his friends privately declared. But a man with a daemon like Keats's does not listen to mere prudent advice. With all writers the compulsion toward achievement remains a mystery in the end, and its motives are many and obscure. The longing for fame that will outlive death is certainly one of them; the desire for love, which seemingly cannot be won any other way; or even, it has been suggested, the need to expiate some imaginary guilt deep in the unconscious. Of these possible motives, Keats had already clearly expressed the first; the second he seems not yet to have admitted to himself; the third was a force whose existence he could not even suspect. Yet it appears that, on a conscious and realistic level, he had calculated the risks in his decision. If he made a name with his *Poems,* he might begin to make a fortune with *Endymion.* Surely it was possible to earn a living by writing if one had the talent and the determination. Reynolds had given up a dull job clerking in an insurance office the year before to write articles and reviews, and was turning out a book of poetry a year. Perhaps when Keats called for "ten years" to devote himself to poetry he had also figured how long his money would last in the effort to prove his powers.

Once he had made his decision, he had to tell his guardian. Abbey, meanwhile, had been laying plans for his future. Partly to spite Hammond, partly because Mrs. Jennings was still remembered in the neighbourhood, he had arranged to set Keats up in practice in Tottenham, only two miles from Edmonton. Keats's reply to this proposal left him fuming with astonishment. Not intend to be a surgeon! What in the world did he plan to do? When Keats answered that he intended to make his career in poetry, Abbey retorted that he was either a fool or a madman to throw over five years' study for such an absurd idea. As calmly as he could, Keats told him he believed that his abilities were greater than most men's, and that he could earn his living by writing. A long argument ensued. Keats held his ground, and Abbey's rage sputtered out at last in calling Keats "a silly boy" and assuring him he would fail. Keats swallowed his anger; Abbey was still the figure of authority, who, though he could no longer legally control his actions, still administered his inheritance. But opposition only hardened his purpose. "In no period of my life have I acted with any self will, but in throwing up the apothecary-profession," he wrote three years later. "That I do not repent of."

Two friends at least cheered him in this decision. A young lady —Jane Reynolds, perhaps—sent him congratulations in the form of a laurel crown, a gesture not unheard of in Hunt's circle. Keats thanked her in the usual sonnet, breathing defiance of Abbey's tyranny and devotion to her gentleness. Haydon also endorsed the plan for *Endymion,* an undertaking much to his mind, on the heroic scale and in the Greek spirit. As a token of his approval, he presented Keats at about this time with a copy of Goldsmith's *History of Greece,* inscribed "from his ardent friend B. R. Haydon." [32] But he did much more: he took Keats at the beginning of March to see the Elgin Marbles, which were now on public view in the British Museum. Like his meeting with Hunt six months before, this marked a new era in Keats's existence. He had a notion of Greek art based, as was then inevitable, on eighteenth-century prints of Roman copies of Hellenistic statues; he had seen Haydon's drawings of the Marbles and perhaps worked a few images from them into his poems; but none of this prepared him for the shock of the reality. He was struck almost at once by the contemporaneousness of the sculpture—the freshness and vitality which made all copies look ancient and lifeless by contrast. Like Haydon, Keats immediately recognized the profound knowledge of anatomy shaping bone and muscle and tendon in these forms. But he was far more deeply moved by the surging energy of the young horsemen, the robust grace of the maidens, the magnificent serenity of the gods and goddesses. This was the Greek spirit made flesh, "the religion of joy," he once called it, an embodiment of a religious attitude which he now realized more clearly than ever was his own. A few months later, on one of his many trips back to the museum, he told Severn, "I never cease to wonder at all that incarnate delight." [33]

His immediate reaction, however, was not delight but speechless astonishment. Somehow he felt that Haydon expected a more vocal response, and on his return home he wrote him a sonnet apologizing for his failure to express what he had felt. It is curious to note that for the moment he lapsed into Haydon's own extravagant rhetoric, borrowing phrases—for lack of any of his own— from Haydon's essay on the Marbles.[34] In a second sonnet, a day or two later, he came much closer to expressing the contrast between his previous notion of greatness and his new vision. In the unassertive strength of Phidias's sculpture, so different from the overwrought effeminacy of the verse he had written under Hunt's influence, he sensed the possibility of a new accent for poetry, embodying the weight, the density of marble itself:

My spirit is too weak—mortality
   Weighs heavily on me like unwilling sleep,
   And each imagin'd pinnacle and steep
Of godlike hardship tells me I must die
Like a sick Eagle looking at the sky. . . .
Such dim-conceived glories of the brain
   Bring round the heart an undescribable feud;
So do these wonders a most dizzy pain,
   That mingles Grecian grandeur with the rude
Wasting of old Time—with a billowy main—
   A sun—a shadow of a magnitude.

The "godlike hardship" of creation, which he had barely glimpsed before—the seas to cross, the pinnacles to scale, the shadowy magnitude to measure and define—now appeared to him in palpable form, with the force almost of a command. Would he be equal to the work he had set himself?

⫸⫷

On Monday, March 3, 1817—a year to the day from the beginning of his term as dresser at Guy's—Keats's first book appeared at last. It was a neat pocket-sized volume, bound in gray boards backed with a white label announcing "Keats' Poems: Price 6s." The title page was embellished with a portrait of Spenser under a Spenserian motto that struck the keynote of "delight with liberty" for the poems that followed—some hundred and twenty crisply printed pages of them, fresh as a new coin. It is not hard to imagine Keats's sensations when he held the first copy in his hands. This was probably an advance copy which Charles Ollier sent him on Sunday, inscribed with a sonnet of congratulation, "Keats, I admire thine upward-daring soul." It is rare for publishers to pay tribute in verse to their own poets, but Ollier was a versifier before he turned publisher, and he was confident that his first publication would win laurels for its author and success for the new firm as well. Ollier was also generous with presentation copies, for Keats had nearly twenty to give away. Almost his first act was to go out to Hampstead with a copy for Hunt. He found him walking in Milfield Lane, on the edge of the Heath; and Hunt, who recalled this meeting vividly a dozen years later, must have accepted the gift as gladly as Keats gave it. In reply to the dedication, he wrote Keats another congratulatory sonnet, foreseeing with Ollier "a flowering laurel" on his brow.[35] On Monday evening the publication was celebrated at a party in Haydon's studio, to which Clarke and Reynolds were invited. Their spirits must have run high. Haydon, who had received Keats's sonnets on the Elgin Marbles that very morning, thanked him with characteristic enthusiasm: "You filled me with fury for an hour, and with admiration forever." A day or two later, on reading "Sleep and Poetry," he wrote Keats in a burst of prophecy: "It is a flash of lightening that will rouse men from their occupations, and keep them trembling for the crash of thunder that *will* follow."

The first peal of recognition came a week later with his fellow poet Reynolds' review in *The Champion*. To the readers of that magazine, who had never heard of Keats before, it proclaimed that he would eclipse the greatest names of the day—Byron, Moore, Samuel Rogers, Thomas Campbell—and compared him with Shakespeare and Chaucer. Reynolds conceded that the earliest poems in the volume fell short of this standard; but the sonnets, he maintained, ranked with Milton's and Wordsworth's. This was audacious praise, of a kind which only one very young man can give to another; yet Reynolds unerringly singled out the very qualities in Keats's early work which later became his distinctive excellences. Keats was dazzled by the review but not blinded. He sat down at once to write Reynolds a few "monosentences" of thanks: "Your Criticism only makes me extremely anxious that I sho^d not deceive you. It's the finest thing by God— as Hazlitt wo^d say However I hope I may not deceive you." Then, realizing that very few of Reynolds' readers would agree with his estimate, he rounded off his thanks with a joke: "There are some acquaintances of mine who will scratch their Beards and although I have, I hope, some Charity, I wish their Nails may be long."

Whoever these acquaintances may have been, Reynolds was becoming one of Keats's most valued friends. A young poet of promise who had gone through three styles in his first three books —the early Byron, Wordsworth, and Hunt—Reynolds was only beginning to find his own voice, that of a dandified romantic who turns away from nature for his inspiration to the green-room, the Garrick Club, and the prize ring. A good-looking young man, with dark eyes, thick lashes, and dark hair combed smooth over his forehead like a fighter's, he had a mobile and intelligent face with

a curiously arch smile. A streak of the sardonic was appearing in
him, which was rapidly to turn against himself. Even if he sensed
that his new friend might displace him as the coming talent, he
was still drawn to Keats, and Keats to him, by a similar zest for
life and sense of humour. They shared enthusiasms for the theatre
and boxing; and Reynolds, as a member of the sporting set known
as "The Fancy," probably took Keats on some of his visits to Jack
Randall's in Chancery Lane to watch the sparring. In the feud
that Shelley stirred up that winter, Reynolds naturally sided with
Haydon and thus heightened the strain on Keats's loyalty to Hunt.
Meanwhile Reynolds was introducing Keats to his own set, where
he found congenial company untrammelled by the claims of discipleship. James Rice, a young solicitor; Benjamin Bailey, a divinity student at Oxford; Charles Wentworth Dilke, an official at
the Navy Pay Office with an active interest in literature; John
Martin, Reynolds' first publisher; John Taylor, his present publisher, with his partner James Augustus Hessey; and Richard
Woodhouse, an old Etonian and barrister who acted as reader in
Taylor's firm—these were to be the friends of Keats's lifetime. It is
not hard to see why. In Reynolds' circle Keats was no longer a
protégé but a man to be met on his own terms, with one promising book already to his credit. In becoming the poet he wanted to
be, he found the friends he had sought but never made for himself
before.

Yet for all their expectations, the crash of thunder which Haydon predicted remained a mere rumble on the horizon. Three
weeks went by after Reynolds' review till another appeared, a
short but favourable notice in the *Monthly Magazine;* then silence. The sale of the book slowed to a halt. As Cowden Clarke
admitted, it might have been published in Timbuctoo for all the
attention it received. Hunt printed three of Keats's new sonnets
in *The Examiner* during March to try to rouse some interest in
the book, but this failed. Indeed, Shelley's friend Peacock told
Mary he was so scandalized by the badness of the sonnet on "The
Floure and the Lefe" that he would petition Hunt not to publish
any more. Keats sent a copy of the book to Mathew, inscribed
with a friendly greeting, but evidently heard nothing in reply.
He also took Abbey a copy, by way of proving his boast of a month
before. His guardian agreed to read it, but only because Keats
had written it. On their next meeting he commented, "Well,

John, I have read your book, and it reminds me of the Quaker's horse—hard to catch and good for nothing when he was caught." The joke stung. Even as Abbey chuckled over it, he sensed that Keats would never forgive him, though he pretended not to notice it. There was nothing for Keats to do but swallow his pride and go back to work—pondering the plan of *Endymion* and extending his close study of the Elizabethan poets. The leading reviews sometimes took months to get around to a book by a new author; in the meantime he would keep his spirits up.

Yet it appears that he was getting restless in London. Now that his responsibilities at the hospital were over, there was nothing to hold him in the city. His rooms in Cheapside were hardly the place for study and work, and the life of literary London, which had seemed so pleasant all winter, was beginning to pall. Around the middle of March he suddenly decided to leave town for a while. Haydon advised him to live alone to concentrate on his work, and Tom and George agreed, though reluctantly. Keats himself was ready to admit that he had had an overdose of City air and late hours. "Banish money—Banish sofas—Banish Wine —Banish Music," he wrote Reynolds in a Falstaffian vein, "But right Jack Health—honest Jack Health, true Jack Health—banish health and banish all the world." Hampstead was the inevitable choice.[36] Keats found rooms near the Heath in the house of the postmaster, Benjamin Bentley, on Well Walk, a pleasant lime-bordered avenue leading to the springs which had been fashionable in the eighteenth century. From here it was only a five-minute stroll to the Vale of Health, where Hunt could read him the latest lines of his new poem or play over his new hymn, "To the Spirit Great and Good." From a letter which Keats wrote to Clarke on March 25, relaying an invitation to take a part in the hymn at Novello's the next evening, it appears that his relations with "Mr. Hunt" were as cordial as ever. Hunt, he reported, had "got a great way" into his new poem, *The Nymphs,* and "said a number of beautiful things"; while he himself had "written a few Lines and a Sonnet on Rimini." Hunt was revising *Rimini* for a second edition, and Keats, on reading it again, had been struck anew by its charm. A few phrases in his sonnet, as well as his mention of writing "a few lines," make it sound as though he was already at work on the opening of *Endymion* and had reread *Rimini* with his own long poem in mind.

Yet this tranquillity was too poetic to last. Unluckily one day Hunt took it into his head to turn his prophecy of a laurel wreath for Keats into a reality.[37] As they sat drinking their wine after dinner, he proposed to Keats that they crown themselves with laurel and ivy "after the fashion of the elder Bards" and write sonnets on their "sensations." Keats agreed but, once the wreaths were produced, found he had nothing to say. While Hunt, delighted with his own whim, dashed off one sonnet and then started on another, Keats sat blankly searching for an idea, then limped through fourteen lines describing his lack of inspiration. At this point three callers were announced. Hunt snatched off his crown before the ladies entered, but not Keats. He refused to disown so abjectly what the laurels stood for. Instead, "in his mad enthusiastic way," he wore his wreath without explanation all through the visit, to the callers' amusement, and when they left he succeeded in writing a second sonnet "To the Ladies Who Saw Me Crown'd." His bravado was more than a match for Hunt's; but soon afterward he began to regret the pretentiousness of the gesture and did what he could to prevent the sonnets from getting into circulation.

For slowly but surely Keats was breaking out of Hunt's orbit. Early in April an invitation came from Shelley, suggesting that he come down with Hunt and his family on a long visit to Marlow, where the Shelleys had taken a house overlooking the Thames. At once Keats realized this would not do. He needed his own "unfetterd scope," as he later put it, to work on *Endymion;* he could not write with Hunt looking over his shoulder and Shelley, who had already made a good start on his poem, pulling ahead of him day after day. Besides, he was increasingly troubled by Hunt's cheerful acceptance of his position as one of Shelley's pensioners —"a Situation which I should be less eager after than that of a galley Slave," as he later remarked to Haydon.

Keats declined Shelley's invitation as gracefully as he could; but meanwhile another awkward situation arose when he and Hunt began talking over their new poems together. *The Nymphs* was turning into a pretty little treatise on the Greek demigoddesses, written with much the same feeling as that with which Hunt had studied the engravings in his schoolbooks of mythology. But Keats's idea of the Greek spirit was rapidly changing, and evidently he now had confidence enough in his own judgment to

question a few of Hunt's phrases. Hunt retorted by casting doubts
on Keats's whole project of *Endymion*. "Why endeavour after a
long poem?" he asked. Perhaps it was a sensible question, now
that the failure of Keats's first volume was apparent, but for Keats
it meant the end of his discipleship. "There is no greater Sin after
the 7 deadly than to flatter oneself into an idea of being a great
Poet," he exploded in a letter to Haydon not long afterward. If
Hunt had flattered him as well as himself into such an idea, Keats
was now undeceived; but if Hunt refused to encourage him with
*Endymion*, Keats refused to be discouraged. As Haydon noted
in his diary at this time, Hunt deprecated any undertaking on the
epic scale because he was too lazy to attempt one himself; but
Keats realized that there was no way to discover whether he could
write a long poem—to him the test of the great poet—but to try,
even at the risk of failure. And, as he later wrote, "I would sooner
fail than not be among the greatest."

Yet he did not make an open declaration of independence.
When Hunt went off to Marlow on April 6, he left Keats with
two commissions which show that he still thought of him as one
of those friends to whom he was glad to be obliged. He asked Keats
to read the proofs of the new edition of *Rimini* when they came
back from the printer, and to go through his study destroying
papers connected with some obscure financial matter. Since Hunt
was over a thousand pounds in debt at this time, it seems likely
that "old Wood," whom Keats in his letter reporting on the affair
described as "a very Varmant—sharded in Covetousness," was a
bailiff with a search warrant whom Hunt was trying to forestall.[38]
Keats, who was clearly embarrassed by the request, decided to lock
the papers up in a trunk instead of destroying them; and perhaps
it was this shabby episode that completed his disillusionment with
Hunt. However this may be, a few days later he made a decisive
move: he broke with Hunt's friends the Olliers and went over to
Reynolds' publishers, Taylor and Hessey—an interesting switch,
since Hunt had just transferred from Taylor and Hessey to the
Olliers with the second edition of *Rimini*.

This change was an important decision for Keats and one which
he never had cause to regret. Taylor promised to keep him in
funds in exchange for "the refusal of his future works." The agreement shows great faith in Keats's talent on Taylor's part, for the
Olliers had understandably become dismayed at the number of

unsold copies of the *Poems* left on their shelves. On April 15 Taylor wrote to his father, a bookseller in Bath, about his new author: "I cannot fail to think that he will become a great Poet, though I agree with you in finding much fault with the Dedication &c. These are not likely to appear in any other of his Productions." Taylor had reasons other than political for regretting the dedication of the *Poems* to Hunt. Six months before, he had advanced him twenty guineas for the collection of mythological poems which Hunt had started with *Hero and Leander;* but though the book was advertised, Hunt never finished it and put off repaying the advance for over a year.[39] Taylor, a man of the world some fourteen years older than Keats, was almost as much amused as impressed by the young poet when he met him in March, for he described his "singular style of dress" in some detail in a letter to his brother. Yet besides his faith in Keats's ability he soon came to feel a very real warmth toward him—"a strange personal interest in all that concerns him," as he once half apologetically put it.

Perhaps Taylor's encouragement helped Keats to make one more decision that week—to get completely away from London in order to work on *Endymion*. He had not found the solitude he needed in his new lodgings. It was not warm enough yet to spend days on the Heath reading and writing, and at Well Walk he was plagued by the Bentleys' carrot-haired children, who filled the house with "horrid rows" and the smell of worsted stockings. Then George and Tom evidently decided sometime in early April to give up their rooms in Cheapside and join him in Hampstead. Perhaps they moved for economy's sake, or to find a better air for Tom; or perhaps it was at this time that George quarrelled with Abbey's junior partner Hodgkinson and left his job in Pancras Lane. Haydon's advice that Keats try living alone in the country was now more to the point than ever. After all the excitements and disappointments and contradictions of the winter he needed to get away—most of all, it would seem, to escape from Hampstead, where his hopes for poetry had soared so high and then collapsed. As he looked back on the events of the winter and spring, Keats was suddenly overcome with consternation and disbelief. How could he have been duped into thinking himself a great poet—even worse, how could he have joined Hunt in the masquerade of the laurel crowning? What an affront to the god of poetry, however he could be imagined to exist! Half in mockery, half in earnest, Keats wrote a "Hymn to Apollo" by way of apology and promised to "put on no Laurels" till he finished *Endymion*. The next six months would tell whether he could claim them in the end. On April 14 he packed up and started out for the Isle of Wight, not to return, so he promised himself, till his poem was done.

*Chapter Five*

---

# A Leap into the Sea

LATE that afternoon Keats climbed up on an outside seat in the Southampton coach and felt the excitement surging up in him as they clattered out of the Holborn innyard. He had said good-bye to friends and brothers, to congratulatory sonnets and laudatory reviews; he was going into self-imposed exile with a great work to be done. Soon after clearing the toll-gate at Hyde Park Corner they reached the open road, speeding south and west between dusty hedges and empty fields in the fading light. The outside seats, cheaper than those within, were usually occupied by smart young gentlemen who cared little about changes in the weather; Keats sat up, trying to look unconcerned, drawing his plaid around him as the evening air grew cold. But after three stages he was glad to take an empty seat inside for the rest of the journey. Here he dozed by fits and starts as they rattled through nameless little towns, where stone fountains and barber poles loomed up and fell away again in the dim light of their lamps. When he looked out again the sun was rising, and yellow furze was ablaze along the roadside. The unaccustomed hour, the brightness, the promise of warmth in the chilly air, sent his spirits soaring with the larks.

Soon they reached Southampton, rolled through an old gate flanked by two lions, and drew up in front of their last inn. Keats climbed down a little stiffly, ordered breakfast, then suddenly felt so lonely that he unpacked a volume of Shakespeare to read with his meal. He found that the boat to the Isle of Wight would not sail till three. The tide was out; the harbor was dank. He spent the morning walking up and down the Southampton streets, noting that the men and women looked no different from those in London; then, beginning to feel a little muzzy, he returned to the inn to dine on a chop and write a letter to George and Tom.

A good sleep at Newport that night and a trip around the island on Wednesday restored his spirits. Spring came early to the Isle of Wight; the fields were already green with young wheat, and the hedges were thick with cowslips and primroses. On the coach from Cowes to Newport they passed a huge army barracks, "a Nest of Debauchery," a fellow passenger told him, which had quite spoiled the people of the island, especially the women. But, said Keats in a letter to Reynolds, "I must in honesty confess that I did not feel very sorry at the idea of the Women being a little profligate." Wondering where to stay, he looked at Shanklin, a fishing village popular with summer visitors, perched over the great wooded cleft of the Chine; but he finally chose Carisbrooke, a hamlet outside Newport in the center of the island. Though less picturesque, it was cheaper, and somehow he felt cheered to see the coast of England from a hill nearby. His landlady, Mrs. Cook, was unexpectedly amiable, for she did not object when he exchanged the print of a French ambassador hanging in his room for one of Shakespeare which had caught his eye in the hallway. After pinning up the Shakespeare with three pictures of his own, Keats arranged his books in a row underneath and told himself he had done a good morning's work. He felt unaccountably restless. After clambering around the ruins of Carisbrooke Castle, he went for a walk by the sea, then began a letter to Reynolds, begging for news of his brothers and Reynolds' sisters and all their friends.

For some reason he could not bring himself to start work yet, though he was all in a tremble, as he told Reynolds, from not having written anything for so long. Instead he turned to his books and began rereading Shakespeare. As he went headlong through his favourite plays he discovered new meaning in line after line that had never struck him before. "I find that I cannot exist without poetry," he wrote Reynolds, "half the day will not do—the whole of it—I began with a little, but habit has made me a Leviathan." Then there was the sea, even vaster and more mysterious than the summer before. As he walked along the shore, scanning the horizon, listening to the ceaseless whisper of the tide, the noise and confusion of London faded from his mind. Thursday evening, haunted by a passage from *King Lear* on the view from the Dover cliffs, he worked out a sonnet "On the Sea." It was the last he was to write for nine months. The sonnet form came almost too easily now; he wanted to say something greater than could be contained in its limits. Yet writing it somehow steadied his nerves, just as, it seems, his walk by the sea renewed the sense of his symbolic journey that had come to him at Margate.* He stood like a diver poised for a moment, then plunged into the timeless world of *Endymion*.

As he first conceived his poem, it was to be a test of his powers of invention—to "make 4000 Lines of one bare circumstance and fill them with Poetry." [1] The legend of Endymion's winning immortal youth through the love of the moon goddess was only the beginning, or rather the ending; he had to fill up his four books with living characters, set them moving in a world of their own, and breathe new meaning into the old legend. The meaning, as he phrased it in his first lines, was quite simple:

> A thing of beauty is a joy for ever:
> Its loveliness increases; it will never
> Pass into nothingness; but still will keep
> A bower quiet for us, and a sleep
> Full of sweet dreams, and health, and quiet breathing.

Such things of beauty are the sun, the moon, daffodils, and clear streams

> That for themselves a cooling covert make
> 'Gainst the hot season; . .

but also the memory of "the mighty dead"—the great names of history he kept constantly before him—and "All lovely tales that we have heard or read." Essentially he still held, with Hunt, that a poet should "simply tell the most heart-easing things." It was the sheer beauty of the story of Endymion, its association with the moon, and its theme of endless youth and love that first appealed to him—both to his worship of nature and to the idealism which still regarded a fair woman as a pure goddess. His head was filled with "lovely tales" from his winter's reading of Eliza-

---

* The image of poetry as sailing recurs in the introductory lines of *Endymion*.

bethan poetry, which had set him an example for retelling the
Greek myths with a wealth of description and adventure and
amorous encounter and an admixture of allegorical significance.
Some idea of a spiritual development to be undergone by his hero
in winning immortal love was also taking shape in his mind, an
expression of the "religion of joy" he had found given tangible
form in the Elgin Marbles. All the varied experiences of the last
year, hope and discovery and discouragement, all the arguments
on poetry and art and religion he had heard at Hunt's and Haydon's, all his own aspirations toward some dimly sensed goal, were
stirring in his mind and gathering around the centre of Endymion's quest.

This ferment of ideas and impressions kept him in "continual
burning of thought," as he called it, in his first week at Carisbrooke and made it difficult to begin. Furthermore, he had no
clear sense of the direction of his story. A year later he confessed,
"Before I began I had no inward feel of being able to finish; and
as I proceeded my steps were all uncertain." But still he struck
out. His plan was to send Endymion on a journey through the
elements in search of his goddess, describing the strange worlds
through which he passes and telling other myths along the way.
"Do not the Lovers of Poetry like to have a little Region to wander
in," he wrote George, "where the images are so numerous that
many are forgotten and found new in a second Reading: which
may be food for a Week's stroll in the Summer?" This is a form-
less design for a long poem, no doubt, the result of starting with
a predetermined length rather than a clearly conceived action.
Yet marvellous adventures and exotic scenery were all to the
taste of the romance-readers of the time: and what better place to
start his poem than the Isle of Wight in mid-April?

> . . . so I will begin
> Now while I cannot hear the city's din;
> Now while the early budders are just new,
> And run in mazes of the youngest hue
> About old forests; while the willow trails
> Its delicate amber; and the dairy pails
> Bring home increase of milk. . . .

He looked ahead, not to the ending of his poem, which was still
unclear, but to the autumn which must come, and laid his plans:

> O may no wintry season, bare and hoary,
> See it half finished: but let Autumn bold,
> With universal tinge of sober gold,
> Be all about me when I make an end.

For a few days all seemed to go well. The first book opened in a forest on the sides of Mount Latmos, and he filled almost a hundred lines with description of the "copse-clad vallies" all around him, the sunrise he had seen on his journey, the murmurings of the sea on his evening walks. Yet after a week, just as he was getting started, he faltered and broke off. The loneliness of Carisbrooke together with the excitement of his work was too much for him. He found himself losing his appetite and unable to sleep at night for thinking of his poem hour after solitary hour. Suddenly he decided he could work better in the familiar surroundings of Margate and wrote Tom to meet him there, then astonished Mrs. Cook by telling her he must leave at once. But as he was packing up she insisted he take the portrait of Shakespeare he had liked so much. It struck him as a good omen.

At Margate Tom's company was a steadying influence. They walked and talked together as they had the summer before, and Keats returned to *Endymion* on a schedule of eight hours of reading and writing a day. Tom, who was deep in Plutarch's *Lives,* sometimes read aloud passages of Pope's Homer from the translation he was reading, and Keats thought Pope's lines seemed "like Mice" compared to his. As he picked up the first book again with his head still full of the lavish beauty of the Isle of Wight, he composed a long "Hymn to Pan" in which the shepherds give thanks to their god for the abundance of their lives:

> O thou, whose mighty palace roof doth hang
> From jagged trunks, and overshadoweth
> Eternal whispers, glooms, the birth, life, death
> Of unseen flowers in heavy peacefulness;
> Who lov'st to see the hamadryads dress
> Their ruffled locks where meeting hazels darken;
> And through whole solemn hours dost sit, and hearken
> The dreary melody of bedded reeds—
> In desolate places, where dank moisture breeds
> The pipy hemlock to strange overgrowth;
> Bethinking thee, how melancholy loth
> Thou wast to lose fair Syrinx—do thou now,

By thy love's milky brow!
By all the trembling mazes that she ran,
Hear us, great Pan! . . .

They were triumphant lines, full of the riches of the earth and touched with the mystery of the vital force binding all living things together. Yet as Keats moved on into the narrative portion of his poem, the most difficult part for him, his old doubts returned. "The high Idea I have of poetical fame makes me think I see it towering to high * above me," he wrote George in a fit of dejection. He was discovering the anxieties of labouring day after day to bring into being a work conceived on a grand scale. He read his lines over; they seemed worthless. His ambitions for *Endymion* were soaring so high, he confessed to Hunt, that he feared he would overreach himself and "drop into a Phæton." Why, he asked, should he think himself a poet more than other men?

Perhaps the first adverse criticism of his *Poems,* which appeared in the *European Magazine* for May, contributed to this mood. Damning the volume with very faint praise, the reviewer found a few promising poems outweighed by "feeble and false thoughts" and a "redundance of poetical decoration." He criticized the Chapman sonnet as "unseemly hyperbole," and predicted that the attack on Pope in "Sleep and Poetry" would bring "ridicule and rebuke" down on the young author. Curiously enough, the only poems he approved were those addressed to the Mathew girls and the sonnets "On Woman," which Reynolds in his review had called "very inferior to the rest." This critic scoffed at Reynolds' praise of Keats and deplored the influence of Hunt. As he warned Keats in conclusion, "the mere luxuries of imagination" can only "inculcate the falsest and most dangerous ideas and refine us into the degeneracy of butterflies that perish in the deceitful glories of a destructive taper." The review was signed simply "G.F.M." [2]

Keats must have been staggered by this obituary notice of his friendship with Mathew, though he never mentioned it beyond remarking offhandedly in a letter to Haydon that "Envy and detraction" were mere "stimulants to further exertion." Evidently it

---

* Keats apparently intended "too high," as appears from an image that haunted him at the time, of trying to scale the Dover cliff—"the Cliff of Poesy": "I am 'one that gathers Samphire dreadful trade,' " as he remarked to Haydon (see *The Letters of John Keats,* ed. H. E. Rollins [1958], I, 131, 139, 141, 169).

reached him around the same time as a gloomy letter from George on May 11 about money matters. What these were is impossible to guess exactly. The country was going through a postwar period of depression and unemployment, and George was having a hard time finding work. Shortly after leaving Abbey, it seems, he became involved in a business venture with a friend named Wilkinson— probably one Thomas Wilkinson, an auctioneer and agent on Bread Street, off Cheapside.[3] George evidently had to put up some capital for the project, and Keats had contributed £40 or £50 of his own. Now, it seems, the plan was heading toward disaster. To make matters worse, George had written a rash note to the Olliers late in April, reproaching them for the slow sale of the *Poems* and asking how many copies were left on hand—perhaps with the idea of buying them out. The Olliers wrote a stinging reply to thank him for relieving them of "any further connection" with the volume and to report that many of their customers considered it "no better than a take in." This news was enough to bring Keats to a complete halt somewhere near the middle of his first book. His cash was running low, and unpaid bills were nagging at him; evidently before leaving London he had run up an account for some new and more presentable clothes. When Taylor and Hessey came to his rescue with an advance of £20, he thanked them in a note of embarrassed jocosity. Was he going to end up like Hunt, sponging on his publishers' confidence?

His uneasiness about Hunt continued. A letter came from Marlow, asking about the commissions Hunt had left him with, but Keats put off answering it for two weeks. He finally replied as best he could in their old easygoing style, commenting on the latest *Examiner* and citing two new passages on the still-vexed question of Shakespeare's Christianity—one for, one against. After asking how *The Nymphs* was progressing and offering a little guarded advice, he admitted his discouragement with *Endymion,* then immediately made a joke about it: "Does Shelley go on telling strange Stories of the Death of kings? Tell him there are strange Stories of the death of Poets—some have died before they were conceived. Does M^rs Hunt tear linen in half as straight as ever? Tell her to tear from the book of Life all blank Leaves." He signed himself "John Keats alias Junkets," but the familiarity was forced. He could write Haydon about his hopes and fears without self-mockery, but to Hunt no longer.

Yet Haydon presented another difficulty. He had written Keats one of his fiery letters, warning him against the "delusions & sophistications" that were ruining Hunt's talent and prescribing his own remedy for discouragement—prayer. From this refuge, he said, "I always arose, with a refreshed fury—an iron clenched firmness, and chrystal piety of feeling, that sent me streaming on with a repulsive power against the troubles of life, as if I were a cannon shot, darting through feathers." Keats replied that Hunt's "self delusions" about being a great poet were "very lamentable," but added uneasily that he hoped he was not deceiving himself in the same manner. Haydon, he felt, was the one person who understood the "turmoil and anxiety" of creation, "the readiness to Measure time by what is done and to die in 6 hours could plans be brought to conclusions." Yet Keats could not "trust in God" in his moments of doubt as Haydon urged him to do. "I never quite despair and I read Shakspeare," he confessed. "I am very near Agreeing with Hazlit that Shakspeare is enough for us." Then, realizing this might lead them into another argument on religion, he desisted.

This casual echo of Hazlitt's remark is a clue to a silent but momentous change that was taking place in Keats's mind that spring. He was discovering in Shakespeare the poet of all poets for him, who not only replaced Spenser and Hunt as his exemplars in poetry but was also bringing to focus his convictions on human experience. All through 1817 Keats's letters echo with Shakespeare's lines, whether he is making a joke or describing his profoundest aspirations. Even his poetry was beginning to show the influence of the dense thinginess of Shakespeare's style, concentrated where his own early verse was diffuse, tough in its sensuousness rather than luxurious. Yet more than this, Keats was drawn to Shakespeare by that most elusive of essences, his outlook on life—the honesty, the saneness, the depth of his humanity in confronting the whole range of human experience. Perhaps Keats first became aware of these qualities in that futile argument at Horace Smith's over Shakespeare's Christianity, for what evidently impressed him then was that neither Haydon nor Shelley could prove his point—that indeed Shakespeare had no point to prove beyond the inexhaustible richness of human character. The portrait of Shakespeare which he had brought from Carisbrooke now hung over his books at Margate, as it was to hang over his writing desk ever afterward. Looking up at it one day after reading over some lines which struck him as bet-

ter than he had thought at the time he wrote them, he recalled
Haydon's belief that a good genius presided over his painting.
Could it be, he asked him, that he too had a good genius? "Is it too
daring to Fancy Shakspeare this Presider?"

Yet, in spite of these flashes of encouragement, Keats found he
had written himself out after three weeks at Margate. The first
book was barely half finished, but his nerves were on edge and his
head swam as though he had been on "a Mental Debauch." Suddenly tired of Margate—"this treeless affair"—he decided to move
again, this time to Canterbury. There the thought of Chaucer, he
wrote Taylor, would "set [him] forward like a Billiard-Ball." Canterbury itself, evidently the first cathedral town he had seen, gave
him a glimpse of the Middle Ages that sank deep into his memory.
With Tom he must have wandered for hours through the narrow
streets and strolled up and down the aisles of the cathedral, marvel-
ling at the royal tombs, the stone tracery, the soaring arches, the
stained glass of the great window. After this breathing space he set
to work again, and by the beginning of June, it seems, he had completed the draft of the first book—over a thousand lines. It was an
achievement. Already he was learning to fill in a large-scale plan
line by line, episode by episode. Still more, he was beginning to
find he could work without the constant encouragement of an older
friend. He refused to copy out a passage for Hunt's approval, and
even told Haydon he could say nothing about his poem till it was
half done. However far the first book fell short of his intentions—
and it was to undergo much agonized rewriting—he had battled
through to the end of his first round.

Now he decided to take a holiday. While Tom returned to
London, Keats went off to a seaside village near Hastings with
the improbable name of Bo-Peep, where Haydon occasionally
went on vacation. And here he had an adventure. For years Keats
had stood in the shadow of his handsome and enterprising brother
George so far as women were concerned; now all on his own he
met an attractive woman several years older than himself and
struck up a flirtation. The affair is shrouded in mystery for us,
and even to Keats the lady remained "an enigma." He referred
to her in several later letters to George merely as "the lady from
Hastings," not because he did not know her name but because
she imposed secrecy on him. Nevertheless her identity can be
gathered from scattered references to her by Keats's friends and

from several of her own letters to Keats's new publisher, John
Taylor, with whom she was on friendly terms. She was Isabella
Jones, the "beautiful Mrs. Jones," as John Reynolds wistfully
recalled her years later.[4] A member of semi-fashionable literary
society in London, she was attached in some undefined manner
to an elderly Irishman of a titled family named O'Callaghan, with
whom she spent summers in Hastings. Intelligent and sophisticated, she was perceptive enough to take an interest in this young
protégé of Taylor's. As for Keats, she was apparently just the
woman he needed to break the bonds of his shyness. If, as seems
possible, the song "Hush, hush! tread softly" was his recollection
of this episode some months later,[5] she had to steal secretly out
of the inn late at night, away from her "jealous old bald-pate," to
meet him in the garden below. How far the affair went in those
few days—Keats said merely that he had "warmed with her"—
can never be known. It may have been only a holiday romance of
strolls along the shore, tea in the garden, and evenings of whist;
it may have been his sexual initiation. They parted after a week,
but Keats must have returned to London with a sense of greater
triumph than he had anticipated. And when he went back to
*Endymion* he began the second book with a hymn to the "sovereign power of love."

The summer now slipped by, leaving almost no trace beyond a
few ripples in the widening circle of his friendships. After Carisbrooke, Keats had quietly dropped his plan not to return to London till the end of the year. Back in Hampstead with George
and Tom, in close touch with his friends in town, he had no
need to write letters, and thus only two short notes survive to
document the summer. In the first, still hard-pressed by duns, he
asked Taylor and Hessey for another loan, this time of £30.
Perhaps it is significant that in this letter he jokingly spoke twice
of losing his virginity—"with respect to money Matters." In the
second note, near the end of August, he told Haydon he had just
finished the second book of *Endymion*. This does not seem like
much to show for ten weeks, but probably much time went in
reworking the first book [6] and in reading. During this summer
he formed the habit of borrowing books from the well-stocked

shelves of Taylor and Hessey's shop. Taylor, one of the most generous and sympathetic of publishers, loaned his young author whatever caught his eye and seems not to have murmured when Keats kept some of his books for over a year. A slight man with a fine intellectual head, Taylor looked more like a scholar than a businessman and had in fact already published several volumes on the authorship of the Junius letters. Hessey, his younger partner, was a round-faced, gregarious, good-humoured man who lived with his wife and young family in rooms over the bookshop at 93 Fleet Street and looked after the firm's business affairs. Taylor and Hessey published some of the best writers of the time— Coleridge, De Quincey, Landor, and Hazlitt among others—and through them Keats's acquaintance in literary London steadily widened. Soon the house in Fleet Street became a kind of club for him, a good place to drop in for an hour of literary or political talk, to browse among the old books in the back room, or occasionally to dine with his publishers and their authors.

The walk into London was a pleasant one in the long afternoons. Keats must have gone many times to visit the Wylies in Romney Street with George, whose interest in Georgiana was now something to speculate about, or to call on the Reynoldses in Little Britain. Here he would match wits with Mrs. Reynolds, listen to Charlotte playing the piano, or tease Jane and Mariane a little; or he would go off with Reynolds and his Oxford friend Benjamin Bailey, who was visiting him that summer, for walks on the Heath or a look at the theatre. On Sundays, Clarke and Severn often came out to Hampstead, and Clarke remembered Keats's once reading them the "Hymn to Pan" with evident pleasure. Severn was getting on well in his work, for his first large oil painting—on a subject from Shakespeare which Keats had suggested to him—had been shown and praised in a review. But this summer Keats's long friendship with his old tutor was cut short when Clarke moved with his parents to the farthest end of Kent. With this break Keats's strongest link with Hunt was snapped. Evidently, of all his friends, Hunt was the one Keats saw least this summer. Hunt returned from Marlow in mid-June and moved from Hampstead to a smaller house in Paddington, on the western edge of London. Early in July he wrote to Clarke rather crossly, "What has become of Junkets I know not. I suppose Queen Mab has eaten him."

This was not far from the truth: Junkets had disappeared for good. The break with Hunt was a painful neccessity for Keats and impossible to explain to the older man. Though he was finding Hunt's influence on his poetry no easy burden to shake off, he was determined to prove his independence in *Endymion*. Perhaps Hunt's review of his *Poems,* which appeared in *The Examiner* in erratic instalments through June and July, had something to do with his resolution. Hunt began his review with a lengthy discussion of the revolt against the school of Pope; when he got around to Keats, a month later, he first examined his faults— those very qualities of superabundant imagery and careless versification which Keats had caught from Hunt himself—reserving the "beauties" of the volume for a final notice. By and large, Hunt's criticism was just; but one or two readers, at least, thought it "done with an air of patronage, not with heart." So Caroline Scott, the wife of the editor of *The Champion,* wrote Haydon, adding a word of caution to Keats against Hunt's undue influence.[7] What Keats thought of the review is not known. But it was about this time that he sent his sonnet "On the Sea" to *The Champion,* where it appeared in the middle of August—his first poem to be printed in a magazine other than *The Examiner.*

Of Keats's other activities this summer we know only indirectly. At about this time, in a flare-up of his schoolboy spirit, he fought and trimmed a great lubber of a butcher-boy whom he found torturing a cat in an alley, and earned a name for himself in Hampstead as a result. Probably also during these months he wrote a little group of love lyrics which express all the moods of a summer romance—excited anticipation ("Hither, hither love"), tender farewell ("Unfelt, unheard, unseen"), dissuasions against remorse ("Think not of it, sweet one, so"), reproaches for coldness ("You say you love").[8] Yet, more than with his other poems, it is difficult to decide how closely, if at all, these verses reflect the moods and events of the time they were written. Even the lady's identity is only a guess, for Keats gave copies of one of these poems to both Isabella Jones and Jane Reynolds.

We can be certain, however, about his growing friendship this summer with Reynolds' friend Dilke, who lived halfway down Hampstead Hill in Wentworth Place, the pleasant double house which he had built on the edge of the Heath. Charles Wentworth Dilke was a man of good family; among his knighted forebears were a distinguished jurist and a leader of the Puritan opposition under Elizabeth. His post at the Navy Pay Office gave him enough leisure to edit early English plays, cultivate an interest—rare for his time—in William Blake, and contribute to the liberal magazines. Dilke was something of a doctrinaire; the theories of William Godwin, Shelley's philosophical father-in-law, provided him with an explanation for almost everything. Yet he was an interesting conversationalist, a keen sportsman, a connoisseur of snuff— and he had a charming wife. Maria Dilke was a close friend of the Reynolds girls and later took a warm interest in young Fanny Keats. Dark-haired, vivacious, unpunctual, and plump, the mother of a badly spoiled seven-year-old boy, she was still something of a flirt and loved an evening of dancing and banter. Keats and his brothers were welcomed at Wentworth Place at all hours and soon were drawn into her Hampstead set.

And always there was the Heath close at hand for long walks through Caen Wood and out into the open fields. Mile after mile they stretched away through meadow and marshland, hawthorn and holly, heather and fern, past willow groves where gipsies sat outside their vans, laughing and chattering in the sun. Keats found that Reynolds shared his taste for reading in the open air, and they used to spend hours on the Heath with Keats's new treasure, a facsimile Folio of Shakespeare.⁹ No doubt they also read their own new verses to each other and talked about the future. Reynolds was deep in love with Eliza Drewe, a young lady he had met in Exeter the summer before, and was already thinking of marriage. With this in view, he was planning to give up journalism to enter the law, even though this would leave him far less time for writing than before. Keats opposed the idea; once or twice he even argued with Reynolds against the whole idea of marriage, and this question must have clouded some hours of their talk. Still, it was summer, they were both young and full of plans, the Heath was still fragrant with clover and honeysuckle, and butterflies fluttered through the sunlit afternoons; it was still time for poetry.

The second book of *Endymion* begins in this summer setting of heath and woodland. Keats had barely got his story under way in the first book, where Endymion confides to his young sister Peona that he has fallen in love with a mysterious bright being— the goddess of the moon, though he does not suspect it. Three times she has appeared to him in his dreams: from the sky, from a well, and in a cave. Now he is bidden to search for her through the regions of earth, water, and air, and he starts by plunging into the depths of the earth. Here he wanders through "one faint eternal eventide of gems," like the interior of a cathedral—Canterbury, perhaps?—on a bright day. This lifeless world miraculously springs into leaf and flower as he approaches the bower of Adonis, where he discovers Venus waking her lover from his winter sleep. Venus then guides him to a mossy bower, where he meets the love of his dreams in a brief but rapturous encounter. Yet she steals away without revealing her identity, and he wanders on forlorn. After meeting two more lovers—Alpheus, the river-god, pursuing the stream-changed Arethusa—and praying for their happiness, Endymion looks up to find "the giant sea above his head": he has completed the first stage of his journey.

In the third book Endymion makes his way across the floor of the sea, past sharks and skeletons and forgotten wrecks. Here he meets Glaucus, a terrifyingly old man who begs Endymion to free him from the doom of endless age by performing a magic rite. Thereupon Endymion changes Glaucus back to his youthful self and not only reunites him with his beloved nymph Scylla but restores to life all the drowned lovers of ten centuries past. In the celebration which follows, Venus promises Endymion that his love will soon be revealed to him and his devotion rewarded in "endless heaven." He faints with joy, then wakes to find himself back on earth again.

By the time Keats had reached the third book, however, the summer was running out and he was left stranded in Hampstead. Haydon, the Reynolds girls, even the Dilkes had all gone off on visits; George and Tom, their finances temporarily recovered, had left for a trip to France, where, it seems, Tom had hopes of meeting his mysterious young lady-friend Amena.[10] Luckily for Keats, Bailey, who had returned to Oxford to read for Schools a month before the start of term, asked him up for a visit at the beginning of September. Oxford, spacious and serene in the first golden days of fall, struck Keats as "the finest City in the world," as he wrote to his sister Fanny, with its "old Gothic buildings—Spires—towers —Quadrangles—Cloisters Groves &c" and "more Clear streams than ever I saw together." Though the university was almost deserted over the long vacation, the sleepy magnificence of the colleges stirred Keats's imagination to a new sense of the past. The air swarmed with bells on the hour; deer nibbled the lawns of the park behind Magdalen, and squirrels darted through the shadows of its oaks. In Bailey's rooms in Magdalen Hall he found snuff and cigars and cordials, a sofa to lounge on with a book, and shelves lined with authors whose names he had never heard before. Under a grim-faced portrait of Jeremy Taylor the two young men worked for four or five hours every morning. Keats had set himself a stint of fifty lines a day, and he astonished Bailey by the ease with which he turned them out. None of the doubts of the spring assailed him; he was now an assured and disciplined writer. Sometimes he finished his task before the morning was up, and read or wrote letters till Bailey was through; then at two they knocked off, dined, and went for a long talkative stroll along the Cherwell.

Bailey opened the door to a new intellectual world. Four years older than Keats, with one year of divinity at Oxford to his credit, he took himself with great seriousness. He impressed Keats as being immensely learned. Plato and Aristotle, medieval commentary and seventeenth-century poetry, Milton's theology and Coleridge's metaphysics, "the relative state of man and woman," "the unity of nature," "the insufficiency of language"—titles of projected essays he hoped to get Taylor to publish—these were the topics revolving in Bailey's mind. "I have seen, from my first glances, an analogy, conformity, & unity in all things," he wrote Taylor that winter, "or, to speak intelligibly perhaps, the two last are perceptible *by* analogy. I have thought that this principle is the governing one of the universe, and that I have equally perceived it in nature, external & internal—in the minds of men as reflected through the best authors—and (as far as we can glimpse) in the eternal mind—of which every thing that exists, it seems to my apprehension, is but the image of the Decree—the word, the Logos. Now all this (which were I to indulge myself I could write on to the end of time almost)—all this, I say, *to me is clear as noonday.*"

Alas for the insufficiency of language! The essays were to remain mostly unwritten; Bailey left Oxford the following spring without a degree and eked out a narrow life as a country parson, colonial chaplain, and finally archdeacon in Ceylon. But in 1817 he represented, however imperfectly, a new and vastly exciting idea to Keats: philosophy. It was the attraction of opposites, for, as Keats confessed, he could never be convinced of a truth by "consequitive reasoning" but only by "a clear perception of its Beauty." Understandably, then, the book on Bailey's shelves which made the most lasting impresson on him was Madame Dacier's *Works of Plato Abridg'd,* which contained several of the early dialogues and the *Phaedo,* that beautiful demonstration of immortality by Socrates on the afternoon of his death. This introduction to Plato added the name of Socrates to Keats's roll of great men; it also posed the questions of knowledge and virtue and happiness in new terms and turned his thought in a new direction—inward, on the activity of the mind itself. Bailey, who had first been drawn to Keats by his "naturalness and simplicity of character," was evidently delighted to play the role of mentor. He has left us an odd image of himself with his hand placed on Keats's head, noting that "the silken curls felt like the rich plumage of a bird." Of his own he had little to teach Keats, but he provided the intellectual companionship which Keats needed most at this time. From Keats's letters a month or two later, we can see a remarkable intellectual flowering has already taken place. In these conversations with Bailey, it seems, his own ideas began to unfold; all that he had read and heard and pondered in the last few years became articulate, fluent, thought linking up with thought.

As the weeks slipped by in an unbroken spell of fine weather, they took a boat out on the Isis every afternoon. Drifting with the stream, they talked of a hundred things—Syriac etymologies and Newton's theory of light, for instance, Coleridge's ideas on the imagination, Hazlitt's essays, Reynolds' decision to enter the law, and their dislike of literary ladies. Love and marriage surely came in for discussion too, for Bailey was giving them much thought. Keats, unaware that he had already started courting Mariane Reynolds, believed that Bailey was suffering the pangs of unrequited love for Thomasine Leigh, a close friend of Reynolds' fiancée. A month later, when he guessed the situation at the Reynoldses', he wrote Bailey circumspectly, wishing him all the happiness of "a little Pæona Wife." This young-sisterly kind of love was not at all what he wanted for himself, for as he later said of the Reynolds sisters, "They do not know what a Woman is." Indeed Bailey was troubled by the importance which Keats attached to physical love. Later he was to accuse Keats of loose moral principles and to lament the "indelicacy" of *Endymion,* though now he had only praise for it. But, as a parson-to-be, he was still more disturbed by Keats's doubts about Christian belief. To Bailey, Christianity could explain all the bitter dilemmas of existence, but Keats was not easily convinced. "Why should Woman suffer?" was one question that vexed these young idealists—innocent and helpless as they believed women to be—and to Keats the third chapter of Genesis was no answer. Bailey later insisted that Keats was "no infidel," but he had to admit that their notions of divinity were very different. He got Keats to promise to give up scoffing at religion, but that was all.

But mostly they talked about poetry, the enthusiasm that had first brought them together, and their pleasantest hours on the river were spent drawn up in a cove of rushes reading aloud to each other. Bailey wrote poetry himself, in a melancholy Wordsworthian vein, which survives in the albums of the Leigh sisters.[11] Together they discussed the metaphysical poets whom Keats had discovered on Bailey's shelves, and Bailey's favourites, Milton and Dante and Wordsworth. Bailey, who had filled his edition of Milton with scholarly annotations, told Keats that he could not claim to be a poet with his sketchy knowledge of *Paradise Lost;* and Keats, evidently convinced, resolved to make a close study of Milton that winter—a decision of consequence. Poetry to Bailey was a matter not of luxuriant description or exquisite sentiment but of moral and philosophic truth. Hunt might think Milton the poet of "love for gentle Lycid drown'd"; to Bailey he was the supreme example of the great poet who "ought himself to be a true poem." So also with Wordsworth: Bailey turned Keats's interest from his early work to the philosophic and religious vein of *The Excursion.*

Keats had evidently been rereading this long meditative poem on nature and the imagination more thoughtfully during his work on *Endymion* that summer and had been more deeply impressed than ever by the discussion of the origin of myth in the fourth book. Here Wordsworth traced the poet's sense of an inward meaning in nature back through the divinities with which the Greeks had peopled their world to the angelic visitations which Adam had received at the beginning of Creation, when he heard "borne on the wind, the articulate voice of God." To Keats the story of Genesis was a myth with no more special claim to belief than the Greek legends; but, discounting Wordsworth's Christian bias, he was profoundly convinced by his theory that the myths were not mere "lovely tales" expressing the changeful beauties of nature, but embodiments of enduring truths of existence. So midway through *Endymion* he tried to convey his own sense of how the Presence brooding over nature spoke with voices that echoed on the wind from cavern to forest to lake and, when caught by the first poets, gave rise at last to myth.[12] A fancy, perhaps; yet the myth, he claimed with increasing conviction, revealed a kind of truth, "the best music in a first-born song." A new sense of the significance of his own legend was growing in his mind as he went on with his poem, a sense which must have deepened in his long afternoon discussions with Bailey on the nature of imagination.

Yet Keats could not keep to Bailey's level of high seriousness indefinitely. In a letter to Reynolds he knocked off a waggish parody of one of Wordsworth's poems, suggested by a prominent feature of Oxford life—"There are forty feeding like one"—which ends:

> There are plenty of trees,
> And plenty of ease,
> And plenty of fat deer for Parsons;
> And when it is venison,
> Short is the benison,—
> Then each on a leg or thigh fastens.

His high spirits spilled over into a series of letters to Jane Reynolds at the seashore, in which he made fun both of himself holding his own in conversation at Magdalen and of Jane trying to make sense out of his foolery, or argued with her about Shakespeare's finest heroine—Juliet, of course—or the best time of day for a walk by the sea. Perhaps without realizing it, Keats was drifting into a kind of platonic flirtation with Jane. With her, as the older sister of his closest friend, he must have thought he was on safe ground, and his inveterate teasing seems clearly intended as a defence against any closer meeting between them.

There was no teasing in the letter he wrote to his own sister from Oxford, however, but a great deal of brotherly tenderness. Fanny's life with the Abbeys was evidently turning her into a sad and spiritless young girl. "Do you ever laugh?" George once asked her, swearing he had not seen her "so undignified" since the age of six—since the time, that is, of her mother's death.[13] Keats quizzed her a little on her reading, gave her a summary of *Endymion,* then added news of George and Tom in France. They had seen "Cathedrals Manuscripts. Fountains, Pictures, Tragedy Comedy," he reported, "with other things you may by chance meet with in this Country such as Washerwomen, Lamplighters, Turnpikemen Fish kettles, Dancing Masters, kettle drums, Sentry Boxes, Rocking Horses &c and, now they have taken them over a set of boxing gloves."

But high spirits and fine weather could not last forever. On September 21 he reported to Reynolds, "I am getting on famous with my third Book—Bailey likes what I have done very much." Five days later, when he reached the end, his mood had changed completely. In exactly three weeks he had written one thousand and thirty-odd lines, day after day without flagging; yet as he looked them over he was profoundly discouraged. Perhaps he had written them too much in the spirit of cramming for an exam—like Bailey, studying his theology across the table; perhaps he now realized how far they fell below his growing sense of the significance of myth. For a moment he thought of tearing up all three books and starting over again, then realized this would not do. "I am tired of it and think the time would be better spent in writing a new Romance which I have in my eye for next summer," he wrote Haydon dejectedly on the twenty-eighth. Already another poem, on a subject much more to Bailey's liking, was taking shape in his mind—the story of Endymion's "lute-voiced brother" Apollo, the god of poetry, in his struggle with Hyperion and the overthrow of the Titans: a theme of almost the scope of Milton's epic of the revolt of the angels and the fall of man. Meantime autumn was setting in and he did not want to face Hunt and Shelley with *Endymion* unfinished. Yet, as he confessed to Haydon, "My Ideas with respect to it I assure you are very low." As he approached the climax of his story, where Endymion was at last to win "immortal bliss" with his goddess, his invention began to flag.

The Oxford long vacation was nearly over, and Keats and Bailey decided to take a holiday before parting. Stratford was forty miles away, and Keats was eager to see Shakespeare's birthplace—Shakespeare whose birthday he had marked alone in Carisbrooke that spring, whose portrait had watched enigmatically over every line of *Endymion*. They approached Stratford with expectations high and were met by what Keats later called "the flummery of a birth place." They visited the half-timbered house in Henley Street, now divided between an inn and a butcher's shop; [14] climbed the narrow stairs and added their names to the thousands of others on the blackened walls of the low attic room where, they were told, Shakespeare was born. When they went to look at his grave in Holy Trinity Church, they were pestered by a custodian who would not let them see it for themselves. Keats was struck by the painted statue in the elaborate sculptured frame over the gravestone. A bald, plump man, his lips slightly parted, stiffly holding his pen and staring blankly ahead: yet this, he realized, was the most authentic of all the likenesses of Shakespeare. Keats said little, Bailey recalled. It was a great moment, but still the gap between expectation and reality must have yawned wide.

→≫ ≪←

The day after his return to Hampstead Keats plunged into the riptide of London life once again. He went into town to call first at the Reynoldses', then on Haydon, who had just moved into a new studio in Paddington, not far from Hunt's. "Every Body seems at Loggerheads," he reported to Bailey. "There's Hunt infatuated"—Shelley was there with Hunt, his long poem *Laon and Cythna* finished within the six-month limit—"theres Haydon's Picture in statu quo. There's Hunt walks up and down his painting room criticising every head most unmercifully—There's Horace Smith tired of Hunt. 'The web of our Life is of mingled Yarn.'" During his absence at Oxford, Hunt had reprinted his "Grasshopper and Cricket" sonnet in *The Examiner,* perhaps as a gesture of reconciliation after Keats's appearance in *The Champion* in August. Now Haydon drew him aside and said, "Keats, don't show your lines to Hunt on any account, or he will have done half of it for you"; while Reynolds told him that on meeting Hunt at the theatre a week before he had reported that Keats was near the end of his four thousand lines and Hunt had replied, "Ah —had it not been for me, they would have been seven thousand!" "Now is not all this a most paultry thing to think about?" Keats exclaimed to Bailey. His independence of Hunt had cost him a struggle; yet for all this, he wrote Bailey, "I shall have the Reputation of Hunt's elevé— His corrections and amputations will by the knowing ones be trased in the Poem." He longed for Oxford again. "I am quite disgusted with literary Men and will never know another." Except Wordsworth, he added; perhaps he had learned from Haydon that Wordsworth was planning to visit London that winter.

With Haydon another storm was blowing up. In September he had written Keats asking him to look up a talented young painter named Charles Cripps whom Haydon had met in Oxford that summer, and whom he now offered to take as an apprentice for a year without the usual fee, if money could be found for his living expenses. Keats and Bailey, delighted with the idea, volunteered to raise a fund by subscription. Back in London, however, Keats found Haydon less interested in the young painter than he had at first seemed. Thereupon Bailey wrote him a reproachful letter; Haydon sent a stinging reply; Bailey then determined to end their acquaintance. At this point Keats stepped in to try to patch things up. He knew that Haydon liked to make generous promises and then hedge on them; but he could not think this was a reason for dropping him, though he also saw why Bailey should. "The best of Men have but a portion of good in them," he pleaded in a later letter. Keeping a friend like Haydon was far more important than being in the right; and the true test of friendship was to recognize a man's faults and then see whether the bond still held. Keats was as convinced as ever of Haydon's greatness as an artist, even while aware that this greatness did not include the "probity and disinterestedness" which he admired in Bailey. He must also have begun to realize that Haydon could be as irresponsible in money matters as Hunt. But how did one balance the claims of genius against ordinary uprightness? Keats was not sure; he only knew that Cripps must not be disappointed, and he set to work on his own to raise the promised funds.

At home there were still more worries. George and Tom had come back from Paris with empty pockets or worse. At the Palais Royal they had discovered the *rouge et noir* tables, plunged, and lost—an unspecified amount, but more than they could afford.[15] George had not yet found a job to his liking. Abbey was trying to persuade him to go into the hat business, but this did not work out. And Tom, in spite of his summer holiday, was looking ill and miserable. After a few weeks Keats became thoroughly alarmed. His trained eye must have noted symptoms that reminded him all too well of his mother's illness—pallor, feverishness, a recurrent cough. For a while he thought of shipping Tom off to Lisbon for the climate; but in another few weeks he seemed well enough so that they decided he should winter in Devon instead. One of the most troublesome aspects of consumption was its unpredictable ups and downs. There was no way of knowing whether Tom was really infected—indeed, the disease was not then thought to be infectious; and, if he was ill, there was no telling when or even whether his condition might become serious. And Keats had his own health to worry about. Toward the end of his stay at Oxford he had picked up a mysterious illness which hung on all through October and which he mentioned a number of times in his letters to Bailey in carefully guarded terms.

The truth seems to be that during his visit with Bailey Keats had contracted a venereal infection, probably syphilis. This point has been hotly denied ever since the story was first told, fifty years later, by a doctor who had it from Keats's friend Henry Stephens, whom he still saw occasionally this fall; [16] but there are several references in Keats's letters at this time which can be explained no other way. He had confided his fears to Bailey before leaving Oxford and wrote him a few days after his return to assure him that the mercury—the specific remedy for syphilis at that time—which he had taken had "corrected the Poison"; though, he added gloomily, he felt he would "never be again secure in Robustness." Apparently on doctor's orders, he spent the next fortnight—a period in which his infection would have been acutely contagious—confined to Hampstead, suffering, as he put it, "for vicious beastliness." And the doctor whom he consulted at this time was evidently not the Hampstead surgeon but one Mr. Solomon Sawrey in London, who in addition to his general practice was a specialist in venereal diseases.[17] By the end of October, Keats felt he was safely over the infection, but he was still troubled enough to keep discussing it with Bailey. The Reynolds sisters had become concerned about his health and wondered whether he was showing signs of consumption like Tom; as Keats wryly remarked, they had a better opinion of him than he deserved. It was a narrow scrape, and one which no doubt affected him more deeply than he could admit. More than any other experience of this year, it must have rubbed the bloom off his idealism and opened his eyes to the unpredictabilities and incongruities of human experience. "Lord! a man should have the fine point of his soul taken off to become fit for this world," he wrote Reynolds a month later, when he had regained his balance. This bravado may express his relief at his escape; it conceals the anxiety which he must have felt about possible after-effects, as well as an inevitable pang of guilt. The immediate effect of this adventure, however, was to plunge him into a numbing depression. For several weeks he could not bring himself even to write Bailey again. A kind of deadness settled over him, in which he began to doubt the genuineness of what he now could only remember feeling.

This was hardly the mood for following Endymion on his quest of "immortal bliss." By the end of October it was clear he had lost his wager with Shelley, for he had written a bare three hundred lines of the fourth book—the equivalent of a single week's work at Oxford. These lines begin with a dejected tribute to the Muse of English poetry, in which he admits his own unworthiness as a poet; they go on with a "Song to Sorrow" sung by a mysterious Indian maiden who makes her entry at this point. Her song builds up into a frenzied hymn to Bacchus, then dies away in the mournful reflection that pleasure cannot lighten the load of sorrow. The first day that Keats was well enough to go to town he had spent the evening with Reynolds' lawyer friend James Rice, in whose rooms a little club was beginning to gather every Saturday to drink and play whist and *vingt-et-un* and crack jokes hardly worth repeating. This gaiety hauled him out of the doldrums for a few evenings, but no more. November came, and in three weeks he dragged out only two hundred more lines.

Perhaps one reason for his despondency was a new worry added to all the others. *Blackwood's,* a magazine recently founded in Edinburgh by three young Tory wits who were determined to outslash even the formidable *Quarterly Review,* came out at the end of October with the first of a series of articles "On the Cockney School of Poetry." It was "a flaming attack" on Hunt, as Keats described it to Bailey, "depreciating his Wife his Poetry—his Habits —his company, his Conversation." Today it is hard to believe the bitterness of the political warfare that raged in the literary reviews of that time, or the absolute power they wielded over writers' reputations. But in the reactionary years after Waterloo, when any kind of intellectual nonconformity was suspect, a man's literary preferences were usually taken as a badge of his political opinions and vice versa. So *Blackwood's,* after proclaiming that only "men of some rank" could qualify as real poets, assailed Hunt's liberal views by describing his poetry as "glittering and rancid obscenities," his style that of "a tea-sipping milliner's girl" who "speaks unclean things from perfect inanition," and so on and so on. This outburst, which was signed only "Z.," hinted that Keats would be the subject of the next instalment. Hunt demanded in *The Examiner* that "Z." reveal his identity, and Keats resolved to send him a challenge. At this Reynolds became concerned and arranged for Keats to meet his friend Jonathan Christie, *Blackwood's* London agent, in the hope of fending off the attack. When the second instalment appeared later in November, "Z." was still pursuing Hunt, and Reynolds must have breathed easier. But Keats could not have been much heartened. Two final reviews of his *Poems* appeared this fall in two of the more influential magazines, *Constable's* and the *Eclectic*, which warned him against the "uncleannesses" of Hunt's poetry and the "affectations" of his style. At last Keats realized that his tributes to Hunt in his *Poems* had succeeded only in damning the book with the general public. But quixotically he felt drawn toward Hunt again, now that a battle was in prospect. He admitted to Haydon that his tributes had been impolitic, but insisted that Hunt had been generous to him and he would stand by him in trouble.[18] Within the next few months he called on and dined with Hunt a number of times and even joined in their old game of versifying on a set subject.

But in November, amid his worries, his glooms, and his "little two penny errands" to raise funds for Cripps, he was being driven farther and farther off course. The "wintry season" was fast coming on, and the fourth book of *Endymion* was still half finished. There was only one remedy—to get away from London again. This time he chose Burford Bridge in Surrey, where he had heard of a pleasant inn at the foot of Box Hill. From the top of this steep chalk scarp, shagged with boxwood and juniper and yew, a magnificent view of the downs stretched away to the Channel, thirty miles distant. At its foot a little weed-choked river, spanned by the three stone arches of Burford Bridge, crept along between the cliff and a deep forest, where the last flames of autumn were swathed in mist. It was a landscape after his own mood. The solitude which had weighed on him at the Isle of Wight was now a miraculous restorative. His first morning there, November 22, he wrote a long and richly reflective letter to Bailey; that evening he climbed Box Hill, watched the moon rise, came down, and added some lines to

*Endymion*—a hundred, more or less [19]—then wrote another letter, to Reynolds. He was himself again.

In this calm the disturbing events of the last two months fell into a new perspective. The passage he added to *Endymion* that evening describes a curious psychological experience which marks a turning point in Endymion's progress and, perhaps, in Keats's own life. Endymion, faced with seeming failure in his quest, enters the "Cave of Quietude," a retreat "of remotest glooms" in the dark depths of consciousness. Here the spirit that has moved beyond all hope of happiness, beyond even the sensation of despair, falls into a dreamless sleep and awakes mysteriously renewed, the fever of self-absorption past, to find the world full of blessings. So, it appears, Keats woke from his own depression at last. The experiences of the fall—Tom's illness and his own, disillusionment with friends and with himself, discouragement about his poetry—had finally shattered his faith in what most young men instinctively assume: that life holds out the promise of happiness to be gained, and sorrow avoided, by one's own efforts. He had learned at last that this was impossible; yet beyond this he had found that life was still good, that indeed there was a kind of beauty revealed through sorrow—the beauty of "light and shade," as he later called it—more intense than mere sunlit delight. "I have the same Idea of all our Passions as of Love," he told Bailey, "they are all in their sublime, creative of essential Beauty." What he had discovered between writing the first and the last books of *Endymion* was a whole new dimension of experience, to be grasped only by surrendering to the wayward and endless richness of the immediate moment. "You perhaps at one time thought there was such a thing as Worldly Happiness to be arrived at, at certain periods of time marked out," he remarked to Bailey. "I look not for it if it be not in the present hour—nothing startles me beyond the Moment. The setting sun will always set me to rights—or if a Sparrow come before my Window I take part in its existince and pick about the Gravel."

This taking part in the existence—or, as he later called it, the identity—of other beings was one of Keats's most important insights as a poet. What he called "essential Beauty" was a sudden realization of the innermost character of a person or thing, won by imaginative identification with it; and through this insight a new universe was revealed to him. So he could become one with the intense absorption of the sparrow picking for its food in the dirt, or with the loneliness of the oyster asleep in its shell at the bottom of the sea; he could even feel his way, as he once said, into a billiard ball delighted with its own smooth motion and perfect roundness.[20] What he described to Bailey was, of course, a quality which he had often achieved in his poetry without being quite aware of it, when his focus shifted from his own response to an object to the imagined inner life of the object itself: the sensations not only of the astronomer discovering a new planet, but of the star itself gazing down on the earth, or of the lazy power of a breaking wave and the delight of the rock weed swirled about in its foam. This ability to enter into the identities of other beings was, he found, not only the source of a great secret joy and the wellspring of his poetry but also the one thing sure among the uncertainy and incompleteness of experience, a faith to replace his earlier longing for some transcendental fulfilment. As he put it to . Bailey, "I am certain of nothing but of the holiness of the Heart's affections and the truth of Imagination—What the imagination seizes as Beauty must be truth—whether it existed before or not." By grasping the essence of a thing through identifying with it, the imagination discovers a beauty in it which lies hidden to the outer gaze; and these essences were to Keats the ultimate reality of existence. "The Imagination," he wrote, in one of those very flashes of perception which he was trying to define, "may be compared to Adam's dream—he awoke and found it truth."

But this new insight into essential beauty and the truth of imagination implied a new idea of poetry, even of the poet himself, very different from the one he had held so long. Poetry was to be found everywhere, not merely in the special experience of luxurious beauty which Hunt cultivated; and to discover it required "Humility and capability of submission" before experience, not the assertion of a special character with special privileges such as Haydon represented. Men of talent who impose their "proper selves" on what they create should be termed "Men of Power," he wrote Bailey, in contrast to the true "Men of Genius," who "are great as certain ethereal Chemicals operating on the Mass of neutral intellect—but they have not any individuality, any determined Character." This receptivity to all experience, sorrow as well as joy, the commonplace as well as the heroic or the exquisite, together with the most self-effacing fidelity of expression, impressed him more and more forcibly as the essence of Shake-speare's greatness. Now in rereading Shakespeare's *Poems*—a copy of which he had just borrowed from Reynolds—he was struck as never before by the poetry of real things which Shakespeare scat-tered so lavishly through his lines. "He has left nothing to say about nothing or any thing," he wrote to Reynolds; "for look at Snails, you know what he says about Snails," and then, after a little thumbing of the pages, he found the stanza in *Venus and Adonis* describing Venus's eyes rolling upward in her anguish over her wounded lover:

> Or, as the snail, whose tender horns being hit,
>   Shrinks backward in his shelly cave with pain
> And there all smothered up in shade doth sit,
>   Long after fearing to creep forth again. . . .

This he thought a superb example of "fine things said uninten-tionally—in the intensity of working out conceits." It was the kind of poetry which he himself was aiming at, that "does not startle the soul or amaze it with itself but with its subject."

So with Shakespeare again his presider, he rediscovered his for-mer spontaneous joy in writing, as proved by the hundred lines he added to *Endymion* on his first day at Burford Bridge. In writ-ing Bailey it occurred to him that this disembodied delight of crea-tion, the "empyreal reflection" of his moments of imaginative identification with other essences, was a kind of immortality achieved in life itself. If there is a hereafter, he mused, it must con-sist of this "happiness on Earth repeated in a finer tone," in which "the simple imaginative Mind may have its rewards in the repeti-tion of its own silent Working coming continually on the spirit with a fine suddenness." So Shakespeare's image of the snail was to return to him a few months later when he described these "si-lent workings" as "the innumerable compositions and decomposi-tions which take place between the intellect and its thousand mate-rials before it arrives at that trembling delicate and snail-horn perception of Beauty." In a great burst of energy he raced through the last five hundred lines of his poem in seven days and signed the manuscript "Burford Bridge, Nov. 28, 1817" to mark the end. His task was done.

⟫⟪

Though he finished *Endymion* with extraordinary speed, it may be wondered whether Keats clearly saw the ending of the poem until he had almost reached it. For in the fourth book the action takes a most unexpected turn, just as the tone changes from joyous idealism to melancholy. Endymion emerged from his adventure under the sea tested in courage and humanity and ready to continue his journey through the region of air to win his promised "immortality of passion." Yet just at this point he meets the dark-haired Indian maid who sings the "Song to Sorrow"; and while reproaching himself for infidelity, he falls passionately in love with her. Together they ascend, dreaming, into the heavens; then Endymion wakes to find Cynthia, the goddess of the moon, bending over him, and realizes at last that she is the love of his visions. But she fades, weeping, from his sight as he turns back to the Indian maid; then she too fades from him in the cold light of the rising moon. In despair, Endymion enters the Cave of Quietude, sleeps, and awakes renewed in spirit on earth again, to find the maiden at his side. At once he decides to renounce his hopeless love for Cynthia:

> I have clung
> To nothing, lov'd a nothing, nothing seen
> Or felt but a great dream! O I have been
> Presumptuous against love. . . .

Then, describing the autumnal beauty of Latmos in lines which Keats might have written on top of Box Hill, Endymion asks the maid to share his life of simple human pleasure in the forest: "Say, is not bliss within our perfect seizure?" But she refuses, mysteriously forbidden to love him on these terms. Endymion then resolves to become a hermit, while the Indian maid reluctantly vows to dedicate herself to Diana, the goddess of chastity. By the end of the day, however, Endymion has found none of the higher pleasures of contemplation he had expected in his solitude, only blank sluggish despair. Now he realizes that his earlier notion of happiness in human love was a trivial one, a thing of "flowers, garlands, love-knots, silly posies"; and the melancholy beauty of the autumn sunset moves him so deeply that he is content to accept his mortal lot and die with the death of the season. Then the will to live and love surges up again. "I did wed Myself to things of light from infancy!" he cries; and when he meets the Indian maid coming to the temple of Diana with his sister to take her vows, he grasps her hand and defies the fate which has separated them. At this a miracle occurs: the dark maiden is transformed into the bright-haired goddess before his very eyes. The love of his dreams has become real at last, and they vanish into the forest together, leaving Peona lost in wonder.

This miraculous ending to a miraculous tale has left many readers as bewildered as Peona herself. Unwilling to take the poem as meaning what it seems to say, most of Keats's critics have moralized it into an allegory of a kind of supersexual love for a supersensuous beauty. Thus Endymion's wanderings become the quest of the poetic soul for "communion with the ideal," and his agonized vacillation between the maiden and the goddess, and the final change of the one into the other, are taken to indicate the seeming conflict and ultimate harmony of the actual beauties of this world with ideal Beauty.[21] Yet this interpretation is hardly convincing. The texture of the poem itself, so richly sensuous and unabashedly sensual, not merely obscures such a meaning, it contradicts it. Moreover, Keats at twenty-one, with his distrust of "consequitive reasoning" and his hunger for "a life of Sensations rather than of Thoughts," was not the kind of young man to prefer abstractions to realities, or the kind of poet to contrive an allegorical system. Indeed, as he later admitted, the development of his tale was "uncertain," lacking a clear plan from the start.

Just as Keats never mentioned an allegory in discussing *Endymion* with his friends, so none of his first readers found any hint of allegory in the poem—not surprisingly, for the allegorical tradition was dead in Keats's time, even for readers of Spenser. Those who enjoyed the poem praised it chiefly for the imagery and accepted the metamorphosis of the Indian maid as the proper fairy-tale ending of a romance.[22] Only Jeffrey in *The Edinburgh Review* sensed Keats's real innovation—to have given the familiar mythological figures "an original character and distinct individuality," that is, a human significance; only Bailey suspected a hidden meaning in the action, which he could not believe Keats really intended: its approach "to that abominable principle of *Shelley's* —that *Sensual Love* is the principle of *things*." This suggests why, in the increasingly literal-minded and prudish age of Tennyson, when the fairy-tale ending was no longer readily accepted, a Victorian lady critic found it necessary to invent the moralistic al-

legory to disguise Keats's naked meaning.[23] For the poem is about
sensual love, like most poems by men of twenty-one. Endymion
represents not the poetic soul but the ideal lover; his adventures
are an assertion of "the holiness of the Heart's affections," and it
is only because the poem expresses such an exalted idea of sexual
love that the Victorian critics felt his quest must have another
goal.

But if there is no allegory in *Endymion,* there is clearly a symbolic significance, one inherent in the events themselves, not imposed on them from without, which might be defined simply as
the young man's discovery of the true nature of love. Keats himself seems to have discovered his full meaning only gradually, in
the very act of writing. He started with "a thing of beauty," and,
like Adam in his dream, "awoke to find it truth." Sexual love, as
Endymion describes it near the end of the first book, is the highest reach of happiness, the richest form of "blending pleasurable," [24] that most completely annuls the division between the self
and the world outside; as such, it is the crown of all other values
and the worthiest goal of our strivings. But even as Endymion set
out on his quest of "endless bliss," Keats's own ideas on the nature of love were changing. His new-won independence of Hunt,
his deepened understanding of Shakespeare, his friendship with
Bailey, his growing sense of tender responsibility for his young
sister, his adventure—whatever it amounted to—with Isabella
Jones, the disillusionments of the autumn, all these profoundly
altered the naïve idealism with which he had begun. By the time
he reached the fourth book, he had come to see the "immortality
of passion" which Endymion pursues as the hollow unreality that
it is. And so an astonishing inversion of the legend takes place.
The hero, on the point of winning his goddess, apparently betrays
her; he wins her in the end only after renouncing her, and not
in her own identity but by discovering her in a mortal maiden.
It is hard not to believe that this unexpected turn of plot was
deeply influenced by Keats's own emotional reversals of the fall.
For up till the very end Endymion's progress parallels Keats's own
feelings as he recorded them in his letters of October and November—disillusionment, depression, recovery; his loss of faith in the
certainty of happiness, his renunciation of idealism, his discovery
that the setting sun could put him to rights.

What of the ending, then? Is it a mere contrivance, a wrenching of the psychological narrative back to the foregone mythological conclusion? Partly so; or rather, the dénouement is presented in highly ambiguous terms and can be read in two quite different ways.[25] On the first, or mythological level, the maid is merely the goddess in a disguise which she has adopted to test Endymion's fidelity—a familiar fairy-tale device which Keats may have borrowed from a version of the legend in one of his Elizabethan poets.[26] So when Endymion seems to renounce human love in reasserting his devotion to "things of light," the maiden turns back into the goddess and rewards him with the "immortality of passion" promised in the myth. On the second, the psychological or symbolic level, the maid represents a new conception of human love, far higher than Endymion's adolescent dream of "endless bliss." So when he finally realizes that to renounce the maid is to deny life itself, he is rewarded by the maid's transformation into the goddess; that is, real love, when accepted for the good it contains, leads to the fulfilment Endymion has sought all along. The ambiguity is inescapable; Keats's legend pulled him in one direction, his experience in another. As between the two interpretations, however, it seems clear that he gravitated toward the second, the human rather than the magical meaning. The last lines of the poem announce that Endymion has been "spiritualiz'd" by "some unlook'd for change" in his final adventure; [27] and—what is not usually noticed—Cynthia herself has changed during the course of the story. She has surmounted her "foolish fear" of yielding to a mortal lover and defied the "decrees of fate" that doomed her to eternal chastity; she has been humanized, has learned to "throw the goddess off," as Keats put it in a later poem, and "play the woman's part." Endymion meanwhile has been spiritualized in a most unexpected fashion by his encounter with the maid, for he wins his goddess at last not through his earlier acts of valour or disinterested sympathy but by learning to love another human being.

Keats's implication, taken in the context of his time, is audacious. He is saying that a man is spiritualized not by self-denial but by self-fulfilment; that a lover becomes perfect in love not by chastity but by the gradual realization of his passionate nature. He gives a hint of this in the first book, in his praise of sexual love as "the chief intensity," the most "self-destroying" of entanglements. This outgoing of the spirit into the identities of others is first experi-

enced in response to the beauties of nature—the intense but
ethereal pleasures of boyhood, when

> every sense
> Of mine was once made perfect in these woods.
> Fresh breezes, bowery lawns, and innocent floods,
> Ripe fruits, and lonely couch, contentment gave.

But with the advent of sexual longing this emotional self-sufficiency
breaks down. Endymion's simple delights give way to troubled
dreams, his boyish ambitions are forgotten in "ardent listlessness."
Significantly, he begins his ascent toward love by plunging into
the depths of the earth and exploring its "silent mysteries" alone
and in darkness. The meaning of his new need becomes clearer
to him as he observes other lovers and learns to give of himself in
friendship. But his rapturous dreams of an ideal love are followed
by desolate awakenings, and often he longs to return to "the old
garden-ground of boyish days." His first actual experience of love
with the Indian maid seems a betrayal of his dreams; thus he can
love her with only "half [his] soul," and discovers in this conflict
his painful lack of "identity." When at last he gives up the dream
for the reality and acknowledges the fact of human incompleteness, he finds the "self-destroying" completion through another
that lies beyond it. So by loving first in guilt and confusion,
then with greater understanding and self-acceptance, he is at
last "spiritualized" and wins his goddess as the legend promised.

Keats's search for a truth underlying "the bare circumstance" of
his legend is the real significance of *Endymion*. He was the first
English poet to sense the possibility of a human meaning implicit
in the myths themselves, rather than to fit them into a precon-
ceived allegorical pattern, as in general the Elizabethans did, or
merely to use them for decorative effect, like the eighteenth-
century poets. His revolutionary attempt—if not his actual achievement—was, as Jeffrey implied, to suggest that the Greek myths
were as relevant to our inner experience as the Christian myth was
to Milton in an age when the pagan gods had lost their hold on
men's imaginations. *Endymion* is a "Song of Innocence and Experience" transposed into the mythic mode. Through Endymion's
adventures Keats attempted to state, however gropingly, his belief
in the necessity of growth, the value of the progression into experience, the impossibility of regression into innocence, the goal
of a more complex harmony of being. The originality of his at-

tempt becomes clear if *Endymion* is viewed against the literary conventions of his time. In romantic fiction, it has been pointed out, the polarities of sexual experience—lawful and lustful, tender and sensual, familial and alien—were usually represented by two heroines, a fair and a dark lady; and the hero, when forced to choose between them, invariably renounced his dark and passionate mistress for his innocent fair-haired love. Keats from the beginning blends these opposites: the bright-haired goddess appears to Endymion by night, the dark maiden by day; and in the end, by ambiguously wedding himself "to things of light," Endymion chooses both women, as one is transformed into the other. In bringing the two parts of his own nature together, he becomes "whole in love" and finds the object of his love has become whole for him.

Still the conflict between Keats's first and final intentions remains embedded within *Endymion,* and he apparently soon became aware of this. The doubts he expressed in September grew deeper. The following January, in the midst of revising the poem, he described it ironically to Haydon as "deep and sentimental"; in February he told Taylor, "I am anxious to get Endymion printed that I may forget it and proceed." By April this weariness had turned into profound dissatisfaction. As he admitted with fanatical candour in the preface he wrote at this time, "There is not a fiercer hell than the failure in a great object." The chief fault of the poem, he realized, was the inexperience of life underlying the original conception. "The imagination of a boy is healthy," he wrote, "and the mature imagination of a man is healthy; but there is a space of life between, in which the soul is in a ferment, the character undecided, the way of life uncertain, the ambition thick-sighted"—and from this sprang the "mawkishness" which he castigated in what is surely the most extraordinary preface any author has written to any poem.

Yet for all its obvious faults of immaturity, *Endymion* is a uniquely interesting work, a Lucretian hymn to the vital force that creates beauty and heroism and love along with life itself, a young man's poem about a central experience of young manhood. Inevitably, and from the very time it was published, it has been compared to Shakespeare's *Venus and Adonis. Endymion* lacks the verbal control and dramatic power of the earlier work; but Shakespeare was twenty-eight when he wrote his first long poem, Keats was twenty-one. He was handicapped not only by his youth but by the sentimental tradition of his time, which left him no acceptable idiom for dealing forthrightly, as Shakespeare could, with physical love, at the same time that it led him to set a much more complex valuation on it. For better, for worse, *Endymion* is a work of romantic art.

And the final value of the poem is a peculiarly romantic one—its value to the poet himself. *Endymion* represents almost half of the poetry Keats published in his lifetime, and occupied him through nearly one-fourth of his poetic career; writing it was a major factor in his creative development. Keats himself was the first to value the poem in this fashion, and this was all the value he eventually allowed it. "It is as good as I had power to make it —by myself," he wrote Hessey a year later. "Had I been nervous about its being a perfect piece, & with that view asked advice, & trembled over every page, it would not have been written." In the end, he saw, his having written it mattered more than what he had written, and for a significant reason: "That which is creative must create itself.—In Endymion," he added, "I leaped headlong into the Sea, and thereby have become better acquainted with the Soundings, the quicksands, & the rocks, than if I had stayed upon the green shore, and piped a silly pipe, and took tea & comfortable advice." *Endymion* made Keats a poet, whatever Keats made of *Endymion*. In the very experience of failure he discovered the truth of achievement: "That which is creative must create itself."

## Chapter Six

# Soundings and Quicksands

K E A T S spent another solitary week in Burford Bridge, putting the final touches on *Endymion,* then returned to town early in December to see George and Tom off for Devonshire and turn his manuscript in to Taylor for approval.[1] There was still much work ahead, recopying his four thousand lines and seeing the book through the press. But for a while it was off his hands, and time lay like a path of gold before him. He was just twenty-two and alone in London; he had completed a long poem which, he still believed, made a confident bid for fame. After months of lonely struggling with *Endymion,* it was pleasant to find himself sought after as the coming young poet. Invitations began flooding in; his cavalier days, as he later called them, had begun.

For the first five or six weeks, it was a rare day that Keats spent at home. In London he was making dozens of new acquaintances in the worlds of literature and art and the theatre. Now (if not before) he caught the eye of William Godwin, the erstwhile leader of London radical intellectual society. There were always old friends in town to pass an evening with, and he now had a standing invitation to Sunday dinner at Haydon's, where he often met Hazlitt. In January he began attending Hazlitt's new course of lectures on "The English Poets," where he usually met the whole circle of his London friends. In Hampstead he dropped in at Wentworth Place almost every day to see Dilke, with whom he began a close reading of *Paradise Lost,* or occasionally to call on Dilke's neighbor Charles Brown, a literary-minded bachelor who occupied the other half of the double house. One Sunday he entertained Severn and Tom's old friend Charles Wells at Well Walk—an occasion for letting off steam. "I pitched upon another bottle of claret—Port," Keats wrote to his brothers. "We were all very witty and full of Rhyme—we played a Concert from 4 o'clock till 10." Claret and high spirits called for music, but the only music they had was what they made themselves. This led to a noisy habit among Keats's friends of making up little bands in which each man imitated a different instrument—Keats usually taking the bassoon. "I said on that day the only good thing I was ever guilty of," he added in his letter. They were talking about the theatre and Henry Stephens's preference for the top gallery— "and I wondered that careful Folks would go there for although it was but a Shilling still you had to pay through the Nose."

Saturday nights he turned up regularly at Jem Rice's now for whist and brag and gin-and-water. Rice, despite chronic poor health, had an irrepressible sense of humour, and Keats livened his letters to George and Tom with some of his bawdy puns. He was picking up some new slang at Rice's too: "They call good Wine a pretty tipple, and call getting a Child knocking out an apple, stopping at a Tavern they call hanging out—Where do you sup? is where do you hang out?" Keats had an ear for lingo of all kinds—the jargon of the boxing ring and the cockpit, the small talk of London drawing rooms, and, later, the short e's of the Devonshire girls—"the prettiest ees in the Language"—and the lilt of the Scots. The slang of his Saturday-night set soon found its way into a song he wrote for Reynolds' amusement called "Sharing Eve's Apple," a deft little piece of *double entendre* addressed to an equivocal young lady and ending with the plea:

> There's a sigh for yes, and a sigh for no,
> And a sigh for I can't bear it!
> O what can be done, shall we stay or run?
> O cut the sweet apple and share it!

Undoubtedly there was talk better worth reporting at Horace Smith's, the stockbroker's, where he was invited to dine in the middle of December. This was a change from Smith's rather condescending notice of Keats as Hunt's protégé the winter before. Smith's set were men who had earned a position in the fashionable literary world or cultivated those who had; and Keats evidently held his own with them, for the evening resulted in a series of invitations. Smith himself had made his name as a wit five years

before with a volume of *Rejected Addresses,* parodies of the leading poets of the day so good that Walter Scott, on reading the
burlesque of his own verse, exclaimed he must have written it
himself. In an age which regarded parody as a fine art, the book
earned Smith a thousand pounds and an entrée into the drawing
rooms of countesses.[2] One topic that must have been discussed
around his table on Keats's visit was the case of William Hone,
the radical journalist, who was being tried that same week for his
Biblical parodies attacking the Ministry. This trial was only the
climax of a year of mounting political and social unrest, which
the Government tried to quell by reviving and extending the
wartime policies of anti-Jacobin repression—suspending habeas
corpus, piling a tax of fourpence on penny newspapers, and prose-
cuting its critics for seditious libel. After a brilliant and witty
self-defence, Hone was found not guilty, and twenty thousand
Londoners cheered him as he emerged from the courtroom. Apparently Keats's elation at his acquittal, and possibly the example
of Smith himself, moved him to write a parody of his own mocking
the Tories—that cryptic sonnet called "Nebuchadnezzar's Dream,"
which echoes some political criticism he had managed to slip into
*Endymion.*[3] Yet his evening with Smith's friends left him bored—
or so he told his brothers. For all their brilliance, "they only served
to convince me, how superior humour is to wit in respect to enjoyment," he wrote, echoing a favorite distinction of Hazlitt's.
They "say things which make one start, without making one feel."
They were all alike; they even had the same style in handling a
decanter. "They talked of Kean & his low company—Would I
were with that company instead of yours said I to myself!"

This remark shows which way his attention was turning. The
week he dined at Smith's he also made his debut as a dramatic
critic for *The Champion,* replacing Reynolds, who was going off
for a Christmas visit with the Drewes. This could not have come
at a better time, for on December 15 Edmund Kean returned in
triumph to Drury Lane after a severe illness. That night Keats
saw him play his greatest role, Shakespeare's Richard III, in top
form, and another deep-dyed villain from Massinger several nights
later. His first review brimmed over with his long-standing admiration of Kean's interpretation of Shakespeare. Kean's greatness
was almost an anachronism in these shabby days of 1817—"Habeas
Corpus'd as we are out of all wonder, curiosity, and fear," Keats

wrote, slashing irrelevantly at the Government; Kean "is a relict of Romance." This tribute suggests the curious temperamental affinity between the two men which Cowden Clarke had noticed in Keats's schoolboy bravado, and which was to grow on Keats himself as the years went by. Kean, like Keats, was very short, but by sheer intensity managed to convey an effect of heroism on a grand scale; as Keats said, "he always seems just arrived from the camp of Charlemagne." What struck Keats most was the gusto or vital force of Kean's art by which he conveyed a character's whole past and future in the present moment. "When he says in Othello 'Put up your bright swords, for the dew will rust them,'" Keats exclaimed, "we feel that his throat had commanded where swords were thick as reeds." [4]

His assignments the following week were very different—a review of a fifth-rate new tragedy, *Retribution,* a fair sample of the wretched melodrama being turned out by the playwrights of his time; and a notice of the inevitable Christmas pantomime, which Keats turned into a parody of some well-known dramatic critics of the day. Standing in the wings at Covent Garden and having some "curious chat" with one of the managers, Keats got his first real smell of greasepaint. Not long afterward Tom's friend Charles Wells took him to one of the small private playhouses that mushroomed in the dank neighbourhood of Covent Garden and smuggled him behind the scenes. Here Keats revelled in the unconscious comedy of the performance as seen from backstage. The musicians had to play the overture three times over and more before the curtain went up. One of the actors was routed by a gibe from the gallery, and another, who stood beside them sweating with anxiety, never got on stage at all when the evening dragged on too long for the third piece in the bill to be played. After being sworn at by grimy stagehands Keats managed to squeeze his way into the green-room with Wells, where they chatted with "a little painted Trollop" dressed in the part of a Quaker and got caught in a quarrel among the actors.

It was a great spectacle, as Keats described it to his brothers. The theatre was in his blood—the lively, lusty, noisy, showy theatre world of the Regency—and was stirring up a new ambition in him. He would write plays. Perhaps in time he could bring the English stage to life again and give Kean some better parts to play than the miserable stuff now provided him. He knew this would be the work of years, but he decided at once to try his hand. So he began rereading Shakespeare with a new eye for the details of dramatic construction—stage directions, characterization, "bye-writing"—and sketched out a satirical verse-drama called "The Castle Builder" and some lyrics for an opera. Nothing came of these two projects, but the ambition took root and grew; and the ambition itself was significant. It is as though in finishing *Endymion* Keats had begun to be released from the preoccupation of proving himself a poet. Now he could turn his gaze outward to the world of other characters, and start to write the more objective and Shakespearean poetry he had glimpsed while reading Shakespeare at Burford Bridge in November.

The Christmas season brought the usual round of parties and visits. Fanny was in town, on vacation from boarding-school, and Keats went to see her as often as he could. Mrs. Abbey, a stupid and querulous woman, always cast a gloom over their meetings, and Abbey himself had decided that Keats was a bad influence on his sister and hinted he was not welcome at Pancras Lane. Christmas Day Keats evidently spent, rather uncomfortably, at the Reynoldses'. The friendship between the Keats brothers and the Reynolds sisters was beginning to cool. George had done something to put himself in their bad books, and Jane Reynolds, her tongue growing a little sharper as she moved, still unmarried, from twenty-five to twenty-six, was beginning to make Keats uneasy in the part of the younger brother which he had chosen to play. But Keats enjoyed himself thoroughly at several dances during the holidays. One especially, at some old friends', the Redhalls', he described in detail in a letter to Devon. Old Mr. Redhall—an innocent well-powdered little man with a lisp, a single topic of conversation, and two outsized nieces—was not used to giving parties and had no idea of how much wine would be consumed. Halfway through the evening his guests discovered he had set out eight dozen bottles on the kitchen stairs, and things thereafter got rather out of hand. They became still livelier when the ladies retired after supper. "On proceeding to the Pot in the Cupboard," Keats reported, "it soon became full on which the Court door was opened Frank Floodgate bawls out, Hoollo! here's an opposition pot—Ay, says Rice in one you have a Yard for your pot, and in the other a pot for your Yard." Keats danced little that evening, perhaps finding himself at a disadvantage with the two large nieces; instead he drank deep and spent most of his time cutting for half-guineas, ending up one to the good. "Rice said he cared less about the hour than any one," he reported to Tom and George, "and the proof is his dancing—he cares not for time, dancing as if he was deaf. Here a happy twelveth days to you," he concluded, "and may we pass the next together."

This greeting, so gaily confident—was Keats whistling to keep their courage up? For Tom was not mending in Devon as he should. New symptoms were appearing—palpitations and spitting of blood. This news must have struck Keats with a chill of foreboding: there could be no doubt now that Tom had consumption. He immediately conferred with Sawrey, the London surgeon he had consulted in October; but Sawrey merely asked that Tom send him a full report of his progress. It is hard to tell whether Keats was reassured by the surgeon's unconcern or was putting up a show of confidence for his brothers' sake. Tom's condition was not yet critical, and in any case there was little to do but keep him in Devon till summer, build up his strength and his spirits, and hope for the best. Meanwhile Keats had his own life to live —a life which he now tried to share with Tom as much as possible through his letters.

One piece of news he did not send. Taylor had evidently read *Endymion* and returned the manuscript to him before the end of December with carefully qualified praise. Though he probably did not tell Keats as much, he was disappointed in the poem as a whole, despite many strikingly beautiful passages; he was puzzled by the ending and downright alarmed by the more passionate episodes.[5] Evidently he spoke firmly to Keats about the need of not offending the ladies, and indicated some lines, especially in the second book, where straightforward references to breasts, legs, "milky toes," "blending pleasurable," and other delights could be toned down. Keats, momentarily taken aback, agreed; he told Taylor he was sorry "that any one should have to overcome Prejudices" in reading his verses. Nevertheless he was irked, as may be gathered from his later sarcastic references to "meretricious romance verse" written to please ladies rather than men; and some of Taylor's suggestions about rewording certain passages he flatly refused to accept.[6] But these disagreements were nothing compared to the troubles which he heard Shelley was now having with his publishers over his long poem. After *Laon and Cythna* had appeared early in December, the Olliers suddenly became alarmed over its atheistic and incestuous aspects. They recalled all the copies they could and made Shelley delete some offending passages and completely change the relationship of the hero and heroine. The revised poem finally appeared late in January as *The Revolt of Islam.* "Poor Shelley I think he has his Quota of good qualities, in sooth la!!" Keats remarked in reporting the blow-up to his brothers, but it may have sobered him into taking at least some of Taylor's advice. So he began recopying *Endymion* on the fifth of January, revising as he went along.

But the news which Keats should have taken the greatest pleasure in sharing with Tom and George was his long-anticipated meeting with Wordsworth, who was in town on one of his rare visits that winter. On December 28 Haydon invited Keats, along with Charles Lamb and Thomas Monkhouse, a relative of Wordsworth, to a small dinner in the poet's honour. Keats found himself introduced to a tall parsonish gentleman near fifty, with eyes like two smouldering coals, a deep rough voice, and the bearing of an Old Testament prophet. They dined in Haydon's studio with the canvas of "Christ's Entry" looming up behind them in the firelight. Wordsworth was at his most oracular, Lamb at his most roguish. The talk began with a debate on Homer, Shakespeare, Vergil, and Milton; but with Lamb getting tipsy, as he usually did, it soon descended from this level. Lamb assailed Wordsworth for condemning Voltaire in *The Excursion;* then turned on Haydon for putting Newton into his picture. Keats joined Lamb in attacking Newton, whom he accused of destroying the poetry of the rainbow by reducing it to a prism. Lamb seized on this as the occasion for another toast, and they drank to "the confusion of mathematics." Haydon, delighted with his own party, thought it was like nothing so much as a scene from Shakespeare, with each man freely expressing his own nature.

After dinner they moved into the sitting room, and other friends began dropping in—John Landseer, the painter; Joseph Ritchie, a young surgeon and African explorer; and John Kingston, a minor dignitary with intellectual pretensions whom Keats had met at Horace Smith's. At Kingston's entrance the evening took a new tack. As Haydon described it, "Into this company a little heated with wine, a Comptroller of the Stamp Office walked frilled, dressed, and official, with a due awe of the powers above him, and a due contempt for those beneath." In Kingston's view, all of the company fell into the latter category except Wordsworth—whose position was ambiguous. Wordsworth held a sinecure in the Stamp Office; as a mere Collector he stood below a Comptroller. Kingston introduced himself in his official capacity, which, according to Haydon, had "a visible effect" on Wordsworth. Then the Comptroller began plying the Collector with observations: "Pray, Sir, don't you think Newton a great genius?" "Don't you think, Sir, that Milton was a very great genius?" Lamb, who had been dozing off by the fire, found this too idiotic to get by. He made Kingston repeat his questions, then seized a candle and staggered across the room on his spindly legs to examine the Comptroller's phrenology and see "Wha-a-at-sort-fello-he-waas." Kingston laughed uncomfortably while Wordsworth tried to smooth things over and Keats and Ritchie struggled to keep a straight face. Finally Haydon had to take Lamb into his studio to sober up, where every now and then he could be heard roaring nonsense rhymes as the Comptroller continued making observations. Keats took refuge in drink, astonishing Kingston at supper, so he told his brothers, by "keeping my two glasses at work in a knowing way." With Ritchie he immediately became friends. Ritchie had already read and admired Keats's poems, and Keats listened with interest to his plans for exploring the Sahara. When they parted, Keats promised to send him a copy of *Endymion* to take and fling into the middle of the desert.

Three days later Keats met Wordsworth walking on Hampstead Heath and was invited to call on him in town. Flattered by the kindness, Keats presented himself on the indicated day, but was kept waiting an uncomfortable while. At last Wordsworth appeared in full dress, knee breeches, silk stockings, and stiff collar, in a hurry to be off. "The thing, Kingston," had invited him to dinner, and Wordsworth had evidently forgotten his young caller. Keats swallowed his anger and accepted Wordsworth's invitation to dine two days later, and this meeting was followed by several others during January. Yet in his letters to his brothers and Bailey, who must have been eager to hear of them, Keats was strangely silent about these occasions. Writing to Haydon on January 10, he affirmed his belief that *The Excursion* was the finest poem of the age; but of Wordsworth himself he was having a bitter revelation.

The great poet of the revolutionary vision was turning into a dogmatic reactionary, driven by repressed hatred of what he had loved before. At home in Westmoreland he could play the role of prophet unchallenged; in London it was a different matter. One afternoon in January, while Wordsworth was dealing out critical judgments in his usual pose, with left hand thrust in his waistcoat, Keats started to make a remark of his own. To his astonishment, Mrs. Wordsworth put her hand on his arm and said, "Mr. Wordsworth is never interrupted." Keats may have remembered this snub when he wrote to Haydon two months later, "He cannot expect his fireside Divan to be infallible he cannot expect but that every Man of worth is as proud as himself." But he may have been recalling other incidents of the winter. One evening at Lamb's, Coleridge had expressed his admiration of Wordsworth's poetry by reciting it at length; Wordsworth responded by quoting not Coleridge's poetry but more of his own. Another time, hearing that Scott was about to publish his novel *Rob Roy*, Wordsworth read aloud his own ballad of the same name and remarked, "I do not know what more Mr. Scott can have to say on the subject." Luckily Keats could not have known that the copy of his *Poems* which he gave Wordsworth this winter inscribed "With the Author's sincerest Reverence," stood uncut and unread thereafter on Wordsworth's shelves.[7]

By mid-January Keats had to confess he had been "racketing too much." He had written almost nothing for a month and had not yet finished revising the first book of *Endymion*. All at once he was tired of dining out, even almost of good talk. Several feuds had broken out in his set—Hunt and Taylor disagreeing about the profits of *Rimini*, Haydon and Reynolds falling out over an unanswered invitation, Hunt and Haydon bickering over some borrowed silver which Mrs. Hunt had failed to return. "Uproar's your only musick," Keats commented ruefully to his brothers. He felt it was somehow his responsibility to bring his friends together again, but this was perplexing, as he saw, when the point of dispute often mattered much less than the disposition to quarrel. At the same time, perhaps without quite realizing it, he was developing a vivid sense of the human comedy with its many-sided clash of differing natures, which he now began watching with the same detached pleasure as he would a play; and this too made intervention difficult.

"The commonest Man shows a grace in his quarrel," he later noted. Two very different outlooks were balancing in his mind—that of the sober moralist and that of the budding dramatist, who, as he later wrote, takes as much delight in Iago as in Imogen.[8] By now he clearly saw the egotism inseparable from the creative temperament such as Haydon's; yet he continued to admire Haydon even while he was coming to value more highly than ever the "probity & dis interestedness" he found in Bailey. Haydon's interest in the young painter Cripps had finally collapsed, though Keats had not yet given up trying to raise the money for his expenses. Haydon had also offered to sketch a head of Keats as frontispiece for *Endymion,* then let the weeks slip by and forgot his promise—just as he had forgotten a similar one to Hunt the year before, and another promise to Bailey to make him copies of his life masks of Keats and Wordsworth.

As for Hunt, the clash of their natures was still something he could not be quite objective about. When, around January 20, Taylor finally approved the revised first book of *Endymion,* Keats took it round to Hunt's before sending it off to the printer. To his surprise, both Hunt and Shelley were a good deal less than enthusiastic. They seemed all too ready to catch him up on small slips, and Hunt, after skimming the book through, objected especially to the "high-flown" conversations between Endymion and his sister. Keats was angry, even though he knew Hunt was wrong: the story of a mortal loved by a goddess could not be written in the style of *Rimini.* At the same time he realized that Hunt and Shelley were hurt, and perhaps justly, because he had not shown them any of the poem before—though they could hardly be expected to understand why he had found this necessary. Keats tried to make amends by staying on that evening and writing an impromptu ode on a lock of Milton's hair which Hunt had just acquired. But this effort merely betrayed his anxiety. For all his "burning and strife," he wrote, his poetry was still bound by "childish fashion"; not for many years, till he had grown "high-rife With Old Philosophy" like Milton himself, would he be able to pay Milton a tribute worthy of his greatness.

This admission reveals Keats's restlessness as well. Already he was impatient to turn his full attention to his next poem, the Miltonic epic on the fall of Hyperion which had occurred to him during his visit with Bailey, and for which he was beginning to prepare himself in his close study of *Paradise Lost*. It also appears that Hunt's criticism of *Endymion* caused him a sudden twinge of dissatisfaction with it. Two days later, writing to Haydon, Keats half-mockingly contrasted the "deep and sentimental cast" of *Endymion* with the "more naked and grecian Manner" he hoped to achieve in *Hyperion*. And shortly afterward he began tinkering with the text of *Endymion*, even though it was already being set up in print. From the first six hundred lines he finally cut about forty—thereby involving Taylor in some extensive charges for resetting. It is significant that all these cuts were aimed at removing as much of the Hunt-like "sentimental cast" of the poem as Keats could at this late stage.[9] Clearly the thought of adverse criticism was beginning to trouble him. "But whose afraid?" he exclaimed. "Ay! Tom! demme if I am."

But a still more sobering experience was in store for him. At a gathering at Haydon's studio one afternoon late in January the painter asked him to recite some lines from *Endymion* for Wordsworth. Keats replied with the "Hymn to Pan"—of all the poetry he had written, the most Wordsworthian in feeling—and repeated it in his characteristic half-chant, walking up and down the room. At the end there was an expectant silence; then the older poet dryly remarked, "A very pretty piece of paganism." Keats was stunned; the party soon broke up.[10] As Haydon savagely commented, "Wordsworth's puling Christian feelings were annoyed"; he rightly blamed Wordsworth both for the lack of tact in his remark and for his literal-mindedness in taking the hymn as "paganism." Keats himself never mentioned the episode in his letters. He suddenly stopped seeing Wordsworth in the last week of January, however, and a month later he told his brothers that he was "sorry that Wordsworth has left a bad impression where-ever he visited in Town—by his egotism, Vanity and bigotry." "Yet," he immediately added, "he is a great Poet if not a Philosopher." The truth was that the Christian philosopher in Wordsworth was slowly strangling the poet—the man who fifteen years before had written in his concern for the England of his day,

> Great God! I'd rather be
> A pagan suckled in a creed outworn;
> So might I, standing on this pleasant lea,

> Have glimpses that would make me less forlorn;
> Have sight of Proteus rising from the sea;
> Or hear old Triton blow his wreathed horn.

Keats, of course, could know nothing of the bitter spiritual struggle that had brought Wordsworth to this point; he did know by a kind of instinct, however, what his own life as a poet required. His disillusionment with Wordsworth was a staggering blow to his conception of poetry itself, and to recover from it he was driven back for the time being on his own deepest resources of poetic vitality.

→»·«←

On January 22, before turning back to *Endymion* to revise the second book, he decided to read *King Lear* again; and on opening his Folio he was overcome as never before by the disparity between his own achievement and Shakespeare's tragic stature—the "Cliff of Poesy" which towered as high above him as it had nine months before. It was a moment to take his bearings and make a new start. "The thing appeared to demand the prologue of a Sonnet," he told his brothers—the first serious sonnet he had written since the day before starting *Endymion*. Looking back and then forward, he took his leave of "golden tongued Romance, with serene lute" to submit himself to the purgatorial sufferings of Lear:

> once again, the fierce dispute
> Betwixt damnation and impassion'd clay
> Must I burn through; once more humbly assay
> The bitter-sweet of this Shakespearian fruit. . . .

As he looked ahead to *Hyperion,* he wondered whether he was yet ready to meet this test of tragic and heroic power; and once again he called on Shakespeare to be his "Presider":

> When through the old oak Forest I am gone,
>   Let me not wander in a barren dream,
> But, when I am consumed in the fire
> Give me new Phœnix wings to fly at my desire.

This sonnet broke the spell. "I think a little change has taken place in my intellect lately," he wrote his brothers shortly afterward, "I cannot bear to be uninterested or unemployed, I, who for so long a time, have been addicted to passiveness." In the next few weeks songs and sonnets came pouring out in exuberant vari-

ety—tributes to Mrs. Reynolds' cat and to the Mermaid Tavern,
a joking attack on a fellow poet and lines in praise of Robin Hood.
He made his first trials of the Shakespearean sonnet—debating
with Reynolds in one whether blue or brown eyes were more beautiful, recalling in two others the mysterious lady "seen for a few
moments at Vauxhall." In one of these ("Time's sea hath been five
years at its slow ebb") he testified to the sway she still held over
him:

> Thou dost eclipse
> Every delight with sweet remembering,
> And grief unto my darling joys dost bring.

What had called her back? If the sonnet is more than a mere exercise, it would seem that his sexual disillusionment in the fall had
paradoxically revived his dream of a perfect love. A more sombre
note is struck in the other sonnet. Written little more than a week
after rereading *King Lear*, it shows his dedicatory mood heightened by a new anxiety:

> When I have fears that I may cease to be
>     Before my pen has glean'd my teeming brain,
> Before high-piled books, in charact'ry,
>     Hold like rich garners the full-ripen'd grain;
> When I behold, upon the night's starr'd face,
>     Huge cloudy symbols of a high romance,
> And think that I may never live to trace
>     Their shadows, with the magic hand of chance;
> And when I feel, fair creature of an hour!
>     That I shall never look upon thee more,
> Never have relish in the faery power
>     Of unreflecting love!—then on the shore
> Of the wide world I stand alone, and think
> Till love and fame to nothingness do sink.

Tom's illness, it seems, had revived the half-repressed sense of his
own mortality that had broken through in "Sleep and Poetry."
Once again, but far more urgently, the thought of all that he hoped
to achieve called up the fear that life would not be long enough.

In this mood he began looking at *Endymion* again more crit-
ically. Wordsworth's brusque dismissal of the "Hymn to Pan"
as merely "pretty" seems to have jarred him into rethinking the
poem's meaning as a whole. One of the passages in the first book
which he had let Taylor emasculate was a statement of his faith
in the value of love—that "blending pleasurable" which is the

most "self-destroying" of all feelings. Now he saw how necessary
these lines were as a preface to his account of Endymion's gradual
ascent toward perfect love. Accordingly he rewrote the passage and
asked Taylor to have it reinserted:

> Wherein lies happiness? In that which becks
> Our ready minds to fellowship divine,
> A fellowship with essence; till we shine,
> Full alchemiz'd, and free of space. . . .[11]

Apparently his conversations with Bailey in the fall had deepened
his sense of what he had tried to express the preceding spring, for
the "fellowship with essence" which he now described as the eventual result and justification of sexual love is clearly related to the
idea of "essential beauty" discovered through "taking part in the
existence" of other identities which he had discussed with Bailey
in November. Only the week before he had written his brothers
that he believed "a very gradual ripening of the intellectual
powers" is the best. It is a striking example of such ripening that
the final meaning of his myth became clear to him only several
months after he had finished his poem.

Keats's experience with Wordsworth seems also to have led him
into news speculations on poetry in general. For a few weeks, indeed, his resentment of his remark on the "Hymn to Pan" led
him to doubt Wordsworth's greatness as a poet, especially when
measured against Shakespeare's. As he asked Reynolds early in
February, "For the sake of a few fine imaginative or domestic *
passages, are we to be bullied into a certain Philosophy engendered
in the whims of an Egotist—We hate poetry that has a palpable
design upon us—and if we do not agree, seems to put its hand
in its breeches pocket." There are echoes here of a comment on
Wordsworth in one of Hazlitt's lectures which Keats had heard
a few days earlier, but the criticism of what he later called "the
wordsworthian or egotistical sublime" reaches farther back into
Keats's own thought. Six weeks before, while walking into town
with his Hampstead neighbour Dilke to see the Christmas pantomime, he had listened to Dilke hold forth in his dogmatic fashion on various subjects. "Several things dovetailed in my mind,"
Keats wrote his brothers, "& at once it struck me, what quality

---

* Perhaps this word is miscopied from Keats's own term "dramatic," which describes Wordsworth's early poetry far better than "domestic."

went to form a Man of Achievement especially in Literature & which Shakespeare posessed so enormously—I mean *Negative Capability,* that is when man is capable of being in uncertainties, Mysteries, doubts, without any irritable reaching after fact & reason." This ability to "remain content with half knowledge"— what today is called "tolerance for ambiguity"—was, as Keats saw it, essential to the poet insofar as he above all men explores the frontiers of human experience and struggles with its endless diversity and contradictions in an effort to extend the limits of human awareness. The lesser poet, such as Coleridge, "would let go by a fine isolated verisimilitude caught from the Penetralium of mystery" because he insists on imposing his own limited interpretation on reality.

But this capacity for suspending judgment in order to report faithfully on experience also involves the "capability of submission," the capacity for "annulling self" and thereby entering into other identities which Keats had previously described to Bailey. As Keats later realized, the ability to "annul self" depended on a very firm sense of self: Dilke, for instance, he came to see was "a Man who cannot feel he has a personal identity unless he has made up his Mind about every thing." [12] At this stage, however, Keats's belief in negative capability seems to have sprung partly at least from his awareness of his own mental growth. His bewildering shifts of allegiance from one poetic influence or intellectual position to another, sometimes in the space of a few weeks, were not contradictions so much as necessary steps in his ever more inclusive development. Still young, still experimenting, he had not yet reached the point where the mind pauses, then begins to exclude, concentrate, harden. He must then have been deeply moved to hear Hazlitt in his January 27 lecture characterize Shakespeare in the very terms which he himself had already set up as his own guidelines in poetry. "He was nothing in himself," Hazlitt remarked; "but he was all that others were, or that they could become." This, of course, was a definition of Shakespeare's dramatic genius; and it is significant that three days later Keats confided to Taylor his new ambition to make his "chief Attempt in the Drama."

For several weeks now he was glad to be mostly alone in Hampstead, revising *Endymion,* studying Milton, and being lazy when he liked. London was full of new people to meet: Peacock, the novelist; Benjamin West, the painter; Peter Moore, a manager of

Drury Lane; Peter Patmore, the journalist; Peter Pindar, the political satirist; Mrs. Opie, a fashionable authoress; and Caroline Scott
*"con occhi neri,"* the beautiful Italian wife of the publisher of *The
Champion* and an especial admirer of Keats's poetry. Crabb Robinson, the friend of Coleridge, a diarist famous for the famous men he
became acquainted with, came out to Hampstead to call. Even
Keats's former publisher was making amends. As he dryly remarked
to George and Tom, honours were rushing thick upon him: "What
think you, am I to be crowned in the Capitol, am I to be made
a Mandarin—No! I am to be invited to a party at Ollier's to keep
Shakespeares birthday Shakespeare would stare to see me there."
But he was learning how to refuse invitations. All through February
his only regular trips to town were to hear Hazlitt lecture each
Tuesday evening.

Hazlitt by now had become, and was to remain, the chief living
intellectual influence on Keats. Hunt's and then Wordsworth's
influence had waned; his discipleship to Haydon had sobered into
friendly respect; from now on his only masters in poetry were "the
mighty dead." With Hazlitt, Keats never became intimate, despite
the affinity of their outlooks; but again and again his critical remarks provided the spark that set off Keats's own most searching
speculations on poetry. Intimacy in any case was not one of Hazlitt's
talents. A shy, unkempt, blunt-spoken man, "brow-hanging, shoe-
contemplative, strange," as Coleridge described him,[13] he carried
with him a heavy load of unhappiness—poverty, ill success, an uncongenial marriage, alienation from his early friends, and the
failure of his political ideals. Hazlitt was one of the few men of his
generation in England to remain outspokenly loyal to the principles of the French Revolution through the wars with Napoleon
and the years after Waterloo. This uncompromising liberalism was
one thing that drew Keats to him; another was his enthusiasm for
the acting of Kean. Hazlitt's first appearance as dramatic critic had
coincided with Kean's debut at Drury Lane in 1814; brilliance
had called forth brilliance, and Hazlitt made his own name as
well as Kean's with reviews of his Shylock and Iago and Hamlet.
Along with his hatred of injustice and cant, Hazlitt had a great
capacity for enjoyment: "gusto," one of his favourite words, he
made a critical term. He admired a great variety of things, from
the painting of Titian to the racquets-playing of the famous John
Cavanagh. Charles Lamb found his conversation the best in Lon-

don, and Reynolds described his *Characters of Shakespeare's Plays* as the only criticism of Shakespeare that was worthy of him. This book, which Keats began reading in the spring of 1817, did much to deepen his understanding of Shakespeare and led him at the beginning of 1818 to class Hazlitt's criticism with Wordsworth's *Excursion* and Haydon's painting as the "three things to rejoice at in this Age."

The audience at the lectures on the English poets was a mixed lot—Quakers, Dissenters, and mind-improvers, along with Keats's set and a sprinkling of Hazlitt's enemies. They gave him an assortment of prejudices to set on edge with his inimitable skill. As a result the lectures were punctuated by murmurs and laughter, irrelevant applause, and shouts of disapproval. Crabb Robinson, one of Hazlitt's detractors, noted in his diary that he quoted "unseemly verses" (John Gay's) to "a congregation of saints" and "even eulogized the modern infidel, so indiscreet and reckless is the man!" [14] The modern infidel was, of course, Voltaire; the eulogy set Keats to rereading him a few days later. When Hazlitt came around to criticizing Wordsworth, Robinson felt called upon to hiss. Hazlitt looked calmly in the direction of the hissing, then turned back his page and repeated the entire passage. Despite their contentiousness, the lectures contained some "fine discriminating criticism," which Keats was to mull over for months afterward.[15] Only one thing disappointed him—the discussion of Chatterton. To Hazlitt he was only "the marvellous boy" of uncertain promise, "the sleepless soul who perished in his pride" when the poems which he tried to pass off as the work of a fifteenth-century monk were found to have been written by himself. Keats apparently protested afterward, and the next week Hazlitt took time to explain his opinion at some length because it had "given dissatisfaction to some persons with whom I would willingly agree on all such matters."

Hazlitt's taking a cue from Keats suggests that their respect was at least partly mutual. A cue which Keats took from one of the earlier lectures was to have more significant results. On February 3, in commenting on Dryden's translations of Boccaccio, Hazlitt had remarked that a rendering of some of his other tales "could not fail to succeed in the present day." Keats at once dug up an old prose translation of *The Decameron,* and in the first tale which Hazlitt had suggested he found what he was looking for. The tragic

story of Isabella and her lover murdered by her own brothers—
here was a subject full of dramatic possibilities, and one which he
could easily turn into another romance while preparing himself
for the much more ambitious *Hyperion*. He roughed out some
stanzas, then mentioned the idea to Reynolds, who was so enthusiastic that they decided to work on a volume of tales from
Boccaccio together.

Keats's friendship with Reynolds was now at its height. In his
new-won independence of Hunt and Haydon, the friendly give-and-
take of rivalry with a man of his own age was just what Keats
needed. In November he promised to send Reynolds a new poem
with every letter he wrote, and from this time on his letters to
Reynolds contain his most thoughtful reflections on poets and
poetry. Reynolds himself was riding high these months. In January his theatre reviews for *The Champion* had earned him a
handsome offer—ten guineas per sheet of sixteen pages—from
Constable, the publisher of the *Edinburgh Magazine,* one of the
best of the literary journals. He turned it down in order to become the mainstay of a new weekly, *The Yellow Dwarf,* which
Hazlitt and John Hunt were starting up. He was already at work
on a long verse narrative when Keats suggested the Boccaccio
project, and eventually he completed two of these tales. His creative outburst that winter must have been partly a consequence of
his engagement to Eliza Drewe. But she had exacted a price: he
must give up writing and become established in the law before
they married. Reynolds agreed only halfway: he entered his uncle's
law office in November and relegated his writing to his spare time,
of which he managed still to find a good amount. On February 14,
probably as a valentine to his fiancée, he wrote a semi-wistful sonnet
of "Farewell to the Muses," which he later gave to Keats—only the
first of many farewells. Three years later he was still unmarried and
still promising

as time increases<br>
To give up drawling verse for drawing leases.[16]

In mid-February, however—perhaps as a sign of the strain of this
conflict—Reynolds came down with a rheumatic fever which kept
him house-ridden for three months. To cheer him up, Keats started
a letter to his friend one sunny morning a few days after he fell
ill. The first hint of spring was in the air; thrushes and blackbirds
were beginning to sing in the bare-branched trees. He had picked

up his regular reading that morning but soon let his book drop and his mind wander. "When Man has arrived at a certain ripeness in intellect," he observed, "any one grand and spiritual passage serves him as a starting post towards all 'the two-and thirty Pallaces.' How happy is such a 'voyage of conception,' what delicious diligent Indolence!" His thoughts circled around the conflicting impressions of the last few months—all the clashes of character he had witnessed, the arguments about poetry, the efforts to win a dispute; then he took a new tack. "Many have original Minds who do not think it—they are led away by Custom—Now it appears to me that almost any Man may like the Spider spin from his own inwards his own airy Citadel—the points of leaves and twigs on which the Spider begins her work are few and she fills the Air with a beautiful circuiting." This required that each man trust to his own "isolated verisimilitudes" but something more: "Man should not dispute or assert but whisper results to his neighbour, and thus by every germ of Spirit sucking the Sap from mould ethereal every human might become great, and Humanity instead of being a wide heath of Furse and Briars with here and there a remote Oak or Pine, would become a grand democracy of Forest Trees." Was he still thinking of Wordsworth, or of his own disagreement with Hazlitt two days before?

A moment later his mind veered back to the mystery of the creative power which he felt growing stronger within him; the old adage of the bee gathering honey came to his mind, and he turned it upside down. "The flower I doubt not receives a fair guerdon from the Bee—its leaves blush deeper in the next spring—and who shall say between Man and Woman which is the most delighted? Let us not therefore go hurrying about and collecting honey, beelike * buzzing here and there impatiently from a knowledge of what is to be arrived at," he added, thinking of Reynolds fretting on his sickbed, "but let us open our leaves like a flower and be passive and receptive—sap will be given us for Meat and dew for drink—I was led into these thoughts, my dear Reynolds, by the beauty of the morning operating on a sense of Idleness—I had no Idea but of the Morning and the Thrush said I was right." And here Keats broke into a blank-verse sonnet which, like the thrush's song, turns back on its own cadence as its thought moves forward.

---

* Following M. B. Forman's punctuation (*The Letters of John Keats*, 2nd ed., revised [1935], p. 104).

O fret not after knowledge—I have none,
    And yet my song comes native with the warmth.
O fret not after knowledge—I have none
    And yet the Evening listens. He who saddens
At thought of idleness cannot be idle,
And he's awake who thinks himself asleep.

"Now I am sensible all this is a mere sophistication, however it may neighbour to any truths, to excuse my own indolence," he ended. "It is no matter whether I am right or wrong either one way or another, if there is sufficient to lift a little time from your Shoulders."

This letter deserves comment, for, though Keats apparently wrote it off without forethought, it conveys one of his most characteristic beliefs. His letters at the time he began writing *Endymion* express all the young writer's sensations as he struggles with his work; but now he could stand back from the struggle and speculate on it. Just as he had begun to observe the interplay of temperament and cross-purpose among his friends with the absorbed detachment of the dramatist, he was learning to watch the ebb and flow of his own creative power with the objectivity of the critic. With no preconceptions about how poetry should be written—"it is no matter whether I am right or wrong"—he realized that for himself at least it required long stretches of drifting with the tide. Perhaps he had come to see this more clearly from silently comparing himself with Shelley—Shelley the indefatigable, full of a dozen political and literary projects at a time; Shelley, who seemed able to turn out a poem in twelve cantos at will. Keats was beginning to recognize in himself a rhythm of energy and indolence, of alternation between the masculine imposition of self upon experience and the feminine surrender to it. This indolence could be a delight, as when he gave himself up to the beauty of an early spring morning; at other times it took the form of a paralysing blankness of feeling and thought, as in the autumn before, when he had wondered whether there was something "radically wrong" with his nature. But now he was beginning to accept these swings of mood, as he did his shifts of intellectual position, as not only inevitable but fruitful in the end. A few weeks later he was to develop this idea in one of his most characteristic metaphors, in a sonnet on "The Human Seasons." Recognizing this fact of his nature, he could now wait more patiently for the "very gradual ripening" of intellect which he realized would be necessary for *Hyperion*—a longer period of "sucking the Sap from mould ethereal." A year or two earlier, he had described the writing of poetry in terms of a journey, a battle, a cliff to be scaled, a vast sea to be explored: now he saw it in images of grain ripening, of wine ageing, of the sun rising and setting, of the flower which

> must drink the nature of the soil
> Before it can put forth its blossoming.[17]

As he wrote to Taylor at this time, "If Poetry comes not as naturally as the Leaves to a tree it had better not come at all."

Yet the indolent fit of the morning of February 19, when he wrote to Reynolds, turned to energy by afternoon. Horace Smith had invited him to dinner; Keats wrote, begging off with the excuse that his brothers were expecting him shortly in Devonshire and he had many days' work still to do. He was recopying the third book of *Endymion* while reading the proofs of the first, and he was increasingly anxious to be done with it. He was restless to get on with *Isabella* and to have more time to read for *Hyperion*. In Devon it appeared that George too was restless. A letter from Georgiana Wylie came addressed to him at Well Walk; it struck Keats that he must have told her he was soon returning to town. By the end of the month George arrived. On February 28 he came of age at last—an occasion, no doubt, for a serious interview with Abbey and a visit to the Wylies. The two brothers spent a few days together in Hampstead, probably discussing George's future, still uncertain, and the family finances, more tangled than ever. Then Tom wrote from Teignmouth that he was feeling much better and might come up to London himself. This could not be allowed to happen. Keats immediately packed up a few books and the remains of his manuscript and boarded the Exeter coach.

Luckily, however, he found time the evening before he left to hear Hazlitt's last lecture—one on "The Living Poets," to which he must have looked forward eagerly. Hazlitt began with a sober reminder that current popularity is no true test of a poet's worth, and that "those minds which are the most entitled to expect it can best put up with the postponement of their claims to lasting fame." After briefly dismissing some lady poets and fashionable rhymesters, he went on to a critique of Wordsworth, Southey, and Coleridge—the poets whose acquaintance he had made in the days of their revolutionary ardour and who had since disavowed him, in private and in print, in the ardour of their reaction. Hazlitt balanced some just praise of Wordsworth's and Coleridge's early poetry against a composite portrait of the Lake Poet of 1818: "He hates all greatness and all pretensions to it, whether well or ill-founded. He hates all science and all art;he hates chemistry, he hates conchology; he hates Voltaire; he hates Sir Isaac Newton; he hates wisdom; he hates wit; he hates prose; he hates all poetry but his own; he hates the dialogues in Shakespeare; he hates music, dancing and painting; he hates Raphael, he hates Titian; he hates the Apollo Belvidere; he hates the Venus of Medicis. This is the reason that so few people take an interest in his writings, because he takes an interest in nothing that others do!" This peroration must have brought the house down, and it was still reverberating in Keats's mind in a letter he wrote to Haydon over two weeks later: "It is a great Pity that People should by associating themselves with the finest things, spoil them—Hunt has damned Hampstead and Masks and Sonnets and italian tales—Wordsworth has damned the lakes—Millman has damned the old drama—West has damned—wholesale—Peacock has damned sattire Ollier has damn'd Music—Hazlitt has damned the bigotted and the blue-stockined how durst the Man?! he is your only good damner and if ever I am damn'd—damn me if I shoul'nt like him to damn me." [18] Hazlitt's critical explosion had evidently cleared the air. More plainly than before, Keats now saw where his own business lay. So with this as postscript to the last two months and a half, he brought his cavalier days to a close and turned his eyes in another direction.

⫸ ⫷

He left London on the night of a gale. Trees were blown down and coaches overturned on the way, and Keats, riding outside as usual, got drenched. This was his first, and prophetic, impression of Devon; his second was a "middle-siz'd Devonshire girl of about 15" waiting at an inn door with "a quartern of brandy." A year and a half later he remembered that "the very thought of her kept me warm a whole stage—and a 16 miler too." This was not enough to keep him from catching cold, however, and he arrived in Teignmouth with a bad sore throat.[19] Tom seemed to be benefiting from

the care of Dr. Turton, a Teignmouth physician to whom he had
taken a fancy, but the Devon climate which was supposed to cure
him had taken a turn for the worse. It rained for a week after
Keats arrived, let up for a day or two, then started again; and it
rained at this rate for most of March and April. Haydon, a Devonshire man, and Reynolds, in love with a Devonshire girl, had made
him eager to see the place; but the weather kept him penned up
indoors for almost two weeks. Their lodgings also were less than
satisfactory—a small airless apartment facing north on a narrow
alley, an unhealthy location for a tubercular patient, and still more
so for anyone shut in at close quarters with him. One night they
went out to the theatre, and Keats—for what reason he never
said—was insulted. Evidently they had ladies with them, for
Keats kept his temper and did not fight, but he was angry that
he could not get redress afterward. In this mood he went doggedly
ahead putting the final touches on *Endymion* and amused himself
in his letters to London by blasting Devon for its "urinal qualifications" and its inhabitants as a race of "dwindled englishmen."

Teignmouth itself offered as few diversions as any seaside resort
in a cold and rainy spring—a deserted promenade, an empty band-
stand, sailboats anchored under tarpaulins. There were a theatre,
where Keats met with his insult, and a ballroom, where waltzing
was banned. But George and Tom had already made some pleasant
acquaintances among the townspeople, especially Mrs. Jeffrey,
their landlady, and her three daughters. With the two elder ones,
"laughing thoughtless Sarah" and "steady quiet Marianne,"
George and Tom had struck up a four-sided flirtation. George as
usual seized the initiative and carried off the prize—a lock of
Sarah's hair, which he took back to London with him. Marianne
evidently withstood his charms, but when John arrived, she seems
to have fallen in love with him at once. Together they all strolled
along the shore and read poetry; and when Keats left Devon in
May, Marianne poured out her feelings in some sentimental verses
of farewell, which were published along with her other poems years
later. Keats was too preoccupied with Tom to reciprocate, and
perhaps the fact that she wrote poetry counted against her. Young
ladies who asked to be taken seriously put him on his guard. Jane
Reynolds sent him a little Tassie seal at this time, showing Leander
swimming the Hellespont in a storm—perhaps as a joking reference to the weather; but Keats never used the seal on any of his

letters, though he thanked her politely in a sonnet. Still dissatisfied with himself as a poet, he evidently could not quite yet accept
himself in the cavalier's role. So he kept the Jeffrey sisters at arm's
length with the same brotherly teasing he used toward the Reynolds girls, and went his own way.

He had other things on his mind at this time besides Tom's
health and his own work—the beginning of a disagreement with
Bailey. Keats had come a long way since his visit to Oxford the
previous fall. Closer contact with Hazlitt's incisive mind and the
sombre realization of Tom's illness made him more sceptical than
before of Bailey's easy assumption that all was well with the world.
Bailey had turned an important point in his career that winter;
he had preached and published his first sermon. This was something of an embarrassment to his friends—to Taylor, who brought
it out, for it did not sell, and to Dilke, who reviewed it in *The
Champion* and found it pedantic and high-flown.[20] Evidently
Keats loaned his copy of the sermon to Wordsworth, who did not
return it, and had to borrow another from Dilke a while later.
When he finally came to comment on it, he must have strengthened Bailey's doubts about his principles. "You know my ideas
about Religion," he wrote rather awkwardly. "I do not think
myself more in the right than other people and [I think] that
nothing in this world is proveable.[21] I wish I could give you a
Page or two to your liking," he added. "I am sometimes so very
sceptical as to think Poetry itself a mere Jack a lanthern to amuse
whoever may chance to be struck with its brillance." What Bailey
replied to this we do not know, for Keats was not in the habit
of keeping his friends' letters. We do not even know what Keats
said in answer to his reply, in a letter he wrote at the end of April
that has not survived—which is curious, for Bailey carefully preserved his other letters from Keats. A slight constraint appears in
Keats's next letter, in May, which he closed with the enigmatic
remark that at their next meeting they would "discover whether
a little more knowledge has not made us more ignorant."

Just as Keats finished his letter commenting on Bailey's sermon,
Tom began to cough a little blood. Then, to Keats's alarm, he
had a severe haemorrhage a day or two later, which seemed to
undo all the good of the last three months. After a few nerve-
shaking days he was out of danger, thanks to Dr. Turton, and

began to mend slowly. Keats put on a cheerful front before the
invalid, like the high fooling he kept up in his letters to his friends;
but secretly he was caught in a terrible conflict between anxiety
for Tom and the depression that overtook him in close contact
with illness, which made him almost angry with himself. A week
later, as Tom's health picked up, the weather relented a little,
and Keats seized the chance to escape on some long walks. He
clambered along the rocky coast, explored the villages on the
Teign and sampled their cockles and cream, then struck inland
through fields already thick with daisies. The first days of the
Devonshire spring swept the gloom from his mind. In a letter
spilling over with verse, he told Haydon that he would stay all
summer:

> Then who would go
> Into dark soho
> And chatter with dack'd hair'd critics
> When he can stay
> For the new mown hay
> And startle the dappled Prickets?

He soon discovered another of the beauties of Devon—the middle-
sized, delicate girls, with their lilting salute, "Well, where be ye
going?" So he added to the doggerel verses he sent to Haydon
some bantering stanzas of "b———hrel"—"Where be ye going, you
Devon maid?"

> I love your Hills and I love your dales
>   And I love your flocks a bleating—
> But O on the hether to lie together
>   With both our hearts a beating.
>
> I'll put your Basket all safe in a nook
>   And your shawl I hang up on this willow
> And we will sigh in the daisy's eye
>   And kiss on a grass green pillow.

Devon was a good field for sowing wild oats, and this was apparently the only relief Keats found from the constant tension
of worry over Tom. For a month or so dairymaids and barmaids,
the girls at the bonnet shop across the way, and the wild young
things at Dawlish Fair all figure in a season of pulling apron
strings and rumpling meadows of fern. But it could not last. Some
weeks later he told Reynolds he was "sick of Venery," and it was

in a verse-letter to Reynolds at the end of March that he gave a hint of an experience that made all such pleasure seem unreal as a daydream.

He had walked down to the shore one evening and sat on a weed-covered rock. The sea at this hour usually brought him peace; but this time he glimpsed it in something he had never seen before:

> 'Twas a quiet Eve;
> The rocks were silent—the wide sea did weave
> An untumultuous fringe of silver foam
> Along the flat brown sand. I was at home,
> And should have been most happy—but I saw
> Too far into the sea; where every maw
> The greater on the less feeds evermore:—
> But I saw too distinct into the core
> Of an eternal fierce destruction. . . .

An abyss suddenly opened up before him. Now at last, it appears, he realized that Tom would not recover; for all his exquisite love of life, nothing could save him in the end. The quiet, unconcerned beauty of nature, which had always been Keats's refuge against unhappiness, now seemed to hold no assurance of any triumph over suffering, or even of any meaning in pain and death:

> Things cannot to the will
> Be settled, but they tease us out of thought.
> Or is it that Imagination brought
> Beyond its proper bound, yet still confined,—
> Lost in a sort of Purgatory blind,
> Cannot refer to any standard law
> Of either earth or heaven?

Neither Bailey's theological explanation of evil nor Hunt's sentimental insistence that evil was unreal, nor even the faith he had absorbed from Wordsworth of some benevolent Power presiding over nature, was proof against this vision of "eternal fierce destruction." The shark and the hawk at prey, even the robin "ravening a worm" in mindless savagery, were as real as the sea and the stars that peaceful evening. Nature itself offered no clue to the riddle of existence: it meant only what the individual himself glimpsed in it. For a moment the whole world reeled in his imagination. Then with an effort Keats wrenched his gaze away from the nothingness he had stared into, turned back to thoughts of Reynolds' recovery and the new poem he had begun writing.

Yet try as he might to forget it, he could not quite blot this glimpse of "Purgatory blind" from his memory.

Keats picked up *Isabella* at this time, it appears, in a deliberate effort to escape from these "detested moods" which he momentarily confided to Reynolds. It was to be, like *Endymion,* a "Romance"—"a fine thing notwithstanding the circulating Libraries," as Keats still felt: a tale combining supernatural plot and essential human emotion, a pair of star-crossed lovers and a *Hamlet*-like ghost who recounts his own murder. Much of Keats's immature sentimentality lingers on in the opening picture of the young lovers; yet as the poem moves ahead, it begins to show a striking new sense of the dramatic at work. Already Keats was learning to submerge himself in the character and feelings of his hero and heroine and to tell his story in flashes of visualized action—the jealous brothers biting their lips in silence, the murderers dipping their swords in the stream, Isabella tossing back her hair as she digs in Lorenzo's grave. Boccaccio set him a good example of concise, straightforward narrative; but even more significant are Keats's additions, where a new note begins to sound in his poetry. In Boccaccio's tale the brothers murder Lorenzo merely because of his illicit passion for their sister; Keats added an economic motive with the brothers' greedy ambition to marry Isabella to a wealthy noble.

> With her two brothers this fair lady dwelt,
>     Enriched from ancestral merchandize,
> And for them many a weary hand did swelt
>     In torched mines and noisy factories,
> And many once proud-quiver'd loins did melt
>     In blood from stinging whip;—with hollow eyes
> Many all day in dazzling river stood,
> To take the rich-ored driftings of the flood.
>
> For them the Ceylon diver held his breath,
>     And went all naked to the hungry shark;
> For them his ears gush'd blood; for them in death
>     The seal on the cold ice with piteous bark
> Lay full of darts; for them alone did seethe
>     A thousand men in troubles wide and dark:
> Half-ignorant, they turn'd an easy wheel,
> That set sharp racks at work, to pinch and peel.

Bernard Shaw once claimed that these stanzas "contain all the Factory Commission Reports that Marx read, and that Keats did not read because they were not yet written in his time." [22] Extravagant, perhaps; but Keats had been reading *The Examiner* for years, he had a stingy guardian, and, as he once said, "you must allow for imagination." Another contrast with Boccaccio comes out in the conclusion. Boccaccio had tried to mute the horror of his story by describing Lorenzo's body as miraculously uncorrupted when Isabella dug it up and reburied his head in her pot of basil; Keats calmly presented the fact of its physical decay in order to heighten the pathos of Isabella weeping over it in her madness.

Perhaps he was aiming at the quality he had praised in *King Lear* a few months before—that intensity which makes "all disagreeables evaporate, from their being in close relationship with Beauty & Truth." But a closer look at the means by which he achieved his effect reveals something still more striking. A string of images of medicine and disease runs through the poem like a dark vein through marble—a description of Isabella as thin and pale as a young mother with a sick child; accounts of stifling and pulsing and hallucinations and fever; pharmaceutical lore of distilling and compounding, of poisonous flowers and strong potions; observations of haemorrhage, psychological shock, and consumption; a metaphor of amputation; and, finally, a detailed picture of a freshly exhumed corpse, perhaps recalled from the dissecting room at Guy's two and a half years before. This imagery implies a more direct confrontation of reality than Keats had yet made in his poetry; and its sudden appearance at this time is strangely significant. The previous spring Keats had told George, "I have forgotten all surgery." Now, it seems, the experience of nursing Tom was bringing this buried self to life again. The doctor he had started to become at the time of his mother's illness and then repudiated, now returned to question the poet he had chosen to be instead. During his months in Devon, Keats spoke repeatedly of his ambition to do some constructive service for the world, even—as he remarked in a sombre moment—of "dying for a great human purpose." In the face of Tom's suffering, poetry began to seem "a mere Jack a lanthern." He told Reynolds he was glad he had kept his medical books and resolved to read them again; even if he made no practical use of it, this study would strengthen his grasp on realities which up to this time he had tried deliberately to exclude from his poetry. Just as, a year or two before, his sense of identity as a poet had widened to include his boyhood vision of life as a

heroic struggle, now it began deepening to include his later awareness as a surgeon of the extent of human suffering and his resolution to relieve it.

But the first effect of Tom's relapse in mid-March was to precipitate all the dissatisfactions Keats felt over *Endymion*. On
March 19 he wound up his labours by drafting a preface that
slashed recklessly at his failure in the poem, admitting all the uncertainties he had felt in writing it and the distance it fell short
of his hopes, and daring his critics to think worse of it than he. "In
duty to the Public I should have kept it back for a year or two,
knowing it to be so faulty," he confessed; "but I really cannot do
so:—by repetition my favorite Passages sound vapid in my ears."
It was an impossible preface. Taylor gave the task of telling Keats
this to Reynolds, who wrote tactfully suggesting that there was
too much of Hunt in its style. "I am not aware there is any thing
like Hunt in it," Keats retorted, "(and if there is, it is my natural
way, and I have something in common with Hunt)." But, he went
on, "a Preface is written to the Public; a thing I cannot help looking upon as an Enemy." He had not laboured for "the thousand
jabberers about Pictures and Books," and he would not humble
himself to them—"or to any thing in existence,—but the eternal
Being, the Principle of Beauty,—and the Memory of great Men. I
never wrote one single Line of Poetry with the least Shadow of
public thought," he added, forgetting for the moment how the idea
of fame had haunted him when he began *Endymion*. Yet even then
he had thought of fame not as the applause of his own time but
as "a light thrown to posterity." Now he had discovered that between him and posterity stood the public—the commonplace people who "read the Edinburgh and the Quarterly and think as they
do," and who would find fault with *Endymion* to prove their own
importance. Kingston criticism! This he had not bargained for.

As he finished his letter to Reynolds it stopped raining
for an hour, and he went out for a walk to let his temper
cool. The lane was banked with primroses on either side,
and he noticed that the hedges were beginning to leaf. Perhaps he remembered the first primroses in the Isle of Wight, the
April before, and the mood in which he had begun *Endymion*. The
next morning he sat down and rewrote the preface. In this second
version he made essentially the same points as in the first, but in a
far different spirit. Again he admitted that the poem was merely

"a feverish attempt, rather than a deed accomplished," and that he regretted publishing it as it stood. But this time he spoke not to the hateful public but to men "who look with a zealous eye, to the honour of English literature." This was what mattered in the end, not the scorn or applause he might win himself; and with this thought he was already plotting and fitting himself, he confessed, "for verses fit to live." With the greater object of *Hyperion* before him, Keats could now accept his failure in *Endymion* with some equanimity. His last act was to dedicate the poem "To the Memory of Thomas Chatterton." The deed was accomplished, the feverish attempt was over.

Now there was the future to deal with. Keats must have spent many hours talking this over with Tom, for his plans were becoming more closely linked all the time to his brother's needs. Tom's illness made another winter in England something to be avoided if at all possible, and George, who still had not found work to his liking, was increasingly restless in London. But there was also Keats's own work to consider. Already his conception of *Hyperion* seemed to be outstripping his power to execute it, even further than his ideas for *Endymion* the year before. He had planned to write the poem in a vein of epic loftiness patterned on Milton; now he felt he must learn Homer and even Dante in the original to master this style. More than this, he realized, the theme of the poem as he envisaged it would require the philosophic mind which, Wordsworth had said, only the years can bring. "I know nothing I have read nothing," he told Taylor, "and I mean to follow Solomon's directions of 'get Wisdom—get understanding.' " Hazlitt would be his guide here, yet Keats felt he needed at least a year's study before he could intelligently ask Hazlitt "the best metaphysical road" to take. But he also realized that he needed something more than "continual drinking of Knowledge" to fit him for the poetry he dreamed of—some actual experience of the world's grandeurs. Slowly his plans took shape. Dilke's neighbour Charles Brown had written from Hampstead suggesting that Keats accompany him on a walking trip through the north of England and Scotland that summer—where, he realized, he would see Wordsworth's own lakes and mountains. Tom must spend the next winter in Italy, and Keats would make the voyage with him in the autumn. Once in Europe, there were "the Kingdoms of the Earth and the glory of them"—"stupendous recollections" to gather for his poetry. He would climb Ben Nevis this summer, Mont Blanc the next. "I will clamber through the Clouds and exist," he wrote Haydon, already drunk with the idea. A life of study and travel, living in Europe at the lowest cost, with his poems bringing in a little money—for the moment Keats forgot the Devonshire rain beating against the window. So at the end of April he announced to Taylor—who had just sent him a copy of the newly published *Endymion*—that he planned to take his books and "retire from the World," meaning London, for some years.

What Keats apparently intended was a period of retirement such as Milton had undertaken after leaving Cambridge with the deliberate purpose of preparing himself for great poetry. Within the last month or two it seems that Milton had begun to take a place beside Shakespeare in Keats's mind, not only as an example of a certain style of poetry but also as a model of the poet himself. It was Milton who first raised the troublesome question of what good a poet could do for the world. From a wildly joking letter to James Rice toward the end of March it appears that Keats was then reading Milton's prose works, in which he had turned from poetry in mid-career to enter the battle between Royalist and Puritan on the side of freedom. "He was an active friend to Man all his Life and has been since his death," Keats commented soberly. In a number of Keats's other remarks this spring there are echoes of Milton's defence of his so far unproductive career in the *Reason of Church Government*. Milton himself had wondered whether he could be "anything worth to his country," and the idea that a poet could serve society in his work, pursue not his own fame or self-fulfilment but what Keats called "the glory of making his country happier," began to take firm root in Keats's mind at this time and grow there. Among the many notes he penned into his copy of *Paradise Lost,* he observed that, like himself, Milton had "an exquisite passion for poetical Luxury," and with this he would have been content "if he could, so doing, have preserved his self-respect and feel of duty performed; but there was working in him as it were that same sort of thing as operates in the great world to the end of a Prophecy's being accomplished." [23] That Milton should have completed his career by writing *Paradise Lost*—one of the works which, Keats thought, "benefit the 'Spirit and pulse of good' by their mere passive existence"—suggested an answer at last to the troubling question that Tom's illness had raised. "I find there is no worthy pursuit but the idea of doing some good for the world," he confided to Taylor. "Some do it with their society—some with their wit—some with their benevolence—there is but one way for me—the road lies through application study and thought."

So, after two months of reading and thinking in Devon, his ideas were beginning to fall into place around a new center. If he could retell the myth of Hyperion to convey the new understanding of things that was taking shape in his mind, he would be serving mankind in the best way he could. On May 3 Keats started a long letter to Reynolds which, along with the usual jokes and new verses, gives hints of what was turning over in his mind as he pondered his theme. Reynolds was now well enough to return to his law studies, and he seemed convinced that this would be the end of poetry for him. Keats tried to persuade him it would not. His own study of medicine had not hindered him in his poetry; he was beginning to see that it had helped. "An extensive knowledge is needful to thinking people," he argued; "it takes away the heat and fever; and helps, by widening speculation, to ease the Burden of the Mystery. The difference of high Sensations with and without knowledge appears to me this," he added, "in the latter case we are falling continually ten thousand fathoms deep and being blown up again without wings and with all the horror of a bare shoulderd Creature—in the former case, our shoulders are fledged, and we go thro' the same air and space without fear."

The echoes of *Tintern Abbey* along with *Paradise Lost* are significant. By now Keats had moved far enough beyond his experience of Wordsworth as a man to reconsider him as a poet, which at this point involved measuring him against Milton's genius. In February he had dismissed Wordsworth as "not a philosopher," at the same time that he was coming to admire Milton for his vast learning and philosophic grasp of the problem of good and evil. By May, Keats was beginning to see an equal value in Wordsworth's more intuitive but perhaps more profound awareness of life, because he himself had begun to explore some of the shadowed depths of experience from which this awareness had sprung. Turning from *The Excursion*, with its lofty philosophizing, back to Wordsworth's early poems of beggars and gipsies, of girls abandoned by their lovers and fathers by their sons, Keats saw where Wordsworth's genius lay—in "thinking into the human heart."

Beside this gift, Milton, for all his brilliance, showed "less anxiety for Humanity." Milton's theology, it struck him, was something that could be learned, and by one "not much advanced in years"; Wordsworth's insight, by contrast, could be gained only by undergoing a similar experience. "Axioms in philosophy are not axioms until they are proved upon our pulses," Keats remarked. He was beginning to understand Wordsworth's central perception—that the nature of the world changes as the individual's growing capacity to experience it changes; and this led him to describe the change as he himself had felt it.

"I compare human life to a large Mansion of Many Apartments," he wrote Reynolds, "two of which I can only describe, the doors of the rest being as yet shut upon me." In the first, "the infant or thoughtless Chamber," we remain "as long as we do not think"; but at length, "impelled by the awakening of the thinking principle—within us," we move into "the Chamber of Maiden-Thought," where "we see nothing but pleasant wonders, and think of delaying there for ever in delight"—the period in Keats's life, we may guess, from his discovery of poetry to the writing of *Endymion.* Yet the awakening of thought has the effect in time "of sharpening one's vision into the heart and nature of Man—of convincing ones nerves that the World is full of Misery and Heartbreak, Pain, Sickness and oppression—whereby This Chamber of Maiden Thought becomes gradually darken'd and at the same time on all sides of it many doors are set open—but all dark—all leading to dark passages—We see not the ballance of good and evil. We are in a Mist—*We* are now in that state," he added, returning to Reynolds. "We feel the 'burden of the Mystery.' " Wordsworth's greatness was in exploring these dark passages: "he is a Genius in so far as he can make discoveries, and shed a light in them." These hidden reaches of the mind, Keats now saw, were the intellectual problem posed by their own times, far more complex than the theological questions with which Milton was absorbed. So Wordsworth was "deeper than Milton," he concluded, though more because of "the general and gregarious advance of intellect, than individual greatness of Mind"—thanks to that "mighty providence" which "subdues the mightiest Minds to the service of the time being."

In sketching this picture of spiritual growth, Keats was not merely measuring Wordsworth's greatness against Milton's; he was stating in a different key one of the meanings he glimpsed in his own myth of Hyperion—mankind's long struggle toward greater understanding. As a child of his age he had almost unconsciously accepted the belief that the spread of enlightenment —the forward thrust of scientific knowledge, the extension of political responsibility, the deepening insight into the mind itself— —must effect " a continual change for the better": [24] the ascent he now saw symbolized in the Olympians' victory over the Titans. It was no mere abstract faith in reason he was trying to express, however, but the great revolutionary struggle of his age against the irrational repressive forces of the old order, in society as well as thought; nor was it an easy faith in progress he held. In his glimpse of "Purgatory blind" that evening in March he had for a moment doubted there was any real goal to the struggle; now he was beginning to sense what the struggle would cost. So, he suggested to Reynolds, if they were to continue as poets, or even to go on living and thinking, they too must explore Wordsworth's dark passages. But, not to leave his friend with too gloomy a picture of the future, Keats ended his letter with the promise, "Your third Chamber of Life shall be a lucky and a gentle one—stored with the wine of love—and the Bread of Friendship."

The lines of verse which he sent in this letter were the beginning of an ode to Maia, the mother of Hermes, which he had started on the first of May. They are different from anything he had written before: they ring with a new resonance, a new maturity. Keats, who had been longing to learn Greek poetry, comes far closer in these lines than anywhere in *Endymion* to the spirit of those

> bards who died content on pleasant sward,
> Leaving great verse unto a little clan.

The sense of a new balance struck, a new peace with himself, and a calm delight in the new season emerges from his prayer:

> O, give me their old vigour, and unheard
>   Save of the quiet Primrose, and the span
>     Of heaven and few ears,
>   Rounded by thee, my song should die away
>     Content as theirs,
> Rich in the simple worship of a day.

In these lines Keats had gone far toward closing the gap between his real nature as it is revealed in his letters—masculine, energetic, straightforward—and the over-intense, half-effeminate idiom into which his early poetry had been lured by the example of Hunt and his contemporaries. At last he was beginning to shake free of the style of other poets and work out his own. Yet it is worth noting that the last line of the ode, so rich in multifold meaning for all its simplicity, echoes the last line of a memorable passage prefacing *The Excursion*—"A simple produce of the common day." Keats had burned through the experience of disillusionment to discover what remained essential and meaningful to him in Wordsworth.

But the ode remained a fragment. The day after Keats sent it off to Reynolds, unexpected news came from London. George had decided to marry and leave England. All at once it was time to return home.[25] Tom had spat a little blood the day before, but seemed well enough to make the trip. They packed hastily, borrowing some money from Mrs. Jeffrey for the journey.[26] Sarah Jeffrey offered to go with them on the first stage, and Tom, under doctor's orders to avoid emotional scenes, made a brief farewell to Marianne and her mother. Then the two brothers climbed into the post chaise with Sarah, to make a dash to Honiton for the Exeter coach which would carry them back to London.

*Chapter Seven*

---

# Mist and Crag

A T Honiton they bade Sarah an affectionate farewell, and Keats sent back a note to Mrs. Jeffrey telling her that Tom had borne the first leg of their journey remarkably well. But twenty miles farther on, at Bridport in Dorset, the worst happened. Tom had another severe haemorrhage. For two or three days they rested in the little coastal town, with Keats in a sweat of anxiety whether to stay or go on. When Tom got some of his strength back they moved on in easy stages and reached London a week after setting out. Here Tom picked up again in one of his unexpected returns of good health and spirits. He insisted he felt better than he had when they left Devon, and his friends managed to cheer him into believing that his illness was "mistaken Fancy." Even Sawrey seemed to find him improved by his winter in Teignmouth and told him that "confinement and low spirits" were his chief worries. Though Sawrey may have suspected, as did Keats, that Tom was "in a lingering state," his advice was to the point, for the emotional condition of a tubercular patient has a considerable effect on his progress. So Tom was encouraged to lay plans for a trip to Italy in the fall. As he wrote to the Jeffrey girls in high good humour, he was thinking of spending the winter in the fine old Lombard town of Pavia, with its ancient university, where he hoped to acquire "a stock of knowledge and strength which will better enable me to bustle through the world."

But both John's and Tom's plans were overshadowed by George's. For months he had been thinking he might emigrate to America, and now at last he had won Mrs. Wylie's consent to marry

Georgiana and take her with him. With a thousand-odd pounds of his inheritance he would buy a farm and strike out on his own. Morris Birkbeck, an enterprising Quaker who had found several large settlements on the frontier, had recently published an account of the opportunities of life in Illinois that aroused great interest in England that year. Yet for George to join Birkbeck's pioneers—knowing nothing of farming and no climate more rigorous than London's—seemed more reckless than enterprising to most of their friends. As Keats told the Jeffrey girls, "They say we are all mad." But George would not be daunted. In a year or two, he believed, he would be earning enough money to support both his brothers and the Wylies. Then they all should follow him to America, with George's old friend Haslam, and Dilke too—the only member of the Hampstead set who approved of his project—and make their fortunes together in the new country.[1]

Keats admitted that this was the best course for George to take, for he saw that his brother was too independent and high-spirited to be happy as a small London merchant. Nevertheless it plunged him ten thousand fathoms deep into gloom again. "I am in that temper that if I were under Water I would scarcely kick to come to the top," he told Bailey in announcing the news. He did not know when he might lose Tom; but now, within a month, he would lose George—his first and in most ways still his closest friend. In the last few years George, who had always appeared to be his older brother, had taken on the major burden of their practical affairs as well; now Keats realized that he must shoulder it himself at the very time that Tom's illness was adding a new load of worry. As for the marriage itself, he told Bailey, he felt almost stony-hearted about it. Beneath his natural but unutterable jealousy of George's happiness were stirring up all his half-forgotten sexual anxieties. This was enough to break through—for the only time in all his letters—his close-guarded reticence about his boyhood. To Bailey he confided that "My Love for my Brothers from the early loss of our parents and even for earlier Misfortunes has grown into a affection 'passing the Love of Women'—I have been ill temper'd with them, I have vex'd them—but the thought of them has always stifled the impression that any woman might otherwise have made upon me."

Writing to Bailey a few months later, Keats was to mock his habit of carrying matters to extremes—"so that any little vexation

grows in five Minutes into a theme for Sophocles." Nevertheless
there were real enough reasons for this lethargy which now
weighed on him like lead. One evidently was the discovery that
his inheritance was dwindling more rapidly than he had thought.
On overhauling his accounts after his return, he decided to transfer
five hundred pounds—most of his remaining resources—to a cash
account at Abbey's, probably to draw on for Tom's extra expenses.
Besides this sobering realization, there were ominous rumblings
from the reviews. The first two notices of *Endymion,* at the end of
May and the beginning of June, were fair-minded and even enthusiastic. But then *The British Critic,* one of the leading Tory magazines, printed a slashing burlesque of a review, which made the
poem out to be both nonsensical and immoral; and meanwhile
*Blackwood's* and the *Quarterly* seemed to be swinging their guns
into position. *Blackwood's* had found a priceless opportunity for
renewing its campaign against Hunt when his new collection of
verse, entitled *Foliage,* appeared early that spring. This contained,
among other things, four sonnets addressed to Keats, two of them
recording the unlucky occasion, a year before, when he and Keats
had crowned themselves with ivy and laurel. So in the May issue
of *Blackwood's* Hunt was set up as "the King of the Cockneys,"
surrounded by a court of would-be poets and crowned with ivy
by "the delicate hand of young Mister Keats—an amiable but infatuated bardling." A few weeks later, the *Quarterly* delivered a
stunning broadside against both *Foliage* and Hazlitt's *Characters,*
along with a clear warning that Keats and Shelley would be their
next targets.[2]

Keats joked about this to Bailey—"I have more than a Laurel
from the Quarterly Reviewers for they have *smothered* me in
'Foliage' "—but the remark was edged with irony. Just when he
wanted to win a hearing for *Endymion* on its own merits, Hunt's
volume had appeared, linking their names more closely than ever.
So he was going to have the reputation of being Hunt's *élève* after
all! In such a mood a fulsome tribute which Bailey published in
an Oxford paper, comparing him to Shakespeare and Milton while
twice mis-citing "Lycidas," [3] could only exacerbate him—"because
the world is malignant enough to chuckle at the most honorable
Simplicity. Yes on my Soul my dear Bailey," he wrote in thanking
him, "you are too simple for the World—and that Idea makes me
sick of it. Were it in my choice," he added, "I would reject a

petrarchal coronation—on account of my dying day, and because women have Cancers."

A savage remark—what had happened to make him lash out at Bailey like this? Not simply his apprehensions about *Endymion* or a momentary impatience with Bailey's plodding appreciation. Even Tom's illness, which no one but himself would admit was hopeless, would not have weighed so heavily on him had he not also been ill himself. His appearance on returning from Devon evidently gave concern to several of his friends. For most of May and June he was not well enough to risk a walk to town in the night air; early in June, in fact, Sawrey ordered him to keep to the house till he got better. What the matter was, Keats did not say. It may have been only a return of the sore throat he had caught in March—which, however, he must have known can be a secondary symptom of syphilis—or he may have noticed symptoms still more disturbing, which with his usual secretiveness he kept to himself. But at this time a strange premonition took hold of Keats. It was unreasonable, and no doubt he told himself so and tried to shake it off. Still it is the kind of idea which, once it gets into a man's mind, is not easy to dislodge. For some reason or other, Keats became convinced that he had only three more years to live. This was an obsession very different from the fear that had gripped him in January, when "the family disease" had reappeared unmistakably in Tom and he realized that his own life might also be cut short before he reached his goal in poetry. Now the thought seems to have shaped itself with a chilling precision: he had three years—a little more than a thousand days—to live. He knew it was unreasonable; he also knew it was possible. Though he made no explicit mention of his foreboding, he let slip half a dozen references to the possibility of his early death in his letters during the next two months.[4] So he must have listened to George's and Georgiana's plans for him to follow them to America with a sense of unreality. Outwardly he agreed to a year's visit; to himself he added the proviso, "If I live to the completion of the three next." "Life must be undergone," he wrote despondently to Bailey; his one consolation was "the thought of writing one or two more Poems before it ceases."

To shake off this mood Keats tried his usual remedy: a few of the old Saturday nights, getting "a little so-so" with Rice and Reynolds; a few Sunday dinners at Haydon's, playing the bassoon in another boisterous "concert" or getting into a political debate with Hazlitt; a few calls at the Reynoldses'—but there the old gaiety was lacking. Mrs. Reynolds openly disapproved of George's plans to emigrate,[5] perhaps regarding his engagement as a defection from Mariane, and conversation with the sisters was growing steadily less enjoyable. Keats found it was more of a pleasure to drop in at Wentworth Place, close at hand, where he could always count on Mrs. Dilke's good humour or the solid masculine talk of Dilke and Brown. One evening in June, Keats went with George and probably Reynolds to the Lyceum, where Charles Mathews, London's favourite comedian and ventriloquist, was holding one of his noisy "At Homes." On the way they unexpectedly met Isabella Jones.[6] One wonders whom she was with or where she was going, and what happened in the sequel. Keats introduced his companions to her, and the meeting may have been extended into a supper party, for at one time, he later noted, the four of them were all in a room together. Whatever the meeting became, it ended as casually as it began, for they parted with no thought of renewing the occasion.

In the end it was another woman who succeeded in lifting Keats out of his depression—unexpectedly, his new sister-in-law. He had liked Georgiana Wylie ever since their first acquaintance, and in their new intimacy he found himself growing fonder of her than he had thought possible. From a sweet but elusive girl of fourteen she had grown in two years into a witty, spirited, and intelligent young woman. She was evidently not pretty and lacked the style conferred by a fashionable upbringing; but she possessed the virtue which counted most with Keats—what he called disinterestedness. She seems to have been the first woman of his age to whom he attributed any kind of moral identity. Up till now, Keats had evidently subscribed to the prevailing masculine belief that "Most women have no character at all"—an attitude which does not, however, preclude idealizing them, but arises from it. Now, on closer knowledge, he discovered that a girl of sixteen could show courage and enterprise. That Georgiana could leave family and friends and the comfortable life of London for a backwoods farm in America, and all for the love of his brother George—he had to admit he was puzzled. "To see an entirely disinterrested Girl quite happy is the most pleasant and extraordinary thing in the world," he wrote Bailey. "Women must want Imagination and they may thank God for it—and so may we that a delicate being can feel happy without any sense of crime." It was the first marriage he had observed from close hand since he was eight, and it gave him much to ponder.

For the time being, however, there were too many other things to occupy him. There had been the wedding itself at the end of May—"I never rejoiced more than at my Brother's Marriage," Keats wrote two months later—and celebrations before and after the event. Now there was the summer ahead to think of. For some reason—perhaps Tom's health, perhaps the state of the family finances—the plans for a winter in Italy were shelved around the beginning of June. For a while Keats wondered whether he should also give up his trip to Scotland. But to confess his worries about his brother would seriously alarm Tom himself, and evidently Tom insisted that he go, since the trip was part of the program for *Hyperion*. "I should not have consented to myself these four Months tramping in the highlands," he wrote Bailey in July, "but that I thought it would give me more experience, rub off more Prejudice, use me to more hardship, identify finer scenes load me with grander Mountains, and strengthen more my reach in Poetry, than would stopping at home among Books even though I should reach Homer." They had neighbours in Hampstead to keep Tom company, and Mrs. Bentley, their landlady, was a kindly woman who could help if needed.

So Keats went ahead with his plans. George and Georgiana were to sail for Philadelphia at the end of June; he and Brown would travel by stagecoach with them up to Liverpool, then from there to the Lakes. Brown, whom Keats had known up till now merely as Dilke's old friend and neighbour,[7] promised to be an excellent companion for the trip—energetic, practical, cheerful, and an experienced traveller. Scottish by ancestry, nine years older than Keats, he was also a writer of sorts and had seen a good deal of the world. On his advice, Keats bought himself a knapsack, then assembled old clothes and new socks, packed up pens, paper and ink, and the manuscript of *Isabella* to mull over. For his summer's reading he chose "a Book Full of vowels," as he described it to Fanny—Carey's translation of *The Divine Comedy*, just published by Taylor and Hessey in three minute volumes which fitted neatly into the remaining inches of space.

The two or three days before leaving were full of the usual last-minute errands. One of these was a financial settling with George. The brothers' accounts had become badly tangled over the last few years, and George had not kept as careful account of his many borrowings from John as he had promised. According to a later statement of Brown's, the sum he finally repaid his brother was less than Keats had expected, and Keats found the settlement less than satisfactory.[8] Money worries were not allowed to spoil their farewell, however. There must have been a flurry of parties at Brunswick Square, where the young couple were spending their honeymoon. To one of these, three days before leaving, George invited Taylor, an amateur phrenologist, to "discover if the lines of [Mrs. Keats's] face answer to her spirit." Abbey's parting words were to call them all Don Quixotes, much to Keats's amusement. He was too busy at the end to say good-bye to many of his friends but swept them all up in a final hurried note to Taylor the night before leaving. Still worried that Tom might be lonely, he asked Taylor to keep him well supplied with books, then to do something he had unaccountably forgotten—send a copy of *Endymion* to Mrs. Reynolds. Signing himself jokingly "John O' Grots," he was ready at last to be off.

At noon on June 22 they boarded the Liverpool coach at the Swan with Two Necks in Lad Lane, near the Guildhall: George, with his thousand pounds of credit; Georgiana, wearing a pretty bonnet; and Keats and Brown with their knapsacks, already dressed for the road. Twenty-five miles from London they stopped for dinner at Redbourn, where, Keats remembered, his medical-school friend Henry Stephens had set up in practice. Keats sent him a note, and Stephens joined them at the inn. If Stephens noticed a change in Keats since his last days at medical school, he did not mention it in recalling the meeting years later; his attention was caught by Georgiana. She was an "original" in his eyes—"not what might be called strictly handsome," "somewhat singular in her attire," but "with an imaginative poetical cast." A man of sensibility might easily fall in love with her, he decided to himself, and observed that Keats introduced his sister-in-law with great satisfaction.

Dinner over, they said their good-byes, and the coach started north again through the long golden afternoon. Almost two hundred miles to their destination—over the Chiltern hills and across the Ouse at Stony-Stratford, through Northamptonshire and War-

wickshire in the brief summer night, and into the quiet cathedral
city of Coventry at dawn; along the borders of Shropshire as the
sun swung high and down into the plains of Cheshire with the
mountains of Wales showing blue toward the west; then across the
Mersey and into Liverpool at last in the early evening.[9] They
were met by a smell of salt and tar, the rumble of drays through
streets lined with tall warehouses, and a forest of masts in the
harbour. George and Georgiana took rooms at the Crown Inn to
wait for the next sailing, and Keats said his last good-byes that
evening. Early the next morning he and Brown were to take coach
for Lancaster, the starting point of their tour. His brother and
sister-in-law were still asleep when he left at dawn, with their farewells and their promises of a reunion in America still fresh in his
ears. He was never to see Georgiana again.

⇒≫ ≪⇐

The walking trip began with bad weather and an unpleasant
surprise. When Keats and Brown reached Lancaster late that afternoon they found the city in an uproar. It was the eve of a parliamentary election in which Henry Brougham, the great Whig lawyer who had defended Hunt in his second trial, was challenging
the Tory incumbent, Lord Lowther. Alarmed by the seething discontent of the industrial population, Lowther had persuaded the
Government to send troops into the district to keep order. The
city was crowded; drink flowed freely while votes were bought
and sold. Keats and Brown had to wait two hours for their dinner,
for the inns were full, then walk the narrow streets looking for
lodgings.[10] Here Keats heard, probably for the first time, "that
most disgusting of all noises," as he described it, the shuttles of the
spinning mills. Lancaster was the first industrial city that he had
seen at close hand, and whatever he glimpsed of the poverty of
the cotton-spinners set him thinking. During the next months, in
the midst of the stupendous scenery he had travelled northward
to see, the image of poverty was to haunt him like an unanswered
question: was all this ugliness and misery necessary? One wonders
whether his outburst against the greedy Florentine merchants who
battened on this misery was added to *Isabella* after his view of
Lancaster.[11]

After putting up for the night in a private house, Keats and

Brown rose early next morning to find it raining hard. For three hours they waited for it to clear, while Brown read aloud from *Samson Agonistes* by way of recommending patience; then at last they strapped on their packs, took their sticks, and set out in a Scotch mist. As they left Lancaster a factory worker jeered at them—gentlemen with nothing better to do than make work for themselves. Perhaps it was at this point that they were struck by the appearance they presented: two nondescript travellers, one tall, heavy-set, and bewhiskered, the other short and lithe, looking like pedlars or sportsmen or neither. Keats was dressed reasonably enough in an old jacket with leather buttons and belt, stout shoes, and the great plaid he usually took on his travels slung over one shoulder—to which he subsequently added a fur cap that caught everyone's eye. Brown had outfitted himself more philosophically in "the best possible dress, as Dr. Pangloss would say": a suit of tartan for warmth, an oilskin cape to keep off the rain, a white hat to protect his bald head from the sun, a plaid over his shoulders, and spectacles on his nose. Keats nicknamed him the Red Cross Knight. Since there was no room in their packs for a change of clothes, they were not taken for gentlemen after their first day's tramp. For it started raining again after their four-mile walk to breakfast, and they walked seventeen miles that day through wet and dry. At the first place they stopped for dinner they were turned away; and twice when they asked for a bed for the night they were refused because the inns were full of Lowther's soldiers. On their third try the landlady took them in grudgingly, and after supper in her whitewashed kitchen a man who had been drinking in the corner staggered toward them and hiccuped at Brown, "Do you—u sell spectacles?" These were still enough of a novelty that Brown's pair was taken as a sign of his trade.

The second day's walk brought them into the Lake Country at last. The morning was fair, though muted by haze, and the larks were singing as they started out on their fourteen miles to Windermere. The road wound upward through fern and furze, and the air grew cool. The Fells of Furness began to show over the hilltops; then suddenly the view opened out, and Windermere lay below them, the Cumbrian Mountains beyond. Keats stopped, wonderstruck. It was a scene which he had described in imagination over and over again in his early poems—the shining lake edged with feathery trees, a green island floating in its midst; the mountains a sombre blue behind, with a silver cloud resting on the lower hills. Now it rose before him, suspended in the strange unreality which scenes long dreamed of wear on their first view, and for a moment blotted out all sense of time and space. "How can I believe in that?" he exclaimed, then, recovering, asserted to Brown that it must beat anything in Italy.

At last they turned down the path to Bowness. Here they found a first-rate inn by the side of the lake, really too luxurious for their tastes, but promising an excellent meal. While waiting for dinner, they rowed out to the island with a man to get trout from wooden cages moored at its edge, then took a swim while the fish were cooking. After dinner they walked five miles up the lake to Amble-side, along a wooded path bordered with fern and purple fox-glove, with the water gleaming through the trees and the moun-tains growing darker behind. That evening Keats wrote to Tom: "The two views we have had [of Windermere] are of the most noble tenderness—they can never fade away—they make one forget the divisions of life; age, youth, poverty and riches; and refine one's sensual vision into a sort of north star which can never cease to be open lidded and stedfast over the wonders of the great Power." He had found what he had come to see.

The next morning he and Brown rose at six and climbed the steep hill behind Ambleside to view the falls, which drop for nearly a hundred feet from a crevice in the rocks. They lost their way in the woods and had to find it by following the roar of the stream. Suddenly the waterfall sprang into sight ahead; they were near the top of the highest fall. Approaching, they watched it plunge like an arrow into a slate-lined pool fifty feet below; then, as they climbed down to the second fall-head, they saw the stream spread out like a fan at their feet and, as it shot over the edge of the third fall, dash itself into a mist. The thunder of the water rang in their ears; its freshness cooled their cheeks. "I cannot think with Hazlitt that these scenes make man appear little," Keats wrote to Tom. "I never forgot my stature so completely—I live in the eye; and my imagination, surpassed, is at rest." They clambered down over moss-covered boulders, grasping at the slender birch and ash trees which grew out of crevices in the rocks, Keats sure-footed, Brown following heavily with a nervous glance at the rapids below; then saw the whole fall from a distance, "streaming silverly through the trees," as Keats described it. "What astonishes me more than any thing is the tone, the coloring, the slate, the stone, the moss, the rock-weed; or, if I may so say, the intellect, the countenance of such places. I shall learn poetry here, and shall henceforth write, more than ever, for the abstract endeavor of being able to add a mite to that mass of beauty which is harvested from these grand materials by the finest spirits and put into etherial existence for the relish of one's fellows." *

This, of course, was the great purpose for which he was making the trip—to "identify finer scenes" and strengthen his reach in poetry. It is significant that in describing it Keats unconsciously echoed one of his favourite passages from Wordsworth:

> Beauty—a living Presence of the earth,
> Surpassing the most fair ideal Forms
> Which craft of delicate Spirits hath composed
> From earth's materials—waits upon my steps. . . .

Even more, his sense of the "countenance or intellectual tone" of Ambleside suggests Wordsworth's description, published years later, of the "workings of one mind, the features Of the same face" he once glimpsed in the Simplon Pass.[12] For the time being, at least, Keats had forgotten his look "too far into the sea" at Teignmouth, when he had caught sight of a nature uninformed by any divine principle, indifferent to any human values. At Windermere and Ambleside it was impossible not to believe in what he once called "the poetry of earth," that mysterious sense of a meaning in nature, or in "the great Power" who expresses His nature through these wonders. Nor could he doubt that somehow from his experience of this sublimity great poetry would be born. A few weeks later, at his first sight of Burns's native countryside of Ayr, with the sea and the black hills of Arran beyond the green valley, Keats wondered, "How is it they did not beckon Burns to some grand attempt at Epic?" Feeling as he did, he found exclaiming over scenery in the usual picturesque terms as distasteful as "jabbering about Pictures and Books." After describing the Ambleside waterfall in his letter to Tom, he apologized—"but how can I help it?" —and promised to send no more descriptions. And after the shock of the first two or three tremendous adventures, his letters contain none of the rhapsodies which Brown, the nearsighted romantic traveller, added to his journal day after day. Keats did not miss

---

* *Letters*, ed. Rollins, I, 301. The last sentence is repunctuated in order to make Keats's meaning clear.

a shade or colour or echo of the wild magnificence all around them, but the true journal of his trip to the north is *Hyperion*.

After Ambleside, their next stop was Rydal, where Keats was to pay a long-planned call on Wordsworth. When he inquired at Bowness about the way to Wordsworth's house, he learned that it was one of the chief landmarks for the fashionable visitors, and that Wordsworth had been in Bowness a few days before, canvassing for Lord Lowther. Wordsworth versus Brougham! This was a jolt, though it might have been less of one had Keats known that Wordsworth was electioneering for Lowther during his London visit the winter before.[13] Nevertheless he kept to his plan and hiked on that morning with Brown to Rydal Mount, at the head of Windermere. Wordsworth was not at home, they were informed, nor any of his family. There was nothing for Keats to do but write a note and leave it on the mantelpiece, propped against what he recognized as a portrait of Dorothy Wordsworth. As he turned dejectedly to go, his eye was caught by the view from the parlour window. Before them Windermere lay at full length, shining under the open sky, reaching ten miles into the silent hills. What a window to sit and read in, or stare out of hour by hour! Keats only half noted it in his hurry to be gone, but the image dropped like a seed into his mind.

Again they set out north, tramping along Rydal Water and Grasmere, then on to Thirlmere at the foot of Helvellyn. Around them on every side rose the green and purple-shadowed mountains whose names Keats had first learned in Wordsworth's poems: Loughrigg, Skiddaw, Scafell, Kirkstone, Silver How, Hammer-Scar, and Helm Crag. He and Brown had planned to climb Helvellyn, the grandest of them all, but the next morning they woke to find it raining. So they started out again, walking eight wet miles to Keswick for breakfast, then tramping ten miles around Derwent Water to climb the Falls of Lodore, then, after returning to Keswick for dinner, trudging another three miles, uphill and down, to see the Druid Temple near the Vale of Saint John. They went to bed "rather fatigued" that night, but not too tired to rise at five the next morning to climb Skiddaw before breakfast. For once the weather promised to be fair, but after they hauled their way nearly to the top, a mist fell over the valleys below. Still they could see beyond the clouds the hills of Lancashire to the south and the coast of Galloway beyond the Solway Firth to the north and west, with the highest peaks of the Cumbrian range all around them. Snow lingered in the crevices of the mountain, and it grew colder and colder as they climbed. "We were glad at about three parts of the way," Keats wrote to Tom, "to taste a little rum which the Guide brought with him, mixed, mind ye with mountain water, I took two glasses going & one returning. We went up with two others, very good sort of fellows, All felt on arising into the cold air, that same elevation, which a cold bath gives one—I felt as if I were going to a Tournament."

The exhilaration of new experience countered any sense of fatigue the first week or two; Keats found that fourteen miles in the Lakes seemed less than the four between Hampstead and London. But even after the first excitement wore off, he and Brown kept to the same routine. Twenty miles a day was their usual stint. The long summer evenings they spent poring over the map and figuring distances, playing cards, reading Milton and Dante, or writing up their journals. Brown kept a diary full of minute details about the scenery and people they passed, with an eye to publishing it later. Keats was more inclined after a long day to sit with his feet up on a chair and laugh at Brown's methodicalness as, evening after evening, he pulled out of his knapsack first, paper; second, pens; and third, ink. Why not vary it a bit? Keats asked— try taking out the pens first. "But I might as well tell a hen to hold up her head before she drinks instead of afterwards." His own journal took the form of long letters to Tom, to which he added a page almost every day. He kept another diary besides this prose one—poems which he wrote, as Wordsworth had done on a similar tour in 1803, to commemorate the places they visited. These sonnets all show a sense of strain, however; writing poetry to order was not one of his real talents, especially when his mood conflicted with what the occasion seemed to demand.

For, in the unpredictable way that all trips do, the journey was turning out different from what he envisaged. He had counted on meeting hardship, fatigue, even hunger, though the actual form of these discomforts—blisters, drenchings, fleas, gadflies, dirty food, a sickening monotony of eggs and oatcake when they reached the Highlands—could not be imagined beforehand. He managed to joke about them all and even to write poetry about some—the gadflies, for instance, that plagued him when he swam in Loch

Fine. But even before the excitement of mountains and lakes and ruins began to wear off, he found an unexpected source of interest in the people they met along the way—a soldier who had fought Napoleon up and down Europe for seventeen years, a Scottish gentleman who cautiously admitted to being a Deist, a pretty Irish chambermaid, a drunken Irish weaver, a provincial playgoer, an Argyllshire innkeeper's family, a schoolmaster in the Hebrides, the shepherds in the Isle of Mull. His first encounter with northern ways was delightful. At the village inn where they stopped in Ireby he and Brown discovered a dancing class in full swing. Half amused, half admiring, they watched the fresh-cheeked boys and girls weaving through the intricate patterns of strathspey and reel. With Burns's "Tam o' Shanter" running through his head, Keats described it to Tom: "They kickit & jumpit with mettle extraordinary, & whiskit, & friskit, & toed it, & go'd it, & twirld it, & whirl'd it, & stamp't it, & sweated it, tattooing the floor like mad.* I was extremely gratified," he added, "to think, that if I had pleasures they knew nothing of. they had also some into which I could not possibly enter I hope I shall not return without having got the Highland fling."

Scotland was in fact still a foreign country to the Englishman of that time. Keats was immediately struck by the broad Lowlands accent—"how is it a' wi' yoursel'?"—and, as in Devon, he tried a poem in the dialect. His eye too was caught by the barefoot Scottish girls, a crowd of whom they passed walking to a horse-fair with their shoes and stockings in hand to put on at the edge of town. Brown was dismayed by their large feet, but Keats noted, with an anatomist's eye, the beauty of the human foot that had been allowed to develop naturally. Yet the farther north they journeyed, the more he was struck by the poverty of the Scottish peasants. Smoke-blackened cottages with no chimneys and often no floors, thatched with turf, picturesque, perhaps, as Brown thought, but very primitive; barefoot girls driving cattle across stony pastures or standing by cowsheds up to their ankles in dirt —he could not look at them as merely part of the landscape. The solemnity of the Scots also began to oppress him. An expressionless

---

* Following F. W. Page's emendation of this sentence from John Jeffrey's transcript of the original letter (*Letters of John Keats*, Oxford World's Classics [1954], p. 133; cf. *Letters*, ed. Rollins, I, 307).

stare usually greeted the two travellers on entering a village; the children played in silence, and even the pretty girls they called out to on the road rarely ventured to smile. Poor little Susannahs, Keats thought, so terrified by the elders of the Scottish Church. "The kirk is greatly to be damn'd," he burst out to Tom. "These kirkmen have done scotland good (Query?) they have made Men, Women, Old Men Young Men old Women, young women boys, girls and infants all careful—so that they are formed into regular Phalanges of savers and gainers—such a thrifty army cannot fail to enrich their Country." Yet also "these kirkmen have done Scotland harm—they have banished puns and laughing and kissing (except in cases where the very danger and crime must make it very fine and gustful)."

When, a few days later, they crossed from Portpatrick to Ireland, the first chambermaid they met in the inn at Donaghadee—"fair, kind and ready to laugh"—proved the difference between the two nations. Yet at the same time the appalling raggedness and dirt of the Irish, cutting peat in bogs or penned up in mills in Belfast, filled Keats with despair. One old woman in a sedan chair whom they encountered near Belfast struck him as the image of Ireland's misery. "The Duchess of Dunghill," he called her, a squalid old woman in a dog kennel, "looking out with a round-eyed skinny lidded, inanity," like "an ape half starved from a scarcity of Buiscuit in its passage from Madagascar to the cape," smoking a pipe with her head nodding like an idiot's while two wretched ragged girls staggered along with their burden. The lot of the Irish seemed far worse than the Scots', but what was there to do about it? According to Malthus, the only economist of the age whom Keats ever mentioned, such poverty was inevitable. "The present state of society demands this," Keats mused, "and this convinces me that the world is very young and in a verry ignorant state—We live in a barbarous age."

He and Brown had expected to spend a week tramping through Antrim and Down. But after their first day's walk though bogs and slums, they found they had miscalculated. Forty-eight Irish miles to the Giant's Causeway came to seventy English ones; worse, the Irish inns charged three times as much as those in Scotland. So they returned to Donaghadee and sailed back to Portpatrick the next day and continued their tramp northward. Reporting this

foray to Tom gave Keats an opportunity to speculate on the differences of national character, a favourite pastime of the traveller.
Yet in the midst of spinning his theories he shrewdly noted that
both the Irish and the Scots are "sensible of the Character they hold
in England and act accordingly to Englishmen." The last thing
an inexperienced traveller expects to find in another land is a
new awareness of himself and his own country, but Keats was making this discovery even while he described travelling to Reynolds
as "one of the pleasantest means of annulling self." Most of the time,
of course, he and Brown might have been traveling incognito; they
were mistaken for "Spectacle venders, Razor sellers, Jewellers,
linnen-drapers and Spies," Frenchmen in Ireland, English soldiers
in the post office at Portpatrick, and excise men in whisky country.
This escape from one's habitual character is one of the pleasures of
travelling; but there comes a time on every journey when a
familiar image glints off the novel surfaces of things and the
traveller is suddenly confronted with himself again.

Keats had caught a glimpse of that image in Dumfries, their
first stop in Scotland, which they reached early in July. Here Burns
was buried, and a visit to the grave of this early hero of Keats was
one of the goals of his pilgrimage. The visit inspired Brown to
make the predictable observations on the value of memorials to
great men; but to Keats it brought something absolutely different
and unexpected, that unsettling sense of dislocation known as
*déjà vu:*

> The Town, the churchyard, and the setting sun,
>   The clouds, the trees, the rounded hills all seem,
>   Though beautiful, cold—strange—as in a dream
> I dreamed long ago, now new begun.

If it is true that in such moments one does in fact dimly recall a
scene already witnessed and repressed, Keats may have been struggling with the memory of another graveyard—St. Stephen's in
London, where his parents lay buried. Or was it that, standing in
this northern churchyard, staring at the large white-painted, iron-
railed mausoleum, overwhelmed by its ugliness—"anti Grecian &
anti Charlemagnish"—and its incongruity with Burns, he had a
vision of still another grave? He had expected to be moved by the
thought of Burns himself—Burns whom Hazlitt had called "as
much of a man, though not a twentieth part as much of a poet, as

Shakespeare." Instead Keats felt only a familiar numbness—"the feel of not to feel it"; and the poetry that came to his mind was not Burns but Shakespeare:

> For who has mind to relish, Minos-wise,
>  The real of Beauty, free from that dead hue
>   Sickly imagination and sick pride
>  Cast wan upon it?

The echo of Hamlet's meditation on death is significant. In May, when Keats told Reynolds, "We read fine—things but never feel them to the full until we have gone the same steps as the Author," he had added, "Now I shall relish Hamlet more than I ever have done." Now as he stood beside the grave of a poet who had died with his promise still unfulfilled, he felt, like Hamlet in the grave-yard, that death makes all great endeavour meaningless; and at the same moment, again like Hamlet, he bitterly reproached him-self:

> Burns! with honour due
>  I oft have honour'd thee. Great shadow, hide
>  Thy face; I sin against thy native skies.

Like Hamlet, he had sinned with the pride of the imagination: instead of "annulling" himself in the occasion, he had let it be sicklied over by his fancy that, for the moment, he stood not by Burns's grave but by his own.

After their tramp westward through Galloway and their hasty trip to Ireland and back, Keats and Brown turned northward again toward Ayr and the birthplace of Burns. These days were full of enough adventure to lighten the burden of the mystery for Keats for a while. He tasted his first whisky—"very smart stuff it is"— and learned how to make a toddy, "very pretty drink, & much praised by Burns." On the boat to Donaghadee he had listened to two old men singing ballads—one on the Battle of the Boyne, an-other on "Robin Huid" with the refrain "Before the King you shall go, go, go." He even made a joke out of his troubling ex-perience at Dumfries in the "Song About Myself" which he wrote two days later to amuse his sister:

> So he stood in
>  His shoes and he wonder'd,
>  He wonder'd,
> He stood in his
>  Shoes and he wonder'd.

Nevertheless the thought of Burns's misery kept haunting him. "Poor unfortunate fellow," he remarked to Tom in the midst of his speculations on the Scottish character, "his disposition was southern—how sad it is when a luxurious imagination is obliged to deaden its delicacy in vulgarity, and riot in things attainable that it may not have leisure to go mad after things which are not." But as they approached Burns's native town he made an effort to put all such thoughts out of his mind.

The first view of Ayr late in the afternoon overwhelmed him with its beauty—the valley rich in every imaginable shade of green, and the silver Doon flowing to the sea, spanned by its famous bridges. He and Brown lingered on the bridge which Tam o' Shanter crossed, then walked on to Burns's cottage in the nearby village of Alloway, which they found turned into a whisky shop. Here something went extraordinarily wrong. An old man who had known Burns was there ready to spin anecdotes and drink a glass with any visitor who happened by, and he filled Keats with unaccountable rage. "He is a mahogany faced old Jackass who knew Burns— He ought to be kicked for having spoken to him," he burst out to Reynolds. "O the flummery of a birth place! Cant! Cant! Cant! It is enough to give a spirit the guts-ache." Part of the reason for his rage was that "the flat dog made me write a flat sonnet." The poem he had intended to write here took still more of an effort than the one at Burns's tomb, and he told Reynolds and Bailey and Tom that it was too wretched to copy for them. Apparently he was so overcome by its badness that he destroyed it several days later—though fortunately not before Brown had made a transcript.

Yet the sonnet is not as bad as all that; and if it were, its badness would not account for the anger and then despair Keats felt at the time. Furthermore, he wrote many poorer poems, both before and after this one, which he let stand; this is the only poem, to our knowledge, that he took the trouble to destroy after burning some of his earliest verses two years before. Why did he single this sonnet out? Perhaps because his own unhappiness and "sick pride" obtruded still more openly here than in his sonnet at Burns's grave:

> This mortal body of a thousand days
>   Now fills, O Burns, a space in thine own room,
> Where thou didst dream alone on budded bays,
>   Happy and thoughtless of thy day of doom!

It struck Keats with a terrible irony that he should be sitting there in Burns's own house, drinking the whisky Burns loved, looking out on the hills of his beloved Ayrshire—that on this summer evening he should be alive and Burns dead.

> Yet can I stamp my foot upon thy floor,
>     Yet can I ope thy window-sash to find
> The meadow thou hast tramped o'er and o'er,—
>     Yet can I think of thee till thought is blind,—
> Yet can I gulp a bumper to thy name,—
> O smile among the shades, for this is fame!

The irony of the poem is summed up in the last line; but the terror is in the first. "This mortal body of a thousand days": again Keats found himself staring at the prospect of his own death, less than three years ahead. The thought he meant never to express had slipped out, and as soon as he regained his balance he tried to expunge it.

This is the only way of accounting for his extraordinary act of destroying his own poem; it is also the only way of bridging a strange hiatus in his letter to Reynolds describing the visit. "I cannot write about scenery and visitings," he went on. "His Misery is a dead weight upon the nimbleness of one's quill—I tried to forget it—to drink Toddy without any Care—to write a merry Sonnet—it wont do—he talked with Bitches—he drank with Blackguards, he was miserable—We can see horribly clear in the works of such a man his whole life, as if we were God's spies.— I should not speak so to you—yet why not—you are not in the same case—you are in the right path, and you shall not be deceived," he continued with a curious emphasis. "I have spoken to you against Marriage, but it was general—the Prospect in those matters has been to me so blank, that I have not been unwilling to die." The thought had been torn from him—that he would go Tom's way and not George's. But immediately he recovered himself: "I would not now, for I have inducements to Life— I must see my little Nephews in America, and I must see you marry your lovely Wife. Believe me," he added, "I have more than once yearne'd for the time of your happiness to come, as much as I could for myself after the lips of Juliet. One of the first pleasures I look to is your happy Marriage—the more, since I have felt the pleasure of loving a sister in Law." He had righted himself by now, and closed his letter with a message to the *vingt-et-un* players. "Tell my friends I do all I can for them, that is drink their healths in Toddy."

—»»·««—

The visit to Burns's cottage marks the turning point in Keats's journey. Here for the first time he allowed himself to express the fear that he had been trying to forget ever since leaving England; at the same time he found himself admitting to a desire which he had tried for several years to deny—for the love which is the best human defence against death. The idea that he should ever wish to marry was a revelation, unexpected and deeply troubling. Perhaps it had come over him only three days earlier, when a wedding party rode past them in Galloway and he found the tears springing to his eyes. Now as he wrote Reynolds he recalled with a pang all the times he had "rodomontaded" against marriage. Some of his reasons for trying to avoid it were fairly clear to him. His devotion to his brothers, deeper for the losses they had suffered together; his warm friendships with a circle of men who shared his interests and ambitions; the opportunities for easy sexual adventures all around him, combined with the general deprecating attitude toward women he caught from his society— that they were for the most part "children to whom I would rather give a Sugar Plum than my time"—all these had left little room of any importance in his life so far for a woman to fill. But there were stronger reasons than the mere absence of need. There were the demands of his work for solitude and for freedom to extend his experience, a freedom which marriage would circumscribe. There was the passionate sensuousness of his nature, which demanded a richer satisfaction than he found, for example, in the Reynoldses' drawing room; there was his own deep-rooted conviction of his physical insignificance. And deeper still, probably far below the level of his awareness, was the fear that to love a woman wholeheartedly meant only to risk betrayal and loss—the legacy of his attachment to his mother.

But in the last half-year he was being forced to wonder whether the challenge of marriage could be argued away. Reynolds' engagement to Eliza Drewe, for whose sake he was almost willing to give up his literary career; George's marriage to a lighthearted girl who was also a disinterested character; even Bailey's heavy-footed pursuit of Mariane Reynolds "with the Bible and Jeremy Taylor under his arm" [14]—all these suggested to Keats that marriage could be the most significant relationship in a man's life. His circle of bachelor friends was beginning to break up; and with George in America and Tom so ill, he was beginning to glimpse the loneliness in prospect for him. Yet at the same time he found himself more and more uncomfortable in the presence of women, especially the young women to whom he was still closest, the Reynolds sisters. Bailey, on learning at Little Britain that Keats had given up his regular calls there before setting out for Scotland, took it on himself to regret this in a letter of July. Keats replied with some asperity. After all, he was a man with "Books to read and subjects to think upon," and moreover he had been able to go out very little in June. But he realized that the truth lay deeper than this, and he went on to give Bailey an extraordinary piece of self-analysis, almost a century before the very idea of such analysis had been conceived:

"I am certain I have not a right feeling towards Women—at this moment I am striving to be just to them but I cannot—Is it because they fall so far beneath my Boyish imagination? I have no right to expect more than their reality." These "pure Goddesses" of his schoolboy dreams were human beings after all; he was also discovering some very human failings in his own reactions to them—that he was "thinking insults in a Lady's Company" which he realized were unjustified. "One who is tender of being insulted does not like to think an insult against another— When among Men I have no evil thoughts, no malice, no spleen —I feel free to speak or to be silent—I can listen and from every one I can learn—my hands are in my pockets I am free from all suspicion and comfortable. When I am among Women I have evil thoughts, malice spleen—I cannot speak or be silent—I am full of Suspicions and therefore listen to nothing—I am in a hurry to be gone—You must be charitable and put all this perversity to my being disappointed since Boyhood," he added. "Mister John Keats five feet high"—how could he expect a woman to take him seriously? Yet in recognizing the cause of his anxiety he still refused to leave it at that. "I must absolutely get over this —but how? The only way is to find the root of evil, and so cure it 'with backward mutters of dissevering Power' That is a difficult thing; for an obstinate Prejudice can seldom be produced but from a gordian complication of feelings, which must take time to unravell and care to keep unravelled."

This admission of a hostility which till now he had successfully concealed suggests that Keats was beginning to look to women for something he had not sought before—the fulfilment not of a single need but of his whole self. Apparently he also felt that, for some reason, he was being unfairly sceptical about their capacity to meet such a demand. The reason was close at hand, whether he realized it or not. Charles Brown, whose company he was sharing hour by hour during these months, must have acted as a solvent of whatever adolescent idealism Keats still preserved. Brown was an enigmatic character, a mixture of Scottish strictness in money matters and Rabelaisian gusto in others; a lover of broad jokes and good poetry; a misogynist who liked to tease pretty young women; a freethinker full of passionate prejudices, who requested before his death to be given a pauper's burial or —to save all funeral expenses—to be consigned to a medical school for dissection.[15] He had lived a far more adventurous life than any of Keats's other friends. After starting work at fourteen in a London merchant's office, he was sent to St. Petersburg at eighteen to manage a branch of the business there. Five years later the firm failed and Brown returned to London, penniless. For another five years he scraped along as a journalist, at one time so poor that he ate at fourpenny ordinaries where the knives and forks were chained to the table. An unexpected inheritance from his brother and the success of his comic opera *Narensky* at Drury Lane put him back on his feet again; a year later he and Dilke, a schoolfellow, built Wentworth Place together. Here Brown settled into a comfortable bachelor existence, living tidily on his small income and continuing to write mainly for his own amusement, his masculine needs satisfied by occasional visits to the shabby side streets off Covent Garden.

Though at first sight they seemed an ill-assorted pair, Brown was eventually to become Keats's closest friend. Better than anyone else he could offer Keats both the brotherly companionship which George had always given him and the fatherly support of an older man which he had sought from Hunt and Haydon. But what Keats seems to have valued in him was that Brown liked him as a man rather than as a poet. Brown's humour was a refuge from his own black moods; his common sense also seemed the antithesis both of Hunt's sentimental falsification of life and Haydon's egocentrical distortions of it. That Brown was, in his own way, as much of an egotist as Hunt or Haydon, incapable of understanding an outlook different from his own, indifferent to the pain his bluntness might cause,[16] Keats had as yet had no time to discover. How far at this point he could share the older man's attitude toward women is another question. Brown's cynicism dated from a romantic setback he had suffered in St. Petersburg in his early twenties. There he had become engaged to an English lady who then turned him down for a compatriot whose business prospects seemed brighter. This gentleman went bankrupt and died shortly afterward, and years later it was hinted to Brown at Hampstead that the widow would be glad to resume their acquaintance.[17] Brown declined the offer, evidently with satisfaction; it certainly confirmed him in his jaundiced view of the sex. Yet the affair kept rankling long enough for him to start an autobiographical novel, thirty years after the event, in which this early defeat is translated into an imaginary victory. The lady is punished for her faithlessness, while Brown himself, in the character of his hero, is both rewarded and vindicated when the lady returns to him, abandoned and ill, and he deserts his wife to live with her, "enduring every slander that the world can heap upon [him]." [18] No better proof could be found of the theory that the cynic is only an inverted sentimentalist.

It is difficult to imagine Keats ever sharing Brown's belief that women are mere sexual objects and no more, though it is clear from his letters on the trip that he enjoyed Brown's bawdy humour. Whether he was aware of a less obvious aspect of his friend's nature is not clear. All the while this sturdy masculine figure was tramping through the Highlands with Keats he was evidently cherishing the image of a fresh-faced boy at Eton—Henry Snook, the thirteen-year-old nephew of his friend Dilke. A few sentences from one of Brown's long letters to Henry reveal a "complication of feelings" equal to if different from Keats's own: "I have thought of you, and your brother, and my two nephews, every day on my walk," Brown wrote. "To have left you all, after so long having been your companion, sometimes comes across my mind in a painful manner, and the farther I have travelled away the stronger has been the feeling. There may be many who cannot understand why I should think of you so much, but my dear boys know how much I have loved them. But let the proof of this remain till some future day, for in the meanwhile I can have nothing to offer but assurances of affection. God keep you well, my dear Boy," he ended, "and believe me your more than brother-friend." [19] Whatever the actual nature of Brown's attachment to the young Snooks, it seems clear that the older man's deep-grained dislike of women helped to bring to the surface all Keats's ambivalent feelings toward them this summer. Yet there was nothing to do about the problem for the time being but to postpone it. So Keats wrote to Tom at the end of July to describe the snug life they would lead together at Well Walk next winter, studying hard, visiting Fanny, going to the theatre every now and then, and added, rather cryptically, "With respect to Women I think I shall be able to conquer my passions hereafter better than I have yet done."

The thought of Tom alone in Hampstead kept troubling Keats, the more so because, after receiving one letter from him at Portpatrick, he could not expect another till he reached Inverness a month later. Uncertainty about his brother's health and a nagging sense of guilt about going off on his adventure added to his uneasiness, and the thought of Hampstead kept coming to his mind more often as the excitement of the trip began to wear off. "I assure you I often long for a seat and a Cup o' tea at well Walk— especially now that mountains, castles and Lakes are becoming common to me," he confessed to Tom. "Yet I would rather summer it out for on the whole I am happier than when I have time to be glum." This mood reflects more fatigue than boredom, however. Day after day, with Brown checking off the distances on the map, they trudged twenty miles, sometimes more, between sunrise and late afternoon; only a hard rain was allowed to slow them down.

From Ayr they walked north to Glasgow, then headed northwest into the Highlands. Loch Lomond on a bright summer evening was "grand in excess," yet they were disappointed to find it, like Windermere, overspread with "the miasma of London." "Steam Boats and Barouches take a little from the Pleasure of such romantic chaps as Brown and I," Keats remarked wryly to Tom. They had looked forward to climbing Ben Lomond but found the guides too expensive. The wild country farther west, around Loch Fyne and Loch Awe, was more to their liking. Here they could walk for miles through the heather and hear no sound but mountain streams, or see no living thing but a few sheep on the hills or an eagle soaring overhead. The Highlanders spoke Gaelic, the first foreign language Keats had heard; they were intelligent and friendly, with nothing of the Lowlanders' suspicion of the English, but their living conditions were still more primitive. At Newton Stuart early in July, Keats found a sofa and some hair-bottomed chairs worth mentioning in his journal; evidently they were the last he encountered for over a month. The Highland fare—eggs and oatcake, meal after meal, washed down with water and a gill of whisky—became sickening. "Sometimes when I am rather tired," Keats wrote Mrs. Wylie, "I lean rather languishingly on a Rock, & long for some famous Beauty to get down from her Palfrey in passing; approach me with—her saddle bags—& give me—a dozen or two capital roast beef sandwiches."

One of the goals of their journey was a visit to Staffa in the Inner Hebrides, a tiny island built on pillars of basalt rising sheer out of the sea. At Oban, finding that the boat fare to Staffa was an exorbitant seven guineas, they almost decided to give the visit up when an obliging fellow offered to take them at a bargain. This involved walking thirty-seven miles across the Isle of Mull instead of sailing around it. They agreed; then, as they started on their tramp through the island, the weather turned bad, and the track through the mountains proved as good as none at all. For two weary days they climbed up hill and down, in wind and rain, jumping from boulder to boulder, fording streams with their breeches tucked up and their shoes in hand, wading ankle-deep through bogs a mile long. They spent the night in a shepherd's hut with no floor or chimney, the air thick with peat smoke; and here, sleeping on the ground in damp clothes, Keats caught a violent cold. At the far end of Mull, however, an adventure waited them: a visit to Iona. Keats had heard nothing of this fabled island, where, thirteen centuries before, Saint Columba had founded the first Christian settlement in Great Britain and where through the Dark Ages all the Kings of Scotland were buried. A stunted little old schoolmaster showed them over the ruins of the cathedral and cloisters. Keats was most stirred by the narrow rows of royal graves in the churchyard, and the moss-covered tombs of Highland chieftains with their effigies in armour lying at full length on top.

From Iona they took a boat to Staffa. As they approached it on a gently swelling sea, the honeycomb of purple-black columns on which the island is based seemed to rise out of pure crystal. The rare good weather allowed them to land and explore Fingal's Cave at the head of the island—a stupendous work of natural architecture which immediately struck Keats as the setting for a scene from *Hyperion*. "Suppose now," he wrote to Tom, "the Giants who rebelled against Jove had taken a whole Mass of black Columns and bound them together like bunches of matches—and then with immense Axes had made a cavern in the body of these columns—of course the roof and floor must be composed of the broken ends of the Columns—such is fingal's Cave except that the Sea has done the work of excavations and is continually dashing there—the roof is arched somewhat gothic wise and the view into the sea through the large Arch at the entrance for solemnity and grandeur far surpasses the finest Cathedrall."

After Staffa and Iona, Scotland could hold few wonders more. They rested a few days in Oban, then started north again with the rain dogging them; and when they reached Fort William on the first of August, Keats's cold had turned into a flaming sore throat. But he was determined to climb Ben Nevis with Brown—the more so for having missed both Helvellyn and Ben Lomond. Ben Nevis, the highest mountain in Great Britain, rose nearly four and a half thousand feet from sea level at Loch Linnhe, where they started —as much as climbing "10 Saint Pauls without the convenience of Stair cases," Keats figured. They set out at five on a grey morning with a guide in tartan, a dog, and a good supply of whisky. Rise after rise they climbed through the mist, with the head of the mountain still hidden behind the next ascent; heath soon gave way to loose stones and patches of snow; then chasms a thousand feet deep, filled with clouds, opened suddenly before them. On one of their brief stops they amused themselves by tumbling rocks into the chasms and setting the echoes at work; then, after a glass of whisky apiece, they started on again. Over the loose stones the going was very rough—"sometimes on two sometimes on three, sometimes four legs, ringing changes on foot, hand, Stick, jump boggle, stumble, foot, hand, foot, (very gingerly) stick again, and then again a game at all fours." Near the top the fog lifted and they were surrounded by swirling clouds, which parted every now and then to give them a burst of sunshine or a glimpse of the crags below. On they crawled, through sun and mist and cold wind;

then at last they reached the summit. Keats found himself standing on a stony plain, which appeared to be low ground but
dropped off into nothing at the edge; at a great distance, the tops
of other mountains rose below. Some artillerymen had piled the
stones near the summit into a neat pyramid; Keats climbed this
mound and thus, to his delight, "got a little higher than old Ben
himself." Then he sat down to write a sonnet.

It was the peak of the summer's adventure, and suddenly there
was nothing to say. Looking out into the clouded emptiness ahead,
he forced this nothingness into a poem—one of the lamest of the
five lame sonnets he wrote on the trip, yet significant as summing
up the summer's meaning:

> Read me a lesson, Muse, and speak it loud
>     Upon the top of Nevis, blind in mist!
> I look into the chasms, and a shroud
>     Vaporous doth hide them,—just so much I wist
> Mankind do know of hell; I look o'erhead
>     And there is sullen mist,—even so much
> Mankind can tell of heaven; mist is spread
>     Before the earth, beneath me,—even such,
> Even so vague is man's sight of himself!
>     Here are the craggy stones beneath my feet,—
> Thus much I know that, a poor witless elf,
>     I tread on them,—that all my eye doth meet
> Is mist and crag, not only on this height,
> But in the world of thought and mental might!

He had come all this way to discover that adventure is not life;
that the finest scenes and the grandest mountains do not of themselves make poetry; and that at the farthest reach of his journey
the familiar spectre of his own impotent bewilderment stood facing him. At the top of Ben Nevis lay the "Purgatory blind," the
vision of the meaninglessness of existence which he had first confronted on the shore at Teignmouth and that was waiting for him
at Hampstead. From now on the road lay downward and backward.

" 'T was the most vile descent—shook me all to pieces." But
once again they shouldered their packs and struck out, through
Glen More and the Great Glen, seventy miles along Loch Lochy
and Loch Ness. When they reached Inverness four days later,
Keats had a burning fever. The doctor whom Brown summoned
looked grave; Keats's throat was ulcerated, and he was too thin

and worn to keep on with the journey. Reluctantly he agreed to return home. It was a blow, but only to Keats's pride; Brown decided at once to complete the trip alone. The two men stumped on for two more days to Cromarty, where they said good-bye and Keats boarded the smack to London.

A nine days' trip—his first sea-voyage—was marred by rough weather and poor food and a toothache at the end; but he reached Hampstead in good humour, glad to be home at last. Stopping in at Wentworth Place before climbing the hill to Well Walk, he startled Mrs. Dilke half out of her wits. She noted in her diary on August 19: "John Keats arrived here last night, as brown and as shabby as you can imagine; scarcely any shoes left, his jacket all torn at the back, a fur cap, a great plaid, and his knapsack." He must have heaved this off his shoulders with relief before dropping into a comfortable stuffed chair—the first since Newton Stuart—and exclaiming with a grin, "Bless thee, Bottom! bless thee! thou art translated!" [20] Then he learned the news they had to tell him.

*Chapter Eight*

---

# The Shores of Darkness

T o m was not better but much worse. Early in August he had had a relapse so serious that Sawrey asked Dilke to send for Keats at once. Dilke's letter reached Inverness after Keats had already sailed, and its news had to be broken that night at Wentworth Place. With a sinking heart Keats climbed the hill to Well Walk, where Tom lay waiting—pale, feeble, pitiably thin, and seized now by the uncontrollable nervousness of the last stages of consumption. All the brave pretences of the months before were shattered. Neither one could now deny the truth to the other: Tom was dying. Keats had known this would come in time; he can hardly have guessed how soon. His first act the next morning was to write to Fanny. His toothache still throbbed; his throat still burned with fever. A letter she had written him at Inverness called for answers on half a dozen irrelevant topics—the death of her canary, the pebbles she had asked him to bring from Scotland, the flageolet she wanted him to buy for her. But she must be told the news, and, still more, Abbey must be talked into allowing her to come to see Tom. His letter was as tender as ever but distracted, and he cut it short with a promise to visit her soon.

But this meeting did not take place for two weeks. His own sore throat kept hanging on, and, a few days after his homecoming, Tom took another turn for the worse. Keats was now left almost entirely alone to take care of his brother. Tom became so agitated by visitors that when the Reynolds sisters offered their help Keats had to refuse it as politely as he could. His close friends seemed to have vanished. Brown was still in Scotland; Dilke, who fell ill himself in August, went off to Brighton to convalesce; Haydon and Rice and Reynolds and Taylor were all off in the country. Severn came down with an attack of typhus later in September; only George's faithful friend Haslam stood by week after week. Keats's regular company now consisted almost entirely of his land-lady, Mrs. Bentley, Mrs. Dilke, and old Mr. Lewis, a Hampstead neighbour who had called on Tom daily during the summer with presents of fruit. To add to his sense of isolation, day after day went by with no letter from George. Uncertain of where to ad-dress him, Keats held off writing for weeks, then could not bring himself to start a letter because of the news of Tom he must send. Fanny was grudgingly allowed to visit Well Walk once or twice in September; but Tom found it so hard to let her go at the end of the day that Keats wondered whether she should come again. Ab-bey soon took this matter out of his hands, however. On one of these visits, Keats took Fanny to see Mrs. Dilke without thinking to ask Mrs. Abbey's permission in advance.[1] When she learned of this infraction of the rules, Fanny was forbidden to come again for several months.

So Keats returned to his long watch by Tom's bedside, nursing him through chills and coughing fits, trying to calm him in spells of despair, reading to him in his comfortable hours, and keeping up as cheerful a front as he could. One Sunday evening, while rereading *King Lear* as his brother lay asleep, his eye was caught by the words "poor Tom"; suddenly overcome, he underlined them and added the date in the margin of his Folio. Once or twice he tried to surmount his anxieties by writing, but found himself plagued by an uneasy feeling of guilt about his brother. "If I think of fame of poetry it seems a crime," he confessed in a letter to Dilke. "Yet I must do so or suffer." Caught between his desire to ease Tom's suffering and his instinct somehow to escape from it, he felt a "hateful siege of contraries" burning in him like a fever. Then something happened that made all writing impossible for several weeks. Early in September the storm of criticism that had been threatening ever since June broke at last. *Blackwood's* came out with the fourth of its "Cockney School" articles, this one de-voted to *Endymion*.

It was a blow aimed squarely below the belt. The reviewer be-gan by gibing at the poetry-writing mania which had turned foot-men and retired governesses to scribbling verses in imitation of

Robert Burns and Joanna Baillie. The latest victim of this malady, he continued, was a young man who had been destined by his friends for a useful career as apothecary but who had fallen under the unfortunate influence of Leigh Hunt—"the most worthless and affected of all the versifiers of our time." Encouraged by Hunt, this "Johnny Keats" has deserted his gallipots and written a long poem on the subject of Endymion, which can only be described as "calm, settled, imperturbable drivelling idiocy." After sneering at Keats's education and slashing at Hunt's politics, the review quoted some of the poem's weakest passages, then wound up with this advice: "It is a better and a wiser thing to be a starved apothecary than a starved poet; so back to the shop, Mr. John, back to the 'plasters, pills, and ointment boxes,' &c. But, for Heaven's sake, young Sangrado, be a little more sparing of extenuatives and soporifics in your practice than you have been in your poetry."

All this was in "Z.'s" usual style of insult, especially bitter to a man as proud and reserved as Keats. To be dubbed "apothecary's boy" and classed with governesses and footmen had an added sting. It was, after all, not a trade he had been trained to but a profession; and in the circle of his friends, he was counted a gentleman among gentlemen. Yet at the same time Keats had "a fierce hatred of rank," as Haydon tells us, of the arrogance with which the aristocracy flaunted its privileges during the bitter years after Waterloo. It has been said that Keats was ashamed of his background— the livery stable, the Clarke school, the apprenticeship to a village apothecary. But this seems to have been not Keats's attitude so much as that of his more class-conscious friends, including even Brown and Hunt; [2] Keats's reticence about his boyhood had other, very different causes. Yet he could do nothing about the *Blackwood's* affront, not even challenge the reviewer to a duel as he had once resolved, for "Z." still refused to reveal himself, despite all the efforts to force him into the open.

In the middle of September an invitation came from Taylor's partner, Hessey, to dine at Fleet Street, along with Woodhouse, the firm's literary and legal adviser, Hazlitt, and some other friends. It was almost the first break in Keats's long exile in Hampstead, and he mustered up what good spirits he could for the occasion. He must have been especially glad to see Hazlitt, for *Blackwood's* had opened a campaign against him in the same issue as the review of *Endymion*. After sneering at him as "pimpled

Hazlitt," a slander too pointless to refute, "Z." had launched into a long outrageous assault on his education and critical opinions, which Hazlitt promptly answered by initiating a suit for libel. But at the time of Hessey's dinner Hazlitt was more aroused by his treatment in the *Quarterly,* an older and far more influential review than *Blackwood's.* The second edition of his immensely successful *Characters of Shakespeare's Plays* had not sold a single copy for the last three months. For this only one thing was responsible—William Gifford's review in June in the *Quarterly,* jeering at Hazlitt's style as borrowed from washerwomen, and attacking him for "senseless and wicked sophistry" and even "sedition." [3] A year ago it seemed that the *Characters* had earned Hazlitt his fame as a critic at last; now the *Quarterly* had blasted it.

Hazlitt's fighting spirit was up, as Keats knew; but he said nothing about the reviews that evening, and Keats followed his example. Still he could not keep from dropping a bombshell of his own. He announced that he had given up poetry. To the astonishment of most of his listeners he began arguing that there was nothing new or valuable left to be done in poetry; all its riches had long since been exploited, and he for one would write no more. Woodhouse, who was a logical man as well as a warm admirer of Keats's work, tried to dispute his point and left at the end of the evening still disturbed by the conversation. Hessey, more practical and less argumentative, also more familiar than Woodhouse with Keats's "rodomontade," did not take him so seriously. A day or two later he reported to Taylor, who was still on vacation in Bath, that their young author was "studying closely, recovering his Latin, going to learn Greek, and seems altogether more rational than usual." For all of Keats's fits and starts, Hessey was still convinced that "sometime or other he will do something valuable." [4]

As for the *Blackwood's* review, if Hessey had told Keats what Taylor already knew about it, he would only have deepened his discouragement. Keats must have wondered how the account of his early years had reached the enemy camp; for a while he and his friends suspected Ollier of being somehow responsible. Not until some time later is it likely that he connected the article with a curious letter he had received from Bailey during his trip in Scotland. Bailey was now a country curate near Carlisle, where, he told Taylor, he was "endeavoring to *humanize* a set of boors." [5] Through a Cambridge friend, George Robert Gleig, he had been meeting the *Blackwood's* set in Edinburgh that summer and thus had an opportunity to forward to Keats an invitation from Mr. Blackwood himself. The editor, who had been impressed by his friend Christie's favourable report on Keats the winter before, had asked him to call when he reached Edinburgh, and Bailey advised Keats that he would do well to conciliate the Tories by accepting. According to Brown, Keats indignantly refused; whereupon Bailey at the end of August wrote not Keats but Taylor a carefully censored account of what followed.

On a visit to Gleig at Stirling, Bailey had met John Gibson Lockhart, a dark, good-looking young Oxford graduate and contributor to *Blackwood's*. After listening to him abuse Keats at dinner, along with Hunt and his set, Bailey put in a word or two on his friend's behalf. Lockhart then talked the slow-witted Bailey into telling him what he knew of Keats's early life—the "respectable family," "the small but independent patrimony," the apprenticeship to Hammond, and all.[6] Once the story was out, Bailey had a sudden misgiving, but as he looked up and down the table he must have realized he was in an awkward spot. His friend Gleig was now working for Blackwood himself; Gleig had a sister who had already caught Bailey's eye; and at the head of the table sat Gleig's father, the Bishop of Brechin, Primus of the Scots Episcopal Church. It was not the moment for an ambitious curate to rise to the defence of a young poet of obscure origins and disreputable connections who had just published a long poem in praise of physical love. Bailey did what Bailey could. He begged Lockhart not to use his information against Keats, and Lockhart sardonically agreed that it would not be used "by *him*." Bailey, taking alarm, then wrote Taylor warning him that *Endymion* might be "dreadfully cut up in *Blackwood's*," recounting Lockhart's abuse of Keats but saying nothing of his own share in the discussion.

Taylor, who had been taking steps of his own to win Keats a fair hearing in the Tory reviews, must have been thunderstruck. One wonders also how much that sharp-eyed scholar read of Bailey's real part in the conversation between the lines of his letter. For Bailey, who three months earlier had praised the "beauty and power" of *Endymion* in an Oxford review, now found its "indelicacy" indefensible—especially in its implication that *"Sensual Love* is the principle of *things."* Bailey then spoke of Tom's relapse. "I do not know well what to think, whether good or bad, of the death of this young man, if it happen. It looks harsh to say it is happy; and yet from his character he must have lived a life of discomfort to himself and those with whom he was connected, if the character I have heard of him be just. Happen as it will, I am *religiously* persuaded, all *is* for the best." So, after a change of heart, does one find oneself on the right side once again. Bailey's next letter to Taylor in October, inquiring about some theological works recommended by Bishop Gleig, was noticeably cooler; and his correspondence with Keats came to a sudden halt at this time. But from several mentions of the conversation in his letters to Taylor, it is clear that it still lay on his conscience—so much so that three years later he wrote Taylor a guarded memorandum defending his part in it, supplemented by a fuller account some thirty years afterward, trying to prove that the use of his information in the review was merely a coincidence.[7]

Taylor can hardly have repeated Bailey's words on Tom to Keats, and it is uncertain how much he told Keats of his friend's unlucky conversation with Lockhart. Keats himself never mentioned Bailey in connection with the *Blackwood's* article; yet it is significant that by the end of 1818 "parson" had become a term of contempt with him. By this time Hazlitt's suit against *Blackwood's* had had the indirect effect of forcing his assailant to identify himself, and so at last the world learned that the infamous "Z." was none other than Bailey's dinner companion, Lockhart himself. In September, however, Keats could have guessed none of this. A week or two after "Z.'s" attack appeared, he spoke of Bailey in a letter to Dilke merely to say that he had heard Bailey was in better spirits than usual, and to note also that his name was not often mentioned at the Reynoldses' now.

His own calls at Little Britain were of course less frequent than ever, with Reynolds in Devon and Tom still too weak to be left for long; and Keats was probably glad enough to be relieved of this obligation. Wentworth Place was much nearer, and Mrs. Dilke was not only a helpful neighbour but a good-humoured companion as well. Keats was a frequent caller at the Dilkes' during the first month or two after his return from Scotland, and it was most probably at this time that he met the family who had taken Brown's half of the house for the summer—a widow with a young son and two daughters. Mrs. Brawne, he wrote to

George in December, "is a very nice woman—and her daughter
senior is I think beautiful and elegant, graceful, silly, fashionable
and strange we have a little tiff now and then." Thus casually,
and three months or more after the event,[8] Keats recorded a meeting which at the time threatened to throw him completely off
balance. Fanny Brawne, just eighteen, graceful, silly, and strange,
had walked into the Dilkes' drawing room and with a word, a
gesture, a glance of her blue eyes, assailed his entire being as no
woman had ever done before. As he later wrote her, "If you should
ever feel for Man at the first sight what I did for you, I am lost."
Clearly, then, his laconic introduction of the Brawnes to George
in December was an elaborate camouflage of his real feelings. He
confessed a little more of them in a letter to Reynolds in September, not long after the encounter: "I never was in love—Yet the
voice and the shape of a woman has haunted me these two days—
at such a time when the relief, the feverous relief of Poetry seems
a much less crime—This morning Poetry has conquered—I feel
escaped from a new strange and threatening sorrow—And I am
thankful for it—There is an awful warmth about my heart like
a load of Immortality." [9]

It was a narrow escape, so he must have thought. Several days
after meeting Fanny, Keats had written her an impetuous letter
declaring himself her "vassal"; but a few days later he burned the
letter instead of sending it because, at their next encounter, he
felt she had taken a dislike to him. This was probably the time
that he took Severn with him to the Dilkes'—Severn, whom
Fanny Brawne remembered as never serious for ten minutes together.[10] Perhaps his friend's good looks and high spirits made a
visible impression on Fanny; perhaps Fanny herself, who had a
reputation as a flirt, set out to impress Severn. Whatever happened, Keats, who had been roused to new anxiety by their first
encounter, felt rebuffed and withdrew. Fanny's beauty was a
threat, his response to it a "crime"; in relief he turned back to the
activity in which he could assert the identity she threatened.
"Poetry has conquered," he told Reynolds. That morning he
copied out the first poem he had written since the day he stood on
Ben Nevis—a free translation of a sonnet by Ronsard—and enclosed it in his letter with an apology for leaving off the last two
lines, which he had forgotten:

Nature withheld Cassandra in the skies,
  For more adornment, a full thousand years;
She took their cream of Beauty's fairest dyes,
  And shap'd and tinted her above all Peers:
Meanwhile Love kept her dearly with his wings,
  And underneath their shadow fill'd her eyes
With such a richness that the cloudy Kings
  Of high Olympus utter'd slavish sighs.
When from the Heavens I saw her first descend,
  My heart took fire, and only burning pains,
They were my pleasures—they my Life's sad end;
  Love pour'd her beauty into my warm veins. . . .

"Poor Tom—that woman—and Poetry were ringing changes in my senses—now I am in comparison happy." Torn between anguish over Tom's growing weakness and this answering upsurge of sexual vitality, he had to escape. "I have relapsed into those abstractions which are my only life," he told Reynolds. This was important news. At last he had started to write *Hyperion*.

—»»·«««—

"Abstract" is the word Keats always used to describe *Hyperion* —a word full of meaning for this poem. Abstract, first, in the sense that the action takes place on a level far above the actualities of human life. Byron, Keats once said, "describes what he sees— I describe what I imagine—Mine is the hardest task." *Hyperion* is abstract also in seeming to follow no one source, but drawing on a few hints scattered through classical poetry of the primeval struggle between the Olympian gods and their forebears, the Titans.[11] It is abstract too in its apparent remoteness from the experiences that were pressing on him at the moment. But while most abstractions are fairly described as lifeless, this epic of the Titans, written at the bedside of his dying brother, became to Keats his "only life," a world of its own intense reality in which he could breathe freely again.

Deep in the shady sadness of a vale
Far sunken from the healthy breath of morn,
Far from the fiery noon, and eve's one star,
Sat gray-hair'd Saturn, quiet as a stone,
Still as the silence round about his lair;
Forest on forest hung above his head

Like cloud on cloud. No stir of air was there,
Not so much life as on a summer's day
Robs not one light seed from the feather'd grass,
But where the dead leaf fell, there did it rest.
A stream went voiceless by, still deadened more
By reason of his fallen divinity
Spreading a shade: the Naiad 'mid her reeds
Press'd her cold finger closer to her lips.

  Along the margin-sand large foot-marks went,
No further than to where his feet had stray'd,
And slept there since. Upon the sodden ground
His old right hand lay nerveless, listless, dead,
Unsceptred; and his realmless eyes were closed;
While his bow'd head seem'd list'ning to the Earth,
His ancient mother, for some comfort yet.

From these first lines we are confronted with a mystery, a muta-
tion, what Auden once called "the strange event of qualitative
change." The chord that Keats struck for a moment in his "Ode
to Maia" is sounded again and again as the music goes gravely forward, sustained in every line. The emotion is severely controlled;
the poem seems to have been chiselled with great deliberation out
of pure imaginary experience. It is written not in Keats's earlier
fluent style but in what he later described as "an artful or rather
artist's humour," in an idiom carefully modelled on *Paradise Lost*.
But how can one account for a miracle? Keats had been reading
Milton closely for months, and much of the measured nobility
of his verse is echoed from his master. He had studied the Elgin
Marbles hour after hour till the silent eloquence of the Parthenon
friezes spoke through every gesture of his fallen gods. He had
tramped through the Lakes and the Highlands, and the rugged
grandeur of their mountains and cataracts shines out in the imagery of the poem. But perhaps the closest one can come to an
answer is to say that Keats had become a different person from the
man who had written *Endymion* a year ago; in fact the theme of
*Hyperion* is the struggle of spiritual growth itself.

  This was the meaning that had been gathering round the original core of his story since the spring—"the grand march of intellect" which he had described to Reynolds, now projected into the
whole creation. In the second book of *Hyperion* the Titans debate
the reason for their fall, much as do Milton's rebel angels; and
Oceanus, the wisest, gives the answer which Keats seems to have

intended at the start. Growth is the law of life; and in the sum of time its direction is upward—from chaos to order, from darkness to light. The Titans, though fairer than their progenitors Earth and Heaven, who themselves sprang from Chaos and Darkness, are now challenged by a new generation of gods "more strong in beauty." In the contest the older gods have proved as frail as mortals, subject to all the human emotions of "fear, hope, and wrath." But for the higher forms of life to appear, the lower must be left behind, and the height of wisdom is to acquiesce in this progress, no matter what its cost to the individual:

> to bear all naked truths,
> And to envisage circumstance, all calm,
> That is the top of sovereignty.

But this conception had grown immensely complicated in the months since Keats began pondering his epic. Not the glory but the cost of the struggle preoccupied him now. Something had driven him off his course—Tom, with his exquisite love of life, dying before his eyes. The horror of undeserved suffering, of useless and degrading pain—the knowledge that made Keats fling at Bailey the reminder that women have cancers—broke through his plan and aligned him with the defeated. All the calm beauty of the new Olympian gods—Neptune scudding the waves in his chariot, young Apollo on Delos discovering his gift of song—could not justify the agonies of the supplanted Titans, too vivid to Keats in what Tom was enduring,

> pent in regions of laborious breath, . . .
> Heaving in pain, and horribly convuls'd
> With sanguine feverous boiling gurge of pulse.

Indeed, the keenest emotion recorded in the first two books is that flash of guilt the healthy person feels when he realizes that the ill person looking at him sees his own illness reflected in the other's eyes. As Hyperion, not yet overthrown, approaches the fallen Titans in all his original brightness, a light "made terrible" by the darkness in which they lie, he sees

> The misery his brilliance had betray'd
> To the most hateful seeing of itself.

So for Keats the hourly contact with his dying brother forced on him a new and painful self-awareness and with it a still more painful sense of self-division. Hyperion in his golden palace, gloomily previsioning his own downfall, recalls Keats the spring before, looking into the dark passages ahead of him; while Saturn in his overthrow, "smother'd up And buried from all godlike exercise," divided from "his strong identity, his real self," conveys the bewildering sense of loss of identity which assailed Keats that autumn when his own "godlike exercise" of poetry came to seem a crime.

This sense of being hemmed in and almost smothered recurs again and again in Keats's letters during these months.[12] At the time of starting *Hyperion* he confessed to Dilke that Tom's identity "pressed" on him so unremittingly that he had to go out or try writing "to ease myself of his countenance his voice and feebleness." He told George that Fanny's identity, being still unformed, did not "press" on him like his own. A letter to Woodhouse in October suggests the real pain the sensation caused him: "When I am in a room with People if I ever am free from speculating on creations of my own brain, then the identity of every one in the room begins so to press upon me that, I am in a very little time annihilated." His capacity for entering into the existence of others, once a delight to him, now became a suffocating weight on his consciousness, almost as heavy as his brother George pinning him down in their battles long ago at school. As Tom grew weaker Keats felt his own "real self" dissolving in his awareness of what his brother was enduring. This feeling is probably not a rare one, though rarely analysed—a sense of dissociation between one's familiar self and a new self, hardly yet one's own, emerging from troubled experience which the self has not yet assimilated; or between the inner self in this state of conflict and the social self habitually assumed in contact with the world. "There I am a child—there they do not know me not even my most intimate acquaintance," Keats wrote George, trying to describe his sensations in company. His frequent repetition of the word "identity" during this autumn suggests how deeply the conflict unsettled him. "Until we are sick, we understand not," he had remarked to Reynolds the spring before. Now he lived "in a continual fever" of spirit which, when it subsided some months later, was to leave him with an extraordinary insight into the struggle for identity; but meanwhile he had to endure a sense of alienation still keener than that he had felt in his year at medical school.

It would seem that in this autumn of 1818 the feeling of self-

hood which Keats had painfully achieved in the last two years—
that of the hopeful young poet of his first two volumes—was
broken down and the ground laid for the building of a new self.
Within himself, Keats had been thrown into a turmoil by Tom's
relapse. The approaching death of a member of one's family poses
a deep unconscious threat to the ego—the deeper for Keats because for years his sense of his own being had been bound up
intimately with Tom's.[13] It was a part of himself that was dying
before his eyes, at a time when he had begun to suspect that he
too had not long to live. His time for poetry was growing shorter;
yet Tom's illness made Keats feel it "a crime" even to think of the
ambition on which he had staked his whole being. Besides this
inner conflict, his sense of identity in the outer world also was
threatened. Months ago he had repudiated the youthful poet of
*Endymion;* now a caricature of that self mocked him from the
reviews and made him feel "little and rediculous in society." In
that world of drawing rooms George had always smoothed his way
and also helped keep young ladies at a safe distance; now his marriage and emigration knocked out the other chief prop to Keats's
security and raised the question of sexual commitment which he
had evaded before. More anxious than ever about his ability to
win a woman's love, he had been overwhelmed by Fanny Brawne
on their first meeting; yet on the point of declaring his love to her
he was—or so he thought—rebuffed. In her eyes he caught again
the reflection of "Mister John Keats five feet high." It was only
part of the truth about himself, he knew, but the one that mattered most in her presence.

It was a time to try all Keats's courage. Day after day he watched
at Tom's bedside, tending to his wasted body and doing what he
could to keep his spirits up; and day after day, in spite of all the
"interruptions to a train of feeling" around him—Tom's demands, the noisy Bentley children—he went on with *Hyperion.*
It was hard work and slower than anything he had ever done, demanding as much dogged endurance as tramping across Mull or
climbing Ben Nevis. The manuscript itself shows the many laborious "compositions and decompositions" it cost him.[14] For a
while he thought of giving it up and trying something easier and
more distracting, perhaps even in prose. But something in him
would not be distracted; for he was creating a new self, groping
his way out of "Purgatory blind," in the very act of writing *Hy-*

*perion*. And from week to week he grew more confident. On the day he began his epic he left the ranks of the "marvellous boys"; as he neared the end of the first book he remarked soberly in a letter to George, "I think I shall be among the English Poets after my death."

It was confidence wrested from something close to despair. For only a few days after Keats started *Hyperion* the *Quarterly* finally exploded with its review of *Endymion*. This was the verdict which would decide, as it had already done for Hazlitt, whether the "common place people" of the book-buying public would read his book or leave it to gather dust on Taylor and Hessey's shelves. The judgment was pronounced: *Endymion* had broken all the rules of poetry as the *Quarterly* thought the game should be played. "There is hardly a complete couplet enclosing a complete idea in the whole book," snorted John Croker—that "cobbling, carping, decasyllabic, finger-scanning criticaster," as Woodhouse called him. *Endymion* was damned as merely another effusion of Cockney verse—"which may be defined to consist of the most incongruous ideas in the most uncouth language"—and Keats was dismissed as "a copyist of Mr. Hunt," but "more unintelligible, almost as rugged, twice as diffuse, and ten times more tiresome and absurd than his prototype."

The *Blackwood's* attack could be shrugged off as beneath contempt, but the *Quarterly* was too powerful to be ignored. Keats's friends leaped to his defence. Hunt, who had not mentioned *Endymion* in *The Examiner*—whether out of tact or pique it is hard to say—immediately inserted a note on the front page congratulating Keats on the *Quarterly* notice as an "involuntary homage paid to his undoubted genius, in an article of grovelling abuse." Keats was touched by this gesture, coming as it did after a year of virtual estrangement. He called on Hunt shortly afterward and gave him the two best sonnets he had written since March to publish.[15] Meanwhile Reynolds in Devon wrote a counterblast to the *Quarterly* for a local paper, which Hunt later reprinted in *The Examiner* along with another defence of *Endymion* from *The Chester Guardian*. For a while it appeared that the *Quarterly* had cut its own throat, as Keats put it, by stirring up wider interest in *Endymion* than it would otherwise have received. A Devonshire admirer who signed himself "P. Fenbank, Teignmouth," sent Keats a laudatory sonnet, enclosing a twenty-five-pound note. Keats was amused by the sonnet's high-flown style—all "empyreal soarings" and "mild light and loveliness"—though rather galled by the gift; yet when he wrote a letter of thanks, hoping for a chance to return the money, no reply came.

Meanwhile two other anonymous admirers sent letters of protest to *The Morning Chronicle,* which Hessey, kindly and methodical as ever, forwarded to Well Walk. Keats's letter of thanks shows that, with his progress in *Hyperion,* he had already recovered his equanimity. "Praise or blame," he wrote, "has but a momentary effect on the man whose love of beauty in the abstract makes him a severe critic on his own Works. My own domestic criticism has given me pain without comparison beyond what Blackwood or the Quarterly could possibly inflict. and also when I feel I am right, no external praise can give me such a glow as my own solitary reperception & ratification of what is fine." So much for criticism; as for the writing of poetry itself, the *Quarterly* critic knew nothing about it. "The Genius of Poetry must work out its own salvation in a man: It cannot be matured by law & precept, but by sensation & watchfulness in itself—That which is creative must create itself."

It was a superb flash of insight into the meaning of his struggles, his discouragements, his exaltations. Six months before, Keats had seen little other reason for publishing *Endymion* than that he must put it behind him in order to move on. Now, though more aware than ever of its shortcomings, he saw more clearly what purpose the writing of it had served for him. This was well, for the reaction against the *Quarterly* article brought him an embarrassing reminder of his own reaction, several weeks earlier, to the *Blackwood's* review. Around the middle of October Woodhouse, who had been brooding over Keats's announcement in mid-September that he had given up poetry, saw the *Quarterly* review and was alarmed. He sat down in his rooms in the Temple and wrote Keats an impassioned letter, arguing that the poet has a responsibility even to the society that rejects him, and encouraging him to keep on undaunted. Keats, who by this time had nearly reached the middle of the second book of *Hyperion,*[16] must have felt a pang of remorse. Had he ever really said he would give up poetry—and meant it too? He could answer Woodhouse only by warning him not to place such faith in the poetic character—because, as he explained, essentially "it has no character," no settled view of things. "What shocks the virtuous philosopher, delights the camelion

Poet," he confessed—light and shade, fair and foul, one side of an argument as well as another. So the poet "is the most unpoetical of any thing in existence; because he has no Identity—he is continually informing and filling some other Body—The Sun, the Moon, the Sea and Men and Women who are creatures of impulse are poetical and have about them an unchangeable attribute—the poet has none. If then he has no self, and if I am a Poet," he continued, warming to his logic, "where is the Wonder that I should say I would write no more? Might I not at that very instant have been cogitating on the Characters of saturn and Ops?" But, he assured Woodhouse, he would continue writing "from the mere yearning and fondness I have for the Beautiful even if my night's labours should be burnt every morning and no eye ever shine upon them."

It was an important point he had reached. He had left the struggle to become a poet far behind, along with the lesser hopes of winning fame and fortune through his poems. Being a poet, he now realized, was no glorious thing in itself but merely a fact of his own nature. What alone mattered was the activity of writing, the kingdom of his own creation which he entered every time he sat down to work. Beside this solitary delight the world's applause or contempt meant nothing. He had not forgotten his ambition, which he mentioned to Woodhouse, "of doing the world some good"; but, perhaps from his long pondering of Milton's career, he saw that to write a poem that might in some way benefit the world would require many years of schooling his powers and gaining knowledge and experience—if he should live that long, he added thoughtfully. "In the interval," he concluded, "I will assay to reach to as high a summit in Poetry as the nerve bestowed upon me will suffer."

Fortunately, in this new abstracted state he met a "creature of impulse" whose poetical quality he felt free to relish as never before. Sometime near the middle of October, on one of his rare trips into town, he had dropped in at Little Britain—probably to see Reynolds, just back from Devon—and was introduced to a niece of Mrs. Reynolds who, as he had already heard, was visiting them during a falling-out with her grandfather and guardian.[17] Miss Jane Cox was a beauty of a kind that Keats did not often meet, an

Anglo-Indian heiress with "a rich eastern look," fine eyes and fine manners, who walked into a drawing room with the grace of a leopardess. Not quite a Cleopatra, Keats decided, but at least a Charmian. He recognized at once the self-absorbed and theatrical quality of her beauty, saw, too, that the Reynolds sisters hated her for it; yet he found pleasure in surrendering to her spell. "I always find myself more at ease with such a woman," he wrote George and Georgiana a few days later; "I am at such times too much occupied in admiring to be awkward or on a tremble. I forget myself entirely because I live in her." He also realized immediately that she was beyond his reach; she accepted his admiration gracefully because it meant nothing to her. "She is a fine thing speaking in a worldly way: for there are two distinct tempers of mind in which we judge of things—the worldly, theatrical and pantomimical; and the unearthly, spiritual and etherial—in the former Buonaparte, Lord Byron and this Charmian hold the first place in our Minds; in the latter John Howard, Bishop Hooker rocking his child's cradle and you my dear Sister are the conquering feelings. As a Man in the world I love the rich talk of a Charmian; as an eternal Being I love the thought of you. I should like her to ruin me, and I should like you to save me."

This contrast between two types of women—the good and the bad angel—raises some familiar echoes from the past; but it would also appear that Keats was gaining enough self-assurance to find the Jane Coxes of the world less a threat than a delight. His tenderness for Georgiana, however, was brimming over at the moment he wrote, for at last, in mid-October, the long-awaited letter from America had arrived. They had reached Philadelphia safely after a rough crossing. George had found a chance to play a game of cricket before they started on their westward journey; and Georgiana was already expecting a child. Their happiness was at the full, and they tried to persuade Keats he too should marry. But it was heavy news he had to send them in reply. He told them briefly of Tom's relapse and begged them to "bear up against any Calamity for my sake as I do for your's." He mentioned the adverse reviews only to dismiss them as "a mere matter of the moment," then went on to give them news of the Wylies and all their friends, talk about politics, recount his meeting with Jane Cox, and scribble some verses in prophecy that their child would be the first American poet. Though it would be several weeks before the next sailing to America, he promised to add a sheet of news—or, failing that, of his "Whims and Theories"—to his letter every day.

There was little to report for another week, however—a visit from Georgiana's brothers and small talk at Wentworth Place with Dilke and Brown, now back from Scotland at last, "of Euclid, of Metaphisics of the Bible, of Shakspeare of the horrid System and consequences of the fagging at great Schools." The next week Tom's condition improved somewhat; he seemed less nervous and slept better at night. This allowed Keats to get into town several times, where he dropped in on Taylor and Hessey and the Wylies and their cousins the Millars, walked with Hazlitt on his way to a game of racquets at Covent Garden, and called on Hunt, where unluckily he met Ollier. And on one of these days—October 24— he had an adventure. Walking down Theobald Road in an abstracted mood, he passed a lady, suddenly realized it was Isabella Jones, his acquaintance from Hastings, and turned back to greet her. She replied cordially and invited him to go with her to call on a friend of hers who had a boarding school in Islington. "As we went along, some times through shabby, sometimes through decent Streets I had my guessing at work, not knowing what it would be and prepared to meet any surprise," Keats wrote George. On leaving her friend's, he asked to accompany her home. "She consented and then again my thoughts were at work what it might lead to, tho' now they had received a sort of genteel hint from the Boarding School. Our Walk ended in 34 Gloucester Street Queen Square—not exactly so for we went up stairs into her sitting room —a very tasty sort of place with Books, Pictures a bronze statue of Buonaparte, Music, æolian Harp; a Parrot a Linnet—A Case of choice Liquers &c &c &. she behaved in the kindest manner—made me take home a Grouse for Tom's dinner—Asked for my address for the purpose of sending more game—As I had warmed with her before and kissed her—I thought it would be living backwards not to do so again—she had a better taste: she perceived how much a thing of course it was and shrunk from it—not in a prudish way but in as I say a good taste—She contrived to disappoint me in a way which made me feel more pleasure than a simple kiss could do —she said I should please her much more if I would only press her hand and go away. Whether she was in a different disposition when

I saw her before—or whether I have in fancy wrong'd her I cannot tell."

It was a tantalizing encounter: he was not sure what she wanted. "She has always been an enigma to me—she has ~~new~~ been in a Room with you and with Reynolds and wishes we should be acquainted without any of our common acquaintance knowing it." It was a curious suggestion, yet he met it at least halfway: "I expect to pass some pleasant hours with her now and then: in which I feel I shall be of service to her in matters of knowledge and taste: if I can I will—I have no libidinous thought about her—she and your George"—that is, Georgiana—"are the only women à peu près de mon age whom I would be content to know for their mind and friendship alone."

As with Charmian two weeks before, he tactfully refrained from referring to her by name; but the lady from Hastings evidently touched a deeper chord than Jane Cox had done. Charmian's beauty was "a passtime and an amuzement"; Isabella's charm added an intellectual attraction, and something more. It was not a simple matter of entering into her being and imaginatively "living in her"; clearly Mrs. Jones wished to enter his. Astute as she was, she must have sensed a change in Keats from the eager boy of two summers before; as a friend of Taylor's and a lady of liberal tastes, she would have read *Endymion* and formed a new opinion of its author. There is no doubt about her deftness in handling the occasion which presented itself so unexpectedly; however, there is much to wonder about in her situation at the time. Game, for instance, with which she seemed to be well stocked, could not be had legally in those days unless one was a landowner—or the friend of a landowner.[18] There was no visible evidence of "the jealous old Bald-pate" in her surroundings: was this in Keats's mind when he confessed that he may have wronged her in his imagination? He did not like to "think insults in a Lady's Company," yet he could not help sensing the ambiguity of the situation. Isabella Jones, a woman of some taste and wit and beauty, whose acquaintance (did Keats know it at the time?) was enjoyed by John Taylor, offered him her friendship and let a hint of other possibilities trouble the air. Nevertheless—and he must be credited with knowing his own feelings in the matter—Keats insisted that he had "no libidinous thought about her." [19] With Jane Cox also he had told George that he was not in love; she merely kept him awake one night "as a tune of Mozart's might do." Perhaps he instinctively sensed that neither woman could give him what he wanted: Jane Cox he could never possess, and Isabella Jones wished in some obscure way to possess him. But there was another reason, of which he was more fully aware. Poetry had conquered, for the third time in little more than a month: for him there could be no greater fulfilment. Since meeting Fanny Brawne he had probably written the first book of *Hyperion* and started the second, and he knew what they were worth.

And so he closed his account of this adventure by telling his brother and sister-in-law that, despite their recommendation, he hoped never to marry. "Though the most beautiful Creature were waiting for me at the end of a Journey or a Walk; though the carpet were of Silk, the Curtains of the morning Clouds; the chairs and Sofa stuffed with Cygnet's down; the food Manna, the Wine beyond Claret, the Window opening on Winander mere, I should not feel—or rather my Happiness would not be so fine, as my Solitude is sublime. Then instead of what I have described, there is a Sublimity to welcome me home—The roaring of the wind is my wife and the Stars through the window pane are my Children. The mighty abstract Idea I have of Beauty in all things stifles the more divided and minute domestic happiness—an amiable wife and sweet Children I contemplate as a part of that Beauty. but I must have a thousand of those beautiful particles to fill up my heart." For the time being, at least, the world that sprang to life as he added line after line to *Hyperion* seemed a complete one. "I feel more and more every day, as my imagination strengthens, that I do not live in this world alone but in a thousand worlds—No sooner am I alone than shapes of epic greatness are stationed around me—then 'Tragedy with sceptr'd pall, comes sweeping by' According to my state of mind I am with Achilles shouting in the Trenches or with Theocritus in the Vales of Sicily. Or I throw my whole being into Troilus and repeating those lines, 'I wander, like a lost soul upon the stygian Banks staying for waftage,' I melt into the air with a voluptuousness so delicate that I am content to be alone." In such a mood the sensation of seeming someone other than himself which assailed him in the Dilkes' drawing room mattered little. "Some think me middling, others silly, others foolish—every one thinks he sees my weak side against my will;

when in truth it is with my will—I am content to be thought all this because I have in my own breast so great a resource."

By the end of October it was time to send his long journal-letter off to catch the Boston post. Keats closed with a few anxious words of advice to his brother and sister-in-law, who were by now crossing the Alleghenies: George, the young pioneer fresh from a counting-house stool; and Georgiana, carrying her first child as their wagon jounced through the wilderness. "Take it calmly— and let your health be the prime consideration," he begged them. He thought for a moment of asking Tom for a message to send them, then decided against it. "Tom is still so nervous that I cannot speak to him of these Matters—I did not like to write before him a Letter he knew was to reach your hands—his heart speaks to you—Be as happy as you can." As he signed the letter he realized what day of the month it was—something he rarely remembered—and added a postscript: "This day is my Birth day." He was now twenty-three years old.

-»»-«««-

The month of November 1818 would be a blank in the narrative except for three short letters—one to Rice on a broken engagement, one to Mrs. Davenport, a Hampstead neighbour who had asked after Tom's health, and a hopeless little note to his sister. Three calls on Abbey in the City had not persuaded him to allow Fanny more visits to Well Walk, and Tom was too ill for Keats to leave him for a trip to Walthamstow. Perhaps one more visit before Christmas—that was the best they could hope for. He made one or two trips into town to see Reynolds and probably several short calls a week at Wentworth Place; more we do not know. After his rally at the end of October, Tom took another turn for the worse: this one, it seemed, would be the last. Keats was with him almost constantly now, nursing him through the crises of his fever, watching his body grow more helpless, his features more shrunken each day, searching for words to nerve him for what lay ahead. George's old friend Haslam, who came regularly to help, was alarmed at how haggard Keats appeared. He told Severn privately that he had heard that a person who took care of a dying consumptive often came down with the same disease afterward.[20] But he could not persuade Keats to move into other lodgings, or even to let him take his place for more than an hour or two at a time. "Poor Tom looks upon me as his only comfort," Keats had told George. Day and night he watched without hope, remembering—could he have helped it?—the long nights, nine years before, when he fought off despair at his mother's bedside. On November 18 Tom had his nineteenth birthday; on December 1, early in the morning, he died.

Keats's first act after Tom's death was to write a note to his sister. The one visit she was to have been allowed before Christmas, Keats had put off through November because he knew it would be too painful for both Fanny and Tom. Now he wrote only to tell her briefly that Tom was much worse, to prepare her for the news he would bring her himself, and begged her to keep up her spirits for his sake. He took the letter to the post, then turned down the hill to Wentworth Place in the half-light of the winter morning. Brown was still asleep; he awoke to find Keats standing at his bedside. Keats took his hand, unable to speak, but Brown knew why he had come. After a few minutes he broke the silence: Keats must come and live with him at Wentworth Place. Keats agreed, glad to put Well Walk and its memories behind him at last. Brown at once stepped in to write his friends the news and shoulder other burdens. Haslam took over the task of writing George. On every side his friends stood by ready to help.

"The last days of poor Tom were of the most distressing nature," Keats wrote to George two weeks later; "but his last moments were not so painful, and his very last was without a pang—I will not enter into any parsonic comments on death"—the adjective suggests that an old wound had been opened and probed that fortnight—"yet the common observations of the commonest people on death are as true as their proverbs. I have scarce a doubt of immortality of some nature or other—neither had Tom." It seems a hope as wan as the English sun in December. A deep primitive need to believe that Tom lived on struggled against his dogged rejection of the formulas of Christianity. As the bells tolled in St. Stephen's the day Tom was laid beside his father and mother and grandparents, did Keats remember the angry sonnet he had written two years ago when they were living within the sound of those bells? Tom was dead—Tom with all his joy in life, Tom who, George said, "understood Keats better than any other human being."

The thought of his brother's death was to haunt Keats for months afterward, but he did not allow himself to give way openly to sorrow, even in writing to George. Two days before Tom's funeral, in fact, he drove down to Crawley Hurst in Sussex with Reynolds and all the sporting crowd to see the prizefight of the decade, the great battle in which Jack Randall defeated Ned Turner after thirty-four bare-fisted rounds.[21] And immediately after the funeral on December 7, he plunged into a round of activity to clear his mind of the memory of the last three months. It was the healthiest antidote to grief; and a week or so was all he needed. "I have been every where," he told George and Georgiana in mid-December: to call on the Reynoldses, the Dilkes, the Wylies, the Millars; to see Hunt, Haydon, Novello, Martin, and Lamb; even to meet up with Kirkman and Archer, friends from the Mathew days. Mrs. Dilke went with him to see Fanny at the Abbeys'. The following Sunday he walked with Haslam over the ten frozen miles to Walthamstow for another visit to his sister, then back into London with his friend. Dilke took him shooting on the Heath one morning—a rare pleasure for Keats, though all he bagged was a tomtit. With Brown he went to see Kean play Brutus in top style in a "very bad" new tragedy—his first trip to the theatre since George's departure. One of his pleasantest trips into town was a call on Hazlitt in his bare untidy rooms at 19 York Street, a house that had once been Milton's, from which Keats carried away the manuscript of the lectures on the English comic writers which he had missed in November. At least one other time, though he did not mention it to George, he paid a visit to Isabella Jones for a few hours' good conversation and perhaps a glass or two of her prize Farentosh whisky.

A less amusing occasion was a party at the Novellos', which Hunt induced him to attend with Brown. With Hunt's knack for "making fine things petty and beautiful things hateful," even Mozart seemed tiresome for once, and Keats agreed with Brown never to get trapped into another such affair. Then Woodhouse forwarded him an invitation that must have tempted him for a moment at least. Mary Frogley—it turned out that Woodhouse was her cousin—had loaned her copy of *Endymion* to the Misses Porter, two of the most successful novelists of the day, and through her Keats was offered an introduction to their set. He was wryly amused that his "meretricious romance verse" should appeal to those lady romancers; he must also have wondered whether Mary Frogley—who, Woodhouse discreetly hinted, was engaged—was still as lovely as ever. But, on the point of accepting, he suddenly changed his mind. "Look here Woodhouse," he wrote, "I have a new leaf to turn over —I must work—I must read—I must write—I am unable to affrod time for new acquaintances—I am scarcely able to do my duty to those I have."

For after a week or two of distraction he was ready to pick up and start forward again. In fact he was beginning to feel stifled in drawing-room crowds by a sense of "everlasting restraint"—"because I feel my impulses given way to would too much amaze them." So it was a relief at last to start his long-deferred letter to George and Georgiana on December 16. A sentence or two was all he could write about Tom's death; a few more about the closeness he felt to them across the Atlantic. "There you are with Birkbeck —here I am with brown—sometimes I fancy an immense separation, and sometimes, as at present, a direct communication of spirit with you. That will be one of the grandeurs of immortality— there will be no space and consequently the only commerce between spirits will be by their intelligence of each other—when they will completely understand each other." He suggested they each read a passage of Shakespeare every Sunday at ten o'clock—"and we shall be as near each other as blind bodies can be in the same room."

The next morning, clear, cold and quiet, he found himself alone at Wentworth Place and suddenly anxious to start writing again. The Dilkes were away; Brown had taken a pair of visiting nephews to see the lions at the Tower; and his old landlord Bentley had just brought him a clothes basket full of books from Well Walk. Yet he found it impossible to pick up where he had left off with *Hyperion*. He opened one of his books, a copy of Beaumont and Fletcher, inscribed "Geo. Keats to his affectionate Brother John"; read a little; then with the thought of "immortality of some nature or other" and the "direct communication of spirit" springing to his mind again, he worked out a little poem on "the double immortality of Poets." [22]

> Bards of Passion and of Mirth,
> Ye have left your souls on earth!
> Have ye souls in heaven too,
> Double-lived in regions new?

It fell into a new form, a kind of free-running "rondeau" which pleased him; he tried another. Hunt had just given him a copy of his latest production, a little Christmas gift-book, half diary and half anthology, in which he had printed the two sonnets Keats had given him in the autumn. "Full of the most sickening stuff you can imagine," Keats had decided after a glance at the twelve descriptive essays which Hunt himself had contributed, one for each month of the year. Yet evidently they started the theme of the seasons turning over in his head,[23] and this, compounded with his idea of the immortality of the imagination, rhymed itself into a second poem, an Ode on "Fancy," full of the fluent joy he felt at his new freedom to write again.

Yet his thoughts were veering in another direction that bright winter noon, away from an ideal season of the imagination to an ideal companion:

> Let, then, winged Fancy find
> Thee a mistress to thy mind:
> Dulcet-eyed as Ceres' daughter,
> Ere the God of Torment taught her
> How to frown and how to chide;
> With a waist and with a side
> White as Hebe's, when her zone
> Slipt its golden clasp, and down
> Fell her kirtle to her feet,
> While she held the goblet sweet,
> And Jove grew languid. Mistress fair!
> Thou shalt have that tressed hair
> Adonis tangled all for spite,
> And the mouth he would not kiss,
> And the treasure he would miss;
> And the hand he would not press,
> And the warmth he would distress.

One wonders whether there was a model for this "mistress of the mind" who emerges through Proserpina's petulance and Venus's abashment by a no less petulant Adonis. Perhaps a clue to her identity—and Adonis's as well—may be found in a passage which Keats added to his journal-letter only the day before. Here at last

he broke his three months' silence about Fanny Brawne by introducing her, a little awkwardly, to George and Georgiana, along
with her mother. "We have a little tiff now and then," he immediately added, "and she behaves a little better, or I must have sheered
off." At once he did sheer off in his letter, Adonis-like, to report
that he had been invited to a birthday dance by the much sought-
after Miss Mary Millar, to which he planned to go as a complete
dandy, "purple Hat and all—with a list of the beauties I have conquered embroidered round my Calves." He could mention Fanny
only while denying the effect she had on him.

> Break the mesh
> Of the Fancy's silken leash;
> Where she's tethered to the heart. . . .

Some kind of leash had begun to tug at him, and already he was
straining away from it.

In spite of his three months' silence on the subject of the
Brawnes, Keats had met them at least several times at the Dilkes'
after Brown's return in October, when they moved into a house
nearby on Downshire Hill. How much Fanny had driven him to
insist to George that he hoped he would never marry, we cannot
know. Quite clearly his first encounter with her had troubled him
too much to let him record it with the keen but detached interest
with which he described his meetings with Charmian and the lady
from Hastings. It is probably also significant that, once he did mention Fanny to George, he felt it necessary to introduce her by name:
she was a real person, not a character in an imaginary drama. Two
days later he ventured a little further: "Shall I give you Miss
Brawn? She is about my height—with a fine style of countenance
of the lengthen'd sort—she wants sentiment in every feature—she
manages to make her hair look well—her nostrills are fine—though
a little painful—her mouth is bad and good—her Profil is better
than her full-face which indeed is not full but pale and thin without showing any bone—Her shape is very graceful and so are her
movements—her Arms are good her hands badish—her feet toler-
able—she is not seventeen—but she is ignorant—monstrous in her
behaviour flying out in all directions, calling people such names—
that I was forced lately to make use of the term *Minx*—this is I
think not from any innate vice but from a penchant she has for

acting stylishly. I am however tired of such style and shall decline any more of it."

There are several things worth noting here. First, and significantly: "She is about my height." Again, he was a year and a half off in estimating her age. Like her mother, who had married a man six years younger than herself, Fanny appeared younger than she was. This suggests that her sense of style did not damp down an energy and spontaneity unusual in most young ladies of her day. She was no Charmian; she was far closer to Juliet. Evidently she felt no need to restrain her impulses for fear of amazing her company, and Keats evidently felt this impulsiveness as a challenge. It succeeded in freeing him from his usual constraint long enough to call her "Minx" to her face, and this "little tiff" seems to have startled them both into a new relationship. "She behaves a little better," Keats noted with satisfaction: on her, as not on Charmian, he could have some effect. Finally, "she wants sentiment in every feature." To an anti-sentimentalist, this was a recommendation. It is clear that, for all his offhandedness, he was being drawn again to Fanny by the same deep attraction he had felt on first meeting her. That it should have flared up with new intensity so soon after Tom's death is no surprise. For over three months his own vital impulses had been held in check with the long ebbing of Tom's life; now they flooded back as through a breaking dam.

Yet it was a desire for life in all its fullness—the "thousand particles" of beauty—that surged up in him. An afternoon or two with Haydon was enough to remind him of the plans for the future which he had put out of his mind during Tom's illness—the kingdoms of the earth and the glories thereof. At one of these meetings Haydon showed him a letter from the young explorer Ritchie, now in Tripoli, "among Camels, Turbans, Palm Trees and sands"; and Keats thought with pleasure of one copy of *Endymion* travelling westward into the wilds of America, another going eastward into the Sahara on a camel's back. Together he and Haydon talked of literary matters and the cartoons of Raphael, which Haydon was then arranging to have exhibited in London for the first time; and Keats looked through a book of prints of the frescoes by Bennozzo in the Campo Santo at Pisa. This first glimpse of early Italian art, so different from the sentimental Guido Reni then in fashion, filled Keats with astonished delight, as it did the young Pre-

Raphaelites thirty years later: "finer to me than more accomplish'd works—as there was left so much room for Imagination."

Haydon, however, was burdened with his usual problems and hinted he was so deep in debt that he must sell some of his drawings to keep going. Keats protested heatedly against this idea, then wrote Haydon impulsively the next morning to offer him more positive assistance. He must have known how endless his friend's demands were, set beside his own resources. But he was concerned about Haydon's recurrent eye trouble, which made it necessary for him to stop painting for weeks at a time; and unwisely he alluded to a fact which Haydon must have suspected, that some money would be coming to him from Tom's estate. This was in fact money which he had been lending Tom out of his own funds for some time, and which he was now counting on to tide him over for three or four more years of "study and travel," even if his own poems brought him nothing.[24] Yet once he was in funds again, Keats could think only of sharing his money with a friend: "Believe me Haydon I have that sort of fire in my Heart that would sacrifice every thing I have to your service—but let me be the last stay—ask the rich lovers of art first—Try the long purses."

The future was opening out before him once again; yet still the silken leash was pulling him another way. In mid-December he had been invited to go down to Hampshire with Brown on his annual Christmas visit to Dilke's brother-in-law, John Snook. Keats accepted tentatively, wishing rather to stay home and write; then, a few days before Christmas, he seized on the excuse of his recurrent sore throat to put off the visit. This involved him in a slight awkwardness with the Reynolds family, whose invitation to Christmas dinner he had declined in good faith the previous week. Mrs. Reynolds renewed her invitation, and Keats wrote her an embarrassed note to decline again. For in the meantime he had accepted a third invitation, which he was determined to keep a secret, and which may have been his real reason for postponing his trip to Hampshire. On Christmas Day he went to dine at Elm Cottage, Mrs. Brawne's house on Downshire Hill.

What happened that day is something of a mystery. Keats never mentioned the occasion, even to George and Georgiana. In fact he let a week go by without picking up his journal to America, then resumed it with no explanation for the lapse—though a few days later he unguardedly confessed, "I never forget you except after seeing now and then some beautiful woman." So the events of that day must be left mostly to the imagination. Yet there are a few tangible pieces of evidence. Sometime during these weeks he presented Fanny Brawne with *The Literary Pocket Book*, the little red leather poetic diary for 1819 which Hunt had given him, and no time seems likelier than Christmas Day. Whatever Keats may have thought of Hunt's sentimental prose, the book was a charming gift for a young lady whose mother had invited him to Christmas dinner, and, still better, it contained the only poetry of his own that had been published since *Endymion*. Fanny seems to have been pleased, for she signed her name in it forthwith and noted some birthdays in the diary spaces. It also seems very probable that she gave Keats a present in return that pleased him still more. For, immediately after Christmas, Keats began sealing his letters with a device he had never used before—a Greek lyre with half its strings broken, circled by the motto "Qui me néglige me désole." [25] This was one of the famous "Tassie gems," then in high fashion, and one which seems especially appropriate for a flirtatious young lady to pick out for a standoffish young man—though in another two years the device was to take on a very different meaning for Keats.

But what else happened that day? The surest clue, though still tantalizing, is Fanny Brawne's remark to Fanny Keats, three years later, that the Christmas of 1818 was the happiest day of her life up to that time. It is impossible not to conclude that somehow or other that day the distance between Keats and Fanny Brawne was bridged: he told her that he loved her and learned that she loved him in return.[26] It is significant, then, that a few weeks after this day Keats began a long poem in celebration of young love, set against a background of good food and music, revelry and rich attire, in which the lovers steal away from a midwinter festivity to reveal their love to each other. *The Eve of St. Agnes* is Keats's commentary on the hidden drama of his life at this time. In the terms of his allegory of human existence, he had emerged at last from the dark passages into the Third Chamber of life, stored with the bread of friendship and the wine of love.

---

## Chapter Nine

# The Melancholy Storm

O<small>N</small> January 1 Keats dined again at the Brawnes', this time with Mr. and Mrs. Dilke. He still kept silent about Christmas and mentioned this New Year's visit to George only to comment, "Nothing particular passed." On Sunday, the third, he dined with the Dilkes and was invited (since Brown was still away) to join them for tea that evening. The next morning he closed his long letter to America with a brief note on that event: "When the tray came up M<sup>rs</sup> Dilke and I had a battle with celery stalks." This poses a problem: from now on Keats's letters, even to George, record the trivia rather than the significant facts of his experience. From the time Fanny Brawne claimed the centre of the stage, a curtain of secrecy drops around the central situation of Keats's life, and only a few stray facts and random observations in his letters, and the still more cryptic record of the poems, give a hint of the drama behind. The last few pages of his journal to George are filled with a barrage of small talk, ranging from an account of a newly discovered kingdom in Africa to the plight of Caroline Mathew, who had just been left high and dry by their old friend Archibald Archer after a two-year courtship. Keats even went so far as to ask his brother what topics he should discuss in his letters: "Whether the affairs of Europe are more or less interesting to you —whether you would like to hear of the Theatre's—of the bear Garden—of the Boxers—the Painters—The Lecturers—the Dress —The Progress of Dandyism—The Progress of Courtship—or the fate of Mary Millar—being a full true and très particular account of Miss M's ten Suitors."

Certainly the outward surface of his life during the first few weeks of January seemed placid enough. Hampstead now provided all the company he wanted; after another return of his "plaguy sore throat" he made few visits to London. One or two parties in town at holiday time were not even dull enough to keep him awake, as he complained to George: "All the evening's amusement consists in saying your good health, *your* good health, and YOUR good health—and (o I beg you pardon) your's Miss ——. Let my eyes be fed or I'll never go out to dinner any where." His new quarters at Wentworth Place pleased him immensely, especially his comfortable sitting room lined with bookshelves, and French windows opening out on the garden shared with the Dilkes. From Brown's upstairs bedroom one could see clear across the Heath to Highgate; and the basement was fitted up with a large brick-binned well-stocked wine cellar. For a few weeks Keats must have been glad to be alone, untroubled by Brown's misogynous presence, free to read and work as he pleased, to call at the Brawnes' and look each day for a letter from George and Georgiana. As he told them, it was only "seeing now and then some beautiful woman" that could put them out of his mind, "but that is a fever—the thought of you both is a passion with me but for the most part a calm one."

Fanny Brawne, then—alternately a feast and a fever—is the key to these first quiet weeks of January. Was she such a beauty as Keats implies? Some of his friends seem not to have thought so. Keats later wrote her, "I cannot conceive any beginning of such love as I have for you but Beauty"; but the casualness of his first appraisal—"beautiful I think"—leaves it an open question. The only portrait of her that survives—a miniature done in her early thirties, regarded as an almost worthless likeness by her family [1]— shows a face too long and thin, a nose too aquiline for a conventional beauty; a childhood ailment—asthma, perhaps—had made her habitually pale, and the oversensitive nostrils and the changeable mouth which Keats described to George in December suggest a bewildering variety of expression. It is interesting to put beside this first catalogue of her points, good and bad, in his letter to George, a later portrait of a woman drawn from the same model:

> Deep blue eyes, semi-shaded in white lids,
> Finish'd with lashes fine for more soft shade,
> Completed by her twin-arch'd ebon brows;

White temples of exactest elegance,
Of even mould, felicitous and smooth;
Cheeks fashion'd tenderly on either side,
So perfect, so divine, that our poor eyes
Are dazzled with the sweet proportioning,
And wonder that 'tis so,—the magic chance!
Her nostrils, small, fragrant, faery-delicate;
Her lips—I swear no human bones e'er wore
So taking a disguise. . . .*

Fanny Brawne's beauty differed from the self-possessed "unchange-able attribute" of a Charmian's, which left less room for the im-agination to work on; it was more like love itself, as Keats once described it—"semireal," requiring "a greeting of the Spirit," some meeting of imagination or sympathy between subject and object, to make it wholly exist.

What, then, was the spirit that greeted Keats from under those enigmatic white lids? "Elegant, graceful, silly, fashionable and strange"; impulsive as well as beautiful—"flying out in all direc-tions"; yet the nickname which Keats gave Fanny was not Juliet (that would have revealed too much) but Millamant. It was her wit and gaiety and sense of style that dazzled him at first, and other young men as well. Fanny Brawne had received the upbringing of a young lady of good family and had the intelligence to carry it off. Her father's ancestors had been knights and lawyers and ab-bots for more than five centuries. Her grandfather, Samuel Brawne, who like John Jennings had prospered in the coaching business, was an early believer in women's independence, for he left ap-prenticeship fees to his daughters so that they could learn trades in case of need. Her forebears on her mother's side had served in government and acquired considerable property in London and Kent. Fanny's mother—"a very nice woman," to Keats's mind—had married for love without her parents' approval, like Keats's own mother. There were other points of resemblance: Mrs. Brawne spoiled her children (according to her daughter), enjoyed merry company, and had a warm, hospitable nature. Her sister had mar-ried Lord North's secretary, William Brummell, who gave Fanny an unusually stylish cousin, George—the famous Beau Brummell; and a great-aunt and great-uncle had acted with Garrick at Drury Lane.[2] This heritage helps to explain Fanny's "penchant for acting

---

* *Otho the Great*, V. v. 61 ff.

stylishly" and her keen sense of comedy. It may also account for
an unusual degree of feminine initiative. Jane Austen's Elizabeth
Bennet incurred the scorn of the neighbouring ladies by walking
three miles in muddy weather, but Fanny Brawne used to walk
five or six miles into town alone to meet her brother at the theatre,
and home again with him at night when they ran through their
quarter's allowance and could not afford the coach.[3]

The theatre was one of Fanny's passions; another was costume,
and in later years she became a skilful and inventive dressmaker.
She also came to be known as a lively and intelligent conversationalist, keenly interested in politics as well as literature.[4] But her occupations at eighteen were only what one would expect of a modish
young lady: singing, waltzing, reading "trumpery novels," chat-
ting in French with the *émigrés* of the Hampstead colony, flirting
with the officers from the barracks in St. John's Wood. She once
described herself as "not at all bashful and hardly modest," but
she was too realistic to be vain. Knowing that "a person must be
a great beauty to look well without them," she set great store by
"dress manners and carriage," accomplishments which she believed were "within the reach of anybody of understanding."
Hardly a romantic heroine; certainly a Regency one. Keats may
have given her a Restoration nickname because she wore her hair
in an original style copied with some care from the age of Charles
II.[5]

His nickname "Millamant" suggests another side to Fanny's
character, or rather the stage of development she had reached
when Keats met her. Fanny at eighteen, at the height of her youthful vivacity, enjoyed the life of a Hampstead belle to the full. Elm
Cottage was a favourite meeting place of the Dilke set, and Keats
could have been only one among many callers there. He was also,
as he must have suspected, one of the least eligible—an unsuc-
cessful young poet with unconventional manners and no money,
often moody and silent in company, handsome enough but too
short and self-conscious to cut a figure on a ballroom floor. That
Fanny did fall in love with him suggests unexpected depths in her
nature, even though Keats had as yet only begun to trouble them.
Privately she thought most men rather stupid, and it is significant
that she was first impressed by Keats's conversation—"in the highest degree interesting," she later recalled.[6] Her mind was keen
enough to recognize Keats's for what it was worth. But the real

attraction went deeper: in Keats's own phrase, she had "a fire in her heart" like the one that burned in his, some superabundant vitality answering to his own hunger for life in all its fullness. But she was still only eighteen; she had some silliness to outgrow, and much frivolous experience that, like any pretty young woman, she wanted to live through.

Even these first few weeks of their affair cannot have been mere tranquil happiness, then. Nor could they quite blot out Keats's usual worries. At the end of December he had loaned Haydon thirty pounds as a stopgap [7]—borrowed, as usual, from Taylor; but now, when he went to Abbey to raise the large amount he had promised Haydon, he began to run into difficulties. *Hyperion* also was giving him trouble. "I have been writing a little now and then lately," he told Haydon on January 12, "but nothing to speak off—being discontented and as it were moulting." His "new Phoenix wings" of the autumn before were failing him, leaving him for a while only to recopy and revise what he had already written.[8] "I see by little and little more of what is to be done, and how it is to be done, should I ever be able to do it," he added despondently to Haydon. What was lacking was the right spirit. He had returned to *Hyperion* in mid-December, the evening after he had finished "Fancy," and at that time the joyous mood of his ode spilled over into the beginning of the third book. A correction in the eighth line, describing the Titans—"Many a fallen old divinity"—reveals something of his difficulty. What Keats wrote in December was first "lonely," then "mateless" [9]—a clue to his state of mind at the time which he immediately struck out. Still his thoughts kept running away from his theme, and after a few weeks' struggle he decided to give up *Hyperion* for a while. It seemed a good time to make his long-postponed visit to Hampshire. So on January 18 [10] he boarded the coach for Chichester to join Brown at Dilke's parents', where he had been staying several days, then round out his fortnight with a visit at the Snooks' in Bedhampton, ten miles away.

Chichester pleased him more than he expected. A prosperous city of graceful Georgian houses, it was full of reminders of its medieval past—the old walls which still enclosed the town, the eight-sided Gothic cross which marked the central square, the ancient buildings which lined the cobblestoned streets around the twelfth-century cathedral. Keats's elderly hosts, Mr. and Mrs.

Charles Dilke, Senior, had been warned by their daughter-in-law that they would find him "a very odd young man, but good-tempered and very clever indeed." They were eager to provide entertainment, chiefly in the form of "old Dowager card parties." Brown, with his bachelor's knack for charming old ladies, had already won the dowagers' hearts, or so he found it amusing to believe; and Keats had to sit through two evenings of their fooling. Miss Mullins, the leader of the card-playing set, managed to persuade Brown to shave off his whiskers at last. Keats took advantage of Brown's transformation to effect one himself—to start wearing his neckerchief in the accepted style, "up to my eyes," as he put it; and this change, probably due to Fanny, is the last we hear of his Byronic habits of dress. If his Chichester evenings were dull, in the daytime he was free to explore the old city and the cathedral, feasting his eyes on stone carving and stained glass, buttress and pillar and arch. When a letter came from Fanny Brawne shortly after his arrival, he took it to read walking up and down the aisles during the service in the choir, to his great and secret delight.

On Saturday, the twenty-third, he and Brown said their good-byes and walked the ten miles to Bedhampton on a fine windy morning. The Snook household was a livelier one than the senior Dilkes'; Keats had been promised he would be very much amused there. John Snook was a stout, cheerful country squire who lived with his hospitable wife and two sons in a charming old millhouse overlooking a quiet pond. The Snooks' larder was well stocked with game, and their cellar (we may assume) with wine; Keats, Brown noted, was now rationing himself to two glasses a meal. Together they spent Sunday morning chaffing Mrs. Snook and filling up a joint letter to the young Mrs. Dilke with a series of risqué puns. Keats rounded off his portion of the letter with a note in the margin: "Remember me to Wentworth Place and Elm Cottage—not forgetting Millamant."

On Monday he and Brown with young John Snook took a carriage and went on a strange excursion for two freethinkers—to attend the consecration of a chapel. Lewis Way, a wealthy eccentric, had recently bought up Stansted, one of the show places of Hampshire, and turned it into a College for the Conversion of the Jews. The house, originally a medieval structure, had been lavishly rebuilt by a seventeenth-century earl; the new chapel was

furnished with stained-glass windows designed by Way himself
to illustrate the unity of the Jewish Law and the Christian Gospel. Keats was bored by the visit. After a five-mile journey uphill
behind an obstinate horse in stormy weather, they arrived late
and got poor seats. The ceremony, led by "the two Big-wigs of
Gloucester & St Davids," lasted two or three hours and was "not
amusing." Yet as Keats's attention wandered around the neo-
Gothic chapel, there was much to catch his gaze. The side windows, high above him, were triple-arched and diamond-paned,
set with stained-glass scutcheons of the arms of Fitzalan and
Arundel, the early proprietors of Stansted. The sun, flashing out
from behind the wind-driven clouds, cast pools of light, blue,
amber, and blood-red, on the white lawn of the attendant priests.
After the consecration he and Brown and the boy paid a call at
Stansted House, now "crammed with Clergy," for whom a sumptuous feast had been laid. Keats did not enjoy the company, but
the house itself roused his imagination. Wide stairways and long
halls with panelling of oak carved in fruits and flowers by Grinling
Gibbons, Arras tapestries and gold-embroidered chairs, fringed
carpets and gold and silver service—it was a banquet for the eye.[11]

The first apparent result of this wet and windy expedition was
a return of Keats's sore throat. After Brown left for London the
next morning, Keats remained for another week at Bedhampton
without going beyond the garden gate. His hosts left him to his
own devices, and Keats came to "like them very much." In the evenings they talked religion and politics, and John Snook, who was
much interested in George's venture, offered to write up "all the
best part of his experience in farming" to send on to America.
During the day Keats was free to work. He had brought down
some thin paper which Haslam had given him for his long letters
to America, but he still found it impossible to begin his new journal. Instead his thoughts turned finally in the direction toward
which they had been veering ever since Christmas. On Haslam's
"thin genteel sheets" he drafted a poem into which he poured all
the feelings and sensations of the last month. From his impressions
of Chichester and Stansted—light and shadow, sumptuous colour
and texture and intricate architectural line—he built up a great
dusky-galleried house in which two young lovers, beset by a dark
and hostile world, meet and escape to their freedom together.

*The Eve of St. Agnes* is Keats's "Epithalamion" in narrative

form, celebrating the joys of a first love fulfilled in a runaway marriage. The abstract tone and superhuman drama of *Hyperion* are
exchanged for a medieval world, remote enough for romance but
as real as the cathedral and cloisters of Chichester, and peopled
with beings of flesh and blood—the Beadsman telling his rosary
with numb fingers, the dim-sighted Angela groping for the balus-
trade, Madeline unclasping the warm jewels from her white throat.
The actual germ of the story seems to have been a recent suggestion
of Isabella Jones's—the superstition that a maiden would see her
future husband in a dream if she fasted on St. Agnes' Eve. And
if one listens for them, echoes of the whole gamut of Keats's reading may be heard throughout the poem, from Spenser and Shakespeare and Milton to Boccaccio and Mrs. Radcliffe and the Arabian Nights. Still, these are not the real sources of the poem.
What matters in *The Eve of St. Agnes*, as in all Keats's other
work, is the poetic intention at the front of his mind which called
up the words and images from his memory—the felt emotion,
the actual experience, the sense of reality which he wished to
express. We can only surmise his adventure with Fanny Brawne,
though we know something of the actual circumstances of these
weeks, from which he could not as yet disentangle his feelings:
the frozen fields and the Christmas festivities at Hampstead; his
elderly companions and medieval surroundings in Chichester; the
baroque splendour of Stansted and the remote quiet of Bedhampton. And yet these very circumstances of warmth and cold, youth
and age, sound and silence, all counterpointed against each other,
perfectly project the emotion he felt at the unexpected birth of a
new love in his time of sorrow after Tom's death. *The Eve of St.
Agnes* is Keats's first great achievement in what he later called
"the knowledge of contrast, feeling for light and shade" which
he thought essential to a poem: the stillness of Madeline's room,
"silken, hush'd, and chaste," balanced against the noisy celebrations in the hall below; the warmth of her bed contrasted with the
chilly night; the pallid moon outside the triple-arched window
casting soft amethyst and rose on Madeline's breast as she knelt
in prayer. The light almost without shade of *Endymion* and the
deep shadows of *Hyperion* here vivify and brighten each other.
It is significant that *Romeo and Juliet* is the source echoed most
frequently in this poem—knowing what symbolic value Keats
set on Juliet. Yet the contrast between the fever heat of midsum-

mer Verona and the aching cold of Keats's castle is striking, for he chose to intensify the passion of his story by an almost Spenserian insistence on its purity. In the authentic feeling of his first master, this is a "song made in lieu of many ornaments" in honour of his love.

**»»«**

With *The Eve of St. Agnes* completed, Keats returned to London on February 2 and settled down prosaically to nurse his sore throat. He was determined this time to shake it off, and for ten days he kept to Hampstead. On the thirteenth he went into town, ran into Woodhouse scowling nearsightedly into a bookshop window, dropped in on Taylor, and met half a dozen other people "from all parts and of all sets." This gave him enough news to start his long-deferred letter to George the next morning. On the seventeenth he went into town again on business and had an uncomfortable interview with Abbey. On the eighteenth he wrote to Haydon to apologize for the delay in sending him the money he had promised; on the nineteenth he resumed his letter to America.

From the beginning this journal sounds a strange new note, stiff and impersonal, especially for a letter to George, with none of the usual play of Keats's "whims and theories." Rather it gives a dry, almost frozen account of his doings, and as the letter goes on an extraordinary note of bitterness creeps in. He states he is "almost tired of Men and things"; he refers to Chichester and Bedhampton only to insist that "nothing worth speaking of happened at either place"—a comment repeated on several other occasions; he mentions old friends either to give bad news or to say he has not seen them; he speaks with distaste of an essay on Valentine's Day which Lamb had just published in *The Examiner,* but quotes with pleasure a grotesque tale of a witch and the Devil that Brown was writing; he admits that he has not been in a mood for poetry lately and mockingly describes the titles of his two latest poems as "fine mother Radcliff names." All this within two weeks of his return from Hampshire; and the same tone holds for the month that followed, through an unflattering description of Henry Wylie's fiancée, an acid comment on Miss Millar's birthday dance, a satirical account of the London theatres, a catalogue of his literary dislikes, and several diatribes against parsons. One phrase of self-characterization which he quotes from Hazlitt and marks approvingly sums up this new mood—"a sour mal content." Nothing could be further from the gusto with which he reported the trivia of life at Wentworth Place and the small talk of London in his last letter, or strung together a series of puns on "bed" to send Mrs. Dilke from Bedhampton. The change must be accounted for.

There were enough worries nagging at Keats in February to bring on his old "blue devils." After two months of expecting a letter from George, he began to fear something had gone wrong in America. He was also concerned about his sister. The Abbeys had decided to take her out of school this winter, to her great distress. Subdued and delicate, backward in her manner and tastes for a girl of fifteen, Fanny needed the stimulus of schoolmates, and Keats hated to think of her mewed up alone in the gloomy household at Walthamstow. His expostulations were useless, however—though when Abbey tried to forbid visits or even letters, Keats protested angrily enough to win the concession of a letter every fortnight. His own affairs with his guardian were also at a crisis. In January, when he tried to persuade Abbey to turn over more of his capital to him for the loan to Haydon, the old man became suspicious. Keats's plan necessitated a close look into his financial affairs, for evidently he had promised to lend Haydon five hundred pounds for two years—which, he figured, would leave him just enough from his patrimony to live on in the interval.[12] But Abbey soon produced a stumbling block. The money owing Keats from Tom's estate, on which he had been counting for the loan, could not be touched till Fanny came of age. This was alarming news, for it meant that Keats's "moderate two years subsistence" mut now do for almost six. "Should it be so I must incontinently take to Corderoy Trowsers," he wrote to Haydon on February 18; "but I am nearly confident 't is all a Bam." He refused to accept Abbey's construction of the will and began a number of weary trips into town to wrestle with his lawyers. The only immediate outcome of these visits, however, was a mock petition which he drew up in his journal, addressed in the best legal language to the Governors of Saint Luke's, a charity hospital for lunatics, asking to be admitted as a confirmed poet and signed the "Count de Cockaigne."

Keats's use of Lockhart's nickname for Hampstead—Cockney-land—is another straw in the wind. The campaign of abuse in

*Blackwood's* had shown no signs of letting up since the fall. The *Quarterly* was silent, but now that the flurry of interest aroused by its attack on *Endymion* had died down it was clear that it had stopped his sales as effectively as it had Hazlitt's. Cowden Clarke, who paid an unexpected visit to Hampstead at this time, remembered Keats's talking angrily for half the night about the injustice of the review.[13] He managed to put on a brave face about it in his letter to America, however, admitting the poem had failed but resolving to try again for George's and Fanny's sake—though, he added, "in a selfish point of view I should suffer my pride and my contempt of public opinion to hold me silent." Yet he could not keep his bitterness from slipping out in several hits at Byron, whose latest canto of *Childe Harold,* he learned, had had an advance sale of four thousand copies. One of these hits suggests that another angry nerve had recently been touched. Mrs. Brawne had evidently been asking discreet questions about him, and his neighbour Mr. Lewis had described him to her as "quite the little Poet" —an unfortunate remark which soon got back to Keats. "Now this is abominable," he burst out to George, "you might as well say Buonaparte is quite the little Soldier—You see what it is to be under six foot and not a lord." As for the reviews, he complained, they had stopped men from thinking for themselves. Readers of the *Quarterly* "are like the spectators at the Westminster cock-pit —they like the battle and do not care who wins or who looses."

Yet Keats cannot have been surprised at the outcome of the attacks, and he had refused to be cast down when they first appeared. "Difficulties nerve the Spirit of a Man," he had remarked when starting *Endymion,* then proved it by finishing the poem in the very teeth of discouragement. Something else must have happened to cause his extraordinary change of mood in February and March. Something, it appears, had gone wrong in his relations with Fanny Brawne. Nothing else can quite account for his profound depression during these months, his inability to write, his increasing concern about money. He even began thinking—and this is significant—of giving up poetry and going to Edinburgh to complete his training as a physician. The idea did not appeal to him, but, as he remarked savagely to George, "it is not worse than writing poems, & hanging them up to be flyblown on the Reviewshambles." What exactly occurred between him and Fanny can only be guessed, however—something which, in his usual secrecy about his deepest feelings, Keats never directly mentioned in his letters.

This could have taken many forms. The most obvious one is that he now realized that their love could be kept a secret no longer, and that he must make some kind of proposal. His comment on Archer's "abominable behaviour" to Caroline Mathew shows that he was well aware of his responsibilities in such a situation. But what in fact could he do? His unlucky offer of a loan to Haydon had revealed that his funds were too low for him to marry unless he changed his whole way of life. He was facing the dilemma which Eliza Drewe had forced on John Reynolds, a choice between poetry and marriage. Mrs. Brawne, in spite of her amiability, had all the usual mother's ideas about a daughter's happiness. Her remark to her neighbour Mrs. Rodd, that Keats was "a mad boy," [14] shows what little encouragement she could have given him. Keats's gloomy remark about Edinburgh also implies that returning to medicine would cause him far deeper conflict than turning to the law had done for Reynolds. All the plans which he had confided to Haydon three days before Christmas—a life dedicated to writing and travel, unhampered by the need to earn a living—were now threatened. So he apparently began to wonder, uncomfortably, whether poetry would not always be more important to him than marriage, even to Fanny Brawne. Fanny's beauty was also beginning to stir up a familiar anxiety—the deepseated conviction that no woman could ever love him for himself. A few months later, in the midst of praising her beauty, he confessed this galling sense of his physical insignificance: "I hold that place among Men which snub-nos'd brunettes with meeting eyebrows do among women." Now an anguished jealousy assailed him whenever in her old lighthearted way she smiled or even glanced at another man.

Still, what happened to produce an estrangement between them is a matter of speculation. Brown's presence at Wentworth Place may well have been disquieting. He resented several of Keats's close friendships with other men and, it seems clear, with women still more. Against young ladies he devised a characteristic stratagem to prevent their borrowing his books of manuscript copies of Keats's poems: he took to writing indecent verses and inserting them among the transcripts.[15] It seems that he quickly took a dislike to Fanny Brawne, which he did not conceal from Keats, and which he expressed in an attitude of amused contempt thinly disguised as flirting. A set of mocking valentine verses which he wrote to her in mid-February, though they amused her, must have exacerbated Keats, and were perhaps intended to do so. By an unlucky coincidence the Reynolds sisters came to spend a week with the Dilkes at just this time. "All very dull," Keats commented. But they, on the lookout as usual, evidently noticed the tension between Keats and Fanny and Brown and at once decided she was "an artful bad-hearted girl," [16] an opinion which they passed on to many of Keats's friends. Fanny at eighteen was undeniably a flirt, perhaps even less ready for marriage than Keats. She can hardly have guessed the emotion she had kindled in him, born of deep loneliness and the experience of death as well as his passionate adoration of beauty. Keats himself was unprepared for the surge of possessiveness which she had stirred up in him—a possessiveness which, it seems, some thoughtless word or act of hers now touched off into a jealous mistrust that was never afterward quite extinguished. But all that is certain is that Fanny, who had started copying his poems into the diary he had given her for Christmas, now suddenly stopped; and Keats remarked to George on Valentine's Day that he and Fanny had "every now and then a chat and a tiff." And with that she disappeared completely from his letters to America.

But February brought Keats still another disillusionment. During the Reynolds sisters' visit to Wentworth Place he learned some news of Bailey which was to estrange him permanently from Keats and his friends. At last Bailey had become engaged. From Thomasine Leigh to John Martin's sister (quite without Keats's knowing it), from Miss Martin to Mariane Reynolds (whom he had asked, the summer before, to take time to think over his proposal), his affections had winged and finally alighted—on Miss Hamilton Gleig, the sister of his college friend and daughter of the Bishop of Brechin. Once accepted, he broke off his London connections with a brusque note to Mrs. Reynolds and, after showing Mariane's letters to Gleig, asked her to return his own to him. "The great thing to be considered," Keats remarked soberly to George on February 19, "is—whether it is want of delicacy and principle or want of Knowledge and polite experience— And again Weakness—yes that is it—and the want of a Wife—yes that is it—Marians obstinacy is some excuse—but his so quickly taking to miss Gleig can have no excuse—except that of a Ploughmans who wants a wife." Bailey, the metaphysician and moralist, come to this! But it also appears from a number of signs that Keats now knew something at least of Bailey's part in the *Blackwood's* affair.[17] Out of pride or some not-quite-extinguished loyalty, he did not mention this incident to George; but his friendship with Bailey was over. "I begin to hate Parsons," he confessed to George a few days earlier while describing his visit to Stansted. As for Bailey, he had not written Keats since his conversation with Lockhart, though from his references to the incident in his subsequent letters to Taylor it appears that he was struggling to maintain a good opinion of himself. As Keats observed to George, the need to keep up an appearance of righteousness makes a parson "fester in himself"—"his features get a peculiar diabolical self sufficient iron stupid expression—He is continually acting—He must be either a Knave or an Ideot."

Yet he cannot have missed the irony of the situation: not only the Reynoldses' adulation of Bailey—"noble fellow—fine fellow! was always in their mouths"—but his own admiration. This was the friend in whom he had confided most openly, with whom he had shared his most searching speculations on the mystery of things. And it is on such a note of speculation that Keats ended his comment on Bailey and the Reynolds girls: "This may teach them that the man who redicules romance is the most romantic of Men—that he who abuses women and slights them—loves them the most—and above all that they are very shallow people who take every thing literal." Then, suddenly soaring away from his shabby story, he added, "A Man's life of any worth is a continual allegory—and very few eyes can see the Mystery of his life—a life like the scriptures, figurative—Lord Byron cuts a figure—but he is not figurative—Shakspeare led a life of Allegory; his works are the comments on it." It is a fine statement of a truth that his own life was proving: that the most significant experiences are often revealed in haphazard and trivial circumstance, and that it requires all the energy of the imagination to grasp their meaning and translate it into poetry.

Yet at just this moment a new friend stepped forward, a man whose first motive for seeking Keats's friendship was his own sense of the allegorical drama underlying Keats's work. Richard Woodhouse has remained in the background of Keats's acquaintance up till now—a scholarly and self-effacing young lawyer, slight, red-haired, and nearsighted. He had been impressed by Keats's conversation at Hessey's dinner in September and still more by the letter Keats wrote him in October on the character of the poet. "Such a genius, I verily believe, has not appeared since Shakspeare & Milton," he wrote to his cousin Mary Frogley shortly afterward, "and if his Endymion be compared with Shakspeare's earliest work (his Venus & Adonis) written about the same age, Keats's poem will be found to contain more beauties, more poetry (and that of a higher order) less conceit & bad taste and in a word much more promise of excellence than are to be found in Shakspeare's work." With this, Woodhouse quietly decided to become Keats's Boswell. Again with Shakespeare in mind and the riddle of the Sonnets, he started to compile a set of notes to Keats's poems. "There is a great deal of reality about all that Keats writes," he observed, "and there must be many allusions to particular Circumstances, in his poems: which would add to their beauty and interest, if properly understood." He ordered copies of the *Poems* and *Endymion* interleaved for annotating, and began gathering Keats's unpublished poetry into a notebook, starting with some early verses culled from Mary Frogley's album.[18] His meeting with Keats on February 13 was a lucky coincidence; he carried him off to his coffeehouse, ordered a bottle of claret, and tactfully persuaded him to talk.

Evidently Keats responded good-naturedly to Woodhouse's prompting, for he gave him information about some of his early poems—those relating to his grandmother and the mysterious Vauxhall lady—which he had never confided to anyone. Certainly he enjoyed the claret. He mentioned the bottle, though not the boswellizing, in his journal to America on February 19, and at this point the gloom of his letter lifted for a moment and his prose took wings. "Now I like Claret whenever I can have Claret I must drink it.—'t is the only palate affair that I am at all sensual in. For really 't is so fine—it fills the mouth with a gushing freshness —then goes down cool and feverless—and the more ethereal Part of it mounts into the brain, not assaulting the cerebral apartments like a bully in a bad house looking for his trul and hurrying from door to door bouncing against the waistcoat *; but rather walks

---

* Keats seems to have intended "wainscot.'

like Aladin about his own enchanted palace so gently that you do not feel his step—Other wines of a heavy and spirituous nature transform a Man to a Silenus; this makes him a Hermes—and gives a Woman the soul and imortality of Ariadne." His prose ran on; one thing led inescapably to another. "I said this same Claret is the only palate-passion I have I forgot game I must plead guilty to the breast of a Partridge, the back of a hare, the backbone of a grouse, the wing and side of a Pheasant and a Woodcock *passim*." He hesitated, thought of a pun, and went on: "Talking of game (I wish I could make it) the Lady whom I met at Hastings and of whom I said something in my last I think, has lately made me many presents of game, and enabled me to make as many—She made me take home a Pheasant the other day which I gave to M⁗ Dilke—The next I intend for your Mother."

The association of ideas is significant; so is the information which he let slip out. On that busy February 13 he had gone to call on Isabella Jones.[19] A sudden impulse to see her at this time is understandable, and moreover he had a reason for calling. There can be little doubt that he took *The Eve of St. Agnes* to show her, and that she was delighted by the unexpected outcome of her suggestion. It is quite possible that she then told him a second legend to use as the framework of another poem.[20] It is certain that she sent him back to Hampstead with a pheasant, and that on that same evening he began what he described to George as "a little thing call'd the 'eve of Sᵗ Mark.' "

It is an enchanting fragment of a poem, a series of vignettes as brightly coloured and lovingly detailed as a fifteenth-century Book of the Hours. "I think it will give you the sensation of walking about an old county Town in a coolish evening," Keats told George when he copied it for him some months later. The first half of the poem gives the rain-washed streets of a medieval city—Chichester, perhaps—filled with pious folk on their way to evensong, the bells ringing and the rooks wheeling above the elms behind the cathedral square, where a bright-haired girl sits reading alone in her room till the light fails. As the scene shifts to the interior of her house, the poem itself moves from the Middle Ages to the early nineteenth century, from Chichester to London—to what seems to be Mrs. Jones's square-panelled room in Gloucester Street with its firescreen and parrot cage.[21] The heroine herself, reading till her eyes ached, leaning forward to stir the fire with her shadow dancing on the wall behind, may indeed have been drawn from life. Yet a few lines further on, just as it is well begun, the poem breaks off abruptly—at the same time that all mention of Isabella ceases in Keats's journals. From the reference to the game he intended to give Mrs. Wylie, it is clear that Keats planned to see Mrs. Jones again. Yet with this brief hint of another visit, she drops from sight as suddenly as Fanny Brawne—the one on a note of anticipated pleasure, the other with "a chat and a tiff."

After the February 19 entry, Keats dropped his letter to America for two weeks. One is left wondering why he also broke off *The Eve of St. Mark* after such a promising start. It has been suggested that he was seized with foreboding by the legend itself— the superstition that whoever watches all night by the church door on St. Mark's Eve will see the ghosts of those who are to die the next year. It seems more likely that he felt both *The Eve of St. Agnes* and *The Eve of St. Mark* were distractions from the real task of *Hyperion,* for he referred to each of them as "little" things and, once having dropped the new poem on February 17, he felt no incentive to go back. What probably interrupted him that day was Abbey's announcement that the money due him from Tom's estate could not be touched for six years. With this alarming glimpse into the future, Keats must have realized that if he were to salvage his reputation as a poet he must get on with *Hyperion* and lose no time. The next entry in his letter to George, on March 3, gives only a stream of rather acid small talk, and when this ran dry he copied out whole pages of Hazlitt's "Letter to William Gifford Esq."—his superbly abusive counter-blast to the *Quarterly's* attack on his *Characters*—for George's amusement. Looking back over February, Keats could not recall anything worth writing about, even though, the week before, he had spent two or three days in town with Taylor, calling on friends and seeing a few plays as well as arguing with his lawyers about family finances. On March 8 he wrote Haydon to assure him he had not forgotten his promise about the loan and to apologize for not having come to see him since his return from Chichester. "I am mostly at Hampstead, and about nothing; being in a sort of qui bono temper, not exactly on the road to an epic poem." Five days later he wrote his sister to tell her his life was as dull as hers. His letter to America went on for a few days, describing a state of "uneasy indolence" rare for Keats—sleeping late, seeing none of his old friends, letting whole days slip by with nothing to show for them; then the journal broke off till mid-April.

The two months from mid-February to mid-April are the blankest and most puzzling period of Keats's creative life. It must be remembered that the record of his letters is often fragmentary and undependable, and so, though almost nothing seems to have happened all this while, even this is uncertain. Moreover, there are times in a man's life when his most important activity is to sit in a chair and think. This two months' blank would matter little, were it not that, looking back on this time from the months that followed, one can catch glimpses of a silent but far-reaching spiritual struggle taking place. Outwardly Keats seems to have sunk into the deepest of all his depressions. Several possible causes of this "qui bono temper" have been described; one effect appears certain—that from mid-February to mid-March he wrote not a single line of poetry. Another result seems to have been a long stretch of sleepless nights. Still another is hinted at here and there in his letters: that Keats now began drinking fairly heavily for the first time in his life. His rhapsody on claret, his attempt to ration himself to two or three glasses a meal, his getting tipsy at a claret feast for Dilke in March—all support Haydon's statement that Keats, in his depression after Tom's death, "flew to dissipation as a relief." One further expression of his "what's-the-use" mood is more speculative—that he began visiting Isabella Jones at this time more regularly than before.

These visits, if in fact they occurred, may be at the center of the mystery of these months; but this is far from certain.[22] There is no real evidence for the theory that Keats carried on a secret love affair with Isabella this winter, though it is likely that she took an interest in him which he can hardly have helped reciprocating. The only tangible proof of this, however, is a flirtatious note she wrote to John Taylor in May from Tunbridge Wells, begging him to write her and to go look at her portrait in the Royal Academy exhibition. In this letter she mentioned with a slightly proprietary air *"our* favourite *Endymion";* but in the same breath she referred to a more fashionable young poet with the pointed inquiry "Who is Barry Cornwall?" [23] Evidently Mrs. Jones enjoyed collecting young men of literary promise, and for a while this winter she seems to have collected Keats. They were well enough acquainted for Taylor to send her news of Keats in his last illness, and for Brown to give her one of Keats's books after his death. But a close attachment between them is another question. Even Taylor, who occupied a special place in Isabella's drawing room for several years, in the end grew tired of her provocative charm. She elicited two sonnets from him, one pondering her motives in sending him a bust of Cupid, the other reproaching her for surrounding herself with so many admirers.[24] Keats's reactions to her gatherings may be inferred from the fact that he developed a distaste for "hateful literary chit-chat" at about this time. "Conversation is not a search after knowledge but an endeavour at effect," he remarked to Haydon early in March. "I will not mix with that most vulgar of all crowds the literary." It may well have been Mrs. Jones he had in mind in a later hit at women who "would like to be married to a Poem and given away by a Novel."

Perhaps, then, his disenchantment with "the beautiful Mrs. Jones," or the conflict of his feelings over both Isabella and Fanny Brawne, had something to do with Keats's dark mood at this time. This conflict, as has been suggested, may have been the origin of a mysterious daydream he had one March morning, of "three figures on a greek vase," a man and two women, which he described to George but refused to elucidate.[25] But there is another possible cause for his depression—the steady company of Charles Brown. When Keats at last started writing poetry again in the middle of April, one of his first productions was an impromptu satire on his friend. This little poem, an elaborate private joke, catalogues Brown's traits by listing their opposites, in a mock-Spenserian style which is itself a joking comment on this full-blooded Regency gentleman. The last stanza hits off to perfection the slang and the entertainment to be found in the "obscured purlieus" of London where Brown went dodging the watchmen in search of damsels "hoarse and rouge of cheek," or

> curled Jewesses with ankles neat,
> Who as they walk abroad make tinkling with their feet.

These stanzas, taken with his portrait of the "bully in a bad house," give at least a hint that Keats may have kept him company on these adventures. Perhaps, then, the note of self-digust that begins to appear in his letters at this time was Keats's unacknowledged reaction to the friend who had by now replaced Haydon and

Bailey and Reynolds and his brothers at the centre of his life.

But there is another clue to the inner drama of these months: the sore throat which Keats told his sister in February had haunted him "at intervals nearly a twelvemonth." After his return from Bedhampton it lingered on for several more weeks, even though he was taking strict care of himself all this time under Sawrey's orders. His health did not improve during March; instead, he began feeling inexplicably fatigued. On Sunday, March 14, he dined with his neighbours the Davenports in Church Row, and came home to take a nap afterward. "I cannot bare a day anhilated in that manner," he wrote George—"to have nothing to do, and to be surrounded with unpleasant human identities; who press upon one just enough to prevent one getting into a lazy position; and not enough to interest or rouse one." Far better to sit at home alone, with his own speculations, "even of an unpleasant colour." "I do not know what I did on monday," he continued, "nothing —nothing—nothing. I wish this was any thing extraordinary." On Tuesday he roused himself sufficiently to go into town to see Abbey on business, walked back to Hampstead for dinner with Taylor and the painter Hilton, smoked a cigar after dinner, and walked back with his guests as far as Camden Town. These eight or nine miles exhausted him so much that he slept late the next morning, Wednesday the seventeenth, and did little with the rest of the day but read a play of Beaumont and Fletcher's and add a desultory page to his journal. The next day he played a game of cricket, got a black eye, and lay abed the next morning till eleven. This lassitude in an energetic young man of twenty-three is suspicious, especially when combined with certain other symptoms which Keats was showing at this time—chronic hoarseness, general irritability, insomnia, inability to concentrate. Today they would be recognized as early signs of tuberculosis.[26]

There can be no doubt that, whether he knew it or not, Keats had contracted the disease. In close hourly contact with Tom during the spring and fall of 1818, he could have escaped infection only by a miracle—if indeed he had not already been infected through nursing his mother years before. The depression and inertia of May and June 1818 may have been an early warning of this infection; certainly the loss of weight, high fever, and ulcerated throat of August 1818 showed something badly wrong. Yet no doctor in Keats's time could diagnose the onset of tuberculosis with any certainty, lacking thermometers, stethoscopes, X-rays, even the simplest technique of auscultation. In fact the first symptom then recognized was a cough, a sign of an advanced stage of the disease, and this was regarded not as a symptom but as a cause. As treatment various remedies were prescribed to allay the cough; wearing warm clothes and keeping out of cold damp air were recommended, as well as moderate exercise, a vegetable diet, and a sea voyage or a mild climate; while emotional agitation was to be avoided as much as possible.[27] From several remarks it is clear that Keats believed he was predisposed to tuberculosis by heredity and constitution and even temperament, given as he was to emotional extremes. The regime he was following this winter—treating his sore throat and avoiding the night air—shows that he at least suspected that he might be developing what he called "the family disease" and was doing what he could to scotch it. Even more significant is a plan he considered later in the spring, of becoming a ship's surgeon on an Indiaman—a sea voyage in southern waters. He could not have regarded his ulcerated throat as a doctor would today, as a secondary symptom showing tuberculosis of the lungs already well advanced. Yet from the fall of 1818 on Keats frequently mentioned an uncomfortable sense of pressure in his chest, almost like suffocation, in moments of anxiety—"the violence of my temperament continually smothered down," as he once described it—which indicates some constricted functioning of the lungs.[28] He also began keeping close watch on his young sister. Fanny was growing up thin and listless, more and more resembling Tom; and Keats's regular questions about her health show that he feared she too might be a consumptive type.[29]

These, then, were the "speculations of an unpleasant colour" from which he tried to escape in drink or sleep or sex or meaningless sociability, but which still waited for him at home at the end of each day. The vital tide that had lifted him up in December had ebbed again, and he was left contemplating what was still the most intense experience of his life up to that point—Tom's death, drawn out over three and a half months of suffering which Keats had shared with him day by day. The middle of March brought him to a crisis: the accumulated nothingness of his existence become intolerable. A few hours spent with people like the Davenports, "who have no light and shade," had come to seem an annihilation of life to which any reality, however painful, was preferable.

On March 17, after one of these evenings, he wrote a sonnet, his first poetry for a month.[30] It is not one of his good sonnets, but it is a revealing one. It asks the same question that posed itself on Ben Nevis the summer before, but in a mood far closer to despair:

> Why did I laugh tonight? No voice will tell:
>   No God, no Demon of severe response,
> Deigns to reply from Heaven or from Hell.
>   Then to my human heart I turn at once.
> Heart! Thou and I are here sad and alone;
>   I say, why did I laugh? O mortal pain!
> O Darkness! Darkness! ever must I moan,
>   To question Heaven and Hell and Heart in vain.
> Why did I laugh? I know this Being's lease,
>   My fancy to its utmost blisses spreads;
> Yet would I on this very midnight cease,
>   And the world's gaudy ensigns see in shreds;
> Verse, Fame, and Beauty are intense indeed,
> But Death intenser—Death is Life's high meed.

Once again the sickening suspicion overwhelmed him that nowhere in the world would he find an answer in his search for some meaning in existence—not even, for the moment, one summoned up from within his own consciousness. Yet in the very act of confronting this suspicion he managed to stare it down. As he told George, "I went to bed, and enjoyed an uninterrupted sleep— Sane I went to bed and sane I arose."

But Keats wrote with a meaning, not merely to rid himself of a mood. As he described it when copying the sonnet for George, "it was written with no Agony but that of ignorance; with no thirst of any thing but knowledge when pushed to the point though the first steps to it were through my human passions." This agony—an overwhelming doubt of the purpose of his life in the face of death—was "a great darkness" to him, in which he wrote "at random—straining at particles of light—without knowing the bearing of any one assertion of any one opinion." The thought of death, it seems, had momentarily paralysed his drive toward "Verse, Fame, and Beauty," the three great impulses of his nature. Yet he was renewing the struggle in another direction: "Give me this credit," he asked George, "Do you not think I strive—to know myself?" From the beginning his poetry had been shaped by his attempt somehow to escape from the realization of death; now he was finally relinquishing the attempt as meaningless. If the pros-

pect of death was faced squarely, he saw, it could be not the negation of all the struggles of life but the supreme experience, "in-
tenser" than all the others, in calling out all a man's heroism to
meet it. More than this, it might become "life's high meed," the
resolution of all those doubts which can never be settled in life
itself. Intensity—which he had described a year ago as a degree of
imagination in which "disagreeables evaporate" by being brought
into relationship with "Beauty and Truth"—he now saw could
not be attained except by admitting these disagreeables; and a life
without intensity, without light and shade, was hardly worth living. Darkness itself was preferable, the darkness of his own unanswered questions in which he still groped toward the light which
he still believed was there.

-»»  «««-

Discouragement, lassitude, disillusionment, the ever-growing
conviction that time was running out—all had acted to silence
Keats's poetry during these weeks; yet he had another reason for
not writing. By January he had reached a crucial point in his epic,
where Apollo was to emerge as the new god of poetry in Hyperion's place. This brought Keats up against the central question
of his life—the making of a poet—at a time when he felt his greatest doubts about his own purposes. His theme is one of the largest
he could have set himself, and one that since his time has become
a central preoccupation of literature: the nature of the artist, the
validity of his insight, and the purpose his art serves in society.
In the English poetry of his time it was only beginning to emerge
as a theme for the poet himself to explore; yet it is characteristic
of Keats to have sensed immediately the central problem of his
age and attempted to solve it in his work even as he was grappling
with it in his own experience. "I would sooner fail than not be
among the greatest," he had said of the failure of *Endymion* at
the time he started *Hyperion*. Now, half a year later, he decided
to write no more till the answer to his own question became clearer
to him.

So he announced to Haydon, early in March, that he had resolved "never to write for the sake of writing, or making a poem,
but from running over with any little knowledge and experience
which many years of reflection may perhaps give me—otherwise

I will be dumb." This was more than a resolution, it was a defiance; for Haydon never saw Keats or wrote to him without urging him on with *Hyperion*. Yet the more Keats struggled with his
poem, the more he realized that great poetry could not be written
out of mere great ambition or even some gift of noble language,
but only out of a knowledge of life which he had not yet achieved.
He had enough to do for the present, he told Haydon, with "looking upon myself, and trying myself at lifting mental weights, as
it were." "I am three and twenty," he added, "with little knowledge and middling intellect. It is true that in the height of enthusiasm I have been cheated into some fine passages, but that is
not the thing."

The thing was evidently philosophy. It seems that, as he pondered his theme of "the grand march of intellect" in *Hyperion*,
Keats was turning with new interest to the philosophic classics,
those mental weights he tried lifting in these otherwise idle
months. Quoting Milton's line "How charming is divine Philosophy!" he explained to George that he now appreciated it as never
before; and his journal at this time shows a new concern with
the perennial questions of the nature of the good, the limits of
reason, and even the pre-existence of the soul. A discussion at
Taylor's evidently fired his interest in Plato again. The Socratic
motto "Know thyself" echoes in his letters during March; perhaps the Socratic paradox that the goal of the true philosopher
is death helped shape his line "Death is Life's high meed." His
imagination had been captured by the character of Socrates, who,
it now appeared to him, embodied the supreme virtue of disinterestedness more completely than any other men in history except
Jesus. And this led him off onto another train of thought. "What
I heard Taylor observe with respect to Socrates, may be said of
Jesus," he remarked to George, "—That he was so great a man
that though he transmitted no writing of his own to posterity, we
have his Mind and his sayings and his greatness handed to us by
others. It is to be lamented that the history of the latter was written and revised by Men interested in the pious frauds of Religion.
Yet through all this I see his splendour."

Inevitably his reading of philosophy led him back to the problems of religious faith—or his lack of it. Perhaps, on closer study
of *Paradise Lost,* he was revising his earlier judgment that Milton's theology could be grasped by one "not much advanced in

years." He was trying at any rate to extend his knowledge of religion, for he began reading Church history in March; and it may have been at this time that the works of Bishop Beveridge and Saint Ambrose and a folio Prayer Book found their way onto his shelves.[31] These excursions into theology did not lessen his distaste for Christian dogma; yet, along with a glance at earlier religions, Zoroastrian and Hindu, they helped widen the range of his speculation.

The year before, Keats had thought of Hazlitt as his guide along "the metaphysical road," and during this winter his admiration for Hazlitt's incisive mind reached its height. It seems likely that his recurrent concern with the idea of disinterestedness owed much to his reading of Hazlitt's early essay on *The Principles of Human Action* at this time. Yet Hazlitt's recent debate with the editor of the *Quarterly,* some of which Keats had copied out for George, struck him more forcibly. The essay raised a troubling question, however. In it Hazlitt maintained, citing Shakespeare's *Coriolanus* as an example, that the poet naturally leans to the aristocratic, or "arbitrary," side of the question rather than to the democratic, because it appeals more to the imagination, even though it may violate our rational and moral sense. Not "the cause of the people," he argued, but "the triumphant progress of the conquerors and mighty Hunters of mankind" provides poetry with its greatest themes. This idea implied a conflict between Keats's political convictions and a view of poetry which he found hard to refute; it also posed a dilemma for *Hyperion.* How could he reconcile Hazlitt's defense of the "poetry of power" with his own epic theme of the "general and gregarious advance" of mankind? It was his aim, as he remarked half-mockingly to George, to "tell truth unto the men of this generation, & eke to the women"; but Hazlitt seemed to force him into the position that "poetry is not so fine a thing as philosophy—For the same reason that an eagle is not so fine a thing as a truth."

The problem was not one to be solved by logic. A few days after copying the passage from Hazlitt on March 13, Keats wrote the sonnet "Why did I laugh tonight?" in his "Agony of ignorance"; then on March 19 he resumed his letter to George. He had just heard from Haslam that his father was on the point of death, and resolved to go to town the next day to see him. "This is the world," he mused. "Circumstances are like Clouds continually gathering and bursting—While we are laughing the seed of some trouble is put into the wide arable land of events—while we are laughing it sprouts it grows and suddenly bears a poison fruit which we must pluck—Even so," he added, "we have leisure to reason on the misfortunes of our friends; our own touch us too nearly for words." He realized how far he fell short of truly disinterested sympathy for his friend, and yet, he reflected, there was in the very intensity of most men's absorption in their immediate feelings a kind of "essential beauty." "The greater part of Men make their way with the same instinctiveness, the same animal eagerness as the Hawk—The Hawk wants a Mate, so does the Man—look at them both they set about it and procure one in the same manner. I go among the Feilds and catch a glimpse of a stoat or a field-mouse peeping out of the withered grass—the creature hath a purpose and its eyes are bright with it—I go amongst the buildings of a city and I see a Man hurrying along—to what? The Creature has a purpose and his eyes are bright with it." In another flash of detachment he saw himself as he sat writing, "pursueing the same instinctive course as the veriest human animal you can think of. May there not," he wondered, "be superior beings amused with any graceful, though instinctive attitude my mind may fall into, as I am entertained with the alertness of a Stoat or the anxiety of a Deer? Though a quarrel in the streets is a thing to be hated, the energies displayed in it are fine. By a superior being our reasonings may take the same tone—though erroneous they may be fine—This is the very thing in which consists poetry." This was the problem Hazlitt had posed; but as Keats pondered it the dilemma seemed to dissolve. Perhaps an eagle is not so fine a thing as a truth; yet the eagle, the lion, the hawk—all agents of the "eternal fierce destruction" that had sickened him to contemplate a year before—had the beauty of intensity to the mind that could see it, and this was the wellspring of poetry.

At this point, it seems, Keats turned back to *Hyperion*. By some mysterious force his long creative paralysis was broken at last. The lines he added to *Hyperion* sometime near the end of March, depicting the young Apollo's birth into godhead, describe the same struggle against darkness, the same mood of agonized questioning, as his sonnet of mid-March;[32] but now they are resolved. Where Keats had shown Hyperion—his younger self—waiting for his overthrow with dread, uncomprehending, unconsenting, he now made Apollo seek out the ordeal of his transformation. Alone on Delos, he has found its unshadowed beauty turning into "painful vile oblivion." The self-engrossed delights of the days of his first discovery of song, when he was content merely to sing his own name over and over in wonderment, now seem meaningless: he "aches" with his ignorance of the universe of which he is now aware. In answer to his distress, Mnemosyne appears to him—the mysterious goddess of Memory, repository of all the experience of the human race. Apollo has known her before as in a dream; now he is ready to confront the reality of knowledge she represents. At first she gives no answer to his troubled questions; but at the height of his anguish he finds he can read "a wondrous lesson" in her silent face. In an electric flash of insight he learns all he lacked before, and his despair yields to exultation:

> "Knowledge enormous makes a God of me.
> Names, deeds, gray legends, dire events, rebellions,
> Majesties, sovran voices, agonies,
> Creations and destroyings, all at once
> Pour into the wide hollows of my brain,
> And deify me. . . ."

This is no knowledge that philosophy could teach, but the wisdom born of the fullness of experience—the awareness of all the sufferings of mankind, the acceptance of "creations and destroyings" together. And as he receives this wisdom of Mnemosyne, Apollo undergoes a change almost beyond description. Keats's search for a metaphor to express this transformation is revealing:

> Soon wild commotions shook him, and made flush
> All the immortal fairness of his limbs
> Into a hue more roseate than sweet pain
> Gives to a ravish'd Nymph when her warm tears
> Gush luscious with no sob. Or more severe,—
> More like the struggle at the gate of death;
> Or liker still to one who should take leave
> Of pale immortal death, and with a pang
> As hot as death's is chill, with fierce convulse
> Die into life: so young Apollo anguish'd.[33]

All the most self-annulling experiences of life—the crises of sexuality, both masculine and feminine, of birth and ecstasy and death —are seized on here to convey an experience beyond themselves which in the end he could only describe literally as "dying into life."

> At length
> Apollo shriek'd;—and lo! from all his limbs
> Celestial Glory dawn'd: he was a god! [34]

Here Keats laid his poem down again. The long passage on Apollo's deification, as he later told Woodhouse, had seemed to come to him from some unknown source outside himself—"as it were something given to him." [35] Once the astonishing flow had ceased, there was nothing more to say, at least for the present. But these lines marked the end of a long struggle for Keats. The annihilation of his old identity was complete. The solitary youthful singer had emerged from the ordeal of innocence into the fullness of life at last, to become "the Father of all verse," a god of poetry indeed.

*Chapter Ten*

---

# The Temple of Delight

AFTER this continuation of *Hyperion,* Keats lapsed into silence again. Following the long meditative entry of March
19, his journal shows a blank for four weeks; only a few brief
letters and a single sonnet fill the interval. As he wrote his sister
on April 12, idleness was becoming a habit with him that would
be hard to break. Yet the only reason he would give was his worry
over not hearing from George. Everything seemed at a standstill;
only the season moved on. As the days grew warmer he started
tramping over the Heath again, but evidently still made little
effort to see his friends in town. With Rice in poorer health than
usual, the card-playing set had fallen apart. Haslam was on the
brink of marriage. Reynolds was completely "limed in the law,"
as Keats noted—not only reconciled to it but making a hobby-
horse of it. His visits to his sister at Walthamstow were still
strictly rationed, but he made a point of sending her a little
present from town every week or so—Goldsmith's poems, a Tassie
seal, drawing paper, seeds for her garden, and, since she was about
to be confirmed, a brief treatise on the Catechism. When Fanny
wrote him a long list of questions which the curate had put to her,
he answered them with a flourish of his new theological knowledge and signed himself, wryly amused, "Your affectionate Parson
John." In another letter he gave her a fanciful portrait of himself in his favourite pose, sunk in an armchair by a globe of gold-
fish, staring out of a window shaded with japonica: "I should like
the window to open onto the Lake of Geneva—and there I'd sit
and read all day like the picture of somebody reading."

Outwardly this unproductive interval seems one of those fallow periods of "delicious diligent indolence" which Keats himself realized were the necessary prelude to intense creative effort. Yet from several signs it appears closer to the uneasy inaction of his continued depression. One clue, though a baffling one, is the hint of a crisis in his financial affairs at this time. After three months of wrangling with Abbey and the lawyers, it seems that at last he received some definite statement on his funds. It was worse even than he had feared. His grandmother's bequest had mysteriously dwindled down to almost nothing. His generosity in lending money to friends had cost him over two hundred pounds, a sum which he knew there was small chance of being repaid. When these loans were reckoned up with still larger ones to his brothers, his medical school expenses, lawyers' fees, and his drafts on his principal, he was left with little more than the hundred-odd pounds remaining in his cash account. Of the five hundred pounds he had deposited at Abbey's the preceding June, nearly half had vanished in loans to Tom and George that summer and a large withdrawal in March evidently to settle Tom's bills. The five hundred pounds, more or less, which he had been expecting from Tom's estate would, it now finally appeared, be withheld till his sister reached twenty-one. This meant that his supply of money had virtually run dry, and for more than five years he could count on nothing but what he could beg from Abbey. Keats must have been staggered. Abbey himself had nothing more constructive to suggest than that Keats enter a hatters' firm in which he had an interest; and he managed to convince him that he had only his own negligence to blame for the situation. Grimly Keats resolved to keep more careful accounts in the future. It did not occur to him that Abbey—as now seems probable—had quietly borrowed his ward's capital for his own use; for this is the only possible explanation of his failure to make over or even mention to Keats some seven or eight hundred pounds still due him from his grandfather's estate.[1] Not till four years later was the existence of these funds discovered, and Abbey's handling of his trust investigated by the Court of Chancery;[2] but by then it was too late.

Why Keats reacted to this revelation by drawing out the £106 remaining in his cash account on April 3 is not clear. But now at last he realized he could not meet his promise to Haydon. The painter, who had been pressing him for the loan all through March,

replied to this announcement on April 12 with a letter reproaching Keats for deceiving him and thus preventing him from obtain-
ing money elsewhere. At this, remembering all the trips to town,
the harangues, the worry, the time wasted, Keats flared up in sudden anger. He had acted in good faith, he told Haydon, and gone
to far more trouble than he would have done for himself. "I cannot
do two things at once," he retorted heatedly, "and thus this affair
has stopped my pursuits in every way. Now you have maimed me
again; I was whole I had began reading again—when your note
came I was engaged in a Book—I dread as much as a Plague the
idle fever of two months more without any fruit." The unexpected
note of petulance in these accusations suggests a deeper strain on
their relationship than either man would have admitted, similar
perhaps to that which had undermined Keats's friendship with
Hunt. Yet for Keats this was only a momentary flash of irritation.
Already his financial predicament seems to have jolted him out of
the doldrums into a new determination to act. His money would
last, he figured, for another six months. So, he decided, when
Brown went off for the summer he would take cheap lodgings in
Westminster, close to a good supply of books in the Abbey Library,
and try to finish *Hyperion*. Then, as he announced to George on
April 15, he would see what he could do "without poetry." It
seems he was thinking of earning his living by journalism, as
Reynolds had done; but if worse came to worst, he could always go
back to medicine. "I have no doubt of making by some means a
little to help on or," he added sardonically, "I shall be left in the
Lurch—with the burden of a little Pride." [3]

There was more to this decision, however, than the low ebb of
his funds. For more than a month he had known that his pleasant
life at Wentworth Place would soon be over, and not just for the
length of Brown's vacation. Ever since mid-February the Dilkes
had been planning to leave Hampstead. Dilke, like a true Godwin-
ian, was giving much anxious thought to his child's education.
Though Charley at nine was quite old enough to be sent away to
school, his father wanted to watch over his schooling himself and
so decided to move into town and send his son to Westminster as
a day pupil. This extravagance of concern first amused then irritated Keats; Dilke will ruin the boy with too much care, he
thought to himself. But he must have heard the sequel to this plan
with a rush of emotion. Mrs. Brawne, it now appears, had decided

to buy the Dilkes' half of Wentworth Place and move in after they left at the beginning of April. Immediately Keats realized this would be the end of his comfortable arrangement with Brown. He made up his mind apparently at once to leave Wentworth Place by the first of May, when Brown planned to rent his house for the summer as he usually did to eke out his income; but for some time Keats could not decide where to go. First Edinburgh occurred to him, then Westminster; then, for another few months, his mind was to run all over the world looking for a place.[4] Only one thing seemed certain: he could not live and work in peace with Fanny Brawne next door.

So matters stood on April 3, when the Dilkes left for Westminster and the Brawnes moved in [5]—a move which, significantly, Keats never mentioned to George. The next day, a Sunday, Mrs. Brawne invited him to dinner. Keats must have accepted with some uneasiness, but he managed at the same time to forget that he had asked his brothers-in-law Charles and Henry Wylie a few weeks before to dine with him that afternoon. When he remembered and tried to excuse himself, Mrs. Brawne insisted that they all come; and so a new chapter of his life at Wentworth Place began. As on New Year's Day, Keats noted in his journal only the mere fact of dining at the Brawnes'; so, as with his Christmas dinner at Elm Cottage, we are left to surmises. Did Fanny set out to dazzle the two good-looking young Wylies, or did she play Millamant to Keats's reluctant Mirabel? Or did she look a little paler than usual? Keats did not record even the impression that "Nothing particular passed"; but that something extraordinary did happen appears from the sonnet he wrote a few days later—the first since the troubled outburst of "Why did I laugh tonight?"

This sonnet sprang not out of the sleepless anxiety of mid-March but from a dream so beautiful that, as he exclaimed in his journal, he wished he could dream it every night. The dream itself was touched off by his rereading the fifth canto of the *Inferno,* where Francesca describes the fateful day she and Paolo read the story of Launcelot together and he "kissed her mouth all trembling." "I had passed many days in rather a low state of mind," Keats wrote to George, "and in the midst of them I dreamt of being in that region of Hell. The dream was one of the most delightful enjoyments I ever had in my life—I floated about the whirling atmosphere as it is described with a beautiful figure to whose lips

mine were joined as it seem'd for an age—and in the midst of all
this cold and darkness I was warm—even flowery tree tops sprung
up and we rested on them sometimes with the lightness of a cloud
till the wind blew us away again—I tried a Sonnet upon it—there
are fourteen lines but nothing of what I felt in it—"

> As Hermes once took to his feathers light,
>     When lulled Argus, baffled, swoon'd and slept,
> So on a Delphic reed, my idle spright
>     So play'd, so charm'd, so conquer'd, so bereft
> The dragon-world of all its hundred eyes;
>     And, seeing it asleep, so fled away,
> Not to pure Ida with its snow-cold skies,
>     Nor unto Tempe, where Jove griev'd that day;
> But to that second circle of sad hell,
>     Where in the gust, the whirlwind, and the flaw
> Of rain and hail-stones, lovers need not tell
>     Their sorrows,—pale were the sweet lips I saw,
> Pale were the lips I kiss'd, and fair the form
> I floated with, about that melancholy storm.

A sense of mysterious release and reunion is evoked so delicately
in these lines that one hesitates to link them to any actual experience. Still there are strange echoes in this sonnet, of the calm
beyond despair Keats had described in the Cave of Quietude and
the warmth of love in Madeline's chilly room, and others far more
remote—recollections of a pale and beautiful woman found in a
shadowy world of faithless lovers, of a nameless "fair form" to
which he remained joined in endless mute satisfaction. Some of
these overtones can have sounded only faintly in Keats's mind;
but, out of the wordless depths of feeling, the dream must have
spoken unmistakably to him of one desire which he had struggled
for months to deny. Fanny Brawne had returned after her mysterious disappearance, the hundred-eyed world had been lulled into
heedlessness, and his long winter was yielding to spring.

This realization was born in another uneventful week at Wentworth Place, in which, for all we know, Keats did nothing but
read and dig in the garden. On Saturday, April 10, Hunt and
Burridge Davenport, his Hampstead neighbour, came for dinner;
and Davenport, in an effort to impress Hunt, "never ceased talking and boaring," while Keats sat on the sidelines watching with
amusement Brown's irritation and Hunt's pleasure at the compliment. On Sunday he took a long walk over the Heath and met his

anatomy demonstrator from Guy's, Joseph Green, strolling with a portly middle-aged gentleman with a strange gleam in his eye—that "archangel a little damaged" whom he recognized at once as Samuel Taylor Coleridge. Keats joined them for two miles of leisurely conversation in which they discussed everything from nightingales and "a dream accompanied by a sense of touch"—was this Keats's contribution?—to mermaids and metaphysics. Two days later he wrote his angry reply to Haydon's reproaches about the loan; two days after that, on April 15, he started up his journal to America again after his month's lapse. And almost at once his letter records an extraordinary change of mood. In a sudden spurt of energy he had begun going into town again, six times within eight days—dining here and calling there, visiting the newly opened Leicester Gallery with Hunt, attending a rout where he talked with a dazzlingly pretty girl, inspecting a panorama of a polar expedition in Leicester Square, spending an entire pleasant Sunday at Taylor's with Woodhouse, going to "a new dull and half damnd opera" with three of his cronies, and all with evident enjoyment. On Monday, the nineteenth, he invited Taylor, Woodhouse, and Reynolds out to Hampstead for dinner, and, when a storm came up to keep them from returning, they played cards till daylight. Tuesday, he was "not worth a sixpence," but the next day he picked up his letter to America again to report a magnificent hoax which he was helping Reynolds perpetrate. Hearing that Wordsworth was about to publish another long-winded rustic narrative called "Peter Bell," Reynolds had written a parody of it, sight unseen, in a five-hour stretch, which he had persuaded Taylor to print under the same title a few days before Wordsworth's own was to appear. Keats, delighted, agreed to crown the joke by reviewing the pretended "Peter Bell" for *The Examiner,* and on Wednesday he roughed out a notice of it in his journal for George's amusement.

A number of things could have spurred him to this burst of activity—a return of good health with the good weather, a visit from Brown's two nephews with "little voices like wasps stings" which made him anxious to escape the house, or perhaps the disturbing new presence next door. But it is also possible that his sudden high spirits resulted from a reprieve on his departure from Wentworth Place. Evidently about this time Brown decided not to let his house till the end of June, and evidently this change of plan pleased Keats more than he would admit. Whatever it was that roused him out of his depression, it also tapped a new spring of poetry. "I am still at a stand in versifying—I cannot do it yet with any pleasure," he told George in starting up his journal on April 15. Yet as he wrote on, late into the evening, with the house quiet at last, his pen began running away with him; three pages of nonsense verse, full of private family jokes, came tumbling out. The next morning, after the nephews left, he went on filling up his letter with gossip for Georgiana and added the mock-Spenserian stanzas lampooning Brown. The following week he drafted a little ballad into his journal; a few days later he wrote a "Chorus of Four Faeries," one for each of the four elements. Then he did a series of experimental sonnets, one on sleep, two on fame, a sonnet on the sonnet itself—all written within a week and ringing unexpected new changes on the form. Nothing could be farther from the bitter satisfaction he had described to Haydon, early in March, "of having great conceptions without the toil of sonnetteering." He had given up his struggle with *Hyperion,* for the present at least, and now found himself absorbed in problems of craft with a delight he had never felt before.

Yet the most unexpected poetry of these two weeks sprang from a strange and troubling adventure. On April 15 Keats called at the Bentleys' to collect the last of the belongings he had left at Well Walk, including some of Tom's papers. Here he found something that brought back his young brother, pale and miserable, with almost unbearable vividness. It was a packet of love letters from the mysterious Amena, written supposedly at the dictation of Tom's friend Charles Wells, and strange letters they were too —such a mixture of high-flown sentiment and downright vulgarity that it is hard to believe that Tom could have taken them seriously, even at sixteen. "It is a wretched business," Keats wrote George that evening; "I do not know the rights of it—but what I do know would I am sure affect you so much that I am in two Minds whether I will tell you any thing about it." The next day, as he reread them, it dawned on him that Tom had been not simply jilted but hoaxed: Amena had never existed, and Tom's visit to France to meet her had been a wild-goose chase—"a cruel deception on a sanguine Temperament, with every show of friendship." Whether Keats caught some overtones of parody of his own early poetry in the letters is another question; [6] but he grew almost incoherent with

anger against Wells as he wrote: "I do not think death too bad
for the villain. I will hang over his head like a sword by a hair.
He is a rat and he shall have ratsbane to his vanity—I will harm
him all I possibly can." This rage seems excessive unless we remember what Keats and all his contemporaries believed—that emotional agitation, especially that of an unhappy love, could bring
on consumption.[7] Wells's hoax, it now appeared, had helped to
kill his brother. The thought of Tom, racked by a passion that was
not only hopeless but unreal, was almost too painful to bear. Keats
turned at once to something else—to copying the sonnet "On a
Dream" into his letter.

The sonnet and the adventure reappear, strangely linked, in
the little ballad that Keats wrote down in his journal five days later
—"La Belle Dame sans Merci." One hesitates to press this poem
for any meaning beyond itself, for it is poetry of a kind that, as
Keats said of his favourite passage in Shakespeare, "One's very
breath while leaning over these pages is held for fear of blowing
these lines away." [8] Yet it seems to have sprung from two recent
experiences, miraculously transformed: his own dream encounter
wth a beautiful woman in a sorrowful world of pale-lipped lovers,
and his discovery of his brother's miserable secret. Keats's corrections in the draft suggest all too clearly how the image of the
knight "palely loitering" by the wintry lake, "so haggard and so
woe-begone," sprang from his painful reminder of Tom the week
before:

> a
> I see death's lilly on thy brow,
>     With anguish moist and fever dew,
> a
> And on thy cheeks death's fading rose
>     Fast withereth too.

The link between the beautiful lady the knight meets in a flower-
strewn meadow and the "beautiful figure" Keats dreamed of floating with in magical blossoming warmth is more delicate but still
perceptible. What matters, of course, is not Keats's actual dream or
recollection but his reshaping of it in the poem. For when the
knight falls asleep in the "elfin grot" he dreams not of love and
warmth but of betrayal and death:

> I saw pale kings and princes too,
>     Pale warriors, death-pale were they all;

> They cried—'La Belle Dame sans Merci
> Hath thee in thrall!'

The dream has changed significantly since early in April; it has turned into a "horrid warning" and comes to an abrupt end. The Knight awakes to find himself alone "on the cold hill side"; the lady herself, he realizes, was a delusion.

So Tom had been deluded and died; so Keats himself had loitered through the winter. And it is hard not to believe that the lady who appeared and then vanished into the wintry air was not also partly real:

> I met a lady in the meads,
>     Full beautiful—a faery's child,
> Her hair was long, her foot was light,
>     And her eyes were wild.

Fanny Brawne on one of her walks across the Heath has been caught up in the process—vision or waking dream—which made this poem.

> She took me to her elfin grot,
>     And there she wept, and sigh'd full sore,
> And there I shut her wild wild eyes
>     With kisses four.

Of course the poem gives no account of what actually happened in that uncertain April, and it is immeasurably better than any literal record of his experience Keats could have left. Still it is a fact that somehow, sometime this month, he and Fanny met and broke through the barrier that had separated them since February; and it is hard not to listen for even a faint echo of that encounter. Was it Fanny herself who made the first move? Two statements which she wrung from Keats a few months later may be taken as comments on their reconciliation if not on the poem itself. "Ask yourself my love whether you are not very cruel to have so entrammelled me, so destroyed my freedom," he wrote Fanny on the first of July. He was enthralled, then, by a lovely lady without mercy—a fate he had reason to fear. A week later he exclaimed, "I never knew before, what such a love as you have made me feel, was; I did not believe in it; my Fancy was affraid of it, lest it should burn me up." He was torn between doubt that such a feeling could be real and dread that it would be his undoing; yet its intensity was such that he could no longer deny it. As Fanny later complained, he had "been an age" in letting her take possession of him; now at last he gave himself up to loving her, though with a foreboding of what might follow—the pale fever, the dream of death, the lonely awakening on a cold hillside.

Yet the poems that began pouring forth a few days after "La Belle Dame sans Merci" show none of his lingering fear of involvement. The "Chorus of Four Faeries" celebrates the joys of a delicate and fanciful sensuality, while the two sonnets on fame mock his own long struggle to win a name with a great poem. The first sonnet, in stating that fame comes only to the man who has learned to be indifferent to it, paints a curious picture of two young lovers at cross purposes:

> Fame, like a wayward girl, will still be coy
>   To those who woo her with too slavish knees,
> But makes surrender to some thoughtless boy,
>   And dotes the more upon a heart at ease. . . .

It also implies an ironically happy ending in the advice to "love-sick Bards" to "repay her scorn for scorn":

> Make your best bow to her and bid adieu,
>   Then, if she likes it, she will follow you.

The second sonnet, which Keats dashed off one morning while Brown was copying out some of his earlier poems, suggests another view of himself at this time. Fame he calls a "fierce miscreed" of salvation, a fever and vexation, from which he turns toward the serenity of growing things: a rose unfolding, a plum ripening with no thought of being plucked or tasted. These images of unforced growth recall his former axiom, "If Poetry comes not as naturally as the Leaves to a tree it had better not come at all"; but Keats was thinking here not of poetry but of life itself. In its full meaning— that all the conditions of growth must be accepted by a man as unconcernedly as a plant accepts them—the sonnet harks back to Keats's meditation on "animal eagerness" that had produced his addition to *Hyperion* toward the end of March; it also echoes the most richly reflective passage in all his letters, which Keats had written to George only a few days before the sonnet.[9]

For the end of April brought a rare moment of calm in which Keats once again could "look upon his mortal days with temperate blood." His poetry, his ambition, his love, and all the contingencies that hedged them about, now fell into a perspective suddenly intelligible and acceptable. At last he felt he could meet the challenges of life squarely on all fronts, without trying to rise above them in the privileged role of poet or taking refuge from them in philosophic abstraction. All his reading and thinking this spring had served only to sharpen his own conception of existence, wrested from his own bitter experience. The vision of "creations and destroyings" which had made the young Apollo into a god of poetry he now saw as giving meaning and value to all human experience, not merely the poet's—just as he now saw himself as a man who must suffer and act, not merely a poet who creates. This sense of things emerges in his journal to George as one evening he let his mind play over two very different books he had recently been reading—Robertson's *History of America* and Voltaire's *Age of Louis XIV*. From Peru to Versailles, he saw, the record of history everywhere refutes the fashionable belief in perfectibility, Shelley's youthful faith that the advance of civilization will eventually eliminate human suffering. "The nature of the world will not admit of it," Keats mused; first "let the fish philosophise the ice away from the Rivers in winter time." The inhabitants of the world will correspond to itself, he saw; and yet his awareness of the limitations on human possibility imposed by man's inescapable link to nature did not preclude a belief in something by which man rises above mere "animal eagerness" and approaches disinterestedness. Even while glimpsing the beauty of destructive animal vitality, Keats recognized "an ellectric fire in human nature tending to purify." [10] So the inevitability of human suffering was no argument against a carefully qualified faith in spiritual progress—such benefit to mankind as might result from "the persevering endeavours of a seldom appearing Socrates." Still less was it a proof of the Christian belief that this world is a vale of tears which will be redeemed by the joys of heaven. No, there was another reason for suffering, a positive value to be realized in this very world.

"Call the world if you Please 'The vale of Soul-making,' " he wrote to George. "Then you will find out the use of the world. I say *'Soul making'* Soul as distinguished from an Intelligence—There may be intelligences or sparks of the divinity in millions —but they are not Souls till they acquire identities, till each one is personally itself." It is significant that, after once viewing the lack of identity as the special exemption of the poet, Keats now saw the achievement of identity as the highest goal of human development. It was a new "system of salvation" he was trying to describe, a process of "Spirit-creation" from "three grand materials acting the one upon the other for a series of years"—the intelligence, the heart, and the "world of Circumstances." How, then, he asked, are souls to be made, to have identity given to them, "but by the medium of a world like this? I can scarcely express what I but dimly perceive," he confessed, "—that you may judge the more clearly I will put it in the most homely form possible—I will call the *world* a School instituted for the purpose of teaching little children to read—I will call the *human heart* the *horn Book* used in that School—and I will call the *Child able to read, the Soul* made from that *school* and its *hornbook*. Do you not see how necessary a World of Pains and troubles is to school an Intelligence and make it a soul? A Place where the heart must feel and suffer in a thousand diverse ways! Not merely is the Heart a Hornbook, It is the Minds Bible, it is the Minds experience, it is the teat from which the Mind or intelligence sucks its identity."

This last image is supremely characteristic of Keats in implying that the assimilation of experience beyond all conscious endeavour is what makes wisdom in the end.[11] The identity or "identical soul," as he now calls it, is not formed by taking thought: for it is the intelligence that must be sent to school, not the heart—the intelligence which must be "fortified and altered" by submitting itself to the world of circumstances and its lesson of perplexity and pain and death. Keats here moves beyond the Platonic idea of soul-making which seems to have tempted him at least briefly— the belief that with death the soul will slough off the imperfect knowledge of bodily life for the perfect knowledge of the intellect. Wisdom, like good, must be attained in this life if it is to be attained at all; and it is won by slow perfection not in knowledge but in experience. "As various as the Lives of Men are—so various become their souls," he concluded; and in the end the achievement of identity is good, however much suffering it entails, because—he can appeal only to experience—it brings "a bliss peculiar to each ones individual existence," the acceptance of one's self and one's destiny as the very condition of being. Whatever experience had brought him to this insight, one thing seems clear:

from his struggle with the world of circumstance, heart and mind together, he had emerged at last, altered and fortified, with the firm sense of his own identity which had eluded him so long.

The last week of April and the first week or two of May seemed lifted out of time. The fine weather in mid-April had hurried the season forward; then for a few days the spring seemed to stand still. "This is the 3ᵈ of May & everything is in delightful forwardness," Keats wrote before closing his journal to George; "the violets are not withered, before the peeping of the first rose." He had another month at Wentworth Place to enjoy his pleasant sitting room opening on the garden, the garden itself coming into full bloom, the cellar under the garden path—and now the sight of Fanny strolling over the grass plot, and the chance of a meeting with her stolen from a walk on the Heath. For this little while the future must wait. "O there is nothing like fine weather, and health, and Books," he exclaimed in a letter to his sister, "and a fine country, and a contented Mind, and Diligent-habit of reading and thinking, and an amulet against the ennui—and, please heaven, a little claret-wine cool out of a cellar a mile deep."

After closing his journal to America on May 3, Keats wrote no real letter till May 31. Several friends came out from town to visit him, but he apparently remained rooted to Hampstead all this while. He was making a close study of Dryden's poetry and walking daily on the Heath with Fanny Brawne; otherwise we know nothing of his life during this month but what can be read from the four Odes of May—"On Indolence," "On a Grecian Urn," "To a Nightingale," and "On Melancholy"—to which should be added his "Ode to Psyche," written in the last week of April. In these odes Keats reached his own full ripeness as a poet at last. With the resolution of his struggle to understand himself, both as the poet represented in Apollo and as the human being of achieved identity, he was now free to express his own inner experience through his poetry with a sense of speaking for all mankind. At the same time his long discipleship to Shakespeare and Milton, masters of the concentrated phrase and long line, had brought him to the command of a new lyrical form, longer than the sonnet but as deliberately wrought—as "interwoven and complete," as he put it—in which every syllable carries its freight of meaning. The order in which the odes were composed is largely conjectural; [12] but even if their dates could be fixed, it is not so much they which cast light on Keats's life this spring, as all of Keats's life that illuminates the odes. For these few weeks he stood at a point of perfect balance, confident in his ability to meet the future, able to contemplate his past with calm, and rejoicing in the beauty of the season, the joy of an answered love, the delight of a mastered craft—the themes of the odes as well as his incentives to writing them.

The "Ode to Psyche" is the first product and the happiest in mood of this interval of peace. Keats told George as he copied it into his journal that it was the first poem with which he had taken "even moderate pains—I have for the most part dash'd off my lines in a hurry," he added. "This I have done leisurely—I think it reads the more richly for it." This comment is curious, for at first sight this ode seems an improvisation. Yet closer study reveals a highly conscious experimentation with stanzaic patterns: like the "Sonnet on the Sonnet," written during the same week, it evolves a form of its own that eludes all traditional symmetries. And while the sonnet takes as its theme the pattern-making faculty that gives a poem form, the ode is concerned with the imagination itself, the visionary faculty that provides its substance. Keats had been reading Apuleius's story of Cupid and Psyche in an Elizabethan translation of *The Golden Asse,* a tale of young love set in a magic palace in an enchanted valley, which blended with the images of spring outside his window, the

> hush'd, cool-rooted flowers, fragrant-eyed,
> Blue, silver-white, and budded Tyrian, . . .

the actual flowers he loved and the human beauty they inevitably suggested. But Psyche, he knew, was also the goddess of the soul in late classical legend, who had been deified too late to receive her proper worship in antiquity. As Keats mused over her story, she became the figure "of all Olympus' faded hierarchy" who held most meaning for the modern world, in which nature was no longer god-haunted. The sacred region was now, as Wordsworth had seen, the mind of man, and the poet its self-appointed priest; Psyche, as a woman who had had to submit to the trials of "a world of Circumstances" before her own soul was formed, was its tutelary goddess.[13] Only a few days earlier Keats had sketched out his own system of salvation in his theory of soul-making; now in this ode he described the ritual of his worship of the imagination. From the opening vision of the two legendary lovers asleep in a forest, the poem circles away to an imaginary woodland altar where Psyche is worshipped as a goddess in a sacred grove which is in fact the poet's own "working brain," which Keats touched in with a skilful suggestion of the physiology of the brain recalled from his days at Guy's.[14] The last few lines, while returning to the legend, bring the poem back to the here and now:

> And there shall be for thee all soft delight
> That shadowy thought can win,
> A bright torch, and a casement ope at night,
> To let the warm Love in!

Out of the meetings of these lovers in the dark mysterious palace, Keats has evoked a lighted window seen from a garden outside— no part of Apuleius's story—and his own longing to enter it. For a brief moment the joys of reality and imagination strike a balance: perhaps because his happiness still lay in a future of anticipated delight.

Keats copied the "Ode to Psyche" out in his journal just before closing it on May 3 and hurrying off to Walthamstow to collect his sister's letter to George. One of Birkbeck's sons was leaving for Illinois shortly and would carry their letters direct. As he jumbled the sheets together, Keats's eye was evidently caught by his description of the daydream he had had one lazy morning in March. "Neither Poetry, nor Ambition, nor Love have any alertness of countenance as they pass by me," he had written; "they seem rather like three figures on a greek vase—a Man and two women —whom no one but myself could distinguish in their disguisement." The image struck him as he looked at it again, and he tried working it out in another ode. The result, the "Ode on Indolence," [15] was not a success. His original idea had cooled for almost two months and could no longer give vital shape to the poem [16] or significance to the allegorical figures, who merely appear and reappear in a vain effort to rouse him from his daydreaming; and the conclusion, in which he dismisses Love and Poetry as well as Ambition, seems to ring false to his change of mood in the interval. Still the image haunted him, and he tried working it into another poem. When the vision first came to him in March, the immobility of the three figures had seemed a kind of reproach, an image of the paralysis which had overtaken the three central impulses of his life; in the first ode he tried, he was still separated from the figures—now slowly moving, but with averted glance— by his own determined indolence. Now, in the "Ode on a Grecian Urn," they are quickened into new life as Keats the perceiver becomes one with the thing perceived. As he questions the figures on the urn and seeks to enter into their existence, allegory becomes symbol and the vase takes on a meaning of its own—the relation between the imagination and its creations, the illusions and realities of art and life together.

The ode begins with a topic which Keats had debated many times at Hunt's and Haydon's, the contrast between the visual arts and poetry. In one of his most extraordinary metaphors— "Thou still unravish'd bride of quietness"—Keats invokes not only the immortal freshness of all great art, but also the enigmatic silence of the urn, which still can tell its tale "more sweetly than our rhyme," and the serenity it preserves amid the scene of Bacchic frenzy it depicts. These antinomies at once suggest another paradoxical aspect of pictorial art, its representation of movement through action arrested at its most dynamic moment. As the bride of quietness reaches the fullness of her beauty while "still unravish'd," the bold lover is most passionate while "winning near the goal." At first the poet finds the unenacted desire of the youth on the urn an incompletion, for which he must console him:

> do not grieve;
> She cannot fade, though thou hast not thy bliss,
> For ever wilt thou love, and she be fair!

Immediately he realizes that by this very arrest of impulse the lovers achieve a perfect bliss, "All breathing human passion far above," which escapes the satiety implicit in all fulfilment. Yet even this unchanging perfection of art—that of the unwearied melodist "for ever piping songs for ever new"—is realized, paradoxically, for only a brief moment. In the fourth stanza, as the poet turns to another scene, the eternity becomes a desolation. As his wondering imagination follows the procession to the woodland altar, it suddenly calls up the town they have forever deserted, its streets forever silent; the beauty immortalized at one point now

implies an emptiness perpetuated at some other. At the farthest
limits of this timeless world of art—that

> little town by river or sea shore,
> Or mountain-built with peaceful citadel, . . .

which is not even represented on the urn [17]—his enraptured contemplation is suddenly chilled by this discovery of the antinomies
of experience. The timeless perfection of art, he now sees, contains
its own imperfection, its immortality is in fact lifelessness—just
as truly as the converse that joy may be won in the world of time
only at the cost of the sorrow which time also brings in its revolu-
tions. With this insight, the illusion of the urn's vital existence
begins to collapse. The vase is only a vase, he remembers at last
—a shape, an attitude, a form empty of meaning till the imagination fills it; and the human imagination cannot rest even in a
dream of endless bliss. But at this moment, as he turns wearily
back to the world of time, the urn breaks its silence with a message
of consolation for him:

> Beauty is Truth,—Truth Beauty,—that is all
> Ye know on earth, and all ye need to know.*

With this dramatic reversal of the dialogue, the illusory nature
of the poet's own quest is finally revealed. He began by seeking in
the world of art that perfect happiness and unshadowed beauty
which Keats had long before rejected as a goal of life; and in exploring this world he finds in the end the joy and sorrow, the
"light and shade" together that make up the world of actual experience. So at last he is ready to hear the enigmatic message of the
urn and understand it for the first time. The imaginary world of
art and the real world of experience, which he tried at first to dis-
join, are in fact complementary and necessary to each other, for
each serves to reveal the value of the other. If the real or "true"
world is viewed as intensely and disinterestedly as the poet contemplates the imaginary world of the urn, it yields up its own
beauty; if the beauty of art is searched to the very depths of speculation, truth will be found there. The true beauty is not the merely
beautiful beauty of "an endless bliss," but the difficult beauty of
light and shade; so also the truth that this is "a World of Pains

---

* Following Keats's original punctuation, as given in all four contemporary
transcripts (see Alvin Whitley, "The Message of the Grecian Urn," *Keats-Shelley
Memorial Bulletin*, V [1953], 1–3).

and troubles" becomes beautiful when it is recognized as not merely necessary but desirable, as the truth that this world is also a "vale of Soul-making." So the urn's message is not, as it has often been called, a meaningless tautology, or, at best, a needless appendage to the poem, but rather its dramatic fulfilment and reason for being, a glimpse of the "knowledge enormous" which made the young Apollo a god of poetry, the wisdom of Keats's own widest experience of life.

The "Ode on a Grecian Urn" seems to have been written at that precarious moment of fulfilment conveyed through its own images of the bride, the lover, the melodist. The mood could not last: in the two remaining odes the shade overbalances the light. From the very beginning of May, Keats knew that he must start "buffeting it" again in another month; in the middle of May he received a poignant reminder of all the contingent world outside the garden of Wentworth Place. On May 13 the letter from America for which he had been waiting ever since December arrived at last. It contained unexpected news—only "tolerably" good. George and Georgiana, far gone in her pregnancy, had reached the end of their long and fatiguing journey by horse and wagon as far as Pittsburgh, then by boat down the Ohio to Henderson, Kentucky.[18] What troubled Keats was George's decision not to take a farm in Birkbeck's colony but to put his money into a Mississippi steamboat. George had great hopes for a quick return on his investment; but Keats, with his habit of "suspecting everybody," had misgivings about the backwoods *entrepreneur* and itinerant painter who had talked George into the plan—one John James Audubon. He took the letter to Mrs. Wylie and tried to put his doubts out of his mind, but the clouds of circumstance were beginning to gather again.

The garden at Wentworth Place was still enchanted, however; a pair of nightingales had built their nest there, and the May nights were flooded with music. One morning after breakfast Keats took his chair out into the garden and sat writing under the plum tree for two or three hours. When he returned to the house Brown noticed him thrusting several sheets of note paper among his books and asked to see what he had written. It was another ode, "To a Nightingale," written in a flow of song as sustained and almost as unfaltering as the nightingale's itself.[19] The poem has often been contrasted with the "Ode on a Grecian Urn," but the similarities are more significant. In each the poet attempts to escape the limitations of actuality by projecting himself into an essence outside him, the nightingale's song or the scenes on the urn; but at the farthest limit of this imaginary world he meets a reminder of the unhappiness he is trying to forget; the spell of identification is broken, and he returns to reality again. At last he realizes that the joy he seems to find in this other world is the product of his own imaginative activity: the lovers turn cold as marble, the happy nightingale's song becomes plaintive. This turning point is marked in each poem by a poignant image of desolation—the empty-streeted town, Ruth standing in tears "amid the alien corn," or the

> magic casements, opening on the foam
> Of perilous seas, in faery lands forlorn.

This last image casts a spell. It calls up one of Keats's favourite paintings, "The Enchanted Castle" of Claude Lorrain, which he had described in his "Epistle to Reynolds" in the spring of 1818; and the view of Windermere from Wordsworth's study window that summer—a sight which moved Keats so deeply that twice afterward he described his idea of perfect happiness as reading in a window looking out on a lake.[20] Behind this image loom two others—the lake and island of his first poem, and Keats himself sunk in the window-seat of his medical-school lodgings, staring moodily out into space. And if we note that "forlorn" means primarily "abandoned" or "lonely," and that Keats first described the seas not as "perilous" but as "keelless," [21] empty or unexplored, we catch another glimpse of Keats standing alone on the cliffs at Margate, gazing out over the ocean with the sense of embarking on a voyage of discovery. The sea has taken on many meanings for Keats in the three years since that summer, however; now, as it reappears in this frame of desolation and unreality, it suggests in the faintest of overtones that his quest may prove an illusion in the end.

In the "Ode on a Grecian Urn" for a brief moment the worlds of permanence and change were reconciled, the lifeless immortality of art balanced against the transitoriness of realized love; in the "Ode to a Nightingale" the balance is tipped. Beyond the knowledge that love and beauty must pass lies the awareness that they give way to misery insurmountable by joy:

> Where youth grows pale, and spectre-thin, and dies;
>> Where but to think is to be full of sorrow
>> And leaden-eyed despairs,
> Where Beauty cannot keep her lustrous eyes,
>> Or new Love pine at them beyond to-morrow.

This ode is an effort not so much to reach a new awareness as to escape from awareness itself—a struggle inevitably doomed, as the very movement of Keats's stanzas seems to suggest.[22] For a moment the poet loses himself in the tranced beauty of the May night; then, as he realizes his own happiness, he longs for death at such a moment—an annulment of consciousness at a time when he would not be aware of it. But life exacts consciousness. Though the nightingale is hailed as deathless—immortal in the sense that its song recurs unchanged from generation to generation—its immortality, like that of the figures on the urn, is won at a price, not of life but of full human awareness. By imagination man can escape momentarily the burden of self-awareness; yet the same imagination causes him to look too far into the sea, as Keats had written Reynolds the year before:

> It is a flaw
> In happiness to see beyond our bourn—
> It forces us in Summer skies to mourn:
> It spoils the singing of the Nightingale.

The nightingale has no imagination, no individuality, and is doubtless happier for it; but, when pushed to the point, man would no sooner give up awareness or identity than life itself—nor, indeed, can he as long as he lives. So the poem returns to the real scene at the end, the meadows, the stream, the hillside; the poet comes to himself with a familiar sense of the unreality of his musings.

> Was it a vision, or a waking dream?
> Fled is that music:—Do I wake or sleep?

With the end of his flight, no such insight remains as at the end of the "Ode on a Grecian Urn"; only the weariness, the fever and the fret, to be faced once more.

For May was fast slipping by, and June would bring decisions to be made and acted on. The weather itself, so perfect earlier in the month, began to cloud over, and Keats had to put off a long-promised visit to Walthamstow for three weeks. His cash was too low for coach-hire, as he explained to Fanny, and he was unwilling to risk being caught in the rain by walking across the fields. These two hints of his recurrent worries about his health and his dwindling finances suggest the reason for an otherwise incomprehensible plan he began considering near the end of May. As he broached it to his sister, he was afraid he would be "forced to take a voyage or two" at the end of the summer, to take a post as ship's surgeon on an Indiaman or a South Sea whaler, or even to emigrate to South America. These are such extraordinary answers to the question of where he might live after leaving Wentworth Place that one cannot help wondering whether he consulted a doctor at this time about his troublesome sore throat and was advised to move to a warm climate for a while to shake it off. It was a choice of poisons, as he put it, even though the idea of becoming a ship's surgeon, which struck him as less appalling than the other, would have been a strange fulfilment of his two youthful ambitions. He could not agree to the suggestion, wherever it came from. The thought of leaving Fanny Brawne for such a length of time was evidently too much to face; but what could he do? The world was taking on "a quakerish look," he admitted—light and shade confounded in a landscape of greys.

This mood of dejected indecision underlies the ode—apparently the last of the five he wrote this spring—"On Melancholy." [23] An epitaph to the month of May, it carries the meditation of the two preceding odes to its ultimate conclusion. Beyond the awareness that all joy passes, and that life brings sorrow insurmountable by joy, this ode explores the thought not only that joy and sorrow are inextricable, but that the deepest joys hold the deepest sorrows. Where the "Grecian Urn" and the "Nightingale" odes recorded an attempt to transcend the world of circumstances, the "Ode on Melancholy" starts by condemning this attempt and turns to meet the consciousness of light and shade full-face, even to advance toward it. Only the melancholy man can fully savour the most poignant beauty—the morning rose, the rainbow in the breaking wave, the flash of anger in his mistress's eyes—because he alone realizes, in the very moment of seizing this beauty, that its perfection is "but a little moment." Melancholy is not only the result but the condition of the greatest intensity of experience:

> She dwells with Beauty—Beauty that must die;
> And Joy, whose hand is ever at his lips

> Bidding adieu; and aching Pleasure nigh,
>   Turning to poison while the bee-mouth sips. . . .

The honey of life, it seems, was turning bitter for Keats. It is easy
to guess that his longing for Fanny Brawne, so close and still ultimately denied to him by the confines of circumstance, had become unbearable after a month.

> Ay, in the very temple of Delight
>   Veil'd Melancholy has her sovran shrine,
>     Though seen of none save him whose strenuous tongue
> Can burst Joy's grape against his palate fine;
>   His soul shall taste the sadness of her might,
>     And be among her cloudy trophies hung.

Joy's grape—the sour-sweet fruit—is the final taste of life and the
conclusive image of the odes: a poignant beauty achieved through
a palpable act of possession, in which taste and touch, the most
intimate of the means of sensuous discovery, unite in the final
conquest. Yet at this moment of symbolic achievement the flush
of exultation chills, and the poet finds himself face to face with a
mysterious veiled figure waiting at the center of his experience.
Like the young Apollo at Mnemosyne's approach, he does not
recognize her at first; he knows only that there is "purport in her
looks for him," of a revelation still to come, some final experience
of her might. And so the odes, like the month which produced
them, end on a note of troubled foreboding.

⋙⋘

On May 30 Keats began to prepare for leaving Wentworth Place
by sorting out books to be returned and burning old letters. Here
he turned up a forgotten bundle from the Jeffrey sisters in Teignmouth, their last letter unanswered since Tom's death. At once
Devon occurred to him as the alternative he was desperately
searching for, a mild climate in which he might give himself one
more chance to finish *Hyperion*. The next day he wrote to Sarah
Jeffrey, asking her to inquire for cheap lodgings in some nearby
village. After a painful apology for not sending her any news since
last autumn, he inquired politely after Marianne (who was now
married) and described the alternatives before him—serving as
ship's surgeon or "leading a fevrous life alone with Poetry." Be-

tween the two, he told her, "I would rather conquer my indolence and strain my nerves at some grand Poem—than be in a dunderheaded indiaman." Yet it was a question not of preference but necessity—the inescapable need to start earning his living by one means or another. "My Brother George always stood between me and any dealings with the world," he explained. "Now I find I must buffet it—I must take my stand upon some vantage ground and begin to fight—I must choose between despair & Energy—I choose the latter."

Sarah answered at once, arguing against the Indiaman and suggesting Bradley as a pleasant and inexpensive place to stay. But almost as suddenly as he had thought of Devon, Keats changed his mind. The memory of Tom which it stirred up was still too painful; and perhaps the very friendliness of Sarah's reply posed another problem. A lucky chance brought him a good excuse a few days later, when James Rice came out to Hampstead for a visit. Though they had seen little of each other all the previous year, Keats found Rice as droll and sensible as ever, despite his usual poor health. So when he suggested they spend part of the summer together on the Isle of Wight, Keats immediately agreed. He not only liked but admired Rice, who he knew had been extremely generous in helping Reynolds get started in the law, and whose fair-minded judgment on Bailey's engagement Keats had valued highly in forming his own. Rice assured him that Shanklin would fit their purses, and it struck Keats as just the thing for the present—and perhaps for next winter too. On June 9 he wrote Sarah Jeffrey again, explaining his change of mind with the candour which, whether he knew it or not, was his best defence against any charge of fickleness. By now he had given up the idea of the Indiaman; yet he insisted on defending it to her as a good one. Rather than deaden his abilities, as she feared, he thought it would strengthen them: "To be thrown among people who care not for you, with whom you have no sympathies forces the Mind upon its own resources, and leaves it free to make its speculations of the differences of human character and to class them with the calmness of a Botanist." England has produced the greatest writers in the world, he argued, because it has ill-treated them rather than honouring them while they were alive. Look at Ben Jonson, a common soldier in the Low Countries, who fought and killed a French trooper in single combat; look at Shakespeare, "a miserable and mighty Poet of the human Heart," whose own life was clouded over as much as Hamlet's. Yet once he stated his belief, Keats felt obliged to contradict it: "For all this I will not go on board an Indiaman, nor for examples sake run my head into dark alleys: I dare say my discipline is to come, and plenty of it too."

It came sooner than he expected. On settling his accounts with Brown the next week, Keats found he had run out of cash. On the sixteenth he went into town to ask Abbey for money for his trip to Shanklin. His guardian greeted him with two letters. One, from George, announced at last the birth of his child, a little girl; the other, from their aunt, Mrs. Midgley Jennings, notified them that she was filing a claim in Chancery against a disputed share in their grandfather's estate. The thin trickle of money that had been drying up for six months was now stopped at the source—or so Abbey maintained. So long as the suit was pending, he said, Keats could not touch even the small sum left from his own inheritance, and even if Mrs. Jennings lost her action there would be heavy legal expenses to pay. Here again it seems that Abbey was playing on Keats's ignorance of money matters for his own private reasons.[24] But by the time he reached Hampstead that evening, Keats had decided there was only one thing he could do: give up his summer plans and look for an apothecary's position at once.

At this news, Brown exploded. It was folly to give up now, he argued, with three long poems on hand that would fill up more than half a volume: *Isabella, The Eve of St. Agnes,* and *The Eve of St. Mark* if he would finish it. Keats should drop *Hyperion* for a while and work up a volume to catch the public's fancy, and Brown would lend him some money to help him through the summer. Keats was reluctant, for he had decided months ago not to publish anything till it could be above even the *Quarterly*'s criticism; yet at another suggestion of Brown's, it seems, he caught fire. Brown had been reading Burton's *Anatomy of Melancholy,* a seventeenth-century miscellany of psychology, classical lore, and curious anecdote, perhaps with an eye for plots for his own satirical fairy tales. Evidently he pointed out several of these anecdotes to Keats on which he might base another verse narrative to round off his volume.[25] One immediately caught Keats's eye—the story of a young Greek philosopher named Lycius, who falls in love with a lamia, or vampire, who has taken the form of a beautiful woman and vanishes on their wedding day with her beautiful house, wedding feast and all, when his master, the philosopher Apollonius, penetrates her disguise. A strange tale, and likely to give the public the "sensation of some sort" which Keats was aiming at; strangely reminiscent, too, of the mysterious beauty who has appeared and disappeared in so many of his earlier poems.

The next day he wrote a number of friends to try to collect on his loans, as now seemed absolutely necessary—reluctantly including Haydon, who still owed him thirty pounds from December. "My purpose is now to make one more attempt in the Press," he announced; "if that fail, 'ye hear no more of me' as Chaucer says." A tactful misquotation: Chaucer had actually said, "Ye gete no more of me." He followed these with a letter to his sister telling her of his plan and regretting there would be no time for another visit before he left. But almost at once he postponed his departure with Rice, for Brown came up with a still better scheme. He proposed that he and Keats write a tragedy together, aimed at a Drury Lane production in the fall with Kean in the lead. He would provide the plot, and Keats would turn it into poetry. With one successful play to his credit, Brown could feel confident about another, and apparently it did not take much to persuade Keats. His old dream of making his "chief Attempt in the Drama" sprang to life again. If the play succeeded, it would send his new volume off to a flying start. Still, Keats was sober enough to realize that the reputation of his poems might spoil the play's chances, and he insisted that his part in it be kept a secret till after it was produced. For their subject they hit on the reign of Otto the Great, first of the Holy Roman Emperors and the scourge of the Hungarians, a period of history remote enough to give Keats full scope in a Shakespearian style. At once they set to work. Brown began sketching a plot of disguises and machinations and tragic misunderstandings, and Keats stayed on in Hampstead another week to wrestle over the scenario of the first act. They agreed that Brown would join Keats at Shanklin at the end of July, when Rice left, and they would continue the play together.

This plan to take both Drury Lane and Fleet Street by storm seems like a hopeless gamble, but Keats undertook it with remarkable coolness. It would demand the utmost of his energy and ability; yet of all the ways in which he might pull himself out of his financial difficulties, this was the one best suited to his talents. But there was far more to his decision than this. In finally giving up the plan of the Indiaman, whatever its recommendations, he appears also to have decided he could not separate himself so completely from Fanny Brawne. All through May they seem to have grown closer together; and now in June the prospect of his leaving Wentworth Place had evidently brought them at last to the point of discussing marriage. An engagement was still out of the question, for his situation needed to improve dramatically before Mrs. Brawne would give her consent. One can only wonder whether Keats sensed that Fanny herself was not yet ready for a binding commitment, or whether he, in the very intensity of his longing for her, hesitated at the idea of a long engagement. Their promises to each other were conditional: everything was staked on the summer. For him to win Fanny in the end, Keats realized, he must make a success of the new volume; and for that he must find the kind of solitude he always needed to work on a long poem, even if it meant exile from Fanny for the time being.

It was a difficult decision to make, and difficult to explain to Fanny herself. Both his pride and his love for her were involved. He felt he must warn her against "the unpromising morning" of his life; yet he wanted to offer her something better than the life of a small suburban doctor. "Do understand me, my love, in this," he wrote her from Shanklin a few weeks later. "I have so much of you in my heart that I must turn Mentor when I see a chance of harm beffaling you. I would never see any thing but Pleasure in your eyes, love on your lips, and Happiness in your steps. I would wish to see you among those amusements suitable to your inclinations and spirits; so that our loves might be a delight in the midst of Pleasures agreeable enough, rather than a resource from vexations and cares." It is a young man's dream of married love, perhaps, now joined to his earlier dream of a life of poetry and travel. "We might spend a pleasant Year at Berne or Zurich—if it should please Venus to hear my 'Beseech thee to hear us O Goddess.' " But he knew well enough what the odds against it were, and a day or two before he left Hampstead he discussed them soberly with her. He would not return to London, he told her, "if my Fate does not turn up Pam or at least a Court-card." In these circumstances she must continue with her usual life in Hampstead; for himself, he would "live upon hope and Chance."

*Chapter Eleven*

>>> ———————————————————————————————————— <<<

# Between Despair and Energy

O N a chilly Sunday, June 27, Keats left for the Isle of Wight at
last. The day-long trip to Portsmouth was marked only by
two small incidents, each in its way prophetic. His fellow passengers included some down-at-the-heel French refugees, one of them
a woman, all courtly in their manner, despite their poor clothes.
Once, when they climbed down from the coach to walk uphill, one
of the Frenchmen picked a rose and gave it to the woman with a
flourish—"Mam'selle, voilà une belle rose!" Keats was amused at
the gesture of this ragged exile, "more gallant than ever I saw
gentleman to Lady at a Ball," as he told his sister; and his amusement was tinged with a curious detachment. The second incident
was a heavy shower of rain. Riding outside as usual, he caught cold
again and arrived in Portsmouth with another sore throat, which
was to hang on for the next two months.

The Isle of Wight was not as enchanting as he remembered it
from the spring of 1817. Shanklin, the little fishing village over-
hanging the Chine, was now crowded with summer visitors; the
hills behind it looked tame after the crags of Scotland. But the
sandy beach below promised fine swimming, and beyond it the
coast stretched for miles of walks along the rocks. He and Rice
found a cottage in the village with a glimpse of the sea over the
other rooftops. "We have Hill and Dale forest and Mead and
plenty of Lobsters," Keats wrote his sister a few days later. Here,
it seems, were the makings of a good summer. But Tuesday evening, the second night after his arrival, he was seized with such
loneliness on going up to his narrow room that he could not keep

from pouring out his feelings in a letter to Fanny Brawne which, he realized the next day, was too Rousseau-ish to send. On Thursday, July 1, he wrote her again in a more balanced mood, and with this, the first of Keats's letters to Fanny that has survived, the drama of their love affair emerges into our full gaze at last. "The morning," he said, "is the only proper time for me to write to a beautiful Girl whom I love so much: for at night, then believe me my passion gets entirely the sway, then I would not have you see those Rapsodies which I once thought it impossible I should ever give way to, and which I have often laughed at in another, for fear you should [think me] either too unhappy or perhaps a little mad." He begged her to send him a letter immediately. "Make it rich as a draught of poppies to intoxicate me—write the softest words and kiss them that I may at least touch my lips where yours have been." He was falling into another rhapsody: he immediately checked himself by reminding her of the task he must accomplish before returning to London. Yet for all his love and resolution, he could not keep a note of jealousy from creeping in at the end of his letter. Though he was trying to be as unselfish as he could about Fanny's happiness, the thought of a possible rival kept haunting him. "In case of the worst that can happen, I shall still love you," he told her—"but what hatred shall I have for another!"

In hope or despair, the thought of Fanny was a torment; only by plunging into work could he forget her and begin to resolve his dilemma. "When I am inclined I can do a great deal in a day," Keats once remarked to his sister; and the next ten days were probably the most concentrated working days of his life. By July 11 he had finished both the first act of *Otho* and the first part of *Lamia*—almost nine hundred lines.[1] When he first sat down to work, it struck him as odd that he was writing for money and not out of the sheer superabundance of poetry within him. But, as he wrote to Reynolds, "The very corn which is now so beautiful, as if it had only took to ripening yesterday, is for the market: So, why sho^d I be delicate?" He was sure he would succeed, too, for he now wrote more deliberately than before, with as much judgment as imagination. He had traded the wings of inspiration for "a pair of patient sublunary legs."

Yet from the beginning circumstances seemed to be against him. Mists drifted in from the sea and stayed bottled up in their valley for days; the air became stifling. His sore throat kept him from swimming and tethered him to a few miles' walk along the coast. Then, though he struggled against it, he began to find Rice a melancholy companion. Whatever Rice's chronic illness was— probably an arrested case of tuberculosis—he had always appeared to be surmounting it cheerfully; but now, living at close quarters with him, Keats realized how much of his humour was a cour- ageous bluff. On July 6 disturbing news came from George. His partner wanted him to put still more money into the steamboat venture, for which he must sell what remained of his holdings. With the Chancery suit pending, this posed difficulties. Keats immediately despatched letters to his stockbroker and to Abbey and Sandell, his other guardian, in Holland, asking for power of attorney,[2] then wrote George as reassuring a reply as he could. George, it appears, was reproaching himself for his failure to make both their fortunes at once. So Keats reminded him that if worse came to worst he would always turn apothecary again. It was a cheerless prospect, but, as he said, he had "spent too many thought- ful days & moralized thro' too many nights" to let it dishearten him. Of course he would not mention his own thoughts of mar- riage to George; better let him think the only stakes he was playing for were books, travel, and the leisure to write. And, for the time being, his hopes were high.

The mails were slow at Shanklin, and Fanny Brawne's answer to his first letter did not reach him till the following Thursday, July 8. At once his passion flared up again. "All my thoughts," he wrote immediately in reply, "my unhappiest days and nights have I find not at all cured me of my love of Beauty, but made it so intense that I am miserable that you are not with me: or rather breathe in that dull sort of patience that cannot be called Life." Fanny, like many another young belle, wanted to be loved for something other than her beauty, and had reproached him ac- cordingly; but, he answered, how else could he have loved her to begin with? "There may be a sort of love for which, without the least sneer at it, I have the highest respect, and can admire it in others: but it has not the richness, the bloom, the full form, the enchantment of love after my own heart." She had also asked him, with a hint of petulance, whether certain "horrid people" would keep him from seeing her again—perhaps Brown, perhaps Abbey —and wondered whether he might think she did not love him because she had agreed to their separation. It was a gambit, and he accepted it with fervour: "In saying this you make me ache the more to be near you," he exclaimed. As for her love for him, he told her, "I love you the more in that I believe you have liked me for my own sake and for nothing else." Keats could have paid her no greater tribute than this. Fanny's love had helped him surmount, for the time being at least, the last barrier to self-acceptance —his old doubt that he could ever be loved as a man rather than a poet.

Desire and determination were balanced in this second letter; with his work going well, he could afford to dwell on the thought of his love. Yet in the following week he had to slack off against his will. With the first act finished, *Otho* had to be laid aside till Brown came; and for some reason Keats decided not to go on with *Lamia* for a while. Instead he turned back to the other poems he had brought with him to work up for publication and mulled over them for a few days. But a feverish restlessness soon took hold of him—"an irritable state of health," he called it—which made it difficult to work. His daily contact with Rice was stirring up all the irrational aversion to illness which he had never succeeded in conquering. Then after two short weeks he found he was tired of Shanklin. The cottages covered with honeysuckle and roses seemed like settings for a sentimental opera; even the wild beauty of the Chine was spoiled by the tourists with spyglasses who came "hunting after the picturesque like beagles."

Some of this restlessness comes out in his third letter to Fanny, on July 15, which he wrote, against his own resolution, late in the evening. Her letter the day before hinted she had been ill; he guessed that she missed him and could not help feeling a little glad of it. That night, in a fit of loverlike behaviour, he put her letter under his pillow; in the morning he found the wax had softened, obliterating her seal—a bad omen. Yet even as he laughed at himself he realized it was a bad habit of his "to bode ill like the raven," to suspect everyone and everything. He had been reading a melancholy story from a collection of Oriental tales, curiously like his own "Belle Dame sans Merci," about a beautiful lady who, seen once, vanishes, to leave her lovers disconsolate ever afterward, and he could not help thinking of it as symbolic of his own apprehensive love for Fanny. A sudden desire to see her overwhelmed him. She had been pressing him to visit Hampstead, perhaps for her birthday on August 9, and rashly he suggested he might steal a brief visit sometime within the next month. The thought of London and its "hateful literary chitchat" made him uneasy, but still more did her absence. He begged her to write again at once—"for your letters keep me alive. My sweet Girl I cannot speak my love for you. Good night!"

The next day he shook himself out of this mood by writing a stiff note to Abbey, asking why he had not replied to his letter about George's affairs, then went off for a ramble about the island. On his return, it seems, he picked up not *Lamia* but his long-neglected *Hyperion*. He was growing dissatisfied with the poem as well as uncertain how to continue it. Just as with *Endymion*, it appears, his idea of it was changing even as he wrote: his epic of human progress was beginning to express his intensified aware-ness of the necessity of suffering. Yet with this shift in the meaning of the action, his hero Apollo—who receives the gift of poetry not by actual experience of suffering but through a godlike flash of insight—came to seem no more satisfactory a protagonist than the shadowy Hyperion, who is broken by his knowledge. For a few days Keats evidently pondered whether to go on with his original conception or rewrite the poem completely, as he had once thought of doing with *Endymion*.[3] Then on the twenty-second he was in-terrupted by Brown's arrival with Reynolds' old friend, the jocular Johnny Martin. In their wake came Martin's sister and three of her friends, who took the cottage opposite theirs for a short house-party. Between dining with the young ladies and playing cards with the men far into the night, Keats found no time for work or even a letter to Fanny. Not till Sunday evening, the twenty-fifth, after Rice and the visitors had left for London, did he sit down in his narrow coffin of a room, looking out over the sea, to write her at last.

In his fourth letter, the hidden battle between his longing and his resolution finally broke out into the open. "Forgive me if I wander a little this evening," he began, "for I have been all day employ'd in a very abstract Poem and I am in deep love with you —two things which must excuse me." He was troubled not only by the alien world which had intruded on his solitude but also by her last letter, which had come three or four days before. Fanny, it seems, was pretending not to be convinced by his reasons for go-ing into exile, and reproached him for having taken so long to fall in love with her that winter. Keats could only reply in anguish that he had been the first to fall in love. Evidently she had mentioned that unlucky meeting with Severn, the gay and good-looking, almost a year ago; and though she said that she had admired him more than Severn even then, at once Keats lost faith in what he had begun to believe—that she loved him for his own sake. "I cannot be admired, I am not a thing to be admired," he insisted. "You are, I love you; all I can bring you is a swooning admiration of your Beauty." She had thrown him into a turmoil: "You absorb me in spite of myself—you alone," he burst out: "for I look not forward with any pleasure to what is call'd being settled in the world; I tremble at domestic cares—yet for you I would meet them." His mind seemed to swarm with a thousand anxieties, in which only two thoughts could bring him peace. "I have two luxuries to brood over in my walks, your Loveliness and the hour of my death. O that I could have possession of them both in the same minute." It was getting late, and, as he looked outside his window, a planet was growing bright against the sky. For a moment he was lifted out of himself as he had been on his first view of Windermere. Doubt and distraction left him: it was only beauty, Fanny's and the star's, that mattered. He closed his letter with the farewell: "I will imagine you Venus tonight and pray, pray, pray to your star like a Hethen. Your's ever, fair Star, John Keats."

From this moment a sonnet was born,[4] of a beauty so serene that for a while at least no other thought but poetry could have possessed him:

Bright star! would I were steadfast as thou art—
   Not in lone splendour hung aloft the night
And watching, with eternal lids apart,
   Like nature's patient, sleepless Eremite,
The moving waters at their priestlike task
   Of pure ablution round earth's human shores,
Or gazing on the new soft fallen mask
   Of snow upon the mountains and the moors—
No—yet still steadfast, still unchangeable,
   Pillow'd upon my fair love's ripening breast,
To feel for ever its soft fall and swell,
   Awake for ever in a sweet unrest,
To hear, to feel her tender-taken breath,
Half-passionless, and so swoon on to death.*

---

* Quoting the final version, except for the last two lines, which are left in their original form; see p. 379.

All the conflicts expressed in his letter to Fanny—the passion which absorbed him against his will, the longing to be assured of her love yet untroubled by the anxieties of marriage—are projected and momentarily resolved in the imagery of the sonnet. The contrasts so precariously balanced in the odes—between the timeless but unreal perfection of art and the time-bound realizations of life, between the unselfconscious joy of natural existence and the self-awareness of human experience—are repeated in a key of passionate urgency and pushed toward a synthesis of contradictions, an eternal calm within perfect sensuality, the ideal moment made actual. Knowing his desire was unattainable, yet still driven by it, Keats tried to resolve his dilemma not by finally submitting to the claims of consciousness, as in the odes, but by eluding them in a vision of death at the moment of supreme happiness. Yet metaphorically he did surmount his dilemma in the first half of his sonnet, which creates, in the imagination at least, an eternal joy.

This joy—a timeless disinterested contemplation of a tranquil unconscious beauty—is a state of being for which all his poetry had groped for an adequate symbol. The contemplating conciousness here imaged in the star, the abstract calm of some "superior being" looking down on the vicissitudes of earth, is implicit in all Keats's most searching remarks on poetry—on negative capability, the poetic identity, the ultimate vision in which truth and beauty become one. Again, the object of this contemplation—all the changes of nature which take place apart from human notice—is a special kind of beauty which had preoccupied him from his earliest poems: the blossoming of unseen flowers, the silent leafing of trees, the sweetening of fruit within its own skin, the ebb and flow of tides on deserted shores. The attempt to magically arrest this changing beauty through the self-annihilating intensity of his contemplation is the theme underlying and unifying the odes of May. But each of the odes turns on the dilemma that the human observer is capable only of brief and intermittent moments of self-transcending awareness. Not until this sonnet of July did Keats find an image for this consciousness which fuses it unchangeably with the object of its contemplation. The star looking down on the sea through all time thus becomes his supreme metaphor, the formula of a state of awareness toward which his own life moved by successive stages of "annulling self."

In tracing his steps toward this image, we may note that even in Keats's earliest poetry the heavens are not remote from human affairs but a vast field in which he searches for a lost but benevolent presence. In the Chapman sonnet the new planet embodies the beauty of the unobserved natural identity only to lose it immediately in the astronomer's triumphant discovery of its existence —a discovery so tremendous that his own identity, like that of Cortez staring at the Pacific, is momentarily annihilated. Yet gradually this "speculation of the stars" changes direction: the stars are no longer watched but become the watchers. The mortal who tries to read the "huge cloudy symbols" upon "the night's starr'd face" sees no such wonders as the stars themselves have seen in gazing eternally upon the earth, as Keats describes them—remote yet absorbed, patient or smiling, throbbing with joy or holding their breath in excitement. The image of the stars' unblinking contemplation first occurred to Keats in his letter from Windermere, as a symbol of the poetic insight he hoped to gain on his trip—the refinement of his "sensual vision" into "a sort of north star" watching "open-lidded and stedfast over the wonders of the great Power"; and the "lone splendour" of this vision is what he momentarily found in his sublime solitude when he began *Hyperion*.

But the vision, to be complete, requires its own perfect object. The sea which the star contemplates,

> The moving waters at their priestlike task
> Of pure ablution round earth's human shores. . . .

is the climactic metaphor of the sonnet, the unpremeditated leap across the void which every new metaphor must take. In Keats's earlier descriptions of the sea, there was always Keats himself, the solitary watcher on the cliffs, gazing out at this vast symbol of his own poetic enterprise or, later, of the unfathomable cruelty of life. Now the scene is empty; there is only the sea with the star looking down—the sea-in-itself as nearly as it can be imagined. And yet from this vision beyond all human notice an extraordinary humanity emerges. Keats no longer projects his own thoughts and feelings into the sea; yet he senses a vital interchange between sea and shore as only the star can observe it, along thousands of solitary miles—a relationship which is somehow human, even benevolent, in its priestlike act of purification. "Everything we look upon is blest," Yeats concluded of one of his triumphant moments of insight; but this is the real triumph of the disinterested vision, a universe that does not require the blessing of human awareness for its perfection.

Yet things fall apart as the sonnet moves toward the end. The delicate links by which Keats tried to bind the star and the lover, each in his own rapt contemplation, are snapped in the final plunge toward unconsciousness. His fair love's breast, as white and soft as new-fallen snow, rising and falling like the sea, holds only an illusion of calm. The sonnet in fact implies a turning point in Keats's own direction. He had gone to Shanklin to write a volume of poetry whose success would make it possible for him to marry Fanny Brawne; now he realized he could accomplish this only by somehow stifling his passion for her. "You absorb me in spite of myself!" he had cried in his letter. In the sestet of the sonnet the human observer reappears, and at this the disinterested vision falters. The object it contemplates, the breathing body of the beloved woman, is the one in all the world most inimical to the vision; in the relinquishment which inevitably follows possession, Keats could imagine no return to the sustaining reality of the concrete world such as he found at the end of the odes. His momentary longing in May "to cease upon the midnight with no pain" now seemed the logical completion of his desire. To surrender to his longing for Fanny meant, in imagination at least, turning toward death; rather than succumb to despair, he chose energy.

＞＞＞ ＜＜＜

The day after writing Fanny, Keats was hitched again to the dogcart, as he called *Otho,* with Brown pulling in the lead. Sitting across the table from Keats, Brown gave him a synopsis of each scene as they came to it; then Keats, after some questions, arguments, and wisecracks, turned the outline into verse without knowing what was to follow. Little wonder that the result reads like an improvisation, and hardly an improvisation of genius. Brown's plot is a jumble of mislaid letters, mistaken identities, and characters who never quite come to life—a father who unjustly suspects his son, a lover who mistakenly trusts his mistress, a villain who repents too late. Yet every now and then an authentic feeling flashes through Keats's lines, most often in those he gave to the betrayed lover Ludolph. "The Lover is madder than I am," he told Fanny: "he has a figure like the Statue of Maleager and double distilled fire in his heart." This was the role he was tailoring to Kean, the part which would make or break the play, and as he went on, Keats poured more and more of himself into the character. Many of Ludolph's speeches echo phrases of letters describing his own feelings that summer.[5] His imagination was catching fire, and he completed three more acts in less than three weeks.

Brown was a welcome change of company from Rice. Away from the disquieting presence at Wentworth Place, their friendship was mellowing into a deeply congenial companionship in which Keats came to accept a certain dependence on Brown in much the same way as he had with George; and their common interest in poetry provided a mutual stimulus. Brown, always full of projects, helped Keats begin his study of Italian, in which he himself was proficient, then dragged him out on painting expeditions in the intervals of their work on *Otho*. "The Art of Poetry is not sufficient for us," Keats reported to Dilke after a morning of sketching Shanklin Church, "and if we get on in that as well as we do in painting we shall by next winter crush the Reviews and the royal Academy." Brown was an expert draftsman, and could draw a head as well as a church. To judge from a set of seventy-two miniature portraits copied from Hogarth, now at Wentworth Place, he was a literal copyist. But this is the very reason for valuing so highly the drawing of Keats in profile, brawny fist to cheek, which Brown made this summer *—the closest likeness of all Keats's portraits, far closer than Severn's sentimental miniature. The two men also trudged over the island together as far as Steephill; but whether Keats kept Brown company on other expeditions there is room to wonder. Within a week of arriving in Shanklin, Brown had taken up with a young woman of the town named Jenny Jacobs. "Open daylight! he don't care," Keats remarked dryly to Dilke on July 31. "I am affraid there will be some more feet for little stockings." "Of Keats' making. (I mean the feet.)," Brown put in. The wit was lame enough. But from signs that appear a few weeks later it seems that Brown's roughshod approach to sex was beginning to batter down Keats's hard-won self-restraint.

Eleven days after his passionate and melancholy letter of July

---

* Reproduced as Plate IX.

25, Keats wrote Fanny Brawne again, and his tone was greatly changed. She had answered his letter by saying he must not write any more like the last; he promised to be obstinate and run the other way. "I am not idle enough for proper downright love-letters," he countered. "Thank God for my diligence! were it not for that I should be miserable." He was utterly absorbed by *Otho*, and told her so; he already regretted his promise of a visit some-time in August. "I shall keep it with as much sorrow as gladness," he remarked, "for I am not one of the Paladins of old who livd upon water grass and smiles for years together." These were brutal words to a girl in Fanny's situation, and more is needed to account for them than an intense physical longing constantly aroused and its satisfaction indefinitely postponed. His smouldering jealousy had flared up at a hint in her letter that she had gone to a dance in his absence: "Late hours will do you great harm," he reproved her. "What fairing is it?" But his churlishness may also be a disguised form of self-reproach if, as seems possible, he had already suc-cumbed to Brown's example of self-indulgence. Some mysterious poison was combining with all his other irritations and anxieties to make the very purpose of his summer's labours turn sour in his imagination. To wander through Europe with Fanny, spend a year in Switzerland—this had been his dream of marriage; but now the reality of living in Hampstead began to seem a kind of life im-prisonment. "God forbid we should what people call, *settle*," he exclaimed in his letter, "turn into a pond, a stagnant Lethe—a vile crescent, row or buildings. Open my Mouth at the Street door like the Lion's head at Venice to receive hateful cards Letters messages. Go out and wither at tea parties; freeze at dinners; bake at dances, simmer at routs. No my love, trust yourself to me and I will find you nobler amusements; fortune favouring."

Yet fortune did not seem to be favouring. Brown's funds were running low; Keats had received no answers to the letters he had written in June to collect on his debts. He wrote again, and still no reply—except from Haydon, who refused with such seeming unconcern that Keats angrily concluded that their friendship was ended. All summer he had not risked swimming because of his throat; now he became convinced that the mists of Shanklin were as unhealthy for him as the London smoke. Little things began to irritate him beyond measure—the shrill voice of the old lady across the way, the stolid unchanging face of a neighbouring fisherman, the very names and doorposts of the cottages. When Brown returned from a few days' hike round the island, his presence broke "like a Thunderbolt" on Keats's comfortable solitude. At last he persuaded Brown they should move. They needed to settle some points of history in *Otho,* and Shanklin had no library. So they decided to go to Winchester—Keats's choice, not only for the books but also for the peace of a cathedral town.

The trip back on August 12 was an adventure after six dull weeks at Shanklin. When they took the ferry at Cowes they found that the Regent's yacht had anchored off the mainland opposite, and the entire fleet of the island was sailing out to meet it. Keats was enchanted by the silent gracefulness of the regatta, circling and tacking in every direction. But in the crowded channel they had an accident. As a small naval sloop cut across their bows, the top of its mast was caught in their bowlines and snapped off close by the board—luckily, for if the mast had been stouter the boat would have overturned. "In so trifling an event I could not help admiring our seamen," Keats wrote to Fanny four days later. "Neither Officer nor man in the whole Boat moved a Muscle—they scarcely notic'd it even with words." A trifling event, but one to compare with the incident on his trip down in the Portsmouth coach. There he had been amused by the Frenchmen's gallantry; now he found the Englishmen's imperturbability something to admire. And in the weeks to come the images of his letters show him time after time half-consciously casting himself in the role of a naval officer as he tried to summon up all his resolution for his work.

He liked Winchester at once, with its wide-windowed cathedral and quiet streets filled with old timbered houses: "A respectable, ancient aristocratical place," he described it to George, with "not one loom or any thing like manufacturing beyond bread & butter in the whole City." The capital of England before the Conquest, Winchester echoed with great names of the past—Sir Walter Raleigh, William of Wykeham, William the Conqueror, Alfred the Great, and the still more legendary Arthur. Keats and Brown found lodgings near the cathedral that were entirely satisfactory except for the fiddling of the landlady's son. Keats now had a room large enough to stroll in and a view of "a beautiful—blank side of a house," which for some reason pleased him immensely. On his walks through the city he discovered Winchester College, a Roman Catholic school, a nunnery, a chapel, and, half a mile outside the city gate, the ancient charitable foundation of St. Cross, where bread and ale were still doled out to passers-by. The air blowing across the downs was worth sixpence a pint after Shanklin, he wrote Taylor, and the clear chalk-bedded streams interlacing the meadows were the most beautiful he had ever seen.

After clearing the decks by writing another batch of irksome letters—including a very belated one to Bailey congratulating him awkwardly on his marriage—Keats turned back to *Otho* again. At once he objected that Brown's plans for the fifth act were too melodramatic and insisted on completing the play himself. Within eight or nine days the act was finished. It is hard to imagine how Brown's ending could have been more melodramatic than the one Keats actually wrote; it is still harder to understand why Keats apparently found greater satisfaction in writing the last act of *Otho* than in composing any of his other poems. As he confessed to Bailey, he hoped to "make as great a revolution in modern dramatic writing as Kean has done in acting"; and with each scene he felt more certain he would succeed. Day by day he became more convinced that "fine writing is next to fine doing the top thing in the world." This alone mattered to him now; this was the identity he had achieved. "My own being which I know to be," he wrote Reynolds exultantly the day after finishing *Otho,* "becomes of more consequence to me than the crowds of Shadows in the Shape of Man and women that inhabit a kingdom. The Soul is a world of itself." Yet for once Keats was completely mistaken about his work. *Otho* is a lumbering failure of a play, and in the last act the dramatic machinery breaks down completely. While the other actors stand helplessly by, the mad prince Ludolph plots to kill his faithless bride at his wedding banquet; Auranthe foils his plan by killing herself first, and he dies broken-hearted. All Keats's poetry could not redeem the hysteria of this ending, which provides an alarming clue to his own state of mind at the time.

On August 16, a day or two after starting the last act, Keats had written Fanny Brawne again. She had evidently answered his previous letter at once and in some pique, denying that she wanted to force him to a visit and telling him he could do as he pleased. To his question about her late hours, she apparently replied that she had attended a ball given by the Royal Artillery Mess at Woolwich—one of the most popular parties of the London summer season.[6] With the shock of this news, Keats could not bring himself to answer her letter for four or five days. When at last he did, a familiar numbness had settled down over his feelings, like a fog from the sea. She appeared to him now through a mist, he wrote, growing strangely unreal to him as he became more absorbed in the imaginary world of *Otho*. He refused to return to Hampstead now. "I would feign, as my sails are set, sail on without an interruption for a Brace of Months longer," he explained; "I am in complete cue—in the fever; and shall in these four months do an immense deal." Moreover, he retorted, he could not do what he pleased, for he was living on borrowed money. All this was most unloverlike and ungallant, but he could not help it: "I am no officer in yawning quarters; no Parson-romeo. My heart seems now made of iron. I can no more use soothing words to you than if I were at this moment engaged in a charge of Cavalry." It was a flint-worded letter, he admitted, and he begged her to forgive him. "Even as I leave off—it seems to me that a few more moments thought of you would uncrystallize and dissolve me—I must not give way to it—but turn to my writing again—if I fail I shall die hard." And with this, his correspondence with Fanny apparently broke off for four long weeks.*

"My heart seems now made of iron": so Ludolph makes his tongue "iron-stern" to denounce Auranthe, and so Keats now steeled himself against Fanny Brawne. Driven to choose between love and ambition, he flung himself into his work with all the intensity of his passion. "I look upon fine Phrases like a Lover," he confessed to Bailey on starting the last act of *Otho,* and on finishing it he told Reynolds that "Poetry is all I care for, all I live for." It is an extraordinary reversal, and cannot be explained simply by the fact that his longing for Fanny had become an unbearable distraction from a task which required all his energies. The stresses of their separation were bringing out all Fanny's wilfulness and all Keats's still unresolved ambivalence toward women. Probably Brown also helped to persuade Keats that, as he wrote not long afterward, "A Man in love cuts the sorryest figure in the world,"

---

* This break may well be apparent and not real, however, for there is no indication of a long silence between them in Keats's next letter to Fanny in mid-September. In reading these love letters it must be realized that the series is certainly incomplete, for around 1878 Sir Charles Dilke (Dilke's grandson) bought the letters from Fanny's son and burned a number of them (*More Letters and Papers of the Keats Circle,* ed. H. E. Rollins [1958], p. 102 n. 2)—presumably the most angry and passionate ones.

as well as convincing him that he was not one to live "upon water grass and smiles for years together." After a month in Brown's company, Keats began to describe his summer's work as fagging "to buy Pleasure"—a significant phrase, which he used twice again before the summer was over.[7] Yet degrading love in his mind to a pleasure to be bought and sold also degraded his poetry to the coin with which to buy it. So even as he became convinced that his work would win a popular success, Keats found himself filled with contempt for the reading public. Writing to Taylor on the day he finished *Otho*, he exploded: "I equally dislike the favour of the public with the love of a woman—they are both a cloying treacle to the wings of independence." It was a hateful situation to be caught in, and he confessed he was "a man fill'd with hatreds." But, he insisted, "this Pride and egotism will enable me to write finer things than any thing else could."

Keats himself realized this hatred was irrational and begged Taylor to forgive him "for hammering instead of writing." But he was gripped by forces he could not understand. In view of the extraordinary satisfaction he found in writing the last act of *Otho*, one wonders how much he unconsciously felt the killing of Auranthe as a symbolic revenge on Fanny Brawne. Yet it seems clear that this emotional disturbance had a physical cause as well: the silent spread of disease within him. Phrase after phrase in his letters this summer suggests his symptoms: the fever of his excitement about *Otho*, the ache of his longing for Fanny, the hammering of his quickened pulse, the taste of poison in his mouth, the giddy rise and fall of his emotions, with boundless confidence in his work followed by irritability and depression once he put it down. A year later Keats became convinced that "the too great excitement" of his writing had undermined his constitution. Rather it seems that his amazing productivity this summer was fueled by the low-burning fever of early tuberculosis, which often has the effect of heightening ambition, intensifying sensation, and releasing subconscious creative processes. Perhaps Keats was describing literally his own fevered perceptions in Ludolph's ravings at his bright-lit banquet in *Otho*:

> This is darkness,—when I close
> These lids, I see far fiercer brilliances,—
> Skies full of splendid moons, and shooting stars,
> And spouting exhalations, diamond fires,

And panting fountains quivering with deep glows!
Yes—this is dark—is it not dark?

As he told Reynolds near the end of August, his whole life had become "a history of sensations, and day-night mares."

It was in a mood of feverish optimism that Keats finished *Otho*
and then, swept along by his own elation, decided to write another
tragedy. Brown had been reading an account of the reign of
Stephen, the hapless grandson of William the Conqueror, and was
struck by its dramatic possibilities. He was starting to sketch a
scenario when Keats stopped him: this play he would write for
himself. He saw at once that Stephen would make a superb part
for Kean, even better than the hysterical Ludolph—a role combining the energy of Richard III with the eloquence of Richard II.
In three days he completed three scenes.[8] They make a brilliant
beginning, full of bold strokes of character and powerful verse;
Keats, it seems, had already far outdistanced Brown in dramatic
construction. But on August 27 or 28 they heard news that threatened to cancel half the summer's work in a single stroke: Kean was
planning to leave Drury Lane for a winter's tour of America. No
other actor in England, Keats was convinced, could play the part
of Ludolph; their work was thrown away. Brown, the practical,
suggested sending the play in to Covent Garden; but Keats thought
the Covent Garden company "ranting, coxcombical, tasteless" and
was sure that *Otho* would be damned if put on there. It was useless to go on with *King Stephen;* everything, he realized, now depended on the volume of poetry which he had neglected for over
a month. And time was running out, as well as money. Keats had
sent Taylor a bombastic letter the week before, asking for a loan
on his expectations of *Otho,* but no reply came. Suddenly sobered,
he despatched another request in a more level-headed vein and
turned resolutely back to *Lamia.*

In the second book of *Lamia,* Keats displayed the most remarkable poetic stamina of the whole remarkable summer. He
completed it in about six days against staggering odds of ill health,
worry, and discouragement, and in it he accomplished two miracles—transmuting history into poetry and magic into reality.
From a musty volume of Greek archaeology [9] he brought ancient
Corinth to life again in all its sounds and smells, its perfumed
temples and crowded colonnades, its banquets and garlands and
torches and the shuffling of sandals over its marble pavements in

the cool hours of night. At the same time he turned Burton's tale of demonic influence into a drama of love and disenchantment that poses a riddling allegory of sexual passion. Is love a fatal illusion or a vital reality without which we cannot live? The question is left unanswered in the poem, perhaps because Keats intended the riddle as part of his poetic effect, perhaps because in his own mind he found no answer. The question is, in fact, the dilemma which he had tried all summer to solve—his longing for Fanny Brawne and his struggle to escape.

The extent to which *Lamia* reflects Keats's own predicament becomes clear in his additions to Burton's story. Keats made the philosopher Apollonius not merely one of the wedding guests, as in Burton, but Lycius's friend and teacher. In Keats's poem it is not Lamia herself but Lycius who tries to silence Apollonius, and —most significant of all Keats's changes—dies when Lamia vanishes. Lycius is caught, in fact, between the perilous enchantment of Lamia and the inhuman rationalism of Apollonius, just as Keats was torn between Fanny's beauty and Brown's cynicism.[10] But then is Lycius's death the result of heeding Apollonius's wisdom or of denying it? of loving Lamia or of losing her? Or perhaps of Keats's own despair of resolving his contradictory feelings about both Brown and Fanny? The equation of Lycius, Lamia, and Apollonius with Keats, Fanny, and Brown is too tidy; the poem is much more of a riddle than this. For one thing, Keats chose his subject and wrote the first part of *Lamia* a month before Brown joined him in Shanklin and the tension appeared in his letters to Fanny; it seems he cannot have intended this meaning at the start. Yet the poem contains some surprising links with Keats's previous work. The parallel with *Otho* is striking: in both the play and the poem there is a father-figure who tries to win the infatuated lover back to the truth; in both the woman deceives her lover and is punished by death; and in both the man dies on his wedding night, broken-hearted at the exposure of his bride's falsity. But this pattern of warning, betrayal, and death also resembles that of "La Belle Dame sans Merci," though there the knight is merely brought to the edge of death by the lady's betrayal and is warned by "Kings and princes" from beyond the grave. Auranthe's suicide in *Otho* is not directly presented; but Lamia is shown horribly transformed under Apollonius's stare in a kind of living death.

While the underlying situation remains the same, the terror of the climax mounts from poem to poem.

But there is another set of parallels which reach close to the very springs of Keats's creativity. It has been pointed out that in all three of these poems the revelation of the woman's falsity is prefaced by a scene of feasting and music—a scene anticipated, in far happier tones, in *The Eve of St. Agnes,* where Porphyro sets a banquet and plays the lute before revealing himself to Madeline.[11] But this same scene occurs several times in Keats's earlier poetry and may be traced back to still earlier events in his life; and the elements are not two but four: first sleep, then awakening, followed by a union of lovers and a feast with wine and music. In this, their original order, the experience is a joyful and health-giving one—as in *The Eve of St. Agnes* and, with a significant reversal of roles, in the second book of *Endymion,* where Venus wakens the sleeping Adonis from his winter sleep to the music of lyres in a chamber stocked with fruit and wine. A similar scene occurs in the third book of *Endymion,* when Scylla is revived by Glaucus and a celebration ensues, recalling the conclusion of "I Stood Tiptoe"—the earlier *Endymion*—in which the sick are wakened to health and reunited with the watchers by their bed-side in a joyous festival on the eve of Cynthia's wedding. It is significant that all through his poetry Keats uses images of feasting —on honey, fruit, wine, even milk—as metaphorical equivalents of love. "Gorge the honey of life," he had advised Reynolds on his engagement; and "the very 'yes' and 'no' " of a beautiful woman's lips, he told George, were "a Banquet" to him. Two unabashed images from *Endymion* describing sexual pleasure as feeding at the breast suggest the origin of the metaphor, which also occurs in his letters to Fanny Brawne when Keats twice speaks of trying to wean himself from her.[12] This identification of food with love is rooted in our biological nature, of course; but its constant recurrence in Keats's poetry suggests that the biological process had an unusually deep significance for him. Keats's mother, a woman fond of eating and drinking and a "doting parent" who, we are told, loved and indulged him even more than she did her other children, had withdrawn her love from him in a shocking way shortly after his father's death. When she later returned home, he had reaffirmed his love for her by nursing her in her illness—feeding her, reading to her, watching at her bedside as she slept. This never-to-be-forgotten experience of his boyhood seems clearly to be the origin of the feast scenes in *The Eve of St. Agnes* and his earlier poems.

But the feast of love was followed in reality not by the happy awakening to new life which Keats had dreamed of, but by the disaster of his mother's death. And gradually, during the spring and summer of 1819, the scene changes in Keats's imagination. The feast and the love-making are followed, not preceded, by sleep, which is now not health-giving but deathlike, or filled with ominous dreams. The man, who provided the feast in the earlier scenes, is now fed by the woman, and dies afterward; she too dies or disappears or, more terrifying still, turns into a dying woman before his eyes, cold, blank of sight, and horribly pale. This recurrent image suggests the early fear of a surrender to love, from which Keats had not yet successfully freed himself; and the resurgence of this fear must underlie the transformation of the love feast that takes place between *The Eve of St. Agnes,* written in the first confident flush of his love for Fanny Brawne, and the later poems, produced in a period of intense anxiety and jealousy. Love, as Keats had once learned, is the prelude to death; and the death following the moment of possession, for which he had longed in the Bright Star sonnet, now seemed to him not so much the only assurance of unchanging love he could imagine as the consequence of a love that is inevitably an illusion or betrayal.

Keats finished *Lamia* on the first or second of September with a surge of elation. As he wrote to Reynolds the week before, "I feel it in my power to become a popular writer—I feel it in my strength to refuse the poisonous suffrage of a public." *Lamia* proved this power. Looking it over afterward, he decided with satisfaction that it had "that sort of fire in it which must take hold of people in some way—give them either pleasant or unpleasant sensation." But even now there was no letting up: on he went, like so many strokes of a hammer. There were his earlier poems to revise; he turned back to them and decided at once they would not do. He was determined not to publish anything which could be laughed at again, and *Isabella* now seemed to show too much innocence of life—" 'A weak-sided Poem' with an amusing sober-sadness about it," he called it. There was almost the same objection to *The Eve of St. Agnes,* but this could be remedied. Adding a stanza, rewriting a few verses at the climax, Keats made it clear that his two young lovers became lovers in fact during the magic storm, then changed the ending to describe the Beadsman's death in grotesque detail. The poem now suited his new mood: it too would give people a "sensation of some sort."

But by now he and Brown were down to their last shillings, and still no money was in sight. No letters had been forwarded to them since Shanklin, not even a newspaper to confirm the rumor of Kean's trip to America. With their credit running out, the Winchester jail loomed up as a menacing possibility. Then, on September 5, in the nick of time, help arrived in a deluge—£30 from Hessey for Keats, another £30 from a friend of Brown's, and a £40 repayment from Keats's absent-minded friend Haslam, who had sent it to Chichester by mistake, along with a note from Taylor. They were jubilant. Keats dashed off a note of thanks to Hessey, adding, "To be a complete Midas I suppose some one will send me a pair of asses ears by the waggon." He may have wondered why Taylor had delayed in writing; he could not have guessed that Taylor, piqued by the arrogance of his first request for a loan, had sent it on to Woodhouse for his opinion. Keats's would-be biographer had risen loyally to his defence: "I wonder how he came to stumble upon that deep truth that 'people are debtors to him for his verses & not he to them for admiration.'—Methinks such a conviction on any one's mind is enough to make half a Milton of him." Then, digging down into his own pocket, Woodhouse came up with £50 which he sent to Taylor to be used for Keats's benefit. "Whatever People regret that they could not do for Shakespeare or Chatterton, because he did not live in their time, that I would embody into a Rational principle, and (with due regard to certain expediencies) do for Keats."

With his pockets full, Brown went off for several weeks to visit at Bedhampton, and Keats found himself alone again. Almost two months remained of the four he had allowed himself, and if he continued working at his summer's rate he would, as he promised Fanny, accomplish "an immense deal." The clear weather held unbroken, and his health began to improve. "I adore fine Weather as the greatest blessing I can have," he wrote his sister. "Give me

Books, fruit, french wine and fine whether and a little music out of doors, played by somebody I do not know—and I can pass a summer very quietly without caring much about Fat Louis, fat Regent or the Duke of Wellington." What or even whether Fanny Brawne replied to his flint-worded letter of August 16 we do not know; but it apparently had the effect of cancelling the understanding they had reached in June.[13] Yet, once the turmoil of this break subsided, Keats turned to his solitude with relief. In the midst of the world he lived as quietly as a hermit, he told George, content merely to write, study Italian, and walk a mile or two after dinner each day. If during his morning's work he found himself getting vaporish, he got up, doused his head in cold water, put on a clean shirt, brushed his hair, retied his shoes, "and in fact adonize as I were going out—then all clean and comfortable I sit down to write."

Yet Keats was no real hermit; this peace was bought at a price. A clue to his state of mind during these quiet weeks in September may be found in the book he was reading at the time—that farrago of donnish ribaldry and learning which Brown had given him in June, *The Anatomy of Melancholy*. Keats read it, as with other books that fascinated him, underscoring and annotating as he went, and the marginal jottings in his Burton form a curious private journal of these weeks, the only real diary he apparently ever kept.[14] At first his notes were mainly literary reminiscences, but as he went on they became more and more personal. For instance, beside a passage describing precious stones as a remedy against a melancholy, he noted wryly, "A valuable diamond would effectively cure mine." The section that drew his closest attention, however, was Burton's long penultimate discourse on Love-Melancholy, one of the most erudite, detailed, and scathing attacks on women ever penned. Keats was so delighted by the Rabelaisan gusto of a long description of an ugly woman that he copied out the entire page for George, adding a few flourishes of his own. But at the beginning of this section, where Burton describes the intellectual love which men share with God and the angels, Keats's marginal comment suddenly lays bare the real anguish of the summer. "Here is the old plague spot: the pestilence, the raw scrofula," he wrote in despair. "I mean that there is nothing disgraces me in my own eyes so much as being one of a race of eyes, nose and mouth beings in a planet called the earth who all from Plato to Wesley have always mingled goatish, winnyish, lustful love with the abstract adoration of the deity. I don't understand greek—is the Love of God and the Love of women expressed by the same word in Greek? I hope my little mind is wrong—if not I could—Has Plato separated these loves?" Hurrying on to the next page, where Burton introduces a distinction between them, he exclaimed, "Ha! I see how they endeavour to divide—but there appears to be a horrid relationship."

What crisis wrung these words from Keats we shall never really know—a moment of self-disgust so naked that we instinctively turn our eyes away. The physiological metaphor of "the old plague spot" somehow links this outburst with his sexual misadventure of two years before, and its recrudescence seems also somehow linked with his alienation from Fanny Brawne since mid-August. Another revealing annotation occurs farther on in Burton, beside some verses of Ausonius, where Keats misquoted a line of Tasso in the margin, *"Cogliam la rosa d'amore"*—an echo of Spenser's "Gather the rose of love"—then added and underscored the Latin word *ubique,* "everywhere." The only possible interpretation of this cryptic addition is that Keats had in fact followed Spenser's advice and joined Brown on his sexual expeditions in August. Certainly remorse for such a lapse would help account for his diatribe against "goatish, winnyish, lustful love"—a remorse which he had felt before, but never so keenly as now. Yet even this mood gave way to cynicism as he read further in *The Anatomy.* Page after page he went on, as Burton added detail to detail of his monstrous indictment. From Keats's approving comments—"Good!" "Aye, aye!" "Extraordinary!"—gradually emerges a portrait of "a man fill'd with hatreds" indeed, hatred of sex, of self, seemingly of all that he had felt and believed before.

Yet from this mood of morbid self-dissatisfaction an important resolution was born. He decided at last to give up *Hyperion,* to which he had devoted most of his thought and effort for over a year—not to discard it completely, but rather to rewrite it from the start on a new plan.[15] By now it seems he clearly saw that the conflict between his first optimistic theme and his increasingly tragic view of the individual's destiny could no longer be resolved in the character of Apollo. But he was also growing restless under his long tutelage to Milton as his own intentions clarified. "Miltonic verse cannot be written but in an artful or rather artist's humour," he explained to Reynolds in telling him later of his decision. "I wish to give myself up to other sensations." One of these sensations was the grave and disciplined clarity of Dante's verse.[16] During August, Keats had gone back to reading the *Inferno* in translation, while also attempting a few lines in the original as his Italian progressed—an effort "well worth the while," as he remarked to George. Dante's austere music echoes in the prologue to the new version of his poem, which he now entitled *The Fall of Hyperion—A Dream;* more than this, Dante's allegorical plan suggested a solution to his structural problem. To recast his epic as a vision in which he himself appeared as the poet witnessing the fall of the Titans, as Dante himself had wandered through the kingdoms of the dead—this would give scope both to his own bitter meditations and to Apollo's struggle for godhead.

> Fanatics have their dreams, wherewith they weave
> A paradise for a sect; the savage too
> From forth the loftiest fashion of his sleep
> Guesses at Heaven: pity these have not
> Trac'd upon vellum or wild indian leaf
> The shadows of melodious utterance.
> But bare of laurel they live, dream and die;
> For Poesy alone can tell her dreams,
> With the fine spell of words alone can save
> Imagination from the sable charm
> And dumb enchantment. Who alive can say
> 'Thou art no Poet; mayst not tell thy dreams?'
> Since every man whose soul is not a clod
> Hath visions, and would speak, if he had lov'd
> And been well nurtured in his mother tongue.
> Whether the dream now purposed to rehearse
> Be Poet's or Fanatic's will be known
> When this warm scribe my hand is in the grave.

So he began; and the poem moved serenely on, into the garden and the temple of his vision, with a terse and sober grace he had never achieved before.

For three or four days he continued; then his solitude was interrupted again. On September 10 a desperate letter came from George. Business had taken a bad turn throughout America. Pressed for credit, he had discovered that his partner was already deep in debt, contrary to the impression of prosperity he had originally given; in fact, Audubon was being sued by five creditors at the time he had persuaded George to invest in the steamboat.

With his cash run out, George's entire investment was threatened unless the rest of his holdings could be sold and the money forwarded at once.[17] Keats now found his worst suspicions of Audubon's honesty confirmed. All summer long Abbey had done nothing about their affairs; Sandell had not yet replied from Holland; the Chancery suit still blocked the road. At once Keats decided to go up to London to extricate George's money and try if he could to get an advance on his new volume of poems. For a moment he thought of approaching Byron's publisher, Murray, then decided that his stock stood too low in the literary market. He would appeal to Taylor and Hessey, even though he sensed they would be unwilling to take another gamble on him. Hastily he gathered up his manuscripts and set off for London in the night coach.

Going straight to Pancras Lane the next morning, a Saturday, Keats found Abbey about to leave for Walthamstow for the weekend and had to put off their interview till Monday evening. In Fleet Street he learned that Taylor was still not back from vacation and had to face the cautious Hessey instead. Hessey listened to his plan to bring out the new volume in time for Christmas, then told him it would not do. The final decision rested with Taylor, of course; but Hessey as business manager could remind Keats that the firm was over a hundred pounds out of pocket on *Endymion*. This was a third blow to his hopes, coming hard on the heels of George's misfortune and the news of Kean's departure. Keats took his leave and wandered up Fleet Street. Suddenly he felt he was in a foreign city, a stranger among the anonymous hurrying crowd. A year ago London had been the battlefield of his struggle for fame; now he was filled with bitterness toward the unseen enemies who had thwarted him. I am a weaver-boy to them, he thought— one of the cotton-spinners who struck for higher wages only to be starved into submission. He made a few calls and found nobody at home; Reynolds and Dilke, he knew, were still away in the country. He tried not to think of Hampstead: that would be venturing into a fire. For hours he drifted about the streets, trying to shake off the sensation of strangeness, then luckily found Rice in at Poland Street, where he managed to round off the day pleasantly enough.

Sunday morning Keats breakfasted at the Temple with Woodhouse, who had dropped in at Hessey's the morning before and was leaving for a holiday in Bath that afternoon. Woodhouse gave him a warmer welcome than Hessey had. He was full of a new discovery, Provençal poetry, and even had a plan for taking Keats with him on a prospecting tour of Provence next summer.[18] He also wanted to hear the new poem. Keats read *Lamia* aloud to him, rather badly, as Woodhouse thought: he sensed its drama but was puzzled about its meaning. Why, for instance, did Lamia consent to marry Lycius when she would thereby lose her immortality? Because, Keats answered, "Women love to be forced to do a thing, by a fine fellow." Still less could Woodhouse understand why Keats refused to include *Isabella* in the projected volume. He thought its simple pathos would have a strong appeal, but Keats insisted it was too mawkish to print. But when he produced the revised version of *The Eve of St. Agnes,* Woodhouse abused it "a full hour by the *Temple* clock." As publisher's reader, he saw at once that turning the dream marriage into a reality made the poem "unfit for ladies." Keats replied heatedly that he wrote not for ladies but for men. As Woodhouse reported with some amusement to Taylor, "he sh^d despise a man who would be such an eunuch in sentiment as to leave a maid, with that Character about her, in such a situation: & sho^d despise himself to write about it &c &c &c— and all this sort of Keats-like rhodomontade." Still, Keats knew what he was up against and probably appreciated the irony of Woodhouse's position. As they walked from the lawyer's rooms to the coachyard together, Keats begged him to write him in Winchester. Woodhouse agreed, then added, "All the reciprocity should not be on one side." Keats laughed; they shook hands at the coach door with a warm sense of fellowship, then Woodhouse rolled off on his journey, mulling over their conversation.

Keats went on to dine at the Wylies' with an uncomfortable sense of constraint. He could not show them George's latest letter, though Mrs. Wylie was full of news from Georgiana, who had just sent her a lock of the new baby's hair and her exact measurements— "the little span-long elf." So Keats joined Charles and Henry in the usual "quizzing"—of Mrs. Wylie's new gown, of Charles's whiskers, of Henry's fiancée, of their fat, smiling new cook, even of the passers-by in the street; but he was glad to escape at last. Monday morning the question he had evaded for two days became insistent. Would he go out to Hampstead? Would he even let Fanny know he had come to London? His equanimity began to collapse; quickly he wrote to explain why he could not come. "If I were to see you to day it would destroy the half comfortable sullenness I enjoy at present into downright perplexities. Knowing well that my life must be passed in fatigue and trouble, I have been endeavouring to wean myself from you: for to myself alone what can be much of a misery? I am a Coward, I cannot bear the pain of being happy." Even then he could not bring himself to mail the letter. He stuffed it into his pocket and took a coach out to Walthamstow to see his sister, putting Hampstead a dozen miles out of reach.

Back on Monday afternoon, he found the city in a hubbub of excitement. Henry Hunt, the Radical orator, was returning to London from Manchester for trial. A month before, a meeting for Parliamentary reform led by Hunt at St. Peter's Fields near Manchester had turned into a massacre when the local cavalry, sent to arrest him for disturbing the peace, charged the crowd with drawn sabres. Eleven men and women were killed and four hundred wounded. A cry of outrage went up from the Liberal press, which the Government answered by passing the infamous "Six Acts." It was the pattern of 1817—misery, protest, violence, repression—repeated in still darker tones. These were the events which added the word "Peterloo" to the English vocabulary; they also inspired Shelley in Italy to write his stirring "Mask of Anarchy," with the refrain

> Rise like Lions after slumber
> In unvanquishable number—
> Shake your chains to earth like dew
> Which in sleep had fallen on you—
> Ye are many—they are few . . .

which Leigh Hunt, in London, put off publishing till 1832. When Henry Hunt reached London in the afternoon of September 13, a crowd of nearly three hundred thousand lined the street from Islington to the Strand to greet him in the greatest triumphal entry the city had seen. At the head of the procession came chariots and barouches drawn by red-ribboned bay horses with red-cockaded outriders, followed by bands playing, men bearing oak branches, a red flag with the motto "Universal Suffrage," a blue flag reading "A Free Press," a white flag emblazoned "Trial by Jury," and rank after rank of marchers; then at last, riding in a landaulet with a banner proclaiming "Liberty or Death," came Hunt himself, looking pale and tired, bowing gravely to the throngs.[19] Somewhere in the clapping, cheering, handkerchief-waving crowd Keats wandered, caught up in the surge of revolutionary ardour. This was an hour to make him forget the sense of estrangement that had gnawed at him since his arrival in London on Saturday, even to cancel out the cynicism and despair of weeks past. Some things in the world were real after all. Weeks later, deep in discouragement again, he was to remember this day: "I have no cause to complain," he wrote Haydon, "because I am certain any thing really fine will in these days be felt. I have no doubt that if I had written Othello I should have been cheered by as good a Mob as Hunt."

Monday evening Abbey received him with unexpected good humour and offered him tea. He looked grave at George's news and promised to do everything possible: send George a remittance immediately and press the lawyers to get rid of Mrs. Jennings' suit. But when Keats hinted he needed money himself, Abbey was less sympathetic. The sober truth had to be faced that Keats had now anticipated most of the small sum remaining from his inheritance by his borrowings over the summer. Abbey ended their interview with a well-aimed dig. After blowing up Byron's poetry, he added slyly, "The fellow does say true things now and then," and picked up a magazine to read a stanza from *Don Juan* hitting at the folly of literary ambition. Keats said good-bye, started aimlessly up Cheapside, then decided to mail the letter to Fanny Brawne which he had been carrying around all day and turned back toward the Lombard Street post office. In Bucklersbury he met Abbey again. As they walked down the Poultry together, Abbey hinted, to Keats's surprise, that he could have a position in his hatter's shop for the asking. Despite his discouragement, Keats saw the humour of it. Abbey was trying to help in the only way he knew; as for himself, he told George, "I do believe if I could be a hatter I might be one."

Tuesday he called on Haslam, whom he found completely absorbed in new business and his approaching marriage—much to Keats's amusement. From Severn's portrait of his fiancée, Keats decided she was "though not very cunning, too cunning for him." "Nothing," he exclaimed in his letter to George, "strikes me so forcibly with a sense of the rediculous as love." That evening he had nothing better to do than go to the second half of the program at Covent Garden, where he met Abbey's junior partner Hodgkinson, George's old enemy, who, Keats noted with amusement, treated him with deference now he had become an author. On Wednesday he returned to Winchester at last. George's fate still hung in the balance, and his own prospects looked even blanker than they had three months before. He tried to pick up his work, but for a day or so his anxiety got the better of him. Then on Friday he pulled himself up short: rather than waste any more time in fretting, he would begin another long letter to George, as encouraging as he could make it. There was no blinking the mess they were in, he wrote—for "mess it is as far as it regards our Pockets." Yet, he added, "I assure you you shall more than share what I can get, whilst I am still young—the time may come when age will make me more selfish." It was a difficult promise to make, since it implied giving up all hope of marriage for the time being. But with George in need, there was nothing else he could do. As for himself, he admitted, he knew of no one whose friends were more generous—though, unfortunately, none of them could well afford their generosity. So he promised George he would send him what he could—if not hundreds, then tens; if not tens, then ones. "I have forgot how to lay plans for enjoyment of any Pleasure," he added. "I feel I can bear any thing, any misery, even imprisonment —so long as I have neither wife nor child."

The next morning his spirits began to rise. He reread *Lamia* and realized that in spite of Hessey's hedging and Woodhouse's bewilderment it was certain to succeed if ever he could get it published. He went back to his letter, rambling on with news, copying out Burton to amuse George, then embarked on the subject that was smouldering in his mind—the recent turn of political events. Trying to put Peterloo in the long perspective of the English struggle for liberty, he began to see hopeful signs in the dark record of the last few years. Henry Hunt's defiance of the Ministry, the solidarity of the London crowd that cheered him, the courage of the Radical pamphleteers and publishers such as Richard Carlile, whom the Government had indicted more than a dozen times but still feared to prosecute—all these were tokens of a new spirit of freedom stirred up by the Tories, which must come to good in the end. Of Carlile he exclaimed, "They are affraid of his defence: it would be published in all the papers all over the Empire: they shudder at this: the Trials would light a flame they could not ex-

tinguish." In his excitement the great words of the martyred
Latimer facing death at the stake went ringing through his head.*
There were still blows to be struck for freedom; the future was
still full of possibility.

Yet even as he wrote, his mind was turning backward. Looking
through some old papers that morning, he had turned up two reminders of the past: one of his letters from Scotland, describing his
trip to Iona and Staffa; and a page from his journal of March which
he had overlooked in sending it off in May. Rereading them, Keats
was struck by the immense amount of time he had lived through
since George had left. From the wonder and expectancy of his
summer in Scotland through the paralysed despair of the following spring to his present state of frustrated indecision, the distance
seemed almost incalculable. How differently things turn out from
one's expectations, he mused, how often had he acted against his
own resolves, how rarely did he speak in his letters of the things
he thought of and felt most deeply. Uneasily he realized that George
must have changed as much as he in the last fifteen months. "Every
man does—Our bodies every seven years are completely fresh-
materiald," he wrote, remembering in a flash the angry boy who
seven years ago had clenched his fist against Hammond. On the
edge of an unpredictable future, he realized his youth was drawing
to a close. The abundance of energy without responsibility which
he had squandered so heedlessly was running out with his hopes
and his money. The loss was irrecoverable; but was there no gain
as well? "Some think I have lost that poetic ardour and fire 't is said
I once had—the fact is perhaps I have: but instead of that I hope
I shall substitute a more thoughtful and quiet power. I am more
frequently, now, contented to read and think—but now & then,
haunted with ambitious thoughts. Quieter in my pulse, improved
in my digestion; exerting myself against vexing speculations—
scarcely content to write the best verses for the fever they leave
behind. I want to compose without this fever. I hope I one day
shall."

The season itself was retrospective. The walk which he took

---

* "Be of good comfort, Master Ridley, and play the man, we shall this day light
such a candle, by God's grace, in England, as I trust shall never be put out." (John
Foxe, *The Book of Martyrs;* see *The Letters of John Keats,* ed. H. E. Rollins [1958],
II, 194 n.)

every day before his solitary dinner led him out past empty fields that a month before had been thick with full-grown wheat. At the beginning of the summer he had reflected ironically that his poetry was destined for the market, like the grain; for weeks he had watched it ripening while he went on with his own work. Now, with the harvest in, he felt a profound satisfaction. In his imagery, gold was always the colour of poetry, autumn the season of fulfilment; now, as he wandered through the mellow countryside, he could forget the uncertainties of his own summer's labour in the serenity of the harvest landscape. "How beautiful the season is now," he wrote Reynolds on the twenty-first, "How fine the air. A temperate sharpness about it. Really, without joking, chaste weather—Dian skies—I never lik'd stubble fields so much as now —Aye better than the chilly green of the spring. Somehow a stubble plain looks warm—in the same way that some pictures look warm—this struck me so much in my sunday's walk that I composed upon it."

What he wrote that Sunday afternoon was his most perfect and untroubled poem:

> Season of mists and mellow fruitfulness,
>     Close bosom-friend of the maturing sun;
> Conspiring with him how to load and bless
>     With fruit the vines that round the thatch-eves run;
> To bend with apples the moss'd cottage-trees,
>     And fill all fruit with ripeness to the core;
>         To swell the gourd, and plump the hazel shells
> With a sweet kernel; to set budding more,
>     And still more, later flowers for the bees,
>     Until they think warm days will never cease,
>         For Summer has o'er-brimm'd their clammy cells.
>
> Who hath not seen thee oft amid thy store?
>     Sometimes whoever seeks abroad may find
> Thee sitting careless on a granary floor,
>     Thy hair soft-lifted by the winnowing wind;
> Or on a half-reap'd furrow sound asleep,
>     Drows'd with the fume of poppies, while thy hook
>         Spares the next swath and all its twined flowers:
> And sometimes like a gleaner thou dost keep
>     Steady thy laden head across a brook;
>     Or by a cyder-press, with patient look,
>         Thou watchest the last oozings hours by hours.

Where are the songs of Spring? Ay, where are they?
　Think not of them, thou hast thy music too,—
While barred clouds bloom the soft-dying day,
　And touch the stubble-plains with rosy hue;
Then in a wailful choir the small gnats mourn
　Among the river shallows, borne aloft
　　Or sinking as the light wind lives or dies;
And full-grown lambs loud bleat from hilly bourn;
　Hedge-crickets sing; and now with treble soft
　The red-breast whistles from a garden-croft;
　　And gathering swallows twitter in the skies.

It is Keats's most characteristic because most impersonal poem. The poet himself is completely lost in his images, and the images are presented as meaning simply themselves: Keats's richest utterance is the barest of metaphor. The fullness of life, the joy of completion which the poem celebrates emerge directly from what he once called the rise, the progress, the setting of the imagery, as natural and magnificent as the sun's. All the hours of an autumn day are implied in this progression—misty morning, drowsy noon, and chilly sunset; all the characters, properties, and stages of the autumnal drama, in a scene that slowly widens from cottage yard to neighbouring fields and distant hills and skies; all the senses by which it is apprehended; all its varieties of action—motionless growth, unhurried toil, langour after harvest, restless stirring before flight. The poem is a garnering of perception, a summary of achievement, a half-conscious gesture of farewell.

The premonition of departure that concludes the poem, the hint of darker and colder days to come, was prophetic. For a day Keats went on, absorbed in his work, picking up *The Eve of St. Mark*—that little poem begun seven months before "quite in the spirit of Town quietude," as he described it to George—and adding a dozen lines or so.[20] Monday evening he filled up another long sheet in his journal with jokes and gossip, including some astonishing news of Severn. "I have to make use of the word Mum! before I tell you that Severn has got a little Baby—all his own let us hope—He told Brown he had given up painting and had turn'd modeller. I hope sincerely tis not a party concern; that no M^r—— or **** is the real *Pinxit* and Severn the poor *Sculpsit* to this work of art—You know he has long studied in the Life-Academy." Tuesday morning he continued in a more sober mood, with a hint of uneasiness under the surface. He could not wait much longer for the fate of his play and his poems to be decided. The question he had put off since spring must now be faced. If he could earn nothing from his writing, what should he do with his life? Restlessly he started a letter to Reynolds, then, after announcing that he had given up *Hyperion,* broke off impatiently. He needed time to think; he decided to go for a late-afternoon walk.

His usual route took him out the back gate of his house into the cathedral yard, past the cathedral, through two collegiate squares, then out the city gate and over the meadows to St. Cross. As he cut through the fields he came to a rail fence and absent-mindedly stooped under it. At once he asked himself why he had not climbed over it instead, and answered, "Because no one wanted to force you under." He was amused at the thought of his own wilfulness, yet, as he walked on, a mood of self-dissatisfaction dogged him. It was a selfish life he had led for the past two or three years, he mused, swept this way and that, anchored to nothing. All of a sudden he felt the lack of a purpose outside himself, of a meridian to measure his course by. Devoting himself selfishly to poetry had meant drifting with the tide of his own moods; now both he and George faced shipwreck unless he changed course. Should he head back toward a safe profession, as Reynolds had done? Three months before, he had been ready to return to medicine when it seemed the only way to marriage; but now, with that hope apparently abandoned, what would he gain? As he walked back along the river after sunset, an autumnal chill was in the air. At the edge of town the clangour and warmth of a blacksmith's shop stopped him. He stood for a while at the open door, watching almost with envy the free, unanxious energy of the men swinging their hammers at the anvil, then returned to his room to finish the letter to Reynolds. His purpose was forged.

The next day he wrote three letters—to Brown, Woodhouse, and Dilke—to announce his decision. He must start earning his living, like everyone else, he told them; but still he would not be sidetracked into medicine. Since he could no longer hope for success with *Otho,* he would return to London to take lodgings and try "prosing for awhile in periodical works." He would speak to Hazlitt, who might recommend him to the *Edinburgh Review* as he had Reynolds; meanwhile he would try to get the theatre reviews of a newspaper. He knew well enough that his friends would regard such hack work as a prostitution of his talents, even if only temporary; but he did not care. "Yea I will trafic. Any thing but Mortgage my Brain to Blackwood," he remarked cynically to Dilke. Yet, from his statement to Brown that he would write "on the liberal side of the question" for whoever would pay him, it is clear that Keats's decision had an idealistic motive as well as a practical one. For the present, poetry would have to wait. "When I can afford to compose deliberate poems I will," he told Brown, and they would be the better for the discipline he imposed upon himself. At the end of another year, he promised, "you shall applaud me,—not for verses, but for conduct."

His plan meant giving up not only poetry but his close relationship to Brown, and announcing it stirred Keats for a moment out of his usual reticence about his deepest feelings. He told Brown that he must break his vicious habit of looking toward him "as a help in all difficulties" and leave him free for the pleasures which, Keats assured him, it was his duty to procure while still in the prime of life. Brown's happiness was one of his chief anxieties: "I wish you could see my heart towards you," he added, apologizing for the word which he never used except in poetry. As for himself, he insisted he was as far from being unhappy about the turn of events as possible. "Imaginary grievances have always been more my torment than real ones," he admitted; real ones only roused him up to action. Journalism was no great calling like poetry; yet in days like these it could serve a great cause, the very one for which Henry Hunt was fighting. The example of Hazlitt stood before him, and the image—which he would not mention directly even to Brown—of Milton laying down the first sketches of his epic to become pamphleteer for the Puritans. "I hope sincerely," he wrote in all earnestness to Dilke, "I shall be able to put a Mite of help to the Liberal side of the Question before I die."

## Chapter Twelve

# Unmeridian'd and Objectless

T H E day of decision was followed by over a week of inaction. Keats did not plan to start for London till he heard from Brown. But when Brown replied from Bedhampton on the twenty-third, he told Keats to do nothing till he rejoined him in Winchester, and in a sudden return of irresolution Keats decided not to send his impulsive letter announcing his decision to Dilke. He resumed waiting for word from Abbey to send to George; but none came. He added a few pages to his journal, teasing Georgiana, describing a wildly successful practical joke he had played on Brown's summer tenant and another played on himself and the young wife of an elderly major in the next apartment at Winchester, but saying nothing of his new plan. George would suspect that it was his own setbacks that had forced Keats to the decision, and this he wished to avoid. On the twenty-seventh another urgent appeal came from George, who was growing desperate at the delay. Keats wound up his letter to send off immediately, adding a bit of good news of his own: he had heard that Kean might not go to America after all. If the rumour was true, there was some hope for *Otho*. He was still surrounded by "uncertainties east west, north, and south," but he would not admit it to George.

The only real record of his uneasy frame of mind at this time is found in *The Fall of Hyperion*. It is impossible to tell just where Keats laid it down when he hurried up to London on September 10, but the most probable point is at the dreamer's entry into the temple of Saturn. His ensuing conversation with the mysterious goddess Moneta appears to have been written after Keats's return, for it is a striking echo of the disillusionment with poetry Keats expressed in his letters all through the following weeks.[1] He told Dilke that he marvelled that people read as much poetry as they did, and remarked even more cynically to Haydon that he had done nothing with his life so far "except for the amusement of a few people who refine upon their feelings till anything in the ununderstandable way will go down with them." This section of *The Fall of Hyperion* thus seems clearly a comment on his resolution to give up writing poetry: now, if never before, Keats was writing a deliberate allegory of his inner life. The dreamer's progress from the garden into the temple corresponds to the poet's growth from unreflective delight in all the beauty of the world to his first awareness of the misery which life holds for the sentient man—the development which Keats previsioned in "Sleep and Poetry" and *Endymion* and underwent in reality with Tom's last illness. What the dreamer sees in the temple of Saturn are, literally, the relics of the wars of the Titans, but in their vastness and antiquity they suggest the whole sum of human experience environing his span of years. His journey through this temple of consciousness is also symbolic; for he moves not from west to east, as through a Christian cathedral, but from east to west, in the direction of earthly time itself. Near the altar he meets the veiled priestess who is to be the Beatrice of his journey—Moneta, the Roman goddess of admonition, sometimes identified with the Greek goddess Mnemosyne who appeared to Apollo in the first *Hyperion*. She bids him ascend the steps to her side or die at once at the altar's foot. He starts to climb, but it costs him an agony as great as death itself:

> Suddenly a palsied chill
> Struck from the paved level up my limbs,
> And was ascending quick to put cold grasp
> Upon those streams that pulse beside the throat:
> I shriek'd; and the sharp anguish of my shriek
> Stung my own ears—I strove hard to escape
> The numbness; strove to gain the lowest step.
> Slow, heavy, deadly was my pace: the cold
> Grew stifling, suffocating, at the heart;
> And when I clasp'd my hands I felt them not.

But miraculously, "one minute before death," he sets foot on the lowest step and finds strength to climb the stairs to Moneta's side. There he begs her to tell him why he should have been saved, and she answers that he has already learned "What 'tis to die and live again before Thy fated hour." The reward of such an experience —the "dying into life" of *Hyperion*—is insight into human suffering: and, she explains,

> "None can usurp this height, . . .
> But those to whom the miseries of the world
> Are misery, and will not let them rest.
> All else who find a haven in the world,
> Where they may thoughtless sleep away their days,
> If by a chance into this fane they come,
> Rot on the pavement where thou rotted'st half."

Astonished, he then asks why he should be there alone, for surely there are thousands of his fellow beings in the world who not merely "feel the giant agony of the world" but also "labour for mortal good." The priestess explains that he is different from these "slaves to poor humanity":

> "They are no dreamers weak,
> They seek no wonder but the human face;
> No music but a happy-noted voice—
> They come not here, they have no thought to come—
> And thou art here, for thou art less than they—
> What benefit canst thou do, or all thy tribe,
> To the great world?"

The poet differs from ordinary "thoughtless" mortals, then, since he at least can share imaginatively the suffering of others; yet he also differs from the truly disinterested, who not only "love their fellows even to the death" but work effectively to relieve their suffering, as the poet does not. At this the dreamer protests that not all poetry is useless: is not the poet "a sage, A humanist, Physician to all men?" Moneta's answer implies that this is true of a few great poets, but certainly not of himself:

> "Art thou not of the dreamer tribe?
> The poet and the dreamer are distinct,
> Diverse, sheer opposite, antipodes.
> The one pours out a balm upon the world,
> The other vexes it."

Apparently Keats later cancelled these lines and made a fresh start; but, it is important to note, he left unqualified his original dismissal of most poetry as useless and of himself as "a dreaming thing," whose imagination merely "venoms all his days." [2] Like Dante, then, who began his spiritual journey aware of how far he had fallen from the good, Keats started *The Fall of Hyperion* with a devastating indictment of his own previous achievement in poetry as well as of the selfish passivity and indulgence in "imaginary woes" which his life as a poet had encouraged.

The comparison he draws here between the true poet and the physician is especially significant, for it shows this aspect of Keats's identity once more emerging into consciousness at a time of crisis. Images of sickness, it is not surprising to note, are scattered everywhere in *Otho the Great,* and do much to establish its tone of fevered frenzy; but in *The Fall of Hyperion* illness is used not simply as a metaphor for various emotional states but as a symbol of the poet's own consciousness. "Until we are sick, we understand not," Keats had written Reynolds over a year before; but there is more to it than that. The dreamer is a sick man, "a fever of himself," when he enters the temple, but in his encounter with Moneta he looks for health:

> "By such propitious parley medicin'd
> In sickness not ignoble, I rejoice."

The self-cured physician here becomes Keats's image of redemption through poetry. By confronting his own sickness, Keats implies, the dreamer may at last surmount it, become a true poet who does not "vex" mankind with dreams of unreal happiness but heals it through his own understanding of "the giant agony of the world." But his debate with Moneta also illuminates Keats's decision to turn to journalism till he was ready for this kind of poetry. The "ambition to do the world some good" which had dogged him ever since he had given up medicine was now to be translated into action; by writing on the liberal side Keats hoped humbly to join the ranks of those who "labour for mortal good."

By the end of September, Brown had returned to Winchester. At once, it appears, he tried to persuade Keats to give up his plan. The prospects for *Otho* looked bright again; why not wait till Elliston, the manager of Drury Lane, read the play and passed judgment? At this Keats may have wavered, but on one point he was adamant. He would not go back to live at Wentworth Place. "I like Miss Brawne and I cannot help it," he was driven to admit. Two weeks before, he had realized that even a short visit to Fanny would disrupt his plans to remain hard at work in Winchester till his four months were up. Living next door to her through the winter was unthinkable: any resolution would be shattered. Accordingly, on October 1 he wrote another letter to Dilke, asking him to find cheap lodgings for him in Westminster, where he would be "in reach of books"; then, two days later, to Haydon, requesting that he get him another ticket to the British Museum Reading Room —without, however, mentioning to either his plan for trying journalism. On October 8 he packed up and returned to town. The lodgings which Dilke had found for him at 25 College Street, near his own house in Great Smith Street and the Westminster Library, were a pleasant set of rooms with a view of the Abbey gardens, as cloistered and quiet as Winchester itself. With his books and pictures moved in, Keats could settle down in complete comfort. Accordingly, on Sunday the tenth, summoning up all his courage, he went out to Wentworth Place to collect his belongings and make his farewells. He took one backward look—and all was lost.

It was a new Fanny who awaited him, as beautiful in his eyes as ever, but schooled to a new tenderness. In the last two months she must have learned much she had never known before—stung pride, bewildered anger, then the long ache of loss. This time she was the one to fear the withdrawal of love, and evidently she welcomed Keats with a passion newly wakened by uncertainty. Keats was overwhelmed, dazzled, driven almost speechless. The old unassuageable desire gripped him again, and the subtler torture of a lingering doubt. Was it true? Could he believe in her kindness? Fanny remained self-possessed enough to threaten to "be cruel" if he ever again allowed his work to come between them, and Keats was helpless. He returned to Westminster in a turmoil. His promise to George, his peace of mind, his plans for the future were threatened. He struggled to blot out her image for an hour—the light of her glance, the touch of her lips, the warmth of her breath on his cheek: it was no use. He tried to steady himself by writing; the tumultuous "Lines to Fanny" were the result.[3]

> What can I do to drive away
> Remembrance from my eyes? for they have seen,
> Aye, an hour ago, my brilliant Queen!
> Touch has a memory. O say, love, say,
> What can I do to kill it and be free
> In my old liberty? . . .

The next morning, against his will, each scene of the day before played itself over and over in his head. There was nothing to do but to write Fanny confessing he was at her mercy, begging her to find a day they could pass alone together.

Two days went by while Keats tried to put his resolution into effect. It seems altogether likely that he went to York Street to ask Hazlitt's advice about entering journalism, though there is no record of such a visit. But if we can assume that the interview took place, we can also infer that it was a discouraging one. Hazlitt was facing a depressing crisis of his own that fall, with the final breakdown of his miserable marriage, a new low in his finances, and the apparent collapse of his own career.[4] Keats, whose first glimpse of York Street the year before had left him with a vivid impression of Hazlitt's son as a "little Nero," may well have been daunted by a closer view of Hazlitt's private life at this time—his contempt for his wife, his unconcealed promiscuity, the sordid bleakness of his living habits—and still more by his despair over what he called "this trade of authorship." Though Hazlitt had become a top-ranking journalist a few years after starting, he had been muzzled, libelled, underpaid, and unceremoniously dismissed every step of the way. And in the fall of 1819, he hardly needed to remind Keats, the rewards of writing "on the liberal side of the question" were not a modest livelihood but the possibility of indictment for sedition. Perhaps he tried to persuade Keats to "try the press once more" with his poems, for only a month later he complimented his work by quoting "Sleep and Poetry" in the first of his new series of lectures. But Hazlitt later recorded his opinion of Keats as a poet lacking "masculine energy" and "hardy spirit";[5] one wonders whether this impression sprang from a glimpse of Keats's desperate conflict at this time.

One friend, as we do know, came to visit Keats in Westminster this week—Severn, full of excitement at his own latest project. He had entered the Royal Academy competition for historical painting, in spite of his lack of experience in this genre, and by now he had nearly finished his canvas on the subject set, the scene at the "Cave of Despair" in *The Faerie Queene*. Keats quoted from memory the central stanza of the episode, to Severn's delight; he then read *Lamia* to him and talked about his other poems, though with no mention of journalism. Yet Severn was troubled by Keats's appearance. Four months in the country had evidently not improved his health. Under an air of confident resolve his friend sensed a deep uneasiness.

By Wednesday, Keats's indecision had become more than he could bear. He could not write; he could not even keep his mind on the drudgery of copying what he had already written. At last he started a letter to Fanny. "The time is passed when I had power to advise and warn you against the unpromising morning of my Life. I am forgetful of every thing but seeing you again—my Life seems to stop there—I see no further. You have absorb'd me. My sweet Fanny, will your heart never change? My love, will it?" At this moment her note of reply to his Monday letter arrived. She assured him she loved him; she had threatened to "be cruel" only in jest. His love flowed over: "I have been astonished that Men could die Martyrs for religion—I have shudder'd at it—I shudder no more—I could be martyr'd for my Religion—Love is my religion." For a moment he had a sensation of dissolving; his resolution was giving way. "You have ravish'd me away by a Power I cannot resist; and yet I could resist till I saw you; and even since I have seen you I have endeavoured often 'to reason against the reasons of my Love'. I can do that no more—the pain would be too great—My Love is selfish—I cannot breathe without you."

The sequel to this letter was another visit to Wentworth Place. On Friday the fifteenth Keats went out to Hampstead to spend three days at Brown's, once more under the same roof with Fanny, surrendering completely to her fascination. One would like to think that for these three days Keats tasted for once in his life the "unalloyed happiness" of the ordinary thoughtless man. Yet from the sonnet "The day is gone," which he probably wrote over this weekend, it appears that even while drugged with joy in his love he ached with the sense of its incompleteness:

> Faded the sight of beauty from my eyes,
> Faded the shape of beauty from my arms,
>    Faded the voice, warmth, whiteness, paradise—
> Vanish'd unseasonably at shut of eve,
>    When the dusk holiday—or holinight
> Of fragrant-curtain'd love begins to weave
>    The woof of darkness thick, for hid delight. . . .

"Only the dreamer venoms all his days," Moneta had warned him; and when he woke from his "three days dream" on Monday to face the consequences of his decision, it was with "a cry to dream again."

What followed was a sudden reversal of his plans. All at once he gave up his rooms in College Street and went to stay with the Dilkes for a few days. He had decided to return to live in Hampstead, even if it meant giving up the idea of journalism. The acutely physical anguish that separation from Fanny now caused him—"I cannot breathe without you"—had grown too great. Dilke was evidently astonished at the sudden collapse of an intention which he must have heartily endorsed. Yet Keats could not explain his behaviour to anyone's satisfaction without betraying the secret of his love; much worse, even to himself he could not justify it. For one miserable night he considered what he had done—the responsibilities shirked, the new distraction risked. The next morning, Tuesday the nineteenth, he wrote Fanny to announce his decision: "I must be busy, or try to be so. I must impose chains upon myself—I shall be able to do nothing—I shold like to cast the die for Love or death—if you ever intend to be cruel to me as you say in jest now but perhaps may sometimes be in earnest be so now—and I will—my mind is in a tremble, I cannot tell what I am writing." *

On Wednesday he returned to Hampstead and the die was cast for love. Mrs. Brawne was finally persuaded to consent to their engagement. As she confided to Mrs. Dilke, she had done all she could to prevent it, and agreed at last in the hope it would "go off." [6] With Keats's prospects still so uncertain, no date for the marriage could even be considered. The engagement was therefore to be kept a secret. Probably at this time Keats gave Fanny a garnet ring that may have belonged to his mother, but she did not wear it openly as a sign of their betrothal till a year and a half later.[7] Keats did not even tell Brown his secret for many months,[8] and with other friends he formed the habit of never mentioning Fanny's name. His deepest joys, like his deepest sorrows, were beyond confiding.

→»» «««←

Back at Wentworth Place, as an act of imposing chains upon himself, Keats gave the script of *Otho* a final polishing before submitting it to Drury Lane. This provided at least a shadow of an excuse for returning to his old quarters with Brown, though Keats's

---

* The complete letter is reproduced as Plate XIII.

part in the tragedy was still an official secret. In the hope of gaining a fair reading, the play was to be sent in signed only by Brown.
Keats's plan for a new volume of poetry seems to have been shelved,
perhaps when he learned of Taylor's reactions to his changes in
*The Eve of St. Agnes.* Writing to Woodhouse in reply to his report
on the revisions, Taylor had exploded against Keats's "preposterous
conceit" and "stupid folly" in "flying in the face of all decency
and discretion." "If he will not so far concede to my wishes as to
leave the Passage as it originally stood," the publisher concluded
grimly, "I must be content to admire his Poems with some other
Imprint." Keats met this rejection by turning back to *King Stephen*
after finishing the revision of *Otho.* Yet, after adding one more
scene,[9] he laid it down in discouragement. Aimlessly he picked up
his history books, searching Holinshed for another subject for a
play, starting an index to his copy of Selden, then putting it aside
after making two entries.[10]

One reason for his restlessness was the long-standing excuse of
George's affairs. At the beginning of November he finally received
the power of attorney for which he had been waiting since July.
By this time also the lawyers had evidently got far enough along
in their efforts to dismiss Mrs. Jennings' claim that the sale of
George's stocks could begin. This was a tedious business, involving
Keats in frequent trips to town, and a discouraging one as well.
The market was very low, and Abbey kept advising him to wait.
By this time Keats had run through Hessey's loan and had to borrow £30 from Haslam. When he told Abbey of his own financial
straits, the tea-broker met him with another well-meant suggestion—that he turn bookseller. Meanwhile the weeks went by and
no word came from Drury Lane. It was a vicious circle of frustration: he could not marry without money, he could not earn money
except by writing, he found it harder and harder to write with all
the anxiety pressing on him. The nautical imagery which keeps
recurring in his letters this fall describes well his sense of helpless
drifting, without a meridian, compass, or rudder, lost in a mist
after the confident course he had been steering two months before.
On November 12 he sent a letter to George, explaining the long
delay in forwarding him his money, then burst out against the
worries that had nagged at him ever since his unlucky promise of
help to Haydon the previous December. "Nothing," he exclaimed,
"could have in all its circumstances fallen out worse for me than

the last year has done, or could be more damping to my poetical talent."

It is an extraordinary indictment of a year of extraordinary achievement—the year in which he produced almost all of his enduring poetry. Yet this November it seemed Keats's old hardihood in meeting adverse circumstance was flagging. His friends began noticing a change in him. He seemed to be losing his old gift of easy friendship, growing more secretive, given over to unpredictable moods. Severn on a visit to Hampstead found him veering between feverish gaiety and apathetic dejection. Despite his frequent trips to town on George's business, he could not summon up the energy to attend Hazlitt's new lectures at the Surrey Institution, and when Severn invited him to see his painting hung at the Royal Academy, Keats put him off with a joke. "I wish you to return the Compliment by going with me to see a Poem I have hung up for the Prize in the Lecture Room of the surry Institution. You had best," he added, "put me into your Cave of despair." Even Taylor was concerned. On November 15 he invited Keats to dinner and evidently questioned him about his work, for two days later Keats wrote him to say that he had decided not to publish any of the poems he now had ready. His one ambition when he felt ambitious—"I am sorry to say that is very seldom"— was to write "a few fine Plays"; and for that, he was now convinced, he would not be ready for some years yet. Nevertheless, he told Taylor, he planned to bring out a poem before long—"and that I hope to make a fine one."

The new work to which Keats referred so cryptically may have been *The Fall of Hyperion*, on which he was still working sporadically, or perhaps another project which Brown had encouraged him to start not long before. Brown, seeing Keats at closer hand than any of his friends, was the most troubled by his depression. After a chance conversation one day on an idea he had for "a comic faery poem," he urged Keats to try working it out himself as a relaxation from his other labours. The subject was the royal scandal which had been rocking the kingdom since August—the Regent's threat to bring Princess Caroline to trial for adultery; the style indicated was Brown's own blend of Byronic satire and Ariostonic fantasy. Brown suggested entitling this jest at royalty *The Cap and Bells;* Keats preferred to call it *The Jealousies.* Evidently the idea chimed with his mood at the moment, for he began turning out ten or twelve stanzas a morning, and soon his imagination began running away with the original theme. Here and there the poem showed flashes of a real satiric gift, as in the description of nightfall in the City end of his fairy capital—the one glimpse of Pancras Lane we get in all Keats's poetry:

> It was the time when wholesale houses close
> Their shutters with a moody sense of wealth,
> But retail dealers, diligent, let loose
> The gas (objected to on score of health),
> Convey'd in little solder'd pipes by stealth,
> And make it flare in many a brilliant form. . . .*

But the strained relations between the elfin monarch and his unwilling bride began to echo strangely of Byron's scandalous break with the unhappy Annabella Milbanke, while the courtiers took on suspicious resemblances to figures of literary London.[11] Brown had doubts about where the poem was really headed, but Keats assured him that all the confusions would be ironed out in the end and went gaily ahead.

Yet this new interest soon flagged. The fairy machinery began to creak and after eighty-eight stanzas broke down completely; but long before that the poem lost all sense of direction. For no apparent reason Keats began throwing in material from his earlier poems, chiefly *The Eve of St. Mark,* and his satire ends like a parody of the poet he had been. His elation gave way to another depression. Then Brown made an alarming discovery: Keats was taking laudanum. At once Brown intervened. Keats should know better than anyone else, he argued, that he risked ruining his health, and Keats agreed not to touch the drug again.

This is the point he had reached within a month or two of his engagement to Fanny; and the account Brown gives of him this fall is not the picture of a happy man. The paralysis of February and March was now compounded with the bitterness of August; and yet this time Keats was neither estranged nor separated from Fanny Brawne but living as her fiancé under the same roof with her. Part of his depression may have had a very simple cause—the

---

* This stanza should be set beside Shaw's comment on Keats as "the sort of youth who calls a window a casement": "If Keats had ever described a process so remote from Parnassus as the taking down and putting up of the shop shutters, he would have described them in terms of a radiant sunrise and a voluptuous sunset, with the red and green [apothecary] bottles as heavenly bodies and the medicines as Arabian Balsams" (*The John Keats Memorial Volume* [1921], p. 174).

physical strain which any man of twenty-four would have felt in his situation; another part, the blow to his pride which the situation itself represented. He had failed to achieve the decisive success by which he had hoped to claim Fanny as his own; he had broken a deeply considered resolution in returning to her; and he had accepted an indefinite postponement of their marriage for reasons of prudence and respectability which were antithetical to his whole nature. Yet none of this quite accounts for the form which his frustrated desire took at this time—a jealousy inflamed rather than allayed by Fanny's constant presence.

Here we are as much in the dark about their relations as any of Keats's friends. No record remains from the autumn of 1819, beyond two or three tortured poems, to suggest whether his jealousy had any real foundation. Indeed, the only clear insight we have into Fanny Brawne's nature and behaviour—for Keats's letters and poems hardly give us that—comes from the long series of letters she began writing to Fanny Keats a year later. These reveal her as a warmhearted, humorous, fair-minded, and straightforward young woman gifted with great control over her own feelings as well as insight into others'. It was the experiences of the coming year that were to prove her as a person; yet the girl of nineteen cannot have been fundamentally different from the young woman she became at twenty. Fanny at eighteen was no doubt a minx, as giddy and lighthearted as any girl of her position was expected to be; Fanny at nineteen had at least started to grow a character. Love is a great educator, and Fanny must have learned much from her first year of involvement with Keats. After the estrangement of the summer, when she might well have been reduced to bewilderment or mere injured vanity, she not only received him with new love but also succeeded in overcoming her mother's opposition to their engagement. It is hard to believe that she did not feel her commitment to Keats with all the intensity of her nature. Yet from the jealous outburst in the "Ode to Fanny," which he wrote probably this November or December,[12] it appears that Fanny continued going to dances even when Keats was not well enough to go himself. Perhaps this shows too great a love of pleasure on her part, or a lingering trace of girlish self-absorption; but with Keats's insistence that their engagement be kept a secret, Fanny can hardly have been expected to withdraw from Hampstead society. And the agonized mistrust of the "Ode to Fanny" seems to have sprung from one of those "imaginary grievances" which Keats admitted were more his torment than real ones. "He doesn't like anyone to look at or speak to her," Mrs. Dilke noted apprehensively around this time. At a word, a smile, a glance between Fanny and another man, his old tendency to "suspect everybody"—the lingering effect of his mother's faithlessness years before—returned with new virulence.

But this suspicion apparently concealed another more devastating jealousy, born of his sense of the contrast between Fanny's radiant health and his own failing energy, between her gaiety and the hatred of the world growing like a cancer within him. Behind his doubt of Fanny's fidelity was gathering a far more terrible uncertainty—the sensation of "dissolving" as a personality which he mentioned in his letter of October 13. In the sonnet to Fanny beginning "I cry your mercy—pity—love!" which he probably wrote soon after the "Ode," Keats cried out to be reassured not simply of her love but also of his own continuing identity:

> Yourself—your soul—in pity give me all,
>   Withhold no atom's atom or I die,
> Or living on perhaps, your wretched thrall,
>   Forget, in the mist of idle misery,
> Life's purposes,—the palate of my mind
> Losing its gust, and my ambition blind! *

Such reassurance—that he remain the person and the poet he was before disease had started to undermine his very existence—was impossible for anyone to give him, even Fanny herself, at least under the conditions of their engagement. Yet, from a few lines written one morning in the midst of his work on *The Cap and Bells,* it appears that it was now not love but life itself which he demanded of Fanny Brawne:

> This living hand, now warm and capable
> Of earnest grasping, would, if it were cold
> And in the icy silence of the tomb,
> So haunt thy days and chill thy dreaming nights
> That thou wouldst wish thine own heart dry of blood
> So in my veins red life might stream again,
> And thou be conscience-calm'd—see here it is—
> I hold it towards you.

---

* Following De Selincourt's reading of "without" as "withhold" in line 2 (*Poems of John Keats,* ed. Ernest de Selincourt, 5th ed., revised [1926], p.287).

Only one thing can finally explain this despair—that Keats was now convinced that he was succumbing to tuberculosis. After his brief spell of good health in September, all the feverish sensations of the summer returned with new force. As yet, it seems, there was no dramatic proof of illness requiring drastic remedy. Yet on October 20, the very day that he moved back to Wentworth Place, Keats dropped a hint of his fear in a letter to his sister. He announced that he had "left off animal food that my brains may never henceforth be in a greater mist than is theirs by nature." The explanation is a joke, of course. He could have had only one conceivable reason for giving up meat—that a milk and vegetable diet was recommended to bring down a consumptive fever.[13] A month or two later he had a warm greatcoat and a pair of thick shoes made for him at his doctor's advice. When these items are added to the list of all the steps he had taken during the previous year to shake off his sore throat—staying at home in wet or cold, refraining from swimming all summer long, leaving Shanklin for more healthful air, even considering a move to a warm climate— one suddenly realizes that Keats had followed every detail of the treatment then prescribed for the early stages of consumption.[14] In the four months after his return from Winchester he felt strong enough for only one visit to Walthamstow. One wonders whether his sudden abandonment in October of his plan to become a journalist was motivated not only by his longing to be near Fanny again but also by a premonition that he was not well enough to carry the plan through—though this makes it seem half-suicidal for him to have risked another winter in London, apparently against his doctor's recommendation.

As he felt himself drifting toward illness in spite of all his efforts, Keats's whole life became the kind of "day-night mare" he mentioned to Reynolds in August. Little of this is directly expressed in the few letters he wrote during this fall, except for one or two outbursts of macabre humour. Later, however, he told Rice that every day since the end of July had been a battle against a kind of angry gloom or passionate longing—"or if I turn'd to versify that acerbated the poison of either sensation." Yet all during the fall he kept up the struggle and even managed to make supreme poetry from his profoundest despair. Evening after evening, alone in his sitting room, Keats pored over the manuscript of *The Fall of Hyperion,* weaving fragments of the first version into the new poem, adding line to line with the greatest difficulty. Something of his own battle against inertia may be read in the dreamer's struggle to climb the altar steps in the very grip of death. As the poem goes on it turns from an indictment of his own earlier poetry into what seems a record of the almost superhuman effort it cost him to continue writing at all—as when the dreamer watches with Moneta the grief-stricken Thea kneeling before Saturn:

> Without stay or prop
> But my own weak mortality, I bore
> The load of this eternal quietude,
> The unchanging gloom, and the three fixed shapes
> Ponderous upon my senses a whole moon.
> For by my burning brain I measured sure
> Her silver seasons shedded on the night
> And ever day by day methought I grew
> More gaunt and ghostly—Oftentimes I pray'd
> Intense, that Death would take me from the vale
> And all its burthens—Gasping with despair
> Of change, hour after hour I curs'd myself.

With this consciousness, as crushing as that which made a god of Apollo, the dreamer has at last become a poet with "power of enormous ken, To see as a god sees"; what Keats himself seems to have struggled to express in these lines was the final realization of his own mortality.

Yet this revelation came to him in an image overpowering in its beauty as well as its terror, the most compelling image in all his poetry, in which Keats summoned up all that remained of his poetic energy. The veiled priestess promises the dreamer a vision of the primeval warfare between the Titans and the rebel gods— the vision which will make him a poet. Yet he is too overwhelmed to speak in his terror of her presence,

> And chiefly of the veils, that from her brow
> Hung pale, and curtain'd her in mysteries
> That made my heart too small to hold its blood.

Seeing this, Moneta parts her veils to reassure him:

> Then saw I a wan face,
> Not pin'd by human sorrows, but bright blanch'd
> By an immortal sickness which kills not;
> It works a constant change, which happy death
> Can put no end to; deathwards progressing
> To no death was that visage; it had pass'd

The lily and the snow; and beyond these
I must not think now, though I saw that face—
But for her eyes I should have fled away.
They held me back, with a benignant light,
Soft-mitigated by divinest lids
Half closed, and visionless entire they seem'd
Of all external things—they saw me not,
But in blank splendor beam'd like the mild moon,
Who comforts those she sees not, who knows not
What eyes are upward cast.

It is still the face of the Goddess of Memory, who has gazed for
ages with infinite compassion on the sufferings of the world; it is
also the Goddess of Melancholy whom he had met, still mysteriously veiled, in the Temple of Delight. Yet it is also the pale lady
of the disastrous wedding feast, La Belle Dame, Auranthe with
eyes "semi-shaded in white lids," Lamia staring at her lover without recognition—though now her visage is softened to benignance;
it is the open-lidded star and the moon "floating through space
with ever-loving eye" that presided over his earlier poetry, but
whose gaze is now recognized at last and forever as sightless. In the
end it is the face of death itself, in the most beautiful and terrifying aspect in which Keats had met it—the face of his dead mother,
shrouded for her coffin. It is the ultimate image of Keats's poetry,
that "one scene, one adventure, one picture" which Yeats called the
image of a man's secret life, which, "if he would but brood over it his
life long," would bring him in the end to an understanding of all his
experience.[15] It is the very foundation of Keats's poetic structure,
the metamorphoses recurrent throughout his poetry of the "Beauty
that must die" and the dead miraculously brought to life again;
it suggests the driving force behind the metamorphoses of his own
identity. The boy whose heroic assertiveness was formed in protest
against his mother's faithlessness, the adolescent who became a
doctor in half-conscious expiation of his failure to save her from
death, the young man who first turned to poetry to escape the
memory of her suffering but became a true poet in facing and accepting the burdens of his own identity—now at last in his fullest
self he confronts the experience that so greatly shaped him and
regards it with love and pity, not with terror. In his discovery of
beauty in the face of death Keats emerged as the poet who is
"Physician to all men." Here he finally proved himself capable of

the poetry he had dreamed of writing; yet these were almost the last lines he ever wrote.

➤➤ ◄◄

In the second week of December, when Keats's hopes were at their lowest ebb, suddenly the tide turned. After almost two months' silence word came from Drury Lane: *Otho* was accepted. This must have lifted Keats high out of his gloom: at last he had proved to all his doubting friends that he could write an actable play. Still the news was only semi-good, for Elliston would not promise to put it on before next season. In thus accepting *Otho* for performance the following year, he unwittingly balked Keats's main purpose in writing it—to shore up his sinking reputation as a poet and bring in some money at once. Brown voted to withdraw the play and send it to Covent Garden instead, but Keats still objected. Elliston's postponement was not final; and, better yet, Kean had evidently been pleased with the role of Ludolph. So they decided to force the manager's hand by threatening to submit the script to Covent Garden unless he would commit himself to an immediate production. This was a gamble, but it seemed worth taking. Meanwhile Keats set to work revising the play once more, in case Elliston should call their bluff.

A few days later he had another stroke of luck. Taylor, evidently impressed by Elliston's approval of the tragedy, decided to take the risk of bringing out the new collection of poems after all. This time poet and publisher reached a satisfactory understanding. *Lamia* was to be included, substantially revised,[16] along with *Isabella* and *The Eve of St. Agnes*, which Keats agreed to let stand in its original and respectable version. The volume was scheduled for the spring, to coincide, if all went well, with the production of *Otho* at Drury Lane. Now the success which had eluded Keats for months looked near enough to grasp. And within the same week two other events seemed to show the tide running steadily in the right direction. The first was Severn's unexpected success. To his own surprise, and his friends' as well, his painting won the Gold Medal at the Academy. This was a special distinction, since in twelve previous competitions no painting had been judged good enough for the award. The second good omen was another propo-

sition from Abbey, that Keats become a tea-broker. Keats, leaping
to the conclusion that Abbey meant to offer him the brokerage of
his own firm, replied that he might be interested. The work could
be done with little trouble and good profit, he decided to himself,
and he might be able to turn it over to George afterward. In the
rush of his new confidence, everything seemed possible. Yet a few
days later, when he questioned Abbey about the business, his enthusiasm veered round. Abbey described the responsibilities of
the position in detail, and Keats realized it was more work than
he had bargained for.

Christmas drew near in a season of close, muggy weather. Keats
had promised his sister a holiday visit but had to renege in the end.
His new greatcoat and thick shoes made no difference: after even
a short walk in the cold his throat burned with fever. Moreover,
he was hard at work on revisions and begrudged the time for the
trip after so many weeks of idleness. For Christmas Day he accepted
an invitation to dine at the Dilkes' with Brown, Reynolds, Rice,
and Taylor. No doubt Mrs. Dilke and her five bachelors made as
merry as ever, though Keats on this occasion remained in the background. Dilke and Brown got into an argument over fairy tales,
with Dilke, the rationalist, maintaining they were nonsense that
anyone could write. whereupon Brown challenged him to a contest. When their tales were read a few weeks later, however, Dilke's
won the wager, and Brown had to pay up as promised—a punch-
and-beefsteak supper for the whole set.

So far all seemed to be well. But shortly after Christmas two
setbacks came in quick succession. First Elliston refused Brown's
gambit. *Otho,* he decided at last, could not be put on this season.
There was nothing to do but try patching it up again and submitting it to Covent Garden. This was a bitter disappointment. Keats
tried hopefully to visualize Macready—whom he once thought
"execrable"—playing Ludolph instead of Kean: "I am *not* affraid
it will be damn'd in the Garden," he insisted, but he was whistling
in the dark. The second disaster came in a letter from George,
announcing that he was on his way back to England. He was close
to bankruptcy and needed to raise capital immediately.[17] He had
not even waited for Abbey's September remittance to reach him
but had borrowed some money from a Kentucky neighbour and
set out for London, determined to pry loose the remainder of his
inheritance without further delay.

Hard on the heels of his own letter, George arrived at the end of the first week of January. The brothers' meeting must have been a strange one. In spite of their happiness at seeing each other again, the unspoken contrast of this reunion with their hopeful leavetaking a year and a half before must have sharpened in each of them an awareness that the other had changed. Even at first glance, there was a difference: George was balder, John thinner and less energetic. George had become disillusioned about America, but bragged endlessly about his baby girl, impervious to his friends' teasing; Keats, by contrast, was reserved and sarcastic as George had never known him. In each the experience of defeat was accentuating certain traits previously held in check: in George, a ruthless energy of purpose; in John, a moody secretiveness. Another irritant was a budding antagonism between George and Brown, who, it must have appeared to George, had taken his place in his brother's confidence. But for the first week these differences were submerged in a round of parties for the returned pioneer, including a family reunion at the Wylies', a trip to the theatre, dinner at Taylor's, "a pianoforte hop" at the Dilkes', a visit to Haslam's fiancée at Deptford, which Keats managed to shirk, and a gathering of their old set at Wentworth Place.

Yet George must have noticed that Keats showed none of his old gaiety at these occasions. At the Dilkes' he sat on the sidelines. bored or ill-tempered. "There was very little amusement in the room but a Scotchman to hate," he reported in a letter to Georgiana back in Kentucky. "Threepenny parties, halfpenny Dances," the theatre, even the company of his friends, now filled him with unconquerable ennui. "I know the different Styles of talk in different places: what subjects will be started how it will proceed, like an acted play, from the first to the last Act—If I go to Hunt's I run my head into many-times heard puns and music. To Haydon's worn out discourses of poetry and painting: the Miss Reynolds I am affraid to speak to for fear of some sickly reiteration of Phrase or Sentiment. At Dilkes I fall foul of Politics. All I can say is that standing at Charing cross and looking east west north and south I can see nothing but dullness." Then, with almost a pang of revulsion, he added, "I hope now soon to come to the time when I shall never be forc'd to walk through the City and hate as I walk."

With the parties over, the brothers turned to business, and at once it became clear how far apart they had drifted. What had been a tangle in their finances two years ago was now a hopeless snarl of miscalculations and misunderstandings. George evidently succeeded in cutting through the legal difficulties which Keats had found impenetrable, for he persuaded Abbey to give him not only the rest of his own inheritance but his share of Tom's estate as well—something around £300. But he needed more than this and therefore asked Keats to lend him the money which he was to inherit from Tom.[18] On the surface, George's request was reasonable. Keats still had *Otho* to count on, which he had told George would be "a bank" to him if it were produced, and *The Cap and Bells,* which all his friends believed would score a great success when finished, even if the new volume of poems did not.[19] George himself was confident that he could repay at least half of the loan by the next summer. But Keats was caught in a dilemma. He had offered to help George at a time when he had no hope of marrying Fanny and when his health seemed good enough for him to turn to medicine or even journalism if he failed with poetry. Now all this was changed. He was gloomy about *Otho*'s prospects at Covent Garden; he was in debt to several of his friends; he could not tell George of his fears for his health, and he would not tell him of his commitment to Fanny Brawne. Even this put another barrier between them, for George, sensing some strain in Keats's behaviour toward Fanny, accepted the Reynoldses' opinion of her as "an artful, bad-hearted girl." But if Keats could no longer confide in his brother as he used to do, he could not yet break a promise. With the superior strength of insensitivity, George had pinned him to the ground, as he had done time and again in their schooldays. Only to Fanny could Keats hint at his resentment, remarking that "having a family to provide for makes a man selfish." [20]

The long journal-letter to Georgiana which he started during George's visit gives only an intimation of this conflict. It is the wittiest letter Keats ever wrote, affectionate and full of fun—"and if Scandal happens to be fun," he noted, "that is no fault of ours." Georgiana's disenchantment with America seems to have drawn them closer together. To prove that London was as dull as Louisville could possibly be, he drew a gallery of satirical sketches of their acquaintance, lit up with flashes of Shandean nonsense. Haslam's fiancée at Deptford, for instance, filled him with something livelier than mere ennui—a magnetic repulsion that drove him metaphorically across the whole map of southeastern England. He

dashed off a comparison of the three greatest wits of his acquaintance—Rice, Reynolds, and Richards—in a parody of Hazlitt's
"fine discriminating criticism" of Swift, Voltaire, and Rabelais
which had delighted him two winters ago, then capped it with an
account of the three greatest bores he knew, then blew it all up
with an anatomy of nonsense stretching around the globe. "Upon
the whole I dislike Mankind," he concluded; "whatever people
on the other side of the question may advance they cannot deny
that they are always surprised at hearing of a good action and never
of a bad one." "Thank God," he said, "there are a great many who
will sacrifice their worldly interest for a friend: I wish there were
more who would sacrifice their passions. The worst of Men are
those whose self interests are their passion—the next those whose
passions are their self-interest." It is a curious distinction. One
wonders whom Keats would have chosen to illustrate the first
class. The second class seems to be as near as he could come to
criticizing George to his sister-in-law.

So Keats began to smoulder with suppressed rage at the world;
but only once during these weeks did he let it blaze out. One
afternoon he was invited to dine in town at Hilton's, the painter
and friend of Taylor. The party was made up mostly of other
painters, and the talk soon turned to the recent Academy award
of the Gold Medal. None of the Academy set had ever heard of
Severn before, and none of them liked his painting. The general
critical comment, as a matter of fact, had been fairly scathing:
Haydon's own magazine, *The Annals of the Fine Arts,* described it
as a "humble mediocrity." One of Hilton's guests came up with
the tale that Severn was an elderly incompetent who had tried
for the prize so many times that the council gave it to him in the
end out of pity. Keats sat glowering while the others laughed at
the story, waiting for Hilton to deny it. But Hilton said nothing.
Keats then rose from his seat in one of those rages that made him
look like a tall man. It was a lie, he shouted. Severn was a young
painter who had never tried for the prize before; he knew the man
himself and admired the painting. And he would not sit at the
same table with men willing to believe such falsehoods. Then he
stalked out of the house.[21]

So January passed and George's visit drew to a close. On the
twenty-eighth Keats dashed off one last page to Georgiana before
posting his letter in a hurry to catch up with George, who had left

London for Liverpool at six that morning. This postscript adds
a few jokes and gives one piece of news. Keats was planning once
again to move away from Hampstead into the country. Whether
it was the state of his pockets or of his health that persuaded him,
he gave no hint, nor did he say anything of George's departure.
That had been no joking matter. George, who set out in too great
a hurry to say good-bye to Fanny in Walthamstow, carried with
him the remainder of his brother's inheritance—all except a few
pounds to tide Keats over till he started repaying the loan. His
visit had been a success, for he managed to raise some £700 in all.
Yet, as he said good-bye, George wondered whether he should have
pressed his brother so hard. He tried to reassure himself out loud:
after all, John had many friends to fall back on. His words must
have echoed ironically in Keats's ears, for they were the very reassurance he had given George in his letter from Winchester. They
parted at the inn-yard in the chilly gloom of the January morning,
and Keats returned to Hampstead with the anger swelling inside
him. When at last he reached Wentworth Place he pulled out of
his pocket a bundle of notes and handed it to Brown. It was all
the money he had left in the world. Brown counted it over at once:
it came to £60. After subtracting his borrowings and unpaid bills,
Keats was worse than penniless: George had left him £20 in debt.[22]

"Brown—he ought not to have asked me." So Brown reported
Keats's words—his first open criticism of his brother.[23] In astonishment, Brown asked Keats why he had agreed to the loan. The
story of his unlucky promise to George came out. Brown was in-
dignant that Keats had kept the promise a secret from him, but
Keats merely replied that he knew Brown would have opposed
the loan if he had told him about it. It was too late to argue, but
it was time enough to regret Keats's act. A few days later [24] *Otho*
was sent back from Covent Garden with a note of rejection in a
boy's handwriting. Brown suspected that the manuscript had not
even been opened. Now there was nothing to hope from the
tragedy for the time being at least—and thus little from the new
volume of poems.

A few days after George's departure a long spell of cold snowy
weather broke and a thaw set in. On February 3 Keats went into
town for the day without his greatcoat, the weather had turned so
warm. When he came to take the evening coach back to Hampstead, it was frosty again. As usual, he could afford only an out-

side seat, and, riding back full against the wind, he was chilled to the bone. All day long he had felt fevered; now, as he walked down Pond Street, his head whirled. When Brown saw him come staggering into Wentworth Place he thought at first that Keats was drunk. At second glance he saw he was seriously ill, flushed and trembling, hardly able to speak. Immediately Brown told him to go to bed. As Keats groped his way up the cold staircase and climbed into bed, a fit of coughing seized him. Brown, who followed him with a glass of spirits, heard him gasp, "That is blood from my mouth."

As Brown hurried to his side, Keats hitched himself up on the pillows and told him to bring the candle close. In the wan circle of light Brown saw a spot of blood on the sheet, bright red against the white. Keats muttered, "This is unfortunate." Then, according to Brown's account, he looked very steadily up into his friend's face and said, "I know the colour of that blood. It's arterial blood. There's no mistaking that colour." As calmly as he could, he added, "That blood is my death-warrant. I must die."

## Chapter Thirteen

# A Wrecked Life

I T had come at last, the proof of the suspicion that had been growing within him for months. And when it came, his only thought was of Fanny Brawne. The blood rushed up in his lungs so violently that for a few minutes he felt almost suffocated; as it seethed within him, he was sure he was dying and could think only that if he died he lost Fanny forever. Slowly the tide ebbed, and still he thought of her. The first minute he could leave him, Brown ran for Mr. Rodd, the Hampstead surgeon, and, according to the best medical practice of the day, Keats was bled. Hour after hour he lay awake, while Brown watched anxiously by his bedside; then toward morning he fell asleep at last. The next day his first request was to see Fanny. Brown told him that she had gone to town. Keats insisted on writing a note to send as soon as she returned, begging her to come to see him. The hours crawled by. All afternoon Keats lay straining for a glimpse of the London coach through the window or studying the pattern of the bed curtains. At last Brown admitted he had been telling a tale: the Brawnes had been at home all the time.

One hopes that Fanny was allowed to come that evening, as she did almost every day in the weeks that followed. Her visit at the end of the afternoon became the centre of his day, her existence his reason for fighting his way back to health. At first he made good progress. On February 6, the third day after the attack, he was well enough to receive a few visitors and sit up to read the papers—full of news of the death of George III—and write a letter to his sister. His own illness filled him with new anxiety for her. He dropped a hint of this to Fanny Brawne, "My Sister would be glad of my company a little longer"; but to Fanny herself he could speak only of his concern for her health. "You must be careful always to wear warm cloathing not only in frost but in a Thaw," he warned her. He made light of his own illness, blaming it on the treacherous weather; then, for lack of news, described the view out of his window. "The half built houses opposite us stand just as they were and seem dying of old age before they are brought up. The grass looks very dingy, the Celery is all gone, and there is nothing to enliven one but a few Cabbage Staks that seem fix'd on the superanuated List." Two days later he was well enough to go downstairs, supported by Brown and their Irish housekeeper, to sit wrapped up in blankets on the sofa in the front parlour. In high spirits, he wrote Fanny again, sketching the passers-by: a pot-boy with the one-o'clock beer, colliers and brick-makers and gipsies, a fellow with a wooden clock under his arm, the old French emigrant "whith his hands joined behind on his hips, and his face full of political schemes," and two old ladies from Well Walk, coaxing their fat little dog along with an ivory-tipped cane.

Like most invalids in the first days of recovery, he saw everything around him shining with a new light. "How astonishingly does the chance of leaving the world impress a sense of its natural beauties on us," he wrote to Rice on the fourteenth. "Like poor Falstaff, though I do not babble, I think of green fields. I muse with the greatest affection on every flower I have known from my infancy—their shapes and coulours are as new to me as if I had just created them with a superhuman fancy." Rice had written Keats to warn him against the "haunting and deformed thoughts and feelings" that often assailed him after one of his own relapses. Yet to Keats his illness seemed to have the opposite effect. "As far as I can judge in so short a time," he wrote, "it has relieved my Mind of a load of deceptive thoughts and images and makes me perceive things in a truer light." There can be no doubt that he was thinking of Fanny Brawne. The brooding jealousies of the previous months had lifted like a mist. For the time being he could demand of her only what she could fully and gladly give— a wave of her hand from the garden, a half-hour of chatter at the end of the afternoon, a kiss at parting, a good-night note each evening before he slept. But for Fanny also the shock of his illness must have marked the end of thoughtless girlhood at last and the start of her own soul-making. For weeks she refused to leave Wentworth Place, in order to be there whenever he wanted her. Brown, jealous of his position as head nurse, objected to her calls and had them cut down to a few minutes at a time; but still she stood by. The summer before, Keats remembered, she had complained that he loved her only for her beauty; now he could prove he had other reasons. "Do not I see a heart naturally furnish'd with wings imprison itself with me?" She convinced him of her love all over again by this tribute; as he exclaimed, "I could build an Altar to you for it."

Yet after the first week his recovery slowed down to a discouraging pace. On the tenth the morning was mild enough for a walk in the garden; but this experiment was not repeated for quite a while. For one thing, the weather turned cold and raw again; for another, his strength was not returning at the rate he hoped. Keats blamed it on the diet ordered for him, so little food that "a mouse would starve upon it." Then the medicine he was taking began to set his nerves on edge. Brown, while sitting with Keats, amused himself by copying grotesque heads from his collection of Hogarth prints; and one of these—"a damn'd melancholy picture" of a Methodist meeting—gave Keats "a psalm singing nightmare" which made him almost faint away in his sleep. Yet when Mr. Rodd examined him at the end of the second week he found no signs of injury to the lungs. "Quietness of mind and fine weather," he told his patient, were all he needed to cure him.

To an extent this prescription was right, for there is little doubt that Keat's first haemorrhage had been brought on largely by the crisis of his anger against George.[1] Yet, as he told Fanny, his mind had always been "the most discontented and restless one that ever was put into a body too small for it." And knowing as much about his disease as his doctor did, and how little could really be done for it, he could not be cheered by Rodd's encouragement. As the weeks went by and the weight and tightness in his chest did not lift, he became certain that his lungs had been damaged. As for quietness of mind, he was now ordered to give up the two things that mattered most in the world—poetry and his love. "My dearest Girl," he wrote to Fanny in dejection, "According to all appearances I am to be separated from you as much as possible. I am reccommended not even to read poetry much less write it. I wish

I had even a little hope. I cannot say forget me—but I would mention that there are impossibilities in the world."

This oblique reference to "impossibilities" was as close as he could come to saying what he realized must be said, once the first shock of his illness had passed. He must release Fanny from their engagement. At this her love and pride and suspicion flared up all at once. Evidently she sensed this was not so much Keats's idea as someone else's suggestion; but she also took Keats's gesture of renunciation half childishly as a rejection. "My dearest Girl," he replied in distress, "how could it ever have been my wish to forget you? The utmost stretch my mind has been capable of was to endeavour to forget you for your own sake. Believe too my Love that our friends think and speak for the best, and if their best is not our best it is not their fault." Who these friends were is a guess—perhaps Brown or possibly Reynolds, who came to see Keats around this time. Fanny evidently accepted his explanation and promised him she would wait for as long as was necessary. This reassurance was "as much a wonder to me as a delight," [2] he told her, not quite able to believe it entirely. Soon afterward she gave him a ring, engraved in true-love style with both their names inside, and for a day he was as happy as illness would let him be. "Health is my expected heaven," he wrote her, "and you are the Houri—this word I believe is both singular and plural—if only plural, never mind—you are a thousand of them."

Yet there was one thought of surpassing bitterness that even the assurance of Fanny's love could not drive from Keats's mind. He had lost his gamble against time; he was now convinced that he had failed to win the immortality as a poet on which he had staked his whole life. The new volume of poems was still not ready to send off to the printer; but even if he got back his strength to complete the revisions, it would be a poor thing beside what he had aimed at achieving. For with *Hyperion* still only half started, all the work of the last two years went for nothing. "I must make myself as good a Philosopher as possible," he told Fanny, and this conviction of failure called out all his stoicism. Night after night he lay awake, looking back over his life and trying to sum it up in some fashion he could accept. " 'If I should die,' said I to myself, 'I have left no immortal work behind me—nothing to make my friends proud of my memory—but I have lov'd the principle of beauty in all things, and if I had had time I would have made myself remember'd.' " It was a noble assertion of identity, a moment of recognition such as is demanded of the great tragic hero in his hour of defeat. Yet in the same breath Keats asked Fanny to forgive him for thinking of fame instead of herself alone, and the words of Milton nerving himself against the possibility of an early death flashed across his memory. "Thoughts like these," he wrote her, "came very feebly whilst I was in health and every pulse beat for you—now you divide with this (may *I* say it?) 'last infirmity of noble minds' all my reflection."

So February went by, a silent battle for peace of mind waged amid the trivialities of an invalid existence. Friends came out from London to call; Hampstead ladies showered him with jam and black currant jelly, which he spilled on Brown's Ben Jonson; Fanny kept him stocked with oranges. Hunt, who had recently moved to nearby Kentish Town, walked over several times, bringing with him the fashionable poet "Barry Cornwall"—Bryan Waller Procter, who brought Keats his latest books. Keats must have been ironically entertained by his *Sicilian Story,* for Procter had also taken Hazlitt's recommendation and retold the tale of Isabella and her pot of basil in a sentimental and decorous version that immediately became popular. His milksop diet of reading also included some of Rousseau's correspondence with lady friends, which it amused him to compare with his own and Fanny's. Otherwise there was little more to mark one day from another than the first thrush singing over the fields, the news of Cobbett's campaign for election to Parliament, an occasional good night's sleep, and a glimpse of Fanny as she went walking over the Heath.

Early in March he took an unexpected turn for the worse. His rapid pulse and starvation diet combined to bring on an attack of palpitations which left him so shaken that for several days he could not endure the sound of an unexpected voice or the sight of a newly arrived letter. On March 8 Mr. Rodd decided to call in Dr. Robert Bree from London for consultation. Bree was a Fellow of the Royal College of Physicians, one of the country's leading respiratory specialists, and doctor to one of the royal dukes. Yet after examining Keats he merely repeated Rodd's verdict that there was "no pulmonary affection and no organic defect whatever" and told Keats that his disease was all "on his mind." He cautioned him against worrying and recommended a more robust diet as well as a little fresh air and exercise. Accordingly Keats was walking in the garden a few days later and picking up the revision of his poems. On the fourteenth he made an ill-advised trip into town to dine with Taylor, and the next day the palpitations returned. More than a week later he was still too upset to write more than a scrap of a letter to his sister. He could not trust Bree's diagnosis. To Fanny Brawne he wrote, "God alone knows whether I am destined to taste of happiness with you: at all events I myself know thus much, that I consider it no mean Happiness to have lov'd you thus far—if it is to be no further I shall not be unthankful—if I am to recover, the day of my recovery shall see me by your side from which nothing shall separate me."

But Brown, hovering in the background, took Dr. Bree's pronouncement at face value. Two days after the physician's visit, he wrote jubilantly to Taylor that Keats was now "perfectly out of danger"—even though he was still too nervous to read his mail— and began talking with Keats about their making a trip to Hampshire together. With the unconscious insensitivity of many robust people, Brown seemed unwilling to admit that Keats was seriously ill. It was unfortunate, this illness, but Brown was also beginning to find it inconvenient. To his credit it must be said that he had nursed Keats faithfully for over a month; but now, as he began to think ahead to the summer, he must have wondered how much more would be required of him. Furthermore, he had problems of his own to concern him—those pleasures which, as Keats had told him in September, it was his duty to procure while still in the prime of life. This pursuit of duty was bearing unexpected fruit, for sometime during the autumn Abby, the Irish housekeeper, had become pregnant.

Just how much of a problem this posed to Brown is uncertain. He had been taken with Abby's lively humour and robust good looks, but he apparently had no intention of becoming involved with her. In his eyes a mistress was as much of an encumbrance as a wife,[3] and he wanted neither; besides, Abby was an ignorant peasant girl and a fanatical Catholic. Nor did Brown seem at this point to have any interest in a child as such, even though years later the son himself testified that Brown had deliberately seduced Abby "for the sake of the offspring." [4] If this story is true, as seems doubtful, Brown's way of providing himself with an heir is curious, to say the least. It was an age in which illegitimacy was an accepted fact of life, and Keats's comment on Severn's by-blow shows that he and his friends took it in their stride. Brown seems to have been concerned this spring mainly with getting Abby out of sight to bear her child and with being at a safe distance himself when the time came.[5] For this he must convince Keats that he was getting well—well enough, at least, to spend the summer away from Wentworth Place, for Brown also needed the money which his summer rental always brought in.

Keats's own reaction to Brown's situation is also uncertain. Several months later the thought of Brown living next door to Fanny "with his indecencies" became too bitter for him to stomach; but during the spring his loyalty to Brown remained unshaken. When Brown learned from Sam Brawne, Fanny's brother, that a neighbour of theirs was spreading malicious gossip about his behaviour in another matter, Keats begged Fanny to tell him what she had heard, for he felt "the least attaint on the disinterested character of Brown very deeply." Yet for whatever cause, the old tension between Brown and Fanny began to be felt again. Between Brown's scorn of women in general or jealousy of Fanny in particular and Fanny's habit of rising gaily to every occasion, Keats was caught once more in an exacerbating conflict. In his own depressed moods, the sight of Fanny good-humouredly meeting Brown's over-hearty badinage began to rasp his nerves unendurably. "To see you happy and in high spirits is a great consolation to me," he wrote with unexpected coolness one day; "still let me believe that you are not half so happy as my restoration would make you." The best he could do was try to keep them apart; so one morning he stiffly suggested to Fanny that she wait till Brown went out before coming to see him. She took this as a reproach, and once again he capitulated in anguish. "Sweetest Fanny," he wrote back, "You fear, sometimes, I do not love you so much as you wish? My dear Girl I love you ever and ever and without reserve. In every way—even my jealousies have been agonies of Love. I have vex'd you too much. But for Love! Can I help it?" [6] She found this argument unanswerable, but for several weeks they kept up the strategem: she waited till she saw Brown disappearing down the lane, then slipped next door for her visit.

Toward the end of March it seemed Keats had reached firm ground at last. Day by day his chest felt freer, his pulse steadier;

his short walks in the garden became more regular. His spirits picked up; he began to suspect that he had worried too much about his illness. Now one visit with Fanny a day was not enough. "I imagine you now sitting in your new black dress which I like so much," he wrote at the end of one afternoon, "and if I were a little less selfish and more enthusiastic I should run round and surprise you with a knock at the door. I fear I am too prudent for a dying kind of Lover. Yet, there is a great difference between going off in warm blood like Romeo, and making one's exit like a frog in a frost." Best of all, perhaps, he could now pick up his poems where he had left off revising them. He still had to take it slowly, but the task heartened him as nothing else could do. "Let me have another oportunity of years before me," he wrote, "and I will not die without being remember'd."

On the twenty-fifth he made his first public appearance at a long-awaited occasion. Haydon had at last finished "Christ's Triumphal Entry into Jerusalem" and was exhibiting it, complete with a frame weighing six hundred pounds, at the Egyptian Hall. The word had already got around that the painting was a masterpiece; and on the afternoon of the opening Piccadilly was blocked with carriages. Ministers, ambassadors, bishops, beauties, all crowded into the great hall to see and be seen. For a while the verdict was uncertain. The weak yet unconventional portrayal of Christ riding an ass puzzled some and displeased others. One sardonic Academician, James Northcote, quipped, "Mr. Haydon, the ass is the Saviour of your picture." But the day was saved for Haydon when Mrs. Siddons swept in at her most majestic. Suddenly silencing the room, she stared at the painting for a minute, then "in her solemn and sublime tone" declared, "It is perfect!" [7] From this moment Haydon's fame was secure, and for a while his fortunes too: the exhibition brought him almost £1800. Keats, caught in the kind of crowd he hated most, retreated to a corner, where he found Hazlitt, who was present as art critic for The Edinburgh Review. It was the first time in months that they had seen each other, and for Keats the day was made.

A few days later, at Keats's request, Brown wrote to George, whom Keats had decided not to send any news of his illness till it could be good news. Brown had reasons of his own for pretending that Keats was making better progress than he was, and gave George far too rosy a picture of his brother's health—that he was eating, drinking, and sleeping as well as ever and walking five miles without fatigue. This letter was not written at Keats's dictation, for it mentioned a matter about which he knew nothing. Dr. Bree had recommended that Keats be sent to Italy in the fall. This was a standard prescription for English consumptives, but with Keats's finances in the state they were, it also posed a problem. So Brown reminded George of his promise to repay his brother £200 by the summer. It is odd, however, that he did not discuss the matter with Keats himself.[8] The inference seems plain—that Brown suspected Keats would ask him to go to Italy with him, and that he had no intention of doing so. Accordingly he kept the proposal a secret and proceeded with his own plans.

So April started for Keats with the prospect of returning health, of walks on the Heath with Fanny and a visit to his sister in Walthamstow. He could work more steadily now at preparing his poems for the press. The weather turned fine; his spirits rose; then suddenly the spring clouded over. Brown announced that he must rent his house again and had found a tenant to take it from early May to late October. With his usual single-mindedness, he had decided to go on another walking trip in Scotland for the summer, leaving Abby to bear her child in July alone in London, and Keats to fend for himself through the summer. Though Keats could not have been completely unprepared for this announcement, he was badly shaken by it nevertheless. He realized he could not ask Brown to stay on in Hampstead for his sake, but he could not talk or even think of leaving Wentworth Place without becoming unbearably anxious. Yet his depression merely confirmed the doctor's opinion that he needed a change of scene—perhaps the voyage up to Scotland with Brown and then back. "The Doctor assures me," he wrote gloomily to his sister on April 21, "that there is nothing the matter with me except nervous irritability and a general weakness of the whole system which has proceeded from my anxiety of mind of late years and the too great excitement of poetry—Mr Brown is going to Scotland by the Smack, and I am advised for change of exercise and air to accompany him. They tell me," he added, "I must study lines and tangents and squares and circles to put a little Ballast into my mind."

Geometry and sea air—it is a pitiful prescription. Yet Keats considered the voyage with Brown for over a week before deciding he could not bear so great a separation from Hampstead. As he told his sister, he was endeavouring to avoid all melancholy or anxious thoughts as "pernicious to health." He tried not to think of George, who had not written him since his good-bye note from Liverpool. But he could not help worrying about Fanny in her imprisonment at the Abbeys'. They had forbidden her to visit him all spring; they made her give away her spaniel and kept her short of pocket-money, then nagged at her for ingratitude. Mrs. Abbey even hinted that she was living on their charity, a remark which drove Fanny to ask Keats to look into her financial affairs. He sent her some money which he could hardly spare, for he was now running hopelessly into debt. On paying his doctors' bills and settling accounts with Brown at the beginning of May, Keats found his obligations added up to £25 more than he possessed— not including his previous debts or allowing for the immediate future.[9] As a last service to his friend before leaving, Brown borrowed £50 at interest from his lawyer to tide Keats over the summer. On May 6 Keats sailed with him down the Thames as far as Gravesend, then got off the smack with the pilot. No doubt Brown was as jocular as ever as they said good-bye, for he urged Keats to finish *The Cap and Bells;* Keats was more constrained. One wonders whether it occurred to either man that he might not see the other again.

—»»·«««—

Keats had decided to spend the summer in Kentish Town, a pleasant little village on the edge of the Heath about two miles from Hampstead. This was close enough for frequent visits to and from Wentworth Place, though one wonders why he did not choose lodgings in Hampstead, where he could see Fanny every day. Still, in Kentish Town he would have Hunt as a neighbour. The spring had brought a renewal of their friendship, on terms very different from the old uneasy relationship of master and disciple. Keats on his side had grown far beyond the intolerance of untried youth for the failures of its elders. He had learned something of defeat and betrayal since his break with Hunt, and could value the older man's warmth and generosity more truly than before. Hunt was still struggling cheerfully under the burdens of debt, poor health, a large family, and an ailing wife. But he now gladly accepted Keats as an equal and evidently suspected nothing

of the younger man's battle against his domination three years
before. As a gesture of friendship Keats gave him some of the
shorter poems which he had not included in his new volume, and
Hunt immediately published "La Belle Dame" in his new literary
weekly *The Indicator*. And it was Hunt who found lodgings for
Keats in May, a set of quiet, airy rooms in Wesleyan Place, only
a few doors from his own house in Mortimer Terrace.

Here Keats was comfortable enough, though hardly happy, and
May went by without event. "I am well enough to extract much
more pleasure than pain out of the summer, even though I should
get no better," he wrote Brown after moving into his new quarters.
Reading the proofs of the new volume kept him busy for a while.
He did not yet feel equal to going ahead with *The Cap and Bells*,
however—"being willing," as he explained, "in case of a relapse,
to have nothing to reproach myself with." Still he was well enough
to go walking alone, though unexpected showers kept him dodging from shelter to shelter. Several times he journeyed into town
to visit friends, and for daily companionship he could always drop
in at Hunt's. There he would have found the same set-tos of
punning and music as before, the same picnics on the Heath complete with cold ham, salad, ginger beer, children, and poetry.
Though he remained a rather silent spectator on these occasions,
they kept him from real loneliness. At Hunt's too he found a
shelf of the Waverley Novels, which provided him with hours of
good reading. And one especially fine summer afternoon Hunt's
stockbroker friend Horace Smith invited him to dinner at his
country house in Fulham with his literary cronies. They ate early,
sitting out under the trees, and—perhaps in honour of Keats's
forthcoming book—drank a dozen bottles of his favourite Château
Margaux.

Yet slowly isolation from Fanny began to have its poisonous
effect on Keats again. At the end of his occasional visits to Hampstead he found parting from her almost more than he could bear.
Day after day, as May wore into June, he remained alone in his
rooms, thinking back over the happiness they had shared, racked
with longing for what was still denied him. "I see you come down
in the morning," he wrote her, "I see you meet me at the Window
—I see every thing over again eternally that I ever have seen."
For one whole day he was haunted by a memory of Fanny in a
moment of triumph, wearing a shepherdess dress at some costume

ball. Yet these images led inexorably to others—Fanny as gay and brilliant as ever in his absence, beautiful to other eyes than his own. Without the daily reassurance of her presence, she became to him more and more the projected image of his old irrational suspicion of the beloved woman. Three months before, he had begged her not to remain at home for his sake; now the news that she had gone to a party at the Dilkes' filled him with savage possessiveness. "Do not live as if I was not existing," he burst out when he learned she had gone into town alone, *"promise me you will not for some time, till I get better."* It was unreasonable, he knew; but he could be convinced of her love only if she was as unhappy as he. "You must be so if you love me—upon my Soul I can be contented with nothing else," he stormed. "If you can smile in peoples faces, and wish them to admire you *now,* you never have nor ever will love me. You must be mine to die upon the rack if I want you."

It was a terrible letter, and one which can be understood only as the outcry of a man of twenty-four against the slow approach of death. He was in a state of mind, as he wrote his sister, that "makes one envy Scavengers and Cinder-sifters." As week after week dragged by with no further improvement in his health, Keats began to lose faith—in his own eventual recovery, in Fanny's love if he should recover, even in a life after death if he should not. This last doubt was to grow more terrifying as the months went by. "I long to believe in immortality," he wrote Fanny in despair in mid-June. "I shall never be able to bid you an entire farewell. If I am destined to be happy with you here— how short is the longest Life—I wish to believe in immortality— I wish to live with you for ever." This was an anguish which Fanny, with her simple religious faith, could understand even less than his jealous rages. Stunned by his previous letter, she had written back to protest that he had wronged her "in word thought and deed." He replied in a rush of remorse: "If I have been cruel and injust I swear my love has ever been greater than my cruelty which lasts but a minute whereas my Love come what will shall last for ever. Do muse it over again and see into my heart," he added; "my Love to you is 'true as truth's simplicity and simpler than the infancy of truth.'"

Yet it was not as simple as all that; for, in echoing the words of Shakespeare's Troilus, Keats implied again the suspicion which, in February, he told her he had "dismissed utterly"—"of you being a little inclined to the Cressid." His copy of Shakespeare's Sonnets gives a revealing glimpse into his mind during these lonely weeks, for he was rereading them with the same brooding intensity with which he had read and marked his *Anatomy of Melancholy* the autumn before. The theme of all his markings now was "the pangs of dispriz'd love"—remorse, reproach, doubt, jealousy, weariness, despair, all the welter of his feelings about Fanny:

> If that be fair whereon my false eyes dote,
> What means the world to say it is not so?
> If it be not, then love doth well denote
> Love's eye is not so true as all men's: no,
> How can it? O, how can Love's eye be true,
> That is so vex'd with watching and with tears? . . .*

And in the turmoil of his distrust of Fanny he began to be consumed with another suspicion—that his friends were spying on their attachment and trying to come between them. It is possible that Mrs. Dilke began inviting Fanny to parties in town out of real concern for her future; it is likely that the Reynolds girls were discussing their affairs behind his back. Whatever happened, Keats was driven to fury. "My friends laugh at you!" he exploded. "I know some of them—when I know them all I shall never think of them again as friends or even acquaintance." His long-smouldering resentment against the Reynolds girls—"these Laughers, who do not like you, who envy you for your Beauty, who were plying me with disencouragements with respect to you eternally"—now flamed out in the open. "Do not let my name ever pass between you and those laughers," he begged Fanny. "Your name never passes my Lips—do not let mine pass yours."

This suspicion evidently provoked some kind of outburst at the Dilkes' on one of his visits around the middle of June. Writing to Brown shortly afterward, Keats alluded to the incident but refused to apologize for it.[10] "I know that they are more happy and comfortable than I am; therefore why should I trouble myself about it? I foresee I shall know very few people in the course of a year or two," he commented acidly. Going on to tell Brown about an exhibition of portraits he had recently seen in Pall Mall, he betrayed his mood by picking out only the unpleasant faces to

---

* Sonnet CXLVIII, marked by Keats in his copy of Shakespeare's *Poetical Works*, in the Keats House at Hampstead.

describe. "There is James the first,—whose appearance would disgrace a 'Society for the suppression of women;' there is old Lord Burleigh, who has the appearance of a Pharisee just rebuffed by a gospel bon-mot. Then, there is George the second, very like an unintellectual Voltaire, troubled with the gout and a bad temper." To Brown himself he was curiously cool in his letter, ending with a brusque "Good morning to you" very different from his usual affectionate closing. But he gave one clue to what was going on in his mind: "My book is coming out with very low hopes, though not spirits on my part. This shall be my last trial; not succeeding, I shall try what I can do in the Apothecary line."

The new volume was due to appear at last toward the end of June, and already he was convinced it would fail. Taylor kept fretting over the conclusion of *Lamia* and asking Keats to bowdlerize it here and there; [11] he also insisted on including *Hyperion* —the two and a half books of the original version. Keats had protested vehemently against printing the poem in its unfinished state, but without success. Now, he realized, the work by which he had hoped to be remembered would stand forever as an abortive fragment, falling even further short of his intentions than *Endymion*. And, try as he might, he could not keep from worrying about the reviews to come. On June 22, the day before the book was expected to appear, a note arrived from his sister, begging him to come see her. Evidently her affairs at the Abbeys' had reached a crisis. Keats started out at once but turned back a few minutes later. He had begun to cough again, and his mouth was filled with the rusty taste of blood.

It was not a haemorrhage but only a premonition of one that pulled him up short. He returned to his rooms to spend the rest of the day alone. At the end of the afternoon he pulled himself together to go to the Hunts' for tea, where he found they had guests —a Mr. and Mrs. William Gisborne, friends of the Shelleys in Italy. Keats said nothing of his attack but remained pale and silent while the conversation ran on. The talk soon turned to singing, an interest which Mrs. Gisborne shared with Hunt. She described the great Italian tenor Farinelli, who had the art of holding a note almost indefinitely while taking imperceptible breaths. At this Keats was evidently overwhelmed by his recurrent nightmare of suffocation. In a voice so low he could hardly be heard, he observed that it must be as painful to listen to this prolonged note as to wait for a diver who has disappeared into the depths of the sea to emerge above the surface at last. Mrs. Gisborne at first had not believed that this insignificant-looking young man was the author of *Endymion;* but she was so struck by this remark that she wrote it down in her journal that night. Tea over, Keats dragged himself back to his lonely rooms, and there, a few hours later, a real haemorrhage set in.

Dr. Lambe, the local physician, was called and found Keats's condition so serious that Hunt insisted he be moved into Mortimer Terrace the next day. The house was small and untidy, overrun with five dirty, ill-disciplined children, but it offered Hunt's companionship and Mrs. Hunt's care. Keats could do nothing but agree. On the twenty-third he was settled in an upstairs room, where he lay with Fanny Brawne's ring on his finger and some flowers she had sent on the table, hardly speaking, struggling to be patient. And so began a seven-week imprisonment during which he never once saw Fanny, a period which he could not remember afterward without shuddering. A spell of stifling heat set in on the twenty-fourth. The cries of ballad singers and street venders drifted up from the road below, while the children shouted and scuffled through the house. Hunt, though unwell himself, did his best to take Keats's mind off his illness, getting him to help in writing an essay on the hot weather for that week's *Indicator,* and dedicating his newest volume, a translation of Tasso's *Amyntas,* to him. Yet, as the sun beat mercilessly down on the roof over his room, Keats's blood-spitting continued. Soon Lambe found it necessary to call in Dr. George Darling, a well-known London physician who had attended Taylor, Haydon, and a number of Keats's other friends, and under their combined care Keats began to regain strength. He ordered a copy of Spenser to give to Fanny and went through it, marking his favourite passages for her. For another week he continued to mend; then he learned something which at once destroyed the little hope he had left for the future. Darling and Lambe had prescribed the final remedy, a voyage to Italy. The news was broken to Keats on July 5. He must leave England at the end of the summer.

To Keats this meant one thing only. "They talk of my going to Italy," he wrote Fanny shortly afterward. " 'Tis certain I shall never recover if I am to be so long separate from you." Now at last he was convinced that he would die. He became so nervous that having to speak to a stranger half choked him. Severn came out to see him and was shocked by the change in Keats's appearance. Emaciated, dejected, he had begun to look startlingly like Tom in his last months. His hands already resembled an old man's, the colour faded, the veins swollen. When the Gisbornes next called, Hunt drew Gisborne aside and asked him to write Shelley asking him to befriend Keats in Italy. Keats was aware of this well-intentioned plotting but too numb with hopelessness to protest. It was not merely that he felt he could not survive the separation from Fanny: he could not convince himself that she would be faithful to him in his absence. Yet to explain to Hunt why he could not go to Italy would mean confiding the secret of his engagement. So he put off consenting to the plan, though every morning the thought of it woke him up at dawn and haunted him throughout the day.

Hunt was quick to sense that Keats was deeply disturbed and guessed that he was worrying about the fate of the new volume. This was certainly one reason for Keats's depression.[12] The book had finally appeared on July 1 with an "Advertisement" which roused him to fury. Without consulting him, Taylor had apologized for the unfinished *Hyperion* by explaining that it was printed "contrary to the wish of the author" and that it was "intended to have been of equal length with *Endymion,* but the reception given to that work discouraged him from proceeding." In the first copy that came to hand, Keats savagely crossed out the entire Advertisement and wrote above it "I had no part in this; I was ill at the time." Beneath the statement that he had given up *Hyperion* because of the adverse reviews of *Endymion,* he scrawled "This is a lie." Yet in his growing despondency the lie began to appear a truth. Since February he had gradually come to believe with his doctors that anxiety and disappointment were the real causes of his illness; [13] now his hatred of the reviewers who had killed his hopes brimmed over. Thanks to them, he would be remembered as a failure, his works a mockery; Lockhart's sneers had doomed his chances not only of worldly success but even of marriage, of life itself—or so he began to think. And for the first six weeks after the new book's appearance, it seemed it might receive the same treatment as *Endymion.* Except for two enthusiastic reviews by Lamb and Hunt and a favourable notice in *The Sun,* it was either damned with faint praise or dismissed as another Cockney effusion, "a nosegay of enigmas." [14] Week by week Keats's anger smouldered till in a letter to Brown in mid-August he exclaimed in a moment of scalding bitterness, "If I die you must ruin Lockhart." *

Yet it was the thought of Brown himself and Fanny that drove Keats to the edge of sanity in these weeks at Hunt's. In his obsession with keeping their love a secret, he forbade Fanny to come to visit him in Mortimer Terrace. His letters to her were addressed to her mother to avert all notice; he even waited till he reached the end of one of his letters before writing the salutation "My dearest Girl" at the top—"that no eye may catch it." Day after day he sat looking toward Hampstead, waiting for Fanny's letters to come, or surrendering in desperation to the fantasies that now raged uncontrollably across his mind. The thought of the last two years became an acutely physical sensation—the taste of brass on his palate. "I cannot forget what has pass'd," he wrote her in agony. "When you were in the habit of flirting with Brown you would have left off, could your own heart have felt one half of one pang mine did. Brown is a good sort of Man—he did not know he was doing me to death by inches. Though I know his love and friendship for me, though at this moment I should be without pence were it not for his assistance, I will never see or speak to him until we are both old men, if we are to be." Then in a great eruption of fury he blazed out, "How have you pass'd this month? Who have you smil'd with? I appeal to you by the blood of that Christ you believe in: Do not write to me if you have done anything this month which it would have pained me to have seen. Be serious! Love is not a plaything—I would sooner die for want of you than—"

And so the letter broke off in an anguish beyond expressing. Beyond answering too, perhaps. Yet Fanny by now had apparently passed beyond indignation at his injustice. Years later she stated that even in the worst of his illness Keats "never could have addressed an unkind expression, much less a violent one, to any human being" [15]—a loyal transcendence of the truth. Eventually, it seems, she learned from these letters to understand his violence

---

* This remark, recorded by Woodhouse in his Commonplace Book (Claude Lee Finney, *The Evolution of Keats's Poetry* [1936], II, 746), evidently belongs in the letter of August 14, 1820, to Brown, who discreetly truncated this sentence in transcribing it (cf. *The Letters of John Keats*, ed. H. E. Rollins [1958], II, 321).

toward her as only a kind of delirium brought on by his fever. On his side Keats maintained his own queer loyalty still, by refusing to speak of Fanny to anyone. Yet in the end he was driven from this position. One afternoon Hunt saw him looking out the window with "a manner more alarming than usual" and suggested a drive to distract him. Keats agreed, and they took a coach over the country roads for an hour. Reaching Hampstead, they stopped at the end of Well Walk and sat down on the bench where Keats used to lounge with Tom in the spring of 1818. Suddenly rocked with the memory of Tom and all his grief, Keats buried his face in his handkerchief. After a few minutes he raised it again, his eyes full of tears, and told Hunt he was dying of a broken heart. He did not mention Fanny's name, but Hunt, in his tact, could guess it. Yet he was amazed by Keats's breakdown. "He must have been wonderfully excited to make such a confession," Hunt wrote afterward, "for his spirit was lofty to a degree of pride." [16]

After this, Keats seemed approaching the exhaustion of despair. In one last letter to Fanny in early August, he wrote, "Every hour I am more and more concentrated in you; every thing else tastes like chaff in my Mouth. I hate men and women more. I see nothing but thorns for the future—wherever I may be next winter in Italy or nowhere Brown will be living near you with his indecencies— I see no prospect of any rest. I am glad there is such a thing as the grave." To think of her merely as living apart from him, smiling with friends, going about her own pursuits, was intolerable. Seared with jealousy, he exclaimed, "Hamlet's heart was full of such Misery as mine is when he said to Ophelia 'Go to a Nunnery, go, go!' " He sent the letter off with a passage from one of her letters which he asked her to express less coldly and resumed his waiting at Hunt's window.

A day went by, then another; no reply came. On the third day young Thornton Hunt produced a letter with the seal broken. It had arrived two evenings before, but the maid instead of taking it up to Keats had maliciously kept the letter back and read it. According to Mrs. Hunt, it contained "not a word of the least consequence"; but it was from Fanny. When she gave it to Keats he broke down completely. He wept for several hours, then pulled himself together and announced he must leave. All Hunt's entreaties could not shake him. That evening he started back to

Hampstead, determined to live in Well Walk again. But halfway up the long hill to Hampstead, drawn by a force he could not withstand, he turned off toward Wentworth Place.

→»·«←

Mrs. Brawne must have been overcome by the sight of his wretchedness when he appeared on her doorstep that evening, for she drew him in and insisted that he stay with them. Keats had come home at last. His remaining days in England were to be spent at Wentworth Place under her nursing, and for this brief spell he was secure in the motherly tenderness he had lacked so long. Fanny later wrote that Keats and her mother became deeply attached in these weeks; to Severn he seemed like a child in his surrender to her care. As for Fanny, the nightmare of the summer was over. She was now simply and truly herself to him again, his young love, his beauty, his own, no longer a figure of bale. From this time on, every word Keats wrote or spoke of her turned on one thought alone—that she had been life to him and parting from her now would be death. For now he finally admitted the necessity which he could not bear to face at Hunt's. He realized at last that he must agree to the plan for sending him to Italy.

The plan itself had been taking shape behind his back all during July. Shelley had been alerted; inquiries were made about doctors and bankers in Rome. Taylor, still confident that the new volume would succeed, agreed to advance money for the passage to Italy and back.[17] Brown's loan was running out by now; at this point, it seems, Haslam stepped forward with another.[18] All Keats's friends apparently believed with the doctors that the Italian climate would save him, and that the change would do his spirits good too. Jane Reynolds, whom he had suspected of gossiping about Fanny, wrote to Maria Dilke that she hoped his absence from England would "weaken, if not break off a connexion that has been a most unhappy one for him." [19] Keats found himself "cheveaux-de-frised with benefits," trapped by the good intentions of his friends. In the end it was the thought of Fanny that decided him. It would be better for her if he went; she must be spared the experience of his death.[20] Two months before, he had grasped at her like a drowning man—"You must be mine to die upon the rack if I want you." Now, convinced that his death was inevitable, he turned to meet it with all the soldierly courage he still possessed. He would go to Italy, he told Taylor, "though it be with the sensation of marching up against a Batterry."

The image is revealing, and it occurs twice in the letters in which he announced his decision, a day or two after his return to Wentworth Place. His nerves were still badly shaken; with each line he penned, the tightening in his chest increased. In a brief note to his sister he broke the news as gently as he could: " 'T is not yet Consumption I believe, but it would be were I to remain in this climate all the Winter." To Hunt he sent an apology for leaving his house as he did, thanking him for his "many sympathies." Then Keats wrote to Taylor, asking him to find out the cost of the journey and a year's residence in Italy. The next day he added a postscript, a scrap of paper containing his will. "All my estate real and personal consists in the hopes of the sale of books publish'd or unpublish'd. Now I wish *Brown* and you to be the first paid Creditors—the rest is in nubibus—but in case it should shower pay my Taylor the few pounds I owe him. My Chest of Books divide among my friends." It was a declaration of worldly bankruptcy. Four years had been enough to run through his inheritance and his hopes of success. In the same spirit of casting his accounts and facing his failure, he wrote to Shelley two days later.

Shelley had invited Keats to spend the winter with him in Pisa in a letter combining tact and grace with the unconscious patronage that had stung Keats's pride at their first meeting.[21] The offer was generous; yet Shelley managed to add some double-edged praise of *Endymion* while recommending his own tragedy *The Cenci*, which he had lately sent to Keats, and *Prometheus Unbound*, which had just been published. The two men's careers had run curiously parallel ever since 1817, with each matching the other in romantic narrative, Elizabethan-style tragedy, allegorical epic, and satirical extravaganza. Keats now had to watch Shelley pull ahead of him in the race for fame, with the four splendid acts of *Prometheus* forever towering above his unfinished *Hyperion*. So Shelley's tribute—"I feel persuaded that you are capable of the greatest things, so you but will"—must have rankled cruelly. He answered the invitation to Pisa circumspectly, for he was still undecided where to go. But he met Shelley's implied criticism of *Endymion* squarely with a trenchant comment on Shelley's own work. "There is only one part of it I am judge of; the Poetry, and dramatic effect, which by many spirits now a days is considered the mammon. A modern work it is said must have a purpose, which may be the God—*an artist* must serve Mammon—he must have 'self concentration' selfishness perhaps. You I am sure will forgive me for sincerely remarking that you might curb your magnanimity and be more of an artist, and 'load every rift' of your subject with ore." It is telling criticism of Shelley's hortatory bent; yet Keats, remembering their first conversation three and a half years before, was also struck with the irony of it. "I remember you advising me not to publish my first-blights"—his first fruits—"on Hampstead heath," he added. "And is not this extraordinary talk for the writer of Endymion? whose mind was like a pack of scattered cards— I am pick'd up and sorted to a pip."

The cards were dealt, he had picked up a good hand—and suddenly, for no reason, the game was called off. Only a hint of the injustice of it all escapes in a remark to Haydon who, as he heard, had started a new painting: "Go on—I am affraid I shall pop off just when my mind is able to run alone." Yet even as Keats wrote, another ironic twist was being given to his destiny. Critical opinion was beginning to turn in his favour. In mid-August at long last the *Edinburgh Review* spoke out. The mighty Jeffrey himself wrote a lengthy critique of *Endymion*—so long, in fact, that he had little space to discuss the *Lamia* volume; but he praised the earlier poem, two years too late, as the surest touchstone of "a native relish for poetry." Shortly afterward the *Edinburgh Magazine* followed suit with another belated appreciation of *Endymion*, concluding "If this be not poetry, we do not know what it is." Their highly favourable notice of the *Lamia* volume did not appear till October, but by that time most of the other reviews had fallen into line. Even the Tory critics were to retract some of their earlier ridicule. The *Quarterly* remained silent, but *Blackwood's* conceded, still with some mockery, that there was much merit in the new volume. But for all this the book sold very slowly—only a few hundred copies by the end of the summer. It did not do nearly as well as the poems of Taylor's latest protégé, the peasant poet John Clare, or Barry Cornwall's newest work, *Marcian Colonna*. The timing was bad, for one thing. The royal scandal had erupted in full view with George IV's indictment of Queen Caroline before Parliament, and for several months pamphlets and lampoons on this subject elbowed other books out of the public's attention.[22]

And here is the final irony; for if Keats had ever finished *The Cap and Bells* he might have made some money as well as a name for himself.

As things now stood, he depended completely on his friends for support. No word had yet come from George. Abbey had promised Keats to lend him some money if George did not remit, but when Keats asked him for it he replied with chilly self-righteousness that he had warned Keats not to lend his money to George and that he himself was harassed by bad debts and could spare nothing. Except for Taylor's generosity, Keats could not have left for Italy at all. Early in September the publisher made a liberal settlement of their accounts which, reckoning all Keats's borrowings against the assignment of the three copyrights, left him with enough money at least to pay for his passage to Italy. Then, though Taylor was short of cash himself and still some £200 out of pocket on both *Endymion* and *Lamia*,[23] he arranged a credit of £150 for Keats's expenses abroad, counting rather doubtfully on George to reimburse him. He also arranged—since Keats had now decided not to go to Pisa—an introduction to Dr. James Clark in Rome, a young English physician with an excellent reputation as a specialist in phthisis.

All Keats needed now was a travelling companion. On August 14 he had written Brown an urgent letter in which he broke the news of his relapse and evidently asked him to return before he left for Italy, adding the secret of his engagement to Fanny and the savage request to "ruin Lockhart." A few days later, having decided against going to Shelley's, he wrote again more anxiously, begging Brown to accompany him on the trip. With luck he might have a reply in eight or ten days, but none ever came. According to Brown, the letters were misdirected and never reached him till September 9 at Dunkeld, whereupon he promptly returned to England. But it is strange that Brown deleted this and subsequent requests from Keats's letters when he later transcribed them into his *Life of Keats*,[24] and that he returned to England at last by the slowest rather than the fastest means available. It is hard not to suspect that he was dodging the issue. Knowing that Keats's physician had recommended he be sent to Italy in the fall, Brown had, as it seems, arranged to be conveniently out of the way when Keats would leave. He had stood by Keats in the spring, it is true, but now clearly wished to do so no longer. Keats, however, put off his departure several weeks in the vain hope that Brown would return in time to go with him. But as September drew on with no word from Scotland, he had to face the prospect of going to a strange country alone, convinced that he would die there. In desperation he asked Mrs. Brawne to accompany him. For a while she wavered; then Fanny begged to go too. It was unthinkable. He withdrew his request, and it was agreed that if he was well enough to return in the spring they would be married at last.[25] It was the dimmest of all hopes; but Keats must have resolved that Fanny at least should have something to hope for.

Under this mounting anxiety he had another haemorrhage on August 30. It was clear that his leaving could not be postponed much longer. Summer was over; a spell of chilly rain set in, and the winds were turning cold toward evening. Taylor got passage for him on the brig *Maria Crowther*, which was to sail from London for Naples around the middle of September, and Keats's friends began to pay their farewells. Haydon came out to the Brawnes' to find him in bed, fevered and irritable. "He seemed to be going out of Life with a contempt for this world and no hopes of the other," Haydon recorded. Evidently he tried to console him with thoughts of the life after death—the last thing in the world Keats wanted to hear about. Angrily he muttered that if he did not get well soon he would kill himself. Haydon tried to argue with him, then left, "deeply affected" by what seemed to him Keats's spiritual disintegration—the result, he thought, of Hunt's renewed influence.[26] Keats's despairing mood seems to have had a similar effect on Reynolds, who was not on hand to bid a final farewell. After his departure, Reynolds wrote Taylor with misplaced facetiousness that he was glad to hear that Keats had escaped the "vain and heartless" company of Leigh Hunt and had left for "a better Lungland," "so comfortably, so cheerfully, so sensibly." As for leaving Fanny, Reynolds chose to believe that Keats could only benefit by "absence from that poor idle Thing of Womankind to whom he has so unaccountably attached himself." [27]

The old circle was breaking up. From a remote parish in Northamptonshire, Bailey wrote Taylor his grave doubts about Keats's character and chances of literary success. By keeping the wrong society, Keats had picked up mistaken notions of morals and religion which, Bailey feared, would prevent him from realizing his promise as a poet. When Taylor replied that he disagreed,

Bailey answered some months later that he found a few traces of intellectual progress in the *Lamia* volume, and sent his kindest remembrances. For himself, Bailey admitted that his literary interests were waning; he still hoped to get something published in the Tory *New Monthly Magazine,* but "if they espouse any freethinking notions I have done with them." A stranger in Scotland, however, one John Aitken, who had admired the *Lamia* volume and been distressed to read in *The Indicator* of Keats's illness, wrote inviting him to come and stay at his country house, offering a good library and freedom in which to write. Of all Keats's friends in London, it was Haslam who, just as two years before, stood by him most faithfully, writing George when Keats could not, and making most of the arrangements for the voyage.

Yet none of these partings mattered to Keats in the face of his separation from Fanny. His whole existence was now concentrated in her. They had never been closer; yet his longing for her, now never to be slaked, had never been more painful. Weeks later it wrung from him a confession of pure despair in a letter to Brown: "I should have had her when I was in health, and I should have remained well. I can bear to die—I cannot bear to leave her." After his haemorrhage at the end of August he could hardly keep up the deception that he might recover in Italy, though Fanny herself accepted the doctors' assurances, like everyone else. He still struggled, however, against his growing conviction that death would be the final and irreversible parting. "Some of the phrases she was in the habit of using during my last nursing at Wentworth place ring in my ears," he wrote Brown at the end of September. "Is there another Life? Shall I awake and find all this a dream? There must be we cannot be created for this sort of suffering." With his whole being he longed to share Fanny's simple faith in immortality, yet the anguish of his incommunicable doubt continued.

The date of his sailing approached with still no companion in sight. No word had yet come from Brown, and all Keats's other friends were bound to England by their families or their work. Yet Haslam, though he could not go himself, was determined that Keats should not go alone. On Tuesday, September 12, the day before Keats was to leave Hampstead, Haslam thought of asking Severn. He was hardly the man for the responsibility, a cheerful young fellow but naïve and inexperienced; still, his company would be better than none. Severn himself was taken aback by the idea. A trip to Italy meant leaving his adoring mother and sisters and a secure career as a miniature painter, all on the shortest possible notice. Yet he could see a possible advantage in accompanying Keats. As the winner of a Royal Academy Gold Medal, he was eligible to apply for its travelling fellowship, which carried a comfortable three years' income; and after a winter of study in Rome he would have a better painting to submit to the jury next summer than if he remained drudging away in England. While Severn puzzled over his decision, Haslam hurried out to spend Tuesday night in Hampstead. His suggestion was a great relief to Keats, whose only plan had been to spend some time in Naples, waiting for Brown to catch up with him. He still expected that Brown would follow him to Rome as soon as he returned from Scotland, and now he would have a companion for the voyage. It was with a courageous show of calm that he made his farewells and set out to town with Haslam the next morning.

After the closeness of the weeks before, there could have been little left for Keats and Fanny to say to each other. She recorded the event simply in her diary with the note, "Mr. Keats left Hampstead." As his final gifts Keats had presented her with his miniature by Severn and his most treasured books—Dante, Spenser, and his Folio Shakespeare. They exchanged locks of hair, after the sentimental custom of the time; each still wore the other's ring. Fanny had lined his travelling cap with silk and given him a new pocket diary and a penknife. To her younger sister Margaret, Keats gave an amethyst brooch [28]—perhaps the last of his mother's relics. To his own sister he sent a last message, dictated to Fanny Brawne. She had been forbidden to visit him up to the very end. Keats had dreaded the thought of their final parting and was relieved to be spared it; yet he was haunted by the thought of her unhappiness with the Abbeys. He asked Fanny Brawne to write to her regularly and do everything she could for the younger girl. In his last letter he reassured her about his health as best he could; then after it was sealed he thought of one word more, which he asked Fanny Brawne to send her. She must avoid chills and coughs and remember never to go out into the cold air from the warmth of the greenhouse. As he later wrote to Brown, she "walks about my imagination like a ghost—she is so like Tom."

In town Wednesday morning Keats went to Taylor's while Has-

lam hurried off to get Severn's final word. At noon the message
arrived: Severn had agreed to go. He had a busy time ahead of him,
packing for the voyage, getting his passport, visiting his family, and
collecting £25 due him for a miniature—all the cash he had to
start the trip on. Fortunately, they learned Wednesday noon, the
*Maria Crowther* would not sail till Sunday morning, though for
Keats this meant only a few more weary days of farewells, which
he had done all he could to avoid.[29] One and all, his friends reassured him that he would return the next year, miraculously recovered, to pick up his interrupted work. If anyone had a suspicion
to the contrary, he succeeded in hiding it from the others. Yet each
man revealed something of himself in his manner of farewell: not
only Reynolds with his ill-concealed pleasure that Keats was escap-
ing from the bondage of his engagement, and Haydon in his recriminations against Keats's failure of nerve, but Taylor with his
kindness carefully spelled out in business terms, and Woodhouse,
the most self-effacing of all in his generosity. Saturday night he sat
down in his rooms and wrote an affectionate letter to give to Keats
the next day with his last handshake. Without mentioning his
anonymous loan the summer before, he explained a little awkwardly that he was glad to know that Keats was well supplied with
money for the time being, since his own funds were low at present.
In about six months, however, he promised they would have recovered enough to answer any draft that Keats might make on
them. Then, quoting from the sonnet which Keats's mysterious
benefactor "P. Fenbank" had sent him from Teignmouth two years
before and which Woodhouse had duly copied into his Keats scrap-
book, he signed himself

> —one, whose hand will never scant
> From his poor store of fruits all *thou* canst want.

Leigh Hunt also wrote a letter of farewell to Keats, to be published
in *The Indicator* the week after he left. Sentimental, even flam-
boyant, still it did what only Hunt could do—remind a still indifferent public of its loss. "Thou shalt return with thy friend
the nightingale, and make all thy other friends as happy with
thy voice as they are sorrowful to miss it," he ended. "Farewell
for awhile: thy heart is in our fields: and thou wilt soon be back to
rejoin it." [30]

»»»———————————————————————————————«««

## Chapter Fourteen

# End of the Voyage

IT dawned pale and chilly on Sunday the seventeenth as a little group gathered at the London docks near the Tower to see Keats off. Taylor, Woodhouse, and Haslam planned to sail down the river to Gravesend with him; a young assistant of Taylor's and one or two other friends made up the rest. Severn arrived late, wan and shaken from parting with his family, for his father in one of his overbearing rages had tried forcibly to prevent his leaving in the end. Keats looked feverish and dejected but made his good-byes with apparent calm. Their trunks were loaded, the last hand-shakes exchanged, and Keats boarded the ship with his four companions to wait the turn of the tide. By mid-morning it reached its height, and they cast off. With the sights and sounds of the Thames traffic and the fresh air of the river, Keats's spirits soon picked up. Suddenly Severn realized he had forgotten his passport. Luckily they were to stop over for a day at Gravesend, where Haslam promised to have it sent. They reached Gravesend early in the afternoon and dropped the pilot. Haslam drew Severn aside to beg him to keep a regular journal of the trip, while Keats asked Taylor to send his sister an account of his departure. Taylor gave him a Greek and Latin Testament in parting,[1] and Woodhouse took a lock of his hair. Then at last they were gone.

Taylor wrote Fanny at once that Keats was comfortably settled and looking forward to an agreeable month's voyage, but this was putting a cheerful front on the affair. The *Maria Crowther* was small, a two-masted brig of less than 130 tons, built for coasting on the Cardiff-Liverpool run; she turned out to be cramped as well as poorly provisioned for a journey of over 2600 miles. There was one cabin of six berths for the captain and the passengers. Two of their fellow voyagers were women—Mrs. Pidgeon, a robust middle-aged lady who seemed affable enough on first acquaintance, and a Miss Cotterell, who was to get on at Gravesend the next day. Captain Walsh was a good fellow, anxious to please, but his resources were limited. Severn, who had recently had a bout with his liver and was a poor sailor, began to look melancholy, but Keats was determined to make the best of a bad situation. At tea in the cabin he cracked one joke after another, amusing Mrs. Pidgeon and bringing Severn round again. That night Severn kept waking up in his narrow berth, unable to think where he was—once, it seemed, in a shoemaker's shop, another time in a wine-cellar; then, restless and upset, he lay awake, listening to the others' snores, while the ship gently rocked and creaked around him. Outside in the quiet river a smack from Dundee drew up and anchored nearby. She carried another sleeping passenger, Charles Brown. At dawn, as the tide turned, she weighed anchor and started up-river for London.

The next morning Severn was alarmed by Keats's low voice; but he ate a good breakfast, as if to prove he was well. When the captain invited Severn to go ashore with him to help lay in his last supplies, Keats gave him a list of medicines to buy at the apothecary's. Included was a bottle of laudanum, a standard remedy for seasickness at that time. Severn obligingly returned with all his commissions and an extra supply of apples and biscuits. That afternoon at dinner Keats was "full of his waggery," by Severn's report. At six the missing passport arrived, and Miss Cotterell soon after. Keats was brought up short at the sight of her. Young, pretty, with gentle manners, she was obviously in an advanced stage of consumption, and a winter in Italy had been prescribed as a last resort. She had a brother in business in Naples, whom she would join there, but she was desolate at the thought of the long journey ahead. Keats, who had never conquered his uneasiness in the presence of illness, was now to be faced with a living image of his own disease for the whole voyage. But at once he tried cheering Miss Cotterell up, dragging Severn along with him in a wild rush of badinage. Severn suspected nothing of her effect on his friend; instead he was struck by the fact that each invalid confided to him that he was in much better health than the other. Severn himself was still feeling "done up" and evidently showed it, for a lady companion of Miss Cotterell asked as she left, a little too audibly, which was the dying man.

Late that night they sailed. Tuesday, Severn rose to watch the sunrise, then had to walk up and down with Miss Cotterell, who was already upset by the roll and pitch of the ship as it reached the Channel. At breakfast Severn himself began to feel "a waltzing in the stomach"; at once he groped his way to the deck, followed by Miss Cotterell and shortly by Keats, who was sick, according to Severn, "in a most gentlemanly manner." Mrs. Pidgeon stayed behind, laughing at them, but a few minutes later joined them at the rail; then Miss Cotterell fainted. This was only the first of many times. Keats helped her below and brought her round, after which all four passengers took to their bunks. There they remained all day as the ship went bucking through the Strait of Dover, and the air in the small cabin became stifling. But they were too shaken even to get out of their clothes that night. Mrs. Pidgeon turned surly and uncooperative; Miss Cotterell became ill again and again, and Keats, showing only a pale profile from his upper berth, dictated instructions to Severn to assist her. Wednesday morning was fair enough for breakfast on deck, but by early afternoon they ran straight into a gale. Once that evening Severn managed to get up on deck, where he watched the ship staggering from crest to trough of the waves, and clambering up again, the sea flooding across the foredeck with each plunge. He groped his way back to the cabin to find their trunks sliding over the floor and water seeping through the planks. The women were terrified, but Keats remained cool enough to joke with Severn about it. For hours they lay in the dark, listening to the groan of the pumps, the shouts of the crew, and the crash of the waves outside; then at last the captain decided to abandon their course and make for shelter.

For another day they hugged the coast of Kent, tacking slowly forward, but soon the wind died down into a mere breeze. On the twenty-first they put in at Dungeness, where Severn and Keats were glad to get ashore and stretch their legs. Then they returned to another week of contrary winds, and Keats's patience began to wear thin. Seasickness brought on fever, and once or twice the terrifying thought crossed Severn's mind that Keats might die on the voyage. At the week's end Captain Walsh decided to anchor at

Portsmouth till the wind changed, and on September 28 Keats
and Severn went ashore again to spend the night. Keats, realizing
that Bedhampton was only seven miles away, was seized with an
impulse to drive over with Severn to surprise his friends the
Snooks with a visit. They were delighted to see him and hear him
abuse the captain's seamanship and Mrs. Pidgeon's manners in a
fine show of cheerfulness. But they had bitter news for him. Brown
had returned from Scotland and come down to Hampshire for a
month's visit; he was at the senior Dilkes' in Chichester that very
day. Keats must have been thunderstruck to realize not only that
Brown had reached London only a day after he left but, still more,
that he seemed to have no plans to follow him to Italy. Twenty
miles to Chichester and back—the distance was too great for the
time he had before returning to Portsmouth. All at once his resolution cracked; he was ready to give the voyage up and return to
London. He almost persuaded Severn, then with a great effort got
himself in hand again. Next morning they drove back to the ship
and started off with a favouring breeze. But soon the wind changed,
and they found themselves becalmed off Yarmouth.

After almost a fortnight at sea they had gone barely two hundred
miles. Severn was disturbed to see Keats's dogged gaiety give way
to silent brooding. This was hardly remarkable, for both captain
and passengers were bad-tempered and weary after their ordeal
with the weather. But Severn had no inkling of Keats's real
thoughts. He had never been one of his intimates, and he was not
a perceptive young man; it seems he literally believed all the assurances he heard that Keats would recover in Italy. As the voyage
wore on and his first resolution flagged, Keats began to withdraw
more into himself, to turn over and over in his mind the anguish
of his parting with Fanny, his growing doubt that Brown would
join him, his terrible conviction that he would die in Italy. He had
put off writing Brown till he might send him good news of his
health; but now it struck him as useless to wait any longer. On
the morning of the thirtieth he started a letter to him in a collected
spirit, expressing his disappointment at missing him in Bedhampton. "I should have delighted in setting off for London for the
sensation merely," he added; "for what should I do there? I could
not leave my lungs or stomach or other worse things behind me."
At this his wild longing for Fanny broke through at last. "The very
thing which I want to live most for will be a great occasion of my

death," he exclaimed. "Were I in health it would make me ill, and how can I bear it in my state? I wish for death every day and night to deliver me from these pains, and then I wish death away, for death would destroy even those pains which are better than nothing. Land and Sea, weakness and decline are great seperators, but death is the great divorcer for ever."

He had fought to put Fanny out of his mind, but failed completely. For the last two weeks he had been able to think of no one else, not even his sister, or George and Georgiana: only Fanny, whom he had lost forever, as from the first he had dreaded he might. "The thought of leaving Miss Brawne is beyond every thing horrible," he confessed to Brown—"the sense of darkness coming over me—I eternally see her figure eternally vanishing." The irrational suspicions of the summer had receded into the past, but he could not forget the hostility which still divided the two people he loved the most, or what he in his weakness had done to add to it. "I think without my mentioning it for my sake you would be a friend to Miss Brawne when I am dead," he begged Brown. "You think she has many faults—but, for my sake, think she has not one —if there is any thing you can do for her by word or deed I know you will do it." For himself he could not even ask whether Brown intended to come to Italy. "I will say nothing about our friendship or rather yours to me more than that as you deserve to escape you will never be so unhappy as I am." A bitter truth was concealed in this remark, which Brown probably did not recognize. Gloomily Keats concluded, "I feel as if I was closing my last letter to you."

Keats had resolved to write Fanny that day but could not find the courage; he could not even bring himself to send his letter to Brown, so naked in despair, but put it back in his writing case.[2] Next morning there was still no wind in sight, and the captain decided to put in at Lulworth Cove, where Keats and Severn went ashore again. As they rambled along the rugged coast, Keats's spirits rose, and for a few hours he seemed to Severn his old self once more. Memories of Margate and Devon and the Isle of Wight must have come flooding back—those days when he had watched and listened endlessly to the sea in all its tones and colours and changes of mood. It was a beautiful evening when they returned to the ship, at the hour Keats had always liked best, with "a few white Clouds about and a few stars blinking—the waters ebbing and the Horison a Mystery." Back on board he got out his copy of Shakespeare's *Poems* and turned over the leaves till he found a blank page. There, opposite Shakespeare's boldly printed title "A Lover's Complaint," he wrote down a sonnet. It was the final version of the one he had written at Shanklin the summer before, wrought from the same elements of sea and evening and longing for Fanny, but with the last two lines reshaped to a more dramatic ending:

> Still, still to hear her tender-taken breath,
> And so live ever—or else swoon to death.

No longer the mingling of love and death in a half-drugged confusion of their separate natures, but all too clear a sense of their tragic antithesis—this was the final meaning he wrung from the contrast between the eternal calm watchfulness of the star and his own eternal restlessness, and in effect his final message to Fanny. And to the end of his life Severn thought that "Bright Star" was the last poem Keats ever wrote.[3]

It was their last evening in England, at any rate. Next morning the wind freshened and shifted, and soon they were scudding across the Channel. After rounding the tip of Brittany and turning into the Bay of Biscay, they ran into another severe storm. With her constant seasickness, Miss Cotterell grew weaker every day. When the portholes were closed, she fainted continually from lack of air; but when they were opened Keats began to cough uncontrollably. Slowly it began to dawn on Severn that he had taken charge of a desperately ill man. More and more he noticed "a starved haunting expression" on Keats's face that bewildered him. As for himself, Severn was proving a good enough sailor to spend most of the time on deck, wrapped in his greatcoat and watching the sea with delight. When the wind dropped again off Cape St. Vincent he made water-colour sketches or leaned over the side, watching strange fish circle below. Together he and Keats read *Don Juan* aloud; but Keats soon grew annoyed with Byron's unflagging cynicism and tossed the book aside. Once they saw a whale shoulder through the placid surface of the sea. Another time they sighted a few warships. To their alarm a four-decker approached them and fired a shot to bring the *Maria Crowther* about. It was a ticklish moment, for pirates still prowled in these waters; but the commander claimed he was a Portuguese admiral and only wanted information about rebel privateers. Captain Walsh had none to give him, and slowly the huge ship, its decks swarming with ragged sailors, drifted off. Later in the day they learned from an English naval sloop that the Portuguese fleet was supporting the Carlist rebellion in Spain and trying to intercept loyal shipping.

By mid-October they reached Gibraltar. They passed through the straits early in the morning and saw the Rock lit up by the first rays of the sun, glowing like a vast topaz, as Severn described it. He sketched while Keats lay watching, glad to have passed this milestone in their journey. Hopeful as always, Severn decided that the Mediterranean air was working a miracle, for Keats was showing signs of recovery. But a day or two later he took an unexpected turn for the worse and began to vomit blood. Severn was terrified. Luckily the vomiting soon ceased, but for several days his fever hung on, with violent sweating at night. Yet as they sailed along through perfect weather and Keats's fever subsided, Severn's optimism returned. It was easy enough to blame any illness on the bad weather, poor food, and lack of exercise, their airless cabin and damp beds, the distressing sight of Miss Cotterell day in and day out. And they were approaching the end of the journey. On October 21 they entered the Bay of Naples at sunrise. Italy at last, most glorious of all the kingdoms of the earth Keats had dreamed of seeing. Around them in a vast semicircle, flanked by islands like cliffs floating in light, rose the shadowed hills of Campania. Before them the white villas of Naples gleamed in the dawn, with terraced vineyards and olive orchards, bronze-green and grey-green, climbing tier on tier over the slopes behind. From the summit of Vesuvius drifted a long purplish cloud of smoke, edged with the gold of the rising sun; to the southeast the cliffs of Sorrento shone like lapis lazuli. As the morning advanced, the blue of the sea deepened to an intensity Severn had never seen before, catching and concentrating the light of the sky like an immense sapphire.

For an hour at least all memory of the surly Atlantic was blotted out in the radiance of the scene. But as they entered the harbour of Naples they learned they could not land for another ten days. There had been a epidemic of typhus when they left London, and they were required to round out the six weeks of quarantine. After more than a month at sea, this was a maddening disappointment. Yet for the first day the stir and bustle of the port provided endless amusement. The *Maria Crowther* anchored off the tiny island

of the Castel dell' Ovo, once the site of the villa of Lucullus, now
of a stolid Norman fortress. Here they could watch ships of all rigs
and sizes coming and going, the fishing boats returning with their
catch, little skiffs loaded with supplies weaving between the larger
craft. Keats sat looking at it, half in a dream. In his mind's eye he
could see the harbour as it had been two thousand years ago,
crowded with Greek galleys and Tyrrhenian sloops carrying merchants or colonists with their wares and their legends from the
East. But the reality was as good as the imagination. Boatloads of
singers, sunburnt and gaily dressed, rowed out to greet them, and
pedlars came by with wine in straw-covered bottles and flowers
and baskets of fruit piled to their gunwales—melons, peaches, figs,
and grapes. The air rang with the singsong of the hawkers, the
tinkling of guitars, and ceaseless Neapolitan laughter.

The adventure soon turned into a nightmare. Out in the Bay
a British naval squadron lay anchored, standing guard against
the recent liberal uprising in Naples; and shortly a young lieutenant was sent to make inquiries of the British arrival. Instead
of remaining alongside the *Maria Crowther,* he blundered aboard
with his six men, and there they had to stay till the quarantine
was up. Their quarters, close enough before, became unspeakably
crowded when after the first day it began to rain, driving them all
into the cabin. Soon the air was almost too foul to breathe. Miss
Cotterell became pitiably ill, and Keats suffered more from bad
air and poor digestion than he had during the entire voyage. Severn, for all of his gaiety and good health, once broke into tears
under the strain. Before the week was up, Miss Cotterell's affable
brother joined them on board. Though his coming left them still
shorter of space, Cotterell's good humour helped speed the time.
He flung jokes back and forth with the boatmen swarming around
them, persuaded them to sing, and translated their gibes for the
passengers' benefit. And Keats, out of the energy of despair, summoned up more puns in a week—so he wrote Brown—than in any
year of his life.

While they were penned up Keats wrote a letter to Mrs. Brawne
which, when compared to the gloomy note Severn scribbled to
Haslam at the same time, is a triumph of cheerfulness. "I would
always wish you to think me a little worse than I really am," he
remarked; "if I do not recover your regret will be softened if I
do your pleasure will be doubled.—Yet you must not believe I

am so ill as this Letter may look," he added, "for if ever there was a person born without the faculty of hoping I am he." He tried to write a message to Fanny but failed: "I dare not fix my Mind upon Fanny. I have not dared to think of her," he continued to Mrs. Brawne. "The only comfort I have had that way has been in thinking for hours together of having the knife she gave me put in a silver-case—the hair in a Locket—and the Pocket Book in a gold net—Show her this." He began to describe the life around them and was overwhelmed by a sense of unreality. "There is enough in this Port of Naples to fill a quire of Paper—but it looks like a dream—every man who can row his boat and walk and talk seems a different being from myself. O what an account I could give you if I could once more feel myself a Citizen of this world— O what a misery it is to have an intellect in splints!" He sent messages to all at Wentworth Place, to Brown and the Dilkes as well. "Tell Tootts [Fanny's younger sister] I wish I could pitch her a basket of grapes—and tell Sam the fellows catch here with a line a little fish much like an anchovy, pull them up fast." He closed his letter affectionately to Mrs. Brawne, then, just before sealing it to go, added a postscript in a small and very ragged hand: "Good bye Fanny! god bless you." [4] These were his last words to her.

⁂

At last their term in quarantine was up. On October 31—his twenty-fifth birthday—Keats stepped ashore with Severn in a cold driving rain. The fresh air revived them a little, but the first encounter with the smells and squalor and confusion of Naples was overwhelming—beggars and ballad-singers elbowing each other in the crowded streets, fish-pedlars and macaroni-venders shouting their wares, women washing and cooking in the doorways of their houses, and children swarming everywhere in the filthy gutters. Cotterell took them to the Villa di Londra and gave them a good dinner; but, in spite of comfortable rooms with a superb view of Mount Vesuvius, both Keats and Severn were depressed. All night the shouts and singing and clatter in the streets below made it impossible to sleep.

The next morning they hurried off some letters to catch the English courier. To Brown, Keats wrote what he hoped would be a short calm letter; but after two sentences describing their quarantine, the compulsion to speak of Fanny swept him off his course again. "As I have gone thus far into it, I must go on a little," he apologized cryptically; "perhaps it may relieve the load of WRETCHEDNESS which presses upon me. The persuasion that I shall see her no more will kill me. I cannot q—" He broke off, unable to finish the sentence or even the word; then the flood of his emotion carried him on. "Oh, God! God! God! Every thing I have in my trunks that reminds me of her goes through me like a spear. The silk lining she put in my travelling cap scalds my head. My imagination is horribly vivid about her—I see her—I hear her. There is nothing in the world of sufficient interest to divert me from her a moment. This was the case when I was in England; then there was a good hope of seeing her again—Now!—O that I could be buried near where she lives!" He hardly dared think of the exile ahead of him and could barely bring himself to remind Brown of his still unanswered request.[5] "If I were in better health I should urge your coming to Rome," he remarked; but even that seemed useless. "I fear there is no one can give me any comfort." After asking about his brother and sister, he begged Brown to let Fanny Brawne know somehow that he did not forget her, and to promise for his sake to "be her advocate for ever."

That night at last Keats broke down and told Severn something of his misery. Severn wrote Haslam the next day that he had persuaded Keats to talk to him about "a heavy grief that may tend more than anything to be fatal"; but what Keats actually said Severn did not make clear. Years later Severn recalled that Keats insisted his greatest misfortune in leaving England was "being cut off from the world of poetry"; but it seems likelier that this time Keats told him, as he told Hunt, of some thwarted love which he left nameless. The one thing certain is that in his stubborn pride he never mentioned Fanny's name. Severn knew of Keats's close friendship with the Brawnes, and even that Fanny was "Keats's favourite" in the family; and from several hints in Brown's letters he might easily have guessed the real relationship between them. But Keats himself never let Severn suspect he was engaged to Fanny.[6] Whatever it was that he confided to Severn that evening, however, it did Keats good; he went to bed much calmer and slept till nearly ten the next morning.

The next day Keats's spirits picked up again: Severn took it as a hopeful sign that he made an Italian pun. They decided to take a week to rest up for the difficult journey to Rome and began en-joying a cordial reception from the little English colony in Naples. Cotterell, in his gratitude for their care of his sister, could not do enough for them. He took them driving to see the sights of the city, then out into the country through the vineyards to Capo di Monte and the Ponte Rossi. It was still glorious autumn; the sun was warm, and late roses bloomed in front of the cottages by the road. The last of the grapes were being harvested, and the sight of heavy-laden carts lumbering off to the presses and the fragrance of the air must have been a joy to Keats. On their way back to the city he stopped the carriage at the Capuan Gate to watch a group of workmen standing around a cauldron, eating spaghetti by im-mense handfuls without knives or forks. The unrestrained vitality of the peasants delighted him, but he was unimpressed by the Neapolitan troops whom they saw in grand review the day they landed. "No backbone," he commented to Severn, and events soon proved him right. The very week of their visit, the King of Naples was conspiring with Metternich to betray the newly established constitutional government to the Austrians, and four months later the Army was to surrender without a fight.[7] When Keats and Severn went to the opera they found sentinels standing under the proscenium arch, whom they took as part of the scenic effect until they realized they were real soldiers, posted there to quell any disturbance. At this symbol of submission to tyranny Keats flared into anger. The air of Naples suddenly became stifling; he wanted to leave at once. A letter came from Shelley in Pisa, full of advice about diet and climate, urging him to come to Pisa but not re-peating his earlier invitation to stay at his own house.[8] But Keats by now had set his mind on Rome. There Severn would find the opportunities for study that were his reason for the trip, and Keats himself was anxious to make contact with his new physician, Dr. Clark. So they collected their visas and, on the morning of Nov-ember 8, set out for the Papal States.

The journey to Rome, a distance of a hundred and forty miles over rough country, usually took two or three days. The little car-riage which Keats and Severn hired for the trip stretched it out to eight. The inns at the regular stopping-places were poor enough, but in the primitive villages where Keats and Severn were forced to spend the nights they were "villainously coarse" by Severn's account. The vile food followed by hours of jolting over bad roads left Keats continually queasy. Severn, however, was enchanted with the flower-strewn hillsides, the festooned vineyards, and the lucent blue of the Mediterranean in the distance. It was a good thing that, as Keats had written Mrs. Brawne two weeks before, Severn's nerves were "too strong to be hurt by other peoples illnesses." He walked alongside the crawling *vettura* for most of the way, which put him in excellent health by the end of the trip, and he managed to cheer Keats up by bringing him armfuls of wild flowers. After Terracina, the midpoint of their route, they entered the vast malarial wasteland of the Campagna, where the only sights were an occasional goatherd with his flock, a few skeletons of horses by the road, a stretch of ruined aqueduct, and, impaled on posts along the way, the shrunken arms and legs of bandits, who still infested the roads. Once they passed a red-cloaked cardinal out shooting songbirds, with an owl tied to a stick with a mirror round its neck used as lure; as Severn observed, the real sport was in not shooting the owl.

After this unexpected adventure came the unimaginable actuality of Rome itself. On November 15 at last they caught sight of the crumbling mass of the Aurelian Wall looming up before them; then entered the city by the Lateran Gate and drove past the Colosseum and the Forum to the Piazza di Spagna, which even at that time was a center for English visitors. Keats went at once to call on Dr. Clark, who had been anxiously awaiting his arrival. Clark had already found them an apartment immediately across the square from his own, in a house at the foot of the wide marble stairs leading up dozen by dozen to the tawny-coloured church of Santa Trinità dei Monti. The rooms were narrow but neat and comfortably furnished. The windows facing south and west looked down two stories to the steps and the square below, where the Barcaccia, Bernini's boat-shaped fountain, splashed in the sun. The piazza itself was an endless spectacle. Lined with the shops of print-sellers and artisans in mosaic, it was crowded with loungers and flower-venders and artists' models, who gathered for hire on the steps in their costumes. Flocks of goats or cattle jostled with the passers-by over the cobblestones, and carriages of English "milords" which were too large for the dank mews below the square stood drawn up in the open. Their landlady, Anna Angeletti, was a lively, smart little woman with two well-brought-up daughters.[9] She asked nearly five pounds a month for the apart-

ment—a price at which Keats apparently demurred, for one of the
first things that struck Clark was his uneasiness about money matters. But prices were high in Rome, at least for English visitors,[10]
and there was nothing to do but give in.

Dr. Clark turned out to be as good a friend and neighbour as
he was a physician. Unknown to Keats, he wrote to England shortly
after his arrival to urge that Keats's friends reassure him about his
financial situation. "I wish I were rich enough that his living here
should cost him nothing," he added. "I feel very much interested
in him." He not only called on Keats at least twice every day but
also watched the English magazines for reviews of *Lamia* and got
his wife to cook special dishes for the patient. Clark's bedside manner, which was later to recommend him to the King of the Belgians
and Queen Victoria, sprang from a genuine warmth of heart. A
personable young Scot in his early thirties, he had served as a surgeon in the Royal Navy and trained as a physician at Edinburgh.
He gave Keats the most skilful and devoted care that was obtain-
able at the time, even though by present-day standards his diagnosis was tragically inadequate. On first examining Keats he was
cautiously hopeful. He had only a suspicion that Keats's lungs
were affected and perhaps also his heart; the chief trouble, he
thought, was his stomach. There is no doubt that the tubercular
infection had now spread to Keats's digestive tract, but it still seems
incredible that Clark, a specialist in phthisis, was not overly concerned about his lungs. As for the cause of the disease, Clark laid
it to his "mental exertions." Fresh air, moderate exercise, and
avoidance of worry above all were his prescription: relieve Keats's
anxiety and "throw medicine to the dogs." Accordingly he recommended that Keats go riding and hired a horse for him—at six
pounds a month, to Severn's indignation. When Keats said he
wanted music and Severn rented a piano (for another thirty shillings a month), Clark loaned him a number of volumes of music,
including a prized set of Haydn's sonatas.

So for a few weeks all ran smoothly. Keats really appeared to be
convalescing, as Severn wrote in a hopeful letter to Haslam.[11] They
settled down into a comfortable round of activity, dull for Severn,
Keats feared, but within the limits of his own strength. They began
to explore the city, loitered along the Corso or strolled up the
fashionable Pincian Hill. Here they met another young English
consumptive, one Lieutenant Elton, who kept Keats company

11 GEORGE KEATS

From a miniature by Joseph Severn,
Keats-Shelley Memorial House, Rome

11 TOM KEATS

From a drawing by Joseph Severn,
Keats-Shelley Memorial House, Rome

IV BENJAMIN ROBERT HAYDON

From the 1828 portrait by Georgiana
Margaretta Zornlin, National Portrait
Gallery, London

V LEIGH HUNT

From the 1821 portrait by B. R. Haydon, National Portrait Gallery, London

VI JOSEPH SEVERN

From an engraving after a pencil drawing by Seymour Kirkup, 1822, reproduced in William Sharp's *Life and Letters of Joseph Severn* (1892)

VII CHARLES BROWN

From the 1828 bust by Andrew Wilson, Keats Memorial House, Hampstead

PHOTOGRAPH BY
CHRISTOPHER OXFORD

VIII JOHN KEATS, 1816

From a drawing by Joseph Severn, Victoria and
Albert Museum, London
CROWN COPYRIGHT

IX JOHN KEATS, 1819

From a drawing by Charles Brown, National Portrait Gallery, London

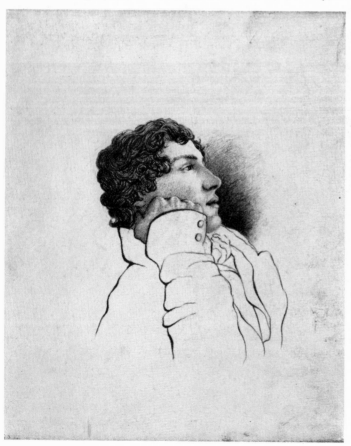

On the first looking into Chapman's Homer.

Much have I travell'd in the Realms of Gold,
And many goodly States, and Kingdoms seen;
Round many Western islands have I been,
Which Bards in fealty to Apollo hold.
Of one wide expanse had I been told,
Which deep brow'd Homer ruled as his Demesne;
Yet could I never judge what Men could mean,
Till I heard Chapman speak out loud and bold.
Then felt I like some Watcher of the Skies
When a new Planet swims into his Ken,
Or like stout Cortez, when with wond'ring eyes
He stared at the Pacific, and all his Men
Look'd at each other with a wild surmise —
Silent upon a Peak in Darien —

XI FANNY BRAWNE

From a silhouette cut by Auguste Edouard, reproduced
in H. B. Forman's edition of *Letters of John Keats to
Fanny Brawne* (1878)

XII WENTWORTH PLACE, HAMPSTEAD

PHOTOGRAPH, RADIO TIMES HULTON PICTURE LIBRARY, LONDON

Great South Street

My sweet Fanny,                                    Tuesday Morn

                    On awakening from my three days dream
("I cry to dream again") I find one and another astonished
at my idleness and thoughtlessness. I was miserable
last night—the morning is always restorative. I
must be busy, or try to be so. I have several things
to speak to you of tomorrow morning. Mrs Dilke
I should think will tell you that I propose living at
Hampstead. I must impose chains upon myself. I shall
be able to do nothing. I should like to cast the die for
Love or death. I have no Patience with any thing
else—if you ever intend to be cruel to me as you
say in jest now but perhaps may sometimes be
in earnest be so now—and I will—my mind is
in a tremble, I cannot tell what I am writing.

                                    Ever my love yours
                                        John Keats

XIII A LETTER FROM KEATS TO FANNY BRAWNE,
19 OCTOBER 1819

From the original in the Houghton Library, Harvard University

xiv KEATS ON
HIS DEATHBED
Rome, 1821

From the drawing by Joseph
Severn, Keats-Shelley
Memorial House, Rome

xv THE HOUSE IN
WHICH KEATS
LODGED
Piazza di Spagna, Rome

PHOTOGRAPH BY THE AUTHOR

while Severn went off to sketch the ruins or study the Raphaels in the Vatican. Elton was tall and good-looking and soon caught the eye of a famous beauty among the promenaders—Pauline Bonaparte, the Princess Borghese, a sister of Napoleon. Her languorous stares irritated Keats so keenly that they gave up walking on the Pincio thereafter. But when the three young Englishmen went to see Canova's notorious statue of the princess lying half nude on a sofa, propped on one elbow, with an apple in the other hand, Keats gave it a nickname, "The Aeolian Harp," which has stuck ever since. Evenings at home Keats read while Severn sketched or played the piano. The Haydn sonatas delighted Keats: he told Severn that Haydn was like a child, "for there is no knowing what he will do next." They practised Italian together, and Keats went on studying Italian poetry. Their one real complaint against Rome was the abominable food sent up from a *trattoria* in the square, at four shillings a dinner. Though Keats's Italian was still far from fluent, he soon found an effective way of protesting. One evening when their meal appeared, tasteless as ever, Keats sniffed the dishes, then emptied them one by one out the window—fowl, cauliflower, macaroni, pudding—and motioned to the porter to take the basket away. The man laughed and returned fifteen minutes later with an excellent dinner, at no extra charge. From that time on they ate well.

Severn had good reason to think Keats was on the mend, for he started talking about poetry again. The idea had come to him of writing a long poem on the story of Sabrina, the river-nymph of Milton's *Comus* and tutelary goddess of the Severn—no doubt as a gesture of thanks to his friend. Thoughts of Milton and English legend and Spenser's lovely Una ran together in his mind as he discussed it—and perhaps also of Fanny, whose faith had endured as many trials as Una's. Keats also encouraged Severn to get to work on his painting for the Academy fellowship, uneasily remembering the gossip about him at Hilton's the winter before. At his urging Severn went and presented his letters of introduction and soon made some valued acquaintances among the connoisseurs and a crowd of young English architects and painters of good family. Severn seems to have had a good eye for the main chance; he had started on the trip thinking that Keats's company in Rome would prove a solid advantage to him, and he later promised his family never to know anyone who was not his superior in talent or fortune or position so that he would be constantly "raising myself and improving." [12] Yet he was so ingenuous in his eagerness to get on with people that no one could dislike him, and he did not resent the fact that his new friends took a greater interest in Keats than in himself.

It was a good show that Keats put on, and in the first month he faltered only once. One day he started reading a copy of Alfieri's tragedies, but at the second page unexpectedly broke down and threw the book aside. The lines

> *Misera me! sollievo à me non resta*
> *Altro che'il pianto, ed il pianto è delitto* *

had touched the nerve which he had managed till then to guard. Severn was upset; he still could not guess the anguish that underlay Keats's resolute control. Even in his last letter to Brown on November 30—the last he ever wrote—Keats kept carefully to the surface of things. "My dear Brown," he began, " 'Tis the most difficult thing in the world to me to write a letter. My stomach continues so bad, that I feel it worse on opening any book,—yet I am much better than I was in Quarantine. I have an habitual feeling of my real life having past, and that I am leading a posthumous existence. God knows how it would have been—" he hesitated, thinking if only Brown had come with him; [13] started again, "but it appears to me—however, I will not speak of that subject." Grasping at calm, he tried instead to speak of some of the matters which Brown had mentioned in a letter that had recently arrived from him, but found he could not even look at the letter again: "I am so weak (in mind) that I cannot bear the sight of any hand writing of a friend I love so much as I do you." He tried to give a little news of himself, but there was nothing worth saying. "There is one thought enough to kill me—I have been well, healthy, alert &c., walking with her —and now—the knowledge of contrast, feeling for light and shade, all that information (primitive sense) necessary for a poem are great enemies to the recovery of the stomach." For one perilous moment he nearly lost his balance, then recovered it. "There, you rogue, I put you to the torture,—but you must bring your philosophy to bear—as I do mine, really—or how should I be able to live?" He added a few messages to friends in London, explaining his

---

* *Filippo*, I.i.19 f.: "Unhappy me! No solace remains for me but weeping, and weeping is a crime."

failure to call before leaving England or promising to write before the next post. The farewell to Brown was almost too much. "I can scarcely bid you good bye even in a letter," he ended. "I always made an awkward bow."

Partly by Keats's fortitude, partly by Brown's careful deletions, the letter conceals Keats's sickening realization that he would probably never see his friend again. The letter of Brown to which he was replying, written from Chichester during Brown's visit there at the end of September, has not survived; but in it he no doubt explained his delay in returning from Scotland by the accidents of the mails and told Keats of the unlucky coincidence of their ships passing at Gravesend. Apparently he also rationalized his refusal to start for Italy by praising Severn's rather doubtful virtues as a companion and by insisting that Keats would be well enough to return in the spring.[14] How much he said of his real preoccupation this fall can of course only be guessed. But it must have been about this time that Brown decided to acknowledge Abby's child as his own son and heir. In order to conciliate Abby, it would be necessary to go through the formality of a Roman Catholic marriage—which, as Brown knew, had no legal force in England at that time—and take her back under his roof.* Once he gained safe possession of the boy, however, he evidently planned to get rid of the mother and go his own way as usual.[15]

Whatever the content of Brown's letter from Chichester, its tone may be gauged by the jocularity of a later letter which has survived, written from Wentworth Place in reply to Keats's "posthumous" letter of November 30. On December 21 Brown wrote a long screed of gossip about their friends, a new literary feud, a lucrative evening of poker—and Abby and the child. "O, I must tell you Abby is living with me again, but not in the same capacity,—she keeps to her own bed, & I keep myself continent. Any more nonsense of the former kind would put me in an awkward predicament with her." These arrangements, he assured Keats, "prevent the affair from giving pain next door." As for the child,

---

* The objections of Brown's friends to his behaviour are an interesting reflection of the double standard of the time. According to Brown, Rice later told him that "As for getting the woman with child, there was no harm in it; but there is harm in taking the child into your own house," if only because Brown was "pretending to have more feeling" than his neighbours while in fact ruffling their sensibilities. (Charles Brown, *Some Letters and a Miscellanea*, ed. M. B. Forman [1937], p. 26.)

he was thriving gloriously—"but between you and me, I think an infant is disagreeable,—it is all gut and squall."

Once again he refused Keats's request that he join him in Rome, pleading the heavy extra expense—an expense which, it may be noted, he afforded without difficulty two years later when the trip was not necessary.[16] It is significant that Brown later deleted this request when he transcribed Keats's November 30 letter for publication. He similarly omitted without indication Keats's offer to meet the costs of his trip out of George's expected remittance—an offer which Brown indignantly refused even though the sum was clearly owing to him. At the end of September a much-delayed letter, written in mid-June, had come from George, who in response to the news of his brother's illness promised to sell the steamboat and send him the expected £200 in a few weeks. If Keats ever read this letter, he would have learned from it the astonishing fact that Brown had written to George without his knowledge about sending him to Italy as long ago as March. But it seems clear that Brown opened it in Chichester and decided merely to summarize it in his own letter to Keats rather than forward it.[17] Yet this fact may also help to explain the inward uneasiness that drove Brown to insist in a letter to Taylor that "the indulgence of his friends" had actually harmed Keats and that the bad weather and company and accommodations of the voyage were "good physic" to his mind, as well as to impel him to tamper with the record of this chapter in Keats's life when he came to write it years later. Brown then rationalized his refusal by stating that he was "preparing to follow [Keats to Italy] very early in the spring, and not return, should he prefer to live there"; but he nowhere mentioned this plan in any of his letters during this winter.[18] Yet this is the friend whom Keats told that he would think of him in his dying moments.

Keats's "posthumous existence" dated from the receipt of Brown's letter from Chichester, and not long afterward it turned in the inevitable direction. On December 10 Severn went out for his early-morning walk and posted some letters; when he returned, Keats was awake and ready for breakfast, in good spirits. Then, without warning, a fit of coughing seized him. Gasping for breath, he vomited nearly two cupfuls of blood. Severn, in terror, ran downstairs and across the square for Dr. Clark, who came at once and took another cupful of blood from Keats's arm to arrest the haemorrhage. Faint with bleeding, Keats lapsed back into bed;

but as soon as Severn left the room he staggered out and began groping among his belongings for the bottle of laudanum which Severn had unsuspectingly bought for him at Gravesend. Severn returned a moment later and in a flash of comprehension snatched the bottle away. Keats pleaded, then flew into a rage, but it was no use. Back in bed, with Severn watching him with a new and startled anxiety, he stared in blank despair at the prospect before him. Only the last painful stage of disease lay ahead—the steady sapping of each vital power, the slow breaking of the spirit. He had gone each step of the way with Tom, and before he left England he had resolved to kill himself rather than accept this final defeat. Now once more he found himself trapped by his friends, impaled on their very kindness.

The next morning he had another attack as violent as the first, then three more in one terrible week. Between the haemorrhages and the blood-letting, all his carefully hoarded strength ebbed away. His fever soared, his eyes turned glassy and staring; but worse still was the hunger he suffered. His power of digestion was nearly gone, and Dr. Clark ordered him onto a starvation diet, as little as one anchovy and a piece of toast a day, to keep down the bleeding. Day after day he begged the anguished Severn for more food; night after night he could not sleep. By the end of the week all his courage and self-control had been battered down. He talked for hours in a delirium of discomfort—about Brown and the Brawnes, George and Fanny and most of all Tom, with every memory or foreboding twisted by his despair; of the friends whose hopes he had disappointed and the enemies who had ruined his career. In his extremity, it seems, he suspected that someone in London had poisoned him.[19] Severn feared Keats was losing his mind. Day and night he watched by his bed, hardly leaving him to sleep. The servants refused to wait on them any longer, out of the Italian superstition that consumption was contagious. "Little did I dream on THIS when I left London," Severn exclaimed to Brown in horror. Yet now he manfully shouldered all the burdens of lighting fires, cooking meals, sweeping and washing up, tending to Keats's bodily needs, then reading to him for hours from *Don Quixote* and Maria Edgeworth, old favourites which Keats had brought with him as convalescent reading.

Two weeks later the crisis subsided, leaving them to face the wreckage of their hopes. Dr. Clark told Severn privately that consumption would set in soon and that Keats could never return to England—indeed, that he should never have left it. Yet not until an Italian physician was called in on consultation did he decide that Keats's lungs were affected as well as his stomach. Meanwhile Clark's kindness to Keats was unflagging. He now called on his patient four or five times a day; once he went all over Rome looking for a special kind of fish which he could eat. Mrs. Clark prepared all Keats's food herself and baked mince pies for Severn. His new acquaintances called regularly, though the sight of a strange face usually made Keats miserable. One of them, the young sculptor William Ewing, spelled Severn at the invalid's bedside and searched the city for ice jellies when they were recommended for Keats.[20]

But once Keats's fever abated he settled down into an unshakable depression which frightened Severn still more. On Christmas morning, when he saw Severn writing to Taylor, he joked, "Tell Taylor I'll soon be out in a second edition—in sheets—and cold press." It was a bad joke. His relapse had brought back his old longing to believe in immortality with a still wilder despair, and Severn, who was a simple believing Christian, found the sight of Keats "dying in horror" unspeakably painful. He tried to convince Keats there would be some kind of reward for his suffering, but Keats was only exacerbated by the piety he could not accept. Yet he desperately wished to believe in something—not the Christian faith, which he found impossible, but in some philosophy that would ease the task of dying for him. In anguish he made Severn write down a list of books—Jeremy Taylor's *Holy Living and Holy Dying, Pilgrim's Progress,* and Madame Dacier's translation of Plato. His mind was turning back to the old arguments with Bailey, and to the noble example of Socrates, who had led him to grapple for his own system of soul-making. Yet none of these books could be found. In his anguish he groaned against the "malignant being" which denied him faith—that "last cheap comfort, which every rogue and fool may have," as Severn was appalled to hear him call it.

Christmas for Severn, his first away from home, was "the strangest and saddest" he ever spent. Yet the day was lightened by a shower of letters from England. Three came for Keats—one from Hessey, another from Brown, which "gravely answered" Keats's despairing letter from Naples with, no doubt, the familiar advice to "keep your mind easy, my dear fellow, and no fear of your body." The third was from Fanny Brawne. The sight of that slender slanting hand was too much. Keats, "affected most bitterly," handed the letters back to Severn, the one from Fanny still unopened, and said, "No more letters for me." By now the pattern of the events of the last year must have been clear to him. The voyage to Italy had been useless from the start, as he had suspected all along; the friend whom he held dearest had intended all along not to go with him; and he would die now cut off both from the woman he loved and from the friend on whose loyalty he had counted to the end. In the weeks ahead, as Severn recalled, it was "the kindness of his friends" that Keats brooded over with the greatest bitterness.[21] Later on Christmas Day, in a desperate gesture of self-destruction, he asked Severn as his last request that his death not be mentioned in the newspapers and that no engraving be made from any picture of him. In his last days in England, Fanny Brawne recalled, "his most ardent desire was to live to redeem his name from the obloquy cast upon it." [22] Now, in what seemed to him the failure of everything for which he had hoped in life, he wanted the record to be wiped clean, his very name forgotten. Only the thought of annihilation could give him peace.

Back in England the members of Keats's circle went each his own way, each one concerned with Keats's progress in his own fashion. Hessey, kindly and conscientious, copied out almost every letter from Rome to send around to Keats's friends, while Brown took his own next door to read to the Brawnes with discreet omissions. Meanwhile he was dickering with John Scott to publish his journal of the Scottish trip and waiting with rising irritation for George to send the promised £200. But George's hopes for selling the steamboat had been dashed when the purchaser disappeared; his only news this fall was the completion of his lumber mill and the birth of his second daughter. In a dejected letter to his brother in November, he suggested "Marriage might do you good," then offered to send Miss Brawne "an India crape dress or merino shawl or something scarce with you but cheap with us." Haslam, whom Brown had already persuaded that George was responsible for all Keats's worries, wrote Severn in deep anxiety never to mention George to Keats but to urge him to unburden his mind.[23] He still counted on the Italian spring to work a miracle, for he could not bear the thought of losing his friend: "If I know what it is to love,

I truly love John Keats." Only Haslam was allowed to call on Fanny Keats at Walthamstow with news of her brother; Mrs. Dilke and Mrs. Brawne were still refused. Yet Fanny Brawne started writing her regularly the day after Keats sailed—tactful, affectionate letters which the girl managed to hide from the terrible eye of Mrs. Abbey. The news which Fanny sent was never bright, for she was more convinced by Keats's hoplessness about his condition than any of his friends. She tried not to expect to hear from Keats herself for a long time—knowing what an effort each letter cost him. Yet two months went by with no word except the "God bless you!" he sent her from quarantine; then a third. "If I have a right guess, a certain person next door is a little disappointed at not receiving a letter from you," Brown observed in mid-December, "but not a word has dropped." Fanny kept her proud silence up; even to Fanny Keats she was no more than her brother's next-door neighbour. At the end of December she was rewarded, briefly, with the good report Severn had sent Haslam from Rome at the beginning of the month.

The three or four weeks that lapsed between the sending and receiving of letters made Fanny very impatient, as she once confessed; [24] they also make for ironic discrepancies in the narrative of these months. The dark December in Rome was a time of rising hopes in London; then early in January, just as the news of Keats's relapse reached Hampstead, Severn was watching a change in Keats which gave him a flicker of hope. A new calm succeeded the black despair of the weeks before. Severn sensed that Keats had at last given up not only the thought but even the desire of recovery. Yet it seemed that this quietude relieved him as no medicine had done. Accordingly on January 11 Severn wrote Mrs. Brawne that he now hoped to bring Keats back to England in the spring; for "if anything will recover him it is this absence of himself."

Outside their window the Roman spring was already starting; in the mild sunshine the fruit trees opened their blossoms to the delicate air. The day before Keats had seemed well enough to get up. Severn put fresh clothes on him and helped him into the sitting room, where he stretched out on the sofa and began to talk with Severn about his own concerns. Keats was anxious about Severn's health, and kept prescribing medicines, rest, exercise, even change of air for his friend. "He is my doctor," Severn told Taylor.[25] But especially since his relapse Keats had worried that Severn would lose his precious chance of the R.A. fellowship by taking care of him. For a month Severn had found hardly an hour or two together for sketching in the back room, but Keats managed to rouse him up to write Sir Thomas Lawrence about his progress. That evening, as he finished his letter to Mrs. Brawne, Severn looked in at Keats: he was sleeping peacefully, looking more like himself than he had for weeks. From somewhere, for a while at least, he had got his courage back, his hard-won sense of identity. The poet was dead in him, the discontented, restless, and eloquent self who had fought for an immortal name and failed. Yet at this crisis his other earlier selves reappeared and buoyed his spirit up: the doctor who, mastering his own distress, sought patiently to do some good for others; and the proud image of his boyhood, the young officer who faced death with wordless fortitude.

By January 15 this brief respite was over, and Keats turned into the last stage of his journey. There were no more haemorrhages, only the relentless advance of the final symptoms: a high fever and a hammering pulse; cold sweats at night that set his teeth chattering; a constant dry cough, with the noose inside his chest slipping a little tighter each time; a thicker and thicker expectoration of mucus, clay-coloured and blood-streaked. By the end of January his digestion had failed and he could live only on milk. The flesh began wasting away from his limbs, his knees growing knobbled, his hands shrinking to a ghastly thinness which once brought him to tears to look on. And each step in this slow destruction of the athletic body in which he had once taken such delight, Keats recognized with dreadful clarity. At last Severn acknowledged there was no hope: Keats's death was only two or three weeks away.

It was a terrible time for Severn. Besides his daily sharing of Keats's sufferings, which bound him closer to his friend every day, he now had several growing anxieties. At the end of December he learned that the landlady had reported Keats's illness to the police. Under Roman law Severn was threatened with heavy additional expenses—not only an autopsy but also a complete refurbishing of every room Keats had entered, in which everything would be destroyed down to the paper on the walls and the varnish on the floor. With his English conviction that this fear of contagion was nonsense, Severn was enraged, but also alarmed: Keats's books, his own painting materials, even the hired piano would be sacrificed. Another anxious secret he had to keep from Keats was a sudden crisis in their finances. In December, on the advice of his banker, Torlonia, Keats had drawn the entire remaining sum in his letter of credit to deposit in Rome, not realizing that the London bankers would not honour drafts above a certain small figure. When the bill for £120 was presented in London, it was promptly returned; and, early in January, Severn found their credit refused at Torlonia's and his supply of cash reduced to a few crowns. Dr. Clark immediately loaned him some money and wrote an explanation to London, but several weeks went by before the misunderstanding was cleared up. Severn meanwhile was paralysed with frustration: he could easily earn money by going out to paint miniatures, but Keats was too nervous to endure a strange face at his bedside. Gallantly he continued his day-and-night watch, performing all the most menial tasks, reading to Keats until, dizzy with fatigue, he hardly understood the words he uttered. Many nights he sat up with him almost till dawn, writing letters or sketching Keats's head on the pillow to keep himself awake,* and stringing the candles together with thread to keep one lit if he fell asleep. His letters to his family were always resolutely cheerful; only to Haslam and Brown did he confide his troubles. Inevitably he fell ill himself, toward the end of January. Keats insisted that a nurse be found to give Severn a respite. Luckily Dr. Clark found an English nurse whom Keats seemed to like, and for two hours every other day Severn had a little precious freedom.

Under this testing, Severn's thoughtless gaiety and simpleminded piety were being transmuted into a resilient and selfeffacing devotion that none of his friends in England could have predicted. It was sorely tried in these last weeks of January as Keats's irritability became uncontrollable. He would ask for food, then refuse it when Severn prepared it for him, five or six times a day. For a while he was too nervous even to be read to; then a great desire for books came on him, and Severn read steadily for three days. The longing for some faith in a life after death still

---

* Severn's sketch, with the inscription "28th Jan. 3 o'clock Mg. Drawn to keep me awake—a deadly sweat was on him all this night," is reproduced among the illustrations as Plate XIV.

tormented him. By good fortune Severn located a copy of *Holy Living and Holy Dying,* but it did not bring Keats the solace he hoped for. Instead, as the weary days and restless nights wore on, he began to accuse Severn of the blackest cruelty in thwarting his attempt at suicide. He could think only of the long sleep of death with any comfort. "He talks of it with delight," Severn wrote Taylor in wonder, "the strangeness of his mind every day surprises me—no one feeling or one notion like any other being." One morning on his early walk Severn saw the first roses blooming and reported them to Keats when he awoke. To Severn's dismay, Keats wept at the news. He had always been able to escape from suffering, he told Severn, in watching the silent growth of flowers; now —he had hoped to be dead before the spring came round again.

Since Christmas, when the mere sight of Fanny Brawne's handwriting had been too much for him, Keats had not been able to read any of his letters from England. Early in February a letter arrived from Hampstead, addressed in Brown's robust hand, and Keats summoned up the courage to open it. In a searing flash of recognition he saw the letter inside was from Fanny Brawne. His nerves, already taut as fiddle strings, now must have snapped. "The effects were on him for many days," Severn noted. When he could bring himself to mention it again, Keats asked Severn to put the letter in his coffin, along with his sister's, after his death. In a day or two he changed his mind and told Severn that only his sister's letters should be buried with him. One last fit of anger choked him at the thought of the desire forever unfulfilled. "He found many causes of his illness in the exciting and thwarting of his passions," Severn wrote Brown in mystification, "but I persuaded him to feel otherwise on this delicate point." But the greatest torment in these last weeks was the thought of the nameless friends who had sent him to a lonely death in Rome. Severn, always unsuspecting, wrote Brown that Keats was dying a martyr to "these infernal scoundrels," "a thousand miles from his dear home, without one comfort but me when—" then broke off in anguish. "I cannot bear to think of it." Neither, apparently, could Brown, for he later deleted this passage in transcribing Severn's letter for publication.[26]

Meanwhile the news of Keats's relapse had reached England, shattering at once all the cheerful expectations of the autumn be-

fore. Brown, who first heard it, was stunned almost to speechless-
ness. For a week he could not bring himself to write Severn,
haunted as he was by a vision of Keats constantly at his side, looking intently into his face. "So much as I have loved him," he cried
out, "I never knew how closely he was wound about my heart."
But at once he defended himself by leaping to the attack. Keats's
disease, he reminded Severn, was all in the mind, all the result
of George's cruelty—an accusation which he repeated not only
to Haslam but also to Taylor and Hessey. "I sit planning schemes
of vengeance upon his head," he wrote—that "canting, selfish,
heartless swindler—who will have to answer for the death of his
brother." Yet two weeks later he was compelled to confess to
Severn his remorse that "I did not, at all hazards, and in spite of
apparent difficulties, follow you both to Italy, and relieve you in
your distressing attentions." [27] Taylor, on learning the news, wrote
Severn to read the Book of Job to comfort Keats; then, after sending
George a stiff letter demanding to be reimbursed for the £150
letter of credit, he began raising a second fund to meet Keats's
further needs. Reynolds informed Taylor that he had already sent
£50 to Keats, though it turned out a few months later that he had
only intended to and never did in fact. Another friend sent a £50
credit to a banker in Florence for Keats to use there in the summer—Woodhouse, perhaps, honouring a little belatedly his farewell promise. Hessey, deeply concerned for Keats's spiritual wel-
fare, urged Severn to convince Keats of God's forgiveness through
Christ and "pray with him—pray by him—pray for him." [28] Bailey, in a letter of literary chit-chat to Taylor, found some consol-
ing "dispensation of a kind Providence" in the thought that Keats
would be spared many inevitable disappointments by his death.
"Poor Fellow," he added, "my heart bleeds for him; but human sorrow is very unavailing." Leigh Hunt, from whom Bailey
thought Keats had learned the "fatal error" of irreligion, sent
Severn a letter whose tenderness redeems all that Keats or his
friends could ever blame him for. Hunt begged Severn to remind
Keats that recovery was still possible if he would only hope stead-
fastly for it; but if he was beyond all hope, Hunt wrote, "tell him
that we shall all bear his memory in the most precious part of our
hearts, and that the world shall bow their heads to it, as our loves
do. Tell him," he added, "that the most sceptical of us has faith
enough in the high things that nature puts into our heads, to

think that all who are of one accord in mind and heart, are journeying to one and the same place, and shall unite somehow or
other again face to face, mutually conscious, mutually delighted.
Tell him he is only before us on the road, as he was in everything
else, and that we are coming after him." [29]

The greatest anxiety among Keats's friends was borne in the
greatest silence. Fanny Brawne took care, as she later told Fanny
Keats, "never to trouble them with any feelings of mine"; and
Brown himself wondered at her firmness. Mrs. Brawne tried to
soften the blow of the bad news, but Fanny replied, "I know he
must die soon: when you hear of his death, tell me immediately—I
am not a fool." [30] For a while she tried to shield Fanny Keats from
the news, writing her a collected letter saying nothing of her
brother's relapse; then, on February 21, she decided she must be
told. Yet, as she wrote, her emotion began to break through, half
against her will. For months she had silently watched Brown, next
door, playing the part of Keats's dearest friend while dodging the
responsibility which she had expected from the first he would fulfil, of following Keats to Italy. Now the news that Keats no longer
wished to live overwhelmed her: he was being killed, she wrote
Fanny Keats, not only by the malignity of an indifferent world
but also by "want of feeling in those who ought above all to have
felt for him." [31] Driven by her grief, she started to take Fanny
into her confidence. "And now my dear Girl, my dear Sister for
so I feel you to be, forgive me if I have not sufficiently softened
this wretched news. Indeed I am not now able to contrive words
that would appear less harsh—if I am to lose him I lose everything,
and then you, after my mother, will be the only person I shall feel
interest or attachment for—I feel that I love his sister as my own."

By the middle of February, Keats had fallen back into the calm
of sheer exhaustion. Slowly his body was relaxing its hold in its
unconscious wrestling against death, and his mind lapsed into a
new peace. He now could talk easily to Severn for hours, and at
night he fell into comfortable sleep. Even his dreams were pleasant. The fresh milk on which he was subsisting came to seem
beautiful to him—its sight and smell and taste. He began to tell
Severn of his last wishes, one by one. Severn was to have his seven-
volume set of Shakespeare's plays and his treasured volume of
Shakespeare's *Poems*. The purse which Fanny Keats had made

for him as a final gift was to be placed in his coffin, along with all his unopened letters and a lock of hair—Fanny Brawne's, though Severn did not know it. And on his gravestone he asked that no name or date should be written, only the legend "HERE LIES ONE WHOSE NAME WAS WRIT IN WATER." Above it was to be carved a Greek lyre with four of its eight strings broken—"to show his Classical Genius cut off by death before its maturity," as Severn later interpreted it. He knew that Keats had had this thought for a long time, for in Hampstead the spring before he had asked Severn to sketch the lyre for him, without telling him the reason. But there was more in Keats's mind than Severn guessed. The lyre was the device of the Tassie gem which Fanny Brawne had evidently given him that Christmas Day of 1818. Not his name, then, but her seal was to mark his resting place.[32]

After making these requests, Keats lay quietly in bed for several days, staring up at the white cross-beams of the ceiling with its yellow rosettes set in blue squares, shifting from one hand to another a white carnelian—Fanny's seal, though Severn did not recognize it.[33] Outside his window the Roman artillery rumbled through the streets; Rome lay in the path of the Neapolitan advance against the Austrians, and it was feared that the city might be ransacked. But Keats hardly noticed the disturbance. He was thinking of the open meadow outside the Aurelian Wall near the Pyramid of Caius Cestius, where a few Protestant graves were scattered between the cypresses in the long grass. Severn had visited the cemetery at his request and returned to tell him of the flocks of sheep that grazed there, with their tinkling bells the only sound to break the silence, and the early daisies and violets already in bloom.

Meanwhile Keats's Roman friends stood by as best they could. Dr. Clark called as regularly as ever and now tried to steady Severn against the event to come. William Ewing also came to help out from time to time. Once he brought a handsome young Spanish gentleman, a romantic novelist and revolutionary-in-exile named Valentine Llanos Guiterez, whose brief meeting with Keats was to be a turning point in his life. But for Keats now it was only Severn's presence that mattered. For long hours he slept as Severn dozed at his bedside by a solitary candle. Sometimes Keats would wake in a moment of terror, wondering where he was or who was with him; then his eyes wandered over the dim room till they fell on Severn and closed again in sleep.

Around February 19 or 20 Clark told Severn to expect Keats's death any day. His face now showed the same emaciation as his body, the cheeks hollowed, the nose beaked, the ridges of the forehead jutting out over the eyes, which still glittered with fever. Yet for all his longing for death, his body fought stubbornly against it up to the end, holding out weeks after Clark thought it possible. Even out of his despair Keats managed to make a joke: he greeted Clark one morning with the question, "How long will this posthumous life of mine last?" His mind still stood over and above the ruin that was overtaking his body, and in two of his last conversations with Severn he was thinking only of his friend. Still fearful that Severn might lose his fellowship, Keats now thought that Hilton should request an extension for him at the Royal Academy—if only for Keats's sake. He made Severn promise to write to Taylor and ask him to take up the matter with Hilton; Severn agreed, and Keats was satisfied.[34] But one more subject had to be discussed, the most painful of all. It took all that was left of the hero in Keats to tell Severn what, as a doctor, he knew his friend must be prepared for. With a calmness that astonished Severn, he asked him if he had ever seen anyone die. Severn answered no; then Keats replied, "Well then I pity you— poor Severn, what trouble and danger you have got into for me." But he must be firm, Keats told him, for it would not last long, and he did not think he would be convulsed at the end. He must have been remembering Tom's last moments, which—so at least he had told George—were "not so painful"; and the very last was "without a pang." So much hope, at least, Keats tried to hold out to his friend.

On the night of February 21 Severn thought the end had come. Keats breathed with such pain that Severn had to prop him up on the pillows, where, hour after hour, he struggled against suffocation; yet he was still alive when the windows turned pale with dawn. Another day and night Severn watched while Keats coughed the breath in and out of his body. On the twenty-third the English nurse came and stayed all day while Severn snatched a little sleep. The nurse left, and the afternoon sank toward evening; then Keats gasped out to his friend, "Severn—I—lift me up—I am dying." Severn took him in his arms and held him close, but Keats broke out into a sweat and cried, "Don't breathe on me—it comes like ice." The phlegm was boiling in his throat, and he gripped Severn's hand very hard as he fought for breath. He was face to face with death, but even at this moment he did not lose his awareness of his friend. Clinging to Severn, he whispered, "Don't be frightened—I shall die easy—be firm, and thank God it has come!"

He did not die easy: for seven hours he fought against slow drowning. Severn listened to the mucus gurgling in his throat as slowly Keats lost the strength to cough. Still he kept his eyes fixed on Severn, watching him with fierce wordless consciousness but seemingly without pain. Toward eleven o'clock the struggle grew quieter; Severn thought he had fallen asleep. Then he realized that Keats was dead.

# Epilogue

T H E next day Dr. Clark took the shattered Severn over to his house to begin a long recovery from grief and fatigue. Then the machinery of death was put in motion. Casts were taken of Keats's face, hand, and foot. The following day an autopsy was performed. Keats's lungs were entirely destroyed; it was the worst consumption Clark had ever seen, and a miracle that he had lived so long. The third day, Monday, February 26, Keats was buried at dawn, with the last gifts and unopened letters of Fanny Brawne and Fanny Keats sealed in his coffin. The English chaplain at Rome and eight mourners followed his body to the grave, which lay near that of Shelley's third child, within the shadow of the Pyramid of Caius Cestius. When the service was over Dr. Clark and his friends heaped turfs of daisies on the grave. Immediately afterward the police took charge of the apartment at the Piazza di Spagna, burning all the furniture, scraping the walls and floors and even making new doors and windows. Severn, though still too shaken to be left alone for almost a fortnight after Keats's death, wrote a brief letter to Brown on February 27 to break the news.

For weeks Brown had tried to pretend he wished Keats's sufferings at an end, but as each letter came from Rome he read it "in a horror" lest his wish had been realized. Now, when the news reached Hampstead on March 17, he was overcome. The next day he sent off four or five notes to pass on the word, then went next door to tell the Brawnes. Writing Severn a few days later, he could not describe the first shock of his announcement, but merely reported that Fanny was "now pretty well,—and thro' out she has shown a firmness of mind which I little expected from one so young." At once she and her family went into mourning. The reactions of Keats's other friends are not recorded. Each man grieved in his own way, then sooner or later returned to his inevitable preoccupations. Haslam broke the news to Fanny Keats. Taylor sent the obituary notices to the papers, then began laying plans to write a biography of Keats and trying once again to collect from George and Abbey some of the funds which he himself had raised for Keats. Bailey, on hearing the news, wrote Taylor that Keats's death seemed a visitation of Providence—"a merciful severity." Haydon recorded Keats's death in his diary almost as an afterthought to that of his friend the journalist John Scott, who had just been killed in a duel arising from a quarrel with the *Blackwood's* set; a month later he wrote Miss Mitford that Keats died a victim of "want of nerve" to bear abuse.[1] Brown in July executed Keats's will by dividing his books among his friends, carefully omitting any gift to George. In Rome, Severn slowly climbed back to health and returned to his painting. In May he wrote Haslam that Keats's grave was now overgrown with daisies, and that he often visited it "with a most delicious melancholy."

But Fanny Brawne, after steeling herself so long against the news of Keats's death, broke down a few weeks after its arrival. She fell ill and her hair was cut short; after her recovery she took to wearing a widow's cap and weeds. Grown alarmingly thin, she shut herself up in her room to pore over Keats's letters, or wandered alone over the Heath day after day and often far into the night, so the watchmen had to be sent with lanterns to find her.[2] As she wrote to Fanny Keats near the end of May, "All his friends have forgotten him, they have got over the first shock, and that with them is all. They think I have done the same, but I have not got over it and never shall—it's better for me that I should not forget him, but not for you."

From the first, it was only to Keats's sister that Fanny Brawne unburdened herself. "For myself, I am patient, resigned, very resigned," she wrote her a week after receiving the news of his death. "I know my Keats is happy, happier a thousand times than he could have been here, for Fanny, you do not, you never can know how much he has suffered. All that grieves me now is that I was not with him, and so near it as I was. And yet it was a great deal through his kindness for me for he foresaw what would happen, he at least was never deceived about his complaint." Once again

she was overwhelmed by the thought of his being sent to "that
wretched country" to die when his recovery was impossible "and
he might have died here with so many friends to soothe him
and me *me* with him." With this she broke through her reticence
at last and told Fanny the secret: "Had he returned I should have
been his wife and he would have lived with us. All now in vain—
could we have foreseen—but he did foresee and everyone thought
it was only his habit of looking for the worst." Then, remembering Keats's dread of gossip, she begged Fanny never to mention
her name in connection with his, and told her she allowed no one
to speak of him to her. A month later, reading *As You Like It*
in Keats's folio Shakespeare, she pencilled the words "Fanny April
17 1821" beside the FINIS at the end.[3]

⋙ ⋘

Keats's friends had not forgotten him that spring, as Fanny
thought; but even then his memory and reputation were entering
a long eclipse. At the end of March, Taylor had made a public
announcement of his intention of writing Keats's biography and
began gathering the manuscripts of his poems and letters from
Woodhouse, Bailey, and Keats's other friends. But Brown immediately opposed the idea, thinking Taylor "a mere bookseller," and
persuaded Severn to send all of Keats's papers to him instead.
Thus began a long many-sided rivalry among Keats's friends—
including Reynolds, Cowden Clarke, and even Shelley—for the
honour of being his biographer, which only served to hasten the
breakup of his circle, while the life remained unwritten. Meanwhile, in Rome, Severn worried about the gravestone. He was uncertain whether to use the bitter inscription which Keats had
dictated to him, and had to write Brown several times asking his
advice in the matter.[4] He also had to nudge Brown to send him
the sketch of the lyre he had made in Brown's copy of *Endymion*
the year before at Keats's request. Not till a year and a half later
did work begin according to his design; then, over two years after
Keats's death, the gravestone was erected at last, at Severn's expense. His friends honoured Keats's dying wish that his grave be
nameless, but Brown thought that his inscription should be prefaced by an explanation.[5]

This Grave
contains all that was Mortal
of a
YOUNG ENGLISH POET
Who
on his Death Bed,
in the Bitterness of his Heart
at the Malicious Power of his Enemies,
Desired
these Words to be engraven on his Tomb Stone
"Here lies One
Whose Name was writ in Water"

The first real memorial to Keats was Shelley's elegy *Adonais*, published in June 1821—the most enduring and yet in some ways the most misleading of all the tributes to him. Shelley had picked up a few hints from Hunt about Keats's brooding over the reviews during his illness at his house the previous summer, and, smarting as he was over his own treatment by the Tory critics, decided that the *Quarterly* article had actually brought on Keats's fatal haemorrhage.[6] As a living poet, Keats mattered little to Shelley; as a martyr to Tory injustice and a symbol of neglected genius, he inspired some of Shelley's most fervent lines.

> He has outsoared the shadow of our night;
> Envy and calumny and hate and pain,
> And that unrest which men miscall delight,
> Can touch him not and torture not again;
> From the contagion of the world's slow stain
> He is secure. . . .

Though Shelley did much to rescue Keats from Lockhart's caricature of the Cockney bardling, "the amiable Mister Keats," he succeeded only by substituting another distorted picture, the poet of fragile, almost feminine sensibility who could not face adverse criticism. This in turn provoked some deserved ridicule from Byron in *Don Juan,* along with a little grudging appreciation of the promise shown in *Hyperion:*

> John Keats, who was killed off by one critique
> Just as he really promised something great
> If not intelligible, without Greek
> Contrived to talk about the gods of late
> Much as they might have been supposed to speak.
> Poor fellow! His was an untoward fate;

'Tis strange the mind, that fiery particle,
Should let itself be snuffed out by an article.

Yet for many years the myth of Adonais was the only alternative
to Lockhart's gibes. Even many of his friends who knew Keats in
health as well as in sickness repeated Shelley's story in one form
or another, out of their own varying needs to blame the tragedy
of his death on someone. Hazlitt, who had his own reasons for
attacking the Tory critics, described Keats again and again as " 'a
bud bit by an envious worm,' " "a little western flower" on which
the reviews had dropped their poison.[7] Hunt, writing the first real
memoir of Keats in 1828 in a sketch included in his volume of
reminiscences of Byron, helped fix this impression of his weakness
even while trying to correct the Lockhart portrait. He managed
also to hint at Keats's dependence on Brown and himself in a way
that enraged George Keats, and described his morbidity during his
illness in detail that distressed both Brown and Fanny Brawne; [8]
but Keats's other friends either would not or could not refute these
implications.

For some years it seemed that Keats's own despairing wish to be
forgotten might well be realized. Almost all his friends took him
at his own final estimate—that he had left "no immortal work"
behind him, though he would have made himself remembered
if he had lived. Even the most sympathetic reviewers of the *Lamia*
volume saw it as full of poetic promise rather than achievement.
Long after 1820 most readers remained puzzled or offended by
Keats's innovations—his original use of mythology, his complex
and concentrated imagery, his range through the whole spectrum
of the English language. In 1846 De Quincey spoke with a heavy
weight of critical authority in protesting that "upon his mother
tongue, upon this English language, has Keats trampled as with
the hoofs of a buffalo." [9] The year before, Taylor had sold all his
copyrights of Keats's poems and rights in his unpublished manuscripts for a mere fifty pounds. The firm of Taylor and Hessey
had long since failed and dissolved; there was no demand for a
reprint of Keats's works in England until 1840, and when one
appeared that year it was soon remaindered.[10] In 1836, when Severn
suggested that a monument be raised to Keats in England, Brown
replied that his fame was not great enough to warrant it.[11]

Meanwhile the years had moved on, carrying each of his friends, as Keats had foreseen, farther in his own separate direction. There is a tragic fitness in the fact that the first and indeed the only one to escape the touch of "the world's slow stain" with him was Shelley. A year after writing *Adonais,* Shelley was drowned in a shipwreck in the Bay of Spezia after sailing to Leghorn to welcome Leigh Hunt to Italy. When his body was washed ashore near Viareggio, a sea-soaked copy of *Lamia* was found doubled back and thrust into a pocket of his jacket.[12] Hunt himself was to subside comfortably into the Victorian age, his foibles smiled away, his old critical rallying-cries accepted as articles of poetic belief. Yet he continued to do good service to Keats's memory by discussing and occasionally reprinting his poetry in his literary journals. Haydon, who had reached the height of his ambition and prosperity at the time of Keats's death, married soon afterward and found, to his disgust, that he must turn portrait-painter to support his wife and family. In and out of debtors' prison, his reputation declining, he stubbornly continued to paint larger and larger canvases,[13] for which there was less and less room in Victorian England. Finally, at the age of sixty, after the failure of an exhibition of two huge paintings at the Egyptian Hall, where the famous Tom Thumb was drawing crowds of a hundred thousand to Haydon's hundred, he lost his nerve, as he once accused Keats of doing, and shot himself. John Reynolds married the beautiful Eliza Drewe at last, in 1822, but could not give up playing the gay blade in the London clubs and theatres and magazines, even though his law career suffered as a result. They had one child, whom they lost, much to Reynolds' grief. Ten years after his marriage he was in financial straits, with a reputation for hard drinking and sharp card-playing. After slowly losing ground, he ended as an assistant clerk at the County Court in the Isle of Wight and died at fifty-two, a broken and forgotten man.

Jane Reynolds, the serious and sentimental, eventually married Thomas Hood the wit—to the surprise of George Keats, who wondered how she ever "captivated so facetious a genius." The cheerful but ailing James Rice took Reynolds into partnership and with his aid mismanaged Fanny and George Keats's legal affairs for a while before dying after a long lingering, in his mid-thirties. The self-effacing Haslam lived out the rest of his days in obscurity and hard work. Woodhouse continued to help Taylor to collect materials for his life of Keats; then he too developed consumption.

His last good deed for Keats was to visit Brown, by then living in Italy, shortly before his death in 1834 and make him promise to start his much-delayed memoir. Hessey turned schoolmaster after failing as a bookseller, and Taylor pursued a long career as editor and scholar. Dilke had as long and more noteworthy a career as a man of letters, while also looking after the interests of Fanny Brawne and George and Fanny Keats. This involved him in a painful quarrel with his old friend Charles Brown when Brown, in gathering materials for his biography of Keats, tried to pin the blame for much of Keats's suffering on George's selfishness. Dilke at once came to George's defence, and the friendship finally ended with bitter words on both sides. Brown, after some difficulty in gaining possession of his boy from "his obstinate mother," went to Italy a year and a half after Keats's death and remained there for twelve years, occupying himself pleasantly in journalism. Having returned to England, he finally wrote his biographical sketch of Keats under curious emotional stress, oppressed by headaches or weeping like a child, haunted by the image of Keats watching him as he wrote. The life was given a public reading in Plymouth at the end of 1836, but Brown could not find a publisher to take it. Five years later he emigrated with his son to New Zealand, where he died in 1842.

Meanwhile George Keats worked hard and prospered in Louisville, raising a large family, paying off his brother's debts, and trying without success to find someone to print Keats's unpublished poems with a brief memoir, for which he was willing to assume the publisher's losses. In his early forties he suffered another financial setback, developed consumption with startling suddenness, and died a few months later. Fanny Keats was the only member of the family to become—as John once promised he and she both should—fat and old "with triple chins and stumpy thumbs." She had to wait patiently for her release from the Abbeys at twenty-one, then go to law, with the help of Dilke, to wrest her inheritance from her guardian—"that consummate villain," as she came to regard him. These were the proceedings that revealed Abbey's mishandling of his trust, and from them Fanny emerged with a portion of £4500—of which about £1200 would have gone to Keats if he had been alive. A year later she married the romantic young Spaniard who had called on Keats a few days before his death, and lived more or less happily ever after as Señora Valentin

Llanos of Madrid. In her late fifties, on a visit to the Piazza di Spagna, she unexpectedly met Joseph Severn for the first time in the very house where Keats died. It was like a reunion of long-lost brother and sister; yet, as a friend of Severn's recalled, Señora Llanos had nothing to say of "her wizard brother," of whom she spoke "as a mystery." [14] But the most unforeseeable change wrought by the years was in Severn himself. Keats's dying advice, that he request Hilton to intercede with the Royal Academy for him, achieved its purpose; in spite of arriving in London three months late, his painting of "The Death of Alcibiades" won him the three-year fellowship as he had hoped. After Keats's death he was taken up by the leaders of the English colony in Rome, and seven years later he married the ward of his patroness, the Countess of Westmoreland. He lived long and happily, though without gaining any distinction as a painter, and in 1860 was appointed British Consul in Rome—a post in which he charmed everyone, according to John Ruskin, from the cardinals in council to the brightest English belles on picnics in the Campagna.

"What fools we mortals are," wrote George Keats on the squabbles over his brother's biography, "how we are straining for ever so small a niche in the temple of Fame." It was not his friends' failings, or lack of them, that mattered to Keats, but some quality that continued to draw him toward them after these failings were recognized; so also it is his gift for friendship that is remembered long after the friends themselves are forgotten. If they are remembered a century or more after their deaths, it is largely in the measure of their loyalty to Keats. Severn, who was honoured to the end of his life as Keats's devoted friend in his last hour, repeatedly acknowledged how much his career owed to this accident of their friendship. But Fanny Brawne, who kept the secret of her engagement for years, as Keats wished, received no such reward for her loyalty. When she recovered from her illness after Keats's death, her beauty had lost all its colour and freshness. She remained in mourning for several years and continued to wear Keats's ring till the end of her life. In 1829 a friend of Valentin Llanos described her as looking very thin and sadly worn, though dazzling in her manner despite her pale looks. She was the same Fanny still. She kept writing gay, affectionate letters to Keats's young sister during her long imprisonment in Walthamstow, full of gossip about books, clothes, their common acquaintances, and Fanny Keats's pet pigeons. When she began going to parties in Hampstead again, her wit was sharp as ever. Sometime after 1825 when she appeared at a ball in a dress trimmed with bugles, John Reynolds punned, "It's good to wear bugles and be heard wherever one goes"; whereupon Fanny Brawne retorted, "And it's good to be a brother-in-law of Tom Hood's and get your jokes for nothing." [15] Her life was darkened again when her brother died of tuberculosis in 1828 and her mother from burns in a tragic accident the following year. Finally in 1833, in her early thirties, she decided to marry, and there is poignant meaning in the fact that she chose a man who, twelve years younger than herself, was close to Keats's own age at the time she first met him in 1818. The rest of her sixty-five years she spent living quietly on the Continent with her husband, Louis Lindon, and their three children.

In 1829, however, four weeks after the death of her mother, Fanny received a disturbing letter from Charles Brown, asking permission to mention her affair with Keats—though not her name—in his projected biography and to quote some of Keats's last bitter poems and letters referring to her. Fanny's reply has often been cited against her to prove she never really loved Keats; yet it is an extraordinary revelation of her honesty and complexity of feeling.[16] Characteristically she said nothing to Brown about her mother's death nor even hinted her possible doubts as to his qualifications as Keats's biographer. After some hesitation she granted Brown's request to mention their story, realizing unhappily that many people both within and without her circle of acquaintance would blame her for a lack of womanly reticence. For herself, she admitted, she did not want to give away the key to her own feelings, or even be connected with all the old abuse of Keats; * and, remembering Keats's desire to be forgotten, she thought it would be kinder "to let him rest for ever in the obscurity to which unhappy circumstances have condemned him." Yet at the same time she hated the picture that had been given to the public—first by Shelley, then by Hazlitt and Hunt—of a "weakness of character that only belonged to his ill health." Though she feared nothing could be done to prove his unfulfilled

---

* Fanny crossed out this sentence in the draft; not, I think, because she feared Brown would think less of her for speaking so forthrightly (as she herself said, "I was more generous ten years ago"), but because on second thought she realized that by surrendering some of her privacy she might help in the vindication of Keats's name.

promise as a poet, she thought his character should be rescued from the misrepresentations of his friends as well as of his enemies. For that reason in the end she approved Brown's intention of telling the full truth of Keats's life; though for herself, she added, "Without claiming too much constancy I may truly say that he is well-remembered by me and that satisfied with that I could wish no one but myself knew he had ever existed."

—&#8250;&#8250;&#8250;&#8249;&#8249;&#8249;—

Fanny's wish was not to be realized. Unknown to her and to most of Keats's friends, a new generation was already springing up to whom his work spoke with the authentic voice of poetry. In the very month that Fanny Brawne wrote her troubled letter to Brown the Cambridge Union maintained in debate against Oxford that Shelley was a greater poet than Byron—sign of an undergraduate cult in which every ardent reader of *Adonais* was also a champion of Keats.[17] In 1834 Severn wrote Brown from Rome that a group of Cambridge men there wanted to perform *Otho*. Even as early as 1826 the discovery of Keats and Shelley fired the fourteen-year-old Robert Browning with the ambition to become a poet himself. Still it was very slowly that, as the age of George IV gave way to the age of Victoria, old battles were forgotten and new allegiances formed; it was largely the success of another Cambridge admirer and close student of Keats's poetry, young Alfred Tennyson, that won Keats a wide audience at last.

It was to Richard Monckton Milnes, the most brilliant of Keats's champions at Cambridge, that Brown eventually turned over his memoir and collection of Keats manuscripts in the hope of getting them published. After Brown's unexpected death, Milnes decided to write the biography of Keats himself—a task for which he was well fitted as poet, politician, and man of the world. He managed to conciliate all the rival biographers and collect their materials; and his *Life, Letters and Literary Remains,* published in 1848, at last presented Keats in something of his true stature, though heavily draped in Victorian respectability. Though Milnes himself thought the book—"the biography of a mere boy"—would rouse little interest, it scored a wide success, and from this time Keats began to be acknowledged as one of the greatest poets of his generation—or even greater. In the wild-eyed enthusiasm of the young Pre-Raphaelite poets he came to be ranked only one step below Shakespeare, in the immortal company of Homer, Dante, Chaucer, and Leonardo da Vinci.[18] A poignant echo of this sudden adulation of a near-forgotten genius is found in the epitaph inscribed on Reynolds's gravestone at his death in 1852—"The Friend of Keats."

Inevitably a new sentimental appreciation of Keats sprang up alongside the respectable. It was the sentimentalists who raised a fund to have Severn's body reinterred in 1881, two years after his death, by the side of Keats in Rome, with a matching gravestone commemorating his devotion. The respectable tradition received a severe jolt at this time, however, when Keats's letters to Fanny Brawne first appeared in print. Dilke's grandson, Sir Charles, had done all he could to prevent this by buying up and even burning an undisclosed number; and most Victorian readers regarded their publication as an outrage, a revelation of the great poet as a snivelling, sensuous, badly bred surgeon's apprentice. But the condemnation of Fanny Brawne that the letters stirred up was far more scathing. She was reviled as unlovely, she took the place of Lockhart as the person whose cruelty had unfaithful, totally unfitted to have been Keat's wife, and soon killed Keats—"as surely as ever any man was killed by love," [19] it was averred. Remembering the reticence of those two proud characters, no reader of Keats's letters to Fanny can help feeling a pang at some point over the violation of their privacy. Yet Fanny was right when she wrote Brown in 1829 that "if his life is to be published no part ought to be kept back." She was a century ahead of her time in her dedication to the whole truth, however, and, as she had never troubled people with her real feelings, she had to wait until 1936 for something of the real truth of her life to be told. Then, with the publication of her letters to Fanny Keats, she was at last allowed to speak for herself and quietly refute the legend that she was unworthy of Keats's love.

With the centenary of Keats's death in 1921, the tide of his reputation reached its flood. Since then he has received all the varieties of recognition that can be heaped on a poet today—from the publication of edition after edition of his work and volumes of critical analysis and biographical research to the dedication of his living places in Hampstead and Rome as memorials to his name; from translations of his poems into some twenty languages to fictionalizations and dramatizations of his life. Much of this activity would astonish if not also amuse him, one suspects, remembering his wry comment on receiving an invitation to a Shakespeare birthday party—"Shakespeare would stare to see me there." Yet the kind of tribute which would please him most—the comments of a fellow craftsman on his craft—has been the least frequent. In fact the spread of Keats's influence on Victorian poetry ended by making him a symbol of the poet which the new talents of the 1910's and 1920's were determined to repudiate. The Victorians had fastened on the more imitable and less valuable aspects of Keats's work, his sensuousness without his objectivity, his melancholy without his "knowledge of light and shade." Our sense of Keats has changed; yet what now seems most significant in his art—the sureness of ear and firmness of structure, the dialectic of imagery, the tragic vision of life—remains a lesson which every poet must learn for himself.

Nevertheless, Keats's work has survived better than that of any of his contemporaries the long devaluation of romantic poetry that began about the time of Auden's appearance on the scene. Eliot has paid tribute to the Shakespearean quality of Keats's greatness, especially as it appears in his letters; and his best poems have stood up well under the most rigorous analysis of recent criticism. When these critical assessments are added to the evaluations of Keats in recent scholarship—those focused on his interest in ideas, his concern with technique, his absorption in the whole range of the English language and the whole tradition of English poetry —his place in the tradition begins to be seen more clearly. Each new discovery about his life helps disprove Byron's quip that he was "snuffed out by an article," or indeed by anything else than tuberculosis, and to reveal him as a man uniquely gifted with the stamina needed to translate the vision of poetry into performance. And for all one's regret at the poems he never lived to write, every new critical insight into his actual accomplishment sets him further apart from "the inheritors of unfulfilled renown" with whom Shelley classed him.

Yet even the most generous assessment of Keats's stature implies another devaluation—an inversion in effect of Byron's joke about Keats's ignorance of Greek. To an extent it is true that, as Middleton Murry put it, what Keats achieved in four years against heavy disadvantages can only be described as a miracle—one greater even than Shakespeare's achievement, which has had so many doubters.[20] Yet it is more than a miracle. It is a fact of poetic growth which can be traced step by arduous step through Keats's poems and letters, where he may be watched laboriously reshaping the language and the sensibility he inherited into an instrument adequate to his own ideal of poetry and his own vision of human experience; it is a living proof of that continual interanimation of tradition and original talent which is the life force of poetry. In an age in which, by its best critics at least, originality was exalted far above tradition, Keats's special originality was his sense of dedication to the whole tradition of English poetry and his attempt to recover it for the use of poetry in his time. And, as Eliot has said, "Tradition cannot be inherited; if you want it you must obtain it by great labour." Keats earned his place in the tradition of English poetry by his courage to take the great dare of self-creation, his willingness to accept failure and move beyond it, his patience in learning his craft from those who could teach him. His sober prophecy as he started *Hyperion*—"I think I shall be among the English Poets after my death"—has been fulfilled; as Matthew Arnold confirmed it, sixty years later, "He is—he is with Shakespeare."

# Notes

All references to Keats's poems are to the second Oxford edition, *The Poetical Works of John Keats* (1958), by H. W. Garrod, cited as *Works*. All references to Keats's letters are to the Harvard edition, *The Letters of John Keats* (2 vols., 1958), by Hyder Edward Rollins, cited as *Letters*. Where more than one item by a single author is cited, subsequent references are given with the initials of the title: thus, for a book, "Gittings, JKLY" stands for "Robert Gittings, *John Keats: The Living Year*"; for an article, "Gittings, 'KSR' " stands for "Robert Gittings, 'Keats's Sailor Relation,' TLS, 15 April 1960." In addition, the following abbreviations are used throughout:

Hampstead   *The Poetical Works and Other Writings of John Keats,* ed. Harry Buxton Forman, revised by Maurice Buxton Forman (Hampstead Edition), 8 vols., 1938–1939.

HBF   *The Poetical Works and Other Writings of John Keats,* ed. Harry Buxton Forman, 4 vols., 1883.

HLB   *Harvard Library Bulletin.*

KC   *The Keats Circle: Letters and Papers 1816–1878,* ed. Hyder Edward Rollins, 2 vols., 1948.

KHM   *Keats House and Museum: Historical and Descriptive Guide,* 4th ed., Hampstead, n.d.

KSJ   *Keats-Shelley Journal.*

KSMB   *Keats-Shelley Memorial Bulletin.*

LFBFK   *Letters of Fanny Brawne to Fanny Keats 1820–1824,* ed. Fred Edgcumbe, 1937.

LJKFB   *Letters of John Keats to Fanny Brawne,* ed. Harry Buxton Forman, 1878.

MBF   *The Letters of John Keats,* ed. Maurice Buxton Forman, 2nd ed., revised, 1935.

MLPKC   *More Letters and Poems of the Keats Circle,* ed. Hyder Edward Rollins, 1955.

PMLA   *Publications of the Modern Language Association.*

PQ   *Philological Quarterly.*

SP   *Studies in Philology.*

TLS   *Times Literary Supplement.*

## I. CLOSE TO THE SOURCE

1. Dorothy Hewlett, *A Life of John Keats* (2nd ed., revised, 1949), p. 21.

2. Richard Abbey: KC, I, 303. On Abbey's general reliability as a witness, see Rollins, KC, I, xli–xlii.

3. Garrod, *Works,* p. lxxix n.; H. E. Briggs, "The Birth and Death of John Keats," PMLA, LVI (1941), 593–94.

4. Jean Haynes, "John Jennings: Keats's Grandfather," KSMB, XIII (1962), 18.

5. Leigh Hunt: HBF, IV, 275.

6. Jean Haynes, "Elizabeth Keats," KSMB, IX (1958), 21.

7. KC, I, 305.

8. William Sharp, *The Life and Letters of Joseph Severn* (1892), p. 5 n.

9. Hewlett mentions this fact in her discussion of John Jennings' will (pp. 375–76) but does not comment on it.

10. HBF, IV, 276; KC, I, 309 and II, 208.

11. Edmund Blunden, *John Keats,* Supplement to *British Book News* (1950), p. 10.

12. Robert Gittings, "Keats's Sailor Relation," TLS, 15 April 1960, p. 245.

13. *The Autobiography and Journals of Benjamin Robert Haydon,* ed. Malcolm Elwin (1950), p. 10.

14. Gittings, "KSR," p. 245.

15. R. Y. Keers and B. G. Rigden, *Pulmonary Tuberculosis* (1953), p. 57.

16. *The Diary of Benjamin Robert Haydon,* ed. Willard Bissell Pope (1960), II, 107.

17. KC, I, 328; also II, 147 and 165.

18. Fourteen is the usual age for confirmation in England, as Keats himself noted in a letter showing a thorough knowledge of the catechism (*Letters,* II, 49).

19. The bearded man in a helmet (the seal which appears, e.g., on his letter to Taylor and Hessey of 21 March 1818) has been identified as King Alfred by Mr. A. W. Wheen, Keeper of the Library at the Victoria and Albert Museum.

20. *The Autobiography of Leigh Hunt,* ed. J. E. Morpurgo (1949), pp. 76–77, 98, and cf. Douglas Bush, *Mythology and the Romantic Tradition in English Poetry* (1937), p. 86 n. 5, which suggests that Keats shared Hunt's interest. Clarke in 1846 merely "suspected" that Keats's familiarity with classical mythology could "be traced" to his reading of Lemprière, Tooke, and Spence (KC, II, 147–48), though the two latter works are not listed among Keats's books; in 1861 Clarke, then seventy-three, recalled that Keats "appeared to learn" Lemprière by heart ("Recollections of Keats," *Atlantic Monthly,* VII [1861], 87). See Chapter IV, note 8 below.

21. Joanna Richardson, "New Light on Mr. Abbey," KSMB, V (1953), 26–31.

22. Gittings, "KSR," p. 245.

23. HBF, IV, 312; Charles W. Hagelman Jr., *John Keats and the Medical Profession,* unpublished dissertation, University of Texas (1956), pp. 11–18.

24. Ibid., pp. 21–26, 153.

25. Ibid., p. 21.

## II. THE WIDENING STREAM

1. E. L. Woodward, *The Age of Reform, 1815–1870* (1938), p. 17.

2. A. S. Turberville, ed., *Johnson's England* (1933), II, 266–70.

3. KHM, nos. 16, 17.

4. Despite his later scorn for Pope's poetry, it is Pope's translation of Homer, not Chapman's, that Keats quotes in his letters (I, 354 n., 404 n.; II, 205 n.).

5. The statements to this effect by Clarke (HBF, IV, 338), Severn (KC, II, 132), and Bailey (ibid., 283; see also Hunt, A, pp. 79–80) are borne out by Ernest de Selincourt's study of the influences on the diction of Keats's early poetry (*The Poems of John Keats* [5th ed., 1926], pp. xxxii–xxxiii, 607 ff.).

6. Clarke's conventional tastes are indicated by Keats's "Epistle to Charles Cowden Clarke," ll. 53 ff. Clarke's own mentor, Leigh Hunt, was contemptuous of Wordsworth's poetry until 1814 (Edmund Blunden, *Leigh Hunt and His Circle* [1930], p. 67).

7. G. Pederson-Krag, " 'O Poesy! For Thee I Hold My Pen,' " in *Psychoanalysis and Culture: Essays in Honor of Géza Roheim*, ed. G. W. Wilbur and W. Muensterberger (1951), p. 445.

8. KC, II, 169, 177.

9. HBF, IV, 306.

10. Claude Lee Finney, *The Evolution of Keats's Poetry*, 2 vols. (1936), I, 36–38; George D. Stout, "The Political History of Leigh Hunt's *Examiner*," *Washington University Studies (New Series) in Language and Literature*, no. 19 (1949), pp. 29–35. "Horrors," the reading of W[3] (*Works*, p. 527; see Hampstead, IV, 17), not only makes better sense than "honours" but also echoes Hunt's editorial.

11. *Works*, p. 531. It is significant that in Mary Frogley's copy, evidently the only early transcript, the poem is dated 1816, not 1814.

12. As appears from the fact that the sonnets to Byron, Chatterton, and his grandmother and the stanzas "To Hope" were not transcribed at the time Keats wrote them, in contrast to other poems of 1814 and 1815, considerably lighter in tone, which were copied by his friends.

13. Neither autograph nor transcript of the sonnet survives; and when Hunt met Keats a year and a half later, he did not recall reading any of his poetry before that time (HBF, IV, 277).

14. The three sonnets "On Woman" have been attributed on very slender evidence to the spring of 1816 by Finney (I, 111); but Keats's grouping of them with his poems of 1814 and 1815 in his first volume and Mathew's praise of these sonnets in his review suggest that they belong to the previous year.

15. James R. Caldwell, "Woodhouse's Annotations in Keats's First Volume of Poems," PMLA, LXIII (1948), 759.

16. Quoted by Catherine MacDonald MacLean, *Born Under Saturn: A Biography of William Hazlitt* (1944), p. 325.

17. Stout, "PHLHE," p. 30.

18. The only indication of the date of this poem is Woodhouse's note, "Written probably when much in company with Leigh Hunt." The spring of 1815 seems far more likely than that of 1814, when Keats was celebrating constitutional monarchy in his sonnet "On Peace," or the spring of 1816, when he turned to non-political themes.

19. Hagelman, p. 59.

## III. THE DARK CITY

1. Edward B. Hinckley, "On First Looking into Swedenborg's Philosophy," KSJ, IX (1960), 15–16.

2. On the probable date, see John Middleton Murry, *Studies in Keats* (1930), pp. 2–5.

3. Hagelman, pp. 148–52.

4. Ibid., pp. 155–56.

5. Mathew's recollections of Keats some thirty years later (KC, II, 184–88) contain several inconsistencies which evidently represent the several stages of their friendship from early 1815 to late 1816. An attempt is made to separate these stages in Chapters II, III, and IV.

6. George A. R. Winston, "John Keats and Joshua Waddington," *Guy's Hospital Reports,* XCII (1943), 101.

7. Hinckley, pp. 22–23.

8. KC, II, 206 n. 2.

9. Hagelman, pp. 130–31.

10. Ibid., p. 263 n. 117.

11. John Flint South, *Memorials* (1884), p. 52.

12. Ibid., p. 54.

13. Hagelman, p. 316.

14. Keats explicitly discussed his lack of identity in a number of later letters; in his early poems he expressed this feeling of "annihilation" as a sense of being "smothered" or "overwhelmed" or "borne along to nothingness" by experience (cf. e.g., "I Stood Tiptoe," 1. 132; "Sleep and Poetry," l. 157; *Endymion* IV, 471 ff.). The term "identity" had some philosophic currency in Keats's time, going back as far as Locke (see *An Essay Concerning Human Understanding,* Book II, Chap. XXVII, especially sects. 9–10), and Keats probably met with it in Hazlitt's *Essay on the Principles of Human Action.* But for Hazlitt as for Locke the term "personal identity" meant primarily the continuing unchanging unique sameness of the individual consciousness, the product of the sum of his perceptions (*Works,* ed. P. P. Howe [1930–1934], I, 28–32; see also XII, 230–41; XVII, 264–75; XX, 171–86 and 376–86). It could also refer to the object of the individual's self-love, which serves to isolate him from other identities (XVII, 264); or to an "internal, original bias," physiologically given, which is born with him and not changed by experience (XVII, 23–34). Hazlitt's conception is thus very different from Keats's notion of a gradually developing sense of self which emerges as the individual matures, in reaction to the crises of his emotional experience and from imaginative interaction or identification with the identities of others. See Chapter X, pp. 276–78.

15. This count excludes purely platonic poems to young ladies, such as his sonnet to Georgiana Wylie; doggerel verses on sex, such as those he wrote in Devon; long narrative poems on love, which are not addressed to a real woman; and the sonnets written to the Vauxhall lady four years after their meeting. The "brief interlude" refers to a few short lyrics written probably in the summer of 1817 (see p. 124 above).

16. Woodhouse's note, quoted by Mabel A. E. Steele, "The Woodhouse Transcripts of the Poems of John Keats," HLB, III (1949), 242.

17. J. Burke Severs has suggested that it is a fairy speaking in this poem,

not a human being ("Keats's Fairy Sonnet," KSJ, VI [1957], 109-13). But this reading does not preclude Keats's use of the fairy imagery as a metaphor for his own feelings of inadequacy (on which Woodhouse commented in his note on the poem, quoted by Caldwell, p. 759); and in other poems written about this time Keats suggested a similar contrast between himself and a magnificent knight to whom he feels somehow inferior.

18. Preface to *Immaturity*, quoted by Erik H. Erikson, "The Problem of Ego Identity," *Journal of the American Psychoanalytic Association*, IV (1956), 58.

19. Haydon, D, II, 101; Winston, p. 105; Sir Benjamin Ward Richardson, *The Asclepiad* (1884), p. 142.

20. I. Peter Glauber, "A Deterrent in the Study and Practise of Medicine," *Psychoanalytic Quarterly*, XXII (1953), 382.

21. *Letters*, I, 245; II, 123, 126, 134, 349.

22. Haydon, D, II, 107.

23. Otto Rank, *Art and Artist: Creative Urge and Personality Development* (1932), pp. 43-50.

24. Ibid., 27-28, 41 ff.

25. HBF, IV, 321; and cf. p. 97 above.

26. Sharp, p. 20.

27. See *Works*, e.g., p. 3, l. 17; p. 8, l. 144; p. 12, l. 17; p. 45, "demesne—mean"; p. 41, "uproar"; and the last line of "To a Friend Who Sent Me Some Roses," p. 41, which in Tom Keats's copy book has not merely six feet (as do five or six of Keats's other sonnets) but seven.

28. There is no reason for thinking that Keats had the time or the motive for starting "Calidore" immediately after the appearance of Hunt's *Rimini* in February, as Sir Sidney Colvin suggests (*John Keats: His Life and Poetry, His Friends, Critics and After-Fame* [1917], p. 34). A more probable incentive was Hunt's publication of Keats's sonnet "O Solitude!" in May, as Keats implies in his "Induction," ll. 57 ff. Furthermore, several poems of the summer of 1816 indicate that he was working on a long poem in the style of *Rimini* at that time: "To one who has been long in city pent," ll. 7-8; "As late I rambled in the happy fields," ll. 3-4; "Epistle to My Brother George," ll. 15-18, 23-44; and "Epistle to Charles Cowden Clarke," ll. 42-48.

29. Sir William Hale-White, *Keats as Doctor and Patient* (1938), p. 31.

30. Pederson-Krag, p. 445.

31. Evidently not the two-volume third edition of the *Lyrical Ballads*, as Rollins suggests (KC, I, 253 n. 3), but the octavo *Poems in Two Volumes* of 1807, which contained all the poems of Wordsworth which influenced Keats most deeply, and whose section-headings Keats twice quoted in his letters (I, 263, 287).

32. "I Stood Tiptoe," ll. 114ab (*Works*, p. 7): lines which suggest the approximate point at which Keats picked up the poem at Margate, especially when it is noted that this section of the poem is written on a sheet of laid paper of a larger size than the wove paper on which Keats started and later finished the poem in London. No one has yet attempted to assign the various sections of this poem to the six months in which it was composed. But a close study of the deletions and insertions in the manuscript noted by Garrod (*Works*, pp. lxxxiv-lxxxviii) and of the paper on which various sections now in the Harvard University Library were written suggests that the first main section (ll. 1-60, 107-14) was written mostly in London and finished in Margate; then in the middle of page 5 (f. iii r.) Keats ran into difficulties, can-

celled some lines (missing in the MS. after 114b: recto of the draft of ll. 65–69), and decided to double back. Starting on the back of the same sheet, Keats then wrote a second section (ll. 61–106), which seems to be as far as he carried the poem at Margate. The third section (ll. 116 to probably 192) picks up in the middle of page 5 again and, after a number of false starts, modulates into a section on mythology influenced by Hunt or Wordsworth, and probably written in October or November (see pp. 80–81 above). The fourth section (ll. 193 to the end), in which the poem begins to turn into "Endymion," was evidently written in several "attacks," as Keats described it, in early December (*Letters*, I, 121).

33. As George Keats, who was still living with Abbey, reported (KC, I, 277).

34. Hagelman shows (pp. 12–20) that Keats did not express his dislike of medicine to Clarke till the fall of 1816.

35. The closings of Keats's letters are a clue to the warmth of his friendships. He did not sign himself "Your affectionate friend" to Reynolds till fourteen months after their meeting, though he began using this or a similar intimate style almost at once with Haydon and Bailey (*Letters*, I, 190; 117, 145, 168, 175).

36. Following the autograph version in the Harvard Library, which, from the marginal guide-lines, the correction in l. 6, and the "wond'ring eyes" of l. 11, appears to be the first draft, rather than the copy in the Morgan Library as Garrod thinks (*Works*, p. 45).

## IV. THE GREEN SHORE

1. Haydon, D, II, 107.

2. B. W. Procter ("Barry Cornwall"), *An Autobiographical Fragment* (1877), pp. 195–200.

3. Haydon, D, II, 136; see also W. B. Pope, " 'Leigh Hunt and His Companions,' " KSJ, VIII (1959), 90 n. 3.

4. HBF, IV, 376.

5. A. H. Beavan, *James and Horace Smith* (1899), p. 137.

6. See *Works*, p. 5, l. 64a; p. 406, xxxi, l. 9; p. 459, l. 13.

7. Edmund Blunden, *Keats's Publisher: A Memoir of John Taylor* (1936), pp. 40–41; G. D. Stout, "Leigh Hunt's Money Troubles: Some New Light," *Washington University Studies, Humanistic Series*, XII (1925), 223–26.

8. Keats's sudden new interest in Greek mythology in the fall of 1816 (see Chapter I, note 20 above) is evident from a study of his allusions. Up to this time, his references to classical legend are infrequent and perfunctory; in fact, his significant allusions are to an English tradition—King Lear, Calidore, the Red Cross Knight, "the sweet mountain nymph" Liberty, King Alfred, William Wallace, Robert Burns, Byron, Chatterton, Sydney, Russell, and Vane. Keats's absorption in Greek myth first appears in "Sleep and Poetry" and the second half of "I Stood Tiptoe," and was evidently due to Hunt's influence rather than to Wordsworth's, as usually stated, since it appears that Keats had barely started reading *The Excursion* at this time. Despite occasional echoes of *The Exucrsion*, IV, 847–87 in "I Stood Tiptoe," ll. 125–92, Keats's view of mythology in the fall of 1816 was far closer to that expressed by Hunt in his review of Keats's *Poems* in 1817—"lovely tales" (De Selincourt, p. 390)—or even in his preface to "The Nymphs" in *Foliage*, 1818—"embodied essences of all the grand and lovely qualities of nature"

(quoted by Bush, p. 175). For the transforming influence of *The Excursion* on Keats's work in 1817, see Chapter V, note 12 below.

9. James Augustus Hessey: MLPKC, p. 117.

10. KC, II, 281; W. B. Pope, "Haydon's Portraits," TLS, 25 January 1947, p. 51.

11. Clark Olney, *Benjamin Robert Haydon, Historical Painter* (1952), pp. 56, 85 n. 10. Haydon nowhere mentions Blake in his *Diary* or *Autobiography*.

12. Ibid., p. 46; A. H. Smith, *The Sculptures of the Parthenon* (1910), pl. 17, Fig. 29.

13. Eric George, *The Life and Death of Benjamin Robert Haydon* (1948), pp. 82–87.

14. *Letters*, I, 118 n. 4.

15. Haydon, D, II, 101; Henry Stephens, KC, II, 211–12.

16. Blunden, LHHC, pp. 57–58, 112.

17. Ian Jack, " 'The Realm of Flora' in Keats and Poussin," TLS, 10 April 1959, p. 212.

18. De Selincourt, p. xxxix.

19. The dash at the end of "I Stood Tiptoe" is noteworthy, for it indicates that Keats intended to let it stand as what J. M. Murry calls, in speaking of *Hyperion*, "a finished fragment" (*Keats and Shakespeare* [1925], p. 82). Compare the endings of "Calidore," "Imitation of Spenser," "Nature withheld Cassandra," "The Eve of St. Mark," and *Hyperion*, where the punctuation gives a similar indication of their fragmentary character.

20. Hampstead, I, 25 n.

21. Beavan, pp. 137–38.

22. *The Complete Works of Percy Bysshe Shelley*, ed. Roger Ingpen and W. E. Peck (1926–1930), IX, 211–13. On the veracity of this letter, which has sometimes been questioned, see Newman Ivey White, *Shelley* (1940), I, 484–85 and 723, n. 45 and 46.

23. HBF, IV, 296; Shelley, Preface to *Prometheus Unbound*.

24. This story evidently originated in Canon Dix's recollection of someone's statement, thirty years after the event, that Shelley visited Charles Richards in 1817 to ask about printing "a little volume" of Keats's poems (John Dix, *Pen and Ink Sketches* [1846], p. 144). The volume was evidently a pamphlet of his own (see White, I, 504, 515); as for Keats's poetry, Shelley either ignored or disparaged it while Keats was alive (HBF, IV, 247–50; White, II, 543) and apparently never read the 1817 volume (see *Letters of Mary W. Shelley*, ed. Frederick L. Jones [1944], II, 344 n. 11).

25. See Hewlett, pp. 24 and 375–77, where the wills of Alice and John Jennings are summarized. It appears that Keats should have received approximately £2000 from his grandmother, £250 from his grandfather, £415 from his mother, £125 from the estate of his great-aunt Mary Sweetingburgh, and some share of the estate of his uncle Midgley Jennings (this was later contested), not counting either the expenses of his medical training or the accumulation of interest. On what he actually received, see George Keats: KC, I, 277–78; also Marie Adami, *Fanny Keats* (1937), pp. 118–19.

26. Charles Brown, in a letter to C. W. Dilke of 6 September 1824 (KHM, no. 80), spoke of £200 as "a moderate two years' subsistence" for Keats. The record of his cash account at Abbey's shows that Keats was in the habit of drawing £20 every two months, £30 when travelling (*Letters*, I, 42–49).

27. Lawrence E. Tanner, "The Library and Muniment Room," *Westmin-*

*ster Abbey Papers,* no. 1 (1935), pp. 7–9. It should be noted that Keats thought of moving to Westminster several times for the express purpose of "being in the reach of books" (*Letters,* II, 52, 179, 225).

28. Edmund Blunden, *Shelley and Keats as They Struck Their Contemporaries* (1925), p. 87.

29. The draft of "I Stood Tiptoe," for instance, shows Keats eliminating such Huntisms as "gently," "gentlest," "little," "nestling," "embower," "dainties," "soft," "tender," "peep," "delicious," "swoonlike," and "elegance" (*Works,* pp. 3–11; Neville Rogers and Mabel A. E. Steele, " 'I Stood Tiptoe Upon a Little Hill': A Hitherto Uncollated Fragment," KSJ, X [1961], 13).

30. Thomas Medwin, *Life of Percy Bysshe Shelley,* ed. H. B. Forman (1913), pp. 178–79. Colvin questions this story (p. 73), but all the circumstantial evidence seems to corroborate it (see *Letters,* I, 170; *Endymion,* I, 39–57; and Shelley, *Works,* IX, 237). Both poems came to over 4000 lines, each far longer than any previous work by either poet.

31. Mr. W. R. LeFanu, Librarian of the Royal College of Surgeons, reports that Keats's name is not listed among any of the candidates who appeared for the monthly examinations of the college during the first half of 1817, and adds that the candidates must have reached the age of twenty-two to qualify for the examination.

32. Willard B. Pope, *Studies in the Keats Circle,* unpublished dissertation, Harvard University (1932), p. 237.

33. Sharp, p. 29.

34. Stephen A. Larrabee, *English Bards and Grecian Marbles* (1943), p. 213.

35. The December 1816 date usually assigned this sonnet is, as Garrod points out (*Works,* p. lxxxi), very doubtful. From its echoes of Keats's dedicatory sonnet it seems to have been written as a reply, and therefore at about the time of the *Poems'* appearance.

36. Keats's decision in mid-March to leave town in order to live alone in "the country" seems to refer not to his visit to the Isle of Wight (see Rollins, *Letters,* I, 125 n. 2) but to his move a few days later to Hampstead (which he repeatedly described as "country" in contrast to London or "town" [*Letters,* I, 172, 175 and II, 52, 56; cf. II, 37]). There is nothing to indicate that his brothers moved with him to Hampstead in March; it seems clear, however, that he decided to go to the Isle of Wight rather suddenly in mid-April, sometime after Hunt's departure for Marlow on April 6 (*Letters,* I, 137).

37. Finney (I, 180–81) dates this episode as occurring before the publication of Keats's *Poems* at the beginning of March. But his argument is not convincing, since it was not Keats himself but George Keats and Thomas Richards who transcribed Hunt's sonnets on the crowning episode into their presentation copies, obviously some time after receiving them. Keats's transcription of his own sonnets into Reynolds' copy (in the Harvard University Library) appears to have been made at a different and therefore later date than that of the inscription and the Elgin Marbles sonnets. The March 1 date on Hunt's autograph (*Works,* p. 529) also suggests that the crowning took place before the appearance of Keats's *Poems;* yet it seems unlikely that the event occurred during the Shelleys' stay at Hunt's from late January till mid-March (*Mary Shelley's Journal,* ed. F. L. Jones [1947], pp. 70–77).

38. See *Letters,* I, 137 and note. Nothing in the *Examiner's* account of the trial of R. G. Butt supports Rollins' inference that "Old Wood" was

Sir George Wood, the presiding judge in the case; and Keats's linking of the papers which Hunt requested him to destroy with "Receipts" suggests they were financial records.

39. Stout, "LHMT," pp. 226–28.

## V. A LEAP INTO THE SEA

1. *Letters*, I, 169–70.

2. Hampstead, I, 129–36.

3. So listed in the London Post Office Directory for 1818; and the Olliers' letter of 29 April 1817 was addressed to George at 62 Bread Street, evidently his business address at the time (see MBF, p. 101 n. 3). On Keats's loan, see MLPKC, pp. 28–29. It seems improbable that Wilkinson was a lawyer (*Letters*, I, 129 n. 2); Keats never mentioned a law career for George, but did refer to his inability "to get on in trade" (I, 287). "C. Wilkinson," Keats's friend, may have been the son or younger brother of Thomas.

4. KC, II, 469; see also I, 253 n. 2 and 260 n. 68; Blunden, KPMJT, pp. 96–98; Garrod, *Works*, pp. xxxviii–xxxix n.; Joanna Richardson, *Fanny Brawne* (1952), pp. 20 and 172, where Mrs. Jones is identified as the lady from Hastings; and Robert Gittings, *John Keats: The Living Year* (1954), pp. 30–33, 59–60, and 230–35 (also Gittings, *The Mask of Keats* [1956], pp. 45–53).

5. Probably January 1818, not, as Mr. Gittings argues (JKLY, pp. 57–64), January 1819: see Aileen Ward, "Christmas Day, 1818," KSJ, X (1961), 17–20.

6. Even after his fair copy was sent to the printer in January 1818, Keats made numerous revisions in the text of Book I (Garrod, *Works*, pp. xxxi–xxxii).

7. MBF, pp. xvi–xvii; cf. *Letters*, I, 169.

8. These lyrics are usually assigned to November 1817 because the transcript of "Think not of it, sweet one, so" is dated "Nov. 11, 1817" by Reynolds (*Works*, p. 432), and the other lyrics appear to belong to the same period (Colvin, pp. 157–58). But the November dating is very doubtful, for several reasons. First, Reynolds usually dated his transcripts by the date on which he copied them, not the date of the poem itself (see *Works*, pp. 262, 264, 268, 481). Second, Woodhouse dated "Think not of it, sweet one, so" April 1817 in W[1]: a date which he probably got from Keats himself two years later. Third, Reynolds quoted a line from "Unfelt, unheard, unseen" in *The Champion* of 17 August 1817 (Leonidas M. Jones, "Reynolds and Keats," KSJ, VII [1958], 48 n. 6), which shows that this poem and, presumably, the others must have been written some time before mid-August. On the connection with Mrs. Jones, see Finney, I, 191.

9. This Folio, which Keats acquired in 1817, seems most likely to be the volume which Keats later recalled reading with Reynolds (*Letters*, I, 274, 276).

10. Hewlett, p. 51.

11. KHM, no. 104.

12. *Endymion*, II, 827–53: the first clear parallel to *The Excursion* in all of Keats's writings (*Exc.*, IV, 631–41; cf. also 718–62, 846–87). The idea of the "legend-laden" wind—an epithet which especially pleased Keats (*Letters*, II, 171)—recurs in *The Fall of Hyperion*, II, 1–6. Other echoes worth noting are "the poor patient oyster" (*End.*, III, 66–68) with the "contented" mole (*Exc.*, IV, 428–30); the "Hymn to Pan" with *Exc.*, IV, 879–87; and "the lidless-eyed

train Of planets" (*End.*, I, 598–99) with "the polar star that never closed His steadfast eye" (*Exc.*, IV, 694–700)—the ultimate source, if one is needed, of Keats's recurrent image of the "open-lidded and stedfast" star (*Letters*, I, 299; *Hyperion*, I, 350–53; "Bright Star," ll. 1–3, and compare "the moving waters" of line 5 with *Exc.*, IX, 9). The full force of the influence of *The Excursion* was slow in appearing in Keats's work, but—as J. M. Murry amply proves (*Keats* [1955], Chapter IX)—it was of central and enduring importance.

13. MLPKC, p. 34.

14. *Leigh's New Picture of England and Wales* (1820), p. 520.

15. Letter of Charles Brown to C. W. Dilke, 20 January 1830 (KHM, no. 80).

16. B. W. Richardson, pp. 138–43; see Rollins, *Letters*, I, 186 n. 5. Miss Lowell's discussion (Amy Lowell, *John Keats* [1925], I, 512–14) overlooks Richardson's highly circumstantial account; and Hale-White's point (p. 46) that mercury was later prescribed for Keats's sore throat likewise fails to disprove it—in fact, a persistent sore throat is a secondary symptom of syphilis. If promptly recognized, syphilis could be cured "with a fair degree of success" in Keats's time with mercury compounds, though a two-year moratorium on marriage was strongly recommended (Morris Fishbein, *Modern Home Medicine Adviser* [1956], pp. 736–39).

17. *Letters*, I, 196 n. 6. With Keats's remark on "vicious beastliness" (I, 175), compare his later comment on being "sick of Venery" (I, 279); on the effect of this experience, see F. W. Bateson, *English Poetry: A Critical Introduction* (1950), p. 222 n.

18. Haydon, D, II, 463.

19. *Endymion*, IV, 496 to about 590, according to Miss Lowell (I, 527).

20. *Endymion*, III, 66–68; KC, I, 59.

21. See, e.g., De Selincourt, pp. xl, 428, 444, 566–67. The variety of goals which De Selincourt attributes to Endymion's quest ("self-realization," "beauty," "truth," "the ideal"), and the various means by which he is said to achieve his end (from a synthesis of opposites to an upward progression from lower to higher), suggest the difficulty in interpreting *Endymion* according to any coherent allegorical scheme.

22. KC, I, 54 and II, 270, 283. The disguise, which was passed over without comment by Hunt and Reynolds, was accepted by *Blackwood's* as a device "to vary the intrigue" (Hampstead, II, 252); Bailey described the ending as a "catastrophe" in the Aristotelian sense (Hampstead, II, 241), and defended its abruptness by comparing it to *Paradise Regained* (KC, I, 25). On Spenser, see *The Poets and Their Critics*, ed. H. S. Davies, Penguin Books (1943), pp. 49–54.

23. On Mrs. F. M. Owen's study, see Colvin, p. 544, and De Selincourt, pp. 566–67; for Jeffrey's praise, see Hampstead, II, 278; and Bailey's comment, KC, I, 35.

24. The original form of "fellowship with essence," *Endymion*, I, 778.

25. Two crucial lines near the end of Book IV are both capable of a double interpretation. In lines 957–58 Endymion may be renouncing either the Indian maid or his recent vow to lead a hermit's life; in lines 975–76 he may be either defying the fate which bars him from the maid or protesting against the fate of mortality which he has incurred through loving her.

26. On the much-discussed question of whether Keats borrowed the device of Phoebe's disguise from Drayton's *Endimion and Phoebe,* it will be noted here merely that Keats could without difficulty have had access to this extremely

rare book in the Westminster Abbey Library (see Chapter IV, note 27 above), and that the three important parallels between Keats's poem and Drayton's (which De Selincourt thinks "can hardly be mere coincidence," p. 568) are limited to Book IV of *Endymion*. It is at least possible, then, that Keats discovered Drayton's *Endimion* after returning from Oxford in a mood of dissatisfaction with his own poem and decided that Drayton's device would solve the problem of his own ending.

27. Lines 988–93 clearly imply that Endymion's "unlook'd for change" took place after his defiance of the "decrees of fate" in freeing Glaucus from his doom of endless age and Phoebe from her doom of eternal chastity (III, 1022 ff.; II, 776 ff.): that is, in Book IV, in which the action does in fact take an unexpected new direction.

## VI. SOUNDINGS AND QUICKSANDS

1. Taylor's agreement with Keats in April mentioned "the refusal of his future works" (Blunden, KPMJT, p. 42); it seems clear that the manuscript was being read prior to its final acceptance and revisions.

2. Beavan, pp. 111–18.

3. See Aileen Ward, "Keats's Sonnet, 'Nebuchadnezzar's Dream,' " PQ, XXXIV (1955), 177–88. Keats's biting reference to habeas corpus in his review of "Edmund Kean as a Shakespearean Actor" (Hampstead, V, 227), written on December 19 or 20, suggests that the issue was much on his mind that week.

4. Hampstead, V, 227–30.

5. See Bailey's replies to Taylor's comments to him, KC, I, 11, 19, 25; also Taylor's letter to James Taylor of 14 June 1818 (KHM, no. 50): "Endymion does not by any means please me as I had expected."

6. See *Endymion*, I, 311, 315, 598 (*Works*, pp. 74, 83). Taylor's bowdlerizing may be seen in I, 157 and 777–80; II, 27–30, 67, 96, 271, 526–34, 948.

7. Hewlett, pp. 144–45; Colvin, p. 246; Clarke, p. 97; Lowell, I, 543.

8. Bernice Slote, *Keats and the Dramatic Principle* (1958), Chaps. 2, 3.

9. Garrod, *Works*, p. xxxii; for the cuts, see pp. 65, 76–81, 85–86.

10. KC, II, 143–44; Sharp, p. 33. On Wordsworth's presumed opinion of *Endymion* as a whole, see *Letters*, I, 270 n. 4.

11. For the original form of the passage, where "blending pleasurable" stood for "fellowship with essence," see *Works*, p. 88, and De Selincourt, p. 427. The original four lines were excised and patched over, evidently at Taylor's suggestion, in the copy sent to the printer on January 22, and the omission troubled Keats for a whole week before he restored them in revised form (*Letters*, I, 218). The fact that Keats was satisfied with the original version till Taylor deleted the lines in January shows that Keats had the idea of "blending pleasurable" in mind when he referred to his first book as an illustration of his idea of "essential beauty" created by passion in his letter to Bailey of 23 November 1817.

12. *Letters*, I, 184, 323 and II, 213.

13. P. P. Howe, *The Life of William Hazlitt* (Penguin Books, 1949), p. 96.

14. Ibid., p. 250.

15. Compare Keats's remark on "compositions and decompositions" (*Letters*, I, 265) with Hazlitt, *Lectures on the English Poets* (Everyman's Library, 1910), p. 51; on "subject" in poetry, *Letters*, I, 223–24 and *Lectures*, p. 53; on the poet's gusto for all experience and his lack of a proper character, *Letters*,

I, 387 and *Lectures*, p. 47. Still further echoes are found in the "Ode on a Grecian Urn" (III, 3–4; *Lectures*, p. 98), *Lamia* (II, 234; *Lectures*, p. 9); and Keats's description of "three witty people" in January 1820 (*Letters*, II, 245; *Lectures*, pp. 111–12).

16. John Hamilton Reynolds, *Poetry and Prose*, ed. George L. Marsh (1928), p. 94.

17. "To Spenser," ll. 11–12; see also *Letters*, I, 214, 232, 238, 288, and "When I have fears," ll. 3–4; and cf. *Endymion*, II, 40–41.

18. Quoting the original version of the last sentence, which was censored not by Keats (see Rollins, *Letters*, I, 252 n. 7) but evidently by Haydon himself, who bowdlerized many passages in his *Diary* and *Correspondence* (see a similar excision by Woodhouse's clerk, *Letters*, I, 263 n. 3). It should be noted that Haydon's paraphrase of the censored passage—"I should like him to damn me" keeps the meaning of Keats's original—"Damn me if I shouldn't like him to damn me."

19. *Letters*, I, 241 and II, 38.

20. KC, I, 7–8, 20 n. 6.

21. *Letters*, I, 242. The meaning of this sentence is badly tangled, as is frequently the case when Keats is embarrassed. The statement as it stands—"I do not think that nothing in this world is proveable"—contradicts the following assertion about his scepticism and the whole direction of his thought at this time. (See "Epistle to Reynolds," ll. 72–82, and *Letters*, I, 185, 193, 243.)

22. *The John Keats Memorial Volume* (1921), p. 175.

23. Hampstead, V, 292. The passage from *The Reason of Church Government* was quoted by Hazlitt in his lecture on Shakespeare and Milton (*Lectures*, pp. 57–58).

24. *Letters*, II, 193.

25. They left hastily, for Keats had written George only a few days before to send him his folio Shakespeare (*Letters*, I, 274); but it is improbable that they left because Tom had taken a turn for the worse, as Miss Lowell suggests (I, 631). The reason for their departure must then be the crystallization of George's plans.

26. Woodhouse's note, quoted by Finney, II, 746.

## VII. MIST AND CRAG

1. Naomi J. Kirk, "Memoir of George Keats," Hampstead, I, lxxxv.

2. The January issue, which did not appear till early June (J. R. MacGillivray, *Keats: A Bibliography and Reference Guide with an Essay on Keats's Reputation* [1949], p. xxiv).

3. Hampstead, II, 239.

4. *Letters*, I, 281, 293 (three references), 325, 343, 387. Hunt stated in 1828 that "Keats felt that his disease was mortal, two or three years before he died" (HBF, IV, 293), echoing a similar statement by Keats to his sister (*Letters*, II, 309). See also his resolutions to take better care of his health at this time (I, 325, 343).

5. KC, II, 15.

6. Not on April 23, as Gittings suggests (JKLY, p. 204); but probably during the third week of June, when the programs of the English Opera House announce "Mr. Mathews At Home" (Harvard Theatre Collection).

7. Dilke's comment to this effect (KC, II, 104–105) is confirmed by Keats's

own letters, in which Brown is mentioned far less frequently and more casually than Dilke till he began sharing Brown's house in December 1818.

8. See *Letters*, I, 248, and Brown's letter to Dilke of 17 December 1829 (KHM, no. 80).

9. *Leigh's New Pocket Road Book of England and Wales* (1825), p. 184.

10. I have drawn freely on Brown's journal of the trip (KHM, no. 87, reprinted in part in *Letters*, I, 421–42) to supplement Keats's own account in the following pages.

11. Though Keats told Reynolds he had finished *Isabella* at the end of April 1818 (*Letters*, I, 274), the MS. draft indicates much reworking. There are numerous revisions, additions, and deletions, and the sections of the manuscript now in the Harvard University Library are written on two different kinds of paper; some sections appear to be a fair copy, others a first draft; and the stanzas are not numbered. This appearance lends support to Woodhouse's note "Finished about the latter end of 1818 or the beginning of 1819" (*Works*, p. 215).

12. *Prelude*, VI, 636–37; Prospectus to *The Excursion*, ll. 42–45 (Murry, K, p. 287).

13. George M. Harper, *William Wordsworth* (1916), II, 287.

14. *Letters*, II, 67.

15. Letter to Charles Brown, Jr., 22 September 1839 (KHM, no. 80).

16. See Brown's letters to his son regarding Dilke (15 March 1839) and a woman named Fanny whom his son apparently wished to marry (11 November 1838, 15 March 1839, 10 March 1840, and 16 April 1840; KHM, no. 80).

17. KC, I, lv.

18. From the synopsis of *Walter Hazlebourne*, inserted in the first MS. volume of the novel (KHM, no. 82) and cast in the first person. Brown's letter to his son of 27 January 1839 (KHM, no. 80) makes it clear that the novel is autobiographical in large part.

19. HBF, III, 354–59.

20. KC, II, 137.


## VIII. THE SHORES OF DARKNESS

1. Not to the Brawnes' (Lowell, II, 126), since Fanny Keats did not know of their existence till September 1820 (LFBFK, p. 3), or to the Hunts' (Gittings, JKLY, p. 28), since they had moved away from Hampstead the year before (*Letters*, I, 168). Keats mentioned Mrs. Dilke in a letter he wrote Fanny soon after her visit (I, 386).

2. Brown protested to Dilke in a letter of 17 December 1829 (KHM, no. 80) that Hunt's account of Keats's origins—"of the humblest"—in *Lord Byron and Some of His Contemporaries* was "indecent."

3. Howe, pp. 266–68, 271–76, 262 and note.

4. Blunden, KPMJT, p. 56.

5. KC, I, 36.

6. Ibid., 246.

7. KC, II, 288, 299.

8. All the evidence points to a meeting in early September, rather than November or December as frequently stated. First, Dilke noted in his copy (now in the Morgan Library) of Richard Monckton Milnes's *Life, Letters, and Literary Remains of John Keats* (1848), with reference to Keats's letter to

Reynolds of 22 September 1818: "About this time, he met *Miss Brawne* for the first time at my house, . . . soon after his return from Teignmouth" (for "Scotland": I, 240-41). Dilke clearly links the letter to Fanny; there is no ground for H. B. Forman's inference that it refers instead to Jane Cox, or that Keats met Fanny "very soon after" writing it (MBF, p. 217 n.). Second, Fanny herself stated that she met Keats at "about the time" of his return from Scotland, and that his spirits were good "except when anxiety regarding his brother's health dejected them" (Medwin, p. 296)—a comment which can hardly refer to a first meeting in November. Gittings argues for a November meeting on the grounds of Severn's "typhoid" fever that fall (JKLY, p. 40). But Keats stated that Severn was ill not with typhoid but with "typhous" fever in October (*Letters*, I, 393), an affair of two or three weeks rather than five or six (cf. *Encyclopaedia Britannica*, 6th ed. [1823], "Medicine," XIII, 268); it is possible, therefore, that Severn visited the Brawnes with Keats during September.

9. *Letters*, II, 132; I, 132 and n. 5. There is no reason to link this letter to Jane Cox (see note 8 above), whom Keats met at the Reynoldses' sometime before the middle of October. His lengthy description of this meeting in his journal for October 14 (*Letters*, I, 394-95) suggests, first, that he did not actually meet her on his first call at the Reynoldses' after his return, in early September; and second, that he was describing a very recent encounter, since his account is cast in the present tense and given in fresh detail. It also seems unlikely that Keats would have mentioned meeting Jane Cox in a letter to Reynolds, who could all too easily have guessed her identity.

10. *Letters*, II, 133; LFBFK, p. 13.

11. So it has always been described by Keats's critics, from Woodhouse on (see De Selincourt, pp. 485-86). Keats did in fact draw on a wide range of reference to the story of the Titans, from Homer to Milton; but one source which has been overlooked in this connection gives extended treatment to the legend and brings together most of the details, such as proper names, mentioned by Keats in *Hyperion*. This is the *Pantheon* of William Godwin ("Edward Baldwin"), a compendium of classical mythology which Keats still possessed at his death (KC, I, 258) and which was probably the handbook which Clarke remembered his learning by heart. Its account of the wars of the Titans and Olympians in Chapters 6 and 7, together with the later war of the Giants, would then have long been familiar to Keats in general outline. It even suggests the theme of *Hyperion* as set forth in Oceanus's speech (II, 206 ff.), in the statement that Saturn was reconciled with his sons Jupiter, Neptune, and Pluto because he was "so struck with their beauty and hopeful qualities, that he forgave his wife [Cybele, who had saved them from being devoured by Saturn at birth] and took them into his favour" (*Pantheon* [1806], p. 45)—an interpretation not to be found in Keats's classical sources.

12. *Letters*, I, 369, 387, 392, and cf. Chapter IX, note 28 below.

13. That Keats identified much more closely with Tom than with George is seen in the fact that in his letters written to both his brothers he addressed Tom directly almost three times as often as George (compare *Letters*, I, 196, 197, 199, 200, 201, 214, and 217 with 129, 196, 235).

14. See Chapter IX, note 8 below.

15. "Ailsa Rock" and "The Human Seasons," which appeared in Hunt's *Literary Pocket Book* in December.

16. Compare his mention of Saturn and Ops on October 27 (*Letters*, I, 387) and *Hyperion*, II, 78, 113, 129 ff.

17. See notes 8 and 9 above.

18. David Thomson, *England in the Nineteenth Century* (1955), p. 17.

19. Gittings thinks otherwise (JKLY, pp. 25–36); but see Murry, K, pp. 116–23, and Aileen Ward, "The Date of Keats's 'Bright Star' Sonnet," SP, LII (1955), 82–84.

20. Sharp, p. 37.

21. Lowell, II, 121; H. D. Miles, *Pugilistica* (1906), I, 328–46.

22. The poem is drafted in Keats's copy of Beaumont and Fletcher (KHM, no. 21): perhaps suggested by Beaumont's song "Mirth," in *The Knight of the Burning Pestle.*

23. Gittings, JKLY, pp. 49–50. On the suggestion that "Fancy" was patterned on the introductory verses in Burton's *Anatomy of Melancholy,* and that Keats started reading Burton at this time, see Aileen Ward, "Keats and Burton: A Reappraisal," PQ, XL (1961), 539–40.

24. Between £400 and £500, according to Brown (letters to C. W. Dilke of 17 December 1829 and 20 January 1830. KHM, no. 80).

25. Ward, "CD1818," pp. 21–24. Miss Lowell reproduced the lyre seal on the title page of *John Keats* but failed to notice its significance.

26. Murry, K, pp. 33–36.


## IX. THE MELANCHOLY STORM

1. H. B. Forman, LJKFB, p. lxvii.

2. J. Richardson, pp. 2–7; C. E. Baker, *Manuscript History of the Brawne Family* (KHM, no. 76).

3. LFBFK, p. 59.

4. H. B. Forman, LJKFB, p. lxvi.

5. MLPKC, pp. 30–31.

6. Medwin, p. 296.

7. See *Letters,* I, 417, II, 206, and note 12 below.

8. De Selincourt suggests (p. 494) that the autograph manuscript of *Hyperion* ("A" in Garrod's apparatus; cf. *Works,* pp. xli–xlii) was "intended to be a fair copy" of an earlier draft, and that Keats made "numerous alterations" on it "when he came to view his work a second time." The excellent quality of the paper, the flourish of the title, and the generally fair handwriting of the MS. (British Museum Add. 37000) support this inference. Evidently this "fair copy" or second draft, which contains many revisions made in the process of recopying, was made sometime between December 1818 and April 1819, when Keats gave it to Woodhouse to transcribe. The most likely date for these revisions is early January.

9. *Works,* p. 300. On the date of the first section of the third book, see Gittings, JKLY, pp. 46–47.

10. Not on January 21, as Gittings suggests (JKLY, p. 62): see H. E. Rollins, "Keats's Misdated Letters: Additional Notes," HLB, VIII (1954), 243–45, and Murry, K, pp. 132–33.

11. On Keats's visit to Stansted, see Gittings, JKLY, Chapters 7 and 8.

12. *Letters,* I, 415 and II, 31, 32, 39–40. Brown's letter to Dilke of 6 September 1824 (KHM, no. 80) describes the sum in question as £500.

13. MacGillivray, p. 101; KC, II, 151.

14. J. Richardson, p. 30.

15. KC, I, 98 and II, 103.

16. MLPKC, pp. 20, 23 n. 4; LFBFK, p. 49.

17. This seems indicated by the sudden break in their correspondence that fall, after Keats's extremely warm and confidential letter that summer (*Letters*, II, 7, 139; cf. I, 369), and by his repeated outbursts against "ideot Parsons" that winter; see also Brown's mention of Bailey's "guilt" and his harsh criticism of him (though not by name) in the draft of his *Life of Keats* (KC, II, 64). Bailey's behaviour to Mariane Reynolds could hardly have been sufficient reason to Keats for the rupture of their friendship.

18. Steele, "WTPJK," p. 244; KC, I, 65–66.

19. Not on February 17 (cf. Rollins, *Letters*, I, 48), which Keats described as a day of business (II, 66), and which on February 19 he referred to as "day before yesterday" in contrast to February 13, "the other day" (II, 64, 65)—which he described as a day of seeing many people.

20. Gittings, JKLY, p. 86.

21. Ibid., pp. 87–91.

22. See Gittings, JKLY, Chapters 3–10, and compare Murry, K, Chapter 3, and the articles by Ward cited above, Chapter V, note 5 and Chapter VIII, notes 19, 23.

23. Blunden, KPMJT, pp. 96–97.

24. Mabel A. E. Steele, "The Authorship of 'The Poet' and Other Sonnets," KSJ, V (1956), 75–76.

25. Gittings, JKLY, p. 102.

26. R. L. Cecil and R. F. Loeb, *A Textbook of Medicine* (1951), pp. 254 ff., 269 ff. Gittings' contention (JKLY, p. 4) that Keats was "in robust health during most of the year" from September 1818 to September 1819 is refuted by Keats's own frequent references to his poor health (especially his sore throat) during this time. Nor does Hale-White's account of Keats's health (pp. 69, 73, 79) bear out Gittings's statement; rather, it implies that Keat's pulmonary infection had already "progressed considerably" (p. 79).

27. *Encyclopaedia Britannica,* 6th ed. (1823), "Medicine," XIII, 225, 349–55.

28. See Chapter VIII, note 12 above; and *Letters*, II, 12, 77, 81. This sensation of weight and tightness in his chest became greatly intensified after his illness, especially in moments of anxiety (ibid., 264, 281, 283, 314, 315, 321). His most vivid expression of the sensation occurs in his marginal comment on *Paradise Lost,* IX, 179 ff., where Satan entered the body of the serpent "but his sleep Disturbed not": "Whose spirit does not ache at the smothering and confinement, the *waiting close?* No passage of poetry ever can give a greater pain of suffocation" (Hampstead, V, 305). A comparison with *Hyperion*, I, 259 ff., suggests this note was written in the fall of 1818.

29. Dilke's note in his copy of Milnes's *Life* (Morgan Library), I, 215; *Letters,* II, 42, 52, 77, 149 et seq.

30. The date of the sonnet is uncertain. It cannot have been written on the morning of March 19, when Keats copied it out fair and referred to it in the past tense (*Letters*, II, 81), and probably not on the evening of the eighteenth, when Keats was laid up with a black eye; the evening of the seventeenth is quite possible, however, and the sonnet fits the mood of utter negativism expressed in his journal for that day.

31. KC, I, 256, 258.

32. The parallelism between "Why did I laugh tonight?" and *Hyperion* III, 86–107 has been noted by Murry, KS, pp. 89 ff., and Gittings, JKLY, pp. 100–101.

33. The third, fourth, and fifth lines were omitted from the printed version, presumably on Woodhouse's initiative, for they were left uncancelled in Keats's

autograph but cancelled in pencil in Woodhouse's transcript, now in the Harvard University Library (cf. *Works,* pp. 304-305).

34. The ending pencilled by Woodhouse into his clerk's transcript (W[1], now in the Harvard University Library; cf. *Works,* p. 305): "probably a subsequent amendment," as Murry describes it (KS, p. 230). Keats's autograph draft (A) provides another ending, "Apollo shriek'd, and lo! he was the God!" The truncated ending of the printed version seems to have been devised to give the effect of "A Fragment," as Taylor and Hessey decided to publish it in 1820.

35. KC, I, 129.

## X. THE TEMPLE OF DELIGHT

1. See Chapter IV, note 25, above, and Hewlett, pp. 255 and 340 n. 1.

2. Rollins, MLPKC, pp. 3-5.

3. *Letters,* II, 52, 84.

4. Ibid., 61 and 46; 70, 52, 83, 111, 113, 114, 115, 123.

5. Dilke's note in his copy of Milnes's *Life* (Morgan Library), I, 288.

6. Hewlett, p. 381; Gittings, JKLY, pp. 120-23.

7. See *Letters,* II, 257, 261, 285, 287, 288, 309, 330; also Keats's comment, recorded by Woodhouse, "Wells should have brothers and sicker than I even had" (Finney, II, 746).

8. Marginalia to *Troilus and Cressida,* I.iii.316 ff., Hampstead, V, 271.

9. Rollins assigns "La Belle Dame," the "Chorus of Four Faeries," and the "vale of Soul-making" passage to a single evening, April 21 (*Letters,* II, 95-104). But the manuscript of the letter, now in the Harvard University Library, shows clear breaks after "La Belle Dame" and the "Chorus," suggesting that these three sections were written on three different occasions.

10. *Letters,* II, 80.

11. Compare this image of suckling (*Letters,* II, 103) with *Endymion,* II, 869 and III, 456; the sonnet "To Spenser," ll. 11-12; and *Letters,* I, 232.

12. Lowell arranges the odes according to a progression of mood (II, 244 ff.), Finney by the development of the ode stanza (II, 610 ff.), H. W. Garrod by the development of a single theme, the search for a transcendent joy (*Keats* [1926], pp. 97 ff.), and Gittings by their connection with Keats's reading, presumably of Burton (JKLY, pp. 136-46; but cf. Ward, "KBR," pp. 535-42). The following analysis draws on all these methods but departs from all the schemes cited above by putting the "Ode on Indolence" immediately after "Psyche" and before "On a Grecian Urn," for reasons noted below.

13. Robert Wagner, "Keats's 'Ode to Psyche' and the Second *Hyperion,*" forthcoming in KSJ.

14. H. J. Pettit, "Scientific Correlatives of Keats's 'Ode to Psyche,'" SP, XL (1943), 560-67; Charles W. Hagelman, Jr., "Keats's Medical Training and the Last Stanza of the 'Ode to Psyche,'" KSJ, XI (1962), 73-82.

15. The "Ode on Indolence" was probably not written early in June, for Keats referred to it then as written some indeterminate time ago and confessed also that he had been "very idle lately" (*Letters,* II, 116). More likely it was written early in May, since it closely echoes the March 19 section of the letter to George (ibid., pp. 78-79), which Keats probably reread before sending it off on May 3. It also echoes the two sonnets on Fame and the "Ode to Psyche," written at the end of April or beginning of May; and the last lines of "Indolence" closely parallel a sentence from *The Golden Asse*

(quoted by Colvin, p. 412 n. 1), which Keats was reading at the time he wrote "Psyche."

16. The order of the stanzas is a matter of dispute, and the versification lacks force: four stanzas (nos. 1, 2, 4, and 5 in *Works*, pp. 447–48) follow a pattern of almost monotonous regularity, which is then altered in the third and sixth stanzas for no discernible reason.

17. Cleanth Brooks, *The Well-Wrought Urn* (1947), p. 148.

18. HBF, IV, 387 ff.

19. Gittings dates the "Ode to a Nightingale" April 30 (JKLY, p. 132), but it is improbable that Keats wrote it on the same morning as his two sonnets "On Fame" and in the same week as the "Ode to Psyche." Stanza v gives the date as mid-May—the time when nightingales usually start nesting in the vicinity of London (H. F. Witherby, *Handbook of British Birds* [1949], II, 188).

20. *Letters*, I, 307, 403 and II, 46.

21. Newell F. Ford, "Keats's Romantic Seas: 'Ruthless' or 'Keelless'?" KSJ, I (1952), 11–22.

22. In contrast to the preponderantly regular versification of the "Ode on a Grecian Urn," the "Ode to a Nightingale" shows a great variety of irregular verses within the first seven lines of each stanza, subsiding, after the truncated eighth line, into two regular lines at the end. The greatest metrical irregularity is concentrated in the first line of each stanza, suggesting a violent effort to break out of the recurrent pattern confirmed in the last two lines.

23. The only clues to the date of the "Ode on Melancholy" are its similarity in mood to the letter of May 31 to Miss Jeffrey and its position as the last of the odes in the 1820 volume.

24. Hewlett, p. 255.

25. Ward, "KBR," pp. 542–43.

## XI. BETWEEN DESPAIR AND ENERGY

1. Keats may have started *Lamia* in June at Hampstead, as De Selincourt suggests (p. 453), and possibly *Otho* as well; but the letter which De Selincourt cites (II, 128) is very inconclusive on this point. In any event, the long first scene of *Otho* was extensively rewritten (*Works*, pp. 312–18).

2. *Letters*, II, 228–29. The emendation of "Holland" to "Holt and" (n. 4) is unnecessary, for Brown speaks of "a trustee being in Holland at the time" (i.e. in the fall of 1819) in a letter to Dilke of 6 September 1824 (KHM, no. 80). Keats's handwriting frequently shows spaces between letters within a word.

3. Keats could not have begun the revised version at this time, as is usually suggested (*Letters*, II, 139 n. 3). Though he was working on "a very abstract Poem" on July 25, a day or two later he resumed writing *Otho* with Brown (ibid., p. 135), and evidently was completely occupied with Acts II–IV of *Otho* between July 26 and August 11 and with Act V of *Otho*, scenes i–iii of *King Stephen*, Part II of *Lamia*, and the revision of *The Eve of St. Agnes* between August 13 and September 5—a schedule which left no time for his epic. Therefore his reference to "writing parts of my Hyperion" on August 14 cannot be taken to mean he had started *The Fall of Hyperion* at this time—especially when it is noted that he was describing the work of the entire previous year in this letter to Bailey (ibid., p. 139). Furthermore, Keats gave up *Hyperion* because, as he stated on September 21, he was dissatisfied

with its Miltonic quality (ibid., p. 167); but several times during August he expressed fervent admiration for *Paradise Lost* (ibid., pp. 139, 146). All of this suggests that Keats was working on the original *Hyperion* at the end of July but did not decide to give it up till early September (see note 15 below).

4. On the date of this sonnet, see Ward, "DKBSS," pp. 75–85.

5. Compare *Otho*, I.III.115 and V.v.146 and *Letters*, II, 141 and 146; *Otho*, II.I.4 and *Letters*, II, 140; *Otho*, II.I.135 and *Letters*, II, 133; *Otho*, III.II.98 and *Letters*, II, 141 and 144; *Otho*, IV.I.13 and *Letters*, II, 144; *Otho*, V.IV.26 and *Letters*, II, 113 and 142.

6. Colvin, pp. 330–31 n.; Gittings, JKLY, p. 162.

7. *Letters*, II, 144, 176–77, 179.

8. KC, II, 67; cf. Gittings, JKLY, p. 164. Scenes 1–3 of *King Stephen* come to 135 lines, but they are followed by a fourth scene 58 lines long: it therefore seems likely that Keats wrote the first three scenes in August, as Brown suggests (KC, II, 67), then added the fourth scene in November on learning that Kean had decided against going to America—when he told Taylor that his ambition was to write "a few fine Plays" (*Letters*, II, 234). This addition would account for the discrepancy between the August date in Brown's *Life* and the November date on his transcript.

9. Potter's *Archaeologia Graeca*: Douglas Bush, "Notes on Keats's Reading," PMLA, L (1935), 785–806.

10. Murry, KS, pp. 157 ff.

11. Gittings, JKLY, pp. 172–73.

12. *Endymion*, II, 868 and III, 456; *Letters*, II, 160 and 257; Chapter X, note 11 above.

13. Fanny Brawne stated that Keats "was not engaged to me" when he offered to lend George "any assistance or money in his power," in September 1819 (LFBFK, p. 33; *Letters*, II, 185, 210; and see note 17 below).

14. The annotations are reprinted in Hampstead, V, 306–20; on their date, see Ward, "KBR," pp. 543–48.

15. Keats's remark to this effect in his letter to Reynolds of 21 September is usually taken to refer to giving up *The Fall of Hyperion* (*Letters*, II, 167 n. 1), because in writing to Woodhouse on the same day he quoted a passage near the end of *The Fall of Hyperion* (De Selincourt, p. 582). Yet this evidence is not at all conclusive. The passage itself (II, 1–4, 6) may be only an isolated fragment which Keats later fitted into place, since it forms an abrupt transition from the preceding passage and is immediately followed by forty-two lines of unbroken quotation from the first *Hyperion* and, after a five-line interpolation, eight more lines from the first version, after which *The Fall* breaks off. Since Keats was working on *The Fall of Hyperion* in November and December (KC, II, 72), it seems unlikely that all his work then added merely five new lines (II, 49–53) to the poem. Several other considerations suggest that Keats in fact gave up the original, not the revised, *Hyperion* at this time. First, since he most probably did not start work on *The Fall* till early September (see note 3 above), he could hardly have written the entire First Canto—containing some of the most concentrated poetry in all his work—in the eight or nine working days between Brown's departure and Keats's letter to Woodhouse. Second, the Miltonic quality which Keats cited as his reason for "giving up Hyperion" is much more pronounced in the first than in the second version (as De Selincourt admits, pp. 519, 582). Third, the passages from *The Fall* which Keats quoted to Woodhouse were later

revised (ibid., p. 582), and Keats quoted them in a manner clearly indicating he was pleased with them (*Letters*, II, 171). Fourth, Keats told Reynolds to reread *Hyperion* and mark it (*Letters*, II, 167): but Reynolds could not yet have seen the revised version, though he had access to Woodhouse's copy of the original version at the time. Fifth, the central passage in *The Fall of Hyperion* (I, 147-210) echoes a disillusionment with poetry that Keats began to express in his letters near the end of September (See Chapter XII, note 2, below).

16. John Livingston Lowes, "*Hyperion* and the *Purgatorio*," TLS, 11 January 1936, p. 35; Gittings, MK, pp. 33-44.

17. *Letters*, II, 185. None of George's three letters between May and September has survived, but their contents may be reconstructed from Keats's replies. In the letter which arrived in May, he told Keats of the steamboat scheme but expressed no need of money at this time (II, 228); Keats presumably replied to this in June in a lost letter (II, 217), congratulating him on the birth of his daughter and telling him of the Chancery suit (II, 121). Evidently Keats next wrote from Shanklin in July (cf. I, 11) in reply to a second less optimistic letter from George, in which he asked Keats to sell his remaining holdings (II, 131-32, 184, 211-12). Not until September did his situation seem so precarious that Keats offered to lend him money of his own (II, 185, 210). Gittings' conjecture (JKLY, p. 138) that Keats offered to lend George money in a letter of May, which he later forgot having written, seems unwarranted. As for Audubon's unreliability, Miss Kirk points out that he ultimately bankrupted six business partners—though George's later belief that Audubon tricked him into investing in the steamboat after it had already sunk cannot be substantiated (Kirk, pp. lxxxvii-lxxxviii; cf. *Letters*, II, 185, 211).

18. KC, I, 88.

19. *The Times*, 14 September 1819; *The Examiner*, 19 September 1819.

20. It seems probable that the two Chaucerian passages were added in September from the fact that Keats copied out lines 1-98 for George on September 20 with the prefatory remark "I will give it [as] far as I have gone," and then added the second Chaucerian passage (ll. 99-114) after a distinct break (*Letters*, II, 201, 204), but did not include the first Chaucerian passage (ll. 98a-p; *Works*, p. 452), which was evidently added later, as were the last four lines (115-19). See also the references in his letters to Venice (II, 201) and to Chatterton (II, 167, 212) and the repetition of the phrase "kepen in solitarinesse" (II, 166, 209), all of which link the poem with this period. The appearance of the rough draft of "The Eve of St. Mark" in the British Museum (Egerton 2780) also suggests a similar break between the first 98 lines and the remaining portion.

## XII. UNMERIDIAN'D AND OBJECTLESS

1. This conjecture is supported by the fact that when Reynolds made a copy of *The Fall of Hyperion* sometime after Keats's return to London, he transcribed only as far as I, 326—presumably the point which Keats had reached at that time.

2. Murry (K, pp. 238-46) and De Selincourt (pp. 517-19, 583-84) have disagreed as to whether the passage from which these lines are quoted (I, 187-210) should stand, since it was cancelled by Woodhouse in his two

transcripts with a pencil mark and a note (though not in the Reynolds transcript); they agree, however, that Keats's intention in this section of the poem was to glorify his own role as a "true poet." This writer disagrees with this interpretation. De Selincourt oversimplifies Keats's argument by reducing it to the Shelley-like contrast between the poet and "the practical unimaginative man" (p. 519), thus overlooking the higher type of the disinterested man of action who is Keats's true ideal. But Murry reads something into Keats's argument of which the text gives no hint if the disputed passage is dropped, as he recommends: that Keats counted himself "a true poet," one who had "utterly rejected dreams," and thus exempt from Moneta's condemnation (p. 242). Keats may have cancelled the disputed passage, not because he disagreed with Moneta's condemnation (which remains in ll. 166–70), but because in his temporary disillusionment with poetry he overstated his case and thus apparently nullified his intention in the poem as a whole. If the dreamer was eventually, like Apollo in *Hyperion,* to be transformed into a true poet, he must maintain his faith in this possibility, rather than accept Moneta's reproof as an irreversible indictment (as in ll. 202–10). When Keats returned to the poem later in the fall, he must have realized the inconsistency and, at least provisionally, cancelled the digression.

3. Murry, K, p. 50.

4. Herschel Baker, *William Hazlitt* (1962), pp. 260–63.

5. Ibid., p. 250.

6. Sir Charles W. Dilke, ed., *Papers of a Critic,* 2 vols. (1875), I, 11, where no date is given. Murry's conjecture that the formal engagement took place in October 1819 (K, pp. 33–36) best fits the few known facts of the matter.

7. KHM no. 67; J. Richardson, p. 87.

8. *Letters,* II, 321 n. 4.

9. See Chapter XI, note 8 above.

10. MBF, p. 513 n.

11. Gittings, MK, pp. 122–39.

12. Murry, K, pp. 51–52.

13. *Encyclopaedia Britannica,* 6th ed. (1823), "Medicine," XIII, 355; compare Keats's own recommendation of a light diet, *Letters,* II, 252.

14. See above, p. 258.

15. W. B. Yeats, *Collected Works* (1908), VI, 109–10.

16. KC, I, 97; *Works,* pp. xxxiv–xxxvi.

17. Not because of the supposed sinking of his steamboat (Hewlett, p. 269; Gittings, JKLY, p. 180), for George mentioned the steamboat twice in the following year (*Letters,* II, 295–96, 356; cf. II, 256–57).

18. Jack Stillinger states the facts of this transaction as clearly as they can be gathered in "The Brown-Dilke Controversy," KSJ, XI (1962), 39–45.

19. LFBFK, p. 34.

20. Ibid.

21. Sharp, pp. 65–66.

22. KC, I, 217; LFBFK, p. 33; Brown, letter to Dilke, 6 September 1824 (KHM, no. 80).

23. KC, II, 102 n. 3.

24. The date is conjectural; but *Otho* was submitted to Covent Garden soon after the middle of January (*Letters,* II, 241) and "speedily returned" (KC, II, 67), and it was evidently shelved by February 11 (MBF, pp. 461–62 n.).

## XIII. A WRECKED LIFE

1. It is significant that George Keats, in whom tuberculosis was evidently latent for years, suffered his first haemorrhage at the time of a desperate financial crisis (KC, I, cviii).

2. This letter (No. 223) appears to follow rather than precede Nos. 225, 226, and 227, all of which refer to breaking the engagement, since Keats here alludes to the subject as closed. On Reynolds' disapproval of his engagement, see *Letters*, II, 258 n. and 292 n. and KC, I, 156.

3. Brown's unpublished letters (British Museum Add. 38109 *passim*) are full of expressions of his derogatory attitude toward women. Writing to Leigh Hunt on 28 November 1829, he commented that their friend Kirkup was "a lucky fellow" to have got rid of "two incumbrances" at the same time by the death of his wife and the marriage of his mistress to an actor (fol. 62).

4. KC, I, lxvii. Brown's rather casual suggestion about leaving the child with his friend Thomas Richards while he went abroad (*Some Letters and a Miscellanea*, ed. M. B. Forman [1937], p. 10) indicates his attitude.

5. On the probable date of Brown's illegal marriage to Abby, which is completely a matter of conjecture (see *Letters*, II, 159 n. 7), see Chapter XIV, note 15 below.

6. This letter (No. 244) seems linked fairly clearly with No. 238 by the mention of the prohibition against visiting when Brown was at home and Keat's allusion to watching when she went out for her walk on the Heath.

7. Haydon, D, II, 265; Baker, p. 238; Sharp, p. 34.

8. Keats evidently did not learn of this plan till July 5 (*Letters*, II, 305); and his report of his own health at the end of March is much less optimistic than Brown's (compare II, 295 and 283-84).

9. Brown's letter to Dilke of 2 May 1826 (KHM, no. 80).

10. The quarrel was evidently not with Bailey (see *Letters*, II, 298 n. 6), with whom Keats had not been reconciled, but probably with Dilke, who noted in his biographical sketch of Keats in his copy of *Endymion* (KHM, no. 47A), "The very kindness of friends was at this time felt to be oppressive to him."

11. *Works,* pp. xxxiv-xxxv.

12. Hunt spoke of Keats's suffering from "critical malignity" during his illness (HBF, II, 536); see also KC, I, 232 and II, 95 n. 77.

13. See Chapter X, note 7 above.

14. Hewlett, pp. 324-27.

15. Medwin, p. 297.

16. HBF, IV, 293-94; Lowell, II, 438.

17. Letter to James Taylor, 10 August 1820 (KHM, no. 50). The date shows that plans were being laid for the trip before Keats finally agreed to go.

18. The difference between his loan of £30 in November 1819 (*Letters*, II, 226) and Keats's debt of £50 at the time of his death (MLPKC, pp. 26-28).

19. Dilke, PC, I, 11.

20. HBF, IV, 294; LFBFK, pp. 25-26.

21. See also MBF, p. 506 n. 1, and compare p. 525 n. 1.

22. Hewlett, p. 306.

23. KC, I, 215.

24. *Letters*, II, 329 and n. 3; compare 321, 327, and see also II, 364 and 359-360.

25. LFBFK, pp. 25–28.

26. HBF, IV, 358–61.

27. KC, I, 155–56.

28. KHM, no. 74.

29. Dilke's note in his copy of *Endymion* (KHM, no. 47A).

30. HBF, IV, 200.

## XIV. END OF THE VOYAGE

1. Blunden, KPMJT, p. 79.

2. *Letters*, II, 350. The letter was never sent (KC, II, 130); Severn evidently opened it after Keats's death and sent Brown a copy. A comparison of the autograph (now in the Harvard University Library) with Brown's transcript (KC, II, 80–82) reveals that Brown occasionally omitted entire sentences without indication (cf. *Letters*, II, 345 n. 2, 4).

3. As he told Milnes, who printed this account of the sonnet in his 1848 *Life* (II, 72)—even though, as M. B. Forman noted (Hampstead, IV, 235–36), he had seen and quoted the earlier version of the sonnet in Brown's transcript, which is clearly dated 1819. Severn's detailed reminiscences of the trip from London to Rome are printed in Sharp, pp. 58–64.

4. KHM, no. 14; cf. *The Keats Letters, Papers, and Other Relics Forming the Dilke Bequest in the Hampstead Public Library*, ed. George C. Williamson (1914), pl. XLVII.

5. Brown may have deleted a reminder, however, as he did in transcribing Keats's letter of 30 November (see note 13 below).

6. KC, II, 130; *Letters of Joseph Severn to H. B. Forman* (1933), pp. 7, 9, 11, 18–19.

7. Harold Acton, *The Bourbons of Naples* (1956), pp. 681–87.

8. MBF, p. 525 n. 1.

9. "Keats's Roman Landlady," from "A Correspondent," *The Times* (London), 2 February 1953.

10. KC, I, 183–84. Severn later found he could live on three shillings a day in Italy (ibid., p. 273). For his reminiscences of his stay with Keats in Rome, see Sharp, pp. 64 ff.

11. This letter has not survived, but its contents can be reconstructed from Fanny Brawne's recapitulation of it (LFBFK, p. 16); Severn evidently mailed it on December 9 (*Letters*, II, 363).

12. KC, I, cxxxiii.

13. These breaks may mark a deletion, since this letter was clearly censored: compare Keats's letter (as transcribed by Brown) and Brown's reply, *Letters*, II, 359–60 and 364.

14. See KC, II, 77, 80.

15. The date and place of Brown's marriage to Abby is conjectural (*Letters*, II, 159 n. 7). From all the contemporary references to Brown's relations with her, it appears to have taken place after the birth of the boy "Carlino," not before, as usually assumed; cf. Rice and other friends' protests to Brown that the boy's birth was "a heinous crime" (Brown, p. 26); Brown's description of his arrangements with Abby in December 1820 as recent (*Letters*, II, 365); and his reproach to Carlino for "wincing under the circumstances of [his] birth" (letter of 12 June 1840, KHM, no. 80). Brown always spoke of Abby "with the utmost callousness" (Rollins, KC, I, lxvii); he was estranged from

her six months after Carlino's birth, and separated finally from her a year later.

16. Rollins, *Letters,* II, 364 n. 2.

17. Since Brown opened and endorsed this letter (now in the Harvard University Library), he evidently withheld it from forwarding, as with George's letter of 8 November 1820 (cf. KC, I, 168 n. 1).

18. KC, II, 80. See also *Letters,* II, 329 n. 3; and KC, I, 159, 160, 173, 174, 186, 200 ff., 228 ff.; also Severn's letters to Brown, KC, I, 175 ff. and II, 90 ff. and 94 ff., which are silent on this point.

19. From a conjectured reading of Severn's mutilated letter in the Harvard University Library which appears necessary from the context and which fits into the gaps: "His dreadful state of mind turns to [per]secuti[on and some] times even murder—he is now under the [terrible de]lusion [that poison] was administered to him by an individual in London" (cf. KC, I, 180).

20. HBF, IV, 362.

21. KC, II, 92.

22. Medwin, p. 297.

23. Sharp, pp. 72–73; KC, I, 168, 201.

24. LFBFK, p. 17.

25. KC, I, 182.

26. Brown's omission may be found in Fanny Brawne's transcript of this letter (compare KC, II, 93 and HBF, IV, 214).

27. KC, I, 201, 207; Sharp, p. 76. It should be noted that Keats's last references to George in his letters were extremely affectionate.

28. MLPKC, p. 117.

29. HBF, IV, 221–22.

30. Sharp, p. 75.

31. LFBFK, p. 20. Fanny implies in a later letter to Fanny Keats that it was Keats's assurance that Brown would go to Rome that kept her from going herself (p. 25).

32. Ward, "CD1818," pp. 24–25. The lyre, as sketched by Severn in Brown's copy of *Endymion* (now in the Keats House at Hampstead), is reproduced in the device on the title page of this volume.

33. Ward, "CD1818," pp. 25–26; Sharp, pp. 91–93.

34. KC, I, 251; HBF, IV, 364.

## EPILOGUE

1. HBF, IV, 358–59.

2. Sharp, p. 109; H. B. Forman, LJKFB, p. lxv.

3. J. Richardson, p. 89.

4. HBF, IV, 366–68; Sharp, pp. 110–12.

5. Colvin, p. 524. On the actual date of Keats's death, incorrectly given on his tombstone as February 24, 1821, see KC, I, 226.

6. MacGillivray, pp. xxxii–xxxvi.

7. Baker, p. 250.

8. MBF, pp. lxi, lxiv; KC, I, 313–14, 326–27.

9. Colvin, p. 529.

10. Ibid., p. 528.

11. D. H. Bodurtha and Willard B. Pope, eds., *Life of John Keats by Charles Armitage Brown* (1937), p. 10.

12. Leslie A. Marchand notes that this is one of the few undoubted details amid the legends surrounding Shelley's death ("Trelawny on the Death of Shelley," KSMB, IV [1952], 17).

13. George, pp. 171–72; Haydon, D, II, 499.

14. Colvin, p. 536.

15. J. Richardson, p. 113.

16. Both letters are printed in MBF, lxi–lxiv.

17. MacGillivray, p. xlv.

18. Ibid., pp. lviii–lx.

19. Dilke, I, 7.

20. Murry, KS, p. 13.

# Selective Bibliography

Adami, Marie. *Fanny Keats,* 1937.

Altick, Richard. *The Cowden Clarkes,* 1948.

Baker, Herschel. *William Hazlitt,* 1962.

Beavan, A. H. *James and Horace Smith,* 1899.

Beyer, Werner William. *Keats and the Daemon King,* 1947.

Blunden, Edmund. *John Keats.* Supplement to *British Book News,* 1950.

————. *Leigh Hunt and His Circle,* 1930.

————. *Keats's Publisher: A Memoir of John Taylor,* 1936.

————. *Votive Tablets,* 1931.

Brown, Charles. *Some Letters and a Miscellanea,* ed. M. B. Forman, 1937.

Bush, Douglas. *Mythology and the Romantic Tradition in English Poetry,* 1937.

Caldwell, James R. "Woodhouse's Annotations in Keats's First Volume of Poems,"
PMLA, LXIII (1948), 757–59.

Clarke, Charles Cowden. "Recollections of Keats," *Atlantic Monthly,* VII (1861), 86–
100.

Colvin, Sir Sidney. *John Keats: His Life and Poetry, Friends, Critics, and After-
Fame,* 1917.

Dilke, Sir Charles Wentworth, Bart., ed. *The Papers of a Critic,* 2 vols., 1875.

*Encyclopaedia Britannica,* 6th ed. (1823), art. "Medicine," XIII, 349 ff.

Erikson, Erik H. "The Problem of Ego Identity," *Journal of the American Psychoanalytic Association,* IV (1956), 56–121.

Finney, Claude Lee. *The Evolution of Keats's Poetry,* 2 vols., 1936.

George, Eric. *The Life and Death of Benjamin Robert Haydon,* 1948.

Gittings, Robert. *John Keats: The Living Year,* 1954.

————. "Keats's Sailor Relation," TLS, 15 April 1960, p. 245.

————. *The Mask of Keats,* 1956.

Hagelman, Charles W., Jr. *John Keats and the Medical Profession,* unpublished dissertation, University of Texas, 1956.

Hale-White, Sir William. *Keats as Doctor and Patient,* 1938.

Harper, George MacLean. *William Wordsworth,* 2 vols., 1916.

Haydon, Benjamin Robert. *Autobiography and Journals,* ed. Malcolm Elwin, 1950.

————. *Diary,* ed. Willard Bissell Pope, 2 vols., 1960.

Hazlitt, William. *Complete Works,* ed. P. P. Howe, 21 vols., 1930–1934.

————. *Lectures on the English Poets,* Everyman's Library, 1910.

Hewlett, Dorothy. *A Life of John Keats,* 2nd ed., revised, 1949.

Howe, P. P. *The Life of William Hazlitt,* Penguin Books, 1949.

Hunt, Leigh. *Autobiography,* ed. J. E. Morpurgo, 1949.

*Keats House and Museum: A Historical and Descriptive Guide,* 4th ed., revised; n.d.

Keats, John. *Anatomical and Physiological Notebook,* ed. Maurice Buxton Forman,
1934.

————. *Letters,* ed. Hyder Edward Rollins, 2 vols., 1958.

————. *Letters,* ed. Maurice Buxton Forman, 2nd ed., revised, 1935.

————. *Letters to Fanny Brawne,* ed. Harry Buxton Forman, 1878.

Keats, John. *Poems,* ed. Ernest de Selincourt, 5th ed., revised, 1926.

——. *Poems and Verses,* Edited and Arranged in Chronological Order by John Middleton Murry, 1930.

——. *The Poetical Works,* ed. H. W. Garrod, 2nd ed., 1958.

——. *The Poetical Works and Other Writings,* ed. Harry Buxton Forman, 4 vols., 1883.

——. *The Poetical Works and Other Writings,* ed. Harry Buxton Forman, revised by Maurice Buxton Forman, Hampstead Edition, 8 vols., 1938–1939.

Kirk, Naomi J. "Memoir of George Keats," in *The Poetical Works and Other Writings of John Keats,* ed. H. B. Forman and M. B. Forman, 1938–1939, I, lxxiii–xcviii.

Lindon, Fanny Brawne. *Letters to Fanny Keats, 1820–1824,* ed. Fred Edgcumbe, 1937.

Lowell, Amy. *John Keats,* 2 vols., 1925.

MacGillivray, J. R. *Keats: A Bibliography and Reference Guide,* 1949.

Medwin, Thomas. *Life of Percy Bysshe Shelley,* ed. H. B. Forman, 1913.

Milnes, Richard Monckton. *Life, Letters, and Literary Remains of John Keats,* 2 vols., 1848.

Murry, John Middleton. *Keats,* 1955.

——. *Keats and Shakespeare,* 1925.

——. *Studies in Keats,* 1930.

Olney, Clark. *Benjamin Robert Haydon, Historical Painter,* 1952.

Pederson-Krag, Geraldine. " 'O Poesy! For Thee I Hold My Pen,' " in *Psychoanalysis and Culture: Essays in Honor of Géza Roheim,* ed. G. W. Wilbur and W. Muensterberger, 1951, pp. 436–52.

Pope, Willard Bissell. *Studies on the Keats Circle,* unpublished dissertation, Harvard University, 1932.

Quennell, Peter. *Byron: The Years of Fame,* 1935.

Rank, Otto. *Art and Artist: Creative Urge and Personality Development,* 1932.

Reynolds, John Hamilton. *Poetry and Prose,* ed. George L. Marsh, 1928.

Richardson, Sir Benjamin Ward. *The Asclepiad,* 1884.

Richardson, Joanna. *Fanny Brawne,* 1952.

Ridley, Maurice Roy. *Keats's Craftsmanship,* 1933.

Rollins, Hyder Edward, ed. *The Keats Circle: Letters and Papers, 1816–1878,* 2 vols., 1948.

——. *More Letters and Papers of the Keats Circle,* 1955.

Severn, Joseph. *Letters to H. B. Forman,* 1933.

Sharp, William. *Life and Letters of Joseph Severn,* 1892.

Shelley, Percy Bysshe. *Complete Works,* ed. Roger Ingpen and W. E. Peck, 10 vols., 1926–1930.

Slote, Bernice. *Keats and the Dramatic Principle,* 1958.

South, John Flint. *Memorials,* 1884.

Spurgeon, Caroline. *Keats's Shakespeare,* 1929.

Steele, Mabel A. E. "The Woodhouse Transcripts of the Poems of John Keats," HLB, III (1949), 232–56.

Stout, George Dumas. "Leigh Hunt's Money Troubles: Some New Light," *Washington University Studies, Humanistic Series,* XII (1925), 221–32.

——. "The Political History of Leigh Hunt's *Examiner,*" *Washington University Studies (New Series) in Language and Literature,* no. 19, 1949.

Trilling, Lionel. "The Poet as Hero: Keats in His Letters," in *The Opposing Self,* 1955.

Ward, Aileen. "Christmas Day, 1818," KSJ, X (1961), 17–27.

——. "The Date of Keats's 'Bright Star' Sonnet," SP, LII (1955), 75–85.

——. "Keats and Burton: A Reappraisal," PQ, XL (1961), 535–52.

White, Newman Ivey. *Shelley,* 2 vols., 1940.

# Index

**443**

# Making God's Word Work

D1205504

# *Making God's Word Work*

## A Guide to the Mishnah

## JACOB NEUSNER

continuum
NEW YORK • LONDON

In Memory of
**RAFI ZAIMAN**
**(1968–1980)**

2004

The Continuum International Publishing Group Inc
15 East 26 Street, New York, NY 10010

The Continuum International Publishing Group Ltd
The Tower Building, 11 York Road, London SE1 7NX

Printed in the United States of America

*Library of Congress Cataloging-in-Publication Data*

Neusner, Jacob, 1932-
    Making God's word work : a guide to the Mishnah / Jacob Neusner.
        p. cm.
    Includes bibliographical references.
    ISBN 0-8264-1556-3 (hc : alk. paper) — ISBN 0-8264-1557-1 (pbk. :
    alk. paper)
    1. Mishnah—Criticism, interpretation, etc. I. Title.
    BM497.8.N4764 2004
    296.1'2306-dc22
                                                      2003015423

# Contents

5

# Preface

## A Personal Note

One time [after the destruction of the Temple in August 70] Rabban Yohanan ben Zakkai was going forth from Jerusalem, with R. Joshua following after him. He saw the house of the sanctuary lying in ruins.

R. Joshua said, "Woe is us for this place that lies in ruins, the place in which the sins of Israel used to be atoned for."

He said to him, "My son, do not be distressed. We have another mode of atonement, which is like [atonement through sacrifice], and what is that? It is deeds of loving kindness.

"For so it is said, 'For I desire mercy and not sacrifice, and the knowledge of God rather than burnt offerings' (Hos. 6:6)."

—THE FATHERS ACCORDING TO RABBI NATHAN IV:V.2

A S I WRITE THESE WORDS, I turn seventy-one. I have lived out my allotted seventy years, spending most of my time from age twenty-two on in the study of the Mishnah and the documents that carried it forward. These are the Tosefta, the two Talmuds, and the Midrash compilations of late antiquity, the first six centuries of the Common Era (C.E.). I have walked an absolutely straight path, each step directly linked to the one before and leading to the one following. That choice of a life's work came about as a direct consequence of the formation of a young Jew's consciousness in the shadow of the Holocaust and in the light of the sequential, and consequential, creation of the State of Israel. Mine has been a life lived in response to the age in which it took place.

I celebrated becoming a bar mitzvah at age thirteen on Shemini Aseret of 5706, the 29th of September of 1945. At that very season the concentration camps still harbored Jews, and death factories were just cooling down. The Jewish world had not yet transformed the catastrophe into its mythopoeic event. A whole generation would pass before Jewry in the exilic communities formulated its identification around what came to be called the Holocaust. For me, the murder of the Jews of Europe by Germany and its allies was vastly overshadowed and outmatched by the drama of the creation of the State of Israel and its difficult War of Independence in 1948-1949. As to what only much later, around 1960, we learned to call the *Shoah*, I had only the vaguest sense.

But then, in autumn 1953, I found myself profoundly changed by my initial intellectual encounter with the horror. That took place when, as a student at Oxford, I found at Blackwells in Oxford Gerald Reitlinger's *Final Solution*. It had just appeared. That was in my first weeks there, separated from home and family by three thousand miles of ocean. At that age I would read anything Jewish—from my earliest years, as early as I can remember, I aspired to become a Reform rabbi—and here was something about a subject of acute interest. As a boy, I had heard of the matter, though I knew of no one lost in the calamity. My family had long ago lost all touch with whatever relatives we might have had in Europe. Nor was there anyone I knew in the State of Israel. Now, here I was back in Europe where it had happened.

I spent the next days reading Reitlinger's book and doing little else, and for weeks afterward I found it difficult to speak to any gentiles. I went off as soon as I could to see Germany and meet people who had done such things. But my main perplexity concerned the future: how were we Jews to respond, to rebuild? My reading on the German war against the Jews of Europe, as further memoirs and historical accounts appeared, then led me to ask how prior generations had coped with catastrophe, rebuilding broken hearts and ruined lives. I concluded that the age closest in its principal issues to the one in which I would make my life, an age of reconstruction and renewal, was late antiquity, when the Temple of Jerusalem was destroyed and Jewry reconstructed its life on the foundations of hope. I saw the world as "before" and "after," and I saw myself as one among the fortunate few who had survived to find solace.

It was then that I discovered the question that would define my life: What next? Can there be another chapter in the biography of God's people? I wanted to know, what do people do after the old world ends, in the shadow of disaster, but as survivors? The human situation is captured by Joshua's question to his master, Rabban Yohanan ben Zakkai, what do we do now? Most generations need not ask, because they are nurtured by answers long ago worked out and well established in the social order. But ours did—and does—ask.

To pursue my question, I needed an education in Judaism, which my upbringing in a Reform temple in West Hartford, Connecticut, had not amply provided. To learn how to read the pertinent writings I spent the next six years of study in a U.S. rabbinical school (1954-1960), including a year at the Hebrew University of Jerusalem and at an Israeli yeshivah. In the last of those years, at a nearby university I also completed my doctoral studies in the academic study of religion. For my doctoral dissertation I chose the life of Yohanan ben Zakkai, because he was universally represented as the man who in the summer of 70 C.E. had led the circle of Torah-sages and their disciples out of Jerusalem on the very eve of its destruction. He and his disciples had formed for Judaism the foundations of its long and vital life thereafter. There I found my model for the new age. One thing led to another, and now, five decades later, I am still engaged by the same documents, trying to solve the same problems of rebuilding, reconstruction, and renewal.

Here is what I have found out. In the pages of this book I show how the law, religion, theology, history, and literature of formative Rabbinic Judaism speak a single message. I define that message. But the medium of the Torah's theological message and religious encounter would be, and is, mainly law: norms of conduct realizing norms of conviction.

When, therefore, I say in the opening lines of the Introduction that the Mishnah is the crown jewel of Rabbinic Judaism in its formative age, I maintain a bold claim. It is that that document, in partnership with Scripture, provides a model and a guide for generations beyond catastrophe. It addresses the age of survivors of the end of the old era and the beginning of what we have power to define by ourselves.

God lives in the details of the law of the Torah. The Mishnah does not make its statement in so many words, but in so many deeds of action or restraint. Furthermore, to ask the Mishnah to address the agenda of our issues —those of theodicy, for example, or even of theology, history, and eschatology— is to deny it its own integrity and authentic hearing. The Mishnah's law focuses our attention on other matters altogether, matters of normative behavior and of the theory of Israel's social order lived in the aspect of eternity. We are the ones who intuit the context of calamity and recovery that we think brought into being these long-ago writings, the Torah and the Mishnah alike.

But to reduce the legal system and the social theology set forth by the Mishnah to its historical setting is to misrepresent as a matter of history what was a system of ahistorical, logical thought. The Mishnah aimed at transcending the transient world of time and circumstance. Actions cohered with attitudes, behavior with belief, the whole a statement of the human condition when sanctified in God's model: "You shall be holy, for I the Lord your God am holy" (Lev. 19:2).

And that account of matters describes the intent of the shank of this book, which is to show precisely how theology inheres in law, each component of the religious system of the Halakhah embodied in its full and detailed particularity.

I regard as a singular *Zekhut* that my lifelong friends Rabbi Joel H. and Mrs. Ann Zaiman have accepted this book as a memorial for their son, Rafi. These eighteen chapters plus one are meant as a living monument to his memory.

Jacob Neusner
Bard College
Annandale-on-Hudson, New York, USA

July 28, 2003

# Introduction

I

THE MISHNAH IS THE CROWN JEWEL of Rabbinic Judaism in its formative age, the first six centuries of the Common Era. It also addresses the principal problem of our own time, the age of *Shoah uGevurah*, Holocaust and Empowerment. That is, what can an Israelite do in the age beyond annihilation, an age of restoration and reconstruction? First, not to despair. Second, rebuild, restore, renew. That is what the generations beyond the Holocaust have found themselves called upon to accomplish. And that is what they have done.

It is natural to look for precedents to our circumstance. These come in the law of the Torah. Responding to the critical issues that endure in the life of Israel—the Jewish people—Judaism makes its systematic theological statement through norms of conduct that constitute acted-out statements of conviction. After Scripture, the Mishnah, a philosophical law code of ca. 200 C.E., forms the best example of that fact, and in these pages I show in detail how that is so.

The critical issues of calamity and renewal became acute for Israel in the Land of Israel by reason of historical events. In August of 70 C.E. the ancient Israelite Temple of Jerusalem was destroyed, the climactic event of a great war against Rome. Three generations later, in 132–135, defeat in a second war aimed at restoring the Temple rendered final the consequence of the first one. Responding to that protracted crisis in the established order, the Rabbinic sages undertook a great labor of reconstruction through law (Hebrew: *halakhah*). They set forth a design for the restoration of Israel to its Land, the Levites to their platform, the priests to the altar of the Lord, in rebuilt Jerusalem.

To do so, the Rabbinic sages formed of the laws of the Torah, the ancient Hebrew Scriptures set forth by God to Moses at Sinai, together with laws deriving from tradition, a system of norms embodying a theological system and structure. It was a system to regulate Israel's social order. The Mishnah, a

11

philosophical law code that came to closure in ca. 200 C.E., results from that enterprise of recovery from that crisis and responds to the issues of reconstruction defined by calamity.

Thus the issue of the age in which the Mishnah emerged—the first two centuries of the Common Era—is captured in the story of Yohanan ben Zakkai and Joshua in the ruins of the Temple. As seen some generations later, when *The Fathers according to Rabbi Nathan* came to closure, the critical issue found definition in calamity and rebuilding. In these pages we shall see how the Rabbinic sages form the best guide to the Rabbinic writings of the formative age of normative Judaism.

## II

As we shall see in chapter 1, the Mishnah is represented by Rabbinic theology as the oral part of the Torah revealed by God to Moses at Sinai. That representation is apt, for in an entirely historical framework the Mishnah compares to the written part of the Torah, namely, the Five Books of Moses. Both documents, Scripture and the Mishnah, came to closure in the aftermath of calamity and marked the culmination of the process of reconstruction. What is the basis for such a comparison? The Pentateuch, the Five Books of Moses, came to closure in the aftermath of the destruction of the First Temple in 586 and emerges within the restoration that followed from 530 forward—such is the view that much scholarship maintains. Along these same lines, the Mishnah is the product of the comparable age of catastrophe and an enterprise of reconstruction: "We have another mode of atonement. . . ."

But there is this difference. The first reconstruction produced the Torah, which came to realization in the rebuilt Temple of Jerusalem. The second reconstruction produced the other half of the Torah, the Mishnah, which made its statement not in a concrete building but in intangible patterns governing the lives of the people, Israel,[1] in the Land of Israel. The second time around, that was accomplished even without the restored Temple and its concrete cult of sacrifice.

## III

What makes the Mishnah Judaism's most important document after the Torah? The reason is simple. The Mishnah sets forth the foundations of the law, or Halakhah, of Judaism, defining in the here and now the knowledge of God contained in the divine imperatives of the Torah. That is what I mean by the phrase "making God's word work." Most of the theology of Judaism is

---

[1] Not to be confused with the contemporary State of Israel. Before 1948, "Israel" referred only to the people of Israel, wherever located. That is the usage that governs in all pre-1948 Judaic writings and pertains here.

embodied in the Halakhah. On the categories defined by the Mishnah and on the exposition of the details of the selected legal categories (tractates) rest the Mishnah's representation, recapitulation, and reconstruction of the entire system of law of the Torah. So the Mishnah glistens; its light illuminates; it is the crown jewel of Rabbinic, that is, normative, Judaism in its formative age, the first six centuries of the Common Era.

The Mishnah therefore should not make its mark as just a source of interesting information, nor does its importance depend on its practicality in shaping the everyday life of Judaism. It is a law code in form, a work of philosophy and theology in substance, and a work of natural history in execution. Its medium of expression and mode of thought mark the book as close to unique among philosophical and theological writings. The point is, the Mishnah not only tells people what to do or refrain from doing; Scripture does that on its own. For the practice of Judaism as the law requires, there are later, more broadly authoritative law codes than the Mishnah.

What the Mishnah does is systematize, regularize, and order details of law into a cogent and coherent whole. The Mishnah undertakes to link one deed or act of restraint with some other act of commission or omission and to pattern all of them together into an utterly coherent message. The Mishnah forms of details a cogent statement, and of statements that cohere the Mishnah yields a working system, one that says the same thing about nearly everything. That system turns out to elevate the workaday transactions to which it refers. Making the word of Scripture work means that exchanges in the everyday and here and now realize large theological truths—and not a great many truths at that, but one truth said many times in many forms.

The Mishnah's legal system talks of eternal issues of guilt and innocence, but only as these emerge in everyday transactions. It rules on matters of the clean and the unclean, the holy and the ordinary. It inductively lays out the rules that govern and their exceptions—matters of classification and hierarchy of classes and the norms that pertain. I claim that throughout the laws in all their categories (tractates), beneath the surface of detail is to be discerned a pattern of governing principles. These both define and transcend details and impart coherence to superficial matters. When we penetrate beneath that surface, we see how philosophy and theology animate law and show how the whole mass of diverse rulings forms a coherent account of a well-ordered, sanctified society.

⌐Together with Scripture, the Mishnah through the law it sets forth makes God's word in the Torah work. That law has sustained the Jewish people, corporate Israel wherever located, in ways I shall spell out, with results for all to see. The Mishnah through the law sets forth the lesson to explain why and how that people should live, transcending the end-times designated for it by one generation of enemies after another, enduring not for inchoate eternity but to the specific, particular end-time designated for all humanity by God: "All Israel has a portion in the world to come" (Mishnah-tractate Sanhedrin 10:1).

The upshot is simply put. The law of the Torah as organized, amplified, extended, and then put forth in the Mishnah explains in God's terms, in the Torah's categories of sanctification and salvation, not just how Israel endures but why it should continue to endure, holy to God, unique in humanity.

## IV

There are three responses to the questions, Why claim attention to this presentation of the Mishnah? To whom does the document matter not as a historical curiosity but as the account of the Torah's theological structure and system realized in law?

First, I address students of Rabbinic Judaism, including those who practice Judaism. For them, the answer is, because that structure and system have embodied Judaism until modern times and form the foundation of most Judaic religious systems of modern times. There is no possibility of understanding Judaism without grasping its particular medium of thought and expression, which is through norms of behavior, not only through belief.

Second, I turn to those interested in the history of religion. For them the answer is, because those who wish to understand religion in the social order—whether Islamic, Christian, Judaic, Buddhist, or Hindu—will find in the Mishnah a concrete example of the interplay of theology and law, attitude and action. There is no hope of grasping religion if we know what the books say but do not know how what the faithful do realizes the teachings of the faith. In that context, those who study the formative history of Christianity will gain perspective on the way taken by Christianity from the path followed by Rabbinic Judaism, which clearly attracted the greater part of the people of Israel for whom Christianity and Judaism competed.

Third, among those interested in the history of religions, I address those who find illuminating the comparison of religions and of cognate systems of a single religion. For them, it is because, as I said at the outset, like the Pentateuch, the Mishnah represents Judaism in the very same situation that the faith confronted when the Torah came to closure—the same situation it confronts today in the context of catastrophe and reconstruction. The two foundation documents of Judaism, then, the Torah and the Mishnah, address the same historical crisis of destruction and renewal as pertains in the present moment.

The comparison of Judaic religious systems is uncommon. Most people know the one, the Torah, while few see the other, the Mishnah. If they see it at all, they perceive it as a dry and dull collection of arbitrary laws and nitpicking rules. But the Torah and the Mishnah belong together, sharing a single pattern. The Torah comes to closure in the setting of the return to Zion under Persian sponsorship. The Mishnah marks the restoration of Israel's government in the Land of Israel, the patriarchate of Judah, under Roman sponsorship. Both documents represent the victory over despair, form statements of high hope, and represent epochs bearing obvious, and striking, relevance to the age of the restoration of the Jewish State in the Land of Israel. The relevance to the contemporary age then is self-evident.

But there is a fourth audience, the one formed by those in quest of religious truth and meaning, guidance in theological reflection and spirituality. For them there is a fourth response, which makes urgent confronting the Mishnah at this particular moment in history. The Torah and the Mishnah represent the few generations of Jews who have faced the world that we confront, the world of Shoah uGevurah, Holocaust and Empowerment, destruction and restoration. We do well, then, to take a close look at the record and response to a condition comparable to ours that comes down to us in the Torah. The age that produced as its monument the Mishnah, the oral part of the Torah of Sinai recorded by the Rabbinic sages of the first six centuries C.E., is one such time like ours: an age in which everything changed, yet Israel, God's people, endured.

Like other Jews, I see the world through the aspect of the Holocaust and the renewal of the life of the Jewish people that followed in both the Land and State of Israel and in the Diaspora. No wonder that I identify with the formative age of Rabbinic Judaism and find in its sources wisdom and guidance for the age of reconstruction. The first and most important of those sources beyond Scripture is the Mishnah, the cornerstone of the law of Judaism.

## V

In the pages of this book I shall show how the law of the Mishnah formulated a system and a structure, brought to concrete expression through the detailed rules of the holy way of life lived by the community of Israel, the holy people. This book demonstrates that the principal parts of the Mishnah's law realize a theological system embodied in the norms of the Israelite society contemplated by the Rabbinic sages. That theological system formed the script for conduct in everyday life. In this book, therefore, I read the Mishnah as a document of religion, rather than of law, and identify the theological response to the issues of calamity and renewal that the law realizes in patterns of behavior, as much as theology does in patterns of belief.

This guide to the Mishnah, then, forms a systematic demonstration of how law forms the medium for theological reflection and expression. Specifically, through law (chapters 2 and 3) the Rabbinic sages expressed their conviction that God is one, omnipotent and merciful, and above all just. Through law they conveyed their theology of Israel amid the gentiles. Through law (chapters 4–8) they sorted out relationships between the community—which I call "corporate" or "holy Israel," the entire holy community seen whole—and the individual Israelite. Through law (chapters 9–11) they defined the mediating social institutions, the family and the household, and through law they meditated on the issues of responsibility and intentionality that permeated the life of both. Through law (chapters 12–15) they set forth the reality of God's real and material presence in Israel's social order. Through law (chapters 16–17) they realized their convictions about God's relationship to the individual Israelite and to Israel in history and eternity, encompassing also their beliefs concerning the Messiah.

In chapter 18, I then relate the law to the historical circumstance in which it took shape and spell out the theology that animates the whole legal system, showing why I regard it as a response to the historical crisis of the age—and I add some words on why I believe the Mishnah forms a guide for our response to the crisis and reconstruction that define the challenge to Judaism in our own day.

## VI

I do not merely refer to, but quote at some length, passages of the Mishnah that are essential to my exposition of matters. The argument based on this detailed evidence is not a set of generalities, and the evidence is not merely alluded to, as though it were widely available and part of common knowledge. Asking the reader to work through sometimes tedious and always detailed laws, however, imposes a task some may find onerous. But it is essential to my representation of the Mishnah and of the Judaic religious system put forth through its laws. For three reasons, I beg the reader's indulgence.

First, the Mishnah does not form a familiar chapter in general culture. Few know it at all; fewer still know it sufficiently well to grasp a mere reference to a passage as a clear signal of text and context. Even in the Jewish community, the Mishnah and its companions do not form part of generally known holy books, as do the Five Books of Moses, for example. I should guess that not one percent of Jewish households possess a copy, whether in the original Hebrew or in English. I therefore have chosen not merely to refer to passages but to quote them. Not only so, but I quote many passages at some length, explaining the course of a given passage as I proceed. Readers may find this, if informative, still a bit excessive. The alternative is still less desirable. The result would have been an opaque exposition, referring to texts few know and fewer still read.

Second, my account of the religious world of the Mishnah ("making God's word work") not only derives from particular texts. This picture is built on my reading of them, which, in the aggregate, is not commonplace. My interpretation is everywhere in play. Therefore I owe the reader a clear account not only of what the words of the text say but also of how, in this context, I read them. Only with the texts in hand can readers grasp why I claim that they mean in historical, social context what I say they mean. That is why I make the texts easily accessible to the reader in the pages of this book.

Third, the texts bear the weight of the argument; they form the evidence and presenting them defines my purpose and shapes my statement. This is a book about a principal holy book of a religion that speaks through books. The texts, accordingly, are integral to the religious presentation of the document.

In the context of Judaism, the direct encounter with the texts classified as part of the Torah, even if only through repetition of the words without much amplification, bears religious meaning. It is an expression of spirituality. Even today, entire Judaic religious communities encourage the faithful to recite chapters of the Mishnah as an expression of piety. I should have erred had I not made accessible—in intelligible context—sizable abstracts of the document that forms the center of this study.

My view is that it is better to err on the side of citing too much, rather than deprive interested readers of a direct encounter with the language of the text at hand. That decision reflects my insistence, as a teacher, that my students on their own engage the texts that sustain my presentations to them. Judaism mediates religious encounter through particular language and its use. That is so not only in prayer but also in study of the Torah.

Readers are therefore urged to find the patience to work their way through the nitty-gritty details of the texts adduced here in evidence. Everything should be clear; the information required to make sense of the Mishnah's statements and of my reconstruction of them should be clearly set forth.

In Judaism, God communicates through speech, not only or mainly through action or attitude, and most of God's speech concerns conduct. So God lives in the details—and speaks through them. The theological task then is to master the details—and to discern the encompassing truths embodied in them. Here is the realized Torah of Sinai: how the Israelite acts out convictions concerning what it means to be holy, "For I the Lord your God am holy" (Lev. 19:2).

# Bibliography

I have chosen as much as possible to avoid the use of footnotes, which in the current context serve no necessary purpose. That is because I have translated most of the texts cited here, and most of the research on which this project is built is my own, and the monographic foundations are listed presently. In connection with the following Mishnah-tractates, I draw upon the published work of others, which I sometimes paraphrase. The published work on which I depend is as indicated.

BIKKURIM (CHAPTERS 4 AND 14): Margaret Wenig Rubenstein, "A Commentary on Mishnah-Tosefta Bikkurim Chapters One and Two," in William Scott Green, ed., *Approaches to Ancient Judaism*, III, *Text as Context in Early Rabbinic Literature* (Chico, Calif.: Scholars Press for Brown Judaic Studies, 1981), pp. 47–88; and David Weiner, "A Study of Mishnah Tractate Bikkurim Chapter Three," in ibid., pp. 89–104. The Tosefta translation is by Margaret Wenig Rubenstein for chapter 1; by Richard S. Sarason for chapter 2, 2:1–7; and by David Weiner for chapter 2, 2:8–16—all taken from Jacob Neusner and Richard S. Sarason, eds., *The Tosefta, Translated from the Hebrew*, I, *The First Division (Zeraim)* (New York: Ktav, 1985). For the Yerushalmi, see *The Talmud of the Land of Israel: A Preliminary Translation and Explanation*, Volume 10, *Orlah and Bikkurim*, translated by Jacob Neusner (Chicago: University of Chicago Press, 1991).

SHEBIʿIT (CHAPTERS 6 AND 13): Louis E. Newman, *The Sanctity of the Seventh Year: A Study of Mishnah Tractate Shebiʿit* (Chico, Calif.: Scholars Press for Brown Judaic Studies, 1983); and Alan J. Avery-Peck, *The Talmud of the Land of Israel: A Preliminary Translation and Explanation*, Volume 5, *Shebiʿit*, Jacob Neusner, General Editor (Chicago: University of Chicago Press, 1991).

DEMAʿI (CHAPTER 7): Richard S. Sarason, *A History of the Mishnaic Law of Agriculture*, Section 3, *A Study of Tractate Demaʿi*, Part 1, *Commentary*, Studies in Judaism in Late Antiquity 27, edited by Jacob Neusner (Leiden: E. J. Brill,

1979); and *The Talmud of the Land of Israel: A Preliminary Translation and Explanation*, Volume 3, *Demaᶜi*, translated by Richard S. Sarason (Chicago: University of Chicago Press, 1993).

ᶜORLAH (CHAPTER 13): Howard Essner, "The Mishnah Tractate 'Orlah: Translation and Commentary," in William Scott Green, ed., *Approaches to Ancient Judaism*, III, *Text as Context in Early Rabbinic Literature* (Chico, Calif.: Scholars Press for Brown Judaic Studies, 1981), pp. 105-48; and, for the Yerushalmi, see my *The Talmud of the Land of Israel: A Preliminary Translation and Explanation*, Volume 10, *ᶜOrlah. Bikkurim* (Chicago: University of Chicago Press, 1991).

KILAYIM (CHAPTER 13): Irving J. Mandelbaum, *A History of the Mishnaic Law of Agriculture: Kilayim* (Chico, Calif.: Scholars Press for Brown Judaic Studies, 1982); and Irving J. Mandelbaum, *The Talmud of the Land of Israel: A Preliminary Translation and Explanation*, Volume 4, *Kilayim*, Jacob Neusner, General Editor (Chicago: University of Chicago Press, 1990).

MAᶜASEROT (CHAPTER 13): M. Jaffee, *The Mishnah's Theology of Tithing* (Chico, Calif.: Scholars Press for Brown Judaic Studies, 1982).

HALLAH (CHAPTER 13): Abraham Havivi, "Mishnah Hallah Chapter One: Translation and Commentary," in William Scott Green, ed., *Approaches to Ancient Judaism*, III, *Text as Context in Early Rabbinic Literature* (Chico, Calif.: Scholars Press, 1981), pp. 149-85; Jacob Neusner, *The Talmud of the Land of Israel: A Preliminary Translation and Explanation*, Volume 9, *Hallah*, With an Introduction by Abraham Havivi (Chicago: University of Chicago Press, 1991).

MAᶜASER SHENI (CHAPTER 14): Peter J. Haas, *A History of the Mishnaic Law of Agriculture: Tractate Maᶜaser Sheni* (Chico, Calif.: Scholars Press for Brown Judaic Studies, 1980); and for the Yerushalmi, *The Talmud of the Land of Israel: A Preliminary Translation and Explanation*, Volume 8, *Maᶜaser Sheni*, translated by Roger Brooks (Chicago: University of Chicago Press, 1993).

## TRANSLATIONS OF THE MISHNAH

The translation of the Mishnah reproduced here is my own. There are many others. That is because all translations of the Talmud of Babylonia and of the Talmud of the Land of Israel include translations of the Mishnah-tractates to which that Talmud provides a commentary. In addition, the two systematic, complete translations of the Mishnah into English are H. Danby, *The Mishnah*

(Oxford: Oxford University Press, 1933), and this writer's *The Mishnah: A New Translation* (New Haven: Yale University Press, 1987). The Hebrew text most commonly consulted is H. Albeck, *Shisha Sidré Mishnah* (Tel Aviv and Jerusalem, 1954-58), in six volumes. I followed it in my translation, checking it against the more important manuscript testimonies.

The definitive study of the text of the Mishnah is J. N. Epstein, *Introduction to the Text of the Mishnah* (in Hebrew; Jerusalem: Magnes Press of the Hebrew University, 1948, 1964). No definitive Hebrew text for the entire Mishnah has ever been published. But collections of manuscript variants have been made.

### Further Bibliography on the Mishnah

Baruch M. Bokser, Joel Gereboff, William Scott Green, Gary G. Porton, and Charles Primus, "Bibliography on the Mishnah," in J. Neusner, ed., *Study of Ancient Judaism* (New York: Ktav, 1979), 1:37-54.

John Bowker, *The Targums and Rabbinic Literature: An Introduction to Jewish Interpretations of Scripture* (Cambridge: Cambridge University Press, 1969), pp. 46-48 (the Mishnah's origin in exegesis), pp. 53-61.

Abraham Goldberg, "The Mishna-a Study Book of Halakha" (origins and development, R. Aqiba and his pupils, the four layers, principles of editing, arrangement, the more important teachers, language, text, reduction to writing, authority, bibliography, manuscripts—by Michael Krupp), in Shmuel Safrai, ed.; Peter J. Tomson, executive editor, *The Literature of the Sages*, First Part, *Oral Tora, Halakha, Mishna, Tosefta, Talmud, External Tractates*, Compendia Rerum Iudaicarum ad Novum Testamentum, Section 2, The Literature of the Jewish People in the Period of the Second Temple and the Talmud (Assen/Maastricht: Van Gorcum; Philadelphia: Fortress Press, 1987), pp. 211-62.

Hyam Maccoby, *Early Rabbinic Writings* (Cambridge: Cambridge University Press, 1988), Volume 3 of *Cambridge Commentaries on Writings of the Jewish and Christian World, 200 BC to AD 200*, edited by P. R. Ackroyd, A. R. C. Leaney, and J. W. Packer, pp. 30-35, selected passage, pp. 49-133.

Jacob Neusner, "The Modern Study of the Mishnah," in J. Neusner, ed., *The Study of Ancient Judaism*, 2 volumes (New York: Ktav, 1981), pp. 3-26.

H. L. Strack and Günter Stemberger, *Introduction to the Talmud and Midrash* (Minneapolis: Fortress Press, 1992), translated by Markus Bockmuehl, pp. 119-66: bibliography in general and by tractates; explanation of terms; survey of contents; structure of the Mishnah; origin of the Mishnah; biblical interpretation as the origin of the Mishnah; prehistory of the Mishnah; redaction of the Mishnah; text: manuscripts, editions, translations; the interpretation of the Mishnah.

Ephraim E. Urbach, "The Mishnah," in *Encyclopaedia Judaica* 12:93–109: the sources of the Mishnah, how the Mishnah was produced and arranged, how the Mishnah was published (orally or in writing), the division of the Mishnah, the text of the Mishnah, editions, commentaries, and translations.

## Manuscript Variants

With the cooperation of the Bibliotheca Apostolica (Vatican), the Bibliothèque nationale de France (Paris), the British Library (London), the Hungarian Academy of Sciences (Budapest), and the Valmadonna Trust (London), the Jewish National and University Library at Hebrew University has published on the Internet, at http://jnul.huji.ac.il/dl/talmud/index.htm, a set of facsimile reproductions of the Kaufman Mishnah manuscript and manuscripts of several chapters of the Talmud Bavli. This facilitates some ready comparison of early sources for variant readings.

## Prior Books of Mine that Deal with the Mishnah and with the Theology of Rabbinic Judaism

This book depends on the results of a variety of prior monographs of mine, each of which encompasses its own bibliography as well.

*The Economics of the Mishnah* (Chicago: University of Chicago Press, 1989).
*The Four Stages of Rabbinic Judaism* (London: Routledge, 2000). E-book edition, London: Taylor and Francis, 2001.
*The Halakhah of the Oral Torah: A Religious Commentary: Introduction*, and Volume 1, Part 1, *Between Israel and God: Faith, Thanksgiving: Tractate Berakhot. Enlandisement. Tractates Kilayim, Shebiʿit, and ʿOrlah* (Atlanta: Scholars Press for South Florida Studies in the History of Judaism, 1997). [The remainder of this project, originally planned for twenty-four volumes, was recast as *The Halakhah: An Encyclopaedia of the Law of Judaism*.]
*The Halakhah: An Encyclopaedia of the Law of Judaism*, Brill Reference Library of Ancient Judaism (Leiden: E. J. Brill, 1999), Volume 1, *Between Israel and God*, Part A, *Faith, Thanksgiving, Enlandisement: Possession and Partnership*; Volume 2, *Between Israel and God*, Part B, *Transcendent Transactions: Where Heaven and Earth Intersect*; Volume 3, *Within Israel's Social Order*; Volume 4, *Inside the Walls of the Israelite Household*, Part A, *At the Meeting of Time and Space. Sanctification in the Here and Now: The Table and the Bed. Sanctification and the Marital Bond. The Desacralization of the Household: The Bed*; Volume 5, *Inside the Walls of the Israelite Household*, Part B, *The*

*Desacralization of the Household: The Table. Foci, Sources, and Dissemination of Uncleanness. Purification from the Pollution of Death.*

*The Handbook of Rabbinic Theology: Language, System, Structure* (Leiden: E. J. Brill, 2003). Epitomization of *Theological Grammar of the Oral Torah*, *Theology of the Oral Torah: Revealing the Justice of God*, and *Theology of the Halakhah.*

*A History of the Mishnaic Law of Purities; A History of the Mishnaic Law of Holy Things; A History of the Mishnaic Law of Appointed Times; A History of the Mishnaic Law of Women; and A History of the Mishnaic Law of Damages*, 43 volumes (Leiden: E. J. Brill, 1975–84). Provides a systematic translation of the second through the sixth divisions of the Mishnah and the Tosefta, side by side, showing the relationships of the two documents, and descriptions of the history and system of the Mishnah pertaining to its principal categories.

*Judaism as Philosophy: The Method and Message of the Mishnah* (Columbia: University of South Carolina Press, 1991).

*Judaism: The Evidence of the Mishnah* (Chicago: University of Chicago Press, 1981; paperback edition, 1984; second printing, 1985; third printing, 1986; second edition, augmented, Atlanta: Scholars Press for Brown Judaic Studies, 1987). Hebrew translation: *Hayyahadut le'edut hammishnah* (Tel Aviv: Sifriat Poalim, 1987). Italian translation: *Il Giudaismo nella testimonianza della Mishnah*, trans. Giorgio Volpe (Bologna: Centro editoriale Dehoniane, 1995).

*The Midrash: An Encyclopaedia of Bible-Interpretation in Formative Judaism*, edited with Alan J. Avery-Peck, 2 volumes, Brill Reference Library of Ancient Judaism (Leiden: E. J. Brill, 2003).

*The Mishnah in Contemporary Study*, 2 volumes, edited with Alan J. Avery-Peck (Leiden: E. J. Brill, 2002, 2003).

*The Mishnah: Religious Perspectives* (Leiden: E. J. Brill, 1999; paperback reprint, 2002).

*The Mishnah: Social Perspectives* (Leiden: E. J. Brill, 2002; paperback reprint, 2002).

*The Perfect Torah* (Leiden: E. J. Brill, 2003).

*The Presence of the Past, the Pastness of the Present: History, Time, and Paradigm in Rabbinic Judaism* (Bethesda: CDL Press, 1996).

*Rabbinic Political Theory: Religion and Politics in the Mishnah* (Chicago: University of Chicago Press, 1991).

*Scripture and the Generative Premises of the Halakhah: A Systematic Inquiry*, Academic Studies in Ancient Judaism (Binghamton: Global Publications, 2000), I, *Halakhah Based Principally on Scripture and Halakhic Categories Autonomous of Scripture*; II, *Scripture's Topics Derivatively Amplified in the Halakhah*; III, *Scripture's Topics Independently Developed in the Halakhah: From the Babas through Miqvaot*; IV, *Scripture's Topics Independently Devel-*

oped in the Halakhah: From Moed Qatan through Zebahim (second printing, revised and condensed: under the title *The Torah and the Halakhah: The Four Relationships* [Lanham: University Press of America, 2003]).

*The Social Teaching of Rabbinic Judaism*, Brill Reference Library of Ancient Judaism (Leiden: E. J. Brill, 2001), I. *Corporate Israel and the Individual Israelite*; II, *Between Israelites*; III, *God's Presence in Israel*.

*The Theological Grammar of the Oral Torah* (Binghamton: Dowling College Press/Global Publications of Binghamton University [SUNY], 1999), I, *Vocabulary: Native Categories*; II, *Syntax: Connections and Constructions*; III, *Semantics: Models of Analysis, Explanation and Anticipation* (epitomized in *Handbook of Rabbinic Theology*, above).

*The Theology of the Halakhah*, Brill Reference Library of Ancient Judaism (Leiden: E. J. Brill, 2001; epitomized in *Handbook of Rabbinic Theology*, above).

*The Theology of the Oral Torah: Revealing the Justice of God* (Kingston/Montreal: McGill-Queen's University Press; Ithaca: Cornell University Press, 1999). Also *Rabbinic Judaism: Theological System* (Boston/Leiden: E. J. Brill, 2003) (condensation of *The Theology of the Oral Torah*).

# The Mishnah
# in Religious Context

# 1 Making God's Word Work

## *Tractate Abot*

THE MISHNAH SETS IN ORDER the details of what we do in the here and now, forming of them a pattern for a life that reaches out to God. The Mishnah shows how to meet God even—or especially—in small gestures, in the corners of community life and of individual conduct and consciousness. The Mishnah lays out in practical terms how the spirit of God animates the details of the good, the Godly, life lived by the community of Israel, the people of the Torah. That is because when we reflect on the Mishnah's messages, we become more thoughtful, more alert, better able to live a life of well-considered action.

Stated simply, the Mishnah is the second most important book in Judaism, coming after Scripture alone. Through detailed law, the Mishnah explains how Jews form the holy community of Israel to which God speaks in the Torah. It provides models of how to carry out Scripture's imperatives to form a "kingdom of priests and a holy people" (Exod. 19:6). The Mishnah explains how Israel, the holy people, can form the community of those "in whose midst God dwells" (Exod. 29:45). Scripture defines the goal; the Mishnah's law sets forth the way. Scripture provides details; the Mishnah organizes the details into coherent topical expositions. Through the Mishnah, the law of the Torah makes a coherent statement. So it is fair to say that the Mishnah makes God's word work.

### The Second Most Important Book of Judaism, after Scripture

That may seem a rather extravagant claim for a book that does not occupy the center of the Judaic conversation in the way Scripture does. After all, declaiming Scripture forms the centerpiece of synagogue worship; the Mishnah has no corresponding role. To be sure, chapters of the Mishnah-tractate Abot, the Mishnah's introduction and initial apologetic, which we meet in this chapter, are studied in some synagogues in a cycle lasting over a few weeks. But few Jews outside the circle of the faithful know, and fewer still acknowledge, the centrality of the Mishnah and its laws.

The upshot is simple. Everyone engaged by Jewish culture knows that

Judaism is the religion of the Torah. Only people of some education hear about the Mishnah, and among them fewer still know why the Mishnah and its laws make a difference. So too, many study Scripture, but only rarely do people open the Mishnah. Even the adult study courses of many synagogues rarely penetrate beneath the surface of the Mishnah. Recently a synagogue organization published a Jewish calendar illustrated by passages of the Mishnah without a word of explanation of how these passages speak to us or even relate (if they do relate) to the month in which they are cited. Hung on display on the wall, the facts of the Mishnah—its tractates (discourses or treatises) and topics—seem merely decorative. Such knowledge without understanding characterizes even those who can recite Mishnah-tractates from memory but do not derive useful knowledge from them.

The traits of the Mishnah's language and contents of law explain why the Mishnah seldom wins immediate recognition when people speak of Judaism. The Mishnah is not a document you can just open and read, the way you can open and read a narrative of Scripture or a Hasidic story or a crystal-clear passage of Maimonides. The Mishnah's messages lie hidden beneath the surface. The Mishnah, after all, is a code of laws, and a code of laws does not yield easy reading. Nor do its laws—descriptions of the normative conduct pertaining in large part to another place, another time—seem to relate to our here and now, for while some deal with actions we still perform, much of the Mishnah concerns matters that simply do not relate to the contemporary world of Judaism. They are—and many were even in the time the Mishnah took shape—matters of theory, not fact.

The Mishnah collects centuries of traditions going all the way back to Sinai and continuing to the time when the Mishnah itself was closed, about 200 C.E., more than one hundred years after the destruction of the Temple of Jerusalem in 70 C.E. So its contents on the surface speak about an age remote from our own times, and many of its topics have no bearing on the world we inhabit. But the Mishnah's laws concern a world that did not exist in 200. For example, nearly a quarter of the Mishnah addresses issues of ritual impurity and purity, only a few of which relate to contemporary practice of the law then or now; and a sixth of the Mishnah contains rules for the conduct of the Temple and its offerings, which even when the Mishnah was published were matters of theory, not everyday practice. Another sixth deals with the conduct of agriculture in the Land of Israel. More than half of the Mishnah therefore relates to an ideal community of Israel farming the Land of Israel and worshiping at the Temple of Jerusalem—a world much prayed for but quite unrealistic even in 200 C.E. Yet the Mishnah, whole and complete, is the second most important book of Judaism.

## The Priority of the Mishnah

There are two reasons for the priority of the Mishnah over all other holy writings of Judaism except for the written Torah: the one narrative, the other substantive. The narrative reason for the Mishnah's importance appears in the story that the Mishnah tells about itself. Since we naturally respond to narrative and see truth in tales, that story supplies the laws of the Mishnah with a context and position that appeal to contemporary sensibility.

The story is told about the Mishnah that when God gave the Torah to Moses at Sinai, it was in two parts. One part was written, and that is the Torah set forth in the scrolls declaimed in synagogue worship and studied as the record of God's instruction. The other part was not committed to writing, but was formulated and handed on in memory, then passed down from one generation to the next orally. The Mishnah recorded in writing the spoken oral part of the Torah—the oral tradition of Sinai. It began a tradition of recording the oral teachings. We shall presently come back to encounter in detail the Mishnah's own narrative of its origin and importance.

The substantive reason is that the Mishnah is essential to the well-examined life of Judaism because the Mishnah shows us not only what to do but how to think about what we do. It sets forth laws, some of them practical, most of them not, but it does so in such a way that the details form a coherent whole. That matters because, when the Mishnah's detailed laws are properly grasped, they turn out to constitute a philosophy of life, a mode of thought about the everyday. That philosophy, moreover, gives us a guide not only to how we should think in abstract terms but also to how to reflect on what we should do—and everyday action is the ultimate focus and goal of the Torah. Accordingly, in dialogue with the Mishnah, thinking as the Mishnah teaches us how to think, we ask more penetrating questions than otherwise we could. In dialogue with the Mishnah we produce answers that change the way we see life and act in everyday matters. That is because, while the Mishnah speaks of small things, little gestures, norms of local conduct, it shows how details come together to form a grand design—the Torah's design, systematically recapitulated.

Studying the Mishnah represents the climactic step in studying the Torah, because it shows how the Rabbinic sages turn aspiration into action. How does the Mishnah make God's word given in the Scripture work in concrete terms? The Torah commands, "Choose life" (Deut. 30:19), and the Mishnah lays out the choices. The Torah demands, "Seek justice" (Deut. 16:20), and the Mishnah defines justice in humble exchanges of the workaday world. The prophet declares, "The righteous person will live by his faith" (Hab. 2:4), and the Mishnah specifies the meaning of true trust in God. Above all, as we shall see later in this chapter, Scripture says, "You will love your neighbor as yourself" (Lev. 19:18), and the Mishnah defines what loving the neighbor as oneself requires in attitude and action.

Where Scripture sets the principle in general terms of ideals, the Mishnah lays out the particularities of behavior and belief. These concrete instructions on how to act—these *laws*—make the ideals a matter of practical conduct. The Mishnah turns Scripture's moral and theological imperatives into laws that everyone can obey. Studying the Mishnah yields not only knowledge of laws but also access to their pattern and hence their purpose.

Why does patterning matter? This capacity to speak about universal principles through small details renders the law of the Mishnah boundlessly portable. For the universals embodied in detail pertain to transactions in worlds other than the immediate world of the Rabbinic sages of the Mishnah. That is the function of a well-ordered system of law: to realize philosophy in concrete ways and, in the case of a religiously based system of law such as that of the Mishnah and of the Judaism that flows from it, to translate theology into action. The Mishnah and the legal system animating it provided the community of Israel with the ability continually to reproduce itself in succeeding ages and in locations distant from the time and place of its origin. It could reconstruct its life patterns in one culture after another and in one region, territory, and locale after another.

Because of its legal foundations in the Mishnah, Judaism was and remains the most universal, the most fungible, of religions. One can form a community of Judaism along the lines set forth by the Mishnah's law in any language and in any political system that tolerates difference. No one language—not Russian, English, Spanish, or Yiddish—enjoys priority, so long as access to classical Hebrew sources is sustained. No one region is required as the setting, apart from the Land of Israel in the Messiah's time. A community of Jews sent off to plant a colony on Mars would and could replicate the main lines of structure and order—not to mention religious practice—familiar from Judaism anywhere on earth. The Mishnah's law focuses on what pertains everywhere and all the time: the essentials of relationships, not ephemeral issues of culture and custom.

Why then does the Mishnah matter to Israel the holy community (as the Jewish people is called in the Mishnah), and why to the individual Israelite (as the Jew is called in the Mishnah)? To the community of holy Israel the law of the Mishnah matters because that community defines itself not only by what people profess but by how they practice their professions, how they conduct their everyday affairs. The Torah defines Israel at Sinai, calling it a mixed multitude in the wilderness. To form them into a community of faith, the Torah commands that Israel make of itself a "kingdom of priests and a holy people." The law of the Torah, articulated by the Mishnah, explains in detail the regulations that sanctify. To the individual Israelite it matters because through the laws and commandments of the Torah the inner spirit is changed. The commandments are meant to purify humanity, so the Rabbinic reading of Genesis says explicitly:

**GENESIS RABBAH XLIV:I.1**

"After these things the word of the Lord came to Abram in a vision" (Gen. 15:1):

"As for God, his way is perfect, the word of the Lord is tried" (2 Sam. 22:31).

If his way is perfect, how much the more so is he!

Rab said, "[Since the word for 'tried' yields the meaning 'purify,' we may conclude that] the religious duties were given only to purify humanity. For what difference does it make to the Holy One, blessed be He, if one slaughters a beast at the throat or at the nape of the neck? Lo, the sole purpose is to purify humanity.

So too: "the All-Merciful craves the heart" (Bavli Sanhedrin 106b).

The Mishnah then organizes and amplifies the laws that God revealed to Moses at Sinai. For example, Moses says, "You shall be holy, for I the Lord your God am holy" (Lev. 19:2), and forthwith lays out laws governing practical matters: respect for parents, care for the poor, not stealing, not dealing deceitfully, not defrauding someone, not insulting the deaf, not hating kinsfolk—above all, "loving your neighbor as yourself." The Mishnah's law spells out what care for the poor requires and defines what not stealing means—and how one makes amends if one has stolen. The Mishnah does this work of re-presenting the law of the Torah by collecting the details of laws and forming of them large topical expositions. For example, it treats support for the poor in a single coherent unit. It spells out the responsibilities and rights of private property in a massive exposition of civil law. These expositions of large topics set forth the governing principles by specifying concrete cases. So the Mishnah turns the Torah's narratives and rules into an encompassing program of rules applicable everywhere, for private life and public policy in holy Israel.

### The Universe in a Grain of Sand

To understand the inner traits of the Mishnah properly and so to appreciate its commanding voice, we have to see the work whole. Then we perceive it as a sequence of topical expositions, each with its own clear purpose. Each chapter of this book does exactly that, beginning with the exposition of God's absolute justice in the presentation of the (superficially unjust) laws of Numbers 5 governing the wife accused of adultery (chapter 2). That legal exposition turns into a huge and wide-ranging demonstration of the perfect justice of God. For another example, as we shall see at some length, the Mishnah collects the laws of torts and damages. In presenting those laws, the document expounds a doctrine that both dwells upon, and also vastly transcends, the specificities of those laws. It spells out the meaning of responsibility and negotiates the effects of intentionality. In thus collecting and organizing the topics of the laws into systematic expositions, the Mishnah treats profound questions, the answers to which pertain to many topics, not only the one that is presented in context. So the law shades over into a philosophy of life such as I invoked at the outset.

That capacity to set forth a transcendent message out of the display of concrete and near-at-hand details explains the power of the Mishnah to shape mind and imagination, hope and aspiration. It places on display the capacity of ordinary people living workaday lives to participate in the grand enterprise of sanctification through law that the Torah sets forth. Thus the Mishnah, though a law code, does much more than collect, arrange, and amplify details of laws—though it does those things. The Mishnah takes the imperatives of

Scripture and organizes them into comprehensive, encompassing demonstrations of religious truth: theology that is practical and practiced as a legal construction of norms. The Mishnah makes the details all fit together into a coherent whole, forms them into a system and a structure for a holy society.

## Turning Facts into Truth

Why is it important to make details compose a coherent picture, to turn facts into truth, as the Mishnah does with the facts of the law of the Torah? People think that what we lack is information, and they bemoan their—or others'—ignorance. But information on its own answers no urgent questions, solves no pressing problems. Only information that makes a point, that shapes our consciousness and conscience, makes a difference. So the priority of the Mishnah, after Scripture and in response to Scripture, rests on its power to form particularities into patterns. It shows the way to transform laws into social principles. These then bear concrete consequences beyond the bounds of mere information. Accordingly, the Mishnah turns out to say the same few things about a great many things. It has the power to find the whole in the parts, the universe in a grain of sand. Then as reworked by the Mishnah into patterns of laws, the conduct of everyday life realizes in the here and now the great moral and theological truths that, in narrative, commandment, and exhortation, Scripture sets forth from Sinai. Once more, therefore, we can say, the Mishnah makes God's word work.

The Mishnah's special power, then, is the capacity to show how coherent statements of law can stand for more than themselves. That power to treat small things as metaphors for large matters is what poetry does. The Mishnah captures the depths of the human condition in slight gestures and fragile words, turning the pathos of the particular into the power of a pattern. That patterning is what music does with sound, dance with gesture, and art with artifacts. No wonder, then, that the very language of the Mishnah is patterned, with the fixed forms guiding us to the meaning of what is said. But the art of the Mishnah differs from poetry, music, dance, and visual arts, because it speaks to an entire society, while the others speak to the heart, the soul, and the eye of the individual. The Mishnah speaks specifically to the community of Israel, the holy community.

What is at stake in the laws of the Mishnah, and why do they form a social imperative of Judaism? The Torah states that at Sinai God called into being a moral entity responsible for its individual constituents, a community that encompasses individual persons. It forms of them a people unique among nations by reason of its responsibility: each for himself or herself, but also all for each and each for all. That is what the election of Israel means: "You alone have I known among all the families of humanity, therefore I will visit on you all your iniquities" (Amos 3:2). Individuals bear the burden of their own failures; and the community for those of individuals viewed as a whole. That is why on the Day of Atonement everyone says the collective confession, even though not everyone has committed the sins that are listed: "For the sin that we have sinned against you by this and by that. . . ."

So the power of the Mishnah to form a system of law out of a corpus of laws, to make a coherent statement out of a mass of details, matches the pathos of Israel, a collection of individuals who are also all together subject to the divine imperative: "You shall be holy, for I the Lord your God am holy" (Lev. 19:2). That commandment is spoken in the plural—you, all of you, all together, all at once, saying in one voice, "We shall do and we shall obey" (Exod. 24:7).

### The Story That the Mishnah Tells about Itself: Tractate Abot

So much for the substantive reason for my claim that, after Scripture, the Mishnah is the most important book of Judaism. What about the story that conveys the same message? How does a law book qualify as a document of religion, a holy writing, as the Mishnah surely does?

The story is a narrative of origins. A law code must have a claim to authority to explain why people should willingly conform to the rules. For the Mishnah that claim is framed in the story that the Mishnah tells about itself, a story found in a tractate called Abot, the "Fathers," or the "Founders," which serves as an introduction to the Mishnah. Its collected wise sayings concerning issues of theology and virtue, study of the Torah, and right attitude and action toward one's fellows reached closure about a generation after the conclusion of the Mishnah itself. Thus, making an educated guess, if the Mishnah was closed in ca. 200 C.E., then tractate Abot concluded in ca. 250 C.E. But tractate Abot always appears in editions of the Mishnah and serves as a kind of prologue to it.

Tractate Abot records the origins of the Mishnah's traditions in a chain of tradition beginning with God's revelation of the Torah to Moses at Sinai, by specifying the Mishnah's pedigree, the chain of tradition commencing with Moses and continuing through specified figures who received and handed on that same tradition. The list of names ends up with sages important in the Mishnah itself. Implicitly, then, the rulings of the Mishnah's own sages derive from a chain of receiving and handing on laws and teachings that began with God's revelation to Moses at Sinai. Hence—so the list we shall consider implies —the laws of the Mishnah come from sages who through a process of discipleship transmit an essential part of the revelation of the Torah at Sinai. The names of the authorities in the chain of tradition by implication situate the Mishnah *within* the Torah, or Instruction, revealed at Sinai.

The implicit story of the origins of the Mishnah at Sinai is told in the opening chapter of tractate Abot. At first glance, this chapter is basically a list of authorities and their wise sayings. In the case of each link in the chain of tradition, however, two facts register. First, the named authority received the

Torah from a specific master, and, second, each handed it on to a specific disciple. So a chain of tradition—receiving, handing on—links generations of sages to Sinai.

Before we examine the text itself, let us consider its context. When does tractate Abot take shape, and what do we know about the authorities it cites? Who are these authorities, and what was the basis for their prominence in the community of Israel in the Land of Israel? The answer starts with the person of the Patriarch, or Nasi, who governed the Jews of Palestine and who sponsored and is credited with producing the Mishnah itself. The Nasi, or Patriarch, responsible for the Mishnah was Judah the Patriarch, who held office in the decades before and after 200 C.E.

At the time that the Mishnah was completed, in ca. 200 C.E., the Jews in the Land of Israel were governed by Rome through a Jewish agency headed by the Nasi. He handled the many matters that the Roman imperial government preferred to leave in the hands of local authorities, including most of the affairs of everyday life in the Jewish community. The Nasi claimed to have descended from Hillel, the great first-century C.E. authority; moreover, the family of Hillel claimed descent from the house of David.

Who are the other names on the list of the links in this chain of tradition of Sinai? They are the Rabbinic sages upon whom the Nasi relied as authorities of the law of Judaism—*hakhamim* in Hebrew. On the side of the sages, what was the basis of their authority? It was not descent from the Davidic household but knowledge of the Torah or Sinai. The Rabbinic sages' authority depended not only on political appointment by the Nasi but, in their view, on their knowledge of the Torah of Moses at Sinai.

In the opening chapter of tractate Abot, an unbroken chain of tradition is traced from Moses forward to the first and second centuries C.E., ending with the names of the Patriarch as well as of the leading sages. So the two sources of authority over the Jewish people in the Land of Israel at the time of the completion of the Mishnah—the Patriarchate and the Rabbinic sages—are joined together. Each finds its place in the chain of tradition stemming from Sinai.

We come to the story implicit in the chain of tradition with which tractate Abot commences its account. The opening part of the list at the beginning of the chapter is the key to all the rest: Moses received the Torah at Sinai and handed it on to Joshua, and thence to Joshua and elders, then the prophets, onward to the men of the great assembly. This simple statement carries us through an obscure period. We have very little solid information on the identities or the dates of those who are listed, but the names themselves make a statement. To the various authorities on the list are attributed wise sayings, Torah-sayings. *These are not verses of Scripture*, but they still form links in the chain of the Torah commencing at Sinai. So teachings revealed by God to Moses at Sinai included more than those in the written Torah. There is an additional, oral or memorized Torah given by God to Moses at Sinai, and the

Rabbinic sages form links in the chain of tradition extending backward to Sinai.

We shall explore the implications of that fact in a moment. First let us examine the text.

**TRACTATE ABOT CHAPTER 1**

1:1 Moses received (Hebrew root: QBL, thus *qabbalah*, tradition) the Torah at Sinai and handed it on (Hebrew root: MSR, thus *masoret*, tradition) to Joshua, Joshua to elders, and elders to prophets.

And prophets handed it on to the men of the great assembly.

They said three things:

(1) "Be prudent in judgment.

(2) "Raise up many disciples.

(3) "Make a fence for the Torah."

So far we are on familiar ground, since Scripture identifies Moses, Joshua, and those who continued the governance of Israel, here called "elders," onward to the prophets. The latter prophets handed the tradition on to "the men of the great assembly," who are not otherwise identified except by their saying. What is important in this saying is that here, at the very early links of the chain of tradition, the work of forming those links is described. The three elements concern making judgments, teaching disciples, and protecting the boundaries of the law. The teachings therefore describe the future of Rabbinic Judaism, with its stress on the Rabbinic sage as authority, teacher, and master of the law of the Torah. Prudence, provision for coming generations, and protection of the Torah by secondary provisions to avoid primary violations—these prefigure the program of the Rabbinic sages later on, as the Mishnah itself will show us.

1:2 Simeon the Righteous was one of the last survivors of the great assembly.

He would say: "On three things does the world stand:

(1) "On the Torah,

(2) "and on the Temple service,

(3) "and on deeds of loving kindness."

1:3 Antigonos of Sokho received [the Torah] from Simeon the Righteous. . . .

He would say,

(1) "Do not be like servants who serve the master on condition of receiving a reward,

(2) "but [be] like servants who serve the master not on condition of receiving a reward.

(3) "And let the fear of Heaven be upon you."

Simeon the Righteous was high priest of the Temple. Destroyed by the Babylonians in 586 B.C.E., the Temple had been rebuilt in the time of Cyrus by the Israelites who returned to Zion when permitted by the Persian conquers of the Babylonians. Simeon's program contrasts with that of the men of the great assembly, with their stress on Torah-study and application. Now the emphasis is on the Torah, along with the Temple service and deeds of loving-kindness. Study of the Torah, sacrifice to God, and generosity toward others form the principal parts of his Judaic system.

Antigonos stresses right attitude: sincerity in serving God, reverence, fear of God. Here again, we are struck by the capacity of each of the participants in a chain of tradition to say something fresh and innovative. While all participate and join the chain by serving as a disciple to a prior master, each makes his own contribution to the tradition, which is not only renewed but made new generation by generation.

From this point, we come upon five pairs of authorities. One of each pair is held to be the *Nasi*, or Patriarch, the other the *Av bet din*, head of the sages' court. Here is where the Patriarchate begins to register its presence on the list. Each is given a set of sayings, which speak for themselves by their diversity. What concerns us is only the list of names, so we shall ignore what is attributed to them:

> 1:4 Yosé b. Yoezer of Seredah and Yosé b. Yohanan of Jerusalem received [it] from them.
>
> Yosé b. Yoezer says
>
> 1:5 Yosé b. Yohanan of Jerusalem says
>
> 1:6 Joshua b. Perahiah and Nittai the Arbelite received [it] from them.
>
> Joshua b. Perahiah says
>
> 1:7 Nittai the Arbelite says
>
> 1:8 Judah b. Tabbai and Simeon b. Shatah received [it] from them.
>
> Judah b. Tabbai says
>
> 1:9 Simeon b. Shatah says
>
> 1:10 Shemaiah and Abtalion received [it] from them.
>
> Shemaiah says
>
> 1:11 Abtalion says
>
> 1:12 Hillel and Shammai received [it] from them.

The first four pairs—the two Yosés, Joshua and Nittai, Judah and Simeon, Shemaiah and Abtalion—name sages and attribute specific sayings. They lead us to two of the greatest figures in the history of Judaism, Hillel and Shammai. At this point we enter the pages of the Mishnah itself, since Shammai and Hillel play important roles in the exposition of the laws of the Mishnah. Moreover, they founded houses, or schools, the traditions of which form the foundation of the law of some of the tractates of the Mishnah, the House of Shammai and the House of Hillel.

Tractate Abot does not tell us much about the sages it names, only giving their wise sayings. But other Rabbinic sources provide stories about Shammai and Hillel, comparing and contrasting them. The most famous ends in the climactic saying of Hillel about what is at the heart and soul of the Torah. It is worth turning aside from the Mishnah for a moment and considering the moral context in which its sages are presented by the later Rabbinic writings. Here is the most famous of them all, the story of how the entire Torah was taught by Hillel while he was standing on one foot. The story occurs in the Talmud of Babylonia, a commentary to thirty-seven tractates of the Mishnah's sixty-two tractates produced in Babylonia under Iranian rule and completed in ca. 600 C.E. The story captures the golden rule based on Leviticus 19:18: "You shall love your neighbor as yourself." Hillel frames the rule in negative terms, "Don't do to your fellow what you don't want done to yourself":

### TALMUD OF BABYLONIA TRACTATE SHABBAT 30B-31A/2:5 I.12

I.12 A. There was another case of a gentile who came before Shammai. He said to him, "Convert me on the stipulation that you teach me the entire Torah while I am standing on one foot." He drove him off with the building cubit that he had in his hand.

B. He came before Hillel: "Convert me."

C. He said to him, "'What is hateful to you, to your fellow don't do.' That's the entirety of the Torah; everything else is elaboration. So go, study."

That concluding instruction, "Everything else is elaboration, so go, study," is often omitted when the story is told. But leaving out the climactic statement misses the mark. For the view that the whole Torah forms an articulation and elaboration of Leviticus 19:18 and that therefore the whole Torah is to be assiduously studied forms the center of the story for the Rabbinic sages. They see all of life as an elaboration of the Torah's teachings. The law of the Mishnah as a whole forms that elaboration of the "entire Torah" taught while standing on one foot, the details that embody the main point.

## The Mishnah as the Oral Part of the Torah of Sinai

I have explained how tractate Abot implicitly states that the Mishnah's laws originate at Sinai, that is, with God. This claim is made explicit in another account of the Mishnah, one that speaks of an oral tradition of Sinai ultimately written down in the Mishnah in particular. This story has a specific, verbal revelation at Sinai coming down through the generations in an unbroken chain of memorization and ending up in the Mishnah:

### TALMUD OF BABYLONIA TRACTATE ERUBIM 54B/5:1.I.43

What is the order of Mishnah-teaching? Moses learned it from the mouth of the All-Powerful. Aaron came in, and Moses repeated his chapter to him and Aaron went forth and sat at the left hand of Moses. His sons came in and Moses repeated their chapter to them, and his sons went forth. Eleazar sat at the right of Moses, and Ithamar at the left of Aaron.

Rabbi Judah says, "At all times Aaron was at the right hand of Moses."

Then the elders entered, and Moses repeated for them their Mishnah chapter. The elders went out. Then the whole people came in, and Moses repeated for them their Mishnah chapter. So it came about that Aaron repeated the lesson four times, his sons three times, the elders two times, and all the people once.

Then Moses went out, and Aaron repeated his chapter for them. Aaron went out. His sons repeated their chapter. His sons went out. The elders repeated their chapter. So it turned out that everybody repeated the same chapter four times.

Here is an explicit account of how Moses received the Torah from God. In that model the disciples received the Torah from their masters in that same chain of tradition. The Torah that is under discussion is orally formulated and then orally transmitted. It is not written down on tablets. It is recorded in the word-for-word dictation of God to Moses, Moses to Aaron, Aaron to his sons Eleazar and Ithamar, then to the whole people, to the elders, and so on down; and the orally formulated and orally transmitted teaching is called "the Mishnah." The root of the word is *SH N Y*, meaning, "repeat." Generically, mishnah with a small *m* would mean, "that which is repeated," that is, from memory.

So in this story the Mishnah is defined as the outcome of a chain of tradition beginning at Sinai and transmitted in a process of discipleship—memorizing the words of the master and handing them on to a new generation of disciples. When God gave the Torah at Sinai, then, included was the oral tradition ultimately embodied in the Mishnah and, by extension, in other teachings of the Rabbinic sages who form links in the chain of tradition from Sinai. Within that story is encompassed the teachings of all those generations of men and women who have acquired learning in the Torah and form links in the chain of tradition to Sinai. The religion that the world calls "Judaism" calls itself "the Torah"—oral and written. The Mishnah, then, is represented by the Rabbinic authorities as the first part of the Oral Torah of Sinai to be written down.

## How Does the Mishnah Do God's Work?
## God's Presence in the Words of the Torah

Now that we have a clear picture of both the substantive and the narrative bases for the claim of the priority of the Mishnah beyond Scripture in Judaism, it is time to ask, Why does that claim matter? What specifically does the Mishnah offer in the setting of the Torah?

The answer depends on what the Torah provides and on how in that context the Mishnah participates in the work of the Torah, of which, as we have seen, it forms a principal part. In the view of Judaism, the Torah conveys God's purpose in creating the world and God's will for humanity, and the Torah tells humanity whatever humanity is going to know about God. That view of the Torah—that the Torah makes explicit what is implicit in God's activities in the world—is expressed in tractate Abot in the name of Aqiba, in the following way:

TRACTATE ABOT 3:14

R. Aqiba would say, "Precious is the human being, who was created in the image [of God].

"It was an act of still greater love that it was made known to him that he was created in the image [of God],

"as it is said, 'For in the image of God he made man' (Gen. 9:6).

"Precious are Israelites, who are called children to the Omnipresent.

"It was an act of still greater love that they were called children to the Omnipresent,

"as it is said, 'You are the children of the Lord your God' (Deut. 14:1).

"Precious are Israelites, to whom was given the precious thing [the Torah].

"It was an act of still greater love that it was made known to them that to them was given that precious thing with which the world was made,

"as it is said, 'For I give you a good doctrine. Do not forsake my Torah' (Prov. 4:2)."

The key language, repeated three times, is "It was an act of still greater love . . . ," meaning that while God acted out of love in making humanity, in calling the Israelites children of God, and in giving them the Torah, it was an act of still greater love that God let people know what God was doing. What is implicit, then, is that whatever we know about humanity, about Israel, and about the standing of the Torah, we know because God has told us. When, therefore, we confront the claim that the Mishnah forms an integral part of the Torah of Sinai, we want to know how the Mishnah participates in revealing God's program, plan, and purpose for humanity.

What is at stake in the Mishnah, as much as in Scripture, is God's will. That is why Yohanan ben Zakkai can say we were created to study the Torah. He does not mention praying or performing deeds of loving-kindness and righteousness—other principal modes of serving God that are specified by the Torah—but study of the Torah itself. That emphasis provokes the question, How does the Mishnah, a humble law code, do God's work? Is there in tractate Abot a claim in behalf of the Torah that God is present in the words of the Torah, encompassing the part of the Torah of Sinai embodied by the Mishnah itself? The question matters to our generation of Jews who, like every prior generation, seek the face of God and ask the Torah to show them the way. That is what it means to take up the religious tradition of Judaism and to search and find God in that tradition in particular.

So the question is urgent to us, Does the Mishnah speak of God? Indeed, tractate Abot contains the allegation that, in the encounter with the actual words of the Torah, as much as in reciting Psalms or declaiming Scripture or saying prayers, faithful Israel encounters God's word. Given the place within the Torah that is attributed to the Mishnah-teachings as just now defined—oral tradition of Sinai—we should not find it surprising that tractate Abot will frame the matter in terms of "words of the Torah" encompassing the Mishnah and much more. But we also should not miss the implicit allegation in that same Mishnah-tractate (Abot), that identifies the Mishnah's teaching with the Torah of Sinai that, in encountering God's words in the Mishnah as much as in Scripture, one meets God. Here is the explicit allegation:

### TRACTATE ABOT 3:6

Rabbi Halafta of Kefar Hananiah says, "Among ten who sit and work hard on the Torah-study the Presence comes to rest, as it is said, 'God stands in the congregation of God' (Ps. 82:1) [and 'congregation' involves ten persons].

"And how do we know that the same is so even of five? For it is said, 'And he has founded his vault upon the earth' (Amos 9:6).

"And how do we know that this is so even of three? Since it is said, 'And he judges among the judges' [a court being made up of three judges] (Ps. 82:1).

"And how do we know that this is so even of two? Because it is said, 'Then they that feared the Lord spoke with one another, and the Lord hearkened and heard' (Mal. 3:16).

"And how do we know that this is so even of one? Since it is said, 'In every place where I record my name I will come to you and I will bless you' (Exod. 20:24) [and it is in the Torah that God has recorded His name]."

The claim that God is present when Israelites pray and invoke the holy Name of God in prayer and supplication is easily grasped. Then there is a "you," referring to God, in what is said, in what is intended. But why studying the Torah, encompassing the laws of the Mishnah, should impel a response of divine attendance is not self-evident. Had the Rabbinic sage not made such a claim that God is present among those who labor at the study of the Torah, we should have found it difficult to say so. But here is an explicit claim of direct encounter with God in the words of the Torah.

## How Is God Present When the Torah Is Studied?

The claim that God is present when people gather for Torah-study comes to us in a famous story in the Talmud, about how Heaven (a euphemism for God) tries to intervene when the great sages engage in disputes about the law of the Torah. Involved are the disciples of Yohanan ben Zakkai, the very master who took over the tradition from Shammai and Hillel and transmitted it to the age beyond the destruction of Jerusalem in 70. Eliezer and sages (identified in due course as Joshua, Eliezer's contemporary and another principal heir of Yohanan ben Zakkai) differ on a rule governing whether or not a certain kind of oven is subject to the rules of uncleanness. The details need not detain us. It suffices to know that we deal with a case that can go either way. It involves the status of a certain kind of oven as to susceptibility to uncleanness in line with the laws of Leviticus. The general rule is that what is useless and broken down is not susceptible to uncleanness, what is useful and whole is. What is the rule governing a clay oven that has been broken down but then reconstructed—a case right in the middle? Eliezer and sages debate the two possible positions: it is susceptible to uncleanness, having been reconstructed; it is insusceptible to uncleanness, having been dismantled, even though it was then reconstructed.

### TALMUD OF BABYLONIA TRACTATE BABA MESIA 59A-B/4:10 I.15

I.15 A. There we have learned: If one cut [a clay oven] into parts and put sand between the parts,

Rabbi Eliezer declares the oven broken-down and therefore insusceptible to uncleanness.

And sages declare it susceptible.

Now comes the part relevant to our question: How does Heaven participate? Eliezer invokes nature to give evidence that his position is correct:

On that day Rabbi Eliezer produced all of the arguments in the world, but they did not accept them from him. So he said to them, "If the law accords with my position, this carob tree will prove it."

The carob was uprooted from its place by a hundred cubits—and some say, four hundred cubits.

They said to him, "There is no proof from a carob tree."

So he went and said to them, "If the law accords with my position, let the stream of water prove it."

The stream of water reversed flow.

They said to him, "There is no proof from a stream of water."

So he went and said to them, "If the law accords with my position, let the walls of the school house prove it."

The walls of the school house tilted toward falling.

Rabbi Joshua rebuked them, saying to them, "If disciples of sages are contending with one another in matters of law, what business do you have?"

They did not fall on account of the honor owing to Rabbi Joshua, but they also did not straighten up on account of the honor owing to Rabbi Eliezer, and to this day they are still tilted.

So R. Eliezer went and said to them, "If the law accords with my position, let the Heaven prove it!"

An echo came forth, saying, "What business have you with Rabbi Eliezer, for the law accords with his position under all circumstances!"

Heaven [God] could not be more explicit: Heaven itself reveals the law. Now comes the great moment in the presentation of the Torah: revealed truth is subject to reasoned argument and criticism. Heaven has joined in the discussion of the law of the Mishnah—and it has laid down its ruling. Is this not a moment of revelation equivalent to the revelation of Sinai? Well, no, it is not. For the Torah has already been given to humanity, and the Rabbinic sages have mastered its rules. These rules form regular and orderly principles; they accord with a logic and are not arbitrary but reasonable. Then the Rabbinic sages can and do master the logic of the Torah and make it their own. When the Rabbinic sages do their work, conduct their debates, and set forth the consequent rulings, they enter into those very same paths of thought and argument that God has made known in the Torah. The Rabbinic sages then are in the position of Abraham arguing with God at Sodom and Gomorrah: "Will not the Judge of all the world not do justice" (Gen. 18:25), meaning, God too is bound by the rules that govern. God is not arbitrary but reasonable, and humanity has access to the same rules of reason—which the Torah to begin with conveys. That is what is set forth in the astonishing response of Joshua to Heaven's intervention into the sages' debate:

Rabbi Joshua stood up on his feet and said, "'It is not in heaven' (Deut. 30:12)."

Lest we miss the point, the Talmud explicitly asks, What is the meaning of Joshua's rebuke in citing Deuteronomy 30:12?

What is the sense of, "'It is not in heaven' (Deut. 30:12)"?

Said Rabbi Jeremiah, "[The sense of Joshua's statement is this:] For the Torah has already been given from Mount Sinai, so we do not pay attention to echoes, since you have already written in the Torah at Mount Sinai, 'After the majority you are to incline' (Exod. 23:2)."

So far God has taken a back-row position in the narrative. But the real issue now emerges: How does God respond to the Rabbinic sage's insistence that once the Torah has been given and is mastered by the Rabbinic sages, then God cannot intervene and contravene the rules of reason already revealed? Now, at the end, we are told that God is present and participating, the Heavenly voice or echo representing the divine stake in the dispute:

> Rabbi Nathan came upon Elijah and said to him, "What did the Holy One, blessed be He, do at that moment?"
>
> He said to him, "He laughed and said, 'My children have overcome me, my children have overcome me!'"

Just as God accepts the rule of justice when Abraham, in pleading for Sodom, raises the principle that even God, judge of all the world, must do justice, so God accepts the rule of reason here. The sages' study of the Torah takes over the exposition of the Torah from Heaven, and their knowledge of the rules of regularity and order that the Torah itself yields when properly studied validates their participation. They carry forward through study of the Torah the work of the very giving of the Torah, finding truth in the Torah by the Torah's own rules. In chapter 2 we shall see a concrete example.

This story conveys that attitude of independent judgment and criticism based on sound reasoning that is implicit in the character of the beginning of tractate Abot. That statement—Torah but not quotation, a chain of tradition in which each participant personally contributes something new to the tradition—assigns to the contemporaries an active part in the definition of that which is handed over, that which is received. Tradition is not the gift of history but a creation of intelligence. Study of the Torah leads sages deep into the mind of God, who gives the Torah and further accords to humanity the intelligence to penetrate into the meanings of the Torah. That is why in studying the Torah the sages meet God—and all Israel participates in this encounter along with them.

Now it is equally clear that intelligence requires nurture. Each figure in the chain of tradition has served as a disciple to a predecessor and is going to serve as a master to many disciples to come. So tradition stands for discipline, and what is handed on is two things: the model of how to enter into dialogue with God and also the increment of insight and learning that earlier links in the chain have set forth as eternal truth. What is handed on is what is treasured and true. It is more than merely a record of how things used to be and to be done. At stake is eternal verity, not only historical fact. When we meet God in the Torah, it is not an encounter with a moment out of time past, but an event in an eternal present, shaped by rules of dialogue that pertain through permanent truth.

On what basis, specifically, do the Rabbinic sages make that claim? The reason God is present among those who study the Torah is that God's own words are set forth in the Torah, just as Aqiba says in the passage cited above. The Torah affords access to the mind of the Creator—and says so. The notion that there is a reason, a rationality, a plan in creation will not surprise the great scientists and mathematicians who have found order in nature. The counterpart conception—that the Torah reveals God's will and purpose—is then readily understood, but contemporary Jews impute to that statement diverse meanings. Within Orthodox Judaism it is often taken literally: God dictated the Torah in its exact wording to Moses (and here we see through Moses onward to the Rabbis of the Mishnah). Reform and Conservative Judaisms interpret the claim in a figurative or poetic framework, for example, speaking of divine inspiration. That is how they tell the story. But all those who practice an expression of Judaism concur that in one way or another, we meet God in the Torah. In more theological language, the Torah contains the record of God's self-manifestation to humanity through Israel. As Aqiba says, it is a mark of God's grace that the story of the Torah is set forth within the Torah too.

It comes down to this: What we know about God begins with what God reveals in the Torah. That is not the only occasion of encounter, but it is the ultimate one. True, we meet God in nature, creation, and in history, divine activity among humanity; we meet God in community and in solitude. But we know what God wants us to know about the divinity through the Instruction of Sinai, and the Torah forms the enduring account of the encounter with God that the prophets of Scripture and the sages of the Mishnah record. Through the study of the Torah the community of Israel recapitulates the revelation of Sinai and relives the initial encounter with God: in those words and in the principles and truths they embody.

### Imitating God in Everyday Life

What then does God most value, and how do we imitate God in everyday life? This last question in my initial exposition of how the Mishnah makes God's word work is once more best addressed to tractate Abot. That section of the Mishnah's tradition presents the most systematic account of the meaning of the encounter with God that the Mishnah sets forth. Tractate Abot sets forth a simple catalogue of virtue. It specifies feelings and emotions and attitudes that the Torah prizes: How do we feel, not only what do we think, in our quest for God? That list—in line with the virtues and vices listed by Yohanan ben Zakkai's disciples—comprises humility, generosity, self-abnegation, love, a spirit of conciliation of the other, and eagerness to please. A list of impermissible emotions or vices of attitude and feeling—as Yohanan's disciples compile the matter—is made up of envy, ambition, jealousy, arrogance, sticking to one's opinion, self-centeredness, a grudging spirit, vengefulness, and the like. People should aim at eliciting from others acceptance and good will and should avoid confrontation, rejection, and humiliation of the other. This they do through conciliation and giving up their own claims and rights.

So both catalogues form a harmonious and uniform whole, aiming at the cultivation of the humble and malleable person, one who accepts everything and resents nothing. Here are some representative sentiments:

**TRACTATE ABOT 2:4**

He [Rabban Gamaliel, son of R. Judah the Patriarch] would say, "Make his wishes into your own wishes, so that he will make your wishes into his wishes.

"Put aside your wishes on account of his wishes, so that he will put aside the wishes of other people in favor of your wishes."

**TRACTATE ABOT 3:10**

He [R. Haninah b. Dosa] would say, "Anyone from whom people take pleasure-the Omnipresent takes pleasure.

"And anyone from whom people do not take pleasure, the Omnipresent does not take pleasure."

God favors those who please others. Disciples of sages show their mastery of the Torah when they are accommodating, forgiving, hard to anger, and easy to appease. The virtues appreciated by human beings prove identical to the ones to which God responds as well. And what single virtue of the heart encompasses the rest? Restraint, the source of self-abnegation or humility, serves as the anecdote for ambition, vengefulness, and above all for arrogance. It is restraint of our own interest that enables us to deal generously with others, humility about ourselves that generates a liberal spirit toward others.

## What Is to Be Done?

How am I to show in detail what sustains these broad claims in behalf of the Mishnah?

First, as I said in the Introduction, readers have to accept the discipline and mode of discourse of the document. It speaks in detail about rules and laws, so we have to find the patience to cope with legal detail. I will translate and explain the selected passages so that they are accessible.

Second, for my part I have to show, also in detail, how tractates of the Mishnah set forth large principles through law, turn details into means for the expression of encompassing truths. That requires a clear picture of how I move from the detail to the governing principle. Readers must stand in judgment at every point: Have I made my case, or have I merely imputed to the Mishnah what I wish to find there?

I claim that the Mishnah organizes its facts by topics so as to ask compelling questions about the topics and answer those questions through articulating details of the law. In asking and answering those questions, the Mishnah introduces principles that cross topical boundaries and form of the details a large and cogent construction of transcendent truth. The only way to sustain that claim lies in following the path of the Mishnah itself as it wends its way through the rules to discover the law, as it asks the law to speak of transcendent questions of God's imperatives for Israelite sanctification in the here and now, yielding salvation from the grave in time to come. That path leads through this book, as I show, text by text, the large ideas that inhere in the small details of the laws, which, in the Torah and the Mishnah, embody norms of belief in norms of behavior.

# Monotheism and Justice

# 2 God's Justice and the Ordeal of the Accused Wife

## *Tractate Sotah*

### Why God's Justice Logically Forms the Heart of Monotheism

The laws of the Mishnah transform random facts into regular rules. The rules determine practical transactions, transforming theological statements into concrete deeds. To see this process in action, consider the first principle of the Torah, the declaration of monotheism, that God is one: "Hear, Israel, the Lord our God, the Lord is one" (Deut. 4:6). That theological affirmation of monotheism, which implies that all things cohere, forms the centerpiece of Jewish life, prayer, and piety; and on it all opinion concurs. One power, one cause, one will animates all creation; just as creation in turn realizes the intent of the one God. First, let us examine the theological principle and then ask how the laws of the Mishnah, in reflection upon the laws of the Torah, set forth that principle.

Israelite monotheism as set forth in Scripture encompasses a fundamental truth—namely, that the one, unique, and only God willingly accepts the discipline of justice. The Torah is explicit. In the negotiation with God in the matter of Sodom and Gomorrah (Gen. 18:25), Abraham asks: "Will not the Judge of all the world do justice?" God assents. So Abraham's challenge leaves no doubt that the Judge of all the earth is bound by the rules of justice.

The upshot is, the religion set forth by the Torah of Sinai announces that one God, who is just, has created the world and governs not arbitrarily but rationally. Rules that God affirms and humanity can intuit prevail. This distinguishes monotheism—belief in one just and merciful God—from polytheism—belief in many, often capricious gods. According to monotheism, whatever happens reflects the working of God's justice. Here is the crux of the problem that preoccupies monotheistic religions: how to cope with manifest injustice, for example, the prosperity of the wicked or the penury of the righteous. The Book of Job is only one instance of elucidating that disruptive question; indeed, every generation finds its indictment—and its way to cope with the ethical anomalies formed by the monotheist dilemma.

God's justice measured against humanity's fate forms the heart of the matter of monotheism when it is reflected upon in abstract philosophy as well. Humanity sees anomalies—the wicked prosper, the righteous suffer. For philosophical monotheism, the question is pressing: Are things merely arbitrary or does a higher power govern—and govern rationally, in accord with rules? A religion of numerous gods finds many solutions to one problem, a religion of only one God seeks one solution for the many problems. Both address the same mordant reality: life is seldom fair; rules rarely work. Diverse gods do various things, so it stands to reason that ordinarily outcomes will conflict. Monotheism has no such option. By its nature it must explain the many anomalies in a single way. One God rules. Life is meant to be fair, and just rules are supposed to describe what is ordinary, all in the name of that one and only God. So in monotheism a simple logic should govern.

But no one in any age of history needs reminding that the wicked *do* prosper and the righteous *do* suffer. So where is the justice of an all-powerful God in that? Monotheistic logic must account for opposites—like God's omnipotence and God's justice—that immediately affect one another. Thus, monotheism must contain its own dialectics. If one true God has done everything, then, since God is all-powerful and omniscient, all things are credited to, and blamed on, God. In that case, logically, God must be either good or bad, just or unjust—but not both.

With this problem of monotheistic theology framed, we turn to the laws of the Mishnah to see how the abstract principles of religious narrative and philosophy are realized in rules governing concrete action: the norms of behavior and belief. The first task of the Mishnah's law is to show how God is just, that is, fair and rational. The Mishnah carries out that task through its presentation of the single truly unjust transaction that the Torah sets forth, the ordeal inflicted upon the wife accused of adultery. When the Mishnah presents that law, it does so in such a way as to underscore the perfect justice of God. Thus, the Mishnah turns an unjust case—the rite of the accused wife—into a broad rule concerning God's justice in dealing with transgression. The broad rule then becomes a theological fundamental of monotheism. In short, the definition of God's justice flows from the Mishnah's examination of injustice.

### How Does the Mishnah Prove That God Is Just?

In Numbers 5, the Mishnah found its concrete evidence for the principle that the world is reliable and orderly by reason of justice. This narrative describes God's test for the fidelity of the wife accused of adultery. Scripture speaks both of the wife who has actually committed adultery and whose husband is made jealous, and of the woman who is guiltless but whose husband expresses jealousy. Scripture focuses upon the rite at the Temple that accommodates the situation. The pertinent verses follow (Num. 5:11–31):

And the Lord said to Moses, "Say to the people of Israel, If any man's wife go astray and act unfaithfully against him, if a man lie with her carnally and it is hidden from the eyes of her husband, and she is undetected though she has defiled herself and there is no witness against her, since she was not taken in the act, and if the spirit of jealousy comes upon him, and he is jealous of his wife who has defiled herself; or if the spirit of jealousy comes upon him and he is jealous of his wife, though she has not defiled herself, then the man shall bring his wife to the priest, and bring the offering required of her, a tenth of an ephah of barley meal; he shall pour no oil upon it and put no frankincense on it, for it is a cereal offering of jealousy, a cereal offering of remembrance, bringing iniquity to remembrance.

"And the priest shall bring her near and set her before the Lord, and the priest shall take holy water in an earthen vessel and take some of the dust that is on the floor of the tabernacle and put it into the water.

"And the priest shall set the woman before the Lord and unbind the hair of the woman's head and place in her hands the cereal offering of remembrance, which is the cereal offering of jealousy. And in his hand the priest shall have the water of bitterness that brings the curse. Then the priest shall make her take an oath, saying, 'If no man has lain with you, and if you have not turned aside to uncleanness, while you were under your husband's authority, be free from this water of bitterness that brings the curse. But if you have gone astray, though you are under your husband's authority, and if you have defiled yourself, and some man other than your husband has lain with you, then (let the woman take the oath of the curse and say to the woman) 'the Lord make you an execration and an oath among your people, when the Lord makes your thigh fall away and your body swell; may this water that brings the curse pass into your bowels and make your body swell and your thigh fall away.' And the woman shall say, 'Amen, Amen.'"

Ironically, it is the injustice done to the innocent wife who, by the husband's mere whim, is required to undergo the humiliating ordeal of the bitter water, which serves as the occasion for the Mishnah's legal system to make its definitive statement that God's justice is perfect. Here, in law they prove that the wicked get their exact punishment; the righteous, their precise reward. For the Rabbinic sages that statement becomes possible *only* here. For in their view it is not enough to show that sin or crime provokes divine response, that God penalizes evildoers. Justice in the here and now counts only when the righteous also receive what is coming to them. Scripture's casual remark that the woman found innocent will bear more children provokes elaborate demonstration, out of the established facts of history that Scripture supplies, that both righteous and wicked are subject to God's flawless and exact justice.

Here, then, is where narrative and philosophical monotheism intersect. Both ways of formulating the ethical monotheism that insists on God as not only unique but all-powerful and just come together in the tractate devoted to the accused wife, the tractate called *Sotah*, "Errant Wife." The penalty must fit the crime, measure must be given for measure, and the more exactly the result matches the cause, the more compelling the proof of immediate and concrete justice in the world order that the Rabbinic sages would put forth out of Scripture. Justice is transformed from a vague generality—a mere sentiment—to a precise and measurable dimension of morality: how things hold together when subject to tension at the pressure points of structure, not merely how they are arrayed in general. Here, in fact, is how God made the world, and what is good about the creation that God pronounced good. To make that point, the Rabbinic sages select this rite that reeks of injustice. Their presentation of the rite is framed so as to demonstrate God's perfect justice—not only in the public life of Israel's social order, but in the here and now of home and family. It is hard to conceive of a less likely candidate for demonstrating God's justice than the subject before us. But, for reasons that soon become clear, the Rabbinic sages identified this topic as the ideal proof.

When the Rabbinic sages examined the facts of Scripture to establish that principle of rationality and order in conformity to the requirements of justice and equity, what impressed them was not the inevitability of divine justice, which they took for granted, but the precision. Scripture portrays the world order as fundamentally just and reasonable, and it does so in countless ways, even while incorporating the complaint of Job and the reflection of Qoheleth. The Rabbinic sages, for their part, identified those cases that transcended generalities and established that proportionate justice lies beyond all dispute. That is why they treat the case at hand as not only exemplary but probative. They set forth their bold proposition, then amassed evidence in support of it.

## Justice Made Explicit

God is not only God but also good. In the system of the Mishnah, what is good, as in the creation narrative of Genesis, is well ordered, proportionate, and trustworthy. In Mishnah-tractate Sotah 1:6ff., the facts of the Torah are shown to convey the orderliness of a world based on God's justice and equity. Remarkably, the Rabbinic sages' account of God's consistently commensurate justice—both for reward and punishment—permits us to know the future with certainty. This is possible because the sages identify the precision of justice, the exact match of action and reaction, each step in the sin, each step in the response, and above all the immediacy of God's presence in the entire transaction. They draw general conclusions from the specifics of the law that Scripture sets forth, and that is where systematic "thinking about" takes over from exegetical "learning about," or, in our own categories, philosophy flows from history:

### Mishnah-tractate Sotah 1:6–7

1:6 [If] she was clothed in white clothing, he puts black clothes on her.

[If] she had gold jewelry, chains, nose-rings, and finger rings on, they take them away from her to put her to shame.

Then he brings a rope made out of twigs and ties it above her breasts.

And whoever wants to stare at her comes and stares, except for her boy-slaves and girl-slaves, since in any case she has no shame before them.

And all women are allowed to stare at her, since it is said, "That all women may be taught not to do after your lewdness" (Ezek. 23:48).

1:7 By that same measure by which a man metes out [to others], do they mete out to him:

> She primped herself for sin, the Omnipresent made her repulsive.
>
> She exposed herself for sin, the Omnipresent exposed her.
>
> With the thigh she began to sin, and afterward with the belly, therefore the thigh suffers the curse first, and afterward the belly.
>
> But the rest of the body does not escape [punishment].

We begin with the Rabbinic sages' own general observations based on the facts set forth in Scripture. The woman accused of adultery drinks of the bitter water that is supposed to produce one result for the guilty, another for the innocent. Scripture describes the process in this language: "If no man has lain with you . . . be free from this water of bitterness that brings the curse. But if you have gone astray . . . then the Lord make you an execration . . . when the Lord makes your thigh fall away and your body swell; may this water . . . pass into your bowels and make your body swell and your thigh fall away" (Num. 5:20–22). The Mishnah amplifies and expands on the entire rite, where and how the woman is disheveled; then on the order—thigh, belly—which shows the perfect precision of the penalty. What Scripture treats as a case, sages transform into a generalization, a process that causes Scripture to yield governing rules.

## Turning the Case into the Exemplification of a Rule

The same passage of the Mishnah proceeds to further cases, which prove the same point: where the sin begins, there the punishment also commences; but also, where an act of virtue takes its point, there divine reward focuses. The mere list of names, without details, will make the point: Samson, Absalom, Miriam, Joseph, and Moses. Knowing how Samson and Absalom match, also Miriam, Joseph, and Moses, suffices to establish the paired and matched general principles:

### MISHNAH-TRACTATE SOTAH 1:8–10

1:8 Samson followed his eyes [where they led him], therefore the Philistines put out his eyes, since it is said, "And the Philistines laid hold on him and put out his eyes" (Judg. 16:21).

Absalom was proud of his hair, therefore he was hung by his hair [2 Sam. 14:25–26].

And since he had sexual relations with ten concubines of his father, therefore they thrust ten spear heads into his body, since it is said, "And ten young men that carried Jacob's armor surrounded and smote Absalom and killed him" (2 Sam. 18:15).

And since he stole three hearts—his father's, the court's, and the Israelite's—since it is said, "And Absalom stole the heart of the men of Israel" (2 Sam. 15:6)—therefore three darts were thrust into him, since it is said, "And he took three darts in his hand and thrust them through the heart of Absalom" (2 Sam. 18:14).

Since justice requires not only punishment of the sinner or the guilty but reward of the righteous and the good, the sages find ample, systematic evidence in Scripture for the reward side of the equation, too:

1:9 And so is it on the good side:

Miriam waited a while for Moses, since it is said, "And his sister stood afar off" (Exod. 2:4), therefore, Israel waited on her seven days in the wilderness, since it is said, "And the people did not travel on until Miriam was brought in again" (Num. 12:15).

1:10 Joseph had the merit of burying his father, and none of his brothers was greater than he, since it is said, "And Joseph went up to bury his father . . . and there went up with him both chariots and horsemen" (Gen. 50:7, 9).

We have none so great as Joseph, for only Moses took care of his [bones].

Moses had the merit of burying the bones of Joseph, and none in Israel was greater than he, since it is said, "And Moses took the bones of Joseph with him" (Exod. 13:19).

We have none so great as Moses, for only the Holy One blessed be He took care of his [bones], since it is said, "And he buried him in the valley" (Deut. 34:6).

And not of Moses alone have they stated [this rule], but of all righteous people, since it is said, "And your righteousness shall go before you. The glory of the Lord shall gather you [in death]" (Isa. 58:8).

Thus, the sages adduce from Scripture the main probative evidence for the anticipation that when God judges, the judgment will match the act of merit with an appropriate reward and the sin with an appropriate punishment. Their proposition actually begins at Mishnah-tractate Sotah 1:7, however, with general observations as to how things are and not with specific allusions to prooftexts. They begin by reflecting on the character of the law as set forth in Scripture, subsequently adducing the cases that yield the generalization.

## Measure for Measure in the Extreme Case of the Wife Subjected to the Ordeal

Let me now set forth a systematic statement of the starting and main point: When God judges and sentences, not only is the judgment fair but the penalty fits the crime with frightening precision. So too, when God judges and awards a decision of merit, the reward proves equally exact. These two together—the match of sin and penalty, meritorious deed and reward—explain the point and purpose of one detail after another, and all together they add up to the portrait of a world order that is fundamentally and essentially just—the starting point and foundation of all else.

The theme of how the righteous are rewarded and the wicked punished through the reliable working of God's justice permeates the Mishnah's exposition of the topic at hand. Still more to the point, the sages choose this particular topic—justice in the household, justice for the accused wife—as the centerpiece of its presentation of evidence that, in the end, God does justice for all to see. The Rabbinic sages recapitulate the rite only to recast it into a juridical transaction, one involving procedures that protect the woman's right and secure, so far as possible, her dignity under her husband's accusation. They do not allow the husband lightly to sever the marriage without paying the marriage settlement, and they do insist on the normal rules of evidence, so far as these pertain.

As the Rabbinic sages present the ordeal imposed on the accused wife, they underscore the exact justice that the ordeal executes. The exposition of the topic in the Mishnah (also in the Tosefta, therefore also in the Talmuds) lays heavy emphasis on how, measure for measure, the punishment fits the crime—but the reward matches the virtue as well. What the guilty wife has done, the law punishes appropriately, but the sages also point to cases in which acts of merit receive appropriate recognition and reward. Why have the Rabbinic sages chosen the law of the accused wife as the venue for their systematic exposition of the divine law of justice? It is not difficult to explain.

The law of the accused wife forces upon us the questions of whether and how justice governs in the household. Scripture, as we note, imposes the ordeal not only upon the adulteress but on the faithful wife. A husband's spirit of jealousy suffices, whether or not the wife warrants suspicion. Surely the entire procedure seems unjust, and the promise of future offspring hardly compensates for the public humiliation that the innocent wife must undergo. It is in the context of presenting that very law that the Mishnah systematically lays out the evidence that, especially here, justice prevails. They make the point that rules of justice prevail, with reward for goodness and punishment for evil the standard, in the household as much as in public life. And that means not only that the wicked woman is punished, but that the righteous one is rewarded. What Scripture tacked on as an afterthought becomes in the Mishnah and its companions a principal focus of exposition.

How do the Rabbinic sages know that God's will is realized in the moral order of justice, that reward and punishment are always just? The sages turn to Scripture for the pertinent facts, for it is in Scripture that God is made manifest. But of the various types of scriptural evidence—explicit commandments, stories, prophetic admonitions—that they had available to show how the moral order prevailed in all being, what type did they prefer? Exact matches between sin and punishment. Here is their starting point and from here all else flows in smooth and orderly fashion. Justice is best embodied when sin is punished, merit rewarded. One without the other does not suffice.

That body of evidence, the exact matches that Scripture supplied, recorded human action and divine reaction, on the one side, and meritorious deed and divine response and reward, on the other. It was made up of consequential cases drawn from both private and public life, all underscoring the Rabbinic sages' insistence that all things, personal and public, are subject to the same simple rule. Demonstrating not only the principle but the precision of measure for measure from Scripture's own record of God's actions takes priority of place in how the Rabbinic sages examined the rationality of the universe. It permeates their system and frames its prevailing modes of explanation and argument. The principle that *all being conforms to rules that embody principles of justice through exact punishment of sin and precise reward of virtue* defined the starting point of all rational thought and the entire character of the Rabbinic sages' theological structure and system. It is therefore of special interest that, when sages wish to show the justice of God, they turn to the case of injustice before us.

It is here in particular that the Rabbinic sages identify the sources for their conviction of the order of society, natural and supernatural alike. What captures our attention is not the conviction but the way in which sages set forth that conviction. Did everyday life cast doubt on the existence of moral order? Not according to the facts of Scripture as the sages ordered those facts. Now, when we open Scripture, we too can locate the pertinent evidence that God is just and the world God made conforms to rules of equity. It is not merely that when God contemplated the world that God had made, God pronounced it good; Scripture leaves no doubt about God's definitive trait of justice, justice understood even as we understand it.

## Proof for God's Justice in the Mishnah's First Commentary, the Tosefta

The second response to the Mishnah's treatment comes in the Tosefta, meaning, "supplements," that is, supplements to the Mishnah. The Tosefta hangs like a vine upon the Mishnah's trellis. It follows the division of the Mishnah into topical tractates and expounds the same agenda of legal topics. Like the Mishnah, the Tosefta, sets forth freestanding propositions, not merely exegeses of verses of Scripture. True to its role as the Mishnah's first systematic commentary and amplification in the Mishnah's own order and style (the second and third commentaries are the Talmuds of the Land of Israel, ca. 400 C.E., and of Babylonia, ca. 600 C.E., which take a very different form), when taking up the topic of the Sotah, the "errant wife," the Tosefta contributes further cases illustrating the exact and appropriate character of both divine justice and divine reward.

What is important here is what is not made explicit; it concerns a question that the Mishnah does not raise: What about the gentiles? Does the principle of world order of justice apply equally to them? The answer given through cases here goes beyond the Mishnah's application of the primary statement to Israelites, to show that the same rules of justice do apply to gentiles. The cases are Sennacherib, who besieged Jerusalem after destroying Israel comprised by the northern tribes, and Nebuchadnezzar, who seized and destroyed Jerusalem in the time of Jeremiah. Now the sin is the single most important one, arrogance or hubris, and the penalty is swift and appropriate, the humbling of the proud by an act of humiliation:

### TOSEFTA-TRACTATE SOTAH 3:18–19

3:18 Sennacherib took pride before the Omnipresent only through an agent, as it is said, "By your messengers you have mocked the Lord and you have said, "With my many chariots I have gone up the heights of the mountains . . . I dug wells and drank foreign waters, and I dried up with the sole of my foot all the streams of Egypt" (2 Kgs. 19:23-24).

So the Omnipresent, blessed be He, exacted punishment from him only through an agent, as it is said, "And that night the messenger of the Lord went forth and slew a hundred and eighty-five thousand in the camp of the Assyrians" (2 Kgs. 19:35).

And all of them were kings, with their crowns bound to their heads.

3:19 Nebuchadnezzar said, "The denizens of this earth are not worthy for me to dwell among them. I shall make for myself a little cloud and dwell in it," as it is said, "I will ascend above the heights of the clouds, I will make myself like the Most High" (Isa. 14:14).

Said to him the Omnipresent, blessed be He, "You said in your heart, 'I will ascend to heaven, above the stars of God I will set my throne on high'—I shall bring you down to the depths of the pit" (Isa. 14:13, 15).

What does it say? "But you are brought down to Sheol, to the depths of the pit" (Isa. 14:15).

Were you the one who said, "The denizens of this earth are not worthy for me to dwell among them"?

The king said, "Is not this great Babylon, which I have built by my mighty power as a royal residence and for the glory of my majesty? While the words were still in the king's mouth, there fell a voice from heaven, O King Nebuchadnezzar, to you it is spoken, The kingdom has departed from you, and you shall be driven from among men, and your dwelling shall be with the beasts of the field, and you shall be made to eat grass like an ox" (Dan. 4:29–32).

All this came upon King Nebuchadnezzar at the end of twelve months (Dan. 4:28–29).

Does the Tosefta's authorship believe that reward is measured out with the same precision? Not at all, reward many times exceeds punishment. So if the measure of retribution is exactly proportionate to the sin, the measure of reward exceeds the contrary measure by a factor of five hundred. Justice without mercy is incomplete; to have justice, mercy is the required complement.

**TOSEFTA-TRACTATE SOTAH 4:1**

I know only with regard to the measure of retribution that by that same measure by which a man metes out, they mete out to him [Mishnah-tractate Sotah 1:7A]. How do I know that the same is so with the measure of goodness [Mishnah-tractate Sotah 1:9A]?

Thus do you say:

The measure of goodness is five hundred times greater than the measure of retribution.

With regard to the measure of retribution it is written, "Visiting the sin of the fathers on the sons and on the grandsons to the third and fourth generation" (Exod. 20:5).

And with regard to the measure of goodness it is written, "And doing mercy for thousands" (Exod. 20:6).

You must therefore conclude that the measure of goodness is five hundred times greater than the measure of retribution.

With that general point in hand, we revert to the specifics of cases involving mortals, not God, and now we wish to show the simple point that reward and punishment meet in the precision of justice. When the life is Abraham's, for example, justice extends beyond the limits of a single lifetime. Justice requires that Abraham's heirs participate in Abraham's virtue, and God remembers Abraham's generous actions in favor of Abraham's children into the long future, an intimation of a doctrine involving a heritage of grace that will play a considerable role in the theological system, as we shall see in due course. Here is how, point by point, Abraham brings benefit to his heirs:

### TOSEFTA-TRACTATE SOTAH 4:2

Of Abraham it is said, "He bowed himself to the earth" (Gen. 18:2).

So will the Omnipresent, blessed be He, respond graciously to his children in time to come, "Kings will be your foster-fathers, and their queens your nursing mothers. With their faces to the ground they shall bow down to you and lick the dust of your feet" (Isa. 49:23).

Of Abraham it is said, "Let a little water be brought" (Gen. 18:4).

So did the Omnipresent, blessed be He, respond graciously and give to his children a well in the wilderness, which gushed through the whole camp of Israel, as it is said, "The well which the princes dug, which the nobles of the people delved (Num. 21:18) teaching that it went over the whole south and watered the entire desert, which looks down upon the desert" (Num. 21:20).

Of Abraham it is said, "And rest yourselves under the tree" (Gen. 18:4).

So the Omnipresent gave his children seven glorious clouds in the wilderness, one on their right, one on their left, one before them, one behind them, one above their heads, and one as the Presence among them.

The same theme is expounded in a systematic way through the entire account. It is instructive to read it in full:

### TOSEFTA-TRACTATE SOTAH 4:3–6

4:3 Of Abraham it is said, "While I fetch a morsel of bread that you may refresh yourselves" (Gen. 18:5).

So did the Omnipresent, blessed be He, give them manna in the wilderness, as it is said, "The people went about and gathered it . . . and made cakes of it, and the taste of it was like the taste of cakes baked with oil" (Num. 11:8).

4:4 Of Abraham it is said, "And Abraham ran to the herd and took a calf, tender and good" (Gen. 18:7).

So the Omnipresent, blessed be He, rained down quail from the sea for his children, as it is said, "And there went forth a wind from the Lord, and it brought quails from the sea, and let them fall beside the camp" (Num. 11:31).

4:5 Of Abraham what does it say? "And Abraham stood over them" (Gen. 18:8).

So the Omnipresent, blessed be He, watched over his children in Egypt, as it is said, "And the Lord passed over the door" (Exod. 12:23).

4:6 Of Abraham what does it say? "And Abraham went with them to set them on their way" (Gen. 18:16).

So the Omnipresent, blessed be He, accompanied his children for forty years, as it is said, "These forty years the Lord your God has been with you" (Deut. 2:7).

The evidence is of the same character as that adduced in the Mishnah: cases of Scripture. But the power of the Tosefta's treatment of Abraham must be felt. Finding an exact counterpart in Israel's later history for each gesture of the progenitor, Abraham, shows the match between the deeds of the patriarchs and the destiny of their people. Justice here is given dimensions we should not have anticipated, involving not only the individual but the individual's family, that is, the entire community of holy Israel. Once more we note that a systematic effort focuses on details. Justice is not a generalized expectation but a very particular fact, bread/manna, calf/quail, and so on. In explicit cases, the sages find the kind of detailed evidence that corresponds to the sort suitable in natural history.

Before proceeding to the Tosefta's extension of matters in a quite unanticipated direction, let us turn to further amplifications of the basic point concerning the exact character of the punishment for a given sin. The fact is, not only does the sinner lose what he or she wanted, but the sinner also is denied what formerly he or she had possessed, a still more mordant and exact penalty indeed. At Tosefta-tractate Sotah 4:16, the statement of the Mishnah, "Just as she is prohibited to her husband, so she is prohibited to her lover" [Mishnah-tractate Sotah 5:1], is transformed into a generalization that is spelled out and then demonstrated by a list lacking all articulation; the listed items themselves serve to make the point. The illustrative case—the snake and Eve—is given at Tosefta-tractate Sotah 4:17–18. The list is at Tosefta-tractate Sotah 4:19.

### TOSEFTA-TRACTATE SOTAH 4:16

Just as she is prohibited to her husband, so she is prohibited to her lover:

You turn out to rule in the case of an accused wife who set her eyes on someone who was not available to her:

What she wanted is not given to her, and what she had in hand is taken away from her.

The poetry of justice is not lost: what the sinner wanted is not achieved, and what the sinner had is lost.

### TOSEFTA-TRACTATE SOTAH 4:17–18

4:17 And so you find in the case of the snake of olden times, who was smarter than all the cattle and wild beasts of the field, as it is said, "Now the serpent was smarter than any other wild creature that the Lord God had made" (Gen. 3:1 ).

He wanted to slay Adam and to marry Eve.

The Omnipresent said to him, "I said that you should be king over all beasts and wild animals. Now that you did not want things that way, 'You are more cursed than all the beasts and wild animals of the field' (Gen. 3:14).

"I said that you should walk straight-up like man. Now that you did not want things that way, 'Upon your belly you shall go' (Gen. 3:14).

"I said that you should eat human food and drink human drink. Now: 'And dust you shall eat all the days of your life' (Gen. 3:14).

4:18 "You wanted to kill Adam and marry Eve? 'And I will put enmity between you and the woman' (Gen. 3:15)."

You turn out to rule, What he wanted was not given to him, and what he had in hand was taken away from him.

The Rabbinic sages' mode of thought employing classification and hierarchy to uncover patterns does not require the spelling out of the consequences of the pattern through endless cases. On the contrary, they are perfectly happy to list further examples of the same rule, knowing that we can reconstruct the details once the facts of Scripture have been shown to follow a common paradigm:

TOSEFTA-TRACTATE SOTAH 4:19

And so you find in the case of Cain, Korah, Balaam, Doeg, Ahitophel, Gahazi, Absalom, Adonijah, Uzziah, and Haman, all of whom set their eyes on what they did not have coming to them.

What they wanted was not given to them, and what they had in hand was taken away from them.

Were we given only the first part of Tosefta-tractate Sotah 4:19, a construction lacking all explanation, we should have been able to reconstruct their conclusion in the latter part of Tosefta-tractate Sotah 4:19! Here is a fine example of how a pattern signals its own details, and how knowing the native categories allows us to elaborate the pattern with little further data. But whether we should have identified as the generative message the principle that what the sinner wanted was not given and what the sinner had in hand was taken away is not equivalently clear. I am inclined to think that, without the fully exposed example, we could not have done what the compositor has instructed us to do: fill out the *et cetera*. What a passage of this kind underscores is the Rabbinic sages' confidence that those who would study their writings would see the paradigm within the case and would possess minds capable of conceiving generalization and objective demonstration.

## Law and Lore Concur: The Demonstration of God's Justice in the Exegesis of Scripture

The precise match of punishment to sin and of reward to virtuous deed may be further pursued, beyond the limits of the law of the Mishnah and the Tosefta. How Scripture sustains the conviction that the one God who is omnipotent is also just goes beyond the limits of the law of the Mishnah to the context in which that law took shape. The discourse on the theme of divine justice occurs in Leviticus Rabbah, a commentary to the book of Leviticus that came to closure in ca. 450 C.E. Here the fact that punishment proceeds directly from the sinner is discussed:

LEVITICUS RABBAH XVIII:II.1FF.:

1. "Dread and terrible are they; their justice and dignity proceed from themselves" (Hab. 1:7).

"Dread and terrible" refers to the first Man.

Following this broad statement, we seek matched opposites, pairs that belong together to show how justice is exacted from the wicked and brings reward to the righteous. The first match is Esau and Obadiah. For the sages, Esau stands for the wicked people of Edom, while the prophet Obadiah represents their exact opposite:

2. Another interpretation: "Dread and terrible" refers to Esau.

That is in line with the following verse of Scripture: "And Rebecca took the most coveted garments of Esau, her elder son" (Gen. 27:15).

"Their justice and dignity proceed from themselves" (Hab. 1:7).

This refers to [the prophet] Obadiah.

The next pair is formed by Sennacherib and his sons, the latter of whom killed his wicked father:

3. Another interpretation: "Dread and terrible" refers to Sennacherib.

"Who among all the gods of the lands has saved their country from my hand" (Isa. 36:20).

"Their justice and dignity proceed from themselves" (Hab. 1:7).

This refers to his sons: "And it came to pass, as Sennacherib was worshiping in the house of Nisroch, his god, [that Adrammelech and Sarezer, his sons, smote him with the sword]" (2 Kgs. 19:37).

Even the wicked sometimes carry out God's justice; here Nebuchadnezzar does God's work in Tyre, punishing Hiram's arrogance:

4. Another interpretation: "Dread and terrible" refers to Hiram, king of Tyre.

"Son of man, say to the prince of Tyre, thus says the Lord God, 'Because your heart was lifted up, and you said, I am God . . .'" (Ezek. 28:2).

"Their justice and dignity proceed from themselves" (Hab. 1:7).

This refers to Nebuchadnezzar.

Yet Nebuchadnezzar also embodied arrogance; hence, he too was brought down by an evil force commanded by God:

5. Another interpretation: "Dread and terrible" refers to Nebuchadnezzar: "And you said, I shall go up to heaven" (Isa. 14:13).

"Their justice and dignity proceed from themselves" (Hab. 1:7).

This refers to Evil Merodach.

At the end and climax is Israel, which brings punishment upon itself, from its own body, and this, too, is made explicit:

6. Another interpretation: "Dread and terrible" refers to Israel.

"I said, You are God[-like beings]" (Ps. 82:6).

"Their justice and dignity [or swelling] proceed from themselves" (Hab. 1:7).

For Israelites may be smitten with flux and with leprosy [which punishes them for their sins, and comes from their very bodies].

Therefore Moses admonished Israel, saying to them, "When any man has a discharge from his body" (Lev. 15:2).

That the punishment is exacted directly from the sinner, and so too the reward, is thus shown in a sequence of cases, but the emphasis is placed on cases that show the former, a requirement of the context.

Time and again sages extended matters by treating the case as exemplary. In the next excerpt, they named the archetypal sinners as the Generation of the Flood, the Generation of the Dispersion (from the Tower of Babel), the Sodomites, the Egyptians, Samson (and, in the list that follows, Amnon and Zimri). The cases turn into a general rule before us that proves of special importance, since the sages' listing also clarifies a major issue, the standing of gentiles in the world order. The six cases yield this generalization: the same God who exacted punishment from the archetypal sinners will exact punishment from anyone who does as they did—and with Samson, Amnon, and

Zimri, we move from the world of gentiles to include the world of Israel. Justice, then, is equal for all of humanity, both those within and those beyond the limits of the Torah defined by Israel:

### LEVITICUS RABBAH XXIII:IX

1. R. Ishmael taught, "'You shall not do as they do in the land of Egypt, where you dwelt, and you shall not do as they do in the land of Canaan . . . I am the Lord your God' [Lev. 18:3–4].

"And if not, it is as if I am not the Lord your God."

The key point is now introduced: the case supplies a rule, and here it is phrased, "I am going to exact punishment from anyone who does as they did:"

2. R. Hiyya taught, "[The text states,] 'I am the Lord your God' two times [Lev. 18:4, 5].

"I am the one who exacted punishment from the Generation of the Flood and from the men of Sodom and Gomorrah and from Egypt.

"'I am going to exact punishment from anyone who does as they did.'"

Once more, a list of names with little elaboration will serve to prove the proposition at hand:

5. "I am the Lord" (Lev. 18:4):

"I am he who exacted punishment from Samson, Amnon, and Zimri, and I am going to exact punishment from whoever does as they did.

"I am he who rewarded Joseph, Jael, and Palti. I am going to reward whoever does as they did."

I see nothing surprising in this list, until we reach Samson, at which point Israel joins the gentiles in the domain of justice.

The Rabbinic sages naturally distinguish the realm of the Torah from the realm of idolatry, Israel from the gentiles, but they also treat the two realms as subject to one and the same rule, justice. But then what difference does the Torah make for holy Israel, the Torah's sector of humanity? As the Tosefta passage that we first met at Sotah 4:1ff. proceeds, discussion shades over into a response to this very question. The point concerning reward and punishment is made not at random but through the close reading of Scripture's record concerning not only the line of Noah—the Generation of the Flood, the men of Sodom and Gomorrah, the Egyptians—but also the founder of God's line on earth, Abraham. Abraham here, often head of the line with Isaac and Jacob, is deemed the archetype for Israel, his extended family. What he did affects his heirs. His actions form models for the right conduct of his heirs. What happened to him will be recapitulated in the lives and fate of his heirs.

If we know how someone has sinned, we also know not only that but exactly how the sinner will be penalized. The same goes for rewards either in this world, as in the case at hand, or in the world to come. Not only individuals but classes of sinners and of sins will be penalized in a manner appropriate to the character of the sin. That accounts for the certainty that justice will always prevail and that the one who is punished bears full responsibility for the resulting fate. All the more urgent, then, are the concepts of judgment, resurrection, life after death, and the world to come, which address the necessary corollary of the perfection of divine justice: the manifest injustice of the worka-day fate of perfectly righteous people. In due course, we shall have much more to say about that matter.

Here it suffices to take note of a further corollary of the axiom of the exact, proportionate character of punishment. All things match; complementarities govern. But then, having identified Israel as that sector of humanity subject to a relationship with the just God that is different from that of the idolators, a further point of commensurate response is raised: sin, punishment, but then atonement, repentance, reconciliation, and conciliation. The same principles apply, but the context expands.

When it comes to Israel, the principle of commensurate response to each action extends to God's response to Israel's atonement. Israel is punished for its sin, but when Israel repents and God forgives Israel and restores the holy people's fortunes, then that same principle that all things match takes over. Hence we should not find surprising the logical extension of the principle of measure for measure to the character of God's forgiveness and comfort of Israel. When, specifically, Israel sins, it is punished through that with which it sins, but it also is comforted through that with which it has been punished.

What is important to us is not only the logical necessity of the sages' reach-ing such a position. It also is the character of their demonstration of that fact. Here is a remarkably successful exposition of the way in which the sages assem-ble out of Scripture facts that, all together, demonstrate the moral order of reward and punishment, along with the merciful character of God and God's justice. Here is a fine case in which a single pervasive logic coordinates a mass of diverse data of both law and lore into a cogent statement of a position that prevails throughout. A passage such as the following can be understood only in light of the insistence at the outset that sages conduct their inquiries in the manner of natural philosophy, the raw data—the cited verses of Scripture—being recast into a coherent demonstration of the desired proposition:

**PESIQTA DE RAB KAHANA XVI:XI.1**

1. "[Comfort, comfort my people, says your God.] Speak tenderly to the heart of Jerusalem and declare to her [that her warfare is ended, that her iniquity is pardoned, that she has received from the Lord's hand double for all her sins]" (Isa. 40:1–2).

When they sinned with the head, they were smitten at the head, but they were comforted through the head.

When they sinned with the head: "Let us make a head and let us return to Egypt" (Num. 14:4),

they were smitten at the head: "The whole head is sick" (Isa. 1:5),

but they were comforted through the head: "Their king has passed before them and the Lord is at the head of them" (Mic. 2:13).

The construction is pellucid, the triplet of sin, punishment, and comfort, applied first to the head and predictably to the other principal parts. Why pre-dictably? Because the sages wish to match nature with supernature, the com-ponents of the natural world with the parts of the body, as we saw in the Prologue, the components of the body with the paradigmatic actions of Israel through time. All things match in exact balance: the natural world and the human body, the human body and the actions of Israel. From the head we now proceed to the eye, ear, nose, mouth, tongue, heart, hand, foot—the agencies of the expression of human will. Once more what is important is not the end product, which is a tedious and repetitious demonstration, but the way in which the facts of Scripture ("proof texts") are coordinated, selected, and organized to form a pattern that, left on their own, they do not establish at all.

The entire passage follows along these same lines, covering the eye, ear, nose, mouth, and so on: when they sinned through . . . they were smitten at . . . but they were comforted through. . . . The basic proposition—when they sinned with this, they were smitten at this—but they were comforted through this—maintains that an exact match unites sin and punishment; through that with which one sins, one is punished. But then that same match links the modes of consolation as well; that is, through that trait through which one is sinned, one also will be comforted. So the conviction of an orderly and appropriate set of correspondences setting forth a world in balance and proportion generates the details. The proofs for the proposition involve an extensive survey of both the media of sin and the character of the resultant punishment.

## Turning Facts into Truth

This survey of how the law and the lore of Scripture are joined to sustain the Mishnah's law and its theological statement on God's omnipotence and justice brings us back to the main point. It is this: the Mishnah makes God's word work by turning facts into truth. What exactly does that mean? What facts? Which truths? The answer is now clearer. The Mishnah takes the facts of Scripture and finds in the detailed cases rules that transcend the details at hand and that extend to other cases. These rules cohere and prove consistent. They withstand tests of criticism. Not only so, but when these facts are transformed into truth, they speak of more than practical matters. They contain transcendent convictions about God: what God does and why. The rest of this book spells out in detail precisely the meaning of these twin allegations concerning how the Mishnah's law embodies theological truths.

These represent large claims in behalf of the Mishnah. That is so even though, taken on its face, the Mishnah scarcely displays them to the naked eye. For what I allege is that the framers of the Mishnah spoke on two levels: at the surface they set forth details, and at the depths they offered universal truths. So the Rabbinic sages took up workaday cases and laws, but shaped the law to express transcendent convictions about God's imperatives for humanity set forth to and through Israel. Above all, in many of its detailed discussions the Mishnah expresses through its transcendent laws of justice and sanctification profound judgments concerning human intentionality: how what we want to make happen affects the outcome of what actually has happened. To that matter we shall turn only at the end, chapter 18, when we ask about the Mishnah's message overall.

# 3 God's Justice: Israel and the Gentiles

## Tractates Sanhedrin-Makkot and Abodah Zarah

## Israel and the Gentiles:
## Justice in the Division of Humanity

The law of the Mishnah divides humanity into two parts, male and female, and accords justice to both parts. The Mishnah also classifies humanity as either Israel or not-Israel and, through the laws governing each half, renders its judgment of divine justice. Matters are straightforward when we ask concerning the accused wife, Where is the justice in the disposition of the husband's jealousy? In that case, both components of humanity–(Israelite) males and (Israelite) females–come under a single legal rubric, Israel, those who know God through the Torah. In cases concerning Israel and not-Israel, by contrast, matters concerning Israel come under one legal category, those concerning the gentiles, a different legal category. What the law wants to know about the Israelite–the questions raised concerning Israel–does not on the surface intersect with the questions that the law asks about the gentile.

Two tractates set forth the justice of this division of humanity. The first is Sanhedrin-Makkot, on Israelite sinners and criminals and how they are and are not penalized. Who is an Israelite and what is the corporate community of Israel reaches articulate definition in the setting of criminal justice. The gentiles find their place in tractate Abodah Zarah, idolatry, which is devoted to interactions with the nations on the part of Israelites, with special reference to relationships in which Israelites, through what they do not do, exercise some control.

The law defines Israel in the setting of the death penalty inflicted on Israelite sinners or criminals for specified sins or crimes. In that setting of life or death, the law makes a statement on resurrection, accorded even to (most) Israelite sinners or criminals. So to be Israel is defined in the context of criminal justice within the Israelite community.

When, as we shall see presently, the law of the Mishnah comes to the gentiles, issues are strikingly different and, by comparison, trivial. For while the Israelite is defined as the portion of humanity that rises from the grave to eternal life, the gentile is defined solely in practical terms of how the Israelite intersects with the gentile on specified occasions or in particular transactions. The statement that the law of the Mishnah makes concerning the gentiles is not only practical; it is also scarcely articulated. That registers yet another, equally striking contrast to what we saw in chapter 2. For the law of the Mishnah explicitly responds, in the matter of the (Israelite) woman, to the issue of how God does justice by identifying apparent injustice done to the feminine half of humanity. But to the comparable issue—What is justice for the portion of humanity excluded from life eternal and left to rot in the grave?—the law speaks only implicitly. Nevertheless, the Mishnah's theology of Israel accounts also for the status of the gentiles. When it comes to the norms of behavior as distinct from belief, that theology is fully exposed, wholly realized. All of this emerges when we contrast Mishnah-tractates Sanhedrin-Makkot and Abodah Zarah, dealing respectively with criminal justice in Israel and idolatry among the nations.

To begin with, the laws on Israel and the gentiles concern the division of humanity between Israel and everybody else. But the anticipated question—How is it just to divide humanity in such a stark way?—is not addressed in so many words. Rather, the consequence of the division yields a rule on one topic for Israel and a rule on an unrelated topic for the gentiles. And the issues scarcely compare: the rule concerning Israel is fundamental and theological; the rule disposing of the nations or the gentiles is trivial and practical.

Still, while the issues and their consequences do not match, the rules do yield a single message. The issue is God's perspective, and the message serves to explain two matters. First, why is all humanity divided by the law of the Mishnah into two sectors? The answer is, one sector, Israel, knows God through the Torah, and the other sector, the nations, does not know God but instead worships idols. As to Israel, the issue concerns the status of Israelite sinners and criminals and whether and how they remain Israelites. When, second, the law of the Mishnah turns to the gentiles, the sole concern is how Israel interacts with gentiles but avoids their idolatry. These issues do not seem to intersect, yet the distinction between Israelite and gentile makes a vast and decisive difference to the law of the Mishnah: the difference between life and death. The gentile, who is an idolater, does not rise from the grave, and even when alive, like the idol itself, is a source of cultic uncleanness just as the corpse is a source of cultic uncleanness (in line with Numbers 19).

Then of what does justice consist? How shall we explain the distinction within the genus, humanity, into two species, Israel and gentiles? Both Mishnah-tractates before us, Sanhedrin-Makkot for Israel, Abodah Zarah for the gentiles, address that question.

In addition, a practical issue of justice in Israelite–pagan relationships flows from the distinction between life and death, Israel and the nations, and should not be missed. How shall we find justice in the present status of Israel, subordinated as it is to the gentiles? For if God rules as sovereign over all humanity, and if the two species of humanity compete, where is the justice in the fact that one species, the gentiles, presently dominates the other, Israel? It follows that to make sense of and to justify world order, the subordinated status of both species, the gentiles in the age to come, Israel in the present age, has to be explained—and the same explanation must govern both. Here too the law does not explicitly ask that question, familiar though it is from Israelite prophecy. But an implicit judgment is rendered that dismisses the question altogether, as we shall see at the end.

To reach that conclusion, we take up the theology framed by narrative in Rabbinic writings other than the Mishnah. As we shall see, both tractates of the Mishnah function within this larger theological context. In passages of narrative and their implicit theology, not explicit law, the issue of justice plays itself out. So there is no understanding the law of the Mishnah without invoking the system of theology that animates and sustains the law of the Mishnah and the documents that embody that system. But any promise already made that the Mishnah guides contemporary public policy for Israel, the community of Judaism, is kept here only in the negative. When we understand the Mishnah's legal theology of Israel and the gentiles, we shall confront a model insufficient to contemporary sensibility—so I argue at the end.

## How Israel Is Defined within the Mishnah's System of Criminal Justice

The definition of "Israel" depends on what category is in focus. For example, "Israel" can be and is defined in genealogical terms as the children of Abraham, Isaac, Jacob, Sarah, Rebecca, Leah, and Rachel. This definition prevails in the Torah's story of Israel. Israel also can be and is defined in theological terms; for instance, Israel is comprised of those who live under God's sovereignty and accept the authority of the Torah and Jewish law, inclusive of the Mishnah. In exegetical contexts, when Scripture is amplified and applied, that definition prevails. But when it comes to the law of the Mishnah, "Israel" is defined with reference to the end of days: Israel is comprised of all those who will emerge victorious over death. An Israelite, then, is one who shares the fate of Israel, which is to rise from the grave for judgment and eternal life. For the Mishnah, this is both the legal definition of Israel as a corporate entity and the meaning, for individual Israelites, of belonging to Israel.

What follows is the Mishnah's legal definition of who and what is Israel. As we shall see, this forms the climactic statement of the Mishnah's laws governing judicial penalties and sanctions for sins and crimes:

### MISHNAH-TRACTATE SANHEDRIN 10:1

All Israelites have a share in the world to come,

as it is said, "Your people also shall be all righteous, they shall inherit the land forever; the branch of my planting, the work of my hands, that I may be glorified" (Isa. 60:21).

I maintain that this passage provides a juridical, practical definition of "Israel" on which courts will act in practical ways. So one may fairly ask, Exactly how does this statement that all Israel has a portion in the world to come serve to define "Israel"? We may in response manipulate the opening declaration, reversing (1) the subject "all Israelites" and (2) the predicate, "have a portion in the world to come" as follows: (2) "all who have a share in the world to come" are (1) "Israelites." And—simple logic requires—all who do *not* have a portion in the world to come logically cannot fall into the category "Israelites" as framed in that same sentence.

What is the meaning of "a portion in the world to come"? It is eternal life, specifically, resurrection from the grave—death having been vanquished—and restoration to the Garden of Eden. That sense emerges from interpreting the quoted verse of Isaiah. "Your people shall be all righteous" meaning, vindicated in judgment, justified, and found righteous; "the land they inherit forever," that is, the Garden of Eden. Since death came into the world by reason of Adam's and Eve's rebellion against God, the end of death implies a return to the Garden. The following shows how Adam acknowledged that he bore full responsibility for his own fate, which is death, thereby rendering death a necessary part of the human condition. We begin with a verse from the prophet Jeremiah:

### PESIQTA DE RAB KAHANA XIV:V.1

It is written, "Thus said the Lord, What wrong did your fathers find in me that they went far from me and went after worthlessness and became worthless?" (Jer. 2:5).

Said R. Isaac, "This refers to one who leaves the scroll of the Torah and departs. Concerning him, Scripture says, 'What wrong did your fathers find in me that they went far from me.'

"Said the Holy One, blessed be He, to the Israelites, 'My children, your fathers found no wrong with me, but you have found wrong with me.'"

Now a case—the archetypal one, Adam himself—will illustrate the generalization contained within the statement of Rabbi Isaac. People who violate the Torah do so of their own volition, not by reason of a tradition of rebellion. They therefore bear responsibility for their own sins. Adam's rebellion brought death into the world:

"'The first Man found no wrong with me, but you have found wrong with me.'

"To what may the first Man be compared?

"To a sick man, to whom the physician came. The physician said to him, 'Eat this, don't eat that.'

"When the man violated the instructions of the physician, he brought about his own death.

"[As he lay dying,] his relatives came to him and said to him, 'Is it possible that the physician is imposing on you the divine attribute of justice?'

"He said to them, 'God forbid. I am the one who brought about my own death. This is what he instructed me, saying to me, "Eat this, don't eat that," but when I violated his instructions, I brought about my own death.'"

Adam is the archetype; he brings upon himself his own death. The lesson may now be applied:

"So too all the generations came to the first Man, saying to him, 'Is it possible that the Holy One, blessed be He, is imposing the attribute of justice on you?'

"He said to them, 'God forbid. I am the one who has brought about my own death. Thus did he command me, saying to me, 'Of all the trees of the garden you may eat, but of the tree of the knowledge of good and evil you may not eat' (Gen. 2:17). When I violated his instructions, I brought about my own death, for it is written, 'On the day on which you eat it, you will surely die' (Gen. 2:17)."

Adam brought about his own death. But the lesson may also be reversed. Israel, by framing the right relationship to God, may restore humanity to Eden. So justice governs, and people may apply this knowledge of the fitting penalty for the sin to explain what happens in ordinary, everyday affairs. The promise includes "all Israelites," even those who have already died. Then the message is clear. To be "Israel" means to rise from the grave and enter eternal life, to be restored to Eden.

Accordingly, behind the statement at hand is the conviction that, at the end of days, the dead will be raised and all humanity judged. Then most Israelites will "stand in judgment," except for a few whom we shall meet in a moment. "To stand in judgment" thus means that, in the balance, a person is found worthy of resurrection and eternal life; while to be denied a "share in the world to come" means, a person is found to have lived so evil a life as not to merit a place in the Garden of Eden but only a grave for all eternity.

This brings us back to our starting point: at the most profound level to be "Israel" means to live forever, to be one of the company of the saints destined to rise from the dead and to enjoy the world to come. And corporate Israel comprises all those destined to rise from the grave and return to Eden.

## Why the Resurrection of the Dead Finds Its Place within the Mishnah's Law of Criminal Justice

The criminal justice law of the Mishnah demonstrates the exact match between crime and punishment, virtuous deed and its reward, in the Israelite context. This is analogous to the exposition of punishment and reward in chapter 2. Why, then, should the promise of eternal life be found in Mishnah-tractate Sanhedrin-Makkot in the context of discussing the death penalty and how it is inflicted? What has that theological conviction about Israel being comprised of those who will enjoy eternal life to do with criminal justice, and why is the resurrection of the dead at the end of days classified as a matter of criminal justice and law?

The reason emerges within the very exposition of criminal justice. The order is (1) the earthly court and property cases; (2) the earthly court and capital punishment; (3) the heavenly court and the denial of life eternal; and, appended, (4) the earthly court and corporal punishment. We move from the procedures in adjudicating property cases to capital cases to corporal punishment (an add-on in Makkot). Within capital cases, we progress through the penalties for catalogues of crimes from the lightest through the heaviest. Each of these sins or crimes is tried before the earthly court, which inflicts the appropriate form of capital punishment. At the end, we turn to the most severe penalty of all. It is one that the earthly court cannot inflict but that only the Heavenly court can impose. That is the *denial,* to certain classes of sinners or criminals, of resurrection and restoration to Eden, the permanent extinction of the person. The auxiliary tractate Makkot, on flogging, then proceeds from capital to corporal punishment.

To say this directly, the Rabbinic sages come to the topic of criminal justice bearing in mind a profound theological issue: how God's justice is to be administered in such a way as to express God's mercy—even for sinners and criminals. It is only in dealing with this topic that the Rabbinic sages could make the statement they wished to set forth concerning God's merciful justice. What they wished to say is that even criminals condemned to the death penalty are able to atone for their sin through their death and may therefore look forward to eternal life. (The only exceptions to this rule are of a theological character, as will be seen.) Death atones for sin, however one dies; and ultimate justice entails divine forgiveness of nearly all sins and sinners.

But let us press the matter further: Why in *this* context and in no other? First, essential to the Rabbinic sages' thought is the conviction that all creatures are answerable to their Creator. Second, absolutely critical to their system is the fact that at the end of days the dead are raised for eternal life. What happens in this life and in this world does not tell the whole story of a human life. The virtuous may suffer in this world. The wicked may not stand in judgment in this world; and the death penalty expiates heinous crimes or sins, so that even the criminal or sinner gains a portion in the world to come. Therefore the criminal justice system encompasses paradoxes that require serious thought regarding the interplay of God's justice and God's mercy.

The Mishnah asks: How are God's justice and God's mercy reconciled in the case of the flagrant sinner or criminal? Specifically, does the sin or crime, which has estranged the sinner or criminal from God, close the door to life eternal? If it does, then justice is implacable and perfect. If it does not, then God is merciful—but what of justice? Where, specifically, is the atonement? The Mishnah answers that death forms the atoning event in the individual's life but not the end of that life, not personal extinction. It must follow that neither does the death penalty mark the utter annihilation of the sinner or criminal. On the contrary, having paid the penalty in this life, the sinner or criminal is situated with all of the rest of supernatural Israel, ready to "stand in judgment," meaning, to enter into the life of the world to come along with nearly everyone else.

What the law of the Mishnah explores therefore is, How is the Israelite sinner or criminal rehabilitated, through the criminal justice system, so as to rejoin Israel in all its eternity? The answer is that the criminal or sinner remains Israelite. So the law of the Mishnah-tractate Sanhedrin-Makkot embodies three theological principles:

(1) Israel endures forever, encompassing (nearly) all Israelites.

(2) Sinners or criminals are able to retain their position within that eternal Israel by reason of the penalties that expiate the specific sins or crimes spelled out by the law of the Mishnah.

(3) It is an act of merciful justice that is done when the sinner or criminal is put to death, for at that point he or she is assured of eternity along with everyone else.

God's justice comes to full expression in the penalty, which is instrumental and contingent; God's mercy endures forever in the forgiveness that follows expiation of guilt through the imposition of the penalty. That explains why the governing religious principle of Sanhedrin-Makkot is the perfect, merciful justice of God, and it accounts for the detailed exposition of the correct form of the capital penalty for each capital sin or crime. The punishment must fit the crime within the context of the Torah in particular so that, at the resurrection and the judgment, the crime will have been correctly expiated. Because the law of the Mishnah rests on the premise that God is just and that God has made us in the image of God, the law of the Mishnah cannot deem sufficient that the punishment fit the crime. Rather, given its premises, the law of the Mishnah must pursue the issue of what becomes of the sinner after the punishment. And the entire construction of the continuous exposition of Sanhedrin-Makkot aims at making this simple statement: the criminal, in God's image, after God's likeness, pays the penalty for crime in this world but therefore, like the rest of Israel, will stand in justice and, rehabilitated by having paid the penalty, will enjoy the world to come.

## Paying the Penalty for Crime in This World, Then Enjoying Eternity with (Nearly) All Israel

All this comes to play in Mishnah Sanhedrin-Makkot in the description of the death penalty of stoning. The ritual of stoning involves an admonition that explicitly declares the death penalty to serve as the means of atoning for all crimes and sins, leaving the criminal blameless and welcome into the kingdom of Heaven. I italicize the key language:

### MISHNAH-TRACTATE SANHEDRIN 6:2

[When the convicted criminal, condemned to stoning,] was ten cubits from the place of stoning, they say to him, "Confess," for it is usual for those about to be put to death to confess.

For whoever confesses has a share in the world to come.

For so we find concerning Achan, to whom Joshua said, "My son, I pray you, give glory to the Lord, the God of Israel, and confess to him, [and tell me now what you have done; hide it not from me]. And Achan answered Joshua and said, Truly have I sinned against the Lord, the God of Israel, and thus and thus I have done" (Josh. 7:19).

And how do we know that his confession achieved atonement for him? For it is said, "And Joshua said, Why have you troubled us? The Lord will trouble you this day" (Josh. 7:25)—

*This day you will be troubled, but you will not be troubled in the world to come.*

And if he does not know how to confess, they say to him, "Say as follows: 'Let my death be atonement for all of my transgressions.'"

The exposition is stunning. In the midst of the law of inflicting the death penalty comes the theological principle that the death penalty opens the way for life eternal! What follows in the tractate Sanhedrin-Makkot is a systematic demonstration of how God mercifully imposes justice upon sinners and criminals. But the law of the Mishnah also specifies where the limits to God's mercy are reached.

## Within the Mishnah's System of Criminal Justice, Who Is Not-Israel and Why?

An expansion of the rule that the death penalty opens the way for life eternal yields the exceptions—classes of persons excluded from resurrection and life eternal. Applying the principle articulated in the law of tractate Sotah, of measure for measure, in a predictable way, any among Israel who do not believe in the resurrection of the dead will be punished by being denied what they do not accept. Some few others bear the same fate, but note that only those are excluded from resurrection and the world to come who, by their own sins, have denied themselves that benefit. Specifically, they are those who deny that the teaching of the world to come derives from the Torah, those who deny that the Torah comes from God, or those who are hedonists. Exegesis of Scripture also yields the names of three kings and four commoners who will not be resurrected; also specified are the Generation of the Flood, the Generation of the Dispersion, the men of Sodom, the Generation of the Wilderness, the party of Korah, and the Ten Tribes. We return to the passage begun a bit earlier and consider it in full:

### Mishnah-tractate Sanhedrin 10:1

All Israelites have a share in the world to come,

as it is said, "Your people also shall be all righteous, they shall inherit the land forever; the branch of my planting, the work of my hands, that I may be glorified" (Isa. 60:21).

And these are the ones who have no portion in the world to come:

He who says, the resurrection of the dead is a teaching which does not derive from the Torah, and the Torah does not come from Heaven; and an Epicurean.

R. Aqiba says, "Also: He who reads in heretical books,

"and he who whispers over a wound and says, 'I will put none of the diseases upon you which I have put on the Egyptians, for I am the Lord who heals you' (Exod. 15:26)."

Abba Saul says, "Also: He who pronounces the divine Name as it is spelled out." All parties concur on the normative law. The idiosyncratic additions need not detain us. The working of pure justice is embodied in the denial of resurrection to those who deny the resurrection.

From classes of persons, we turn to specified individuals who are denied a place within Israel and entry in the world to come; all but one are Israelites, and the exception, Balaam, also has a special relation to Israel, as the gentile prophet who came to curse but ended with a blessing:

### MISHNAH-TRACTATE SANHEDRIN 10:2

Three kings and four ordinary folk have no portion in the world to come.

Three kings: Jeroboam, Ahab, and Manasseh.

Four ordinary folk: Balaam, Doeg, Ahitophel, and Gehazi.

Then come entire generations of gentiles before Abraham, who might have been considered for eternal life outside of the framework of God's self-manifestation first to Abraham and then in the Torah. These are the sinful generations in the history of humanity before Abraham and Sarah: the Generation of the Flood, the Generation of the Dispersion (following the destruction of the Tower of Babel), and the men of Sodom:

### MISHNAH-TRACTATE SANHEDRIN 10:3

The generation of the flood has no share in the world to come,

and they shall not stand in the judgment,

since it is written, "My spirit shall not judge with man forever" (Gen. 6:3)

neither judgment nor spirit.

The generation of the dispersion has no share in the world to come,

since it is said, "So the Lord scattered them abroad from there upon the face of the whole earth" (Gen. 11:8).

"So the Lord scattered them abroad"—in this world,

"and the Lord scattered them from there"—in the world to come.

The men of Sodom have no portion in the world to come,

since it is said, "Now the men of Sodom were wicked and sinners against the Lord exceedingly" (Gen. 13:13).

"Wicked"—in this world,

"And sinners"—in the world to come.

But they will stand in judgment.

R. Nehemiah says, "Both these and those will not stand in judgment,

"for it is said, 'Therefore the wicked shall not stand in judgment nor sinners in the congregation of the righteous' (Ps. 1:5).

'Therefore the wicked shall not stand in judgment'—this refers to the generation of the flood.

'Nor sinners in the congregation of the righteous'—this refers to the men of Sodom."

They said to him, "They will not stand in the congregation of the righteous, but they will stand in the congregation of the sinners."

The spies have no portion in the world to come,

as it is said, "Even those men who brought up an evil report of the land died by the plague before the Lord" (Num. 14:37).

"Died"—in this world.

"By the plague"—in the world to come.

So much for the three archetypal generations before and after the flood. The Generation of the Flood exceeded all bounds in its wickedness; the Generation of the Dispersion was arrogant toward Heaven; the men of Sodom practiced collective injustice (so the Rabbinic reading of the story goes). What about counterparts in Israel, from the Torah forward? The issue subject to contradictory opinion concerns the Generation of the Wilderness, which rejected the Land; the party of Korah, which rejected Moses' leadership; and the Ten Tribes, which sinned grievously. These match the gentile contingents.

Scripture thus contributes the details that refine the basic proposition; the framer has found the appropriate exclusions. But the prophet, in Scripture, also has provided the basic allegation on which all else rests, that is, "Israel will be entirely righteous and inherit the land forever." Denying the stated dogmas removes a person from the status of "Israel," in line with the opening statement.

To summarize: to be Israel means to rise from the grave, and that applies to all Israelites. That is to say, the given of the condition of Israel is that the entire holy people will enter the world to come—will enjoy the resurrection of the dead and eternal life. "Israel" then is anticipated to be the people of eternity. What of the gentiles, the other part of humanity that is comprised of idolaters?

### How the Gentiles Are Defined within the Mishnah's Laws: Living in the Midst of the Gentiles and Their Idolatry

It is by contrast with Israel that the gentiles are defined as idolaters; and the Mishnah makes its statement concerning them in the contrast of the law on how Israel is to relate to idolatry. That is the sole point at which the Mishnah's law takes an interest in gentiles. The Torah's policy toward idolatry is captured in passages such as the following:

> The graven images of their gods you shall burn with fire; you shall not covet the silver or the gold that is on them or take it for yourselves, lest you be ensnared by it; for it is an abomination to the Lord your God. And you shall not bring an abominable thing into your house and become accused like it. (Deut. 7:25-26)

But how Israel is to relate to the gentiles or the nations in general is not to be inferred from the implacable prohibition of idolatry in any form. So it is noteworthy that, while the Torah concerns itself with the disposition of idolatry—destroying idols and tearing down altars and the like—for its treatment of the same subject Mishnah-tractate Abodah Zarah takes as its problem the relationship of the Israelite to the gentile. Without further differentiation, whether Persian or Roman, Canaanite or Babylonian or Assyrian, the gentile is defined by the practice of idolatry. "Gentile" and "idolater" are synonymous, and "idol-worshiping" and "gentile" are equivalents.

The Mishnah's rules for interaction presuppose cohabitation of Israel and gentile individuals. They do not recognize gentiles as nations or communities, and they do not differentiate between and among gentile nations or communities. The law sets forth the way in which the Israelite can interact with the individual gentile while remaining uncorrupted by idolatry. Thus, the Torah provides instruction on destroying idolatry, assuming that Israel has the opportunity to do so, the law of the Mishnah explains how Israel is to coexist with idolatry, on the assumption that there is no alternative.

But the definition of the gentile as idolater pure and simple proves necessary but insufficient. For the interplay of Mishnah-tractates Sanhedrin-Makkot and Abodah Zarah should not be missed. Each defines its subject in opposition to the other: Sanhedrin-Makkot tells who is the Israelite and, by implication, the not-Israelite; and Abodah Zarah, what is the gentile and the not-gentile. At their intersection the tractates render blatant the theological proposition realized in legal terms: Israel stands for life; the gentiles, for death. The category "the nations" encompasses all persons who do not belong to Israel and therefore do not live in the kingdom of God. Israel encompasses the sector of humanity that knows and serves God by reason of God's self-manifestation in the Torah. "The nations" encompass all those placed by their own intention and active decision beyond the limits of God's self-revelation. Guided by the Torah, Israel worships God; without its illumination gentiles worship idols.

## The Issues Addressed by the Law of Idolatry

These theological propositions, however, do not allow us to predict what issues of a concrete nature will be addressed. Nor could we anticipate the way in which the law of the Mishnah addresses the theme of paganism. With issues of life and death in play, we should expect meditation on deep things. But, while Israelite sinners and criminals precipitate profound thought on the nature of God's response to atonement at death, pagans do not. The law of the Mishnah disposes of the gentiles in a practical way, theology rarely coming to the surface. It answers the question, How are the Israelites to conduct themselves in accord with the Torah so that at no point and in no way do they give support to idolatry and so betray the one and only God?

The issues that the law neglects are blatant. There is no accounting in the law of the Mishnah for the idolatry of the idolater. The same profound thinkers who are able to speak, through the legal discourse concerning capital punishment, of repentance, reconciliation, resurrection, restoration, and life eternal, disappoint in their treatment of the nations. Counterpart issues not only do not surface but also do not lurk at the foundations of their legal program.

The accounting for paganism and idolatry missing from the law is found in other forms of Rabbinic expression, especially in narratives of how the gentiles were offered the Torah and rejected it because it contradicted their very essence. Two examples given later will suffice to show how Rabbinic Judaism in its narrative theology demonstrated the justice of the fate of the gentiles. Many examples could be brought, and all of them supplement and underscore the limited and quite practical focus of the Mishnah's presentation of the gentiles and their idolatry—and how justice is done to them.

The Mishnah does not say, but surely takes for granted, that the gentiles are responsible for their own condition—another instance of divine justice being realized. That is because the gentiles deprived themselves of the Torah, which they rejected, and, showing the precision of justice, they rejected the Torah because the Torah deprived them of the very practices or traits that they deemed characteristic, essential to their being. That circularity marks the tale of how things were and how things always are; it is not historical but philosophical. But can the law of the Mishnah make such a statement? After we consider the narrative message, we shall take a look at how the law of the Mishnah explicitly sets forth the same judgment concerning the depravity of the idolaters.

The basic theory of gentiles, all of them assumed to be idolaters, is, first, gentiles always and everywhere and under any circumstance are going to perform an act of worship for one or another of their gods. Second, gentiles are represented as thoroughly depraved (not being regenerated by the Torah), so they will murder, fornicate, or steal at any chance they get; they routinely commit bestiality, incest, and various other forbidden acts of sexual congress. Here is how the Mishnah's law expresses these premises:

MISHNAH-TRACTATE ABODAH ZARAH 2:1

> They do not leave cattle in gentiles' inns,
> because they are suspect in regard to bestiality.
> And a woman should not be alone with them,
> because they are suspect in regard to fornication.
> And a man should not be alone with them,
> because they are suspect in regard to bloodshed.

The law then takes as its problem how Israel is to protect itself in a world populated by utterly immoral persons who exist wholly outside of the framework of the Torah and its government. Basically, the law embodies the principle of compromise where possible, but rigid conformity to the principles of the Torah under all circumstances at whatever cost. Israel must avoid anything more than routine courtesies and necessary exchanges with idolaters.

So, one must avoid entering into situations of danger that might provide opportunities for gentiles to carry out their natural instincts of murder, bestiality, and the like. Cattle are not to be left in their inns; a woman may not be left alone with gentiles, nor a man, the former by reason of probable fornication, the latter murder. Their physicians are not to be trusted, though when it comes to using them for beasts, that is all right. One also must avoid appearing to conduct oneself as an idolater, even if this is only an appearance. Thus, if while you are in front of an idol, you get a splint in your foot, you should not bend over to remove it, because it looks as though you are bowing down to the idol. But if it does not look that way, you are permitted to do so.

But there are objects that are assumed to be destined for idolatrous worship, and these under all circumstances are forbidden for Israelite trade. Israelites simply may not sell to gentiles anything that gentiles are likely to use, or that they explicitly say they are intending to use, for idolatry. That includes wine and the like. Whatever gentiles have used for idolatry may not be utilized afterward by Israelites, and that extends to what is left over from an offering to idols—for example, meat or wine. Israelites also may not sell to gentiles anything they are going to use in an immoral way—including wild animals for the arena, materials for the construction of places in which gentile immorality or injustice will occur, ornaments for an idol, and the like.

The gentiles' own character, the shape of their conscience then, now, and always, accounts for their condition—which, by an act of will, as we have noted, they can change. What they did not want, that of which they were by their own word unworthy, is denied them. And what they do want condemns them. So when each nation comes under judgment for rejecting the Torah, the indictment of each is spoken out of its own mouth, its own self-indictment is at the core. Given what we know about the definition of Israel as those destined to live and the gentiles as those not, we cannot find surprising that the entire account is set in that age to come to which the gentiles are denied entry.

When they protest the injustice of the decision that takes effect just then, they are shown the workings of the moral order, as the following quite systematic account of the governing pattern explains:

TALMUD OF BABYLONIA TRACTATE ABODAH ZARAH 1:1 I.2/2A-B:

> R. Hanina bar Pappa, and some say, R. Simlai, gave the following exposition [of the verse, "They that fashion a graven image are all of them vanity, and their delectable things shall not profit, and their own witnesses see not nor know" (Isa. 44:9)]: "In the age to come the Holy One, blessed be He, will bring a scroll of the Torah and hold it in his bosom and say, 'Let him who has kept himself busy with it come and take his reward.' Then all the gentiles will crowd together: 'All of the nations are gathered together' (Isa. 43:9). The Holy One, blessed be He, will say to them, 'Do not crowd together before me in a mob. But let each nation enter together with its scribes,' 'and let the peoples be gathered together' (Isa. 43:9), and the word 'people' means 'kingdom': 'and one kingdom shall be stronger than the other' (Gen. 25:23)."

We note that the players are the principal participants in world history: the Romans first and foremost, then the Persians, the other world rulers of the age:

> "The kingdom of Rome comes in first.
>
> "The Holy One, blessed be He, will say to them, 'How have you defined your chief occupation?'
>
> "They will say before him, 'Lord of the world, a vast number of marketplaces have we set up, a vast number of bathhouses we have made, a vast amount of silver and gold have we accumulated. And all of these things we have done only in behalf of Israel, so that they may define as their chief occupation the study of the Torah.'

"The Holy One, blessed be He, will say to them, 'You complete idiots! Whatever you have done has been for your own convenience. You have set up a vast number of marketplaces to be sure, but that was so as to set up whorehouses in them. The bathhouses were for your own pleasure. Silver and gold belong to me anyhow: "Mine is the silver and mine is the gold, says the Lord of hosts" (Hag. 2:8). Are there any among you who have been telling of "this," and "this" is only the Torah: "And this is the Torah that Moses set before the children of Israel" (Deut. 4:44).' So they will make their exit, humiliated."

The claim of Rome—to support Israel in Torah-study—is rejected on grounds that the Romans did not exhibit the right attitude, always a dynamic force in the theology. Then the other world rule enters in with its claim:

"When the kingdom of Rome has made its exit, the kingdom of Persia enters afterward.

"The Holy One, blessed be He, will say to them, 'How have you defined your chief occupation?'

"They will say before him, 'Lord of the world, We have thrown up a vast number of bridges, we have conquered a vast number of towns, we have made a vast number of wars, and all of them we did only for Israel, so that they might define as their chief occupation the study of the Torah.'

"The Holy One, blessed be He, will say to them, 'Whatever you have done has been for your own convenience. You have thrown up a vast number of bridges, to collect tolls, you have conquered a vast number of towns, to collect the corvée, and, as to making a vast number of wars, I am the one who makes wars: "The Lord is a man of war" (Exod. 19:17). Are there any among you who have been telling of "this," and "this" is only the Torah: "And this is the Torah that Moses set before the children of Israel" (Deut. 4:44).' So they will make their exit, humiliated.

"And so it will go with each and every nation."

As native categories, Rome and Persia are singled out, "all the other nations" play no role. Once more the law's theology reaches into its deepest thought on the power of intentionality, showing that what people want is what they get.

But matters cannot be limited to the two world empires of the Rabbinic age, Rome and Iran, standing in judgment at the end of time. The theology values balance and proportion, seeks complementary relationships, and therefore treats beginnings along with endings, the one going over the ground of the other. Accordingly, a recapitulation of the same event—the gentiles' rejection of the Torah—chooses as its setting not the last judgment but the first encounter, that is, the giving of the Torah itself. In the timeless world constructed by the Rabbinic sages, what happens at the outset exemplifies how things always happen, and what happens at the end embodies what has always taken place. The basic thesis is identical: the gentiles cannot accept the Torah because to do so they would have to deny their very character. But the exposition retains its interest because it takes its own course.

Now the gentiles are not just Rome and Persia. There are others. The claim is, it is natural for the gentiles (not just Rome and Persia) to violate some of the

Ten Commandments—specifically, not to murder, not to commit adultery, not to steal—yet these are essential to the Torah. So the reason that the gentiles rejected the Torah is that it prohibits deeds that the gentiles do by their very nature. The subtext here is that Israel ultimately is changed by the Torah, so that Israel exhibits traits nurtured by God and imparted by their encounter with the Torah. Once more a single standard applies to both components of humanity, but with opposite effect:

### SIFRÉ TO DEUTERONOMY CCCXLIII:IV.1FF.:

1. Another teaching concerning the phrase, "He said, 'The Lord came from Sinai'":

When the Omnipresent appeared to give the Torah to Israel, it was not to Israel alone that he revealed himself but to every nation.

First of all he came to the children of Esau. He said to them, "Will you accept the Torah?"

They said to him, "What is written in it?"

He said to them, "'You shall not murder' (Exod. 20:13)."

They said to him, "The very being of 'those men' [namely, us] and of their father is to murder, for it is said, 'But the hands are the hands of Esau' (Gen. 27:22). 'By your sword you shall live' (Gen. 27:40)."

At this point we cover new ground: other classes of gentiles who reject the Torah. Here the Torah's own narrative takes over, replacing the known facts of world politics presented in the earlier account and supplying instead evidence out of Scripture as to the character of the gentile group under discussion:

So he went to the children of Ammon and Moab and said to them, "Will you accept the Torah?"

They said to him, "What is written in it?"

He said to them, "'You shall not commit adultery' (Exod. 20:13)."

They said to him, "The very essence of fornication belongs to them [us], for it is said, 'Thus were both the daughters of Lot with child by their fathers' (Gen. 19:36)."

So he went to the children of Ishmael and said to them, "Will you accept the Torah?"

They said to him, "What is written in it?"

He said to them, "'You shall not steal' (Exod. 20:13)."

They said to him, "The very essence of their [our] father is thievery, as it is said, 'And he shall be a wild ass of a man' (Gen. 16:12)."

And so it went. He went to every nation, asking them, "Will you accept the Torah?"

For so it is said, "All the kings of the earth shall give you thanks, O Lord, for they have heard the words of your mouth" (Ps. 138:4).

Might one suppose that they listened and accepted the Torah?

Scripture says, "And I will execute vengeance in anger and fury upon the nations, because they did not listen" (Mic. 5:14).

The condition of the gentiles, pagans, then reveals God's justice: their own character explains their condition. The various gentile nations rejected the Torah for specific and reasonable considerations concretely, because the Torah prohibited deeds essential to their being. This point is made in so many words.

## How the Law of the Mishnah Provisionally Solves the Gentile Problem

For the Torah, the community at large forms the focus of the law, and the collectivity of holy Israel is not to negotiate with idolatry. In its Land, Israel is to wipe out idolatry, even as a memory. The Torah is clear that Israel is to obliterate all mention of idols (Exod. 23:13), to refuse to bow down to gentiles' gods or serve them, but to overthrow them and break them into pieces (Exod. 23:24): "You shall break down their altars and dash in pieces their pillars and hew down their Asherim and burn their graven images with fire" (Deut. 7:5). Israelites are commanded along these same lines:

> You shall surely destroy all the places where the nations whom you shall dispossess served their gods, upon the high mountains and upon the hills and under every green tree; you shall tear down their altars and dash in pieces their pillars and burn their Asherim with fire; you shall hew down the graven images of their gods and destroy their name out of that place. (Deut. 12:2–3)

Since the Torah supplies the foundations for the treatment of the matter by the Mishnah, the focus of discourse concerning the gentiles is idolatry. Scripture's law does not contemplate Israel's coexisting in the land with gentiles and their idolatry.

But the law of the Mishnah transforms the entire topic of idolatry into an essay on Israel's relationships with the nations, an undifferentiated realm of idolatry. The law of the Mishnah, then, centers on the negotiation between Israelites and the pagan world in which they live: How can Israelites conduct themselves in accord with the Torah so that at no point and in no way do they give support to idolatry?

Thus, the Mishnah uses the occasion of idolatry to contemplate a condition entirely beyond the imagination of Scripture, which is the hegemony of the idolatrous nations and the subjugation of monotheistic Israel. Rather, the law of the Mishnah deals with this-worldly, practical matters: commercial relationships, matters pertaining to idols, and finally the particular prohibition of wine, part of which has served as a libation to an idol. A single example of its law suffices for each of the three concerns:

MISHNAH-TRACTATE ABODAH ZARAH 1:1

> Before the festivals of gentiles for three days it is forbidden to do business with them.
>
> (1) To lend anything to them or to borrow anything from them.
>
> (2) To lend money to them or to borrow money from them.
>
> (3) To repay them or to be repaid by them.

The point is that in commercial relations the Israelite may do nothing to enhance the idolater's practice of idolatry. As to matters pertaining to idols:

MISHNAH-TRACTATE ABODAH ZARAH 3:1–3, 5

> 3:1 Images are prohibited that have in its hand a staff, bird, or sphere.
>
> 3:2 He who finds the shards of images—lo, these are permitted.
>
> [If] one found [a fragment] shaped like a hand or a foot, lo, these are prohibited, because objects similar to them are worshiped.

3:3 He who finds utensils upon which is the figure of the sun, moon, or dragon, should bring them to the Salt Sea. One breaks them into pieces and throws the powder to the wind or drops them into the sea.

Also: they may be made into manure, as it is said, "And there will cleave nothing of a devoted thing to your hand" (Deut. 13:18).

3:5 Gentiles who worship hills and valleys—these [hills or valleys] are permitted [for Israelite use], but what is on them is forbidden [for Israelite use], as it is said, "You shall not covet the silver or gold that is upon them."

On what account is an *asherah* prohibited [for Israelite use]? Because it has been subject to manual labor, and whatever has been subject to manual labor is prohibited. The Israelite must destroy idols and may not derive benefit from them.

What are the operative distinctions in play? They are three categories of relationship to gentile property: prohibited, tolerated, and wholly neutral transactions. There are relationships with gentiles that are absolutely prohibited, particularly occasions of idol worship; the law of the Mishnah recognizes that these are major commercial events. When it comes to commerce with idolaters, Israelites may not sell or in any way benefit from certain things, may sell but may not utilize certain others, and may sell and utilize yet others. There are these unstated premises within the law of the Mishnah: (1) what a gentile is not likely to use for the worship of an idol is not prohibited; (2) what may serve not as part of an idol but as an appurtenance thereto is prohibited for Israelite use but permitted for Israelite commerce; (3) what serves idolatry is prohibited for use and for benefit. Scripture makes no such distinctions; it deals with a simpler world. The Mishnah's laws cope with a much more complex situation. But the premises are the same as those of Scripture.

## What Is Central in the Mishnah's Law on Relationships with Idolaters?

Gentiles are idolaters, and Israelites worship the one, true God. In the Mishnah, that is the difference, the only consequential distinction, between Israel and the gentiles. What is central here, as in Mishnah-tractate Sanhedrin, is that Israel stands for life; the gentiles, like their idols, for death. An *asherah*-tree, that is, a tree that has served for idolatrous worship, like a corpse in Numbers 19, conveys uncleanness to those who pass underneath it. One may derive no benefit from the wood of such a tree:

**MISHNAH-TRACTATE ABODAH ZARAH 3:8**

3:8 [One should not sit in [an *asherah*'s] shade, but if he sat in its shade, he is clean.

And he should not pass underneath it, but if he passed underneath it, he is unclean.

If it was overshadowing public domain, taking away property from public use, and one passed beneath it, he is clean.

3:9 [If] one has taken pieces of wood from [an *asherah*], they are prohibited for benefit.

[If] he lit a fire in the oven with them, if it is a new oven, it is to be overturned. If it is an old oven, it must be allowed to cool down.

[If] he baked a loaf of bread in [the oven heated by the wood of an *asherah*], it is prohibited for benefit.

[If] the loaf of bread was mixed up with other loaves of bread, all of them are prohibited as to benefit.

The law of the Mishnah then serves as the means for the translation of theological conviction into social policy. As we saw earlier, the gentiles are assumed to be ready to murder any Israelite they can get their hands on, rape any Israelite women, and commit bestiality with any Israelite cow. The Mishnah cites few cases to indicate that that conviction responds to ordinary, everyday events; the hostility to gentiles flows from a theory of idolatry, not the alleged facts of everyday society, which the sages recognize is full of neighborly cordiality.

Then why take for granted that gentiles routinely commit the mortal sins of not merely idolatry but bestiality, fornication, and murder? It is because the law of the Mishnah takes as its task the realization of the theological principle that those who hate Israel hate God, those who hate God hate Israel, and God will ultimately vanquish Israel's enemies as God's own—just as God too was redeemed from Egypt. So the theory of idolatry, involving alienation from God, accounts for the wicked conduct imputed to idolaters, without regard to whether, in fact, that is how idolaters conduct themselves.

## God's Justice, the Gentiles' Hegemony, and the Mishnah's Law on the Gentiles: The Power of the Weaker Party

For the prophets of the Torah, gentile rule over Israel forms the point of tension, the source of conflict attracting attention and demanding explanation. They ask, How can justice order the world if the gentiles rule over God's people? They answer, gentiles rule as the instrument by which God punishes Israel for its sins. That is entirely familiar. Not so familiar is the Mishnah's empowerment of Israel, the weaker party. That is because the law of the Mishnah asks a different question from that of the Torah's prophets and answers its question in a different manner altogether. It asks about how Israel is to cope with facts that Israel cannot change, and it answers (as it does consistently) by setting forth rules that embody principles in concrete actions.

The law of the Mishnah therefore makes its own point. It presupposes not gentile hegemony but only gentile power. The prophets accord a role in God's plan to the gentile conquerors of Israel. The Rabbinic sages do not challenge that view, but they also do not go back over it. The Mishnah's law simply takes for granted that Israelites may make choices. They may specifically refrain from trading in what gentiles value in the service of their gods and may hold back from gentiles what gentiles require for that service. Tractate Abodah Zarah legislates for a world in which Israelites, while subordinate in some ways, control their own conduct and govern their own destiny. Israelites may live in a world governed by gentiles, but they decide what to sell and what not to sell, whom to hire for what particular act of labor and to whom not to sell their own labor; and, above all, Israelite traders may determine to give up opportunities denied them by the circumstance of gentile idolatry.

The law of the Mishnah therefore makes the formidable statement that Israel exercises freedom to make choices within the realm of reality dictated by God. Israel possesses the opportunity within the context of everyday life to preserve a territory free of idolatrous contamination, just as Israel in entering the Land was to create a territory free of the worship of idols and their presence. In the world at large, Israel may find itself subject to the will of others; but within the house of Israel, Israelites can be free of idolatry. They can and should establish a realm for God's rule and presence. And if to establish a domain for God Israelites must practice self-abnegation, refrain from actions of considerable weight and consequence, well, much of the Torah concerns itself with what people are not supposed to do, and God's rule comes to realization in acts of restraint.

The law of the Mishnah focuses on an inner world of an Israel in command of itself, responsible for its own condition, as the prophets maintained, but responsible in a different framework, for a different situation from that contemplated by the prophets. The Mishnah sees that world as being within Israel's dominion, the realm for which Israel bears responsibility. It is there that the Rabbinic sages legislate.

## The Gentiles Reconsidered: The Commandments to Which Gentiles Are Subject

This stark division leaves open the critical question, Are gentiles wholly outside of God's kingdom, and are they subject to no divine imperatives at all? Not at all. God does not neglect the gentiles or fail to exercise dominion over them. For even now, gentiles are subject to a number of commandments or religious obligations. God cares for gentiles as for Israel, God wants gentiles as much as Israel to enter the kingdom of Heaven, and God assigns to gentiles opportunities to evince their acceptance of God's rule. In fact there are seven religious obligations that specifically apply to the "children of Noah," meaning, of course, all the nations. In spelling them out, the Tosefta supplements Mishnah-tractate Abodah Zarah:

### TOSEFTA-TRACTATE ABODAH ZARAH 8:4–6

Concerning seven religious requirements were the children of Noah admonished: [1] setting up courts of justice, [2] the prohibition of idolatry, [3] the prohibition of blasphemy [cursing the Name of God], [4] the prohibition of fornication, [5] the prohibition of bloodshed, and [6] the prohibition of thievery, [7] the prohibition of consuming a limb cut from a living being.

As in the case of Israelites, so the death penalty applies to a Noahide (Talmud of Babylonia Tractate Sanhedrin 7:5 I.4-5/57a): "On account of violating three religious duties are children of Noah put to death: on account of adultery, murder, and blasphemy."

When dealing with the gentiles, the law of the Mishnah speaks of Israel, not the gentiles; what precipitates the formation of the law concerns Israel's response to gentile conduct, and that is all that matters. The Mishnah thereby constructs, indeed defines, the interiority of an Israel sustaining God's service in a world of idolatry: life against death in the two concrete and tangible dimensions by which life is sustained: trade and the production of food, the foci of the law of the Mishnah. No wonder that, at Mishnah-tractate Abodah Zarah 1:1, Israel must refrain from engaging with idolatry on days of the festivals for idols that the great gentile fairs embody—especially then! The presentation of the law of the Mishnah commences with the single most important, comprehensive point—as usual.

### Israel and the Gentiles

In the law of the Mishnah, Israel does not constitute an ethnic group, a nation or people defined by culture or measured by this-worldly matters of practical consequence. Status as an Israelite, part of "Israel," comes about by reason of the Torah, Israel forms the holy community of those destined for life eternal, and that constitutes not an ethnic group, nation, or people, but a social entity that is *sui generis*. To offer the gentiles less than life eternal within eternal Israel is to promise them nothing and to betray the Torah that offers them resurrection and restoration. Taken together, Mishnah-tractate Sanhedrin and Mishnah-tractate Abodah Zarah offer a response that today, as for two millennia past, the Mishnah has made to the world beyond the Torah: there is God, one and unique, made known only through the Torah, and there is nothing else. That is why, too, there is life or there is death, but nothing in between.

# Corporate Israel and
the Individual Israelite

# 4 CORPORATE ISRAEL AS A MORAL ENTITY

## Tractates Sheqalim and Bikkurim

FOR HUMANITY IN GENERAL, according to the law of the Mishnah, individuality is the norm. The paradigm is Adam and Eve. Individuality means that everyone, Israelite or gentile, bears responsibility one by one for his or her moral standing before God. Thus, for example, each gentile is individually answerable for idolatry and, comparably, each Israelite is individually responsible for rebellion against God. But while gentiles in the law of the Mishnah do not coalesce into larger communities, do not become, for example, nations or peoples responsible *collectively* for their joint character and conduct, Israelites do. This exception, constituted solely by Israel, forms a collective that bears responsibility for the enduring community in family and in society. In perhaps too simple a formula, humanity (the children of Noah) is individual by nature, whereas humanity (solely in its Israelite sector) forms a social entity by nurture. That is, by the nurture of the Torah.

But precisely how does Israel form a corporate body, one that transcends its individual components? And how does the shared, communal status of Israelites as Israel come to concrete expression in the law of the Mishnah? The mechanisms for realizing Israel, that whole that transcends the individual Israelite parts, are few but serve well.

### Individual and Personal Autonomy

Before proceeding, let me define the terms and categories that govern in chapters 4 and 5. The first and foremost has just occurred: "individuation." By "individuation" I mean the power of persons deliberately to distinguish themselves from one another, each from all others. The Mishnah describes individuation as follows:

Therefore man was created alone . . .

. . . to portray the grandeur of the Holy One, blessed be He. For a person mints many coins with a single seal, and they are all alike one another, but the King of kings of kings, the Holy One, blessed be He, minted all human beings with that seal of his with which he made the first Adam, yet not one of them is like anyone else.

Therefore everyone is obligated to maintain, "On my account the world was created." (Mishnah-tractate Sanhedrin 4:5)

All of humanity is minted with God's seal ("in our image"), yet each person is unique. That is the theological doctrine of individuality effected by processes of legitimate individuation. By "personal autonomy," by contrast, I mean the right of individuals to define themselves in terms that are idiosyncratically generated, not in relationship to others at all. Personal autonomy, then, distinguishes an individual from all others and validates his or her insistence upon the right of radical isolation: for example, by allowing an individual to place personal conscience above other considerations and obligations. Rabbinic Judaism legitimates individuation but categorically denies the utter autonomy of persons.

In this context individuation represents a claim to form of oneself a distinctive personality, one possessed of that "my" in "On *my* account the world was created." Individuation is contextual: in the setting of other persons, this is what makes me into *me.* "Personal autonomy" represents a much more extreme position. It goes beyond the mere allegation of legitimate, even commendable, individual difference. It would seek to free the individual from having to answer to others at all. Personal autonomy, for the purposes of this inquiry, represents the definition of the individual out of all relationship to the social order: his or her right to defy all social norms in the name of individual integrity, his or her right to claim absolute autonomy in the cause of truth. In common contexts, rights of religious freedom, free speech, freedom of the press, and above all freedom of conscience exemplify the ways in which the legal expression of a social culture accords to members of society the status and right of "personal autonomy." In our context, this is more than a matter of comparing and contrasting. Individuation is the celebration of the "I" over any "we"; but personal autonomy stands for the celebration of the "I" and the annihilation of the "we" altogether.

Keeping this distinction in mind clarifies the next step in the analysis. All humanity—Israelite, not-Israelite—in accordance with the law of the Mishnah—possesses the right of individuation. As to personal autonomy, within remarkably broad limits, all not-Israelites may claim close to complete personal autonomy, there being no boundaries of a social order to limit them. One single social entity—Israel—forms a corporate body that imposes its boundaries, its shape, and its structure upon individuals. And it goes without saying that the whole thereby exceeds the sum of its parts. Being "Israel" imposes on individuals rights and responsibilities vastly in excess of the basic obligations incumbent upon other individuals. To these others, classed as "the children of Noah," seven duties pertain—to establish courts of justice, refrain from murder and adultery, practice humane treatment of animals, and the like. To Israel, hundreds of imperatives—613 it is alleged—pertain: "Only you have I known of all the families of man, therefore I will visit upon you all your iniquities" is how Amos put it (Amos 3:2). The other side of the coin is expressed in the following:

### MISHNAH-TRACTATE MAKKOT 3:16

R. Hananiah b. Aqashia says, "The Holy One, blessed be He, wanted to give merit to Israel.

"Therefore he gave them abundant Torah and numerous commandments,

"as it is said, 'It pleased the Lord for his righteousness' sake to magnify the Torah and give honor to it' (Isa. 42:21)."

## The Plural "You": Corporate Israel as Moral Entity

Viewed communally, the Romans, the Persians, and the Canaanites bear collective traits. But they are not considered collective communities in relationship to God. The Mishnah knows Israel as *the* social order that bears moral obligations to God. Corporate Israel alone transcends the grave, and that is so for the community and the individual: Israel is eternal. Accordingly, corporate Israel, addressed as a collectivity in the plural "you," is uniquely subject to divine imperatives. Belonging to Israel bears uniform consequences for each Israelite ("All Israelites . . ."), no matter how they differ as individuals.

How then does the law of the Mishnah distinguish corporate Israel from corporate Rome or corporate Iran or corporate Canaan? The answer is, by the contrast between its treatment of corporate Rome and corporate Israel. The Mishnah does not legislate for Rome distinguished from Iran or Canaan: all gentile communities are characterized by idolatry. Not a single rule, let alone a sizable category of rules, pertains solely to Canaanites or Babylonians or Medians or Greeks or Romans or any other nation or people, all of which, in the mythic framework of the Rabbinic reading of Scripture, have distinctive roles. But, as we noted in reference to tractate Abodah Zarah, "the idolaters" form an undifferentiated mass in the law.

When viewed in contrast to "the gentiles," always and only treated as singular individuals, corporate Israel does not break down into individual Israelites. That is the very mark of its uniqueness. That trait, in God's view, forms of Israel an entity larger than its parts, since it imposes the status of the entire group upon every single person in it. How that is effected remains to be seen. But even at the outset the question of the relationship of the Israelite to corporate Israel presents itself. The Israelite bears responsibility not only for what he or she does as a private person, like any gentile, but also for what all Israel does collectively. Two issues then demand attention, and, driven by its own powerful logic, the Mishnah's law system, in two tractates, responds to them.

First, how does the law of the Mishnah deal with the Israelites' ambiguous status—both individual answerability and shared responsibility? The answer emerges in the law of tractate Sheqalim, which defines collective atonement for all Israel. Here the individual Israelite forms an integral part of corporate Israel through participating in the daily rite of atonement of all Israel.

Israel forms a moral entity as a community that requires atonement: an atoning community.

That leads to the second question: Precisely how does the individual in full
individuality identify with corporate Israel? What differentiates and expresses
the particularity of the Israelite within the community of Israel? Here the individual Israelite defines himself or herself not only as a member of a natural family, genealogically, but also as a party to corporate Israel, a social entity that
both encompasses and transcends the natural family. Each Israelite does this
by telling, about himself or herself personally, the common narrative of all
Israel. And the details count: this is not a mere fabrication or generic identification. The law of the Mishnah provides an actual occasion for the Israelite
male householder to position himself by reason of unique genealogy within the
larger story of all Israel. This weaving of the threads represented by the lives
of individuals in families into the tapestry of the whole Israelite social order
takes place in the law of tractate Bikkurim.

These are the two means by which the law of the Mishnah provides the
individual in Israel with a standing and a grounding in corporate Israel. Israel
is a singular entity within humanity, distinguished from, though comparable
to, the rest of humanity. In mythic-narrative terms, Israelites are among the
children of Noah, to be sure, but they are also the children of Abraham and
Sarah and as such are part of a covenantal family.

## Corporate Israel: Unique in Its Peoplehood

The law of the Mishnah provides for the condition of corporate Israel as
a moral entity with no counterpart in the rest of humanity. Surprisingly, what
marks Israel in community as distinct is that Israel as corporate community has
sinned all together and all at once. The Mishnah does not specify the occasion,
but the Torah does: the narrative of the Golden Calf made at the moment God
was giving Moses the Torah tells the tale. Having sinned as a community,
Israel is required to atone all together as well. So, individual Israelites belong
to community that begins with Abraham and Sarah and lives eternally, an
Israel that transcends its individual parts. Nevertheless, each Israelite endures
in full individuality within corporate Israel. Israelites collectively live forever,
but are judged and stand in judgment individually, a very subtle notion indeed.

Contrast the condition of humanity at large, the gentiles. In a profound
sense they are *un-social-ized*. That is to say, gentiles are deemed not to form a
society. Neither by nature (genealogy) nor by nurture (culture) are they formed
into social, corporate moral entities, with each person bearing responsibility
for the whole and with culpability for the acts of the whole imposed upon each.
The law does not differentiate among gentiles' "families," "societies," "peoples," "nations," and the like. Groups of gentiles—families or communities
bound by culture or nationality—constitute only collections of individuals, not
something more, something morally other. The collectivities, however classi-

fied, represent a mere happenstance, bearing no standing in the divine scheme of things. It is standing in relationship to the divine that is the critical determinant.

Individuality defines the natural condition of humanity, inclusive of Israel. But corporate Israel is formed by reason of God's intervention and Israel's response. That theological principle is expressed in the Torah in narrative and in the Mishnah in law derived from that narrative. The Torah accounts for the community of Israel as a result of God's activity in the repair of the flawed world: God's self-manifestation in the call to Abraham; in the liberation of Israel from Egypt; at the Sea; at Sinai; in the acquisition of the Land. For that reason, God judges Israel as a whole, not only severally but jointly. That captures the mythic formulation by the Torah of how individuals—the descendants of the patriarchs and the matriarchs and the mixed multitude that went out of Egypt—became the corporate community, unique Israel. It is through divine activity: revelation, engagement, intervention. Again, it is standing in relationship to the divine that is the critical determinant.

### The Radical Individuality of Gentiles and the Corporate Israel

The law of the Mishnah defines the normative conduct of gentiles in negative terms. It defines Israelite norms, at once individual and collective, in positive ones. In both cases, the Mishnah begins with the conception of eternal and corporate Israel as set forth in the Torah.

The negative definition comes first. The law of the Mishnah holds that gentiles—by reason of being idolaters—do not even constitute families, the smallest social unit beyond the individual that can be imagined by the Torah. Gentile parents have no children recognized by the law, not even for purposes of inheritance or marriage. Gentile individuals in the Mishnah have no ancestry and produce no descendants. They thus do not possess family relationships of legal standing or material consequence. Their utter individuality is underlined by that fact: the gentile family is deemed null. It is an adventitious grouping, nothing but individual members.

Thus, in the law of Judaism, gentile family ties bear no implications for either consanguinity or inheritance. If a gentile becomes an Israelite, his or her prior family ties are null. He or she is viewed as a newborn child; the father and mother of every convert are Abraham our father and Sarah our mother. These are explicitly not the natural parents. In the law of the Mishnah, therefore, a gentile mother and her son, or a brother and a sister, after conversion to Judaism may marry without violating the Torah's laws against incest. A convert who dies without Israelite heirs (produced in a union with an Israelite after conversion) cannot bequeath property to gentile natural relations. Lacking an Israelite heir, the property is deemed ownerless. The convert to Judaism thus has no natural heirs by law. In these concrete ways, the distinction between Israel as a social order and gentiles as masses of individuals bearing no traits of socialization (in the sense just now defined) comes to expression.

The definitions for Israel's obligations are positive. They are found in how the law of the Mishnah defines the relationship of the Israelite to Israel—the individual to the community. First, precisely how does an individual by obligation take his or her place within Israel and with what consequence? The answer to that, at a fundamental level, defines the character of "Israel." It indicates for what purpose Israel is so constituted as to act in common, thus, what links individuals into Israel. Along these same lines, second, we ask how the individual defines his or her place within the group and with what outcome.

Our task, therefore, is to follow the social theory of the law of the Mishnah as it affords definition of the individual embedded in the Israelite social order (Sheqalim) *and* differentiated therein (Bikkurim).

## How the Individual by Obligation, Not Volition, Takes a Place within the Social Construct Israel: Tractate Sheqalim

Tractate Sheqalim deals with the collection and disposition of the half-sheqel collected from all Israelite males, wherever they are located, in support of the Temple's daily whole offerings. This is not a votive gift but an obligatory one, and in that context all males are required to donate the same (paltry) sum. The Torah describes the half-sheqel in this language, in which I have italicized the critical clause:

> The Lord said to Moses, "When you take the census of the people of Israel, *then each shall give a ransom for himself* to the Lord when you number them, that there be no plague among them when you number them.
>
> "Each who is numbered in the census shall give this: half a sheqel, according to the sheqel of the sanctuary . . . half a sheqel as an offering to the Lord. Every one who is numbered in the census, from twenty years old and upward, shall give the Lord's offering. The rich shall not give more, and the poor shall not give less, than the half-sheqel
>
> "*when you give the Lord's offering to make atonement for yourselves. And you shall take the atonement money from the people of Israel and shall appoint it for the service of the tent of meeting; that it may bring the people of Israel to remembrance before the Lord, so as to make atonement for yourselves*" (Exod. 30:11–16).

From this passage of Scripture, we may derive the answer to the question that preoccupied the law of the Mishnah in the present matter: At what point is all Israel viewed as a moral entity, with individual Israelites formed into a corporate body, responsible collectively? The answer must be found in the facts elicited by the question, What must every Israelite head of household, without exception or variation, do *because, and only because, he belongs to Israel?* That is a fundamental marker of the corporate community's encompassing individuals and making them add up to something more than they are one by one.

The answer is blatant. What every Israelite male is obligated to do solely because he belongs to the collectivity of Israel is annually to contribute the half-sheqel to support the public offerings of the Temple. Each Israelite male must contribute his share of those offerings, which are described from the Torah forward as collective atonement—atonement for all Israel. That view is expressed in so many words in the Tosefta's complement to the Mishnah's law, once more with the critical language italicized:

**TOSEFTA-TRACTATE SHEQALIM 1:6**

They exact pledges from Israelites for their sheqels, so that the public offerings might be made of their [funds].

This is like a man who got a sore on his foot, and the doctor had to force it and cut off his flesh so as to heal him.

*Thus did the Holy One, blessed be He, exact a pledge from Israelites for the payment of their sheqels,*

*so that the public offerings might be made of their [funds].*

*For public offerings appease and [collectively] effect atonement between Israel and their father in heaven.*

Likewise we find of the heave offering of sheqels which the Israelites paid in the wilderness, as it is said, "And you shall take the atonement money from the people of Israel and shall appoint it for the service of the tent of meeting; that it may bring the people of Israel to remembrance before the Lord, so as to make atonement for yourselves]" (Exod. 30:16).

This is concise. Every Israelite male is obligated to contribute equally to the provision of the daily whole offerings, which atone for all Israel collectively. These have no bearing on the status of the individual donor, other than that he be an Israelite male. Selected other classes of Israel—women, for example—may join in as well. So in the daily whole offerings Israel is incorporated. Corporate Israel forms an atoning community, readying itself to stand in judgment and enter the Garden of Eden for eternal life.

The daily whole offerings are presented at dawn and dusk to atone for the sins of all Israel. These and certain counterpart offerings, like those of the Day of Atonement (Lev. 16), are explicitly designated to effect atonement for the community as a whole. They are not to be confused with the atonement offerings (sin offerings, guilt offerings, and the like) that the Torah provides for individual expiation of personal sins committed inadvertently. Individual atonement for inadvertent sin is attained through the sin offering and the guilt offering:

**MISHNAH-TRACTATE KERITOT 1:2**

For those [thirty-six classes of transgressions] are people [individually] liable, for deliberately doing them, to the punishment of extirpation,

and for accidentally doing them, to the bringing of a sin offering,

and for not being certain of whether or not one has done them, to a suspensive guilt offering (Lev. 5:17).

The individual suffers personally for what he or she has inadvertently done to violate the law of the Torah. The individual atones through death for deliberate sin; the Day of Atonement serves to suspend the penalty, the moment of death completes it. One cannot deliberately sin and trade off with an animal sacrifice; God wants the heart, so an act of rebellion not followed by a change of heart is indelible. But if a sinful act is not deliberate, then a sin offering suffices, along with an unconditional guilt offering.

Two other methods of atonement for sin (as mentioned above) are death, on the one side, and the advent of the Day of Atonement, on the other, which accomplishes atonement: "For on this day atonement shall be made for you to cleanse you of all your sins" (Lev. 16:30). Death marks the final atonement for sin, which bears its implication for the condition of the person at the resurrection. Because one atones through death (accompanied at the hour of death by a statement of repentance, "May my death be atonement for all my sins," in the liturgy), when one is raised from the dead, the atonement for all one's sins is complete. For almost all, the judgment after resurrection becomes a formality. That is why "all Israel has a portion in the world to come," with the few exceptions we know from the last chapter. The Day of Atonement provides atonement, as the Torah makes explicit, for the sins of the year for which one has repented, and that accounts for the elaborate rites of confession that fill the day. Here is how the methods of atonement—of death for a lifetime, and the Day of Atonement for the year just past—are sorted out:

MISHNAH-TRACTATE YOMA 8:8

> A sin offering and an unconditional guilt offering atone.
>
> Death and the Day of Atonement atone when joined with repentance.
>
> Repentance atones for minor transgressions of positive and negative commandments.
>
> And as to serious transgressions, [repentance] suspends the punishment until the Day of Atonement comes along and atones.

So much for the condition of individuals. But daily, morning and night, all Israelites atone for what all Israel has done—that is the contrast that the passage of the Tosefta cited above draws.

Then what is the theology of Israel realized in the law of the Mishnah? It is that the social entity of corporate Israel represents a sinful community. Individual Israelites, party to the community of Israel, all together sinned and all together share in the task of collective atonement. This theology is symbolized in the half-sheqel, paid by all Israelites. It serves as the principal means by which all males are obligated, and women permitted, to participate in the public atonement offerings. So all Israelites everywhere relate to God through support of the public offerings that expiate collective guilt. In the obligation to provide that support all are equal, rich and poor, priest and convert, resident of the Land and of the Exile alike.

## How the Individual Situates Himself within Israel: Tractate Bikkurim

The story implicit in the Mishnah's law of tractate Sheqalim tells of corporate, undifferentiated Israel before God, atoning for collective sin with a collective sacrifice. But how *in the very context* of the corporate community do individuals define their role in the collectivity of Israel. Through the rite of presenting Firstfruits described in Mishnah-tractate Bikkurim, male landholders in the Land of Israel link themselves to corporate Israel in an act of individual amalgamation with the community at large. The Israelite male householder tells the story of corporate Israel in connection with *his* personal fate and condition.

We begin with the Torah, for the law of the Mishnah amplifies the law of the Torah into normative conduct. The presentation of the Firstfruits[1] defines the occasion for declaring who in his person, individually, is and who is not that Israel of whom the Torah speaks in defining the terms of the Declaration made with the presentation of the Firstfruits. That is the one to whom reference is made in the statement, to which we shall return. I italicize the relevant language:

> "A *wandering Aramean* was my *father,*
>
> and he went down into Egypt and sojourned there, few in number; and there he became a nation, great, mighty, and populous. And the Egyptians treated us harshly and afflicted us . . . and the Lord brought us out of Egypt . . . and he brought us to this place and gave us this land. . . .
>
> *And behold, now I bring the first of the fruit of the ground that* thou, O Lord, *have given* me" (Deut. 26:5, 10)

Thus, as articulated in the cited language, the narrative moves from "we" to "I." The transaction is between you, singular, and me, singular. Israel's story becomes the individual Israelite's story. He is now a person fully embodying the community of which he is an integral part, entirely absorbed within that community—yet with a distinct and personal identity. That is how the individual Israelite incorporates himself within Israel. *His* father went down to Egypt few and became a nation. Israel, that nation, is his own family. But the story then proceeds to further chapters, not only the servitude of Egypt and the Exodus but also the advent to the Land and the division of the Land. By the language, "the first of the fruit of the ground that *you* have given *me*," the whole is transformed into a personal transaction, one between the singular "you" and "me." And the articulation of the statement by the law of the Mishnah underscores the individuality of the participants: God and the Israelite.

Accordingly, resorting to the Torah and adopting its tale for themselves, individual Israelite males tell their personal story within Israel's collective story. In that way, in the story that the individual Israelite tells in his own regard, in the first person singular, the individual Israelite finds a place for *himself* in particular in the corporate body of Israel. Then the narrative shifts from the first person singular ("what happened to me when I went forth from

---

[1] We are dealing not with the generic first fruits, but with the particular offering Bikkurim, translated here as Firstfruits, a specific designation, hence the capital throughout.

Egypt") to the first person plural ("we shall do and we shall obey" [Exod. 24:7]). That is not the only rite that links the living generation with the experience of the ancestors. The Passover Narrative or Haggadah contains another such rite of identifying the private person—here the family—with the generality of all Israel:

> We were the slaves of Pharaoh in Egypt; and the Lord our God brought us forth from there with a mighty hand and an outstretched arm. And if the Holy One, blessed be He, had not brought our fathers forth from Egypt, then surely we, and our children, and our children's children, would be enslaved to Pharaoh in Egypt. And so, even if all of us were full of wisdom and understanding, well along in years and deeply versed in the tradition, we should still be bidden to repeat once more the story of the exodus from Egypt; and he who delights to dwell on the liberation is one to be praised.
>
> For ever after, in every generation, every Israelite must think of himself as having gone forth from Egypt.

The story of Israel then is spelled out, and in the course of the narrative, Israel comes to definition: a family become a people, saved by God from bondage.

### Israel, the Israelite, and the Land of Israel

The Israelite is not alone in incorporating his (and, by extension, her) personal story into the collectivity of Israel. The Land itself plays a functional role in the act of incorporation, of transformation, which takes place through the rite of telling a story. The Land joins in defining this occasion, designated by the Torah, the presentation of the Firstfruits, and the recitation of the Declaration. The point of the Declaration is to link the Israelite to the Land, and the meeting of the Israelite with God, in the presentation of the Firstfruits, takes place in the venue of the Land.

The intent is transparent: the individual Israelite male "I" attains recognition of "you," God, not only on his own but also within corporate Israel. This he does, in line with the Torah, through his situation and his possession of a share in the Land of Israel. The Land links family to family and all families (situated thereon) into corporate Israel. It is unique among lands by reason of God's perpetual concern for it. That is what enchants the Land and makes it party to the lives of those who live upon it, whether the Canaanites whom it vomited up by reason of their corruption (Lev. 18:28) or the Israelites, in perpetual danger of the same fate (Lev. 26:32ff.). The full force of that assertion becomes clear only in the encounter with the Torah's narrative, which is told along with the specification of actions required to confirm that narrative set forth in the law of the Mishnah.

The Torah treats the act of separating Firstfruits as acknowledgment of God's faithfully keeping the promise to give God's people the Land. It further encompasses the first harvest of wheat within the calendar of the cult. Of the three pertinent passages of the Torah, Deuteronomy 26:1–11, Leviticus 23:9–21, and Numbers 28:26, the first, part of which we met just now, is the most important in this context:

When you come into the land that the Lord your God gives you for an inheritance and have taken possession of it and live in it, you shall take some of the first of all the fruit of the ground that you harvest from your land the Lord your God gives you and you shall put it in a basket and you shall go to the place that the Lord your God shall choose to make his name dwell there.

And you shall go to the priest who is in office at that time and say to him, "I declare this day to the Lord your God that I have come into the land that the Lord swore to our fathers to give us."

Then the priest shall take the basket from your hand and set it down before the altar of the Lord your God.

And you shall make response before the Lord your God: "A wandering Aramean was my father, and he went down into Egypt and sojourned there, few in number; and there he became a nation, great, mighty, and populous. And the Egyptians treated us harshly and afflicted us and laid upon us hard bondage. Then we cried to the Lord the God of our fathers, and the Lord heard our voice and saw our affliction, our toil, and our oppression; and the Lord brought us out of Egypt with a mighty hand and an out-stretched arm, with great terror, with signs and wonders; and he brought us to this place and gave us this land, a land flowing with milk and honey. And behold, now I bring the first of the fruit of the ground that thou, O Lord, have given me."

And you shall set it down before the Lord your God and worship before the Lord your God; and you shall rejoice in all the good that the Lord your God has given to you and to your house, you and the Levite and the sojourner who is among you. (Deut. 26:1-11)

The law of the Mishnah along this line requires Firstfruits to be presented annually out of the produce native to the Land of Israel. The produce is presented on Pentecost, when the required Declaration is made; it is carried in a basket that is waved by the priest before the altar. What is important in the law of the Mishnah is simple. (1) Only the householder presents Firstfruits. The "householder" refers to (2) an Israelite male who owns and farms land in the Land of Israel. He and he alone embodies in his person united by inheritance to the Land the whole of Israel's story. The Israelite who is the bearer of Israel's narrative in his person then is the male who has inherited land in the Land of Israel and who farms that land and produces a crop; he returns to God the Firstfruits of the crop produced by the Land, the outcome of the partnership between the Israelite family and the Land of Israel.

## Genealogy and Individuality Realized through the Land

The aspect of genealogy and family history that matters is possession of the Land. The emphasis on personal genealogy and family history, on the one side, and enlandisement—possession of a share of the actual holy Land—as essential to the character of corporate Israel, on the other, is not to be missed. It is within the corporate, enlandised community that the Israelite householder distinguishes himself. Israel as a collectivity is actualized by the encounter with God through possession of the Land.

What is the meaning of the Declaration, "and he brought us to this place and gave us this land, a land flowing with milk and honey. And behold, now I bring the first of the fruit of the ground that thou, O Lord, have given me"? The householder's is a remarkable statement, bringing what he calls his own but what he merely possesses on God's sufferance—and then speaking of *himself* and *his* fathers. It is this rite that defines in acutely individual terms the relationship of God and Israel, and of Israel to the Land by reason of God's gift. This is made actual in the person of the Israelite individual and his family.

The rite of the Firstfruits makes the relationship between God and Israel personal and immediate, familial and genealogical—wholly through the nexus of the Holy Land. The "I" is representative of the "we," the story that is recapitulated is the story of everybody subject to the Land that formed Israel's promised destination. Therein and thereby, corporate Israel and the individual Israelite (male householder) are identified and joined: this particular householder, owner of a plot of land in the Land, which he inherited from his family and will bequeath to his sons.

## The Corporate Dimension of the Story of Israel Repeated in the Offering of Firstfruits

But if it is everybody's story, then how is the individual singled out in full personality? The law of the Mishnah insists that Firstfruits are presented and their purpose and standing explicated only by the *specific* Israelite householder born to inherit the Land. The Firstfruits come out of crops raised in his *own* fields and presented only by him personally to the priesthood only in the Temple. Now, when the law of the Mishnah wishes to state that Israel in its fleshly embodiment of families through genealogical ties relates to God at the Temple through the gifts of grace presented by the Land, it can make no more particular and concrete statement than that.

That is how the law of the Mishnah through its systematic definition answers the question, Who is Israel and who is not? The question is answered in terms of who does not present Firstfruits at all. Those who do not own the land that has produced the produce do not present Firstfruits or make the Declaration that celebrates possession of the Land. One does not present Firstfruits from produce that has grown on land he does not own.

MISHNAH-TRACTATE BIKKURIM 1:1–2

1:1 There are [those who] bring [the] Firstfruits [of the produce of their land] and recite [the Declaration, "I declare this day . . ." (Deut. 26:3–10)], those who bring [Firstfruits] but do not recite, and there are [those] who do not bring [Firstfruits at all].

These are the [people] who do not bring [Firstfruits]: (1) he who plants [a tree] on his own [property] and bends [a branch of the tree and sinks it into the ground so that it grows on private [property] or on public [property, as an independent plant];

(2) [as well as] he who bends [a branch of a tree which is growing] on private [property] or on public [property, and sinks the branch into the ground so that it grows] on his own [property];

(3) he who plants [a tree] on his own [property] and bends [a branch of the tree and sinks it in the ground so that it still grows] on his own [property], but a private road or a public road [runs] in between [the tree and its offshoot], lo, this one does not bring [Firstfruits from the offshoot]—R. Judah says: "Such a one does bring [them]."

1:2 For what reason does he not bring [them]? Because it is written, "[You shall bring] the first of the Firstfruits of your land" (Deut. 26:2). [You may not bring Firstfruits] unless all of their growth [takes place] on your land.

(1) Sharecroppers, (2) tenant farmers, (3) a holder of confiscated property, and (4) a robber do not bring Firstfruits, for the same reason: because it is written, "the first of the Firstfruits of your land."

It would be difficult to make a more explicit or articulate statement of matters with the classifications defined and explained. So much for those who present and recite the Declaration. The excluded classes of male Israelites leave no unexplained cases. Genealogy in relationship to possession and inheritance of the Land provides the key to the message that the law of the Mishnah conveys.

That brings us to the logical next question. It is the one that attracted our interest to tractate Bikkurim to begin with: Where does the individual then enter in? The answer is contained within the rule governing who presents Firstfruits but does not recite the Declaration. This is where the particularities of the narrative take over and impose their definition:

**MISHNAH-TRACTATE BIKKURIM 1:4**

These [people] bring [Firstfruits] but do not recite [the Declaration]: a proselyte brings but does not recite, because he is not able to say, "[I have come into the land] which the Lord swore to our fathers to give us" (Deut. 26:3).

But if his mother was an Israelite, he brings and recites. And when he [the proselyte] prays in private, he says, "God of the fathers of Israel."

And when he prays in the synagogue, he says, "God of your fathers." [But] if his mother was an Israelite, he says, "God of our fathers."

The convert who possesses a share in the Land presents the Firstfruits. God wants his share of the Land's crop. So the convert is equal to all other Israelites in his obligations to God. But while the convert's children may marry home-born Israelites and so through ethnic and territorial assimilation enter into normative Israel, the convert himself cannot fully participate in the rite. He may present his Firstfruits to the priest, but he does so in silence. He enjoys full equality as God's partner in the ownership of the Land; the priest receives on God's behalf the Firstfruits that he therefore presents. So in practical terms the convert forms one with all Israel. But the facts that differentiate do register. With what outcome of identification? The Israelite householder who presents Firstfruits and who makes the required Declaration is distinguished from the proselyte. This is the only rite of the law of the Mishnah that in any way differentiates the home-born from the newcomer.

How is that the case? The law of the Mishnah declares in its reading of Scripture, having been Israel from the moment at which Israel set foot in the Land is not the same thing as having become part of Israel later on. In the end, the enchantment of the Land by the long-term presence of Israel upon it, the imposition of the sanctity of the one upon the sanctity of the other—these represent a dimension of being Israel that only time and future genealogical integration may bring about: more time within Israel, more time on the Land. So the reading of the language of the Declaration that sages undertake requires them to reflect upon what it means to live on the Land, be nurtured by the Land, and be changed in the passage of time, in the intersection of the two sanctified entities, Land and People.

Those whose status, history, and current situation contradict the statements do not make the Declaration. A principal mode of individuation therefore involves genealogy. But it is a very specific criterion that comes into play. What makes all the difference here is how one has acquired the land: by inheritance from forefathers and ultimately from the original, correct division of the Land by God—or by purchase. The former mode of acquisition denotes possession of the portion of the Land to genealogy within the Israelite family; the latter does not.

Others who control the Land but do not come within the tradition of inheritance—such as executors, agents, and so on—present Firstfruits but do not celebrate their possession of the Land. Those who are not definitively male do not make the Declaration. Those who owned the field when the crop came in and separated Firstfruits but then sold the field do not make the Declaration. Not only so, but the Firstfruits that are presented must be the ones originally designated, or the householder makes the presentation but not the Declaration.

Finally, the law asks, Who presents Firstfruits and recites the Declaration? The answer is now predictable. It is those who come at the proper time, who separate Firstfruits from the correct species, and who own all the Land that has yielded the crops—these present the Firstfruits and make the Declaration. The presentation and Declaration may take place from Pentecost to Tabernacles. Place, time, circumstance: all join together to confirm the language of the Declaration.

### Firstfruits and the Half-Sheqel

Note at the end the contrast between the two parts of the law that defines the corporate character of Israel and its individual components. The half-sheqel identifies the individual as part of corporate Israel. It does not individuate. The Firstfruits offering also defines the individual as part of corporate Israel. But it does so while recognizing the individuality of the Israelite within corporate Israel.

All Israelite males, wherever they live, whatever the source of their living, are required to take a share in the public offerings of atonement. Women are permitted to do so.[2] But once the Land enters into the law, it introduces a vari-

---

[2] That does not conclude the matter of votive acts of atonement. Any Israelite—man or woman—may atone through a personal, votive offering of expiation in the Temple. He or she may thus declare the

able and imposes its own traits on the definition of Israel. Then only the native-born male householder in the Land of Israel counts as fully Israel. He alone may present the produce as Firstfruits with an explicit Declaration. This act of both individuation and personal incorporation at one and the same moment is accomplished through the union with the Land. The individual Israelite attains recognition within corporate Israel through his possession of a share in the Land of Israel.

Is Israel a family or the community subject to God's dominion in the Torah? The ambiguity of the Israel-ness of Israel conveyed in the dual narrative, the one of the family of Abraham and Sarah, the other of the formation from the mixed multitude that left Egypt of the unique people of Israel at Sinai, is preserved in the two offerings. The one defines the people through the shared rite of atonement. The other forms the family through the union with the Land. Both stories are required. The atonement rite invokes the narrative of Sinai; the Firstfruits rite invokes the narrative of entry into the Land. The one pertains to individuals formed into a corporate community; the other to families joined into a larger society by inheriting the common property promised by God to the family of Abraham and Sarah with possession thereof subject to the stipulations of the Torah. Israel in both definitions—individual, corporate community—is preserved and embodied in the two rites that define corporate Israel as unique, and the Israelite as part of corporate Israel, a particular part.

---

classification of a beast or bird or cereal, for example, a sin offering, a guilt offering, a freewill offering, a peace offering.

# 5 | Personal Autonomy

## Tractates Arakhin and Nedarim-Nazir

### The Individual Israelite

What does the law of the Mishnah provide in recognition of the particularity of the individual Israelite? After all, the Israelite enjoys the same rights of individuation as the rest of humanity. So, do we discern in the law of the Mishnah *foundations within the framework of corporate Israel* for the personal autonomy of the Israelite? Where and how are the Israelite's personal autonomy and predilections afforded normative legal recognition in concrete terms?

First, the question is, What in theory individuates Israelites in the context of Israel? By this I mean, How do Israelites exhibit traits or adopt qualities that differentiate them as individuals from one another? Tractate Bikkurim distinguishes the native-born Israelite householder only from converts, the landless, and the like. But that point of differentiation is gross and generic. Ordinarily, people distinguish themselves by a repertoire of personal choices, each in his or her own way. For the answers to these questions, we turn to tractate Arakhin, which, also in the setting of the Temple, provides for Israelites a way to distinguish themselves.

Second, as parts of that whole community, Israel, we wonder whether Israelites can legitimately assert if not personal autonomy then at least individual traits of taste, temperament, and judgment. This overlaps the first question, but places the emphasis squarely on the matter of personal autonomy. The answers to this are in the paired tractates, Nedarim-Nazir, Vows and the Special Vow of the Nazirite.

### How the Individual Israelite Is Differentiated: Arakhin

The law of the Torah as amplified by the Rabbinic sages affords to individuals the opportunity of expressing their personal piety, so marking them off as distinguished from all other persons. This they do in pledges or Valuations. Exercising personal initiative, individuals may consecrate to the cult something of value not directly enjoined by the sacrificial program of the cult. The matter of Valuations derives from the Torah, as follows:

> The Lord said to Moses, "Say to the people of Israel, When a man makes a special vow of persons to the Lord at your valuation, then your valuation of a male from twenty years old up to sixty years old shall be fifty sheqels of silver according to the sheqel of the sanctuary. If the person is a female, your valuation shall be thirty sheqels. If the person is from five years old up to twenty years old, your valuation shall be for a male twenty sheqels and for a female ten sheqels. If the person is from a month old up to five years old, your valuation shall be for a male five sheqels of silver and for a female your valuation shall be three sheqels of silver. And if the person is sixty years old and upward, then your valuation for a male shall be fifteen sheqels, and for a female ten sheqels. And if a man is too poor to pay your valuation, then he shall bring the person before the priest and the priest shall value him; according to the ability of him who vowed the priest shall value him." (Lev. 27:1-8)

I can think of no more concrete evidence of the possibility of personal initiative than this matching of donor and donation. Such supererogatory acts of sanctification of what is not in its essence pertinent to the holy altar at all may pertain either to persons ("the value of Mr. So-and-so") or to movables or to real estate. These in general are covered within the normative legal category formation of *Arakhin*, "Valuations." When someone takes such a vow of Valuation, the value of persons or movables or real estate that has been specified— "Lo, I pledge the Valuation of Mr. So-and-so"—is estimated, and the cash is paid to redeem from the sanctuary the pledged value of the person or the thing that has been sanctified. The scarce resource is thus turned into fungible cash, which goes to the Temple for its upkeep.

Individual acts of dedication via the vow of Valuation represent, then, the recognition of private persons not only as components of corporate Israel but as individuals of distinction. The Torah explicitly makes provision for such votive offerings of not only animals but abstract personal worth, specifying the requisite number of sheqels that measure the worth of a person of a given classification. The individual, acting autonomously, then selects another individual, also viewed autonomously, and pledges to the Temple that individual's worth. The law of the Mishnah spells out how such a procedure is carried out, and in the details of its exposition, we discern a single tendency. It is to accord very broadly the rights of individuation through personal donation to the Temple. Thus the Mishnah states in so many words:

### MISHNAH-TRACTATE ARAKHIN 1:1

> All pledge the Valuation [of others] and are subject to the pledge of Valuation [by others], vow [the worth of another] and are subject to the vow [of payment of their worth by another]: priests and Levites and Israelites, women and slaves. A person of doubtful sexual traits and hermaphrodites vow [the worth of another] and are subject to the vow [of payment of their worth by another], pledge the Valuation [of others], but are not subject to the pledge of Valuation by others, for only [a person of] clear masculine or clear feminine [traits] is subject to the pledge of Valuation [by others].
>
> A deaf-mute, an imbecile, and a minor are subject to the vow [of payment of their

worth by another], and are subject to the pledge of Valuation by others, but do not vow the worth, and do not pledge the Valuation, of others, for they do not possess understanding.]

One who is less than a month old is subject to the vow [of payment of worth by another], but is not subject to the pledge of Valuation.

This specifies that no class of Israelites capable of forming a valid intention (thus omitting children, for example) is excluded from the right of individuation. It is for the Israelite to single himself or herself out at the very point of the incarnation of corporate Israel, the Temple altar itself. All normal Israelites, including women and slaves, may pledge the valuation of third parties and may be subjected to such a pledge of their worth by third parties. And any one who possesses value, even lacking a capacity of intention, may form the object of such a pledge.

What about gentiles? Since we deal with individuals, not "all Israel," gentiles are not to be excluded. Since the pledge is one of volition, and since gentiles may sanctify offerings for thanksgiving or freewill donations to the cult, they may also pledge the value of others and are subject to such a vow. The details, however, are open to dispute:

**MISHNAH-TRACTATE ARAKHIN 1:2**

The gentile—

R. Meir says, "He is subject to the Torah's pledge of Valuation [by others], but he does not pledge the Valuation [of others]."

R. Judah says, "He pledges the Torah's pledge of Valuation [of others] but is not subject to the pledge of Valuation [by others]."

And this one and that one agree that they vow and are subject to the vow [of payment of worth, if not under the Torah's provision for Valuations].

The point of agreement underscores the fundamental principle: any human being has the right to claim individual standing in the divine service. Those in a special class of persons may do so as well, but only within their own class. That class is formed of individuals whose volition is unclear, or whose indicative traits are not certain. That is to say, a person of doubtful sexual traits may participate in his own class, but may not cross the lines to be valued on the pledge of third parties, for only a person of clear masculine or clear feminine traits is subject to the pledge of Valuation by others. Persons of imperfect senses, minors, and imbeciles may be the object of a Valuation but may not undertake a vow of Valuation, being assumed not to possess understanding.

When it comes to Valuations, everyone in an assigned category is worth the same as everyone else in that category. The minimum payment of a vow of Valuation is a sela, so Leviticus 27:8, and the maximum, fifty. One's status at the moment of valuation dictates what is owing. But within the stated limits— age, condition—all persons are worth the same fifty selas, and that is without regard to looks or skills or social standing or genealogy or other gifts. A priest is not worth more, a *mamzer*—the child of parents who may never legitimately wed, for example, brother and sister, or a married woman and a man other than her husband—is not worth less.[1] The same rule applies to one who pledged the Valuation of "the most beautiful among Israelites and one who pledged that of the ugliest among Israelites—he gives fifty selas in either case." If, however, he said, "Lo, his *actual* value is incumbent on me," he gives his actual value. The important point, then, concerns a vow of Valuation. Pledges of personal worth, by contrast, involve actual, individual assessment.

The actual payment is assessed in terms of the governing variables: the status of the person concerning whom the vow of Valuation is made *and* the net worth of the person who takes the vow of Valuation. The former governs what is to be paid, depending on age, sex, and so on; the latter, the matter of ability to pay, depending on the ability of the one who takes the vow. A poor man who pledged the Valuation of a rich man gives the Valuation required of a poor man. And a rich man who pledged the Valuation of a poor man gives the Valuation required of a rich man.

The vow of Valuation, as defined by the Torah, is not the only means of self-differentiation in acts of piety. In addition to the vow of Valuation, the law of the Mishnah recognizes, in its own category and subject to its own rules, the vow of personal *worth*. That further individuates the one who takes it. Vows of Valuation pertain solely to persons, as the Torah indicates. By contrast, vows to pay the worth apply to anything—individuals or animals, live or slaughtered beasts, whole persons and limbs—and ability to pay is not an issue. Now the individual is singled out according to his or her actual traits, not subject to the fixed value defined by the Torah. One may vow to give one's weight to the sanctuary, even in silver or in gold. A person may pledge to give the worth of a hand, in which case the difference is paid between one's value with and without a hand. If the pledge is for a person's own Valuation and the person dies, the estate pays; the obligation takes effect forthwith. But if the pledge is for a person's worth and the person dies, the estate pays nothing. At the moment of payment, when the obligation takes effect, the person is worth nothing.

But if someone pledges the Valuation of a third party and dies, or the person concerning whom the pledge is made dies, the estate of the one who took the vow pays. If it is not the Valuation but the *worth*, the situation changes. If one said, "The price of so-and-so is incumbent on me" and the one who makes the vow dies, the heirs must pay the vow. If the one concerning whom the vow is made dies, the heirs do not have to pay—corpses have no price or value. The same conception emerges in the following: One who says, "This ox is a burnt-offering," or "This house is *Qorban* [meaning, in the status of a Temple offering]," if the ox died or the house fell down, the person is not liable to pay. If

---

[1] It is interesting to note that the sage does not figure in any of the reckoning, e.g., as worth more than the priest; nor is a *mamzer*-sage deemed worth more than an ignorant high priest. Why the sage does not constitute a subset in the present context is not clear to me.

the person said, "The price of this ox is incumbent on me for a burnt-offering," or "the price of this house is incumbent on me as *Qorban*," if the ox died or the house fell down, that person is liable to pay.

## Variations among Individuals

Individuals may contribute their scarce resources, whether movable property, realty, or personalty (property in the form of persons), to the upkeep of the Temple buildings. They have the right to do this, because they possess and may dispose of goods and land and also themselves, their own market value. They may dispose of these in accord with their own will; in doing so they make God's will their will, their property God's. In that, they really are distinguished from one another, since they willfully distinguish themselves in Godly dedication.

But here in the context of Arakhin, Valuations, the law of the Mishnah maintains that God's perspective differs from ours. When it comes to God's Valuation of persons, all are equal; when it comes to human valuation, the beautiful are worth and give more, the ugly less. That underscores the fact now established: when the law of the Mishnah takes the measure of individuals within corporate Israel, all weigh equally and give appropriately. When, however, the law of the Mishnah accords to individuals the right to distinguish themselves, it carefully defines that by which they take their own measure. It furthermore restricts to appropriately corresponding purposes that to which they then may donate. That is why, when moved to volunteer to God something of personal value, individuals within Israel have every right to pledge the value of their persons or property. In line with the Torah, the law of the Mishnah deemed it entirely rational to devote scarce resources to the upkeep of the Temple; it was entirely proper for individuals to provide for this on their own.

That fact brings us to a further answer to the question, Why is it that individuals have the right voluntarily to contribute to the Temple? To answer that question out of the law of the Mishnah, we ask another: Under ordinary circumstances, who must support the priesthood and its activities? The answer is, the householder, out of the produce of his land. Then in permitting individuals to pledge personal Valuations of themselves for the support of the Temple, the law of the Mishnah treats the population without land, including the population outside of the Land, as equal in all ways to the enlandised householder. The entire population of Israel, not only at home but also scattered in the Exile, finds itself in a position of equality vis-à-vis the holy place and its staff.

The stress on the equalization of all Israel in the matter of personal Valuations is explicit: wealth and poverty, beauty and its opposite—these play no role in assessing the worth of a person who pledges his, hers, or another's Valuation to the upkeep of the Temple and its priesthood. And just as the householder may contribute more than the prescribed minimum or may decorate his firstfruits and contribute the supplementary decorations, for example, so every individual enjoys the same option. He or she has every right to pledge not the fixed Valuation but the actual worth, and the law of the Mishnah takes pains to differentiate the fixed Valuation from the actual worth and dictate how the latter is assessed.

### Idiosyncrasy: Nedarim-Nazir

What happens if an individual adopts for himself or herself restrictions pertinent in general to the holy sacrifices of the Temple? It is an act of personal individuation. Since the offerings of the Temple altar are prohibited for ordinary use, the individual states that, so far as he or she goes, such and such an object is equivalent to an offering, a *Qorban*, as we just saw. Then, on that subjective basis, the specified object is forbidden to that person alone and not to anybody else. Such a statement indicates the intent radically to isolate the speaker from all others through personal adoption of special rules of sanctification that apply only to him or her in particular.

That is done by taking a vow that declares, "Such and such"—a person or an object—"is *Qorban* to me," that is, "so far as I am concerned that person or object is forbidden to me in particular as would be a sacrifice on the altar of the Lord in the Temple of Jerusalem." The sense, "May what I eat of your food be prohibited to me as is a sacrifice prohibited to me," is conveyed by the word "*Qorban*." Having said that word, the person may not eat the food of the other, concerning whose cooking it is spoken. The reason is that the other person's food has been declared by the individual who took the vow to be in the status of a sacrifice. The law of the Mishnah of Nedarim-Nazir, devoted to the vow taken by an individual (*Nedarim*) the special vow of the Nazirite set forth at Numbers 6 (*Nazir*) investigates the power of a person through invoking the name of Heaven to affect the classification in which he or she alone is situated. Involved are not intangibles alone, however, but rather concrete and material relationships with other people.

In recognizing the power of a statement of personal intent to affect tangible matters, the law carries beyond the walls of the Temple the principle that individuals' statements of intention and attitude take effect in the material world. To be more specific: we know that what makes an ordinary beast into a holy beast, subject to the laws of sacrilege and set aside for the altar, is a verbal designation of that particular animal as a sacrifice. Here too what makes ordinary food into food in the status of Holy Things, so far as the given individual is concerned, is the verbal designation of that ordinary food as Holy Things. The difference is that designating an animal as a beast for sacrifice is a public act, affecting society at large. No one then can make use of that animal. Declaring that a dish of oatmeal is in the status of a *Qorban*, by contrast, has no effect on the cereal, except for the person who made that declaration.

The point is that if a man or woman says a certain set of words, Heaven hears. The man or woman thereby adopts certain restrictions or prohibitions, whether, as in Nedarim, not to eat certain foods of any sort or not to derive benefit from a given person, or, as in Nazir, not to eat grapes, not to cut hair, not to attend funerals (something the husband cannot ever prevent the wife from doing, but the Nazirite vow prevents the Nazirite from doing). These restrictions, announced in that language, serve to provoke Heaven's interest in and intervention into the conduct of the individual man or the woman. So Nedarim and Nazir form a continuous exposition of the law of the Mishnah.

### Private Language and Public Language

Then in Nedarim-Nazir the problem arises of how to mediate between private use and public comprehension and expectation. And that brings us to the center of the issue of individuation: private use of public speech.

The law of the Mishnah deems language the mirror of the soul; the words we use expose our heart, articulate and give effect to our intention. But that most private transaction involving self-expression also takes place in the public square, for shared language forms the foundation of the social order. The key to the entire system comes to expression in the language that individuals use as an expression of their own will and intention—which directly affects the public interest as embodied by third parties. Then the power of intention, which defines individuals as apart from the social collectivity, signals the law of the Mishnah's recognition of the legitimacy of individuality. Language is empowered by the people who use it; it bears little power on its own. So individuality defines a dimension in sorting out the effects even of something so critical to the social order as common speech.

Take the extreme case of a verbal act of sanctification. Phrases such as "This beast is sanctified," "as an offering in expiation of such-and-such an inadvertent sin that I now discover I have committed," or "as a thank offering" or "a whole offering" or "this beast substitutes for that already consecrated beast" (Lev. 27:9–10)—any such expression suffices to classify the animal as God's. All Israelites, not only the one who spoke the words referring to the beast, are bound by the language that has been used. But these formulas take effect only when they match the will of the person who utters them. An act of consecration done in error is not binding, and the beast remains unconsecrated. Language does not bear objective force *eo ipse,* so merely declaring something sacred without regard to one's intention is not enough. From the viewpoint of the law of the Mishnah, what we intend makes all the difference: God responds to what we want more than to what we do, as the distinction between murder and manslaughter shows in an obvious way.

Language makes public, and attracts public attention to, the intention of the private person. It forms the point of intersection ("the interface") between the individual and the community. If used only idiosyncratically, it ceases to carry out its task. Now, as I have explained, the law of the Mishnah of Nedarim-Nazir takes up the theme, the power of language to impose changes in status. By using certain language, a man or woman effects an alteration in his or her condition—for instance, in relationships with other people, or in food that may or may not be eaten, or with regard to situations that may or may not be permitted. Words affect the world of tangible substances and real relationships. But there is nothing so open to idiosyncrasy as language, even as there is no aspect of culture so public and collective as language.

## Public Recognition of Personal Individuality: The Nazirite in Particular

The Torah deals with two topics, the restrictions self-imposed by the Nazirite vow, and the offerings required in connection therewith. Of interest here first of all is the self-imposed restriction, the relevant verses of the Torah occurring at Numbers 6:10ff.:

> And the Lord said to Moses, "Say to the people of Israel: when either a man or a woman makes a special vow, the vow of a Nazirite, to separate himself to the Lord, he shall separate himself from wine and strong drink; he shall drink no vinegar made from wine or strong drink, and shall not drink any juice of grapes or eat grapes fresh or dried. All the day of his separation he shall eat nothing that is produced by the grapevine, not even the seeds or the skins.
>
> "All the days of his vow of separation no razor shall come upon his head; until the time is completed for which he separates himself to the Lord, he shall be holy; he shall let the locks of hair of his head grow long.
>
> "All the days that he separates himself to the Lord, he shall not go near a dead body. Neither for his father nor for his mother nor for brother or sister, if they died, shall he make himself unclean, because his separation to God is upon his head; all the days of his separation he is holy to the Lord."

From the perspective of the Torah, once the Nazirite vow takes effect, prohibitions are invoked against wine, hair-cutting, and contact with the corpse; the other point of interest is the offerings that are required if the Nazirite is defiled by being near a corpse and when the Nazirite completes the vow in a state of cleanness. The Nazirite, whatever his or her caste status, is comparable to a *Kohen*, or Temple priest: subject to certain prohibitions and assigned a particular position in the conduct of the Temple cult. The priest cannot serve if he is drunk or contaminated by a corpse or bald (a bald-headed man is invalid to serve as a priest, so Mishnah-tractate Bekhorot 7:2A). A single paradigm pertains to the priest and the Nazirite.

The Nazirite is an Israelite who wishes to be distinguished in holiness by pretending to be a priest ready to serve at the altar. That is because two of the three restrictions adopted by the Israelite who takes the Nazirite vow are comparable to the restrictions that apply at all times to the priest (*Kohen*)—drunkenness and corpse uncleanness. The priest, to be sure, cannot appear unkempt. But as in the case of Samson, not cutting one's hair is deemed an act of devotion to Heaven. So the three components of the Nazirite vow come down to the same thing, the intent to mark oneself off as holier than others. As is the priest to the family of Israel, so is the Nazirite to the household of Israel, a particular classification of persons, distinguished in consequential and practical ways as to nourishment and comportment. The vow does not encumber all Israel in relationship to God. It is not an obligatory act of service, as an offering is, but a votive one. And while other votive acts of service, such as the thank offering or the peace offering, engage the priesthood in the Temple, the vow does not; and the Nazirite vow brings about offerings given to the priest at the door of the tent of meeting, in the manner of the offerings of the person afflicted with the skin ailment described in Leviticus 13 and 14; and there he stays at the door, not entering the Temple proper.

## The Dubious Virtue of the Nazirite

What is the attitude of the Rabbinic sages toward the layperson pretending to be a priest? The law here gives way to a narrative that answers the question outside the framework of a ruling. To understand the story, a fact is required. A Nazirite completing the term of the vow is required to present offerings, including some that yield meat for the sacrificer (the Nazir in this case) and the officiating priest. The details of the Nazirite vow and its execution need not detain us. The only point of interest is how the sages evaluate this individual who has spent a month conducting himself by the rules that govern a status to which he has otherwise no claim. The answer occurs in a story about the attitude toward the Nazirite that is expressed by Simeon the Righteous, high priest of unblemished virtue, whom we met in chapter 1:

SIFRÉ TO NUMBERS XXII:VI

". . . to the Lord:" (Num. 6:1–4).

The religious obligation in taking the vow of the Nazirite must be for the Name [and sake of God, and not for any lesser purpose].

Said Simeon the Righteous, "In my entire life I accepted a share of the guilt offering brought in connection with the Nazirite vow only one time [for in all other cases I regarded the vow as having been taken for improper motives].

"Someone came from the south, a man of beautiful eyes and handsome visage, with flowing curls. I said to him, 'Why in the world did you decide to take a vow to destroy that lovely head of hair [by shaving it all off in the completion of the Nazirite vow? You should not have taken the Nazirite vow that would require you to cut off your hair as an offering.]'

"He said to me, 'I was a shepherd in my village, and I went to draw water from the well and I looked at my reflection in the water. My heart took hold of me and sought to drive me out of the world [by taking pride in my looks]. I said to [my hair], "Wicked one, you take pride in something which does not belong to you, but which belongs to the dirt and the worm and the maggot. Lo, I shall shave you off for the sake of Heaven."'

"Forthwith I patted his head and kissed him on his head, saying to him, 'May people like you become many in Israel, who carry out the will of the Omnipresent.'

"And in you is fulfilled the verse: 'When either a man or a woman makes a special vow, the vow of a Nazirite, to separate himself to the Lord.'"

The sages' judgment of the Israelite counterpart to the Narcissus story is clear in the exemplary case of Simeon the Righteous: here was the only case of a Nazirite of whom the high priest Simeon approved. That is because when the Nazirite made it clear, his motivation was pure. The vow was genuinely "to the Lord." So, while the Rabbinic sages accepted the institution of the Nazirite vow, they looked dubiously at those that took the vow, seeing the rite as a possible occasion for self-aggrandizement, along the lines I have suggested. We shall presently encounter a similar judgment concerning those that take vows: they are not regarded as truly virtuous Israelites.

## Private Language and Public Meaning

The Rabbinic sages take a special interest in the matter of idiosyncratic use of shared language. Does the law accommodate private formulations of thought in words, or does it impose upon individual usage a general rule of meaning?

MISHNAH-TRACTATE NAZIR 1:1–2

1:1 All euphemisms for [the form of words for] a Nazirite vow are equivalent to a Nazirite vow [and binding]. He who says, "I will be [such]"—lo, this one is a Nazir. Or: "I shall be comely"—he is a Nazir. [If he says,] "Naziq" or "Naziah" or "Paziah"—lo, this one is a Nazir. [If he says,] "Lo, I shall be like this one," "Lo, I shall curl [my hair]," "Lo, I shall tend [my hair]," "Lo, it is incumbent on me to grow [my hair] long"—lo, this one is a Nazir. [If he says,] "Lo, I pledge myself [to offer] birds"—he is not a Nazir.

1:2 [He who says,] "Lo. I shall be an abstainer [Nazir] from grape pits" or "from grape skins" or "from haircuts" or "from uncleanness [of corpses]"—lo, this one is a Nazir [in all regards]. And all the details of a Nazirite vow pertain to him. [He who says,] "Lo, I shall be like Samson" or "like the son of Manoah" or "like the husband of Delilah" or "like the one who tore down the gates of Gaza" or "like the one whose eyes the Philistines plucked out"—lo, this one is a Nazir in the status of Samson.

Language emerges from the depths and speaks out of what is intensely personal and private. But language also conveys meanings of general intelligibility. It is by definition a public act. With what result for the individual's personal preferences? What is private (mumbled, unintelligible, gibberish) bears no consequence; what is intelligible by a commonsense standard takes effect. That is how the law of the Mishnah sorts matters out. Thus, when it comes to euphemisms, all of them take effect; for what matters about language is not adherence to the governing formula, though it matters. What makes all the difference is the perceived and publicly comprehensible intent. If the intent conveyed by the language is clear and unmistakable, then the language has done its task of embodying intention. And then the language is affective. If the intention is not vividly conveyed, however indirectly, then the language is null.

The main problem addressed by the law of the Mishnah pertaining to the language of the vow to be a Nazirite is how to standardize matters, so that private meanings and personal stipulations do not corrupt discourse. Then the prevailing solution is to identify what is general and intelligible and dismiss the rest. One example serves. If a person specifies even a single detail as incumbent, then all the details of a Nazirite vow pertain. Language is such that everything begins, but nothing remains private, personal, idiosyncratic. Even what affects the household in particular is framed for effect for all Israel.

## The Effects of the Vow in General: Nedarim

The law of the Mishnah insists that Israel has a stake in the speech of private persons. This rule extends from the special vow of the Nazirite to vows in general. As we saw just now, a vow in the law of the Mishnah ordinarily depends on an individual's self-confirming statement that such and such is in the status of an offering, is sanctified as a *Qorban*. That is quite subjective. The fact is, the thing is not sanctified for anyone else, but is holy only for the person who has used that language. But, as with the Nazirite vow, so with vows in general, others are directly affected by the change in status of that thing to that particular person. Here we confront in acute form the ambiguity of language, especially in vowing, at the intersection of the private and the public. Nothing is more individual than language—and nothing is more public!

First, then, how is the idiosyncratic use of language interpreted? It is interpreted within the paradigm of the conventional use of language. If someone uses euphemisms or other odd formulations, these are interpreted against the common background of ordinary speech. So adopting for oneself an individual status or in peculiar, private ways imposing, so far as one is concerned, the status of sanctification upon persons or objects yields a single common result:

MISHNAH-TRACTATE NEDARIM 1:1

All euphemisms [substitutes for language used to express] (1) vows are equivalent to vows, and [all euphemisms] for (2) bans (*herem*) are equivalent to bans, and [all euphemisms] for (3) oaths are equivalent to oaths, and [all euphemisms] for (4) Nazirite vows are equivalent to Nazirite vows. He who says to his fellow [euphemisms such as], (1) "I am forbidden by vow from you," (2) "I am separated from you," (3) "I am distanced from you," "if I eat your [food]," [or] "if I taste your [food]," is bound [by such a vow]. [He who says], "As the vows of the evil folk . . . ," has made a binding vow in the case of a Nazir, or in the case of [bringing] an offering, or in the case of an oath. [He who says,] "As the vows of the suitable folk" has said nothing whatsoever. "As their [suitable folks'] freewill-offerings" . . . he has made a binding vow in the case of a Nazir or in the case of [bringing] an offering.

It is elegant. A single repertoire of public meanings governs the interpretation of diverse expressions of private language. At the same time, we note how the law of the Mishnah recognizes in objective ways the private language of the one who has vowed. A uniform result follows. If something can be understood to refer to an act of sanctification, however idiosyncratic the words, that objective reality takes over and defines the transaction. So singular sounds take effect when they sufficiently resemble what is generally intelligible in one context, rather than in some other.

Here, then, we enter the world encompassing subjective will and usage that the law of the Mishnah constructs to accommodate the expression of personality. It is not a kind of self-expression that the law of the Mishnah admires. The dismissive judgment of the law of the Mishnah upon the vow is fully exposed in the rule given above, "He who says, '[Lo, I vow a vow] as the vows of the suitable folk' has said nothing whatsoever." Such a statement does not constitute a euphemism for a vow. Why not? Because "suitable folk" (*kesheyrim*) do not take vows. And the rest follows. But most people do take vows, and they are particularly common in the life of the household, that is, in relationships between husband and wife.

The vow is the weapon of the weak, the way by which the lesser party to a transaction exercises power over the greater. If the wife says to the husband, "By a vow, I shall not derive benefit from you," or "What food you feed me is *Qorban*," she removes from herself her husband's control; so too, the guest to the host. But vows often stem from the release of discipline, as expletives and outcries, as acts of temper—no wonder sages do not respect those who take vows.

In what way do the laws governing vows accord recognition to the individual and his or her use of language? And how do they do this even while honoring the public interest in discourse that is objective, common, and valid everywhere? On one side, there is the normative legal confirmation that a quite personal formulation of matters takes effect. Even if someone uses the language of a vow in an unconventional manner, the vow counts. The reason is that the result pertains only to the person who has used that language. That person's intention governs, even where others are affected. Where there is genuine ambiguity in the language, to be sure, that fact is taken into account, as in the following case:

#### MISHNAH-TRACTATE NEDARIM 2:5

[If] one vowed by "herem," but then he said, "I vowed only concerning that which is a herem [a net] of the sea," [or if he vowed] by "*Qorban*," but then he said, "I vowed only concerning Qorban [offerings] to kings,"

[if he said,] "Lo, *asmi* [my bone] is *Qorban*," and explained, "I vowed only concerning the *esem* [bone] which I placed before me by which to vow,"

[if he said,] "Qonam is that benefit which my wife derives from me," and he said, "I vowed only concerning my first wife, whom I have already divorced"—

they find an opening for them in some other place [by some pretext]. And they instruct them that they not treat vows lightly.

The ambiguity—the fact that words can have, and often do have, more than one meaning—is objective: "*herem*" can stand for "devoted to God" or "a fishing net," and so with the other examples. In such unclear settings, where the language can sustain more than one intent, we pay attention to the person's claim, but we also take account of the facts of public speech. Hence, while the vow is null, the sages' intervention—finding an opening for publicly releasing the vow—is required.

## The Objective Facts of Human Nature and the Individual's Vow

The Rabbinic sages also take account of objective facts of human nature in interpreting what a private person can have meant in his or her subjective expression. The facts of human nature form part of the setting for interpreting the meaning and effect of what someone has said. Intention is weighed against context. Someone can use language without the remotest intention of being taken literally. In such an instance the vow is null. Examples of this occur when people use exaggerated language, vow in error or under constraint, or take a vow to add emphasis to their language in a situation of conflict. None of these is found legally binding:

### MISHNAH-TRACTATE NEDARIM 3:1–4

3:1 Four [types of] vows did sages declare not binding: (1) Vows of incitement, (2) vows of exaggeration, (3) vows made in error, and (4) vows [broken] under constraint.

Vows of incitement: How so? [If] one was selling something and said, "Qonam if I chop the price down for you to under a sela," and the other says, "Qonam if I pay you more than a sheqel," [then] both of them agree at three denars.

3:2 Vows of exaggeration: [If] he said, "Qonam if I did not see [walking] on this road as many as went out of Egypt," ". . . if I did not see a snake as big as the beam of an olive press." Vows made in error: ". . . if I ate," or ". . . if I drank," and he remembered that he ate or drank; ". . . if I shall eat," or ". . . if I shall drink" and he forgot and ate and drank. [If] he said, "Qonam be any benefit my wife gets from me, for she stole my purse" ". . . for she beat up my son," and he found out that she had not beaten up his son, or he found out that she had not stolen it. [If] he saw people eating figs [belonging to him] and said, "Lo, they are Qorban to you!" and they turned out to be his father and brothers, and there were others with them—these and those [men] are permitted [to eat the figs].

3:3 Vows [broken] under constraint: [If] one's fellow imposed a vow on him to eat with him, but he got sick, or his son got sick, or a river [overflowed and] stopped him—lo, these are vows [broken] under constraint.

3:4 They take a vow to murderers, robbers, or tax collectors that [produce] is heave offering, even though it is not heave offering; that [property] belongs to the state, even though it does not belong to the state, even in the form of an oath. One [voluntarily] takes a vow at the outset. [One takes a vow] only in the matter concerning which the vow is imposed also: Concerning that in which the vow is not imposed. How so? [If] they said to him, "Say: 'Qonam be any benefit my wife has with me!'" and he said, "Qonam be any benefit my wife and children have with me!"—these and those are permitted.

In the cases reviewed here, an assessment of human nature in general governs, and sages do not take the expression of the individual seriously. The objective facts of language take over and impose their implications on the statement the person has made as an individual.

Finally, we take account of what the individual who takes the vow anticipates and does not anticipate. The basic principle is, if the person had known the facts not only as they were but as they would turn out to have been, the vow would not have been taken. Therefore the vow was taken in error and is null.

MISHNAH-TRACTATE NEDARIM 9:9–10

9:9 They unloose a vow for a man by reference to his own honor and by reference to the honor of his children. They say to him, "Had you known that the next day they would say about you, 'That's the way of So-and-so, going around divorcing his wives,' "and that about your daughters they'd be saying, 'They're daughters of a divorcée! What did their mother do to get herself divorced' [would you have taken a vow]?" And [if] he then said, "Had I known that things would be that way, I should never have taken such a vow," lo, this [vow] is not binding.

9:10 [If one said,] "Qonam if I marry that ugly Miss So-and-so," and lo, she is beautiful, ". . . dark . . . ," and lo, she is light, ". . . short . . . ," and lo, she is tall, he is permitted [to marry] her, not because she was ugly and turned beautiful, dark and turned light, short and turned tall, but because the vow [to begin with] was based on erroneous facts.

This, then, is the final, normative manner of disposing of the vow, and it suffices to show the balance between objective language and subjective intention that is maintained. But we must not lose sight of one simple fact: The law of the Mishnah does secure for the private person a considerable range of personal power in relationship to Heaven. All vowing (including the special vow of the Nazirite) concerns matters of personal status: what may a person do or not do by reason of a self-imposed vow, which is to say, by reason of the intent to express personal will.

The sages here are legislating for that which they do not hold in esteem. They maintain that people who take vows show their weakness, not their strength. Vows represent the power of the put-upon. They open the easy way to defend oneself against the importunities of the overbearing host, the grasping salesman, the tormenting husband or wife. But sages do not honor those who take the easy way, asking God to intervene in matters to which on their own Israelites ought to be able to attend.

## The Vow as a Disreputable Action

We have seen that language used for vows, so the Rabbinic sages portray matters, does not sanctify; it contaminates. Really, language ought to express reflected-upon intention—as in the designation of an animal to expiate an inadvertent, newly realized sin. Instead, as we shall see in a moment, it often conveys the outcome of temper and frustration. Designating a beast as consecrated realizes a noble, godly intention; designating benefit one receives from one's spouse as "*Qorban*" uses language to embody a lowly and disreputable intention, meant to cause humiliation, rejection, and disgrace. The sages treat language as dangerous because it realizes intention, which had best, therefore, be expressed with probity and restraint.

The Rabbinic sages in the law of Nedarim do not treat respectfully of the person who takes vows. They regard the vow as an act of disrepute. The reason reflects a profound bias in favor of rationality that animates the law of the Mishnah. Vow takers yield to the undisciplined will, to emotion unguided by rational considerations. But intention must (ideally) take form out of both emotion and reflection. Vows explode the fuel of emotion ignited by the heat of the encounter. "Qonam (a euphemism for *Qorban*, thus, "forbidden as holy") be any benefit I get from you" hardly forms a rational judgment of a stable relationship. It bespeaks a loss of temper, a response to provocation with provocation. Right at the outset the law of the Mishnah gives a powerful signal of its opinion of the whole: suitable folk to begin with do not take vows; only wicked people do.

People who take vows are deemed irresponsible; they are adults who use words even as children swing fists. They possess the power of intention but use it foolishly. So, while they are given openings toward the unbinding of their vows, they are forced at the same time to take seriously what they have said. Vows are treated as a testing of Heaven, a trial of Heavenly patience and grace. Sanctification can affect a person or a mess of porridge, and there is a difference. Expletives, with which we deal here, make that difference; these are not admired.

But because the law of the Mishnah begins and ends with the conviction that language is power, the law of the Mishnah also takes account of the sanctifying effect even of language used stupidly. That is the message, and it is only here in the law of Nedarim that the sages could set forth this message concerning the exploitation and abuse of the power of language, the disreputable use of the holy.

### MISHNAH-TRACTATE NEDARIM 9:1, 9

9:1 In a matter which is between him and his mother or father, they unloose his vow by [reference to] the honor of his father or mother.

9:9 They unloose a vow for a man by reference to his own honor and by reference to the honor of his children. They say to him, "Had you known that the next day they would say about you, 'That's the way of So-and-so, going around divorcing his wives,' "and that about your daughters they'd be saying, 'They're daughters of a divorcée! What did their mother do to get herself divorced' [would you have taken a vow]?" And [if] he then said, "Had I known that things would be that way, I should never have taken such a vow," lo, this [vow] is not binding.

The normative law rejects unforeseen events as a routine excuse for nullifying a vow; foresight on its own ("had you known . . . would you have vowed?") plays a dubious role. But when it comes to the intention involving honor of parents or children, that forms a consideration of such overriding power as to nullify the vow.

Expletive vows are a means used on earth by the subordinated to coerce the more powerful by invoking the power of Heaven. They are taken under emotional duress and express impatience and frustration. They do not follow a period of sober reflection. They come into play at crucial, dangerous points, disrupting important relationships, particularly marriage and hospitality. They jar and explode. By admitting into human relationships the power of intention, they render the predictable—what is governed by regularities—into a source of uncertainty, for who in the end will penetrate what lies deep in the heart, as Jeremiah reflected, which is beyond fathoming? It is language that often brings to the surface, in a statement of will best left unsaid, what lurks in the depths, and the result, Heaven's immediate engagement, is not to be gainsaid. That is why vows form a source of danger. In marriage, in hospitality, in the household, in the public square—vows rip open the fabric of sacred relationships.

## A Judgment on the Individual Seeking Distinction

To reach the positive side of the issue, let me expand the negative to its utmost: Language represents power and it is a power not to be exercised lightly. The weaker party takes a vow—whether the milquetoast husband or the abused wife. The vow is taken by the wife against the husband, the harried guest against the insistent host, the seller against the buyer, the boastful storyteller against the dubious listener, the passive against the active party. The strong incites, the subordinated reacts; and the language of reaction, the vow, contains such power as is not to be lightly unleashed even against the one who gives and therefore dominates, whether in sex or food or entertainment. Vows are the response, the mode of aggression exercised by the less powerful party to the relationship. The inferior party will invoke Heaven; the strong do not have to. A vow will be spit out by a guest who has been importuned to take a fourth portion in a meal he does not want to eat. A wife will exclaim that she will derive no benefit whatsoever from her husband. A whole series of cases emerge from a vow taken by a person not to derive benefit from his friend, with the consequence that the friend, who wants to provide some sort of support for the dependent person, does so through a third party. The dependence then is less obtrusive. So, once more: who gives, dominates, and the vow is the instrument to escape earthly domination in the name of Heaven.

The law of the Mishnah then asks, What can a man or a woman say so as to become obliged to do or not do a specified range of deeds? The answers to that question respond to yet another, still more profound question: How is Heaven mindful of man and woman on earth? The law of the Mishnah speaks large and simple truths in conveying a remarkable vision of humanity in God's image. Man and woman are so like God as to be able through what they say to provoke, and even encumber, God's caring and concern. That is because man and woman know how to say the ordinary words that make an extraordinary difference on earth and in Heaven. The message of the law of the Mishnah of the Oral Torah is that persons are responsible for what they say—there is no such thing as "mere words"—because what they say brings to full articulation what they want, words bearing the burden of intention. After all, the first act of intention, the first act of creation, is contained in words: "And God said. . . ."

## Individuation and Personal Autonomy:
## Relative or Absolute?

Let us return to the starting point of chapters 4 and 5, the matter of how Israelites both enjoy individuation, just as do gentiles, and also form corporate Israel. To do so, they relinquish all possibility of defining a realm of absolute autonomy of the person. Their freedom is limited to the choice: live in God's kingdom or no, find freedom incised upon the Torah or no.

Clearly, individual Israelites enjoy important options of personal individuation. They may distinguish themselves in virtue. This they do by generosity toward the Temple and its cult, transforming wealth into divine service. They do so by giving of themselves, undertaking onerous religious duties in behalf of the community, or through expressions of individual conscience (if we may use a word grossly anachronistic for the period of which we speak). We have now seen how the law of the Mishnah even recognizes the legitimacy of dubious methods of individuation involving the idiosyncratic manipulation of language through vows and the special vow of the Nazirite. Any conception of Israelites as faceless automatons of the law grossly violates the letter and spirit of the Torah as mediated by the Rabbinic sages. So, within the definition of individuation with which we began in chapter 4—"the power of persons deliberately to distinguish themselves"—a rich repertoire of opportunities and occasions for individuals to embody God's grandeur in creation by showing themselves different from all others beckons.

But does the law of the Mishnah provide a foundation for the autonomous individual? The simple answer is, it does not. The law of the Mishnah does not recognize the total autonomy of persons, whether Israelite or not-Israelite. All children of Noah, by definition, are subject to divine imperatives, and these apply to all without variation. Within the framework of the seven commandments applying to all humanity, a range of personal autonomy extends outward in all directions to the farthest horizons. Gentiles can eat anything they want, and they can do nearly anything they want, except for murder, theft, and fornication.

But Israel's situation is different, and while Israelites may shape for themselves traits of individuality, these are limited to those means of self-differentiation that the law of the Mishnah can endorse (Arakhin) or at least tolerate (Nazir, Nedarim). In narrative terms, Israelites accepted God's dominion at Sinai and so they are God's slaves; they cannot take a valid oath that violates the Torah they have sworn to do and to obey. If they take such vows or oaths contrary to the Torah, they need not seek remission from a sage, for the vow or oath to begin with never was valid. So Israelites possess full rights of individuation, but only as slaves indentured to God they have surrendered part of their rights of free and unfettered will. Their freedom is within the Torah; the Torah frees them to choose within the repertoire of choices God in the Torah has already defined.

In short, Israelites may differentiate themselves from one another, but they may not distinguish themselves as individuals from the body of corporate Israel. That is what I meant when I said, they have the right of individuation but no access to a claim of complete personal autonomy, which, in the law of the Mishnah, is incomprehensible. Individual Israelites always form integral components of corporate Israel; it is within that boundary that Israelites express their individuality. Those Israelites who cross the outer limits of Israel lose what being part of Israel promises, which is eternal life. This is expressed in the unambiguous language that I find at the heart of the entire system of the law of the Mishnah: "All Israel have a share in the world to come" (Mishnah-tractate Sanhedrin 10:1).

# 6 Ownership and Possession

## Tractates Shebi*it
## and Shabbat-Erubin

## The Context for Understanding Ownership and Possession

We have seen how the individuality of Israelites is expressed through personal piety in offerings and how individual idiosyncrasy is expressed in vows. But the Israelite community is realized not only in the Temple and in relationship to God. It also encompasses the Israelite individual in the Israelite village, in relationships of family and household. When, in the law of the Mishnah, does the incorporation of individual Israelites into the community—the moral entity Israel—make a concrete difference in ordinary affairs? We find the answer when we take up the theory of ownership of property that animates the law of the Mishnah. The individual forms part of a supernatural community, and that leads us to wonder whether his or her property reflects that ambiguous status: private individual but also participant in the commonwealth Israel.

Specifically, how does the law of the Mishnah both (1) accord to the individual (householder, head of family) rights of ownership of private property and (2) abridge those rights in favor of shared ownership by corporate Israel? The question of ownership is answered when the Mishnah distinguishes ownership of property from possession and usufruct—rights of utilization—of property. Specifically, there are points at which the law imposes a collective claim that overrides the exclusive ownership of the individual Israelite, and there are points at which the law encourages relinquishing exclusive rights of private property in favor of sharing title with the community of local Israel, or of all Israel in the Land (in the case of real property, the law of the Mishnah does not legislate for Israelites living in the Diaspora).

First, Israelite householders in the Land of Israel do not own their real estate free and clear. They cannot fully realize their unfettered will in regard to their property. In the Land of Israel they are subject to the will of another, a partner: God. So they do not actually own real property in the way in which they own movables—say, a bench or a sofa, of which they are free to dispose for any purpose at all. In general, householders possess and may use their property and individually enjoy its fruits, but in significant ways they are subject to their divine partner's claim on it. That fact is best expressed, the context most clearly delineated, in Shebiʿit, the law of the Mishnah having to do with the Seventh Year of the sabbatical cycle. In the Seventh Year, all the real estate of the Land of Israel is declared ownerless, its crops free for all; its fields are left fallow, and debts are remitted. That assertion of God's overriding ownership of the Land of Israel distinguishes the radically isolated Israelite individual from the communitarian collectivity of Israel.

Second, while the law of the Mishnah differentiates ownership from possession, it also nurtures an unusual Israelite communitarian policy. It provides for individuals to surrender their property in favor of symbolic, but effective, collective ownership of the households of a given village. That process takes place on a regular schedule, one day a week. It is no rare exception; it is a cyclical norm, for the Sabbath day in particular. The law fosters communitarian conceptions of possession by setting forth incentives for the sharing of ownership on the Sabbath—partnerships formed for mutual benefit, comfort, and convenience. Households, each deemed private domain, are joined into collective courtyards to form a large, shared domain. In sharing ownership on the Sabbath day of what during weekdays is private domain, the whole is accessible to, and subject to the usufruct of, all partners in the shared domain. The shared domain may be alleyways, courtyards, and, indeed, entire villages or towns. Through fictive rites—the provision of a shared meal open to all or the construction of a symbolic boundary marker—community domains are formed out of individual property. The prohibitions against transporting objects from one domain to another (private/public or private/private) are turned into rules for the Sabbath in the law of the Mishnah of Shabbat, and the manner of creating ad hoc partnerships—shared domain out of individual property—is spelled out in the law of the Mishnah of Erubin, "Boundaries." In what is essentially a continuous exposition, the incentives to create community itself are fully exposed.

These two category formations of the law of the Mishnah, tractates Shebiʿit for the Seventh Year, and Shabbat-Erubin for the formation on the Sabbath of shared domain to permit transportation of objects, express in practical terms the balance—individuation, not personal autonomy—that the law of Bikkurim, Arakhin, and Nedarim-Nazir realizes in the context of the Temple and its rites.

To restate what is now familiar: (1) Because they are part of the entirety of humanity, Israelites are individuals, each a distinct moral entity subject to God's will, just as were Adam and Eve. But (2) because they constitute, all together and all at once, "Israel" as well—a moral entity responsible for its collective conduct and answerable for the actions of individuals—Israelites cannot claim utter autonomy as freestanding persons, responsible only for themselves and (besides God) only to themselves. (3) Israelites may distinguish themselves from one another. By their nature they are accorded full rights and opportunities of individuation, including those of possession of private property. But (4) by their situation within Israel, they bear other bonds. These are bonds of connection and responsibility, which abridge the condition of personal autonomy and define the range of permitted individuation, including limitations on the exercise of full autonomy in the disposition of private property.

Within that large theory of matters, beginning with the definition of Israel as *sui generis* in the context just now spelled out and of the Israelite as fundamentally different from the not-Israelite in the very definition of the social order constituted by each, everything else follows.

## Ownership and Possession: Tractate Shebiᶜit

From the entry of Israel into the Land of Israel, the Land was accorded a Sabbath, counting by years, not by days of the week. This septennial cycle decreed that every Seventh Year private ownership of the Land of Israel be nullified, the crops declared free for all. As a mark of relinquishing all claim to private ownership of the land, none may hoard the prior years' crops for personal use. Private ownership of land in the Land of Israel is radically abridged by the Torah's cyclical cancellation—*tout court!*—of all claim to private possession of the land and its produce in favor of shared access accorded to all Israel.

It would be difficult to point to a more dramatic statement that individual ownership is contingent upon God's grace and is not an absolute right. It is a gift, not a given. God, acting upon corporate Israel in the Land of Israel, also registers a claim even to share in the ownership of what appears to represent private property. The law of the Mishnah thus does not regard ownership of the Land as absolute. By extension, by making sure the crops of the Seventh Year are free for all, that policy seeks to link individuals together into a community of common domain, to underscore the stipulated character of possession as against the absolute status of ownership. The reason is that God ultimately owns everything—"the earth is the Lord's, and the fullness thereof" (Ps. 24:1) and even more specifically the Land of Israel, which Israel possesses on sufferance. So the individual's rights of ownership to begin with are subject to God's claim. Israel in the Land evokes the paradigm of Adam and Eve in the Garden of Eden. In Eden everything was—explicitly—free to all, within the limit set by God's will for matters. No one owned Paradise.

Within that model the Israelite householder who possesses land in the Land of Israel never is the absolute owner of either the land or its crops. Israelites hold them; they may use them as they like (also within limits). But possession for usufruct is different from absolute ownership. The difference corresponds to the distinction between individuation and personal autonomy, so important to our analysis in chapters 3–5. Through imposing the distinction between possession and rights of usufruct, which the law favors, and absolute ownership, which it wishes to abridge, the law of the Mishnah in practical terms reinforces the bonds of community. It is how Israel is incorporated. Mishnah-tractate Shebiᶜit bases itself on and elaborates the Torah's commandment at Leviticus 25:1–8:

> When you enter the land that I am giving you, the land shall observe a Sabbath of the Lord. Six years you may sow your field and six years you may prune your vineyard and gather in the yield. But in the Seventh Year the land shall have a Sabbath of complete rest, a Sabbath of the Lord; you shall not sow your field or prune your vineyard. You shall not reap the aftergrowth of your harvest or gather the grapes of your untrimmed vines; it shall be a year of complete rest for the land. But you may eat whatever the land during its Sabbath will produce—you, your male and female slaves, the hired-hand and bound laborers who live with you, and your cattle and the beasts in your land may eat all its yield.

The language of the Torah, assigning a Sabbath to the Land, dictates the topic and the way in which the law of the Mishnah will actualize the topic, start to finish. But in the Mishnah's realization and secondary amplification of matters, the prevailing issues and concerns of the law of the Mishnah will make their mark as well.

A second, correlative commandment at Deuteronomy 15:1–3, invokes the Sabbatical Year in connection with rights of ownership, and it is also treated in Mishnah-tractate Shebiᶜit:

> Every Seventh Year you shall practice remission of debts. This shall be the nature of the remission: every creditor shall remit the due that he claims from his neighbor; he shall not dun his neighbor or kinsman, for the remission proclaimed is of the Lord. You may dun the foreigner, but you must remit whatever is due you from your kinsmen.

Mishnah-tractate Shebiᶜit concerns how, in the Sabbatical Year, God exercises rights of ownership along with the Israelite householder. It sets forth the law that, in relation to the Land of Israel, embodies the conviction of God's partnership in all things. It bears the message that Israelites never own the Land and fungible assets, but are custodians and stewards of their possessions, subject always to God's interest in them. The Mishnah's law systematically works through the Torah's rules, treating (1) the prohibition of farming the land during the Seventh Year; (2) the use of the produce in the Seventh Year solely for eating; and (3) the remission of debts. During the Sabbatical Year, Israel relinquishes its ownership of the Land of Israel. At that time Israelites in farming may do nothing that in secular years effects the assertion of ownership over the land. Just as they may not utilize land they do not own, in the Sabbatical Year, farmers relinquish ownership of the land that they do own. What the law of the Torah as elaborated by the law of the Mishnah prevents is clear: householders, landowners, or lenders are reminded that ownership is not absolute. People possess land or wealth. They do not own it outright.

Not only may landowners not reserve for their own use the produce of their fields, but they also may not hoard the crop. When a crop has ceased to appear in the fields, moreover, householders must remove from their household and leave for public utilization that same crop that they may have in storage. This rule is expressed in the following language, concerning the law of removal:

MISHNAH-TRACTATE SHEBIʿIT 9:2-3, 4, 8

9:2-3 Three regions [are delineated] with respect to [the laws of] removal: Judah, Transjordan, and Galilee.

And why have they stated [that the three main areas are each divided into] three regions? That they may eat [produce of the Sabbatical Year] in each region only until the last [produce] of that region is gone [without regard to whether or not such produce remains in the other regions]. [At that point people may not hoard the produce but must remove it from their homes, affording all Israelites equal access to the limited food supply.]

9:4 They may eat [produce of the Sabbatical Year which they have gathered into their homes only] by virtue of the fact that ownerless produce [is available in the fields], but [they may] not [eat such produce] by virtue of the fact that [it is found] in protected [places, where it is inaccessible to the animals of the field].

9:8 One who has [in his possession] produce of the Sabbatical Year when the time for removal [of that produce] arrives, allots food [enough for] three meals for each [member of his household and then removes any remaining produce; that is now ownerless and not to be hoarded].

Enforcing the law of removal equalized community access to the now-ownerless crops for all Israelites, each person receiving a share "in accordance with the size of his [or her] household":

TOSEFTA-TRACTATE SHEBIʿIT 8:1

In the past, agents of the court would sit near the gates of the cities. [From] each person [who harvested produce of the Seventh Year and] who carried it [to them, these agents] would take it from him and return to that person [enough] food for three meals [cf. Mishnah-tractate Shebiʿit 9:8A-B], and the remainder they would deposit in the city's storehouse.

When the time for [harvesting] figs arrived, the agents of the court would hire workers [to harvest them], harvest [the figs], press them into cakes of pressed figs, place them in jars and deposit [these jars] in the city's storehouse.

When the time for [harvesting] grapes arrived, the agents of the court would hire workers [to harvest them], harvest the grapes, press them in presses, place the wine in jars and deposit [these jars] in the city's storehouse.

When the time for [harvesting] olives arrived, the agents of the court would hire workers [to harvest them], harvest the olives, pack them in a vat, place them in jars and deposit [these jars] in the city's storehouse.

And they would distribute [portions] of this [stored-up produce] on the eve of the Sabbath [and] each person [would receive an amount of produce] in accordance with [the size of his household].

The law of removal, which prevents hoarding, is part of the larger account of who may eat the produce of the ownerless fields in the Land in the Sabbatical Year, and how people are to obtain food during the Sabbatical Year. A passage of Sifra, the normative commentary to the book of Leviticus, produced about 300 C.E. in response to the Mishnah, expands on that theme.

### SIFRA CCXLVI:I.12

"The Sabbath of the land shall provide food for you . . . for yourself and for your male and female slaves":

What is the point of Scripture here?

Since it is said, "[For six years you shall sow your land and gather in its yield, but the seventh year you shall let it rest and lie fallow,] that the poor of your people may eat; and what they leave the wild beasts may eat. You shall do likewise with your vineyard and with your olive orchard" (Exod. 23:10–11),

I might have supposed that produce of the Seventh Year may be eaten only by the poor alone.

How do I know that even the rich may eat it?

Scripture says, "for yourself and for your male and female slaves."

Lo, wealthy landowners are covered, bondmen and bondwomen are covered.

The passage thus stresses that the common ownership of the Land is not a means of supporting the poor alone. It is a shared circumstance that all Israel enters: the fields are left fallow and untended; whatever crops they yield on their own belong to no one in particular but to everyone in general. The matter of removal of the stored (hoarded) crops from the household to the fields or streets, where they are accessible to everyone, is the key. This is a way of underscoring the common circumstance confronting all Israel in the Sabbatical Year.

The remission of debts at the advent of the Seventh Year makes a still more extreme statement of the stipulative character of ownership, here of wealth as much as of property. The law of the Mishnah, with the Tosefta's complement, states matters in this way.

### MISHNAH-TRACTATE SHEBI'IT 10:1
### AND TOSEFTA-TRACTATE SHEBI'IT 8:4

M. 10:1 The Sabbatical Year cancels a loan [which is secured] by a bond and [a loan which is] not [secured] by a bond. A debt [owed to a] shopkeeper is not canceled [by the Sabbatical Year]. But if [the debt] was made into a loan, lo, this [loan] is canceled [by the Sabbatical Year]. The [unpaid] wage of a hired laborer is not canceled [by the Sabbatical Year]. But if [the amount of the wage] was made into a loan, lo, this [loan] is canceled [by the Sabbatical Year].

T. 8:4 A woman's marriage contract [which stipulates the amount of money which her husband owes her if he either divorces her or dies]—[if] she accepted partial payment [of this sum of money from her husband before the Seventh Year] and converted to a loan [to him the remaining amount], lo, the Seventh Year cancels [this loan]. [But if] she accepted partial payment and did not loan [the remaining amount to her husband, or if] she loaned [to her husband the full amount specified in her marriage document] and did not accept partial payment [of this sum], lo, the Seventh Year does not cancel [this loan].

Note that, while the law of the Mishnah does not legislate in terms of property owned by Israelites living outside of the Land, the remission of debts is tied to the Land, even though it is practiced outside of the Land as well. I cannot imagine a more eloquent statement of the communitarian ideal than that which is contained within the law of the Mishnah of the Seventh Year.

What story is embodied in the law of the Mishnah before us, corresponding to the story that is told of genealogical, enlandised Israel, in Bikkurim? The generative paradigm has already made its appearance: Adam and Eve in Eden, compared with Israel in the Land of Israel. The logic may be stated simply, since the Torah itself declares that analogy to govern. The Land is to have its Sabbaths just as Israel does; and if the Land is denied its Sabbaths, Israel will lose the Land. The Torah states this negatively:

> Then the land shall enjoy its Sabbaths as long as it lies desolate, while you are in your enemies' land; then the land shall rest and enjoy its Sabbaths. As long as it lies desolate, it shall have rest, the rest that it did not have in your Sabbaths when you dwelt on it. (Lev. 26:34–35)

So the comparison of Israel's loss of the Land and Adam and Eve's loss of Eden is not merely to be imputed, it is made explicit. The Sabbatical Year recovers in the Land's repose that perfect time of Eden when the world was at rest, all things at peace. Before the rebellion, human beings did not have to labor on the land; they picked and ate their meals freely. In the nature of things, everything belonged to everybody; private ownership in response to individual labor was nonexistent since there was no need to work. Reverting to that perfect time, the Torah maintains that the land will provide adequate food for everyone, including the flocks and herds, even if people do not work the land. That brings us back to our point of interest: the realization of Israel's corporate character, nurturing the communitarian sense among individual Israelites.

The comparison of the Land to Eden is made equally explicit in the law that the Sabbatical Year takes effect at the moment of Israel's entry into the Land. Then Israel reenacts the drama of creation, the seventh day marking the perfection of creation and its sanctification and a Sabbath of the Seventh Year observed for the Land as much as for its human inhabitants. Observing the commandments of the Sabbatical Year marks Israel's effort at keeping the Land like Eden, six days of creation, one day of rest; six years of labor, one year of rest. We find the critical ties in Sifra, where the commentary engages in a dialogue with the Mishnah and its laws:

**SIFRA CCXLV:I.2**

> "When you come [into the land which I give you, the land shall keep a Sabbath to the Lord]":
>
> Might one suppose that the Sabbatical Year was to take effect once they had reached Transjordan?
>
> The Torah says, "into the land."
>
> It is that particular land.

This is the key point: the Sabbatical Year takes effect only when Israel enters the Land, which is to say, Israel's entry into the Land marks the counterpart of Adam's entry into Eden at the creation. But a further point will register in a moment. What is the climactic moment of Eden? It is when Eden or, for Israel, the Land enters into stasis that the process of the formation of the new Eden comes to its climax. For Eden that is when God pronounced the work complete and sanctified the Sabbath day. What about the counterpart moment for the Land? It was when the families of Israel received their inheritance in the Land promised by God. And then each Israelite bears responsibility for his or her share of the Land. That is when the Land has reached that state of order and permanence that corresponds to Eden at sunset on the sixth day:

> Might one suppose that the Sabbatical Year was to take effect once they had reached Ammon and Moab?
>
> The Torah says, "which I give you,"
>
> and not to Ammon and Moab.
>
> And on what basis do you maintain that when they had conquered the land but not divided it, divided it among familiars but not among fathers' houses so that each individual does not yet recognize his share—
>
>> might one suppose that they should be responsible to observe the Sabbatical Year?
>>
>> The Torah says, "[Six years you shall sow] your field,"
>>
>> meaning, each one should recognize his own field.
>>
>> ". . . your vineyard":
>>
>> meaning, each one should recognize his own vineyard.
>
> You turn out to rule:
>
> Once the Israelites had crossed the Jordan, they incurred liability to separate dough offering and to observe the prohibition against eating the fruit of fruit trees for the first three years after planting and the prohibition against eating produce of the new growing season prior to the waving of the sheaf of new grain [that is, on the fifteenth of Nisan].
>
> When the sixteenth of Nisan came, they incurred liability to wave the sheaf of new grain.
>
> With the passage of fifty days from then they incurred the liability to the offering of the Two Loaves.
>
> At the fourteenth year they became liable for the separation of tithes.

The Sabbatical takes over only when the Israelite farmers have asserted their ownership of the land and its crops. Then the process of counting the years begins.

> They began to count the years of the sabbatical cycle, and in the twenty-first year after entry into the land, they observed the sabbatical year.
>
> In the sixty-fourth year they observed the first Jubilee [Tosefta-tractate Men. 6:20].

So, the Sabbatical cycle commences when Israelite householders have asserted their will to own and utilize the Land. At that point, the individuals take their place within all Israel and their exercise of will takes place as part of the collective intentionality, to which God responds. Corporate Israel then entered into the situation of Adam on the day of his creation, when, joined by Eve, the first man and the first woman entered into Paradise—and, through an exercise of will, lost everything.

### Relinquishing Private Ownership in Favor of
### Communitarian Possession on the Sabbath Day:
### Tractates Shabbat-Erubin

The world of space is divided into public and private domain, meaning, property assigned corporate, communal ownership, and property belonging to and subject to the will and control of a private person, a householder. For purposes of Sabbath observance, the distinction makes a difference. The Torah defines the Sabbath in part by sending Israel to its tents on that occasion. Repose of the Sabbath involves entry into a stationary condition, because, on the Sabbath one is expected to remain in place, not to transport goods from private domain to public domain or vice versa. What is located in public domain on the Sabbath may be transported only four cubits, that is, within the space occupied by a person's body. What is in private domain may be transported within the entire demarcated space of that common domain. The laws of Mishnah-tractate Shabbat expound that principle.

This division of real estate into public and private domain is based on the Rabbinic reading of the statement of the Torah concerning remaining in one's place on the Sabbath:

> See! The Lord has given you the Sabbath; therefore on the sixth day he gives you bread for two days; remain every man of you in his place; let no man go out of his place on the seventh day. So the people rested on the seventh day. (Exod. 16:29–30)

To remain in one's place—within property one owns or controls, a domain subject to one's own will—means to eat at home and also not to transport objects from that private domain to the public domain ("out of his place"). How an Israelite establishes the dimensions of "his place" and secures access to a larger space than specifically owned private property, or a different space altogether, is worked out in the laws of Mishnah-tractate Erubin.

### Dividing Public from Private Domain:
### Tractate Shabbat

The law of the Mishnah of Shabbat sets forth the division of domains. On the Sabbath the household and village divide into private and public domain, and it is forbidden to transport objects from one domain to the other. Private domain is defined as, at the very least, an area ten handbreadths deep or high by four handbreadths wide. Public domain is defined as an unimpeded space open to the public. In public domain, one is liable for carrying an object more than four cubits. In private domain, there is no limit other than the outer boundaries of the demarcated area, for instance, within the walls of the household. What is worn for clothing or ornament does not violate the prohibition against carrying things from private to public domain. It is even permissible for one to transport an object from private domain to private domain, for example, by tossing it from one private domain to another, so long as the object is not brought into public domain. Here is how the law of the Mishnah formulates the basic conception of the division of space into public and private domain:

### MISHNAH-TRACTATE SHABBAT 1:1

[Acts of] transporting objects from one domain to another [which violate] the Sabbath (1) are two, which [indeed] are four [for one who is] inside, (2) and two which are four [for one who is] outside.

How so? [If on the Sabbath] the beggar stands outside and the householder inside, [and] the beggar stuck his hand inside and put [a beggar's bowl] into the hand of the householder, or if he took [something] from inside it and brought it out, the beggar is liable, the householder is exempt.

[If] the householder stuck his hand outside and put [something] into the hand of the beggar, or if he took [something] from it and brought it inside, the householder is liable, and the beggar is exempt.

[If] the beggar stuck his hand inside, and the householder took [something] from it, or if [the householder] put something in it and he [the beggar] removed it—both of them are exempt.

[If] the householder put his hand outside and the beggar took [something] from it, or if [the beggar] put something into it and [the householder] brought it back inside, both of them are exempt.

The point of the division into private and public domain emerges in the exposition of the distinction that concerns transporting objects. One may cross the line but not carry anything in so doing—hence the concern for what may or may not be worn as clothing. The same point emerges in the rule that one may move an object from one private domain to another, so long as public domain does not intervene. Carrying within public domain forms an equally important consideration; one may do so only within the space occupied by one's body or person. But the four cubits a person occupies in public domain may be said to transform that particular segment of public domain into private domain, so the effect is the same. The advent of the Sabbath day then imparts enormous consequence to the status of what is private. There, and only there, on the Sabbath, is life to be lived ("remain in place"). The Sabbath assigns to private domain the focus of life in holy time: the household is at the center on the Sabbath.

## Fusing Domains: Tractate Erubin

By sharing ownership, therefore, individual householders gain access to a much larger space for the conduct of everyday life on the Sabbath. How the Israelite defines "his [or her] place" forms the touchstone of all else. Spending the Sabbath in public domain—that is, domain not designated for one's place or residence for this holy span of time—means sitting in place and doing nothing. Private domain is where one may, within the broad limits of Sabbath propriety, do what one likes. As long as there is no conflict with the laws of the Sabbath, it is in the private domain that Israelites may handle what they wish, carry what they wish from spot to spot, conduct all licit actions, and perform actions within the spirit of the Sabbath—actions that are not constructive with enduring results and that are consonant with the sanctity of the time. Beyond "his [or her] place," householders may not conduct themselves as if they owned the territory, meaning, handle whatever they want, move about whatever they wish, do whatever they choose. Apart from walking about, for all practical purposes on the Sabbath, all householders may do in public domain by their mere presence is establish private domain, meaning, a space of four cubits; from that point they cannot budge.

Accordingly, establishing residence defines a key point at which the law of the Mishnah trades ownership for possession, so reinforcing the communitarian definition of Israel and diminishing the isolated individuality of the Israelite. We have now seen that the law of the Mishnah encourages relinquishing private ownership of real property in favor of participating in the joint possession, with other neighbors, of a much larger, shared area. Let us turn to the way in which the law nurtures the communitarian spirit.

The Mishnah's law of fusing domains, Erubin, provides for the union of numerous private domains, individually owned, into a large domain, also classified as private, now subject to joint ownership by all who willingly join their private domain to the larger property. This is a roundabout but precise way of saying: setting up an imaginary domain with imaginary boundaries.

With real estate classified as private domain, the householder gives up to the collectivity sole ownership of what is uniquely his or hers in exchange for a share in the property of all others within the pertinent boundaries—the whole retaining the established classification of private domain. That fact bears the implication of a redefinition of what is meant by private and personal. The individual releases control of private property, sharing control with other individuals of their private property, and gains in consequence access to property over which, during ordinary time, the individual bears no power of will whatsoever. The laws of Mishnah-tractate Erubin—"the means of fusing domains"—specify the way in which that is done.

That is what I mean by reinforcing the bonds of community through relinquishing ownership in favor of possession: usufruct of a common domain, shared among many individuals, who now own less but use more. By sharing ownership of one's private domain with others in one's district, the individual also acquires a share in the private domain of others, and the whole forms a single, augmented private domain, subject to the mingled ownership of many householders. That is effected by mingling ownership: giving up sole, total control of one's own to one's neighbors in the courtyard, alleyway, or entire village, in favor of gaining from them communitarian rights.

Establishing this shared ownership happens in several ways. First, the law of the Mishnah provides for a meal of commingling—a fictive meal, theoretically available for all residents of the now-augmented private domain. Second, householders who share a common courtyard or alleyway made up of many courtyards may erect a fictive boundary of commingling of property that demarcates that same domain; such a fictive boundary forms the physical counterpart of the meal of commingling.

The law takes for granted a number of propositions, upon which all else is founded. These are as follows:

(1) Remaining in one's place does not mean one may not leave his or her house; one may move about his or her own property, to the limit of two thousand cubits from one's own residence.

(2) Through a fictive meal or an *'erub*—a boundary marker or a meal of fusion—one may commingle ownership of a courtyard or still larger space that is shared with others. Similarly, through a fictive meal, or a *shittuf*, a meal of partnership, an alleyway into which a number of courtyards debouch may be formed into a common courtyard; this is signaled by marking the alleyway as a single domain by establishing a gateway, and then the shared meal establishes that all of the private domains are commingled as to ownership. In consequence of the fictive meal or boundary, the householders and their families and dependents may utilize on the Sabbath a much larger space than they own on weekdays.

(3) One must remain in his or her own village, that is, the settled area and its natural environs. The village space is demarcated as generously as possible through surveying techniques.

(4) One may establish residence at some place other than his or her own household by making provision for eating a meal at that other place. The meal must be located in its place by sundown on the Sabbath, but a verbal declaration accomplishes the same purpose. That fictive residence permits the area of permitted travel to be measured from that other place. How then does the meal in particular take shape? One party acts on behalf of all:

### MISHNAH-TRACTATE ERUBIN 7:6

How do they make a partnership [through a fusion-meal, or a *shittuf*] in an alleyway? One [of the residents] sets down a jar [of food or drink] and states, "Lo, this belongs to all the residents of the alleyway."

And thus he effects possession for them through his adult son or daughter, his Hebrew slave boy or slave girl, or his wife.

But he does not effect possession on their behalf by means of his minor son or daughter, or by means of his Canaanite slave boy or slave girl, because their hand is as his hand.

Once the institution of the fictive fusion-meal is established, the various participants are assumed to take their share, even when the physical condition of the meal changes.

### MISHNAH-TRACTATE ERUBIN 7:7, 8

7:7 [If] the food diminished in volume [to less than the prescribed quantity], one adds to it and effects possession for the others. And he need not inform them. [But if] the number [of residents of the alleyway] became larger, one adds to the food and effects possession for them. And he does need to inform them.

7:8 What is its prescribed volume? When the [residents] are numerous, food sufficient for two meals for all of them. When they are few in numbers, a dried fig's bulk—such that may be taken out on the Sabbath—for each and every one.

Given the premises of the rite of preparing a fictive fusion-meal, we should not be surprised that all parties to the fused domain have to concur in commingling the ownership of their domains with all the others. How that yields a valid fusion when one party neglects or rejects the rite is treated in the following. The issues are spelled out in laws that stress the individuality of the householder and his or her responsibility willingly to give up rights to a private domain in order to form a partnership in a much broader, still-private domain.

**MISHNAH-TRACTATE ERUBIN 6:3**

> The men of a courtyard, one of whom forgot and did not participate in the fictive fusion-meal with the others—his house is prohibited, both for him and for them, from bringing things in and from taking things out. And theirs are permitted both for him and for them.
>
> [If] they gave him their right [of access], he is permitted, and they are prohibited. [If] they were two [who forgot], they prohibit one another. For one person gives or takes the right of access. But [while] two can give the right of access, they cannot take it.

The failure of the individual to join in the fictive fusion-meal brings serious inconvenience and underscores the incentive that the law of the Mishnah presents to relinquish autonomous ownership in favor of joint control.

Thus, by means of the fictive fusion-meal or boundary, a householder gives up unlimited power over a particular share of private domain in order to acquire limited power over a much larger share of land that is in that same status. By the same means, one may not only commingle rights of ownership; one may also remove oneself from the property that is usually his or her private domain and establish another domain. It comes down to the same thing. The advent of the Sabbath, then, redefines what is meant by private domain. The Sabbath, like the Seventh Year, brings about a reorganization of the division of property and society alike.

## The Sabbath of Creation in Shebiʿit, Erubin, and Shabbat

Shabbat-Erubin, in its sustained exercise of thought on the commingling of ownership of private property for the purpose of Sabbath observance and on the commingling of meals to signify shared ownership, accomplishes for Israel's Sabbath what Shebiʿit achieves for the Land's Sabbath. On the Sabbath inaugurated by the Sabbatical Year, the Land, so far as it is otherwise private property, no longer is possessed exclusively by the householder. So too, the produce of the Land consequently belongs to everybody. Both categories of Sabbath law define the Sabbath of the Land in exactly the same terms: the Land is now no longer private, and the Land's produce belongs to everybody. Indeed, sharing is so total that hoarding is explicitly forbidden, and what has been hoarded has now to be removed from the household and moved to public domain, where anyone may come and take it.

The implication is not to be missed. The Sabbatical Year bears the message that, on the Sabbath, established arrangements as to ownership and possession are set aside, and a different conception of private property takes over. What on ordinary days is deemed to belong to the householder and to be subject to the householder's exclusive will on the Sabbath falls into a more complex web of possession. The householder gives up exclusive access to private property, gaining in exchange rights of access to other peoples' property. Private property is commingled; everybody sharing in everybody's. On the Sabbath, as a result, private property takes on a new meaning, different from the secular one. To own, on the Sabbath, is to abridge ownership in favor of commingling property—to own is to diminish, but to possess is to share. And that explains why the produce of the Land belongs to everyone as well, a corollary to the fundamental postulate of the Sabbath of the Land.

Clearly, the law of the Mishnah of Shebiʿit appeals to the metaphor of the first Sabbath, the one celebrated in Eden. If we wish to understand how the sages thought about the Sabbath, we have to follow suit. What qualities of Eden impressed the sages? First, Adam and Eve are free to move in Eden where they wish, possessing all they contemplate. God has given it to them to enjoy. If Eden then belongs to God, as God's private domain, it is God who freely shares ownership with Adam and Eve. And—all the more so—the produce of Eden is ownerless. With the well-known exception, fruit of a tree subject to God's particular attention, all the fruit is theirs for the taking. The Sabbatical Year recovers that perfect time of Eden when the world was at rest, all things in place. As if reverting to that perfect time, the Torah maintains that the Land (even if people do not work it) will provide adequate food for everyone, including the flocks and herds. That is, on condition that all claim of ownership lapses; that the food is left in the fields, to be picked by anyone who wishes; and that it not be hoarded by any landowner in particular.

It is in this context that we return to the law of the Mishnah of Shabbat-Erubin with special reference to the division of the world into private and public domains, the former the realm of permitted activity on the Sabbath, the latter not. If we may deal with a fusion-fence or a fusion-meal, how are we to interpret what is at stake in these matters? It is to render private domain public through the sharing of ownership. The fusion-fence, for its part, renders public domain private, but only in the same sense that private domain owned by diverse owners is shared, ownership being commingled. If the fusion-fence signals the formation for purposes of the sanctification of time of private domain, then what is "private" about "private domain" is different on the Sabbath than it is in secular time. By definition, for property to be private in the setting of the Sabbath, it must be shared among householders. For property to be private the rest of the time, ownership cannot be shared among all comers. And along these same lines, radically private ownership is not liberating but limiting. That is, on the Sabbath, domain that is totally private, its ownership not commingled for the occasion, becomes a prison, the householder being unable to conduct normal manners in the courtyard beyond the door, let alone in other courtyards in the same alleyway, or in other alleyways that debouch onto the same street.

What happens, therefore, through the fusion-fence or fusion-meal is the redefinition of proprietorship: what is private is no longer personal, and no one totally owns any property, but then everyone (who wishes to participate, along with his or her household) owns a share everywhere. So much for the "in his place" part of "each man in his place." If constructing a fence serves to signify joint ownership of the village, now turned into private domain, or constructing the gateway in an alleyway and its courtyards, what about the meal? The *ʿerub*-meal signifies the shared character of what is eaten. It is food that belongs to all who wish to share it. But it is the provision of a personal meal, also, that allows individuals to designate for themselves a place of Sabbath residence other than the household to which they belong.

In that the Sabbath loosens the bonds of the householder to property, it forms of Israelites nothing less than corporate Israel. The householders of a courtyard form a community of shared ownership of the entire courtyard; individuals enter into a community other than their household or family. Indeed, the law provides for a variety of communities. There can be the community of disciples of a given sage or the community of a family other than that in residence in the household, to cite two examples common in the law of the Mishnah. Just as the Sabbath redefines ownership of the Land and its produce, turning all Israelites into a single social entity, "all Israel," which all together possesses the Land in common ownership, so the Sabbath redefines the social relationships of the household, allowing persons to separate themselves from the residence of the household and designate some other, some personal, point of residence instead.

The meaning of "private domain" is redefined. Ownership is rendered both public and collective. Why is this so? Taking as our model Shebiʿit, we note that in the year that is a Sabbath, the land is held to be owned by nobody and everybody, and the produce of the Land belongs to everyone and no one, so that one may take and eat but thank only God. The Sabbath recapitulates the condition of Eden, when Adam and Eve could go where they wished and eat what they wanted, masters (along with God) of all they contemplated. Israel on the Sabbath in the Land, like the first humans on the Sabbath of Eden, which celebrates creation, shares private domain and its produce. And that is only appropriate, for Israel forms a moral entity, a corporate body, comparable to Adam and Eve, moral entities of an individual character: the people Israel, the corporate Israel, not just Israelites.

## When the Individual Israelite Is Wholly Subordinated to Corporate Israel

When does the individual have to accept his or her place within corporate Israel to the exclusion of all individuality—even to its extinction? We now know. Under particular circumstances, the individual Israelite must identify himself or herself with Israel, specifically, for sharing in the collective atonement for collective sin, so we read in Sheqalim. In addition, the individual must relinquish claim to ownership of his private domain, so far as productive agricultural lands are concerned, in the Seventh Year, so we find in Shebiʿit. Along these same lines, a particular class of individuals—householders who trace their genealogy back within Israel and receive their land-holdings by inheritance—narrates a family story that recapitulates Israel's history, so we read in Bikkurim. Further, the individual Israelite may, is encouraged to, identify himself with that Israel that is embodied in the community where he or she lives, relinquishing ownership of singular property in favor of possession through sharing a much wider space, so we read in Shabbat-Erubin. But the question remains, at what point *must* the individual give up all semblance of individuality—life itself, the ultimate realization of individuality—and submit to the public interest? That is the final question to be answered in an account of how corporate Israel is actualized by the adherence of individual Israelites.

In the first place, it is a public occasion, not a private one. The law upon which the Mishnah rests makes a critical distinction between one's obligation in private and one's duty in public. When in private, the individual Israelite represents only himself or herself. But when in public, *the same individual embodies corporate Israel.* That distinction forms the foundation for a body of law not articulated in the Mishnah. Nevertheless, attention to it is required for a full understanding of absolute, outer limit of the Mishnah's laws of individuation. It is this law that determines the point at which the individual must surrender his or her very being, accept extinction for now, in favor of resurrection and eternal life within all Israel in the end of days.

In the second place, on specific occasions, when an Israelite is faced with the choice of betrayal of God or martyrdom in God's name, one's duty in public is to accept martyrdom, sanctifying God's name in behalf of all Israel. Faced with the same choice in private, martyrdom is not demanded. The absolute choice, in this case, arises in relation to blasphemy (denying God's name) through an act of idolatry.

These matters are so self-evident to the sages of the Mishnah, that no systematic tractate on the law of martyrdom exists in the law of the Mishnah. Once more, we turn to Sifra to see the matter expounded. Predictably, Sifra itself takes up a secondary issue, assuming the primary affirmation as a given. The secondary issue concerns miracles in the rite of martyrdom. Surrendering oneself, one's individuality, one may not expect a miracle to be done on such an occasion; miracles are done only on worthy occasions. But God exacts vengeance for the blood of the martyrs, as we shall now see in the exposition of Sifra:

SIFRA CCXXVII:I.4–8

4. "And you shall not profane [my holy name]:"

I derive the implication from the statement, "you shall not profane," that sanctification is covered.

And when the Torah says, "but I will be hallowed," the sense is, "Give yourself and sanctify my name."

Might one suppose that that is when one is all alone?

The Torah says, "among the people of Israel."

5. In this connection sages have said:

Whoever gives his life on condition that a miracle is done for him—no miracle will be done for him.

But if it is not on condition that a miracle be done for him, a miracle will be done for him.

For so we find in the case of Hananiah, Mishael, and Azariah, that they said to Nebuchadnezzar, "We have no need to answer you in this matter, for if so it must be, our God whom we serve is able to save us from the burning fiery furnace, and he will save us from your power, O king. But even if he does not, be it known to you, O king, that we will not serve your god or worship the statue of gold that you have set up" (Dan. 3:16–18).

And when Marianos seized Pappos and Lulianos, brothers in Laodicea, he said to them, "If you come from the people of Hananiah, Mishael, and Azariah, let your God come and save you from my power."

They said to him, "Hananiah, Mishael, and Azariah were worthy men, and Nebuchadnezzar was a king worthy of having a miracle done on his account.

"But you are a wicked king, and you are not worthy of having a miracle done on your account, and, for our part, we are liable to the death penalty inflicted by Heaven, so if you do not kill us, there are plenty of agents of punishment before the Omnipresent, plenty of bears, plenty of lions, plenty of panthers, plenty of fiery snakes, plenty of scorpions, to do injury to us.

"But in the end the Omnipresent is going to demand the penalty of our blood from your hand."

They say that he did not leave there before orders came from Rome, and they chopped off his head with axes.

6. "who brought you out of the land of Egypt":

"I brought you out of the land of Egypt on a stipulation that you be prepared to give yourselves to sanctify my name."

7. "I shall be your God":

like it or not.

8. "I am the Lord":

"I am faithful to pay a reward."

As we have stated, the law defining martyrdom does not surface in the exposition of the Mishnah. Why the Rabbinic sages did not translate the exposition that is before us into a set of generalized laws is difficult to say without a long excursus in the principles that govern in choosing the topics of the

Mishnah's topical tractates. Nevertheless, the exposition yields normative rules of conduct, not just suggestions on self-sacrifice beyond the measure of the law.

The focus is not directly on the rules and regulations of attaining martyrdom. Rather, what is explained is the right attitude for martyrdom. It is one that accepts death for the sake of sanctifying God's name, without the expectation that God will miraculously intervene. It also provides a reasonable explanation for why God intervenes at some times and not at others. But the main point comes at the climax. When corporate Israel is present, then God is engaged and God's name must be sanctified, and when not, not. When corporate Israel is present, the Israelite must surrender to Israel—for God's sake.

Can a more extreme case of individual self-abnegation be imagined than the act of voluntarily giving up one's life? That, in the case of Israel, is called not martyrdom but the act of *qiddush hashem,* "sanctifying the divine name," accepting (even courting) martyrdom in God's service. That is how Israel's ultimate calling, to bear witness to the unity and dominion of God in the world, is realized. It is the point, therefore, at which the individual Israelite completely surrenders to the calling and mission of corporate Israel.

Here is how the Rabbinic exposition of the Torah mediates between the natural instinct of Israelite individuals to live, and the divine imperative addressed to all Israel to embody God's share in the world: those who know and affirm the unity of God, made manifest in the Torah. The martyred will live, too, at the resurrection at the end of days. Giving up one's life to sanctify God's name is for a brief interim. In his or her person, at the occasion of martyrdom, the Israelite martyr incorporates Israel. But—and here is the heart of the matter—that takes place *only in the presence of Israel.* Then, by its presence corporate Israel defines the reference point, the template, for the individual Israelite. Corporate Israel defines the occasion and sets the norm; the individual Israelite represents the anomaly. What I see here is this: Israel is truly Israel all together, in community.

## Individuality and Community: The Natural Condition of Humanity, the Normative Condition of Israel

We began with the assumption that the natural condition of humanity is individual, that human beings, both gentile and Israelite, *by nature* are individuated. Then corporate Israel, a moral entity, appeared unnatural, a huge anomaly to the rule of individuated humanity. We thus treated Israel as part of humanity, so that Israelite individuality simply represented a continuity with the norm for everybody. So we found the corporate character of "all Israel," its constituting a moral entity out of individuals, to represent the exceptional, the differentiating quality of Israel in particular.

But that premise does not hold for corporate Israel. Corporate Israel comes prior to individual Israelites and imposes imperatives on its own, which individual Israelites cannot accomplish, represented by the requirement to give up life for the sanctification of God's name: in public, but not in private, in the context of Israel, but not otherwise. The conclusion is this: Israel is Israel corporately, the individual Israelite enters into his or her *Israelness*—in this case, the obligation to sanctify God's name through martyrdom—only via corporate Israel. Then the norm for Israel is its corporate existence; only in Israel is the individual an anomaly. The natural condition of the Israelite is within corporate Israel. That is why, on his or her own, the Israelite need not submit to martyrdom. In private, there is no question of sanctifying God's name. God's name is only sanctified in the corporate body, Israel. That is what "in public" means. Then and there the individual Israelite surrenders individual existence altogether, even his or her very being, within, for the sake of, corporate Israel.

The accumulation, the collectivity, of Israelite individuals is necessary, but not sufficient, to define Israel. What does define Israel? It is that corporate Israel never dies. It is an enduring component of humanity, the part of humanity that knows God through God's own self-manifestation in the Torah, the sector of humanity that accepts the law of the Torah as the will of God. This Israel, integral to the perfection of creation, is eternal in the same sense that God is. For Israel, the people, resurrection categorically does not pertain—it is pertinent only to individual Israelites.

# 7 | The Norm and the Exception

## Tractates Dema<sup>c</sup>i and Tohorot

*Tractates Dema<sup>c</sup>i and Tohorot*

### Corporate Israel at the Apex

The law of the Mishnah subordinates the individual Israelite to corporate Israel. In cases where the individual Israelite's interests intersect with those of corporate Israel, those of the latter take priority. Corporate Israel imposes on all Israelites the requirement to obey the law: do what the Torah requires, refrain from doing what it prohibits. These imperatives are many and detailed, far exceeding those incumbent on non-Israelites. But corporate Israel also accords toleration to erring Israelites by identifying areas in which meeting lower than the optimal standards bears consequences but no sanctions.

How does corporate Israel deal with deviancy? What we wish to find out concerns areas in which the community tolerates less than perfect conformity to the law of the Mishnah. We know that all Israelites are expected to tithe food produced in the Land of Israel and consumed by them. As we shall see, the law assumes that most people give some of the required tithes but that only a minority give all of them. Then there is produce that has been tithed but only partially—doubtfully tithed produce. Mishnah-tractate Dema<sup>c</sup>i deals with the disposition of doubtfully tithed produce. It responds then to the simple fact that not all Israelites conduct themselves in accord with the strict requirements of the Torah. Then the law takes upon itself the task of arranging matters within Israel so as to preserve the correct relationship between Israel and God. The specific answer is, the trustworthy Israelites within Israel, those who give all the required tithes, so far as they are able, undertake responsibility for the condition of all Israel.

Recognizing the diversity of Israelites within corporate Israel, the law of the Mishnah estimates the probabilities of law conformity. This assessment of the social realities of Israelites, as they constitute corporate Israel in practice, is not in theory alone. The answer to this in Mishnah-tractate Tohorot once again recognizes that the system imposes its norms in a nuanced way, negotiating the gap between the ideal and the real. In both Dema<sup>c</sup>i and Tohorot the law presupposes good will and a desire to do the right thing even on the part of deviant Israelites. On that basis the law finds ample grounds for leniency.

## Accommodating Acceptable Difference and Tolerated Law Breaking: Tractate Dema'i

To begin with, the law of the Mishnah does tolerate widespread individual deviation from the highest standards of corporate Israel. How is this act of legerdemain to be accomplished? In practice, of course, the law legislates for a social order in which standards of conformity to laws of marginal importance vary among individuals. It does so by devising an elaborate system for mediating the relationships between the perfectly punctilious and those who mean to keep the law but do so in a less than meticulous manner.

The legislation itself is intended to instruct fully observant Israelites in how to accommodate themselves to the realities of the imperfect social world around them. What the law of the Mishnah requires is that the faithful take account of the failure of neighbors to observe details of the law and so act as to secure broad adherence to the requirements of the law. Such provision for the facts of life represents not compromise but remediation. From the very particular case at hand, we can readily extrapolate the policy of the Mishnah that would cover comparable circumstances. It is: identify acceptable deviance, but provide for realizing the norm so far as is feasible.

Mishnah-tractate Dema'i presents a complicated solution to a simple problem. The issue concerns proper tithing of the agricultural produce of the Land of Israel by the Israelite householder. Law breaking enters in, because, while everybody separates some classifications of the tithes—obeying the law to the letter—many are also assumed not to separate other classifications of tithe. All Israelites, the law of the Mishnah takes for granted, separate heave offering for the rations of the priesthood. But other pertinent agricultural offerings are designated only by those most faithful to the rule.[1] So the premise of the law of the Mishnah is that people do generally keep the law, but there are those who do so imperfectly.

The laws themselves dictate how a responsible person makes certain that what is purchased in the marketplace and eaten or given to another to eat will be properly tithed. In other words, what marks the outer limit of responsibility of the Israelite toward corporate Israel for the conduct of third parties? The specific problem that provokes the formation of this law of the Mishnah concerns the heave offering of the tithe given to the Levite, of which a further share goes to the priest. Produce that has not certainly yielded that offering of

---

[1] These are (1) first tithe, a tenth of the crop remaining when heave offering has been removed, given to the Levite, (2) heave offering of the tithe, that is to say, a tenth removed from the Levite's tithe and given to the priest, and (3) second tithe or (4) poorman's tithe (depending on the year of the Sabbatical cycle, first, second, fourth, and fifth, or third and sixth, respectively).

the tithe to the priest is called Dema⁀i, doubtfully tithed produce, that is, produce that has been only partially tithed. We shall not trouble ourselves with the details, since what is important here is only the main point: most Israelites separate some of the tithes, but only some Israelites present all of the required portions of their crop to the appropriate recipients.

The broad issue is how those who properly separate tithes are to relate to those who do not. The recurrent questions are, what is their responsibility for produce that they transfer to others? What is their obligation in regard to produce that they receive from others? The law responds that all Israelites by definition belong to corporate Israel. Each is responsible, within limits, for the standing of all others. Corporate Israel imposes upon Israelites that obligation to the commonwealth. No one is excluded, excommunicated, shunned, or boycotted; there are no children of darkness in Israel, as distinct from the children of light of Israel, so far as the law of the Mishnah is concerned. Everyone is obligated to take account of everyone else's condition.

The law of the Mishnah-tractate Dema⁀i emphatically states that Israelites who do not fully tithe their produce must respect the convictions and conduct of those who do. Other components of the law of the Mishnah—in tractate Tohorot, which we meet presently—stress that those who do not observe cultic cleanness in the household will not wantonly or deliberately impart cultic uncleanness to the food of that component of Israel that does eat everyday food as though it were priestly rations in the sanctuary and subject to the Temple's purity laws on that account. The premise of the law of the Mishnah in both tractates is one and the same: all Israel keeps some of the law of the Mishnah, and some of Israel keeps it all—and all together, the two kinds of Israelites form a single, corporate Israel. The observant make provision for the unobservant, doing so, however, without intruding into their affairs in a haughty or hostile manner. Of such intrusion in the spirit of holier-than-thou, I can identify not a trace in the law of the Mishnah.

That does not mean everyone is as good as everyone else. Corporate Israel is differentiated from within. That is accomplished by the action of self-selected individuals who undertake to keep the law in a trustworthy manner, bearing responsibility for those who do not fully keep the law. The one undertakes a discipline that does not bind the other. The trustworthy Israelite is called a *Haber,* variously rendered as "fellow," "member," or "associate," and the one who does not undertake to tithe as the law of the Mishnah requires is called an ⁀Am Ha²ares, "one of the people of the land," "a boor." The former tithes whatever is intended to be transferred to others and, through this responsible action and attitude, ensures that everyone will eat properly tithed produce. Here is how the law of the Mishnah lays matters out:

**Mishnah-tractate Dema⁀i 2:2–3**

2:2 He who undertakes to be trustworthy [one who is assumed to tithe all of his produce] tithes (1) what he eats, and (2) what he sells, and (3) what he purchases, and (4) does not accept the hospitality of an ⁀Am Ha²ares.

R. Judah says, "Also one who accepts the hospitality of an ʿAm Haʾares is trustworthy."

They said to him, "[If he is not trustworthy concerning himself [viz., concerning food which he himself eats], how should he be trustworthy concerning that of others [viz., concerning food which he feeds or sells to others]?"

There are two levels of undertaking, the one who pledges to be "trustworthy," described just now, and the one who pledges to be a *Haber*, at a higher level of meticulous observance, as follows:

2:3 He who undertakes to be a *Haber* [member of a group which scrupulously observes the laws of Levitical cleanness] (1) does not sell to an ʿAm Haʾares wet or dry [produce, either produce which has been rendered susceptible to uncleanness or produce which has not been rendered susceptible], and (2) does not purchase from him wet [produce, produce which has been rendered susceptible to uncleanness], and (3) does not accept the hospitality of an ʿAm Haʾares, and (4) does not receive him [the ʿAm Haʾares] as his guest while he [the ʿAm Haʾares] is wearing his [the ʿAm Haʾares's] own clothes.

R. Judah says, "Also (1) he should not raise small cattle, and (2) he should not be profuse in [making] vows or in levity, and (3) he should not defile himself for the dead, and (4) he should minister in the study house."

They said to him, "These [rules] do not enter the category [under discussion, viz., they do not deal with matters of cleanness]."

We see that the point of differentiation registers in public life, at the marketplace; not only or mainly in private life, in the household. Samaritans—regarded by the law of the Mishnah as not authentic Israelites by reason of improper conversion but also as not excluded from Israel as gentiles are—and Israelites who are not trustworthy in the governing sense are assumed to honor the requirements of those who are. Reciprocally, the *Haber*, to whom the law of the Mishnah speaks, takes responsibility not only for what is personally eaten but also for what is provided to others. Each Israelite bears responsibility for the condition of corporate Israel, so the differentiation distinguishes a hierarchy of accountability that one personally assumes.

One who advances to a higher level of responsibility takes responsibility also for the cultic cleanness of produce. Those who discard vegetables must tithe them first; those who purchase vegetables in the market and return them must tithe them first. One who finds produce in the road and takes possession of it must tithe it before putting it aside. But not everybody bears the same responsibilities. One also may not take for granted the reliability of third parties, for example, a person who gives already tithed produce to the mistress of an inn so that she may prepare it for him or her to eat, tithes that which is given to her and that which is received back from her, since she is suspected of exchanging her own doubtfully tithed produce for the tithed produce. Bakers do not have to separate second tithe and carry huge volumes of stale bread to Jerusalem; wholesalers enjoy the same leniency. The premise throughout underscores the good will imputed to all parties to the Israelite commonwealth.

Complexities abound. For example, the law asks, How about relationships between partners, one of whom separates, the other of whom does not separate tithes? To what extent does the common ownership permeate the whole, so that the faithful one of the two is responsible for tithing, out of his or her share, the entire crop? The answer is contained in the following group of rulings:

### MISHNAH-TRACTATE DEMA⁽I⁾ 6:6–10

6:6 Two [men] who gathered [the grapes of] their vineyards into a single winepress—one [who] separates tithes and the other [who] does not separate tithes—the one who separates tithes, tithes his own [share of the wine] and his portion [of the grapes] wherever it may be.

6:7 Two [men, viz., one who separates tithes and one who does not separate tithes] who [jointly] sharecropped a field, or inherited [a field], or became joint owners—he [the one who separates tithes] may say to him [the one who does not separate tithes], "You take the wheat in such-and-such a place and I [will take] the wheat in such-and-such a place; "you [take] the wine in such-and-such a place and I [will take] the wine in such-and-such a place." But he may not say to him, "You take the wheat and I [will take] the barley; you take the wine and I will take the oil."

The *Haber* also can participate in the division of the crop, but the *Haber* may not consign an entire component of the crop to the ownership of the one who does not properly separate all the tithes. What about a common inheritance?

6:8 A *Haber* and an ⁽Am Ha⁾ares who inherited [the property of] their father, [who was] an ⁽Am Ha⁾ares—he [the *Haber* brother] may say to him [the ⁽Am Ha⁾ares brother], "You take the wheat in such-and-such a place and I [will take] the wheat in such-and-such a place; "you [take] the wine in such-and-such a place and I [will take] the wine in such-and-such a place." But he may not say to him, "You take the wheat and I will take the barley; "you take the wet produce [susceptible to uncleanness] and I will take the dry [insusceptible] produce."

6:9 A proselyte and a gentile who inherited [the property of] their father, [who was] a gentile—he [the proselyte brother] may say to him [the gentile brother], "You take the idols and I [will take] the coins; "you [take] the wine and I [will take] the produce." And if [he said this] after it [the property] came into his possession, this [arrangement] is forbidden.

The same basic rules govern. In numerous particular cases the principle is uniform: the *Haber* seeks to control for the nonobservance of the ⁽Am Ha⁾ares, without impugning the good will and good faith of the ⁽Am Ha⁾ares. The latter does not rebel against God, even though the ⁽Am Ha⁾ares does not practice the law in the prescribed manner.

6:10 He who sells produce in Syria and said, "It is from the Land of Israel [and thus liable to tithing]"—he [the purchaser] must tithe [the produce]. [If the vendor subsequently said,] "It is tithed," he is believed, for the mouth that forbade is the mouth that permitted.

[If the vendor said,] "It is from my [field, and thus liable to tithing]"—he [the purchaser] must tithe [the produce]. [If the vendor subsequently said,] "It is tithed," he is believed, for the mouth that forbade is the mouth that permitted.

But if it was known that he [the vendor] owns a field in Syria, [the purchaser] must tithe [the produce].

The Israelite who is meticulous about matters thus bears responsibility both personally and for the other, but the range of responsibility is not unbounded.

In sum, those who do not meticulously tithe are not deemed deliberate law violators. They do not place themselves outside the pale. Rather, Israelites exert themselves, each according to his or her sense of matters. The more observant, where they appropriately are able to do so, conduct themselves so as to take responsibility for the presence of the less observant. This has the effect of diminishing the occasion for the less observant to err. Nevertheless, the law of the Mishnah imputes the same obligations to all and presupposes that everyone maintains a relationship with God, a relationship characterized by conscientious observance of the law. But it recognizes that differences of opinion will divide Israel and accommodates that fact. In that complex law, the Mishnah preserves the autonomy of corporate Israel while accommodating the presence of individual Israelites of diverse customs.

In fact, the Mishnah's recognition of the heterogeneity of Israel forms a religious judgment. Everyone is Israel, and everyone is equal, responsible to both God and the corporate community of Israel. Even Samaritans and even the less meticulously observant Israelites are assumed to exhibit integrity and good will, since they are held to keep the law correctly. Thus we note: "He who leaves [his tithed] produce in the keeping of a Samaritan or an ʿAm Haʾares— [the produce remains] in its presumed status with regard to tithes and with regard to Seventh-Year produce." Where they err, they err; where not, not. That latitudinarian definition of the holy people, corporate Israel, emerges in the laconic character of the rules that instruct those who are more observant on how to deal with those who are less so. The law of the Mishnah sets forth no recriminations and pronounces no exclusions. Those who keep the tithing law relate to those who do not in three ways.

In the first place, they form a single community. Failure to keep the law does not bring about exclusion from Israel. Given what is at stake—eternal life— that is a critical concession. Nor do the *Haberim* separate themselves from the rest of ordinary Israelites. Those deemed reliable do not aspire to segregate themselves in public life from others, though when it comes to home hospitality that is another matter. But that underscores the public focus of the law, which is upon all Israel. And the law of the Mishnah presupposes, as we noted, that Israelites (here including Samaritans) respect the convictions of those who keep the law differently, more strictly than they do. So the more reliable may rely on the honesty of the less observant. That is the norm, the law of the Mishnah rules, it is not merely a matter of whim or will.

In the second place, they take precautions to preserve the integrity of their observance. They keep the rules among those who do not. That is why they can participate in public life—in the market or the synagogue, for example. They properly tithe what they are given or, more to the point, what they give away. So the more reliable within Israel do make provision for the failure of the others to tithe in the correct manner; they do not adapt themselves to a lower requirement of the Torah but preserve their own integrity.

In the third place, the more observant make provision for the observance of those who do not observe. They regard themselves as "their brothers' keepers." That is what is at stake in properly tithing all food that goes back into the market or passes into unknown hands. So far as they can correct the prevailing situation, they do so, tithing properly what they introduce into common usage, whether in the market or in transfer payments through gifts. The *Haber* prepares for others food that meets the highest standards, but does not thereby impose that practice on others.

If, therefore, we had to identify the religious principle that animates the law of the Mishnah-tractate Dema'i, it is to affirm the integrity of all Israel, to make a statement of the fundamental coherence of the Israelite community in the Land. All Israelites now are shown to bear responsibility for one another; and without regard to their situation in relationship to the Land, all engage with God. And that points toward what the law of the Mishnah does not nurture—a sentiment of superiority by reason of higher standards of tithing. That absent attitude complements the engagement with the other that the law of the Mishnah does mean to foster, which is the unobtrusive provision for the less observant. All Israel bears mutual responsibility for one another; in the matter at hand no Israelite may interfere in the affairs of the other—a neat balance.

All Israel enters into a covenanted relationship with God through possession (by only some) of the Land, and the conduct of all Israel upon the Land, in respect to its produce, bears heavily on Israel's enduring possession of the Land. So when it comes to doubtfully tithed produce, the practice of all Israel is taken into account and the condition of all Israelites registers. That is why the law insists that the faithful shop in the same market as the less or the nonobservant, diminishing so far as possible the occasions for the less faithful to misuse produce. It is the very insistence of the law of the Mishnah upon rules for dealing with the marketplace, the public square of Israel, that makes the most eloquent statement: All Israelites, when it comes to relating to God through the produce of the Land, form a single Israel before the one and only God. Sanctification overspreads Israel wherever situated, however a particular individual behaves.

## Assessing Probabilities of Conformity: Tractate Tohorot

Some Israelites fail to tithe meticulously, but that does not exempt corporate Israel from responsibility for separating the crops' full tithe. So too, when it comes to matters of cultic cleanness, outside of the Temple, where everyone was obligated to keep the purity laws, some observe the law, but all are responsible to keep it. The law of the Mishnah presupposes that Israelites observe the Temple purity rules in connection with eating their meals at home, not only in the Temple; but it also recognizes that some Israelites conform, and some do not. Here again, corporate Israel finds a way to legislate past what is clearly widespread indifference to the requirements of the law. Mishnah-tractate Tohorot, "Purities," covers relationships between those who keep the purity laws within the domestic household and those who do not, and it governs how ambiguities are resolved in that connection. This program correlates with that of Dema'i but makes its own points.

In addressing the topic of the uncleanness affecting food and drink, Mishnah-tractate Tohorot offers guidelines on how to resolve cases in which the status of food as to uncleanness is subject to doubt. The matter of doubt further encompasses relationships between those who keep the cleanness laws at home for the domestic table and those, also Israelites, who do not keep those laws and hence are subject to cultic uncleanness.

Once more we see how the sages reckon with individuals who do not measure up but who nonetheless belong to corporate Israel. Now the problem is not how to take responsibility for the effects of their recalcitrance, but how to prevent one's being affected by it. Since day-to-day relationships are assumed to be close and constant, the issue arises of: how to sort out cases in which an outsider, an 'Am Ha'ares, has had access to things belonging to an observant person and, in the status of a person afflicted with flux (zab) imparts uncleanness to what he or she touches, and therefore may or may not have imparted to them cultic uncleanness. The principal statements of the law of the Mishnah follow.

### MISHNAH-TRACTATE TOHOROT 7:1–8:5
### TOSEFTA-TRACTATE TOHOROT 8:1–9:12

M. 7:1 The potter who left his pots and went down to drink—the innermost ones are clean. And the outermost ones are unclean. He who gives over his key to an 'Am Ha'ares—the house is clean, for he gave him only [the charge of] guarding the key.

The premise here is that the 'Am Ha'ares follows orders. He will not maliciously impart uncleanness in violation of the householder's instructions. But the less observant Israelite may inadvertently cause contamination. So the law of the Mishnah presupposes both responsibility and good will on the part of the Israelite individual. The Tosefta's amplification refines matters.

T. 8:1 He [the context requires: the *Haber*] who gave a key to an 'Am Ha'ares—the house is unclean. [If] he gave him the [key to the] outer [room] and did not give him [the key to] the inner [room], the outer one is unclean. And as to the inner, unclean is only [the space] up to the place to which he can stretch out his hand and touch.

[If] there were there shelves ten handbreadths high and niches ten handbreadths high, unclean is only [the space] up to the place to which he can stretch out his hand and touch.

[If] the outer room belongs to one [person] and the inner room to another [person], even though the clean things are placed on the side of the door of the inner [room], lo, they are clean.

He who enters without permission, even though he stands at the side of clean things—they are clean. And so in the case of a gentile: one does not take into consideration [the possibility of his touching things] in connection with wine used for purposes of idolatry.

Now we turn to the principle: We confirm the status quo, and in a case of doubt we resolve matters accordingly. Within the same context, we furthermore assume that the nonobservant Israelite will not deliberately impart uncleanness hither and yon. That principle is expressed in the following:

M. 7:2 He who leaves an ʿ*Am Haʾares* inside his house awake and found him awake—

asleep and found him asleep—
awake and found him asleep—
the house is clean.

[If he left him] sleeping and found him awake—unclean is only [the space] up to the place to which he can stretch out his hand and touch.

T. 8:2 A *Haber* who was sleeping in the house of an ʿ*Am Haʾares*, with his clothing folded up and lying under his head, and his sandals and his jug before him—lo, these are clean because they are in the presumption of being guarded.

In the next case, Israelite tax collectors, assumed to search through property for seizure, impart uncleanness to the house. But they will not go out of their way to impart uncleanness to objects used for sitting or lying, which would involve a special effort (in purposely sitting or lying down on beds or couches). In this case, too, they are not assumed to deliberately or maliciously impart uncleanness.

M. 7:6 The tax collectors who entered the house—the house is unclean. If there is a gentile with them, they are believed to state, "We did not enter." But they are not believed to state, "We entered, but we did not touch [anything]."

The thieves who entered the house—unclean is only the place [trodden by] the feet of the thieves. And what do they render unclean? The foods, and the liquids, and clay utensils which are open. But the couches and the seats and clay utensils which are sealed with a tight seal are clean. If there is a gentile with them, or a woman, everything is unclean.

T. 8:5 The tax collectors who went into the house—if they said, "We entered the house, but we did not touch anything," lo, these are believed, for the testimony which prohibited is the testimony which permitted.

If there were others giving testimony concerning them that they entered the house, and they said, "We did not touch anything," they are not believed. When the pledge is in their hand, even though others do not give testimony about them, they are not believed, because the pledge gives testimony about them.

If there was a gentile with them, even though the pledge is in their hand, even though the gentile gives testimony concerning them that they entered, and they said, "We did not touch anything," lo, these are believed, because the fear of the gentile is upon them.

Attitude is everything, as we see in the following case. If a person was clean but no longer preserved the intention of remaining clean for the eating of heave offering in a state of cultic cleanness, that change of attitude marks the person as unclean.

M. 7:8 He who was clean, and changed his mind about eating [heave offering]— they [the foodstuffs] are unclean. [If] his hands were clean, and he changed his mind about eating, even though he said, "I know that my hands have not been made unclean," his hands are unclean, for the hands are busy.

M. 7:9 The woman who entered in to take out a piece of bread for a beggar, and she came out and found him standing by the side of loaves [of bread] of heave offering—and so, the woman who went out and found her girl friend stirring up coals under a pot of heave offering—it is clean.

How do the *Haber* and *ʿAm Haʾares* share a common courtyard? As with the matter of the fictive fusion-meal or boundary (*ʿerub*), the law of the Mishnah makes provision for the diversity of Israelite observance, at the same time making possible the maintenance of the high standards of sanctification demanded of corporate Israel:

M. 8:1 He who lives with an *ʿAm Haʾares* in a courtyard, and forgot utensils in the courtyard—even jars tightly sealed with a stopper, or an oven tightly sealed with a stopper—lo, these are unclean.

Where the *Haber* has no total control, we assume that the *ʿAm Haʾares* will thoughtlessly contaminate what is left in common property, since the *ʿAm Haʾares* has every right to walk about there and to touch what is located in the shared domain. But this is not an act of malice, only of ordinary routine. In fact, as we shall now see at some length, we do not impute to the *ʿAm Haʾares* any malice whatsoever. If property is signified as private, the *ʿAm Haʾares* will not go to lengths to contaminate it at all. He will honor the practices of his neighbor.

At issue for us is the relationship of the Israelite who observes purity in connection with ordinary food and the one who does not. That area of the law allows sages to spell out their deepest convictions about how to live in a diverse society. The law of the Mishnah intends more than to take account of the diversity of the Jews, a merely ethnic group defined every which way; it intends to confirm a basically affirmative reading of the intentionality of all parties to the Israelite social order, fully and partially observant alike.

Essentially we discover the sages' estimate of how people concern themselves with issues of cultic contamination. That, in the end, testifies to the intentionality of the concerned parties. If they want to preserve the cultic cleanness of their food and utensils, we translate that intention into fact: we assume they have accomplished their goal. If they do not form such an intentionality, then we dismiss the possibility that purity has been maintained.

The matter of intentionality is expressed in so many words, not only implicitly, in the following (the pertinent phrase is italicized):

### Mishnah-tractate Tohorot 7:7

He who leaves his clothing in the wall niche of the bathhouse—they are not clean unless one give [the attendant] his mind
the key, or a seal, or unless he will make a mark.
He who leaves his utensils from one vintage to the next vintage—his utensils are clean.
And in the case of an Israelite, they are not clean *unless he should testify: "In my heart was the intention to guard them."*

On the other hand, if someone had the intentionality of eating food in the status of priestly rations and so was in a state of cultic purity, as soon as he or she changes his or her mind about doing so, we classify that person as unclean. Clearly, once the intention changes, the consequent attitude and activity no longer suffice to preserve, by happenstance, the cleanness of the person. Either the person intends to keep the purity rules and so is assumed to succeed, or does not intend to keep them, and, sources of contamination being abundant, we simply assign the now-thoughtless person to the status of uncleanness.

We should not miss what is subject to doubt. It is not only whether or not a pot has contracted uncleanness when it was not watched. It is how persons are likely to behave in situations when they are unsupervised. The problematics of the law finds definition in the question: To what extent do those at the upper side of the hierarchy of sanctification impute good faith to people at the lower end of the same hierarchy, that is, those who in the household observe purity laws only at specified times and occasions but not all the time? What the law of the Mishnah has shown is now self-evident.

People will not touch and so contaminate what is not theirs, especially if they are warned not to do so: The woman who entered in to take out a piece of bread for a beggar, and she came out and found him standing by the side of loaves of bread of heave offering still has cultically clean loaves. That is so in certain transactions. But if someone takes the view that he or she has every right to utilize an area, then it is assumed that he or she has handled whatever is lying about—as in the case of a courtyard shared with an ʿAm Haʾares. If, by contrast, the ʿAm Haʾares is warned of the concerns of the observant one, the ʿAm Haʾares is assumed to take ordinary precautions.

## Dealing with Matters of Doubt: Tractate Tohorot

Resolving cases of doubt involves an assessment of what is likely to happen, that is, forming a theory of probabilities. The governing principles in determining matters of probability prove few, but sufficient for a broad variety of cases.

First, as we have already noted, we confirm the status quo whenever possible. So too, we rely on evidence interpreted in a commonsense way. We deal with ordinary people, not scholars or priests. In the present context, we deal

with those who most of the time do not observe the purity laws in their households as these extend to the cultic status of food and drink. How such people
are assumed to conduct themselves in relationship to the food and utensils of
observant ones who do keep those laws is at issue. A fine example of how that
works is in the following:

### MISHNAH-TRACTATE TOHOROT 7:4

> The wife of a *Haber* who left the wife of an ʿAm Haʾares grinding [grain] in her
> house—[if the sound of] the millstones ceased—the house is unclean. The millstones did
> not cease—unclean is only [the space] up to the place to which she can reach out her
> hand and touch. [If] they were two, one way or the other [whether or not the grinding
> ceased], unclean is only [the space] up to the place to which they can reach out their
> hands and touch.

If the wife of the ordinary person stops grinding, we assume she touches
whatever is at hand anywhere in the house. If she keeps grinding, we assume
she touches only what she can reach from her place at the grindstone.

Second, where ordinary people have no instructions, they will not take
heed of concerns important to those who observe cultic cleanness even in connection with everyday food. But where there are instructions, ordinary people
will follow instructions faithfully and may be relied on. That distinction,
between ordinary people who are under no charge and those who have been
given a responsibility, is expressed in simple and in complex rulings. We recall
the simple case: "He who gives over his key to an ʿAm Haʾares—the house is
clean, for he gave him only the charge of guarding the key." Now what the law
of the Mishnah expresses is confidence in the good faith of the ʿAm Haʾares.
But where no one is in charge, then we take for granted that what can contract
cultic uncleanness ordinarily will do so. Thus if the potter leaves the pots, the
ones that people might handle, at the outside, are assumed to be unclean; the
ones that people cannot reach retain their prior status. Through the law of the
Mishnah the sages set forth their confidence that people exhibit good will for
the concerns of their neighbors, and if informed, they will avoid imparting
uncleanness to their neighbors' property. Now let us broaden the discussion
of matters of probability beyond the limits of the judgment as to the character
of Israelite individuals who are not fully observant by the standards of sages'
theory of corporate Israel. For it is in reckoning with how to sort out and
resolve cases of doubt affecting food that the sages lay forth their judgments
on matters of probability.

The first principle, confirm the status quo, governs most of the time. Food
and utensils subject to uncleanness are adjudged in accord with their condition
at the moment that they are found. When an unclean thing has an accustomed
place, a matter of doubt affecting its no longer being in that place is resolved
as unclean; when it is found in its normal place (the status quo), it is clean.

The second, and comparable, principle is, where one may find grounds for
a ruling in favor of cleanness, the decision should rest on those grounds.

Where there are grounds to assume something is unclean—proximity, for instance, to a grave area, to dirt that comes from abroad, to clothing of an Israelite who does not keep the purity laws, and the like—we treat what is subject to doubt as having been contaminated. If the contaminated thing is food in the status of heave offering, we burn the food. On the other hand, the sages resolve as "clean" conditions of doubt concerning a variety of less weighty matters: unconsecrated food (not heave offering), matters of doubt concerning the hands, matters of doubt concerning rulings of the scribes (at a lower level of authority than those of the Torah itself), and the like. This is a variation of the first principle.

Third, we rely on the most likely outcome; we assign a doubtful case to the condition of the majority of pertinent cases or persons. Where one doubt piles up upon another, we resolve doubt in favor of cleanness when public domain is involved and uncleanness when private domain is involved. This too refines our opening criterion.

But, fourth, we take full account of peoples' sensibility, meaning that they are assumed to pay attention to what they touch and where they walk or sit. If they can be interrogated and cannot give a reason to assume something has not been contaminated, that testimony to thoughtlessness suffices to rule unclean the matter subject to doubt. They must be prepared to state in positive terms that they have grounds for maintaining that food has not been contaminated, as in the following exemplary instance:

**TOSEFTA-TRACTATE TOHOROT 4:8**

> A person went into an alley and made dough, and afterward a creeping thing was found—and the person said, "If it were here, I would have seen it"—it is unclean, until he will state, "It is clear to me that it was not here beforehand."

Here again, what intervenes is the householder's own attitude toward these matters: Is the person alert and careful, or mindless and careless? Now attitude and intentionality form the foundation for assessing probabilities on what might have happened.

The same basic tendency to confirm the status quo explains the principle that what is dragged is assumed to have been contaminated, but what is thrown, not. But other considerations enter in. The first of these is the distinction between public domain and private domain. A matter of doubt concerning what is in public domain is resolved as clean, in private domain, unclean. That is to say, within the household itself, people are expected to pay extra care to avoid sources of uncleanness. In the public domain, where matters are more difficult—but the stakes much lower—matters of doubt are resolved as clean. That decisions are guided by circumstance and relationship, not by intrinsic considerations, is made explicit time and again, in one case after another: A place which was private domain and became public domain and once again was made private domain—when it is private domain, a matter of doubt concerning it is deemed unclean. When it is public domain, a matter of doubt concerning it is clean. So again we find no trace of a fixed and physical foundation to the matter of uncleanness; all things are relative, each in its context.

Here is the law's account of the resolution of cases of doubt in matters of uncleanness:

### MISHNAH-TRACTATE TOHOROT 3:5

All unclean things [are adjudged] in accord with [their condition] at the moment that they are found. (1) If they are [appear to be] unclean, they are unclean; and (2) if they appear to be clean, they are clean; (3) if they are covered up, they are assumed to have been covered up; and (4) if they are uncovered, they are assumed to have been uncovered. A needle which is found full of rust or broken is clean.

For all things subject to uncleanness [are adjudged] in accord with [their condition] at the moment that they are found.

Status quo governs wherever plausible. We resolve doubt as to the classification of food and drink by appeal to a variety of probabilities. It is more probable that the status quo has prevailed than that it has not; it is more probable that what is dragged, and so can touch something, has touched the unclean thing than what is tossed, and so cannot touch it. The former has made contact with something the status of which is uncertain. Common sense about the more or the less probable, however, is joined to certain principles that appear to be arbitrary.

Because we want the householder to maintain a high state of alertness concerning sources of uncleanness, we declare that cases of doubt in private property are treated as unclean. Because the public domain contains many imponderables and cannot be closed off to the faithful, we declare cases of doubt in public property to be treated as clean. Now that position is counterintuitive, for, given the distractions of crowds, one is more likely in public to step on unclean spit or urine than in the private domain. Reason therefore suggests that a case of doubt in public domain should be resolved in favor of uncleanness, and in private, cleanness. So here the system concerns itself with its larger goal—sanctifying the household and its table—and mitigates its more extreme possibilities. Where people can and should take care, they are held to a high standard. Where circumstances make difficult a constant state of alertness amid a barrage of occasions for contamination, they are not.

## Sanctifying Israel by an Act of Will

The law of the Mishnah rests on the foundations of a single condition: Israel is holy, wherever located; that is its natural condition. What removes Israel from its status as sanctified is unnatural to Israel, but a given of the world. But individual Israelites may or may not be sanctified, and what removes them from their status as clean is common to their condition. Sanctification is the established condition for family and property (food, drink, clothing, utensils). What removes the family, its food, drink, clothing, and utensils, from the status of sanctification interferes with what ought to be natural. Sources of uncleanness also come about by nature; sages adhere rigidly to the definition of those sources that Scripture establishes and do not add a single new source or extend an existing source in any consequential way.

Corporate Israel, then, confronts round about the sources of contamination; its task is constantly to remain alert and watchful, lest those sources of contamination affect Israel. And, we now see, that means individual Israelites must watch not only what they eat and drink and wear and where they stand and sit and lie. Israelites must pay attention also to what the food they eat may have touched and to who may have stood or sat upon the clothing that they wear and the beds on which they take a rest. To preserve the condition it ought always to enjoy, which is, the state of sanctification, Israelites have to maintain a constant surveillance of the present and past of the world in which they live and the people among whom they make their life. Marrying without carefully investigating the genealogy of the Israelite family into which one marries can produce *mamzerim*; sitting on a bench without finding out who has sat there before can produce uncleanness that can contaminate much else; and eating a piece of bread without knowing where it has been and who has touched it can diminish one's standing in the hierarchy of sanctification.

Intentionality marks a person as alert to the possibilities of contamination. This is the context in which the texts that invoke intentionality find their place, the reason that the entire system treats cleanness and sanctification, or uncleanness and desacralization, as relative to the individual Israelite's attitude and will. What the Israelite values as food receives or conveys uncleanness as food. What the Israelite does not value does not contract or transmit uncleanness; only that to which an Israelite to begin with pays attention counts for anything in the system of watchfulness with which we deal. What the Israelite values as a useful utensil may contract uncleanness. What the Israelite deems an essential part of a piece of fruit or vegetable is integral to the fruit or vegetable, adds to its volume, contracts such uncleanness as takes effect from the fruit or vegetable or transmits it to that produce. What the Israelite holds to be inedible or disgusting even for dog food does not contract uncleanness as food. When the Israelite subjects to the cleanness regulations of consecrated food what is merely everyday edibles, the rules of consecrated food pertain—even though the substance of the food is unchanged. In these and numerous other details the relativity of all things to intentionality comes to full and rich instantiation. So the law of the Mishnah manages to say the same thing about many things.

## Intentionality: Tractates Demaʿi and Tohorot

The details of the law of Demaʿi and Tohorot as we have examined them, yield a massive generalization:

*The law of the Mishnah tolerates personal deviation from the norms of corporate Israel when deviant actions (1) do not express a rebellious attitude and (2) do not embody the intention to defy the Torah.*

The law accommodates idiosyncrasy and difference of opinion on matters of ambiguity. That is where individuality reaches the outer limits of the system's norm. Beyond is the line of rebellion against God, setting one's own will in opposition to God's, as Adam and Eve did in Eden; and that deliberate conflict of wills the law of the Mishnah will not tolerate. Where Israelites within corporate Israel do not conform to the law, it is in details of an otherwise obedient pattern of life, on the one side, or within a pattern of amiable good will, on the other.

The law of the Mishnah-tractate Dema'i illustrates the former matter; that of Tohorot, the latter. As to Dema'i, we have seen that the law affirms that Israelites generally tithe. Some individuals, *Haberim*, distinguish themselves by meticulous provision of the last details of the priestly share of the crop. They, moreover, attain the virtue of attending not only to their own food but also to that which they supply to others; they distinguish themselves individually by the responsibility that they undertake for the community at large. Here corporate Israel figures in the definition of virtue. Some individuals—a great many, the law takes for granted, called *'Ammé Ha'ares*—conform to the law in general and give the principal offerings, but they do not necessarily give the tithe of the Levite's tithe to the priest that the law requires. That they keep the basics indicates an attitude of responsibility for the condition of not only themselves but corporate Israel in the Land. Not doing so is to be regretted, but it is not a brazen violation of the law of tithing. So the law of the Mishnah-tractate Dema'i focuses not on violation of the law by the individual but on the way in which other individuals virtuously take responsibility for others. No one imputes to the *'Ammé Ha'ares* an attitude of rebellion against God, only slovenliness, ignorance, or benign indifference.

When matters of probable contamination are investigated, the governing principles derive from an assessment of the attitude of the other-than-fully-observant Israelite individuals. They are known not to eat their secular food with concern for cultic cleanness. But the law of the Mishnah takes for granted that they are motivated by good will and respect for those who do. They exhibit no malice and will not deliberately contaminate food or utensils of those who keep the law. They are indifferent but not hostile. The supervised *'Am Ha'ares* will contaminate nothing. The unsupervised *'Am Ha'ares* will contaminate only by inadvertence. Left in charge, the *'Am Ha'ares* will contaminate that which is subject to his or her charge. Here, too, therefore, the law of the Mishnah works out in detail the principle that Israelites respect the law even when they do not keep it in every detail.

In that same setting we address the resolution of matters of doubt. The theory of probabilities transcends the judgment of prevailing good will in a setting of uneven adherence to the law of the Mishnah's marginal details—for eating secular food as though one were a Temple priest is represented as an activity that distinguishes the individual Israelite, not that characterizes, or is supposed to characterize, all Israel as a corporate body. At issue is the same notion we have just met: the less-than-fully-observant Israelite will not maliciously violate the law of the Mishnah, but does so only through indifference. That is why the law can insist on confirming the status quo, a principle that comes to expression in diverse ways. The single most pertinent rule is, when a person can say, "It is clear to me that . . . ," we accept this judgment of the case. So too, if we can find grounds for resolving doubt in favor of cleanness, we do so: "For I say, 'Someone else gathered them and gave them to him.'"

So imperfectly observant Israelites remain part of corporate Israel. That is because at no point are they accused of rebelling against the Torah, that is, so acting as to indicate through their violation of the law the will to sin. At every point where attitude enters in, we impute to the individual Israelite an obedient attitude and interpret the violation of the law in a context of general conformity to the law of the Mishnah. Corporate Israel is made up of Israelites who accept the will of God and so live in God's kingdom.

That observation brings us back to the recognition that the law of the Mishnah affords legitimate media for the expression of individuality. That turns out to encompass not only the singularity of persons but even their nonconformity to the law of the Mishnah. As a result, the individual enjoys a wide range of possibilities of personal expression. But, we now realize, that is because of the governing premise, which is that Israelites participate in corporate Israel, which, all together and all at once, has declared its acceptance of God's will embodied in the Torah. Remissions then are afforded and nonconformity is tolerated where God is not defied. This is expressed in positive language in the following way:

**MISHNAH-TRACTATE ABOT 2:4**

Rabban Gamaliel, son of R. Judah the Patriarch, would say, "Make his wishes into your own wishes, so that he will make your wishes into his wishes.

"Put aside your wishes on account of his wishes, so that he will put aside the wishes of other people in favor of your wishes."

What the Torah demands, then, is that individual Israelites conform their wills to God's will.

At that point we reach the resolution of the tension between the Israelite and corporate Israel. It is in the matter of will that the Israelite and corporate Israel come together. Will and intentionality express what is private and personal—by definition. For nothing so distinguishes one person from another as intentionality. The definition, for law's purposes, of the Israelite individual is: one who has the power to form an autonomous act of will, not being subject a priori to the will of some other person (parent, master, husband). That is why the Israelite is responsible for what he or she does, and therefore is subject to sanctions for doing wrong. Not only so, but within the mythic statement of monotheism, it is possession of an autonomous will, the favor of which God can crave but not coerce, that marks human beings as "in our image, after our likeness." That defines, as we shall see, the one way in which humans are like God.

In brief, God and the individual human are, so far as attitude and emotion register, consubstantial. The intentionality of the one is comparable to the intentionality of the other. In this matter, attitude and intention form both singularly individual exercises and occasions for the uniform affirmation of corporate Israel, a moral entity that encompasses and transcends the individuality of Israelites. That is because Israelites find their being within corporate Israel; and because, I cannot overstress, corporate Israel constitutes a moral entity subject to judgment just as does the individual Israelite, intentionality also defines the corporate character of Israel. "We shall do and we shall obey" expresses the intention of not only individuals who met that day but the enduring corporate community at Sinai. Israel's collective attitude therefore reigns supreme; the individual Israelite cannot opt out. Within that given, which is not negotiable, two positions are formalized.

First, when the individual Israelite does not conform to the law, if the nonconforming act does not express the attitude of defiance of the Torah, the assertion of individuality (however passively, even through nonactivity) finds toleration. The faithful sector of Israel accommodates the happenstance of difference of opinion on marginal matters. That is what we have learned about Israelites who do not live up to the norms of corporate Israel.

Second, when the individual Israelite does not conform to the law, if the act in violation of the law expresses an attitude of rebellion against God's will to which corporate Israel, as a moral entity, is answerable, then corporate Israel asserts its interest and attends to the aberrant individual. We now turn to the way in which deliberate violation of the Torah is addressed, and the purpose accomplished in doing so.

# 8 When Israelites Deliberately Violate the Norms

## Tractates Sanhedrin-Makkot Keritot, and Horayot

THE MISHNAH, AS WE HAVE SEEN in tractates Demaᶜi and Tohorot, assumes that when entire classes of Israelites are less than perfect in their observance, their failure conveys no malice, no hint of rebellion against God. But within Israel there are aberrant individuals, for whose sins or crimes corporate Israel bears responsibility. These are persons who deliberately violate the Torah. So there are times when the community must intervene to punish individuals who in acts of intentional violation transgress the norms.

When an individual sets his or her will over against God's—that is, intentionally rebels against God's will—the integrity of corporate Israel is threatened and the community intervenes forcefully. Accordingly, in Mishnah-tractates Sanhedrin-Makkot, Keritot, and Horayot, we encounter the final component of the law as it focuses on corporate Israel and the Israelite: how to deal with the willful violation of the Torah by the Israelite.

### Corporate Israel Penalized as a Moral Entity: Tractate Sanhedrin-Makkot Once More

The law of the Mishnah begins with the problem on the collective level, that is, the way in which corporate Israel inflicts punishment for corporate sin or crime. Corporate Israel itself is subject to sanction by reason of collective rebellion, the rejection of God's dominion. That is the case even when the law of the Mishnah itself differentiates the individual Israelite from corporate Israel, deeming the latter to form a moral entity subject to its own rule—a subtle distinction indeed. That distinction is made explicit, and corporate Israel is punished collectively, in the case of an entire town that has committed apostasy:

### MISHNAH-TRACTATE SANHEDRIN 11:4

The townsfolk of an apostate town have no portion in the world to come,

as it is said, "Certain base fellows [sons of Belial] have gone out from the midst of thee and have drawn away the inhabitants of their city" (Deut. 13:14).

And they are not put to death unless those who misled the [town] come from that same town and from that same tribe,

and unless the majority is misled,

and unless men did the misleading.

[If] women or children misled them,

or if a minority of the town was misled,

or if those who misled the town came from outside of it,

lo, they are treated as individuals [and not as a whole town]

and they [thus] require [testimony against them] by two witnesses, and a statement of warning, for each and every one of them.

The distinction between the community and the individual is explicitly articulated as the rule proceeds:

This rule is more strict for individuals than for the community:

for individuals are put to death by stoning.

Therefore their property is saved.

But the community is put to death by the sword,

Therefore their property is lost.

The Talmud of Babylonia (Tractate Sanhedrin 111b) explicitly identifies the crime or sin of the "base fellows": they are "those who have broken the yoke of the Torah from their shoulders," that is, who have rejected the dominion and kingdom of God. That is the circumstance in which corporate Israel intervenes against the embodiment of corporate Israel in some one place. The fact that we distinguish individual from corporate sin is spelled out in the words, "This rule is more strict for individuals than for the community." Both are punished, each in a different way. What they have in common is rejection of God's rule: the sinful exercise of the freedom of will that all humanity possesses.

Israelites have the power to make uncoerced, deliberate choices and must bear responsibility for the outcomes of their choices. Individuals, Israelite and otherwise, match God in possessing utter freedom of will. In exercising free will, they carry forward the narrative of Adam and Eve in their loss of Eden. The will of the human being is the sole power in the world that in any aspect matches the power of God. That variable in creation accounts for the present imperfection of the world. This is so because it was by an act of will that God created the orderly world of justice, a world that exhibits abundant, indicative marks of perfection. And God's Torah, a part of that orderly creation, teaches Israel how to tame the unruly spirit of man and woman.

Because corporate Israel possesses the Torah and committed to obey and observe it at Sinai, corporate Israel bears responsibility for its condition before God. Indeed, at this moment, Israel is already in a compromised condition: its Temple is in ruins and its means of atonement compromised. So corporate

Israel cannot ignore the deliberate rebellion of individual Israelites against God. God judges what we do by reason of the exercise of our free will. Set forth in many ways, the simplest statement is made when R. Aqiba says, "Everything is foreseen, and free choice is given; in goodness the world is judged; and all is in accord with the abundance of deeds" (Mishnah-tractate Abot 3:15). Alongside God's judgment, then, comes the engagement of corporate Israel with the conduct and conviction of the Israelite.

## Legitimate Violence: How Sanctions are Differentiated by Intentionality: Again Tractate Sanhedrin-Makkot

It is to sustain the social structure of corporate Israel that the Mishnah's law designs enduring structures, institutions for the governance of Israel as a godly realm. In its very doctrine of how corporate Israel is governed, intentionality forms the critical point of differentiation even of institutional politics—the power legitimately to inflict violence. When the sages describe the government of corporate Israel, they differentiate, indicating what agency or person has the power to precipitate the working of politics as legitimate violence. Through the provisions that they make for various institutional foci of power to carry out diverse tasks, it is at the point of intentionality, with the story of Eden in hand, that sages accomplish their goal. Were we to ignore Eden, we could make no sense of their concrete provisions for government. The very politics set forth by the Mishnah embodies the doctrine that when Israelites deliberately violate the norms of the Torah, their intention is matched by the outcome.

The encompassing political framework of rules, institutions, and sanctions is explained and validated by appeal to God's shared rule. That dominion, exercised by God and God's surrogates on earth, in Mishnah-tractate Sanhedrin-Makkot, is focused partly in (1) the royal palace (the king), partly in (2) the Temple (the priesthood), and partly in (3) the court (the sages). The system answers the question of who imposes which sanction and why.

Mishnah tractate Sanhedrin-Makkot contains four types of sanctions, each deriving from a distinct institution of political power, each bearing its own narrative explanation. The first comprises what God and the Heavenly court can do to inflict legitimate violence. The second comprises what the earthly court can do to people. This type of sanction concerns the legitimate application of this-worldly and physical kinds of violence, of which political theory ordinarily speaks. The third comprises what the administration of the Temple and its cult can do. The priesthood through its requirements can deprive people of their property as legitimately as can a court. The fourth comprises conformity with consensus—self-imposed sanctions.

Across these four types of sanction four types of coercion are brought to play. They depend on legitimate violence of various kinds—psychological and social as much as physical. Clearly, then, the sanctions that are exercised by agencies other than judicial-political ones prove violent and legitimately coercive, even though the violence and coercion are not the same as those carried out by courts. On this basis we can differentiate among types of sanctions—and hence trace how the differentiation is explained, why the various types of sanctions are put into effect by diverse political agencies or institutions.

The exercise of power is invariably undertaken in the name and by the authority of God in Heaven to be sure. So the distinctions in this case signal important differences. The salient points of differentiation require a bit of explanation. Concrete application of legitimate violence (1) by Heaven covers different matters from parts of the political and social world governed by the policy and coercion of (2) the this-worldly political classes. And both sorts of violence have to be kept distinct from the sanction effected by (3) the community through the weight of attitude and public opinion. Likewise, we find a distinct set of penalties applied to a particular range of actions.

These governing questions then apply: Where Heaven intervenes, do other authorities participate, and, if so, what tells us which party takes charge and imposes its sanction? Is the system differentiated so that where earth is in charge, there is no pretense of appeal to Heaven? Or do we find cooperation in coextensive jurisdiction, such that one party penalizes an act under one circumstance, the other the same act under a different circumstance? So we wonder whether each of these three estates that enjoy power and inflict sanctions of one kind or another—Heaven, earth, Temple in between—governs its own affairs, without the intervention of the others, or whether, working together, each takes charge in collaboration with the other, so that power is parceled out and institutions simultaneously differentiate themselves from one another and also intersect. The politics works in such a way that all three political institutions, God, the court (sage) and the Temple (priest), the three agencies with the power to bestow or take away life and property and to inflict physical pain and suffering, work together in a single continuum and in important ways cooperate to deal with the same crimes or sins.

We may divide sanctions just as the authorship of the Mishnah did, by simply reviewing the range of penalties for infractions of the law as they occur. These penalties fall into four classifications: (1) what Heaven does, (2) what political institutions do, (3) what religious institutions do, and (4) what is left to the coercion of public opinion, that is, consensus, with special attention to the definition of that "public" that has effective opinion to begin with. The final realm of power, conferring or withholding approval, proves constricted and, in this context, not very consequential. When we catalogue and classify the correlation of crime or sin and penalty as inflicted by the four foci of politics, we find a startling result:

Some of the same crimes or sins for which the Heavenly court imposes the penalty of extirpation are those that, under appropriate circumstances (for example, sufficient evidence admissible in court) the earthly court imposes the death penalty.

That is, the Heavenly court and the earthly court impose precisely the same sanctions for the same crimes or sins. The earthly court therefore forms below the exact replica and counterpart, within a single system of power, of the Heavenly court on high. But this is not the entire story. There is a second fact, equally indicative for our recovery of the substrate of story. We note that there are crimes for which the earthly court imposes penalties, but for which the Heavenly court does not, and vice versa. The earthly and Heavenly courts share jurisdiction over sexual crimes and over serious religious crimes against God. The Heavenly court penalizes with its form of the death penalty religious sins against God, in which instances a person deliberately violates the taboos of sanctification.

That fact calls our attention to a third partner in the distribution and application of power, the Temple with its system of sanctions that cover precisely the same acts that are subject to the jurisdiction of the Heavenly and earthly courts. The counterpart on earth is now not the earthly court but the Temple. This is the institution that, in theory, automatically receives the appropriate offering from the person who inadvertently violates these same taboos of sanctification. The juxtaposition involves courts and Temple, and the result is that both are equally matters of theory. In the theory at hand, then, the earthly court, for its part, penalizes social crimes against the community that the Heavenly court, on the one side, and the Temple rites, on the other, do not take into account at all. These are murder, apostasy, kidnapping, public defiance of the court, and false prophecy. The earthly court further imposes sanctions on matters of particular concern to the Heavenly court, with special reference to taboos of sanctification (as found, for instance, in the negative commandments). These three institutions, therefore, exercise concrete and material power, utilizing legitimate violence to kill an individual, exacting penalties against property and inflicting pain. The sages' modes of power, by contrast, stand quite apart, apply mainly to their own circle, and work through the intangible though no less effective means of inflicting shame or paying honor.

The facts draw us back to our analysis of the differentiation of applied and practical power. Power flows through three distinct but intersecting dominions, each with its own concern, all sharing some interests in common. How are the agencies differentiated? (1) The Heavenly court attends to deliberate defiance of Heaven. (2) The Temple pays attention to inadvertent defiance of Heaven. (3) The earthly court attends to matters subject to its jurisdiction by reason of sufficient evidence, proper witnesses, and the like; and these same matters will come under Heavenly jurisdiction when the earthly court finds itself unable to act.

Accordingly, we have a tripartite system of sanctions—Heaven cooperating with the Temple in some matters, with the court in others, and each bearing its own distinct method of enforcing the law as well. The forms of power and the modes of mediating legitimate violence form a single, simple political story. It is the story of God's authority infusing the institutions of Heaven and earth alike, based on a single source and origin of power, God's law set forth in the Torah. But the story has not performed its task until it makes clear who tells whom to do what—case by case, who judges, who suffers, and what is the sanction or penalty? In the end, it is the attitude of the human being who has erred: did he or she act deliberately or unintentionally? The point of differentiation within the political structures, supernatural and natural alike, lies in the attitude and intention of a human being exercising free will.

We differentiate among the application of power by reference to the attitude of the person who comes into relationship with that power. A person who comes into conflict with the system, rejecting the authority claimed by the powers that be, does so deliberately or inadvertently. The story accounts in the end for the following hierarchy of action and penalty, infraction and sanction: (1) If the deed is deliberate, then one set of institutions exercises jurisdiction and utilizes supernatural power. (2) If the deed is inadvertent, another institution exercises jurisdiction and utilizes the power made available by that same supernatural being.

A sinner or criminal who has deliberately violated the law has, by this action, challenged the world order of justice that God has wrought. Consequently, God or God's surrogate imposes sanctions—extirpation (by the court on high), or death or other appropriate penalty (by the court on earth). A sinner or criminal who has inadvertently violated the law is penalized by the imposition of Temple sanctions, losing valued goods. People obey because God wants them to and has told them what to do, and when they do not obey, a differentiated political structure appeals to the issue of intention. The components are two: God's will, expressed in the law of the Torah, and the human being's will, carried out in obedience to the law of the Torah or in defiance of that law.

The sages find their referent in the story of the Garden of Eden, the story of power differentiated by the will of the human being in communion or conflict with the word of the commanding God. We cannot too often reread the following astonishing words:

> The Lord God took the man and placed him in the garden of Eden . . . and the Lord God commanded the man, saying, "Of every tree of the garden you are free to eat; but as for the tree of knowledge of good and bad, you must not eat of it; for as soon as you eat of it, you shall die."
>
> . . . When the woman saw that the tree was good for eating and a delight to the eyes, and that the tree was desirable as a source of wisdom, she took of its fruit and ate; she also gave some to her husband, and he ate . . .

The Lord God called out to the man and said to him, "Where are you?"

He replied, "I heard the sound of You in the garden, and I was afraid, because I was naked, so I hid."

Then He asked, "Who told you that you were naked? Did you eat of the tree from which I had forbidden you to eat?"

. . . And the Lord God said to the woman, "What is this you have done!"

The woman replied, "The serpent deceived me, and I ate."

Then the Lord said to the serpent, "Because you did this, more cursed shall you be than all cattle. . . ."

So the Lord God banished him from the garden of Eden. . . . (Gen. 2:15ff.)

Now a reprise of the exchange between God, Adam, and Eve tells us that what was at stake was responsibility: not who has violated the law, but who bears responsibility for deliberately violating the law. Each blames the next, and God sorts things out, responding to each in accord with the facts of the case: Whose intentionality matches the actual deed?

"The woman You put at my side—she gave me of the tree, and I ate."

"The serpent duped me, and I ate."

Then the Lord God said to the serpent, "because you did this . . . ."

The ultimate responsibility lies with the one who acted deliberately, not under constraint or on account of deception or misinformation, as did Adam because of Eve, and Eve because of the serpent.

True enough, all are punished, the serpent, but also woman ("I will make most severe your pangs in childbearing"), and Adam ("Because you did as your wife advised and ate of the tree about which I commanded you, 'you shall not eat of it,' cursed be the ground because of you"). But the punishment is differentiated. Those who were duped, Adam by Eve, Eve by the snake, are distinguished from the one who acted wholly on his own volition, The serpent himself is cursed; the woman is subjected to pain in childbearing, which ought to have been pain-free; and because of man, the earth is cursed—a diminishing scale of penalties, each in accord with the level of intentionality or free, unco-erced will involved in the infraction. Then the sanction applies most severely to the one who by intention and an act of will has violated God's intention and will.

The operative criterion in the differentiation of sanction—that is, the exercise of legitimate violence by Heaven or by earth or by the Temple—is the human attitude and intention in carrying out a culpable action. So it is the story of Adam and Eve in Eden that is constantly being rehearsed. The social teaching finds its dynamic in the correspondence between God's will and humanity's freedom to act however it chooses, thus freely incurring the risk of penalty or sanction for the wrong exercise of freedom. At stake is what Adam and Eve, Moses and Aaron, and numerous others intend, propose, and plan, for that is the point at which the teaching differentiates between and among its sanctions and the authorities that impose those penalties. We now have the answer to the question, When does corporate Israel sanction the individual

Israelite for violating the Torah's law? It is when he or she acts maliciously and intentionally to violate the Torah.

Power flows from two conflicting forces, the commanding will of God and the free will of the human being. Power expressed in immediate sanctions also flows from these same forces, Heaven above, human beings below, with the Temple mediating between the two. Power works its way in the interplay between what God has set forth in the law of the Torah and what human beings do, whether intentionally, whether inadvertently, whether obediently, or whether defiantly. When we consider sins that are penalized, at every point we are reminded of the most formidable source of power, short of God, in all, the will of the human being. And that is why only human beings have the power to disrupt that world order so painstakingly created and maintained by God. Only human beings are sufficiently like God to possess the utterly free will to corrupt perfection. In free will, the critical issue is intention. The critical question is, Did the transgressing Israelite cross the line deliberately or inadvertently?

### Expiation of Inadvertent Sin: Tractate Keritot

In a violation of law that is inadvertent, the action does not mean to express an attitude of defiance or an intention to rebel against God's will. The Israelite, to be sure, bears responsibility for what he or she does even without the intention to rebel against God. That is why the law of the Mishnah provides the individual with the opportunity to atone. The Torah explicitly imputes guilt even for actions committed inadvertently and not with the intention of violating the Torah. The Torah further provides for means of atonement in such an instance. It follows that the law of the Mishnah has to provide for penalties to expiate sin or crime, whether deliberate or otherwise. A sin offering or its counterpart atones for inadvertent action; extirpation or premature death atones for deliberate sin; a suspensive guilt offering (an offering presented on condition that it is required) is specified in a case of doubt, as we shall now see. The Torah contributes to the topic the following statement at Leviticus 5:17–19:

> If any one sins, doing any of the things that the Lord has commanded not to be done, though he does not know it, yet he is guilty and shall bear his iniquity. He shall bring to the priest a ram without blemish out of the flock, valued by you at the price for a guilt offering, and the priest shall make atonement for him for the error that he committed unwittingly, and he shall be forgiven. It is a guilt offering; he is guilty before the Lord

The governing principle is stated by the Mishnah and amplified by the Tosefta as follows:

#### MISHNAH-TRACTATE KERITOT 1:2

> For those [thirty-six classes of transgressions] are people liable, for deliberately doing them, to the punishment of extirpation, and for accidentally doing them, to the bringing of a sin offering, and for not being certain of whether or not one has done

them, to a suspensive guilt offering [Lev. 5:17]–[except for] the one who blasphemes, as it is said, "You shall have one law for him that does anything unwittingly" (Num. 15:29)–excluding the blasphemer, who does no concrete deed.

**TOSEFTA-TRACTATE KERITOT 1:6**

This is the general principle: [For violation of] any negative commandment containing within itself a concrete deed do [violators] receive the penalty of forty stripes. And for the violation of any which does not contain within itself a concrete deed they do not receive the penalty of forty stripes. And as to all other negative commandments in the Torah, lo, these are subject to warning. He who transgresses them violates the decree of the King.

Premature death or extirpation is inflicted for deliberate violation of the Torah; presentation of a sin offering is the sanction for inadvertently committing any of the thirty-six classes. These are the pertinent transgressions:

**MISHNAH-TRACTATE KERITOT 1:1**

Thirty-six [classes of] transgressions set forth in the Torah are subject to extirpation: he who has sexual relations with (1) his mother, or (2) with his father's wife, (3) with his daughter-in-law; he who has sexual relations (4) with a male, or (5) with a beast; and (6) the woman who has sexual relations with a beast; he who has sexual relations (7) with a woman and with her daughter, and (8) with a married woman; he who has sexual relations (9) with his sister, and (10) with his father's sister, and (11) with his mother's sister, and (12) with his wife's sister, and (13) with his brother's wife, and (14) with his father's brother's wife, and (15) with a menstruating woman (Lev. 18:6ff.); (16) he who blasphemes (Num. 15:30), and (17) he who performs an act of blasphemous worship (Num. 15:31), and (18) he who gives his seed to Moloch (Lev. 18:21), and (19) one who has a familiar spirit (Lev. 20:6); (20) he who profanes the Sabbath day (Exod. 31:14); and (21) an unclean person who ate a Holy Thing (Lev. 22:3), and (22) he who comes to the sanctuary when unclean (Num. 19:20); he who eats (23) forbidden fat (Lev. 7:25), and (24) blood (Lev. 17:14), and (25) remnant (Lev. 19:6-8), and (26) refuse (Lev. 19:7-8); he who (27) slaughters and who (28) offers up [a sacrifice] outside [the Temple court] (Lev. 17:9); (29) he who eats leaven on Passover (Exod. 12:19); and he who (30) eats and he who (31) works on the Day of Atonement (Lev. 23:29-30); he who (32) compounds anointing oil [like that made in the Temple (Exod. 30:23-33)], and he who (33) compounds incense [like that made in the Temple], and he who (34) anoints himself with anointing oil (Exod. 30-32); [he who transgresses the laws of] (35) Passover (Num. 9:13) and (36) circumcision (Gen. 17:14), among the positive commandments.

In a case of doubt whether or not a sin has inadvertently been committed, a suspensive guilt offering is presented, counterpart of the sin offering, illustrated by the following:

**MISHNAH-TRACTATE KERITOT 3:1; 4:1**

3:1 [If] they said to him, "You have eaten forbidden fat," he brings a sin offering. [If] one witness says, "He ate," and one witness says, "He did not eat"–[or if] a woman says, "He ate," and a woman says, "He did not eat," he brings a suspensive guilt offering.

[If] a witness says, "He ate," and he says, "I did not eat"–he is exempt [from bringing an offering]. [If] two say, "He ate," and he says, "I did not eat"–he is exempt.

4:1 It is a matter of doubt whether or not one has eaten forbidden fat, And even if he ate it, it is a matter of doubt whether or not it contains the requisite volume—Forbidden fat and permitted fat are before him, he ate one of them but is not certain which one of them he ate—His wife and his sister are with him in the house—he inadvertently transgressed with one of them and is not certain with which of them he transgressed—The Sabbath and an ordinary day—he did an act of labor on one of them and is not certain on which of them he did it—

[in all the foregoing circumstances] he brings a suspensive guilt offering.

As we see, the key language is that which delineates inadvertence from deliberate violation of the law. For us the important point is that, if someone has transgressed unintentionally, a sin offering suffices. That underscores the social teaching, its focus on intentionality. Extirpation, by contrast, is inflicted by Heaven for one's deliberately doing the sins specified above, and that is matched by the sin offering, required when the sins are inadvertent. The second penalty for inadvertent sin is the offering of variable value, and once more, we list those who are required to present such an offering and special situations in that regard. The third is the suspensive guilt offering, presented when one has some reason to suppose that he or she has carried out a sin but lacks adequate, positive grounds for confessing inadvertent commission of a sin. That addresses cases of doubt and how they are resolved.

But atoning through offerings or premature death, as the case requires, is not the sole means. The law of Mishnah-tractate Keritot furthermore encompasses the atoning power of the Day of Atonement:

**MISHNAH-TRACTATE KERITOT 6:4**

Those who owe sin offerings and unconditional guilt offerings for whom the Day of Atonement passed [without their making those offerings] are liable to bring [the offerings] after the Day of Atonement.

Those who owe suspensive guilt offerings are exempt. [The Day of Atonement has atoned for those transgressions that may or may not have taken place.]

He who is subject to a doubt as to whether or not he has committed a transgression on the Day of Atonement, even at twilight, is exempt. For the entire day [of atonement] effects atonement.

The effect of the Day of Atonement comes under consideration. It functions as does a suspensive guilt offering, that is, to make atonement in cases where whether the sin has been committed is in doubt. That accounts for the role of the Day of Atonement in the atonement process; it has no bearing on the requirement of sin offerings or unconditional guilt offerings; these must be paid for the specified deed.

What is the point of all these details? The key doctrine once more concerns the distinction between an act that is deliberate and one that is inadvertent. In its principal divisions—the sin offering as against extirpation, the suspensive guilt offering as against the unconditional guilt offering—the law of the Mishnah treats in concrete terms the distinction between deliberate, intentional sin and unintentional violation of the law.

Nowhere else in the law of the Mishnah do we find so sharp a line distinguishing the unintentional sin, penalized by an offering, and the intentional one, penalized by extirpation. The reason that that critical distinction concerns us is self-evident. Here is where God intervenes, and it is God above all who knows what is in a person's heart and can differentiate intentional from unintentional actions. It also is God who has the heaviest stake in the matter of intentional sin, for intentional sin represents rebellion against the Torah and God's rule through the Torah.

Offerings, we have seen, expiate those sins that are not committed as an act of rebellion against God. These God accepts graciously as an appropriate act of atonement where there was no defiance of God intended. Acts of rebellion, by contrast, can be expiated not through the surrogate, the blood of the beast, but personally through the sinner, who is put to death by the court here on earth or flogged by the court's agents. So Mishnah-tractate Keritot translates into law the theology that holds that God sees into the heart. That conception is translated into a great many laws of the Mishnah. It is how God's word is made to work in Israel's social order.

## Restoring the Deliberately Sinful Individual to the Community of Eternal Israel: Tractate Sanhedrin-Makkot Yet Again

By design, the death penalty imposed by the earthly court is the restoration of the deliberately sinful individual to the life of corporate Israel, which is to say, to eternal life, which is promised to corporate Israel. That point, which we first met in chapter 3, is stated in so many words: "All Israel possesses a portion in the world to come," meaning, life after the grave (Mishnah-tractate Sanhedrin 10:1A).

Certain sins or crimes that affect the social order, those carried out by individual Israelites (in the main) that endanger the health of the commonwealth, come to trial in the court conducted by sages and are penalized in palpable and material ways: death, flogging, and the like. Here God does not intervene, because humans on earth bear responsibility for this-worldly transactions. But just as we shorten the life of the criminal or sinner in the matters specified in Sanhedrin and exact physical penalty in the matters covered by Makkot, so, as we saw in Keritot, God shortens the life of the criminal or sinner in matters of particular concern to God. These are matters that, strictly speaking, concern only God and not the Israelite commonwealth at large: sex, food, the Temple and its cult, and the laws of proper conduct on specified occasions. Where the community does not and cannot supervise, God takes over. Israel tends to Israel's business, God tends to God's.

Both operate on the same ground: sin or crime is not indelible. An act of rebellion is expiated through life's breath, an act of inadvertent transgression through the blood of the sacrificial beast, with the same result: all Israel, however they have conducted themselves in their span of time on earth, will enjoy a portion in the world to come: all but the specified handful enter to eternal life beyond the grave. The most profound question facing Israelite thinkers concerns the fate of the Israelite at the hands of the perfectly just and profoundly merciful God. Two principles come to bear. First, essential to their thought is the conviction that because they enjoy freedom of will and make choices on their own, all creatures are answerable to their Creator. Second, absolutely critical to the entire system is the fact that at the end of days the dead are raised for eternal life. Accordingly, the criminal justice system encompasses deep thought on the interplay of God's justice and God's mercy: How are these reconciled in the case of the sinner or criminal?

Within Israel's social order, the law of the Mishnah wrestles with a theological issue, the profound question of social justice. Specifically, does the sin or crime, which estranges an Israelite from God, close the door to life eternal? If it does, then justice is implacable and perfect, but who can survive? If it does not, then God shows mercy—but what of justice? We can understand the answer only if we keep in mind that the law of the Mishnah takes for granted the resurrection of the dead, the final judgment, and the life of the world to come beyond the grave. From that perspective, death becomes an event in life but not the end of life. And it must follow that neither does the death penalty mark the utter annihilation of the person of the sinner or criminal.

On the contrary, once an individual pays for a sin or crime in this life, when laid to rest in the grave, the sinner or criminal is situated with all of the rest of supernatural Israel, ready for the final judgment. Having been judged and having atoned in this life, the individual will "stand in judgment," meaning, find a way to the life of the world to come along with everyone else. Within the dialectics formed by those two facts—punishment now, eternal life later on—we identify the critical passages in the law found in Mishnah-tractate Sanhedrin 6:2, familiar from chapter 3:

**MISHNAH-TRACTATE SANHEDRIN 6:2**

A. [When the convicted criminal, condemned to stoning,] was ten cubits from the place of stoning, they say to him, "Confess," for it is usual for those about to be put to death to confess.

B. For whoever confesses has a share in the world to come.

C. For so we find concerning Achan, to whom Joshua said, "My son, I pray you, give glory to the Lord, the God of Israel, and confess to him, [and tell me now what you have done; hide it not from me.] And Achan answered Joshua and said, Truly have I sinned against the Lord, the God of Israel, and thus and thus I have done" (Josh. 7:19).

D. And how do we know that his confession achieved atonement for him? For it is said, "And Joshua said, Why have you troubled us? The Lord will trouble you this day" (Josh. 7:25)—

E. *This day you will be troubled, but you will not be troubled in the world to come.*

F. And if he does not know how to confess, they say to him, "Say as follows: 'Let my death be atonement for all of my transgressions.'"

Achan pays the supreme penalty in this life, on earth, but secures his place in the world to come, where all Israel, with only a few exceptions, is going to stand in judgment and enter—a world to come that explicitly includes all manner of criminals and sinners who have made atonement.

## The Israelite and Corporate Israel Once More

Here is the ultimate point of resolution of the tension between the Israelite and corporate Israel. Corporate Israel enters eternal life, carrying within it all Israelites over all time with the stated exceptions. Corporate Israel takes pains to secure a place within its limits for every Israelite. What the law of the Mishnah wishes to explore is how the Israelite sinner or criminal is rehabilitated through the criminal justice system so as to rejoin Israel in all its eternity. The answer is, the criminal or sinner remains Israelite, no matter what he or she does—even though he or she sins—and the death penalty exacted by the earthly court atones. So the law of Mishnah-tractate Sanhedrin embodies these religious principles: (1) Israel endures forever, encompassing (nearly) all Israelites; (2) sinners or criminals are able to retain their position within that eternal Israel by reason of the penalties that expiate the specific sins or crimes spelled out by the law of the Mishnah; and (3) it is an act of merciful justice that is done when the sinner or criminal is put to death, for that death assures the wayward of sharing eternity along with everyone else. God's justice comes to full expression in the penalty, which is instrumental and contingent; God's mercy endures forever in the forgiveness that follows expiation of guilt through the imposition of the penalty.

That explains why the governing religious principle of Sanhedrin-Makkot is the perfect, merciful justice of God, and it accounts for the detailed exposition of the correct form of the capital penalty for each capital sin or crime. We recall the same emphasis in the law of Mishnah-tractate Keritot on the exact match between the sin offering and the particular sin for which the offering atones. All the more so here, where the death penalty atones! The punishment must fit the crime within the context of the Torah in particular so that, at the resurrection and the judgment, the crime will have been correctly expiated. Because the law of the Mishnah rests on the premise that God is just and that God has made us in God's image, after God's likeness, the law of the Mishnah cannot deem sufficient that the punishment fit the crime. Rather, given its premises, the law of the Mishnah must pursue the issue, What of the sinner once he has been punished? The entire construction of the continuous exposition of Sanhedrin-Makkot aims at making this simple statement: the criminal, in God's image, after God's likeness, pays the penalty for crime in this world but like the rest of Israel will stand in justice and, rehabilitated, will enjoy the world to come. That is why the climactic moment in the law of the Mishnah comes at the end of the long catalogue of those sins and crimes punished by the death penalty: "all Israel has a portion in the world to come, except . . . ." The exceptions pointedly do not include any of those listed in the long catalogues of persons executed for sins or crimes.

The exceptions, indeed, pertain to persons who classify themselves entirely outside of the criminal justice system: those who deny that the resurrection of the dead is a teaching of the Torah or (worse still) deny that the Torah comes from God. As we realize, these classes of persons hardly belong in the company of the sinners and criminals catalogued here. Then come specified individuals or groups: three kings (Jeroboam, Ahab, and Manasseh) and four ordinary folk (Balaam, Doeg, Ahitophel, and Gehazi) have no portion in the world to come. There follows the standard trilogy, the Generation of the Flood, the Generation of the Dispersion, the Generation of Sodom and Gomorrah. We noted at the outset the difference between the individual who commits an act of idolatry and the entire community, the townsfolk of the apostate town, that does so. God punishes and forgives the individual, but not an entire generation, not an entire community. That is the point at which the criminal justice system completes its work.

The legal exposition and the theological principle are one and the same. The death penalty opens the way for life eternal. The tractate Sanhedrin-Makkot is a systematic demonstration of how God mercifully imposes justice upon sinners and criminals, and also of where the limits to God's mercy are reached: rejection of the Torah, the constitution of a collectivity—an "Israel"—that stands against God. God's merciful justice, then, pertains to private persons. But there can be only one Israel, and that Israel is made up of all those who look forward to a portion in the world to come, who will stand in justice and transcend death. In the broader humanity, idolaters will not stand in judgment, and entire generations who sinned collectively—as well as Israelites who broke off from the body of Israel and formed their own Israel—do not enjoy that merciful justice that reaches full expression in the fate of Achan: he stole from God but shared the world to come. And so will all Israelites who have done the dreadful deeds catalogued here.

This is also true for collective guilt that is deliberately incurred, by an entire tribe that willfully and knowingly violates the law or a city that all together opts for idolatry. But when the community collectively errs, what penalty is exacted from the individual who participates in the communal sin?

### The Responsibility of the Individual When the Community Collectively Errs: Tractate Horayot

What happens when corporate Israel errs and thereby causes individual Israelites to do so as well? Mishnah-tractate Horayot deals with collective sin through erroneous decisions made by instruments of government, as distinct from those of individuals or towns. Cultic penalties for official instruction—that of the anointed priest—in error and the consequent sin are specified at Leviticus 4:1–5. The entire congregation's doing so is taken up at Leviticus 4:13–21. Leviticus 4:22–26 moves on to the ruler. Finally, at Numbers 15:22–29, the unwitting sin of the entire community is addressed (the deliberate sin of the entire community, in the case of idolatry, already having been taken up elsewhere). Scripture makes provision for collective expiation of guilt incurred on account of collective action effected through public institutions of government or instruction. The Torah refers to a sin committed in error. A court instructs the community to do something that should not be done, thus the erroneous instruction to which the law of the Mishnah pertains. Leviticus 5:1-5; 13:21; 22:26; and Numbers 15:22-26 deal with that situation.

So the ruler, the high priest, or the people all are subject to the sanction invoked by the erroneous ruling that has caused this unwitting sin. Conversely, individuals are not. Interstitial issues—did the court and the public act together, did the court issue the ruling while the public carried it out, and the like—are addressed. The court, the ruler, and the high priest embody the community at large, the body of political institutions that, each in its own realm, bears responsibility for the whole. This tripartite division of political power dictates the organization of the exposition before us. As usual, the center of interest is divided between the crime and its penalty. In the present instance of inadvertent crime for which the penalty is a particular offering, the careful specification of which sort of beast matches which condition of inadvertent sin demands close attention. The basic principle is expressed at the very outset:

### MISHNAH-TRACTATE HORAYOT 1:1, 3, 4

[If] the court gave a decision to transgress any or all of the commandments which are stated in the Torah, and an individual went and acted in accord with their instructions, [so transgressing] inadvertently, (1) whether they carried out what they said and he carried out what they said right along with them, (2) or whether they carried out what they said and he carried out what they said after they did, (3) whether they did not carry out what they said, but he carried out what they said—he is exempt, since he relied on the court.

[If] the court gave a decision, and one of them knew that they had erred, or a disciple who is worthy to give instruction, and he [who knew of the error] went and carried out what they said, (1) whether they carried out what they said and he carried out what they said right along with them, (2) whether they carried out what they said and he carried out what they said after they did, (3) whether they did not carry out what they said, but he carried out what they said—lo, this one is liable, since he [who knew the law] did not in point of fact rely upon the court.

This is the governing principle: He who relies on himself is liable, and he who relies on the court is exempt.

The main point is clear: the individual who has violated the law relying on the instructions of the court is exempt from having to present an offering on account of this inadvertent sin. The individual is in no way responsible. What links the individual to the community, so assigning to the collectivity the consequence of private behavior? Here we turn to the matter of where and how the public bears responsibility for private, individual conduct—collective guilt for individual action. The individual is subsumed within the community when personal action results from a common misconception fostered by the community's representative agencies. What triggers the application of the collective penalty provided by the law of Mishnah-tractate Horayot is reliance on the community's court. One who relies on oneself personally is liable, and one who relies on the court is exempt. Here is a case, then, in which "they told me to do it" represents a valid claim; but the case is carefully restricted. The law of the Mishnah ordinarily does not accept such a claim, as we noted in the explicit statement that ordinarily no one can blame a third party for damages that he or she does, with the allegation that so-and-so told me to do it:

### MISHNAH-TRACTATE BABA QAMMA 8:7

Even though [the defendant] pays off [the plaintiff], he is not forgiven until he seeks [forgiveness] from [the plaintiff]. He who says, "Blind my eye," "Cut off my hand," "Break my leg"—[the one who does so] is liable. [If he added,] ". . . on condition of being exempt," [the one who does so] is liable [anyhow].

"Tear my cloak," "Break my jar," [the one who does so] is liable. [If he added,] ". . . on condition of being exempt," [the one who does so] is exempt.

"Do it to Mr. So-and-so, on condition of being exempt," he [who does so] is liable, whether this is to his person or to his property.

So the law of the Mishnah is clear in a variety of contexts: people are responsible for their own deeds. Then when does the person who does a deed validly assign guilt to a third party? It is when the court speaks in the name of the Torah—erroneously. But even here, the conditions under which such a claim may register are narrowly defined. The only case in which the community at large does not deliberately violate the Torah and incur the penalty of death now and the loss of eternity at the last judgment involves erroneous instruction on the part of the court. Then, when an individual sins in ignorance, he or she is exempt from penalty, having relied on the court. Even though an individual knows the law, relying on the court renders the individual exempt. The court is liable. But the error of the court must pertain to details, not to the basic rule, which the court is expected to know.

The individual, as much as the community, bears responsibility to know the Torah's explicit laws. Inadvertent errors in detail based on court instruction alone allow the individual to assign guilt to the community at large. Scripture then provides for a means of expiating the collective sin. But inadvertence affects both the community and the court, so a range of possibilities comes under consideration: for example, if the court gave an incorrect decision inadvertently and the entire community followed their instruction and did the thing in error; if the court gave an incorrect decision deliberately but the community, following their instruction, did the thing in error inadvertently; if the court gave incorrect instruction inadvertently and the community followed their instruction and did the thing in error deliberately; and so on.

What is the import of the law of Mishnah-tractate Horayot? It is not so much the distinction between the community and the individual as the inter-relationship of the Israelite with corporate Israel as an autonomous moral entity. Israel is represented by the high priest or the ruler or the court—the three foci of politics that serve to govern Israel and inflict the this-worldly sanctions that pertain. When the law of the Mishnah deals with the deliberate sin or crime of the individual, it inflicts capital or corporal punishment, as the case requires. The law of the Mishnah is mostly silent in the face of the deliberate sin or crime of the individual or of the community. Here God intervenes, and (outside of the framework of prophecy) we have little in the law of the Mishnah that spells out the rules for divine intervention: we know who is subject to extirpation but not how extirpation is imposed upon the individual, and only a handful of rules pertain to how extermination or exile is imposed upon the community.

What sages wished to say through the law of Mishnah-tractate Horayot is, when it comes to deeds performed in good faith by the individual at the instance of the community and its authorities, the community, not the individual, bears collective guilt, and the individual is atoned for within the offerings of the community at large. Horayot in its way bears all of the messages that Sanhedrin-Makkot or Keritot, respectively, delivers, each in its manner. All insist upon an exact match between inadvertent sin or crime, whether personal or public, and the animal offering that expiates the sin or crime and that accomplishes Israel's atonement. On that basis, eternal life must come to (nearly) all Israel, one by one and all together.

## Eternal Israel and the Individual Israelite's Conquest of Death

There can be no doubt that the basic logic of the legal system of the Mishnah requires the doctrine of personal resurrection. The entire system of criminal justice involving corporal and capital punishment revolves around the conception of life beyond the grave, which requires punishing sinners or criminals in this world so that they may be fully at one with God at the resurrection and the last judgment. Indeed, without the conception of life beyond the grave the system as a whole yields a mass of contradictions and anomalies: injustice to the righteous, prosperity to the wicked, never recompensed. Without resurrection and judgment, the system cannot account for the very being of the private person. That explains why, at one point after another, the path to the future passes through, and beyond, the grave and the judgment that, for all Israel leads to eternity. The principal continues and yields interest, or punishment may take place in this world, while eternal punishment goes onward as well, especially for the trilogy of absolute sins—idolatry, incest (or fornication) and murder—capped by gossip. But how all of this squares with the conception of "all Israel"—that autonomous, unique moral entity, corporate Israel, which transcends individual Israelites—remains to be seen.

The individual Israelite is the focus of resurrection and judgment, for people die one by one. "Israel" the holy people, by contrast, never dies. It is the enduring component of humanity, that part of humanity that knows God through God's own self-manifestation in the Torah. The sector of humanity that accepts the law of the Torah as the will of God, corporate Israel cannot die any more than God can. Then, to corporate Israel, resurrection categorically does not pertain. True, judgment does. Corporate Israel is subject to judgment as much as individual Israelites are, but for Israel the people, judgment is not left to the end of days, when the dead will rise from their graves. For corporate Israel judgment takes place in this world and in this age. Of that Scripture leaves no doubt. The Torah laid down the principle that Israel suffers for its sins, and everything that has happened since the closure of the Torah only confirms that principle. The very continuation of Scripture beyond the Pentateuch and the account of the inheritance and subsequent loss of the Land makes that point. The explanation of Israel's subjugation to the gentiles and their idolatry carries within itself a profound statement about corporate Israel's identity, its enduring presence, from this age to the world to come, without interruption.

Corporate Israel is judged and suffers its punishment in the here and now. That conviction animates the entire theological system, which in turn animates the Mishnah's law. Then that same Israel, the never-dying people, emerges in the world to come fully at one with God. Indeed, that is the meaning of the advent of the world to come, as it said, it will arrive "today if all Israel will it," "today if all Israel keeps a single Sabbath." To corporate Israel, a moral entity without counterpart, the resurrection of the dead therefore bears no categorical relevance. The advent of the world to come and eternal life bears its own meaning for Israel the holy people. To the Israelite, the resurrection of the dead forms the beginning of the restoration of Eden, which we can now see has a clear meaning: the restoration of corporate Israel to the Land of Israel, representing the restoration of humanity to Eden. All this the Torah makes possible, the life of sanctification leading to the end of salvation.

# Israel: The Family
and the Household

# THE ISRAELITE FAMILY

*Tractates Qiddushin, Ketubot,*
*Sotah, Gittin, and Yebamot*

## The Family and the Household

To this point I have presented the account of the Israel set forth by the law of the Mishnah as if "Israel" in that system were composed only of corporate Israel and the individual Israelite. But that is misleading. The law conceives that two countervailing social formations intervene between the individual Israelite and corporate Israel: the family and the household, the one a genealogical, the other an economic, entity.

When the law of the Mishnah confronts the dynamics of conflict and social tension—which is to say, produces practical law for the everyday community—that focus is on neither corporate Israel nor the individual Israelite. The former, corporate Israel, is intangible, a function of abstract theology: a collectivity realized in no one place, in no single transaction. The latter, the individual Israelite, as we saw in some detail, is recognized principally in the Temple cult, on the one side, and is disposed of for personal behavior in judgments of the criminal justice system broadly construed, on the other. Here too, then, is no source of social tension in those transactions of the social order, again broadly construed.

What requires attention is the everyday social reality of Israel, the mediating institutions of family and household. In the law system, these took their place between the private individual and the corporate body viewed as a whole. It was a capacious, central position, for the system of law was especially meant to legislate for, to regularize and realize, those two intermediate units of the social order. The family and household thus form the principal source of tension and conflict addressed by the law of the Mishnah.

By definition, the law of the Mishnah considers the family—a palpable, genealogical construction—and the household—a collectivity of persons who engage in productive work together—as the building blocks of society. The household is treated in the law of the Mishnah as the smallest whole unit of production. While craftsmen and traders occasionally figure, the household is

**175**

deemed equivalent to what we should call a farm peopled by an extended family and its dependents, unskilled workers and craftsmen, for example. These two social entities transcend their individual participants and, like corporate Israel, impose the mark of the whole on the individual parts. The family and the household for their part should not be too sharply distinguished from one another, although in the organizing categories (tractates) of the law, they are to be differentiated, the one as a genealogical-cultural entity, the other as an economic entity.

Here, then, the law of the Mishnah finds its energy and movement. The definition of both the family and the household begins in the delineation of each in contexts of conflict. Where one family intersects with another, there the outer bounds of each result in competing claims, always bearing material consequences. The unfaithful wife suffers the loss of the marriage settlement that provides alimony and restoration of the dowry. The abusive husband is forced to divorce the wife and pay off the promised alimony and return the dowry. To be sure, the family also forms an indicator of personal status, placing each individual into a continuum with all others, fore and aft, generations past and those to come. Then conflicts will emerge in those same matters of personal status. In the nature of things, these concerned women as principal media of family articulation, as we shall soon see. Property is generally at stake, but not always.

So too, when households enter into disputes, the claims of each define the respective household's outer limits. These claims are ordinarily material in character, for land or payment of damages, for example. As the unit of production entering transactions of an economic character, the household involves conflicts also over property. Disputes about movables, for example, ordinarily are framed in the language of conflict between householders. The household is also taken for granted as a unit of ownership and possession of real property, even without an economic function such as a means of production. On the household as the building block of the economic order of corporate Israel, the law of the Mishnah constructs further disquisitions on contention and conflict. These we shall defer to chapter 10.

Note the match between the Mishnah's topics and the type of questions that are addressed to those topics. When attending to the individual Israelite, the law provides the means for individuation and sets the limits thereof, in the context, as we note, of the Temple and its offerings. Both expositions sort out fixed relationships. Neither introduces the dynamic of tension and conflict, for instance, contending claims for property or personal status. Indeed, even where we should anticipate laws to regulate conflicting claims, we find none. For example, conflict rarely figures in the recognition of issues of ownership and possession, which concern cooperation in common ventures. Without addressing relationships that create strife, the law of the Mishnah further defined how the individual legitimately deviates from the norm, and it outlined the outer limits of tolerance for deviancy. Indeed, the emphasis lay on honest, agreeable disagreement, not malicious action on the one side and an attitude of arrogant self-righteousness on the other. In the context of the law's treatment of individuation, conflict between individuals is not investigated, and large-scale conflict within corporate Israel is not contemplated. In treating Israel and the Israelite, the law treats corporate Israel as a society unaffected by tension and strife; and as to the Israelite, his or her relationships subject to the law of the Torah concern God. That leads to a point of productive interest: Why does sorting out conflict define the treatment of the twin topics of family and household?

## Why Conflict Matters in the Mishnah's Law of Family and Household

When it comes to the family and the household, the law confronts conflict between the building blocks of the Israelite social order and brings about a just resolution of conflicting claims. These concern personal status and property. Both by nature generate conflicting claims, the one for social standing, the other for class status defined in material terms. Amid the myriad relationships and engagements of the family and the household, claims as to genealogy or property indicate where the law finds the cases it wishes to investigate in any given topic. In the adjudication of conflict, the law realizes that abstract commitment to justice that defines its purpose, that is to say, God's purpose in forming Israel. Beyond the altar of the Temple and its local analogies, the individual finds his or her position in Israelite society as member of a family or household. Indeed, the Mishnah's legal system ordinarily deems the extended family to form, also, a household. What renders that intermediate unit, interposed between corporate Israel and the individual Israelite, remarkable is its dual definition in both genealogical and economic terms. Though the two are not sharply delineated, the language of genealogy dominates when family is at issue (this chapter), and that of property dominates when household is at stake (chapter 10).

Which one takes priority? As between "family" and "householder," words that refer to the entities that overlap, it is "family" that defines the governing metaphor. "Family" extends upward and outward to "corporate Israel." Another way of saying this is that corporate Israel comprised first the children of Jacob, then downward and inward to the individual Israelite, the child of an Israelite mother, whose caste status is determined by an Israelite father. With its account of the formation of Israel out of the generations of Abraham, Isaac, and Jacob, Israel as a large holy family, the narrative ("mythic") theology of monotheism accomplishes the selection for us. Stated simply: "Israel" is "the children of Israel," portrayed by generations, the descendants of the same forebears, ultimately Abraham and Sarah. Converts to Judaism receive a genealogy when they become children of Abraham and Sarah, joining the family *ab initio*. All Israel therefore is deemed an extended family. It is a family defined by a genealogy of a supernatural character to be sure, for idolaters may join the family by renouncing idolatry and worshiping the one true God. Then corporate Israel is the composite of Israelite families.

The social building block "household" is subordinate to "family." That secondary standing is shown by the fact that the family is primary to the narrative that the law invokes and embodies: the story of God and Israel worked out through the life of Israel on the Land. The Torah links corporate Israel's possession of the Land of Israel to the Israelite families present at its division. It seeks to preserve the possession of the Land in the hands of those who originally divided it and their heirs. These, for the Mishnah, are represented by those who possess the Land through inheritance. Thus, by "Judah" is meant both the (genealogical) family of Judah and the portion of the Land of Israel assigned to the family of Judah, and the same holds for all the families of the children of Jacob.

That is why the Mishnah's law, deriving from the Torah, determines the status of real property by how it is acquired. One type of real estate in the Land of Israel is that received as an inheritance, which cannot be permanently sold or alienated from family possession. In the Jubilee it reverts to the representative of the initial family assigned the plot at the original division of the Land of Israel. Separate, there is property purchased with funds and not inherited. Property in the Land of Israel acquired not by inheritance but merely by purchase is not subject to the special rules governing restoration of property to those that originally received it in the conquest of the Land under Joshua. That distinction makes the point. Genealogy governs the disposition of the Land of Israel as much as it defines the composition of the people of Israel.

After it is established that the smallest whole unit of construction of corporate Israel must itself constitute a corporate entity—individuals viewed as a collectivity for moral purposes—the family takes center stage. It follows that the systemic interest in quarrels between families derives from the definition of corporate Israel as a conglomerate of families. "Family" as metaphor not only takes priority over "householder"; it also subordinates the individual Israelite, establishing his position within the social order both locatively and genealogically ("father's house"). "Family" forms the ground of being of the individual, who, though responsible on his or her own before God, still is conceived in functional terms in relation to others, past, present, and future, through family identification and genealogical position. The Mishnah's concept states in abstract, categorical terms three tangible reference points: (1) the concrete scriptural narratives of the formation of Israel out of the patriarchal and matriarchal progenitors, (2) the conquest and division of the Land by and among social groups defined along those original lines of family and genealogy (now: by tribes made up of families), and (3) the continuing possession of, and transactions concerning, ownership of real property in the Land divided by tribes and, within the tribes, by families. That brings us to the Mishnah's laws concerning the formation (Qiddushin, Ketubot), maintenance (Ketubot, Sotah), and dissolution (Gittin, Yebamot) of families.

## Disputes in the Union of Families through Marriage: Tractate Qiddushin

The law of the Mishnah addresses conflict in the family relationships of the husband, the wife, and the wife's father. The husband represents his family; the wife and her father, the wife's family. Omitted categorically are relationships between and among siblings (except insofar as the wife's brothers enter the position of the father upon his death, or the brothers of the husband in the case of the husband's death without children). The extended family—including other daughters of the same family, co-wives of the same widow, and other relationships in prohibited marriages (see Lev. 18)—plays only a circumstantial role. Explicit points of contentious intersection are few, and, in due course, we shall see why these, and no other conflicts, are subjected to an exposition by the law of the Mishnah.

While Israelite individuals marry, what counts is that families merge and emerge from the marriage, and that is where conflict is generated. The reason is that the merger of families requires the woman's family to assign to the daughter her share of the patrimony, which the man's family takes over, just as the man's caste status defines the caste status of the offspring of the union. The interest of the law of the Mishnah, then, is how the relationship of the individuals in the formation of a marital union links two families, enriching the one that receives the bride and compensating the one that gives her up. Indeed, the act of betrothal forms a particular detail of the larger theory of how a man acquires title to, or possession of, persons or property of various classifications. It is thus the this-worldly side of the law of the Mishnah; the transcendent side emerges through the marriage, the sanctification of the relationship between a particular woman and a particular man so that she is consecrated to him and to no other. (No one deemed the relationship reciprocal; a particular man was not consecrated to a particular woman, since the law of the Mishnah presupposes polygamy.) In effect, just as a farmer acquires a slave or an ox or real estate, so the householder-husband effects possession of, and gains title to, a woman.

But while the slave or ox or field could never be called "consecrated" to that particular farmer, and the language of sanctification never operates in such transactions, the act of acquisition of a woman has also transformed the relationship of the woman not only to that man who acquired her but to all other men. The woman, to begin with, is deemed by the Torah to form a property belonging to her father, to be transferred to the ownership of her husband. In that regard, the governing analogy for the acquisition of a woman as consecrated wife derives from the rules of the transfer of title to property. But the woman must concur in the transaction, and that separates her from all others subject to the ownership–the free will–of others. And there is a second difference. The language that is used here, the language of sanctification, derives from the Temple, and, as I said, when we speak of sanctifying or consecrating a woman to a specific man, we are using the language of the altar, which speaks of sanctifying an animal to the altar for a particular purpose. This, then, is the context in which conflicts take place.

We will examine only the laws of tractate Qiddushin on betrothing or "sanctifying" a woman to a particular man. I will not reproduce the many compositions that yield a picture of how two or more parties can have set forth claims against one another. Qiddushin is quintessential because it details only this one articulated conflict:

MISHNAH-TRACTATE QIDDUSHIN 3:10–11

> He who says to a woman, "I have betrothed you," and she says, "You did not betroth me"–he is prohibited to marry her relatives, but she is permitted to marry his relatives.
>
> [If] she says, "You betrothed me," and he says, "I did not betroth you"–he is permitted to marry her relatives, and she is prohibited from marrying his relatives.
>
> "I betrothed you," and she says, "You betrothed only my daughter," he is prohibited from marrying the relatives of the older woman, and the older woman is permitted to marry his relatives. He is permitted to marry the relatives of the young girl, and the young girl is permitted to marry his relatives.
>
> "I have betrothed your daughter," and she says, "You betrothed only me," he is prohibited from marrying the relatives of the girl, and the girl is permitted to marry his relatives. He is permitted to marry the relatives of the older woman, but the older woman is prohibited from marrying his relatives."

Under dispute in the above is whether the betrothal has taken place, and if so, between which parties. In the first instance (3:10) the conflict concerns the consequence of opposed claims that a betrothal has taken place. There is no issue of a transfer of property. At stake is only the consequences concerning further unions. We impose upon the claimant the implications of his claim. Since the man claims to have betrothed the woman and she denies it, he is believed vis-à-vis her female relatives and may not marry any of them. But she is believed vis-à-vis his male relatives and may marry any of them. The same issue works itself out in variations. We note that the testimony of the mother that the man has betrothed the daughter has no effect upon the daughter. So the issue is not the determination of the facts subject to contention, only the resolution of the implications of the several claims. That yields the anomaly that lies at the heart of the matter. The governing principle is: a person's claim in his own regard is affirmed so far as he, but no one else, is concerned. A person cannot on his own define another person's status. The context does not encompass the transfer of property or the formation of a family unit, only the consequences of the self-ascribed status. These have to do with the prohibitions of consanguineous relationships as defined by the Torah at Leviticus 18. That is the sole interest in the transaction expressed by the Mishnah's law.

The resolution of the conflict accepts the conflicting claims and simply turns them back upon those who enter the claims. But the claim of one party has no bearing on the standing of the other party. No institutional intervention is contemplated. The law simply declares the standing of the two parties vis-à-vis those affected by their claims in their own behalf. The obvious premise is, further intervention beyond a declaration of fact is not required. So the sages' court is not instructed on how to reach a decision on the conflicting claims, only on how to work out the consequences of these claims, none of which can be verified and all of which bear implications for relationships with third parties.

How does the interest of corporate Israel come to realization in the disposition of the conflict? Corporate Israel concerns itself with ensuring that the relationships prohibited by Leviticus 18 not be entered into within the community. The particular class of conflicts that is addressed—conflicting claims as to personal status—is resolved in the simplest possible way. The range of issues demanding attention could not be defined more narrowly. Property does not enter in, because the law of the Mishnah does not contemplate affirming that a betrothal in actuality has taken place. There are no transfers of property involved in the resolution. That is self-evident since the party denying the betrothal is unaffected by the claim of having been betrothed. The point of the law of the Mishnah is, *what one says about oneself affects one's own standing but no one else's.* An entire category formation Nedarim, "Vows," is built on that point (see chapter 5); indeed, the principle extends to a variety of topics of the law.

What is Heaven's interest in the transaction? The sanctification of a particular woman for a particular man is exposed in the intersection of the language of acquisition with the language of sanctification. When a householder buys a cow, acquiring it does not *sanctify* it (unless it is explicitly meant for an offering on the altar in Jerusalem), so a person who utilizes that same cow, milking it or using it for plowing, does not offend God. The issue of sanctification does not enter the transaction. But a householder who acquires a woman thereby consecrates the woman as his wife. Another person who utilizes the same woman, having sexual relations with her and producing children by her, enormously outrages God (not to mention the husband). The category sanctification and its opposite applies. Yet in both instances the fact is acquiring title—whether to the cow or the woman. What follows from this observation? The law of the Mishnah does devote attention to the meaning of the declaration of sanctification in regard to the law of Scripture, here Leviticus 18, with special concern to avoid violating the Torah's law.

## Disputes in the Union of Families through Marriage: Tractate Ketubot

A "written marriage contract," the Ketubah, is required to validate the relationship that families establish through the union of their offspring. In it, the husband undertakes to support the wife, should he divorce her or predecease her, to permit her time to remarry. The stipulated amount of the settlement depends on the status of the wife—virgin or not—at marriage. But the obligation for actual payment of the settlement may depend on the conduct of one or another party to the union, particularly, the husband's abuse of authority in the relationship or the wife's violation of the implicit obligations of an Israelite woman. In the former case, the husband has to pay off the marriage settlement and issue a writ of divorce; in the latter, the wife loses all claim to alimony. These are the instances in which articulated conflicts demand attention within the Mishnah's system.

The marriage transaction encompasses an exchange of wealth between the families of bride and groom. The husband's family gains the daughter as wife for its son and mother of future generations; and property pledged in support of the woman changes hands. The wife's family loses an asset but also ceases to have to support the daughter; and she further has a claim on an inheritance out of her father's household's property that has to be honored through the payment of a dowry. Nearly the whole of the law of the Mishnah of Ketubot, devoted as it is to the transaction in property in a marital union, covers such conflicting claims.

But only at specific points are the conflicts articulated, and to these I restrict my account. The three parties to potential conflict—wife, husband, and wife's father—all enjoy material rights. The husband is entitled to the dowry. The wife's father is entitled to certain fees and fines under conditions specified by the Torah. And, most pertinently, the wife is entitled to protection during the marriage and alimony or support in the event of divorce or widowhood. The basic question facing the law of the Mishnah is how to spell out the reciprocal and corresponding rights and obligations of all parties to the marriage as it unfolds. The marriage contract defines the locus for working out those rights and obligations. Within it, each party has an interest in the orderly formation of the social and economic fact of the marriage and in its fair and orderly dissolution as well.

One important source of conflict concerns what is owing in the marriage settlement called for by the Ketubah.

### Mishnah-tractate Ketubot 2:1

The woman who was widowed or divorced—she says, "You married me as a virgin"—and he says, "Not so, but I married you as a widow"—if there are witnesses that [when she got married], she went forth to music, with her hair flowing loose, her marriage contract is two hundred [zuz].

Thus, the status of the bride determines the answer. At the time of the marriage was she virgin or otherwise (widow, divorcée)? If the former, she collects twice the sum owing for alimony or support should the husband divorce her or die. The law of the Mishnah provides for the resolution of the claim long after the first act of intercourse.

The law of the Torah on which this is based is concerned with the issue of sexual misconduct as opposed to defamation. The law of the Mishnah, however, sidesteps this matter entirely. Instead, the conflict is resolved judicially, through the provision of witnesses. If the woman claims to have been a virgin at marriage and circumstantial evidence sustains her claim, she is awarded the appropriate alimony for a virgin. The case is not parallel to the Torah's law; it is defined as a contest concerning property, not status. The sages take for granted that the case occurs only in the absence of an explicit marriage contract, which would have otherwise settled the matter before any dispute arose.

But not all family conflicts concern property transactions. In those involving relationships between husband and wife, the sages have to balance the husband's authority against the wife's human rights. In the following, the husband prohibits the wife by vow from doing something. It is implied, though not stated, that she appeals to the sages for relief.

#### MISHNAH-TRACTATE KETUBOT 7:1–5

He who prohibits his wife by vow from deriving benefit from him for a period of thirty days, appoints an agent to provide for her. [If the effects of the vow are not nullified] for a longer period, he puts her away and pays off her marriage contract.

He who prohibits his wife by vow from tasting any single kind of produce whatsoever must put her away and pay off her marriage contract.

He who prohibits his wife by a vow from adorning herself with any single sort of jewelry must put her away and pay off her marriage contract.

He who prohibits his wife by a vow from going home to her father's house—when he [father] is with her in [the same] town, [if it is] for a month, he may persist in the marriage. [If it is] for two, he must put her away and pay off her marriage contract. And when he is in another town, [if the vow is in effect] for one festival season he may persist in the marriage. [But if the vow remains in force] for three, he must put her away and pay off her marriage contract.

He who prohibits his wife by a vow from going to a house of mourning or to a house of celebration must put her away and pay off her marriage contract, because he locks the door before her. But if he claimed that he took such a vow because of some other thing, he is permitted to impose such a vow. [If he took a vow,] saying to her, (1) "On condition that you say to So-and-so what you said to me," or (2) "what I said to you," or (3) "that you draw water and pour it out onto the ash heap," he must put her away and pay off her marriage contract.

At issue is whether the husband may impose his will upon the wife concerning matters in which she has the right to exercise her own will and autonomous judgment. The husband then claims the right to control personal details of his wife's conduct, and the wife resists that claim. The sages' judgment is clear: the husband may not interfere with long-standing relationships of an autonomous character that the wife maintains. She retains personality and autonomy in the marriage. If he does interfere, the costs are enormous.

The law of the Mishnah does not contend with the husband's claim, it resolves the conflict by dismissing that claim. The wife is paid off, the husband incurs the costs of the marriage settlement called for in the marriage contract; and the conflict that he has precipitated is tantamount to an act of divorce. In brief, the law of the Mishnah examines the claim of the husband for control of the wife and not only rejects that claim but summarily dismisses it and the marriage that embodies it.

There is a counterpart for the wife. She has the obligation to conduct herself in accord with the law of the Torah and penalties are inflicted on her if she does not.

#### MISHNAH-TRACTATE KETUBOT 7:6

And those women go forth without the payment of the marriage contract at all: She who transgresses against the law of Moses and Jewish law. And what is the law of Moses [which she has transgressed]?

[If] (1) she feeds him food which has not been tithed, or (2) has sexual relations with him while she is menstruating, or [if] (3) she does not cut off her dough offering, or [if] (4) she vows and does not carry out her vow.

And what is the Jewish law? If (1) she goes out with her hair flowing loose, or (2) she spins in the marketplace, or (3) she talks with just anybody.

This establishes the limits on the wife's claim to conduct herself any way she wishes. The conflict arises from the wife's conduct and the husband's implicit application to the sages. The issue again turns on property: Does the husband have to pay the marriage settlement stipulated in the marriage contract in the present circumstance? Once more, the law of the Mishnah does not seriously confront the wife's implicit claim to collect. It declares that she has no such right. This is so, since she has no right to violate the law of the Torah, which overrides all property claims she may have in mind.

So in both instances—the husband's overreaching in one direction, the wife's in another—the law of the Mishnah recognizes no conflict that requires adjudication. But while the husband's offense is against the wife, the wife's is against the Torah, and the husband is joined, in the conflict, by the Torah itself.

The final instance concerns the collection of the marriage settlement. The wife wishes to collect from the husband or his estate the stipulated sum. Implicit is the husband's or the estate's claim that she already has done so. Here again, the issue is how to resolve conflict when the facts cannot be established, that is, when the husband has no receipt, or quittance, to show that he has paid the stipulated sum, or the wife has the marriage contract but no writ of divorce to show that she has a legitimate claim on alimony. Given the range of uncertain transactions, where each party enters a plea, we must ask, Why was this particular conflict chosen to be included? The answer is that here is where Heaven becomes a party to the dispute. In this case, an oath is taken, alerting God to the truth claim and asking God to validate it, and the only issue in resolving the conflict is who gets to take the oath and so validate the claim.

### MISHNAH-TRACTATE KETUBOT 9:7–8

She who impairs her marriage contract collects it only through an oath. [If] one witness testified against her that it had been collected, she collects it only through an oath. From (1) the property of the heirs [orphans], or from (2) property subject to a lien, or (3) in his [the husband's] absence should she collect [her marriage contract] only through an oath.

"She who impairs her marriage contract." How so? [If] her marriage contract was worth a thousand zuz, and he said to her, "You have collected your marriage contract," but she says, "I have received only a maneh [a hundred zuz]," she collects [the remainder] only through an oath.

[If] one witness testified against her that it had been collected: How so? [If] her marriage contract was worth a thousand zuz, and he [the witness] said to her, "You have collected the value of your marriage contract," and she says, "I have not collected it," and one witness testified against her that it had been collected, she should collect the marriage contract only through an oath.

"From property subject to a lien" How so? [If the husband] sold off his property to others, and she comes to collect from the purchasers, she should collect from them only through an oath.

From the property of the heirs [orphans] How so? [If the husband] died and left his property to the orphans, and she comes to collect [her marriage contract] from the orphans, she should collect from them only by an oath.

"In his absence" How so? [If the husband] went overseas, and she comes to collect [her marriage contract] in his absence, she collects [what is due her] only by an oath.

In the oath, the legal procedures of the Torah and Mishnah merge. The Torah attaches the most solemn importance to the oath, since it invokes God's name. The law of the Mishnah articulates the dispute over the collection of the marriage settlement to indicate whether or not an oath is required for the plaintiff to collect what is owing to her. The specified cases, involve the husband's provision of witnesses for his claim; these are overridden by the wife's oath. God's name is introduced with the oath. The system provides for the oath when the evidence is insufficient to sustain a decision on any other basis. Then the person who is allowed to take the oath also collects what she claims. The invoking of God's name represents an absolute validation. Then the conflict between the parties to the marriage and property settlement concerns whose claim is established by the right to take the oath. It is the plaintiff, the wife; not the defendant who does not wish to transfer the property.

We should not miss the source of the legal system's dynamism. What animates the law here and everywhere is God's presence and God's active engagement with certain transactions within Israel. The language of the document provides the key. The law of the Mishnah rests on the premise that Heaven takes seriously the language of human transactions, in oaths and vows as other formularies in which Heaven has a special interest, so that if a man violates his commitment to a woman, or vice versa, God intervenes. The entire relationship of betrothal and marriage, fidelity in marriage on the part of the woman, and the dissolution of marriage—all of these transactions are effected through Heavenly supervised formularies. That is the lesson that we learn from the matter of the husband's excessively controlling the wife's relationships, on the one side, and of the provision for the wife to take an oath where the document is somehow impaired, on the other. Here the conflict that requires articulation involves Heaven's particular interest, in the one case because the husband's or the wife's conduct overrides all the protections of the document; in the other because of the engagement of God's name via the oath.

The question of who takes the oath and so secures his or her claim will arise again when conflicts between individuals over property come to resolution in that same manner. The law then has to determine who has the right to collect by taking an oath—who is the presumptive owner of contested property. The issue in the present context is who is favored by the power of the oath; here it is the wife who seeks to collect the marriage settlement. So while the marital relationship presents numerous occasions for conflicting claims, where the law of the Mishnah identifies a conflict and resolves it, it is where Heaven's interest, for one reason or another, proves paramount.

## When Marriages Break Down:
## Tractate Sotah Once Again

From Qiddushin and Ketubot, we return to Sotah, the wife accused of adultery, whom we discussed in chapter 2, and also take up Gittin, writs of divorce—both tractates dealing with the dissolution of the marriage. Both rest on the foundation of a breakdown in the family unit—conflict by definition.

In the case presented in Sotah, the Torah's identification of the subject of contention entails also a device for resolving the matter: the rite of the bitter water imposed upon the wife accused of infidelity and carried out in the Temple. The conflict and the method for working out the conflict are specified by the Torah. That is not to suggest that the sages of the Mishnah do not reshape the law of the Torah, for within their framework they do. The Torah speaks both of the wife who has actually committed adultery and whose husband is made jealous, and the woman whose husband expresses jealousy but who is guiltless. The Torah focuses on the rite at the Temple that accommodates the situation. The law of the Mishnah takes the ordeal and encases it in juridical procedures, rules of evidence, guidelines meant to protect the woman from needless exposure to the ordeal to begin with. The law of the Mishnah radically revises the entire transaction when it says, if the husband expresses jealousy by instructing his wife not to speak with a specified person, and the wife spoke with the man, there is no juridical result: she still is permitted to have sexual relations with her husband. But if she went with him to some private place and remained with him for sufficient time to become unclean, she is prohibited from having sexual relations with her husband and if the husband is a priest, she is prohibited from eating heave offering.

The law of the Mishnah thus conceives of a two-stage process, two kinds of testimony. In the first kind, she is warned not to get involved, but she is not then prohibited to the husband. In the second kind, witnesses attest that she can have committed adultery. Not only so, but the law of the Mishnah wants valid evidence if it is to deprive the wife of her marriage settlement. The provision of the law of the Mishnah certainly closes off the possibility of conflict, except as to facts. If a single witness to the act of intercourse is available, that does not suffice. People who ordinarily cannot testify against her do not have the power to deprive her of her property rights in the marriage, including her mother-in-law and the daughter of her mother-in-law, her co-wife, the husband's brother's wife, and the daughter of her husband. The accused wife still collects her settlement. But because of their testimony, she does not undergo the rite; she is divorced in course and the transaction concludes there.

Before the ordeal is invoked, the Rabbinic law of the Mishnah therefore wants some sort of solid evidence (1) of untoward sexual activity and also (2) of clear action or at least the possibility, confirmed through a specific case, that adultery has taken place. The Torah law left everything to the husband's whim, the "spirit of jealousy." But in the law of the Mishnah, if the husband gives his statement of jealousy and the wife responds by ignoring the statement, the ordeal does not apply. By her specific action the wife has to indicate the possibility that the husband is right. This is a far cry from the Torah's "spirit of jealousy." For the Torah, the ordeal settles all questions. For the Mishnah, the ordeal takes effect only in carefully defined cases where (1) sufficient evidence exists to invoke the rite, but (2) insufficient evidence to make it unnecessary: well-established doubt, so to speak.

Here, in addressing a raw and blatant conflict, the law of the Mishnah thus identifies not a single point at which to augment, with its own exposition of conflict and resolution, the situation of contention that the Torah resolves through the imposition of the rite of the bitter water. That negative result contributes to the unfolding thesis that where Rabbinic Judaism takes up conflict between Israelites is where the Torah for one reason or another has defined a systemically consequential controversy but requires the sages' intervention to restore Israel's wholeness. A similar result occurs for a different reason in the dissolution of the household union, the writ of divorce.

## When the Union of Families through Marriage Dissolves: Tractate Gittin

Every line of Mishnah-tractate Gittin, "Writs of Divorce," announces the presence of conflict in Israel. But much of the tractate deals with the sages' disposition of the writ of divorce under various circumstances. As with Ketubot, so here the issue engages sages in their scribal role and involves questions of correct procedure. The social tensions represented by the transaction do not generate the Mishnah's program. While implicit in the sages' discussion is the status of the woman who has relied on the writ of divorce and now finds that it is invalid (the man can marry more than one wife, so his situation differs), here again, conflict between Israelites—the husband alleges the writ is null, the wife demands its confirmation—does not surface.

Note the contrast with Sotah. In the matter of the conflict between a husband and the wife accused of infidelity, Scripture has identified the conflict demanding attention and has also provided for its resolution. In the case of Gittin, Scripture contributes minimal information (Deut. 24:1-4). The Torah emphasizes the prohibition of a divorced woman, once remarried, to return to the husband who has divorced her. The law of the Mishnah, by contrast, finds its focal point in the subordinated details of the transaction set forth in the Torah.

The law of the Mishnah takes as its principal problem the delivery of the writ of divorce to the wife. The husband may send it through his agents, in which case they must give testimony that they have witnessed the writing and the signing by witnesses of the document. That guarantees one of the main requirements, that the document has been prepared for this particular woman by this particular man. These and comparable requirements make certain that the writ is valid and takes effect, so that all parties to the transaction know that the woman's status has changed irrevocably. But that means, even an imperfection without any bearing on the substance of the transaction, such as entering the wrong date or misidentifying the locale of the husband, suffices to invalidate the writ. So too, if the scribe erred and gave the writ of divorce to the woman and the quittance to the man, rather than giving the writ to the man to give to his wife and vice versa, it is a complete disaster. Both cases and comparable ones bring to bear the most severe penalties. Then, if she should remarry on the strength of the impaired writ of divorce, her entire situation is ruined. She has to get a new writ of divorce from the first husband and from the second; she loses her alimony; she loses many of the benefits and guarantees of the marriage settlement. And the offspring from the marriage fall into the category of those whose parents are legally unable to wed, that is, the offspring of a married woman by a man other than her husband. Everything is lost by reason of the innocent actions of the wife in remarrying on the strength of an impaired writ, and that means that the wife has an acute interest in, and bears full responsibility for, the validity of the writ.

The husband's only unique power is to direct the writing and delivery of the writ; otherwise the wife bears equal responsibility for the accurate preparation of the document, the valid delivery (hence the insistence that she be alert to the transaction), and the fully correct details inscribed therein. While these provisions make the correct provision of the writ an urgent matter, they do not articulate conflict between Israelites as the focus of the Mishnah's category formation—only the outcome of conflict as definitive in forming that Mishnah's category.

## Disputes in the Dissolution of the Union of Families through Marriage: Death without Offspring: Tractate Yebamot

What happens if the husband's goal in consecrating the woman—engendering children in his name ("name," here, standing for household or extended family)—has not come to fruition? Then, the Torah maintains, the original act of consecration has not accomplished its goal. The purpose of the act of sanctification of a woman in marriage is to produce the new generation. That purpose not having been achieved, the act of sanctification remains in play. The woman therefore remains consecrated for the as-yet-unrealized purpose embodied in the intention of betrothal and the action of consummation of the union. Then, so far as is possible, the widow bears the obligation to accomplish the intention that effected the original act of consecration. Any act of sanctification, whether a woman to a man or an animal to the altar, has formally to be resolved, either through realization—the woman producing offspring, the animal being offered on the altar—or its nullification—the man issues a writ of divorce, the animal is redeemed from the altar through a specified process.

When the husband dies without offspring, circumstance intervenes. Since the future of the household is uncertain, the Torah holds, if brothers survive the deceased, then a surviving brother of the childless deceased may take his place as husband of the widow. The law of Levirate marriage—marriage of the widow to a brother of the childless deceased husband for purpose of procreation—aims at bringing about the realization of the original act of consecration. That is the explicit view of the Torah , which expresses the desire to maintain the deceased's "name" in Israel. The pertinent verses of the Torah (Deut. 25:5-10), is as follows:

> If brothers dwell together and one of them die and have no son, the widow of the dead man shall not be married to a stranger outside the family; her husband's brother shall go in to her and take her as his wife and perform the duty of a husband's brother to her. And it shall be that the firstborn son which she bears will succeed to the name of his dead brother, that his name may not be blotted out of Israel. But if the man does not want to take his brother's wife, then let his brother's wife go up to the gate to the elders and say, "My husband's brother refuses to raise up a name to his brother in Israel; he will not perform the duty of my husband's brother." Then the elders of his city shall call him and speak to him. But if he stands firm and says, "I do not want to take her," then his brother's wife shall come to him in the presence of the elders, remove his sandal from his foot, spit in his presence, and answer and say, "So shall it be done to the man who will not build up his brother's house." And his name shall be called in Israel, "The house of him who had his sandal removed."

The match of the penalty (the deceased's brother is labeled with a demeaning name) to the failure (not preserving the deceased's name) rests on the premise that the original act of consecration of this woman to this man meant to bring a new generation into being. The Torah deems the widow's role in realizing the initial intentionality, to which she has acceded, to be active; she is the one who demands the realization of the original transaction. The surviving brother forms a mere instrumentality in the fulfillment of the deceased husband's and now widowed wife's agreement. The surviving brother(s) may then prevent the transaction, in which case the woman is freed of her status of sanctification; *halisah*, or the rite of removing the shoe, then forms the counterpart to the presentation of a writ of divorce. But there is this obvious difference: now the unwilling brother takes the passive role, the outraged widow, the active one. She has willingly accepted for herself the responsibility entailed in the original act of consecration, taking the place of her now-deceased husband. Her brother-in-law, however, has failed in his Heavenly task.

When Heaven intervenes in a consecrated relationship and severs it, no writ of divorce is required to free the woman from the marriage. In the Levirate connection, Heaven may also have arranged matters so that a union of a surviving brother with the widow contravenes other laws of the Torah. So Heaven bears responsibility for a complication of the Levirate connection when the deceased childless man's widow is related to the surviving brother in a relationship prohibited by the Torah, that is, if she is the sister of the surviving brother's wife. The potential conflict between the prohibition of consanguinity (and incest) and the requirement of Levirate marriage is worked out in the Yerushalmi. If Heaven may be said to intervene, the Levirate connection may prove null. No rite of removing the shoe is carried out, just as, at the death of a husband who has produced offspring, no writ of divorce is necessary to sever the marital bond.

Neither of the two issues is immediately central to the law of the Mishnah at Yebamot. Nevertheless, they are of special interest to us in this discussion. The first concerns issues arising among the brothers as to the selection of the particular Levir. The second concerns issues arising in establishing the fact of the husband's death. A representative treatment is as follows:

### MISHNAH-TRACTATE YEBAMOT 4:5–6

It is the duty of the oldest surviving brother to enter into Levirate marriage. [If] he did not want to do so, they pass in turn to all the other brothers. [If] they [all] did not want to do so, they go back to the oldest and say to him, "Yours is the duty! Either undergo the rite of removing the shoe or enter into Levirate marriage."

[If the Levir proposed to] suspend [his decision, waiting] for a youngster to grow up, or for an adult to come from overseas, or for a deaf-mute or an idiot [to recover sound or sense], they do not listen to him. But they say to him: "Yours is the duty. Either undergo the rite of removing the shoe or enter into Levirate marriage."

The Torah leaves open the question which of the surviving brothers bears the responsibility of Levirate marriage. The law of the Mishnah then articulates conflict among them ("if he did not want to do so . . ."). Its resolution is through the rules of process. The oldest comes first here as in other matters, for instance, the right of a double portion in inheritance. Others in sequence address the obligation. But it is, in the end, the responsibility of the eldest. The systemic interest is in carrying out the rite, and it is realized when the priority of the eldest surviving brother is carried over from one transaction, inheritance, to the other, Levirate connection. If that is the correct consideration, then what the sages have done is simply extend the metaphor of Levirate connection—inheriting the deceased, childless brother's relationship—to the broader framework of rules of primogeniture.

The principal issue of conflict set forth in Yebamot is whether the husband actually died, and, if so, whose testimony suffices to establish the fact of the matter. The conflict, we see, is between the wife and other women in relationship to the same man: his mother, his sister, his other wives, and others whose status or property are affected by the husband's alleged death.

#### MISHNAH-TRACTATE YEBAMOT 15:4

All are believed to testify in her behalf [that her husband has died], except for (1) her mother-in-law, (2) the daughter of her mother-in-law, (3) her co-wife, (4) her sister-in-law [who will enter Levirate marriage in case the husband has died childless], and (5) the daughter of her husband [by another marriage]. What is the difference between evidence for [severing a marital relationship] through a writ of divorce and [evidence for doing so] through death? The written document [of divorce] proves the matter. [If] one witness says, "He died," and she remarried, and then another witness comes and says, "He did not die," lo, this woman does not go forth [from the second marriage]. [If] one witness says, "He died," and two witnesses say, "He did not die," then even though she has remarried, she goes forth. Two witnesses say, "He died," and one witness says, "He did not die," even though she has not remarried, she may remarry.

When it comes to matters of personal status, a person is believed to be truthful so far as he or she is concerned, but not with regard to other parties; hence the matter of status permits anomalies, as we saw in Qiddushin. Here too, what a woman says is accepted for herself, but the implications for others who are affected by her status are not realized. Any conflict of interest between the various female relatives of the deceased requires resolution. A woman may not testify with the result that her co-wife is freed from the marital bond; she is believed about herself, but not about her co-wife. A woman also may not give unsupported testimony that frees her of the Levirate bond. Then who are the parties to the dispute? A woman who wishes to be free of the Levirate obligation clearly takes one side. But, since others are not affected by her testimony, the nay-sayer can only be the sages responsible for the proper maintenance of the standards of the Torah for Israel.

The conflict is between the woman who wishes to free herself of the Levirate obligation and other women with an interest in their status by reason of her claim. But that is not the center of the matter; that is a mere matter of rules of evidence. What is at the heart is conflict between the Torah's law and the woman's interest. Here the law of the Mishnah introduces conflicts among Israelite women to register its concern that the Torah's law be realized in an honest and conscientious manner.

I believe we can identify the following points of conflict between Israelites in their family units: (1) brothers equally obligated to undertake the Levirate obligation; (2) co-wives (and other women) affected by a change in the status of one of the set. In the former case, the law of the Mishnah invokes primogeniture—as a matter of principle, the firstborn bears the ultimate responsibility. In the latter, it assures that the Levirate obligation is not lightly disposed of, preventing a woman from avoiding it merely on her own say-so. As to the conflict among the women attached to the deceased, the law of the Mishnah invokes the familiar principle that we believe a person as to what she says about herself, but not about the implications of that statement for the status of third parties.

The spirit of matters is expressed in a famous passage that asserts that, despite differences of opinion, the protagonists of conflicting viewpoints nonetheless conducted themselves in a spirit of amity. What that means is, marriages deemed unlawful by one or another party would produce offspring deemed lawful by both—a profound anomaly indeed. The position of the House of Hillel, which is the normative law, is given first. Then Mishnah Yebamot 1:4 proceeds to reflect on the consequences of the conflict of opinion between the two Houses in Israel. The consequences are alleged to have been nil.

### Mishnah-tractate Yebamot 1:1, 4

1:1 Fifteen women [who are near of kin to their deceased, childless husband's brother] [because they cannot enter into Levirate marriage with the deceased childless husband's brother also] exempt their co-wives, and the co-wives, from the rite of removing the shoe [*halisah*] and from Levirate marriage, without limit. And these are they . . . —lo, these exempt their co-wives and the co-wives of their co-wives, from rite of removing the shoe and from Levirate marriage, without limit.

1:4 The House of Shammai declare the co-wives permitted [to enter into Levirate marriage with] the other brothers. And the House of Hillel declare [them] prohibited. [If] they have performed the rite of removing the shoe, the House of Shammai declare [them] invalid [for marriage with] the priesthood. And the House of Hillel declare [them] valid. [If] they have entered into Levirate marriage, the House of Shammai declare them valid [for marriage with the priesthood]. And the House of Hillel declare them invalid.

Even though these declare prohibited and those permit, these declare invalid and those declare valid, the House of Shammai did not refrain from taking wives from the women of the House of Hillel, nor [did] the House of Hillel [refrain from taking wives from the women] of the House of Shammai.

[And despite] all those decisions regarding matters of cleanness or uncleanness in which these did declare clean and those unclean, they did not refrain from preparing things requiring preparation in a state of cleanness in dependence on one another.

The difference of opinion between the Houses concerns the rule (stated in 1:1) on the standing of the co-wives as to Levirate marriage, in a case in which one of the co-wives cannot enter into Levirate marriage while the others may. The normative law is, if one of the co-wives cannot carry out the Levirate connection, *all of the co-wives* are exempt. Now if one does not accept that view, then the co-wives do enter into Levirate marriage. But, from the Hillelite viewpoint, that is an illegal marriage; the parties to it are not legally permitted to wed. The allegation before us is, even in so serious a violation of the law, the Houses not only treated one another with dignity and respect but intermarried. Clearly, those who framed matters in this way deemed the resolution of conflict to constitute the transcendent interest, even at the expense of observance of the law of the Torah!

## Where Conflict Is Resolved by the Law of the Mishnah, and Why Conflict Is Neglected

This survey yields a short list of conflicts between families that are addressed by the law of the Mishnah:

| | |
|---|---|
| Qiddushin: | the laws of consanguinity (Lev. 18) |
| Ketubot: | the bride price (Deut. 22:13–21); proper conduct of the husband and the wife vis-à-vis the Torah of Moses; oath-taking |
| Sotah: | none |
| Gittin: | none |
| Yebamot: | which brother is Levir (Deut. 25:5–10); the laws of consanguinity, now with regard to Levirate obligations of the childless widow |

This little catalogue produces an obvious point. The kind of conflict taken up in the law of the Mishnah is one that has a bearing upon the law of Scripture. For that reason it is a kind of conflict that mars the perfection of corporate Israel—perfection defined as realization of the imperatives of Scripture. Where the law of the Mishnah spells out conflict and its resolution, at stake will be the perfection of Israel from the perspective of the Torah.

How then do we explain the silence of the law of the Mishnah on conflict in connection with Gittin and Sotah? In the former case, the Torah scarcely figures (Deut. 24:1–4 hardly generates the program of Gittin or even relates to it). In the latter case, the Torah itself defines the conflict and decrees the rite that resolves it. So the condition that should signal an interest in the definition and resolution of conflict is a detail of the law of Scripture that yields contention not resolved by the mechanisms provided by Scripture itself. The interest of corporate Israel governs in the broadest and most general way: Israel's inner strife demands attention at those points at which Israel's embodiment of Scripture's vision of the kingdom of priests and the holy people is affected.

Thus, when classes of Israelites contend, what matters above all is that the contending parties subordinate their dispute to that larger obligation incumbent upon them, that is, that they remember the interest of corporate Israel—the realization, by the Israelite social order, of the rules of sanctification of God's name that form the imperative of Scripture. Just as corporate Israel transcends the interest of individual Israelites, while affording full opportunity for legitimate individuation, so corporate Israel will interest itself in conflicts between classes of Israel, that is, when God's name is at stake. So much for the intermediate building block, the family. What about the household—the family at work?

# 10 THE ISRAELITE HOUSEHOLD: RESPONSIBILITY AND INTENTIONALITY

## Tractates Baba Qamma and Baba Mesia (Chapters 1-5)

### When Households Come into Conflict

The law of the Mishnah fosters cooperation and sharing between and among households and families. The central idea is that Israel attains perfection when all things are in place, at rest, and in proportion as at creation. The Mishnah's sages deem indicative of perfection traits of the social order such as consistency, immutability, coherence, and stability. Conflict mars the stability, hence the perfection of Israel. The kind of conflict addressed by the law of the Mishnah comes about principally in connection with property, subject to intersecting claims among Israelites in their family or in their household units. Corporate Israel produces no interior conflict, only strife with gentiles and idolaters; and the Israelite individual not within family or household on his or her own engages in no conflict that registers socially.

That is shown by a simple fact of the organization of the law of the Mishnah. Of the six divisions that form the principal parts of the Mishnah, only the third, Nashim ("Women," "Families"), and the fourth, Neziqin ("Damages"), explicitly spell out and resolve conflicts between and among Israelites. These concern families (Nashim) or households (Neziqin). In the law of the Mishnah the locus of conflict rarely centers upon collisions between isolated Israelites. Conflict takes place between householders. The other four divisions focus on issues other than conflict in the construction of corporate Israel. True, the legal exposition in the divisions of Zeraᶜim ("Agriculture") and Moᶜed ("Appointed Times") refers to points of conflict between priests and Israelites or between (in context) meticulously observant and generically observant Israelites. The differences concern details, but not main points, of the law of the Torah. The observant sector of Israel constructs its response to the less-than-perfectly observant sector within the prevailing assumption that the non-observant Israelite expresses good will for the peculiar convictions of the observant sector and behaves responsibly.

A good example was seen in Mishnah-tractate Erubin. When Israelites of diverse convictions concerning the importance and effect of the fictive meal or boundary share the same courtyard, some participating, others not, in the fictive fusion-meal that forms of the whole a single domain, the law of the Mishnah controls for that complication. It does so by telling those who rely on the domain-fusing power of the fictive meal or boundary line how to go about their business. The law of the Mishnah does not acknowledge the conflict or resolve it as it does when it tells how to deal with a man who claims to have betrothed a woman, while the woman denies the matter. No hint suggests that the non-participating Israelite can be coerced to conform. But when it comes to conflict over personal status, the court acts.

Another evasion of conflict was seen in Tohorot, where the same mixtures of populations interact in matters concerning cultic cleanness of food and drink, some households observing the taboos, others not. Here is an obvious occasion for conflict: whether or not a given law is efficacious or even applies, in the respective cases. But the law of the Mishnah does not portray such conflict or suggest that it requires resolution. No one suggests coercing or penalizing the Israelite who does not observe purity laws at home. The law of the Mishnah simply devises rules for confessing Israelites to accommodate their circumstance as best they can. These rules embody presuppositions about what such a nonobservant Israelite can be assumed to do or not to do. They provide for the observant Israelite to take responsibility for the action of the other, but never contemplate coercing him or her to keep the law.

The law of Mishnah-tractate Demaʿi, to take another instance of the matter, works out rules governing relationships between Israelites who tithe properly and those who do not. It negotiates the givens; it does not portray conflict resulting from them. The law of Demaʿi makes an entire class of Israelites responsible for the conduct of another entire class, without ever articulating cases or exemplifications of conflict between those two classes. When it comes to Purities, even the differences between those who meticulously observe the purity laws for secular, domestic meals and those who keep them only in Temple pilgrimages yield no contention of legal consequence. The law of the Mishnah simply assesses what the nonconfessing Israelite is likely to do and shapes rules accordingly. The conduct of the Temple rites in Holy Things show priesthood and laity in partnership for a shared activity. So when it comes to public disagreements on the law, the Mishnah's response is to assess the intention of those who do not affirm as required the observance of the indicated details of the law.

The Torah makes clear God's intense interest in the justice and equity of the Israelites' ordinary transactions among themselves. The Israelites are to form the kingdom of priests and the holy people. Their conduct with one another—the Torah's civil law insists in every line—shapes God's judgment of them and therefore dictates their fate. So the Mishnah's sages demonstrate what householders can do actively to participate in perfecting the social order through the results of their own and their chattels' conduct. Here the consideration of free will proves paramount: what the householder by an act of will has upset, the householder by an act of will must restore. With these general observations in hand, let us turn to the specifics.

### The Two Principal Parts of the Civil Law: Where Intention Does, or Does Not, Register

When it comes to the disposition of conflict over property in the civil law, intention is taken into account at some points and not at others. In *restoring* the status quo disrupted by damages or torts, the intentionality of the one who has done the damage or the tort comes into consideration in assessing responsibility, therefore damages. When, however, the law that serves to *maintain* the status quo is concerned, intentionality simply does not register.

That point of differentiation, between *restoring* and *preserving* the status quo, defines the governing criterion in the construction of the system of civil law—the civil law of the Mishnah stresses restoring and preserving the status quo. The first part aims at securing for all parties to a transaction a proper exchange so that value remains constant. The second undertakes designing and sustaining a social order aimed at an equitable structure and secured by ancient custom. We treat them separately. I have divided into two the civil law pertaining to conflict within Israel. In this chapter, I deal with the resolution of conflicts that necessitate restoring Israel's social order. In chapter 11, I will deal with maintaining that same social system in perfect stasis. As I said, intentionality figures in the former component of the system of civil law, not in the latter.

Called by Aramaic names, the three tractates of the civil law, Baba Qamma, "The First Gate," Baba Mesia, "The Middle Gate," and Baba Batra, "The Last Gate," consist of ten chapters each.[1] Among these thirty chapters the first fifteen (all of Baba Qamma and the first half of Baba Mesia) involve the *restoration* to stasis of the Israelite household's property and material condition, which through injury done to an Israelite householder by another Israelite householder has been set into imbalance—that is, done deliberately or accidentally by an act of overreaching, aggrandizement, or a tort. In that connection matters of malice and other issues of intentionality intervene, for culpability is proportionate to intentionality. The second set of fifteen chapters involves the *preservation* of Israel's steady-state condition. There, issues of inten-

---

[1] Internal, formal evidence validates the chapter divisions, not only printers' conventions imposed centuries after the document came to closure.

tionality simply do not register. Here, in brief is the picture of the whole, by tractates and chapters.

### I. ILLICIT TRANSACTIONS; RESTORING ORDER.
### INTENTIONALITY REGISTERS
#### Baba Qamma
    i. Damage by Chattels 1:1–6:6
    ii. Damages Done by Persons 7:1–10:10
#### Baba Mesia
    iii. The Disposition of Other Peoples' Possessions; Bailments (property left on deposit with a guardian, or bailee, by the owner) 1:1–3:12
    iv. Illicit Commercial Transactions. Overcharge, misrepresentation, usury 4:1–5:11

### II. LICIT TRANSACTIONS; PRESERVING ORDER.
### INTENTIONALITY DOES NOT MATTER
#### Baba Mesia
    v. Hiring Workers. Rentals and Bailments 6:1–8:3
#### Baba Mesia, Baba Batra
    vi. Real Estate B.M. 8:4–10:6, B.B. 1:1–5:5
#### Baba Batra
    vii. Licit Commercial Transactions 5:6–7:4
    viii. Inheritances and Wills. Other Commercial and legal Documents 8:1–10:8

The entire repertoire lays itself out as a huge essay on the role of humanity's intentionality—the exercise of will, the making of private plans—in the ordering of Israel's households. All topics that I have grouped as illicit transactions involve righting the wrongs done by people on their own account. When free will is taken into consideration, encompassing negligence and malice, the social order requires forceful intervention to right the balance upset by individual aggression. Some licit transactions permit individual intentionality to register, specifically, those freely entered into and fairly balanced among contracting parties. And some licit transactions leave no space for the will of the participants and their idiosyncratic plans. Considerations of fairness take over and exclude any engagement with the private and the personal. So Israel's social order takes account of intentionality, especially controlling for the damage that ill will brings about.

Intentionality or attitude matters in situations of conflict when the attitude of both parties makes all the difference, since to resolve conflicting claims, we have in the end to conciliate all parties to a common outcome. In such cases intentionality or attitude forms the critical determinant for restoring and sustaining balance and order. Parties to an exchange—householders and their property—are now responsible to one another, and they must intend the outcome to be a proportionate and equal exchange of value. Both parties must accept the outcome, that is, form at the end the same attitude toward the transaction. A claim of ownership ends in any act of despair. Once the owner of property despairs of the possibility of recovering it, the law holds he has relinquished title. Responsibility is proportionate to the attitude of the bailiff, that is, to the degree of accountability that he has accepted to begin with. Such is the use of intentionality in the restoration and maintenance of the social order.

But in what instances do we dismiss all considerations of will or attitude as null, even when parties to an exchange concur? In market transactions true value overrides the attitude of the players. Whether or not the parties can agree on the price, the Torah too must approve. So too usury is never permitted, even when the borrower consents to pay it. Broadly held expectations govern: whether those of custom or of the Torah's own law. The Torah's law is not relative to the will of humanity. Established custom defines the norm for humanity. In these two matters, intentionality possesses no power, since attitude or personal will serves no purpose in restoring or sustaining the balances of a well-ordered society.

What message emerges as we move from the illicit to the licit, the abnormal to the normal? The transactions that all together form the ordinary life of inner Israel, Israel in its households, yield two matching propositions. First, when it comes to acts that disrupt the social order, the householder is responsible for what he does. But, second, when we turn to transactions that sustain the ordinary relationships within Israel, the householder's proper intentionality takes over. Then personal will forms only one element in a complex transaction. Where wills clash, compromise is invoked. Where the Torah imposes its own rule, intentionality is null. Publicly accepted custom and procedure take the paramount position. In cases of negligence or malfeasance, people bear responsibility for what they have done—so much for the first half of the Babas, the ten chapters of Baba Qamma and the first five of the ten chapters of Baba Mesia, which are treated in the rest of this chapter.

## Where Intention Registers in Context: Tractate Baba Qamma

The message of the law of the Mishnah on householders taking responsibility for their own and their property's actions cannot be missed in the ringing opening words of the following, which I have italicized:

### MISHNAH-TRACTATE BABA QAMMA 1:4

What they [various animate and inanimate causes of damages] have in common is that they customarily do damage and taking care of them is your responsibility. And when one of them has caused damage, the [owner] of that which causes the damage is liable to pay compensation.

*In the case of anything of which I am liable to take care, I am deemed to render possible whatever damage it may do. If I am deemed to have rendered possible part of the damage it may do, I am liable for compensation as if [I have] made possible all of the damage it may do.*

That remarkably eloquent formulation contains the entire message of Baba Qamma and the first half of Baba Mesia. Since householders undertake to assume responsibility for what they do, their liability is assessed always in just proportion to causation. Within Israel's social order, what God wants a person to do is take responsibility for his or her own actions, accountability for the results of what chattel belonging to him or her has done—no more, no less. Responsibility begins in right attitude. To watch over their chattel, people must form the intentionality of taking responsibility for their actions; this they must do by an act of will. That is why the whole of Baba Qamma plays itself out as an exercise in the definition of the valid intentionality in transactions involving damage and conflict. Where people diminish others, they must willingly take responsibility for their deed of omission or commission (as the tractate unfolds).

But several principles intersect, and intentionality or will is only one of them. The law of the Mishnah holds that we are responsible for what we do and what we cause, but we are not responsible (or not responsible in the same degree) for what we cannot control or even foresee. So the law asks, How does our action or lack of action relate to the consequence of what we do or do not do? If we do not know that an act has caused a result, we cannot hold responsible the person who has done the act for the consequences he or she has brought about. The law works out these gradations between total culpability or blame, by reason of one's forming the efficient cause without mitigating considerations, and total absolution from culpability and blame, by reason of one's bearing no responsibility whatsoever for what has happened: (1) responsibility for *all* damages done, because the event that has caused loss and damage is voluntary and foreseeable, not the result of overwhelming external force; preventable; brought about by willful action; the result of culpable knowledge; consequent upon deliberate choice, not mere negligence; (2) responsibility for *the greater part* of the damages that are done, because the damage is foreseeable; not the result of overwhelming external force; preventable; thus in the event the ignorance is classified as culpable; but not voluntary; (3) responsibility for *the lesser part* of the damages that are done, because the damage is foreseeable; but the result of overwhelming external force and not preventable, thus: involuntary, but the result of culpable ignorance and negligence; (4) no responsibility *at all*, the event being involuntary, the result of overwhelming external force, not foreseeable; hence, inculpable ignorance and possibly even pure chance.

We therefore identify three operative criteria in the law—points of differentiation in the analysis of events and the actions that produce them, which form a cubic grid, with, in theory, nine gradations of blame and responsibility and consequent culpability: (1) an event produced by an action that is voluntary as opposed to one that is involuntary; (2) an event that is foreseeable as opposed to one that is not foreseeable, or an action the consequences of which are foreseeable as opposed to one where the consequences are not foreseeable; (3) an event that is preventable as opposed to one that is not preventable; or an action that is necessary and therefore blameless as opposed to one that is not.

Thus we may construct a layered or dimensional grid: one layer formed of considerations of what is voluntary vs. involuntary; the second layer, of what is foreseeable vs. not foreseeable; the third layer, of what is preventable vs. not preventable. That permits us to identify an efficient cause that is voluntary, foreseeable, and preventable; voluntary, foreseeable, and not preventable; involuntary, foreseeable, and preventable; involuntary, not foreseeable, and not preventable; and so on. What is voluntary, foreseeable, and preventable imposes maximum liability for restoration. The householder cannot blame his or her ox, nor impose upon passersby in the public way the responsibility to accommodate the obstacles he or she has set up. Here, then, is a case of conflict that is articulated, the resolution of which is fully worked out in a manner particular to the case at hand, not resolved by imposition of standard rules that are merely instantiated.

### MISHNAH-TRACTATE BABA QAMMA 3:1–3

He who leaves a jug in the public domain, and someone else came along and stumbled on it and broke it—[the one who broke it] is exempt. And if [the one who broke it] was injured by it, the owner of the jug is liable [to pay damages for] his injury. [If] his jug was broken in the public domain, and someone slipped on the water, or was hurt by the shards, he is liable.

He who pours water out into the public domain, and someone else was injured on it, is liable [to pay compensation for] his injury. He who put away thorns or glass, and he who makes his fence out of thorns, and a fence which fell into the public way—and others were injured by them—he is liable [to pay compensation for] their injury.

He who brings out his straw and stubble into the public domain to turn them into manure and someone else was injured on them—he is liable [to pay compensation for] his injury. But whoever grabs them first effects possession of them.

The conflict, "he who leaves his jug," focuses on the classification of causality: direct or efficient. Who is the responsible party—the one who left the jug or the one who stumbled on the jug and broke it? Each has a defense, the one who left the jug is not the direct cause of the breakage, and the one who is the direct cause is not the efficient cause. In this classification of causation, the efficient cause is assigned full blame.

The following two segments continue the exposition, but in these added rules there is no doubt as to who is responsible for the injury; it is the person who has taken over public domain for private use. The explicit adjudication of conflicting claims of responsibility is made on the basis of diverse classes of causation—direct as opposed to indirect, proximate as opposed to efficient. The Mishnaic system takes the position that the efficient cause bears full responsibility. The Tosefta introduces a further distinction: one may save one's property at someone else's expense only when one fears that the property will be damaged at some point in the future. If the damage has been done, one may not injure someone else to save one's own property from further damages.

MISHNAH-TRACTATE BABA QAMMA 3:5–7

This one comes along with his jar, and that one comes along with his beam—[if] the jar of this one was broken by the beam of that one, [the owner of the beam] is exempt, for this one has every right to walk along [in the street], and that one has every right to walk along [in the same street]

Two who were going along in the public domain, one was running, the other ambling, or both of them running, and they injured one another, both of them are exempt.

He who chops wood in private property, and [the chips] injured someone in public domain; in public domain, and [the chips] injured someone in private property; in private property, and [the chips] injured someone in someone else's private property—he is liable.

The injured party claims damages. But the defendant counters that he or she had every right to be in that particular place and do that particular thing, namely, utilizing the public domain for a licit purpose. The one who suffered the damage bears responsibility for his or her own loss. If, by contrast, one chops wood, the licit activity produces a secondary effect (the chips) which must be taken into account; and for what they do, he or she is responsible under the stated condition. So this set of cases, in the aggregate, makes the point that all have equal rights to utilize public domain; none but the householder has unrestricted rights in private domain; where what one does in one domain has secondary effects for the other domain, the householder is responsible for those effects. There are two matters here: responsibility and the distinction between private and public domain. The former retains its primary standing. But the latter leads to complications that limit complete freedom of action. If licit action in a householder's own domain produces secondary effects in the public domain, the householder is held responsible.

MISHNAH-TRACTATE BABA QAMMA 3:11

An ox which was running after another ox, and [that latter ox] was injured—this one claims, "Your ox did the injury," and that one claims, "Not so, but it was hit by a stone"—he who wants to exact [compensation] from his fellow bears the burden of proof. If two [oxen] were running after one [ox]—this one says, "Your ox did the damage," and that one says, "Your ox did the damage"—both of them are exempt. [But] if both of them belonged to the same man, both of them [oxen] are liable [to pay compensation].

[If] one of them was big and one little—the one whose ox has suffered an injury says, "The big one did the damage," but the one who is responsible for the damage says, "Not so, but the little one did the damage"—

one of them was deemed harmless, and one was an attested danger—

the one whose ox has suffered an injury says, "The one which was the attested danger has done the damage," but the one who is responsible for the damage says, "Not so, but the one which had been deemed harmless did the damage,—

he who wants to exact [compensation] from his fellow bears the burden of proof.

Here is a well-articulated dispute, perhaps the most common type that the law of the Mishnah adjudicates: a conflict as to actualities. When the mere facts of the matter are subject to dispute, then the principle that is invoked is straightforward: prove your case. The same was true of the law in Qiddushin, where a person's claim affects that person but, absent adequate proof, no one else. The system demands that the claim be proved. The status quo shifts only in response to establishing what has actually taken place.

### MISHNAH-TRACTATE BABA QAMMA 5:2–3

(1) The potter who brought his pots into the courtyard of the householder without permission, and the beast of the householder broke them—[the householder] is exempt. (2) And if [the beast] was injured on them, the owner of the pots is liable. (3) If [however], he brought them in with permission, the owner of the courtyard is liable, (1) [If] he brought his produce into the courtyard of the householder without permission, and the beast of the householder ate them up, [the householder] is exempt. (2) And if [the beast] was injured by them, the owner of the produce is liable. (3) But if he brought them in with permission, the owner of the courtyard is liable.

(1) [If] he brought his ox into the courtyard of a householder without permission, and the ox of the householder gored it, or the dog of the householder bit it, [the householder] is exempt. (2) [If] that [ox] gored the ox of the householder, [the owner] is liable. [If] it fell into his well and polluted its water, [the owner of the ox] is liable. [If] his father or son was in [the well and was killed], [the owner of the ox] pays ransom money. (3) But if he brought it in with permission, the owner of the courtyard is liable.

The owner of the pots claims that the householder is responsible for the breakage. The householder claims that the pots were located in his or her courtyard without permission. If so, the householder has not accepted responsibility for the pots; he or she is not in the status of a bailiff, and the pots do not constitute a licit bailment—deposit of goods left for storage. The issue of responsibility is worked out by appeal to the matter of responsibility for what happens in the location controlled by the householder, a key consideration in assigning culpability. The potter had no right to put his pots where they were; the potter is responsible for what has happened to them. The system concerns itself with assigning responsibility, now demanding that the circumstance of ownership enter in once more. Here, if the one who owns the location of the transaction has assumed responsibility for what is situated in his or her property the householder is responsible, otherwise not. So the resolution of conflict once more focuses upon types and degrees of culpability, measured against the exercise of will by the one whose intentionality governs: the householder.

### MISHNAH-TRACTATE BABA QAMMA 5:6; 6:1–3

A pit belonging to two partners—one of them passed by it and did not cover it, and the second one also did not cover it, the second one is liable. [If] the first one covered it up, and the second one came along and found it uncovered and did not cover it up, the second one is liable.

[If] he covered it up in a proper way, and an ox or an ass fell into it and died, he is exempt. [If] he did not cover it up in the proper way and an ox or an ass fell into it and died, he is liable.

[If] it fell forward [not into the pit] because of the sound of the digging, [the owner of the pit] is liable.

[If] it fell backward [not into the pit] because of the sound of the digging, [the owner of the pit] is exempt.

[If] an ox carrying its trappings fell into it and they were broken, an ass and its trappings and they were split, [the owner of the pit] is liable for the beast but exempt for the trappings.

[If] an ox belonging to a deaf-mute, an idiot, or a minor fell into it, [the owner] is liable.

[If] a little boy or girl, a slave boy or a slave girl [fell into it], he is exempt [from paying a ransom].

He who brings a flock into a fold and shut the gate before it as required, but [the flock] got out and did damage, is exempt. [If] he did not shut the gate before it as required, and [the flock] got out and did damage, he is liable. [If the fence] was broken down by night, or thugs broke it down, and [the flock] got out and did damage, he is exempt. [If] the thugs took [the flock] out, [and the flock did damage], the thugs are liable.

[If] he left it in the sun, [or if] he handed it over to a deaf-mute, idiot, or minor, and [the flock] got out and did damage, he is liable. [If] he handed it over to a shepherd, the shepherd takes the place of the owner [as to liability].

[If the flock] [accidentally] fell into a vegetable patch and derived benefit [from the produce], [the owner must] pay compensation [only] for the value of the benefit [derived by the flock]. [If the flock] went down in the normal way and did damage, [the owner must] pay compensation for the [actual] damage which [the flock] inflicted.

He who stacks sheaves in the field of his fellow without permission, and the beast of the owner of the field ate them up, [the owner of the field] is exempt. And [if] it was injured by them, the owner of the sheaves is liable. But if he had put his sheaves there with permission, the owner of the field is liable.

Since both partners are responsible for keeping the pit covered, in theory they share equally in the obligation to compensate the claimant damaged by the pit. But the abstract theory of the matter conceals a complicated reality. Both partners had the opportunity to prevent the accident. The first of the two to pass by, however, is not responsible if the second went by later. The last to pass the pit is deemed the efficient cause, through negligence, of what has happened. What if the second had not come by? Then the first owner would bear responsibility. If the first owner covered it up and, while he or she was standing there watching, it became uncovered, he or she is liable for not covering the pit again. Here the direct cause is also the efficient cause. One carries out one's responsibility by making adequate provision.

Once the owner hires someone else to do the work, the latter takes over the responsibility. In these circumstances, the injured party has no claim on the householder. If, as in the case of the flock, suitable provision was not made, the householder, of course, is responsible. Where the householder has not accepted responsibility, the householder is not in the status of bailiff. If responsibility was accepted, then the responsible person is in the status of an unpaid bailiff. Causality once more enters the fray.

The conflict between the two owners is resolved by appeal to the efficient cause, which is the failure of the second, not the first of the partners to come by. Much depends on covering the pit in the proper manner; here too, negligence involves a haphazard provision for the danger. Responsibility is, moreover, for primary damages, to the beast, but not secondary ones, to the trappings or the yoke.

### MISHNAH-TRACTATE BABA QAMMA 9:3–4

[If the householder] gave [something] to craftsmen to repair, and they spoiled [the object], they are liable to pay compensation.

[If] he gave to a joiner a box, chest, or cupboard to repair, and he spoiled it, he is liable to pay compensation.

A builder who took upon himself to destroy a wall, and who smashed the rocks or did damage is liable to pay compensation.

[If] he was tearing down the wall on one side, and it fell down on the other side, he is exempt. But if it is because of the blow [which he gave it], he is liable.

He who hands over wool to a dyer, and the [dye in the] cauldron burned it, [the dyer] pays the value of the wool.

[If] he dyed it in a bad color, if [the wool] increased in value more than the outlay [of the dyer], [the owner of the wool] pays him the money he has laid out in the process of dyeing.

But if the outlay of the dyer is greater than the increase in value of the wool, [the owner] pays him back only the value of the improvement.

The householder gives the craftsman materials for processing, for example, an object to repair, or a wall to dismantle, or wool to dye. Here again the conflict of claims is deemed resolved: the craftsman is responsible to the householder. The only issue is, How, in the case of poor craftsmanship, is the householder compensated? A craftsman who destroys the materials has to pay the householder their value. At issue is the disposition of the bailment—property left on deposit—assigned by the householder to the craftsman. The conflict is resolved by the imposition upon the craftsman of the defined status, paid bailiff, with the consequences for the case at hand. The systemic interest seems to me to narrow down to the identification of the pertinent metaphor: To what established classification of transactions does the present set conform? Issues of balance and fairness are set aside. There is, for example, no provision for the craftsman to show absence of negligence but presence of due diligence.

### MISHNAH-TRACTATE BABA QAMMA 10:2

[If] excise collectors took one's ass and gave him another ass, [if] thugs took his garment and gave him another garment, lo, these are his, because the original owners have given up hope of getting them back.

He who saves something from a river, from a raid, or from thugs, if the owner has given up hope of getting them back, lo, these belong to him.

And so a swarm of bees: If the owner had given up hope of getting it back, lo, this belongs to him.

And one may walk through the field of his fellow to get back his swarm of bees. But if he did damage, he pays compensation for the damage which he did. But he may not cut off a branch of his tree [to retrieve the swarm, even] on condition that he pay damages for it.

Who owns property forcibly seized from one owner and handed over to another? The conflict is between the two owners, the one who has lost property and the one to whom it has been handed over. If we have reason to suppose that the original owner has given up hope of getting the property back, then the new owner holds on to what has been given, establishing title to the object to which title has been relinquished. The key language is given in the Tosefta (10:24): If the owner continued to go looking for them, or if they were in some other place, then, these remain the possession of the owner. Invoking the consideration of attitude, the system resolves the conflict in such a way that the will and expectation of the parties to the conflict over the ownership of the stolen property are realized. So long as the original owner maintains his or her claim, that claim preserves his or her title to the property; once he or she abandons hope of recovering the property, the one who then holds it gains title.

#### MISHNAH-TRACTATE BABA QAMMA 10:4

This one is coming along with his jar of wine, and that one is coming along with his jug of honey—the jug of honey cracked—and this one poured out his wine and saved the honey in his jar, he has a claim only for his wages. And if he said, "I'll save yours if you pay me back for mine," [the owner of the honey] is liable to pay him back.

[If] the river swept away his ass and the ass of his fellow, his being worth a maneh and his fellow's worth two hundred [zuz] [twice as much], [if] he then left his own and saved that of his fellow, he has a claim only for his wages. But if he said, "I'll save yours, if you pay me back for mine," [the owner of the better ass] is liable to pay him back.

The dispute concerns the claim of one party that he or she has incurred a loss so as to save the property of the other. The defendant rightly denies responsibility. Where no agreement in advance has been reached, the sole claim is to wages for the plaintiff's effort. But if there is an agreement to compensate for the loss, then that agreement prevails. The conflicting claims are settled by appeal to the status of any preexisting agreement. One may not invoke an unstipulated agreement that exceeds the limits set by established custom. One has an established right to be compensated for labor, which the beneficiary has implicitly affirmed. Any further claim, without prior negotiation, is overreaching.

#### MISHNAH-TRACTATE BABA QAMMA 10:5

He who stole a field from his fellow, and bandits seized it from him—if it is a blow [from which the whole] district [suffered], he may say to him, "Lo, there is yours before you." But if it is because [of the deeds] of the thief [in particular], he is liable to replace it for him with another field.

[If] a river swept it away, he may say to him, "Lo, there is yours before you."

If the land-grabber can claim, "Had I not taken your land, you would have lost it in the general conflagration (in which I have, in fact, lost it, too)," the defendant need not pay compensation. But if the land-grabber bears particular responsibility for the matter, and the land-grabber himself then lost the land, the land-grabber must compensate the original owner by replacing the lost land with another field. The issue is, has the thief personally become a victim, in which case the thief does not have to compensate the original owner? Only in the case of a general catastrophe, has the thief become a victim. Otherwise, the thief has to make up the loss of the original owner. The land-grabber is not responsible for what affects everyone, but is certainly responsible for what takes place by reason of his or her personal intervention.

### MISHNAH-TRACTATE BABA QAMMA 10:7–8

He who says to his fellow, "I have stolen from you . . . ," "You have lent something to me . . . ,"You have deposited something with me . . . ," ". . . and I don't know whether or not I returned [the object] to you"—is liable to pay him restitution.

But if he said to him, "I don't know whether I stole something from you," ". . . whether you lent me something," ". . . whether you deposited something with me," he is exempt from paying restitution.

He who steals a lamb from a flock and [unbeknownst to the owner] returned it, and it died or was stolen again, is liable to make it up.

[If] the owner did not know either that it had been stolen or that it had been returned, and he counted up the flock and it was complete, then [the thief] is exempt.

If the person concedes having in hand property belonging to the other party but does not know whether or not the property has been returned, he or she is liable to pay restitution for the other's claim to that property. But if the person does not concede the claim and is doubtful about whether the claim is a valid one, he or she does not have to pay restitution. So too, if someone stole property and returned it and the property was lost or stolen again, the thief must make up the loss. But if the owner knew nothing of the transaction, then the owner has not laid claim, and the thief is exempt. The Tosefta's cases, not cited, underscore the issue of responsibility and intentionality. If the thief has informed the owner of the transaction, then he or she has restored the property and the owner is responsible for his property. If not, then the thief continues to bear responsibility. The main consideration is the awareness of the victim of the fact that he or she has lost property. If the owner is informed, then the thief who restored the property is exempt from having to pay restitution. The owner has responsibility for his property. But if the victim is uninformed as to the transaction, then the thief bears responsibility for the property that has been taken, whatever becomes of it.

Clearly, conflicts involving issues of responsibility and causation, will and intentionality, predominate. These, moreover, form a congeries of closely connected analyses. In short, disputes involving considerations of causation, translated into rulings on responsibility, predominate in the consideration of contentious relationships between householders or between householders and other categories of society—land-grabbers, craftsmen, and the like. Stated differently: the conflict that the law of the Mishnah deems systemically consequential involves the resolution of claims as to who bears responsibility for loss or damage. The issues in general terms contain no surprises; what govern are considerations of responsibility or causation or intentionality. These considerations prove particular to the kinds of conflict between householders that predominate in Baba Qamma. Once the principle is adopted, *In the case of anything of which I am liable to take care, I am deemed to render possible whatever damage it may do*, the focus of consequential conflict upon issues of responsibility, encompassing intentionality, extending outward to considerations of causality, is predetermined.

## Where Intention Registers in Context:
## Tractate Baba Mesia Chapters 1–5

Mishnah-tractate Baba Qamma concludes with analysis of the law of restoring what has been stolen; Baba Mesia starts with restoring what has been lost. Then it shifts to a new topic, the law governing transactions of an equitable character between buyer and seller, then, employer and employee. In the former case the law of the Mishnah focuses on the counterpart to theft, which is overcharging and usury. In the latter, we proceed to an account of what each party owes the other. With the matter of overreaching, we come to the end of the exposition of how the social order is restored to the condition of stasis—stability, order, balance—that signifies perfection. The corpus of compositions pertinent to our inquiry is modest, but right from the outset, the points of contention are vividly portrayed.

### MISHNAH-TRACTATE BABA MESIA 1:1-2

Two lay hold of a cloak—this one says, "I found it!"—and that one says, "I found it!"—this one says, "It's all mine!"—and that one says, "It's all mine!"—this one takes an oath that he possesses no less a share of it than half, and that one takes an oath that he possesses no less a share of it than half, and they divide it up. This one says, "It's all mine!"—and that one says, "Half of it is mine!" the one who says, "It's all mine!" takes an oath that he possesses no less of a share of it than three parts, and the one who says, "Half of it is mine!," takes an oath that he possesses no less a share of it than a fourth part. This one then takes three shares, and that one takes the fourth.

Two were riding on a beast, or one was riding and one was leading it—this one says, "It's all mine!"—and that one says, "It's all mine!"—this one takes an oath that he possesses no less a share of it than half, and that one takes an oath that he possesses no less a share of it than half. And they divide it. But when they concede [that they found it together] or have witnesses to prove it, they divide [the beast's value] without taking an oath.

Faced with conflicting claims to title to an object, the law of the Mishnah immediately raises the issue of the oath, its principal means for resolving conflicts as to the facts of a case. But who takes the oath? Each legitimate claimant does so, and the only issue is, concerning what portion of the disputed object does the oath pertain? Here the conflict is articulated, but the resolution is made to depend on the mechanism of the oath. That is to say, the law of the Mishnah does not settle the conflict; it administers it. Since the oath is assigned in the presumption that the oath taker tells the truth and will not take God's name in vain, the systemic interest lies in defining what portion of the disputed object is subject to the person's oath. That represents a detail, and the main point is not to be missed: procedure predominates when facts do not clearly establish themselves.

### MISHNAH-TRACTATE BABA MESIA 1:3–4

[If] one was riding on a beast and saw a lost object, and said to his fellow, "Give it to me," [but the other] took it and said, "I take possession of it"—[the latter] has acquired possession of it. If after he gave it over [to the one riding on the beast], he said, "I acquired possession of it first," he has said nothing whatsoever.

[If] he saw a lost object and fell on it, and someone else came along and grabbed it, this one who grabbed it has acquired possession of it. [If] he saw [people] running after a lost object—after (1) a deer with a broken leg, (2) pigeons which could not fly, and he said, "My field has effected possession for me,"—it has effected possession for him. [If] (1) the deer was running along normally, or (2) [if] the pigeons were flying, and he said, "My field has effected possession for me," he has said nothing whatsoever.

The issue turns to how title is acquired to a lost object. The answer is, only by taking physical possession of the object; a mere declaration has no bearing. The second case complicates the matter. On the one side, if the moving object has come to rest in his or her domain, the owner of the domain may effect rights of possession by a declaration that the property has acquired possession on his or her behalf. If the object did not come to rest in his or her domain but merely passed over it, that has no effect. Again, mere words settle nothing, only an act effects valid claim to possession of ownerless objects. The dispute over the object is settled by assigning ownership to the one who actually takes hold of the object and declares possession. This is a variation on the norm of affirming the status quo.

### MISHNAH-TRACTATE BABA MESIA 2:11

[If one has to choose between seeking] what he has lost and what his father has lost, his own takes precedence. [If he has to choose between seeking] what he has lost and what his master has lost, his own takes precedence.

[If he has to choose between seeking] what his father has lost and what his master has lost, that of his master takes precedence. For his father brought him into this world. But his master, who has taught him wisdom, will bring him into the life of the world to come. But if his father is a sage, that of his father takes precedence. [If] his father and his master were carrying heavy burdens, he removes that of his master, and afterward removes that of his father. [If] his father and his master were taken captive, he ransoms his master, and afterward he ransoms his father. But if his father is a sage, he ransoms his father, and afterward he ransoms his master.

The dispute concerns rights of priority, here with regard to seeking a lost object. First of all, a person takes personal priority as against all others. As between a father and a master, by contrast, the master takes priority, unless both the master and the father are of equal standing. Then the father's claim comes first. The conflict concerns the claim of a relationship established by nature (the father's) as against that established by Heaven (the master's), and the resolution is in favor of Heaven. The supernatural family takes priority over the natural family.

### MISHNAH-TRACTATE BABA MESIA 3:2

He who rents a cow from his fellow, *and then lent it* to someone else, and it died of natural causes—let the one who rented it take an oath that it died of natural causes, and the one who borrowed it then pays compensation to the one who rented it out.

The dispute concerns who pays and receives compensation for the cow: the one who rented it or the one who borrowed it, on the one side, and the one who owned the cow and rented it out as against the one who rented it and then lent it, on the other. The oath once more resolves the conflict, by settling the facts of the matter and permitting the operative principles to enter in. The one who rented the cow takes the oath as to the facts of the matter: the cow has died of natural causes. The one who borrowed it then has to pay compensation. The original owner receives the compensation. The one who rented the cow and then lent it out has fulfilled his or her duty in establishing the facts; he or she did not rent the cow out and so has done nothing wrong.

### MISHNAH-TRACTATE BABA MESIA 3:3–5

[If] one said to two people, "I stole a maneh [a hundred zuz] from one of you and I do not know from which one of you it was." "The father of one of you deposited a maneh with me, and I do not know the father of which one of you it was," [he] pays off a maneh to this one and a maneh to that one, for he has admitted it on his own.

Two who deposited something with one person, this one leaving a maneh [a hundred zuz], and that one leaving two hundred [zuz]—this one says, "Mine is the deposit of two hundred [zuz]," and that one says, "Mine is the deposit of two hundred [zuz]" —he pays off a maneh to this one, and a maneh to that one, and the rest is left until Elijah comes.

And so is the rule for two utensils, one worth a maneh, and one worth a thousand zuz—this one says, "The better one is mine," and that one says, "The better one is mine"—he gives the smaller one to one of them. And from the [funds received from the sale of] the larger one, he gives the cost of a smaller one to the other party. And the rest of the money [received for the sale of the larger one] is left until Elijah comes.

The dispute is, to whom is the money or bailment owing? In the first case, since the householder has admitted to owing, the householder pays all possible claims. There is no fraudulent claim of one of the alleged victims to be avoided. But if two or more parties lay claim to the same funds, then both are paid the lesser claim, and the disputed sum is left over. Where the debt certainly is owing, the one who confesses to it pays all parties to the debt. Where, in the other cases, there are conflicting claims, the payoff is to the limit of the lower of the two claims. The result is, we resolve the conflict by fulfilling the minimal claim of all parties.

### MISHNAH-TRACTATE BABA MESIA 3:9–10

He who deposits a jar with his fellow, and the owner did not specify a place for it, and [someone] moved it and it was broken—if in the midst of his handling it, it was broken, [and if he moved it to make use of it] for his own needs, he is liable. [If he moved it] for its needs, he is exempt. If after he had put it down, it was broken, whether he had moved it for his own needs or for its needs, he is exempt. [If] the owner specified a place for it, and [someone] moved it and it was broken—whether it was in the midst of his handling it or whether it was after he had put it down, [if he had moved it] for his own needs, he is liable.

He who deposits coins with his fellow—[if the latter] (1) wrapped them up and threw them over his shoulder, (2) gave them over to his minor son or daughter, or (3) locked them up in an inadequate way, he is liable [to make them up if they are lost], because he did not take care of them the way people usually take care [of things]. But if he did take care of them the way people usually take care of things, he is exempt.

At issue is compensation for the loss of the bailment, the responsibility of the person in charge for the bailment. The bailment is moved and broken. If the bailee, with whom the property has been left, moved the bailment for his or her own convenience, the bailee is liable; but if it is moved for the better protection of the bailment, he or she is not liable since the trust has been kept. So too, if the bailee has met the normal standards of care of a bailment, he or she is not liable for damages. The conflict between bailer and bailiff is resolved by reference to the bailiff's meeting the normal standard. If things have been done in the usual way, the obligation has been carried out and there is no liability for damages. If not, there is. So too, if the priority has been placed on the protection of the bailment, the bailee is exempt; if the priority has been placed on the bailee's needs, liability exists. The systemic interest then is in securing the good faith of all parties: meeting the normal standards, keeping the faith with the one who has entrusted his goods to the bailiff.

## The Household: Responsibility and Intentionality

To review briefly: the goal of the system of civil law is the restoration of the just order that characterized Israel upon entry into the Land. The law aims at the restoration and preservation of the established wholeness, balance, proportion, and stability of the social economy realized at that moment. The civil law in both aspects pays closest attention to how the property and person of the injured party so far as possible are restored to their prior condition, that is, to the state of normality disrupted by the damage done to property or injury done to a person. So attention to torts focuses upon penalties paid by the malefactor to the victim, rather than on penalties inflicted by the court on the malefactor for what has been done. So much for the characterization of the legal system viewed whole for Baba Qamma and Baba Mesia 1–5. If I had to state, in broad and general terms, the principal point of concern, it is with (1) issues of causation, encompassing attitude and responsibility, on the one side, and (2) procedure in resolving disputes, on the other.

## Causation

Baba Qamma and the first half of Baba Mesia identify as consequential conflict those cases that concern issues of responsibility, causation, will, and intention. In the fifteen chapters conflicts are resolved by assessing, for torts and bailments alike, the limits of the defendant's responsibility, on the one side, and the extent to which one who has caused loss must make restitution, on the other. One is responsible for damages caused in the public domain, which may not be freely converted to private use. But when both parties have the same right of use of public domain, the injured party has no claim for restitution; but when it comes to private domain, the householder is not responsible for damages incurred by an intruder. The law of the Mishnah works out the distinction between levels of causation. The matter of responsibility comes to the surface in disputes concerning bailments, for example, when the householder of raw materials gives them over to be processed by a craftsman. The matter of intentionality reappears when an owner of a property loses title through despairing of recovery of the property. But the law does not recognize implicit agreements. One cannot take for granted that a loss suffered in saving another's property will be compensated; that depends on prior stipulation.

### Resolving Conflict: Oath Taking
The primary, though not sole, occasion for the presentation of conflict and the resolution thereof involves oath taking as the means for establishing facts. (In chapter 12 we will address the religious implications of the reliance on oath taking.) When it comes to conflicts over the facts of a case, the claimant bears the burden of proof. Where both parties have a valid basis for their respective claims, one or another is permitted to establish the truth of his claim through taking an oath. When it comes to the methods for resolving conflict, they are two: restitution or compensation, where called for, and appeal to Heaven via the oath to establish the facts, where necessary. The former presents no surprises; it expresses the essence of the legal program in the present division of the law.

What has the oath—the other focus of conflict representation in Baba Qamma and the first half of Baba Mesia—to do with will and intention and responsibility? A person who takes an oath invokes God's name. The oath is taken as an act of free will and total personal commitment to, responsibility for, the claim as to facts that the householder avows. Who takes the oath forms a variable, but the standing and effect of the oath do not. So, viewed in this perspective, the interest of corporate Israel comes to the surface. The conflicts between householders that the law of the Mishnah portrays are those involving questions of the exercise of will or intentionality: types of causation differentiated by levels of responsibility. Then the key is responsibility, just as the law of the Mishnah says time and again. I state my conclusion with heavy emphasis:

*The legal system finds particularly interesting those relationships between householders, or between a householder and another class of Israelite society (for instance, the craftsman), that embody in one way or another the exercise of the householder's autonomous will.*

That is hardly surprising, since the Rabbinic sages read the Torah as an exercise in purifying the heart of humanity. It is conflict that defines the measure of the Torah's work that is yet to be done in Israel. It follows that, when the building blocks of the Israelite social order engage in contention, the conflict is going to be explained in terms of will, attitude, intentionality, and responsibility. That carries us as far as we can go until we have taken up the other half of the matter of conflict between households: the maintenance of social order and the role of contention in the representation of that program.

# THE ISRAELITE HOUSEHOLD: WHEN INTENTION DOES NOT COUNT

## *Tractates Baba Mesia (Chapters 6–10) and Baba Batra*

### Corporate Israel's Interest: Where Intentionality Does Not Count

Will, attitude, intention—these figure prominently in disrupting, and therefore in restoring, the social order. But they play no important role in maintaining it. For if intentionality forms a critical determinant in the restoration of the social order of corporate Israel, as in Baba Qamma and the first half of Baba Mesia, when it comes to preserving that social order, the householder's attitude or intention no longer plays a principal, or any, role. In Baba Mesia 6-10 and Baba Batra 1-10, the emphasis is on preserving order. Individual attitude or will in that context does not form a governing criterion of analysis.

The transition from restoring to preserving the social order occurs in the very middle of "The Middle Gate," Baba Mesia. There we see a progression. Baba Mesia coherently describes the three dimensions of will or intentionality: (1) where humanity's will defines the norm, (2) where God's will overrides humanity's will, and (3) where custom and the social norm enter into the assessment of humanity's will and turn out to exclude unarticulated idiosyncrasy. Baba Batra concludes with topics of civil law in which intentionality plays no role whatsoever. It completes the picture that commences with the magnificent formula cited in chapter 10 from Mishnah-tractate Baba Qamma 1:4.

The entire exposition from the middle of Baba Mesia through chapter 10 of Baba Batra concerns the interplay between intentionality and value, with specific attention to where the attitude of participants to a transaction governs, where it is dismissed as null, and where it takes a subordinate position in an exchange. These are the three readings of the role of the will of the parties to a transaction: (1) paramount, (2) excluded, and (3) subordinated but effective.

Mishnah Baba Mesia 6:1–8:3 covers the hiring of workers, rentals, and bailments; 8:4–10:6 and Mishnah Baba Batra 1:1–5:5 deal with problems of real estate law. Mishnah Baba Batra 5:6–7:4 covers licit commercial transactions, and finally 8:1–10:8 deals with documents important in civil relationships—inheritances and wills, and other commercial and legal documents.

In the preceding chapter the issue was resolving conflicting claims; we focused on the attitudes of the participants to the conflict. First, we wanted conflicts to be resolved in a manner that was not only equitable but also that was *deemed* by all parties to be equitable. Second, in assessing rights of ownership, we took account of the attitude of the original owner, who relinquished title out of despair of regaining the lost property. Third, in assessing liability of a bailiff, we assigned restitution in proportion to the responsibility that the bailiff had accepted. In all three instances, therefore, the variables of the law responded to the attitudes of the participants in a transaction, to acts of will that determined the outcome of untoward consequences.

In Mishnah-tractate Baba Mesia chapter 6 forward, we deal with market transactions. Here, by contrast, other considerations override, so we treat as subordinate (or dismiss outright as irrelevant) the attitude of the players—informed seller, willing buyer. Rather, we impose the criterion of a fixed or true value. That supersedes the agreement of the parties to the transaction, and the law goes out of its way to underscore the fact that, in the face of the fixed and true value that inheres in a transaction, the willingness of the parties to ignore true value is simply nullified. A borrower may willingly pay usury—in the innocent form of a warm greeting for instance or a gesture of friendship—but the transaction is still deemed illegal. Even though a purchaser is willing to pay a premium for an object, attitude does not affect the value of the object. One may be willing to pay a premium for the use of capital, but such a premium is deemed not a return on capital but usury and is illegal. All transactions must conform to a measure of exact exchange of true value, and that extends to exchanges of labor. It follows that prices will be fixed—in terms of market conditions that affect what is immediately available—and private agreements cannot upset public arrangements.

But private agreements can be taken into account in other exchanges. That carries us to what is new in this exposition of conflict. Specifically, in transactions involving labor, rentals, and bailment, the attitude of the participants to an agreement fixes the terms of the agreement, which then cannot be unilaterally revised. Labor—like slaves, bonds, and documents—has no true value in the way in which grain or produce or a pot does; each party bargains in good faith without the constraints governing usury. But then the transaction involving such-and-such a wage for this-or-that span of labor, once agreed upon by both parties, is binding. Here the initial agreement governs, each party having acceded willingly, and the attitude or intention of one party cannot then dictate changes not accepted by the other. In the matter of bailments, liability responds to the level of responsibility imposed by variable compensation of the bailiff; he or she is assumed to be willing to take greater precautions and accept more substantial liability in response to greater compensation.

What about that which is not articulated but only assumed? Here too we impose upon the parties an imputed attitude; that is, we assume that all parties accept the prevailing norms and make those norms their own. Once more individual intentionality plays no role; individuality is null. In resolving conflicts in real estate, certain implicit agreements are assumed. Prevailing attitudes or expectations are imputed to the parties, custom then defining what we assume the players to have accepted. On that basis, I characterize the second half of the Babas as an exercise in maintaining the social order, the restoration of which is covered in the first half. It follows that the law of the Mishnah-tractate Baba Mesia—the mediating component of the civil law—both sets forth information about the topics at hand and also works out a theoretical concern through the presentation of those topics. That concern focuses on the attitude of parties to a conflict or transaction.

To what extent does the intentionality or attitude of a participant in an exchange govern, and to what extent do immutable rules override the will of the individual householder? Baba Mesia provides a good exercise in answering that question.

(1) In certain situations of conflict, we take full account of the attitude of all parties. When two persons claim ownership of the same object, either because both have grabbed it at the same moment or because one has lost what the other has found, or because one has accepted responsibility in proportion to the other's inveiglement (good will, a fee, and so on), then intentionality reigns supreme. That is to say, we settle the conflict by a weighing or a matching of wills. The Torah requires fairness, and, no other considerations intervening, all parties have a say as to what is equitable.

(2) But the willingness of two persons, for example, a buyer and seller, to come to an agreement is set aside by other considerations. The householder's will cannot overcome the law of the Torah. The Torah prohibits usury, which involves the concept of distributive economics that inherent in an exchange is a fixed valuation, which the participants may not set aside. A theory of static wealth comes into play when we maintain that true value inheres in things. God's will overrides humanity's, and what God does not want, humanity cannot legitimate merely by an act of will, even in an exchange involving mutual consent. Intentionality or attitude—willingness to evaluate at a higher or lower value than the intrinsic one—no longer enters into the disposition of a transaction. God's will outweighs humanity's will.

(3) Established custom modifies intentionality, in that people are assumed to conform to a common norm. In exchanges not of conflict nor of fixed value

but of service, attitude or intentionality is subordinated to expectations that are broadly accepted: general considerations of sound public policy. We may formulate matters in the following way: intentionality plays its part, but idiosyncrasy does not. We do not impute to an individual an intention or expectation that diverges from the norm. The parties may willingly enter a valid agreement to exchange service—work, rental of property, and the like—but their agreement cannot violate fixed procedures, any more than a buyer and seller may ignore true value. Custom in intangible relationships matches inherent worth in tangible ones.

### Where Intention Sometimes Registers in Context
### Tractate Baba Mesia 6:1–10:3

Against that background of issues of will and attitude, we now take up conflicts connected with the maintenance of the social order, once more surveying the articulated encounters of contention. We begin with labor law. If workers fail to show up, what do they owe the employer? What if the employer specifies a task and a wage and reneges?

#### MISHNAH-TRACTATE BABA MESIA 6:1

He who hires craftsmen, and one party deceived the other—one has no claim on the other party except a complaint [which is not subject to legal recourse]. [If] one hired an ass driver or wagon driver to bring porters and pipes for a bride or a corpse, or workers to take his flax out of the steep, or anything which goes to waste [if there is a delay], and [the workers] went back on their word—in a situation in which there is no one else [available for hire], he hires others at their expense, or he deceives them [by promising to pay more and then not paying up more than his originally stipulated commitment].

The conflict between householder and hired hands concerns the workers' failure to fulfill their commitment or the householder's failure to provide the promised work. Where there is the possibility of loss, the disappointed householder may deceive the workers into doing the work, promising a higher wage than he or she actually pays. That is the case when the workers did not show up. But if the fault did not lie with the workers, then they are paid their wages.

Breach of contract bears only limited liability for the householder and the worker. In the present case, there has been deception; that is, the workers did not show up. If a contractor causes loss, the householder has the right to defend his or her interest. If there is no loss, the conflict is treated as inconsequential. If there is loss, the householder can protect his or her interest. The workers' good faith—a measure of intentionality—is taken into account; if they failed to do the work through no fault of their own, they are compensated for their time. The systemic interest is in securing compensation where the damage is real and avoiding litigation where it is not. Now we proceed to a case not of deception but of unilateral abrogation of the contract—a case where the terms of the original contract are changed.

### MISHNAH-TRACTATE BABA MESIA 6:2

He who hires craftsmen and they retracted [from the terms of the original con-
tract]—their hand is on the bottom. If the householder retracts, his hand is on the bottom. Whoever changes [the original terms of the agreement]—his hand is on the
bottom. And whoever retracts—his hand is on the bottom.

In conflict between householder and workers involving breach of contract,
the one who fails to keep the agreement in its exact terms loses. The householder cannot add to the stipulated work or change the conditions of labor. If
it is to ease the task, it is permitted. While, as we saw earlier, breach of contract
to perform labor is not actionable, breach of the terms of the contract in the
actual performance of the work is. The employer may not add to the stipulated
assignment or change the conditions of labor. Here the conflict is resolved by
a strict reading of the terms of the agreement. The householder's relationship
to the craftsmen concerns the status of the property left with the craftsman
for processing, for example, cloth into clothing. If the materials are stolen, the
craftsman bears responsibility as paid bailiff, unless he or she has changed that
status in common agreement. Once we can classify the relationship of conflict,
we know how to resolve it. The present case then works itself out easily. The
paid bailiff is responsible to compensate for the loss of the bailment. The plaintiff has to validate his or her claim. These are familiar principles.

### MISHNAH-TRACTATE BABA MESIA 7:1–2

He who hires [day] workers and told them to start work early or to stay late—in a
place in which they are accustomed not to start work early or not to stay late, he has
no right to force them to do so. In a place in which they are accustomed to receiving
a meal, he must provide a meal. [In a place in which they are accustomed] to make do
with a sweet, he provides it. Everything accords with the practice of the province.

And these [have the right to] eat [the produce on which they work] by [right
accorded to them in] the Torah: he who works on what is as yet unplucked [may eat
from the produce] at the end of the time of processing; [and he who works] on plucked
produce [may eat from the produce] before processing is done; [in both instances
solely] in regard to what grows from the ground. But these do not [have the right to]
eat [the produce on which they labor] by [right accorded to them in] the Torah: he who
works on what is as yet unplucked, before the end of the time of processing; [and he
who works] on plucked produce after the processing is done, [in both instances solely]
in regard to what does not grow from the ground.

The householder wants the workers to extend their hours beyond the
norm; the workers appeal to the norm. If the householder imposes exceptional
requirements, and the workers protest, the dispute is readily resolved by imposing the established norm. The workers' claim is upheld. That is because a valid,
unwritten contract covers the transaction. There also is a right explicit in the
Torah that is vigorously upheld. Specifically, the Torah accords the workers the
right to eat produce on which they are working. But the householder also has
customary rights. Workers, for their part, owe their best efforts to their employers and cannot work night and day and so give less than their best effort. These

are fixed obligations, though they are subject to negotiation. The householder may not change the normal conditions of labor and the worker has to be capable of giving a full day's work for a full day's pay. The systemic interest here is in realizing the provisions of the Torah that govern householder–worker relationships and in overriding conflict coming from either side. But it is a stable condition of balance, proportion, and order: both sides must concur.

### Mishnah-tractate Baba Mesia 8:2

He who borrows a cow—[if] he borrowed it for half a day and hired it for half a day, [or] borrowed it for one day and hired it for the next day, [or] borrowed one [cow] and hired another—and [the cow] died—the lender says, (1) "The borrowed one died"—(2) "On the day on which it was borrowed, it died" (3) "At the time that it was borrowed, it died,"—and the [borrower] says, "I don't know"—[the borrower] is liable. The hirer [lessee] says, (1) "The hired one died," (2) "On the day on which it was hired, it died," (3) "at the time that it was hired, it died," and the other party says, "I don't know"—[the hirer] is exempt. [If] this party claims that the borrowed one [died], and that party claims that the hired one [died], the one who rents it is to take an oath that the rented one died. [If] this one says, "I don't know," and that one says, "I don't know," then let them divide [the loss].

The conflict here concerns the responsibility to make up the lost cow. If the borrower cannot ascertain the facts, the lender's claim is allowed. Where both parties lay claim, the one who rented the cow takes the oath to establish his or her position. If neither party has access to the facts, they divide the loss. The systemic interest is in establishing the correct procedure for settling the conflicting claims. Testimony of one or another party or an oath serves, depending on the circumstance. Where there is a direct conflict as to the facts of the matter, the character of the claim makes the difference. If both claim to know the facts, one takes an oath; if neither claims to know the facts, they divide what is at stake. As we have repeatedly seen, throughout the law of the Mishnah, the system assumes that Israelites tell the truth and rarely controls for lying. That is a fixed principle by which intentionality is assessed.

### Mishnah-tractate Baba Mesia 8:4

He who exchanges a cow for an ass, and [the cow] produced offspring, and so, too: he who sells his girl slave and she gave birth—this one says, "It was before I made the sale," and that one says, "It was after I made the purchase"—let them divide the proceeds. [If] he had two slaves, one big and one little, or two fields, one big and one little—the purchaser says, "I bought the big one," and the other one says, "I don't know"—[the purchaser] has acquired the big [slave]. The seller says, "I sold the little one," and the other says, "I don't know"—[the latter] has a claim only on the little one, This one says, "The big one," and that one says, "The little one"—let the seller take an oath that it was the little one which he had sold. This one says, "I don't know"' and that one says, "I don't know"—let them divide up [the difference].

Now the conflict concerns the facts of the matter. Where each party has a valid claim and there is no way of settling the question, the proceeds are divided. Where the purchaser claims to know the facts and the seller does not, the purchaser establishes the claim, otherwise the reverse is true. By now, this should seem natural. The law assesses the weight of conflicting claims. If one party alleges knowledge and the other does not, the former's claim prevails. Once more, the system affirms its confidence in Israelites to tell the truth. But the oath is the mechanism for ascertaining the facts.

### MISHNAH-TRACTATE BABA MESIA 10:5

He whose wall was near the garden of his fellow, and it was damaged [and fell down]—and [the owner of the garden] said to him, "Clear out your stones," but the other said to him, "They're yours!"—they pay no attention to [the latter]. [But if ] after the other party had accepted [the ownership of the stones] upon himself, [the original owner of the wall] said to him, "Here's what you laid out! Now I'll take mine!"—they do not pay attention to [the former].

He who hires a worker to work with him in chopped straw and stubble, and [the worker] said to him, "Pay me my wage," and [the employer] said to him, "Take what you've made for your wage!"—they do not pay attention to [the employer]. But [if,] after [the worker] had accepted [the proposition), [the employer] said to him, "Here's your salary, and now I'll take mine!"—they do not pay attention to [the employer].

The householder has the obligation to clear away the stones of his or her wall that have caused damage to the neighbor. The householder cannot simply assign ownership of the stones to the other. But if the other party concurred, he or she is now owner of the stones, and the householder cannot renege on the agreement. So too, a worker must be paid in the conventional manner. A worker cannot be paid in kind. If the worker agrees, the householder cannot go back on his word. The householder bears fixed obligations under the law. These apply whether stipulated or not. One cannot change the terms of the social compact. But if the other party has agreed to the proposal, it is a valid and enforceable contract.

## Where Intention Does Not Register at All:
## Tractate Baba Batra

Baba Batra begins in the middle of Baba Mesia's concluding topical unit, the rules governing joint holders of a property. It proceeds to further licit real estate transactions: not infringing the property rights of others, establishing title through usucaption (three years of unchallenged utilization of the property, yielding a claim to title through what in the United States we know as squatter's rights), transferring real estate and movables through sale. The next major section turns to licit commercial transactions and unstated stipulations in commercial transactions.

In its topical exposition, therefore, Baba Mesia flows uninterruptedly into Baba Batra. But why cut off the discussion of a topic, such as is done in the break from Baba Mesia chapter 10 to Baba Batra chapter 1? If not topical, the break must derive from some other consideration. Since, we noted, the concluding third of Baba Mesia takes up situations in which intentionality may or may not enter into the adjudication of a case, it becomes relevant to observe that in the opening unit of Baba Batra, intentionality plays no role at all. That is to say, joint holders enjoy certain rights in common, and how they personally wish to arrange matters has no bearing. The same point repeats itself throughout Baba Batra: the established custom overrides intentionality; the right of the community overrides even agreements among individuals; the rights of the other must be respected. If we wish to make the point that certain considerations override intentionality, there is, moreover, no more effective way of making such a statement than to say, as the law does, that even where the owner of a property has not abandoned the hope of recovering the property—even when despair has not nullified his or her title—the property may still be lost. Neglect of rights speaks for itself and overrides any intentionality toward the property; actions here set aside attitude.

There is a marked insistence throughout Baba Batra on the irrelevance of individual intentionality, let alone idiosyncrasy. For example, the private intention of the purchaser is null, if common usage is violated. The buyer may say that he or she assumed that the sale of property encompassed various movables, but that claim is null. People conform to customary usage, including language, and cannot invent their own conditions of sale. The law does not take account of private intentionality. That same matter carries us forward to cases in which unstated stipulations govern when all parties share the same general view; so far as nullifying a transaction, the reasonable expectations of each party are taken into account in accord with a common law. When it comes to inheritances, there is a way for one's intentionality to prevail, and that is through an act of donation (gift); but when it comes to transferring property through the right of inheritance, then the Torah's law takes over, and personal intentionality—which we might commonly place at the very center of dividing an estate—is null. So, seen from this perspective, the entire set of rules forms a sustained essay on where and how intentionality gives way before established procedures and usages.

### Mishnah-tractate Baba Batra 1:2–4

... in a place in which it is customary to build a fence, they require [a recalcitrant owner] to do so. But in a valley, in a place in which it is not customary to build a fence, they do not require him to do so. But if he wants, he may withdraw inside his own portion [of the property] and build it. And he places the facing of the wall outside of [the fence] [on the side of the neighbor, indicating his ownership]. Therefore, if the wall should fall down, the location [on which it had stood] and the stones are his. If they had made it with the consent of both parties, they build the wall in the middle. They place the facing of the wall on this side and on that side. Therefore, if the fence should fall down, the location [on which it had stood] and the stones belong to both parties.

He whose [land] surrounds that of his fellow on three sides, and who made a fence on the first, second, and third sides—they do not require [the other party to share in the expense of building the walls].

The wall of a courtyard which fell down—they require [each partner in the courtyard] to [help] build it up to a height of four cubits. [Each one is] assumed to have given, until one brings proof that the other has not contributed to the cost. [If the fence was built] four cubits and higher, they do not require [a joint holder in the courtyard to contribute to the expenses]. [If the one who did not contribute] built another wall near [the restored one] [planning to roof over the intervening space], even though he did not [actually] put a roof on it, they assign him [his share in the cost of the] whole [other wall]. [He is now] assumed not to have contributed to the cost, until he brings proof that he has contributed to the cost.

In the first instance, local custom prevails. But within one's own property, the individual has the right to act independently. Does the neighbor on the fourth side have to share the cost of building the walls from which he or she benefits? No, the neighbor may reject the claim of the other party, even though benefit is gained from the other's fence. It is optional. Since the courtyard must have a wall, every partner may be forced to contribute to building and maintaining it. The law of the Mishnah balances the claim of the partnership of householders to provide for the common good with the right of the individual to manage privately owned property. As before, local custom prevails. But that custom may encompass the obligation of all householders to pay their fair share of facilities benefiting the group as a whole.

### MISHNAH-TRACTATE BABA BATRA 1:5

They force [a joint holder in the courtyard to contribute to] the building of a gate-house and a door for the courtyard. They force [each joint holder to contribute to] the building of a wall, gates, and a bolt for the town. How long must one be in a town to be deemed equivalent to all other townsfolk? Twelve months. [If] one has purchased a permanent residence, lo, he is equivalent to all the other townsfolk forthwith.

The same issue is carried forward: all parties benefit from the facilities, so each must contribute. The Tosefta, which is particularly rich here, extends the application of the principle (Tosefta-tractate Baba Mesia 11:23–26), allowing for guilds to control their own prices and output. The necessities of the community or its subdivisions take priority over the individual's predilections. Where the public interest intervenes, the community imposes its will on the individual householder.

### MISHNAH-TRACTATE BABA BATRA 2:2–3

A person should not set up an oven in a room, unless there is a space of four cubits above it. [If] he was setting it up in the upper story, there has to be a layer of plaster under it three handbreadths thick, and in the case of a stove, a handbreadth thick. And if it did damage, [the owner of the oven] has to pay for the damage.

A person should not open a bake shop or a dyer's shop under the granary of his fellow, nor a cattle stall. To be sure, in the case of wine they permitted doing so, but not [building] a cattle stall [under the wine cellar]. As to a shop in the courtyard, a person may object and tell [the shopkeeper], "I cannot sleep because of the noise of people coming in and the noise of people going out." One may [however] make utensils [and] go out and sell them in the market. Truly one has not got the power to object and to say, "I cannot sleep because of the noise of the hammer, the noise of the millstones, or the noise of the children."

One cannot maintain a public nuisance, and where there is a dispute (because of the noise, or the traffic, or the like), the intrusive party gives way.

Here again, the public good overrides private interest. All parties have rights to the common facilities, and no one can abridge the enjoyment of others. But if an established custom or facility causes discomfort to newcomers, the system favors the status quo.

The passage before us refers to acquiring title to movables or real property by "usucaption." That is roughly comparable to the American right of acquiring title through "squatter's rights," meaning, utilization of property without any opposition for a specified period of time.

### MISHNAH-TRACTATE BABA BATRA 3:1, 3

3:1 [Title by] usucaption of (1) houses, (2) cisterns, (3) trenches, (4) caves, (5) dovecotes, (6) bathhouses, (7) olive presses, (8) irrigated fields, (9) slaves, and anything which continually produces a yield—title by usucaption applying to them is three years, from day to day [that is, three full years]. A field which relies on rain—[title by] usucaption for it is three years, not from day to day.

3:3 Any act of usucaption [along] with which [there] is no claim [on the property being utilized] is no act of securing title through usucaption. How so? [If] he said to him, "What are you doing on my property," and the other party answered him, "But no one ever said a thing to me!"—This is no act of securing title through usucaption. [If he answered,] "For you sold it to me," "You gave it to me as a gift," "Your father sold it to me," "Your father gave it to me as a gift"—Lo, this is a valid act of securing title through usucaption. He who holds possession because of an inheritance [from the previous owner] requires no further claim [in his own behalf]. (1) Craftsmen, partners, sharecroppers, and trustees are not able to secure title through usucaption. (2) A husband has no claim of usucaption in his wife's property, (3) nor does a wife have a claim of usucaption in her husband's property, (4) nor a father in his son's property, (5) nor a son in his father's property. Under what circumstances? In the case of one who effects possession through usucaption. But in the case of one who gives a gift, or of brothers who divide an estate, and of one who seizes the property of a proselyte, [if] one has locked up, walled in, or broken down in any measure at all—Lo, this constitutes securing a claim through usucaption.

The squatter's claim is spelled out (3:1): three years of undisrupted usucaption of the property, joined to a claim of legitimacy. It is contested by the original owner, as outlined in Mishnah Baba Batra 3:3. Mere utilization of the property does not suffice. The squatter must be able to allege not merely uninterrupted utilization but a valid claim—of sale, gift, or the like. But this applies only to real property. Where the claim would not likely be contested, in the cases of a claim of usucaption by a husband, partner, sharecropper, or trustee, there the claim is null. So a claim of ownership via usucaption is a dispute over the basis of landownership that is not all that different from a claim of acquisition through gift or purchase. The law does not favor promiscuous claims of acquisition of title through usucaption, and that is why the most important detail is that there must be a valid basis for the claim, and not only uncontested use of the property for the requisite three years. Only with such a basis does uninterrupted usucaption bear a solid claim.

### Mishnah-tractate Baba Batra 5:6

There are four rules in the case of those who sell: [If] one has sold good wheat and it turns out to be bad, the purchaser has the power to retract. [If one has sold] bad wheat and it turns out to be good, the seller has the power to retract. [If he has claimed to sell] bad wheat, and it turns out to be bad, [or if he claimed to sell] good wheat and it turns out to be good, neither one of them has the power to retract.

[If one sold it as] (1) dark-colored, and it turns out to be white, white, and it turned out to be dark, (2) olive wood, and it turned out to be sycamore [wood], sycamore wood, and it turned out to be olive wood, (3) wine, and it turned out to be vinegar, vinegar, and it turned out to be wine, both parties have the power to retract.

The dispute here concerns the quality of wheat that the householder has sold, with special reference to who has the right to retract. If the householder claimed the wheat was of good quality and it turns out bad, the purchaser withdraws; if contrariwise, the seller. If the seller has claimed to sell precisely what has been sold and the buyer paid for that, then the deal is final. A transaction becomes permanent only when both parties are satisfied that they have been treated fairly, in accord with the intent of each. The conflict over who can cancel the sale is resolved by appeal to the facts of the transaction and to the presumption of the will of each participant. That is why the final case—dark/white, olive/sycamore—yields an ambiguous result. The overriding interest of the Mishnah is to establish rules that resolve conflicts without confrontation and without the need for adversary proceedings.

### Mishnah-tractate Baba Batra 6:3

He who sells wine to his fellow that went sour is not liable to make it up. But if it was known that his wine would turn sour, lo, this is deemed a purchase made in error [and null]. And if he had said to him, "I'm selling you spiced wine," he is liable to guarantee it [and make it up if it goes sour] up to Pentecost. [If he said it is] old [wine, it must be] last year's. [If he said it is] vintage old [it must be] from the year before last.

Does the seller take responsibility for the future condition of what is sold? The buyer claims the wine went sour; the seller maintains he or she is not responsible—these things happen. On the one hand, if the outcome was known in advance, then the transaction is null. On the other hand, if not, then fixed rules apply. If the wine went sour, the seller is not obligated to make it up. If the seller set a condition that contains an implicit guarantee that it will not go sour until a specified point—by saying the wine was spiced, for instance—the seller is responsible, and so throughout.

This brief survey could be extended several times over. The outcome would be the same. If I had to identify the center of it all, it would be this: *Both parties have a right to a fair deal. Neither may change agreed-upon stipulations arbitrarily, and neither may emerge with more than he or she entered the transaction with.* Apart from the matter of bailment, the issue of intentionality hardly arises when the law of the Mishnah provides for the maintenance of the established relationships of the social order comprised by Israelite householders. Conflict of will or intentionality defines a focus for the legal program of restoring the social equilibrium. The legal system takes account of issues of will and intentionality in assessing responsibility for disrupting the social order since it is the conflict of wills—God's and Adam's and Eve's—that to begin with ruined the perfection of the human condition captured in the word Eden. By contrast, when it comes to maintaining the status quo, what governs are balanced exchanges and considerations of equal responsibility for agreements freely undertaken.

The interest of corporate Israel comes to realization in the disposition of conflicts between classes of society—workers and employers, craftsmen and householders, householders and householders, bailers and bailees, and the like. In all of these transactions, the law of the Mishnah aims not at confronting conflict but rather at imposing the correct principle: dismantling and classifying the components of the transaction, reckoning on the rights and responsibilities of each, and administering the pertinent rule. That is best illustrated by the classifications of bailments and the consequent rules that pertain.

## Intentionality, Conflict, and the Israelite Civil Order Embodied in the Household

The representation of conflicts is not randomly distributed over the topical program of the three Babas. The conflicts that require resolution concern (1) issues of causation, will, and responsibility; (2) affirming the status quo of fairness, balance; (3) methods for deciding the facts of a case; and (4) imposing an oath in specified cases for settling conflicting accounts of the facts of a case. Problems of conflict attract attention in only a modest segment of the Babas' topical program. Entire chapters of Baba Qamma (chapters 1, 2, 4, 6, and 7), Baba Mesia (chapters 4 and 5), and Baba Batra (chapters 4, 7, and 10)—one third of the whole—present no conflict between householders at all. The issues portrayed in the framework of conflict are of two kinds. First come those that encompass issues of responsibility and causation, will and intentionality, and establishing the facts of a case (Baba Qamma and Baba Mesia 1–5). These are followed by instances that insist on confirming established custom or agreed upon contracts, imposing rules of fairness, and the like (Baba Mesia 6–10 and Baba Batra).

So sages here demonstrate what an Israelite can do actively to participate in the perfection of the social order through the results of personal conduct and the conduct of his or her chattels. Here the consideration of the individual's free will proves paramount: what the householder by an act of will has upset, the householder by an act of will must restore. Within Israel's social order what God wants a person to do is take responsibility for his or her own actions (and for the results of actions undertaken on his or her behalf)—no more, no less. And that pervasive point of insistence transforms our view of the civil law. True, it forms an exercise in restoration and stability of the just society, which is a commonplace in most legal systems.

## The Theology of the Babas: God, Eden, and Israel

But the details of the law of the Mishnah comprise a chapter of theology, an answer to the question, What, in the formation of the just society, can a human being do? And the answer is, Israelites can and must take responsibility for not only what they do but also—and especially—what they bring about. They are answerable for the things they may not have done but may have caused to happen. Viewed in this way, the laws of Baba Qamma form a massive essay upon the interplay of causation and responsibility: what one can have prevented but through negligence (in varying measure depending on context) has allowed to take place, a person is deemed in that same measure to have caused. And for that, the householder is held in that same measure to make amends. Not only so, but the classification of types of conflict and their resolution conforms, underscoring the sources of conflict in irresponsibility and overreaching and disrupting the established order.

It may therefore be said that humanity possesses (1) free will to assume responsibility, on the one side, and (2) the power to take action in consequence of responsibility, on the other. That principle assumes religious status in two steps. First, in the words of the Torah, where God framed the laws that link causation and responsibility—negligence and culpability, for instance. It is in the very portrayal of the holy society that Israel at Sinai is commanded to realize, that God's stake in humanity's framing of the social order is made explicit. Consequently, second, Israel in the workaday transactions of one person with another acts out in this-worldly terms its governing principle of transactions with Heaven. The one in palpable terms shows the character of the other in intangible ways.

In a society ordered by God's justice—as Israelite society is supposed to be—the Israelite will acknowledge responsibility and bear the consequences of actions. The negative here makes all the difference. What will Israelites not do? They will not deny or dissimulate. They will not blame others and take no blame themselves. When they have upset the social order by diminishing others and aggrandizing themselves, by altering the terms of an established contract or covenant, they will restore the balance they have upset. Confronted with the result of their own negligence or worse, Israelites cannot shift the burden of blame or avoid responsibility for the consequences of what they personally have caused. And the entire arrangement for restoring the social balance and preserving the social order builds upon that principle.

In a situation of stability, on the other side of the equation, Israelites will keep their word, abide by agreements that are rationally shaped to accommodate the interests of all parties. The social order then becomes a model for humanity's accepting responsibility for human actions.

What, in Israelite context, marks that statement as critical to the worldview of the Torah? To answer, we revert to the initial point at which the world order of perfection was disrupted by an act of Adam and Eve. When we take up that moment of flaw and imperfection, we must examine whether and how the consideration of accepting responsibility for the damage one has done enters in. For the theology of the sages of the Mishnah, Adam and Eve's fall is recapitulated in the setting of Israel's loss of the Land for rebellion against the Torah. Israel's return to the Land marks the opportunity to correct the errors of Eden. The Babas in their sector of the entire law of the Mishnah spell out how this is to be done.

The law of the Mishnah responds both to the challenge of the fall and Israel's response to the restoration: Do right what then went wrong, correct the error of Eden. The story of Adam's and Eve's disobedience in Eden (Gen. 3:11–13) tells why Adam and Eve's accepting responsibility explains these laws of damages and misappropriation. At the center of the story of the human condition after Eden is man's and woman's denial of responsibility for the deed each did, and, implicitly, rejection of responsibility for the consequent loss of Eden that is coming. At the heart of the law of the Mishnah of the Babas is the opposite: the Israelite's explicit acceptance of responsibility for what he or she causes. Why so? Because if corporate Israel wants to show God that it is regenerate, how better to do so than to act out in cases of damages and injury the requirement to bear responsibility for what one does (as in the case of Adam) and causes to happen (as in the case of Eve)? Here in its everyday conduct of the inner affairs of the community, Israel shows how, unlike Adam and Eve, through the instruction of the Torah, Israel has learned what it means to take responsibility for injury and damage to others and, more still, to accept the obligation of preserving the status quo of balance, order, and teleological perfection.

Israel's workaday life, in the very practicalities of conflict and its resolution aimed at restoring and preserving the perfection of the status quo, is conducted as an ongoing exercise. It is one of making explicit one's responsibility for what one has caused, then apportioning damages in proportion to one's negligence or malfeasance. Take the conflicts arising in Baba Qamma and the message of how they are resolved. What is voluntary, foreseeable, and preventable imposes maximum liability for restoration. The Israelites cannot blame their ox, nor in the public way impose upon passersby the responsibility to accommodate the obstacles they have set up. The premise of the exercise is that Israel's inner affairs, the transactions between and among Israelites, in the most practical terms, are conducted as a test of whether regenerate humanity can bear responsibility for their own actions. No excuses ("the woman you put at my side," "the snake duped me") exculpate when one has caused damage, because Israelites assume the burden of their actions and take responsibility so far as possible to restore the world to its original condition, before, in the here and now, some deed or act of negligence of theirs disrupted it. I can think of no more direct response to "the woman . . . the snake . . ." than the language, "In the case of anything of which I am liable to take care, I am deemed to render possible whatever damage it may do."

So much for the first of the Babas. The second and third gates complete the picture. Here the issue is sustaining the social order, as we have seen. Here too attitude and intentionality come into play, but in a different way from before. Sin, crime, torts, and damages—these carry forward bad attitudes; differentiating types and degrees of intentionality when addressing how the social order is disrupted yields nothing of interest. By contrast, in treating ordinary exchanges and transactions, the law of the Mishnah forms an essay on when intentionality matters and when it does not. Intentionality or attitude matters in situations of conflict. The attitude of both parties makes all the difference, since to resolve conflicting claims, we have in the end to conciliate all parties to a common outcome. Now, intentionality or attitude forms the critical means for restoring and sustaining balance and order. Parties to an exchange are responsible to one another, and they must intend the outcome to be a proportionate and equal exchange of value. Both parties must accept the outcome, that is, form at the end the same attitude toward the transaction. Intentionality counts in the restoration and maintenance of the social order.

But then where do we dismiss as null all considerations of intentionality or attitude, even when parties to an exchange concur? In market transactions where, by contrast, true value overrides the attitude of the players. Even where all parties agree, the Torah too must approve. And we impute to all parties the same attitude and deny the pertinence of idiosyncratic or private meanings. Broadly held expectations govern, whether those of custom or of the Torah's own law. In these two ways, custom and the Torah's law, intentionality possesses no power. That is because it serves no purpose in restoring or sustaining the balances of a well-ordered society.

What message emerges when we move from the illicit to the licit, the abnormal to the normal, the first half of the Babas to the second? The transactions that all together form the ordinary life of inner Israel, Israel on its own, yield matching propositions. First, when it comes to acts that disrupt the social order, a person is responsible for what he or she does. But, second, when we turn to transactions that sustain the ordinary relationships within Israel, humanity's proper intentionality takes over. Then the Israelite's will forms only one element in a complex transaction. Where wills clash, compromise takes over—that is the message of the layer of the law devoted to conflict. Where the Torah imposes its own rule, intentionality is null. Publicly accepted custom and procedure take the paramount position. In cases of negligence or malfeasance, people take responsibility for what they have done—this is what happens throughout the first half of the Babas.

In the Babas, these distinct and interrelated forces—(1) humanity's will, (2) God's law, and (3) accepted public practice—are far from abstractions. Each contributes to conflicting relationships between Israelites. In the interplay of individual will, God's absolute law, and ancient, enduring custom, Eden endures in the realization of Israel in the here and now. No wonder the great teacher, Samuel, took the view, "There is no difference between the world to come and the days of the messiah, except the end of the subjugation of the exilic communities of Israel" (Talmud of Babylonia Tractate Sanhedrin 11:12 I.24/91B). That is to say, in context, the Messiah will restore Israel to the Land (one of his two principal missions, raising the dead being the other), the Torah to the government of Israel in the Land. Then, for all eternity marked by "the world to come," Eden once recovered will endure forever.

But what precisely is meant by "Eden"? In the context of the Torah's narrative, Eden is a location. But for the law of the Mishnah Eden is an occasion, a situation, a mode of organization, a condition and not a location. In the statement of the law of the Mishnah, specifically, Eden is a condition that prevails in the here and now of inheritances and wills, real estate and market transactions, a circumstance that comes about in the compromise of conflict and through the fair and just arrangements brought about among the householder and laboring craftsman and farm worker. With the proper intentionality, in full responsibility, maintaining the ancient order and arrangements of the Torah, Israel in the Land will realize Eden—this time around forever. That is the paramount importance of confronting and resolving conflict between Israelites in their household units: possessors of the Land. That too is the evidence for God's perpetual presence within Israel: corporate, individual, family, and household alike.

# God's Presence
# in Israel's Social Order

# 12    GOD'S PERPETUAL PRESENCE IN ISRAELITE CONTENTION: THE OATH

## Tractate Shebu<sup>c</sup>ot

---

### Invoking God's Presence in Israel's Conflicts

Conflict between Israelite families and households comes to resolution in one of two ways. Either the conflict can be sorted out, administered, by the court in accord with established facts and procedures—then the status quo takes over and rights itself. Or one or another party takes an oath in God's name to support a claim as to the facts of the litigated matter—then God intervenes. By definition, God's intervention into this-worldly matters is not an extension of the regular, the orderly, the affirmation of the status quo and its realization, but the very opposite. The oath thus represents an ad hoc intrusion when the status quo cannot be determined.

The Mishnah thereby sets forth a legal system that relies on God to resolve conflicts as to allegations of facts. In every practical context imaginable, God is present at the taking of the oath, knows the truth, and will enforce the commandment against taking God's name in vain, that is, taking an oath to sustain a lie. It follows that although the social order is restored and preserved through a variety of this-worldly principles and procedures, the law constantly invokes an otherworldly consideration, the perpetual presence of God within Israel's social order, ever ready to engage with the Israelites in the ordinary conduct of their everyday affairs. The oath represents something of a paradox. For all the Mishnaic law's powers of regularization and rationalization, Israelite society conducts its affairs in an everyday encounter with God. God is rarely mentioned in the Mishnah, yet God is always present and effective and engaged in the workaday life of Israel.

The oath plays so commonplace a role in resolving conflict that we may simply say, in the face of contradictory claims, the Mishnaic law system cannot function without it. So we have seen especially in chapters 2 (the rite of the accused wife), 10, and 11. The oath is the Torah's contribution to resolving contention in Israel, in particular to resolving conflict between Israelites. The taking of the oath is the point at which the Mishnah's legal system addresses conflicts in Israel in particular, whether in order to restore or to maintain the social order. There, and principally there, the certainties of applying the right rule to the appropriate case give way, and the conflict over the facts of the case is resolved.

### Crossing the Outer Bounds of Conflict Resolution

Chapters 10 and 11 have demonstrated that ordinarily the law of the Mishnah does not really confront conflict. It reorders relationships in accord with prevailing rules. It does not so much settle disputes as close them off. Nor, most commonly, does it rely on an adversarial transaction to resolve contention. In most of the cases we have reviewed, the system prefers to find the correct rule and impose that rule. It carries over into relationships of social contention its theory that all things are subject to rules so that, when we have determined the prevailing pattern, we also know how to sort out the conflicting claims at hand. But that is not always so. At a few significant turnings, Heaven (that is, God) is invoked to participate not in settling scores but in adjudicating claims. When the facts of the case are in doubt, God guarantees them.

Specifically, there are cases in which we know the governing classification of participants and their actions, along lines familiar from the Babas—responsible or not responsible, conforming to established custom or not conforming to custom. What we do not know are the facts of the transaction—Has the widow collected her marriage settlement? Has the bailiff faithfully attended to the bailment? Whether affected by issues of intentionality (chapter 10), or untouched by such intangible considerations (chapter 11), the transaction is the same. The oath is administered to one party or the other, and taking it establishes the truth of the claim. The oath—who takes it, what issues are covered by it—forms the one method for the resolution of social conflict that transcends universals of fairness and faithfulness to agreements. Having been taken in God's name, the oath automatically establishes the facts of the matter and resolves the conflicting claims of the participants to the transaction. God will hear what the oath taker vows—God's presence being invoked by the mention of God's name—and the result is assured.

Therefore, the oath presupposes that God is present, hears the oath, and knows the facts of what has occurred. So here is a legal system that at critical turnings invokes in immediate, concrete contexts an other-than-this-worldly power and presence to make the system work. This way of dealing with practical conflict embodies a theological doctrine in the strictest sense. Israelite society at this particular moment invokes God's very presence in its midst: When an oath is taken, God is in attendance. So the oath may be compared to an act of prayer, which likewise God attends.

## Oaths as Social Policy

Oaths fall into five classifications: the vain oath, the rash oath, the oath of the judges, the oath of testimony, and the oath of bailment. Three of the five serve a single purpose. The oath of the judges, the oath of testimony, and the oath of bailment all serve to introduce the criterion of truth and to exclude the exercise of force. The claimant seeks a just restoration of property or compensation for loss; the defendant insists on a fair adjudication of the matter. For that purpose, words backed up not by deeds but by divine supervision serve. But contention precipitates also the remaining classes of oaths: the taking of the vain and rash oath. The rash oath involves securing credence for a preposterous allegation—one that others deny. The vain oath asks people to believe that one will carry out an implausible resolve, again bearing within itself the implicit motive to secure credibility where there is none. So one way or another, the oath serves, within the Israelite polity, to engage God's participation within the transactions of Israelites, to involve God in Israel's points of inner conflict, to ask God to impart certainty to the points of stress and strain. Let me explain.

Ultimately, God is there to keep Israel's peace. That statement should be understood in palpable and concrete, not intangible ("spiritual") terms. The concrete fact emerges from what we have learned about resolving conflict between Israel's families and households. Heaven has a heavy stake in family ties, God's engagement in securing truth telling in response to the invocation of God's name—these form the foundations of the Mishnah's theory of the social order. God intervenes in transactions that, in all other aspects, are guided by this-worldly rules and exchanges. That is because when God's name is invoked, God responds. God, then, is explicitly called to attest to the truth. Everywhere present, God knows the facts and "will not hold that one guiltless who takes [God's] name in vain" by swearing to the contrary.

## The Torah's Provisions for the Oath

On what basis does the Mishnah's legal system of Israel's social order confidently call upon God to resolve Israelites' own conflicts? The Torah answers that question, specifying the character of oaths in God's name and where they pertain. That the bailiff—the one with whom a bailment is deposited—is responsible to take an oath at the instance of the claim of the one who has left the bailment, the bailer, and is not required to make restitution if he has not committed negligence is indicated in the following:

> For every breach of trust, whether it is for an ox, for ass, for sheep, for clothing, or for any kind of lost thing, of which one says, "This is it," the case of both parties shall come before God; he whom God shall condemn shall pay double to his neighbor. If a man delivers to his neighbor an ass or an ox or a sheep or any beast to keep, and it dies or is hurt or is driven away, without anyone seeing it, an oath by the Lord shall be between them both to see whether he has not put his hand to his neighbor's property; and the owner shall accept the oath and he shall not make restitution. But

if it is stolen from him, he shall make restitution to its owner. If it is torn by beasts, let him bring it as evidence; he shall not make restitution for what has been torn. If a man borrows anything of his neighbor and it is hurt or dies, the owner not being with it, he shall make full restitution. If the owner was with it, he shall not make restitution; if it was hired, it came for its hire. (Exod. 22:9–15)

The bailiff concedes part of the claim ("This is it"), and God settles the matter. So too, the character of the oath that resolves the matter, which responds to the nature of the claim of the competing parties depends, further, on what portion of the property a claimant alleges is his or hers. The will of each party enters into the transaction, therefore, embodied as it is in the extent of each party's claim. As to (1) oaths of adjuration; (2) imparting uncleanness to the Temple and its Holy Things; (3) the rash oath; (4) the false claim in connection with bailments, Leviticus 5:1–6 states as follows:

If any one sins in that he hears a public adjuration to testify and though he is a witness, whether he has seen or come to know the matter yet does not speak, he shall bear his iniquity. Or if any one touches an unclean thing, whether the carcass of an unclean beast or a carcass of unclean cattle or a carcass of unclean swarming things, and it is hidden from him, and he has become unclean, he shall be guilty. Or if he touches human uncleanness, of whatever sort the uncleanness may be with which one becomes unclean, and it is hidden from him, when he comes to know it he shall be guilty; or if anyone utters with his lips a rash oath to do evil to do good, any sort of rash oath that men swear, and it is hidden from him, when he comes to know it, he shall in any one of these be guilty. (Lev. 5:1–6)

Leviticus 6:1–7 on bailments completes the matter, and its distinctions, along with those in Exodus 22:9–15, play a role in the legal exposition:

The Lord said to Moses, "If any one sins and commits a breach of faith against the Lord by deceiving his neighbor in a matter of deposit or security, or through robbery, or if he has oppressed his neighbor or has found what was lost and lied about it, swearing falsely, in any of all the things that men do and sin therein, when one has sinned and become guilty, he shall restore what he took by robbery, or what he got by oppression or the deposit that was committed to him or the lost thing that he found or anything about which he has sworn falsely; he shall restore it in full and shall add a fifth to it and give it to him to whom it belongs, on the day of his guilt offering. (Lev. 6:1–7)

Clearly, the Torah supplies the basic categories and conceptions of the oath. The Mishnah systematizes matters, presenting no surprises, as we shall now see.

## The Mishnah-tractate's Systematization of the Torah's Laws of Oath Taking

The Mishnah-tractate Shebuᶜot, building on the facts supplied by the Torah, defines types of oaths and the counts on which, in the taking of an oath that turns out to be false or that is violated, one incurs culpability. A brief précis of its program suffices to show the practical and worldly context in which the Mishnah calls upon God's intervention.

From rules pertinent to all oaths, the Mishnah's legal exposition proceeds to the subdivision of oaths into the categories noted earlier: rash, vain, testimony, and bailment. A separate category of oaths, those imposed by the judges as part of a court proceeding, is taken up in due course. The first four principal types obviously fall into two distinct categories as well, the former being oaths of a private character, the latter involving public policy—the courts, the protection of property. Once more we distinguish inadvertent taking of such an oath, where an offering suffices, and deliberate lying, where the sanction is corporal. Taking the former two types of oath is itself culpable; in the latter cases, violating the oath or taking the oath under false pretenses is culpable, an important difference. The rash or vain oath takes effect as a general statement; the oath of testimony or of bailment must be particular to the case at hand. One is not penalized for taking a true oath of testimony or oath of bailment, but one is automatically subject to sanctions for taking another that is rash or vain. That difference accounts also for the character of the rules that define the application of the law to men and women, relatives and otherwise, and the like. Oaths pertaining to the court matter only when taken by those qualified to give testimony, thus, men not women, unrelated parties but not relatives of the litigants, and the like. That explains, also, why for these categories of oaths only taking a false oath is penalized. In these cases, too, the oath must be particular to the case, that is, imposed on specific, named persons.

The judges investigate the case by imposing oaths. These form their own category, involving not only private persons but the agency of the community at large. The judges exercise the power to impose an oath upon contesting parties, in the certainty that Israelites will not take a false oath involving God's name or Presence. Here the character of the claim and the concession govern. If the defendant denies that anything is owed, the defendant is exempt from having to take an oath; if the defendant concedes the facts but quibbles about details, the oath is required. Once the oath is taken, the defendant prevails and pays no more than has been conceded. That indicates the power of the oath in court. Five classes of claimant take the oath and collect what they claim. The oaths as they affect bailments are subdivided in terms of the character and quality of the guardianship promised by the bailiff, the unpaid bailiff being held to a lower standard than the paid bailiff, and so on. Here the oath proves effective where there are no witnesses as to the facts.

The facts on which the law of the Mishnah builds derive wholly from the Torah, and even the proportions of the category correspond to those of the relevant passages of the Torah. The law of the Mishnah explores the character of any breach of faith toward God, whether it is done knowingly or not knowingly. When it comes to the penalties for diverse types of oath, the determinant is whether the oath is an inadvertent misstatement or a deliberate falsehood. Often it comes down to what one knew when and with what result. Intentionality comes to the fore. Every case set forth by Moses in the Torah involves a deliberate action, based on firm knowledge of facts and the consequences of one's own intentional deed. That is why someone, guilty in any of these, has the power to confess: he or she knew just what he or she was doing and did it anyhow—all the more so the breach of faith in regard to bailments! We may, therefore, conclude that the law of the Mishnah has identified the animating consideration of the Torah's law, which is the deliberate act of deceit of one sort or another and has recapitulated the character and the results of intended deceit.

Conflict lurks in the background of oath taking, even where it has no speaking part to play. In all cases of the four classifications of oath, the oath taker uses the oath to close (if not to win) an argument. The rash oath attracts attention because it is one that in the end is going to be violated willy-nilly: the oath not to do something that one is highly likely to do. The vain oath is one that is contrary to fact or condition—an oath that one has seen what is impossible, or an oath not to do what one is commanded to do, or something quite similar. These oaths misuse, abuse language; they represent the utilization of the formula of the oath in inappropriate ways, asking by an oath that people believe that one will do the impossible or believe the implausible.

The conflict here is between contradictory opinions; one party strengthens his or her allegation by resorting to the rash or vain oath. In the context of the law of the Mishnah, two things are required: a definition of the sin or crime, and a specification of the penalty for deliberate and for inadvertent commission of the sin or crime. The law of the Mishnah then identifies those whose oaths bear consequences. In the present instance anyone may take such an oath, anyone may be affected by it: men and women, persons not related and those related, and the like. But what distinguishes the classification is that the oath represents an act of one's own volition.

The other two types of oath—oath of testimony, oath of bailment—by contrast may be imposed by the court or by the law, especially, as we saw in chapters 10 and 11, where testimony conflicts. These two types then pertain only to those who, to begin with, are able to give testimony. Men not related to the parties to the conflict, suitable to bear witness, are subject to the oath of testimony. Gentiles, women, children, and others invalid to testify in a Jewish court of law are not. The oath of testimony then serves the process of the courts in the administration of law, imposing the requirement to testify upon reluctant witnesses. The oath of testimony is particular to the person on whom it is imposed; it cannot form a generalized imprecation applicable to all who hear it. The transaction moreover takes a highly personal form, the oath being imposed by the party who requires the testimony upon the party who is supposed to know pertinent facts. The oath of bailment has no bearing on court transactions, so anyone may take it. It must pertain to something of value. Its terms and consequences are defined by the diverse definitions of responsibilities for bailments.

The oath imposed by the judges, finally, embodies the Torah's disposition of the conflicting claims to property—for example, the claim of an undischarged debt in specie or in kind, but one that is tangible and not personal or theoretical (ownership of land)—therefore, claims to money but not slaves, to movables but not real estate.

So the oath, by definition, signals the presence of conflict and provides for its resolution.

## God's Intervention into Conflict Codified

Up to this point we have asked about the interest of corporate Israel in the resolution of conflict. But here we deal with those specific classifications of conflict in the resolution of which God, very present in Israel, has an interest. In the Torah God told Moses precisely that. Accordingly, the social teaching before us introduces God's participation in the resolution of conflicts between Israelites. God is party to the corporate life of Israel, as God made clear many times not only in statements to Moses and the prophets but also through the Torah's provision of the law. Ever responsive to the words of the Israelite and always cognizant of the individual's intentionality, God not only lays down the laws of Israel's social order but also sees to their realization, one by one, case by case.

The Mishnah's legal definition of conflict and how it is resolved by oath taking is addressed in particular in Mishnah-tractate Shebuᶜot, "Oaths" or "Vows." As I said, there are few surprises, only ample cases that organize and illustrate the law.

### MISHNAH-TRACTATE SHEBUᶜOT 5:2

An oath concerning a bailment—how so? He said to him, "Give me my bailment which I have in your hand," "I swear that you have nothing in my hand"—or if he said to him, "You have nothing in my hand," "I impose an oath on you," and he said, "Amen" lo, this one is liable. [If] he imposed an oath on him five times, whether this is before a court or not before a court, and the other party denied it, he is liable for each count.

In line with the Torah, the conflict concerns a claim on a bailment denied by the bailiff. The bailee—who has left the bailment—imposes the oath; the bailiff—who is responsible for the bailment—accepts it. If the bailiff has lied, the bailiff is liable. The law of the Mishnah takes for granted that Israelites take God's name only with reverence and will not lie in that context. It further knows that God is present when called upon, so if the one who takes the oath is lying, God will take note.

### MISHNAH-TRACTATE SHEBUᶜOT 5:3–5

[If] five people laid claim on him and said to him, "Give us the bailment which we have in your hand"—"I swear that you have nothing in my hand"—he is liable on only one count. "I swear that you have nothing in my hand, nor you, nor you"—he is liable on each and every count. "Give me my bailment, loan, stolen goods, and lost property [Lev. 6:2] which I have in your hand"—"I swear you have nothing in my hand"—he is liable on only one count. "I swear that you do not have in my hand a bailment, loan, stolen goods, or lost property"—he is liable for each and every count. "Give me the grain, barley, and spelt, which I have in your hand"—"I swear you have nothing in my hand"—he is liable on only one count. "I swear that you have not got in my hand wheat, barley, or spelt"—he is liable for each and every count.

"You raped and seduced my daughter"—and he says, "I did not rape and I did not seduce" "I impose an oath on you"—and he said, "Amen"—he is liable.

"You stole my ox"—and he says, "I did not steal it"—"I impose an oath on you,"—and he said, "Amen"—he is liable. "I stole it, but I did not slaughter it, and I did not sell it"—"I impose an oath on you"—and he said, "Amen"—he is exempt. "Your ox killed my ox"—and he said, "It did not kill"—and he says, "I impose an oath on you"—and he said, "Amen"—he is liable. "Your ox killed my slave"—and he says, "It did not kill"—"I impose an oath on you"—and he said, "Amen,"—he is exempt. [If] he said to him, "You injured me and made a wound on me," and he said, "I did not injure you and I did not make a mark on you," "I impose an oath on you"—and he said, "Amen"—he is liable. [If] his slave said to him, "You knocked out my tooth and you blinded my eye," and he said, "I did not knock out your tooth or blind your eye," and he said to him, "I impose an oath on you,"—and he said to him, "Amen"—he is exempt. This is the governing principle: Whoever pays compensation on the basis of his own testimony is liable. And whoever does not pay compensation on the basis of his own testimony is exempt [in the case of these oaths].

The issue now is the liabilities incurred for multiple oaths, as spelled out. We note that the discussion proceeds from bailments to conflicts as to the facts of other transactions altogether, including rape and theft. Once the oath is taken, whether imposed by the judges or by the plaintiff, it is enforceable.

### MISHNAH-TRACTATE SHEBUᶜOT 6:2

"I have a maneh in your hand"—before witnesses he said to him, "Yes"—On the next day he said to him, "Give it to me"—"I already gave it to you"—he is exempt [from having to take the oath]. "You don't have anything in my hand"—he is liable [to pay].

"I have a maneh in your hand," and he said to him, "Yes,"—"Don't give it to me except before witnesses"—On the next day, he said to him, "Give it to me"—"I already gave it to you"—he is liable [to pay], because he has to hand it over to him before witnesses.

Here the bailiff has conceded the bailment, but claims that it was paid off. No oath pertains; the claim is accepted. The key lies in the contrast between not establishing the condition that repayment take place before witnesses and imposing that condition. In the latter case, the claim already to have handed over the bailment is null, in the absence of witnesses. There is no issue of an oath. The condition of repayment before witnesses once imposed is enforceable.

### MISHNAH-TRACTATE SHEBUᶜOT 6:3

"I have a litra of gold in your hand"—"You have in my hand only a litra of silver"—he is exempt [from having to take the oath]. "A denar of gold I have in your hand"—"You have in my hand only a denar of silver, a terisit, a pondion, and a perutah, "—he is liable, for all of them are kinds of a single coinage.

"I have a kor of grain in your hand"—"You have in my hand only a letekh of pulse"—he is exempt [from having to take the oath]. "A kor of produce I have in your hand"—You have in my hand only a letekh of pulse"—he is liable, for pulse falls into the category of produce.

[If] he claimed wheat and the other admitted to having barley, he is exempt [from having to take the oath].

He who claims jars of oil from his fellow, and the other confessed to having flagons—this confession is not of the same kind as that which is subject to claim.

In line with the law of the Torah, if the concession involves part of what is claimed—so with a claim of silver and a concession of silver—the oath is imposed. But if the concession concerns something other than what is claimed ("the bailment is not what you claim at all"), the oath is not imposed. The exposition of the matter then works out the speciation of a common genus, such as pulse/produce.

### MISHNAH-TRACTATE SHEBUᶜOT 6:5

And what are matters on account of which an oath is not imposed? [Claims involving] slaves, bonds, real estate, and consecrated property. To these also do not apply the rules of twofold restitution or fourfold or fivefold restitution. [In the case of these] an unpaid bailiff is not subjected to an oath. [In the case of these] a paid bailiff does not pay compensation.

The oath pertains only to tangible movable property, not to personalty (slaves) or realty or to commercial paper (bonds). One is liable to take an oath only in a matter involving a claim which specifies a concrete measure, weight, or number, and in which the claim involves a concrete measure, weight, or number. The oath pertains to a very determinate conflict of property; like all transactions of a sacred character, it must be specific to an object of a particular description. The oath cannot be generalized but must specify that to which it pertains.

### MISHNAH-TRACTATE SHEBUᶜOT 6:6–7

Ten fruit-laden vines I handed over to you"—and the other says, "They were only five"—whatever is attached to the ground is classified as real property.

They are forced to take an oath only in a matter involving a claim which specifies a concrete measure, weight, or number. How so? "A room full of goods I gave you," "A wallet full of money I gave to you," and this one says, "I don't know—but whatever you left is what you can take"—he is exempt [from having to take the oath]. This one says, "[I gave you a heap of produce] as high as the projection," and that one says, "It was only as high as the window," he is liable [to take an oath for denying the bailment].

He who lends money to his fellow on the strength of a pledge, and the pledge got lost—[the creditor] said to him, "I lent you a sela on the strength of it, but it was worth only a sheqel, " and [the debtor] says to him, "Not so. But you lent me a sela on the strength of it, and it was worth a sela"—he is exempt [from having to take the oath].

"A sela I lent you on the strength of it, and it was worth a sheqel, " and the other says, "Not so. But a sela you lent to me on the strength of it, and it was worth three denars"—he is liable.

"A sela you lent to me on the strength of it, and it was worth two," and the other says, "Not so. But I lent you a sela on the strength of it, and it was worth a sela"—he is exempt [from having to take the oath].

"A sela you lent me on the strength of it, and it was worth two," and the other says, "Not so, but a sela I lent to you on the strength of it, and it was worth five denars" —he is liable.

And upon whom is the oath imposed? Upon him with whom the bailment was left, lest this one take an oath, and the other one then produce the bailment.

Here, too, the oath pertains to movables of a certain value, and to a particular corpus, involving a concrete measure, weight, or number. Here, exemption from having to take an oath means that the defendant, the bailiff, is not penalized in any way. The oath serves as the plea of the defendant—the bailiff in the present sequence. If the plaintiff took the oath validating the claim, it leaves open the possibility of the defendant's nullifying the entire procedure by producing the bailment after all.

### MISHNAH-TRACTATE SHEBU⁽OT 7:4

He whose contrary litigant is not trusted [even if he takes] an oath—how so? All the same are an oath regarding testimony, an oath regarding a bailment, and even a rash oath—[if] one of the litigants was a dice player, gave out loans on usury, [was] a pigeon racer, or a dealer in Seventh-Year produce [Mishnah-tractate Sanhedrin 3:3], the other litigant takes an oath and collects [his claim].

Since taking the oath automatically guarantees success in the litigation, who gets to take it makes a considerable difference. In general it is the defendant. What happens if the defendant is untrustworthy? Then the advantage of taking the oath shifts to the plaintiff. If both are untrustworthy, neither takes an oath. The system protects the institution of the oath by assigning the matter to the plaintiff in cases where it is clear that the defendant will abuse it.

### MISHNAH-TRACTATE SHEBU⁽OT 7:5–6

A storekeeper concerning [what is written in his] account book—how so? It is not that he may say to him, "It is written in my account book that you owe me two hundred zuz." But [if the householder] said to him, "Give my son two seahs of wheat," [or] "Give my worker change for a sela," and he says, "I already gave it to him,"—and they say, "We never got it"—[the storekeeper] takes an oath and collects what is owing to him, and [the workers] take an oath and collect what they claim from the householder.

[If] one said to the storekeeper, "Give me produce for a denar," and he gave it to him—he said to him, "Give me the denar,"—he said to him, "I already gave it to you, and you put it in the till"—let the householder take an oath. If he gave him a denar and said to him, "Give me produce"—he said to him, "I already gave it to you and you brought it home"—let the storekeeper take an oath.

[If] he said to the money changer, "Give me small coins for a denar," and he gave them to him—he said to him, "Give me the denar"—he said to him, "I already gave it to you, and you put it in the till"—let the householder take an oath. If he gave him a denar and said to him, "Give me small change," he said to him, "I already gave them to you, and you tossed them into your wallet," let the money changer take an oath.

The disputes are now spelled out. In the former case, the storekeeper takes an oath to collect what is owing and so do the workers. That is to say, the oath ascertains that the storekeeper gave the money or the wheat, and the workers say they never got it. Both can be telling the truth. The oath then secures repayment of the storekeeper and of the workers by the householder, who has initiated the transaction and who is the plaintiff. Next, the plaintiff shifts. The system ordinarily identifies the pertinent plaintiff, to whom is assigned the privilege of validating a claim by taking an oath.

### MISHNAH-TRACTATE SHEBUᶜOT 7:8

And these [must] take an oath even when there is no claim [laid against them]: (1) partners, (2) tenants, (3) guardians, (4) a woman who manages her household, and (5) a manager of a common legacy ("son of the household"). [If] he said to him, "What is your claim against me?" "I want you to take an oath to me"—he is liable.

[Once] the partners have divided up the property, or the tenant farmers, then one cannot impose an oath upon the other. [If the requirement to take] an oath happened to come upon him from some other source [cause], they impose upon him an oath covering the entire [enterprise].

The advent of the Sabbatical Year releases the requirement to take an oath.

The parties listed here take an oath even when not specifically designated as defendants of a claim. The oath then specifies that there has been no overreaching or malfeasance—for instance, the woman who manages her household takes an oath that she has not stolen any property, even though she is not accused of having done so. These are areas to which the oath extends as a means of forestalling suspicion of misconduct.

## The Oath and the Resolution of Conflict: Must One Party to a Conflict Take a False Oath?

What about a case in which two parties take an oath as to the same point of contention, but one must be lying? How, then, can the sages utilize a procedure that guarantees offending God, by one party if not by the other? That question is raised in the familiar context of Mishnah-tractate Baba Mesia 1:1, as expounded by the Talmud of Babylonia (Bavli):

### MISHNAH-TRACTATE BABA MESIA 1:1 AND
### BAVLI BABA MESIA 1:1 I.2/2B

MISHNAH-TRACTATE BABA MESIA 1:1

Two lay hold of a cloak—
this one says, "I found it!"—
and that one says, "I found it!"—
this one says, "It's all mine!"—
and that one says, "It's all mine!"—
this one takes an oath that he possesses no less a share of it than half,
and that one takes an oath that he possesses no less a share of it than half,
and they divide it up.
This one says, "It's all mine!"—
and that one says, "Half of it is mine!"
the one who says, "It's all mine!" takes an oath that he possesses no less of a share of it than three parts,

and the one who says, "Half of it is mine!," takes an oath that he possesses no less a share of it than a fourth part.

This one then takes three shares, and that one takes the fourth.

Here both claimants to the cloak must take the oath, and then the division is prescribed in the assumption that each has told the truth. The Talmud's discussion of the Mishnah-passage raises the question, Are we not guaranteeing that one or the other party is taking a false oath, when both are required to do so? Ben Nannos, a Mishnah-authority himself, asks how the court can be party to the taking of a false oath:

BAVLI BABA MESIA 1:1 I.2/2B

May one claim that the Mishnah-passage before us [in requiring the taking of an oath to settle the matter] does not accord with the principle of Ben Nannos.

For Ben Nannos has said, "How is it possible that this party and that that party should be brought into the state of taking a false oath?" (Mishnah-tractate Shebuᶜot 7:5) [David Daiches, *Baba Mesia* (London: Soncino Press, 1948) *ad loc.*: For does not Ben Nannos express surprise at the decision of the Sages to impose oaths on disputants one of whom is bound to swear falsely?]

The reference is to Mishnah-tractate Shebuᶜot (7:1A, C): "These are the ones who take an oath and collect what is owing to him: . . . a shopkeeper concerning what is written in his account book." Then, Mishnah-tractate Shebuᶜot (7:5): "A shopkeeper concerning what is written in his account book—how so? It is not that he may say to him, 'It is written in my account book that you owe me two hundred zuz.' But if the householder said to him, 'Give my son two seahs of wheat,' 'Give my worker change for a sela,' and he says, 'I already gave it to him,' and they say, 'We never got it'—the storekeeper takes an oath and collects what is owing to him, and the workers take an oath and collect what they claim from the householder. Said Ben Nannos, 'How so? But these or those then are taking a vain oath! Rather, the storekeeper collects what is owing to him without taking an oath at all, and the workers collect what they claim not to have received without taking an oath.'" The Talmud now continues:

[The case before us may accord] even with the principle of Ben Nannos [who will not impose an oath in a case in which it is clear one or another party will be taking the oath falsely].

In the case to which Ben Nannos refers [in stating his principle], there is most assuredly going to be a false oath.

But in the present case, there is the possibility of claiming that there is no false oath.

One may say that the two of them at the same instant raised up the object [and thereby effected possession of it, so both can be telling the truth].

The premise of the question confirms the sages' view that taking the oath guarantees a just result. The remainder of the discussion need not detain us. The point is clear. When I say, at the oath taking, God is tangibly present and intervenes in the administration of justice, I stand on firm ground, indeed. *It* is the law of the Mishnah, not solely the declaration by God to Moses at Sinai, that systematizes God's presence as a principal way of resolving contention.

## The Power of Using the Right Words to Invoke God's Presence

God hears when Israelites call upon God's name or presence. The use of a common language forms the bridge between Israelites and between corporate Israel and God. If the sages wished to make the statement that the Israelite's word is comparable to God's and that, for the Israelite as for God, words form the means of sanctification, they could have found no more suitable occasion for doing so than in their discussion of the oath. And if, further, they wanted to say that God is everywhere present, a sentient being who pays close attention to everyone all the time, to what people say, not only to what they do, and, especially, to what they say upon the invocation of God's presence, God's hearing, in particular—if that is what they wanted to say, then Mishnah-tractate Shebuʿot provides not the ideal occasion but the only really appropriate one.

There are two reasons. First, the oath by definition calls God to witness the transaction; the person who takes the oath invokes God's name and calls upon God to confirm an allegation. So the consequence of asking God to join in one's claims and certify them, the conviction that God is everywhere, all the time, when God is called upon, forms the foundation of all else. Second, the oath represents a purely verbal transaction, not ordinarily confirmed by concrete action. It is the transaction that in the end depends on the integrity of the person who makes the statement in God's name, "By an oath, I shall not eat." Now, who is going to keep watch to see that the Israelite does not eat? And who says, "Amen—to what you have said,"—if not God who knows the truth? But since God knows the truth, that suffices.

The premise of oath taking accordingly involves an assessment of the Israelite's conscience and of God's character. The embodiment of truth, God oversees all things; God will know when God's name has been taken in vain. The Israelite is possessed of conscience. So he or she does not need to be subjected to supervision by a this-worldly force, when, having invoked God's name, the Israelite has called down God's oversight. What remarkable power the sages impute to language! Forceful religious convictions of a theological character come to full expression in the law of the Mishnah regarding oaths. God responds when God's name is invoked and God is not to be deceived—ever. Such convictions provide ample motivation for a detailed definition of the circumstances and formulas that engage God's interest and participation.

Each time an Israelite takes an oath, the householder imitates God. God not only enforces the oath, God himself takes oaths and is bound by them, the Torah being rich in divine oath takings, for example, Genesis 22:15, "By myself

I have sworn an oath, says the Lord, because you have done this and have not withheld your son, your only son, I will indeed bless you. . . ." In formulating matters in that way, God undertakes a perpetual blessing for Abraham's heirs, the taking of the oath securing credence from Abraham and imposing an iron-clad obligation upon God. As such, the oath possesses an integrity, an autonomy of power, such that God as much as the Israelite is bound by it.

## Law and Theology: The Oath in Rabbinic Narrative Context

The Mishnah itself is only one forum in which the Rabbinic sages treated a topic. They also produced a narrative tradition, the *Aggadah*. Here, too, the oath is treated, especially in regard to how God is bound by it (by contrast, as we have seen, the law of the Mishnah always centers on the oath as the Israelite is affected by it). Here is how the Rabbinic narrative tradition of the Oral Torah expresses the conception that God is bound by the oath:

LEVITICUS RABBAH X:I–III.1 = GENESIS RABBAH 39:6

"You love righteousness and hate wickedness, [therefore God, your God, has anointed you with the oil of gladness above your fellows]" (Ps. 45:7).

R. Yudan in the name of R. Azariah interpreted the verse to speak of Abraham, our father:

"When [Abraham] was pleading for mercy for the people of Sodom, he said before him, 'Lord of the world! You have taken an oath that you will not bring a flood upon the world.'

"That is in line with the following verse of Scripture: 'For this is like the days of Noah to me; as I swore that the waters of Noah should no more go over the earth, so I have sworn that I will not be angry with you and will not rebuke you' (Isa. 54:9).

"'Now [Abraham continued], it is a flood of water that you will not bring, but a flood of fire you will bring! Then you turn out to practice deception with regard to the oath.

"'If so, you will not carry out the obligation of your oath.'

"That is in line with the following verse: 'Far be it from you to do such a thing!' (Gen. 18:25).

"He said before him, 'Far be it from you . . . shall not the judge of all the earth do justly' (Gen. 18:25)."

What emerges is that the language of the oath is deemed precise and determinative, so that Abraham can read God's oath concerning the flood to be exclusionary—a flood of something other than water would represent an act of deception, violating the oath in spirit if not in letter.

In the narrative tradition, an oath actually imposes upon oneself restrictions or limitations, strengthens one's own resolve to avoid sin. How abstract! We find ourselves some distance from the representation of the oath in the law of the Mishnah, which, as we know, sees the oath in a different, concrete context of household and family. For example, these three invoked an oath so as to avoid temptation by the impulse to do evil, specifically, sexual sin:

**RUTH RABBAH LXXII:III.1**

Said R. Yosé, "There were three who were tempted by their inclination to do evil, but who strengthened themselves against it in each case by taking an oath: Joseph, David, and Boaz.

"Joseph: 'How then can I do this great wickedness and sin against God' (Gen. 39:9).

"David: 'And David said, "As the Lord lives, no, but the Lord shall smite him" (1 Sam. 26:10).'

"Boaz: 'As the Lord lives, I will do the part of the next of kin for you. Lie down until the morning.'"

To avoid sexual sin, the three principals take oaths, thus gaining fear of God as a buttress against sin. Now these are private transactions, so the oath brings God's oversight into the conduct of the named saints even when they are all by themselves. The oath here governs God's relationship to individuals, just as the oath taken to Abraham governs God's relationship to Abraham and his seed. In the law of the Mishnah, by contrast, matters are otherwise; there the oath is invoked to regulate the Israelite's relationship to the Israelite, God being asked to validate the commitment.

Further, in the narrative representation of the world, the nations are adjured as much as Israelites, and in the same transaction. By an oath, God imposes the arrangement that the gentiles must not rule Israel so harshly that Israel will rebel, and Israel must not rebel against the gentiles but must accept their government as punishment for sin:

**SONG OF SONGS RABBAH XXIV:II.1**

R. Yosé b. R. Hanina said, "The two oaths [Song 2:7: 'I adjure you, O daughters of Jerusalem,' and Song 3:5, 'I adjure you, O daughters of Jerusalem, by the gazelles or the hinds of the field'] apply, one to Israel, the other to the nations of the world.

"The oath is imposed upon Israel that they not rebel against the yoke of the kingdoms.

"And the oath is imposed upon the kingdoms that they not make the yoke too hard for Israel.

"For if they make the yoke too hard on Israel, they will force the end to come before its appointed time."

Thus, for the lore of the exegetical tradition, the oath concerns the Israelite as an isolated individual ("sin") or corporate Israel in relationship to the gentiles. In the law of the Mishnah, by contrast, we find not a single case in which a gentile figures in oath taking to settle conflicting claims to property. Nor are there any cases that invoke corporate Israel, on the one side, or the radically isolated Israelite individual on the other, but mainly householders and families in conflict. The perspective of the law of the Mishnah and that of the lore of the narrative tradition scarcely intersect. That is because, in general terms, the law of the Mishnah covers the intermediate ground, occupied by family and household. It encompasses Israelites and Israel: the social space between Israelites all by themselves and Israel's outer frontiers with the nations.

But the message of the law and the lore coheres. The power imputed to the oath, the context in which the oath exercises its controlling authority, the cogency of the details of the types of oaths—all work together in concrete and detailed ways to say of the law precisely what the abstractions of the lore also express. That is God's intimate, eternal, tangible engagement with what Israelites say to one another. If sages wanted to declare, "God listens carefully to what people say and pays attention to the details of what they do, God knows what you promise and observes how you carry out your promise, God oversees what no one witnesses, God lives among us and abides with us"—how better say so? For if sages wished to underscore the perpetual presence of God within Israel's everyday life, they could have accomplished their goal no more effectively than they have in the law, amplified by its corresponding lore. With God perpetually present and listening, an Israel took shape in law and in lore that was able to trust itself even amid conflict and contention, an Israel whole and at peace. Israel lived in God's house and ate at God's table, and God dwelt in Israel's abode and was nurtured by Israel's gifts. We turn now to the ways in which the law of the Mishnah embodied these fundamental theological convictions, not in words alone but in concrete deeds that defined the entire social order.

# 13 | GOD THE LANDLORD, ISRAEL THE TENANT

## God the Landlord:
### Tractates Shebiᶜit, ᶜOrlah, and Kilayim

## Israel the Tenant:
### Tractates Maᶜaserot and Hallah-Makhshirin

### Where Israel Meets God:
### The Locative Relationship

Israel encounters God in transactions of a concrete character, which God is asked to witness and certify. It is a relationship defined by occasions. But Israel's life with God is not only occasional, a matter of *when*, but locative, a matter of *where*. The Torah identifies the Land of Israel as the location of Israel's meeting with God. Scripture made clear that Israel's possession of the Land indicated Israel's standing with God. This conviction comes to expression not only in the narrative theology of the Torah but in the normative law of the Mishnah.

God in the Torah defines the conditions in which Israel is to work that particular Land. The law of the Mishnah responds to that definition, building on the implications of the Torah's laws. Specifically, the Mishnah's laws governing the management of the Land and the distribution of its produce embody the conviction that God owns the Land and Israel lives from its bounty as sharecroppers of God's Land. The Land is comparable to the Garden of Eden, and it is to be farmed in accord with the procedures of creation.

To treat the Land as holy means to farm it in such a way that order prevails, corresponding to the order of creation. Chaos and confusion must be overcome. The law of tractate Kilayim ordains that the Land recapitulate the perfection of creation, all things in place and in order, everything in its correct category or species, no two species confused. To treat the Land as holy means also that it is to enjoy the Sabbath of creation. Mishnah-tractate Shebiʿit, "the Seventh Year," in line with Scripture, treats the Land as holy, in the model of creation. And that means the Land must enjoy the Sabbath that God ordained to celebrate the sanctification of the perfect, the orderly creation God had made. In ʿOrlah, on the prohibition of fruit until the fourth year after the fruit trees was planted, the issues of creation play a complementary role; here the mythic foundation laid by the creation narrative yields legal consequences.

In these ways the Mishnah has Israel, living on God's Land, make of the Land a counterpart to Eden. The closely aligned tractates of Shebiʿit, ʿOrlah, and Kilayim say the same thing in three cognate ways. Enlandisement encompasses the restoration of Israel to the Land, and the restoration of the Land to replicate Eden, as it was meant by God to be. These tractates lay out Israel's role in the repair of creation.

### Shebiʿit Revisited

Tractate Shebiʿit concerns how, in the Sabbatical Year, God exercises rights of ownership along with the Israelite householder. This God does by decreeing a year in which the Land lies fallow, enjoying a Sabbath rest. The Sabbatical Year is calculated from the time of Israel's entry into the Land, which corresponds to the first day of creation. The Land of Israel is deemed animate and enchanted, sentient really, comparable to Israel. Just as Israel observes the Sabbath of creation, so too does the Land. There Israel bears responsibility for the Land and can bring about a Sabbath of rest for it. Mishnah-tractate Shebiʿit, which we met in chapter 6 and now revisit from a fresh perspective, elaborates the Torah's commandment (Lev. 25:1–8), which explicitly introduces the metaphor of the Sabbath of creation to the law of the Seventh Year:

> When you enter the land that I am giving you, the land shall observe a Sabbath of the Lord. Six years you may sow your field and six years you may prune your vineyard and gather in the yield. But in the Seventh Year the land shall have a Sabbath of complete rest, a Sabbath of the Lord. (Lev. 25:2–4)

The Land is to have its Sabbaths just as Israel does, and if the Land is denied its Sabbaths, Israel will lose it, as is stated in Leviticus 26:34–35:

> Then the land shall enjoy its Sabbaths as long as it lies desolate, while you are in your enemies' land; then the land shall rest and enjoy its Sabbaths. As long as it lies desolate, it shall have rest, the rest that it did not have in your Sabbaths when you dwelt on it.

Observing the commandments of the Sabbatical Year marks Israel's effort at keeping the Land like Eden.

Israel triggers the count. The Sabbatical Year takes effect only when Israel enters the Land. That is another way of saying that Israel's entry into the Land marks the counterpart of the beginning of the creation of Eden: six days matched by six years. When the Land has reached that state of order and permanence that corresponds to Eden at sunset on the sixth day, then the Sabbatical cycle commences, a year per day for the Land.

Sifra, the Rabbinic commentary to the book of Leviticus, articulates matters that the law of the Mishnah presupposes:

**SIFRA CCXLV:I.2**

> Once the Israelites had crossed the Jordan, they incurred liability to separate dough offering and to observe the prohibition against eating the fruit of fruit trees for the first three years after planting and the prohibition against eating produce of the new growing season prior to the waving of the sheaf of new grain [that is, on the fifteenth of Nisan].
>
> When the sixteenth of Nisan came, they incurred liability to wave the sheaf of new grain.
>
> With the passage of fifty days from then they incurred the liability to the offering of the Two Loaves.
>
> At the fourteenth year they became liable for the separation of tithes.

The Sabbatical takes over only when the Israelite farmers have asserted their ownership of the land and its crops. Then the process of counting the years begins.

> They began to count the years of the Sabbatical cycle, and in the twenty-first year after entry into the land, they observed the Sabbatical Year.
>
> In the sixty-fourth year they observed the first Jubilee.

Israel enters the Land and takes possession of it; everything starts at that moment. The key point is that the Sabbatical cycle commences when the Israelite householders have asserted their will to own and utilize the Land. Corporate Israel then entered into the situation of Adam on the day of his creation, when, joined by Eve, the first man and the first woman entered into Paradise—and, promptly, through an exercise of will, lost everything. How Israel, Adam's counterpart and opposite, is regenerated through the Torah comes to expression not only in Mishnah-tractate Shebiᶜit but also in the law of Mishnah-tractate ᶜOrlah.

## ᶜOrlah: The Produce of an Orchard in the Fourth Year after It Is Planted

Mishnah-tractate ᶜOrlah addresses a single detail of the narrative of Creation, specifically, the elaboration of the Torah's commandment:

> When you come to the land and plant any kind of tree for food, you shall treat it as forbidden. For three years it shall be forbidden, it shall not be eaten. In the fourth year all its fruit shall be set aside for jubilation before the Lord, and only in the fifth year may you use its fruit, that its yield to you may be increased: I am the Lord your God. (Lev. 19:23–25)

The produce of the fourth year after planting is treated as equivalent to second tithe, which we meet in the discussion of tractate Maᶜaser Sheni in chapter 14. That is, it is brought to Jerusalem ("for jubilation before the Lord") and eaten there. The religious premise in ᶜOrlah is the same as that which sustains tractate Shebi'it. God relates to Israel through the Land and the arrangements that God imposes upon the Land. What Israel does, how it conducts itself, takes the measure of its regeneration, its remedy for the condition of Adam.

But that theological generalization does not clarify the rule before us, which seems arbitrary and pointless. What, specifically, is the purpose for the prohibition of using the fruit for three years and having the Israelites present themselves with it to Jerusalem in the fourth? The specificities of the law turn out to define with some precision a message on the relationship of Israel to the Land of Israel and to God. These, as articulated in Sifra's reading of Scripture, make explicit matters of religious conviction that we might otherwise miss. The first is that the prohibition of 'Orlah-fruit applies solely within the Land of Israel and not to the neighboring territories occupied by Israelites, which means *that it is the union of Israel with the Land of Israel that invokes the prohibition:*

### Sifra CCII:I.1

"When you come [into the land and plant all kinds of trees for food, then you shall count their fruit as forbidden; three years it shall be forbidden to you, it must not be eaten. And in the fourth year all their fruit shall be holy, an offering of praise to the Lord. But in the fifth year you may eat of their fruit, that they may yield more richly for you: I am the Lord your God" (Lev. 19:23-25)].

Might one suppose that the law applied once they came to Transjordan?

Scripture says, ". . . into the land,"

the particular Land [of Israel].

Here, some trait deemed to inhere in the Land of Israel and in no other territory must define the law, and a particular message ought to inhere in this law. This same point is reached once more: it is only trees that *Israelites* plant in the Land that are subject to the prohibition, not those that gentiles planted before the Israelites inherited the land:

### Sifra CCII:I.2

"When you come into the land and plant":

excluding those that gentiles have planted prior to the Israelites' coming into the land.

Or should I then exclude those that gentiles planted even after the Israelites came into the land?

Scripture says, "all kinds of trees."

A further point of special interest requires that the Israelite plant the tree as a deliberate act; if the tree merely grows up on its own, it is not subject to the prohibition. So Israelite action joined to intention is required; that is what activates the system:

### Sifra CCII:I.4.

". . . and plant . . .":

excluding one that grows up on its own.

". . . and plant . . .":

excluding one that grows out of a grafting or sinking a root.

The several points on which Sifra's reading of the law of the Mishnah and the verses of the Torah that pertain alert us to the religious principle embedded in the law of Mishnah-tractate ʿOrlah.

First, like the Seventh Year, so here too, the law takes effect only from the point at which Israel enters the land. That is to say, Israel's entry into the Land marks the beginning of the time at which the trees produce fruit that are subject to God's concern. To understand, we recall from Shebiʿit that the entry of Israel into the Land matches the restoration of Eden. So there is no missing the essential message. The Land bears that fruit of which God takes cognizance—that fruit that will cause jubilation in the house of God in Jerusalem, when it is presented to God there—only when the counterpart moment of creation has struck. The law of the Mishnah has no better way of saying that the entry of Israel into the Land compares with the moment at which the creation of Eden took place. Israel's entry into the Land marks a new beginning for humanity, comparable to the very creation of the world.

Second, according to the law of the Mishnah, Israelite intentionality is required to subject a tree to the ʿOrlah rule. If an Israelite does not plant the tree with the plan of producing fruit, then the tree is not subject to the rule. If the tree grows up on its own, not by the act and precipitating intentionality of the Israelite, the ʿOrlah rule does not apply. If an Israelite does not plant the tree to produce fruit, the ʿOrlah rule does not apply. And the tree must be planted in the ordinary way; if grafted or sunk as a root, the law does not apply. In a moment, this heavy emphasis on Israelite intentionality will produce a critical result. But, before reaching that juncture, let us ask some fundamental questions.

First, what is the counterpart to Israelite observance of the restraint of three years? Second, why should Israelite intentionality play so critical a role? The answer becomes obvious when we ask a third question: Can we think of any other commandments concerning fruit trees in the Land that—the sages say time and again—is Eden? Of course we can: "Of every tree of the garden you are free to eat; but as for the tree of knowledge of good and evil, you must not eat of it" (Gen. 2:16).

But there is this difference: the law of Mishnah-tractate ʿOrlah imposes upon Israel a more demanding commandment than God's imperative to Adam and Eve. Of the fruit of *no* tree in the new Eden may Israel eat for three years. That demands considerable restraint.

Not only so, but it is Israel's own intentionality—not God's—that imposes upon every fruit-bearing tree the prohibition of use of the produce for three years—not only the one tree of Eden. So once Israel wants the fruit, it must show that it can restrain its desire and wait for three years. By Israel's act of will, Israel has imposed upon itself the requirement of restraint. Taking the entry point as our guide, we may say that, from the entry into the Land and for the next three years, trees that Israelites value for their fruit and plant with the produce in mind must be left untouched. For all time thereafter, when Israelites plant fruit trees in the Land, it is as if they have taken the Land for the first time, so they must recapitulate that same exercise of self-restraint. That is, they are to act—to keep time within the cycle of creation—as though, for the case at hand, they have just come into the Land.

### The Details of the Law of Mishnah-tractate ʿOrlah and the Theological Statement That They Make

To find the context in which these rules make their statement, we consider details, then the main point. First and most important: Why *three years* in particular? The narrative of Creation answers the question. Fruit trees were created on the third day of creation. Then, when Israel by intention and action designates a tree—any tree—as fruit-bearing, Israel must wait for three years, as creation waited for three days for the advent of the fruit-bearing tree.

Second, why fruit trees in particular? Once more the narrative of creation gives a self-evident answer: it is a fruit-bearing tree that was the object of a particular commandment, a prohibition recapitulated now. But there is this difference. It is not one tree alone, but any tree. The regeneration of Adam through Israel reenacts itself without end. So the planting of every tree imposes upon Israel the occasion to meet once more the temptation that the first Adam could not overcome. Israel now recapitulates the temptation of Adam then, but Israel, the New Adam, possesses, and is possessed by, the Torah. And that makes all the difference. So by its own action and intention in planting fruit trees, Israel finds itself in a veritable orchard of trees like the tree of knowledge of good and evil. The difference between Adam and Israel is that, permitted to eat all fruit but one, Adam ate the forbidden fruit, while Israel refrains for a specified span of time from fruit from all trees. This restraint marks what has taken place, the regeneration of humanity. So Israel waits for three years—as long as God waited in creating fruit trees.

Adam picked and ate. But here too there is a detail not to be missed. Even after three years, Israel may not eat the fruit wherever it chooses. Rather, in the fourth year from planting, Israel will still show restraint, bringing the fruit only "for jubilation before the Lord" in Jerusalem. That signals that the once-forbidden fruit is now eaten in public, not in secret, before God, as a moment of celebration. That detail too recalls the fall and makes its comment on the horror of the fall. That is, when Adam ate, he shamefully hid from God for having eaten the fruit. But when Israel eats the fruit, it does so proudly, joyfully, in God's very presence. The contrast is not to be missed, so too the message. Faithful Israel refrains when it is supposed to, and so it has every reason to cease to refrain and to eat "before the Lord." It has nothing to hide, and everything to show.

And there is more. In the fifth year Israel may eat on its own, the time of any restraint from enjoying the gifts of the Land having ended. That sequence provides fruit for the second Sabbath of creation, and so through time. How so? Placing Adam's sin on the first day after the first Sabbath,[1] thus Sunday, we may calculate the three forbidden years as corresponding to Sunday, Monday, and Tuesday. Then Wednesday of the second week of creation, the fourth day corresponds to the fourth year when the fruit is to be brought to Jerusalem. Thursday and Friday provide the equivalent of a double portion for the Sabbath—the second Sabbath of creation. So now, a year representing a day of the Sabbatical week, just as Leviticus says so many times in connection with the Sabbatical Year, the three prohibited years allow Israel to show its true character, fully regenerate, wholly and humbly accepting God's commandment, the one Adam broke. And the rest follows.

By its own act of restraint, the New Adam, Israel, in detailed action displays its repentance in respect to the very sin that the Old Adam committed, the sin of disobedience and rebellion. Facing the same opportunity to sin, Israel again and again over time refrains from the sin that cost Adam Eden. So by its manner of cultivation of the Land and its orchards, Israel manifests what in the very condition of humanity has changed by the giving of the Torah: the advent of humanity's second chance, through Israel. Only in the Land that succeeds Eden can Israel, succeeding Adam, carry out the acts of regeneration that the Torah makes possible.

### Kilayim: Mixed Seeds

God is concerned not only with the use of the Land but with its appearance—in line with the account of creation, which stresses that each species was created in its own framework. Thus, the Land is to be sown in such a way that species are kept distinct, whether vegetable or animal. The law of Mishnah-tractate Kilayim elaborates on the law of Leviticus 19:19:

> You shall not let your cattle mate with a different kind; you shall not sow your field with two kinds of seed; you shall not put on cloth from a mixture of two kinds of material.

It further elaborates on the law of Deuteronomy 22:9–11:

> You shall not sow your vineyard with a second kind of seed, otherwise the crop from the seed you have sown and the produce of the vineyard may not be used; you shall not plow with an ox and an ass together; you shall not wear cloth that combines wool and linen.

Leviticus 19:19 places into the context of the sanctification of Israel the considerations of meticulous division among classes or species of the animal and vegetable world that define the tractate's topic. Sanctification takes place

---

[1] But not all calculations concur; some place the sin on the day on which Adam and Eve were created, the sixth day of creation, and not on Sunday.

in the context of Genesis 1:1–2:3, the orderly creation of the world, species by species. The act of sanctification of creation took place when all things were ordered, properly in place, each according to its kind. Creation takes place when chaos is brought under control and ordered, that is, when the world is made perfect and ready for God's act of sanctification. Creation was orderly, and Israel restores the orderly appearance of the Land to conform to the condition of creation.

This means not mixing classes or species of flora or fauna—plants, animals, fibers—thus, whether plants, crops in a vineyard, kinds of animals, or diverse sources of fabrics, linen from the earth and wool from animals. Mixing them violates the principles of order established in creation, when each species was set forth in its own category ("according to its name"). But what defines a class? The law of the Mishnah takes the view that it is the human being who does. It is the human being's definition of species and perception of their mixtures that governs. What appears orderly is deemed in good order. That explains the stress of the law of tractate Kilayim on appearances, which generates the issues of the law. If plants look alike, they are considered to belong to the same kind. The *appearance* of confusion, not the actual sowing together of two kinds, imposes liability for violating the law.

Take, for example, the issue of growing two or more crops in the same field. The Torah supplies only the rule that this may not be done. But the law holds that if the field would *appear* to contain more than a single crop, then the law is invoked; but if the field would appear to contain one crop only, with other crops growing adjacent but not within the main crop, then appearance takes over and the field does not violate the law. If different kinds of crops appear to be planted in an orderly way, they are deemed sown separately, even within the same field. But if someone cannot with the naked eye distinguish them from one another, they are deemed as mixed in kind.

If in a person's view the field contains mixed crops, it is forbidden, but if from the human perspective it does not, then the law is not violated. If properly distinguished, therefore, wheat and barley may grow in the same field, if they are kept separate within the field, and so on. It follows that if items when mingled together do not appear to confuse diverse species, they may be planted together. When it comes to adjacent spaces, the rule is the same. Sufficient distance to set off one species from another prevents violating the law. How things look, not how they actually are, defines the governing criterion. It is the Israelite who bears responsibility for preventing the mixing of species. If diverse kinds grow without the owner's intent, the crops do not have to be destroyed—for instance, if they are growing among vines—but once the householder finds out, he has to remove the diverse kinds.

From one viewpoint Kilayim takes God's perspective on the Land, imagining the landscape as seen from on high. God wants to see in the Land an orderly and regular landscape, each species in its proper place. God wants to see Israel clothed in garments that preserve the distinction between animal and vegetable exactly where that distinction operates for fabrics. God wants to see animals ordered by their species, just as they were when Noah brought them into the ark (Gen. 7:14). What that means is that grapes and wheat are not to grow together; oxen and asses are not to be yoked together; and wool and linen are not to be woven together in a single garment.

But from another viewpoint, it is not the perspective of God but of the Israelite in particular, that dictates matters. For who bears responsibility for restoring the perfection of creation? The Priestly Code wants the land to be returned to its condition of an unchanging perfection. But the Mishnah's law empowers humanity to impose order upon the world. The Israelite house-holder has the power to do in the Land of Israel what God did in creating the world at Eden, that is, establish order, overcome chaos, perfect the world for the occasion of sanctification. The law thus embodies in the topic at hand the principle prevailing throughout the law of the Mishnah (as formulated at Mishnah-tractate Kelim 17:11): "Everything is according to the measure of the man." The law of the Mishnah that elaborates the commandments on the present topic set forth in the Torah transforms the human individual into God's partner in overcoming chaos and establishing order. It is the individual's perspective that governs, the individual's discernment that identifies chaos or affirms order.

The reason is that the Israelite's and God's perspectives are the same. If a person discerns the confusion of species, so would God, and if he or she does not, then neither would God. But when the law of the Mishnah leaves matters relative to appearance to humanity, the actualities of mixed seeds no longer matter, or do not matter so much as appearances. And that requires a second reason as well. For if God cares that "you shall not sow your field with two kinds of seed and that you shall not sow your vineyard with a second kind of seed," surely the actuality, not the appearance, ought to prevail—unless another consideration should be considered. And that other consideration comes into play when we ask, how, through the shared engagement with the Land, do God and Israel collaborate, and to what end?

## The Law of Mishnah-tractates Kilayim, ʿOrlah, and Shebiʿit

Israel is in charge of the Land of Israel. Israel not only bears responsibility for what happens in the land, but also bears the blame and the penalty when matters are not right. It is Israel that goes into exile for failing to treat the Land as holy in the way God has decreed, e.g., ignoring the Land's right to Sabbath repose every seventh year. God ascends from the Temple through the levels of Heaven, from which God originally descended to the Temple. So

Israel relates to God through Israel's trusteeship of the Land. The tractates that deal with the enlandisement of the relationship of Israel to God, Kilayim, ʿOrlah, and Shebiʿit, present Israel as the trustee of the Land and here assign to Israel the task of cultivating the Land in a manner appropriate to the perfection of creation at the outset. No wonder, then, that Israel's view of matters must prevail, for Israel bears full responsibility on the spot for how things will appear to Heaven—and the liability for failure.

That fact—Israel's responsibility to farm the Land in accord with the orderly rule of Eden—makes Israel not only the custodian of the Land but also God's partner in that vast labor of reform that, in the end, will bring about the restoration of Adam to Eden. For, we recall, it is God's plan at the end to bring to life all Israel and in the world or age to come to restore all Israel to the Land of Israel, completing the return to Eden—with, however, the difference made by the Torah. Armed with the Torah, Israel will not rebel as Adam did. Israel's heart has been purified, its will has been tamed, so that it wants what God wants, loving God with all its heart, all its soul, and all its might. That represents the regeneration of Adam in Israel. That is why, the restorationist theology maintains, the world to come will endure: chaos overcome, order will prevail. How Israel cultivates the Holy Land entrusted to it then makes all the difference—field by field, all must be in its correct configuration.

The restoration of Adam to Eden takes place, at the end, in and through the restoration of Israel to the Land of Israel. So all matters cohere. In assigning to Israel the task of farming the country in a manner appropriate to the principles of its original creation, therefore, the law of the Mishnah asks Israel to do its concrete part in a restorationist teleology. That is, Israel must make the end like the beginning, Eden having been recovered. Once God has assigned the Land to Israel and instructed Israel on how to attain and preserve its condition of perfection as at creation, then Israel's perspective, not God's, must govern, because, for Israel, the stakes are very high: the resurrection of the dead to life, the restoration of Israel to the Land. When we speak of the enlandisement of the relationship of Israel to God, the law of the Mishnah once more permits us to turn the Mishnah's elaboration of the Torah's laws into a considerable formulation of religious conviction and consciousness.

### Israel the Tenant Farmer

The Israelite householder owes a share of the crop to the Landlord, who is God. Two issues in connection with giving God his share of the crop are probed in the law of the Mishnah. First, at what point in the work on the crop does the householder become liable for the separation of God's share of the crop? Second, at what point in the utilization of the sharecropper's portion of the crop does the householder once more become liable for setting aside a portion for God? These are distinct matters—when the crop in general becomes liable and when the householder's portion of the crop must yield a portion to God's designated representative. The one is treated in the Mishnah-tractate Maᶜaserot, the other, Hallah, with its companion, Makhshirin. Each bears its own distinct message.

The main point of the former, reworked in the latter, with special reference to Makhshirin, concerns the response of God to the householder's act of will. That act may involve laying claim to a portion of the crop, as at Maᶜaserot and Hallah; or it may involve deliberately changing the natural condition of produce and inaugurating life-creating processes, as at Makhshirin. In both cases, the interplay of the householder's will with God's presence—as owner of the Land and its crops, as source of the processes that create and sustain life—takes place in immediate terms.

## Maᶜaserot: The Rules That Govern Tithing in General

The rules set forth in Mishnah-tractate Maᶜaserot pertain to all the agricultural tithes and offerings and dictate the procedures—liability, timing, special problems—that pertain to them in general. The main point is simple: when Israel asserts its rights of possession, God's interest is aroused. Then God lays claim to a proper share in the crop of Land held in partnership with the Israelite farmer. So when the Israelite householder signifies his or her taking possession of the crop, that is the point at which God's claim on the crop is activated; then the householder must designate God's share, too. What ensues is a vast exercise in how the will of God and the will of the Israelite meet in concord, Israel obeying God's laws about the disposition of the abundance of the Land. The law of the Mishnah responds to the basics: What is to be subjected to tithing of various kinds, and when is the obligation to do so incurred? As to the former, the Torah is clear:

You shall tithe all the yield of your seed that comes forth from the field year by year. (Deut. 14:22)

All produce of the Land thus is subject to sharing. As to when the removal of God's portion of the crop must take place, the Torah requires an annual donation. The law of the Mishnah is concerned with (1) the point at which produce becomes liable to the designation and separation of tithes, (2) the kind of produce that falls into the category of tithing, and (3) the timing of the act of tithing. In dealing with these issues a single theological conception appears, presenting an essential social teaching.

When does the crop become liable to tithing? The basic principle is that when the produce is suitable for use by its owner, then it becomes subject to tithing and may not be used until it is tithed. The law of the Mishnah then indicates the point in the growth of various species at which tithes may be removed. That is the moment at which the produce is deemed edible. If someone picks and eats unripe produce, that does not impose the obligation to tithe, since the commonality of people do not regard unripe produce as food and do not eat it. Only when people ordinarily regard the produce as edible does consideration of tithing arise. Then there are two stages in the process, votive and obligatory. Crops *may* be tithed when the produce ripens. Then the produce becomes useful, and it is assumed that the farmer values the produce. But crops *must* be tithed when the farmer by a determinate act of will claims the produce as his own.

It is not the condition of the produce that makes the difference but, rather, the attitude toward the produce that is taken by the farmer who has grown it. That attitude takes effect through the farmer's act of ownership, beyond possession. Asserting ownership takes place, specifically, when the householder brings untithed produce from the field to the courtyard or prepares it for sale in the market. At that moment, the farmer having indicated a claim to the produce and intent to use it for his own purposes, God's interest is aroused, God's share becomes due. God responds to the human, specifically, God's attitudes correspond to those of the householder: when the Israelite in the Land of Israel wants to own the crop and dispose of it in some way, then and only then God demands a share.

What produce is subject to tithing? Crops that are ripe, owned by particular householders and valued by them are subject to tithing. Crops that are unripe, not owned by a particular person or valued by him are not. The first principle is, what is ownerless and thus not possessed by a particular farmer as his private property simply is not liable to tithing. Man having laid no claim on the produce, God also is unprovoked to take an interest in that produce and demand his share of it. The second (now familiar) one is, the obligation to tithe pertains once the crop has ripened.

When does the act of tithing matter? Untithed produce that is liable to tithing may not be eaten as a regular meal. That is to say, it may not be eaten in the accepted way, which is in the manner of priests eating their rations or in the manner of commoners eating daily bread. But it may be eaten in a random or informal way. To be made suitable for ordinary, regular meals, the produce must be properly tithed; the sacred offerings must be designated and removed, leaving the produce available for the wish and will of the farmer.

While produce in the field is not liable to tithing, the farmer by his or her actions may show a desire to convert possession into ownership; then the produce must be tithed. If in the field one pickles or boils or salts produce, it must be tithed; if the produce is merely stored for later transport, it need not be tithed. If the farmer merely tests the produce, no tithe is yet required. That fine distinction is shown in the law of Mishnah-tractate Maʿaserot 4:1:

> One who squeezes the oil of olives onto his body is exempt from tithing. If he squeezed the oil and placed it in the palm of his hand, he is required to tithe.

Such distinctions rest upon the foundation of decided law, principles established before the exegesis of the law commences. In different language, Mishnah-tractate Maʿaserot 4:5 makes the same point:

One who husks barley removes the husks from the kernels one by one, and eats without tithing. But if he husked a few kernels and placed them in his hand, he is required to tithe.

Produce is subject to tithing from the time that it ripens through the harvest and up to the point when it is carried into the courtyard, that is, into private property, or sold in the market. So the law of the Mishnah sorts out the cases of when produce subject to tithing but not yet tithed is meant as a snack or as a meal. That depends on the intent of the farmer. If the person eating the food intends it as a snack, it is classified as such; if it is intended as a meal, it is classified as such and tithes must be removed. So the attitude of the owner dictates the status of the untithed but liable produce. M. Jaffee states the matter in this language: "The liability of a particular batch of produce to the removal of tithes is determined solely by what its owner intends to do with it." Actions reveal intentions. If a farmer in the field cooks food, then the food is intended for a meal; if the farmer left produce in the field to ripen, not cooking it, the food is deemed a snack. But the Torah, for its part, may relieve a person of the liability to tithe, such as in cases where, by assigning to him or her ownership of the produce; God has relinquished God's share. That would pertain to produce acquired by the poor in gleaning or to produce received by workers in the course of harvesting the crop: One who is granted eating privileges by the Torah is exempt from tithing what is eaten, while one who is granted no eating privileges by the Torah is required to tithe that which is consumed.

## God Responds to the Israelite's Attitude and Intention

Only when the produce is shown by the actions of the farmer to be valuable to the farmer does God's claim emerge. That principle is expressed in the law that produce that is ownerless is not liable to tithing, such as in regard to the produce of the Seventh Year and the like. The system of obligatory tithing then gets under way when the Israelite proposes to exercise personal will over his or her domain and its produce. Every other party to the system then responds to the intentionality of the farmer. Priests cannot claim their dues whenever they choose, and God does not take an active role in determining when the produce must be tithed. Human actions that reveal human intentions provoke God.

As we see, the law of the Mishnah spins out the implications of the distinction between possession and ownership, on the one side, and of the fundamental affirmation of the message of creation, on the other. That message is, we are like God, as the Torah states, "Let us make man in our image, after our likeness . . ." (Gen. 1:26). The consubstantiality of God and the human individual comes to concrete expression in the law of Mishnah-tractate Maᶜaserot.

## Hallah and Makhshirin: Dough Offering, and When Bread Becomes Dough

Mishnah-tractate Hallah deals with dough offering, a detail in the larger program of sharing the Land's produce with God the landlord. At issue is God's share of the bread when it is being made, the dough offering, or Hallah:

> The Lord said to Moses, "Say to the people of Israel: when you come into the Land to which I bring you, and when you eat of the food of the land, you shall present an offering to the Lord. Of the first of your coarse meal you shall present a cake as an offering, as an offering from the threshing floor, so shall you present it. Of the first of your coarse meal you shall give to the Lord an offering throughout your generations." (Num. 15:17–21)

The sages understand the verses to require the separation of a portion from the bread; a portion of coarse meal, taken to mean unbaked bread dough. It is comparable to the offering of the threshing floor, which sages call heave offering (priestly ration). Since heave offering is given to the priest, so sages assume dough offering is assigned to the priest as well.

The law of Mishnah-tractate Hallah takes as its task, first, to define that bread which must yield dough offering; second, to indicate when the dough offering is to be separated, that is, at what point in the baking of bread does the householder have to remove God's portion, the Hallah; and, third, to consider the applicability of the offering to Israelites outside of the Land of Israel.

What defines bread dough that is liable to the separation of dough offering? In bread we deal with food that humans deem edible. Only that bread that is fit for human consumption is liable to dough offering; bread made for animals is not. But we do not differentiate among humans; if impoverished people will eat the bread, that suffices; it does not have to be bread fit for a king. Only grains that leaven produce dough that is liable to dough offering. They alone—for the same reason—also produce unleavened bread. All dough made from grain in the status of ordinary, unconsecrated produce is liable to dough offering. Rice, sorghum, poppy, sesame, and pulse, which do not leaven, also do not produce dough subject to dough offering. Why the leavening process is key to the message of the Mishnah will become clear presently. Dough is liable to dough offering only if prepared in the manner that is normal for bread, so the character of the processing matters. Dough prepared to serve as leaven is nonetheless liable to dough offering, so intention as to the use of the dough is not at issue here.

When is the obligation to separate dough offering incurred? Dough becomes liable to dough offering as soon as it is prepared as bread. In all cases the operative criterion is the point at which the dough forms a crust in the oven, at which point the dough is liable to dough offering. That is the point at which the dough must be designated as dough offering. People may snack on dough without first separating dough offering from it until the person preparing the dough rolls the dough out or makes the dough into a ball, in the case of dough made from wheat, or until it is formed into a solid mass, in the case of dough made from barley. Once the baker rolls the dough out, in the case of dough made from wheat, or forms it into a solid mass, in the case of dough made from barley, one who eats from it without first separating dough offering is liable to death.

The point is simple. The dough can be rolled out or made into a ball only when flour has been mixed with yeast and water; hence the obligation may be met at the outset of the process of working the dough, when the enzyme is activated and the fermentation process is begun, but must be met at the end, when the enzyme dies and the fermentation process concludes.

There could hardly be a more vivid way of linking the obligation to separate dough offering to the fermentation process. Such a process must be possible—hence the five species but no others—and it must be under way. Then the consideration of God's share in the dough becomes relevant. Or to put it somewhat materially, when the flour is brought to life by water and yeast, then God's claim on the bread registers. The dough, when alive and expanding, encompasses a share belonging to God.

## Dough Prepared by the Israelite in the Land of Israel Yields Dough Offering: What Is at Stake?

Only dough owned by an Israelite in the Land of Israel is liable to the dough offering in its conventional form. However, when grain is brought to the Land of Israel, dough made from it is liable to dough offering. So the critical matter is not the origin of the grain but its location and possession, thus:

MISHNAH-TRACTATE HALLAH 3:4; 6

> A gentile who gave [flour] to an Israelite to make into dough for him—
>
> [the dough] is exempt from dough offering,
>
> One who prepares dough [in partnership] with a gentile—
>
> if [the share of the dough] belonging to the Israelite does not comprise the [minimum] volume [subject to] dough offering,
>
> it is exempt from dough offering.
>
> A convert who converted [to Judaism] and had dough in his possession [at the time he converted]—
>
> [if the dough] was prepared before he converted, it is exempt [from dough offering].
>
> But [if it was prepared] after he converted, it is subject [to dough offering].

The point is that dough offering is owed only by Israelites in the Land of Israel. The fact that Israelites own and eat that grain in the Land of Israel makes all the difference. As to what is required of dough made from grain grown in the Land but consumed abroad, there is a dispute. One authority maintains that produce of the Land, wherever located, is liable. The other holds that the liability takes effect only in the Land and not abroad. The Torah is clear that "bread of the land" would exclude bread produced abroad. The contrary view invokes "into the land to which I bring you" (Num. 15:19-20): "there you are liable, you are not liable abroad." So from all perspectives what registers is the presence of Israel in the Land of Israel, and that (within the present view) is the key to the liability of bread to dough offering: grain, wherever grown, if eaten by Israel in the Land of Israel, is liable to dough offering, while grain grown in the land, if eaten abroad, may or may not be liable.

Dough that has formed a crust within the Land of Israel is liable, whatever the origin of the flour. In the priests' view dough offering may not be brought from outside of the Land of Israel. The priests reject dough offering brought by Israelites from abroad since the liability for dough offering only takes effect when Israelites in the Land of Israel prepare dough. Then the actuality of Israel dwelling on the Land, not the origin of the grain is the determining feature: Israelites living in the Land of Israel separate dough offering from the bread that they are going to eat, from the point at which the bread begins to ferment, and they are obligated to do so from the point at which the bread has ceased to ferment.

## The Fermentation Process: When Bread Lives, God Takes Note

That the whole matter of the dough offering forms an exercise in thinking about the fermentation process is demonstrated, moreover, by the explicit insistence that just as flour produces dough subject to dough offering only if a fermentation process is possible, so flour produces unleavened bread valid for Passover only if a fermentation process is possible but is thwarted. So the bread that the Israelites in the Land of Israel eat to which God establishes claim is comparable in its traits to the bread that the Israelites leaving Egypt, or commemorating their Exodus from Egypt, are required to eat. At the moment of the fermentation process itself, *God takes notice.* The process need not take place, but it must bear the potential to take place. So it may not affect the bread of the Exodus—which is liable to dough offering—but it must affect the bread of Israel in the Land of Israel—which is always liable.

Having come this far, we may readily perceive the broad outlines of a simple message: bread in which God takes an interest is bread subject to living processes of nature: the life of the enzyme (as we should express matters). Leavening, then, is the key to the definition of bread. Taken as a natural process, leavening is animate, or is perceived as animate. It comes about

> through the action of gas bubbles developed naturally or folded in from the atmosphere. Leavening may result from yeast or bacterial fermentation, from chemical reactions or from the distribution in the batter of atmospheric or injected gases.[2]

Nature's process spills over once more into a theological principle. Israel's life in the Land of Israel is nourished through the transformation of grain into bread, that is, through the life process that takes grain and makes it edible and life-sustaining. Then and there God lays claim to a share: when Israel renews

---

[2] Samuel A. Matz, "Baking and Bakery Products," *Encyclopedia Britannica*, 15th ed., 2:597.

its life, meal by meal, its action in invoking the life process of fermentation, start to finish, provokes God's reaction. That is because God has a natural share in the transaction by which life is maintained—but (as the priests clearly maintained) only in the transaction that takes place between Israel and the Land of Israel, there alone.

Does Israel have a say in the inauguration of the fermentation process and the engagement of God therein? In this exchange, this transfer and renewal of Israel's life in engagement with the living processes of nature, Israel's intentionality plays no role. The processes go forward willy-nilly. Then what about intentionality, for instance, that of the baker? In fact, that point is raised explicitly in Mishnah-tractate Hallah 1:5 in discussing whether a third party imposes upon grain the status of that which has been fully processed and is liable to be tithed. One authority maintains that the baker has imposed liability, even though the owner of the pile of grain does not know and approve of the baker's action. That is in line with 1:7:

### MISHNAH-TRACTATE HALLAH 1:7

[As regards] women who gave [dough] to the baker to make [it into] leaven for them—

if [the dough] of each woman comprises less than the [prescribed minimum] volume [subject to dough offering], [the dough] is exempt from dough offering.

If the volume of the dough of all the women all together does meet the requisite amount to impose liability to dough offering, the dough will be exempt, because it was the baker, not the woman who owned the dough who imposed liability. But contrary opinion registers as well. The point is clear: the dough offering is owing whatever the intentionality of the owner of the grain. So Israel becomes liable to hand over God's share of the produce no matter what. The reason that intentionality plays no role in the liability of the dough to dough offering becomes clear when we recall the critical role human intentionality plays in the law of Mishnah-tractate Makhshirin, the counterpart and opposite of the law of Mishnah-tractate Hallah, to which we now turn.

## Makhshirin: When Produce Becomes Susceptible to Uncleanness, and What the Moment of Susceptibility Signifies

Mishnah-tractate Makhshirin is concerned with the centrality of human intentionality in inaugurating the process by which the sources of contamination take effect. Here we deal specifically with the role of the human being in imparting susceptibility to uncleanness in foodstuffs. A person's deliberate will, or intentionality, is what renders food susceptible. That is because of the sages' reading of the law of the Torah, at Leviticus 11:34, 37. There Moses states that food that is dry is not susceptible to uncleanness, but food that is wet is susceptible. Only when produce is wet down is it susceptible. The Rabbinic sages further take as a fact that produce that is wet down by the intent of the owner is affected, but that wet down inadvertently, under duress, or by third parties is not. The pertinent verses are these:

> And these are unclean to you among the swarming things that swarm upon the earth. . . . These are unclean to you among all that swarm; whoever touches them when they are dead shall be unclean until the evening. And anything upon which any of them falls when they are dead shall be unclean. . . . And if any of them falls into any earthen vessel, all that is in it shall be unclean, and you shall break it. Any food in it that may be eaten, upon which water may come, shall be unclean; and all drink that may be drunk from every such vessel shall be unclean. (Lev. 11:29–34)
>
> And if any part of their carcass falls upon any seed for sowing that is to be sown, it is clean; but if water be put on the seed and any part of their carcass falls on it, it is unclean to you. (Lev. 11:37)

The Mishnaic sages maintain then that if the farmer deliberately wets down seed or produce, then the produce is susceptible to uncleanness and is made unclean by any source of uncleanness. The sages take as fact that if produce is wet down by deliberate action, that is, by an informed intentionality confirmed by a concrete deed, then it is susceptible to uncleanness. But if produce is wet down naturally, on the one side, or by some action not initiated by an individual, on the other, then the produce is not rendered susceptible to uncleanness—even though it is wet.

What would be a concrete case. A householder takes flour, which is dry and has not been deliberately wet down. That is because once wet down, the flour molders. The householder further takes yeast. And, putting the yeast and flour together, the householder adds water. Then the process of kneading dough to bake bread commences with the irrigation of the yeast and the dough. That is the moment at which the dough congeals and the yeast buds and ferments, producing its sugar, its carbon dioxide, and its ethanol. Now, at that exact moment, the instant of animation, at which the bread begins to live, the householder goes on the alert for dangers to the bread—and so throughout. So in a cuisine based on bread (not potatoes, not rice, for example) what is at stake in "wetting down seed," based on the analogy of adding water to dry flour and yeast, is the point at which vegetation begins the process by which it becomes maximally edible and useful to the householder.

Then the state of sanctification, which inheres and is normal for the Israelite household, comes under threat from the source of uncleanness, such as corpse-uncleanness and its analogues, that the Torah has identified. The moment of wetting grain down defines the hour of conflict between life and death—and this in concrete ways. No wonder that, at the very time, the act done with deliberation precipitates the conflict. But that is only if the householder cares. If the householder does not intend the dough to congeal and the yeast to rise, nothing of consequence happens. It is the Israelite's will and intention and the act that realizes them that endow with consequence what by nature happens of its own accord.

The really critical and generative question of the law of Mishnah-tractate Makhshirin asks about the relationship of action to intentionality. Do we decide on the basis of what one has done the character of a prior intention, that is, of what was intended to be done? If I take up water in order to pour it out, does my ultimate action in pouring out the water govern the interpretation of my original plan for the water? If it does, then even though for a time I might have wanted the water in its present location, by my final disposition of the water, I have defined that original intention and determined that the water never was wanted; therefore, retrospectively it does not impart susceptibility to uncleanness.

We have a variety of positions: (1) intention without action is null; (2) action is retrospectively determinative of the character of intention—we judge the intention by the result. A further view is that prior intention plays a balancing role in the interpretation of the status of the water. We do not decide solely by what one has done, by the ultimate disposition of the water. So if one's action never was intended to bring down water, the water is not utilized intentionally and does not impart susceptibility to uncleanness. Or the deed dictates the character of the intent, and the result is paramount in interpreting the means. Or what was wanted has to be balanced against what has happened. If one wants the water to fall, that is not the end of the matter; one wanted it to fall in a particular place, and it falls both there and elsewhere; then what has served one's purpose imparts susceptibility, and what does not serve one's purpose does not. What is incidental to one's main purpose is not taken into account, and that is without regard to the ultimate consequence of one's deeds. And then there is the possibility of distinguishing immediate from ultimate result, primary from subordinate outcome, and so on.

(1) Liquids impart susceptibility to uncleanness only if they are useful to human beings, drawn with approval, subject to human deliberation and intention.

(2) Liquids that can impart susceptibility to uncleanness do so only if they serve a person's purpose, are deliberately applied to produce, irrigate something through human deliberation and intention.

## Hallah and Makhshirin: The Single Message of Two Distinct Topical Tractates

Both categories of the law of the Mishnah, Hallah and Makhshirin, take up the same problem, namely, the point at which in the natural processes by which life is sustained, life commences. That point is reached when the process of fermentation starts when life processes commence in the yeast mixed with flour and water and ends when the dough forms a crust, marking the death of the enzymes. At the outset, with the deliberate addition of the water to the yeast, considerations of uncleanness take over (Makhshirin), and at the end, with the formation of the crust and the death of the enzyme (Hallah), considerations of sanctification commence and the dough offering is owing. Makhshirin, then, insists on the centrality of human intentionality in the inauguration of the processes with which it is concerned; Hallah accords no consequence to what the individual wants or does not want to happen.

What we have in the law of Mishnah-tractates Hallah and Makhshirin together is a full account of how holy Israel in the Land of Israel triggers the working of life processes, protecting the natural life within the living dough from the uncleanness deriving from death, protecting that same life force for the sanctification that renews and sustains life, thus in dough offering rendering to God the proper portion of the staff of life.

Makhshirin requires intentionality; Hallah excludes it. Why so? With Hallah the process itself does not depend upon the householder's intentionality. The fermentation process that animates the flour and produces bread goes forward whether or not the householder intended it to. Nothing he or she does can stop it once it has started, and no call upon his or her alertness to prevent uncleanness is issued. That is why God's claim on the dough, for the dough offering for the priesthood, depends not on human intentionality—irrelevant to the process of animation, of bringing life to the inert flour—but on God's own reason for engagement. That has to do with the maintenance of the processes of life, human and natural.

### How God and Israel Meet in the Land

In the law of Mishnah-tractate Makhshirin, which corresponds in an exact way to that of Hallah, we see the way in which the conception that Israel forms God's abode translates into tangible rules. If I had to identify where the everyday meets the Eternal, I should choose the here and now of petty obsessions with tiny events and their intangible, animated histories, down to the moment of adding water to the yeast and dough when making bread: when life renews itself through the life-precipitating touch of water to the flour and the yeast. Here at Hallah and Makhshirin considerations of uncleanness and those of sanctification intersect. That is the point that precipitates concern with the forces of death, prime source of cultic uncleanness. Then, to preserve purity, Israel goes on the alert for the danger of pollution: at the moment when yeast, flour, and water ignite the processes of animation. So too for all of their counterparts: "if water be put on the seed," take care.

Now we see the other half of the story. Unclean or otherwise, the dough congeals, the yeast ferments and yields gas, and so, life-processes having commenced, though death and its surrogates threaten. Then the householder goes on the alert—if he or she cares, if by an act of deliberation he or she has made life happen. And there too, by sharing the outcome of the fermentation with God, the householder acknowledges the opposite of death, which is life, embodied in the living processes by which the bread comes into being, and resulting in the presence, within the dough, of a portion subject to sanctification: donation to the priest in the present instance.

The particularity of dough offering is in the fact that it is paid from bread made from grain from which the heave offering has already been removed. So the critical point of differentiation—an offering from the mixture of flour, yeast, and water, taken from when fermentation starts to when it ends—takes on still greater consequence. Wine and beer ferment, but no counterpart offering from wine, over and above the heave offering and tithes to which all produce is liable, is demanded, nor from beer. In the wine-olive-oil-wheat culture of the Land of Israel, it is only wheat, in the course of its later processing, that becomes subject to a further offering of the present kind, one linked to its life cycle. That is because—so it seems to me—bread stands for life, consumed, to be sure, with oil and wine. Therefore it is the processing of flour into bread to sustain life where fermentation represents life that marks the occasion for the affirmation of God's presence in all life forms and processes: God lays claim to God's share, because God's claim upon the Israelite householder extends to the outer limits of vitality. "All Israel has a portion in the world to come," because Israel transformed by the Torah stands for regenerate humanity, restored to Eden.

# 14    EATING TOGETHER: ISRAEL'S PRESENCE IN GOD'S HOUSE

## Tractates Hagigah, Ma<sup>c</sup>aser Sheni, and Bikkurim (Again)

### Israel's Meals in God's Houses

God meets Israel both in God's house and in Israel's households. In this chapter, we survey the laws of Israel's encounter with God in the Temple and in Jerusalem. This is detailed in the law of the Mishnah-tractates Hagigah ("The Festal Offering"), Ma<sup>c</sup>aser Sheni ("Second Tithe"), and Bikkurim ("First-fruits"). In chapter 15, we examine how the law of the Mishnah provides for God to return the compliment by personally meeting Israel in the Israelite household.

On specified occasions in the year God wants Israel to appear in God's house, to share a meal, and to rejoice. Israel accepts the invitation to appear before and see God. In the Temple, in Jerusalem, Israel eats God's share of the crop. Doing so in God's house places Israel in a special relationship with God. And, as in Eden, food, the means for sustaining life, frames this relationship.

The Torah explicitly declares that God resides in Jerusalem. Israel—journeying from every province of the Land of Israel and from the Exile as well—meets God in this metropolis in several ways. In the Temple, the holiest location in the Land, the highest point in Jerusalem, the place where God's Name abides, Israel provides God with meat, wine, oil, and bread. And God summons all Israel to Jerusalem to eat a portion of the crop sanctified to God. Thus, what belongs to God is brought back to the holy city, there to bring joy to the life of the holy people through the produce of the holy Land.

Once Jerusalem and the Temple are involved, the transaction is one of sanctification, and that involves cultic cleanness. Specifically, Israel eats its meals in Jerusalem in conformity with the purity rules governing God's table in the Temple proper.

Israel is personified by pilgrims who, three times a year, assemble at the Temple. The three celebrations are Passover, the fifteenth of the lunar month of Nisan, with Pentecost fifty days later, and Tabernacles on the fifteenth of the lunar month of Tishré—times at, or calculated from, the new moon following the vernal (March 21) and the autumnal (September 21) equinoxes. Each of the three festivals is devoted to the enjoyment of creation and commemoration of Israel's own formation, in Egypt (Passover), at Sinai (Pentecost), and in the wilderness (Tabernacles).

The act of rejoicing encompasses the eating of meat. God provides Israel with a share of the offering of God's altar; Israel provides its own vegetables out of God's store. God and Israel share a meal, with God as the host (Hagigah). Not only so, but God shares God's portion of the crop, the second tithe (Ma'aser Sheni) with the pilgrims, providing them with wine and vegetables out of second tithe. God further ensures that the priesthood celebrates with the pilgrims, supplying the priests with fruit and vegetables, through Firstfruits (Bikkurim).

### What God Wants for the Israelite

What God wants for the Israelite is for him or her to be happy. That is shown in the fact that God provides the Israelite pilgrim with meat and vegetables and drink to be enjoyed in God's abode. It is further indicated by the disposition of the share of the crop belonging to God that God assigns to the householder and his family. God thereby imposes his will upon the crop. God's will is for the householder and his family, supported by his portion of the crop, to attend upon him in his abode itself, there to celebrate an occasion for rejoicing. Here, then, we meet the Israelite household not only as God's sharecropper but also as his beneficiary.

What makes the transaction consequential is the condition of rejoicing. In order to share God's portion of the crop, the Israelite must leave his or her household altogether and go to God's house. This is yet another act that emphasizes the transient nature of possession, while underscoring the enduring character of relationship. The Israelite householder brings these components of God's share to Jerusalem and consumes them there, as the Torah explicitly states: "where God takes up an abode." That accounts for the condition of purity that the pilgrims are required to enter.

But emotions, not only purity, are engaged in the transaction with God. When we deal with Israel's relationship with God, time and again we find Israel *required* to rejoice, and that takes place through eating God's food in God's place. The character of the relationship—joy consequent upon purity, humility, and obedience—is eloquently precise. In the Torah, God insists that in relating to God, Israel find occasion for rejoicing. God explicitly declares, among the emotions or sentiments or attitudes that animate Israel's relationship with God, the experience of pure joy takes precedence. Israel should not find its ultimate joy in its own enlandisement, in the household, but rather in life with God. That is, in God's locus: eating meals in God's presence. So, eating God's food in God's place accomplishes God's goal, which is for Israel to rejoice.

### Appearing to God, Sharing a Meal:
### Tractate Hagigah

Mishnah-tractate Hagigah, rooted in the laws of Scripture, expounds the three requirements for establishing Israel's presence in God's house: (1) appearing in person before God (Exod. 23:17), (2) keeping a feast to the Lord (Deut. 16:15); and (3) rejoicing (Deut. 16:14). A fourth requirement, expounded in the Mishnah and implicit in Scripture, concerns the purity to be attained for the pilgrimage to the holy place, a requirement for which we have already accounted.

On the pilgrim festivals Israel is seen by God. The Hebrew letters for the passage can be read "be seen by God" or "sees God," and that is the promise of the encounter: in the holiness of the Temple, in the savor of its offerings to heaven, in its music and song and bloody rites in celebration of life, Israel sees God.

A variety of offerings is presented, first of all a whole offering, burned up on the altar. The Israelite is to be seen in the Temple court on the feast with a whole offering (birds or cattle) and that is obligatory: "None shall appear before me empty-handed" (Exod. 23:15). Keeping the feast, second, means presenting a peace-offering when one appears on the first festival day of the feast. That yields meat for the pilgrim and his family. The duty of rejoicing involves a peace offering in addition to the festal peace offering: "the peace offering of rejoicing in the feast," in line with Deuteronomy 27:7: "And you shall sacrifice peace offerings and shall eat there and you shall rejoice before the Lord your God." Thus, three offerings are called for by the pilgrimage: (1) an appearance offering presented as a burnt offering, which yields no food for the sacrifier (the one who derives the benefit of the offering, that is, the one fulfilling an obligation thereby) or sacrificer; (2) a festal offering (Hagigah), which falls under the rules of peace offerings and does yield meat for the sacrifier and the sacrificer; and (3) peace offerings of rejoicing, subject to the same law as the festal offering. The obligatory appearance offering is located by sages in the following verses:

> You shall rejoice in your feast. . . . For seven days you shall keep the feast to the Lord your God at the place that the Lord will choose, because the Lord your God will bless you in all your produce and in all the work of your hands, so that you will be altogether joyful.
>
> Three times a year all your males shall appear before the Lord your God at the place which he will choose: at the feast of unleavened bread, at the feast of weeks, and at the feast of booths. They shall not appear before the Lord empty-handed; every man

shall give as he is able, according to the blessing of the Lord your God which he has given you. (Deut. 16:14-17)

The passages that refer to celebrating a festival (*Hag*) are deemed to pertain to the festal offering (*Hagigah*). The law of the Mishnah is concerned with two matters, first, the details of the pilgrims' offerings; second, the attainment by pilgrims of cultic cleanness to permit their participation in the cult and their eating their share of the Holy Things of the altar.

All persons possessed of autonomy of will are liable to bring an appearance offering, that is, to make the pilgrimage. Excluded is the standard list: those who are impaired in body or mind, and those subject to the will of another: (1) a deaf-mute, (2) an idiot, (3) a minor, (4) one without pronounced sexual characteristics, (5) one who exhibits the sexual traits of both sexes, (6) women, (7) slaves who have not been freed, (8) the lame, (9) the blind, (10) the sick, (11) the old, (12) and one who cannot go up on foot. An unclean person does not appear in the Temple either. So the pilgrim must be ready, willing, and able to be seen by God.

To participate in the cult the pilgrims must be in the state of purity required for entry into the part of the Temple that is open to them. They also will eat a share of the altar meat. Then, like the priests, the ordinary Israelites too must obey the laws of cultic purity that apply to protect that meat from the Torah's designated sources of uncleanness. So entering God's presence entails preparing oneself to participate in the sacrificial cult and enjoy a share of its meat. That is why the law of the Mishnah takes for granted that one does get ready by entering a state of cleanness as decreed by the Torah for the priests in the Temple precincts. When it comes to the festival seasons, ordinary people are assumed to preserve cultic cleanness, even though at other times of the year they do not do so. That is because everyone is assumed to understand that the condition for entering the Temple is cultic cleanness.

The same assumption, that people in general will preserve cultic cleanness where it is required, pertains to the produce destined for the Temple: in Judah people are deemed trustworthy in regard to the preservation of the cleanness of wine and oil for use on the altar—that is, food in the status of Holy Things throughout the year. When it comes to the status of clay utensils that one finds within the locale of Jerusalem, Israelites are assumed to preserve the cultic cleanness of clay utensils, and if they claim that the utensils are cultically clean, that claim is accepted. In Jerusalem, even tax collectors searching a house for valuables are assumed to respect the rules of cultic cleanness.

An unclean person is exempt from the requirement of making an appearance (Exod. 23:14; Deut. 16:16), since it is said, "And you will come there and you will bring there" (Deut. 12:6). The requirement applies to one who is suitable to come into the Temple courtyard, excluding the unclean person, who is not suitable to come into the Temple courtyard. How, then, does one achieve the status of cleanness for cultic purposes? To attain cultic cleanness for eating

Holy Things, people had to immerse in an immersion pool. In that context, the purpose of the act of immersion determines the outcome. One's attitude differentiates, and intentionality governs the effect of the physical act of bathing.

Thus, if a person immerses for eating unconsecrated food, that does not suffice for eating tithe; if a person is confirmed as suitable for eating tithe, the person still has not immersed for the purpose of eating heave offering, and if a person immerses for eating heave offering, that person still has to immerse to eat Holy Things. Whatever the pilgrim's normal practice, in connection with the visit to the cult, immersion must be undertaken with the intention of attaining cleanness sufficient for eating the Holy Things of the altar. Hence, a clear distinction is drawn between cleanness in the household, where only some maintained cultic purity in connection with everyday food, and cleanness in the Temple. The one represented an act of intent and conviction; the other, an act of substance. The two are complementary.

The key to the effect of the immersion, therefore, is the attitude with which the act of immersion takes place. In the matching opposite, the law of the Mishnah differentiates among ordinary folk, those who eat heave offering, and those who eat Holy Things. Here is how the matter is fully spelled out. To understand what is at issue, we recall the lesson of tractate Tohorot: ordinary folk undertake to observe the rules of cleanness even outside of the Temple; they eat their food at home in accord with the laws governing the priests' consumption of their holy rations in the Temple or in Jerusalem. That means that people at home may observe the taboos governing priests when it comes to the priests' eating of their holy rations ("heave offering"). Now what is involved in such a ritualization of the domestic meal is the attitude of the faithful. What they wish to accomplish they can do.

When they immerse to begin the purification process, they do so with the intent of attaining cultic cleanness for a specified purpose. In the present context, it is to eat their food at home as if it were priestly rations, as I explained. But then have they attained cleanness for a more rigorous requirement, e.g., eating meat from the altar of the Lord ("holy things")? No, their attitude has defined the outcome of their act of immersion.

### MISHNAH-TRACTATE HAGIGAH 3:1–3

The clothing of those who are so clean as to be able to eat heave offering is deemed unclean in the status of Pressure-uncleanness for the purposes of Holy Things.

Utensils which are completely processed in a state of insusceptibility to uncleanness [and so when completed are clean] require immersion for use in connection with Holy Things, but not for use in connection with heave offering.

The result of immersion thus is clear. The attitude of the pilgrim governs. If an ordinary person immerses for attaining purity required for the eating of priestly rations—that is, a layman pretending to be a priest, treating his table in accord with the rules governing the table of the priest—that suffices for his purpose. But if actual Holy Things of the Lord's altar in Jerusalem are concerned, he is deemed effectively unclean.

The purpose of the immersion therefore governs its effects, and that is without regard to the physical act of immersion. The effect of the act of purification through immersion is dictated by the attitude with which he or she immerses. If one was unclean and immersed with the intention of becoming clean for eating the pilgrim's share of the meat of the Lord's altar, that serves.

A clear distinction differentiates God's house from the Israelites' households. That is why the intentionality to attain cleanness in the domestic household now does not suffice. Nor do the rules and regulations that pertain when ordinary folk in their homes eat their food as though they were in the Temple in Jerusalem. Not only so, but while one's attitude makes a difference at home, as in the pretense of eating one's domestic meals in the condition of a priest in the altar, attitude on its own makes no material difference in the Temple.

When it comes to the actual pilgrimage, as distinct from the pretense of treating the domestic table as tantamount to the Temple altar, the law of the Mishnah embodies the difference between imagination and intention, on the one side, and actuality, on the other. At home adopting the rules that govern priests' eating of their rations allows the householder to pretend to be a priest. But that does not mean the householder is a priest so far as the Temple is concerned. What suffices in the pretense that one's table forms the altar, the members of the household are the priesthood and its ménage, the home is the Temple—now does not serve. Actuality intervenes: the real Temple imposes its own, very strict rules, and all of the proper intentions in the world are swept aside. The pilgrimage bears its own integrity: God's house is actually different from the Israelite household, and it is in God's house that the Israelite sees and is seen by God, in the act of pure joy.

## God Shares with the Pilgrim People in Jerusalem a Portion of His Share in the Crop: Tractate Maᶜaser Sheni

For the purpose of encouraging the pilgrimage, part of God's share of the crops of the country is assigned by him to the caste of Israelite householders, not just to the priests, Levites, and the poor—the principal beneficiaries of God's fees. Two classes of produce—second tithe and its counterpart, the produce of trees in the fourth year after they are planted (see chapter 13), are subject to the laws of Deuteronomy 14:22-26:

> You shall tithe all the yield of your seed, which comes forth from the field year by year. And before the Lord your God, in the place that he will choose for an abode for his name, you shall eat the tithe of your grain, of your wine, and of your oil, and the firstling of your herd and flock. It is so you may learn to fear the Lord your God always.
>
> But if the way is too long for you, so that you are not able to bring the tithe when

the Lord your God blesses you because the place is too far from you that the Lord chooses for the abode of his name, then you shall turn it into money and bind up the money in your hand and go to the place that the Lord your God chooses, and spend the money there for whatever you want, oxen or sheep, wine or strong drink, whatever your appetite craves; and you shall eat there before the Lord your God and rejoice, you and your household.

Here, then, is an agricultural offering that the farmer designates for God but receives back from God for enjoyment in God's house. In this way God provides food for the pilgrims, not only sharing the meat of the altar with them, but setting aside vegetables and drink. Specifically, among the tithes and priestly rations that the householder sets aside for God's share of the crop is second tithe. Second tithe constitutes ten percent of the net yield of the crop *after* other tithes have been removed (hence, second). It is separated in the first and second, fourth and fifth years of the Sabbatical cycle. A tithe for the poor is separated in the third and sixth years.

Second tithe is sanctified—specifically, set aside to be eaten in Jerusalem in an act of rejoicing before God. To make transporting the gift lighter, the value of the designated produce, rather than the produce itself, is brought to Jerusalem in the form of coins. The coins are then designated to be spent in Jerusalem on food and drink.

What links food in the status of second tithe to the produce of fruit trees in the fourth year after they are planted is the purpose—to give Israel occasion for rejoicing with God's produce. The Torah declares these portions of the crop to be times for God to give Israel occasion to rejoice with God, where God lives. The Torah is explicit in both cases: "you shall eat there before the Lord your God and rejoice, you and your household" (Deut. 14:26) and the produce of a tree in the fourth year after planting must be "set aside for jubilation before the Lord" (Lev. 19:24). In this way, God helps defray the cost of the pilgrimage and secure proper conditions for its realization. All the Israelites have to do is walk.

Three issues define the focus of the law of the Mishnah. First, what, exactly, does it mean to transfer "sanctity" to coins from food, then to food from coins? And how do sages conceive such a transaction between Israel and God to take place? The law of the Mishnah in practical terms takes up the important problems inhering in the conception of holiness. The law spells out exactly what "holiness" entails, a matter of substance or of status.

Then, second, the effect upon what is designated as holy that is exerted at the moment of entry into a place that is holy—the interplay of status and location—has to be explored. Specifically, what happens when the produce of second tithe is brought within the holy space of Jerusalem?

A third concern is introduced by Scripture. That is the final disposition of God's share of the crop, which is embodied in the law of removal. That law requires that by a given point in the year, the householder hand over what is owing to God's designated surrogate. The law of removal assures that the crops designated as holy will not be accumulated in a hoard but will be distributed to those for whom God has assigned them: the priests, Levites, poor, the Holy City, and the like. It forms the counterpart to the rule of the Sabbatical Year, which declares ownerless the entire crop of the Land of Israel in that year; none may hoard any portion of the crop, which all may freely enjoy. What God possesses, he freely gives to all comers. His will, not the householder's, prevails, and that is his will.

## The Meaning of Sanctification

It is here, most succinctly, that we see the law of the Mishnah place its unique imprint on the specifics found in the law of the Torah. Sanctified food may be secularized, with its value transferred into cash. The coins, now bearing the value of sanctified food, are brought to Jerusalem and then converted back into food. This transfer of holiness or the status of sanctification to and from produce, to and from coins, requires the sages to translate into concrete rules their own conception of "the sacred." This they do within their own gifts of analysis, which find in detail implications for the general rule. For the sages may think about abstract questions, but they set forth their results in practical and concrete cases, certain that their disciples will grasp the broader rule inhering in the specific.

At issue is the practical effect of sanctifying produce, declaring it in the status of second tithe, transferring the sanctity of the produce to coins, then transferring the sanctity inhering in the coins back into other produce. The law of the Mishnah makes its statement in both negative and positive ways. Produce that belongs to God must be used for exactly the purpose for which God created that class of produce. The purpose of the produce furthermore finds its definition in ordinary practice and custom. When it comes to produce in the status of second tithe, it must be used, all of it, in accord with the normal usage, which is taken to embody God's natural purpose: it is permitted for eating and drinking and anointing; for eating that which is normally used for eating, for anointing with that which is normally used for anointing. The issue is not mere misuse, for using wine or vinegar for anointing does not degrade the produce. The issue is adhering to the Creator's purpose for the matter, and wine is for drinking, not for anointing, though it may serve such a purpose. Otherwise why object—as the law certainly does—to spicing oil in the status of second tithe, which enhances its flavor?

So much for the positive statement of matters. What about the negative? It is an extension of a familiar notion. Even possession does not bestow upon the householder absolute freedom of will. God has given the produce to the householder for enjoyment, and still the householder cannot do with it exactly what he or she wishes but must adhere to God's regulations for what is, to complete the circle, meant for the householder's own emolument. Designated for the householder's use, the produce and the money that embodies its sanctification belong not to the householder but to God. Therefore the householder may not do business with the coin, that is, may not treat it in partnership as other than a gift: A person may not say to his friend, "Take this produce in the status of second tithe up to Jerusalem in order to divide it between us." But the person may say to the friend, "Take this produce up to Jerusalem so that we may eat of it and drink of it together in Jerusalem." They give produce to one another as a gift. So once more the produce compares with the crops of the Seventh Year; people may derive benefit from the crops of that year, but they may not treat that produce in any way they wish but must conform to God's wishes for it—and, above all, they may not establish private ownership of it.

Produce in the present classification, accordingly, may not be treated as the private property of the householder, it may not be sold or used as capital or traded. It also may not be weighed or measured, in the way in which one's own produce in the market is. Once the produce is designated, it must be treated as God's property, not the householder's. The money may not be used for investments in slaves or in real estate; it may not be used for what cannot be eaten, to buy unclean animals, for instance. It cannot be used for obligatory offerings, meaning for offerings that must come from the householder's, not the public or divine, domain. If, therefore, one makes improper use of the money, the money has to be replaced. Water, salt, unharvested produce, produce that cannot be transported to Jerusalem, do not serve; if the money is used for these, it has to be made up. Water and salt are not deemed food. Unharvested produce is not yet food. What cannot be carried to Jerusalem also cannot be purchased with the sanctified coins. In short, the entire transaction involves issues of sanctity and engages the pilgrim with God, who is the host in God's house. And that fact leads to the next question.

### Is Sanctification a Matter of Substance or of Status?

When it comes to the transfer of the status of sanctification to and from coins and produce, the law of the Mishnah takes an unequivocal position that sanctification is a matter of function not status. Sanctity is extrinsic and imputed; it imposes rules and requirements upon that which is sanctified. Sanctification is not a matter of intrinsic substance; holiness does not inhere in the coins. One does not immerse the coins in an immersion pool to purify them, then preserve them from sources of impurity. The law of the Mishnah leaves no doubt of that fact. That is consistent with the law's position on uncleanness: uncleanness is a matter of status, not substance. Mishnah-tractate Ma'aser Sheni then constructs a vast structure of relationships that dictate for one and the same thing one classification under one circumstance, another classification under a different circumstance.

The denial of intrinsic sanctity to produce in the status of second tithe comes in a variety of specific rules. For example, if unconsecrated coins and coins designated as second tithe were mixed and scattered, all the coins that are recovered are deemed second tithe coins until the amount that was lost has been made up; then the rest are treated as secular. We are not concerned to find the specific coin originally designated as holy. If a person mingled consecrated and unconsecrated coins together and scooped them up by the handful—what is in each handful is deemed to be consecrated or unconsecrated by proportion. What is sanctified is the value of the produce. The coin serves merely as a means for conveying that value. If one wishes to deconsecrate coins that have been designated in place of second tithe produce, the rule is that coins of greater value replace coins of lesser value. That is in line with the principle that treats the more valuable specie as a commodity for barter, not as abstract currency.

But that ruling shows that there are limits to the process of abstraction and relativization that the law of the Mishnah nurtures. In insisting that the more valuable coin can be used to replace the less valuable coin (a coin struck in silver may replace a coin struck in copper), the law of the Mishnah wishes to underscore that second tithe coins represent a commodity, not specie or abstract currency. That accords, then, with the principle expressed in the following Mishnah paragraph:

**MISHNAH-TRACTATE BABA MESIA 4:1**

(1) Gold acquires silver, but silver does not acquire gold. (2) Copper acquires silver, but silver does not acquire copper. (3) Bad coins acquire good coins, but good coins do not acquire bad coins. (4) A coin lacking a mint mark acquires a minted coin, but a minted coin does not acquire a coin lacking a mint mark. (5) Movable goods acquire coins, but coins do not acquire movable goods.

Each example makes the same point—that title is transferred through barter, not through the exchange of abstract value represented by coins for merchandise or for other coins. In a market economy, the law of the Mishnah rejects the notion of specie or money as an abstract indicator of value, a way of keeping score, in favor of concrete barter. Likewise with the second-tithe coins, these must be treated as commodities. So the sanctity inhering in the produce has been transferred to the coins, but, as we have noted, that represents a functional transaction, not an inherent characteristic.

Still, in establishing the selling price of second tithe produce for purposes of transfer of value to coins, the law of the Mishnah takes account of the market mechanism, as against the distributive economics represented by barter instead of money as the medium of trade. That position emerges in the rule imposing the market price on produce to be translated into money. The law of the Mishnah does not insist on true value, as it ordinarily does. Here the law of the Mishnah deals only with market value and is insistent on that point. If the value of the produce went up before the transfer of money took place, the original, lower price prevails. If the value declined, the buyer pays the new, lower price. Once a fixed number of coins is declared to represent the produce, only that number of coins becomes consecrated, no more, no less. But whether a fixed formula is required to accompany the transaction ("Lo, these coins are in place of this produce") is not a settled question; the transfer of sanctity may well take place without a declaration to that effect.

A market mechanism, an auction, also transfers to coins the holiness of produce of a fourth-year planting. It is described in this language: "How many baskets of such produce as yet unharvested and still in the field is one willing to redeem for a sela$^c$, on condition that the purchaser pay the expenses of harvesting the produce out of his own pocket?" Then the one who purchases the produce sets aside money with which to purchase the produce and says, "All produce of this type, that is, the type in the basket which is picked at my expense, is to be deemed deconsecrated with these coins at a rate of so many baskets to a sela$^c$."

A further indication of the working of the market mechanism derives from the case of market fluctuation. One who carries produce in the status of second tithe from a place where it is expensive to a place where it is cheap, or from a place where it is cheap to a place where it is expensive, redeems it according to the market price of his current location. The law of the Mishnah further distinguishes retail from wholesale prices and calculates the value of the produce at the shopkeeper's buying rate and the rate of exchange from money to produce in Jerusalem at the money changer's selling rate. An estimate of true value is not made. So the produce is sold at wholesale prices and coins are evaluated at their premium value. When the household transfers the holiness of the produce in the status of second tithe to coins, the householder is required to pay a fixed indemnity of an added fifth over the selling price of the food; that is in line with Leviticus 27:31: "If a man wishes to redeem any of his tithe, he shall add a fifth to it." But a third party may sell the produce without the surcharge.

If the consecrated money is spent on food but yields also inedible byproducts, say, the hide of a cow, the meat is consecrated but the hide is not; so too, jugs carrying wine are unconsecrated, though the wine is holy.

## The Locative Power of Sanctity: Bringing Produce into Jerusalem

The effect of entry into the holy place upon the consecrated produce and coins transforms them. Entering God's presence effects changes upon the individual who, or that which, makes an appearance. The character of sanctity and of the result of the act of sanctification takes on a substantive quality at a particular moment and location. So appearing before God realizes sanctity that inheres and actualizes the matter of relationship and status, and transforms it into tangible reality. That marks the impact of entry into God's space upon the person or produce of the pilgrim.

Specifically, when the produce itself—not the coins but the fruit and vegetables that have been designated as second tithe—has entered the walls of the Holy City, it becomes holy in substance, not only in relationship, status, or function. Entry into Jerusalem makes all the difference. Outside the wall, the sanctity of the produce had been fungible; inside, it is absolute. Indeed, a specific rule makes that point. Once produce is brought into Jerusalem, it enters the status of sacrificial meat on the altar.

That is, just as once meat suitable for the altar is placed thereon, it may not be removed (Mishnah-tractate Zebahim 9:1), so once produce suitable for eating in Jerusalem has entered the city as second tithe, it may not be removed. That legal ruling bears the clear principle that just as what God eats in the Temple remains sanctified once committed, so the same is the rule for what Israel eats in Jerusalem; then Jerusalem is to Israel as the Temple sanctum is to God.

So too, produce that is in the status of second tithe enters Jerusalem and does not go out. It must remain in the city until it is consumed. That principle precipitates inquiry into a variety of subordinate questions of an interstitial focus, including the status of produce at the boundaries of Jerusalem. But coins, bearers of the sanctity of the originally designated produce, are subject to a different rule. Coins in the status of second tithe enter Jerusalem and may be taken out again.

Now the produce must be *consumed*, not traded for coins, and the coins must be spent. While the status of second tithe is transferred from coins of inferior metal to coins of better metal (thus, as I said, effecting a transaction through barter), inside Jerusalem, the procedure is reversed. Now the farmer gets small change so he can use the coins. No considerations of sanctification intervene, since the coins have accomplished their task, which is the movement of the value of the produce to the Holy City, and, consequently, the coins are treated as secular, within the obvious limitation on what they may purchase. So the character of "the sacred," like the character of "the unclean," is to be inferred from the law of the Mishnah. The important point here is that the produce once sanctified responds to its circumstance, while what bears the value of the sanctified produce does not.

### The Law of Removal and the Confession Covering Disposition of Accumulted Tithes and Offerings

All consecrated produce of a given tithing cycle must be disposed of in the proper manner—to those entitled to it—by the eve of the last festival day of Passover in the fourth and seventh years of the Sabbatical cycle, meaning, at the end of a period of collection of two years of second tithe and a year of poor man's tithe. On the next day in the fourth and seventh years of the cycle, the farmers would recite the confession specified at Deuteronomy 26:12–19. Then the priests get the produce that has been declared heave offering; first tithe goes to the Levites; poor man's tithe to the poor; and, so far as second tithe or Firstfruits are concerned, if the farmer cannot make the pilgrimage to Jerusalem, the produce has to be destroyed. With no Temple, without access to Jerusalem, that provision prevails. So the householder cannot hold back what does not belong to the householder—even at the cost of destroying perfectly good grain or wine.

Scripture speaks of the householder's "clearing out the consecrated portion from the house," and sages take that to mean that, at a given point in the year, the tithes and offerings must be removed from the household and handed over to those designated to receive them:

> When you have set aside in full the tenth part of your yield—in the third year, the year of the tithe—and have given it to the Levite, the stranger, the fatherless, and the widow, that they may eat their fill in your settlements, you shall make the following declaration before the Lord your God: "I have cleared out the consecrated portion from the house; and I have given it to the Levite, the stranger, the fatherless, and the widow, just as you commanded me; I have neither transgressed nor neglected any of your commandments; I have not eaten of it while in mourning; I have not cleared out any of it while I was unclean; and I have not deposited any of it with the dead. I have obeyed the Lord my God; I have done just as you commanded me. Look down from your heavenly abode, from heaven, and bless your people Israel and the Land you have given us, a Land flowing with milk and honey, as you swore to our fathers." (Deut. 26:12–19)

The passage then links the fulfillment of the commandments pertaining to the Land as the basis for God's affirming Israel as "his treasured people who observe all his commandments . . . a holy people to the Lord your God." The effect is stunning. Sages follow the Torah in identifying as a principal expression of Israel's relationship with God the householder's punctilious rendering to God of God's share of the crop. Here intentionality has its role; if the householder cannot do the deed, he or she may make a declaration, confirmed by action later on. The right to make the declaration accords recognition to the householder as an Israelite and assigns to the householder, through this action and declaration, a position within the sacred history of the holy people.

### His Yoke Is Easy and His Burden Is Light

All God asks is that the householder enjoy God's gift in God's presence, in Jerusalem. God calls Israel to gather in God's city and provides food for their enjoyment there. No Mishnah-tractate makes a more concise statement on what Israel's relationship to God comprises than this one, and its message is, to serve God, Israel must rejoice with God, in God's presence, by having a good meal of God's produce in Jerusalem. So the law of the Mishnah orders that Israel relate to God through joy, finding in its act and occasion of rejoicing the realization of Israel's interaction with God.

In its exegesis of Deuteronomy 26:15, the Tosefta, the Mishnah's closest companion, amplifies the Mishnah's law by making clear that the tithes and offerings in general, celebrated in connection with bringing the second tithe or money bearing its value to Jerusalem, define Israel's relationship with God. And that is a relationship of rejoicing: God's purpose is to make Israel happy. God is concerned with Israel's condition, encompassing also its feelings as much as its attitude and intentionality. In carrying out God's instructions and keeping the covenant that governs its possession of the Land, Israel enters into an enduring situation of bliss in its life with God in the Land, all on the analogy of Adam and Eve in Eden. The pertinent passage is as follows:

### TOSEFTA-TRACTATE BIKKURIM 5:27–29

5:27 "Israel" (Deut. 26:15)—all these blessings come through the merit of Israel, as it says in Scripture, "Israel dwelt in safety, the fountain of Jacob alone, in a land of grain and wine, even the heavens of which dripped with dew. Happy are you, Israel. Who can compare to you—a people saved by the Lord?" (Deut. 33:28).

"And the earth" (Deut. 26:15)—all these blessings come through the merit of the altar, as it says in Scripture, "Make me an altar of earth and offer upon it your burnt offerings, your peace offerings, your sheep and your cattle. For wherever I cause my name to be remembered, I will come and bless you" (Exod. 20:24).

5:28 "Which you gave us" (Deut. 26:15)—all these blessings come in proportion to the agricultural offerings which Israel renders to God, as it says in Scripture, "Houses full of all good things which you did not fill, dug out cisterns which you did not dig, vineyards and olive trees which you did not plant and you eat and are satisfied. Watch yourself lest you forget the Lord who brought you out of Egypt" (Deut. 26:12).

5:29 "As you vowed" (Deut. 26:15)—this was the vow made to Abraham our father, as it says in Scripture, "By myself I have sworn, says the Lord, because of what you have done I will surely bless you and increase your progeny like the stars of the heaven" (Gen. 22:16).

"To our fathers" (Deut. 26:15)—all these blessings come through the merit of the tribes, as it says in Scripture, "Were you mad at the rivers, God, was your anger against the sea when you rode upon your horse, your chariot of victory? You stripped bare your bow from its sheath, the oaths of the tribes; say Selah, you gashed the earth with rivers" (Hab. 3:9).

"A land" (Deut. 26:15)—this is the land itself, and it says in Scripture, "These are the names of the tribes . . . from the eastern side to the western side: Naphtali, one portion . . ." (Ezek. 48:3).

"Flowing with milk and honey" (Deut. 26:15)—this teaches that the giving of tithes imparts flavor, aroma, and plumpness and abundance to the crop.

Here we see that the tithes and offerings represent one component of Israel's service to God, the burnt offerings, peace offerings, the presentation of sheep and cattle on the altar, the other component. But the agricultural offerings take priority, since they represent God's share in God's own gifts to Israel.

What marks God's ownership, and Israel's mere possession, of the Land is God's laying claim to two matters. On the one side, it is a share of the crop. On the other side, it is a share of the outcome of particular life processes that render the important part of the crop desirable. The one share represents God's response to people and is owing when people indicate by their action that they wish to possess the now-ripe crops, so God responds to their will by laying claim to God's portion. The other share forms God's response to nature and is owing when the natural processes of life have accomplished their task; then God responds to the moment of fulfillment of God's purpose, to which human intentionality is irrelevant, and God's share once more is owing. Human intentionality, nature's teleology—both come to realization in God's laying claim to what is God's. So requiring what is due, God convenes with human beings when their engagement defines the venue—the harvest in the field, the transport of the crop to the courtyard—and with nature when nature's processes do. It is all the same: God's purpose, not human will or nature's way, governs.

## In His House God Receives a Particular Portion of the Crop: Tractate Bikkurim Briefly Revisited

The pilgrimage at the specified occasion involves the presentation of the Firstfruits of the Israelite householder's crops to the priesthood, set forth in the law of the Mishnah of Bikkurim, which we discussed in chapter 4. Second tithe has now to be placed into the larger context of meeting God in God's house in Jerusalem. We gain perspective through comparison and contrast, in the present case, of Firstfruits, second tithe, heave offering, and other agricultural offerings.

To identify the particular point that Bikkurim registers, we have to classify the offering in relationship to others that are both like and unlike it. How do the Firstfruits compare with other agricultural offerings? They are comparable to, but different from, produce that has been designated as heave offering and second tithe.

Firstfruits and heave offering both are consecrated to the priesthood and eaten only by them; both sanctify any unconsecrated produce with which they are mixed but can be neutralized in proper proportion; both are eaten in a state of cleanness. They are comparable to heave offering in that Firstfruits are to be eaten by the priests and their families, not the householders who present them. They must be eaten in a state of cultic cleanness.

What about Firstfruits and second tithe? They are comparable to second tithe in that Firstfruits, like second tithe, must be presented in Jerusalem and involve the correct recitation; heave offering is presented without a declaration. Like second tithe, Firstfruits must be removed at the designated point in the year. A person in mourning before the burial of the deceased may not eat either second tithe or Firstfruits. Both represent occasions for rejoicing. Once in Jerusalem considerations of neutralization no longer apply. Then the sanctity inheres and is indelible.

How do Firstfruits stand alone? Unlike heave offering and second tithe, Firstfruits do not render prohibited for consumption produce that has been completely processed; there is no prescribed volume that must be designated Firstfruits; only the seven species are covered by the offering; the rite does not apply in the time in which the Temple is in ruins; those who do not own the crops may not designate Firstfruits from them. Not only so, but (1) the status of produce as Firstfruits may be designated even to what has not been harvested; (2) an entire field may be donated; (3) the householder must see to it that the produce is delivered and replace what is designated and subsequently lost; and (4) a Temple rite is involved in the presentation (an ox for meat for the householder and his family as well as for the priesthood, a bird for a burnt offering, Levitical song, waving before the altar); and (5) in the Temple rite, the householder participates.

While the basket is still on his shoulder, the householder recites the entire confession of Firstfruits, beginning from the words "I declare this day to the Lord your God" (Deut. 26:3), and proceeding through the entire passage. In one Rabbinic sage's view, while the basket is on his shoulder, the householder recites only up to the second part of the confession, which begins with the words, "A wandering Aramean was my father" (Deut. 26:6). Having reached these words, the householder takes the basket down from his shoulder and holds it by its rim, and a priest puts his hand beneath the basket and waves it before the altar. Then the Israelite recites the second part of the confession and then places the basket beside the altar and bows down and departs.

The final requirement is the householder's remaining overnight in Jerusalem. To heave offering and second tithe these rulings do not pertain. These are the critical indicators of the legal standing of Firstfruits and yield for us the statement that the law of the Mishnah makes through no other category.

Firstfruits, like second tithe, focus upon the Land as the particular channel for the celebration of life. Once again they draw the householder off the Land being tended to God's place, there to explain the householder's claim upon the nurturing Land. When God and Israel meet for Israel's presentation of the Firstfruits of the Land, the new crops in hand, Israel comes to God's abode and speaks its piece to God. This speech concerns the Land they hold in common. Israel sets forth its claim to possess the Land at the very moment of acknowledging God's ownership.

It does so in the offering of the choice crop to the priesthood—not a mere random sample of the entire crop, such as is represented by heave offering, eaten by the priests wherever located, nor a tithe of the crop reserved for Israel's own enjoyment at God's abode. For the Firstfruits the householder bears responsibility until the priest takes possession in God's behalf in the Temple—just like the animal offerings the householder brings along. But unlike the obligatory offerings presented out of public funds, the obligatory offerings presented out of personal funds in expiation of sin, Firstfruits are both personal and public. They are personal, because—the Declaration stresses—they represent the householder's individual and physical claim to presence and possession of the Land. They are public because they are obligatory and serve no individual aspiration of atonement.

We have already encountered what I call "the genealogization of Israel." Now we see what that means. The negative comes first. *Anyone* may buy a beast or bird or cereal and designate it for a personal purpose. *Only the householder* in the Land of Israel out of his *own* land's produce presents Firstfruits. Anyone may declare the classification of a beast or bird or cereal, that is, a sin offering, a guilt offering, a freewill offering, a peace offering. Only the householder may classify the produce as Firstfruits by an explicit designation.

The householder's is a remarkable statement, bringing what is called his own but is merely possessed on God's sufferance (as we have seen time and again) and then speaking of himself and his fathers. The rite then defines the relationship of Israel and God in acutely personal terms, invoking the "I" and the "my," in giving back to God the first testimonies to God's ongoing benevolence.

Firstfruits localizes the deeply enlandised relationship between God and Israel. It makes that relationship personal and immediate, familial and genealogical—wholly through the nexus of the Holy Land. Note the contrast with other agricultural taxes. Heave offering and tithe are presented whether or not the Temple is standing and they are separated by sharecroppers, tenant farmers, holders of confiscated property, and by robbers. By contrast, Firstfruits are presented, their purpose and standing explicated, only by the specific Israelite householder born to inherit the Land, out of crops raised on his own fields and presented to the priesthood only in the Temple. Now, when the law of the Mishnah wishes to state that Israel in its fleshly embodiment of families through genealogical ties relates to God at the Temple through the gifts of grace presented by the Land, it can make no more particular and concrete statement than that. Here is a striking example of how theology is realized in the Mishnah's law.

### God's Presence in Israel, Meaning Both Land and People

This, then, is the import of sharing the crop with God, the landowner. The meticulous designation of portions of the crop as tithes and heave offering forms a weighty matter of the Torah. Specifically, in disposing of the produce of the Land as God requires Israel to do, Israel recapitulates, with a different ending, that story of the beginning that had closed in disaster. Adam could not refrain from one thing. Israel gives up many. Adam lost it all. Israel gains pure joy, and its relationship with God is one of utter happiness—bliss is not too strong a word. Representing the agricultural dues as a mere formality, an onerous tax, therefore misses and trivializes the point of the law of the Mishnah.

Matters could not be stated more uncomprehendingly than in the language of outsiders to "you people": "Woe to you, scribes and Pharisees, hypocrites! For you tithe mint and dill and cumin and have neglected the weightier matters of the law, justice and mercy and faith; these you ought to have done, without neglecting the others" (Matt. 23:23). That formulation frames the issue disproportionately. The law of the Mishnah does not neglect the weightier matters of the law. It makes ample provision for justice and mercy, and everywhere and always faith. The law of the Mishnah here concerns itself with Israel's relationship with the ever-present, ubiquitous God in God's dwelling in the Land. That is an encounter of bliss attained through obedience to God's always-benevolent will.

To treat as opposites tithing and justice therefore misses the point: tithing in its place, justice in its setting. Each realizes the undivided will of the one God, who is holy and just. The law of the Torah as set forth in the Mishnah whether in connection with civil law or cult and rite speaks of sublimity. Through the Torah as systematized by the law of the Mishnah, "God is with us," *immanu el.*

# 15 DWELLING TOGETHER: GOD'S PRESENCE IN THE ISRAELITE HOUSEHOLD

## Tractates Pesahim, Sukkah, and Yoma

### Reciprocal Hospitality: God's House, Israel's Households

As we have just seen, on the pilgrim festivals Israel meets God in God's house. On comparable occasions God meets Israelites in their households. This domestic engagement comes about on holy days when the Israelite household corresponds to God's house—Passover, Tabernacles, and the Day of Atonement. On these days some aspect of observance causes the home to be purposefully identified with the Temple. In the end, then, it is the occasion and not the location that precipitates the meeting of Israel and God, whether in God's place or in Israel's.

### The Household and the Altar (1): Mishnah-tractate Pesahim

Passover marks the celebration of Israel's redemption, its separation from Egypt in the Exodus. That separation is demarcated by corresponding blood rites: the Egyptians suffer the loss of their firstborn sons and the Israelites sacrifice the paschal lamb. It is also marked by the fact that a Temple offering may be eaten in the very household of the Israelite. On Passover Israel differentiates itself from the nations (Egypt) and chooses as the signification of its identity the attainment of the condition of cleanness in the household, such that Temple meat may be eaten there. Mishnah-tractate Pesahim centers its exposition on preparation of the household for the rite through the removal of leaven, on the one side, and the presentation of the Passover offering in the Temple and its consumption at home in the family—natural or fabricated—on the other.

The basic rules derive from the Torah. The most important passage is found at Exodus 12:1-28. The Torah deals with these topics in order: (1) setting aside and killing a lamb for the Passover (Exod. 12:1-13); (2) unleavened bread and the taboo against leaven and what is leavened, with the festival of unleavened bread (Exod. 12:14-20); and (3) the lamb again (Exod. 12:21-28). Our central concern is with the passage pertaining to the slaying of the Passover lamb and the placing of its blood on the lintel and two doorposts of the house, to keep Israel on the side of life when the angel of death descends upon the Egyptian firstborn. Scripture states the matter in the following language:

> Then Moses called all the elders of Israel and said to them, "Select lambs for yourselves according to your families and kill the Passover lamb. Take a bunch of hyssop and dip it in the blood that is in the basin and touch the lintel and the two doorposts with the blood that is in the basin; and none of you shall go out of the door of his house until the morning. For the Lord will pass through to slay the Egyptians; and when he sees the blood on the lintel and on the two doorposts, the Lord will pass over the door and will not allow the destroyer to enter your houses to slay you. You shall observe this rite as an ordinance for you and for your sons for ever. And when you come to the Land that the Lord will give you as he has promised, you shall keep this service. And when your children say to you, "What do you mean by this service?" you shall say, "It is the sacrifice of the Lord's Passover, for he passed over the houses of the people of Israel in Egypt when he slew the Egyptians but spared our houses." And the people bowed their heads and worshipped. (Exod. 12:21-27)

The purpose of the blood on the lintel will engage us in a moment. First, we note that, contrary to this Exodus, with its assumption that the rite takes place in the home, Deuteronomy 16:1-8 states that the sacrifice of the Passover lamb is to take place only in Jerusalem:

> . . . You may not offer the Passover sacrifice within any of your towns that the Lord your God gives you, but at the place that the Lord your God will choose to make his name dwell in it, there you shall offer the Passover sacrifice, in the evening at the going down of the sun at the time you came out of Egypt. And you shall boil it and eat it at the place that the Lord your God will choose; and in the morning you shall turn and go to your tents. For six days you shall eat unleavened bread and on the seventh there shall be a solemn assembly to the Lord your God; you shall do no work on it. (Deut. 16:1-8)

God's abode is the Temple in Jerusalem, so Deuteronomy assumes that the Passover offering takes place there. The two formulations—Exodus commanding the offering in the Israelite household, Deuteronomy commanding that it take place in the Jerusalem Temple—are harmonized by the Mishnah. The sacrifice takes place in the Temple and provides the meat that is to be eaten at home *within Jerusalem*. With that statement in hand, we should treat the Passover offering as a Temple rite, just as the sacrifice for the Day of Atonement is a Temple rite.

That is more than a general observation, for details of the home rite invoke

Temple rules. The Mishnah explains how freeing the Israelite household from leaven make the household comparable to the house of God:

**MISHNAH-TRACTATE MENAHOT 5:1**

All meal offerings are brought unleavened [Lev. 2:4–5, 6:7–9], except for the leaven[ed cakes] in the thank offerings [Mishnah-tractate Menahot 7:1] and the two loaves of bread [of Shabuᶜot], which are brought leavened [Lev. 7:13, 23:17].

In other words, in the Temple, God's bread is normally unleavened. So removing leaven from the household in preparation for the consumption of unleavened bread (*massah*) aligns the household with the Temple. With the removal of leaven and all marks of fermentation, the Israelite eats only that same unleavened bread that is God's portion throughout the year.

Likewise, requiring the consumption of the Passover offering's meat at home introduces into the household the considerations of cultic cleanness that govern in the Temple. The premise of the legal exposition is that the Passover offering is sacrificed in the Temple and then its carcass is carried home to be eaten there. That provision means that the household must be readied for God's presence as the Temple is, by provision of rites of purification, both those of commission (immersing persons and objects) and those of omission (avoiding sources of contamination). As a result, on Passover the Israelite household, so far as is possible, is analogous to the Temple. The Torah has supplied the facts; the law of the Mishnah has expanded upon them and drawn out what is implicit in them.

Like the law of Mishnah-tractate Yoma, which, as we shall see, is devoted to the Temple rite on that occasion, the law of Mishnah-tractate Pesahim stresses the cultic aspect of the occasion: the disposition of the Passover offering. In volume, nearly half of the law of the Mishnah found in Pesahim is devoted to that one theme—of the tractate's ten chapters, five in all (5:1—9:11). In complexity, by far the best-articulated and most searching legal problems derive from that same theme. But with its attention to removing leaven from the home, the opening unit, and the Passover narrative and banquet held in the home (chapter 10), the law of Mishnah-tractate Pesahim belongs to the realm of the Israelite household. It yields a statement on the character of that household that the law of Mishnah-tractate Yoma does not even contemplate.

The main point is that the offering sacrificed in the Temple yields meat to be eaten in the household, at home, not only in the Temple courtyard. That rule pertains only to Lesser Holy Things, the peace offerings and the festal offering, for example—and to the Passover, so we read in Mishnah-tractate Zebahim 9:14:

Most Holy Things were eaten within the veils [of the Temple], Lesser Holy Things and second tithe within the wall [of Jerusalem].

But even here, among Lesser Holy Things, the Passover offering is unique. Among offerings eaten in Jerusalem in the household but outside of the Temple walls, the Passover offering is the only one precipitated by the advent of a particular occasion (as distinct from peace and festal offerings). The festivals of

Tabernacles and Pentecost, by contrast, do not entail a home rite of a similar character, nor does the celebration of the New Month. Likewise, the law of Mishnah-tractate Yoma describes an occasion that is celebrated at the Temple or in relationship to the Temple, with no corresponding rite in the home. In this context, then, the law of Mishnah-tractate Pesahim alone sets forth an occasion in the life of all Israel that commences in the Temple but concludes at home. On Passover—"the season of our freedom"—the home and the Temple form a single continuum.

The law details how people bring the animals to the Temple, where the beasts are sacrificed, the blood collected, and the sacrificial portions placed on the altar fires. Then the people take the remaining meat home and roast it. This is the continuum of Temple and household in Jerusalem.

But the Mishnah's picture of sacrificing the meat in the Temple and then eating it outside of the Temple in the city, as with Lesser Holy Things in general, places the Passover sacrifice in an intermediate situation. It is not an offering that takes place in a state of uncleanness, like the offering of the red cow, which is presented outside of the Temple, hence in a place by definition subject to uncleanness (Num. 19:1–20), nor is it an offering that is presented and eaten in the Temple in a state of cleanness, with the meat eaten by the priests in the Temple itself, like the sin offering and other Most Holy Things. As to where the sacrifier's share of the Passover offering (and its comparable ones) is eaten, the law of the Mishnah takes for granted that it ordinarily is in a state of cleanness (though Scripture and the Mishnah make provision for those unclean on the fifteenth of Nisan to make the offering a month later). That consideration gains weight when we recall the unleavened character of the bread with which the meat is eaten, for all now falls into the model of nearly every meal offering.

But then we must wonder, where is the altar in the home? The answer depends on what we mean by "altar." What marks the altar is the sprinkling of the offering's blood upon it. Thus, the place in the household where the blood is sprinkled defines the location of the altar. Exodus 12:1–28 treats the offering as a rite for the home, with the blood tossed on the lintel of the house as a mark of an Israelite dwelling. So the answer to the question follows: the lintel serves as the counterpart of the altar. That is where the blood rite takes place, where the blood of the sacrifice is tossed.

## The Passover Offering Analogous to the Sin Offering

The analogy of household to Temple is succinct. The Israelite home compares to the Temple, the lintel to the altar, the abode of Israel to the abode of God. Blood on the lintel marks the dwelling as Israelite. With what meaning, and why the lintel? Seen from the inside to the outside, as the account in Exodus indicates, it forms the point of entry to death. It is the gateway, marking the household apart from the world beyond—the world subject to death outside, the world of life inside. For inside the walls of the Israelite household conditions of genealogical and cultic cleanness pertain, in a way comparable to the space inside the contained space of the Temple courtyard. The rite of sprinkling the blood on the altar, and here on the lintel, is at one and the same time the atonement for sin, which brings death, and the sanctification of the Israelite household, which represents life eternal, with the coming resurrection of the dead.

That what is at stake in the Passover offering's blood rite is atonement for sin is not merely my surmise. It emerges from the law of the Mishnah's answer to the question, in so many words: To what offering may we compare the Passover? The answer is, to the sin offering. This is stated explicitly:

**MISHNAH-TRACTATE ZEBAHIM 1:1**
> All animal offerings that were slaughtered not for their own name are valid [so that the blood is tossed, the entrails burned],
>
> but they do not go to the owner's credit in fulfillment of an obligation,
>
> except for the Passover and the sin offering—
>
> the Passover at its appointed time [the afternoon of the fourteenth of Nisan],
>
> and the sin offering of any time.

The Mishnah's formulation leaves no doubt that the sin offering and the Passover offering are comparable. In both cases the animal designated in one or the other classification must be offered by the priest for the purpose of that particular classification of offering. The animal must be designated as a Passover offering, for a particular family. Or it must be designated as a sin offering to expiate a particular sin inadvertently committed and only later on discovered. Now, if that is not so, then the offering is null, atonement not being attained by the tossing of the blood.

The analogy of domestic lintel to Temple altar is temporal and occasional, not permanent and spatial. The household serves as the venue for an offering comparable to the sin offering. But that analogy takes effect only at a very specific moment. That matches the Sabbath and its effect upon the household. That is, the household compares to Eden only at the specific moment of the Sabbath day, from sunset on the sixth day. Then the invisible wall descends to mark the temporal Eden in the particular space consecrated by the Israelite abode. So too with Passover: the advent of the first new moon after the vernal equinox then compares with the advent of sunset on the sixth day, the beginning of the Sabbath comparing, then, to the beginning of the lunar calendar marked by the first new moon of spring. The Sabbath places Israel in Eden. That is how, as I said earlier, the full moon, the fifteenth of Nisan, when the Passover offering is presented, places the Israelite household into a continuum with the Temple, the lintel with the altar.

The animal that has been consecrated as the Passover offering must be offered within that classification, and an animal not designated as a Passover offering cannot serve as such. This is comparable to the status of an animal designated as a sin offering, as we just noted in Mishnah Zebahim 1:1 ff. The Mishnah's law stresses that the rite is analogous to the sin offering in that the animal that is designated for the rite must be offered for that purpose—and for that particular sacrifier. If it is designated for the benefit of a given party (sacrifier) and offered for some other sacrifier and it is not possible to clarify the situation, the animal is simply disposed of, so, we recall, Mishnah Pesahim 9:9 for example:

> An association, the Passover offering of which was lost, and which said to someone, "Go and find and slaughter another one for us," and that one went and found and slaughtered [another], but they, too, went and bought and slaughtered [one for themselves]—if his was slaughtered first, he eats his, and they eat with him of his. But if theirs was slaughtered first, they eat of theirs, and he eats of his. And if it is not known which of them was slaughtered first, or if both of them were slaughtered simultaneously, then he eats of his, and they do not eat with him, and theirs goes forth to the place of burning, but they are exempt from having to observe the second Passover.

The stress on the specificity of identification of the beast and sacrifier aligns the Passover offering with the sin offering, as opposed to peace or freewill offerings. The theory of the matter is explained in the argument of Eliezer (Mishnah Zebahim 1:1), who holds that the guilt offering should be subject to the same rule. What is important to my argument is not his position but his reasoning, expressed as follows:

> Just as the sin offering is unfit if it is offered not for its own name [meaning, in the category for which the beast was originally consecrated], so the guilt offering is unfit if offered not for its own name].

Eliezer's statement takes for granted that the sin offering is brought in expiation of (inadvertent) sin. And we realize that the Passover offering is in the same classification as the sin offering. That theory of the matter matches the story of the blood on the lintel. The Passover is an offering that expiates Israel's sins and atones for those sins for which, at the same moment, Egypt will atone through the death of the firstborn among men and cattle alike.

Within that theory, how shall we find in the account of the offering the basis for treating it as comparable to the sin offering, which is offered to expiate inadvertent sin? Since the Passover offering signals that Israel is to be spared the judgment of the Lord against the firstborn of Egypt, it is reasonable to suppose that the blood of the Passover lamb, placed on the lintel not only marks the household as Israelite but also expiates inadvertent sin carried out in that household.

As we saw earlier, the Torah itself imposed the requirement of celebrating Passover in two places: Deuteronomy puts it in the Temple, the meat to be consumed in Jerusalem; Exodus puts it at home, the meat to be consumed there. But in joining the two conceptions, with its rules for the household wherever it is located, the law of the Mishnah has made a statement of its own out of the disharmonious facts received from the Torah. That statement is in two parts.

First, we now realize full well that the Israelite dwelling is treated as comparable to the Temple not merely in the aspect of cultic cleanness but also in the aspect of cultic activity: the place where the sacrificial meat was consumed, within the unfolding of the rite of expiation of inadvertent sin itself. It is that analogy, between the Passover on the fourteenth of Nisan and the sin offering at any time, that forms the critical nexus between the Israelite abode and the Temple altar.

Second, why that particular analogy, and to what effect? Or to state matters differently, what statement do we make when we say that the Passover offering is comparable to the sin offering? The answer derives from the occasion itself: Israel on the eve of the Exodus from Egypt is at the threshold of its formation into a kingdom of priests and a holy people. When God executed judgment against Egypt, exacting the firstborn of man and beast as the sanction, God saw the blood, which—the Mishnah's law now tells us—is comparable to the blood of the sin offering. Israel then had expiated its inadvertent sin and attained a state of atonement, thereby entering a right relationship with God. On the eve of Israel's formation, the Passover offered at home, with the blood on the lintel, marked Israel as having expiated its sin. The sinless people was kept alive at the time of judgment—just as, at the end of days, nearly all Israel will stand in judgment and pass on to life eternal.

Sin and atonement, slavery and freedom, death and life—these turn out to form the foci of Passover. If the sages had wished to make the theological statement that Israel differs from the Egyptians as does life from death, and that what makes the difference is that Israel is sanctified even—or especially—within its household walls, not only within the Temple veils, how better to say so than through the law of Mishnah-tractate Passover? Eat unleavened bread as God (ordinarily) does in the meal offerings, consume the meat left over from the blood rite of the Passover offering, analogous to the sin offering in its very particular identification with a given family unit—then the actions speak for themselves.

These are the two facts out of the repertoire of the data of Passover that the legal statement from the Mishnah chooses to explore and articulate. It is Scripture at Exodus that sets forth the facts, and it is then the Mishnah's law that explores their implications for the norms of conduct, while, in doing so, imparting its sense for the proportion, therefore the meaning and significance, of the whole.

The sages will assuredly have maintained that they said in the law of the Mishnah no more than the Torah had implied, and, as we have seen, that claim enjoys powerful support in the content of the law of the Mishnah. But the sages are the ones who framed the law and chose its points of emphasis. In doing so, they shaped the Mishnah's law into a statement congruent with the stresses of their system as a whole. Theirs was a theology of restoration, with

Israel brought back to the Land standing for humanity returned to Eden. They knew full well that the majority of Israel was resident outside of Jerusalem. In point of fact, in the time that the legal statement was being formulated, Israel could not enter Jerusalem, let alone sacrifice on the ruined, ploughed-over Temple mount. Yet the sages chose to make no statement at all concerning the realities of the moment; these meant nothing of enduring consequence to them—the situation of Israel in the here and now did not define the focus of the law of the Mishnah, only its transient venue.

## The Household and the Altar (2):
## Mishnah-tractate Sukkah

Called simply "the Festival," Sukkot, or the festival of Tabernacles ("Huts"), celebrated both in the household and in the Temple, forms the counterpart in autumn of the festival of Passover in spring. Both mark the first full moon after the equinox. The Torah links both to the Exodus-Passover in detail, Sukkot in general terms. In each case, Temple offerings on the pilgrim festival form only one part of the matter. The other part for Passover is the household's freedom from leaven and consumption of the Passover meat at home. For Sukkot, it is the building of a Sukkah, a "booth," and the taking up of temporary residence therein for the holy season. At Passover the activities of the Temple encompass the home. At Tabernacles, the home itself is redefined. Israel is to take shelter by reverting to the wilderness in any random, ramshackle hut covered with what nature has provided but in form and in purpose what we otherwise do not value. Israel's dwelling in the wilderness is fragile, random, and transient—like Israel in the wilderness. Out of Egypt, Israel atoned and lived—but only in the condition of the wilderness, like the generation that, after all, had to die out before Israel could enter the Land and its intended eternal life.

The Torah supplies nearly all of the pertinent facts of Sukkot, though leaving to the Mishnah's law the work of defining details. Leviticus 23:33–43 states with reference to the hut:

> And the Lord said to Moses, "Say to the people of Israel, On the fifteenth day of this seventh month and for seven days is the feast of booths to the Lord. . . . You shall dwell in booths for seven days; all that are native in Israel shall dwell in booths, that your generations may know that I made the people of Israel dwell in booths when I brought them out of the land of Egypt; I am the Lord your God."

Deuteronomy 16:13–15 specifies the use of the hut:

> You shall keep the feast of booths seven days, when you make your ingathering from your threshing floor and your wine press; you shall rejoice in your feast, you and your son and your daughter, your manservant and your maidservant, the Levite, the sojourner, the fatherless and the widow who are within your towns. For seven days you shall keep the feast to the Lord your God at the place that the Lord will choose; because the Lord your God will bless you in all your produce and in all the work of your hands, so that you will be altogether joyful.

As is its way, Deuteronomy assigns the feast to Jerusalem, at the same time arranging for rejoicing in the towns elsewhere. The law of the Mishnah takes as its task the presentation of three topics: (1) Temple rites, (2) home obligations, (3) special methods for and modes of the celebration of the Festival. Our special interest is the hut, the Sukkah.

The Mishnah's highly analytical presentation comes with the matter of the Sukkah itself. There the law is more than merely routine or informative; it amplifies the practical requirements of how the Sukkah is constructed and defines what constitutes an invalid Sukkah. The details add up to one main point. The Sukkah is to resemble but not to replicate a house. It is the abode of the wilderness: impermanent but serviceable under the circumstances. The Sukkah must look like a dwelling, casting a shadow and affording protection from the sun. But whatever its appearance, it is not a real house, because it does not afford Israel shelter from the rain, its covering leaving shade but providing for light to filter in as well—open space to see the stars—and by design a strong wind will knock it over.

Definitive traits distinguish the Sukkah from the house. It must be constructed out of doors, not under a tree; it must be built for that particular holiday, meaning, the roofing (*sekhakh*) must be put up for the occasion. That recalls the rule of the Passover lamb, which must be designated for a particular sacrifier, a particular Passover occasion (and that is by definition, since it has to have been born after the last Passover). The roofing (*sekhakh*), moreover, forms the center of interest, the walls not having to be modeled on conventional housing. As to the roofing, the key, as I said, is that the shade must exceed the light but cannot by definition block out all light. Thus it is like a roof, giving shelter from sun and rain, but not like a roof, allowing sun and rain to pass through but in diminished volume. The main purpose of the impermanent abode, like that in the wilderness, is shelter from the sun. But, as the Tosefta specifies, the form scarcely matters: If one spread Sukkah roofing on top of a bed or on top of a tree ten handbreadths high, if the roofing's shade was greater than its light, it is valid. If not, it is invalid, meaning that the walls may be provided by the most unconventional arrangements. So the ordinary house supplies not so much a model as an analogy.

The Sukkah must derive from human artifice and intent; it cannot be formed of what is attached to the ground, but must be made of what has grown from the ground, what is insusceptible to uncleanness, and what has been cut down. It must come about through deliberate human action, a natural or permanent Sukkah being an oxymoron, and it must represent an occasion, not a permanent arrangement. The Sukkah-roofing must afford shelter by means of what derives from nature but has been detached from nature; human intervention then is required once more.

The roofing must be insusceptible to uncleanness, but that requirement hardly figures routinely, for it is not self-evident why people should build the

Sukkah at home out of insusceptible *sekhakh*. But, as with the law of the Mishnah everywhere, so here too the detail is not arbitrary. The context is everything. What has to be at issue, when questions of susceptibility to cultic uncleanness enter in, involves eating, specifically, eating consecrated food such as the family's portion of an offering for the holy day. The ordinary house in which an Israelite dwells and eats is attached to the ground and therefore insusceptible. By contrast, important components of the Sukkah need not be attached to the ground at all—the walls may even be suspended some handbreadths off the ground. On this basis we may make some sense of the rule. The insusceptibility of the *sekhakh* accommodates the separation of the abode from the earth. The temporary abode of the Israelite—where if in Jerusalem the Israelite's share of the sacrifices to God is eaten—is comparable in its function to the Temple. The Sukkah should therefore be in a cultic state of cleanness, which is possible if it is constructed out of insusceptible materials.

But the definition of the kind of materials to be used adds a dimension to the layers of meaning attached to the Sukkah. Edible vegetation is susceptible to uncleanness as food, for instance, when someone intends to eat it. Insusceptibility to uncleanness in this context finds its definition in what is useless and not edible as food. The Tosefta's amplification makes this clear: If one made a *Sukkah* roofing with sheaves, if the straw was more abundant than the grain, it is valid. If not, it is invalid. Once more the Sukkah crosses lines of definition. The roofing, or *sekhakh*, therefore, is to be the produce of nature, subject to human purpose, but produce of nature that is inedible and deemed useless and therefore insusceptible to uncleanness.

A good case in point is the difference between bundled and loose straw, wood, or brush. Bundled straw or wood or brush may not serve, since in that form the straw, wood, or brush is formed into useful composites; but undone, in their natural state and form, they do serve. In that way the random and fragile character of the dwelling is underscored—Israel, at home but not at home, dwells in a house that is not a house, the whole then recapitulating the situation of the wilderness, after Egypt, before Eden.

While people are encouraged to sleep in the Sukkah, they are required to eat their meals there or at any rate their fixed and formal meals. What is emphasized is the act of eating in the Sukkah. That is the principal obligation on the first two nights of the Festival. Women, slaves, and minors are exempt from the commandment of dwelling in the Sukkah because it is an obligation that is temporally defined. As a general rule, women, slaves, and minors are subject to the will of others and cannot be required to keep a commandment for which a fixed time is set, since at any given moment the householder may legitimately impose upon them some obligation that prevents their complying.

The Mishnah's regulations treat as the counterpart to the Passover offering the *lulab*, the sheaf of branches specified by the Torah, and the *etrog*, the fruit of the citron tree. The lulab and the etrog are utilized in the Temple, just as is the Passover offering. How else do the Temple rites of Sukkot and Passover compare? So too the animal designated for the Passover offering must belong to the sacrifier and be subject to the particular ownership and will of the sacrifier, and likewise the lulab and etrog must belong to the person who utilizes them. They may not be stolen or lost or borrowed, and they must meet a particular standard as to their form, just as the animal for a sacrifice must be free of blemishes. Just as, in connection with eating the Passover meat, the sacrifier recites the Hallel Psalms, so in the utilization of the lulab and other objects, the worshiper recites those Psalms. (The former takes place at home, the latter, it is assumed, in the Temple.)

## Israel between Earth and Heaven, Death and Life

What statement, then, does the Halakhah of the Festival of Sukkot make through the Sukkah concerning God's presence in Israel? It underscores Israel's reliance on that Presence. The temporary abode of the Israelite, suspended between heaven and earth, the Sukkah in its transience matches Israel's condition in the wilderness, wandering between Egypt and the Land, death and eternal life. Sukkot addresses the condition of Israel.

How does this transpire? The context in the narrative that animates the Halakhic structure answers. Since Sukkot is a festival of the wilderness, we deal with the Generation of the Wilderness. That is the generation that must die out before Israel can enter the Land. So, entering the Sukkah reminds Israel not only of the fragility of its condition but also—in the aftermath of the penitential season—of its parlous actuality. That is, it is sinful, yet awaiting death, so that a new generation will be ready for the Land. Then it is that interstitial circumstance, between death in Egypt and eternal life in the Land that Sukkot recapitulates. The now-abode of Israel-in-between is the house that is not a house, protected by a roof that affords no real shelter but is open to the elements—yet serves somewhat: Israel en route to death (for those here now) and later eternal life (for everyone then).

The odd timing of Sukkot and its requirements should not be missed. Sukkot marks the beginning of the autumn rains in the Land of Israel. The fate of the commonwealth for the coming year in nature is settled by the rain. Passover marks the end of that same season. So the Sukkah is not wholly functional to its season. It is built not with the coming of the spring and the dry season, when the booth serves a useful purpose against the sun. Rather, the Sukkah is required at the advent of the autumn and the rainy season, when—by definition—it does not protect against the rain. We deal, then, with an abode that cannot serve in the season that is coming but the one that is concluding. So the message of transience reinforces itself: even what serves is good for just so long.

The Mishnah's law emphasizes also the contemporaneity of the wilderness condition. That is why the Sukkah is constructed afresh every year. Israel annually is directed to replicate the wilderness generation—the Torah says no less. The dual message is not to be missed: Israel is en route to the Land that stands for Eden, but Israel even beyond the penitential season bears its sin and must, on the near term, die; but in death all Israelites (but the few exceptions) enjoy the certainty of resurrection, judgment, and eternal life to come.

What we are dealing with here is a redefinition of the meaning of Israel's abode. All seven days Israelites treat the Sukkah as their regular dwelling and their house as their sometime dwelling. On the occasion of the Festival, Israel regains the wilderness and its message of death but, in the end, also transcendence over death in the entry into the Land. Only in the context of the New Year and the Day of Atonement, only as the final act in the penitential season and its intense drama, does Sukkot make sense. It is the law of the Mishnah that draws out that sense.

True, the Torah tells more about the observance of the Festival of Sukkot than about the occasion for the Festival. What it does say suffices—"that your generations may know that I made the people of Israel dwell in booths when I brought them out of the land of Egypt." The reversion to the wilderness, the recapitulation of the wandering, the return to Israel's condition outside of the Land and before access to the Land, the remembrance of the character of that generation, its feet scarcely dry after passing through the mud of the Reed Sea when it has already built the Golden Calf—that is the other half of the cycle that commences at Passover and concludes at Sukkot.

This brings us to the matter of the matching of Temple occasion and household celebration of the same occasion. The home is abandoned altogether, a new house being constructed for the occasion. During the Festival, Israelites move out of their homes, eating meals and (where possible) sleeping in the Sukkah, making the Sukkah into their regular home, and their home into the random shelter. Just as, in the wilderness, God's abode shifted along with Israel from place to place, the tabernacle being taken down and reconstructed time and again. Thus, in recapitulating the life of the wilderness, Israel's abode shifts, losing that permanence that it ordinarily possesses. What, however, happens in the home that connects the home to the Temple? At first glance, nothing, there being no counterpart to the Passover Seder. But a second look shows something more striking. To see the connection, we must recall that during the Festival a huge volume of offerings is presented day by day. There Israelites will consume the festal offering (*Hagigah*) and other sacrificial meat, for instance, from the freewill offering. So, Israel moves to the housing of the wilderness to eat the Festival meat, doing in the Sukkah what God did in the tabernacle in that epoch.

What, then, does the abode in the wilderness represent? To answer that question within the framework of the law of the Mishnah, we have to introduce two well-established facts. First, I cannot overemphasize that, as the law of the Mishnah knows Sukkot, the Festival continues the penitential season commencing with the advent of Elul, reaching its climax in the season of judgment and atonement of the Days of Awe, from the first through the tenth of the month of Tishré, Rosh Hashanah, the New Year, and Yom Hakkippurim, the Day of Atonement. Sukkot finds its place in the context of a season of repentance for sin and of atonement. And since, as the rites themselves indicate, it celebrates the advent of the rainy season with prayers and activities meant to encourage the now-conciliated God to give ample rain to sustain the life of the Land and its people, the message is vital. Israel has rebelled and sinned, but Israel has also atoned and repented: so much for the first ten days of the season of repentance.

At the new moon following, having atoned and been forgiven, Israel takes up residence as if it were in the wilderness. Why so? Because in the wilderness, en route to the Land, still-sinful Israel depended wholly and completely on God's mercy and good will and infinite capacity to forgive in response to repentance and atonement. Israel depends for all things on God, eating food God sends down from heaven, drinking water God divines in rocks—and living in fragile booths constructed of worthless shards and remnants of this and that. Even Israel's very household in the mundane sense, its shelter, now is made to depend on divine grace: the wind can blow it down, the rain prevent its very use. Returning to these booths, built specifically for the occasion (not last year's), manipulating the sacred objects owned in particular by the Israelite who utilizes them, as the rainy season impends, the particular Israelite here and now recapitulates his or her personal, total dependence on God's mercy.

Accordingly, requiring that everything be renewed for the present occasion and the particular person, the law of the Mishnah transforms commemoration of the wandering into recapitulation of the condition of the wilderness. The Sukkah makes the statement that Israel of the here and now, sinful like the Israel that dwelt in the wilderness, depends wholly on, looks only to, God. Israelites turn their eyes to that God whose just-now forgiveness of last year's sins and acts of rebellion and whose acceptance of Israel's immediate act of repentance will recapitulate God's ongoing nurture, which kept Israel alive in the wilderness. The law of the Mishnah's provisions for the Sukkah underscore not so much the transience of Israel's present life in general as Israel's particular condition. The law of the Mishnah renders Israel in the Sukkah as the people that is en route to the Land, which is Eden. Yes, Israel is en route, but it is not there. A generation goes, a generation comes—Israel will arrive, all together, at the end.

So in defining the Sukkah as it does, the law of the Mishnah also underscores God's presence in providence and God's remarkable forbearance. In a negative way the law of the Mishnah says exactly that:

**MISHNAH-TRACTATE SUKKAH 2:9**

[If] it began to rain, at what point is it permitted to empty out [the Sukkah]? From the point at which the porridge will spoil. They made a parable: To what is the matter comparable? To a slave who came to mix a cup of wine for his master, and his master threw the flagon into his face.

No wonder, then, that in the enveloping lore of the Festival, Sukkot is supposed to mark the opportunity for the Messiah to present himself and raise the dead.

## The Household and the Altar (3): Mishnah-tractate Yoma

The Torah presents the offerings of the Day of Atonement as a narrative, mostly in Leviticus 16:1–34, concluding with a reference to the requirement of affliction of soul in atonement for sin. The law of Mishnah-tractate Yoma simply recapitulates that of the Torah. Of the eight chapters, the first seven provide a narrative, bearing interpolated materials, of the sacrificial rite of the Day of Atonement. The eighth does little more, taking up the rules of affliction of soul, that is, fasting. But at the end, the Mishnah's law links atonement to repentance, and that is the point at which the Temple rite of atonement finds its match in the domestic act of repentance. The pertinent verses of the Torah compare with the Mishnah's treatment of the subject in the following pattern:

| LEVITICUS | | MISHNAH-TRACTATE YOMA |
|---|---|---|
| 16:3 | He shall put on the holy linen coat. | |
| | | M. 3:6–7 |
| 16:6 | Aaron shall offer the bull as a sin offering for himself and shall make atonement for himself and for his house. | |
| | | M. 3:8 |
| 16:7 | Then he shall take the two goats and set them before the Lord . . . and Aaron shall cast lots upon the two goats, the lot for the Lord and the lot for Azazel. | |
| | | M. 3:9; 4:1 |
| 16:9 | Aaron shall present the goat on which the lot fell for the Lord and offer it as a sin offering, but the goat on which the lot fell for Azazel is sent away into the wilderness. | |
| 16:11 | Aaron shall present the bull as a sin offering for himself and for his house. | |
| | | M. 4:2–3 |
| 16:12 | He shall take a censer full of coals of fire from before the altar and two handfuls of sweet incense and shall bring it within the veil. | |
| | | M. 5:1–2 |
| 16:14 | He shall take some of the blood of the bull and sprinkle it with his finger on the front of the mercy seat. | |
| | | M. 5:3 |
| 16:15 | Then he shall kill the goat of the sin offering which is for the people. | |
| | | M. 5:4 |
| 16:18 | Then he shall go out to the altar which is before the Lord and make atonement for it and shall take some of the blood | |

of the bull and of the blood of the goat and put it on the horns
of the altar.

M. 5:5-6

16:20  And when he has made a end of atoning for the holy place
and the tent of meeting and the altar, he shall present
the live goat. And Aaron shall lay both his hands on the head
of the live goat and confess over him all the iniquities of the
people of Israel and all their transgressions and sins . . . and
send him away into the wilderness.

M. 6:2-6

16:23  Then Aaron shall come into the tent of meeting, bathe, and
put on his garments and come forth and offer his burnt offering
and the burnt offering of the people.

M. 6:7-8

16:24  The high priest changes into golden garments and offers the
ram and the ram of the people, so completing the offerings
of the day.

M. 7:3-4

16:31  You shall afflict yourselves.

M. 8:1-7

This final part of Leviticus 16 is pertinent to our problem:

It shall be a statute for you for ever that in the seventh month, on the tenth day
of the month, you shall afflict yourself and shall do no work, either the native or the
stranger who sojourns among you; for on this day shall atonement be made for you, to
cleanse you, from all your sins you shall be clean before the Lord. It is a Sabbath of
solemn rest to you, and you shall afflict yourselves; it is a statute for ever. (Lev.
16:31-34)

The comparison of the legal presentation of the Day of Atonement with
that of Leviticus 16 now becomes self-evident. For that purpose, we turn to the
Mishnah.

What the Mishnah adds are the rules on how the people, in addition to
the priests, observe the holy day—how the household matches God's house.
These provisions are in two parts: first, rules on not eating or drinking, ampli-
fying the Torah's prohibition; second, on repentance—the point at which we
move from the Temple to the Israelite household. I include the Tosefta's complement to the Mishnah, because it is exceptionally interesting here. In the
present context, there is no understanding of the Day of Atonement outside of
the framework of the Mishnah's exposition as amplified by the Tosefta; hence
the somewhat sizable abstract that follows. I indent the Tosefta gloss, to show
its relationship with the Mishnah.

### Mishnah-tractate Yoma 8:6-7,
### Tosefta-tractate Kippurim 4:5-17

M. 8:6 A sin offering and an unconditional guilt offering atone. Death and the
Day of Atonement atone when joined with repentance. Repentance atones for minor
transgressions of positive and negative commandments. And as to serious transgres-

sions, [repentance] suspends the punishment until the Day of Atonement comes along and atones.

T. 4:6 R. Ishmael says, "There are four kinds of atonement. [If] one has violated a positive commandment but repented, he hardly moves from his place before they forgive him, since it is said, 'Return, backsliding children. I will heal your backsliding' (Jer. 3:22).

T. 4:7 [Continuing the foregoing:] "[If] he has violated a negative commandment but repented, repentance suspends the punishment, and the Day of Atonement effects atonement, since it is said, 'For that day will effect atonement for you' (Lev. 16:30).

T. 4:8 [Continuing the foregoing:] "[If] he has violated [a rule for which the punishment is] extirpation or death at the hands of an earthly court, but repented, repentance and the Day of Atonement suspend [the punishment], and suffering on the other days of the year will wipe away [the sin], since it says, 'Then will I visit their transgression with a rod' (Ps. 89:32). But he through whom the Name of Heaven is profaned deliberately but who repented—repentance does not have power to suspend [the punishment], nor the Day of Atonement to atone, but repentance and the Day of Atonement atone for a third, suffering atones for a third, and death wipes away the sin, with suffering, and on such a matter it is said, 'Surely this iniquity shall not be purged from you until you die' (Isa. 22:14)."

M. 8:7 He who says, "I shall sin and repent, sin and repent"—they give him no chance to do repentance. "I will sin and the Day of Atonement will atone,"—the Day of Atonement does not atone. For transgressions done between man and the Omnipresent, the Day of Atonement atones. For transgressions between man and man, the Day of Atonement atones, only if the man will regain the good will of his friend. This exegesis did R. Eleazar b. Azariah state: "'From all your sins shall you be clean before the Lord' (Lev. 16:30)—for transgressions between man and the Omnipresent does the Day of Atonement atone. For transgressions between man and his fellow, the Day of Atonement atones, only if the man will regain the good will of his friend." Said R. Aqiba, "Happy are you, O Israel. Before whom are you made clean, and who makes you clean? It is your Father who is in heaven, as it says, 'And I will sprinkle clean water on you, and you will be clean' (Ezek. 36:25). And it says, 'O Lord, the hope [Miqweh = immersion pool] of Israel' (Jer. 17:13)—Just as the immersion pool cleans the unclean, so the Holy One, blessed be He, cleans Israel."

T. 4:9 The sin offering, guilt offering, and Day of Atonement all effect atonement only along with repentance, since it says, But on the tenth day of the seventh month [is a Day of Atonement] (Lev. 23:27). If [the sinner] repents, atonement is effected for him, and if not, it is not effected for him. R. Eleazar says, "'Forgiving [iniquity, transgression, and sin]' (Exod. 34:7)—He forgives iniquity to penitents, but he does not forgive iniquity to those who do not repent." R. Judah says, "Death and the Day of Atonement effect atonement along with repentance. Repentance effects atonement with death. And the day of death—lo, it is tantamount to an act of repentance."

T. 4:13 R. Yosé says, "[If] a man sins two or three times, they forgive him. [But on the] fourth, they do not forgive him, as it says, 'Forgiving iniquity, transgression, and sin, but he will by no means clear the guilty' (Exod. 34:7). Up to this point he clears [him]. From this point forward he will not clear [him], since it says, 'For three transgressions of Israel—but for four, I will not turn away the punishment' (Amos 2:6). And it says, '[He will deliver his soul from going into the pit. All these things does God do two or three times for a man' (Job 33:28-29). And it says, 'Withdraw your foot from your neighbor's house lest he be weary of you' (Prov. 25:16)."

We see that only when we reach the concluding statements of the law of the Mishnah do we move beyond the legal reprise of the Torah's narrative. And then we shift from the Temple to Israel wherever located.

So the jarring shift in the presentation of the law of the Mishnah tells us what is crucial, which is the prophetic reading of the cult: right, not only rite. The Mishnah's sages understood the prophets' critique not as a repudiation of the cult but as a refinement of it, and in the very context of their account of the blood rite they therefore invoke the prophets' norms alongside the Torah's. Jeremiah's call to repentance, Isaiah's reflections on the role of death in the penitential process, God's infinite mercy, Ezekiel's insistence on purity of spirit—these flow into the sages' exposition of the law of the Mishnah. Above all, the sages underscore God's explicit promise to purify Israel, the promise set forth in Ezekiel's and Jeremiah's prophecies.

So the law of the Mishnah recasts the Torah's presentation of the Day of Atonement. This it does by taking the theme of atonement to require an account of repentance, on the one side, and God's power to forgive and purify from sin, on the other. In short, the rites of atonement in God's house do not work *ex opere operato* but only conditionally. And it is the attitude and intention of the Israelites in their households that set that condition.

Two fundamental lessons are taught. First, the rites atone and so does death—but only when joined with repentance. Then repentance reaches its climax in the cleansing effect of the occasion, the Day of Atonement itself, as is stated in so many words: "A sin offering and an unconditional guilt offering atone. Death and the Day of Atonement atone when joined with repentance. . . ." But the entire system realizes its promise of reconciliation with God only on one condition: the Israelite to begin with must frame the right attitude. And that is an attitude of sincerity and integrity: One who says, "I shall sin and repent, sin and repent"—they give no chance to do repentance. "I will sin and the Day of Atonement will atone,"—the Day of Atonement does not atone.

How do they pertain? These statements change the subject. They relate not to the Day of Atonement nor even to the rites of penitence, but to the spirit in which the person acts when he or she commits a sin. And the message is clear: there is no such thing as preemptive atonement. One cannot contemplate the hypocrisy: atone, then sin. If in the commission of the sin he or she declares a conviction that attitude makes no difference—"I shall do what I want, and then repent in impunity"—that attitude nullifies the possibility of repentance and the Day of Atonement to do their part in the work of reconciliation.

The law of the Mishnah carries the matter still further, when it insists that, in the end, the attitude of the repentant sinner does not complete the transaction; the sinner depends also on the attitude of the sinned-against. I cannot think of a more eloquent way of saying that the entire condition of Israel depends on the inner integrity of Israel: the intentionality that motivates its actions, whether with God or among human beings.

The personal discipline of atonement through repentance on the Day of Atonement and a life of virtue and Torah learning on the rest of the days of the year—these form the foundations of the Israelite society, shaped by God's presence. Just as God can be found in the Holy of Holies, God can be found wherever Israel locates.

## Location, Occasion, the Character of the Encounter

For the sages the critical issue in the law of the Mishnah is the transformation of Israel by time and circumstance. What changes is the relationship: the reconciliation of Israel and God by rites of atonement for sin. It is what takes place in the Holy of Holies on the Day of Atonement. It also takes place within the household of all Israel at home. God's abode overspreads Israel. With what consequence?

Death is transcended when God is at home, where God is at home. The Torah said no less, the sages in the law of the Mishnah-tractates Pesahim, Sukkah, and Yoma say no more. Take Passover for example:

> I will smite all the firstborn in the land of Egypt, both man and beast; and on all the gods of Egypt I will execute judgments; I am the Lord. The blood shall be a sign for you, upon the houses where you are; and when I see the blood I will pass over you, and no plague shall fall upon you to destroy you, when I smite the land of Egypt.

The law of the Mishnah makes the statement that the freedom that Passover celebrates is Israel's freedom from death. Where Israel lives, there life is lived that transcends the grave. When, as is the custom, some people at the Passover Seder wear their burial garment, the gesture says no less than that. Passover places Israel's freedom into the context of the affirmation of life beyond sin.

Sukkot returns Israel to the fragility of abiding in the wilderness. Sukkot as the sages, in line with the Torah, portray the Festival is to be set only in the context of the penitential season. That begins with Elul, the lunar month prior to Tishré in which Sukkot falls, then reaches its climactic moment with the judgment and atonement of the New Year and Day of Atonement, and finally proceeds to its elegant conclusion in Sukkot. In the rhythm of the Torah's time, Sukkot forms a meditation in deeds upon the uncertain life still open to judgment even beyond the penitential season. Israel recapitulates the life of the wilderness, with Israel beyond the death of Egypt, before the eternal life of the Land of Israel. The Sukkah then represents taking up residence in the fragile present and not yet in the perfected life that will take place in the Land when Israel regains Eden.

"God craves the heart," the Talmud says, and there is no more exquisite legal restatement of that theologoumenon than Mishnah-tractate Yoma chapter 8. The Day of Atonement, which the Torah lays out as principally a Temple occasion, now overspreads the world. Leviticus 16 and the first seven chapters of Mishnah-tractate Yoma center the Day of Atonement on the Temple and its offerings. Israel participates as bystanders; but in chapter 8 of Mishnah-tractate Yoma, all Israelites are assigned atonement tasks of the weight and consequence of the rites the high priest uniquely carries out. On the Day of Atonement, holy Israel joins the high priest in the Holy of Holies; this they do by afflicting themselves through fasting and other forms of abstinence, as the Torah requires. What is singular and distinct—the rites of atonement on the holiest day of the year in the holiest place in the world—now makes its statement about what takes place on every day of the year in the ordinary life of holy Israel.

# Israel in God's Context

# 16 GOD AND THE INDIVIDUAL ISRAELITE

## *Tractate Hullin*

WHILE PERTAINING TO THE PRIVATE PERSON, the individual and the meat he or she eats, this enchanting tractate surely marks the high point of the entire legal system of the Mishnah. For Mishnah-tractate Hullin transforms the process of nourishing the individual Israelite into a statement of broad social, historical consequence about the enduring sanctification of Israel, down to the least Israelite individual—wherever living, whenever alive. The power of the Halakhah to make a theological statement comes to its climax here.

To understand why, we begin with the fundamental program of the Mishnah: to make concrete and orderly the encounter of Israel and God. God and corporate Israel, God and the Israelite family, God and the Israelite household—the law of the Mishnah affords concrete occasions for these encounters. But how far into the Israelite interior do these encounters extend? If God also meets the singular, the individual Israelite, we have yet to identify the grounds for them to intersect. Nor do we know where and when; under what circumstances and in what context the meeting regularly takes place. But we already have ample grounds for forming a theory. Since Israel and God meet in Jerusalem, at God's abode in the Temple, the household table, analogous to the table of the Lord in the Temple, presents itself as a likely meeting place. For the outcome of meeting God is life eternal, and it is where life is nurtured that Israel and God should come together. But at stake—so we may expect by now— is no abstraction, "life," but the concrete transactions of which life is composed: the household, the village, the family, corporate society, and what happens to them in history.

Indeed, Mishnah-tractate Hullin, the climax of the legal system of the Mishnah, addresses the preparation of meat for the domestic table. As I shall show, it encompasses what is private and what is public, what endures and what is transient, in a single coherent statement. In doing so, it draws together the routine and the historical, events at home and events on the stage of world history. The encounter of Israel and God takes place in God's context, in nature and in history, in two disparate settings—one private, the other cosmic. The one that takes place in nature comes about when an Israelite takes life to sustain life. The other, the historical, is scarcely congruent; it emerges in the grand, consequential happenings of history.

These two points of juncture, nature and history, private and public, prove risibly incongruous and disproportionate. How the law of the Mishnah regularizes the slaughter of animals for domestic, secular use—not for Temple offerings—and how it sorts out great public moments of time, on the surface scarcely relate, let alone correspond. But as we shall see, they follow a common pattern, matching a moment in nature to a moment in history. The law of the Mishnah treats them within the same program, calling upon the same pattern to define their uniform context, as we shall see in this chapter and the next. A cosmic construction accommodates them both, and once more it is comprised by Temple, Israel, Land.

## Taking Life to Sustain Israel's Life: Tractate Hullin

The individual Israelite is answerable to God for what he or she eats. That never is treated as a private, wholly secular act in the exercise of merely subjective taste. It is a deed governed by public law, an act that carries cosmic significance. The written Torah is clear that God is deeply concerned for what priests and other Israelites eat and how food is made ready for their domestic table. As we have seen, that concern pertains to how crops are raised and disposed of, and it also extends to how animals are killed for meat, doing so for the altar providing the model of doing so for the domestic table. Turning nature to man's nurture defines a dimension of Israel's sanctification. But knowing that the Torah sets forth rules governing what foods Israel may consume and how they are to be brought into being—for example, the rules of Mishnah-tractate Kilayim or Maʿaserot or Hallah—does not prepare us for the topic of Mishnah-tractate Hullin. I cannot overstress: here I find the climax and triumph of the Mishnah's endeavor: stating theology through law, transcendent truth in trivialities.

To gain perspective on the particularity of the matter at hand, we recall that public laws govern other aspects of food preparation. How crops are planted and harvested in the Land, the rhythm of the cultivation of the fields, the disposition of the produce of the Land—all are subject to rules that embody an entire theory of Israel's social order. The laws of tithing and separating priestly rations, exemplifying the whole, represent dietary rules as much as do those considered in Hullin. The dietary rules of Hullin are represented by the taboo against mixing milk and meat, the requirement about covering up the blood of a beast that is slaughtered for domestic consumption, and above all about the proper manner in which to slaughter an animal for the domestic table.

There is, however, an important distinction between the proper slaughter of animals for domestic, secular purposes and all those other concerns. In the preparation of domestic foods, meat is differentiated from vegetables and other produce. Hullin's interest in meat preparation concerns matters that contain no counterpart in the comparable processes of preparing the crops for the table.

We have already reviewed God's claim to a share of the crops of the Land and God's intense interest in how they are grown. A look back tells us, however, that, once God's interest in produce is accommodated, no further rules govern how the food is prepared or utilized. One may not grow grapes and wheat side by side. But one drinks wine and eats bread at the same meal. Produce that grows on its own in the Seventh Year may not be treated as a commercial commodity, but the Israelite at home may prepare grain grown in that year in any number of ways. How the food is produced matters, but what is done with it (within broad limits) does not—it simply does not matter to God. By contrast, apart from the prohibition of hybridization and the requirement of tithing flocks and herds, few regulations of a holy order pertain to producing meat. But when it comes to the individual's consuming meat, precisely how the living beast is killed and prepared engages God's concern.

So while God does not care what kind of a scythe is used for harvesting grain, God does take an interest in the condition of the knife that is used for slaughtering a cow. And God does not take account of whether grapes or wheat are ripe and fat or wizened, but God does care about the health of the beast that is slaughtered for meat, rejecting one that is dying as unfit for Israelite consumption.

I refer to the *terefah*-beast, one that could not have survived but is not killed by the act of slaughter, rather that will die of natural causes but is not yet dead. To explain: Since the main point of the act of slaughter is deliberately to take the life of the living beast, rather than allowing the animal to die of natural causes and only then to use its meat, a category between suitable and unsuitable has to take account of an interstitial case. A suitable act of slaughter kills the beast and attends to its blood. An unsuitable act of slaughter does not. But what about a beast that has not died on its own out of the fullness of life, but that also has not been slaughtered in the ordinary manner?

Such an interstitial case is taken up under the category *terefah*. That word, at Exodus 22:30, refers to a beast clawed by a wild animal: "You shall be men consecrated to me; therefore you shall not eat any flesh that is torn by beasts in the field; you shall cast it to the dogs." *Terefah* then pertains to carrion, a beast that dies without a proper act of slaughter. Exodus 22:30 then refers to a beast that has not yet died but that cannot survive. This yields the notion that beasts that bear some imperfection capable of causing death cannot be eaten by Israelites. Thus both beasts that die on their own, carrion, and those that are going to die by reason of wounds or imperfections, *terefah*-beasts, are prohibited. In these and other ways, meat preparation for the individual responds to God's presence among the people of Israel.

Blood is what is at issue. First, because harvesting meat, not vegetables, involves the shedding of blood. Second, because shedding blood at the altar engages God's intense concern, and shedding blood for the domestic table is analogous. The Torah repeatedly asserts that "the blood is the life." It is deliberate in making provision for the disposition of the blood produced in slaughtering an animal. If killed for God's meal, that is to say, in the Temple courtyard, the animal yields blood for the altar, to be sprinkled at the corners in an act of expiation. The beast further produces the sacrificial parts to be burned up in smoke on the altar fires and thence to ascend to God. The beast may also yield meat for the priests and their families to eat. If the animal is killed for the Israelite's meal, the animal yields blood to be covered with dust, which is to say, returned to the earth.

In transactions involving animals serving Heaven's and Israel's purposes, God and Israel therefore stand in alignment with one another. Here is an act, for the benefit of the individual Israelite, that is subjected to acute public scrutiny, by reason of the analogical context: the slaughter of beasts to produce meat for sale to the Israelite market. Here is the outcome of the imperative, "You shall be holy, for I the Lord your God am holy" (Lev. 19:2)—the concretization of holiness through the proper disposition of the blood, which is the life.

## The Domestic Table Compared with the Temple Altar

The problem for the sages is, then, how far may a metaphor be pushed before it loses its message? Must all the elements of the metaphor be physically present or can the metaphor continue to serve if one or more elements on one side of the equation exist only in memory? The equation—table and altar—tangibly serves only the situation in which the Temple stands, in which Israel itself is located in the Land of Israel, and in which both consecrated and unconsecrated beasts are subject to the rite. Then the analogy between table and altar begins in the palpable and undeniable facts of time, place, and circumstance.

But a sequence of questions comes in the wake of the exploitation of the analogy. The first is this: if the analogy depends on the facts of historical, social reality, does it continue to govern when those facts have changed? What is at issue concerns the age in which the Temple and its altar lie in ruins and vast segments of the community of Israel reside outside the boundaries of the Land of Israel. So too, since the Temple no longer stands, the very status of the consecration of a beast is subject to complications, and hence, the standing of beasts not consecrated for the altar requires attention. In that time and circumstance, no beasts are so consecrated and there is no locus for receiving them even if they were. The governing analogy of table and altar then proves asymmetrical to workaday reality.

One might be tempted to argue that the facts of history and society make no difference to the logic of the law of the Mishnah. But that contradicts the law's basic character. For, to begin with, the laws of the Mishnah flow from Scripture's narrative; they are conveyed by historical documents. These tell what happened to a particular people, corporate Israel, holy Israel, and the sages draw lessons for the design of the social order from these recapitulated events. The laws are portrayed in such a way that they do not take form in an ahistorical vacuum. They respond to a historical context. They are formed if not by circumstance then in response to what Israel has done or what God has done. That represents the affirmation of the scriptural narratives themselves, which persist in linking social imperatives to actualities in formulas like "You shall . . . for you were . . . ," "You shall keep the Sabbath, for you were slaves in Egypt . . . ," "For in six days the Lord made heaven and earth . . . therefore you shall . . . ," and the like. That propensity for systematically thinking about history—the irregularities of the here and now—produces the question faced when the law of the Mishnah addresses how, in the household, individual Israelites secure and prepare food.

Articulated and answered in Mishnah-tractate Hullin, the specific question is, What happens when the fires have gone out on the Temple altar, when Israel locates itself outside the Land of Israel, and when animals no longer are consecrated for divine service at all? Then the material foundation for the balance of the altar and the table, the analogy between slaughter for God and slaughter for everyday food, is lost. If we read Scripture's requirements in connection with taking the life of an animal for God's use and human use as a set of interdependent, categorical actions—Israel is nourished as God is nourished—then what law persists in this time is not self-evident.

### The Particular Laws of Mishnah-tractate Hullin

As usual with the Mishnah's laws, the legal specifics do not easily yield their theological generalizations. The subject of the tractate is the proper modes of killing and dividing the animals that are used for meat at home. The first four chapters of the tractate deal with that subject. Most of the rules for slaughtering an animal for God's table apply also to slaughtering one for the Israelite's. True, we cannot ignore the infinitely more elevated level of sanctification that applies to the holy space of the Temple and the holy caste of the priests than to the Israelite household and the caste of Israelites. But if we control for the fixed differences, we can account for the few consequential differences.

The story does not end with the legal narrative that requires beasts for ordinary Israel to be slaughtered and evaluated as though for use on the altar. Other food taboos pertinent to preparation of meat meals cover the next eight chapters, in each instance spelling out regulations set forth in the Torah. These cover the law against slaughtering the dam and its young on the same day (Lev. 22:28); the requirement to cover up the blood of the slaughtered beast (Lev. 17:13-14); the taboo against consuming the sciatic nerve (Gen. 32:32); and the taboo against cooking meat with milk (Exod. 23:19; 34:26; Deut. 12:21), food uncleanness, and then two chapters on what is owing to the priest from the meat of animals slaughtered at home, for secular purposes (Deut. 18:3); then the gift of first fleece to the priest (Deut. 18:4); and finally, the law of letting the dam go from the nest when one takes the eggs (Deut. 22:6-7).

What holds the whole together is the generative issue throughout, that is, predictably, how the domestic table is like the Temple altar. And that draws in its wake the complementary issue, how is it different? Since the table compares with the altar, how and where and why is it subject to a different rule from that pertaining to the altar? So the process is familiar: it is the work of comparison first, then contrast, that animates the Mishnah's intellectual program.

The analogical-contrastive analysis begins at the head of the tractate by stating the difference between an act of slaughter performed solely by a priest for the Lord's altar and one that is performed by an ordinary person. The requirements for the two settings exhibit striking differences, as is to be expected. In the Temple, priests ordinarily slaughter the beast and are the only ones who can sprinkle the blood on the altar. In the household any Israelite performs the act of slaughter and, as to the blood, anyone may cover up the blood as well. Temple rites take place in daylight, the counterpart act of slaughter in the household may be done at night. And so on. The main point is that, for the table, unlike the altar, any Israelite (here including a Samaritan or an apostate) may perform the act of slaughter and it may be carried out at any time, day or night. This is how it is stated in the law of the Mishnah:

### MISHNAH-TRACTATE HULLIN 1:1

(1) All slaughter, (2) and their act of slaughter is valid, except for a deaf-mute, an imbecile, and a minor lest they impair [the fitness of the carcass] through their act of slaughter). But all of them who performed an act of slaughter, with others watching them—their act of slaughter is valid. The act of slaughter of a gentile [produces] carrion. And it [the meat] imparts uncleanness through being carried. He who slaughters at night—and so too a blind person who slaughtered—his act of slaughter is valid. He who slaughters on the Sabbath or on the Day of Atonement, even though he [thereby] becomes liable for his life—his act of slaughter is valid.

Then how are the two settings comparable? The actual act is the same: a knife is applied to the throat and drawn across the two organs of the throat, windpipe and gullet. But that mode of slaughter applies only to beasts, not to fowl, in the Temple, while in the household or village, it serves for both.

**MISHNAH-TRACTATE HULLIN 2:1**

He who slaughters [cuts] one [organ, either the windpipe or the gullet] in the case of fowl, or two [both the windpipe and the gullet] in the case of a beast—his act of slaughter is valid. And the greater part of one [of the organs] is equivalent to [the whole of] it. [He who cuts through] half of one [organ] in the case of fowl and one and a half [organs] in the case of a beast—his act of slaughter is invalid. [He who cuts through] the greater part of one [organ] in the case of fowl or the greater part of two [organs] in the case of a beast—his act of slaughter is valid.

Beasts are slaughtered in exactly the same way for the altar and for the household. The rule joining household to altar goes a step further. The act of slaughter for domestic use must be intentional and carried out intentionally by an individual, just as in the case of the altar: "If the knife fell and effected the act of slaughter, even if it effected the act of slaughter properly, it is invalid. As it is said, 'And you will slaughter . . . and you will eat . . .' (Deut. 12:21)"—just as *you* effect the act of slaughter, so do *you* eat.

That exegesis carries us back to the metaphor that compares the domestic table with God's altar in the Temple. The introduction of the issue of correct intentionality underscores that the altar and the table form a single genus, the operative traits being dictated by the altar. Just as in the Temple offerings may be presented on behalf of gentiles, so an Israelite may slaughter a gentile's beast on behalf of the gentile. But if the intent is improper, the act is null, just as it would be if the officiating priest declared an improper intentionality in connection with a critical component of the rite, for instance by tossing the blood with the wrong purpose in mind. So the law states:

**MISHNAH-TRACTATE HULLIN 2:7**

He who slaughters [a gentile's beast] on behalf of a gentile—his act of slaughter is valid.

The Mishnah's law does not address the issue of the gentile's intentionality, only the naked facts of the transaction: one may slaughter a gentile's beast on his behalf. But what about the intention involved? If the person who slaughters the beast at the moment of doing so forms and expresses the intention that the beast serve for Zeus, the act is an act of idolatry and the meat is forbidden for Israelite—not only cultic—use or benefit:

**MISHNAH-TRACTATE HULLIN 2:8**

He who slaughters (1) for the sake of mountains, (2) for the sake of valleys, (3) for the sake of seas, (4) for the sake of rivers, (5) for the sake of deserts—his act of slaughter is invalid. [If] two take hold of a knife and perform an act of slaughter, one for the sake of any of the forenamed, and one for the sake of a valid purpose, their act of slaughter is invalid.

The critical point is that improper intentionality invalidates the act of slaughter for the altar and for the table alike. It produces meat of an idolatrous character. But that does not extend to a post facto disposition of the blood with an improper attitude. Further, slaughtering an unconsecrated beast outside of the Temple with the intent of offering up a sacrifice produces carrion.

So a clear distinction differentiates slaughtering in the household and for its purposes from slaughtering in the Temple for its appropriate considerations.

But what links the two venues proves equally striking: what renders an animal unfit for the altar invalidates it for the table as well. Conversely, what the altar will not accept the household table cannot receive either. Simply put, when Israel eats meat, it eats the meat of the same classification and character as the meat that God consumes at the altar. Accordingly, beasts (but not fowl) are slaughtered for the altar and the domestic table in accord with one and the same protocol, and the critical consideration that pertains to the altar—the attitude of the officiating priest—pertains to the table. What counts is the attitude of the person who carries out or supervises the act of slaughter (as the case requires).

But there is yet another striking difference between the household and the Temple. The law of the Mishnah encompasses the Israelite household both in the Holy Land and abroad, and systematically states that prohibitions set forth in the Torah concerning preparation of meat and poultry apply in both settings, and pertain whether or not the Temple is standing, as well as to both unconsecrated and consecrated beasts. The recurrent formula, "(1) in the Land and outside the Land, (2) in the time of the Temple and not in the time of the Temple, (3) in the case of unconsecrated beasts and in the case of consecrated beasts," insists that these rules transcend boundaries of space, time, and circumstance.

That carries us to the centerpiece of Mishnah-tractate Hullin. It is the explicit statement that meat for Israelites is subject to sanctification even when the governing analogy no longer pertains: outside of the Land, when the Temple is in ruins, and for beasts that to begin with have not been sanctified for the altar. Then the eternity of Israel transcends the ephemerality of the Temple; Israel's table remains sanctified and therefore subject to the rules of cultic slaughter, even after God's table has been desecrated.

First, what justifies the distinction between ephemeral and enduring within the legal system of the Mishnah? The principle is well established, that, as between the enduring and the ephemeral, the enduring takes precedence, thus:

#### MISHNAH-TRACTATE MENAHOT 10:1-4

Whatever is [offered] more often than its fellow takes precedence over its fellow:
(1) Daily whole offerings take precedence over additional offerings.

And whatever is more holy than its fellow takes precedence over its fellow:
(1) The blood of the sin offering takes precedence over the blood of the burnt offering, because it makes atonement [for a sin] . . .

Where is the theology in all this? It lies right at the surface. By that same principle of hierarchical classification, then, the Israelite's table takes precedence over "the Lord's table," and Israel is holier than the Temple. That is because *Israel is God's abode even when there is no Temple.* The Mishnah makes that statement in so many words when it says that the laws that apply to the altar and the table apply to the table even when the altar is destroyed. We shall rapidly survey the principal statements of that view, together with the details of the law governing slaughter for secular purposes that the law of the Mishnah encompasses.

Only when we encounter the laws in the language in which the Mishnah portrays those laws does the full power of the system come to expression. That is in its nearly liturgical repetition of the same sacred formula, replicated in topic after topic. Then, working our way through the details, we are shown the regularities and order that yield theological truth. That is why I cite the entire set of topics as the opening statement of each formulates them. Then alone the power of patterned language and thought takes effect. I state very simply that I find this tractate, at these passages, the single most affecting theological writing in the formative canon of Judaism.

#### MISHNAH-TRACTATE HULLIN 5:1

[The prohibition against slaughtering on the same day] "it and its young" (Lev. 22:28) applies (1) in the Land and outside the Land, (2) in the time of the Temple and not in the time of the Temple, (3) in the case of unconsecrated beasts and in the case of consecrated beasts. How so? He who slaughters it and its offspring, (1) which are unconsecrated, (2) outside [the Temple courtyard]—both of them are valid. And [for slaughtering] the second he incurs forty stripes. [He who slaughters] (1) Holy Things (2) outside—[for] the first is he liable to extirpation, and both of them are invalid, and [for] both of them he incurs forty stripes. [He who slaughters] (1) unconsecrated beasts (2) inside [the Temple courtyard]—both of them are invalid, and [for] the second he incurs forty stripes. [He who slaughters] (1) Holy Things (2) inside—the first is valid, and he is exempt [from any punishment], and [for] the second he incurs forty stripes, and it is invalid.

The pattern is established by speaking specifically of the holiness of the Land, the time of the Temple, and consecrated beasts, and insisting that the Israelite table at home takes priority in the level of sanctification over the Land, Temple times, and beasts sanctified for the altar.

#### MISHNAH-TRACTATE HULLIN 6:1

[The requirement to] cover up the blood (Lev. 17:13-14) applies in the Land and abroad, (2) in the time of the Temple and not in the time of the Temple, (3) in the case of unconsecrated beasts, but not in the case of Holy Things. And it applies (4) to a wild beast and a bird, (5) to that which is captive and to that which is not captive. And it applies (6) to a *koy*, because it is a matter of doubt [whether it is wild or domesticated]. And they do not slaughter it [a *koy*] on the festival. But if one has slaughtered it, they do not cover up its blood.

Now the issue is covering up the blood, and the outcome is the same. The other items are self-evident.

#### MISHNAH-TRACTATE HULLIN 7:1; 8:1; 10:1-2; 11:1; 12:1

7:1 [The prohibition of] the sinew of the hip [sciatic nerve, Gen. 32:32] applies (1) in the Land [of Israel] and outside of the Land, (2) in the time of the Temple and not in the time of the Temple, (3) to unconsecrated animals and to Holy Things. It applies (1) to domesticated cattle and to wild beasts, (2) to the right hip and to the left hip. But it does not apply (3) to a bird, because it has no hollow [of the thigh or spoon-shaped hip] and its fat is permitted. Butchers are believed (1) concerning it and (2) concerning the [forbidden] fat (Lev. 3:17; 7:23).

8:1 [As to the separation of milk and meat (Exod. 23:19; 34:26; Deut. 12:21)]: Every [kind of] flesh [i.e., meat, of cattle, wild beast, and fowl] it is prohibited to cook in milk, except for the flesh of fish and locusts. And it is prohibited to serve it up onto the table with cheese, except for the flesh of fish and locusts. He who vows [to abstain] from flesh is permitted [to make use of] the flesh of fish and locusts.

10:1 [The requirement to give to the priests] the shoulder, the two cheeks, and the maw (Deut. 18:3) applies (1) in the Land and outside of the Land, (2) in the time of the Temple and not in the time of the Temple, (3) to unconsecrated beasts, but not to consecrated beasts. For it [the contrary] might have appeared logical: Now, if uncon-secrated animals, which are not liable for the breast and thigh [which are taken from peace offerings for the priests (Lev. 7:31)], are liable for the [priestly] gifts [of the shoulder, cheeks, and maw], Holy Things, which *are* liable for the breast and thigh, logically should be liable to the priestly gifts. Scripture therefore states, "And I have given them to Aaron the priest and to his sons as a due for ever" (Lev. 7:34)—he has a right [in consecrated beasts] only to that which is explicitly stated [namely, the breast and thigh].

11:1–2 [The laws concerning the obligation to donate to the priest] the first shear-ings [of wool from the sheep of one's flock (Deut. 18:4)] apply both inside the Land of Israel and outside the Land of Israel, in the time the Temple [in Jerusalem stands] and in the time the Temple does not [stand]. [And the laws apply] to [the fleece of] uncon-secrated [animals] but not to [the fleece of animals that were] consecrated [to the Tem-ple]. A stricter rule applies to [the obligation to give to the priest] the shoulder, the two cheeks and the maw [of one's animals] than to [the obligation to give to the priest] the first shearings [of wool from the sheep of one's flock]. For [the obligation to give to the priest] the shoulder, the two cheeks and the maw [of one's animals] applies both to the [large] animals of one's herd and to the [small] animals of one's flock.

12:1 [The requirement to] let [the dam] go from the nest [Deut. 22:6–7] applies (1) in the Land and outside of the Land, (2) in the time of the Temple and not in the time of the Temple, (3) to unconsecrated [birds] but not to consecrated ones. A more strict rule applies to covering up the blood than to letting [the dam] go from the nest: For the requirement of covering up the blood applies (1) to a wild beast and to fowl, (2) to that which is captive and to that which is not captive. But letting [the dam] go from the nest applies only (1) to fowl and applies only (2) to that which is not captive. What is that which is not captive? For example, geese and fowl which make their nest in an orchard. But if they make their nest in the house (and so Herodian doves), one is free of the requirement of letting the dam go.

With all this evidence before us, the law of the Mishnah is fully exposed: the analogy to the altar governs—but only within explicit limits. Preparation of meat whether for the Temple altar or for the home table is subject to the same rules, which is why those rules extend the sanctity of the altar to the home. Since the law of the Mishnah treats the altar and the table as forming a single entity as far as sanctification is concerned, differentiated only in that the one is holier than the other, its task is to compare, then contrast, the two realms of the holy when it comes to meat preparation. That logical requirement—showing where and how two entities that are alike differ—accounts for the problematics of the law. Thus, for example, Hullin (M. 5:2) sets up a grid: (1) unconsecrated versus consecrated beasts, (2) inside and outside the Temple courtyard —the grid yields a variety of results as the possible cases are systematically considered. Then another distinction is introduced (M. 6:1): Blood of a consecrated beast is to be tossed on the altar; that of a secular one is to be buried. But that distinction only underscores the main point, which is to compare and contrast the two realms of sanctification in connection with the consumption of meat.

The topical program of the law of the Mishnah is in two parts: first, what pertains to preparation of meat, covering up the blood, the prohibition of the sciatic nerve, separation of meat from dairy products ("cooking meat in milk"), and the cultic uncleanness of food; and, second, what involves gifts of meat or animal by-products to the priests. Letting the dam go from the nest when taking the young is placed at the end, because it has no bearing on the altar at all ("to unconsecrated birds but not to consecrated ones"). That the concern for general uncleanness should enter the picture presents no surprise; the law of the Mishnah takes for granted that Israelites will eat their meat not only in accord with the requirements of the Torah, such as are specified, but also in accord with the rules of cultic cleanness that govern, to begin with, in the Temple itself.

What about cultic cleanness in the household? The law of the Mishnah does not state that meat consumed at home is to be eaten in the state of cultic cleanness as it is in the Temple (whether by the altar, whether by the priests). But, as a matter of fact, the exposition in chapter 9 rests on that premise. It begins:

#### MISHNAH-TRACTATE HULLIN 9:1

The (1) hide, and (2) grease, and (3) sediment, and (4) flayed-off meat, and (5) bones, and (6) sinews, and (7) horns and (8) hooves join together [with the meat to which they are attached to form the requisite volume] to impart food uncleanness, but [they do] not [join together to impart] uncleanness of carrion. Similarly: He who slaughters unclean cattle for a gentile—while it yet is writhing, it imparts food uncleanness, but [it does] not [impart] uncleanness of carrion—(1) until it dies, or (2) until one cuts off its head. [Scripture thus] has [prescribed] more [conditions] to impart food uncleanness than uncleanness of carrion.

These principles form the foundations of the rules. The law of the Mishnah compares and contrasts two categories of uncleanness that affect meat: food uncleanness and carrion. Food contracts uncleanness from various specified sources, including a corpse or a dead creeping thing. Meat untouched by a corpse or dead creeping thing falls into one category; meat classified as unclean as carrion into another. The consequences of the one kind of uncleanness differ from those of the other. The law of the Mishnah is generated by the labor of hierarchical classification—that is characteristic of the Mishnah. It exhibits a systematic concern for asking how different species of the same genus (two different sources of uncleanness affecting meat) join together or function together to produce the same result—if they do.

As usual, we find particulars at the core of the Mishnah's discussion. A minimum volume of food is required for contracting uncleanness—a negligible volume is deemed null and outside of the system altogether. Therefore, in estimating whether that requisite volume of food has been formed, do we differentiate food that has become unclean by reason of a corpse from food that has become unclean by reason of being declared carrion? It is the volume of food that is in question.

Another way of asking the same question is, Do we regard the semi-attached or distinct components of the carcass to form part of the carcass for purposes of assessing whether or not the requisite volume for receiving uncleanness has been reached? Thus, the issue is framed in terms of "connection," meaning, treating as a single entity distinct parts of the beast, that is, the hide (which separates from the flesh), the grease or sediment or bones or sinews or horns or hooves. If we do treat these as part of the beast, they contribute to the formation of the requisite volume to contract uncleanness. Otherwise, they do not.

The governing distinction is stated at the outset, namely, the specified, distinct components of the carcass do join together, when attached, to form the requisite volume to impart food uncleanness; for that purpose they are deemed integral to the carcass. But they do not join together to impart uncleanness by reason of carrion, meaning, in a beast that has died of natural causes, the specified components of the carcass are not assigned an integral part in the carcass. Clearly, the entire discussion presupposes a domestic venue and not a setting in the Temple, where, for example, no one is going to slaughter unclean cattle for a gentile. And what follows is that the law of the Mishnah everywhere takes for granted that considerations of uncleanness, not only those of suitability (proper slaughter and the like) pertain. So the law of the Mishnah makes sense only if its fundamental premise—comparing the altar to the table—extends even to imposing cleanness taboos of the former upon the latter.

## Gradations of Sanctification

Herein there are gradations of sanctification. The sanctity that encompasses Israelites one by one is distinct from the sanctity that permeates the Land of Israel. And the sanctity of the Land of Israel itself is distinct from the sanctity that is embodied in the Temple and on upward to its altar—and beyond. For the law of the Mishnah, the hierarchy is expressed in three realms or levels of sanctification: (1) the Land, (2) the Temple, and (3) Israel, each with its own place on the ladder of holiness that rises from earth to heaven.

The law of the Mishnah here states in so many words what it wants to know. That is whether (1) the destruction of the Temple and cessation of the offerings, (2) the degradation of the Land of Israel—its loss of its Israelite residents—and (3) the exile of the holy people, Israel, from the Holy Land, affect the rules of sustenance in the model of the nourishment of God, The question pertains to three venues: (1) in the Temple, (2) in the Land, (3) among the holy people.

The answer is, whatever the condition of the Temple and its altar, whatever the source—the Holy Land or unclean gentile lands—of animals, and whatever the location of the people Israel—whether in the Holy Land or not—one thing persists. And that is the sanctification of Israel, the people.

That status of holiness imputed to the social entity (Israel) and to each individual (Israelite) therein endures (1) in the absence of the cult, (2) in alien, unclean territory, and (3) whatever the source of the food that Israel eats. Israel's sanctity is eternal, unconditional, absolute. The sanctification that inheres in Israel, the people, transcends the Land and outlives the Temple and its cult.

Since the sanctity of Israel the people persists beyond the Temple and outside of the Land, that sanctity stands at a higher point in the hierarchy of domains of the holy that ascend from earth to heaven and from humanity to God. The result of our inquiry concerning corporate Israel and the individual Israelite and their relationship, now comes into play. The social given is corporate Israel. That fact is now recapitulated in the issues before us: the status of Israel—in the Land or abroad, possessed of the Temple or excluded therefrom—in preparing meat, whether for God or for Israel itself. These issues address the condition of corporate Israel. But they play themselves out on the domestic table of the individual Israelite man, woman, and child, whether formed into families or not, whether constituting households or not.

How are we asked to hear that remarkable statement of the eternal sanctity of Israel, corporate and individual? The law of the Mishnah, to make its statement about the eternal sanctification of the people Israel explicitly responds to three facts: (1) Israelites live not only in the Holy Land but abroad, in unclean lands; (2) the Temple has been destroyed and not yet rebuilt; and consequently (3) animals are slaughtered not only in the Temple in the Land but in unconsecrated space and abroad, and the meat is eaten not only in a cultic but in a profane circumstance.

Holy, corporate Israel's sanctification endures beyond the Land, the Temple, and the age in which the active source of sanctification, the altar, functions. It continues when the others do not, and in line with the principles of Mishnah Menahot 10:1ff., cited earlier, we know what that means. How then do we hierarchize Temple, Land, and corporate Israel? The desuetude of the one, the abandonment of the other—neither ultimately affects the standing of the Israel. The Land and the Temple have lost that sanctity that infused them when Israel dwelt on the Land and the Temple altar was nourished by Israel's priesthood and produce. But the sanctification of Israel itself endures through history, eternal and untouched by time and change. When Israel returns to the

Land and rebuilds the Temple, the sanctification of the Land and the Temple will once more be realized.

That returns to the agendum the question of history. Anyone who wonders whether the law of the Mishnah that applied to the Temple and the home when the Temple was standing and Israel was in the Land of Israel continues to apply with the Temple in ruins and Israel in exile here finds the answer. Every meal at which the Israelite eats meat embodies that answer in a most active form: the menu itself. Although the sanctity of the Temple stands in abeyance, the sanctity of the Israelite table persists. Although Israel is in exile from the Holy Land, Israel remains holy. Although in the Temple rules of uncleanness are not now kept, they continue in force wherever Israelites may be. Birds and animals that flourish outside of the Land, when prepared for the Israelite table, are regulated by the same rules that apply in the Land and even (where relevant) at the altar. So Israel the people not only retains sanctity but preserves it outside of the Land, and the sanctity of Israel transcends that of the Temple and its altar. Corporate Israel is endowed with a higher degree of sanctity than the Temple and the Land—and, in the hierarchy of the sacred, stands at the apex, closest to God.

The law of the Mishnah does not treat as an all-or-nothing proposition either sanctification or cultic cleanness. That is the advantage of seeing all things as matters of degree, location within a continuum. In the present case, the law of the Mishnah works out in detail the general theory of the gradations of sanctification matched by those of uncleanness. We can understand the law of Mishnah-tractate Hullin only within the nurturing context of the general theory of sanctification, spatial (locative), temporal, and circumstantial, involving answers to the questions of where, when, and whom. The outcome is that when it comes to the preparation of meat, the law of the Mishnah deals with three locative settings: (1) the Temple, (2) the Land of Israel, and (3) foreign land. These correspond to two temporal periods: (1) when the Temple stood and (2) now, when the Temple lies in ruins.

For all three settings and for both periods, the Mishnah insists, the same rules pertain, even despite the considerable differences that apply. Since all territory outside of the Land of Israel is by definition unclean, the premise of the law is that, in spite of that fact, Israel is to consume its secular meat in accord with those rules of sanctification that pertain to food and its preparation. The laws of cultic cleanness may apply to the household in the Land of Israel but cannot pertain abroad; nonetheless, the other principal admonitions apply everywhere. The metaphor is persistent: the existence of the Temple or its destruction makes no difference.

### Why Hullin in Particular?

Why is it particularly the law of Mishnah-tractate Hullin that makes the statement that Israel—the person, the people—is holier than the Land and even than the Temple, even to endowing with sanctity the animals slaughtered to nourish the people? That theological proposition comes to the fore in particular here because the written Torah supplies the law that contains the entire message. It does so when it imposes the same requirements that pertain to slaughter of an animal sacrifice for the altar in Jerusalem and to killing an animal for the use of Israel at home, specifically, burying the blood or draining it. That means that the meat Israel eats is subject to the same regulations that apply to the meat that God receives on the altar fires. That very law states that meat for those who are not holy, that is, for gentiles or idolaters, is not subject to the same rules (Exod. 22:30; Deut. 14:21). So it is unmistakable: food for God and for Israel must be prepared in comparable manner, which rule does not apply to food for gentiles.

History enters in when we ask how that principle affects animals raised abroad. The laws of Hullin apply to them, because the laws apply to unconsecrated animals as much as to consecrated ones. The purpose in nature—nourishing Israel—is alone what counts. The beast intended for Israelite consumption at the table even in a foreign country must be prepared as though for God on the altar in Jerusalem, and that can only mean, since the beast is intended (by the act of correct slaughter) for Israel, the use of the beast by Israel sanctifies the beast and necessitates conformity with the rules of slaughter for God in the Temple. Israel, even abroad, renders the food that it eats comparable to food for the altar.

Then comes the matter of the Temple and its condition. We ask, What has food preparation to do with the consideration of location? The rule that permits slaughter of meat outside of the Temple (Deut. 12:20-24) explicitly states that it speaks of corporate Israel outside of the Temple in Jerusalem. So, even if the act of slaughter does not take place in Jerusalem, the act must conform, because the focus is on Israel, wherever Israel is located—even far from Jerusalem (for so the law is formulated in Scripture). The law of the Mishnah before us simply carries the same conception forward in a logical way: the same considerations govern even so far from Jerusalem as territory that to begin with is laden with corpse uncleanness, that is, foreign soil; and even in an age in which Jerusalem is no more; and, it goes without saying, even in connection with a beast that has not been consecrated for the altar.

Since Scripture itself has separated the act of slaughter from the rite of sacrifice in the Temple, the law of the Mishnah has done little more than explore the consequences of that rule when it states that the requirements of slaughter in the cult pertain also outside of the cult—thus, wherever Israelites are located, and whenever the act takes place, even outside of the Land altogether, even during the time that the Temple is no longer standing. If an Israel outside of Jerusalem is contained within the logic set forth by the Torah at Deuteronomy 12:20-24, then the next step, and it is not a giant step, is to contemplate an Israel outside of the Land altogether, not to say a Temple in ruins.

The integral connection of slaughter of animals and sacrifice at the altar having been broken when all cultic activity was focused by Deuteronomy within Jerusalem, all that the law of the Mishnah has done is to address in so many words the extreme consequences of that situation. If the rules apply even to unconsecrated beasts, and even to the Land beyond Jerusalem, and even outside of the Temple, then by the same token, logic dictates a utopian consequence. The same laws apply even when no animals are being consecrated at all, and they apply even when the Temple no longer stands, and they pertain even abroad.

So the Torah sets the stage by addressing the situation of slaughter not in behalf of the transaction at the altar and not in the setting of the holy place. Consequently, the law of the Mishnah worked out in the critical details of the sustenance of life the conviction that Israel the people forms the locus of sanctification. What follows is that this allegation about the enduring, ubiquitous sanctification inherent in Israel the people—even outside of the Land, even in the time of the Temple's destruction—pervades the exposition of the laws in detail. It is an amazing statement in its insistence on the priority and permanence of the sanctity of Israel—whatever may become of the holiness of the altar and of the Land.

## Location, Occasion, the Character of the Encounter, in God's Context, of God and the Israelite

Affirming the unique holiness of the Temple and the Land of Israel, Mishnah-tractate Hullin still wants to show how the holiness of the people Israel retains its own integrity. Israel's enduring sanctification transcends location and occasion because it is realized at the moment at which life-blood is spilled in the preservation of life. Thus, the law of the Mishnah establishes in practical ways that Israel remains holy even outside of the Land, even in the age without the Temple. Meat prepared for Israel, wherever the meat has itself been nourished, even on gentile ground, must be prepared as though for the altar in Jerusalem. Then Israel's sanctity persists, even when that continuum in which it stood, the chain of continuity with the Temple altar in Jerusalem (as the formulation of Deuteronomy 12:20-24 framed matters), has been disrupted. Israel's sanctity endows with sanctity even animals raised in unclean ground, so powerful is the sanctification that transforms Israel. The liturgy, stating in its way what the law of the Mishnah sets forth in its manner, explains this in the Afternoon Worship for the Sabbath, speaking to God: "You are unique and your name is unique, and who is like your people, Israel, a unique people on earth?" That society where God is present then, in social terms, must sustain that condition of sanctification imposed by the standing of uniqueness. Israel is *sui generis,* so the prayer says, a mark of sanctification.

Precisely what social response God's presence invokes remains to be specified. It is expressed in two parts. First, when Israelites recite prayers and blessings, God is present to hear them. An entire tractate, Mishnah-tractate Bera-khot, which we have not surveyed, defines the effects of God's presence in hearing and answering prayers. At the table, the public occasion at which the laws of Hullin apply, that is certainly the case, as Berakhot shows with its rules for blessings recited before eating food, and the Grace recited afterward. So the location is clear: wherever Israelites eat, individually or corporately. But, second, God is present not only at the table of the Israelite but wherever animals are killed to provide meat for the Israelite's table. And that is a presence not in response to what is said but what is done: God responds when blood is shed.

Then God's presence is not only locative but temporal and occasional. God is present when the slaughterer takes up the knife and cuts the vital organs of the throat. That occasion is defined by an Israelite, not a priest alone, not a male alone, not an adult alone:

##### MISHNAH-TRACTATE HULLIN 1:1

All slaughter except for a deaf-mute, an imbecile, and a minor lest they impair the fitness of the carcass through their act of slaughter. All are valid to carry out an act of slaughter even a Samaritan, even an uncircumcised man, and even an Israelite apostate.

In light of that startling fact, much becomes clear. The act of any Israelite capable of deliberate action in slaughtering an animal for meat suffices to win God's attention. The character of the encounter is defined by the action, not by the person, and the transaction resembling the blood rite is possible solely by reason of the status of all individual Israelites: God responds to every one of them engaged in an action of the specified sort. The encounter of God and the individual Israelite, not defined by caste status, gender, or age, then comes about because, at this particular action, the Israelite matters by reason of what he or she validly does, which is take a life for Israelite benefit, as the priest at the altar takes a life for God's.

So we must ask, Is the act of slaughter for the domestic table comparable to the act of slaughter for the altar? As we have seen, formally that is explicitly the case. But, categorically, we cannot maintain that food preparation for the altar always is comparable to food preparation for the domestic table. Grain, oil, and wine, not only meat, comprise God's meals. As a matter of fact, other topics concerning dietary laws, for example, removing from grain and produce, including olives and grapes, the share that belongs to God and is assigned to God's protected castes—including the priests and the poor—are treated in their own terms and are not comparable, as we noted at the outset. That fact comes to expression in the categorical organization of the law of the Mishnah, which deals with meat preparation in the context of Holy Things, otherwise devoted to God's table; and produce preparation in the setting of agricultural law, generally devoted to the agricultural rules for farming the Land.

What we see is that through one aspect of dietary laws, the law of the Mishnah makes a statement of one sort, through another aspect, a statement of another sort. In the division pertaining to Agriculture, the dietary rules recapitulate the overarching statement that division of the law makes about the standing and sanctity of the Land, and in the division pertaining to Holy Things, the rules pertinent to the Israelite's food recapitulate a statement that can be made only in the context of Holy Things and nowhere else. The division of Agriculture speaks of the interplay of the realms of sanctification of the Land and of the people, Israel, in relationship to God as coproprietor of the Land with Israel. There we find the sharing of the gifts of the Land with its proprietors, God and Israel. The division of Holy Things in the present part of the law speaks of the interplay of the realms of sanctification of the altar of God and the table of Israel. Here we find the issue of location made specific in the matter of enlandisement—precisely the opposite issue from the one that animates the division of Agriculture.

Both deal with the generic category sanctification, but do so distinctively: it is sanctification that is enlandised or locative (Agriculture) versus utopian (Holy Things). But what joins the two statements together should not be missed, since both concern the same generative principle, the inherent sanctification of Israel and the consequent requirement that Israel sustain itself in accord with the rules of sanctification of food that is offered to God. In brief, Israel is holy and God is holy and where pertinent, the same rules dictate the appropriate source and correct preparation of food for both. But the conception—Israel's sanctification in a continuum with God's holiness and with the Land's holiness—provokes reflection on one set of issues here and another set in connection with the division of Agriculture.

For the law of Mishnah-tractate Hullin the sanctification of Israel, corporate and personal, pertains, as it states time and again, in the Land and outside, in the time of the Temple and afterward, in connection with consecrated and secular beasts. And so, at an infinitely higher point in the hierarchy, does God's—wherever, whenever God is present—even in history, especially in history, to which we now turn.

# 17    ISRAEL IN HISTORY AND IN ETERNITY: THE MESSIAH

## Tractates Rosh Hashanah, Ta'anit, Zebahim, and Sotah

## From Analysis to Synthesis

To this point we have conformed to the Halakhic discipline of the Mishnah by asking its topical expositions or tractates to answer our theological questions. In quest of the implicit social theology, specifically, the realization of Israel's sanctification in the details of ordinary life, we focused on the systematic exposition of the Halakhah. We found guidance in the foci and tensions of topical analysis. That approach is essential, because of the character of the Mishnah, which speaks in particular details about large, general, and abstract issues. We have found in the topical expositions fundamental theological principles. The analysis of topics as set forth in the several tractates yielded a systematic account of how the Mishnah designed a social order to make God's word work. After these chapters, chapter 2 through 16, as we approach the central issue of the interrelation of God, the Land, and Israel, and the nature of salvation in history itself, we find a mismatch between our theological questions and the Mishnah's systematic Halakhic answers.

The reason is a disjuncture between the Mishnah's system and the critical center of our theological program. The Mishnah's statement of the Halakhah is timeless and transcends change. But we want to situate the Mishnah in time. The Halakhah regularizes the occasional and systematizes the episodic. But we ask about how the system as a whole responds to historical turning points, the destruction of the Temple, the cessation of the service of God through blood rites, and the loss of control over large parts of the Land of Israel.

In more general terms: the Mishnah systematically speaks of sanctification, tractate after tractate exploring the issues implicit in that protean conception: "You shall be holy, for I the Lord your God am holy." But only episodically, and neither Halakhically nor analytically does it address the issues of salvation. No tractate sets forth the Halakhah governing a Messiah and his activities, or, more generally, regularizes history, the end of days, the coming of a Messiah, the resurrection of the dead, and the advent and character of the world to come. These do not form categories for Halakhic presentation, and they do not present occasions for analytical inquiry. Yet these issues do inhere in the Judaic system and structure that is built on the Mishnah, the system of the dual Torah. They are integral to the task of making God's word work. It is natural for us to want to interrogate the Mishnah about categories important in the structure built upon the Mishnah and, not only about the Mishnah's own topics.

The Mishnah legitimates the inquiry, because it does contain discussions of topics that pertain to salvation, not only to sanctification. It responds explicitly to facts of history. It refers to a Messiah, not only to Temple, Land, and people. To address the Mishnah's position on those themes, I take a synthetic approach to a theme, rather than an analytic approach to a well-construed topic of the Mishnah itself. I look at the whole constellation of Halakhic treatments of the pertinent topics, rather than at individual topical expositions. I interweave Halakhic and narrative materials from several tractates, as I reach the climactic themes of history, eternity, and Messiah: the integration of eschatological salvation in a system of restorationist sanctification.

### From Theology to History

God acts in history, so the Torah teaches. Then God sets the place and time when Israel encounters him. These encounters may take place at moments of sublime elation: at the Sea, at Sinai, at the entry into the Land. But they are also at moments of loss: the loss of the ten tribes of northern Israel, the counterpart exile of the southern tribes of Judea and Benjamin, the destruction of the Temple, the loss of Jerusalem. To this list we must add the moment of the restoration of Zion.

The Torah leaves no doubt that it is through historical events that Israel lives in the cosmic political context defined by God. The character of the events—what makes them eventful—is their grounding in issues of salvation: salvation from Egyptian bondage, salvation for restoration to the condition of Eden realized in the Land—the whole prefiguring salvation from the grave and entry into life eternal. The narrative of the Torah defines God's actions in terms of Israel's relationship to the Land, so history consists of chapters in that parlous connection. History recapitulates Israel's relationship to the Land, abandoned, recovered, lost, and restored.

It is the way of the Mishnah to respond to Torah by regularizing the irregular. But these axial events, by their nature, cannot be regularized by the law of the Mishnah. They are one-time, to be remembered and memorialized; they are not accessible of everyday reenactment. On the negative side, then, they can define no topic for a tractate. That is because, as a matter of definition, world-historical happenings defy ordering. They disrupt the timeless serenity of everyday life and its orderly transactions of sanctification through purification. That is what marks such events as eventful: as history-making. The law of the Mishnah provides for the regular, orderly, predictable, reliable life of the Temple with its penumbra of sanctification encompassing the secure life of the Israelite household. But that life was lived above the serrated surface of history, with its irregular, disorderly, never-certain consequences for the Israelite social order.

Awaiting salvation, anticipating restoration, the Mishnah's framers could not ignore disruptive history. They formed the earliest generations after events of millennial consequence, whether viewed backward or (as we now know) forward. The loss of Jerusalem, confirmed in 135, defined the context of the Rabbinic sages' work, and they made that fact explicit in tractate Hullin, as we just saw. They had no reason to anticipate the near-term restoration of the sacrificial system that had functioned for many centuries and had defined Israel's service of God: the medium for atonement, as Joshua says to Yohanan ben Zakkai in the story cited at the head of the Preface.

But momentous happenings express God's will—so the prophets, including Moses in the Torah, made clear—and therefore they define God's context for Israel. The law of the Mishnah could not ignore history. The issue for the Mishnah was how to process the consequential facts of history. Here the sages embraced Scripture's convictions (1) that God has a plan for humanity, (2) that history has a purpose, and (3) that history leads to a foreordained conclusion, the coming of a Messiah at the end of days. Accordingly, salvation, not sanctification alone, presented to the sages of the Mishnah a program of inquiry. The high priest on the Day of Atonement, bringing about the sanctification of Israel through the atonement for sins effected by the rite and by the Day of Atonement itself, ministered through time without boundary, so long as history did not intervene. But history did intervene: the Temple was destroyed, the rites were abandoned.

In Mishnah-tractate Hullin, among other important components, we encountered the program of historical construction that animates the law code. The law of the Mishnah faced happenings that qualify as great historical events—the destruction of the Temple, the cessation of animal offerings of atonement, and the separation of Israel from the Land of Israel. These qualify because they bring about the disruption in the continuities of Israel's perpetual patterns involving Land, People, and sanctification. These massive intrusions of God's judgment of corporate Israel redefined and recast the life of individuals. But the larger events of history affect more than the life of individual Israelites. They affect all Israel. Accordingly, we ask, How does the law of the Mishnah process and regularize and order those disruptive transactions we call historical events? The answers respond to our quest for the religious foundations of the Mishnah—the way in which the Mishnah's law makes the Torah's word work—as we address Israel in God's context: in those world-historical moments that the Torah explicitly defined as God in action, God who not only sanctifies but also saves Israel.

We know how the Mishnah's law sorts out issues of sanctification and eternity. But how does it legislate concerning salvation and history? As soon as history, with its beginning, middle, and end, enters in, should we focus on the end of days and the coming of a Messiah, which the Torah promised too? Or is that a legitimate question to address to the Mishnah at all?

## History in the Torah and in the Mishnah

In the Torah events bear unique meaning and deliver God's message and judgment. Every event, seen as unique, must be interpreted on its own terms, not as part of a cyclical pattern but as significant in itself. What happens when God intervenes is singular and therefore is identified as consequential, an event to be noted. The one-time event thus points toward lessons to be drawn for where things are heading and why. Events, being unique, do not conform to patterns. They form patterns. That pattern is preserved through the narrative of what has happened, and prophets and sages interpret the meaning of events.

So the writing of history served as a form or method of understanding prophecy, an applied theology. Just as prophecy takes up the interpretation of historical events, so historians retell these events in the frame of prophetic theses. Out of the two—history writing as a mode of reflection, prophecy as a means of theological construction—emerged a picture of future history, that is, what is going to happen. In short, history consists of a sequence of one-time events, each of them singular, all of them meaningful. These events move from a beginning somewhere to an end at a foreordained goal. History moves toward the end of history—the teleology of the narrative.

One has every right to expect such a view of matters to lead people to write books of a certain sort, rather than of some other sort. In the case of the written Torah people wrote sustained narratives, history books that teach lessons or apocalyptic books that through pregnant imagery predict the future and record the direction and end of time. In antiquity that kind of writing proves commonplace among all kinds of groups and characteristic of all sorts of Judaic systems except one, the Mishnah. Here we have a system of thought that does not appeal to history as a sequence of one-time events, each of which bears meaning on its own. Rather, the Mishnah seeks to classify events, to discover what they have in common.

The framers of the Mishnah explicitly refer to very few events, treating those they do mention within a focus quite separate from what happened—the unfolding of the events themselves. They rarely create sustained narratives. More probative still, historical events do not supply organizing categories or taxonomic classifications. We find no tractate devoted to the destruction of the

Temple, no complete chapter detailing the events of Bar Kokhba, nor even a sustained celebration of the events of the sages' own historical life. These are matters alluded to episodically, not foci of systematic analysis.

When things that have happened are mentioned, it is neither in order to narrate nor to interpret and draw lessons from the event. It is either to illustrate a point of law or to pose a problem of the law—always *en passant*, never in a pointed way. So when the sages refer to what has happened, this is casual and tangential to the main thrust of discourse. Famous events of enduring meaning, such as the return to Zion from Babylonia in the time of Ezra and Nehemiah, gain entry into the Mishnah's discourse only because of the genealogical divisions of Israelite society into castes among the immigrants (Mishnah-tractate Qiddushin 4:1).

Moreover, where the Mishnah provides little tales or narratives, they more often treat how things in the cult are done in general rather than what in particular happened on some particular day. It is sufficient to refer casually to well-known incidents. Narrative, in the Mishnah's limited rhetorical repertoire, is reserved for the narrow framework of what priests and others do on recurrent occasions and around the Temple. That staple of history, stories about dramatic events and important deeds, in the minds of the Mishnah's jurisprudents provide little nourishment. Events, if they appear at all, are treated as trivial. They may be well known, but are consequential in some way other than is revealed in the detailed account of what actually happened. Let me now show some of the principal texts that contain and convey this other conception of how events become history and how history teaches lessons.

The most striking difference appears right at the surface. The Mishnah contains anecdotes but no sustained narrative whatsoever. For example, it portrays relationships of patriarch and sage in a perfect story, at Mishnah-tractate Rosh Hashanah 2:8–9, but contains no sustained and systematic narrative account of matters—and little legislation. The Mishnah sets forth very few tales, but undertakes to portray no large-scale conception of history. It organizes its system in ahistorical terms.

Historical events are absorbed into the pattern of classification, as we saw in Mishnah-tractate Hullin and shall see still more elaborately in a moment. That effort to regularize and order disruptive moments is underscored by what the Mishnah does not contain. As to meaning, no effort goes into setting it into historical context: a particular time, place, or circumstance defined by important events. At most there will be a notation of the occasion on which such-and-such a decision was reached, but not the provocation, beyond the purities of legal logic, for the conclusions drawn.

More to the point, the Mishnah's legal system is set forth outside of all historical framework. Viewed whole, the Mishnah proper (the sixty-two Halakhic tractates) contains no story of its origin and authority; that story was left to one small tractate, Abot, to tell, and then in its own unusual way, as we saw in chapter 1. Even there, historical narrative plays no role. The issue is other than an event.

Compare the Pentateuch's presentation of its law. The law codes of Exodus and Deuteronomy are set forth in a narrative framework, and the priestly code of Leviticus, for its part, appeals to God's revelation to Moses and Aaron at specific times and places. In the Mishnah we have neither narrative nor setting for the representation of law. The Mishnah admits no sustaining story, recognizes no before or after, begins in no particular locale and ends in the middle of a legal exposition. No narrative logic governs the ordering of its topics.

Instead of narrative, which as in Exodus spills over into case law, the Mishnah gives an atemporal description of how things are done in general and universally; that is, it supplies without context strictly descriptive cases. These are not episodic or anecdotal cases, but they form patterns that yield laws. Instead of reflection on the meaning and end of history, it constructs a world in which history plays little part. Instead of narratives full of didactic meaning, the Mishnah's authorship provides lists of events so as to expose the traits that they share and thus the rules to which they conform. The definitive components of a historical system of Judaism yielding a theory of the end of history and its goal are not set forth in the Mishnah. The law of the Mishnah rarely resorts to the description of events as one-time happenings, to analysis of the meaning and end of events, and to interpretation of the end and future of singular events.

None of these commonplace constituents of all other systems of Judaism of ancient times is found in the Mishnah's system. So the Mishnah has no precedent in prior Israelite writings for its mode of dealing with things that happen. The Mishnah's way of identifying happenings as consequential and describing them, its way of analyzing those events it chooses as bearing meaning, its interpretation of the future to which significant events point—all those in the written Torah's context are unique. In form, the Mishnah represents its system outside of all historical framework.

Then how does history come to full conceptual expression in the Mishnah? History as an account of a meaningful pattern of events, making sense of the past and giving guidance about the future, begins with the necessary conviction that events matter because they form series, one after another. When we put a series together, we have a rule—just as when we put cases together, we can demonstrate the rule that governs them all. The Mishnah's authors therefore dispose of historical events just as they sort out the traits of clay pots or the regularities of anything else of interest—the correct composition of contracts, the appropriate disposition of property, proper conduct on a holy day. The upshot is, all things imputed to specific events—exemplary anecdotes—and concrete transactions—illustrative cases—are formed so that we can derive, out of the concrete, the abstract and encompassing rule.

That is why we may not find surprising the Mishnah's framers' reluctance to present us with an elaborate theory of events, a fact fully consonant with their systematic points of insistence and encompassing concern. Events do not matter, one by one. The Mishnah's philosopher-lawyers exhibited no theory of history either. Their conception of Israel's destiny in no way called upon historical categories of either narrative or didactic explanation to describe and account for the future. The small importance attributed to the figure of a Messiah as a historical-eschatological figure, therefore, fully accords with the larger traits of the system as a whole. If what is important in Israel's existence is sanctification, an ongoing process, and not salvation, a one-time event at the end, then no one will find reason to narrate history. In the Mishnah no one did—hence no tractates on historical themes or problems, even when, as in Mishnah-tractate Hullin, historical issues framed the governing problematics.

Although the theology of the Mishnah encompasses history and its meaning, history and the interpretation of history do not occupy a central position on the stage of Israel's life portrayed by the Mishnah. The critical categories derive from the modalities of holiness; that is what, in chapter 16, Hullin, the climax of the Mishnah, has shown us with great force. What can become holy or what is holy? These tell us what will attract the close scrutiny of our authors and precipitate sustained thought that is expressed through very concrete and picayune cases.

If I had to identify the two most important foci of holiness in the Mishnah they would be (1) in the natural world, the land, but only the Holy Land, the Land of Israel, and (2) in the social world, the people, but only the People of Israel. In the interplay among Land, people, and God, we see how Israel figures in God's context, in God's good time. These are the abstractions. In what follows one can discern how the concrete texts illuminate them.

## How the Mishnah Configures Israel in the Context of History Defined by God. How the Destruction of the Temple Figures in Misnhah-tractate Rosh Hashanah 4:1–3

The Mishnah's system may be ahistorical, but concluding that it is non-historical or antihistorical could not be more mistaken. The Mishnah presents events in a different way, producing a different kind of history. Specifically, it revises the inherited conception of history and reshapes that conception to fit into its own system. Since the greatest event in the century and a half, from ca. 50 to ca. 200, in which the Mishnah's materials came into being, was the destruction of the Temple in the year 70, we must expect the Mishnah's treatment of that incident to illustrate the document's larger theory of history: what is important and unimportant about what happens.

The destruction of the Temple thus constitutes a noteworthy fact in the history of the law, because various laws about rite and cult had to undergo revision on account of the destruction. The following provides a stunningly apt example of how the Mishnah regards what actually happened as simply marking changes in the law.

### MISHNAH-TRACTATE ROSH HASHANAH 4:1–3

> The festival day of the New Year which coincided with the Sabbath—
>
> in the Temple they would sound the *shofar.*
>
> But not in the provinces.
>
> When the Temple was destroyed, Rabban Yohanan ben Zakkai made the rule that they should sound the *shofar* in every locale in which there was a court.
>
> Said R. Eleazar, "Rabban Yohanan b. Zakkai made that rule only in the case of Yabneh alone."
>
> They said to him, "All the same are Yabneh and every locale in which there is a court.

The Halakhic issue, predictably, concerns the hierarchical comparison of Jerusalem and Yabneh, the locus of Yohanan ben Zakkai's circle of disciples, continuators of the oral tradition. So in this version of matters, the center of Torah-study forms the counterpart to the center of divine service through sacrifice. Placed on a continuum with Jerusalem, Yabneh served as the embodiment of the tradition of Sinai, the activities of learning carried on there as the continuation of the divine service now suspended—an amazing claim. It is continued in the following language:

> And in this regard also was Jerusalem ahead of Yabneh:
>
> in every town which is within sight and sound [of Jerusalem], and nearby and able to come up to Jerusalem, they sound the *shofar.*
>
> But as to Yabneh, they sound the *shofar* only in the court alone.

What about rites formerly carried on only in the Temple? The issue of how these are adjusted to the new age is raised in the following:

> In olden times the *lulab* was taken up in the Temple for seven days, and in the provinces, for one day.
>
> When the Temple was destroyed, Rabban Yohanan ben Zakkai made the rule that in the provinces the *lulab* should be taken up for seven days, as a memorial to the Temple;
>
> and that the day [the sixteenth of Nisan] on which the *omer* is waved should be wholly prohibited [in regard to the eating of new produce]. (Mishnah-tractate Sukkah 3:12)

The point is, the loss of the Temple requires adjustments in the rites, but does not justify dropping them altogether.

What we see is that the destruction of the Temple in the law of the Mishnah is recognized and treated as consequential—but only for the organization of rules. The event forms division between one time and some other, and, in consequence, we sort out rules pertaining to the Temple and synagogue in one way rather than in another. Hullin has prepared us for such a disposition of historical events. That is the conclusion drawn from the destruction of the Temple, which is to say the use that is made of that catastrophe: it is an indicator in the organization of rules. What we perceive is the opposite of an interest in focusing on the one-time meaning of events. Now it is the all-time significance of events in the making of rules. Events are treated not as irregular and intrinsically consequential but as regular and merely instrumental.

## Patterning Events:
## Mishnah-tractate Taʿanit 4:6–7

The Mishnah's sages surely mourned for the destruction and the loss of Israel's principal mode of worship, and certainly responded to the event of the ninth of Ab in the year 70. But in the Mishnah they did so in their characteristic way: they listed the event as an item in a catalogue of things that are like one another and so demand similar responses. Then the destruction no longer appears as a unique event. It is absorbed into a pattern of like disasters, all exhibiting similar taxonomic traits, events to which the people, now well schooled in tragedy, know full well the appropriate response. History yields rules, just as nature does, just as the Torah does. The work of regularization and ordering was not to be abandoned in the face of catastrophe; it was, rather, to be intensified and renewed.

So it is in demonstrating regularity that the sages reveal their way of coping. Then the uniqueness of the event fades away; its mundane character is emphasized. The power of taxonomy in imposing order upon chaos once more does its healing work. The consequence was reassurance that historical events obeyed discoverable laws. In this way Israel's ongoing life would override disruptive, one-time happenings. So catalogues of events, as much as lists of species of melons, served as brilliant apologetic by providing reassurance that nothing lies beyond the range and power of an ordering system and a stabilizing pattern. Here is yet another way in which the irregular was made regular, orderly, and subject to rules:

MISHNAH-TRACTATE TAʿANIT 4:6–7

4:6 Five events took place for our fathers on the seventeenth of Tammuz, and five on the ninth of Ab.

On the seventeenth of Tammuz

(1) the tablets [of the Torah] were broken,

(2) the daily whole offering was cancelled,

(3) the city wall was breached,

(4) Apostemos burned the Torah, and

(5) he set up an idol in the Temple.

On the ninth of Ab

(1) the decree was made against our forefathers that they should not enter the land,

(2) the first Temple,

(3) the second [Temple] were destroyed,

(4) Betar was taken,

(5) the city was ploughed up [after the war against Emperor Hadrian led by Bar Kokhba, 132–135].

When Ab comes, rejoicing diminishes.

I include M. Ta$^c$anit 4:7 to show the context in which the list of M. 4:6 stands.

> 4:7 In the week in which the ninth of Ab occurs it is prohibited to get a haircut and to wash one's clothes.
>
> But on Thursday of that week these are permitted,
>
> because of the honor due to the Sabbath.
>
> On the eve of the ninth of Ab a person should not eat two prepared dishes, nor should one eat meat or drink wine.

The calamities catalogued in the list form groups and reveal common traits, so they are subject to classification. Then the laws (Mishnah-tractate Ta$^c$anit 4:7) provide regular rules for responding to and coping with these untimely catastrophes, all (fortuitously) in a single classification. So the raw materials of history are absorbed into the ahistorical, supernatural system of the Mishnah. The process of absorption and regularization of the unique and one-time moment is well illustrated in this passage from Ta$^c$anit.

## Patterning the History of the Sacrificial Cult: Mishnah-tractate Zebahim 14:4–10

A still more striking example of the reordering of one-time events into all-time patterns derives from the effort to put together in a coherent way the rather haphazard facts that form the history of the cult inherited from the Torah, with sacrifices made here and there and finally in Jerusalem. Now, the entire history of the cult, so critical in the larger system created by the Mishnah's lawyers, produced a patterned, sensible, and intelligible picture. This is, we now realize, typical of their disposition of events. Everything that happened turned out to be susceptible of classification once the taxonomic traits were specified. An exercise in sorting out periods and their characteristics took the place of narrative, to explain things in its own way: first this, and then that, and, in consequence, the other.

So in the neutral turf of holy ground, as much as in the trembling earth of the Temple Mount, everything was absorbed into one thing—all classified in its proper place and by its appropriate rule. Indeed, so far as the Mishnah's lawyers proposed to write history at all, they wrote it into their picture of the long tale of the way in which Israel served God: the places in which the sacrificial labor was carried on, the people who did it, the places in which the priests ate the meat left over for their portion after God's portion was set aside and burned up. This "historical" account forthwith generated precisely that problem of locating the regular and orderly that the philosophers loved to investigate: What happens when a given set of cases is governed by two distinct rules, so that we do not know how to classify the cases? We see the intersection of conflicting but equally correct, taxonomic rules in this passage from Mishnah-tractate Zebahim. The passage is history, so far as the Mishnah's creators proposed to write history: finding meaning in the reduction of events to rules that form compositions of regularity.

I reproduce the entire disquisition, even though it is of formidable length, because that is the only way for the reader to see the full extent of the pattern that is adumbrated. A single example will not serve, when centuries of history are reduced to a few taxonomic indicators, realized in a tiny repertoire of concrete actions; the whole then differentiated by whether or not a given action pertains to a given circumstance. What we have is a triumph of that process of ordering and regularization that transforms the chaos of the everyday into the patterned construction that the Mishnah's law seeks to bring into being.

#### MISHNAH-TRACTATE ZEBAHIM 14:4–10

14:4 Before the tabernacle was set up, (*1) the high places were permitted, and (2) [the sacrificial] service [was done by] the firstborn (Num. 3:12–13; 8:16–18).

When the tabernacle was set up, (1) the high places were prohibited, and (2) the [sacrificial] service [was done by] priests.

Most Holy Things were eaten within the veils, Lesser Holy Things [were eaten] throughout the camp of Israel.

14:5 They came to Gilgal.

The high places were prohibited.

Most Holy Things were eaten within the veils, Lesser Holy Things, anywhere.

14:6 They came to Shiloh.

The high places were prohibited.

(1) There was no roof-beam there, but below was a house of stone, and hangings above it, and (2) it was "the resting place" (Deut. 12:9).

Most Holy Things were eaten within the veils, Lesser Holy Things and second tithe [were eaten] in any place within sight [of Shiloh].

14:7 They came to Nob and Gibeon.

The high places were permitted.

Most Holy Things were eaten within the veils, Lesser Holy Things, in all the towns of Israel.

14:8 They came to Jerusalem.

The high places were prohibited.

And they never again were permitted.

And it was "the inheritance" (Deut. 12:9).

Most Holy Things were eaten within the veils, Lesser Holy Things and second tithe within the wall.

14:9 All the Holy Things which one sanctified at the time of the prohibition of the high places and offered at the time of the prohibition of high places outside—

lo, these are subject to the transgression of a positive commandment and a negative commandment, and they are liable on their account to extirpation [for sacrificing outside the designated place (Lev. 17:8–9)].

[If] one sanctified them at the time of the permission of high places and offered them up at the time of the prohibition of high places,

lo, these are subject to transgression of a positive commandment and to a negative commandment, but they are not liable on their account to extirpation [since if the offerings had been sacrificed when they were sanctified, there should have been no violation].

[If] one sanctified them at the time of the prohibition of high places and offered them up at the time of the permission of high places, lo, these are subject to transgression of a positive commandment, but they are not subject to a negative commandment at all.

14:10 These are the Holy Things offered in the tabernacle [of Gilgal, Nob, and Gibeon]:

Holy Things which were sanctified for the tabernacle.

Offerings of the congregation are offered in the tabernacle.

Offerings of the individual [are offered] on a high place.

Offerings of the individual which were sanctified for the tabernacle are to be offered in the tabernacle.

And if one offered them up on a high place, he is free.

What is the difference between the high place of an individual and the high place of the community?

(1) Laying on of hands, and (2) slaughtering at the north [of the altar], and (3) placing [of the blood] round about [the altar], and (4) waving, and (5) bring near.

R. Judah says, "there is no meal-offering on a high place [but there is in the tabernacle]"—

and (1) the priestly service, and (2) the wearing of garments of ministry, and (3) the use of utensils of ministry, and (4) the sweet-smelling savor and (5) the dividing line for the [tossing of various kinds of] blood, and (6) the rule concerning the washing of hands and feet.

But the matters of time, and remnant, and uncleanness are applicable both here and there [by contrast to M. 14:3F-I].

All possible cases are dealt with. A few comments suffice to highlight the pattern that imparts coherence and rationality to the particular rules.

In the first case, both sanctification and offering up take place at the time that prohibition of high places applies. There is transgression of a positive commandment and a negative commandment. The negative is Deuteronomy 12:13; the positive is Deuteronomy 12:14: "Take heed that you do not offer your burnt offerings at every place that you see; but at the place which the Lord will choose in one of your tribes, there you shall offer your burnt offerings . . . ." The mixtures (Mishnah-tractate Zebahim 14:9) then go over the same ground. If sanctification takes place when it is permitted to sanctify animals for use in high places, but the offering up takes place when it is not allowed to do so (that is, the former for Mishnah Zebahim 14:4, the latter for 14:6), then extirpation does not apply (Lev. 17:5-7). When we reverse the order (as at Mishnah Zebahim 14:6 and 14:7), there is no negative (Deut. 12:13), but the positive commandment (Deut. 12:14) has been transgressed. However, matters do not stop there. The rule making out of the raw materials of disorderly history continues unabated.

The inclusion of Mishnah Zebahim 14:9, structurally matching Mishnah Ta'anit 4:7, shows us the goal of the historical composition. It is to set forth in a system and pattern the rules that intersect and otherwise produce confusion. The typology may now be stated briefly. The authorship at hand had the option of narrative, but chose the way of natural philosophy: generalization through classification, comparison, and contrast.

The Mishnah thus absorbs into its encompassing system all events, small and large, that it deems consequential. With what happens the sages accomplish what they do with everything else: an immense construction of the order and rules governing the classification of everything on earth and in heaven. One-time events of ineluctable significance scarcely impress the Mishnah. The authors find no difficulty in showing that what appears unique and beyond classification has in fact happened before and so falls within the range of trustworthy rules and known procedures. Once history's components, one-time events, lose their distinctiveness, then history as a didactic intellectual construct, as a source of lessons and rules, also loses all pertinence. Instead, lessons and rules come from sorting things out and classifying them, that is, from the procedures and modes of thought of the philosopher seeking regularity.

For this labor of taxonomy, the historian's way of selecting data and arranging them into unique patterns of meaning to teach lessons beyond their own limits proves inconsequential. One-time events are not what matters. The world is composed of nature and supernature. The repetitious laws that count are those to be discovered in heaven and, in heaven's creation and counterpart, on earth. Keep those laws and things will work out. Break them and the result is predictable: calamity of whatever sort will supervene in accordance with the rules. But precisely because it is predictable, a catastrophic happening testifies to what has always been and must always be, in accordance with reliable rules and within categories already discovered and well explained.

The sages possessed not an antihistorical conception of reality but a deeply historical one, even though it is a different conception of the meaning of history than what is familiar to us. It was in a single word social-scientific, not historical in the traditional sense of history writing. For history writing, what is important is to describe the unique and the individual, not what is ongoing and unremarkable. That explains the requirement of narrative: histories are the story of change, development, movement, not of what does not change, develop, or move. For the thinkers of the Mishnah, historical patterning emerges as today scientific knowledge does, through the classification, the ordering by rule of the unique and individual. Learning proceeds through the organization of change and movement within unchanging categories.

## A Messiah in the Mishnah:
## Mishnah-tractate Sotah 9

The Mishnah's framers found it possible to present a statement of goals for their system entirely separate from appeals to history and eschatology, the end of history. Theirs was a teleology without an eschatological formulation thereof. They would restore and renew Eden—the opposite of an eschatological teleology. Time and change, accordingly, took a subordinated role to enduring patterns, built upon the sanctification of Israel.

Since the Mishnah's sages certainly knew and even alluded to long-standing and widely held convictions on eschatological subjects, they from time to time utilized the terms "Messiah" and "Messianic." In the Mishnah the words "the" and "Messiah" violate the rules of semantics. "Messiah" referred to a classification of priest, for example, a Messiah anointed for war. There were several classifications of Messiahs, and any number of representatives within those classifications. Messiahs played a part. But these "anointed men" had no historical role. They undertook a task quite different from that assigned to Jesus by the framers of the Gospels. They were merely a species of priest, falling into one classification rather than another.

If we ask the Mishnah to answer the questions concerning a Messiah, When will he come? To whom, in Israel, will he come? What must, or can, we do while we wait to hasten his coming?, to these questions we find no answers. Answering these questions out of the resources of the Mishnah is not possible. As we saw in Rosh Hashanah, Ta'anit, and Zebahim, the Mishnah presents no large view of history. It contains no reflection whatever on the nature and meaning of the destruction of the Temple in 70 C.E., an event that surfaces only in connection with some changes in the law explained as resulting from the end of the cult. The Mishnah pays no attention to the matter of the end-time. The word "salvation" is rare, "sanctification" commonplace.

In one of its few historical-narrative passages, the Mishnah sets forth the decline of generations, in which the destruction of the Temple and the death of great sages mark the movement of time and impart to an age the general rules that govern life therein. Here is how the Messiah theme is treated by the Mishnah within an explicitly eschatological framework. The decline of generations leaves no choice but salvation through divine intervention:

### MISHNAH-TRACTATE SOTAH 9:15

When R. Meir died, makers of parables came to an end.

When Ben Azzai died, diligent students came to an end.

When Ben Zoma died, exegetes came to an end.

When R. Joshua died, goodness went away from the world.

When Rabban Simeon b. Gamaliel died, the locust came, and troubles multiplied.

When Eleazar b. Azariah died, wealth went away from the sages.

When R. Aqiba died, the glory of the Torah came to an end.

When R. Hanina b. Dosa died, wonder-workers came to an end.

When R. Yosé Qatnuta died, pietists went away.

(And why was he called *Qatnuta*? Because he was the least of the pietists.)

When Rabban Yohanan b. Zakkai died, the splendor of wisdom came to an end.

When Rabban Gamaliel the Elder died, the glory of the Torah came to an end, and cleanness and separateness perished.

When R. Ishmael b. Phabi died, the splendor of the priesthood came to an end.

When Rabbi died, modesty and fear of sin came to an end.

R. Pinhas b. Yair says, "When the Temple was destroyed, associates became ashamed and so did free men, and they covered their heads.

"And wonder-workers became feeble. And violent men and big takers grew strong.

"And none expounds and none seeks [learning] and none asks.

"Upon whom shall we depend? Upon our Father in heaven."

R. Eliezer the Great says, "From the day on which the Temple was destroyed, sages began to be like scribes, and scribes like ministers, and ministers like ordinary folk.

"And the ordinary folk have become feeble.

"And none seeks.

"Upon whom shall we depend? Upon our Father in heaven."

With the footprints of the Messiah: presumption increases, and dearth increases.

The vine gives its fruit and wine at great cost.

And the government turns to heresy.

And there is no reproof.

The gathering place will be for prostitution.

And Galilee will be laid waste.

And the Gablan will be made desolate.

And the men of the frontier will go about from town to town, and none will take pity on them.

And the wisdom of scribes will putrefy.

And those who fear sin will be rejected.

And the truth will be locked away.

Children will shame elders, and elders will stand up before children.

For the son dishonors the father and the daughter rises up against her mother, the daughter-in-law against her mother-in-law; a man's enemies are the men of his own house" (Mic. 7:6).

The face of the generation in the face of a dog.

A son is not ashamed before his father.

Upon whom shall we depend? Upon our Father in heaven.

R. Pinhas b. Yair says, "Heedfulness leads to cleanliness, cleanliness leads to cleanness, cleanness leads to abstinence, abstinence leads to holiness, holiness leads to modesty, modesty leads to the fear of sin, the fear of sin leads to piety, piety leads to the Holy Spirit, the Holy Spirit leads to the resurrection of the dead, and the resurrection of the dead comes through Elijah, blessed be his memory, Amen."

What we learn from this elegy is that the Messiah theme in the Mishnah does not stand at the forefront of the framers' consciousness. The framers of the Mishnah do not resort to speculation about a Messiah as a historical-supernatural figure. So far as that kind of speculation provides the vehicle for reflection on salvific issues or—in mythic terms—narratives on the meaning of history and the destiny of Israel, we cannot say that the Mishnah's philosophers take up those encompassing categories of being: Where are we heading? What can we do about it?

That does not mean that questions found urgent in the aftermath of the destruction of the Temple and the disaster of Bar Kokhba failed to attract the attention of the Mishnah's sages. But they treated history in a different way, offering their own answers to its questions. So lessons and rules come from sorting things out and classifying them from the procedures and modes of thought of the philosopher seeking regularity. Within the framework of well-classified rules, there could be Messiahs, but no single Messiah.

## The Messiah Theme Naturalized into the Mishnah's System: The Talmud of the Land of Israel

The story of the Mishnah does not conclude here. Continuator documents, the Tosefta and the two Talmuds, would receive and carry forward the presentation of the Halakhah organized and set forth by the Mishnah. The Messiah theme, trivial in the Mishnah, moves to the forefront in the Mishnah's continuation and commentary set forth in ca. 400 C.E. by the Talmud of the land of Israel, also called the Yerushalmi.

What is of special interest here is that, in the first of the two Talmuds, the Messiah theme would come to full and detailed exposition. But, as I shall explain, that theme was made to reinforce the theology of sanctification through the Halakhah that we have found paramount in the Mishnah itself. What we see here is how the Messiah theme was naturalized by the Yerushalmi into the legal system of the Mishnah and made to reinforce that system.

If the Mishnah provided a teleology without eschatology, the framers of the Yerushalmi framed matters in historical terms and promised a Messiah at the end of days. Integral to the doctrine of history was the prophetic view that Israel's own deeds defined the events of history. Israel had to learn the lesson of its history in order to take command of its own destiny. But this notion of determining one's own destiny should not be misunderstood.

The narratives chosen by the framers of the Talmud of the Land of Israel were not telling the Jews to please God by doing commandments in order that they should thereby gain control of their own destiny. On the contrary, Israel can free itself of control by other nations only by humbly agreeing to accept God's rule. The nations—Rome, in the present instance—rest on one side of the balance, while God rests on the other. Israel must then choose between them. There is no such thing for Israel as freedom from both God and the nations, total autonomy and independence. That is an arrogant conception, recapitulating the sin of Adam in Eden. There is only a choice of masters, a ruler on earth or a ruler in heaven.

With propositions such as these, the framers of the Mishnah will certainly have concurred. And why not? For the fundamental affirmations of the Mishnah about the centrality of Israel's perfection at rest—sanctification—readily prove congruent to the attitudes at hand. Once a Messiah's coming had become dependent upon Israel's condition and not upon Israel's actions in historical time, then the Mishnah's system will have imposed its fundamental and definitive character upon the Messiah theme.

An eschatological teleology framed through that myth then would prove wholly appropriate to the method of the larger system of the Mishnah. That is for a simple, striking reason. The Messiah theme is made to repeat, in its terms, the doctrine of virtuous attitudes and emotions that prevail throughout; the condition of the coming of a Messiah is Israel's humility, its submission to the tides and currents of history. What, after all, makes a Messiah a *false* Messiah? In the Talmud of the Land of Israel, it is not his claim to save Israel, but his claim to save Israel without the help of God. The meaning of the true Messiah is Israel's total submission, through a Messiah's gentle rule, to God's yoke and service. So God is not to be manipulated through Israel's humoring of heaven in rite and cult.

The notion of keeping the commandments so as to manipulate Heaven and get God to do what Israel wants is totally incongruent to the text. Keeping the commandments as a mark of submission, loyalty, and humility before God is the Rabbinic system of salvation. So Israel does not save itself. Israel never controls its own destiny, either on earth or in heaven. The only choice is whether to cast one's fate into the hands of cruel, deceitful human beings or to trust in the living God of mercy and love. The Rabbinic sages stressed that Israel's arrogance alienates God, and Israel's humility and submission win God's favor. This, too, we shall see spelled out in the setting of this discourse about a Messiah in the Talmud of the Land of Israel.

How does the Mishnah's system figure? The failed Messiah of the second century, Bar Kokhba, above all exemplifies arrogance against God. He lost the war because of that arrogance. His emotions, attitudes, sentiments, and feelings form the model of how the virtuous Israelite is not to conceive of matters. In particular, he ignored the authority of the sages.

**YERUSHALMI TAʿANIT 4:5**

Said R. Yohanan, "There were eighty thousand pairs of trumpeters surrounding Betar. Each one was in charge of a number of troops. Ben Koziba [Bar Kokhba] was there and he had two hundred thousand troops who, as a sign of loyalty, had cut off their little fingers.

"Sages sent word to him, 'How long are you going to turn Israel into a maimed people?'

"He said to them, 'How otherwise is it possible to test them?'

"They replied to him, 'Whoever cannot uproot a cedar of Lebanon while riding on his horse will not be inscribed on your military rolls.'

"So there were two hundred thousand who qualified in one way, and another two hundred thousand who qualified in another way."

When he would go forth to battle, he would say, "Lord of the world! Do not help and do not hinder us! 'Hast thou not rejected us, O God? Thou dost not go forth, O God, with our armies'" (Ps. 60:10).

Bar Kokhba is shown false by his arrogance. So, too, is any Messiah shown false by arrogance. Then the opposite proposition emerges. When Israel humbly accepts God's rule, then a Messiah will come. Until Israel subjects itself to God's rule, the Jews will be subjugated to pagan domination. Since the condition of Israel governs, Israel itself holds the key to its own redemption. But this it can achieve only by throwing away the key. The paradox must be crystal clear: Israel acts to redeem itself through the opposite of self-determination, namely, by subjugating itself to God. Israel's power lies in its negation of power. Its destiny lies in giving up all pretense at deciding its own destiny. So weakness is the ultimate strength, forbearance the final act of self-assertion, passive resignation the sure step toward liberation. Israel's freedom is engraved on the tablets of the commandments of God: to be free is freely to obey.

The Yerushalmi's system, then, has transformed the Messiah theme in its totality into an essentially ahistorical force. If people wanted to reach the end of time, they had to rise above time, that is, history, and stand off at the side of great movements of political and military character. At its foundation, it is precisely the message of teleology without eschatology expressed by the Mishnah and its associated documents. The new mode, the Talmud, a commentary to the Mishnah, highlights the old and enduring message of the Mishnah: Israel must turn away from time and change, submit to whatever happens, so as to win for itself the only government worth having, that is, God's rule, accomplished through God's anointed agent, a Messiah.

Now we should not conclude that the Yerushalmi has simply moved beyond the Mishnah's orbit. The opposite is the case. What the framers of the Yerushalmi have done is assemble materials in which the eschatological, and therefore Messianic teleology is absorbed within the ahistorical and therefore sagacious structure of the Mishnah. The Messiah turned into a sage is no longer a Messiah embodied in the figure of the arrogant Bar Kokhba (in the Talmud's representation of the figure). The reversion to the prophetic notion of learning history's lessons carried in its wake a reengagement with the Messiah theme. But the reengagement does not represent a change in the unfolding system because the climax comes in an explicit statement that the conduct required by the Torah will bring the coming Messiah. That explanation of the holy way of life focuses upon the end of time and the advent of a Messiah—both of which therefore depend on the sanctification of Israel.

So sanctification takes priority; salvation depends on it. The framers of the Mishnah had found it possible to construct a complete and encompassing teleology for their system with scarcely a single word about a Messiah's coming at that time when the system would be perfectly achieved.

The Yerushalmi, heir to the Mishnah, accomplished the Messianization of the system of the Mishnah. The reversion to the prophetic notion of learning the lessons of history carried in its wake reengagement with the Messiah theme. The climax of the matter comes in an explicit statement that the practice of conduct required by the Torah will bring about the coming of a Messiah. That explanation of the purpose of the holy way of life, focused now upon the end of time and the advent of a Messiah, must strike us as surprising. For the framers of the Mishnah had found it possible to construct a complete and encompassing teleology for their system with scarcely a single word about a Messiah's coming when the system would be perfectly achieved. So with their interest in explaining events and accounting for history, third- and fourth-century sages represented in the units of discourse at hand invoked what their predecessors had at best found of peripheral consequence to their system. The following contains the most striking expression of that viewpoint.

**YERUSHALMI TAʿANIT 1:1.X**

"The oracle concerning Dumah. One is calling to me from Seir, 'Watchman, what of the night? Watchman, what of the night?' (Isa. 21:11)."

The Israelites said to Isaiah, "O our Rabbi, Isaiah, what will come for us out of this night?"

He said to them, "Wait for me, until I can present the question."

Once he had asked the question, he came back to them.

They said to him, "'Watchman, what of the night?' What did the Guardian of the ages tell you?"

He said to them, "The watchman says, 'Morning comes; and also the night. If you will inquire, inquire; come back again' (Isa. 21:12)."

They said to him, "Also the night?"

He said to them, "It is not what you are thinking. But there will be morning for the righteous, and night for the wicked, morning for Israel, and night for idolaters."

They said to him, "When?"

He said to them, "Whenever you want, He too wants [it to be]—if you want it, he wants it."

They said to him, "What is standing in the way?"

He said to them, "Repentance: 'Come back again' (Isa. 21:12)."

R. Aha in the name of R. Tanhum b. R. Hiyya, "If Israel repents for one day, forthwith the son of David will come.

"What is the Scriptural basis? 'O that today you would hearken to his voice!' (Ps. 95:7)."

Said R. Levi, "If Israel would keep a single Sabbath in the proper way, forthwith the son of David will come.

"What is the Scriptural basis for this view? 'Moses said, Eat it today, for today is a Sabbath to the Lord; today you will not find it in the field' (Exod. 16:25).

"And it says, 'For thus said the Lord God, the Holy One of Israel, "In returning and rest you shall be saved; in quietness and in trust shall be your strength. And you would not"' (Isa. 30:15)."

The discussion of the power of repentance would hardly have surprised a Mishnah-sage. What is new is the explicit linkage of keeping the law with achieving the end of time and the coming of a Messiah. That motif stands separate from the notions of righteousness and repentance, which surely do not require it. So the condition of "all Israel," a social category in historical time, comes under consideration, and not only the status of individual Israelites in life and in death.

We must not lose sight of the importance of this passage, with its emphasis on repentance, on the one side, and the power of Israel to reform itself, on the other. The Messiah will come any day that Israel makes it possible. If all Israel will keep a single Sabbath in the proper (Rabbinic) way, the Messiah will come. If all Israel will repent for one day, the Messiah will come. "Whenever you want . . . ," the Messiah will come. Now, two things are happening here. First, the system of religious observance, including study of Torah, is explicitly invoked as having salvific power. Second, the persistent hope of the people for the coming of the Messiah is linked to the system of Rabbinic observance and belief. In this way, the austere program of the Mishnah, with no trace of a promise that the Messiah will come if and when the system is fully realized, finds a new development.

Now we find an explicitly Messianic statement that the purpose of the law is to attain Israel's salvation: "If you want it, God wants it too." The one thing Israel commands is its own heart; the power it yet exercises is the power to repent. Yet these will suffice. The entire history of humanity will respond to Israel's will, to what happens in Israel's heart and soul. And, with Temple in ruins, repentance can take place only within the heart and mind.

## The Mishnah at the Foundations

The Mishnah designed a world in which the Temple stood at the center, a society in which the priests presided at the top, and a way of life in which the dominant issue was sanctification. Whether the full realization of that world, society, and way of life was thought to come sooner or later, the system had been meant only initially as a utopia; but in the end it was intended as a plan and constitution for a material society here on earth and specifically here in the Land of Israel.

Two hundred years had passed from the closure of the Mishnah to the completion of the Talmud of the Land of Israel. Much had changed. Pagan rule gave way to the sovereignty of Christian emperors. Israel's history stretched backward, to a point of disaster, and forward, to an unseen and incalculable time beyond the near horizon. Short of supernatural events, salvation was not in sight. The Mishnah's view persisted: Israel lived under its own government, framed within the rules of sanctification and constituted a holy society.

But when would salvation come and how could people even now hasten its day? The Talmud of the Land of Israel expressly links salvation to keeping the law. Its sages maintained that keeping the law now signified keeping the faith: the act of hope. This means that the issues of the law were drawn upward into the highest realm of Israelite consciousness. Keeping the law in the right way is represented as not merely right or expedient. It is the way to bring a Messiah, the son of David. And that meant re-creating the condition of Eden, the Sabbath of creation, one time, perfectly, when God blessed and sanctified the Sabbath day. This is stated by R. Levi, as follows:

YERUSHALMI TAʿANIT 1:1.IX

Said R. Levi, "If Israel would keep a single Sabbath in the proper way, forthwith the son of David would come.

"What is the Scriptural basis for this view? 'Moses said, Eat it today, for today is a Sabbath to the Lord; today you will not find it in the field' (Exod. 16:25)."

And it says, "For thus said the Lord God, the Holy One of Israel, 'In returning and rest you shall be saved; in quietness and in trust shall be your strength. And you would not' (Isa. 30:15)."

Here, in a single saying, we find the entire Talmudic doctrine set forth. How like, yet how different from, the Mishnah's restorationist view. Keeping the law of the Torah represented the visible form of love of God.

What is most interesting is that the hope for a Messiah's coming is further joined to the moral condition of each individual Israelite. Hence the Messianic fulfillment was made to depend on the repentance of Israel, its adherence to the law, its humility—all private and personal virtues—Israel in God's context once more. The coming of a Messiah depended not on historical action but on moral regeneration. So from a force that moved Israelites to take up weapons on the battlefield, the Messianic hope and yearning were transformed into motives for spiritual regeneration and ethical behavior in conformity with the law. The energies released in the Messianic fervor were then linked to the sages' government through which Israel would form the godly society. When we reflect that the message, "If you want it, he too wants it to be," comes in a generation confronting a dreadful disappointment—its full weight and meaning become clear.

Two things follow. First, the Israelites were made to take up the burden of guilt for their own sorry situation. But, second, they also gained not only responsibility for but also power over their fate. They could do something about salvation, just as their sins had brought about their tragedy. This old, familiar message—announced by Jeremiah's prophecies and lamentations but nowhere in the Mishnah—took on specificity and concreteness in the context of the Talmud, which offered a detailed program for reform and regeneration. The message was stern. But it also promised strength to the weak and hope to the despairing.

No one could be asked to believe that a Messiah would come very soon. The events of the day testified otherwise. So the counsel of the Talmud's sages was patience and consequential deeds. People could not hasten things, but they could do something. The law of the Mishnah, amplified and clarified by the commentaries to follow, defined what that something was. The Messiah theme had now been joined to the Mishnah's program and subordinated to it: "Today, if . . . ."

# The Mishnah
## as Model

# 18 | HOW THE TOPICAL, RHETORICAL, AND LOGICAL MEDIA OF THE MISHNAH CONVEY ITS THEOLOGICAL MESSAGE

THEOLOGY VIEWED IN ITS REALIZATION through rules for Israel's social order—set into historical context—has guided this account of the Mishnah as a religious system. But theology not only animates the message; it also shapes the modes of expression that govern the making of that statement.

The Mishnah's organization by topics, its patterned rhetoric, and its governing logic of coherent discourse form well-crafted media for the theological message of the document. The task of this chapter is to show how the main traits of the message of the Mishnah—the modes of expression and rules of coherent thought—are conveyed by the media of topic, rhetoric, and logic.

## The Uniqueness of the Mishnah
## in Judaic Canonical Context

In the context of Judaism, from Scripture forward, the combination of distinctive traits of rhetoric, construction by topic, and logic of coherence, is unique. No prior document, deriving from any venue and any age, offered a model, and none for a thousand years afterward imitated the Mishnah in its indicative qualities. But that does not mark as original to the document's authors the facts utilized by them.

The opposite is the case. The Mishnah forms a pastiche of received laws, customs, and exegeses. Much of the data of the Mishnah derive from Scripture; some originate in law or custom established for millennia in the ancient Near East, even from Sumerian and Akkadian times; some come from a common heritage of Israelite custom—facts of law shared with the Qumran writings, for instance. But these inherited facts constitute part of the raw materials, inert and awaiting a shape and a position dictated by the Mishnah itself. What is new in the Mishnah *is* the Mishnah: the formation of a comprehensive, coherent system and a cogent structure that lack all precedent in prior Israelite times and circumstances and circles.

After Scripture the first document of Rabbinic Judaism, the Mishnah as a piece of writing is absolutely unique. No other Judaic writing, Rabbinic or otherwise, exhibits the same set of indicative traits of rhetoric, logic, and topical organization. None in any Judaic setting prior to the closure of the Mishnah—for example, in the Dead Sea Scrolls—compares in systematic coverage of the entire program of law, topically expounded, logically analyzed, that is encompassed by the Mishnah. And no later canonical writing in antiquity exhibits the indicative traits of writing that characterize the Mishnah. A thousand years would pass before Maimonides in his law code would produce a similarly systematic, freestanding, topically constructed, logical exposition of the Halakhah.

The authors of the Mishnah undertook to match the media of expression and analysis to the message they wished to convey overall and in the individual parts of their document. A review of the way in which the topical, rhetorical, and logical media of the Mishnah convey its message is therefore necessary to complete this guide.

## The Topical Organization of the Mishnah

The organization of data by topics is noteworthy. The traits of the topics form the taxonomic indicators, as in natural philosophy generally. The alternatives to the topical mode of exposition mark the Mishnah as the result of choosing among antecedent alternatives, as I shall stress in a moment. First, let me explain what I mean by "topical organization" and why it matters.

The Mishnah is divided up into six principal divisions, each expounding a single, immense theme. The respective tractates of each division then take up subtopics of that same theme. The chapters of the tractates unfold along the lines of the logic that governs the dissection of the division into its topical parts. Themes unfold in accord with an inner logic we can identify. That claim is proved very simply.

The topical arrangement is intrinsic and not merely formal. The proof is simple. Once we outline the specific assertions of a tractate and then identify the topical units, we may ask why one unit comes before or after some other. In nearly all cases, we can answer that question in a straightforward logical way: question A had to be answered before question B could have been asked, for without the information deriving from the answer to question A, question B is incomprehensible, out of all context. In more general terms: when we examine our topical outline and its principal parts, we immediately see that any other ordering of the units of the tractate will self-evidently have yielded an unintelligible document. Any order other than the one before us ordinarily would have produced gibberish. That trait of ordered, logical exposition marks the respective tractates.

To show that the topical-logical exposition represented a choice and signals a policy, I have now to show the authors of the Mishnah sifted alternative modes of organizing discourse. In fact, even within the Mishnah itself, we see alternatives tried and rejected. There are three other ways of organizing law that are episodically found within the document. These available media of organization other than by appeal to the inherent, indicative traits of things were rejected because they produce confusion and obscure the intrinsic logic of natural philosophy accessible only through topical construction. If people wanted to set forth a legal system that would form a plan for social reconstruction, then the choice of a topical ordering of data would best serve their purpose.

One way is to collect diverse sayings around the name of a given authority. If the principal purpose of the code was to transmit the traditions sponsored by named authorities—a political emphasis, not one meant to facilitate the ordering of society—that was the way to accomplish the purpose. And it does lurk in the background of the Mishnah. The whole of tractate ʿEduyyot is organized in that way. So, too, as we saw in chapter 1, tractate Abot is set forth through sequences of names and their wise sayings, not through expositions of principles of wisdom. The politics of the Rabbinic institution, with its foci of power, patriarchs and sages, comes to expression in the emphasis on organization by authority.

A second way is to express a given basic principle through diverse topics. Here the law illustrates the principle, and one illustration from one topic of law readily adheres to another comparable illustration from some other topic of law. What is presented in this second way is a fundamental and abstract rule cutting across many areas of law. That governing and encompassing principle then will be stated through a miscellany of legal topics, whether deriving from the topics of the second or the fourth or the sixth divisions of the Mishnah. The construction then encompasses all of the diverse types of law through which the rule or principle may be expressed. No tractate is set up in that way, but a chapter or two may find its principle of coherence in a principle of law covering diverse topics, for instance, things done by reason of maintaining the social order (as in the Mishnah-tractate Gittin 5:8–9). The preference of the Mishnah's authors for an inductive presentation of laws through cases accounts for the neglect of the exemplary principle of organization.

A third way is to take a striking language pattern and collect sayings on diverse topics that conform to the given language pattern (examples include Mishnah-tractate Kelim 13:2 and Parah 8:2–7). Very often these patterns may be expressed in abstract symbols. That appeal to language patterns as the organizing medium of thought invites chaos instead of an orderly description of the holy society.

Faced with these possible ways of organizing materials, the framers of the Mishnah chose to adhere to a highly disciplined thematic-logical principle of organization. The appeal to rhetorical and topical order turned the medium of discourse into a pervasive statement of the message of the order inherent in all

of God's creation, the order Israel is to attain to realize the sanctity of that creation, whether in nature or in society.

To summarize: the Mishnah organizes its data by topic. Tractates form
analyses of a given subject, and the chapters of the tractates take up particular
problems that inhere in the subject. Each presentation of a topic is susceptible
of a simple outline, primary matters taking priority over secondary ones. The
order of exposition is ordinarily dictated by the logical requirements of the
topic. Any rearrangement of subdivisions of a given subject from the Mishnah's presentation of them yields gibberish. To state the matter simply, a primary question always is answered prior to raising a subordinate detail that
depends on that answer.

## The Internal Evidence on the Topical Division
## of the Mishnah: The Match of Rhetoric and Topic

I claim, therefore, that the original intent of the document's authors is systematically to expound the subjects they have chosen, doing so through the
orderly presentation of the indicative traits of those subjects. Readers then may
fairly ask, Is the division of the Mishnah into chapters and paragraphs merely
a happenstance, not integral to the document but, perhaps, an invention of the
early printers? So they may wonder whether internal evidence validates the
claim that the Mishnah is organized topically, within the rules of order just
now set forth.

Manuscript evidence does not help to define the initial plan of the document. It is centuries late and therefore inconclusive. Not only so, but in antiquity paragraphing and punctuation were not commonly used. Long columns of
words would contain a text—as in the Torah today—and the student of the text
had the task of breaking up those columns into tractates, chapters, sentences,
large and small sense units. So where is the internal evidence?

A thought experiment answers the question. If we had the entirety of the
Mishnah in a single immense scroll and spread the scroll out on the ground—
perhaps the length of a football field!—we should have no difficulty at all discovering the point, on the five yard line, at which the first tractate ends and
the second begins, and so on down the field to the opposite goal. For from
Berakhot at the beginning to ʿUqsin at the end, the breaking points—the markers of divisions, comparable to the ten- or twenty-yard lines—practically jump
up from the ground like streaks of lime in grass.

Let me state with heavy emphasis: *When the subject of a protracted exposition changes, the exposition of that initial subject is always concluded.*

That is what I mean by claiming that a topical organization of the whole is
integral to the document from its initial definition. That shift is confirmed by
changes in the formal or stereotype syntax that governs. Once the subject
changes, so does the form. The form then not only responds to, but signals,
the integral character of the topical organization.

Then, when the dominant subject changes, in literary terms, a tractate has come to completion and a new one commences. That is, the tractates are readily distinguishable from one another since each treats a distinct topic. So if the Mishnah were to be copied out in a long scroll without the signification of lines of demarcation among the several tractates—no title pages, no tractate headings—the opening paragraph of a new tractate would readily distinguish itself from the prior, closing paragraph of the completed tractate. There never is reason to doubt that one topic had been completed and a new one begun. That is evidence for topical organization based on the character of the document itself, not the imposed markers of copyists or printers at some later point in the transmission of the document.

The same is so within the tractates. Intermediate divisions of these same principal tractate divisions are to be discerned on the basis of internal evidence, through the confluence of theme and form. When a new theme commences, a fresh formal rhetorical pattern will be used.

To spell this out: a given intermediate division of a principal one (in conventional language, a chapter of a tractate) will be marked by (1) a particular, recurrent, formal pattern in accord with which sentences are constructed, and also by (2) a particular and distinct theme to which these sentences are addressed. Within the intermediate divisions, we are able to recognize the components, or smallest whole units of thought, because there will be a recurrent pattern of sentence structure, a syntactic pattern repeated time and again within the unit and a shifting at the commencement of the next theme. Each point at which the recurrent pattern commences marks the beginning of a new cognitive unit. In general, an intermediate division will contain a carefully enumerated sequence of exempla of cognitive units, in the established formal pattern, commonly in groups of three or five or multiples of three or five (pairs for the first division).

## The Rhetorical Repertoire of the Mishnah

Just as the Mishnah's framers say the same thing about many things, so they manage to make their statement in a few fixed forms or syntactic patterns, whatever the topic. That formalization of language conveys a sense for the pattern that imparts cogency upon all transactions. The ordering and regularization, the systematization of the social life of Israel and God find their match in the character of the formal rhetoric that everywhere defines the way things are said.

This brings us to the matter of rhetorical forms. The cognitive units—"paragraphs" or "completed statements of thought"—resort to a remarkably limited repertoire of formulary patterns. The Mishnah in the Division of Purities, representative of the entire document, of which it forms in volume one-fourth, manages to say whatever it wants in one of the following ways:

(1) the simple declarative sentence, in which the subject, verb, and predicate are syntactically tightly joined to one another, for instance, "he who does so and so is such and such";

(2) the duplicated subject, in which the subject of the sentence is stated twice, thus, "he who does so and so, lo, he is such and such";

(3) mild apocopation, in which the subject of the sentence is cut off from the verb, which refers to its own subject, and not the one with which the sentence commences, so, "he who does so and so . . . , it [the thing he has done] is such and such";

(4) extreme apocopation, in which a series of clauses is presented, none of them tightly joined to what precedes or follows, and all of them cut off from the predicate of the sentence, thus, "he who does so and so . . . , it [the thing he has done] is such and such . . . , it is a matter of doubt whether . . . or whether . . . lo, it [referring to nothing in the antecedent, apocopated clauses of the subject of the sentence] is so and so . . .";

(5) In addition to these formulary patterns, in which the distinctive formulary traits are effected through variations in the relationship between the subject and the predicate of the sentence, or in which the subject itself is given a distinctive development, there is yet a fifth. In this last one we have a contrastive complex predicate, in which case we may have two sentences, independent of one another, yet clearly formulated so as to stand in acute balance with one another in the predicate, thus, "he who does . . . is unclean, and he who does not . . . is clean."

It naturally will be objected: Is it possible that a simple declarative sentence may be asked to serve as a formulary pattern, alongside the rather distinctive and unusual constructions that follow? True, by itself a tightly constructed sentence consisting of subject, verb, and complement, in which the verb refers to the subject, and the complement to the verb, hardly exhibits traits of particular formal interest. Yet a sequence of such sentences, built along the same gross grammatical lines, may well exhibit a clear-cut and distinctive pattern. When we see that three or five "simple declarative sentences" take up one principle or problem, and then, when the principle or problem shifts, a quite distinctive formal pattern will be utilized, we realize that the "simple declarative sentence" has served as the formulator of the unit of thought as aptly as did apocopation, a dispute, or another more obviously distinctive form or formal pattern.

The important point of differentiation, particularly for the simple declarative sentence, therefore, appears in the intermediate unit, as I just said, and thus in the interplay between theme and form. It is there that we see a single pattern recurring in a long sequence of sentences, for instance, "the X which has lost its Y is unclean because of its Z. The Z which has lost its Y is unclean because of its X." Another example will be a long sequence of highly developed sentences laden with relative clauses and other explanatory matter, in which a single syntactical pattern will govern the articulation of three or six or nine exempla. That sequence will be followed by one repeated terse sentence pattern, thus, "X is so and so, Y is such and such, Z is thus and so." The former group will treat one principle or theme, the latter some other. There can be no doubt, therefore, that the declarative sentence in recurrent patterns is, in its way, just as carefully formalized as a sequence of severely apocopated sentences or of contrastive predicates or duplicated subjects.

The dominant stylistic traits of the Mishnah, therefore, are the acute formalization of its syntactical structure, and its carefully framed sequences of formalized language—specifically, its intermediate divisions, so organized that the limits of a theme correspond to those of a formulary pattern. The balance and order of the Mishnah are particular to the Mishnah.

### The Matter of Mnemonics

There is no reason to doubt that if we asked the authorities behind the Mishnah the immediate purpose of their systematic use of formalized language, their answer would be to facilitate memorization. For that is the proximate effect of the acute formalization of their document. Much in its formal character can be seen as mnemonic.

First, the formal aspects of Mishnaic rhetoric are empty of content. This is proved by the fact that pretty much all themes and conceptions can be reduced to the same few formal patterns. These patterns are established by syntactical recurrences, as distinct from repeated use of the same sounds. Long sequences of patterned and disciplined sentences fail to repeat the same words—that is, they do not attain syllabic balance, rhythm, or sound—yet by syntactical patterning they do establish a powerful claim to order and formulary perfection. That is why we could name a pattern *he who . . . it is . . .* apocopation: the arrangement of the words as a grammatical pattern, not their substance, is what establishes the pattern.

Accordingly, we have a document composed along what clearly are mnemonic lines. But the Mishnah's mnemonic derives from recurrent syntactical patterns, not the concrete repetition of particular words, rhythms, syllabic counts, or sounds.

This fact—the creation of a pattern through repetition of the grammatical relationships of syntactical elements, more than through concrete sounds—tells us that the people who memorized conceptions reduced to these particular forms were capable of extraordinarily abstract cognition and perception. Hearing peculiarities of word order in diverse topical contexts, their ears and minds perceived regularities of grammatical arrangement, repeated functional variations of utilization of diverse words. They grasped from such subtleties syntactical patterns not expressed by recurrent external phenomena such as sounds, rhythms, or keywords, and independent of particular meanings.

What they heard, it is clear, were not only abstract relationships but also principles conveyed along with and through these relationships. That is, once more, they could notice the match of cases expressing a single principle and rhetorical pattern characteristic of those cases, then take account of a shift in rhetorical pattern, alerting them to a shift in the legal conception subject to illustration. And they themselves could dispense with the articulation of the general rule, which occurs only episodically in the Mishnah; the cases, in their matched forms, suffice to register that a general rule has been set down. Then what was memorized was a recurrent and fundamental notion, expressed in diverse examples but also in recurrent rhetorical-syntactical patterns.

Accordingly, what the memorizing student of a sage could and did hear was what lay far beneath the surface of the rule: the unstated principle, the unsounded pattern. This means that the prevalent mode of thought was attuned to what lay beneath the surface; minds and ears perceived what was not said behind what was said and how it was said.

When it comes to mnemonic qualities, we focus on the Mishnah in particular, because it is the one document among the Rabbinic writings that is consistently written to facilitate ready memorization. The patterns of language, that is, syntactic structures, follow a few simple rules. These rules, once known, apply nearly everywhere. They permit anyone to reconstruct, out of a few key phrases, an entire cognitive unit ("paragraph").

The mnemonics of the Mishnah therefore rests on the confluence of three elements: (1) deep logic, (2) articulated topic, and (3) manifest rhetoric. Working downward from the surface, anyone can penetrate into the deeper layers of meaning of the Mishnah. Then and at the same time, while discovering the principle behind the cases, one can easily memorize the whole by mastering the recurrent rhetorical pattern dictating the expression of the cogent set of cases. For it is easy to note the shift from one rhetorical pattern to another and to follow the repeated cases, articulated in the new pattern downward to its logical substrate.

So syllogistic propositions, in the Mishnah's authors' hands, come to full expression not only in what people wish to state but also in how they choose to say it. The limits of rhetoric define the arena of topical articulation. The completed units of discourse come in sets of three (thus establishing a series, a rule) or five (mnemonic matching the fingers of a hand) or multiples of three or five, joined to topical propositions. Once we ask what these clearly demarcated sets have in common, we state the logic shared among them all. So the mnemonics serves as an exegetical signal: these cases work together to make a point, now determine the point in common among them.

Let me show how this mnemonics works in concrete cases. The smallest whole unit of thought—sentences or paragraphs, in conventional language—is made up of fixed, recurrent formulas, clichés, patterns, or little phrases, out of which whole units of thought, or large complete sayings, are constructed. An example of part of a paragraph composed primarily of formulaic language is as follows:

> *A basket of fruit intended for the Sabbath*
> the House of Shammai
>> declare exempt
>
> And
>> the House of Hillel
>>> declare liable.

The italicized words are not stereotype. *And* is redactional; the formulation of the statement of the problem does not follow a pattern. The Houses sentences, by contrast, are formed of fixed, recurrent phrases, which occur in numerous pericopae. Similarly:

> House of Shammai say . . . House of Hillel say . . .

are fixed small units, whether or not the predicate matches; when it balances, we have a larger unit of tradition composed of two small units. Let me give another such example:

> Statement of the case subject to the rulings that follow
> (1) House of Shammai say,
> (2) it is subject to the provision, when water be put (Lev. 11:34)
> (3) House of Hillel say,
> (4) it is not subject to the provision, when water be put (Lev. 11:34)

In this paragraph, only the statement of the problem or protasis of the propositional composition, which is not given, would constitute other than a fixed unit; *House of Shammai/Hillel* + *say* are complete units, and the opinions in the apodosis are also stereotype.

Another, more complex example of the power of mnemonics to govern formulation of rules in the Mishnah derives from the Mishnah-tractate Berakhot 8:7. First we examine the paragraph as a whole, with the free-hand, unformalized, language given in italics, and the stereotype or patterned language in regular type:

> *[As for] one who ate but forgot and did not recite the grace [after meals]*—
> The House of Shammai say, "He should return to his place and recite the grace."
> But the House of Hillel say, "He should recite the grace in the place in which he remembered [that he had not recited the Grace after Meals]."

If we eliminate the attributives, House of . . . say . . . , we find each statement composed of three elements, which correspond in ascending, then descending order:

(1) He should return (2) to his place and (3) recite the grace.

versus

He should (3) recite the grace (2) in the place in which (1) he remembered.

The two statements, in fact, only differ at (1), *return* vs. *remember;* the Hebrew words are *HZR* vs. *ZKR*, so that, once we know what is at issue and the governing formula, all we need to remember is that one House gets the *H*, the other the *K*; the *H* comes first in the alphabet, so it goes to the House of Shammai, which nearly always gives its opinion first, and the *K* then follows for the House of Hillel.

I cannot imagine a more thoroughgoing effort to formulate at the deepest structure of language a working mnemonics. It is routine in the Mishnah to find counterparts in formalization in mnemonic patterns to this remarkably simple, skillful formulation. So much for the then-clause, the concluding component, the apodosis.

But now we must ask about the statement of the problem, the opening clause or protasis. To answer that question, we double back to our starting point, the topical structure of the document and the logical sequencing of the subdivisions of the topics. Internal evidence has already shown us that the arrangement by topical divisions and their subdivisions ("tractates," "chapters") is fundamental to the redaction of the Mishnah. Once a primary theme shifts, we know that the redactors have completed their treatment of one subject and commenced that of another. Now we repeat the question and ask about the "chapters." What we want to know is whether the dissection into intermediate divisions of these same principal divisions is shown by internal evidence to be equivalently fundamental to the redaction of the document.

So I return to my initial question: What internal evidence permits us to differentiate the intermediate divisions, or sizable aggregations of completed cognitive units? Answers to this question solve the problem of the mnemonics of the protasis, the statement of the problem or the "if"-clause. Two criteria come into play, topic and rhetoric, and they function as partners. To state matters simply: when the topic changes, the rhetorical *pattern* shifts, and, concomitantly, when the rhetorical pattern shifts, look for a change in topic or principle. To wit:

(1) TOPIC: The second of the two criteria derives from the nature of the principal divisions themselves: theme. We know from the football field analogy that it is along thematic lines that the redactors organized vast corpora of materials into principal divisions, tractates. These fundamental themes furthermore were subdivided into smaller conceptual units. The principal divisions treat their themes in units indicated by the sequential unfolding of their inner logical structure. Accordingly, one established criterion for distinguishing one aggregate of materials from some other, fore or aft, will be a shift in theme, or predominant and characteristic concern, of a sequence of materials.

(2) RHETORIC: Normally, when the topic changes, the mode of expression—the formal or formulary character, the patterning of language—will change as well.

These two matters, theme and form, must be asked to delineate for us the main lines of the intermediate segments or subdivisions of the Mishnah's principal divisions, the "chapters." There are, therefore, four logical possibilities for the application of the two stated criteria (with A referring to topic, B to rhetoric) +A+B, +A-B, -A+B, -A-B:

(1) coherent themes expressed through coherent formulary patterns

(2) coherent themes lacking coherent formulary patterns

(3) coherent formulary patterns lacking coherent themes

(4) incoherent themes and incoherent formulary patterns

In the fourth case all depends on context: the random, unformalized language stands out by reason of surrounding formalized units. For in cases of the fourth type the only reason to imagine that we deal with a subdivision is that before and after the set of materials that lacks coherence of theme and form are sets that do exhibit traits of coherent theme and/or form, that is, subdivisions demarcated by one of the first three possible combinations.

What do these facts of interior mnemonic patterns tell us about the history of the Mishnah? It is that the Mishnah was made up in a single generation, not through a long sedimentary process of agglutination and conglomeration. The bulk of the work of giving expression to the Mishnah's paragraphs, so formalized and patterned as they were, was uniformly carried out in the processes of redaction which resulted in the formation—patterning and aggregation—of the intermediate divisions of the several tractates, in their formulation and obviously in their organization and thematic arrangement.

The theological message conveyed by the mnemonic medium concerns, first of all, the mythic claim of the Mishnah to form the originally oral tradition of Sinai. The Mishnah was originally "published" in memory units, as the narrative cited in chapter 1 portrays matters. In this way, the framers of the document acted out the narrative they told about the origins of the traditions now given formal expression.

But there is a second message beneath the surface. The regularity of language underscored the well-organized account of Israel's social order, which the authors intended to set forth. Using the same language to speak of many topics, saying the same thing about many things—these underscore the intent of the writers to construct an account of a world of regularity and order. So far as the medium carried the message, it was a medium that spoke of reliability and stability—the very opposite of the world of chaos that second-century Israel in the Land of Israel confronted.

## The Mishnah's Logic of Coherent Discourse

We turn to the third element in the definition of a document, an aspect of the governing logic, namely, how sentences hold together in coherent paragraphs and what rules govern the composition of cogent thought. The Mishnah's modes of thought, with their philosophical disposition of facts in their native categories signaled by their intrinsic indicative traits, match its media of expression.

What is at issue in the matter of coherent discourse is simple: How do statements cohere, how do the facts contained in those statements cohere? Some Rabbinic documents join propositions to a fixed text, that is, comments to a book of Scripture or a chapter of Mishnah sentences. Others hold sentences together through narrative. The Mishnah's paramount logic of coherent discourse is propositional, philosophical—indeed, most commonly syllogistic. That is to say, the Mishnah's sentences form coherent propositions, claims of meaning or consequence concerning collections of facts.

Once more, we see bits of evidence that show alternatives, ways not taken. Other modes of securing coherence between sentences do occur but play little or no part. For example, making lists of authorities and joining sentences assigned to those authorities not because they formed coherent propositions but merely because the names were formed into a list never presented itself as a dominant option. It is the way chosen only by tractates Abot and ʿEduyyot. Nor the commentary on a received text (such as Scripture) form a routine choice. That is the fact, even though coherence by reference to a common text that is commented on occasionally shows up, in Mishnah-tractate Sotah for instance. And coherence through commentary on a received text predominates in the successor documents of the Rabbinic canon. That logic underscores the claim of writing to form a living tradition.

But the formal logic of coherence through a common text not only does not dominate; it is generally repudiated—and that is the message that emerges from the medium of logic that predominates. The Mishnah on rare occasion does present itself as the outcome of tradition, but it generally responds to a logic of coherence through reasoned proposition, evidence, and argument to the point. Indeed, in this regard its silence makes an eloquent statement. Specifically, in stating most of its laws without citing Scripture as the source for the category or the fact, the Mishnah's authors show their preference for propositional, philosophical principles of coherence. That is how they insisted on the intrinsic regularity of the social order. Nothing arbitrary or episodic characterizes the lines of structure and order of nature or society. Creation is orderly, and humanity has the intellectual power to discern the regular, reliable principles of order that emerge from a proper, inductive sifting of the facts of the social order as God created it.

How the logic functions is readily explained. Generalizations about two or more pieces of data—facts—flow from the classification of things by their intrinsic traits (the topical focus with which we began) and the formulation of the rule governing things of a given class. One classification is then compared and contrasted to others of a like character with the object of setting forth the hierarchy of the classifications. This method of scientific inquiry is called *Listen-wissenschaft*, that is, natural history: classification of things in accord with their intrinsic taxonomic or indicative traits, and (concomitantly) the hierarchization of the classes of things, that is, species of the same genus. These somewhat abstract definitions forthwith require instantiation.

How this logic of coherent discourse in a process of hierarchical classification forms quantities of facts into coherent propositions is illustrated by Mishnah-tractate Sanhedrin 2:2-3. There the authorship wishes to say that Israel has two heads, one of state, the other of cult, the king and the high priest respectively, and that these two offices are nearly wholly congruent to one another, with a few differences based on the particular traits of each. Broadly speaking, therefore, our exercise is one of setting forth the genus and the species. The genus is head of holy Israel. The species are king and high priest. Here are the traits in common and those not shared, and the exercise is fully exposed for what it is—that is, an inquiry into the rules that govern, the points of regularity and order, in this minor matter, of political structure. My outline, imposed in boldface type, makes the point important in this setting. Here I preserve my reference system, which differentiates sentences by assigning them letters; this makes the analytical process transparent.

#### MISHNAH-TRACTATE SANHEDRIN 2

1. **The rules of the high Priest: subject to the law, marital rites, conduct in bereavement**

MISHNAH-TRACTATE SANHEDRIN 2:1

    A. A high Priest judges, and [others] judge him;

    B. gives testimony, and [others] give testimony about him;

    C. performs the rite of removing the shoe (Deut. 25:7-9), and [others] perform the rite of removing the shoe with his wife.

    D. [Others] enter levirate marriage with his wife, but he does not enter into levirate marriage,

    E. because he is prohibited to marry a widow.

    F. [If] he suffers a death [in his family], he does not follow the bier.

    G. "But when [the bearers of the bier] are not visible, he is visible; when they are visible, he is not.

    H. "And he goes with them to the city gate," the words of R. Meir.

    I. R. Judah says, "He never leaves the sanctuary,

    J. "since it says, 'Nor shall he go out of the sanctuary' (Lev. 21:12)."

    K. And when he gives comfort to others

    L. the accepted practice is for all the people to pass one after another, and the appointed [prefect of the priests] stands between him and the people.

M. And when he receives consolation from others,

N. all the people say to him, "Let us be your atonement."

O. And he says to them, "May you be blessed by Heaven."

P. And when they provide him with the funeral meal,

Q. all the people sit on the ground, while he sits on a stool.

## 2. The rules of the king: not subject to the law, marital rites, conduct in bereavement

MISHNAH-TRACTATE SANHEDRIN 2:2

A. The king does not judge, and [others] do not judge him;

B. does not give testimony, and [others] do not give testimony about him;

C. does not perform the rite of removing the shoe, and others do not perform the rite of removing the shoe with his wife;

D. does not enter into levirate marriage, nor [do his brothers] enter levirate marriage with his wife.

E. R. Judah says, "If he wanted to perform the rite of removing the shoe or to enter into levirate marriage, his memory is a blessing."

F. They said to him, "They pay no attention to him [if he expressed the wish to do so]."

G. [Others] do not marry his widow.

H. R. Judah says, "A king may marry the widow of a king.

I. "For so we find in the case of David, that he married the widow of Saul,

J. "For it is said, 'And I gave you your master's house and your master's wives into your embrace' (2 Sam. 12:8)."

MISHNAH-TRACTATE SANHEDRIN 2:3

A. [If] [the king] suffers a death in his family, he does not leave the gate of his palace.

B. R. Judah says, "If he wants to go out after the bier, he goes out,

C. "for thus we find in the case of David, that he went out after the bier of Abner,

D. "since it is said, 'And King David followed the bier' (2 Sam. 3:31)."

E. They said to him, "This action was only to appease the people."

F. And when they provide him with the funeral meal, all the people sit on the ground, while he sits on a couch.

## 3. Special rules pertinent to the king because of his calling

MISHNAH-TRACTATE SANHEDRIN 2:4

A. [The king] calls out [the army to wage] a war fought by choice on the instructions of a court of seventy-one.

B. He [may exercise the right to] open a road for himself, and [others] may not stop him.

C. The royal road has no required measure.

D. All the people plunder and lay before him [what they have seized], and he takes the first portion.

E. "He should not multiply wives to himself" (Deut. 17:17)—only eighteen.

F. R. Judah says, "He may have as many as he wants, so long as they do not entice him [to abandon the Lord (Deut. 7:4)]."

G. R. Simeon says, "Even if there is only one who entices him [to abandon the Lord]—lo, this one should not marry her."

H. If so, why is it said, "He should not multiply wives to himself"?

I. Even though they should be like Abigail (1 Sam. 25:3).

J. "He should not multiply horses to himself" (Deut. 17:16)—only enough for his chariot.

K. "Neither shall he greatly multiply to himself silver and gold" (Deut. 17:16)—only enough to pay his army.

L. "And he writes out a scroll of the Torah for himself" (Deut. 17:17).

M. When he goes to war, he takes it out with him; when he comes back, he brings it back with him; when he is in session in court, it is with him; when he is reclining, it is before him,

N. as it is said, "And it shall be with him, and he shall read in it all the days of his life" (Deut. 17:19).

MISHNAH-TRACTATE SANHEDRIN 2:5

A. [Others may] not ride on his horse, sit on his throne, handle his scepter.

B. And [others may] not watch him while he is getting a haircut, or while he is nude, or in the bath-house,

C. since it is said, "You shall surely set him as king over you" (Deut. 17:15)—that reverence for him will be upon you.

The philosophical cast of mind is amply revealed in this well-formed and highly formalized essay, which in concrete terms effects a taxonomy. That is accomplished through the matching of data of an identical class, a study of the *genus* national leader and its two *species*, (1) king, (2) high priest. How are they alike, how are they not alike, and what accounts for the differences? The premise is that national leaders are alike and follow the same rule, except where they differ and follow each the opposite rule from the one that governs the other. But that premise also is subject to the proof effected by the survey of the data consisting of concrete rules, those systemically inert facts that here come to life for the purpose of establishing a proposition. By itself, the fact that, for example, others may not ride on his horse, bears the burden of no systemic proposition. In the context of an argument constructed for nomothetic, taxonomic purposes, the same fact is active and weighty. The logic of coherence undertakes the search for points in common and therefore also points of contrast. We seek connection between fact and fact, sentence and sentence in the subtle and balanced rhetoric of the Mishnah, by comparing and contrasting two things that are like and not alike.

At the logical level, then, the Mishnah falls into the category of familiar philosophical thought. Once we seek regularities, we propose rules. What is like another thing falls under its rule, and what is not like the other falls under the opposite rule. Accordingly, as to the species of the genus, so far as they are alike they share the same rule. So far as they are not alike, each follows a rule contrary to that governing the other. So the work of analysis is what produces connection, and therefore the drawing of conclusions derives from comparison and contrast: the *and*, the *equal*. The proposition that forms the conclusion concerns the essential likeness of the two offices, except where they are different, but the subterranean premise is that we can explain both likeness and difference by appeal to a principle of fundamental order and unity. The high priest and king fall into a single genus, but speciation based on traits particular to the king then distinguishes the one from the other.

## The Autonomy of the Mishnah within the Torah

So much for the description of the Mishnah, its rhetorical patterns, and logic of coherent discourse. What we see is the independence of spirit manifest in the document's media of topical exposition, rhetorical program, and logic of coherent discourse. That trait of autonomous judgment matched the Mishnah's own example. For the Mishnah sometimes developed Scripture's categories, sometimes defined and articulated topical categories of its own, and occasionally simply recapitulated those of Scripture. But that means, overall, the Mishnah took an independent stance vis-à-vis Scripture's topical program. Its rhetoric in no way imitated that of Scripture. The Mishnah's language takes its leave from biblical Hebrew. Its logic of coherent discourse, with its emphasis on the intrinsic traits of things and its hierarchical classification of things in accord with those traits, finds no counterpart in Scripture.

The topical, rhetorical, and logical program conveyed the message that the Torah reached Israel in two media. The other medium, the oral one, conveyed—from the very data of the social, customary, and natural order—the truths that Scripture set forth in its narratives, episodic laws, and exhortations. The Torah's oral medium invoked society and nature and custom to impose system upon the chaos of the world. In the age of reconstruction, it was that chaos that defined the issue addressed in every line of the Mishnah, form and substance alike.

The Talmudic sages would later claim that, with the loss of Temple, city, and Land, all God had left in this world was the four cubits of the Halakhah. In that judgment they paid tribute to the intellectual achievement of the masters who in the Mishnah formed the law into an instrument of sanctification in the here and now, leading to salvation in the end of days. Their work Halakhic sufficed, and nurtured through the ages it still does. It still does.

# 19 | THE MISHNAH IN CONTEXT: MAKING GOD'S WORD WORK TODAY

. . . one cannot study ferns in the wild without some understanding of why they grow where they do and their relationship to other plants and animals, their habitats.

—Oliver Sacks, *Oaxaca Journal*

## The Mishnah Seen Whole

At the end of the old order, the Mishnah pursues a quest for restoration and renewal. That quest defined both its aesthetic and its theological traits. It explains its preference for carefully calibrated constructions of patterned language, its nurture of balance and proportion. It also accounts for its emphasis, in the face of chaos, on the rationality and structure of Israel's interior reality.

Accordingly, the indicative traits of rhetoric, topical organization, and logical form of the Mishnah match the message that the document sets forth. So too, the details expounded in chapters 2 through 17 make best sense as a response to the generative question answered by the system of the Mishnah viewed whole. Part by part the details deliver diverse messages but produce no pattern. They truly cohere only when taken all together and as a response to a turning, such as I outlined in the Introduction: a cultural crisis of historical proportions confronting the Judaic society and culture.

We grasp the systemic cogency of the Mishnah's theology only when we ask how the Mishnah's system corresponds with, and responds to, the politics defined by Israel's historical context. The Mishnah's theology stressed that Israel, a vanquished and broken-hearted nation, could yet make decisions. It above all assigned to Israel responsibility for its condition. That formed the answer to the historical, political question of the age. Intentionality disabled history. Remaining responsible for its own condition, Israel still could decide its destiny. That is because its will still mattered to God, in command of history. The prophets of ancient Israel had said just that. All the Halakhah of the Mishnah did was repeat the message in the medium of law embodying theology.

So the issues now to be addressed focus on the recurrent questions and the repeated preoccupations, for instance, with matters of intentionality and the power of the human will, as much as of purity and sanctity. These point us toward concrete problems of everyday life that the Rabbinic sages resolved through the law of the Mishnah and its messages. Understanding how they solved their problems, we may ask them to serve as a model for us as we respond to tasks of crisis and renewal two thousand years later.

## What Do We Miss When We See the Mishnah Whole?

That is what we see when we view the Mishnah whole and complete, in context. But what then do we miss? The answer is clear from chapter 17: the Mishnah as a philosophical law code is remarkably unengaged by problems of history and eschatology and rarely entrusts its message to narrative. When we do find narrative, it is principally in connection with the presentation of the Temple and its rites, when the storytelling mode takes over: for example, in the account of the purification rite of Leviticus 14 (Mishnah-tractate Negaʿim 14), or at the account of the high priest's rites on the Day of Atonement in Leviticus 16 (recapitulated in Mishnah-tractate Yoma 1–7). Even here we cannot allege that myth enters in; the narrative involves what the priest would do or did do—not any larger context shaped by a teleological motive.

But that does not mean that the Mishnah's system is constructed outside of the framework of events and is indifferent to great historical moments. Composed in the century after the destruction of the Temple, the Mishnah's system explicitly alludes to that destruction (Mishnah-tractates Rosh Hashanah 3–4 and Hullin 5–12). There the question is raised in concrete legal contexts, Has the law changed by reason of the destruction of the Temple? Implicit in the question is the matter of sanctification.

The urgent issue taken up by the Mishnah was specifically, What, in the aftermath of the destruction of the holy place and holy cult, remained of the sanctity of the holy caste, the priesthood, the holy land, and above all the holy people and its holy way of life? The answer was that sanctity persists indelibly in Israel the people—in its way of life, in its Land, in its priesthood, in its food, in its mode of sustaining life, in its manner of procreating and so sustaining the nation.

The Mishnah's system therefore focused on the holiness of the life of Israel the people and of the Land of Israel by extension—a holiness that had formerly radiated out from the Temple, God's abode. The logically consequent question was, What is the meaning of sanctity and how shall Israel attain or give evidence of sanctification? The answer to the question derived from the original creation, the end of the Temple directing attention to the beginning of the natural world that the Temple had embodied. For the meaning of sanctity the framers therefore turned to that first act of sanctification, the one in creation. It came about when, all things in array and in place, God blessed and sanctified the seventh day on the eve of the first Sabbath. Creation was made ready for the blessing and the sanctification when all things were "very good," that is to say, in their rightful order, called by their rightful name. An orderly nature was a sanctified and blessed nature, so Scripture set forth in the name of the Creator. So to be made holy, all things had to be set in right array.

## The Historical Context

Context is everything, and how the system responds to its context is the main thing. The system seen whole is what defines the Mishnah's context, part by part.

True, details originate hither and yon. Bits of the legal traditions of the Mishnah originated long before the document took shape and came to closure in 200 C.E. The Torah's laws were taken over as facts and form the foundations of all the topical tractates to which they pertain. That is so, even though some Mishnah-tractates claim little or no basis in the written Torah's laws, but by definition rest rather on oral tradition. But details take on full meaning and consequence only when formed into the very particular system constituted by the Mishnah. And whatever components derived from remote antiquity, that system came to realization whole and complete not in remote antiquity but in its categories and structures in the mid-second century. Then all the divisions and their topical tractates came to definition, each in place and in proportion to the whole.

So our question is, How do the topical program and propositional message of the Mishnah match the times in which the Rabbinic sages organized the ancient traditions? The answer is that the Mishnah took shape in the times in which the ancient order of Israelite life—focused as it was on Israel's possession of the Land, the primacy of Jerusalem, the service of the Temple and its sacrifices—collapsed in the catastrophes of the destruction of the Temple in 70 and the failure of the war led by Bar Kokhba some three generations later to regain Jerusalem and restore the Temple. We have already seen how Mishnah-tractate Hullin articulately responds to those events and sorts out their implications.

The explicit statement of Hullin suffices to define the existential issue to which the Mishnah's framers' respond overall, the problem that they solved, and the solution that they set forth for future generations of Judaism. It was a labor of restoration, reconstruction, and renewal—the sanctification of Israel in its ordinary life, aimed at the end outcome of the salvation of Israel from its condition in this age and the restoration of Israel to the Land, embodying the return of Adam and Eve to Eden.

Given the condition of Israel in the aftermath of the catastrophic war against Rome led by Bar Kokhba in 132–135, putting things in order was no easy task. But that is why, after all, the question pressed, the answer proving inexorable and obvious. The condition of society corresponded to the critical question that obsessed the system builders.

## Israel and Adam

The issue now required a second look at the established paradigm that compared Adam and the loss of Eden to Israel and the loss of the Land. For the written Torah had not contemplated what had come about: not only the restoration of the Temple but its destruction a second time. No wonder the Rabbinic sages thought deeply about Israel in comparison with Adam. At issue was whether or not Israel had now gone down the last path to extinction, and what future awaited God's experiment in making humanity in God's image, after God's likeness. Here is how, in later exegetical writing, the comparison was drawn.

### GENESIS RABBAH XIX:IX.1–2

R. Abbahu in the name of R. Yosé bar Haninah: "It is written, 'But they [Israel] are like a man [Adam], they have transgressed the covenant' (Hos. 6:7).

"'They are like a man,' specifically, like the first man. [We shall now compare the story of the first man in Eden with the story of Israel in its land.]"

Now the sage identifies God's action in regard to Adam with a counterpart action in regard to Israel, in each case matching verse for verse, beginning with Eden and Adam. Adam is brought to Eden as Israel is brought to the Land, with comparable outcomes:

"'In the case of the first man, I brought him into the garden of Eden, I commanded him, he violated my commandment, I judged him to be sent away and driven out, but I mourned for him, saying "How . . ."'[which begins the book of Lamentations, hence stands for a lament, but which, as we just saw, also is written with the consonants that also yield, 'Where are you'].

"'I brought him into the garden of Eden,' as it is written, 'And the Lord God took the man and put him into the garden of Eden' (Gen. 2:15).

"'I commanded him,' as it is written, 'And the Lord God commanded . . .' (Gen. 2:16).

"'And he violated my commandment,' as it is written, 'Did you eat from the tree concerning which I commanded you' (Gen. 3:11).

"'I judged him to be sent away,' as it is written, 'And the Lord God sent him from the garden of Eden' (Gen. 3:23).

"'And I judged him to be driven out.' 'And he drove out the man' (Gen. 3:24).

"'But I mourned for him, saying, "How . . ."' 'And he said to him, "Where are you"' (Gen. 3:9), and the word for 'where are you' is written, 'How . . .'"

Now comes the systematic comparison of Adam and Eden with Israel and the Land of Israel:

"'So too in the case of his descendants, [God continues to speak,] I brought them [Israel] into the Land of Israel, I commanded them, they violated my commandment,

I judged them to be sent out and driven away but I mourned for them, saying, "How
. . .'"

"'I brought them into the Land of Israel.' 'And I brought you into the land of
Carmel' (Jer. 2:7).

"'I commanded them.' 'And you, command the children of Israel' (Exod. 27:20).
'Command the children of Israel' (Lev. 24:2).

"'They violated my commandment.' 'And all Israel have violated your Torah'
(Dan. 9:11).

"'I judged them to be sent out.' 'Send them away, out of my sight and let them go
forth' (Jer 15:1).

"'. . . and driven away.' 'From my house I shall drive them' (Hos. 9:15).

"'But I mourned for them, saying, "How . . ."' 'How has the city sat solitary, that
was full of people' (Lam. 1:1)."

We end with Lamentations, the writing of mourning produced after the
destruction of the Temple in Jerusalem in 587 by the Babylonians. Here we end
where we began, Israel in exile from the Land, like Adam in exile from Eden.
But the Torah is clear that there is a difference: Israel can repent, rebuild,
restore, renew. That is where the law of the Mishnah enters in. The Torah of
Sinai endured and retained its power and promise of the regeneration of Israel
through the law.

These persons, Israel and Adam, form not individual and particular, one-
time characters, but exemplary categories. Israel is Adam's counterpart; Israel
is the other model for Man—the one being without the Torah, the other possessing, and possessed by the Torah. Adam's failure defined Israel's task,
marked the occasion for the formation of Israel. Israel came into existence in
the aftermath of the failure of creation with the fall of Man and his ultimate
near-extinction; in the restoration that followed the Flood, God identified
Abraham to found in the Land the new Eden, a supernatural social entity to
realize God's will in creating the world. Called variously a family, a community, a nation, a people, Israel above all embodies God's abode in humanity,
God's resting place on earth.

## Humanity in Crisis: What Can Israel Do?

With the equation of Adam and Israel in hand, we grasp the Mishnah's
solution to the crisis. The human being, "in our image, after our likeness,"
male and female, is God's counterpart and partner in creation. That is
because, like God, the human being has power over the status and condition
of creation, putting everything in its proper place, calling everything by its
rightful name. That brings us to the meeting of theology and law in the Mishnah's judgment of the nature of the human being in relationship to God.

The human being and God are the two beings that possess the active will.
The human being is like God in that both God and the human being not only
act, but form attitudes and intentions. That theory of the human being, a theological issue concerning the nature of will and attitude, meets the theory of

God's relationship with humanity, a theological concern about the correspondence of God's and humanity's inner being. All of this deep thought is precipitated by the critical issue facing Israel, defeated on the battlefield and deprived of its millennial means of serving God in the temple in Jerusalem: What, now, can a human being do? The Rabbinic sages answered that question through the law of the Mishnah: renew, restore, rebuild, now the right way, the Torah's way. That meant, by purifying the heart.

Addressing an age of defeat and despair, in the wake of the destruction of the Temple and a disastrous loss of life and liberty following the Roman war and the subsequent abortive rebellion against Rome, the Mishnah's framers' principal message—which makes the Judaism of this document and of its social components distinctive and cogent—is that the human being is at the center of creation, the head of all creatures upon earth, corresponding to God in heaven, in whose image that human being is made. The way in which the Mishnah makes this simple and fundamental statement is illustrated on nearly every page. It is to impute the power, effected through an act of sheer human will or intentionality, to the human being to inaugurate and initiate those corresponding processes, sanctification and uncleanness, which play so critical a role in the Mishnah's account of reality.

## The Power of the Will

The will of the human being, expressed through the deed of the human being, is the active power in the world. As matters would be phrased in later writings, "Nothing whatsoever impedes the human will." But, of course, looking back on the age at hand, we know that everything did. The Israel of the Mishnah never achieved its stated goals, for example, in *once more* setting up a government of priests and kings, in *once more* regaining that order and stasis that people imagined had once prevailed. But the key is in the "once more," for these were things that in point of fact had not been at all. The will for "once more" encompassed nowhere and never.

So, stated briefly, the question taken up by the Mishnah and answered by Judaism is, What can a person do? The answer laid down by the Mishnah is, the human being, through will and deed, is master of this world, the measure of all things. But the world in which the human being is the measure of all things is within: in intellect, imagination, sentient experience. When the Mishnah thinks of a human being, its authors mean the Israelite who is the subject and actor of its system. This is the Judaism that identifies at the center of things Israel, the Israelite person, who can do what he or she wills. In the aftermath of the two world wars and defeats of millennial proportions, the message of the Mishnah cannot have proved more pertinent—or more poignant and tragic. Yet the power of the message shaped the entire history of Israel, and of Judaism, from then to now. For Israel, understood as the answer to the ineluctable questions of frailty and defeat in society and death for everyone who walked the earth, the self-evident truth is that everything that matters depends on human will and intention: we are what in mind and imagination and sentiment and heart we hope, believe, insist, and above all by act of will persist in being.

## What Then Happened to the Mishnah's System?

The Mishnah's six divisions thus formed a coherent system for Israel's social order. It said the same thing about many things, forming a consistent statement acted out in all kinds of ordinary transactions. The theological statement, complex in legal form, was simple in substance: God made humanity in hope and through the Torah expressed God's yearning and love for what God had made. The world that the Mishnah designed in theory would show how humanity could respond in fact to that yearning and reciprocate that love.

But the Mishnah's six divisions, half of them devoted to the now-ruined Temple, in the aggregate spoke of a world that never was and never would come into being. As a set they responded to the crisis of renewal after the Bar Kokhba debacle, answering the issues of the age. So the Mishnah's system found no sustenance in the social order to which it was addressed. Indeed, that fully articulated system ignored the world meant to realize it and proved remarkably incongruous to its setting. And time's judgment cannot be ignored: the Mishnah's system never attained full realization. And its heirs, in the Talmuds, would form their own judgment of the restoration.

Take the Mishnah's politics, for example. Israel in the time of the composition of the Mishnah was not ruled by high priest, king, and sage, as Mishnah-tractate Sanhedrin laid matters out. It had never been governed in such a manner, and it never would be. Consider the entire division devoted to the upkeep of the Temple house and the conduct of its offerings. The system in the fifth division portrayed a Temple and its sacrificial system, priesthood, and appointed times and seasons. But there was no Temple. The offerings of meat and meal ceased, and most of the rites portrayed in that division awaited restoration. Contemplate the elaborate statement devoted to cultic purity and impurity. In the sixth division the system explained how to attain purity in the Temple or by analogy to it. But the Temple grounds had suffered desecration and contamination.

But there is more. Israel outside of the Holy Land lived in unclean territory, and Israel within the Holy Land resided in the midst of gentiles, who were unclean by definition. So the aspiration to eat ordinary food at home in the state of cleanness comparable to that attained in the Temple proved empty. Is there not at least some reality in the first division? Did not the priesthood endure? Not even here. In the first division the system provided for the support of the priesthood (and scheduled castes), but the priesthood no longer had an altar to maintain, nor did the Levites ascend to their platform to sing their songs. In the second division, the system described the appointed times—New Year, Passover, Day of Atonement, and the rest—mainly though not exclusively as these entailed Temple rites, which were permanently suspended for a long duration. So the entire Mishnaic system took shape in a world to which it was only marginally relevant.

## The Tosefta

Three principal documents form the exegetical continuation of the Mishnah: (1) the Tosefta (ca. 300 C.E.), (2) the Talmud of the Land of Israel (also called the Yerushalmi, ca. 400 C.E.), and (3) the Talmud of Babylonia (also called the Bavli, ca. 600 C.E.). All three depend for structure and order on the Mishnah. Each establishes its independence of the Mishnah as well.

The Tosefta, which follows the program and organization of the Mishnah tractate by tractate, lacks any autonomous standing as a document. Rather, it depends on the Mishnah for topic, rhetoric, and logic of coherent discourse, forming a compilation of legal expositions correlative with those of the Mishnah. Classified in their relationships with the counterpart statements of the Mishnah, these are of three types: (1) compositions of the Tosefta that cite and gloss passages of the Mishnah—these form commentaries in the true sense: citation and gloss of a prior, received text; (2) compositions of the Tosefta that do not cite the Mishnah verbatim but that can be fully and completely understood only in relation to the Mishnah's counterpart legal statements, commentary in a subtle form; (3) a set of compositions that are independent of the Mishnah in principle or problem and can be understood without reference to the Mishnah.

## The Talmuds

In all its patient, loyal expositions, the authorship of the Tosefta recapitulated the system of the Mishnah, attending to detail but making few changes of a fundamental order. The real revolution in the presentation of the law of Judaism took place in the academies of the Rabbinic sages of the Land of Israel, which produced the Talmud of the Land of Israel (completed ca. 400 C.E.) and of Babylonia (in Sasanian Iran), which produced the Talmud of Babylonia, (completed ca. 600 C.E.). The two Talmuds registered the judgment that the laws of the Mishnah governed, even as they dispensed with its system. This they did in two ways, one on the surface, one beneath.

On the surface they set aside the Mishnah's system by selecting for exegesis among the principal parts of the Mishnah's (and Tosefta's) legal construction those components that retained relevance in the workaday life of Israel in Babylonia or Israel in Roman Palestine (which was the Land of Israel now without the Temple, without Judaic Jerusalem). The Talmud of the Land of Israel and the Talmud of Babylonia both took up the work of commenting on the divisions of Appointed Times, Women, and Damages. The household formed a locus for the realization of Appointed Times, the family for Women, and the community at large for Damages.

The Talmud of the Land of Israel in addition commented on the Division of Agriculture, part of the law of which continued to apply to the Land of Israel. The Talmud of Babylonia commented in rich detail on the Division of Holy Things, certainly an anomaly. Neither Talmud attended to Purities, except for the tractate Niddah, which deals with a woman's menstrual period and related matters. The Mishnah would seldom be studied start to finish, and still more rarely would it make its statement whole, complete, and beyond the intervening mediation of the Talmuds, with their selectivity and their practicality. Dropping most of Purities removed a bit more than a quarter of the sheer volume of the Mishnah's detailed system, including its most profound and sophisticated expositions of principles through dense details. So the framers of the two Talmuds made their own decisions on the construction of the law of Judaism, and instead of reinforcing the systemic character of the Mishnah, they chose to dismantle it.

The deeper means for deconstructing the Mishnah's system and using its elements for another systemic construction altogether functioned at the very boundaries where the later generations would meet the Mishnah: the exegesis of words and phrases and, less commonly, of sentences and of entire legal concepts—and never of the Mishnah's system viewed all together and all at once, as we have understood it here. The authorities of the two Talmuds broke the Mishnah up into sense units, and these they subjected to a close reading. They seldom articulated the larger questions implicit in those sense units. It would carry us far afield to describe how the heirs of the Mishnah conducted their analysis of the received law. It suffices here to observe that their exercise of exegesis paid only limited attention to the principles of a theology that the Mishnah had set forth with such exquisite subtlety, case by case.

These facts suffice to make one point. The Mishnah's system formed a model that the heirs and continuators both amplified and also revised. They did not simply take over the Mishnah and extend it; they also reshaped and redefined its system to stress the domestic and communal law and to set aside the Temple's purity regulations. But in their selection and amplification they lost the coherent quality of the Mishnah's legal system. The Mishnah had made a theological statement through its law. The whole construction that the Mishnah set forth, its topical composition and program, had made that statement through the entirety of the law. Now the details of the law would remain, but only where relevant to Israel's present social order.

Since the statement the system had made would be deprived of intrinsic and principal parts, a third of it in each Talmud, what had made the Mishnah work—its power to speak in the voice of law and the inspired energy to set forth a theological message through concrete transactions and activities—was lost. Then the law persisted in the very topical category formations that the Mishnah initially defined for a thousand years—but not as the acted out, embodied, and socially realized theology that the Mishnah's system had set forth. So the theological system that sustained and animated the law and imparted cogency to it, deprived of part of its voice, did not survive—at least not in its original mode of law.

But other means would serve to convey the Torah's message that humanity "in our image, after our likeness" *can* realize God's hopes for creation—and will. And today, the third generation of Holocaust and Empowerment may take for itself the model of the generations of the Torah, who endured catastrophe and undertook to hope: the generation of Ezra, ca. 450 B.C.E., who renewed the Torah, and the generation of Judah the Patriarch, ca. 200 C.E., who made the whole a statement of a sanctified social system in the Mishnah. This takes place when the power to see a future is renewed by an act of daring imagination and the power to hope is renewed by an act of audacious will. The dream then endures, the transcendent vision of humanity in the workaday encounter with the living God that the Mishnah put forth in its sublime vision of holy Israel, meant to live with God forever, rising out of the grave for all eternity, and even in the here and now.

## AN AFTERWORD

The message of the Mishnah matches the moment. The people Israel finds itself in another age of construction beyond catastrophe. In that age of despair, the Rabbinic sages offered hope in the form of a vision conveyed in everyday actions and attitudes. The Mishnah forms a monument to the capacity of the human imagination to transcend calamity, the power of the human will to transform crisis into the occasion of renewal. In their system of norms of sanctifying behavior the Rabbinic sages realized norms of belief that would sustain the people. Their message, beginning to end, told enduring Israel why to rebuild—and how to rebuild. And the work of renewal is possible and right. That is because Israel bears the power to form in the renewed social order the abode for God's dwelling on earth, just as the Torah had said.

The Mishnah shows the way to use that power for God's sake, and eternal Israel responds by adopting this vision of law that sanctifies and fashioning of it the foundations of its sacred society. That is why the Mishnah forms the monument to the power of the human will, and—as Adam learned and Israel would discover—that is precisely how God planned matters from creation.

# Acknowledgments

B IBLICAL QUOTATIONS ordinarily are copied from the Revised Standard
Version of the Bible © 1952 by Division of Christian Education of the
National Council of the Churches of Christ in the United States of America.
My thanks for permission to reproduce them.

Rabbi Seymour Rossel served as manuscript development editor of this
book, and I owe him much, beginning with the title. All the books I have written under his editorship have carried the mark of his astuteness and insight as
editor and rabbi.

Dr. David Altshuler, founding Director of the Museum of Jewish Her-
itage/Holocaust Memorial in New York City and founding President of The
Trust for Jewish Philanthropy, provided many valuable suggestions.

I reviewed the manuscript with Rabbi Joel H. Zaiman as well. The original idea of presenting a guide to the Mishnah was his, and I appreciate his continuing engagement with my work.

From day to day I discuss many problems of interpretation with Professor
Bruce D. Chilton, Bard College, whom I find consistently astute and discern-
ing.

My editor at Continuum, Justus George Lawler, served as the first and
most helpful outside reader. Not only am I indebted to him for his engaged
reading of the first draft, but the readers as well share this debt. I have had
many fine editors in my career as a publishing scholar; none exceeded him in
perspicacity.